# MAHLER

# Henry-Louis de La Grange

# *MAHLER*

## VOLUME ONE

Doubleday & Company, Inc.

GARDEN CITY, NEW YORK

## PICTURE CREDITS

Bildarchiv d. Ost. Nationalbibliothek—1, 2, 10, 13, 14, 15, 16, 17, 28.
Photohaus Eberth—19.
Bilderplest Suddentscher Verlag—30.
A. Huber—41.
I. Heinrichshof—54.
Mertens, Mai & Co.—55.

ISBN: 0-385-00524-5
Library of Congress Catalog Card Number 72–76147
Copyright © 1973 by Henry-Louis de La Grange
All Rights Reserved
Printed in the United States of America

*To my mother*
*Emily Sloane de La Grange*

# CONTENTS

# PREFACE

Gustav Mahler is a paradox without precedent among great composers. He was possessed of two identities, in both of which he achieved international fame. Of itself, this is by no means unprecedented. The paradox is, rather, that he had one pre-eminent identity during his life, quite another after his death. The massive documentation crowded into this pioneering volume by Henry-Louis de La Grange provides, for the first time, exact, exhaustive, and illuminating documentation, not only of why this was, but how it came about.

During his life Mahler was known and admired on both sides of the Atlantic as one of the master conductors of his time—a time in which it was much harder to achieve, and hold, top rank than it has more recently become.

Since his death, as Mahler's fame as a conductor has inevitably receded, his repute as a composer has slowly but ever more irresistibly risen. In the years between 1950 and 1972—which is to say, in the third quarter of the century—no symphonic literature has contributed more to the relief of the belabored Beethoven-Brahms-Tchaikovsky repertory than his.

Nevertheless, the hundredth anniversary of his birth in 1860 came and went without a full length biography of Mahler in English or any other language. Until La Grange addressed himself to this necessary task with unexampled results, the library of Mahleriana has consisted in large part of personal reminiscences, of a compilation of letters (far from complete), and of the kind of anecdotage that is an addendum to a life rather than a life in itself.

For this the reasons are all too plain. Conductors who outlive the influence exerted in their lifetime to merit biographies are all but unknown. By the time the world came to a belated realization of Mahler's worth as a composer, decades had slipped by and the usual sources of biographical minutiae had all but dried up. Unprovidentially, two wars had swept across Europe since Mahler's death in 1911. Not only was the landscape rearranged; lines of national division had been relocated and all too many of the physical surroundings in which Mahler pursued his earthly existence had been erased.

Thus the prospects had become increasingly less likely that anyone disposed to pursue a biographical project out of conventional, customary motivation would elect Gustav Mahler as the subject. But it sometimes happens that difficulties, if they are sufficiently forbidding, have a way of attracting persons peculiarly qualified to surmount them. Stout Cortez, not so stout Edmund Hillary, and far from stout Roger Bannister are synonyms for all those others who have done the impossible. They belong to a breed peculiarly responsive to a hopelessly unpromising challenge because, in John Kennedy's phrase, "it is there."

Dozens of Mahler enthusiasts might have marshaled the interest and the energy to challenge the backbreaking project of regaining enough information about him to bring about a creditable life. It remained for one, Henry-Louis de La Grange, to combine with the interest and the energy, not only the will and the determination to see it through, but also the means to make the research possible. Not since Sir Thomas Beecham drew on his own resources to document the life of Frederick Delius have private means been so unselfishly marshaled to achieve a public benefit for the whole musical community.

What began, in all probability, as a project modestly designed to provide the "creditable life" previously lacking grew year by year, even decade by decade—from its beginning nearly twenty years ago—to the compilation of a staggering dossier of facts about Mahler unequaled in scope and of almost unimaginable detail. The outcome is a source book of a richness to rank with Jahn on Mozart, Thayer on Beethoven, or Newman on Wagner. Doubtless as time accumulates there will be those who will burrow more deeply into this or that aspect of Mahler, but none will be able to make a move or scratch the investigatory surface without profound indebtedness to La Grange.

Thanks to a systematic search, with qualified collaborators, of publications in every community in which Mahler pursued his almost incessant public activity, we follow Mahler from his birth in an obscure Bohemian village through preparatory phases of a progress that made his aspirations to study in Vienna almost laughable. After he had attained that unattainable, we are led, by ways almost too roundabout to be credible, from humble musical duties in a spa to assignments in Ljubljana, Olomouc, and Kassel, beyond which Leipzig, Prague, and Budapest loom as heights almost too lofty to scale. It is thus scarcely strange that Mahler regarded an opportunity in Hamburg—then one of the most important opera centers of the German-speaking world*— as "a stage on the way, but I cannot deny that I am tired of this eternal 'voyage' and hope to find a homeland." This and similar yearnings recaptured by La Grange reveal one of the fundamental faults in Mahler's nature. Satisfactions would ever remain relative to him, because his aspirations were absolute—to be the best conductor, the greatest composer, even the finest husband and father.

Through La Grange's immense documentation, we have all the materials to determine whether, as Mahler contended, "this hell of the theater" was

---

* Berlin, Vienna, Dresden, Munich, Leipzig, Frankfurt, and Stuttgart would have been the others.

thrust upon him because he did not have the luck or persistence to win the grants and prizes that would have enabled him to concentrate on composing, or whether the urge to public performance was a deep-seated, fulfilling part of his artistic impulse.

At the very least his creative activities furthered the physical side of his emotional nature. His first sweetheart, La Grange informs us, was a member of a company in which Mahler was a young conductor, and his later involvements included a descendant of Carl Maria von Weber, the sopranos Anna Mildenburg and Selma Kurz, and even Alma Schindler, whom he married. His recreative activities bore heavily on his creative career.

They were to an extent a distraction but to an even greater extent a stimulation to the impulses from which emerged the enduring works on which his lasting fame is based. That the two careers were in opposition has long been obvious, but we only learn, through La Grange's illumination of Mahler's day by day activities, the extent to which they had an overriding interrelationship.

These revelations take the form of the almost innumerable citations of the orchestral repertory conducted by Mahler. This was an activity he doted on in every city where he had operatic involvement, including Vienna. There are in addition many confidential expressions of opinion to correspondents.

On page after page we find hitherto inaccessible citations of his preferences (often with such soloists as Ferruccio Busoni, Eugen D'Albert, or Carl Friedberg). In a time when the *Symphonie fantastique* was considered inacceptable by most musical right-thinkers, Berlioz ranked high among Mahler's musical enthusiasms. He esteemed Mendelssohn and Spohr, Smetana and Anton Rubinstein no less selectively.

From each new experience, whether it was playing the chamber music of Schubert and Beethoven with fellow musicians in Hamburg, or expressing incisive commentaries on Bruckner and Brahms to his favored correspondents, we derive provocative indices to his determination to produce a different, better result in his own work "next time." It is inescapable because it is encountered more than once in such correspondence, that Mahler's overpowering urge was to achieve, in his own music, a clarity he did not find in that of others. Thus, rather than being entirely an intrusion on his creative activities, his recreative commitments nourished and refined them.

Mahler's search for the "homeland" for which he yearned in Hamburg in his early thirties, should have been rewarded when he achieved the unimaginable eminence of the directorship of the Vienna State Opera at less than forty. His secret objective was to survive long enough to qualify for a pension and have the ease to apply himself to being something other than an off-season composer. This, however, did not reckon with the possibility of an Alma Schindler entering his life, which, with parenthood, escalated his needs to the new objective of a money-making connection with the Metropolitan in New York.

Ever and always, as artfully conveyed by La Grange, there is the feeling of an imminent involvement with something to which all else has been preliminary, yet another stage of the "voyage." As the grinding pressures for more, for bigger, for better close in on his private as well as public being, the causes first for physical and then for spiritual disintegration become all too graphically apparent.

In the aggregate of all that is contained within this mammoth first volume one can only speculate by what connection, link, or impulse does the son of an American woman and a French aviator who attained a position of prominence in the cabinet of Paul Reynaud become entangled with the offspring of a tavern keeper and his village bride in an obscure Bohemian town. Like so much else associated with La Grange, it can be related to something affiliated with Mahler and Mahler lore. I refer to the memoirs of the quixotic but crucial Alma Mahler, which she called *The Bridge Is Love,* a phrase derived from Thornton Wilder's *The Bridge of San Luis Rey.* The whole quotation is:

> There is a land of the living and a land of the dead
> and the bridge is love, the only survival,
> the only meaning.

Henry-Louis de La Grange has known such a love, built such a bridge.

IRVING KOLODIN

# INTRODUCTION

Since I started work on this biography, many years ago, Mahler's position in the musical world has undergone a radical change. Although he is still a controversial figure, his importance as a creator is no longer challenged. Whereas in the forties he was the idol only of a small group of devotees who usually coupled his name with that of Bruckner, he is now performed more and more frequently all over the world and has acquired a large new group of listeners and admirers. Our epoch having at last broken with the nineteenth century's rigid concept of originality, few critics today dare to call his music derivative or "eclectic." In this respect, as in many others, contemporary composers have helped to rediscover Mahler as a highly original creator and a bold yet disciplined revolutionary who rejected traditions and conventions that he appeared to be respecting more faithfully than his flamboyant contemporary, Richard Strauss.

Much is written and said about Mahler's music, yet little is known about his life and personality beyond the simple facts of his career. Few musicians have inspired so many legends and misunderstandings. This is possibly because Mahler cannot be classed in any definite category. Those who consider him a postromantic, late offspring of the Wagnerian tradition, are infallibly disappointed by the neoclassicism of the *Fourth Symphony*, by his naïve use of folk-song material, and by his essentially diatonic harmony. Those who think of him as prolonging Bruckner's monumental neoclassicism, and who admire his prodigious craftsmanship and supreme mastery of form, must concede that his art is more subjective than objective, and that his aim, like the romantics, is to convey a message by awakening his listener's emotions. And finally, those who take him for a modern, forerunner of the Viennese school, and prophet of the future are disconcerted by the "banality" of his themes and by his fidelity to traditional form and diatonic harmony.

Thus, depending on one's point of view, Mahler is either a romantic, a classicist, or a modern. And yet none of these three words describe him as a whole. Countless attempts have been made to analyze and clarify his glaring contradictions. But, vital as the brilliant essays of Schoenberg, Adorno,

Schnebel, etc., are to the understanding of his music, they cover only part of the subject and express essentially personal views. Little or no effort has been made to examine Mahler's life from a new and dispassionate viewpoint and to restore the truths that have been distorted by biographers and commentators. This had to be attempted before it was too late. I have tried to adopt as impersonal and unprejudiced an attitude as possible, deliberately avoiding preconceived theories and aesthetic commentaries. Throughout this long and often harassing task, I have always felt that the mere exposition of facts should be enough to shed light on the sources of Mahler's art and on his unique and complex personality. I believe that these facts should, in any case, be firmly established before any new attempts are made to analyze or interpret his work.

My aim is thus to provide future researchers and commentators with sound new material on which to work. Mahler's music has long seemed to defy all traditions and conventions; it will still be a long time before it can be judged objectively and be placed, like that of the earlier masters, in the historical context that it did so much to change.

Mahler's glaring paradoxes and contradictions have been pointed out many times, and they are indeed unique in the history of music. He was, for instance, a world-famous virtuoso performer as well as a great composer. He spent most of his life conducting operas, yet he never wrote for the stage. Within his music itself, the contrasts are no less startling: Tragedy/Mockery; Pathos/Irony; Nobility/Vulgarity; Gravity/Humor; Folkloric simplicity/Technical refinement; Romantic, visionary mysticism/Critical, modern Nihilism. So strong are these contrasts that many early critics have considered them as evidence of his creative impotence, whereas today it is obvious that they bring to his music an exceptional richness, a unique depth, and an inimitable flavor. I believe that many apparent inconsistencies can be dispelled thanks to a thorough and detailed knowledge of Mahler's private and professional life, and that this knowledge is essential to the understanding of his music. Why, for instance, did he compose no operas, he who spent more time working in the theater than most operatic composers? Because this familiarity with opera houses made him hyperconscious of the problems and difficulties connected with theatrical productions. Why did he never cease to polish and improve his scores? Because, being a performer himself, he was again hyperconscious of the problems of performance and did not conceive his works as abstract entities. The actual sound was, for him, an essential part of the composition as a whole and required testing. In this respect Mahler was the forerunner of such contemporary composers as Boulez, Stockhausen and Berio, who also conduct their own works and revise them constantly. It is a striking fact about Mahler that he nearly always wrote music when he knew that it would be performed, and inversely wrote little until his authority was sufficient to obtain performances.

Thus Mahler's extraordinary ability as a performer is closely linked to his creative genius, which it undoubtedly influenced. All the information about his own performances of his music had to be placed at the disposal of modern interpreters. I have therefore assembled in an appendix all the available details regarding manuscripts, revisions, different versions, programs, etc. With such an amazingly lucid and intelligent composer, it is, to my mind, a sacrilege to play anything but the final version of the works: Mahler knew better than anyone what his music should sound like, and he never ceased to perfect his scores. Early and unpublished compositions should of course be heard occasionally, but more for their documentary than for their musical value, for Mahler's judgment was never at fault concerning his own music.

I have consequently included all the material that could be of use to conductors, stage directors, music historians, and musicians, as well as to music lovers. I have been particularly careful to include, either in text or footnotes, all the surviving descriptions of Mahler's famous opera productions, and also of his interpretation of classical works, if only because none of them have been preserved in a recording.

If the reconstruction of the events in Mahler's life had been an easier task, if there had not been so many obscure episodes, so many gaps and errors in earlier biographies, if so many letters and manuscripts had not inexplicably vanished, this book would have undoubtedly been shorter, for I would not have been tempted to research ever further in my efforts to overcome the many obstacles. Surprising as it may seem, I have always tried to cover the main events as briefly as possible, while still providing future historians and commentators with a sound basis of facts. Whenever feasible, I have allowed Mahler himself or his contemporaries to speak for themselves. All arid discussions concerning dates, probable source errors or discrepancies have been banned from the text and, when essential, placed in footnotes.

The first volume covers a period of forty years. Only ten remain for the second, but, apart from the fact that it seemed logical to end Volume I as Mahler's bachelor life comes to a close, the disproportion in the material included in the two volumes is more apparent than real. On the one hand, Mahler's childhood and youth required much less space than his mature period, and, on the other, his last years in Vienna, his late symphonies, the great Roller productions, and the stormy New York seasons provide ample matter for a second volume. It will also include a complete chronology of Mahler's life and an alphabetical list of all the works conducted by him. Further details about his family and origins, not included in the first volume, will also be found in the second.

Among those who helped me in my work, I must extend posthumous thanks to Frau Alma Mahler Werfel; thanks also to her daughter, Mrs. Anna Mahler, who never ceased to help and encourage me, to Professor Alfred Rosé, who generously gave me access to his huge collection of manuscripts and letters; to Peter Riethus, without whose daily assistance and tireless efforts over many years this book would certainly not have existed; to

Johanna Harwood and Wendela Schurmann, as well as to Mrs. Rudolf Bunzl, who helped me to revise the late Herbert Weinstock's original translation; to the late Alfred Cortot, who read most of my French manuscript and made many useful suggestions; to Jerry Bruck, for his generous help in clearing up many small mysteries and providing important new material; and to all those who sent me information and documents: Notar Hertz (Hamburg) and Dr. Franz Strauss (Garmisch) in Germany; Professor Erwin Ratz, director of the Internationale Mahler Gesellschaft in Vienna; Mr. Josef Szigeti (Clarens) and Mr. Josef Ritter-Tcherv (Melide, Tessino) in Switzerland; Dr. Rabinovitch (Moscow) in Russia; Mr. Dragotin Cvetko (Ljubljana) in Yugoslavia; Mrs. Friedrich Zuckerkandl (Paris) in France; Mrs. Edward Saher (Bilthoven) in Holland; Madame Roskam-Dupuis (Liège) in Belgium; Mr. Franco Serpa (Rome) in Italy; Mr. Deryck Cooke and Mr. Peter Branscombe (London) in England; Professor Nils-Eric Ringbom (Helsinki) in Finland, and finally to Mr. Ernst Rosé (Washington), Mr. and Mrs. Wolfgang Rosé (New York), Professor Edward Reilly (University of Georgia), Professor Adolf Klarmann (University of Pennsylvania), Mr. James Osborn, Mr. Leeman Perkins, and Mr. Howard Serwer (New Haven) in the United States, and many others.

## SOURCES

The sources from which material for this biography have been drawn are so numerous that it is impossible to mention them all here. A few preliminary remarks may however be of interest regarding the relative importance of the principal books and articles written about Mahler.

Four books are indispensable to anyone interested in Mahler's life and personality: (1) his own letters, published by his wife in 1924, which are of such importance that one can only regret that a larger number of them were not included at that time. It is also a pity that the book has not been translated into English. (2) Natalie Bauer-Lechner's fascinating recollections of Mahler's Hamburg and early Vienna years, written in the form of an extended diary that does great credit to the author's modesty and intelligence. (3) and (4) Alma Mahler's two no less absorbing, though often unreliable, books. The English version of *Gustav Mahler, Memories and Letters,* has been republished recently with a new introduction and footnotes by Donald Mitchell. It is unfortunate that such an erudite Mahler scholar has failed to point out some of the more obvious distortions and errors in this highly subjective book—if only those in the dating of the letters included at the end. As for Alma Mahler's memoirs, published in English under the title *And the Bridge Is Love,* they are greatly abridged and therefore much less interesting than in the German original. The same is unfortunately true of *Gustav Mahler,* mentioned above.

Among the many unpublished letters that I have discovered, the most important are those, sent by Mahler to his family, which are to be found in the collection of Professor Alfred Rosé; the many affectionate or passionate notes, written to Anna von Mildenburg during Mahler's last years in Hamburg, which reveal a previously unknown aspect of his personality; and finally his long and fascinating correspondence with his most famous contemporary and colleague, Richard Strauss. Mahler's letters to Strauss are in the possession of Dr. Franz Strauss, but only part of Strauss's to Mahler have survived in various collections. A few others are reproduced in Alma Mahler's book, but most of the originals vanished in the fire that destroyed her library in Vienna at the end of the last war.

Frau Mahler was fully conscious of her husband's importance as an artist and was careful to preserve most of his letters and manuscripts. Nevertheless she was sometimes guilty of carelessness. There is, for instance, among her papers an empty folder that once contained an important manuscript, the memories of Mahler's closest friend in Hamburg, Arnold Berliner, describing the years they spent together there. This manuscript has disappeared.

Thanks to the kindness of Mrs. Anna Mahler, I discovered, after her mother's death, an important new source of information: Alma's original manuscript of *Gustav Mahler,* which contains many passages she later suppressed and numerous unpublished letters from her husband, as well as long and fascinating excerpts from her private diary that shed a new light on the couple's relationship.

Early biographies of Mahler were distressingly incomplete. Those by Guido Adler and Paul Stefan are probably the most valuable, both biographers having obtained firsthand information from the composer himself. Richard Specht's later book contains little biographical data but much precious material about Mahler's theatrical activity and his compositions. Regarding Bruno Walter's book, *Gustav Mahler,* one can only regret its brevity and its lack of details, and also that it was not written at a time when the author's memories were fresher. One of Mahler's favorite confidants, Walter spent many months, and even years, in close contact with him, yet he has contributed little to our knowledge of Mahler's life and has an incomplete image of his personality. His own memoirs, *Theme and Variations,* are luckily of more value to any Mahler biographer.

J. B. Foerster's *Der Pilger* tells us much concerning Mahler's life in Hamburg; Ludwig Karpath's *Begegnung mit dem Genius* is a real mine of information regarding the intrigues and *"Affären"* at the Budapest and Vienna Operas; Alfred Roller's introduction to *Die Bildnisse von Gustav Mahler* contains a description of Mahler's habits, character, and physical appearance which is unique and invaluable in its precision and accuracy. William Ritter's surrealistic descriptions of Mahler's rehearsals and premieres, from 1901 on, and Paul Decsey's moving reminiscences of conversations with Mahler in the last years of his life conclude the list of the main sources.

Hans Holländer must be given credit for being the first to investigate Mahler's youth, background, and origins in Czechoslovakia, and for publishing several magazine articles that put me on the track of further discoveries. Finally, Donald Mitchell's volume on Mahler's youth contributed some precious information. However, although I myself had access to most of the same sources, I was often led to different conclusions.

I have already published articles on the main problems that I have encountered, mentioning the errors that constantly recur in almost all the previous biographies. These articles are listed in my bibliography. Many difficulties arise from the fact that most of Mahler's family and friends fled Nazi Europe, which has led to the disappearance of many letters and documents. Alma Mahler's Vienna house was hit by bombs near the end of the war, and, according to her at least, all the letters written to Mahler were consequently destroyed. Her own letters to her husband she claimed to have burned, as well as some letters that he wrote to her. Some passages of others she has so heavily crossed out as to make them illegible. Before her death some of the manuscripts in her possession inexplicably vanished. It is to be hoped that they will come to light at a later date. Several of the theaters in which Mahler conducted, such as those in Kassel and Leipzig, were also destroyed by allied bombs. The archives of the Hamburg Opera vanished in the same way, as did the score of Mahler's early incidental music to *Der Trompeter von Säckingen*. The archives of the Budapest Opera house have also been burned, but this time during the 1956 Hungarian Revolution. In certain countries such as the U.S.S.R., scholars have been helpful but somewhat careless. Despite countless efforts and frantic letter writing, I have, for instance, been unable to discover the names of the newspapers responsible for publishing Mahler reviews that I received in photostatic form.

Many of Mahler's letters cannot at present be traced because of an unwritten law observed by most autograph dealers, according to which the names of those who buy documents cannot be revealed, even to dedicated researchers. Fortunately the dealer's old catalogues provided excerpts from many unpublished and unobtainable letters. It is my intention to publish in the near future a large new collection of Mahler's letters, and I hope that all autograph owners will contact me in order to enable me to make it as complete as possible.

Concerning Mahler's music, Paul Bekker's comprehensive study of the symphonies remains unrivaled, though Fritz Egon Pamer's thesis on the lieder was more useful to me because of his thorough study of their literary and musical folklore sources. Theodor W. Adorno's writings initiated a whole new epoch in the understanding of Mahler's music. His highly individual and philosophical perspective makes him a difficult writer to read and more difficult still to translate, but he nevertheless contributed more than anyone else to the present Mahlerian renaissance, particularly among postwar European composers, who now regard him as a prophet and pioneer of today's avant-garde.

*Paris. March 1971*

For those who follow the path of the inner
cult, music is essential for their spiritual
development
Sufi Inayat Khan: *Music*

# INTRODUCTION

## *by Karlheinz Stockhausen*

Like the mosaic of a notorious criminal case-book: nothing is irrelevant, anything can become a clue!

One must quite simply take on trust the contents of this book. Who could
find the time to verify it all?

This is one of the first monuments of the new world-era, in which Mahlers
will become scarcer while biography upon biography will be written.

Mahler is a universal being within whom all threads converge. In his music,
the old and the new, the trite and the never before heard, the naïve and the
labored (with every imaginable degree of shading between each of these extremes) are ranged above, beyond, and alongside each other, as though in an
impassioned effort to compress the whole of life into one single experience.

Mahler has no need of the avant-garde to establish him; like every great
name, Mahler is a myth. Mahler is the music, that which we call his and
which in fact belongs to all of us. Mahler is this book. Mahler was only
transitorily a human being.

Even the private—the most intimate—side henceforth belongs to all who
can visualize such a life within these pages, though they themselves may not
be capable of the same frenzy, the same breadth, the same excesses. Readers
of this book will be magically transformed: into Mahler. They will never again
be the same as they were before Mahler, through La Grange, entered into
them.

It is always stimulating to nose into this book one way or another. Because
it takes such a straight course through historical time, it makes it a pleasure
to jump back and forth between the pages whenever you have a spare moment.
However, you must have the appropriate records handy as you read, in order
to hear exactly what Mahler heard at that moment while composing or con-

ducting, while making alterations to a score, or commenting on his music in a letter.

La Grange has said all that can be said by someone who wants his readers to form their own judgment. He wastes no time on the meaning of the works. Thus he is placing in us the same trust that we, by not questioning the accuracy of all his dates and details, place in him. He is confident that free minds will never cease to discover new implications in the music without suppressing or ignoring anything essential. Just as past, present, and future merge in Mahler's music, so also is the transition from this Side to the Other continuous. Death, the healing place between farewell and springtime, never leaves him: "I come to thee, my trusty place of rest!" (*"Ick komm' zu Dir, traute Ruhestätte!"*)

For those who do not accept the message of the poems Mahler used, his music can be only an acoustic toy. "I am from God and will return unto God!" says the *Second Symphony,* and, toward the end of the "Symphony of a Thousand," Dr. Marianus ("prostrate in prayer"), sings, from Goethe's *Faust:* "Virgin, Mother, Queen, Goddess, rest merciful!"

Above all, we must not make the gross error of dismissing as naïve Mahler's deep and supradenominational religiosity. Even if the words are rejected, the music remains imbued with this religious spirit and will be a welcome oasis in coming ages of ice-cold intellectualism.

This book proves that Mahler will become the center of a new spiral for those subjective beings of the future who, while themselves unable to be such a center, yet refuse to be debased by collectivism. A secret net will thus span the globe, linked by music of this nature.

Although the remarkable esoterism of this biography (which, by its scope and manner, bursts the conventional bonds of time and space like one of Mahler's own great symphonies) would seem to preclude all hope of distribution outside dusty libraries, intuition prompts one to believe that it will reach, move, and thus transform men in a unique and fundamental way. Film after film will be made of Mahler's life; so compellingly written are long sections of this book (Mahler's life was such a unique vortex of metamorphoses from spirit into body and body into spirit) that generations of directors will bring Mahler back to life, while television viewers will be rushed at breakneck speed through La Grange's book by means of a sequence of the weirdest scenes.

As for Mahler's physical existence, as here described, with all its joy and sorrow, its pettiness and grandeur, we must never forget to view it as he did himself when he set the following words to music:

| | |
|---|---|
| *Alles Vergängliche* | *Everything transient* |
| *Ist nur ein Gleichnis;* | *Is but a likeness;* |
| *Das Unzulängliche* | *All things imperfect* |
| *Hier wird's Ereignis.* | *Here become whole.* |

Of that which revealed itself through him and through the talent vested in him, of that which used him as an instrument: his music sings unceasingly of that for which he yearned like all transient and imperfect beings.

Mahler was constantly aware, as this book so vividly demonstrates, that he himself was no more than an instrument. His own personality, exceptionally rich and passionate as it was, he knew to be of no consequence compared with that which took form in the best passages of his music. This was why, at crucial moments, he would brush aside all personal matters, even to the extent of being recklessly insensitive to the feelings of those who loved him, so that he might compose the music from which he could not escape. Even his game of hide-and-seek to avoid this task (his traveling and conducting, his administrating and standing around at receptions) was no more than a cleansing purgatorial fire to prepare his works, which then, as soon as he had nursed them through infancy, went their own separate ways.

The same will be true of La Grange, the author of this biography. He, too, is but an instrument. For fifteen years, he has been collecting all this material, and he will spend the rest of his life completing and improving this book and paving its way into the future:

The atoms disintegrate: the spirit becomes free!

Should a higher being from a distant star wish to investigate the nature of earthlings in a most concentrated moment, he could not afford to bypass Mahler's music. He could doubtless find elsewhere music more specialized in each range of mood: in Gagaku music, Balinese music, Gregorian chant, in the music of Bach, Mozart, or Webern, all of which would probably be "purer" and more serene. But in order to discover that which is most characteristic of the earthling, to understand his entire range of passions, from the most angelic to the most animal, to know everything that binds him to the earth and lets him no more than dream of the other regions of the universe, there would be no richer source of information than Mahler.

This book bears witness to the life and music of a man who combined an unusually large number of human traits in a *single* personality, and who was capable of translating them into the eternal medium of music. Mahler's music is one of the last to stem from the old, undivided, "individual" man, as he was before humanity set about taking men apart and rebuilding them in the weirdest new varieties. Mahler's music will now serve as a signpost for all those no longer certain who they really are.

*Kürten, May 1, 1972*
Translated by Wendela Schurmann and Tom Sutcliffe

# MAHLER

"Three times without a country . . ."

# CHAPTER 1

*Background — Family — Origins*

When Gustav Mahler was five years old, he was asked what he wanted to be when he grew up. His reply was as strange as the question was banal: "A martyr."

As one follows the course of Mahler's tragic destiny, there is often reason to marvel at this presentiment. Without attributing either prescience or divination to his reply, his unhappy, lonely childhood more than justifies such a state of mind. Few people can have been so deeply marked from birth by the stigma of suffering. He was born of ill-matched parents, and his unhappy childhood was overshadowed by the successive deaths of eight of his brothers. As a Central European Jew, he inherited at birth many centuries of persecutions, exiles, and massacres.

Though Mahler was Austrian, the Austro-Hungarian Empire of that time was a huge, insecure, and ill-assorted group composed of Magyars and Poles, Ruthenians and Slovaks, Slovenes, Croats, Rumanians, and Italians—all governed by a small German minority. Ever since the end of the eighteenth century, this divided and unwieldy empire had passed through alternating phases of absolutism and liberalism, sometimes bringing relief and sometimes renewed constraint to the Jewish minorities, who suffered from the consequences of political upheavals and were dependent upon the whims of ministers and the good will of emperors.

Both before and after a period of relative tolerance established by Joseph II at the end of the eighteenth century[1]—during which the Jews received almost complete emancipation—first Maria Theresa and later Metternich pursued violently anti-Semitic policies. The Jews were expelled from Vienna and Prague, and there was even question of expelling them from the whole empire. In 1848, however, a new wave of revolution swept across Europe and once more reforms were considered.

An essential factor in Mahler's career, since his first important posts were in Germany, was the fact that at the same time as the star of the Austrian monarchy grew dim, the end of the nineteenth century brought the growing supremacy, in Central and Northern Europe, of the newly formed Prussia, under Wilhelm I and the dynamic Bismarck. After several fruitless attempts by the two empires to reach some compromise agreement, Austria—defeated at Sadowa in 1866—lost both the territory of Venetia and any chance of taking the initiative in the unification of the German states, which took place in 1871 under the hegemony of Prussia.

From 1848 to 1916, the Austro-Hungarian Empire retained its shaky unity entirely due to its last important Habsburg sovereign, Franz Josef, who has been harshly treated by historians, most of whom agree that the difficulties created by the empire's minorities could have been overcome by a more gifted ruler. In fact Franz Josef was a hard-working prince, devoted to his people. But he had a limited and slow-moving mind, that of a bureaucrat rather than of a ruler. A study of the history of his interminable reign (sixty-eight years) shows him switching from clerical absolutism to militant liberalism, from Germanic centralization to an aristocratic Slav federalization, making his lack of system a system in itself. Many historians consider that the immense, complicated, formalist Austrian bureaucracy and its extreme dispersal of power were the two chief reasons for the fall of the empire.

The reign of Franz Josef was marked by an almost regular alternation between constraint and liberty. In 1851, for example, when the danger of revolution seemed over, he abolished the liberal constitution of 1849 and—through the ministry of Baron Alexander Bach—pursued a reactionary policy. On the other hand, after the Italian defeat in 1859, the *Diplom,* or October Diploma, revived the provincial diets and initiated an era of liberalism and decentralization, and the Compromise (*Ausgleich*) of 1867 gave a real charter to the empire's minorities, especially the Jews. Nonetheless the electoral system remained wholly undemocratic and universal suffrage was not proclaimed until 1907.

Mahler was born on July 7, 1860,[2] in a small rural community, Kalischt (Kaliště), near Iglau (Jihlava), on the border of Bohemia and Moravia. We know little about his forebears, but it is possible to guess what their life was like by studying that of Central European Jews in general.

The institution of ghettos dates from the Middle Ages, when the Jewish influence on the Christian faith was feared. For hundreds of years Jewish families had been living in shamefully restricted areas under deplorable conditions of hygiene and health. Deprived of all civil rights and confined to insalubrious slums, this unhappy people had increased steadily in numbers, but misery and sickness had introduced a physical degeneration that may have been partly responsible for the cardiac weakness of Mahler's parents and the early deaths of eight of his brothers. Even after the abolition of the ghettos, the *Familiengesetz* (an iniquitous law that was not even repealed after 1848) allowed only the eldest son of a Jewish family to marry, thus forcing younger sons either to emigrate or to have their children listed as illegitimate. Another law made the Jews liable for special taxes and forced them to wear a yellow arm band in certain localities.

At the end of the eighteenth century, almost one million Jews were living in Poland in relative peace and quiet when the partition of the country forced them to flee en masse from the cruel yoke of Catherine the Great, while at the same time others were leaving Bucovina and Galicia (Polish provinces that had become Austrian) to settle in less thickly populated regions: Austria itself, Bohemia, and Slovakia. Under Maria Theresa, complete expulsion of the Jewish minorities was considered,[3] but they were finally granted the right to settle in a particularly poor and uninhabited region, the Czecho-Moravian hills in southeastern Bohemia. The installation on Czech territory of Jewish families such as those of Sigmund Freud, Franz Kafka, Stefan Zweig, and Mahler is generally attributed to these migrations.

At the beginning of the nineteenth century, living conditions there were relatively favorable. Certainly, a Jew still had no right to choose either his residence or his profession. If he lived in the country, he could not own land. Nonetheless, the influence of Napoleonic tolerance was spreading, and the era of persecutions seemed over. This progress was halted by Metternich, who again curtailed the Jews' hard-won freedom, forbade them to spend more than one night in any town, and once more made them acutely conscious of their race at a time when most of them had become completely assimilated. Nevertheless, in 1848 the ghettos disappeared, the Jewish taxes were abolished, and religious liberty was finally proclaimed throughout the empire.

In 1849, however, another swing of the pendulum removed almost all these benefits, and it was only in 1867, with the Compromise, that Jews were finally accorded full civil and political rights, in particular those of living where they wished and of entering the hereditary nobility. The laws of 1868 and 1874 guaranteed equality to all religions in the empire and freed public education from the exclusive control of the clergy. From 1879 to 1893, however, influenced by his minister, Count Eduard von Taaffe, Franz Josef once more introduced new restrictions, which luckily did not last long.

These stages leading up to the emancipation of the nineteenth-century Central European Jews are important in that these persecutions, this alternation of oppression and clemency, must have provoked severe internal conflicts in Mahler's forebears. Indeed his own childhood was darkened by them, since the final emancipation did not come until 1867, when he was seven years old. In order to complete the picture of his background, it must be remembered that Czech nationalism, resenting Austrian domination, kept the region in which he was born in a constant state of unrest and revolt. The rich, cultivated Czech bourgeoisie considered itself linked to Austria by dynastic union only, and wanted the ancient rights of the Kingdom of Bohemia re-established. These rights were in fact recognized by Franz Josef in November 1871, in a rescript, but as usual he abolished them again the following year. After 1880, however, the Czech nationalist movement did manage to obtain a guarantee that the Czech and German languages should be used equally in government administration.

Thus Gustav Mahler was born into a troubled and uncertain political atmosphere. Not far from Kalischt is the village of Polna, where, as late as the eighteenth century, a Jew was accused of "ritual murder" of a Christian child, which gives a good idea of the mental state of the inhabitants of this region. The American critic Paul Rosenfeld, whose family no doubt originally came from there, has given a striking though somewhat subjective description of the state of mind of the Central European Jew. In an article on Mahler, he asserts that to be born into such conditions was ". . . a circumstance full of baleful encouragement to those who had been hurt, to button tighter and hug ever closer to themselves the ancient gray overcoat of fear. The quick was menaced by the sharp swords of the repressed but very living hostility of the surrounding population; and to expose it was to invite almost inevitable pain; to have more rocks thrown on the wavering column of confidence in self, satisfaction in self, faith in the greenness of life; to have ever heavier chains hung on the arms when they moved of instinct in the great embracing rhythms. For whatever in the growing lad wanted cause for not projecting his interest, his love into the objective world, and fulfilling himself, there waited (as it waits in every land on every child of Jews) the distrust, the antagonism, the exclusiveness of alien peoples, with its gift of the sentiment of inner unworth, of tribal inferiority. And this fact must have helped arrest the already inhibited spontaneity of the heart, with unresting counsel of niggardliness."[4]

This analysis[5] may be justified as regards certain Jewish children, such as its author, but it is far from applicable to Mahler. Further, it forms part of an article that is nothing but a spiteful denial of Mahler's creative genius, based exclusively on racial considerations. It must thus be considered as a flagrant example of Jewish anti-Semitism and more attention should be paid to the point of view of Stefan Zweig, who, himself from a Moravian Jewish family, writes from personal experience: "There the Jewish communities lived in small country villages on friendly terms with the peasants and the petty bourgeoisie. They were entirely free both of the sense of inferiority and of the smooth pushing impatience of the Galician or Eastern Jews."[6]

Far from showing any complex of inferiority due to his race, the adult Mahler displayed a clear awareness of his personal worth. It is, however, impossible to believe that he did not suffer from the position of those of his race in Moravia. The Jews of that area spoke German and considered themselves as the representatives of German culture in Czechoslovakia, though Russian, Lettish, and Polish blood ran in their veins. It has been said that in the seventeenth century, after the suppression of the Hussite heresy, some Czechs preferred to enter the Jewish community rather than become Catholics, which could explain the origin of the Jewish families bearing Czech names.

Whether this is true or not, the Jews of the area were tolerated by the Czechs and, despite their love of German culture, despised by the pure-blooded German minorities among whom they lived. Those who lived in the country and traded with both the rural Czechs and the German town dwellers, spoke both languages. For one brought up in these conditions it is not difficult to understand why Mahler later on declared: "I am three times without a country: a Bohemian among Austrians, an Austrian among Germans, and a Jew among all the peoples of the world."

Recent investigations in Czechoslovakia seem to indicate that some of Mahler's anecdotes about his forebears were somewhat distorted either by his own memory or by that of those to whom he talked. The name Mahler was common in Bohemia-Moravia.[7]

Its origin is not easy to determine. Two different etymologies have been suggested[8]: Meller, Mahler, Miller may be derived from Müller (Miller) or from Mahler (painter); in fact the derivation almost certainly comes from the Czechoslovakian and Hungarian, whose "a" vowel sound is very short, rather like "o"; thus Mohel (Circumciser) has become not only Mahler (at first spelled Mohler or Moller) but also Moll, Mohl, Molling, etc. This explanation seems the most likely, since several families were registered in the Csaslau district under the name of Mohler or Moller (*Judenfamilien-bücher*. Csaslau). The great frequency with which the name is encountered becomes less surprising when one considers the size of its holders' families. Bernhard Mahler, the composer's father, had at least seven brothers and sisters; he himself had fourteen children, and his brothers had respectively not less than five, seven, and ten. The Mahlers might quickly have peopled whole villages if the infant mortality rate had not been particularly high at the time.

Mahlers were to be found almost everywhere. All these families were probably descended from a common ancestor in the eighteenth century, when, under Josef II, the Jews were forced to take German family names.[9] Mahler's grandfather was called Simon. He was born in 1793,[10] and seems to have known nothing about his antecedents: contrary to well-established practice, none of the official documents, not even the birth certificates of his children, give any information about his forebears.

The earliest documents mentioning Simon Mahler date from 1832, later than the birth of his son Bernhard, the composer's father. The archives of Lipnitz contain documents proving that he was expelled from this town, doubtless because he had been living there without official permission. Four years later he had settled in Kalischt, and the following year there was an exchange of letters regarding his departure from this town. Simon managed to get this second expulsion suspended, though perhaps only temporarily.[11] Unfortunately only the file numbers of this correspondence exist. The documents themselves have disappeared. By then, Simon was married to Maria Bondy, daughter of Abraham Bondy, (who was the manager of a tavern and a distillery in Kalischt after having been in Lipnitz

(Lipnice) a merchant and *"Bestandjude,"* a Jew and a lessee of land and of an inn or tavern), and of Sara Anna Meisl, daughter of Abraham Meisl of Ronow.

In the Catholic parochial register of Kalischt,[12] all Simon Mahler's children are not unsurprisingly listed as illegitimate, the *Familiengesetz* having prevented his marrying since he was not an eldest son. In order to obtain the right to marry, it was necessary to get a permit from the authorities, who allowed only a limited number of Jewish families to be formed in each district (8600 in all Bohemia). When this "quota" was full, and it was always full, a young Jew had to wait for the death of the head of his family before he himself could found a new one and obtain a *Familiantenstelle*. Needless to say, some waited all their lives without obtaining this privilege, for as soon as a place became free, the officials would assign it to whichever applicant offered them most. The Jews were therefore secretly married by their rabbis and did not legitimize their union until they were rich enough to bribe their local official. Thus the marriage of Simon and Maria Mahler was not made legal until February 8, 1850, after the birth of their last child, Sophie, who was also listed as illegitimate.

According to the birth certificate of his son Markus, in 1833 Simon Mahler was already a distiller in Kalischt, and this profession was later exercised by his son Bernhard. He had also taken over the tavern run some years earlier by Abraham Bondy, his father-in-law. This was an important concern, at least by village standards: an official description in 1838[13] states that his holding (No. 52) was one of the largest in Kalischt, second only to the farm. A list (probably incomplete) of his children can be derived from the Catholic parish register of Kalischt[14] (see Appendix 1).

Thus the Mahlers, or at least this branch of their family, lived, like most Jews in the region, by trading in small hamlets and villages, since access to the towns, where their profits would have been far greater, was forbidden. It was doubtless for this reason that Abraham Bondy, and later his son-in-law and his grandson Bernhard, became tavernkeepers: from time immemorial, the right to sell liquor and to keep a tavern was one of the few privileges granted to the Jews. They adopted this profession from necessity rather than choice: indeed most of them were teetotalers.

At the time of his daughter Sophie's birth in 1843, Simon Mahler was still a tavernkeeper, but his death certificate, dated July 14, 1865, when he was seventy-two, lists him as a haberdasher. In 1860, Simon and Maria Mahler had left Kalischt for Deutsch-Brod, a small town about fifteen miles away, where they had bought a haberdashery and a house with a garden.[15] There Simon died in 1865; and his wife Maria probably died there also, though her death certificate has not been found.

Mahler described his grandmother as a woman gifted with great virility. He told an anecdote about her that sounds more legendary than factual. She was, he said, a peddler until the age of eighty, going from door to door with a basket on her back. It is hard to believe, however, that Bernhard

Mahler—who, at the time of his father's death in 1865, was settled in Iglau and already living quite comfortably—would have allowed his widowed mother to do such tiring work at her advanced age. It may well have been earlier, while her husband was still alive, that this first Maria Mahler[16] augmented the family income by selling from door to door. This would also explain why her husband, at the age of sixty-five, had followed her advice and exchanged his tavern in Kalischt for a small mercer's shop, less lucrative but doubtless also much less tiring.

Mahler gives us only one anecdote about the first Maria Mahler. One day, when she was already very old, it seems she broke one of the laws regulating her profession, and was condemned by the local tribunal to pay a fine. Not at all abashed, she left for Vienna immediately, and there solicited an audience with the emperor. According to Mahler, the emperor showed himself to be a very democratic sovereign, for he received Maria and canceled the fine. On the basis of this story, most of Mahler's biographers have asserted that his energetic, domineering character was inherited from his grandmother. Her intrepid glance and strong chin have been immortalized in a photograph taken at Iglau.

Maria Mahler's son Bernhard, perhaps born in Kalischt[17] on August 2, 1827, was not less energetic. All his life he strove to better himself socially and intellectually.[18] He began work as a carter, but never abandoned his passion for reading. While driving his cart, he read all sorts of books (including a French grammar), thus winning the nickname of *Kutschbockgelehrter* (literally "cart seat scholar"). This anecdote, which comes from Mahler's family, is confirmed by a *Protokoll* for foreigners in Iglau dated 1858.[19] In it, we learn that in three months Bernhard spent the night at the Czap Hotel in Iglau four times. His profession is noted on these documents as *Branntweinhändler* (liquor dealer) from Kalischt and it is probable that he brought his goods to be sold in a cart.

Family sources inform us that later on he worked in shops and small factories, then he became a tutor while waiting until his savings made it possible for him to acquire a small business. Before he was thirty, he had leased a small *Wirtshaus* at Kalischt.[20]

However modest this business sounds, by the time he was thirty, Bernhard Mahler had already achieved part of his dream. He was a *petit bourgeois;* he was his own master; and he began to think of marrying. His marriage was doubtless a marriage of convenience: it was in line with his decision to climb the social ladder step by step. For a father-in-law, he chose Abraham Hermann, a well-to-do "soap boiler" established in Ledec, some miles from Kalischt. Hermann had at least seven daughters, and for this reason he was probably not too demanding about the financial and social positions of his sons-in-law.[21]

Born of Isaac Hermann (1766–1836) of Sniet and Sara Spitz of Habern, Abraham Hermann married a young widow with the same surname as himself, probably a relation. Theresia Hermann, widow of Joseph Weiner—

a Ledec merchant—was the daughter of Markus Hermann, of Neuzerekwe, and Karoline Netzl. Once again, it was impossible to legalize this union until after the birth of the second daughter, Gustav Mahler's mother: the couple could not obtain permission to marry until December 7, 1837. They had at least seven children (see Appendix 2).

What attracted the exuberant, authoritarian, irascible Bernhard Mahler to the quiet, affectionate, retiring Maria Hermann? Such aberrations are too frequent to be surprising even though it was, as we know, a marriage of convenience. Maria, or Marie, as she was called later on—a lame and probably insignificant-looking girl—was forced by her parents to marry Bernhard though they scarcely knew each other. Though she objected that he was ten years her senior and that she loved someone else, they undoubtedly replied that she "could not hope to make a better match."

The marriage, licensed by the authorities of Csaslau and Humpolec, (the chief towns of the provinces in which were situated Kalischt and Ledec) took place in Ledec in February 1857, after which the couple returned to Kalischt, and moved into that part of the tavern set aside for the manager (to the left of the building). The house was destroyed by fire in 1937, but the walls remained almost intact; reconstructed, it appears today much as it was before the fire.[22] Mahler described this house[23] as a simple cottage without even glass in the windows. According to him, a pond outside the door kept it unhealthily damp. But these details are likely to have been somewhat romanticized by his memory. How could drinks be served to clients in a tavern without glass in the windows? Or did Bernhard and Maria live in some poor cottage during the first year of their marriage and only later move into the tavern?

Marie and Bernhard Mahler were as unlike as fire and water. He was harshness, and she sweetness, personified. Marie was frail and thin and this "aristocratic" delicacy may very well have been the quality that led Bernhard to propose. Ironically known in Kalischt as die Herzogin (the Duchess), she lived a silent, lonely life at her husband's side. Bernhard, also isolated in his pride and reserve, brutalized his wife and sometimes his children. But he was determined to give them the education that he himself had not received.

Kalischt at that time[24] comprised sixty houses and about five hundred inhabitants, including three Jewish families. There was a church, a Lokalisten Wohnung (meeting hall), a schull, a Maierhof (farm), a tavern, connected to a distillery, and a Wirtshaus—the last two kept respectively by Simon and Bernhard Mahler. The old castle had by that time already disappeared. One thing was certain—in so small a village Bernhard would find no way to realize his dreams of grandeur.

Children soon came to enlarge the family. In 1858 the first-born, Isidor, who was killed in an accident the following year. Then came Gustav, the composer, born on July 7, 1860. His new role of parent increased Bernhard's desire to improve his situation, so he could feed and bring up his children well and later give them a standard of living higher than his own. In the autumn of 1860, he obtained a privilege for which he had certainly been maneuvering for some time, a *Heimatschein,* a sort of passport delivered in Humpolec which for four years allowed him to change his domicile as he wished. In order to renew it four years later, he had, on paper, to move from Iglau (Jihlava) while actually, thanks to this, he brought his family there on October 22, 1860. Iglau was located in Moravia, about twenty-two miles from Kalischt (which lies in Bohemia).[25] He immediately took an apartment near the house that he later bought and in which he lived for the rest of his life: 265 (or 4)[26] Pirnitzergasse. In this commercial center, he was able to carry on his trade much more lucratively.

Iglau is an attractive, peaceful little town, set on the slope of a wooded valley. Most of its narrow streets lead into a large market place where the main administrative buildings are to be found. It owes its prosperity to its location, halfway between Vienna and Prague, and to nearby mines. At that time it had about twenty-five thousand inhabitants who lived by trading, by weaving, and by making velvet. An oasis of German culture in Czech-speaking Moravia, it possessed a school, a theater, and even newspapers. It was a musical center of some importance. There, in the sixteenth century, the mastersinger Paul Speratus had founded a school of singing that survived until 1620, combined with that of Nuremberg. The elder Johann Stamitz, Johann Ladislaus Dussek, and Friedrich Smetana had all studied for some time in the school,[27] and the local *Musikverein* was quite active. For the season of 1827, for example, it announced two new important productions: Beethoven's *Second Symphony* and *Fidelio.*[28]

The records of the Iglau police[29] give a detailed account of Bernhard Mahler's business career. They also indirectly tell us about his character—the remarkable tenacity with which he gradually enlarged his business in the face of many obstacles. One day after his arrival in Iglau, on October 23, he applied for a license to run a liquor distillery and premises on which to sell his products. This was refused, on the grounds that there were already many similar businesses in the town. On October 29, however, he was granted the right to open a food store.

Undiscouraged by this first setback, Bernhard tried another approach and announced to the authorities that he was taking over the lease for a tavern already in existence, which belonged to one Katharina Plott. One month later, he was granted a license to make and sell bottled liqueurs, but was again refused the right to sell these products retail. Three months passed, and on June 6, 1861, Bernhard—now listing himself as a food merchant—asked for the annulment of a decree forbidding him to sell bread. But before he obtained official permission he had already added a bakery to his business; in August, a police report mentions the "warnings" and a five-florin fine that had been imposed on him for selling bread without a license. That same year, he requested permission to move his distillery, but once again his request must have followed a *fait accompli,* for he was again fined two florins for having broken the law regarding declarations.

In 1863, Bernhard's financial position suddenly but temporarily worsened. He announced that he was abandoning his distillery and bakery in order not to have to pay the taxes on them. But this move was only for the form, since later on we find the same businesses listed under his own name. From then on, each successive year his enterprises developed and increased. True, he was refused the right to rent a new tavern, that of Antonia Melion, but five years later he arranged to take it over on a sublease, and meanwhile he acquired several others,[30] thus gradually reducing the competition. In 1866, he was fined again, a police inspector having found four prostitutes, who were not allowed on the premises, drinking with his clients. The following year, Bernhard asked for permission to increase his volume of business, since he wished to take in as a partner his brother David,[31] who had come to Iglau two years earlier. Later this request was canceled, but in 1868 Bernhard obtained the right to sell all his products without restriction and without having to keep his various enterprises separate. In 1872, when his business was no doubt doing better than ever, he was granted permission to open another branch in Iglau.[32]

Finally, in 1873, after thirteen years in Iglau, Bernhard Mahler was made a citizen of the town (*Bürgerrecht*). He was so proud that he had the certificate framed and hung it on his living-room wall. From then on, he took his place among the well-to-do bourgeoisie of the town, served on juries, and was a member of several charitable societies. Thanks to his intelligence and perseverance his dream had come true: his children would not go barefoot or be without roots. Like their father, they would at least be *petits bourgeois* in Iglau. Between 1870 and 1875, he opened two new branches of his business and a vinegar factory.

In the light of documents recently discovered in Iglau, it seems clear that Bernhard Mahler's position was more advantageous than has been generally supposed. In 1869 his household included a nurse, a servant, and a cook, as well as the bookkeeper and the waitress employed full time in his tavern. At his death in 1889, his business, including the buildings and complete inventory, was estimated at 28,000 florins, and this estimate was certainly lowered to a minimum in order to reduce the death duties.

Mahler often spoke of his father's irascible and intransigent character. At least one proof of this is to be found in the Iglau police records. On December 7, 1869, Bernhard Mahler was fined ten florins, a considerable sum, for having "spoken insultingly to Schrötter, the police captain of the district."

That the Mahler family did not willingly talk about Bernhard's tavern is not surprising. His son Gustav had reached the height of his fame when people began to ask questions about his background, and an excusable reticence prevented him from indicating the exact nature of his father's business. The Mahlers habitually referred to the distillery as *"die Fabrik,"* but there is no doubt that there were also a liquor store[33] and a tavern from which Bernhard drew a large part of his income. Except at the start, he probably rarely graced the tavern with his presence, leaving it most of the time in the hands of employees. Furthermore, he forbade any consumption of alcohol in his own home, showing that he had little taste for his profession.

Thanks to his unceasing efforts, Bernhard Mahler also realized another of his dreams, by building up a "classical and modern library" which had the place of honor in his living room and was one of the first libraries in Iglau. But all the evidence points to the fact that his children had a difficult childhood, because of a shortage of money and because of their father's rigorous beliefs. The Mahlers had fourteen children in twenty-one years, enough to wear out poor Marie even if she had enjoyed a robust constitution. Of her three daughters and eleven sons[34] most died at an early age:

1. Isidor—born March 22, 1858, died accidentally in Kalischt in 1859.
2. Gustav, the composer—born July 7, 1860, died May 18, 1911.
3. Ernst—born 1861, died April 13, 1875, of pericarditis (*Wassersucht*).[35]
4. Leopoldine—born May 18, 1863, died in Vienna September 27, 1889, of a tumor of the brain or meningitis. Married Ludwig Quittner; two children, Anna and Heinrich.
5. Karl—born August 1864, died in Iglau December 28, 1865. He was not inscribed in the *Jüdische Geburtsmatrikel* in Iglau but figures in the police records.
6. Rudolf—born August 17, 1865, died in Iglau February 21, 1866.
7. Louis or Alois (later Hans Christian), born October 6, 1867, died in 192?. A bookkeeper in Iglau in his father's business, and later in Vienna, he married Bohumila Mergl, born in Willimov on March 18, 1862. He immigrated about 1907 to America, where he represented Heller Candies of Vienna. He undoubtedly died in Chicago, where he had become a baker. This information, given by Anna Mahler, is difficult to verify, police records in Chicago being incomplete.
8. Justine—born December 15, 1868, died in 1938. She married in 1902 the famous violinist Arnold Rosé, by whom she had two children, Alfred and Alma.
9. Arnold—born December 19, 1869, died of scarlet fever about December 14, 1871. News of his death was published in the Iglau paper *Der Vermittler,* and the date is given in the civil records as the fifteenth.
10. Friedrich—born April 23, 1871, died of scarlet fever about December 14, 1871. News of his death was published in the Iglau paper *Der Vermittler.*
11. Alfred—born April 22, 1872, died in Iglau of *"Lungenwassersucht"* (pulmonary congestive heart failure) on May 6, 1873.

12. Otto—born June 18, 1873. He had just begun a career as a theater orchestra conductor when he committed suicide in Vienna on February 6, 1895.

13. Emma—born October 19, 1875. Married in 1898 Eduard Rosé the violoncellist, brother of the violinist; lived in Boston, Vienna, and Weimar; she died on May 15, 1933. Two children, Ernst and Wolfgang.

14. Konrad—born April 17, 1879, died of diphtheria on January 9, 1881.

This long and tragic list sums up the unhappy fate of Marie Mahler, who one after another saw eight of her children die. Her own fragile health could not withstand these trials. She died in 1889, six months after her husband. She had reached the age of fifty-two, living just one year more than her famous son.

"The impressions of the Spiritual
experiences of that period gave my
future life its form and its content . . ."

# CHAPTER 2

## Childhood: In Search of Himself and of the World
### (1860–74)

Upon arrival in Iglau, Bernhard Mahler rented an apartment on the first
floor of No. 265 Pirnitzergasse (later No. 4), quite close to the market
place. Many years later, in 1872, he moved both his family and his business
into the next door house, No. 264 (No. 6), which he bought from the
widow Fischer, née Proksch,[1] the mother of Heinrich Fischer, Musikdirektor
of the Stadtkapelle, to whom Gustav owed his introduction to music. For
some time Bernhard doubtless kept his various businesses on the premises
they occupied when he took over their leases; however, it seems likely that
he rented the shop and warehouses of No. 6 some time before he moved
in with his family.

No. 264 (later No. 6) which was Bernhard's home until his death, is
spacious and comfortable. Then, as now,[2] it consisted of a main section
overlooking the street, which contained the living quarters, from which
two subsidiary buildings ran at right angles, forming an inner courtyard.
In the main section, the ground floor was occupied by the tavern, while the
Mahler family lived on the second floor and the third floor was let. The
distillery and the shops were installed in the two buildings overlooking the
yard, while the servants occupied one of the upper floors. The apartment in
which Mahler spent his childhood consisted of a large kitchen, an entrance
hall, and two living rooms. The "parlor" walls were covered in velvet, as
was usual at that time. A glass case filled with objects of glass and porcelain
had pride of place; there was a glass-fronted bookcase full of books and a
grand piano on which Mahler practiced.

When Gustav was still very young, his parents noticed his attraction
to music: during a journey from Iglau to Ledetsch he ceased howling and
crying only when his parents, taking turns to carry him beside the carriage,

sang to him. Even before he could stand, he would hum tunes he had heard. He soon knew a great many of the local Iglau folk songs by heart[3]; it was a region where everyone was musical by nature; the child heard the sad Slav cradle songs that were to make such an impression on him and later so deeply mark his music. He also heard the gay rounds sung by the peasants and the city dwellers[4] and listened passionately to the stories he was told, especially those of Nanni, the Fischers' nursemaid, who knew a great many; among them was the sinister story, *Das klagende Lied* (The Plaintive Song), upon which he later based his first important work.

Young Mahler was also delighted to discover military music, for there was an infantry regiment based in Iglau and soldiers from the nearby barracks would sing as they marched past his home each day. The children were present when the regimental band rehearsed and got to know their repertoire of light music for the Sunday concerts and funeral marches for sadder occasions. Mahler was also sometimes a spectator at village celebrations, when there was much singing and dancing—in the summer in forest clearings and in the winter in local inns. Iglau also had a village band, made up of three string instruments and a little double bass with a handle and bow which served as an accompaniment.

All those who came in contact with Gustav noticed the speed with which he could reproduce everything he heard; for his third birthday he was given a little accordion, and before long he could play a great many songs and marches faultlessly, as well as the bugle calls from the barracks. He was not yet four when one day a band playing the military music that enchanted his childhood passed the house. Gustav was not even dressed, but he slipped outside in his shirt and followed the soldiers with his accordion. It was only when he reached the market place and began to be frightened at having gone out alone that two neighbors recognized him. The women agreed to take him home, but only after he had played to them, on his accordion, his entire repertoire of military music. Seated on a fruit vendor's counter, he enchanted a large audience of housewives and passers-by. After this, amid applause and laughter, he was taken back to his parents, who were by then considerably worried by his disappearance.

Traces of these two childish musical pleasures are to be found in Mahler's work; in his first lieder, influenced mainly by Bohemian folklore, and also in the symphonies and lieder of his maturity, for which he has drawn so prodigiously and unexpectedly for his effects on the military music that fascinated his youth.[5] Mahler used to tell another amusing story in this respect. One evening on his way back from school he came upon a military band giving a concert. He was so entranced that he stood rooted to the ground, unable to tear himself away even to satisfy a most pressing natural need. Inevitably he soiled his breeches, to the disgust of the rest of the audience.

About the same time, Gustav was sent to spend a few days with his maternal grandparents in Ledec. During a game of hide-and-seek in the attics he came upon an enormous box. Examining it with curiosity, he finally discovered that there was a keyboard under a lid which he could just reach by stretching his arms above his head. Standing in this uncomfortable position, he managed to bang out with his tiny hands a succession of melodies he had heard, so clearly recognizable that the whole family was struck dumb with amazement and pride when they discovered the author of the miniature concert. His grandfather asked him if he would like to take this large toy home with him, and on receiving the little boy's enthusiastic reply sent it next day to Iglau, on an oxcart.[6]

Among the anecdotes about Mahler's childhood, one of the most amusing without a doubt is that in which he relates one of his first visits to the synagogue, where, hidden in his mother's skirts, he interrupted the community's hymn singing with howls, shouting "Be quiet! Be quiet! It's horrible!" Then, when he had finally managed to quiet everyone, he started to sing at the top of his voice one of his favorite songs: *"Eits a binkel Kasi (Hrasi)."*[7]

Lacking more precise details concerning Mahler's first contact with serious music, his first biographers have insisted at length on these and similar anecdotes and on the popular and instinctive origins of his musical vocation. We now know that Mahler was familiar with a certain number of classical masterpieces from childhood, thanks to his friendship with the young Theodor Fischer,[8] his neighbor and contemporary. He visited the house of the Musikdirektor Fischer from an early age, and later received harmony lessons from him. Fischer conducted the parochial choir of Sankt Jacob and the Männergesangverein, who rehearsed every week and gave annual concerts. At that time the Jewish and Christian communities of Iglau lived in peaceful coexistence.[9] Thus Mahler sang in the Sankt Jacob choir and in this way got to know several great masterpieces, such as Beethoven's *Christus am Ölberg,* Haydn's *Die Sieben Worte,* and Rossini's *Stabat Mater.*[10] Mozart's *Requiem,* given on the occasion of the death in 1872 of the burgomaster Peter Ernst Leupold von Löwenthal, particularly impressed the young boy. He sometimes accompanied the choral rehearsals on the piano.

All those who knew the adult Mahler imagined that he had possessed the same quick, lively, restless character as a boy. They were not wrong, since one of his teachers nicknamed him "quicksilver." Even at an early age his tyrannical character showed in his treatment of his brothers, his sisters, and his friends. However, he already had a deep sense of justice; he knew how to be patient, charitable, and sympathetic toward all forms of human misfortune. Far from being always restless, he often daydreamed interminably.

"You cannot imagine to what point I was tormented for that reason," he later told Natalie Bauer-Lechner, his close friend and confidante. "Of course I felt terribly guilty about my brooding and it only occurred to me later how much parents and adults can sin against such a child who evidently

needs this introversion desperately for his spiritual and intellectual development.

"As an amusing example of my silent reveries, I was told that while
I was still a small boy, my parents spent several hours looking in vain
for me while I was in the pigsty. I had wandered in accidentally and,
discovering that I could not open the door, had just stayed there, God
knows for how long, without uttering a word or a cry until someone who
had come to look for me passed nearby. When I heard them call 'Gustav,
Gustav!' I answered quite happily, 'Here I am.'

"Another time, my father took me for a long walk in the woods around
Iglau and ordered me to sit on a bench until I was called. In the meantime
he forgot about me. But I did not get tired waiting and remained in my
place, without moving and very happy. To everyone's great amazement I
was found in just that way several hours later."[11]

Gustav daydreamed endlessly, not only because he needed to concentrate
and to develop his inner potentialities, but also to escape from unpleasant
reality, his parents' quarrels, and the endless bereavements in the family.
Bernhard was often brutal, and Gustav, like his oversensitive mother, was
sometimes treated with excessive severity. For example, his deplorable habit
of leaving his drawers untidy exasperated his father. Almost every day
the latter upbraided him severely and punished him for his carelessness.
Almost every day Gustav would become lost in his daydreams, forget his
father's orders, and there would be another scene.

However, about the age of five, or maybe even younger, this dreamy
and inattentive child began to reveal his real capacities when he started to
take music lessons.[12] According to Heinrich Fischer, his first teacher was a
double-bass player named Jakob Sladky. Right from the start Gustav showed
exceptional keenness, but in the beginning it was to please his mother, who
sat beside him while he practiced. Soon several other teachers had a hand
in his musical education. A violinist named Johannes Brosch gave him piano
lessons at five kreuzer an hour, either before or after the Kapellmeister
Viktorin of the Iglau Theater.[13] Later Mahler probably studied piano
theory and harmony with Wenzel Pressburg, once a pupil of Sechter and
Anton Bruckner and now a teacher in Iglau.[14] Later Pressburg recalled
the enthusiasm which Mahler brought to his studies and the lessons which
generally took place in the Mahler home, under Bernhard's strict surveillance. Finally, at a later date, Mahler studied harmony under Heinrich
Fischer, leader of the parish choir and the Männergesangverein, the father
of his friend Theodor and professor of singing at the Iglau school.

Gustav progressed so rapidly it was decided that he should play in
public at the age of six. This first appearance is not mentioned in the Iglau
papers, but later Mahler told Natalie Bauer-Lechner that, since his legs were
too short, a device had to be found so that he could use the pedals. It is
possible that Mahler's memory had once more played him false, and that
this was in fact the 1870 concert. That day, too, it had been impossible

to persuade him to bow to the audience. He had run straight to the piano, sat down, and started to play immediately. As soon as the piece was finished he ran off again as fast as his legs could carry him, paying no attention to the applause.

At the same time as these first musical experiences, Mahler discovered the joy of reading, which was to become another of the ruling passions in his life. Once again, his parents worried needlessly: "They did all they could to restrain and deprive me of that nourishment so necessary to my young spirit. Suffering terribly from their constant restraint and prohibitions, my most ardent desire was to read day and night without stopping. How many times I swore to do so when I was grown up!

"In order to find a place where I could indulge in this pleasure, I devised the following scheme: with my treasure of books in my pocket, I climbed onto the roof through the attic window. Suspended between heaven and earth on the steep slope, I presumed myself safe from interruptions and punishments. There I read away blissful hours, until someone spied me from the house opposite to ours. Terrified, they informed my father, who ran up to the attic. For perhaps an hour he stood at the garret window in mortal fear, not daring to call, lest I should fall. Finally, I crawled down and was given a terrible beating. To my great sorrow the window was soon walled up.

"I was just as insatiable, if not more so, in my passion for music a little later on. Every week I came back from the library, where we had taken out a subscription, with a brief case full of symphonies, opera arrangements, and salon pieces. All of them filled me with indescribable joy, though I was unable to say which I preferred: at that time I was peculiarly and utterly devoid of judgment. My imagination undoubtedly filled the most junky pieces with all sorts of imaginary beauties, transforming them and perfecting them in my mind.

"One day I asked my teacher which music was more beautiful, that of Beethoven or that of Tausig. He himself had no idea either. As soon as I came home from the library, I played over everything that I had brought, stringing the pieces together one after the other, beginning over again each day of the week so as to get the most out of those marvels. I would not leave the piano, even to eat. One after another my brothers and sisters were sent after me: Emma, Justi, Alois, 'Gustav, you are to come and eat.' In the end my mother came, 'Oh, Gustav, do come!' This did not work either, until finally my father's cane got me to the table. I would scarcely have put down my spoon, before I would rush back to sit before the music until evening. I could not be budged to go to the garden or even for a walk. A pleasure, as you know, so very important to me today. At that time it bored me and I hated it for separating me from the books and scores I was devouring.

"That was the period of the struggle for spiritual absorption which for me continued far beyond into adolescence. My spirit had needed abundant nourishment for its development, and I began to exist and create for myself relatively late. That is natural enough, as one's whole life is fed by what is absorbed and assimilated during those crucial years. Each day I become more conscious of the degree to which the impressions and the spiritual experiences of that period gave to my future life its form and its content."[15]

Several of Mahler's teachers held posts at the Iglau Theater and surely procured tickets at reduced prices for him or invited him to their rehearsals, thus enabling him to discover part of the lyric repertoire. Between 1860 and 1870 the Iglau Theater[16] presented the Offenbach operettas, *Orphée aux enfers, L'Ile de Tulipatan,* the *Savoyards, La Belle Hélène, La Vie parisienne,* and light operas such as Donizetti's *La Fille du régiment* and Flotow's *Martha* and *Alessandro Stradella.* Among the more serious works given there were Meyerbeer's *Robert le diable,* and Lortzing's *Zar und Zimmermann,* which later became one of Mahler's favorite operas, together with Schubert's *Zauberharfe.* After 1870 the little theater's repertoire became more ambitious, and they gave some of the great lyric masterpieces, such as *Der Freischütz, Norma, Il Trovatore, Ernani, Faust,* and even *Don Giovanni* and *Figaro.* In 1875, when Mahler left Iglau for the Vienna Conservatory, his musical knowledge was certainly more extensive than has previously been supposed.

Mahler's teachers quickly realized that he possessed exceptional ability; he was lucky, in that "from the cradle" his vocation was never questioned. In order to pursue it he was not obliged, like Berlioz for example, "to waste a lot of time and effort." In fact, not only was he given the necessary freedom to continue his studies, but he also benefited from considerable sacrifices made on his behalf, at least according to Natalie Bauer-Lechner, to whom Mahler later described his childhood. "Draconian measures were introduced into the Mahler household, with Gustav and his art as the focal point of the entire family. Everyone wished to have some small share in his art. He could not easily overcome his shyness which has remained with him till today. Only after the greatest struggle could he transmit to others what was most personal and sacred to him: music. Those dearest to him, his parents, brothers, and sisters, suffered most from this; they were always hurt since they considered it an insult to be excluded and driven away whenever Gustav played music.

"Between Gustav and Ernst, the brother nearest in age and affection, a charming habit was formed, thanks to which Ernst was 'at his service' all day, fetching things for him, and cleaning his shoes and clothes without a murmur, in return for which Gustav played the piano to him."[17]

About this time Mahler began composing, and little by little his parents managed to persuade him to note down what he composed, in return for a reward. His first composition was a *Polka with Introductory Funeral March* written about the age of six. A strange title, but also a fascinating one to anyone acquainted with Mahler's music, for one of its essential traits is the mixture of gaiety and sadness. His mother had promised him two kronen on condition that he copy out the piece without a single blot. Before starting to work, Gustav recited a prayer. Then, sure that he was protected by the hand of God, he chose an absolutely indelible ink and set to work. He had just reached the last notes when a large blob of ink dropped from his pen and he had to start all over again. "That day," Mahler said when relating the story long afterward, "my faith in God was considerably shaken!"

Some time later it was Bernhard who promised his son a few kronen if he would compose a lied. Gustav chose one of Lessing's poems, and many years later he could still recite it with astonishing accuracy:

### DIE TÜRKEN

Die Türken haben schöne Töchter,
Und diese scharfe Keuschheitswächter;
Wer will, kann mehr als Eine frei'n:
Ich möchte schon ein Türke sein.
Wie wollt' ich mich der Lieb'ergeben!
Wie wollt' ich lieben, ruhig leben,
Und . . . Doch sie trinken keinen Wein:
Nein, nein, ich mag kein Türke sein.[18]

### THE TURKS

How beautiful the Turkish daughters.
Though fierce guards protect their quarters
Who wills can marry one, two, three;
How I should like a Turk to be!
To love I long myself to give,
I long in peace with love to live,
However, wine Turks never drink.
I will not be a Turk, I think!

The choice of this poem hardly prepares us for the somewhat ascetic life of Gustav Mahler.

Later Mahler needed no encouragement and composed more diligently than ever. When he entered the Vienna Conservatory in 1875, he took so much of his own work with him that Hellmesberger (the director) exempted him from the examinations on harmony and counterpoint.[19]

The young Gustav's reputation spread through Iglau, and some parents asked if he would accept their children as pupils. The first of these was aged six or seven, a year younger than Gustav, and throughout the lesson the latter rested his arm on his pupil's shoulder, his open palm next the cheek, in order to be able to slap him as soon as he played a wrong note. If the wrong note was repeated several times, the unfortunate pupil was required to write out one hundred times: "I must play C sharp, and not C." With such radical educational methods it is not surprising that Gustav did not keep this pupil long.

Another was found, however, to brave the wrath of the young teacher, and Gustav was no less severe with him. One day, he came running home to his mother with tears streaming down his face. Astounded, she asked him what had happened. Stamping his feet angrily, and still in tears, Gustav sobbed: "I don't want to give any more lessons to that fool who plays the piano so badly. I won't, I won't, I won't!"[20] Nonetheless the boy remained his pupil for about a year and made progress that satisfied his parents if not his teacher. Gustav behaved toward him with the same tyrannical nature and the same outbursts of enthusiasm that were to characterize his behavior later. He was paid at the modest rate of five kreuzers an hour.

It is significant to note, in view of Mahler's future conception of musical "programs," that from early childhood he would picture in great detail actions to illustrate all the musical works he knew. He would weave whole stories around them, which he would relate to his parents and their friends, after having carefully closed the windows and pulled the curtains in order to create an impressive and mysterious atmosphere. Sometimes he was moved to tears by his own stories. In Beethoven's Trio Variations on *"Ich bin der Schneider Kakadu"* for example, he evoked the whole life of the poor tailor; his poverty, his misfortunes and his sufferings from the cradle to the grave. According to him, the last variation is a parody of a funeral march, informing the listener: "Now the poor beggar is the equal of kings!"[21] The strange conception of a march that is both funereal and caricaturial proves that at the age of eight Gustav Mahler was already Gustav Mahler!

About the same time Mahler unwittingly gave his first lesson in composition. The top floor of the house in the Pirnitzergasse had been taken by a teacher with a seven-year-old daughter named Emma. One evening after dinner she sent her parents' maidservant to ask Gustav how music was composed. Delighted to be of help, Mahler sent back the following advice: Emma should sit down at the piano and play whatever came into her head. After noting the principal melodies she should develop them, improve them, and finally write down the resultant piece of music. The servant carried out her mission faithfully and the next evening came running back again: Emma had composed something but could not transcribe it! Gustav hurried to her rescue and wrote down what Emma had improvised, thus marking both the beginning and the end of her career as a composer. When telling this story later, Mahler would add: "These instructions that I gave at the age of eight are followed by most composers all their lives!"

The only known photograph of Gustav as a child was taken when he was about five or six. He holds a score in his hand.[22] There is a story attached to this photograph. Gustav did not in fact want to be photographed at all, for he was convinced that, before he could appear on the picture, he would have to submit to some strange enchantment in front of the camera, and that afterward he would be forced to remain fixed to the paper forever. The first day he was brought back to the house in tears, unphotographed. But next day a means was found to overcome his resistance: his father was photographed in front of him, and when Gustav saw that he walked away unharmed from the terrifying machine he finally agreed to let himself be photographed as well.[23]

From then on, serious occupations took up more of Mahler's time than childish pursuits, yet Theodor Fischer has described a pale-faced adolescent with piercing eyes and jet black hair, heading a small group of children and organizing their games in the street, in the courtyard, the cellars, and the huge deserted storerooms of the paternal home. The dark attics were particularly suitable for the games of the little group of children, because of their shadowy and mysterious corners, where they could hide, shivering, in a game of "cops and robbers." One day, doubtless in the course of one of these games, Mahler injured his finger badly, and the pain was so great that he yelled for hours. Then suddenly there was complete silence from the direction of his room, soon followed by loud laughter. Wondering if he had gone mad, his family went to investigate and found him deep in a book which his father had just given him to take his mind off the pain. He was laughing helplessly, as he would do all his life, whenever he opened Cervantes' *Don Quixote*.[24]

There is no doubt that Mahler's childhood was overshadowed by his parents' quarrels, and particularly by his mother's suffering, though his filial loyalty, and perhaps also the wish to suppress certain painful memories, prevented him from talking much about this in later years. However, when, at the age of fifty, he went to consult Freud, he told him a most significant incident from his childhood. Once, after his parents had had a particularly violent quarrel, Gustav fled from the house and on the pavement outside met an itinerant musician who was playing the well-known folk song *"Ach, du lieber Augustin"* on a barrel organ.

This incident has far more than psychological importance. Mahler himself considered it to be one of the reasons why, when a moment of deep emotional creation carried him to the heights, a street song would suddenly make itself heard, almost against his will. These intrusions, which so shocked his contemporaries, are now considered as one of the most striking and daring features of his art. It is strange to think that such conscious or unconscious "quotations" sprang from a painful and almost forgotten childhood memory, opened a new chapter in musical history, and were the forerunners of neoclassicism in early-twentieth-century music.

Bernhard Mahler, in addition to possessing a difficult character and a tendency toward senseless brutality, does not seem to have been the most faithful of husbands, since his son watched him paying court to all the servant girls in turn. Such behavior, which was so contrary to the usual puritanism of orthodox Jews, is surprising in a Jew whose religion meant much more to him than his son's biographers have so far led us to believe. Stefan Zweig asserts that the Moravian Jews were "soon emancipated from narrow orthodoxy" and were generally liberal-minded and enthusiastic sup-

porters of the new religion of progress. Yet several documents confirm that
Bernhard was not a freethinker.[25]

In addition to his musical studies, Mahler attended the primary school
in the Brünnergasse and then, at the age of nine in October 1869, went to
the *Gymnasium* or German school in Iglau which was at that time housed
in a building constructed by the Jesuits, behind the church of St. Ignaz.
Though his father already knew he was going to be a musician, he was
nonetheless determined that Gustav should have a normal schooling. At
the end of the first semester a report, dated February 4, 1870, tells us the
result of his first few months work.[26]

Conduct: *Adequate*
Participation: *Satisfactory*

Study Results:
Religion (Mosaic): *Excellent*
Latin: *Satisfactory*
German: *Satisfactory*
Geography: *Adequate*
Mathematics: *Sufficient, quite unsure of himself, shaky*
Natural science: *Adequate, descriptions unsure*
Handwriting: *Satisfactory*
Gymnastics: *Praiseworthy*

Appearance of written work: *Not careful enough*
Number of lessons missed: *Four (excused)*

This report, duly signed by each professor and by the headmaster, is
highly significant. The remarks on conduct and participation indicate a
dreamy and undisciplined child. The only "Excellent" was received for religious teaching and would seem to emphasize Mahler's early interest in
spiritual matters. Any child who did not claim to be an atheist was obliged
to attend religious classes, and it seems that no Jewish child ever received
bad marks for religious studies. Throughout his entire school days he
always received excellent grades for religious studies, while the others were
nearly always only fair. The first term's results for mathematics, natural
science, and geography should not surprise us, since these subjects rarely
interest children who are destined to become artists. Later however, Mahler
became passionately interested in scientific questions and carried on long
conversations with learned friends. The praise Mahler received for gymnastics is proof of his lifelong predilection for sports and physical exercise.
He also discovered at an early age the joys of boating and swimming and
did both enthusiastically with his friend Theodor Fischer.

Daydreaming and lack of attention were not the only reasons for the
low grades Gustav Mahler received in the colleges of Iglau and Prague.
When this "quiet" child became an adolescent, he began to feel within
himself the demons of fanaticism and impatience which later on caused

him to be called a "tyrant" and a "monster." The following anecdote reveals his childish impatience.

One day Gustav was waiting at the door of the Iglau Gymnasium for the distribution of the monthly report cards. The wait seemed endless, for he was eaten up with curiosity to know what his card would say: he felt an urge as if to jump out of his skin. Having withstood this impatience for a long while, he suddenly decided that the time had come for self-control, and addressed his own spirit in the following terms: "Control yourself and drive out this impatient demon! Someday, when this moment will be long past, when you will be an adult, you will often feel as if impatience for some ardently desired event will kill you; then remember this day, and say to yourself: as that moment ended, so the most disagreeable will pass."[27]

Along with his work at school, Mahler's piano studies progressed so rapidly and satisfactorily that, as early as 1870, it was decided that he should play in public for the townfolk. The first trace we have of such an event is a public concert given in Iglau, which the town newspaper, *Der Vermittler,* wrote up in the following terms: "On October 13, 1870, an exceptional concert occurred outside the subscription, during which a nine-year-old child [he was in reality more than ten years old], the son of a Jewish merchant in this town, Mahler by name, was heard at the piano for the first time before a large audience. The future virtuoso's success with his audience was great, and would have been greater still if he had been given an instrument of the same quality as his nice playing. When this artist's former teacher, Herr Kapellmeister Viktorin, hears word of yesterday's success, he may rightly rejoice in his pupil."

Unfortunately the program for this performance is lost, so there is no means of knowing what the young prodigy's repertoire consisted of at this time. Given this brilliant debut, it would have been understandable if Bernhard Mahler had tried to push his son into the role of virtuoso prodigy. Posterity should be grateful to him for having understood the real nature of his son's gifts and for giving him a thorough musical and general education. That same autumn Mahler probably took part in the ceremonies commemorating Schiller's birth which were held in the school on November 10, and in which "some very young pupils played the piano and the violin."

Judging from the Iglau school reports, the level of Gustav's work varied between average and frankly mediocre. It was probably in order to quicken his progress and give him more competition that Bernhard decided, in 1871, that Gustav should continue his studies in the autumn in the Neustädte Gymnasium of Prague. He was to board with a family in the capital, and Bernhard chose that of a very well-to-do leather merchant named Moritz Grünfeld, who was a music lover and the father of eleven children, two of whom—Alfred and Heinrich—later became well-known virtuosos, one as a pianist, the other as a cellist.[28]

Regarding this stay in Prague, some of the details which Mahler later told his wife are hard to believe, but it is nonetheless certain that it was one of his most unpleasant childhood experiences. He complained particularly of hunger and cold, for he was not given much to eat and sometimes the Grünfelds borrowed some of his clothes and his shoes, so that he had to go barefoot. Mahler admitted, however, that he was only half conscious of his surroundings, since, as always, he took refuge in his world of dreams. "I thought it must be quite normal," he explained later to his wife, to justify his passive acceptance of the situation. One day, however, his father heard indirectly about his treatment at the Grünfelds' and went to Prague to see for himself. He took Gustav to a restaurant, so he could eat his fill, and after the meal went back alone to fetch the few things he had left at the Grünfeld house before returning to Iglau; when he returned to fetch his son he found him sitting motionless, in a sort of trance, his eyes staring at some far-off, imaginary world, as once before in the Iglau forest.

Though the Grünfelds' lack of scruples do not seem to have affected Gustav much, one incident that took place during his stay there was to make a considerable impression on him, for thirty years later he still remembered it and related it to his wife. One day he wandered by mistake into a darkened room and surprised Alfred Grünfeld, who was then nineteen, making love to one of the maidservants. Mistaking the young woman's reactions, Gustav hurried to her rescue. Needless to say she showed no gratitude whatever, and the two young people swore the young boy to silence. Many years later Alma Mahler, his wife, states that Mahler never forgave Alfred Grünfeld for causing this awkward scene. What she omits to say is that Mahler never really recovered from this brutal introduction to the facts of life. It is possible that this was one of the causes of the apparent puritanism that Mahler displayed most of his life.

In later years Mahler never alluded to the very second-rate grades he obtained at the Prague Neustädter Gymnasium: there is in existence a report[29] on his progress written after he had been at the college for six months. His participation is classed as "Uneven" and his conduct as "Adequate," which seems to indicate no particular enthusiasm on the part of his teachers. Each of the subjects listed on the report card—Latin, Greek, religion, history, and geography, natural history, and mathematics—is followed by the word "Inadequate." Only his German language studies were "Adequate" and in a class of sixty-four pupils Mahler came sixty-fourth! The following is written in the margin of this lamentable report: "Came from the Iglau college with the following grades": There follows a transcription of a much better report card from the Iglau college (including two "Excellents" for religion and singing).

In the absence of any other information, it is useless to speculate on the reasons for this rapid and radical lowering of the standard of Gustav's work. One thing is certain: he was never what is known as a good student. His absent-mindedness certainly led to negligence, and his independent spirit to a fierce dislike of authority. Like many geniuses, he had to develop according to his own laws and not those imposed from outside. In addition, everything about Prague must have displeased him at that time, starting with the atmosphere and the surroundings in which he lived. Ernestine Grünfeldova, daughter of the youngest of the Grünfeld brothers, defined her father and her uncle's attitude toward him as follows: "The Grünfeld children were real rascals, brimming over with good health: they could make nothing of Gustav, whose terrible shyness only exasperated them."

Heinrich Grünfeld's memoirs throw a rather ironic light on this episode in Mahler's life. Grünfeld starts by describing the environment in which he spent his youth: his father played the accordion; his mother sang, accompanying herself on the guitar, and from the time he was four his brother Alfred received the musical education that his early talent deserved. Soon the two brothers were organizing chamber music séances, to which outside players came, so that the Grünfeld house became one of the musical centers of Prague. "In my parents' house," relates Heinrich, "we often played ensemble music with our friends; among these also was a pale and skinny boy, then boarding with my parents, whom I remember mostly because of his mane of jet-black hair. None of us saw anything particular in him. He was studying music in Prague and was modesty personified. He was called Gustav Mahler."[30]

However, Gustav himself tells us[31] that he did manage to astonish the Grünfelds by playing the most difficult pieces by ear without a mistake. This was an exploit that in later years he was unable to repeat, and it always surprised him that he had once been capable of doing it.

Heinrich Grünfeld makes no allusion to Mahler's sudden departure, which, according to a school report card, took place in March, but it is possible that when he was writing his memoirs fifty years later he had forgotten all about it. His text, however, clearly shows the indifference with which his family treated the "shy" provincial boy whose budding genius passed unnoticed in Prague.

Upon his return to Iglau, Mahler resumed his music lessons and his academic studies, and was once more part of a family torn apart by dissensions and bereavements.

In November 1872, the anniversary of Schiller's birth (November 10, 1759) was celebrated in the brilliantly lit assembly hall of the Iglau Kaiserlich Königliches Obergymnasium, in the presence of eight hundred guests and a garlanded, beribboned bust of the poet. The town Stadtkapelle began by playing three orchestral pieces: Beethoven's overture to *Die Geschöpfe des Prometheus,* a Meyerbeer *Fantaisie,* and a Hummel *Festmarsch.* A spoken "prologue" by a young eighth-grade pupil introduced two piano selections: an eight-handed medley of melodies from *Lucia di Lammermoor* and finally Liszt's Variations on the Wedding March from Mendelssohn's incidental music for *A Midsummer Night's Dream,* played by a young virtuoso "who had already made his name." The Iglau newspaper praised his "admirable technique" and "attractive interpretation" (*Vortrag*). At the end of this performance Gustav Mahler, who was then twelve, received "an interminable and wildly enthusiastic ovation." The evening ended with choral singing and recitations from the works of Schiller.[32]

On April 20, 1873, Gustav again received much applause in the course of a gala evening given at the Iglau Theater in honor of the wedding of the Archduchess Gisela to Prince Leopold of Bavaria. This time Gustav played Thalberg's Fantaisie on Themes from *Norma* during an orchestral concert given by both the Militärkapelle and the Stadtkapelle. The program included the *Kaiserouverture* by Westmeyer and Suppé's *Mein Österreich* (with hunting horn solo). At the end of the evening Heinrich Fischer conducted patriotic choruses and Wagner's *Festmarsch*. Two months later, on May 17, Mahler again played the Thalberg Variations, this time in the salon of the Czap Hotel during a choral concert to commemorate the founding of the Männergesangverein (men's chorus).

Throughout his childhood Mahler's love and affection for his mother never wavered,[33] and if by chance he was momentarily unkind or brusque —for instance, if he caught her listening outside the door when he was playing the piano—he always blamed himself afterward for adding yet another sorrow to all those that filled her life. As for her, she suffered in silence and placed all her hopes in this adored son, in whom she doubtless sensed a force that she could admire blindly. Despite the importance that Mahler attached to family ties—which he later proved by uncomplainingly assuming the heavy responsibility of supporting his brothers and sisters when his parents died—Mahler never spoke of his father with affection. In his youth he no doubt transferred all his capacity for love to his mother and, by a process of identification with her, acquired at an early age a knowledge of human suffering.

In 1874, when Mahler was fourteen, he experienced his first adult sorrow. Of all his brothers and sisters he preferred Ernst, who was his companion in their games and who was always chosen to listen when Mahler played the piano. Theodor Fischer was struck by the almost "maternal" affection that Mahler showed to him and the friendly way he lectured him when he was disobedient. And now this brother, the most intelligent and gifted of his brothers, to whom he had been so close since infancy, died after a long illness. Gustav followed the phases of its progress with terror, and for many months scarcely left the dying boy's bedside. He was always inventing new stories to cheer him up and take his mind off his sufferings. Later he was to say that no other death had ever affected him so deeply.[34]

According to Alma Mahler, Mahler dreamed his way through the places and lands of his childhood, and even in the heart of his family he dreamed away his youthful years. If any one event woke him from this endless dream and plunged him into brutal reality, it was certainly the death of his beloved brother. That day—which was perhaps the last of childhood—was essential for his discovery of the world and of himself. A few months later he left Iglau and took the first step up the difficult ladder that was to lead him to fame.

"... the habitation of the Muses
and ... the land of my desires ..."


# CHAPTER 3

*Mahler in Vienna (I) — His Years at the Conservatory
— Teachers and Fellow Students (1874–76)*


Mahler's first biographers ascribed the discovery of his musical talent entirely to his father. In 1905, however, an important Vienna paper, the *Neues Wiener Journal,* published an article on this subject, written by an elderly man named Gustav Schwarz. No reason for doubting its authenticity exists, since it was accompanied by two letters from Mahler.[1]

In 1874 or 1875, Gustav Schwarz, an administrative manager for the Morawan estates[2] near Iglau, discovered in an attic, among other musical manuscripts, some autographs of unpublished pieces by Sigismund Thalberg. For the task of deciphering the manuscripts, a friend of his named Steiner[3] recommended a young schoolboy who played the piano and could read music perfectly. Through Steiner, Schwarz sent for the young man, and shortly afterwards there arrived in Morawan a small, pale, rather awkward youth, whose unattractive face did not light up until he sat down at the piano. Then all his awkwardness vanished as if by magic, and the adolescent expressed himself on the instrument with an ease and musical maturity quite astounding for his age. After sight reading the music for Schwarz, the young boy played some of his own compositions, in particular extracts from an opera entitled *Ernst von Schwaben,*[4] which greatly impressed his host.

Struck by the boy's gifts, Schwarz immediately advised Gustav Mahler to study music seriously in a large town. Gustav replied that there was nothing he would rather do, but he could not persuade his father to agree. Bernhard Mahler wished his son to complete his college studies and was not willing to let him continue his musical education at the Vienna Conservatory. Mahler hoped that Schwarz could influence his father in this respect.

The following letter from Mahler, published alongside Schwarz's account, is dated August 28, 1875, and is his earliest known letter in existence.

Dear Sir. I want to take advantage of my dear father's letter to you, in order to also thank you for your kind reception and frequent hospitality. I should add that we still have to fight a few battles to get my father to agree to our project. . . . He is now clearly leaning in our direction, but still is not entirely convinced. As in Bürger's *Wilde Jagd*,[5] there are horsemen on both sides of him, pulling in opposite directions. However, I have high hopes that in our case the good horseman will be the one to win.

*Dazu musst du, O Werner, mir verhelfen*[6]

My dear father is afraid that I will either interrupt and neglect my studies or will be corrupted by bad company in Vienna. Even though, I think that he is more favorably inclined, but you must understand that I am all alone in this struggle against the superior strength of "reasonable and sober folk." I therefore ask the honor of your visit on Saturday, September 4, as only you can convince my father. Please give my compliments to Mme Schwarz and to the people at Ronow.

This letter, previously ignored by Mahler's biographers, clearly explains Bernhard Mahler's attitude toward his son's vocation. He wanted Gustav to complete his schooling and hesitated to send him to the capital, where he would be far from his parents' watchful eyes. The fact that, after some hesitation, he finally relented, deserves our admiration, particularly since it entailed a considerable financial effort.

Even though Gustav's exceptional talent had been obvious from an early age, the reader may be surprised that Bernhard Mahler agreed so readily to forgo the possibility of hard-won material comforts, so that his eldest son could follow his musical vocation, when so many other parents might have tried to channel their son's interests in other directions. Yet there was nothing exceptional about Bernhard Mahler's reaction. To understand it, one only has to read Stefan Zweig's memoirs, *The World of Yesterday,* in which he refers to the attitude of even the simplest Jews in this respect:

"It is generally accepted that getting rich is the only and typical goal of the Jew. Nothing could be further from the truth. Riches are to him merely a steppingstone, a means to the true end, and in no sense the real goal. The real determination of the Jew is to rise to a higher cultural plane in the intellectual world. . . .

"Even the wealthiest man will prefer to give his daughter in marriage to the poorest intellectual rather than to a merchant. This elevation of the intellectual to the highest rank is common to all classes; the poorest beggar who drags his pack through wind and rain will try to single out at least one son to study, no matter how great a sacrifice, and it is counted a title of honor for the entire family to have someone in their midst, a professor, a scientist or a musician, who plays a role in the intellectual world, as if through his achievements he ennobled them all."[7]

When Gustav Schwarz used his influence to persuade Bernhard to send his son to the Vienna Conservatory, Bernhard no doubt put up only a token resistance. Schwarz writes that after receiving the letter of August 28, 1875, he visited Mahler's parents, who agreed that Schwarz should take Gustav to Vienna without delay. This is the only strange part of the story, since, after Mahler's death in 1911, several journalists interviewed his former teacher, Julius Epstein, who asserted that Mahler had been brought to him in 1875 by his father, Bernhard Mahler.

According to Schwarz, it was on Saturday, September 4, 1875, when he visited Mahler's parents in Iglau, that the decision was taken to send Gustav to Vienna, where Julius Epstein would be asked to estimate his talent and possible future. But this discrepancy is not enough to invalidate Schwarz's account, for it was published in Vienna while Mahler was director of the Vienna Opera. Furthermore, there is no doubt about the authenticity of the two Mahler letters published by Schwarz. Possibly the aging Epstein made a mistake and confused two visits: a first one when Mahler might have been presented to him by Schwarz, and another made by Bernhard Mahler, anxious to hear from the famous teacher in person that he was convinced of his son's talent.

Two years later, on September 6, 1877, Mahler was to send Schwarz a second letter, in which he said: "When, two years ago, I had the good fortune to meet you, when you received me with such friendliness and helped me perhaps more than I deserved, I never thought that the Neptune who was to smoothe the waves of my destiny with his trident and guide my life's vessel into port would one day have reason to complain of my conduct. . . . Because of your intervention, I later acquired a powerful friend in Vienna,[8] who today still treats me with the greatest good will and sympathy. You were the one who opened for me the doors to the habitation of the Muses and introduced me into the land of my desires. How, you will ask, have I been able to forget for one instant my duty toward you and forgotten to keep you informed of my successes and progress? I cannot understand it myself."

After repeating his excuses and telling Schwarz that Bernhard Mahler was coming to Vienna to look for lodgings for him, Mahler closed by saying: "I can say that I was not mistaken in taking this road, that I satisfy my professors' demands to their utmost satisfaction, and that perhaps, if Providence wills it, you will hear more of me this year." The ceremonious, flowery style of this letter reveals a rather too bookish young man, overfond of figures of speech, but its ending clearly demonstrates that at the age of seventeen Gustav Mahler was already conscious of his capabilities and his mission.

After Mahler's death, Julius Epstein, his old professor, gave a detailed account of their first meeting.[9] He was in Baden, not far from Vienna, when he was told that Bernhard Mahler, a distiller from Iglau, had come to see him with his fifteen-year-old son. "This is my son Gustav, who is determined to be a musician. However, I would prefer to send him to the Handelsakademie[10] and to the university so that later on he could take over my distillery. But my child does not want to hear of it," Bernhard explained somewhat unenthusiastically. Epstein looked at the young man, who did not seem in the least intimidated but gave the impression of being "capable of shaping his own destiny." Epstein thought that his face held unusual character. "Must I decide his future?" he asked, looking at the boy. "That is a very difficult task." And he asked Gustav to play him something.

After a few minutes, Epstein interrupted Gustav and turned to his father. "Herr Mahler, your son is a born musician." Surprised and somewhat disappointed, Bernhard replied: "But Herr Professor, you just said that it was difficult to decide a young man's future, and now you feel able to pass judgment after having heard him play for scarcely five minutes?" "I assure you, Herr Mahler, that I am not as presumptuous as you seem to believe. In this case I cannot possibly be wrong. This young man has *spirit,* but not to take over his father's *spirit* business." Thirty-six years later, in 1911, Epstein still remembered the gratitude in Gustav Mahler's eyes.

In the *Neues Wiener Journal* of May 19, 1911, Epstein published another, slightly different account of this scene, which more closely resembles that given by Gustav Schwarz. Mahler had begun by playing some of his own compositions, which had struck Epstein as "Wagnerian." He then played some classical pieces, and Epstein was amazed by his astounding memory. Schwarz even adds that the celebrated teacher was surprised that he had not been summoned to Vienna by telegram to hear such a prodigy. According to Schwarz, Epstein was more impressed by Mahler's compositions and their Wagnerian character than by his piano playing.

This immediate conquest of one of Vienna's most famous musicians was to prove decisive in young Mahler's career. Epstein had enormous prestige. Thanks to his recommendation, Gustav Mahler (under the number 326) was enrolled on September 10, 1875, as a student at the Vienna Conservatory, where he spent the next three years, though officially still continuing his schooling in Iglau.

The Vienna Conservatory was an offshoot of the *Gesellschaft der Musikfreunde,* or Society of Friends of Music (generally referred to as the Musikverein), one of the oldest and most revered of Viennese institutions. Created in 1812 to provide the city of Vienna with the several musical organizations that it still lacked—a concert society, a music school, and a library—the Musikverein was housed in a pretentious neoclassical structure built in 1870 and situated on the Karlsplatz not far from the opera. The conservatory, founded by Mozart's renowned rival, Antonio Salieri, had been directed since 1851 by Josef Hellmesberger. It occupied one section of the huge building, which also contained several concert halls. The fees for scholars were high, which explains why Mahler was obliged to ask for a reduction the following year. Some scholarships had been established by benefactors of the Musikverein, and Mahler was probably awarded one of them.

Josef Hellmesberger, Sr., who directed the Vienna Conservatory from 1851 to 1893, was a legendary figure in the capital, where he was known simply as Old Hellmesberger, to distinguish him from his two sons, both musicians like himself.[11] Typically Viennese, though over fifty at this time, he tried to look younger by wearing make-up, a grotesque wig, and side whiskers à la Franz Josef. Even at a distance, the old-fashioned cut of his clothes, his top hat, his silver-topped cane, and his jerky walk were quite unmistakable. The same somewhat arch grace was also to be found in his playing, according to both the well-known critic Eduard Hanslick and the violinist Arnold Rosé.[12] Hellmesberger had great success as a violinist and was known for this "honeyed," typically Viennese tone. For a long time he was concertmaster of the opera orchestra, director of the Gesellschafts-Konzerte and the student orchestra, and first violin in the celebrated string quartet that bore his name. One of his chief claims to fame is that his quartet included in its program, from 1850 on, the great quartets of Schubert and Schumann, the last quartets of Beethoven, and finally those of Brahms, who entrusted him with several first performances. According to Karl Flesch, Hellmesberger particularly disliked three things: Jews, nearsighted people, and Jakob Grün, his successor as leader of the Vienna Philharmonic.

Hellmesberger was far from lacking in taste. He had a sure sense of musical value, but his typically light, superficial Viennese nature made him an impersonal and mediocre conductor[13] and sometimes a negligent professor of chamber music. Among other works, he composed *Scène de Ballet,* a long piece in the form of a waltz, which was ideally suited to the charity performances given by Princess Pauline Metternich. This confirmed traditionalist was, needless to say, extremely disturbed by the turbulence of such young students as Hugo Wolf, Hans Rott, and Mahler. The last mentioned was often reprimanded for having "behaved insubordinately," and as for Wolf, he was dismissed outright in March 1877 for breaking one of the rules. Visiting the conservatory one day, the critic Ernst Decsey saw Old Hellmesberger shaking his cane at a wild-looking young man in a high collar who was pursuing him with murder in his eyes. In his panic, Hellmesberger lost both his top hat and the last vestiges of his directorial dignity. His impulsive young pursuer was none other than Hugo Wolf, then a harmony student at the conservatory, where he terrorized his professors.

The authority of the director of the conservatory was backed up by a committee of twelve members, who supervised the teaching and distributed the scholarships. Normally the study of piano lasted for ten years—two years of preparation, three of secondary study, four years of advanced study, and one of virtuoso playing. Thanks to Epstein's recommendation and to his own virtuoso talents, Mahler started in the first year of advanced study. In addition to the piano, which he chose as his "principal subject," he began to study harmony with Robert Fuchs and composition with Franz Krenn.

During Mahler's first two years at the conservatory, his instrumental studies were directed and guided by Epstein, a man of inexhaustible goodness and generosity, whose influence on Mahler's musical development must not be underestimated. In fact, Julius Epstein (1832–1926), editor of Schubert's sonatas and a fervent Mozart lover, was an enlightened musician with taste and discernment well in advance of his time. He was a close friend and great admirer of Brahms, and when the latter arrived in Vienna, Epstein gave a public performance of Brahms's piano quartets, in order to introduce them to the Austrian capital. A born teacher, he trained most of the important musicians of his time and opened Mahler's ears to much music that the young man would otherwise have taken far longer to discover for himself: Mozart, Schubert, and Brahms formed a salutary counterbalance to Mahler's fervent "Wagnerianism."

The great musical esteem and understanding that sprung up between Mahler and Epstein at this time lasted for as long as Mahler lived. Their friendship led Epstein to shut his eyes to many irregularities that others would not have forgiven. For many years he adopted a semipaternal attitude toward the younger man, and, to help him earn a living, he sent him his own son Richard as a pupil.

Like Hellmesberger, Mahler's professor of harmony, Robert Fuchs (1847–1927), also had a nickname, "Serenaden" Fuchs. This referred to the five serenades for strings that he composed, in addition to over a hundred other works. He is considered responsible for making Mahler conscious of the essential problems of musical form. He later declared that his brilliant pupil "was always playing truant," but added that "nothing was impossible for him."[14]

For three years, Mahler's composition teacher was the organist Franz Krenn (1816–1897),[15] an obscure but prolific composer of some twenty-nine masses and many other religious works. Nicknamed "Old Krenn," this dry, taciturn, pedantic, "typical" professor taught harmony, composition, counterpoint, and theory. His composition class was not part of the normal program of studies, but Mahler was admitted to it because of the pieces that he had submitted upon arrival. Mahler's greatest successes were in this field, which is all the more remarkable since he never observed closely the rigorous disciplines of harmony and counterpoint.

Who were Mahler's fellow students in the corridors and on the benches of the conservatory in the autumn of 1875? One of them, Rudolf Krzyzanowski, quickly became his closest friend. A year older than Mahler, he had entered the conservatory in 1872 to study the violin.[16] They attended Krenn's class together, and Mahler was immediately attracted to this gifted and pleasant-looking young man, with whom he had much in common. He often tried to help his career and was for years a close friend both of Krzyzanowski and his brother Heinrich, a writer of modest talent.[17]

In Fuchs's harmony class, Mahler met another musician, much more gifted than Krzyzanowski, and formed a close friendship that lasted for five years. This was Hugo Wolf, future master of the lied, who later became one of the leading figures of the new Austrian school. Mahler also made two other friends, a young Slovene named Anton Krisper, to whom he wrote some of his most important letters, and Hans Rott, son of Carl

Mathias Rott, the well-known Theater an der Wien actor. Rott was strikingly handsome,[18] a remarkable organist and composer, and an extraordinary improviser. Almost immediately Mahler felt a great admiration and
a deep friendship for him.

Mahler may also have met Felix Mottl, a brilliantly gifted young conductor, who later became first *Kapellmeister* at the Munich Theater.[19] At
the age of sixteen, he had founded the Vienna Wagner Society, which
Mahler joined in 1877 together with Krisper and Krzyzanowski. He had
to leave the conservatory when he was twenty, at the end of 1875.
Another contemporary at the conservatory was Franz Schalk, three years
Mahler's junior, who later became one of his two assistants at the Vienna
Opera. These two students doubtless came to know one another through
their common admiration for Bruckner.

Also at the conservatory with Mahler were his two future brothers-in-law,
Arnold and Eduard Rosenblum, who later altered their name to Rosé.
Born in Jassy in northern Rumania, Arnold was three years younger than
Mahler, but in 1875–76 followed more advanced piano and violin classes.
The two certainly met at this time in Fuchs's harmony class. When the
following year Arnold's brother Eduard entered the conservatory, he also
attended one of Epstein's piano classes, though he intended to adopt the
cello as his instrument. When, before leaving the conservatory in 1878,
Mahler gave a public performance of the scherzo of his *Piano Quintet,*
which had just won a first prize for composition, the cellist was Eduard
Rosé—who twenty years later was to marry Mahler's sister Emma.

What were the first impressions of the fifteen-year old provincial boy
when he arrived in the city famous not only throughout the Austro-
Hungarian Empire, but in all of Central Europe? No document survives to
tell us of his wonder or his disappointment. For five years Mahler left
Vienna only for vacations, but he probably profited little from the big city's
joys and the beauty and gaiety of the capital. Entirely absorbed in his
literary and musical studies, he lived in a seclusion interrupted by constant
moves, sometimes due to excessive noise and sometimes to financial difficulties. His daily life was the same as that of many other poor students
from provincial families: he often shared his room either with one of his
fellow students or with his cousin Gustav Frank. The postscript added by
Mahler to a letter Frank sent to an uncle in Ledetsch[20] indicates his chief
concern throughout this period. He proclaims with legitimate pride that he
is "flying with his own wings," and that, except for this month his family
"has no need to send him a penny."

From the time of his arrival in Vienna, Mahler did in fact give piano
lessons to pupils sent to him by Epstein, and these lessons, by increasing
the meager funds sent by his father, enabled him to get by. One undated
letter, written in 1876,[21] petitions the directing committee of the conservatory to grant him the reduction in fees that had been refused the preceding
year. "My Father is unable to support me, and is even less able to pay my

school fees. I myself cannot pay them, as my existence in Vienna is jeopardized by the lack of pupils. My professor, Herr Epstein, has promised to obtain some for me."

At the bottom of this letter, the ever-paternal Epstein wrote: "I permit myself to endorse this request, and I offer a guarantee for half of the tuition fees. Epstein." The last phrase has been interpreted to mean that Epstein was thus offering to pay half of Mahler's fees. It seems more probable that the committee, which this time granted Mahler the requested reduction, simply awarded to Mahler one of the scholarships reserved for the most gifted pupils.

It was very probably during Mahler's second year at the conservatory that for two months he shared a room with Wolf and Krzyzanowski.[22] The three of them got on well together and played their works to one another. Wolf seems to have considered his lieder inferior to those of his two companions.[23] One night Mahler composed a competition piece in this room while the two others slept on benches on the Ring.[24]

Alma Mahler relates that the three friends, and in particular Wolf, had great difficulty in obtaining pupils, and that the end of a month often found them completely penniless. When this happened one of them would announce his departure to one of his pupils—the aim being to obtain immediate payment for lessons. This scheme gave the three friends a few good meals, dearly paid for by the loss of a pupil. Many years later in Vienna, Mahler pointed out to Ludwig Karpath a dairy in which he and Hugo Wolf had bought cheese rinds during those impoverished moments. Another anecdote from this period concerns a package Bernhard Mahler sent to his son at Christmas. It contained a huge green overcoat, selected "to last a long time." Mahler wore it proudly for several days without noticing that it dragged on the ground behind him. He finally realized that the garment made him look ridiculous, and presented it to Krzyzanowski, who was taller than himself.

To judge by this last anecdote, Mahler was still able to escape from his mediocre surroundings by daydreaming. Natalie Bauer-Lechner gives another example of his absent-mindedness while he was at the conservatory. One day Mahler had rehearsed his sonata for piano and violin there. Dissatisfied with the work and the way it had been played, he forgot that it was the middle of the winter and ran off, neglecting to take his coat, his stick, and his hat. Upon reaching the Ring he lost half his manuscript without noticing it. Luckily two of his friends had followed with his clothes, and they gathered up the scattered pages.[25]

The conservatory archives contain no trace of the public performance of a work by Mahler in the student concerts that took place regularly during the school year. Such a performance was, however, planned for 1876 or 1877, according to a joint letter sent by Mahler and Gustav Frank to their uncle in Ledetsch.[26] At the end of December 1875 a quintet in C minor by Krzyzanowski was performed at the conservatory, and the work by

Mahler played by his fellow pupils was doubtless the piano quintet movement with which, in June 1876, he won a first prize for excellence (I +) in composition.[27]

Although Mahler certainly composed pieces for the conservatory, and doubtless for his own pleasure also during his student years, only short fragments have survived to give us an idea of his activity during this period: there is a piano quartet movement from 1876, the opening of a Scherzo for the same ensemble, and fragments of two songs.[28] Mahler himself destroyed all the rest.

The identity of the lost works is difficult to establish, for the information relating to them is sometimes vague and contradictory. Natalie Bauer-Lechner, however, throws considerable light on this subject, thus solving many problems. Mahler told her that *he did not complete a single work* while at the conservatory, having always abandoned them after the first or second movement or, in rare cases, after the third. "It was not only that I was impatient to begin a new piece, but rather that before I finished my work it no longer challenged or interested me, as I had gone beyond it. But who at the time could know whether my trouble was not a lack of ability or of the power to persevere?" Krzyzanowski and Mahler's other conservatory friends had predicted that he would never complete a composition, and Mahler ended his remarks to Natalie by saying how difficult it is to judge a young man while his talent is still maturing.[29] Thus the numerous piano quartets and quintets that all Mahler's biographers mention were never completed. During another conversation with Natalie,[30] Mahler complained that his ideas lacked all originality, and always came to him "from another source." The few fragments that have survived show that he was right on this point and prove once again his astonishing lucidity regarding himself.

The existence of a first symphony is proved by an anecdote related by Natalie Bauer-Lechner, who first met Mahler shortly before he composed it for a competition. Still too poor to pay someone to copy it, Mahler had worked night and day to copy out the instrumental parts himself, and, mainly due to his fatigue, a certain number of mistakes had crept in. At the run-through of the work the day before the competition, Hellmesberger, "who was the sworn enemy of those who were talented but poor,"[31] flew into a black rage and threw the score to the ground, shouting, "Your scores are full of mistakes! Do you think that I am going to conduct a thing like that?" Having made the necessary corrections, Mahler tried to get Hellmesberger at least to play through the piece and allow him to present it for the competition. But Hellmesberger was adamant, and Mahler was forced to compose a piano suite at the last minute. Mahler himself said that this suite was a superficial and hurried work that deserved a prize far less than his other scores.

The fact that no trace of this competition remains throws some doubt on the accuracy of this anecdote, but Natalie Bauer-Lechner and her sister Ellen played in the conservatory orchestra, and their testimony indisputably proves the existence of the symphony. The story is all the more surely true since there are several versions of it. According to Richard Specht,[32] Mahler's fellow-students introduced the mistakes into the orchestral parts to prejudice his work, and what was played at the conservatory—and in Iglau in 1876—was a quintet. Bruckner, on the other hand, usually spoke of a "sonata andante" rather than a quintet, when relating this episode.[33] A sentence in a letter to Mahler's uncle in Ledetsch probably refers to the same work: "They will very probably play one of my works at a conservatory concert, and that means lots of work for me."[34]

In addition to this symphony, the piano quintet, and the quartets,[35] the earliest works of Mahler also included a sonata for piano and violin, played in Iglau in 1876, and mentioned by Natalie in an anecdote: a nocturne for cello also mentioned by her; another symphony, never entirely written out; the piano pieces Mahler played to Epstein and Schwarz: the fragments of the opera *Ernst von Schwaben,* played to Schwarz in 1875; some lieder, of which Alma Mahler possessed two fragments, a suite for piano, and a string quartet, also mentioned by Alma Mahler. But only references made twenty-five years later by Mahler, whose memory was often faulty about details, testify to the existence of the last two works.

Thus Mahler's first year at the conservatory ended brilliantly. In the piano competition of June 23, 1876, he won one of the five first prizes for excellence for his interpretation of the first movement of a Schubert sonata in A minor.[36] The choice of this piece reveals the influence of Epstein, an apostle of Schubert's great works at a time when they were still considered only as flawed masterpieces. That Mahler was particularly fond of the works of this great master is clear from something he said in Natalie's presence in 1901, when he recalled that his greatest and most ardent wish, when he had the pleasure of playing Schubert's works, was to be able to express with as much feeling, and in the same form, everything that he felt stirring inside him.[37] One week later, on July 1, Mahler won another first prize for excellence—this time for composition—with the first movement of a piano quintet.[38]

Crowned with these academic laurels, Mahler returned to Iglau for his vacation. He was at once invited to participate in a concert given on July 31 by the Städtische Musikkapelle, at which he played the Schubert *Fantasy* and his own *Sonata for Violin and Piano,* the latter with a young Iglau violinist, Richard Schraml, who had just graduated from the Vienna conservatory.

Mahler spent the rest of the summer partly in his family's home in Iglau, partly in neighboring Csaslau, Morawan, and Ronow. One passage from the long "literary" letter written to Josef Steiner in 1879 alludes to this summer: "From that gray sea two friendly names appear: Morawan[39] and Ronow! And I see gardens and many good people in them, and a tree into which a name is cut—Pauline. And a young girl with blue eyes leans toward me; smiling she picks a grape off the vine for me. . . . I blush at this

memory. Again I see those eyes which one day made a thief of me—and then
everything disappears again."[40] Of what pilfering had Mahler been guilty?
The letter, written three years after the event, gives us no details but
conjures up a bucolic scene. The incident has no intrinsic value but deserves
retelling because it refers to the first known episode of a vaguely sentimental nature in Mahler's life.

At the end of the summer, Mahler invited Rudolf Krzyzanowski to his
home, to take part in an Iglau charity concert. He took him to Ledetsch to
visit one of his aunts. Frau Freischberger, who, according to the Czech
conductor Josef Stransky,[41] was one of his mother's sisters. According to
him, this tall woman had gray eyes that reflected her innate kindness, and
she was treated with respect in the little town, where it was considered an
honor to be invited to her home. One day the young Stransky was taken
to see her by relations, and she at once told him that her young nephew
Gustav Mahler, who was already the pride of the family, was there with a
friend of his, and that they would soon be back from a walk.

The two young people did in fact soon return, deep in animated conversation. At the tea table Mahler finally noticed the new visitor, ruffled
young Stransky's hair, and demanded his name. He then asked him if he
was the son of the teacher for whom he had written a "Eulogy in memory
of the Empress Maria Anna." Mahler took an enthusiastic part in the
general conversation, but the child noticed that his friend remained gloomy
and silent. Mahler's aunt finally asked Krzyzanowski—for it was he—why
he said nothing, and it was Mahler who replied with a laugh, "You must
take him as he is. He will always be a bulldog."[42]

Mahler had invited Krzyzanowski and two other conservatory pupils,
Eugen Grünberg and August Siebert,[43] both violinists, to take part in the
charity concert he was organizing on September 12, 1876, at the Czap Hotel
in Iglau. The proceeds of this concert were to be used for the purchase
of books and supplies for the Iglau College. The program, published in the
Iglau papers two days before the concert, was as follows:

1. Krzyzanowski: Quartet for Piano, Two Violins, and Viola [sic]
2. Vieuxtemps: First Movement of the Violin Concerto in D minor
   (Siebert, solist)
3. Schubert: Fantasy in C major (Mahler)
4. Mahler: Sonata for Violin and Piano
5. Mahler: Quartet for Piano, Two Violins, and Viola
6. Chopin: Ballade (Mahler)
7. Allard: Concerto for Two Violins and Piano

Far from helping to identify Mahler's youthful works, this program,
published on September 10, complicates matters due to its inaccuracies.
Happily, the criticism that appeared in the *Mährische Grenzbote* a week
later provides some useful details. The program quoted above includes
two "quartets" of unusual instrumentation: piano, two violins, *viola*. But

the criticism published on September 17 speaks clearly of a quintet by Krzyzanowski and another by Mahler, which had "won a first prize for composition at the conservatory." This seems to prove that the pieces played at the concert were quintets and not quartets, as the program states. It also confirms the conservatory archives, which mention that Mahler obtained, on July 1, 1876, a first prize for composition for a piano quintet, and not the 1876 *Quartet in A minor,* as one might have been tempted to believe.

The anonymous critic praises Mahler's composition highly: "It would be difficult to decide which of the two works (Sonata or Quintet) is the better. In both of them one finds impressive richness of invention and adeptness in execution, which mark a composer of genius [*sic*]. The difficult violin part was admirably performed by Herr Siebert from both the technical and the interpretative points of view."

The same critic showed great discernment by considering these works "decidely dramatic"—one of the essential traits in all Mahler's music. Regarding Mahler the pianist, the critic was also generous with praise: "In the Schubert Fantasy we admired his completely original interpretation and conception," in the Chopin Ballade "the excellent playing of this tireless performer, who showed himself worthy of his teacher, Epstein."

Carl Schnürmann, one of Mahler's fellow students at the conservatory, turned the pages for him at this concert and has related how Mahler, having mistakenly begun the Schubert *Fantasy* in the wrong key, transposed the entire piece so as not to have to interrupt it.[44] Was this a real mistake, or was it one of those virtuoso fancies so frequent at the time? We can never know, but the latter explanation seems unlikely in view of the scrupulous respect for the masters which Mahler always showed. In any case, the concert of September 12 was warmly applauded by an audience that the critic of the weekly paper wished had been larger.

That year the conservatory opened on September 20, and Mahler resumed his piano studies with Epstein and his composition classes with Krenn. He dropped the harmony class and put himself down for counterpoint (first year), also with Krenn. Because of the arguments that have been raised concerning this subject, and in view of the importance of counterpoint in Mahler's composition, certain misunderstandings should be cleared up at this point.

The controversy has arisen because of statements made by Mahler's first biographers, who affirmed that he dropped his classes in harmony and counterpoint after having been "exempted" by Hellmesberger. Documents at the conservatory do not entirely confirm this assertion.

In fact, Mahler entered Krenn's counterpoint class at the beginning of his second year, as Robert Hirschfeld stated[45] in a letter of March 15, 1912, addressed to Ludwig Karpath: "Mahler's admirers have always asserted that he skipped his classes in counterpoint and at once entered the composition class. Nevertheless, I have documentary proof that he received a mere third-class grade in counterpoint (that is, a merely passing mark)—

a fact that the final report from the conservatory discreetly does not mention. . . . At the time, Bruckner was teaching counterpoint . . . but without counterpoint it was easier to win a first-class grade in Krenn's composition class."

This insinuating and spiteful letter was written by one of the most violent and unremitting of Mahler's enemies during his final Vienna years. The fact that Hirschfeld, so short a time after Mahler's death, should have sought out documents to contradict statements made by the composer's biographers is enough to make his assertions suspect. The records that he consulted still exist and reveal that Mahler's name is not among Krenn's pupils at the end of the year, despite the fact that he put himself down for the class in September 1876. Hirschfeld's statements are wholly gratuitous concerning his reference to the "third-class grade" obtained by Mahler. As to the conservatory's discretion, it is difficult to imagine a more absurd explanation. Who has ever heard of an institution of this sort discreetly keeping secret the marks obtained by one of its students?

However, when a conservatory student did not obtain an above-average mark at the end of the year, his name did not appear on the register. If Mahler obtained no prize in harmony and counterpoint at a time when his compositions had won prizes twice, this does not necessarily mean that he was weak in these subjects. More probably, his turbulent nature could not accept the severe discipline of his teachers, and, like other geniuses (Wagner for example), he had to acquire by personal experience the science and technique needed for his work.[46] There are too many excellent unknown counterpoint experts, too many who are untalented at the "top of the class" for us to be surprised when a young man of genius refuses to submit to the same disciplines as his less talented fellow students. Later Mahler regretted his neglect of technical studies, saying that it had "done him considerable harm." Yet it would be absurd to accuse the composer of the first movement of Mahler's *Eighth Symphony* of lacking contrapuntal mastery.

"I was a crazy young man who let
himself be blinded by his passions
and obeyed only the impulses of
the moment . . ."

# CHAPTER 4

*Friendship and Admiration—Graduation from the
Conservatory (1876–78)*

At least once during his years at the conservatory the brilliantly gifted
student Mahler was in disciplinary trouble. In a letter written in May
1876[1] he regrets his "hasty decision," which implies that in a moment of
rebellion he had resigned. This letter, no doubt intended for Hellmesberger,
was probably written by Epstein, since the hand is too formed to be
Mahler's.

Epstein used to relate two anecdotes that testify to Mahler's quick wit
during his student days. Mahler arrived at his class one morning with a message from the director: "Herr Professor, Hellmesberger asks you to be good
enough to go to his office after class." Unable to believe his ears, Epstein
made Mahler repeat the sentence, and then indignantly corrected it: ". . .
Herr Director Hellmesberger . . ." After a moment's thought, Mahler replied: "I have often heard you say: "Director Hellmesberger is a genius."
Epstein still did not understand and Mahler continued: "When one speaks of
geniuses, should one say *Herr* Mozart or *Herr* van Beethoven? And if they
have no need of titles, must we really give one to a Hellmesberger?"
This answer may have been implied criticism of the Viennese weakness for
obsequiousness. In any case, it shows that Mahler already possessed an independent character—and greatly disliked the director.

On another occasion, Mahler joined Epstein's nine-o'clock class at eleven.
The kindly professor felt it necessary to remind his pupil somewhat
severely that such unpunctuality was incompatible with school discipline,
and asked for an explanation. Unabashed, Mahler answered that he had
come from the Schillerplatz. "That is not your place [*Platz*]," Epstein
replied. "Your place is the Schülerplatz [student place] here." "An ex-

cellent pun, Herr Professor," Mahler answered calmly, "but you have undoubtedly forgotten that this morning the monument to Schiller's memory was
unveiled." Not offended by this insolence, Epstein shook Mahler's hand, said
he was right, and withheld punishment. It is easy to imagine that Mahler's
other teachers were more severe, and that his passage through the conservatory was sometimes stormy.

We possess two important descriptions of Mahler at the conservatory. One
is by Frau Marie Lorenz,[2] Krzyzanowski's sister-in-law, who knew Mahler
at the time when he lived with Krzyzanowski and Hugo Wolf:

"I knew Mahler from his modest times (when he was a student at the
conservatory) and even at that time he could not bear being put in the shade
in any way. Tyrannical to the verge of heartlessness, stepping on all obstacles in his path, accessible only if one happened to find him in good
humor and at a propitious moment, he could still act obsequiously at times.
Did he have time to devote to Bruckner? If the question of playing a work
was involved! Yes, but for how long? . . ." Frau Lorenz was a close friend
of Bruckner and this friendship greatly influenced her judgments. In giving
this spiteful description, she was probably reproaching Mahler (then a
famous conductor) for devoting so little time to spreading Bruckner's
works,[3] and did not understand that his artistic ambition was far greater than
the egoism that she believed to be his dominant characteristic. Often, throughout his life, Mahler was accused of being tyrannical, ruthless, inconsiderate,
and heartless, but always by people who either knew him only slightly or
did not understand him.

The other description is from the pianist Robert Fischhof, son of Josef
Fischhof, a friend of Wagner and a professor at the Vienna Conservatory.
Robert Fischhof studied with Mahler in Fuchs's and Krenn's classes. "Even
in his youth (he was then 15 or 16), one could form an exact notion of
his basic personality. In that early period, he was always silent and reserved
with his comrades; his deepest thoughts and feelings were obviously
awareness of his own abilities and a quiet contempt for men. His eccentricities as a composer already had elicited explosions of anger from his
professors. His teachers and we, his comrades, had no idea of the number
of enthusiastic disciples and impassioned adversaries who one day were to
argue about his works."

Clearly Mahler was already arousing violent and often hostile reactions.
But certain of these criticisms were extremely unjust. Theodor Fischer, one
of his oldest friends and companions, emphasizes Mahler's lively character
and strong will, even as a child. He adds, however, that he was patient
and generous, and never passed a beggar without giving him something,
even at a time when he himself did not always have enough to eat.

Mahler probably heard a good many concerts during his conservatory
years, but we know little of the works with which he became acquainted
at that time. According to a diary kept by Hugo Wolf, the young conservatory
students could attend rehearsals and buy tickets at reduced prices for con-

certs and performances. In the months of December 1875 and January 1876 alone Wolf attended performances of *Tannhäuser* and *Lohengrin* (conducted by Wagner), as well as *The Flying Dutchman, Don Giovanni, Lucia di Lammermoor, The Huguenots.* He also heard Liszt's oratorio *St. Elisabeth,* a Philharmonic concert, and another given by the Hellmesberger Quartet, Schubert's Quartet in A Minor and Mendelssohn's Octet. Mahler almost certainly heard the latter concert, in the course of which his teacher Epstein played Brahms's Piano Quintet. He certainly attended some Philharmonic concerts, for in a letter written in 1897 he assured Hans Richter of his immense admiration for him, dating from his years at the conservatory, when he had heard Richter conduct the Vienna Philharmonic.

On March 16, 1877, Mahler and Carl Schnürmann[4] attended Liszt's final Vienna concert, which had been organized to raise funds for a monument to Beethoven. The program included the March with Chorus from *The Ruins of Athens* and *"Abscheulicher, wo eilst du hin,"* from *Fidelio,* some *Scottish Songs,* the *Choral Fantasy,* and the "Emperor" Concerto. In 1901 Mahler, when speaking to Natalie, still recalled this memorable occasion. He had forgotten the details of Liszt's performance but remembered how enthusiastic he had been: as always, at that time, he "drank everything in, without thinking, since this seemed natural to him. But if something displeased him, he remembered it vividly and was as shocked as though by some impropriety!"

About the same time, Mahler heard the complete cycle of the Beethoven sonatas, given for the conservatory students by the great pianist Anton Rubinstein. These performances aroused such enthusiasm that sometimes the virtuoso was induced to encore a whole sonata.[5] Thus Mahler was able to compare his interpretation with that of Liszt.[6] This concert confirmed Mahler's conviction that he had not been born to be a pianist. Returning home, he flung down his score of the Beethoven concerto and swore that he would never play another note. The fact remains, however, that during his early years as a conductor Mahler did not entirely abandon the piano but gave several concerts, notably at Laibach. But it was clear that, despite his gifts, he would never be a professional pianist. Epstein said that Mahler worked at the piano regularly, but that his interests and aspirations led him in another direction from then on. He did not attend the piano class after the 1876–77 school year.

Mahler's limited funds certainly prevented him from attending many concerts, but he nevertheless acquired a wide musical culture at this time by reading scores and by attending the rehearsals of the Hellmesberger Quartet and the student orchestra. Also, he certainly saw the operatic performances given by students of the conservatory singing classes. During the period of Mahler's studies these included *Lucia di Lammermoor* and other Donizetti operas, *Fidelio, Faust, l'Africaine,* Lortzing's *Waffenschmied,* and Schubert's *Der häusliche Krieg.*

From that time on, Wagner's art played an essential role in Mahler's life. We have already seen that almost immediately after joining the conservatory he became friendly with Hugo Wolf. In 1877, they both joined the Wagner Verein,[7] whose members were almost all university or conservatory students. It was there that Mahler met, among others, young Guido Adler, five years his senior, and also born in Iglau. Adler, who later became a famous musicologist, was to play a considerable part in Mahler's life and work.[8] The members met in order to play the piano and sing Wagner's operas together, and they followed the sayings and exploits of the Master with all the exultant enthusiasm of youth. Mahler's Wagnerism probably preceded his arrival in Vienna; it is almost certain that he was already familiar with some of the opera scores in Iglau, since Epstein considered Mahler's first piano works Wagnerian, and one early melodic fragment exists that entirely justifies this epithet. Wagner, of course, symbolized modernism, progress, and liberty for the young conservatory students.

Wagner's visits to Vienna during the winter of 1875–76 were undoubtedly events of importance in Mahler's life, especially since at that time the *Wagner Verein* had organized a series of introductory lectures on the *Ring,* followed by enthusiastic discussions in which all the young members took part. The first of Wagner's two visits to Vienna, which lasted from mid-October to mid-December, 1875, made a great stir among the public and in the Vienna papers. Wagner had come to attend the performances of *Tannhäuser* and *Lohengrin,* which Richter was conducting at the opera. Hugo Wolf described these performances enthusiastically in one of his letters. Wolf managed to meet and speak to Wagner several times. Wagner's visits to Vienna were the most important events to mark his early days at the conservatory. To realize this, one only has to read his diary.[9] He dreamed of his beloved Master and one day waited in the hall of his hotel for half an hour in order to open the door of his carriage for him. Then, taking to his heels, he hurried to reach the opera before him and open the door again. The next day, he even managed to enter Wagner's apartment in the Imperial Hotel, hoping to be allowed to play some of his compositions.[10] Wagner dismissed him with some friendly words that filled the young man with emotion. Wagner visited Vienna for the last time in March 1876, to conduct a benefit performance of *Lohengrin* in aid of the opera chorus. The following day, the chorus bade him farewell on the station platform with an excerpt from *Die Meistersinger.* Mahler no doubt participated with equal enthusiasm in the Wagnerian events that winter. But, shyer than Wolf, he did not like to ask for an appointment to meet him. One day he found himself standing behind him in the musicians' cloakroom after a concert. Respect and admiration made his heart beat wildly, but he did not dare to help when he saw the great man fighting to get into his overcoat. All his life he regretted this shyness.[11]

Mahler later told his wife that one day, when he was sharing lodgings with Krzyzanowski and Wolf, the three of them went to the piano to sing the trio of Gunther, Brünnhilde, and Hagen from Act II of *Die Götter-dämmerung.* The incident had tragicomic consequences, for the noise they made was quite unbearable, and their landlady ordered them from the house, refusing to leave the room until they had moved out with their belongings.[12]

The most active Viennese musical circles were divided into two factions —the conservatives, grouped around Brahms; the progressives, around Bruckner. A talented young musician would inevitably be drawn into one camp or the other. Mahler, with his "modern" tendencies, naturally felt the spell of Wagner's art and instinctively turned toward the Bruckner faction. This whole situation was absurd, as neither Brahms nor Bruckner had the character or temperament to lead a party. Brahms himself stated that he was conscious of following a solitary road, far from the crowds. As for the gentle, shy, naïve Bruckner, he was anything but a modern iconoclast. He constructed his symphonic movements in peace and isolation, doomed to failure whenever his works were played: surrounded by his disciples and friends, he lived a quiet and retired life, disturbed only by internal storms. In 1867, and again in 1887–89, he suffered from an obsessional nervous breakdown that forced him to stop working for several months.

The process by which this conformist and old-fashioned musician became the symbol of "progress" is extremely odd. The essential factor was the hostility felt and expressed by the celebrated critic and polemicist Eduard Hanslick toward Wagner. Hanslick never ceased to defend the strict, classic grandeur of Brahms against the Wagnerian "excesses." The relationship between Hanslick and Wagner could provide matter for a whole book; it is one of the most interesting moments in the history of Viennese music. Despite the partisan war that he provoked, Hanslick was a broad-minded and intelligent man, superior in almost every way to his disciples and followers. He was far from being as opposed to Wagner as has generally been supposed. He always preferred the earlier operas, but among the Bayreuth giant's later works he particularly liked *Die Meistersinger,* though he knew quite well that in the original libretto Beckmesser had borne the scarcely disguised name of Hans Lick.

To evoke the violence with which, from 1877 on, the Wagner and Brahms factions in Vienna fought, we need only recall the curious episode of the Putzmacherin letters. In 1864–65, Wagner had sent to Bertha Goldwag, a Viennese milliner, a series of letters ordering artificial roses, pink satin, gay frills, and other decorative items that he considered necessary for creating an atmosphere favorable to inspiration. Needless to say, the discovery of these letters was a windfall for the scandalmongers. They were published in the Vienna *Neue Freie Presse* in 1877, when Wagner was still alive, by a colleague of Hanslick, one Daniel Spitzer, a critic, talented satirist, and long-standing anti-Wagnerian.

How these letters had come into Spitzer's hands was not learned until many years later. They had been taken by the Putzmacherin's husband, Louis Maretschek, who had sold them to an autograph dealer named Kafka.

Kafka had showed them to Brahms, who had not hesitated to read them to several friends before advising Kafka to sell them to Spitzer.[13] This episode clearly shows the hatred aroused on both sides by this stupid "war."

Why did Bruckner finally become the symbol of the Wagnerian party? Doubtless because he admired Wagner's art wholeheartedly and had even introduced some of its characteristic traits[14] into the world of the symphony. Also, undoubtedly, because of Hanslick, who disliked Bruckner even more than Wagner. Thus a factional war sprang up where in reality there were only two great symphonic musicians. The heat of battle was increased by the mutual scorn felt by Brahms and Bruckner on both the artistic and personal levels. Brahms considered that Bruckner had been "invented" solely in order to give a leader to the Wagnerian party after Wagner's death. This personal contempt should not, however, have been enough to explain his active antipathy for Bruckner and his disciples. The gentler, calmer Bruckner could not recognize his rival's greatness, but he expressed his opinions less harshly.[15]

An almost legendary character in Austrian music, Anton Bruckner had already had a long career as organist and teacher at the Abbey of St. Florian, and then in Linz, when he decided, between the ages of thirty-one and thirty-seven, to study his profession again, from scratch, with a well-known Viennese teacher named Simon Sechter, whose teaching methods he later adopted. Shortly afterward, Bruckner moved to Vienna, where in 1867 he was named professor of harmony, composition, and counterpoint at the conservatory, despite the strong opposition of Hanslick, who taught at the university and had sworn to keep Bruckner out. But Bruckner did enter the university in 1875 as a simple lecturer of harmony and counterpoint, for which he received no salary until 1880.

Whatever one may think of Bruckner's music—which, despite its real greatness and its undeniable beauty, demands of the listener a spiritual repose rare west of the Rhine—one must admire the warmhearted man, the teacher, the generous older musician constantly discovering and helping talented younger men, and exercising a beneficial influence on the destinies of Mahler, Hugo Wolf, Rott, and many others.

For a long time Mahler has been counted among Bruckner's pupils. But this direct relationship between them is even more open to discussion than the resemblance, more apparent than profound, that some have tried to read into their works. In order to destroy the "Bruckner-Mahler" myth it is enough to analyze the personalities and styles of the two composers. First, it is necessary to establish the truth regarding an aspect about which the vaguest and most inexact ideas have long been held: that of their personal relationship.

When Mahler entered the university of Vienna on October 1, 1877, he immediately joined Bruckner's harmony class. But later Bruckner's name does not appear on the list of courses that Mahler attended. When, at the end of an academic year, a student wanted to obtain recognition from the authorities for the studies he had completed in a certain field, he had to get the professor in question to sign his study book. Naturally this signature was forthcoming only if the student had followed the course assiduously.

There are two possible explanations for the fact that Bruckner's signature did not appear in Mahler's book. Either Mahler did not ask for it, or it was refused. The first hypothesis seems the more likely. Whatever Bruckner's qualities as a teacher, the childlike simplicity of his nature and his instinctive conformity as an old-fashioned church musician necessarily influenced his teaching methods. It is not surprising that Mahler, one of the liveliest, lucid minds of his time, could not find in such teaching the techniques that he needed and was probably capable of finding for himself by studying the works of the great masters.

Mahler nonetheless liked and respected Bruckner, which was probably why he attended Bruckner's lectures at the university. As he had come to know Bruckner personally under circumstances that we shall see later, and as he had behaved toward him with respect and admiration, it was only elementary courtesy that Mahler, upon entering the university, should attend the old Master's course, which he had failed to do at the conservatory.

The first direct contact between Mahler and Bruckner took place, doubtless thanks to Epstein, in the following way. Bruckner had just revised his *Third Symphony*, intending to conduct its first performance during a Gesellschaft Konzert given by the Vienna Philharmonic Orchestra on December 16, 1877. The few who witnessed this first performance[16] have described the composer-conductor's lack of skill, the public's lack of understanding, and the sabotage of the musicians, who played wrong notes on purpose and added passages of their own. During the finale, the hall gradually emptied, and at the end only seven people remained in the stalls and about twenty-five in the entire hall, mostly young enthusiasts—among them Mahler. The orchestra went out to scattered applause, and poor Bruckner was left to bow from the podium completely alone.

Bruckner was depressed and shaken, not by the lack of success, but by the malevolence of those who had brought it about. His disappointment was, however, alleviated by one thing. None of his works had as yet been published. But the publisher Theodor Rättig, who had attended all the rehearsals and the macabre premiere, was highly enthusiastic about the symphony and decided to issue simultaneously the orchestral score and a piano duet arrangement. Mahler and his friend Krzyzanowski were given the job of preparing the piano arrangement, and later they played it in public, after a conservatory class, in the presence of Josef Schalk and Karl Goldmark. The transcription, published by Bösendorfer and Rättig, has survived.[17] It reveals a scrupulous, almost excessive respect for the orchestral original, often to the detriment of pianistic convenience. The old composer was so delighted that he presented Mahler with the manuscript of the second version of the symphony.[18]

Alma Mahler has related that when Mahler took the transcription of the first movement to Bruckner, the old Master exclaimed: "Now I have no further need for the Schalks!" Josef and Franz Schalk, in fact, made many piano versions of Bruckner's symphonies, but what is surprising about this anecdote is that most of their transcriptions were made after 1877, and that at the time Josef Schalk was only twenty, and his younger brother Franz—later Mahler's assistant at the Vienna Opera—just fourteen.

This anecdote, known to all Mahler's friends, has been distorted over the years. Luckily a passage in Natalie's unpublished manuscript establishes the truth. In fact the hero of this story was not Mahler at all, but Hermann Behn, who told it to Mahler.[19] Behn arrived in Vienna sometime after Mahler, to study composition under Bruckner, and at once suggested correcting or transcribing manuscripts for him. It so happened that the domineering Schalk brothers were beginning to irritate Bruckner. He looked upon Behn as his deliverer and called out triumphantly to his cook: "Leni, Leni, come here! Just think, this gentleman will do all my piano transcriptions in future. We'll never need the Schalks again!"[20]

Bruckner thought highly of the young Mahler. Often after a university class, he would join him at a café and offer him a beer while his young admirer ate bread rolls, unless his pockets were entirely empty. They often went to and from the university together, and Bruckner was in the habit of sending for him to play passages from his works. Later, when Mahler conducted abroad, he always visited Bruckner when he passed through Vienna, and Bruckner never failed to show his esteem by accompanying Mahler from his fourth-floor apartment to the street door, his hat in his hand, which was a typically Austrian form of courtesy.

Mahler enjoyed telling the following story to illustrate Bruckner's teaching methods. The old Master used pieces of cloth to make clear the problem of the resolution of dissonance. Taking a dirty rag from his pocket, he would say: "See, here is a dissonance." Then, showing them a cleaner rag: "See, it has been resolved." And then, holding up a third, immaculate piece of rag, he would proclaim: "This is the tonic." Bruckner's teaching was as traditional as his music was then considered "advanced." He himself realized that there was a certain incompatibility between the two, but his mind did not enable him to co-ordinate his teaching and his work as a composer. Thus he continued to instruct according to Sechter's strictest methods. Only occasionally, as he left the platform, would he wink mischievously at certain chosen students and whisper: "That is the rule. But when I'm at home, I disregard it!" It is not surprising that such methods did not succeed in capturing young Mahler's attention.

Although none of Bruckner's full-time pupils—Ferdinand Löwe, Alfred Orel, Friedrich Eckstein, August Göllerich, Camillo Horn, Franz and Josef Schalk—knew real fame, Bruckner's teaching methods were not without value. He was a solid theoretician and was revered and loved by his disciples. Mahler later wrote to August Göllerich, Bruckner's biographer: "I was never Bruckner's pupil. Everyone thinks that I was because during my years of study in Vienna I was so often with him, and I was always one of his greatest admirers. In fact, I think that at one time my friend Krzyzanowski and I were his only disciples. That was, I think, during the years 1875–81. The letters that he sent me are dated over several different years, and their contents are of little interest. My relationship with him endured up to the completion of his *Seventh Symphony.* I remember to this day that one beautiful morning during a lecture at the university, my friends were amazed to hear him call me from the street so that he could play for me on an old, dusty piano the admirable theme of the Adagio of the *Seventh.*

"Despite the great difference in age between us, Bruckner's invariable happy, juvenile, almost childlike nature made our relationship a true friendship. Due to this I learned little by little to comprehend his life and his ideals. I could not fail to be influenced in my development as a man and as an artist. Thus I think that perhaps I can call myself his pupil with more justice than most other people, and I shall always do so with profound respect and gratitude."[21]

Thus Bruckner and Mahler respected and admired each other, and Bruckner may even have influenced Mahler, but he never really taught him. Up to now no biographer has drawn attention to one essential point that must have determined the personal relationship between the older man and the younger, as well as the basis of their art: that is, their characters. We have seen that Mahler had difficulty in accepting the technical teachings of Fuchs and Krenn. By the time he met Bruckner, he had joined Krenn's counterpoint class. When he began to compose *Das klagende Lied,* he had already acquired the technique he needed. It seems certain that the real reason why he never became one of Bruckner's pupils was that he did not wish to, because his tastes, his beliefs, his intentions, and even his artistic conceptions were all diametrically opposed to those of the Master of St. Florian, despite the "influence" on his own development which he later admitted.[22]

On the other hand, Bruckner told Auer that despite his admiration for Mahler his "Jewishness"[23] worried him. But in fact, Mahler's modern, restless, lucid, inquiring, antitraditional spirit must have worried him still more, as well as the vague realization that he was face to face with a creative temperament completely opposed to his own. Bruckner must nonetheless have followed with interest Mahler's first steps as a conductor. Their meetings were less frequent between 1880 and 1890, though Mahler seems to have played a decisive part in the old Master's decision not to revise his *Third Symphony* in 1884.[24] Later when Mahler conducted Bruckner's *Te Deum*[25] and two of his masses in Hamburg, he informed Bruckner of the fact in a letter in which he once more expressed his admiration.

Except for some visits, faithfully noted down by Bruckner, only one undated postcard from Mahler provides any information about their relationship at this time. The "Kapellmeister Gustav Mahler" writes to his "dear and beloved Master": "I know you have been angry with me for some time, but you misjudge me. I am somewhat buffeted by the waves of life, but I am still on the high seas for the moment. I think of you with all my long-standing friendship and admiration, and one of my aims in life is to contribute to the victory of your superb and masterly art. I hope to be able to prove this to you soon."[26] Later we shall examine the somewhat limited role that Mahler played as a Bruckner interpreter and his attitude toward the older man's naïve, powerful art at various stages in his career.

Bruckner certainly had some artistic and personal influence on Mahler and Krzyzanowski, but much more on one of their friends, Hans Rott, whom tragedy prevented from fulfilling the brilliant career for which he seemed destined at the conservatory. For three years Rott studied the organ under Bruckner, became an excellent improviser, attended Krenn's third composition class with Mahler, and during this time played an essential role in Mahler's life, for they were united by spiritual as well as creative bonds. "We felt ourselves," Mahler later said, "to be two fruits from the same tree, growing from the same earth and breathing the same air. . . . We could have done great things together in our new musical epoch." Mahler always spoke of Rott with affection and admiration and often considered Rott's compositions superior to his own, particularly on one occasion, when he regretted winning a prize in his place. Mahler told his mother of his doubts so movingly that Marie Mahler burst into tears and said, "What injustice! when Rott's work was better than yours!"

Rott's life, like Wolf's and Krisper's, was fated to end tragically. He left the conservatory in 1878 without having won a single award, and accepted a post as organist in a monastery at a starvation wage.[27] Mahler went to see him in his tiny cell, where a supply of sausages hung from the ceiling. Shortly afterward Rott fell victim to a series of disasters. He was driven from the monastery in a particularly humiliating way: the monks, who hated him, accused him of stealing and selling books from their library. With Bruckner's help, he then tried in vain to get another post as organist in Vienna, and finally became choirmaster of the Mulhouse Concordia choral society. Before his innocence was finally proved, Rott went insane and was shut up in an asylum, where he used his manuscripts as toilet paper, saying: "That's what human works are worth!"[28]

According to Mahler, Rott had composed a remarkable symphony at the age of twenty, which should have become the "basis of a new symphonic genre." He always regretted the complete destruction of Rott's works, especially the "Strange Lieder", which Rott had carried in his head instead of writing down. "What music has lost with him cannot be measured," Mahler later said. One detail he recalled that is particularly striking is that Rott, like himself, seems to have devoted himself almost entirely to the lied and the symphony, and this could have been one of the causes of the great artistic sympathy which united the two young men.[29]

Wagner, Bruckner, and Rott—three important figures in Mahler's youth —have led us to anticipate events and somewhat neglect Mahler's actual studies. At the end of his second conservatory year, on June 20, 1877, he received a first piano prize for his playing of Schumann's *Humoreske*.[30] His name does not appear among those of the best piano students, however; no doubt his enthusiasm for the instrument was waning. He left Epstein's class the following autumn.

Mahler won no composition prize in 1877; possibly he did not enter the contest. The following letter, written to Epstein from Iglau, informs us that he had wished to return to Iglau to take his *Matura* (school leaving certificate). "Your 'well-tempered' goodness will forgive me if I modulate after the sweet adagio of my feelings, by way of the dissonances of my wrath, to a savage finale that truly is 'extremely rubato.' I reached Iglau a few measures late for the Concert of my *Matura,* and therefore could not participate in it, but had to postpone it for two months. Nevertheless, I hope to do my vacation work in a manner that will satisfy you." Comparing this undated letter[31] with Mahler's second letter to Gustav Schwarz,[32] we can be certain that it was written in July 1877. In fact, Mahler is not strictly truthful. The Iglau archives and an article published in 1924 in the *Brünner Tagesboten*[33] give a clear picture of the results obtained by him in the different examinations that took place in the middle of May. The first day he was taken ill and had to go home without finishing his mathematics paper. The next day, having recovered, he finished his German paper an hour before the twenty-three other candidates. He dealt less rapidly with the Latin exercises and the translations from Plato and Livy on the following days, but his Latin papers were nonetheless judged satisfactory; so was the mathematics paper that he did again on June 29. Like many musicians he certainly did not lack skill in this subject: in fact the results obtained were so satisfactory that he was exempted from the oral examinations on July 14.

However, the results obtained by Mahler in Greek, German, geography, and physics were sufficiently poor during the oral examinations for him to have to take the examination again in September. He thus had all summer to revise his knowledge.

In September his Greek papers (Homer and Xenophon) were judged "Scarcely adequate" while his Latin translations (Livy and Ovid) were judged "adequate." As for history (the constitution of Servius Tullius, the causes of the French Revolution, and the Tudors), mathematics (logarithms and geometry), physics (resistance of an electric wire, the colors of the spectrum, and communicating vessels), German (eighteenth-century Austrian literature, Goethe's first journey to Italy, and the works of Jean Paul), and religion (Jewish "written and moral law" and "respect and love of man"), they were considered "praiseworthy." Mahler was judged to be ready for the university, where he registered at the end of September.

Since Mahler's preoccupations during the preceding years had been above all musical, the poor results of his examinations should not surprise us. He spent the summer preparing for the second session of the examination, and his success in September is proved by his immediate matriculation to the university. Mahler was always considered a mediocre student at the Iglau college, doubtless because his other interests distracted him from his schoolwork and his inquiring, original mind led him to study certain subjects more fully than others. Not one of the many school reports that have been preserved places him higher than a modest average.

Winter brought certain changes both to Mahler's life and his program of studies. Joining the university meant that he was promoted from the rank of "pupil" to that of "student." Thereafter he gave up Epstein's piano class in order to devote himself entirely to composition and to fairly assiduous study of the history of music, then taught at the conservatory by Adolf Prosnitz.[34] In addition, Mahler, Emil Freund, Rott, Theodor Fischer (a childhood friend from Iglau), and one of his cousins, Gustav Frank,[35] formed a literary club that met weekly at Frank's. During these meetings, the members took turns stating their opinion on some artistic or philosophic question. These speeches were followed by interminable discussions, which often went on late into the night.

The courses chosen by Mahler when he entered the university that autumn reveal his intellectual interests at that time. Ancient literature, Philological studies of Medieval German (*Parzifal* by Wolfram von Eschenbach), history of Greek art, general history (a course crossed out, as was Bruckner's, in Mahler's dossiers), and finally, "practical exercises in the definition and explanation of works of art." It is interesting to note that at this period Mahler was attracted to the plastic arts in addition to subjects such as philology, literature, and history, which interested him all his life. During his youth, he was relatively unmoved by this form of beauty. It was not until the end of his life that, due to the influence of his wife (she came from a family of painters), his eyes were opened onto this new world.

In order to visualize Mahler as he was during the conservatory years, we must take into consideration, besides the two rather spiteful opinions already quoted, another, which we owe to his future admirer and confidante, Natalie Bauer-Lechner, author of a book of memoirs which is of endless interest for every Mahlerian. She met Mahler at the home of a man named Pichler and then heard him play the piano one evening at the house of Richard Kralik,[36] a poet whose sister had been a fellow pupil of Mahler at the conservatory. Natalie admired his "orchestral" handling of the Overture to *Die Meistersinger,* which Wagner's young admirer played enthusiastically for his friends. Nevertheless, Mahler's personality did not at first attract her. He struck her as provincial and uncouth, and it was not until they had a literary conversation about Goethe's *Wilhelm Meister* that she revised her first impression.

Mahler's professors and fellow students at the conservatory looked upon him as "arrogant" and undisciplined. Epstein spoke of his pride (*Übermut*) and his swift changes of mood. Mahler, writing to Epstein from Kassel some years later, alludes to the reproaches that the latter had made to him at that time: "Is it true that I am always as arrogant?" Most of those who knew him then agreed, however, that he was an exceptional person. They admired his lively, agile mind, his quick repartees, and his habit of going straight to the heart of a problem. In the field of music, everyone noticed his remarkable memory and his early maturity both as an interpreter and a composer. According to Alma Mahler, some people even considered him as a kind of "new Schubert."

Surprising though it may seem, Mahler never once conducted at the conservatory. He himself spoke to Natalie of that institution as "the place where one learns everything except the most difficult, that is how to conduct an orchestra, with the result that the novice has to plunge in and then see what happens." For this reason the Vienna Conservatory students were not especially sought after for conducting posts, and most of the first prizes for conducting were "only good for beating time."[37] Thus Mahler's latent and prodigious talent as a conductor was not apparent until he was over twenty and fulfilling his first engagements.

During a public concert given by conservatory pupils on October 20, 1877, Mahler played the first movement of Xavier Scharwenka's *First Concerto,* Opus 32, an entirely new work, which had been premiered in Berlin on April 14, 1875. The choice of this piece shows the skilled instrumental virtuosity that he still possessed.[38] Epstein has asserted, however, that Mahler rarely practiced the piano, adding that for some time his professors had predicted a career other than that of pianist. Toward the end of the year Mahler, with Krzyzanowski's help, arranged Bruckner's *Third Symphony* for a piano duet. That winter, new compositions began to take shape in his head, and his vocation as a composer seemed clear. At the beginning of 1878, he devised from a story by Ludwig Bechstein the text of a dramatic cantata entitled *Das klagende Lied,* to which he first gave a theatrical shape.[39] This "libretto" was completed in its final form on March 18, 1878. In the original autograph score of *Das klagende Lied,* belonging to Alfred Rosé, the text—given in full at the beginning—bears this date. Mahler may have made preliminary sketches from late 1878 on, but the score was completed only two years later. It was to be one of the first, if not *the* first work, that Mahler finished. It is the first complete existent piece that we possess, and is a major work.

On April 25, 1878, Mahler once more enrolled at the university for the summer semester. His courses were much the same as those for the preceding semester, but in addition to the history of the philology of the Middle Ages, he took one on "philosophy of the history of philosophy" (*sic*), one on the history of Germano-Netherland painting, and one on the study of antique sculpture by means of plaster casts. For reasons not known at present, Mahler left the university that autumn and did not return until April 1880. Bruckner's course, noted in Mahler's records, was again crossed out at the end of the year.

On July 2, 1878, Mahler won a first prize for composition with his *Piano Quintet* Scherzo[40] and, at the same time, received his diploma from the Vienna Conservatory.[41] These results were less good than those of 1876. Fräulein von Kralik, the poet's sister, won a special prize for excellence, and, like Mahler and Pichler (doubtless the one at whose home Natalie Bauer-Lechner met Mahler), Krzyzanowski won a first prize. Perhaps the *Quintet* Scherzo contained some of those "modern touches" that aroused the indignation of the judges and prevented them from giving Mahler a first prize for excellence.

A concert of the prize works was given at the conservatory under Hellmesberger's direction on July 11, 1878. After the adagio of a string *Sextet* by Krzyzanowski, Mahler's *Quintet* Scherzo was heard with four string players and the composer at the piano; the cellist was none other than his future brother-in-law, Eduard Rosé.

A short time earlier, Mahler had been unsuccessful in a lieder contest at the conservatory. The two prizes went to Rudolf Krzyzanowski and a student named Ludwig. This new failure seems to prove once more that Mahler's musical idiom more and more frequently outstepped the bounds laid down by the Vienna Conservatory professors.

Twenty years later, when Mahler returned to Vienna as director of the opera, a middle-aged man went up to him in the Café Kremser. "I don't know if you'll remember me," he began. Without a moment's hesitation, Mahler answered, "I know very well who you are. Your name is Ludwig, and you won the first prize in a lieder competition at the conservatory when I myself won nothing. Your lied began like this . . ."[42] Twenty years after his defeat, Mahler could still remember the first notes of a lied that the judges had preferred to his own!

This incident not only is an example of Mahler's prodigious musical memory, but also proves that, far from being indifferent to such failures, the creative force that he felt within him during his years at the conservatory longed for recognition. After some other similar disappointments, he began to realize what insurmountable obstacles faced him as a composer. This painful realization deterred him from embarking on this career until much later, after he had already made his name in a quite different way, as an orchestral conductor.

"May the Devil take this worthless existence."

# CHAPTER 5

*The Intermediate Years — Melancholy, Passion, Literary Flights — Mahler, Socialist and Vegetarian (1878–80)*

At the age of eighteen, Mahler obtained his diploma from the Vienna conservatory and had to face an important turning point in his existence. The year before, he had given up the idea of a career as concert pianist; as for conducting an orchestra, nothing was further from his thoughts. From 1878 to 1880, he was completely taken up by his creative work and forced himself to live on the small allowance sent by his family, supplemented by what he earned from giving lessons.

These intermediate years are the least well known of Mahler's life, since most of his letters from this period remain unpublished and inaccessible. The usual sources of information—the books by Natalie Bauer-Lechner and Alma Mahler—are curiously silent about these two years during which Mahler was vegetarian, socialist, unhappy, nostalgic, and tortured by a hopeless passion, while at the same time conceiving his first great work. Thanks to Hugo Wolf's correspondence and to the few known Mahler letters dating from this period, we can glean a few meager facts about the unsettled and painful life that Mahler led in Vienna from September 1878 to June 1880.

Mahler left the university in the autumn of 1878 and did not return until the spring of 1880. During those two years he spent his vacations in Moravia, with his parents in Iglau, or with his friend Emil Freund in Seelau, which was a three-hour journey away. In Seelau he could enjoy the quiet country life and play the piano for the Freunds. His humor and intelligence won over the entire family, and in particular an eighteen-year-old girl cousin of Emil Freund, with whom Mahler shared a short romantic idyl. But the eighteen-year-old Mahler did not let his feelings run away with him.[1] Conscious of his precarious situation as an unknown and unemployed composer, he was wise enough to act with caution and reserve.

While remaining "warm and friendly" toward the girl, he warned her against "the sorrow that surely would follow her succumbing to an attachment not controlled by reason." Perhaps he sensed in her that lack of balance which, intensified by another disappointment in love, was to drive her to suicide in 1880. Both Mahler's childhood and adolescence were overshadowed by the suicides and mental illnesses that one after the other struck down some of his closest friends.

During his visits to Iglau and Seelau, Mahler undoubtedly went for long walks, wandering for hours over the wooded hills of his native countryside and appreciating the tranquillity of the Moravian landscapes, with the rivers and little lakes, the big farms and extensive forests, scattered with clearings in which, every Sunday, the peasants danced. Sometimes the Bohemian village musicians would make the countryside ring to their wild songs, and echoes of their improvisations can be heard in some of Mahler's music. This open air contact with nature was an inner necessity for him, one of his few pleasures during those difficult, uncertain years.

One of the childhood memories later evoked[2] by Mahler concerned his impressions when he was alone in an Iglau forest and suddenly heard in the distance several harmoniously blended sounds; the singing of thousands of birds, a military band, the peasants' dances. Mahler considered that this memory had a special significance; to him it symbolized the principle of polyphony, with each voice going its own way, while the artist unites and controls the whole. This observation shows Mahler's precise and precocious grasp of counterpoint and reveals his early awakening to artistic sensibility through contact with nature. For a long time Mahler was to draw his inspiration and creative force from these natural sources, which penetrated his work in many different ways.

The *Mährische Grenzbote* tells us of another concert given by Mahler at the Iglau Theater on April 24, 1879. The program again included two of the pieces with which he had won conservatory prizes: the Schumann *Humoreske* and the Schubert *A minor Sonata*, preceded by a *Hungarian Rhapsody* by Liszt. The occasion was a gala concert given at the theater by several local instrumentalists. Though we know little about the external events in Mahler's life during this period, we do have one splendid description of his inner feelings and state of mind at the age of nineteen, thanks to a letter written to his childhood friend Josef Steiner.[3] During the summer of 1879 Mahler took a job with one Moritz Baumgarten, whose country property was in Teteny, Hungary.[4] The following letter was written from Teteny on June 17, 18, and 19, 1879:

"Dear Steiner: Forgive me for having left you so long without an answer, but everything around me is so desolate! Behind me the branches of a wasted and sterile existence are cracking. Much has happened within me since my last letter; I cannot describe it. Only this: I have become a different person. I don't know whether this new person is better, he certainly is not happier. The fires of a supreme zest for living and the most gnawing desire for death alternate in my heart, sometimes in the course of a single hour. I know only one thing: I cannot go on like this! If the hideous coercion of contemporary hypocrisy and deceit have brought me to despise myself, if the unbreakable links that exist between life and art can stir up in my heart only disgust with everything that was sacred to me—art, love, and religion—then there is no solution but self-destruction. I tear violently at the links that bind me to the stale disgusting swamps of my existence, and with the energy of despair I cling to sorrow as my only consolation. Then the sun smiles at me again, gone is the ice from my heart, I again see the blue skies and the swaying flowers, and my contemptuous sneer dissolves in tears of love. And again I have to love this world, with its trumpery, its lightheadedness, its eternal laughter! Ah, how I'd like to see this world all naked, unclothed, unadorned, just as it lay before its Creator! I would approach its Spirit to say: Now, at last, I know you as a liar! You have not deceived me with your hypocrisy, you have not blinded me with your illusions! Behold before you a man strong and unbowed, in spite of your playful gibbering deceits and the terrible strokes of your irony! May you tremble with fear, there where you lie concealed. From the valley of mankind it resounds, toward your solitary, frozen heights. Can you conceive the unspeakable sorrow that through the ages has accumulated here until it has formed mountains? And on their peaks you sit enthroned, and laugh! How then will you reply to all this one day before the Avenger, you who have not allayed the sorrow of a single tormented soul!!!

"June 18 . . .

"I was too exhausted yesterday, too upset to write anymore. A calm moment has followed yesterday's mad agitation. I am like someone who cries tears of relief after prolonged anger. Dear Steiner! You want to know what I do here? A few words will suffice. I eat and drink, wake and sleep, weep and laugh. I have stood high on the mountains, where the Spirit of God breathes; I have walked in the meadows, lulled by the sound of the cowbells. However, I have been unable to flee from my destiny. Doubt pursues me along every road. Nothing makes me really happy and tears accompany my most blissful smile. Meanwhile, I am living here in the Hungarian Pusta with a family that has secured my services for the summer. I am supposed to give piano lessons to the boys and to inspire the family with musical enthusiasm from time to time. I am like a fly in a web—I writhe. Nevertheless, the slave does his duty . . . Toward evening, if I go out into the meadow, I climb the great lime tree that stands there alone, and contemplate the world from its summit. Before my eyes the Danube follows its eternal course and the gleam of the setting sun is caught by its waves. Behind me in the village the bells of evening ring. They are borne to me by a friendly breeze and gently stir the branches of the tree which rock me to sleep like the daughters of the *Erlkönig,* while the flowers and leaves of my beloved lime tree brush against my cheeks! Everything is peaceful. A sacred peace! From a distance only the melancholy call of the frog resounds sadly among the reeds.

"Now the pale figures of my life pass before me like shadows of a long-lost happiness, and the song of longing [*Sehnsucht*] sounds again in my ears. And once more we are wandering together in that familiar countryside, and there we see the organ grinder standing, his hat proffered with his fleshless hands. In the discordant sounds of his instrument I hear *Ernst von Schwaben*'s[5] greetings. He himself seems to appear, trying to embrace me and when I look at him closely, I see it is my poor brother.[6] Veils fall. Sights and sounds grow pale."

Mahler then recalls various people from his childhood: Melion, an assistant professor at the Iglau College; Buxbaum, a professor at the conservatory. He evokes Morawan and Ronow, the Caslau farms, where he had often spent part of his vacations. Finally he recalls a young girl named Pauline: little by little "the clouds become denser, then suddenly, as in a Raphael madonna, an angel's head appears and, below her, Ahasuerus (the Wandering Jew) with all his sufferings. He wants to rise toward it, toward that blissful region of redemption, but the angel takes wing, smiling, with immeasurable grief; he stares after it and then takes up his staff and goes on his way without tears, eternal, immortal!

"O my beloved earth—when, oh when, will you enfold this unhappy and abandoned one? Look, men have cast him away. He flees their cold embraces, their heartlessness—toward you, toward you! Receive this solitary one who knows no rest, oh eternal mother!

"June 19 . . .

"Now I return to you, for the third day, this time to take a cheerful leave. These pages contain the history of my life. A strange destiny sometimes tosses me about on the rough waters of longing, other times it lets me drift happily under the smiling sun. What I most fear is that one day during a storm my boat may strike a reef; my keel has skimmed so many!

"It is six o'clock in the morning. I have already been out in the pasture sitting close to Farkas, the shepherd, so as to listen to the sound of his pipe. Ah! what sadness and still passionate ecstasy was in that folk melody!"[7]

This curious document is likely to surprise anyone not familiar with the style and characteristic tone of German romantic literature. Like many romantic texts, it is a baroque mixture of impressions, ideas, emotions, literary reminiscences, and dramatically evoked personal memories, which, it must be admitted, also have a certain original and attractive charm. It is also an inexhaustible source of wealth for any Mahler biographer, for it shows many essential and different aspects of his psychology and state of mind. Just as *Das klagende Lied* and the *Lieder eines fahrenden Gesellen* reveal the characteristic traits of Mahler's musical style, so this letter illustrates the traits of his personality, the form of his restlessness, and the paths followed by his daydreams.

Obviously such a monologue also reveals the sensitivity of a youth of nineteen, who has just experienced the problems of adolescence, and the pompous, heavy-handed style betrays the influence of the romantic writers on whom Mahler had fed. Fifteen years later he himself was conscious of the excessively "literary" tone of some of his youthful writing: "I remember clearly the time when I tried to cultivate an elegant style and went to a great deal of trouble to write what are known as 'fine letters.' My correspondent was only a pretext, an excuse to express my thoughts . . . One should never assume a pose, nor disguise oneself, inwardly or outwardly . . ."[8] And yet, beneath the overemphasis and excess of imagery lies an unmistakable gift for writing. The graceful, almost overcareful handwriting[9] reveals its author's concern for elegance, and desire for full control over his means of expression, as well as underlining the "literary" nature of the document. To judge by the few erasures and corrections, it seems likely that Mahler first made a rough draft. Later he abandoned this flowery style in favor of a more compact and vigorous one, but he always expressed himself on the art of composing and interpreting, upon his reading, and about his music and the music of others with an ease and a mastery of language almost unique in a musician.

This letter to Steiner is the mental autobiography of a gifted nineteen-year-old and deserves close examination. Its first literary motif is a comparison between the aridity of existence and leafless branches beating together. All the great romantics have known this conflict, in which "the supreme joy of living and the desire for death" alternate in their hearts. It was, for instance, the source of E. T. A. Hoffmann's irony and that of his celebrated hero, Kapellmeister Kreisler; it was also the chief source of Mahler's irony. All Mahler's music contains similar changes of mood from the sublime to the grotesque, from exaltation to depression. Parallel to this, all his life he fought to instill the purity of his inner being into those around him.

"Then the sun smiles on me again, the ice melts around my heart"—thus the traveler in Mahler's first song cycle receives, at the moment of his greatest sorrow, joy and consolation from nature; thus the afflicted father of the *Kindertotenlieder* is consoled, at the end of the cycle, by the thought that his children are now protected by the hand of God. Further on in the same letter come the waves of nostalgia, the joyful sunlight, the sufferings of the Wandering Jew, and his vain longing for the "happy and redeeming place" where angels smile, all feelings later expressed in the "programs" of some of Mahler's symphonies. Most of them begin with suffering and conflict, then gradually reach up toward redemption and eternal life. In the letter to Steiner, Mahler does not turn to God for help, but to the world or, more precisely, the earth, to which he later dedicated one of his last great works. There are two different conceptions of the earth in the letter, a few lines apart: first the earth, a symbol of human hypocrisy and everyday life, then a quasi-pagan conception of the Earth Mother, who offers rest, consolation, and shelter to the lonely. This is the inspiration for *Das Lied von der Erde* (1908). *"Die liebe Erde allüberall/Blüht auf im Lenz und grünt aufs neu! Allüberall und ewig blauen licht die Fernen!/Ewig . . . ewig . . ."*[10]

The whole letter to Steiner breathes a passionate love of nature; not a "literary" love, so often professed, if not practiced, by the romantics, but an indissoluble, profound attachment. This is one of the essential leitmotivs of Mahler's music and often gives it incomparable grandeur. No one else has conjured up the immensity of nature, both friendly and hostile to man, its overwhelming immobility and splendor, more powerfully than the composer of the first movement of the *Third Symphony*. The twilight, the lime tree, the eternal river that has flowed since time began, the cowbells, all these motifs occur both in Mahler's lieder and his letters.[11] More important still, we can sense, at the very heart of his music, this nature that he conceives as a reflection of mankind, a grandiose and tragic entity.

The paradoxical conception of sorrow, "my only consolation," inherited from the romantics, is another essential motif in Mahler's philosophy and work. Sorrow is to be found everywhere; it determines his conception of man and endows his art with depth and richness. When, thirty years later, Mahler reproached his wife because her face had "too few lines," it was because he considered sorrow as an inevitable, sacred experience, vital to both life and art. "Sorrow, my only consolation," a paradoxical conception inherited from the romantics, is essentially Mahlerian. Mahler extolled sorrow as a lonely and exalted moment in man's life and not, as is sometimes held, as an excuse for whispering despairing confidences into his listeners' ears. Sorrow is at the very center of his work and gives it its unique style: through sorrow, man escapes from mediocrity, hopelessness, and the "negative" forces of life.

The sound of the shepherd's pipe, the sad *Volksweise* of Farkas the shepherd, with its "passionate ecstasy," irresistibly recalls the desolate solitude of the last act of *Tristan und Isolde*. This brings us to another essential trait in Mahler's art. Studying the popular musicians whose improvisations fascinated him, Mahler unaffectedly and without false naïveté imitated the style of their folk music, thus finding exactly the right tone for the melodies he composed to texts from *Des Knaben Wunderhorn*. Few have understood the link between the refined, complex Mahler, the alchemist of sound, the eternal seeker and inventor, and Mahler the "folk" musician, perhaps the first to whose work can be applied the term, "imaginary folklore."[12]

Of all the words in the German language, one of the most difficult to translate is *Sehnsucht;* a vague sadness, abstract desire, sorrowful daydreaming. This one word describes the state of mind of the German romantics, and particularly those who were eighteen years old. In Mahler's letter to Steiner, *Sehnsucht* significantly appears with reference to Ahasuerus, the Wandering Jew. From time to time Mahler was haunted by the knowledge that he was without a country and everywhere in exile. To the other previously mentioned reasons for this feeling must be added the conception, common to all romantics, that the artist is an exile in this world, where ideals are nonexistent and where everything is vile, superficial, and hypocritical. Mahler's *Sehnsucht* that summer, however—his ideas of suicide and moments of despair mentioned in the letter to Steiner—undoubtedly sprang from the extreme poverty in which he had been living for a year in Vienna. Another letter written in June 1879, requesting a loan and addressed to Emil Freund, makes it clear that Mahler had not received his monthly salary at the Baumgartens' and was thus penniless.

Six letters written by Mahler to his old conservatory friend Anton Krisper[13] give an idea of what his life in Vienna was like during the winter of 1879 and the spring of 1880. Mahler complained to Krisper[14] about his constant need to move his lodgings, either because of his poverty or because noise made all work impossible. During the three years that Hugo Wolf spent in Vienna, at which time he became a close friend of Mahler (from the autumn of 1876 to that of 1879), the latter moved not less than twenty-one times and almost all of his letters of 1879 and 1880 bear a different address. These constant moves depressed him and awakened all his dormant feelings of anxiety.

Only once did he seem to have discovered the ideal place to live: "I have now made such a cozy home of my room that I can pursue my dreams and musings with the most pleasant contemplation," he wrote to Krisper, no doubt in 1879. "My window faces a large, spacious square, shaded by big old trees. It is surrounded by a complex of village-like houses which fit the landscape in a lovely and natural way. The elder bushes in the small garden immediately in front of my window will scent my room during the summer. Can you imagine a corridor, exactly like the one in the Piaristen Monastery (where Rott lived) only a little longer, even more gloomy and with more atmosphere. My room opens onto it, just like Rott's. It is long, very large and spacious, cheerful and comfortably furnished. Wagner's picture, the one Frank painted for me, is on my desk. I also have a good piano."[15]

Such moments were exceptional in those years and Mahler later illustrated the loneliness and poverty of his daily life in the following characteristic anecdote. Always passionately fond of nature, he one day organized a long walking excursion in the Wienerwald with a friend named Feld, the father of two young girls to whom Mahler gave piano lessons.[16] On the walk, he twisted his ankle, but since he was determined to finish the day's program at all costs, he disregarded his sufferings and continued walking. When he finally reached his lodgings in Vienna, he was in great pain and it was only with difficulty that he was able to climb the stairs to his fourth-floor room in the Franzensring.

Feverish and exhausted, he managed to sleep, or at least fell into a semi-lethargic state that lasted until early the next afternoon. When he regained consciousness he was suffering from hunger almost as much as from the sprain. Nobody, it appeared, was worried about him. He rang for the serving girl, who appeared, sluttish and surly, grumbling because she had been disturbed. She had no time to take care of Mahler or even to go out to find a doctor; nor could Gustav get help from anyone else. He just lay there, a prey to the unpleasant thought that, even if he should die, no one would take any notice.

That evening, Hans Rott's brother Karl happened to visit him. Mahler gave him what little money he had left and asked him to find a doctor and some food. But Karl Rott was an amiable scapegrace who never had a penny. He pocketed Gustav's money and disappeared, while Gustav waited for him in vain until the following morning. By then hunger and exhaustion were making his ankle ache unbearably, and Mahler knew that there was only one thing left to do. In a final burst of energy, he got dressed and went down the four flights of stairs. With his last ten-groschen piece he took a streetcar to the home of the Reichardts, friends who lived on the other side of Vienna, near the Marxer Linie. The Reichardts were far from being well to do. The father was a modest *Militärkapellmeister* with many children. But Mahler's confidence in their friendship was not misplaced. Not only did they at once find a doctor and give Mahler something to eat, they also kept him with them for three weeks, nursing and caring for him affectionately until his recovery was complete. All his life he remembered them with gratitude.

Mahler's instability at the end of 1879 and the beginning of 1880 was not caused entirely by the problems of his daily life. He was also passing through an emotional crisis; his first adult affection, which most probably dated from the preceding summer. Josephine, or Josefa, Poisl[17] was the daughter of the Iglau postmaster. Mahler's letters to Krisper speak of this romance as early as September 1879. "I am the unhappiest of happy men," he wrote, "a new name has entered my heart, near yours, murmuring and blushing, but powerful . . . I am a real fool, and I am too upset to write anymore . . ."

In February 1880, surrounded by open books and late at night, Mahler again wrote to Krisper: "If I had written to you half an hour ago, the old sobs and tears would have run across the paper. Now I am tranquil . . . This is the first time in a long while that I find calmer words within me . . ."

"Dear friend," he wrote at another time, "I am completely caught in the sweet bonds of the Darling of the Gods. And the hero now 'sighs, wrings his hands, moans, supplicates, etc. . . . . etc.' I have really come to suffer most of the time, and have experienced the most diverse sorts of sorrow. I get up with ah! and go to bed with oh! I live in a dream and dream while I'm awake."[18] Some phrases in this letter could have come from Hoffmann's Kapellmeister Kreisler: "While keeping up this detested smile, I have had to adopt a style of pastoral gaiety so as not to fall back into the old trivial lamenting. I no longer wish either to sigh or to smile. In my inner self battalions of curses are held back, and I want to let them out. 'May the devil take this worthless existence!' My eyes are like old dried-up lemons, no more tears in them. I must taste the boredoms of this world one by one;

not a single one is to be spared me." Mahler ended this letter to Krísper by promising to explain the reason for all this mysterious suffering.

Several unpublished documents are now available to throw light on this unhappy love affair of Mahler's. In 1930, Frau Alma discovered them in a little brief case that had been for years among her husband's books and that she had never had the curiosity to open.[19] As well as several letters written by Mahler, his parents, and Justi, she found four letters written to Mahler by Fanni Poisl, Josephine's mother, one from Anna, her sister, two from Josephine herself, and two from a friend named Melion. Finally there were three letters from Mahler—one to Frau Poisl and the others to Josephine —a list of the birthdays and saints' days of various members of the family in Mahler's handwriting, and finally the letter that the young girl's father sent to him to end the idyl.

Josephine and Anna Poisl had studied the piano with Mahler during the summer of 1879. Their life in Iglau was like that of all the young middle-class girls in the town. Anna, who was no doubt the younger, wrote a letter dated February 25 in which she described a carnival ball given in the Czap Hotel, and mentioned the quadrilles and gallops that she had danced with the garrison's officers. Josephine's first letter, which seems to have been written shortly afterward, also mentions the balls and concerts they had attended, and she alludes to the evening before Mahler's departure, when he showed himself to be "such an enthusiastic dancer"—the only testimony we have on this point! The young girl also speaks of her singing and mentions *The Flying Dutchman*, for Mahler had no doubt advised her to study the role of Senta; finally she urges him to return to Iglau and continue giving her piano lessons.

Fanni Poisl's letters of October 17 and November 14 are short and conventional: she several times thanks Mahler for having visited her son Otto in Vienna, for the latter had been "greatly tried by destiny." On November 25 she reproaches Mahler for the gloomy and sad tone of his letters: "From them one might think that you had been abandoned in some gloomy corner of the earth, instead of the gay Imperial city. How can a young man as gifted as yourself let himself be surrounded thus by coldness and convention and long for solitude? Leave such dispositions to the old and have fun with other young people! . . ." According to Frau Poisl, Josephine and Anna were still dancing, neglecting the piano and their singing, admiring the imposing beards of young professors, and often visiting the skating rink. At the beginning of March, Fanni finally sent some conventional good wishes to the young musician and added some more equally banal information about the two young girls, who had by now adopted the Vienna waltz.[20]

All these letters give the impression that those in Iglau ignored or wished to ignore Mahler's sentiments. The "crisis" came to a head in March—the month of *Das klagende Lied* and the three lieder dedicated

to Josephine. On the eighteenth Mahler wrote to Josephine on the occasion
of her saint's day.

"Dear Fräulein, you pitilessly keep mute, and I deduce that you are
ill-disposed toward me. Nevertheless, at the risk of having this page thrown
to the four winds, I have decided to send you with all my heart my good
wishes for tomorrow.

"I should have preferred to bring them in person, and I am still
astonished by the strength of will I have had to expend in order to
resist the temptation to spend my Easter vacation at Iglau despite my
resolution. And now what agitation I feel deep down in myself when I
dream of all my colleagues gaily walking the streets of Iglau while I, shut
up in my room, scarcely can see spring arriving outside the window.
Nevertheless, I'll arm myself against the coolness of the North Pole so as to
send my impertinent wishes back to the place at which they were born.
But it should not surprise you if one or another of these little elves
accidentally penetrates into your room. Have no fear. They will do you no
harm, for they are light, aerial, and affectionate, and will be content with
a tiny place.

"I shall be well repaid for my stoicism at the time of my summer vacation.
Then idleness will begin, and you know that I know how to be idle. You will
be bombarded again with myths, music, and other learned matters.

"We shall sit again in the forest of firs, in that little house, near the
attic window, waiting for rain, and I shall tell you stories of Siegfried
the invulnerable who awoke Brünnhilde from her magic sleep; of Wieland
the Smith, who forged brass wings in order to carry off the Princess
Bathilde through the air; and of old gods, the somber Wotan, the beautiful
Freia with her golden apples which bring eternal youth; of the impetuous
Donner and his hammer, of the Giants of the Ring and the nighttime gnomes,
and of the Nibelungen. Then we shall run through the rain to the house
and scamper to the top of the town watchtower. Suddenly we shall be a
year older, but I hope that otherwise we shall remain the same!

"I picture all this so clearly that I forget my present world while my
desires soar above the flat reality. While I wait, I can only send you all my
wishes for your happiness on the occasion of your saint's day. The few
springtime messengers that accompany this letter announce the arrival of
their master, Spring. He himself will arrive two days later, on March 21 . . ."

Mahler wrote in a jocular, light tone, but his real feelings can be
sensed in the evocation of their walk together the preceding year. On
March 26, Josephine replied to his good wishes in the most conventional
tones: nothing is happening in Iglau, the sleigh rides have ended with the
winter and so have the concerts and entertainments; they have been
replaced by walks in the country; preparations are being made to go fishing,
to search for crayfish, to catch birds. Her mother has made some Easter
cakes for him and he is invited to share them with the young Otto.

Mahler expressed all his sufferings in a poem that he sent to Krisper on March 3,[21] saying it would "show his feelings better than anything."

> How faithful and limpid was once the look in her eyes!
> For her I ceased my endless roaming despite grim winter's malice!

> And when Spring said farewell
> My sweetest decked her golden hair with white orange blossom!

Thus, in his eyes, Josephine had broken her promises.

In addition to indicating Mahler's psychological state during this crisis, the poem is the first example of the simple, naïve literary style used for the three unpublished lieder—*"Im Lenz"* (In Springtime), *"Winterlied"* (Winter Song), and *"Maitanz im Grünen"*—composed that same month and dedicated to Josephine.[22] Besides the conventional expressions of romantic sorrow ("eternal tortures," "solitary heart," "love's sorrow"), these songs contain one significant allusion—the *Wanderstab,* or Pilgrim's Staff, which evokes both the Wandering Jew of the letter to Steiner written in 1879 and the "wandering companion" of the *Lieder eines fahrenden Gesellen* of 1884. To Mahler, this idea, used a great deal by the German romantic writers, assumed the characteristics of a nonmetaphorical obsession that haunted him all his life.

The poems of March 1880 are written in folklore idiom and stem from a common romantic source; the contrast between man's sorrow and the beauty of nature was to be the essential theme of the *Lieder eines fahrenden Gesellen.* Thus, before Mahler's discovery of the *Knaben Wunderhorn,* we can see that the twenty-year-old poet was as fascinated by folklore as was the twenty-year-old musician.

"I am so alone. I would love to see you, to be with you," Mahler again wrote to Krisper on March 14, 1880. "Can I bear this for a long time to come? I feel as if I were about to burst at every moment. I am going through a great struggle that never ends. I have no right to explain this to you for the time being.

"For the first time, the world has seized upon me and shut me up in material things. All those stale phrases, those old wives' tales worn so threadbare—I have always listened to them with a pitying smile. But like witches they have caught me up in their wake, and now the waves come over me."

Despite a certain romantic tendency to exhibitionism, the rejected lover expresses sincere, heartfelt unhappiness. But he is conscious of appearing ridiculous and suffers accordingly. On March 25, one week after writing to Josephine, Mahler received the following letter from Melion.[23]

"Dear Mahler. Things are not going particularly well here. Believe me, however, that they are not going much better for me. More details tomorrow. Melion.

"P.S. J. received the bouquet, but according to what A. told me, she was not especially pleased with it. Ut mihi viditur, Wallner valde amat [It seems to me that she loves Wallner]."[24]

Thus Mahler had asked his former professor for news from Iglau and learned that Josephine was attracted to Wallner, the future director of the Iglau College, whom she was shortly to marry. Two days later, Melion tried to reassure Mahler and to correct the impression made by his card, in the following cable: "Clouds blown away. Write to them."

Mahler did so at once. On the twenty-ninth he wrote to Fanni to thank her for her cake and to complain in a roundabout way of her daughter's coldness: "I really needed someone in the world to remember me; spring has kept its promise to me badly. My state recalls that of someone who, condemned to the pyre by the Inquisition, received the grace of being strangled before being burned; he should acknowledge that which none-theless had spared him the torture of the pyre."

Mahler tells Frau Poisl that he spent Easter on a disastrous walk in the Prater, in the course of which he lost his way, having mistakenly walked along beside the Danube in the direction which led away from the town. He had left at eight in the morning and only returned to the Prater at three in the afternoon. At the end of the letter he asks to be remembered to Josephine and thanks her "for having taken the trouble to write to him."

No doubt Josephine's parents considered that things had gone far enough, and the young girl no longer wished to continue writing in secret, for her silence led to the following explosion:

My Passionately Beloved!

Despair dictates these lines to me.—Is it possible? Have you already forgotten the vows we made to each other?—Alas, I don't know what to say to you? The words emanating from my soul are cold as ice in comparison with the seething within my heart!

Oh, and just at a time when I am closer than ever to the goal of my desires—when that which we (oh, would I could say—we both) so ardently long for, could soon be fulfilled.

I have never humbled myself before anyone. Look! I kneel before you! Oh, by everything that is dear to you,—if ever you have felt only the tiniest spark of love for me,—I implore you—give me a sign, so that I might not despair.—Even if it is only an empty postcard with my address on it—I shall take it as a sign that you have not forgotten me.—Oh, forgive my deranged talk—I can hardly control myself—my blood freezes —I walk around like a corpse!

I saw myself so close to my goal—the day on which I could have asked your parents for your hand would have been so near—and now, just before the gates of heaven, my fate should lure me back into the deepest abyss.—

Have mercy on me! and with one single word let me know that you still love me. Then I shall know whether on Sunday I shall celebrate the day of my resurrection—or . . .

Oh, would you could see my tears, certainly you'd take pity!

—Oh, my dear, dear Josephine!

Must I remind you of what you said to me when, in the pouring rain, we walked in the Seufzerallee; when I quoted you the lines: "And the descendant wanders on the *ruins of old faithfulness.*" And you answered, "One only has to search for it—*whatever one wants,* one can do!" Oh, I have carried these words like a banner; in everything I did or thought, they were my guiding star. They are so deeply embedded in my heart that all the power of hell could not erase them! And now all this is to become lie and sham!? I cannot believe it—Yes! Yes! I know it, you do still love me! Your heavenly countenance—your eyes—they cannot deceive—or has the Lord cloaked the poison of Belladonna in the garments of a lily in order to destroy a human heart.

Oh—I'm so far away from you—you neither see nor hear me.—Would I could speak face to face with you—would that heaven would lend me its eloquence!—Then I would destroy the infernal lies that have crept into your heart!

Yes! Yes! You do still love me!—You must still love me—otherwise I must despair of light, of heaven, yes, of everything that is beautiful and good!—

Oh, my sweet, my passionately beloved! Hear me! Over all the lands and mountains that separate us, I cry to you from the depths of my misery! Give, oh give me a sign!

I fear and despair I shall wait till Monday,—and if nothing has arrived by then,—then oh, Lord, have mercy on my poor soul! Farewell! My salvation! My light, write only a single word to

Your
Gustav
who is faithful to you till death.

*Oh, write!*

There is no longer any trace of literature in this despairing letter. Was it sent direct to Josephine? The envelope has neither stamp nor postmark, which seems to indicate that Melion was asked to deliver the letter and perhaps did not do so. Perhaps he was growing tired of his role as go-between, for he did not even reply to Mahler's urgent questions and, worse still, revealed the whole truth to the young girl's father. On June 14 the latter wrote the following letter to Mahler:

According to Professor Melion, you have asked him several questions, to which he cannot at present reply, since the unhappy man is plunged into grief and sorrow due to the death of his mother, whose funeral is today. 1. We would very much regret it, if the continuation of an already terminated relationship were to deter you from the pursuit of your life's ambition. This relationship took us by surprise, and we parents can never approve of it.

2. Frankly, it does not please us.

3. We cannot permit any communications.

4. Whatever position you took, you would only lose our respect, if you tried, against our will and without our approval, to persuade our child to leave the path which has been indicated to her as being beneficial to her and her interests.

I have learned to respect and esteem you; I am sorry to have to be against you. But believe me, things being as they are, it is best if you give up all thought of my child, both for now and the future. There is not, there never was and there *never* will be any serious affection on her part strong enough to surmount all obstacles.

You will make your way, as a man and as an artist; and very soon you will smile at your youthful mistake.

With the best wishes for your well-being, Yours, I. Poisl.

After such a rebuff, Gustav finally understood that his sufferings and his hopes were equally useless. His work as an orchestral conductor in Bad Hall and Laibach soon helped him to forget this unhappy romance. As for Josephine, she married Julius Wallner, who was twenty years her senior, and led a very bourgeois life with him. This innocent idyl may have progressed further than Josephine's letters imply, for they were written under her mother's severe eye. But its principal interest for posterity is that it brought out the passionately violent reaction that Mahler always had in such circumstances. It plunged him into an intense creative fever. Three songs with piano accompaniment, dedicated to Josephine Poisl[25] were composed in February and March 1880, and also a large part of *Das klagende Lied,* a work of the greatest importance, since it was the first to be completed, after innumerable rough drafts.[26] Except for some fragments of conservatory works in Alma Mahler's collection, these are the earliest Gustav Mahler works known today. To them must also be added a no doubt incomplete and now lost *"Nordic"* Symphony, which Mahler mentions in a letter to Krisper dated December 14, 1879.[27]

Mahler's *Sehnsucht* at the beginning of 1880 was not due to his poverty and his disappointment in love alone. There was another cause, which he ignored: since he had not yet discovered his calling as an interpreter, his occupations were far from satisfying his imperative need to be fully occupied. As far as we know, neither his composing nor the occasional lessons that he gave in order to earn a little money were sufficient to fill his life. True, he had not entirely abandoned the piano, for, according to Theodor Fischer, he often accompanied recitals in the Bösendorfer concert hall. Fischer recalls in particular one concert when, to the singer's fury, Mahler stepped on the train of her dress when following her onstage. Another time he was accompanying a Polish violinist, and, suddenly forgetting where he was, he started daydreaming. The unfortunate soloist had to beat time loudly with his foot, to bring Mahler back to earth. He played in public once again in Iglau on April 24, 1879, on the occasion of a patriotic festival celebrating the twenty-fifth wedding anniversary of the Emperor.[28] With other local musicians he organized a gala concert and played two of his conservatory successes, Schubert's Sonata in A minor and Schumann's *Humoreske,* preceded by one of Liszt's rhapsodies.[29]

Mahler spent the following summer with the Baumgartens in Hungary, with Emil Freund in Seelau, and certainly in Iglau as well. He returned to Vienna in the autumn and first took lodgings with Hugo Wolf.[30] Then, until December 1879, he moved to a nearby suburb, the Cottage-Verein in Währing, where, in a small cluster of English-style villas that the Viennese used as summer residences, he found a very reasonable furnished flat,[31] "consisting of living room, corridor, kitchen, attic, and cellar." When Mahler left on December 18 to spend the Christmas holdidays in Iglau, he turned the flat over to Wolf, along with an excellent grand piano on which the rent was paid up to January 1.

In 1880, Mahler, like Wolf and Krzyzanowski, belonged to a socialist, vegetarian group that met in a restaurant called the Ramharter.[32] Located in a cellar, the small room was dimly lit by tiny windows up by the ceiling, so that gas lamps had to be kept lighted all day. There Mahler ate his melancholy meals, without meat or alcohol, both of which were strictly forbidden in such virtuous surroundings. At the big communal tables he often met a certain number of friends who were vegetarians like himself. A young physician of thirty, a disciple of Freud named Victor Adler, more or less headed the group. He was a Nietzschean, a fervent admirer of Wagner and Ibsen, and later he placed his entire fortune at the service of socialism. The editor of the group's newspaper, *Deutsche Worte,* the bearded Engelbert Pernerstorfer, often presided over the reunions. Around Adler and himself were gathered Hermann Bahr, the young writer[33]; another doctor who was a close friend of Mahler's, Albert Spiegler; Hans Emmanuel Sax, the socialist theoretician, author of a long treatise on the poverty of Thuringian workers; Heinrich and Otto Braun, socialists and social theoreticians (both brothers-in-law to Adler); a doctor-poet, Joseph Winter; the archaeologist Fritz Löhr, who became one of Mahler's best friends, and a painter named Buchbinder.

This society had been formed due to the ideological influence of a curious article by Wagner[34] on the regeneration of the human race through vegetarianism. The group also included back-to-nature faddists like the pianist August Göllerich, Liszt's pupil and secretary, and a future biographer of Bruckner. He was a picturesque and striking character, with an immense beard, a shock of long hair and extraordinarily big hands. The group's mouthpiece was an intellectual young Jewish writer from Galicia, Siegfried Lipiner, a strange, mystical and spiritualist, a *"raté"* genius, to whom Mahler remained attached all his life, and for whom he had a quite unjustified admiration.[35] Lipiner was twenty-four when he had his one moment of glory: his first writings, notably a certain *Prometheus Unbound,* won him a considerable reputation, and in particular attracted the attention of both Nietzsche[36] and Wagner. Wagner sent for him from Bayreuth and asked him to write, for the *Bayreuther Blätter,* a simple and easily understandable version of one of his works. Unfortunately, Lipiner wrote something even more obscure than the original, and his association with the illustrious Master was broken off entirely after a bitter discussion, during which the young man tried to defend Nietzsche, who had become very unpopular in Bayreuth.

Lipiner soon had considerable influence over Mahler: not only was Lipiner several years older, not only did Mahler consider his intelligence and culture inexhaustible, but above all he had the merit of having "expressed himself," as Mahler so desperately wished to do. To him, Lipiner embodied knowledge and erudition, the things he admired most. In the eyes of all the young vegetarians, Lipiner, with his affectations and his incomprehensible works, was genius personified. In fact, his talent lacked originality and did not continue after the brief blaze that sometimes marks the end of adolescence. He never published any of his works, except for his translation of Mickiewicz's ballads, and gradually he was forgotten so completely that his name appears in no history of Austrian literature or reference book.

To what extent did Mahler adopt the ideals of his socialist friends? It seems certain that the bonds that united them were not only those of friendship; they resulted from a shared ideology as well as from tastes and interests in common. Mahler, then, was for at least one period of his life both a socialist and a German nationalist. The Vegetarian Society had begun by recruiting its first members from among the young musicians and music lovers of the Wagner Verein,[37] but Adler gradually gave the group a frankly sociopolitical orientation. Later Adler was in fact the founder of Austrian social democracy.

At this heroic time, the young socialists had not yet passed from talk to action but were content to exchange ideas about the future of humanity while Mahler played the German national anthem, *"Deutschland, Deutschland über alles"* on the restaurant's old upright piano.[38] After Mahler had left Vienna, he still followed the group's activities from a distance. In particular he had its newspaper, *Deutsche Worte,* in which his friend Fritz Löhr published articles, sent to him in Kassel.[39]

Was Mahler a convinced socialist, or did he allow himself to be influenced by his friends? There is no way of telling, for Mahler does not discuss his political views in any of his known letters. An incident that occurred on May 1, 1905, in Vienna, however, indicates that at the age of forty-five he had not disavowed the socialist sympathies of his youth.[40] From June 1883 on, anti-Semitic tendencies began to penetrate the ideology of the socialist-vegetarian group. It was probably for this reason that

Mahler, who was no longer living in Vienna, finally left the group and at the same time returned to a normal diet.

It was during the Vegetarian Society period that Natalie Bauer-Lechner met Mahler again, at the home of the poet Kralik, and heard him play the *Meistersinger* overture. Some time later they met once more, again at Lipiner's house, where she witnessed a violent discussion about Wagner between Mahler and his host. Lipiner had condemned Wagner's attitude toward his father-in-law, Liszt, and, as always happened when anyone attacked Wagner in his presence, Mahler flew into a rage. In the heat of the argument he even began to attack Liszt. The discussion became so violent that the two friends parted, furiously angry with each other, and did not meet again for several years.[41]

The members of the vegetarian restaurant society also frequented the Café Griensteidl (situated on the Michaelerplatz; the Viennese had nick-named it the Café Grössenwahn—Café Megalomania). It was another meeting place for young left-wing artists and intellectuals of the time. One of Bruckner's pupils, Friedrich Eckstein, in the memoirs that he wrote about this period,[42] has left some striking portraits, notably of Hugo Wolf, "slender, blond, pale, always silent and distant, his glance nonetheless revealing his interior ardor," and Mahler: "He is a short man; his extreme irritability is noticeable in the peculiar unevenness of his walk. His narrow, taut, slender, mobile face is framed by a huge brown beard. His heavily accentuated speech is precise and has a strong Austrian flavor.[43] He always carries a pile of books or music under his arm, and all conversation with him takes place amid interruptions and sudden halts."

At the beginning of 1880 Mahler had grown a beard that he kept for several years. It made him look older and, when he started conducting, helped him to impose his authority more easily upon musicians older than himself. As for the "unevenness of his walk," this was not psychological, but a nervous "tic," no doubt of hereditary origin. Some biographers have put it down to his having suffered from St. Vitus's dance[44] as a child, but since no direct proof of this exists, the illness is probably imaginary. The following description of Mahler's celebrated "tic" is by the painter Alfred Roller, one of his closest adult friends.

"It is said that Mahler as a child suffered from involuntary movements of his extremities. These are frequently seen in mentally very advanced children, and if they are neglected, they can degenerate into 'St. Vitus's dance.' That malady, however, disappears when the child's mind and sensibility are suitably occupied later on. With Mahler, these involuntary movements persisted in his right leg throughout life. He never spoke of them, feeling a certain sense of shame. When he was walking, one noticed that at times, perhaps only one, perhaps two or three steps were in a different rhythm from the rest. When he was standing still, there was a slight tapping of his foot on the ground.

"His powerful will usually managed to control this tic, but when by accident the will was relaxed or was concentrated elsewhere, his right foot would again take up its curious habits. Whatever caused the will to relax—surprise or some comic or disagreeable happening—the effect was the same. It is wholly wrong to say, as is so often said, that this tic revealed Mahler's impatience or anger; it appeared just as often, and perhaps with greater energy, when he was laughing, which he did gladly, like a child, and with such good heart that tears streamed from his eyes. He would take off his glasses then, to wipe the moisture from the lenses, and would perform a veritable dance of joy on the spot. The fact that this motion of his feet generally has been considered a mark of impatience and anger demonstrates that Mahler had more often to deal with people who irritated or bored him than with people who made him laugh.

"This tic has been talked about maliciously only because most of those who observed it have not been attentive enough. When Mahler was expounding his thoughts tranquilly, one never saw the tic, nor when his will was being exerted—as, for example, while conducting. On the other hand, one observed it often when he was walking alone, following the development of a musical idea before entering it in his notebook of sketches. Then he generally started to walk again with one or two steps that were too short.

"I have sometimes seen him standing in the middle of his room in a strange posture, immobile on one leg, one hand on his hip and the index finger of the other hand against his cheek, his head bowed, plunged in his thoughts, with the back of his other foot held in the hollow of his knee, his eyes fixed on the floor before him, sometimes for several minutes." Roller claims that this strange position was an exercise invented by Mahler in an attempt to cure the involuntary arhythmic quality of his walk.[45]

Despite this tic, which all Mahler's contemporaries noticed, he had a muscular body, a robust constitution, and exceptional resistance, which allowed him to indulge in prolonged and violent exercise. Many authors have spoken of his "bad health" and after his death his widow did all she could to create the legend of a Mahler who was frail and always ill. If this had been so, he would have been unable to accomplish the herculean tasks that filled almost every day of his life; he would also have been obliged to cancel performances. In fact, there are almost no examples of canceled Mahler performances. He was unusually strong and exceptionally resistant. He suffered from certain chronic conditions, in particular one that he referred to as "my subterranean troubles."[46] He also often suffered from a sore throat, but it rarely prevented him from conducting. One of them was probably responsible for his heart condition, which, contrary to the generally accepted opinion, does not seem to have been hereditary. A recent discovery has shown that certain sore throats (those due to viridans streptococci), often found in children and adolescents, and which seem to clear up quickly, sometimes have serious long-term results: severe rheumatism of the joints, which in its turn brings on a grave heart condition, pericarditis[47] or hard-

ening of the valves of the heart.[48] This latter condition was diagnosed in
Mahler at the age of forty-seven. Roller tells us that Mahler's slender,
fragile appearance when dressed was an illusion, and that the first time he
saw Mahler naked he was surprised by his muscular and perfectly proportioned
frame.

Mahler re-entered the university in April 1880. Classical art, archae-
ology, the history of philosophy, the philosophy of Schopenhauer, the
history of the Renaissance and of the Napoleonic period were the subjects
that attracted him during this final semester, which was to be interrupted
by his engagement at the Hall Theater. They are much the same subjects
as those he had chosen earlier. He also attended a class in the history of
musical forms given by the well-known critic Eduard Hanslick, the friend
of Brahms and sworn enemy of Wagner. That Mahler, the passionate
Wagnerian, attended this class is proof of his unusually broad-minded
lucidity. Despite his *parti pris,* Hanslick was in fact one of the most intelligent and cultivated of all the Viennese musicians. Later, in 1897,
when Mahler became a candidate for the post of director of the Vienna
Opera, Hanslick intervened in Mahler's favor.

There is much evidence of the friendship between Mahler and Hugo
Wolf, which sprang up when Mahler entered the conservatory, and lasted
until 1880, though none of the letters they doubtless exchanged exists to
give us a more detailed picture. According to one anecdote, related by
several different people, Wolf one day asked Mahler what manuscripts
he had under his arm. "A song I've composed," replied the latter. Embarrassed by Wolf's enthusiastic praise, he added, "Yes, I think we've
equaled Mendelssohn now!"[49] The meaning of this story seems obscure,
but probably the two young men did not think highly of Mendelssohn. In
any case it confirms they were close enough at this time to show each
other their works. After 1880, they saw less of each other, and when they
met again in Bayreuth in 1883 they were scarcely on speaking terms. It
was not until 1897, when Mahler became director of the Vienna Opera,
that they were again on friendly terms, but only for a few months. Then
they had a violent scene in Mahler's office, which was instrumental in
bringing to a point of crisis Wolf's latent insanity.

An unfortunate earlier episode hastened this disagreement; a shortened
account of it appears in Alma Mahler's book; another, more complete one
in the unpublished manuscript by Natalie Bauer-Lechner. One day, probably in 1880, Wolf told Mahler that he had discovered an excellent subject
for a musical drama and that he was going to work on the libretto for a
while in the Hofbibliothek. In answer to Mahler's questions, he replied
that it was the famous story of *Rübezahl.* The two friends discussed the
idea, Gustav asserting that such a subject could only be treated humorously,
and Wolf believing the contrary. Without stopping to think that he might
anger or hurt Wolf, Mahler at once set to work on the story to prove that
he was right, and completed a humorous libretto in eight days.

When it was ready, Mahler asked Wolf if his own was finished yet. "I haven't even started yet," Wolf replied, "but I'm enchanted because I've found marvelous ideas during my work at the library." At this point, Mahler took his own libretto from his pocket and showed it to Wolf. He was thunderstruck by Wolf's fury and tried in vain to persuade him to finish his libretto in his own way. But Wolf swore by the gods that he would not write another word.[50]

Neither Mahler's memory nor the accuracy of his chronicler can be doubted on this point, because the libretto of *Rübezahl* is still in Frau Mahler's collection.[51] According to an unpublished letter written in June 1880 to Albert Spiegler[52] Mahler had worked on this score the previous winter; he begs Spiegler to ask Lipiner to return the score, which was his "only copy." He asks if this copy of his work is "still in existence," since he would like to revise it, even though "he is so angry he has almost lost taste of it." So Mahler had become seriously interested in this work, composed it in a fairy-tale opera form, and worked on it for several years. The composition was never finished: in 1900 he told Natalie that only "a few lieder" remained and that his "damned employment as opera conductor had dealt the 'coup de grâce' to this and many other works."[53]

This story is interesting, not only because it shows us one of the chief reasons for the coolness between Mahler and Wolf, but also because it emphasizes the difference between their artistic natures. Mahler, with his genius for parody and the grotesque, is already a modern as compared with Wolf, whose fervent, impassioned sensitivity places him in the great romantic tradition of Schumann and Brahms.

According to Frau Alma, Wolf's fury at Mahler's "theft" was all the greater because in 1880 the idea of writing a fairy-tale opera was still new (despite some precedents by Weber, Lortzing, and Marschner), for Humperdinck's famous *Hänsel und Gretel* was not produced until 1893.[54] However, Mahler, too, abandoned the idea. Ironically the two good friends had fallen out over an opera subject that finally neither of them used.

# CHAPTER 6

## Das klagende Lied — *First Engagements as a Conductor: Hall and Laibach* (*1880–82*)

In the spring of 1880, Mahler had made some pleasing plans for his summer vacation: a walking tour with Krisper, Heinrich and Rudolf Krzyzanowski through the Böhmerwald and the Fichtelgebirge to Eger, the two brothers' home town. He then intended to go on to Bayreuth, Nuremberg, and finally Oberammergau, in order to see the famous passion play.[1] But Providence, or rather Gustav Mahler's personal destiny, intended otherwise. In the late spring of 1880, he was to wield for the first time a conductor's baton—that mysterious, many-voiced instrument that he was to put to such glorious use in the course of his dazzling career.

Mahler spent the whole month of March 1880, including the Easter vacation, in Vienna, but his thoughts were in Iglau with the young Josephine. However, he was not, or was no longer, one of those morbidly anxious people who revel in their own unhappiness. Alongside his dreamy romanticism, a determined, practical character, endowed with an urgent need for action, was taking shape. From that time on he resembled the description of himself he gave, many years later, to Natalie Bauer-Lechner[2]: "We are much alike in that the most terrible blows that life reserves for us do not put us down. I can say on my part that even if I were to die, I should come to again at the end of three days."

In fact, once his sentimental crisis was over, Mahler pulled himself together and completely changed his way of life. On March 21 he finished the sketch of the first part of *Das klagende Lied*. On April 1 he re-entered the university but quickly realized that his poverty-stricken life as an eternal student had already lasted too long. Following the example of many earlier composers, he began to seek a post as conductor. With this aim in view he moved heaven and earth, requesting help from all his friends and acquaintances.[3] He asked for advice from the publisher Rättig,[4] for whom two years earlier he had made the piano duet arrangement of Bruckner's *Third Symphony,* and Rättig put him in touch with the "inevitable" impresario; in this case Gustav Löwy (or Loewy, Lewy),[5] who was to represent Mahler exclusively for almost ten years.

On May 12, 1880, Mahler signed a five-year contract with Löwy. By its terms Löwy had the right to 5 per cent of all remunerations and fees received by Mahler from various theaters. The first job offered by Löwy was of little interest, but undoubtedly was meant to test Mahler's ability. He was to conduct the operettas performed during the summer by a tiny provincial group in Hall, a small spa in Upper Austria. Mahler's parents were unenthusiastic at the idea of their son in so modest a position. However, Epstein, the young man's kind and faithful guardian angel, persuaded him to accept the offer, consoling him for its mediocrity by assuring him that he would "work his way up."

Hall, which later received the more imposing name of Bad Hall, is a small thermal station near Linz, famous for its iodized waters. Leaving the thermal establishment by the road to Priehlaussicht, today's traveler soon reaches a place where a narrow pathway branches off at a sign pointing to the "Villas Hillischer." This path leads to two attractive villas built at the edge of the forest on a plot of land clearly torn from the steep slope rising behind them. Close beside one of the villas is a wooden outbuilding with a notice board on which it is still just possible to make out the word "Theater." It is difficult to believe one's eyes, so modest is the building and so strangely chosen the theater site. Nevertheless it was in this big wooden shed that the future director of the Imperial and Royal Opera of Vienna made his first appearance as a conductor.

For most of the second half of the nineteenth century, Johann Hillischer, administrator of the Hall thermal establishment, considered himself a patron of the arts and was proud of his friendly relations with the famous Austrian poet Franz Grillparzer, who had taken a cure there in 1866. Some years after that memorable event Hillischer had a small one-story wooden theater built in the park of his villa. Four years later he added an upper floor, with two small turrets to flank the entrance, in order to give the building the rustic elegance of a Tyrolean villa, which it had previously lacked.[6]

Thus enlarged, the theater scarcely held two hundred; sixteen boxes with six places each, sixty-six seats in the gallery, sixteen in the pit and some pull-down seats in the balcony.[7] The theater received support from both the local authorities and the thermal establishment on condition that its directors "gave the best and newest operettas and comedies." Because of the risk of fire, performances were not given in artificial light, but instead took place at five o'clock in the afternoon! And the orchestra was the same one that entertained those taking the cure during their morning stroll in the establishment's gardens.

Today this modest structure serves as a henhouse and garden shed. But it still shows traces of its earlier use, though in 1921 it lost its upper floor and ostentatious turrets. On one of the outside doors it is still possible to read "Box 10," and a few of the partitions that formerly separated the boxes are visible from the interior. All traces of the stage have disappeared, but on the back wall there are scraps of wallpaper and two signs reading "It is forbidden to smoke near the hall."

The financial and artistic management of the theater was in the hands of one Viktor Berthal, who signed a "Farewell Souvenir" distributed to the public with the program at the end of the 1875–76 season, and which luckily has been preserved. This interesting document tells us that during that season the theater company consisted of eleven men and twelve women. Their repertoire was considerable: seventeen works in June, fourteen in July, and eleven in August. These included three Offenbach operettas: *Barbe-Bleue, Orphée aux Enfers,* and *La Princesse de Trébizonde,*[8] as well as *Drei Paar Schuhe* by the Austrian composer Karl Millöcker.

There is also in existence an inventory of the Hall Theater dated May 30, 1878. It is endorsed with the word "Accepted" and signed by someone of much greater interest than Berthal, since his name is closely linked with Mahler's first theatrical experience: Karl Ludwig Zwerenz. Born into a theatrical family, Zwerenz began his career as an actor about 1867, before becoming a stage manager and theatrical director, as well as singing leading comic roles in operettas. All his life he was closely connected with the vogue for operetta in Austria. At the start of a long career that in 1889 took him as far as Vienna, he worked in a succession of towns throughout the empire. During the winter season of 1879–80 he directed the theater in Steyr, the town nearest to Hall. The following winter he was in charge of the theater in Iglau, Mahler's birthplace.

Unfortunately we do not know the repertoire of the little Hall Theater during the 1880 summer season, but we can get some idea of it by examining Zwerenz's choice for the previous year's winter season in Steyr, which ended on April 25. This included: Johann Strauss, Jr.'s *Der Karneval in Rom* and *Die Fledermaus;* Lecocq's *Giroflé-Girofla, La Fille de Madame Angot,* and *Cent jeunes filles;* Offenbach's *Le Mariage aux lanternes* and *Les Géorgiennes;* Suppé's *Die Schöne Galatea,* etc.

How long was Mahler in Hall? The information so far provided by his biographers is vague, but some unpublished documents show that he was there as early as May 20 and as late as July 1. There is in existence an unsigned postcard dated May 25, 1880, sent from Vienna to Herr Kapellmeister Gustav Mahler Wohlgeboren, Theaterbegäude, Hall, Ober Österreich.[9] The handwriting and the form of address indicate that the card was sent by Anton Bruckner, as a humorous consolation for the modest post Mahler held in Hall. The card reads:

*"Durch Nacht"* (Through the Night), followed by a quotation from the trio of the March from Suppé's operetta *Fatinitza,*[10] *"Vorwärts"* (Forward), followed by a quotation from the Valhalla theme in *Das Rheingold,* and *"Zum Licht"* (To the Light).

Bruckner certainly had no idea how quickly his prophecy would come true. Only five years later, in Prague, Mahler conducted for the first time *Das Rheingold* and *Die Walküre*.

The granddaughter of Josef Hermann Hillischer still possesses a list of the amounts paid to the Hall Theater personnel in 1880, on which Mahler's name appears. His salary covered the period from June 15 to July 1, which is the last certain date of his stay. This salary is more than modest: thirty gulden a month, less 5 per cent to Löwy, plus a fee of fifty kreutzer for each performance! And this was not one of the lowest salaries paid by the theater!

The Hall orchestra was certainly not made up of more than fifteen musicians (the same size as the Steyr orchestra during the preceding season). Twenty years later Mahler told his wife that his duties had not been solely orchestral: he had also been required to dust the piano, place the parts on the music stands before each performance, and put them away again afterward, while during the intermissions the prima donna—who was Zwerenz's wife—had him wheel her newborn baby around the theater in its carriage.[11] The only service that Mahler felt justified in refusing was that of playing character parts on stage. He later regretted this refusal, remarking humorously that pride had been responsible for his decision, but that he could thus have gained a lot of useful experience.

Only one known letter reflects Mahler's state of mind in Hall. It was written on June 21 to his friend Albert Spiegler: ". . . As for me, my usual state is that of being able to rise to the occasion. I do not yield to discouragement, as you can imagine, without fighting, and I do not try to surmount my difficulties by joking about them. I am still on my feet, and I hope always will be. It would be too absurd to let myself be reduced to despair by dung flies. If I complain, it is for a quite different reason, which you ignore, which is not new and which is not so unimportant that you can just shrug your shoulders."

In fact Mahler had entrusted the score or the text of *Rübezahl* to Lipiner and had had no news of him for some time: he wanted to work on his opera and did not even know if the only copy of the manuscript was still in existence! "When, as well as all the other vexations that I undergo, I must add to them those for which I alone am responsible, I feel myself literally submerged in bile," he adds, and begs Spiegler to remind Lipiner that he exists, and also Krzyzanowski, from whom he had received no news.[12]

According to Alma Mahler, Mahler saw a great deal of a small group of elegant young men from Hall, headed by Heinrich von Angeli,[13] the academic artist and fashionable portrait painter. These young men greatly impressed the young provincial Mahler, who up to then had had no contact with people of culture and taste. According to Frau Alma, their pleasant company once made him forget his duties in the theater. He arrived back there after the start of a performance and was immediately sacked. His young friends, responsible for this misfortune, accompanied him to the Hall railroad station with many protestations of friendship and arranged to meet him again in Vienna. But when Mahler did in fact try to see them there later, he found their doors closed to him, and was bitterly disappointed. Perhaps this incident was one of the reasons for the mistrust and haughty reserve with which Mahler treated the Viennese aristocracy when he was director of the opera there and all the hostesses fought for the honor of receiving him into their homes.

From what we know of Mahler's character, it seems surprising that he could forget his duty for any cause whatever.[14] It was probably lassitude or exasperation that led him to commit this insubordinate act. The story of his dismissal by Zwerenz is perhaps true, but it does not seem to have had any effect on Mahler's later career, since this same Zwerenz at once offered him another engagement.

A letter that Mahler wrote to Löwy from Hall on June 21, 1880,[15] shows that he was not discouraged by the unimportance of this first post.

"Dear Sir, I beg you to try to find me a position as orchestra conductor for the coming winter season. Despite the urgings by Director Zwerenz, I cannot, because of my family, accept the engagement in Iglau, my home town. I take it that you know of my abilities. I have acquired sufficient insight to know that I am capable of filling such a position in any theater whatever. I allow myself, therefore, to offer you a supplementary commission of 50 florins if you succeed in finding me a good engagement as orchestral conductor; perhaps you might be able to find me a position as assistant conductor in a large theater, preferably in Germany."

Thus, after only a few weeks at the unprepossessing Hall Theater, Mahler already knew that conducting was to be both his livelihood and his vocation. When, in April 1898, he told Natalie Bauer-Lechner that his failure in the Beethoven Prize contest of December 1880 had "condemned" him to "the Hell of the Theater," he had momentarily forgotten that this "Hell" had rapidly become as necessary to him as the air he breathed. His desperate need for activity would never have been satisfied by the calm, isolated life led by most of his contemporary composers.

At the end of June 1880, Mahler's career seemed assured. Zwerenz was made director of the Iglau Theater for the winter of 1880–81, and he suggested that Mahler go with him. Why did Mahler tell Löwy that he could not accept a position in his native town? Perhaps his parents' understandable pride led them to consider that their town's little theater was unworthy of their son. Whatever the reason, after his spell in Hall, Mahler returned to Vienna and the uncertainty, poverty, and sadness of his former life. October brought a succession of bad news: Rott had gone mad, and Krisper, for two years Mahler's closest confidant, was also showing signs of mental strain. Into the bargain Emil Freund told him of the suicide of the young girl whom Mahler had met at Freund's home and been so attracted to some years earlier. "There is nothing but sorrow everywhere!" he wrote to Freund on November 1. "And it puts on the strangest disguises in order to mock the sons of men. If you know one happy man on this earth, tell me his name quickly before the little courage that I still have disappears. One who has watched a noble, profound nature flounder after struggling with the most ignoble basenesses and let itself be overcome by them[16] can only with difficulty keep from crying out to himself in his dreams! Today is All Saints' Day." In the same letter, Mahler tells Freund that he has been back on a vegetarian diet for a month and adds that this regime suits him.

This letter to Freund did, however, contain one piece of good news. Once more sorrow had born fruit, and Mahler had just completed his cantata *Das klagende Lied,* his *"Schmerzens Kind"* (Child of Sorrow), on which he had been at work for more than a year. In October 1880, while finishing his great work, he was seized by a strange and powerful feeling of anxiety each time he worked on a certain, seemingly unimportant passage: he thought he could see himself appearing in a dark corner of the room and suddenly felt an unbearable physical pain, as though his double were trying to force a passage through the wall. Each time this happened he had to stop working and leave the room. And one morning, while working on this particular passage, he was seized by a genuine nervous fever.[17]

Later Mahler attributed these incidents to physical weakness brought on by too much work and the vegetarian diet.[18] But the real cause seems to have lain deeper, for from this time on Mahler's composing was always closely linked to his emotional state. He came to consider certain of his works, such as the *Kindertotenlieder* and the *Sixth Symphony,* another "child of sorrow," with a kind of holy terror, as though each time they plunged him back into the suffering that had accompanied their composition. In the same way, in Leipzig, when composing the first movement of his *Second Symphony,* he had a gloomy vision of his own corpse laid out in a coffin.

Mahler always showed remarkable lucidity regarding the relative quality of his own works. Already he had destroyed most of his first efforts, which he judged unworthy to survive, but on the other hand he had no illusions regarding the value of his great cantata and said to Natalie in 1893, "This first work is already completely original."[19] Once it was finished, his next task was to get it performed and, for a young composer who had adopted Vienna as his spiritual home, there was one excellent way, which was to compete for the Beethoven Prize of the Gesellschaft der Musikfreunde.[20] The prize of five hundred gulden, instituted in 1875, was in effect a great encouragement to young composers. Later Mahler made the following statement to Natalie Bauer-Lechner:

"If the conservatory jury, which included Brahms, Goldmark, Hanslick, and Richter, had given me the Beethoven Prize of 600 gulden for *Das klagende Lied,* my whole life would have taken a different course. I was then at work on *Rübezahl.* I would not have had to go to Laibach, and perhaps would thus have been spared the whole vile operatic career. Instead, Herr Herzfeld received the composition prize, while Rott and I left with empty hands. Rott despaired, went insane, and died shortly thereafter, and I—I was and always will be condemned to the Hell of the theater."

Strange though it may seem, Mahler, in relating this episode, is no more faithful to the truth than his least scrupulous biographers. To begin with, he did not present his score to the jury until after his stay in Laibach in 1881. Then the prize was awarded in December and Rott was already insane in October, so his madness cannot have been caused by this reverse. Finally, Herzfeld only won the prize much later, and the amount was five hundred and not six hundred gulden.

Most of Mahler's earlier biographers have stated that *Das klagende Lied* was submitted to the Beethoven Prize jury in 1880, and indeed, in the above quotation, Mahler asserts that he submitted the work before leaving for Laibach—that is, before January 1881. The extreme haste with which he completed the cantata in October 1880[21] seems to indicate that he was indeed working against time. Furthermore, in his November 1 letter to Freund, he speaks of "obtaining the performance of this work by any possible means," and the Beethoven Prize was one of the most obvious. Donald Mitchell[22] was the first to question this usually accepted date. He calls particular attention to the short time between completion of the score (November 1) and the award of the prize (December 8)—not long enough to allow all the members of the jury to examine the score. And, as the archives of the Gesellschaft testify, no prize money was awarded either in 1879 or in 1880.

There is another, more conclusive reason why Mahler cannot have presented his work in 1880, which is that the rules of the contest barred him from entering it that year. At a meeting of the board of directors of the Gesellschaft der Musikfreunde on December 16, 1880, it was decided to alter the rules of the Beethoven Prize, since because of them it had been impossible to award the prize for several successive years. Until that date the regulations stated that every candidate must have attended the conservatory for at least ten years before the contest, and the composition class for at least two years. After 1880, any composer who had studied at the conservatory could enter the contest, whatever classes he had attended and for whatever length of time. Thus Mahler could not have submitted his score before December 1881, the year after the rules were changed.

On December 15, 1881, the Beethoven Prize was awarded to Robert Fuchs, a former professor of Mahler's at the conservatory, for a piano concerto in B minor; at the same time, an overture by Viktor von Herzfeld,[23] *Der Traum ein Leben,* was considered by the jury to be "praiseworthy." It was only in 1884 that Herzfeld finally received the Beethoven Prize. According to Maja Löhr, Fritz Löhr's daughter, Rott submitted, or meant to submit, two of his scores to the jury in 1880, and it was for this reason that he visited Brahms in September, but he went mad before the prizes were dis-

tributed. It must thus be supposed that Mahler, in 1898, confused the Beethoven Prize with the composition contest of 1878, which Rott in fact did
not win.[24]

Despite all these errors of detail, it seems unquestionable that Mahler
did try to obtain the Beethoven Prize. In his view his failure to win it was
due to the hostility of the "conservatives" of the time, that is to say, Brahms
and the critic Hanslick. Let us consider the outward signs of this hostility—
in other words the relationship between Brahms and the young lions of
Austrian music.

It cannot be denied that Brahms was deeply hostile to Bruckner. He
became angry every time anyone spoke of him; in his opinion the whole
"Bruckner affair" was a farce: in two years' time, he said, Bruckner's music
would be dead and forgotten, for it was impossible to take seriously works
that did not even deserve to be called symphonies. Brahms always regretted this absurd antagonism. He felt unable to belong to a faction, and
considered that Bruckner had been invented purely and simply because a
party leader was needed to oppose him.[25]

As well as his scorn for Bruckner's personality, Brahms felt real hostility
toward Bruckner's pupils and disciples. Writing on April 29, 1879, after a
visit from Hugo Wolf, he spoke most scornfully of "the conservatory method
of teaching composition," which he judged "from what he had seen of the
pupils and their work," no doubt alluding to the three most gifted of them,
that is to say, Rott, Wolf, and perhaps Mahler.

Brahms treated Rott with great cruelty. The latter, since the business
of the Piaristen Monastery, had been searching unsuccessfully with the
help of Bruckner for another position as organist in Vienna, and had finally
resigned himself to accepting that of *Musikdirektor* of the Concordia Chorale
of Mulhouse. Before leaving for Alsace he submitted two of his scores, a
Symphony and a Pastoral Prelude to the jury of the Beethoven Prize, and
then went to play them to Brahms in the hope of obtaining his support. But
the latter's judgment was merciless: he advised him without amenity to give
up a musical career.[26] This made Rott so furious that, in his already sick
mind, he imagined that Brahms wished to kill him.

A visit to Richter, whose judgment was less harsh, failed to calm him,
and he went mad in the train that was taking him to Alsace, October 21 or
22, 1880. He tried to stop one of his traveling companions from lighting a
cigar, claiming that Brahms had filled the train with dynamite. He had to be
taken back to Vienna two days later and the following year he was interned
in a psychiatric hospital, where he died on June 25, 1884.[27] Knowing
Brahms's share of responsibility in this tragedy, Bruckner decided to accuse
him at Rott's funeral, but his grief and his peace-loving temperament finally
got the better of him, and he took no action.

Long before Rott's visit, at the beginning of 1879, Wolf had also called
upon Brahms, and the latter's verdict was no more encouraging: "First you
must learn something. Then we shall see if you have any talent." Brahms

advised Wolf to take lessons from Gustav Nottebohm, an authority on counterpoint.[28] From that time on, Wolf, who had been a fervent admirer of Brahms, conceived an implacable hatred for him.

The only sign of Brahms's hostility toward Mahler is in the refusal of his work by the Beethoven Prize jury, but Brahms was not the only member of that jury, which also included Hans Richter, Karl Goldmark, Josef Hellmesberger, the head of the conservatory, Franz Krenn (Mahler's old teacher), the noted conductor Wilhelm Gericke, and Johann Nepomuk Fuchs, professor and conductor, another of Mahler's former professors and the brother of Robert Fuchs, who won the Beethoven Prize in 1881.

Today it seems obvious that *Das klagende Lied* deserved the Beethoven Prize far more than the mediocre works of Herzfeld and Fuchs, but at the time the jury undoubtedly reacted with alarm to the "revolutionary" tendencies of a work already Mahlerian down to the last detail.[29]

There is no reason to think that Brahms's influence was the determining factor in this jury composed entirely of diehard conservatives; the most dangerous was doubtless Fuchs, who had often criticized Mahler's "eccentricities" at the conservatory and who was, into the bargain, the brother of the prize winner. We shall see the favorable and even decisive influence that Brahms had on Mahler's career fifteen years later. Two pieces of music bear witness to his momentary influence on Mahler's style: some passages of the 1876 *Piano Quartet* and the song *"Erinnerung."*

After completing *Das klagende Lied,* Mahler spent his Christmas vacation in Iglau as usual and returned to Vienna at the beginning of January 1881. In a letter of March 1881[30] he draws the attention of his friend Carl Schnürmann to a concert scheduled for April 11 by the Wagner Verein, in which the pianist Raab was to take part: "It is a concert organized by aristocrats, and I think the price of tickets is very high, out of the question for people like us." He also mentions a concert devoted to Liszt and conducted by Gericke, on April 1, with the *Dante Symphony,* and tells Schnürmann that he has moved lodgings again. Friedrich Eckstein[31] mentions two events, organized by the Vegetarian Society early in 1881: a banquet (vegetarian of course) accompanied by speeches, and a concert given by the vegetarians in the salon of an old hotel, now demolished. Cyrill Hynais, a pupil of Bruckner, played his *Ozeansymphonie;* the opera singer Josef Reiff-Heissiger sang Löwe's *Ballades;* and Eckstein himself sang the bass aria from *Die Zauberflöte,* with Mahler at the piano.

Apart from these insignificant details, we know nothing about Mahler's life in Vienna during the first half of 1881. A letter to Emil Freund, written from Iglau in September of that year[32] tells us that he once more spent his vacation in Iglau and Seelau, with his own family and at the Freunds'. During the summer of 1881 Mahler regained some of his optimism, for it seemed that his difficulties were coming to an end. His efforts with Löwy had borne fruit: Alexander Mondheim-Schreiner, director of the Landschaftliches (Provincial) Theater of Laibach (now Ljubljana), had chosen him to be principal conductor for the next season.

Laibach was then a pleasant little town. In Napoleon's time it had had twenty-five thousand inhabitants and had played an important role as the capital of the province of Illyria. By the end of the nineteenth century, the population had risen to about one hundred thousand, and, although the town had been relegated to the more modest position of capital of Carniola, it had a university and preserved a theatrical tradition more than a century old. The theater itself, located on the Congressplatz, had been built in 1765[33] and was used in turn for plays, opera, and operettas. The first performance in the Slovenian language was given in 1789, but for many years Italian and German companies had alternated there until the latter took over entirely.

In 1881, after mixed experiences with various directors, the committee managing the theater had engaged a man resembling Zwerenz, who was both a comedian and a stage producer. This was Alexander Mondheim-Schreiner, who filled the post for more than four seasons. One of his first acts was to engage Mahler. Conditions in the provincial theater at Laibach were scarcely better than those at the little summer theater in Hall. The Landestheater had three stage producers, recruited, as was the custom at the time, from among actors and singers: one was responsible for comedies, one for operas; the director himself bore the title *Oberregisseur*. The chorus was small: seven men and seven women. The orchestra usually consisted of eighteen musicians but was "reinforced" for operas.

As in Hall, many singers were also actors, for the demarcation line between the two genres was ill-defined, especially in the provinces. In a theater of this kind, the staff was kept to a minimum, and everyone's talents were exploited; thus, in Laibach, the director was also a producer and comic actor, while his wife, doubtless little gifted for the stage, took care of the box office and bookkeeping.

Perhaps it was due to Mahler's influence that this mixed group, so lacking in real vocal talent, was strengthened by two "invited" singers, the Italian baritone Alessandro Luzzato and the young tenor Friedrich Erl, son of a "court singer." These two professionals helped to raise the level of the opera performances, in which most of the "singers" were only "helping out."

With these modest means Mahler was required to perform a repertoire consisting of a dozen operas and fifteen operettas, not counting the farces and plays with incidental music, for a six-month season.[34] Mahler's stay in Laibach was of considerable importance to his career, despite the lack of facilities at his disposal. Firstly because his repertoire was much larger and more ambitious than his first biographers believed. *Il Trovatore, Die Zauberflöte, Der Freischütz,* and *Il Barbiere di Siviglia* were key works in the repertoire. Mahler had to discover and conduct them sooner or later, and this responsible apprenticeship enabled him to evaluate his own capabilities.

The season officially opened on September 24, 1881, with a performance of Bauernfeld's *Bürgerlich und Romantisch*. This gala evening started with

Beethoven's *Egmont* Overture, played by the theater orchestra and conducted by Kapellmeister Gustav Mahler, who was conducting classical music in public for the first time. The performance was only described as "accurate" by the Slovenian newspapers, which do not say how it was received. However, ten days later, when Mahler conducted his first opera, Verdi's *Il Trovatore,* before a packed theater, the Laibach German paper[35] mentioned that the performance took place "without special incident." Kapellmeister Mahler made it his business to rehearse this opera very conscientiously. We feel able to state that from today on we can be certain that he is completely equal to his task, and that in the future also greatest care in rehearsing will be evident." Wrting two days later about Lecocq's *Giroflé-Girofla,* the same critic praised the orchestra's verve and spirit.

Thus, from the time of his very first appearance as a conductor, Mahler's enthusiasm and his attention to detail were noticed. Nobody seems to have remarked upon his lack of experience, and there were no reservations after the first performance of *Die Zauberflöte* on October 27. The Slovenian critic Peter von Radics considered the performance excellent, accurate, and well thought out, and said that its success was due to the detailed preparation such a performance required. For the anonymous critic of the German paper, there was no doubt that Mahler was a capable *Kapellmeister* who deserved the public's thanks, for the orchestra rarely carried out its task with such precision; under the circumstances, the chorus had performed prodigies, and the whole performance had been excellent for a provincial theater.

Even though Mahler's memory was not always accurate, some incidents that he later told his wife[36] at least reflect his state of mind during his stay in Laibach. One day, for instance, the absence of a singer necessitated his whistling "The Last Rose of Summer" during a performance of Flotow's *Martha.* On another occasion, instead of the Soldiers' Chorus in *"Faust,"* a single singer marched slowly back and forth across the stage, singing the Lutheran chorale *"Ein feste Burg."* These anecdotes are entertaining but hard to believe. The Laibach chorus contained fourteen singers, so it is unlikely that Mahler would have consented to conduct *Faust* without them. As for "The Last Rose of Summer," the weakest member of the chorus would have replaced the missing prima donna better than a whistling *Kapellmeister.*

Besides *Il Trovatore* and *Die Zauberflöte,* the operatic repertoire that year included *Der Freischütz,* Verdi's *Ernani,* Donizetti's *Lucrezia Borgia, Faust, Il Barbiere di Siviglia,* Flotow's *Martha* and *Alessandro Stradella,* and Nicolai's *Die lustigen Weiber von Windsor.* Mahler very probably conducted most of these performances. He was also responsible for many of the repertoire operettas: Strauss's *Die Fledermaus, Cagliostro,* and *Der lustige Krieg;* Suppé's *Boccaccio,*[37] *Fatinitza, Donna Juanita,* and *Flotte Burschen;* Offenbach's *La Vie parisienne, Barbe-Bleue,* and *La Belle Hélène;* Lecocq's *La Fille de Madame Angot* and *Giroflé-Girofla;* and Planquette's *Les Cloches de Corneville* (*The Chimes of Normandy*). He was probably often replaced by his assistants for the operettas, but they were also kept busy with the incidental music for plays, among which Mahler seems to have reserved for himself only *Egmont* (Beethoven), *A Midsummer Night's Dream* (Mendelssohn), and *Preciosa* (Weber).

In six months, Mahler conducted some fifty performances, and the critics were nearly always favorable to him, especially when he conducted *Lucrezia Borgia, Ernani, Die Zauberflöte, Il Barbiere di Siviglia, Faust,* and *Die lustigen Weiber von Windsor.* The first *Lucrezia Borgia* seems to have been "insufficiently prepared": a few lapses occurred in the ensemble between the singers and the orchestra, but these were corrected by the second performance. Johann Strauss's operetta *Der lustige Krieg* was performed twelve times, doubtless because public enthusiasm was stimulated by the work's novelty. Its first performance had taken place in Vienna the preceding year, on November 25.

In those days it was the custom for orchestral conductors to be given an annual benefit in the form of a performance or concert; it was thus that Wagner often managed to pay his debts in Dresden. When Mahler stepped into the orchestra pit of the packed theater on March 23, 1882, to conduct his own benefit performance of *Alessandro Stradella,* he was greeted by a storm of applause, followed by a fanfare from the orchestra. After the performance he was presented with a big laurel wreath decorated with ribbons, and the next day the critics praised his energy and enthusiasm; they drew attention to the difficult task he had undertaken and the wonders he had accomplished during the season.

To date, no Mahler biographer has mentioned one event that took place during his stay in Laibach. On March 5, 1882, he was soloist in a Philharmonic Society concert. He was "accompanied by a string quartet" in Mendelssohn's *Capriccio Brillant,* Opus 22, displaying the "brilliant technique of which he was master." Then, in order to thank his enthusiastic audience, he played Chopin's *Grande Polonaise* in A flat (with "much bravura") and the *"Jagdlied"* and *"Vogel als Prophet"* from Schumann's *Waldscenen.* Except for a charity concert given in Iglau in August 1883, this was Mahler's last public appearance as a pianist. From then on he played the piano for friends, for chamber music, or for rehearsing singers and occasionally accompanying them during a recital.[38]

Because no letters written by Mahler at this period are available, we have little information concerning his daily life in Laibach. At first he lived at the home of his friend Krisper's parents.[39] In order to appear older than he was, he wore a beard and a mustache. Mahler apparently wanted to do this earlier, but his father had been against the idea. He also wore enormous tortoise-shell spectacles to correct his shortsightedness and to enable him to "see in the theater in all directions at once."[40] His fanaticism and idealism already provoked a somewhat scornful astonishment among his colleagues: Alma Mahler states, for instance, that one day during a rehearsal Mahler reproached a singer for the lightness of her morals. The young woman jumped up onto the piano, slapped her thighs, and advised Mahler to mind his own business, since his own ascetic life struck her as being both grotesque and suspicious.

The Landestheater closed its doors on April 2 with a final production of *Der lustige Krieg,* and Mahler left Laibach after a benefit concert given the same day for the theater's choir, during which he accompanied a violinist named Gerstner in a Vieuxtemps *Ballade* and *Polonaise.*

Unimportant and unpleasant as the Laibach interlude had been for the youthful idealist, it proved a decisive step in his career, for it was there that he began to acquire the theatrical experience and the orchestral control essential for his future success. From then on he knew he would be a conductor: he had discovered his gifts of interpretation and had mastered many scores during those long months of feverish effort devoted not only to rehearsals but also to intensive personal work. All the critics of the period agree that the season conducted by Mahler was the best of all those organized by Mondheim-Schreiner.

Returning home from Laibach, Mahler saw the sea for the first time at Trieste, and enjoyed the Adriatic sunshine. He wrote to Löwy to announce his impending arrival in Vienna, and asked him to think urgently about finding him a new post.[41] For Mahler the dismal years of unemployment and poverty were over at last.

"When a noble steed is harnessed
with oxen . . ."

# CHAPTER 7

## Vienna and Olmütz — Brothers and Sisters — Literary
## Affinities (1882–83)

After leaving Laibach, and despite his success there, Mahler was again forced to return to his inactive Vienna existence. Once more he planned to spend the summer with the Baumgartens in Hungary and was thus the only one of the vegetarian group to miss the premiere of *Parsifal* in Bayreuth. Back in Iglau, he conducted his one and only stage performance there on September 19: Suppé's *Boccaccio,* which he had doubtless also conducted in Laibach. Two days later, the *Iglauer Grenzbote* praised the excellent casting, the good staging, and above all the musical performance: "The ensembles were perfect, bearing witness to the spirited and crisp direction by our townsfellow Herr Mahler, who was on the podium, and who recently initiated his career as *Kapellmeister* with such marked success at Laibach." Writing some months later to Krisper, Mahler complained about the stupidity of the young prima donna, Fräulein Hassmann, who was making her debut that day. "She is the least gifted of all the female creatures who have come to my attention for a long time." Perhaps hoping to persuade Mahler to take a job at the Iglau Theater, the local paper criticized his successor on the podium adversely, regretting, in the subsequent performances, "the lack of energetic control" that had been so remarkable in *Boccaccio.* But, as we know from Mahler's 1880 letter to Löwy, Mahler was determined not to conduct again in Iglau and had no doubt only done it to help out the director.

Mahler returned to Vienna in the fall and continued his monotonous existence as piano teacher and unperformed composer. He wrote some lieder[1] and worked on the first act of *Rübezahl,* the fairy-tale opera he had begun the preceding year. Only one document exists from this autumn—a short letter dated November 30, from the socialist doctor Victor Adler and his wife, inviting him to dinner.

On November 14, Marie Mahler wrote to her son urging him to follow her advice and not treat her "worries" lightly; and on December 15, in a long and charming letter, she suggests that he take advantage of a reduced rate "special train" to visit Iglau for the Christmas vacation. At that time he would not be able to give lessons, and the few days during which he would make no money would cost him more than the journey. He need bring no luggage; just a paper bag containing shirts and socks in need of mending. "Does any other man change his lodgings every two weeks?" she continues. "In the end you'll change addresses as often as your shirt, and have no clothes or underclothes left. I know you well enough to be sure you forget something everywhere, and you'll go on moving until you've nothing! Isn't this so?"[2]

At the New Year, Mahler complained to Krisper about his wandering life: in three months he had occupied no less than five different lodgings, not to mention hotel rooms.[3] When he was in a good mood, he would become lost in his work, only to find that a baby's crying or a nearby piano player would drive away his inspiration. When calm returned, inspiration had fled. Despite these unsatisfactory working conditions, he hoped that Act I of *Rübezahl* would soon be complete.

On December 8, Mahler wrote to the director of the Salzburg Theater, Leopold Müller, asking for the post of conductor at that theater. In his reply, dated the eleventh, Müller says that he has not yet engaged anyone for the following winter: in fact he attaches such importance to the choice that he wishes to see the candidate on the podium before taking a decision. For the moment he is looking for a head assistant who can rehearse the chorus and direct the farces and operettas. If Mahler does not consider such a position too modest, he could thus get to know the theater for the following year.[4] No doubt Mahler preferred to wait until he found a post more worthy of his capacities, for the letter he wrote to Krisper at the beginning of January does not mention his negotiations with Müller.

This letter to Krisper makes no reference to Mahler's engagement in Olmütz, which was wholly unexpected: according to the Olmütz papers, Mahler was in fact called there by telegram on January 10.[5] Once more Mahler's memory was at fault when he told his wife that he went directly from Laibach to Kassel, "after having read in a newspaper that a post as conductor was free there." He also stated that he left the Slovenian town without regret and without saying good-by to his superiors.[6] Mahler remembered feeling "misunderstood and unhappy" there, but he forgot a stay of several months in Vienna afterwards, followed by the Olmütz engagement, which preceded that in Kassel. The latter was in fact negotiated by an exchange of letters between the impresario Löwy and the theater management.[7]

Once an Austrian stronghold, the town of Olmütz, like Jihlava, had remained a small oasis of German culture in Moravia—a Czech province whose national conscience was then awakening. At that time Olmütz had some twenty thousand inhabitants. The German Municipal Theater, built in 1830, stood in the main square. For some years it had been going through an artistic and economic crisis, which became acute in 1880, when Emanuel Raul was made director. He distinguished himself from his predecessors by his pronounced taste for new works, but also by his lack of discernment in choosing them. He staged expensive productions of mediocre operas that bored the public and made large inroads in the theater budget.

Facing financial ruin, Raul naturally had to ask the town authorities for subsidies, which were usually refused. That December he had even delegated several of the theater's actresses to second his efforts to persuade the Municipal Council members to make further grants, but they had turned a deaf ear, replying that "many touring companies had better actors than the Municipal Theater," that "the income from the Olmütz Theatre was extraordinarily high, considering the mediocre quality of its players," and that Raul "was trying the patience of the citizens to the utmost" with his disappointing new productions. A further demand for a subsidy was down on the Municipal Council's agenda the day before Mahler's arrival, that is, January 9, 1883. Raul had been forced to admit that in two years the sale of season tickets had dropped by half, and that the deficit for the present season was already five thousand florins.[8]

To make matters worse, on January 10, 1883, after a performance of Meyerbeer's *L'Africaine,* a quarrel broke out at the theater between the director and his chief conductor, Georg Kaiser,[9] who considered his salary insufficient. The situation became so explosive that the police had to be called in. The next day the press got hold of the story and accused Raul of "shamefully robbing the taxpayers," of "causing scandalous scenes," and of "transforming the Temple of Thalia into a third-class cabaret." It is not known whether Kaiser resigned or was fired, but the following day his departure was announced in the German newspaper *Mährisches Tagblatt.* The announcement continues: "The conducting of the operas for the rest of this season will be entrusted to a young *Kapellmeister* summoned by telegram from Vienna, Gustav Mahler. The latter will take up his task under very difficult circumstances; the forthcoming opera performances will tell if he is capable of fulfilling his duties." Mahler's engagement was almost certainly arranged through Löwy, though Raul may very well have heard talk in Moravia about the brilliant young musician who had been so successful in Laibach and who would surely become a credit to his native province.

Thus conditions at the Olmütz Theater were scarcely better than those in Laibach, and the situation was not helped by the fact that the director had had to resign after the Kaiser affair, because of the subsequent press campaign against him. Raul, like Mondheim-Schreiner, combined the functions of director with those of head producer, while his wife sang alto roles. The forces at Mahler's disposal were slightly superior to those in Laibach: the orchestra consisted of thirty musicians, and the chorus numbered twenty. Most of the singers were actors, too, and not one of them made his mark in the annals of opera. The repertoire seems to have been more limited than in Laibach, but perhaps the level of performance was slightly higher.

However, the report of the theater committee, published in the *Mährisches Tagblatt* on February 8, mentions the "unbelievably dilapidated" décors and the primitive stage machinery and installations in general.

Mahler reached Olmütz on January 10 and three days later announced in the *Mährisches Tagblatt* that he would not conduct that day's performance of *Les Huguenots,* prepared by his predecessor, "because he had not yet had time to familiarize himself with the theater." The real reason for this delay was slightly different, as Mahler later confessed to Natalie Bauer-Lechner. Not only had he not had time to "familiarize himself" with his colleagues, but, more important still, he did not know a single note of the score of *Les Huguenots* and was determined not to admit this fact, since he had recently learned the hard way not to confess to this form of ignorance.[10] One day while waiting in an agent's outside office, he had overheard a contralto singing an aria (*"Ah! mon fils"*) from Meyerbeer's *Le Prophète.* Later Mahler asked the impresario who had composed the aria. Horrified by this ignorance, the impresario refused to help Mahler. This was why, in Olmütz, Mahler preferred to spend several nights learning the score of *Les Huguenots* rather than admit that he did not know it. "It was an excellent performance, and that day Meyerbeer pleased me a lot," he added when he told this story later.

On January 13, *Die Neue Zeit* published a statement to the effect that young Mahler had never before conducted an opera. The writer of the article deplored an engagement that, in his view, was hardly likely to raise the artistic level of the opera. After the performance, on January 15, the *Mährisches Tagblatt* spoke of Mahler's remarkable zeal and talent but comments adversely on a "certain haste" in his conducting, perhaps caused by nervousness. It is surprising to learn from this article that Mahler had to conduct from a piano score. With the exception of a few "incidents," in particular the premature entry of a horn in the Act II *"Choeur des baigneuses,"* the evening proceeded normally, and Mahler seems to have carried off without apparent difficulty the tour de force he had attempted. Three days later, on January 18, he conducted Meyerbeer's *Robert le Diable*[11] in a performance that was praised by the same critic, despite another "incident," which had isolated the wind instruments from the rest of the orchestra in Act IV. The German daily paper, *Die Neue Zeit,* resolutely conservative, was immediately hostile to the young conductor. It again criticized the engagement of a "beginner" and attributed a large part of the success of *Robert le Diable* to the "excellent" chorus and orchestra, as well as to Mahler's predecessor, Kaiser. According to this article, only a long pause had prevented a complete "derailment" in Act V, and the young conductor had to fumble his way back onto the tracks.

Mahler himself was appalled by his working conditions. Already on January 20, on a hurried postcard to his new friend, the philosopher Fritz

Löhr, he writes that he is "in a very bad temper." A month later, on February 12, he explains the reasons for his bitterness:

"I am paralyzed, like one who has just fallen to earth from heaven. Ever since I entered the Olmütz Theater, I have felt like a man who is awaiting the Last Judgment. When a noble steed is harnessed with oxen to a cart, he has no choice but to pull and sweat with them. I scarcely dare to appear before you, I feel so covered with filth . . .

"I am almost always alone except during rehearsals. Up to now, thank God, I have conducted almost nothing but Meyerbeer and Verdi. I have successfully plotted against including Wagner and Mozart in the repertoire, as I could not bear to massacre *Lohengrin* or *Don Giovanni* here. To-morrow, [Méhul's] *Joseph in Aegypten*. It is a charming work that has a little of Mozart's grace; I have rehearsed it with a good deal of pleasure. I ought to say that, despite the incredible insensitivity of my good people, they often do put themselves out for my sake; this time they have been more serious than usual. Unhappily, they do this only out of a sort of pity for my 'idealism,' a term of supreme scorn in this town. They absolutely cannot understand an artist's being entirely absorbed by a work of art. Often when I am burning with the fire of enthusiasm and am trying to carry them along toward a greater involvement, I suddenly see their stupefied faces smiling at each other knowingly. Then my effervescing blood subsides in a flash, and I would like to run away for good. Only the feelings I bear for my masters, and the hope that perhaps after all I shall be able to project into the souls of these unhappy creatures a spark from their fire, steels my courage. I vow during those happier hours to bear with love even their mockery. Perhaps you will laugh at the pathos with which I speak of these insignificant little details. But isn't it really symbolical of our relation to the world?"

This letter, written when Mahler was twenty-three, already indicates his life long attitude toward interpretation. The insignificant *Kapellmeister* of the provincial Olmütz Theater is already the tyrannical idealist, in love with accuracy and perfection, who was to arouse so much anger and resistance when he conducted the Budapest and Vienna opera houses; he spared neither his subordinates nor himself and would rehearse a passage a thousand times if necessary, to bring out a nuance, underline a rhythm, or lighten a tone. What battles his enthusiasm and inflexible sense of artistic quality were to wage against mediocrity, routine, lethargy, and "tradition" in order to defend his well-loved "masters." And how often, during the struggle, Mahler was to suffer from the same solitude and despair in the face of stupidity and indifference!

During his short stay at the little provincial theater of Olmütz, Mahler had at least one satisfaction, that of discussing his depressing work conditions with Karl Muck, an eminent colleague who later became one of the best known conductors of his time. According to the latter, Mahler's idealism already showed in his conversation. Muck wrote: "He attempted to give first-class performances with an orchestra of thirty musicians, and naturally failed, to his eternal sorrow, because of the feeble means at his command. Because of this he put more strain on his nerves than anyone else would have done in his position. However I do not remember his ever falling ill. He was indeed very thin, but he had a strong constitution and amazing energy."

At Olmütz, then, Mahler was lonely and unhappy. He also suffered from hunger, since he was a vegetarian in a district where only meat was eaten. He lodged on the second floor of a vast Renaissance building built by rich shopkeepers—Au Brochet d'Or (At the Sign of the Golden Pike), No. 1 Michalska Street, on the corner of Sarkandrova Street.[12] Moreover—the inevitable curse of Mahler's life—there were two pianos in the house, on which people played for hours at a time, and seemingly always the hours when he was present! Worse still, he had left Vienna so hurriedly that he had not thought to bring books with him, and asked Löhr to send him some. He does not seem to have made friends in Olmütz during his short and trying stay there. Only one anecdote has come down to us to indicate that at least one door was open to him. According to the anonymous article published at the time of Mahler's Death in *Die Neue Zeit* (Olmütz, May 20, 1911), he spent the whole of one Sunday in the house of a man who encouraged the arts, playing *Die Walküre* on the piano and singing all the roles.

What was Mahler's repertoire during the three months in Olmütz? His assistant, Hugo Schenk, in theory conducted the operettas by Offenbach, Strauss, Suppé, etc. At the end of January, after *Les Huguenots* and *Robert le Diable,* Mahler conducted Auber's *La Muette de Portici* and Meyerbeer's *L'Africaine.* In February he prepared a new production of Verdi's *Un Ballo in maschera,* as well as Méhul's *Joseph.* At the end of that month the premiere was postponed, due to the illness of the prima donna, for whom there was no substitute in so modest a company, and this gave him a few days' respite.

The first performance of *Un Ballo in maschera* was warmly praised by the critics of the *Mährisches Tagblatt* and also by *Die Neue Zeit,* which up to then had been severely critical of Mahler. Later the press agreed unanimously that this performance was the highlight of the 1882/83 season. Mahler sent a copy of the two articles to Löwy.[13] According to Mahler the praise was all the more significant because from the time of his arrival in Olmütz— and before he had conducted at all—the papers had adopted a somewhat hostile attitude toward him, due to the influence of a local conductor, offended at not having been offered the post. In his letter to the impresario Mahler states that after Act III he was applauded by the audience. He ended by expressing the hope that Löwy would "remember" him.

Shortly after this important event, on February 13, Mahler learned of the death of Richard Wagner, the greatest contemporary German musician and, in his opinion, second only to Beethoven as a composer.[14] No letter known to be in existence mentions this event, but it is not difficult to guess at Mahler's feelings. In Vienna five years earlier, unlike Hugo Wolf, he had been too shy to visit Wagner, but no doubt he was still hoping to see him in the course of the pilgrimage to Bayreuth he had dreamed of making for so long and that he was to accomplish the following year. With Richard Wagner's death the brightest star, the guiding light of German music, disappeared. Mahler was one of his most fervent supporters; with heart and soul he admired not only the great artist but the great man, and in many ways considered him his spiritual father. Better than anyone he knew the irreplaceable loss that music had suffered.

The Musikverein, Olmütz's German Choral Society, decided to give a memorial concert in honor of the great musician. No doubt wishing to show their sympathy for the previous theater *Kapellmeister* and to condemn the injustice of his sudden departure, they invited Kaiser to conduct. Mahler was probably not sorry: he would not have enjoyed performing Wagner with such mediocre voices and musicians. While waiting to express his Wagnerian enthusiasm, he had to be content with more modest tasks. On February 15 he conducted a benefit evening for the contralto Frau Meyer, which included the first act of Nicolai's *Die lustigen Weiber von Windsor,* the second acts of *Rigoletto* and *Un Ballo in maschera,* and the last act of *Le Prophète.* On February 25 he accompanied on the piano a lieder concert given by some opera singers,[15] and on March 10 he conducted again, this time the first Olmütz production of *Carmen.*

Many difficulties arose during rehearsals. The director, Raul, who was taking less and less interest in theater affairs, allowed the principal soprano to leave, and it was almost impossible to find a replacement among the few remaining singers. The day before the premiere, five members of the chorus left Olmütz without any warning, and an hour before the curtain was due to rise the local school children's chorus was refused permission to appear on stage, though it had taken part in all the rehearsals. Despite these many setbacks, the evening seems to have been entirely successful. According to the *Mährisches Tagblatt,* Mahler had "brought out the beauty and subtlety of the score, while knowing how to conceal the weaknesses of the performance." Even his enemy, the critic of the *Neue Zeit,* laid down his arms before the "technical perfection" of the performance, which "expressed the spirit of the work."[16] The next day *Carmen* was given again, and the day after that, Mahler, as in Laibach, conducted his own benefit concert. His efforts were rewarded by enthusiastic applause and he received an elaborate laurel crown. Before leaving Olmütz, Mahler conducted a repeat performance of *Il Trovatore,*[17] and a third *Carmen* ended the season on March 17.

It is difficult to place an anecdote told to his wife by Mahler. It seems that one evening "in Kassel" he agreed to conduct *Martha* from memory, though the evening before the performance he did not know a single note. However, this most popular of Flotow's operas had figured in his repertoire in Laibach, so it cannot have been Mahler who carried out this tour de force. He must have been referring either to *Les Huguenots,* which he

conducted when he first arrived in Olmütz, not Kassel,[18] or Heinrich Marschner's *Hans Heiling,* which was one of the "tests" to which Mahler was
submitted in Kassel before being given the post.

Another anecdote seems closer to biographical truth. Conducting from memory a brilliant performance of *Carmen* in Olmütz, Mahler was noticed
by the director of the Kassel Theater, who immediately engaged him.
However, it was not Von Gilsa, the director, who heard *Carmen* in Olmütz
in March 1883,[19] but Karl Ueberhorst, a producer at the Dresden Theater.
If Mahler's memory of details is again at fault, he was right in asserting that
the wonders he accomplished in Olmütz with provincial musicians and singers
were instrumental in bringing about his Kassel engagement, for he did in
fact obtain it thanks to Ueberhorst's recommendation.[20]

According to press reports and other documents of the time, it seems clear
that Mahler had, at least temporarily, saved Raul and the theater from total
failure. His talent and enthusiasm had worked wonders, and in consequence
Raul had not completely lost face. The situation was to grow progressively
worse after Mahler's departure, especially since most of the members of the
company left Olmütz at the same time as he did, on March 18, Palm Sunday.
The next day the *Mährisches Tagblatt* announced that he had returned to
Vienna "to continue his studies." In fact, he had already accepted an
engagement as chorus master for a season of Italian opera, organized by
the impresario Marelli at the Carl-Theater, a small house on the outskirts
of Vienna, near the Prater. Mahler's correspondence contains only one
much later allusion to this episode.[21] No detailed information exists concerning his activities during that season, for the Carl-Theater is privately
owned and has kept no records, but a certain amount can be learned from
periodicals of the time.

The performances were given from March 30 to May 2 inclusive, and
the repertoire included Bellini's *La Sonnambula,* Rossini's *Il Barbiere di
Siviglia,* Donizetti's *Lucia di Lammermoor* and *Lucrezia Borgia,* and Verdi's
*La Traviata* and *Il Trovatore.* A young conductor with the high-sounding
name of Cavaliere Oreste Bimboni arrived in Vienna from Italy, as did
most of the singers, on March 22 for the rehearsals. The prima donna,
Etelka Gerster, a Hungarian soprano, a pupil of Marchesi at the Vienna
Conservatory, was at the start of a brilliant international career that had
already taken her to England in 1877 and to New York in 1878.

The opening performance, *Lucia di Lammermoor,* was a great success,
"surpassing all expectations, which for many reasons had been modest."[22]
The male chorus in the first scene was considered highly ridiculous, since it
seemed made up of "candidates for the role of Falstaff," but, thanks to
Mahler perhaps, "they sang passably." On the second day, the whole
future of the season was in jeopardy, since the prima donna fell victim to
"the redoubtable fever that often seizes the most experienced theatrical
people, stage fright." So great was her anguish that she refused to sing,
much to the despair of the impresario and his secretary, who drew up an

announcement canceling the performance: "Because of the unexpected cancellation by Frau Ethelka [sic] Gerster, the theater will remain closed today. Despite the pressing pleas of the Management, Frau Gerster has refused to sing, though Professor Schnitzler has ascertained that no serious indisposition prevents her from appearing on the stage." After reading this notice, the prima donna made a miraculous recovery and at once agreed to perform.

After his work at the Carl-Theater, Mahler rested for a time at Perchtoldsdorf, near Vienna, at the home of Fritz Löhr, the new friend introduced to him by Hans Rott and Rudolf Krzyzanowski. Löhr has described their excursions in the enchanting hills of the Wienerwald. The two young men reveled in the beauties of nature, while discussing art and literature. Sometimes their walks resembled a pilgrimage as they passed through the small village of Heiligenstadt, made immortal by the memory of Beethoven; from there they went on to Nussdorf and climbed the Kahlenberg, from where they could gaze out over the whole of Vienna and the Danube Valley.

Later, at the beginning of summer, upon his return from Kassel,[23] Mahler sometimes played the piano in Löhr's little bedroom, which looked out over the Markplatz of Perchtoldsdorf.[24] Despite the heat, Löhr kept the window closed, as otherwise the passers-by would gather in the street to listen. The words Löhr chooses to describe Mahler's playing recall many later descriptions of his conducting. "Disembodied," "surpassing all human and technical considerations," "transfigured" (entkörpert, entrückt), "magnificently rendering each nuance, each degree in the gamut of sound," with the attention to detail that later struck all those who saw Mahler conducting. Never, according to Löhr, did the storm at the beginning of Beethoven's Opus 111 sonata rumble with such savage violence; never was the end of that sonata interpreted with such clear and disembodied sounds; its clarity seemed "to open the gates of eternity."

On vacation afternoons Mahler also liked to play for his friends preludes and fugues from Das wohltemperirte Clavier and other works by Bach. At that period, the piano was still a familiar means of expression for him. Löhr also heard him playing in lodgings that he occupied near the Karlsplatz in Vienna. On that occasion Mahler played Beethoven's Missa Solemnis from beginning to end, scarcely taking time to breathe, he was so carried away by the grandeur of the music.

Mahler's friendship with Löhr was to prove one of the closest and most lasting in his life. When Mahler's parents died and his brothers and sisters moved from Iglau to Vienna, Löhr kept an eye on their studies, and for many years Mahler was to pass part of each summer with him in Iglau, in Perchtoldsdorf, or in Hinterbrühl. Judging from the style of the abundant notes that Löhr made for the collection of Mahler's letters, Löhr was a fussy, pompous, pedantic, and rather limited man, but his affectionate admiration for Mahler is undeniable. Even before Natalie Bauer-Lechner, he was the confidant of Mahler's youth, about which he has given a multitude of useful details, for he followed each stage in the development of his friend's personality with the greatest interest. Like many other great men, Mahler preferred his friends to be confidants rather than equals. His domineering personality was still in the formative stage, and he needed reliable, peaceful friends like Löhr, Emil Freund, and the Krzyzanowski brothers. Mahler remained attached to most of these confidants of his stormy youth —even after he became aware of their faults and limitations.

Mahler's attitude toward his family is one of the most fascinating and least known aspects of his personality. Most contemporaries have given the same, now classic description of a nervous, impatient, exacting, despotic man, too often merciless in the face of human failings. But the many unpublished letters written by him to his parents and to his sister Justi[25] reveal a quite different aspect of his personality; a Mahler whom neither his theater colleagues nor even, later on, his Vienna friends ever knew: an exceptionally attentive and devoted son[26] who later, as head of the family, showed untiring patience and abnegation toward his four brothers and sisters. Each time that Otto's laziness or Alois's weakness led to a new catastrophe, Mahler—though at first exasperated and furious—would try to save the situation and by good advice get them back onto the straight and narrow path.

Bernhard and Marie Mahler had fourteen children, of whom all but six died in infancy. The eldest girl, Leopoldine or Poldi, was three years younger than Gustav. In 1882 or 1883 she married a Jewish-Hungarian merchant named Ludwig Quittner. It was doubtless a marriage of convenience like her mother's, and Poldi was to regret it for many years. Later Mahler blamed himself for having been "young and ignorant" and not trying to prevent the marriage; he had not realized what suffering it would cause his sister.

During the early years of this marriage, Quittner, who had been born in Palgocz, Hungary, made and sold collars and cuffs in Vienna. Later, having become a "commercial agent," he constantly changed addresses, which seems to indicate that he was poor. Mahler mentions Poldi only three times in his letters.[27] The second shows that a certain coldness had crept into his relationship with his eldest sister: "If Madame Poldi has become so proud, she will have to bear the consequences of her attitude. In any case, I recall that she congratulated me very briefly on my engagement in Leipzig. Perhaps she is waiting for a letter of thanks for that." This pride, which is all we know of Poldi's character, could indicate the reserve of an unhappy woman toward a brother more successful than herself.

In a letter written from Prague on September 6, 1885,[28] Mahler promises to introduce Quittner to a friend named Feld, offers to help him whenever possible, and invites Poldi to stay with him in order to discuss the ways and means of helping. A photograph of Poldi taken before her marriage[29] shows a handsome sad face with large jet-black eyes recalling those of Mahler as a child. During the summer of 1889, Poldi suffered from terrible headaches, and she died after a sudden illness, almost certainly from a brain tumor, on September 27, scarcely fifteen days before her mother's death.[30] She left two children, aged two and four.

Toward his second sister, Justine, Mahler displayed a tenderness and affection that survived a succession of small conflicts and crises. The countless letters that he wrote to her show the solicitude he felt for the sister who was his companion during the most difficult years of his life.

"A simple and completely defenseless human being" was how Mahler described Justi in a letter to Natalie Bauer-Lechner.[31] And in fact it is as a warm, impulsive, somewhat childish person, lacking in culture and common sense, and not above disguising the truth when she feared to irritate her awesome brother, that Justi appears in letters and contemporary accounts. Acting from instinct rather than reason, she frequently irritated Gustav by indulging in family intrigue. But she was devoted to him, heart and soul, as later on she was devoted to her husband, Arnold Rosé.

Alma Mahler relates a curious anecdote that shows that as a child Justi possessed a morbid imagination. One evening, when she was about ten, she had the idea of placing a dozen lighted candles around her small bed. Then she lay down and imagined she was dead. Far from giving rise to amusement, this macabre game makes one's blood run cold when one considers the child's age at the time and realizes how much knowledge she had acquired of death and its rites. Certain tragic childhood memories were probably responsible for the funeral vision that assailed Mahler later on, when he was composing *Das klagende Lied* and the *Second Symphony*.[32]

Emma, Mahler's third sister, was fifteen years his junior. Gentle, shy, rather self-effacing in her youth, she no doubt suffered first from her parents' ill-health and then from Justi's somewhat unorthodox ideas on education. Justi was authoritative, but she was not gifted as a teacher. In the few photographs of Emma that exist she seems to have had more character and personality than her husband. She lived first in Vienna, where she worked for some time in a shop. Later she married Eduard Rosé, the cellist and elder brother of Arnold. She lived with him in Boston and later Weimar. They had two sons. In 1882 she was Mahler's "little sister," only seven years old, and the baby of the family. Later, when their parents died, Mahler watched over her education from a distance.

The elder of Mahler's two brothers, Louis or Alois,[33] born in 1867, was a strange, irresponsible person whose odd ways bordered on mental instability. He resented all forms of discipline, and his chronic carelessness and laziness did not lessen his pride and pretension. One day he hired an old horse and rode it through the streets of Iglau dressed as a German mercenary from the Middle Ages, with one trouser leg blue, the other red. To his astonished and ashamed parents he said, "Just as you see me now, one day I'll ride past the Burg [the Imperial Palace in Vienna], and the Crown Prince, seeing me, will say, 'Who is this handsome horseman?' and will summon me to give me an important position."

Unfortunately, Alois had none of the qualities necessary to realize this dream of glory or even to succeed in his chosen profession of shopkeeper. Neither of Mahler's brothers was a model of virtue, but Alois gave him the most trouble. Just before their father died, he criticized Alois severely, and the future showed that he was right. Careless, extravagant, a compulsive liar and storyteller, lavishly spending money he did not have, Alois tried Gustav's patience sorely.

In the autumn of 1892, after three years' compulsory military service as a private, Alois developed serious lung trouble and Mahler was obliged to send him, with Justi, to recuperate in the mountains. They stayed at a pension in Merano,[34] where all the guests took their meals at a long table d'hôte. One evening the petrified Justi heard Alois boasting that he had served as a volunteer in one of the most elegant and aristocratic Austrian cavalry regiments. An army officer in civilian clothes began asking Alois embarrassing questions about some friends of his who had served in the same regiment, and Alois became more and more tangled up in his inventions. Luckily the meal ended before the discussion became acrimonious, but Justi felt it necessary to leave the town at once in order to save Alois from the embarrassment of a similar conversation.

Though reproaching Alois for his laziness and mythomania, for a long while Mahler remained irreproachably loyal to him. When he went to Hamburg, he tried to get Alois into a large business school there, always hoping that he would reform. But his brother's too frequent misdemeanors, and the evil genius that seemed to inspire his actions, finally discouraged him. One of Alois's obsessions was to be accepted by society. He called himself Hans Christian, considering this name "less Jewish" and more elegant than his own, and he liked to wear a top hat, a flowered waistcoat, and white spats. Incapable of earning the money necessary to realize these dreams of grandeur, he contracted many debts and even seems to have had trouble with the police over a forged check.[35] From 1904 to 1907, Alois (from then on "Hans Christian") was office manager and bookkeeper at the Heller Confectionery in Vienna. He left for New York a year before his brother, to represent the Heller company there. When Gustav in his turn reached New York in 1908, Alois called at his hotel. Later he seems to have moved to Chicago, where he set up as a baker and died some time between 1920 and 1930.[36]

The last reference to Alois in Mahler's correspondence is to be found in a letter to Alma Mahler, dated January 1904, in which Alois is referred to as a "writer" and "chief accountant." The relations between the two brothers at that time were extremely cold: when they met by accident at the Vienna railroad station they did not speak, and Mahler was even afraid that chance might have placed him in the same compartment as his brother, "which would have been embarrassing for both of us."

Unlike Alois, Otto, the youngest of the brothers, seems to have displayed intelligence and marked musical gifts at an early age, and an equally markéd distaste for hard work. While his parents were still alive, Mahler assumed responsibility for Otto's musical education and sent him to study at the Vienna Conservatory. After his parents' deaths Gustav installed his brothers and sisters in an apartment in the capital and put Justi in charge of Otto's studies, which were never brilliant. Like Alois, Otto was lazy, capricious, and lacking in will power; the least temptation distracted him from his studies. Into the bargain he was oversensitive and proud. No matter how many tutors and opportunities he was given, the level of his work remained poor.

During all the time that Mahler spent in Hamburg, in each letter he complains, scolds, storms, and despairs because Otto will not work, has failed to attend an examination, shows no interest in his future, etc. Sermons, remonstrances, calls to order—nothing helped. For a few days Otto would wander about, depressed and melancholic, feeling unloved and misunderstood, but he lacked both the will and the energy to keep from reverting to his bad habits. "One cannot deny," Mahler wrote to Justi in 1893, "that his education has been ruined from the beginning. Fritz Löhr on one hand, the young girls [Fritz's sisters] on the other, and then Nina, have completely spoiled him. We can only hope that his good disposition and the modicum of 'good Mahler blood' running in his veins will finally emerge so that everything will end well."

But that was too much to expect from a young man whose lack of stability prevented him from making the most of his modest talent. Otto was rejected in 1894 by a military examining board when he tried to volunteer for the army, since it was discovered that he was almost blind in his left eye.[37] Shortly afterward, Mahler persuaded Max Staegemann, director of the Leipzig Theater, to give Otto a five-year appointment as Chordirektor. From then on, there is no further mention of Otto in his brother's known correspondence. Since Otto's character and insufficient musical gifts prevented him from succeeding, he probably returned to Vienna almost at once. There he saw a great deal of Nina Hoffmann,[38] a friend of the Mahlers who had married a well-known painter-architect and who had herself published translations of Dostoyevsky. They spent many hours discussing the tragic meaning of life, the fall of man, and other pessimistic themes from the works of the great Russian novelist. Mahler considered that these discussions and Nina's influence played a vital role in Otto's suicide, which took place at her home on February 6, 1895.

This, then, was Mahler's family: the two girls were loyal and devoted wives who led mainly happy, well-organized lives, and the two boys were weak individuals who became victims of their own weakness and instability. It seems that, even discounting his genius—by definition an exceptional, quasi-miraculous gift—nature had concentrated in the oldest brother both the talent and the ability to develop it: that is to say, energy and will power, as well as integrity. What torture it must have been for Mahler to witness the successive setbacks of his brothers, whom he then had to support on his own hard-earned theatrical salary. Most geniuses are generally more egotistical than altruistic; they rarely believe so strongly in the sacred ties of family life. For many years this conviction remained unshaken, despite the fact that his brothers' weaknesses were incomprehensible to someone with his own steely determination.

Although the relationship between Bernhard Mahler and Gustav was never particularly close, Bernhard seems to have sensed his son's future greatness. One day he was walking in Vienna with Julius Tandler, whose own son, then a medical student, later became one of the town's most famous anatomy professors. As they passed the university, Tandler proudly declared to his companion that one day his son would teach there. A few minutes later the two friends reached the Ring, and Bernhard Mahler pointed to the opera house. "At this moment my son is conductor at the provincial theater in Laibach, but one day he will become director of the Hofoper!"[39]

Mahler always felt more respect than affection for his father, but it was from him that he inherited his strong family feeling that so closely resembles the paternalism characteristic of Jewish society; as the head of the family he felt morally and materially responsible for all its members. Right to the end he never refused to assume moral and financial responsibility for his brothers.

Even before he discovered the weaknesses and limitations of those close to him, Mahler had known, from early childhood, how to gather around him a spiritual family that never disappointed him. Other composers have rarely needed literature as a daily source of inspiration. But Mahler's mind, feelings, and indeed whole life were nourished by books, and certain of his favorite authors created or influenced the atmosphere of his works. "I devour more and more books! They are the only friends that I can take with me! And what friends! My God, what would I do without them! I forget all that goes on around me when such a voice from 'our own people' sounds! They are more and more familiar and consoling, my true brothers, and parents, and beloved."[40]

At the age of sixteen Mahler and his friends had founded a literary club that met each week for endless discussions.[41] All of his letters teem with literary allusions and with advice to his correspondents on their choice of reading. He was an enthusiastic reader from childhood on, and his tastes later included philosophy, under the influence of Siegfried Lipiner. In this he showed himself to be heir to the German romantics, and in particular to Wagner, for whom philosophy was an indispensable part of art.

Mahler was familiar with the writings of the great masters of German philosophy, Kant and Schopenhauer,[42] but he was even more interested in lesser known thinkers, especially those who attempted to combine philosophy and science. He read the mystic works of Fechner, for example, on the advice of Lipiner, who had studied under Fechner in Leipzig. The beliefs of this physicist, doctor, experimental psychologist and animist philosopher, who attributed a soul even to stars and plants,[43] no doubt influenced Mahler's conception in the *Third Symphony*. Rudolf Hermann Lotze, his lifelong friend, was closely akin to Fechner as a thinker; he dreamed of a philosophic union of science, art, literature, and religion and formed a theory of the microcosm which anticipated that of the atom. Mahler also read Johannes Reinke, the philosophic botanist, and Hermann Helmholtz, the Prussian philosopher and physicist who wrote a *Philosophic Theory of Music*.

This list of Mahler's favorite thinkers shows his desire to explain and understand everything, even subjects quite foreign to his art. Many romantic German artists tried to create scientific theories at a time when these various spheres of knowledge were much closer than they are today. Mahler was always attracted by the sciences, especially biology, and was delighted to discuss them, even with specialists. Bruno Walter, especially, recalled seeing him deep in discussion with one of his physicist friends,[44] and heard him elaborating with his usual enthusiasm a theory of gravity based on the centrifugal force of the sun; he even wished to go further and adapt it to various celestial phenomena.

Later, in Hamburg, Mahler became dazzled by the prose and philosophy of Nietzsche,[45] revealed to him by Lipiner and Victor Adler. The *Third Symphony* marks the zenith of his Nietzschean period. He first entitled it the *Gay Science* and incorporated Zarathustra's celebrated *Rondo* as a contralto solo. At first attracted by the beauty of the language and the poetic fervor of the work, he later turned away from this glorification of man, so opposed to his instinctive traditional sense of religion. Nietzsche's essential theme, the very quintessence of his thought, which is the conflicting Apollonian and Dionysiac principles, nevertheless influenced Mahler all his life.[46] Nietzsche may have had something to do with his discovery of *Des Knaben Wunderhorn* and his passion for folklore, in which the philosopher saw a union of these two principles. Having completely rejected the influence of Nietzsche, Mahler was later deeply shocked to find his complete works in the home of his fiancée, Alma Schindler: he even tried to persuade her to burn them on the spot.

According to Bruno Walter, who had many literary discussions with him, Mahler read and reread the mystic works of the poet-monk Angelus Silesius, for his medieval antitheses between light and darkness, eternity and time, all and nothing, etc., were for Mahler "as many discoveries of divinity." Among the great romantic writers, he knew Schiller well, but Goethe was always his favorite; not only *Faust,* which he set to music in his *Eighth Symphony,* but also the novels, the conversations with Johann Eckermann[47] and the book of Sulpiz Boisserée,[48] which enabled him to relive the great poet's daily life. During his conservatory years, he discussed

*Wilhelm Meister* at length with Natalie Bauer-Lechner, and toward the end of his life, when he considered abandoning conducting, he delighted in the idea of being able to read Goethe's complete correspondence.

Among the romantics, he preferred Hölderlin, whose two epics, *Patmos* and *The Rhine,* were particular favorites, as were the obscure poems written after the poet went mad. He was always a passionate admirer of Shakespeare, who was as popular in Germany as in England, and he also liked the great Austrian poet Grillparzer.[49]

Mahler's favorite prose writer was probably Jean Paul. His first letters show the influence of the writer's style. They echo Jean Paul's extravagances, his love of nature, his exaltation, and his sudden shifts from the sublime to the grotesque. Mahler considered *Siebenkäs* the "most perfect" work, but his preference went to *Titan,* though he always denied borrowing the title for his first symphonic work.[50] In July 1883, shortly after leaving Olmütz, Mahler took advantage of his first trip to Bayreuth to visit Wunsiedel, the birthplace of Jean Paul, "that extraordinary man, so nearly perfect, so accomplished, whom no one now knows any longer."[51] According to Bruno Walter, the grotesque funeral march in Mahler's *First Symphony* was inspired by Roquairol, the introspective, scornful, dangerous antihero of the *Titan.* Mahler believed that all men of talent contained the seeds of such a character, which they must dominate in order to achieve complete self-mastery.

Another character from German romantic literature—and one related to Roquairol—has often been mentioned in relation to Mahler. This is E. T. A. Hoffmann's famous Kapellmeister Kreisler, the hero of *Der Kater Murr* and of the *Kreisleriana,* who has the same exaltation, quickly changing moods, and idealism as the young Mahler. Grave and lighthearted, sublime and grotesque, nocturnal and naïve, Mahler's music is closely akin to the universe of Hoffmann.

The young Mahler's personality and behavior also in many ways resembled those of a Hoffmann hero; not only Kreisler, but also Anselm in *Der goldene Topf.* Anselm personifies the glorification of the poet, and his apparent madness is only the exaltation of a man enamored of purity. Like Kreisler, like Anselm, like Albano in the *Titan,* too, Mahler sought for the absolute and the meaning of life. Like them, he loathed reality, and, when disappointed, he turned to nature, to the earth, and to children, for purification and liberation. "Men must again become like simple children if they want to open their eyes to what is to be seen in the full light," Hoffmann wrote in *Der goldene Topf.* Mahler too was drawn toward the world of childhood and nearly always chose poems of popular origin for their simplicity and purity.

Like Hoffmann, and most romantics, Mahler was acutely conscious of the distance between the "cesspool" of daily life and the summits where the creator lives alone.[52] It was thus that humor developed as an antidote or counterpoison: "With him it was nothing but a very keen sense that made him discover a discordant note everywhere, an extreme talent that allowed him to make it appear."[53]

At the end of the nineteenth century the public were still charmed by Hoffmann's tales and had appreciated their humor, yet they severely criticized the same humor in Mahler's music, considering it destructive and reprehensible. Hoffmann's humor—satiric, grotesque, extravagant, fantastic, grimacing, linked to the world of sorrow and to that of dreams—came to life again in Mahler's music. "This irony, born of a profound look at humanity, which may be called nature's finest gift, coming as it does from the purest sources,"[54] disconcerted and even exasperated the first audiences who heard Mahler's symphonies and his *Humoresken* (as the songs of *Des Knaben Wunderhorn* were first called). Those "death leaps from one extreme to the other, which break the heart,"[55] are to be found in all his works; *Das klagende Lied,* the funeral march in the *First Symphony,* the Scherzo and Finale of the *Second,* the monumental first movement of the *Third,* right up to the final *Ninth,* whose central movements are one of the most striking examples.

Mahler himself connected these "death leaps" to an unhappy childhood incident,[56] and it is not known whether he ever consciously linked Hoffmann's characteristic style to his own, although he held his work in high esteem. He saw in it "a source of light and inspiration for musicians," as he said notably in a long letter that he wrote later to his wife: "If you examine Hoffmann's works with a well-disposed eye, you will gain new insights into the curious relations that exist between music and reality, music always mysterious and puzzling, but at times illuminating the soul like a streak of lightning. Then you will perceive that the only true reality in this world is our soul [*Gemüt*], and for him who has grasped this fact, everything real is nothing but schema and insignificant shadow. And I beg you *not* to take this for a poetic image, but rather as a conviction that will retain its validity even when confronted by the sober glance of the intellect . . ."[57]

Inspired by the admirable story *"Rat Krespel,"* Mahler evolved this Hoffmannesque conception of the essence of music. According to him, Antonia, the heroine, does not die of consumption; she dies because the demoniacal principle of art forces those possessed of it to abandon their own personalities. In Antonia's case she was only too ready to accept this demoniacal principle, which first leads to her disincarnation and finally snatches her away from life. Few artists have illustrated more clearly than Mahler this possession of the artist by his art, for he literally lived only for and by music.

Mahler also admired several humorous writers. We know that *Don Quixote* by Cervantes was always one of his favorite books. While writing his *Third Symphony* he often read it for relaxation. The humor of the English novelist Laurence Sterne also delighted him. He considered it an antidote to the poison of life, and a means of accepting the tragedy of human existence. He often alluded to the habits and maxims of old Shandy, in *Tristram Shandy*,[58] to the opening of the will in Jean Paul's *Years of Indiscretion* and to Dostoyevsky's short story "A Silly Affair," and each time he would laugh in retrospect.

Although Mahler lived almost entirely immured in his profession, he was always aware of the troubles that beset humanity. He discovered Dostoyevsky when the great Russian novelist was still little known in Western Europe. He found in his writing almost everything he himself was trying to express in music. He read all his works, and they made a deep and lasting impression on him. He urged everyone to read them and knew almost by heart the famous conversation between Ivan and Alyosha and the allegory of the Grand Inquisitor in *The Brothers Karamazov*. He considered that both passages essentially symbolized his own "World Sorrow" (*Weltschmerz*). Paraphrasing that episode, Mahler expressed his own Dostoyevskyan compassion for suffering humanity in a phrase that he often repeated: "How can one be happy on this earth while a single being is unhappy?" Throughout all his youth, Dostoyevsky remained his favorite author and had most influence on him. Early in life, he was greatly concerned by humanitarian and social problems. He was also an ardent reader of Ibsen. One of the most memorable events during his trip to Norway was his wordless encounter with the great dramatist, when, one day, quite by accident, he found himself sitting next to Ibsen in the reading room of a hotel in Christiania.[59]

Unlike most composers, these literary influences played an essential part in Mahler's formation. According to Specht, literature had a greater influence on his formative years than the scores of the great masters. One of the few other composers with such strong literary tendencies was Schumann. But, unlike Schumann, Mahler almost never used for his compositions the poems he admired the most. True, he set the final scene of *Faust* to music, but this was conceived as a kind of cantata in which only the music is lacking. The lyrics of Mahler's songs were taken either from Friedrich Rückert, a minor romantic poet, or from *Des Knaben Wunderhorn*, a folklore anthology. He was too receptive to poetry not to understand that the most beautiful, the most perfect poems are complete in themselves and that, in consequence, the greatest poets are always betrayed by composers.

"I have willingly let myself be
loaded with innumerable chains . . ."

# CHAPTER 8

*Mahler in Kassel (I) — Prussian Bureaucracy and Discipline — Der Trompeter von Säkkingen — Johanna Richter (1883–84)*

Miraculously, the correspondence that led to Mahler's engagement in Kassel still exists in the archives of the old Royal and Imperial Theater, having survived both bombing and fires. The impresario Löwy having learned early in May 1883 that the previous Kapellmeister Matzenauer had resigned and that the management needed a replacement, on May 12 he wrote to the intendant, Baron von Gilsa, praising "a young musician who is musically thoroughly trained, and who is extremely conscientious." He adds that a letter of recommendation is on its way from the chief stage director at the Dresden Theater Royal.[1]

Two days later, Karl Ueberhorst[2] did indeed write an enthusiastic letter to the intendant. "At Olmütz he rehearsed and conducted operas that I heard, displaying great care and remarkable taste despite the mediocrity of the singers at his disposal. I watched him with special care on the podium and saw that he knew how to make the best, cleverly and energetically, of the weak forces at hand, and that he succeeded in uniting them into a harmonious whole. He is an adept reader of scores and an accomplished pianist."

Baron von Gilsa asked Löwy to send him his candidate, and the Royal Berlin Administration, which was responsible for the Kassel Theater, tentatively offered Mahler a three-year contract at an annual salary of two thousand marks, plus living expenses. Mahler was asked to give his answer before May 21. On the nineteenth, his impresario accepted the conditions and signed a contract to act as Mahler's business representative on the same terms as before. Löwy, who was to receive 5 per cent of Mahler's salary, sent von Gilsa Mahler's curriculum vitae, which gives his age as twenty-five instead of twenty-two, for obvious reasons.

Löwy wrote to ask if Mahler's visit was essential to his engagement, since the theater had Ueberhorst's recommendation and his own. The journey from Vienna to Kassel was long and expensive, and the young musician was not rich. The answer must have been affirmative, for Mahler reached Kassel on May 22 and was given a week's trial. First he had to conduct the Overture to Rossini's *Guillaume Tell,* then for several days rehearsed the choruses. For the final test he had to conduct the dress rehearsal of Marschner's *Hans Heiling.* No doubt the intendant was satisfied, since on May 31 Mahler signed a contract, which was accompanied by a long and detailed description of his duties. By the terms of this contract, he would be known from October 1 as "Music and Choral Director" (*Königlicher Musik- und Chordirektor*) of the Kassel Theater.

Mahler returned to Vienna on June 1, having received the sum of two hundred marks to compensate him for the week's hard work, hardly enough to cover the cost of his trip. He spent three more weeks in the capital, and on June 15 he visited Bruckner, who noted in his diary that he had lent Mahler the score of his *Second Symphony.*[3]

Back in Iglau about June 20,[4] Mahler received a letter, dated the nineteenth, which confirmed that his contract had been approved by the Royal Berlin Administration. After an exchange of letters and telegrams sent between July 30 and August 10, it was decided that he would reach Kassel in time for the first chorus rehearsal on August 21.

Since Mahler had not been able to go to Bayreuth the year before with his vegetarian friends for the premiere of *Parsifal,* he used the money earned during the Italian season to visit Bayreuth. Unfortunately, since Wagner had died five months before, there was no longer any hope of meeting him.[5] Upon his return to Iglau, Mahler wrote to Fritz Löhr, to describe his impressions:

"Dear Fritz, I had scarcely returned from Bayreuth when I received your gift at a moment when it fell upon my somber darkness like a ray of light from heaven.

I cannot tell you what your lines and, through them, you yourself have become to me. In that way, with your unshakable love you have seen into the bottom of my heart through the arid aspect of my present life, and you believe in me as today I no longer believe in myself. I can hardly describe my present state to you. When I came out of the Festspielhaus, completely spellbound, I understood that the greatest and most painful revelation had just been made to me, and that I would carry it with me unspoiled all my life. And then, back here at home, I found those I love so sad, so dejected. . . . my parents, with the three iron rings that bind their breasts and their unhappy, tortured hearts, and I myself so hard and cruel toward them. Still, I cannot act otherwise, and I torment them relentlessly. And in three weeks I must leave to take up the duties of my new 'profession.' "[6]

Mahler gives no more details about his reaction to *Parsifal,* but goes on to say that he met Heinrich Krzyzanowski in Eger and went on a walking trip with him in the Fichtelgebirge as far as Wunsiedel, the birthplace of Jean Paul. Unfortunately some lines of this letter have been rubbed out by Fritz Löhr because of their "personal" nature, and it is therefore impossible to know what domestic crises Mahler was referring to. However, we learn that as early as 1883 both Mahler's parents suffered from the heart trouble that was to prove fatal six years later.

Soon after Mahler's return to Iglau, the local Red Cross organized a charity musical evening at the theater on Saturday, August 11, to be given in the presence of the Archduke Eugen in aid of the victims of the Ischia earthquake. The program was made up of music, drama, and recitations. An Iglau musician and contemporary of Mahler's, Hans Bruckmüller,[7] was asked to turn the pages during rehearsals of a one-act operetta by Karl Kuntze entitled *Das Kaffeekränzchen* or *Kaffeeklatsch,* which Mahler was to conduct and accompany on the piano. There was trouble as soon as the rehearsals started, for Mahler, irritated by this artless music, began to make ironic remarks about it to the six charitable Iglau ladies who were participating. He scarcely took the trouble to beat time, and consequently the preparations went ahead amid general bad temper.

On the gala evening, the piano was placed on a small platform in the center of the orchestra pit. As the performance proceeded, Mahler showed more and more signs of irritability. Halfway through he suddenly jumped up, overturning his chair, banged the piano lid, and, glaring furiously at the astonished ladies,[8] said loudly, "Go ahead, Bruckmüller, you accompany this nonsense. It's too difficult for me." It is difficult to believe that Mahler would be so rude, especially in the presence of a member of the imperial family, but Bruckmüller affirms that he had to save the situation by conducting in his place.

That evening was the last time Mahler played for the Iglau public. After a Chopin impromptu and polonaise, he accompanied his friend the violinist Mila von Ottenfeld in Wieniawski's *Fantaisie sur Faust* and the *"Kreutzer" Sonata,* for which the unfortunate Bruckmüller was once more asked to turn the pages. Mahler read the music swiftly, and, fearing the pages would not be turned in time, kicked his friend at the bottom of each page. Exasperated, Bruckmüller finally kicked him back. In the midst of the applause, Mahler called him "a dirty dog," whereupon the violinist, thinking the insult was directed at herself, stared at him in amazement until Mahler burst out laughing.

Before going to Kassel, Mahler sent Liszt, at that time president of the Allgemeiner Deutscher Musikverein, the score of *Das klagende Lied,* then entitled, it seems, *Waldmärchen.*[9] Liszt returned it to him in Kassel on September 13, commenting dryly that he had found "many praiseworthy details" in it, but condemning the text wholeheartedly. Decidedly, the "child of sorrow" had no success with the established masters of German music. Even the "moderns" like Liszt were not interested.

Mahler reached Kassel on August 21, 1883, where he worked temporarily as *Musikdirektor,* while waiting for October 1 and his permanent job. His first impressions of his new life were probably satisfactory. At that time Kassel was an important town of more than a hundred thousand inhabitants, and though its theater, which seated 1600, was used, like the one in Laibach, for both operas and plays, there were almost daily performances during a nine-month season. There were only eight male singers and seven women, but they were professionals. The chorus numbered thirty-eight, twenty men and eighteen women, and the orchestra had forty-nine permanent musicians. It was a great honor for Mahler, who was only just twenty-three, to be nominated to a post of such importance in a theater whose artistic level was far superior to that of Olmütz and Laibach.

Unfortunately, Mahler, though *Musikdirektor,* was not only under the orders of the Theater Administration, which in turn took orders from Berlin, but he was also subordinate to the *Kapellmeister* and several producers. In addition he was bound by the document entitled *Dienst-Instruktion (Employment-Instructions),* which he had signed at the same time as his contract and which submitted all his actions to the control of officials to whom discipline and obedience were not empty words. The two documents in question are enough to explain most of the difficulties that Mahler was to encounter in Kassel.

The contract itself contains nothing particularly remarkable, except that it states that Mahler must know all the theater regulations and conform strictly to the *Dienst-Instruktion* and to any other orders from the intendant. In case of sickness, he was to receive only half pay after two months, and his contract could be canceled on one month's notice. The *Dienst-Instruktion* is much more precise and detailed. It begins by stipulating that Mahler owes obedience to his Royal and Imperial Majesty, whose interests he must serve on all occasions. He was also required to keep professional secrets if necessary. He was responsible for the chorus, which he was to rehearse and conduct to the best of his ability. Not only was he answerable to the intendant, but was under the orders of the *Ober-Regisseur* (head producer).

All necessary precautions must be taken to avoid disputes between the musical direction and the stage producers. All eventual disagreements were to be submitted to the administration for arbitration. The man in charge of rehearsals, which were to be held in small rooms set aside for that purpose, was to make certain that no one was absent without written permission from the director. The choirmaster was expected to inform the administration of any carelessness or unpunctuality, together with the names of those involved. He was to prevent singers from cutting or modifying their parts without prior permission from the administration, even during a performance, except in case of absolute necessity. If a work required a larger orchestra than usual, Mahler must present the administration with a request for supplementary musicians, duly endorsed by the musical director. He was to avoid taking this step whenever possible and with the *Kapellmei-*

*ster's* agreement must try to do away with the small stage orchestras in the operas. All proposed changes were to be submitted in advance to the administration.

The *Musikdirektor* had certain specific duties. One of them was to modify the scores of works chosen for presentation when they demanded more personnel than the Kassel Theater had available. He also had to orchestrate vocal cadenzas, passages added or altered in sung parts, and must compose incidental music when requested by the administration.

If, because of a singer's illness, for example, a last-minute change in the program became necessary, the *Musikdirektor* was expected to propose an alternative solution if asked. Except on Sundays and holidays, he was to devote at least an hour each day to rehearsing the chorus, not only in the current program works, but also those for forthcoming productions. He was also to rehearse singly new choristers and those to whom solos were entrusted, spending at least four hours per week, taken from his free afternoons, if they were not thoroughly familiar with the repertoire works. He was to submit to the administration every Sunday morning the singers' timetables and the rehearsal schedule for the coming week. During rehearsals and performances conducted by his superior, the *Kapellmeister,* Mahler was to supervise the chorus from the wings. He was also in charge of stage music, and in this capacity had to rehearse the orchestra at least two days each month, on dates to be communicated in advance to the administration.

Finally Mahler was to demand maximum punctuality and zeal from all his colleagues and must exercise strict discipline over the orchestra and chorus. He was to apply the rules without personal considerations of any sort and could allow no substitutions among the musicians unless the *Kapellmeister* had agreed to them in advance. He must see to it that rehearsals began promptly. If one of the musicians was excused, the others must be informed at once. During rehearsals, he must prevent any conversation detrimental to the work on hand. If his first call to order produced no result, he must see that the guilty person was listed for disciplinary action. Finally, he was forbidden to give private lessons to the singers. He was required to observe all these instructions to the letter, as well as those which might be given to him later, not forgetting the theater's rules and regulations.

At first sight, this long, meticulous list of regulations seems more appropriate for an administrative or military organization; it is clear proof that the Prussian disciplinary and bureaucratic mind never rests, even in the theater world. It is easy to foresee the penalties that were to be inflicted on Mahler for two years, for, with his impatient and stubborn nature, he was bound to break one or other of the rules. Also, the material conditions of his life were far from brilliant. Of the 2000 marks that he received annually altogether, 10 per cent was withheld—5 per cent for Löwy, 5 per cent for the theater employees' retirement fund.[10] The contract, valid for three years, was to be extended automatically from year to year unless Mahler handed in his resignation three months before its expiration. It was also specified that, for as long as he remained Musikdirektor, his salary could not exceed 2400 marks.

At the end of August the intendant divided between Mahler and Kapellmeister Treiber[11] the repertoire works. The latter was more than twenty years older than Mahler, who was mainly assigned the light operas of Donizetti, Flotow, Lortzing, Nessler, and Rossini. This made him extremely resentful toward his superiors. Luckily his repertoire also included four Kassel premieres: Delibes's *Le Roi l'a dit,* Adolphe Adam's *Le Brasseur de Preston,* Meyerbeer's *Robert le Diable,* and a new production of Verdi's *Un Ballo in maschera.*[12]

On September 19, scarcely a month after his arrival in Kassel, Mahler wrote to Löhr: "Everything has happened as usual. I have willingly let myself be loaded with innumerable chains, and thus have again fallen into the usual humiliating slavery. I am determined to fight valiantly, but sometimes 'night gnomes'[13] whisper to me: 'Go far away from here!!' . . . This evening I conducted *Robert le Diable*—the *Herr Kapellmeister* has leased [sic] the classics for himself. He is the gayest time beater I have thus far encountered. Naturally, he looks upon me as a 'stubborn young man' who refuses to receive the revelation of Art from his lips."

So the conflicts had already begun. By the end of September, Mahler had appeared three times on the official list of sanctions. To begin with, he was taken to task for his "extremely irritating" habit of tapping his heel very loudly during rehearsals and performances; a habit on which the intendant commented politely but dryly in order that Mahler might correct it. On September 10, he conducted *Robert le Diable* but was nonetheless supposed to be backstage during the first scene of Act V to supervise the chorus during the hymn singing with organ accompaniment. Mahler considered this an unnecessary nuisance and did not do it. He was fined twelve marks and fifty-nine pfennigs.[14] Again on September 21, Mahler incurred the wrath of the administration by making the women of the chorus laugh during the dress rehearsal of *Hans Heiling.* But this sin was judged to be venial, and he did not have to pay the usual fine.

During the last months of 1883, Mahler's repertoire in Kassel was almost exactly the same as in Laibach and Olmütz: Meyerbeer's *Les Huguenots* and *Robert le Diable,* Flotow's *Martha* and *Alessandro Stradella,* Maillard's *Les Dragons de Villars,* Boïeldieu's *La Dame blanche,* Marschner's *Hans Heiling,* and finally *Carmen.* In a letter to Löwy written around January 1,[15] Mahler mentioned that he had also conducted *Aïda* and *Rigoletto,* but no trace of the first of these two operas is to be found in the 1883–84 programs. Mahler's days were certainly fully occupied by his work. Moreover, in September he founded a "chorus school for young people wishing to enter the Theater."[16]

The *Kasseler Zeitung* for September 18 mentions one of the first performances that Mahler conducted in the Prussian city: Gounod's *Faust.*[17] After praising the assurance of the chorus and the subtle nuances, the anonymous critic reproaches the young conductor for his restlessness on the podium. But the same journalist was less severe when, on October 10, Mahler conducted a new production of *Alessandro Stradella*.[18] The critic of the *Kasseler Journal,* however, was hostile, reproaching Mahler for having conducted with his nose glued to the score and for moving about too much, thus thoughtlessly "disturbing the orchestra and irritating the audience." Despite this, he praised Mahler's energy and enthusiasm and did not deny his success with the public. In another article published in the same paper at the end of the year, the same critic dealt even more severely with the second performance of *Robert le Diable,* saying that Mahler's excessive movements could not fail to worry the orchestra.[19]

From this time on, many critics were most surprised by Mahler's tempos, which they considered either excessively fast or too slow. He was also sometimes criticized for the violence of his sforzandos and small crescendos. After *Hans Heiling,*[20] the critic of the *Kasseler Zeitung* regretted that the orchestra had not rehearsed sufficiently to be able to follow Mahler and to adopt his untraditional conceptions. But he was always praised for the sureness and precision of his beat. Surprising tempos, particularly marked nuances, unusual conceptions; already critics are reproaching Mahler for these three things and continued to do so all his life.

At the end of November, a note from the administration called Mahler's attention to the fact that the *Dienst-Instruktion* made him responsible for punctuality at rehearsals and the reporting of latecomers to the administration. The principal reason for this call to order is clearly to be found in the final paragraph, which forbids Mahler to rehearse female singers in private. A third person must be present each time, preferably another female singer with whom he could rehearse when the first one was resting. Furthermore, if any infringement of the regulations, which called for disciplinary action, were ignored—either intentionally or through negligence—the fine would be doubled when the infraction was discovered.

By reading between the lines, it is easy to imagine that Mahler, because of his innocence, had already acquired the reputation of a seducer, which was to follow him all the way to Vienna. Perhaps he was already attracted to one of the singers mentioned by Alma Mahler,[21] and had shown his liking for her by ignoring some unpunctuality or other infraction of the opera's despotic regulations.

At the start of his stay in Kassel, Mahler lived in furnished lodgings.[22] He complained to Löhr that he was not visited there by the "mountain spirits" of *Rübezahl,* who no doubt realized that their presence would be useless, since their creator could do nothing with them for the time being. On the other hand, the house was full of "knocking spirits," or, rather, various noises that interrupted and upset Mahler's work. Early in January, he was already tired of Kassel, and on learning that the Graz Opera had just lost its conductor, he asked Löwy to suggest him for the post.[23] Not wishing Löwy to accuse him of lack of stability, he added that he was very pleased with his present position, had conducted nothing but "grand operas" (which was inexact), and—a signal honor for a simple *Musikdirektor*—he was to prepare and conduct a new production, Léo Delibes's *Le Roi l'a dit*.

One of Mahler's rare consolations, in the midst of the difficulties of theatrical life, was to be able to hear some concerts given by famous musicians, for Kassel was a musical center of some importance. In November, he saw Anton Rubinstein conduct his oratorio *Paradise Lost*.[24] The outstanding events that winter were, however, the two concerts of January 24 and 25, 1884, given by Hans von Bülow, who was touring with the orchestra of the Meininger Hofkapelle, which he had formed some years earlier. The Meiningen orchestra had only about forty members, who, like their conductor, performed standing up. Von Bülow had decided that "quality would replace quantity," and that his small orchestra should be without equal. Each concert was given many more rehearsals than was usual in those days, and he constantly improved the standard of his players. In order to be able to engage the best in Germany, he sometimes paid part of their salary from his own pocket and occasionally he would even refuse his own fee if he considered that a performance had not been satisfactory. His mottoes were: "No artistic detail is ever insignificant," and "Long rehearsals, short programs."

In 1880, Bülow had started work in Meiningen by rehearsing Beethoven's works daily for three whole months. Around this nucleus he intended to build the new orchestra's entire repertoire. He rehearsed the different instrumental groups separately, studied each bar, each phrase, each bowing. Not since the famous Paris Conservatoire concerts, which had filled Wagner with such enthusiasm thirty years earlier, had such a level of performance been attained or the smallest details of the score been so perfectly rendered.

Bülow's conducting was calm and controlled, spare to the point of austerity. The orchestra was so well rehearsed that the slightest glance was sufficient for the conductor to express his wishes, and he often placed his baton on the podium.[25] The quality of the performance, the conductor's musical genius, and the beauty of the works all made a tremendous impression on Mahler and brought a sudden, blinding light to bear on the present wretchedness of his own position. He tried in vain to see Bülow at his hotel, and immediately afterward, his heart filled with joy, he wrote to him: "Very Revered Master. Pardon me if after being barred by the concierge of your hotel, I still dare to appeal to you and risk your considering me impudent. When I first asked you for the honor of an interview, I had as yet no conception of the fire that your incomparable art was going to light in me. In a few words, I am a musician wandering without a star to guide him in the arid night of our time's musical life. I am at the mercy of doubt and confusion.

"When, during your concert of yesterday, I felt myself in the presence of that greatest beauty that I had ever divined or hoped for, everything became clear to me. I thought: here is your home, here your master; today or never you must end your search.

"Now I am here and I beg you: take me with you in whatever way possible and let me become your pupil even if I have to pay the tuition with my blood. What I can do and what I could do I don't know, but you will find out very quickly. I am twenty-three years old. I have taken courses at the University of Vienna, as well as composition and piano classes at the conservatory. After wretched wanderings, I have accepted the position of second *Kapellmeister* in the local theater. Whether a man who believes in art with all his strength and love, and always sees it profaned in the most intolerable way, can be satisfied with such a dull existence, you can judge too well yourself. I give myself to you completely, and if you accept this gift, you cannot imagine how happy you will make me. If only you will reply, I shall be ready to do whatever you wish. Ah! at least answer me. Gustav Mahler, who is waiting."

Even if he were not able to take such a proposition seriously, and considered it impulsive and remiss, it might be expected that any great musician or kindhearted man would have looked sympathetically upon this *cri du coeur*. Unfortunately this was not the case. Bülow sent a curt note in reply: "Dear Sir. It is not impossible that in a year and a half your desire could be realized, but before being able to recommend you, I should have to have sufficient proofs of your capacities as pianist, conductor, and choral conductor; at this time I cannot give you the occasion to furnish me with them." Not content with throwing cold water on Mahler's enthusiasm, Bülow, even before replying to the letter, forwarded it to Treiber, who placed it in the theater files, where it can still be seen. It is easy to imagine that from then on Mahler's position in Kassel, never very agreeable, must have become intolerable. The authorities already suspected that he was intractable, but now they had clear, irrefutable proof of his audacity. From that time on, they saw to it that the "chains" of discipline weighed ever more heavily upon him. Mahler was to suffer many humiliations in the remaining eighteen months, before he could obtain his freedom.

The *Kasseler Zeitung* attributed to Mahler most of the credit for the success of Delibes's *Le Roi l'a dit,* which was given its first presentation on February 16, with Mahler conducting. A month earlier, he had conducted for the first time one of the operas that delighted him all his life: Weber's *Der Freischütz.*[26] His repertoire during the early part of that year was completed by Lortzing's *Zar und Zimmermann,* Nicolai's *Die Lustigen Weiber von Windsor,*[27] *Der Rattenfänger von Hameln* by Viktor Nessler,[28] *Le Brasseur de Preston* by Adam, and *Robert le Diable.* Mahler was still living in furnished rooms with a certain Frau Frank.[29] As though the bureaucratic tyranny of the Prussian theater did not complicate his life enough, he became infatuated with Johanna Richter, a Kassel theater singer whose greatest claim to fame is that she was the source of inspiration for the *Lieder eines fahrenden Gesellen.*

Halfway between a lyric and dramatic soprano, and also singing coloratura roles occasionally, Johanna Richter probably came originally from East Prussia, for it was in that region that much of her career took place. She had made her debut in Danzig in 1880, and was engaged by the Kassel Theater at the same time as Mahler, in October 1883. She remained there a year longer than he did, and then sang in Rotterdam, Cologne, Chemnitz, and finally Königsberg and Danzig, where we lose track of her in 1905. Nothing else is known about her. She probably never married. From a professional point of view the Kassel papers do not give a very favorable picture of her. The critics praised her "beauty" more than her performance and complained that she sometimes sang too low. They also mentioned a faulty sense of rhythm and added to this unfavorable picture the coldness of her interpretation and the inadequacy of her high notes. Once or twice they were less severe, but the general impression is that she was a mediocre singer.

During the spring of 1884, Mahler wrote to Löhr: "I have learned from Heinrich, my dear Fritz, of the grief that Christmas Day brought you.[30] You should know that on that same day I experienced a sorrow of the same sort, and that since then I have had each day to undergo interminable struggles with myself. I see no end to it. It makes me live through each day, even each hour, battling anew." This mysterious allusion seems to indicate an amorous confidence: the tone resembles that which he adopted four years earlier when speaking of Josephine Poisl to Krisper. His new passion certainly originated before the summer, for in August or September, Mahler wrote two love poems in which for the first time he used the expression *"fahrende Gesell,"* which later became the title of the cycle dedicated to Johanna Richter.

For a while Mahler seems to have paid lip service to discipline, for the Kassel Theater archives rarely mention him in the winter of 1883 and spring of 1884. But on February 16, at the time of the first performance of Delibes's *Le Roi l'a dit,* there was some trouble between Mahler and the administration on the subject of paying an additional musician, a violinist named Abbau, who had to play onstage. Had Mahler engaged Abbau without consulting the intendant? In any case five marks were paid to Abbau from Mahler's February salary. On April 15, three marks and ninety pfennigs were also withheld from his pay, this time for unpaid taxes (to be repeated in July, August, and September). Doubtless Mahler found it difficult to live on his meager salary and was unable to pay them on time. From then on the intendant automatically deducted them at the source.

In June, Mahler was asked to compose incidental music for a charity gala to be held on the last day of the season, for the theater's pension fund. After two acts from operas chosen from the theater's repertoire, the great attraction of the evening was to be a series of *tableaux vivants* linked together by monologues and inspired by the well-known narrative poem by

Viktor von Scheffel. This form of entertainment was very popular in nine-teenth-century Germany. "In the last few days I have had to write in great haste some music for the 'Trumpeter of Säkkingen,'" Mahler wrote to Löhr, "which will be given tomorrow at the Theater in the form of *tableaux vivants.* I completed this opus in two days, and I must tell you that I am very pleased with it. As you will imagine, my work has not much in common with Scheffel's affectation and goes much beyond the poet."

Mahler's low opinion of Scheffel is not surprising, for his well-known ro-mantic and humorous narrative poem, published in 1853 and reprinted over 250 times, was extremely popular with schoolmasters but universally scorned by German intellectuals. Mahler's incidental music was performed only once in Kassel on June 23. It followed the overture to *Rienzi,* Act IV of *Les Huguenots,* the last act of *Il Trovatore,*[31] and poems and songs given by members of the company.[32] It was acclaimed by the public and the critics, who praised his "magnificent technique" and "dazzling instrumenta-tion." Everywhere "could be seen the sure and skilled hand of the composer who deserved a laurel crown far more than the singer." Mahler told Löhr that the music would be played in Mannheim, Wiesbaden, and Karlsruhe, but no fragment of the score survives in any of these theaters.[33] Mahler still had a copy of it four years later in Leipzig, but the music critic Steinitzer, who transcribed it for the piano, had to promise to destroy it, for the young composer did not want any trace to remain of a work that he considered unworthy of him.[34]

The morning after the gala, Mahler left for Iglau, where he spent some days with his parents. On June 30 he passed through Vienna on his way to Perchtoldsdorf, where, like the year before, he and Fritz Löhr spent a week of relaxing, music sessions and refreshing walking tours. No doubt this was when Mahler, on a visit to Bruckner, persuaded him to give up his idea of revising his *Third Symphony.* The editor Rättig had in fact persuaded Bruckner to rewrite his work, since none of the many conductors to whom he had sent the score would agree to play it.[35] Bruckner had started work on the revision, and about fifty pages were already engraved. Mahler was firmly opposed to this idea, and the old master asked the editor to destroy the new pages, since "an orchestral professional" had convinced him that revision was unnecessary.[36] He did it later, however, in 1890. Mahler returned to Iglau on July 8 and invited Löhr there at the end of the month. The family home was full to overflowing, for Poldi and her husband were also spending their vacation there, and Mahler and Löhr shared a room. Outside their windows a neighbor had set up a pigsty, and its inmate lulled the family to sleep with "songs" and wakened them each morning with a cheerful concert, "while the hens laid eggs and announced the good news with noisy cackling."

On his way back to Kassel at the end of August, Mahler stopped in Dresden to attend performances of *Così fan tutte* and *Tristan und Isolde* conducted by Ernst von Schuch.[37] No doubt Mahler had to fight against a feeling of envy when he saw the quality of the productions and the success obtained by his lucky colleague, who had got everything that Mahler could only hope for in the distant future. His friend and patron, the producer Ueberhorst, introduced him to the already famous *Kapellmeister* during the intermission. Schuch in turn introduced Mahler to the principal singers and promised to go to Kassel to hear him conduct. Mahler had nothing but praise for the technical qualities of the *Tristan* performance, and especially for the performance of Therese Malten,[38] who sang the role of the heroine. But he already had his own precise views on how to interpret the Wagnerian masterpiece, and those of Schuch did not entirely please him.[39]

This same Schuch who was to become one of the most famous nineteenth-century German conductors, was also to be one of Mahler's best and most faithful friends and one of his performers. He also overcame the prejudices of the times and presented in Dresden, one after the other, Strauss's main dramatic works, *Feuersnot, Salome, Elektra,* and *Der Rosenkavalier.*

# CHAPTER 9

*Mahler in Kassel (II) — Conflicts and Passion — The*
Lieder eines Fahrenden Gesellen — *The Münden Festival*
*(1884–85)*

Mahler returned to Kassel at the end of August 1884 and was once more overcome by the theater's depressing bureaucracy and the sterile torments of his liaison with Johanna. He found her "enigmatic as always." "All I can say is: God help me!" He wrote to Löhr, trying to describe his state of mind: "You might have noticed, when we were together lately, that a shadow passed over me occasionally. It was dread of the inevitable. This afternoon I am going to see her, 'to pay my call,' and then my position will be much clearer." But in fact the situation became more confused than ever, and Mahler sounds strangely offhand for a man who has just written for his beloved two love poems filled with grief and passion.

Early in September, a performance of *Die lustigen Weiber von Windsor* pleased the critic of the *Kasseler Zeitung,* who considered it greatly superior to that of the preceding season. He admired the discrete perfection of the orchestra and even praised Johanna Richter for her "inexhaustible humor." He also praised Mahler for having at last restored Nicolai's original Finale. But this initiative brought Mahler a severe reprimand from the intendant. He was also blamed for "deleting, without official permission, a cadence with violin accompaniment" that closes the second-act duet.[1]

Mahler wrote a long letter to his immediate superior, trying to exonerate himself from blame. He pointed out that in every other theater in the world the conductor was allowed to make last-minute changes, cuts, and alterations in special circumstances, and neither of the orchestra's two solo violinists was capable of playing such an exposed cadenza. He claims that "he did not want to trouble the intendant by submitting to him daily changes dictated by circumstances." Mahler asserts that "it is sometimes at the last moment, and in cases of extreme urgency," that such decisions must be made. "When this happens I think of myself as representing the Intendant, and am always ready to account for such decisions," he wrote with splendid unconcern, since he was expressly forbidden, in the famous *Dienst-Instruktion,* from considering any such thing.

As for the last-act Finale, he considered that his action in replacing Franz Abt's air by Nicolai's Finale was praiseworthy in the extreme. In both cases he had "meant well," but he promised to follow the *Dienst-Instruktion* to the letter in future. A few ironic lines from the intendant closed the incident. In them he suggested that Mahler comply less with "custom" and more with the *Dienst-Instruktion.*

In October, Mahler restaged Verdi's *Un Ballo in maschera,* and he invited Ernst von Schuch to the first performance, scheduled for October 30.[2] A few days before the premiere Mahler asked the administration for permission to go every Monday evening to Münden, a small town near Kassel, and rehearse the town choir. Since operas were never given at the Kassel Theater on Mondays, this request was granted. By a set of unforeseen circumstances this unimportant post as a provincial choirmaster was to have a considerable influence on Mahler's future, but it also made his position in Kassel more difficult than ever.

Late in November, Martersteig, the assistant producer, infuriated Mahler by listing him for disciplinary action for no apparent reason, according to Mahler. All we know of this new incident comes from the letter of self-justification that Mahler sent to the intendant. According to Mahler, Martersteig called an orchestral rehearsal of incidental music for Gustav von Moser's play *Der Salon Tyroler* without informing him. At the time, Mahler was rehearsing the *Faust* choruses in a small rehearsal room. Martersteig sent for him, and Mahler hurried down to the main hall only to learn that for the moment he was not needed. He had already resumed his own rehearsal, when he was sent for again, this time by the intendant. He went downstairs once more, and was told that a change in schedule had been necessitated by the late arrival of an actress, and he was therefore needed to rehearse the orchestra. Mahler felt no responsibility for either of these incidents, and "could not believe his eyes" when two days later he saw his name on the list of sanctions. In his indignation and haste, he even forgot to sign the letter that he sent to the intendant.

At the end of 1884, Mahler drew up a long administrative report on the members of the chorus, in which their annual salaries were studied in relation to their respective merits as regards voice, musical accuracy, and enthusiasm. Occasionally his remarks contain a touch of humor. One of the sopranos sings very "out of tune"; another has "a thin, disagreeable voice"; a third is "only average" in every way. A tenor named Paul Fels "is so lazy that he has been nicknamed Faulpelz."[3] Another tenor "has no ear and always sings too low," a third "has a loud voice that is never heard," and a fourth, "completely lacking sight and hearing, passes unnoticed."

In December, Mahler prepared and conducted the Kassel premiere of Adolphe Adam's *La Poupée de Nuremberg* and a new staging of Ferdinand Pillwitz's *Rataplan ou Le Petit Tambour*.[4] His affair with Johanna Richter had reached a particularly difficult and unhappy stage. Was it true, as Alma Mahler suggests,[5] that Mahler was simultaneously courting another singer, and the two young women made fun of him in the best Shakespearean tradition by comparing the letters that he wrote to them? According to a typewritten sheet of paper that precedes the copies of a poem from Kassel and a letter from Johanna[6] in one of Alma Mahler's unpublished manuscripts, the second singer was Frau Naumann-Gungl, the principal dramatic soprano, whose name is to be found in nearly all the cast lists of the Kassel Opera that year. It seems rather surprising that someone as single-minded as Mahler could have become involved in such a situation, but many recently discovered documents show how easily he succumbed to feminine charms and in particular to those of the singers with whom he worked.

Johanna Richter was certainly the principal object of Mahler's affections that year. From the letter she sent to him in 1886[7] it is clear that she was also a friend of Frau Naumann. She gives him news of Naumann's children and adds: ". . . she hasn't changed and one cannot help but love her dearly, in spite of the fact that with her usual naïveté she makes her little blunders in any closer relationship, but I am a good enough friend to ignore them, for I know that she likes me a little more than the others . . ."

No doubt Mahler also felt at least a passing attraction to Frau Naumann, since he spoke of her many years later to his wife. Probably Frau Naumann was "ill-advised" enough to speak of him to Johanna. In a moment of jealousy, the latter may have shown her rival the letters and poems that Mahler had sent to her. According to his letters to Löhr, he was once more living a romantic love affair, though it seems unlikely that it remained platonic. As it was thwarted by real or imaginary obstacles, it seems to have been for him, and perhaps also for Johanna, a source of endless suffering and anxiety. In order to guess at the vicissitudes of this affair, one must try to read between the lines of the poems he wrote to his beloved that year. The first, light in tone and written on August 18, very probably for Johanna's saint's day or birthday, brings her the good wishes of a "traveling companion" (*fahrenden Gesellen*).[8] A second poem, *In der Nacht,* written in September, is more gloomy and anguished. It speaks of Johanna's beauty, of the exquisite last hour the lovers spent together, and mentions the grief of him who must stand aside and disappear into the darkness, asking himself which star in the heavens shines for him.[9]

In October, another poem sings the happiness of the lover who thinks of the "beautiful sun in his life" and who, in a dream, sees a sea of blinding flames and hears sounds of pain and mourning. Anguish, man's most secret terror, fills him; he is seized with an indescribable trembling. However, the conclusion of the poem is optimistic: "Oh no; not to die, not to perish!

Cease to be? God in heaven! To live to live!"[10] Finally a few lines of verse, scribbled on the back of a draft letter,[11] are addressed to the being "rich in grace," to the angel with snowy wings who bends over him with compassion. Two months later Mahler wrote some other poems and at once set them to music. They were the famous *Lieder eines fahrenden Gesellen*.[12]

On January 1, 1885, Mahler described to Löhr the sadness that he had experienced on Christmas and New Year's Day. "My dear Fritz. Today, on the morning of New Year's Day, my first thoughts are dedicated to you. I passed the first minutes of the year in a very strange way. Last night I was at her home alone, and we sat side by side, almost in silence, awaiting the arrival of the New Year. Her thoughts were far away, and when the bells rang, tears came to her eyes. I understood in despair that I could not dry them. She went into the next room, where she stood silently near the window for a moment. When she returned, weeping in silence, that unspeakable sorrow stood between us like an eternal barrier, and I could do nothing but press her hand and leave.

"When I reached my own doorway, the bells rang and a solemn chorale sounded from the top of the tower. Ah, my dear Fritz, it was as if the Great Stage-Manager of the Universe wanted everything arranged by the rules of art. I spent the whole night weeping in my dreams. My only light[13] in that darkness: I have composed a cycle of lieder, six for the time being, all dedicated to her. She does not know them. What can they tell her beyond what she already knows? I am going to send you the last lied, even though the paltry words cannot even express a tiny part of them. The cycle deals with a young *Gesell* ill-treated by destiny, who goes into the vast world and wanders about aimlessly."

Once more Mahler's emotional crisis had borne fruit. This time, at the age of twenty-four, he gave the world a cycle of autobiographical songs that is one of the most striking products of his creative genius and also one of the most moving and accomplished masterpieces in the history of the lied. Once more this desperate confession was written in record time: the last two poems are dated December 15 and 19, so Mahler can have taken only a few days to compose the "six" songs, of which we know only four.[14] To fit the simple, folklore style of the poems, Mahler created a style inspired by popular music, in which the echoes of his childhood lullabies alternate with vivacious interludes, more naïve than parodic. The combination of these two elements forms an extremely personal musical style. For the first time, in Mahler's work, the shape and pattern of these lieder are as perfect as their emotional content.

Shortly before he composed the *Lieder eines fahrenden Gesellen,* Mahler had written another poem,[15] which also speaks of the solitude of a disappointed lover, and his sad journey through the night without a guiding star, surrounded by deceptive voices trying to lead him astray. In it he encounters a sphinx "who gazes at him silently with its gray eyes and threatens him by setting riddles that must be solved on pain of death." A new emotional crisis had been enough to reawaken in Mahler his old obsession, that of being a traveler without a destination, an eternal exile. In Mahler's present situation his anxiety was intensified by the humiliations he suffered at the theater; he longed for an early escape from his "prison" and his "chains," and longed to fly off to some more glorious destiny.

Early in December, Mahler had learned that the well-known impresario Angelo Neumann was about to resume the direction of the Prague Opera. Mahler had written him the following letter: "Dear Director. I take the liberty of introducing and recommending myself to you. I am the second Kapellmeister at the theater in this city, and I conduct *Robert le Diable, Hans Heiling, Freischütz, Rattenfänger,* etc. . . . You can easily obtain information as to my qualifications, either from here or from stage-manager Ueberhorst of Dresden, who knows me very well. I am anxious to leave my present post. I would like more stimulating and responsible work. Here, as second conductor, I will not find activity commensurate with my capabilities. Will you have need, in the near or more distant future, of a young and energetic conductor—I am forced to sing my own praises—experienced and knowledgeable, capable of infusing a work of art and its interpreters with passion and enthusiasm? I shall be brief so as not needlessly to waste your time. I beg you for an early and positive answer."[16]

Unlike Hans von Bülow, who, as a good Prussian, had been ill-disposed toward a young *Kapellmeister* who was guilty of insubordination in writing to him, Neumann, discoverer of new talent, was immediately struck by the unusual tone and content of Mahler's letter.[17] "Without quite knowing why," he was more impressed by it than by any of the innumerable requests he had received. From Bremen he wrote to thank Mahler for his offer, regretting that he could not accept it for the moment, but advising Mahler to write him again as soon as Neumann's appointment was announced in the press.

Thus, despite his passion for Johanna—or perhaps secretly because of it—Mahler was doing all he could to get away. In his letter of January 1 to Löhr, he explains his state of mind: "Dear Fritz. All that you know about her is a misunderstanding. I have forgiven her everything, sacrificing my pride and my egoism. She is everything that is lovable in this world, and I would like to give my last drop of blood for her. Nevertheless, I know that I must leave. I have tried to do so by every means, but have not yet found a way out . . ."

At the same time that he wrote to Neumann, Mahler also contacted Bernhard Pollini, the director of the Hamburg Opera, as well as the director of the Leipzig Opera, Max Staegemann. By January 23 he had received an affirmative reply from the latter and knew that he would be engaged for six years as head conductor in Leipzig, working with Arthur Nikisch.[18]

"As you see, destiny smiles upon me. But believe me, without making me the slightest bit happier. I live like a Hottentot. I cannot exchange one sensible word with anyone. The Kasselers are such terrible blockheads that I prefer to converse with a Viennese cabdriver. I have worked quite a lot, if only for my 'drawers.' Now I should have the possibility and the chance to perform my compositions; yet, because of the absurd conditions in this city, I do not care a bit about a performance and I do not make the slightest effort to get one . . ."

In the same letter, Mahler inquires about his Viennese friends, Sax, Adler, Pernerstorfer, Seraphin Bondi, and suggests that one of them publish in a Viennese newspaper the news of his engagement. "This could be very useful to me in the future, although I no longer have many steps to climb. But my final aim remains Vienna. I can never feel at home anywhere else."

Mahler himself,[19] like most of his biographers, attributed the difficulties he encountered at the Kassel Theater entirely to his excessive zeal. Later on he admitted to Natalie that a full-scale mutiny had almost broken out among the singers because of the length of his rehearsals. One day his friends advised him to feign illness, for the musicians had sworn that they would bring sticks in order to give him a beating. Mahler ignored this advice, and when the time came he was even more severe than usual, but he kept a close watch on the musicians throughout the whole rehearsal, and then departed, after glaring at them furiously and slamming the piano shut. No one had dared to make a move. This story is not surprising in view of all we know of Mahler's authoritative character and his demands in the artistic field. Nevertheless, it is hard to believe that such a rebellion could have taken place in a theater where the discipline was so strict. In any case, no trace of this incident survives in the theater archives, though they do contain ample evidence of Mahler's insubordination.

In January 1885, Mahler was put in charge of a new production of Schubert's opera buffa *Der häusliche Krieg*,[20] presented with Weber's *Abu Hassan* in a double bill on January 31. The *Kasseler Zeitung* once more criticized Mahler for excessive movement on the podium, for his nuances, and for some of the tempos. In February, Mahler resumed acquaintance with an old Hall and Laibach friend—Offenbach, whose *Mariage aux lanternes* was restaged on the twenty-fourth.

Mahler, the *fahrende Gesell,* moved three times that winter. At the start of the season, he lived in a hotel for some days before taking private lodgings (Frankfurterstrasse 22, according to the theatrical almanacs of the period). Then, early in 1885, he moved to a new apartment that must surely have pleased him because of its Weberian connotation: Wolfsschlucht, 13.

Was Mahler's talent starting to be appreciated, or was he being purposely subjected to an increasingly tight schedule in order to curb his desire for independence? Whatever the reason, in March he conducted a dozen operas, almost twice the usual number. Besides *Le Mariage aux lanternes, Un Ballo in maschera, Der häusliche Krieg, Die lustigen Weiber von Windsor,* and *La Poupée de Nuremberg,* these included a new production of Flotow's *Conte d'hiver.*

On February 14, after three and a half months' work with the Münden choir, Mahler conducted a complete performance of Haydn's *The Seasons* in the large Nickel Hall in Münden, with orchestra and soloists from the Kassel Theater. The performance was very well received by the public, and the local critics congratulated him for obtaining such brilliant results in so short a time. They also praised both orchestra and singers, one of whom was Johanna Richter. Public response had been so great that the audience invaded the stage. Thanks to this great personal success, Mahler was about to reach a turning point in his career.

That year, the town of Münden had decided to organize a music festival that would attract music lovers from the nearby provinces. Normal procedure, since the Kassel Theater orchestra was to take part, would have been to engage the conductor, Treiber, also. From the outset, however, the plans for the festival had aroused violent discussion in the press regarding the choice of both location and conductor.[21] There had also been talk of employing Albrecht Brede, director of the Kassel Oratorienverein, one of the societies that were to take part in the choral performance. But he withdrew his candidacy as soon as he realized there was going to be trouble. The battle then broke out between those wishing to prove that the festival could take place without Treiber and the others who considered that, whatever the reasons, it was not possible to insult him by looking elsewhere. However, the majority favored the first point of view, and when it was decided not to engage Treiber, his orchestra loyally refused to take part in the festival.

An article in the *Hessische Blätter* relates the different stages of the battle. Instead of approaching a prominent conductor from elsewhere, which would have poured oil on troubled waters, the organizers had the "unfortunate idea" of approaching Treiber's subordinate, "for whom it was an advantage to be selected," since he was at the start of his career. This choice seems to have displeased nearly everyone, whether or not they were taking part in the festival, not counting the virtuous Christians who were indignant at the idea that a Jew should conduct so Christian a work as Mendelssohn's *Paulus* (these good souls having conveniently forgotten that this "Christian" oratorio was the work of a Jew).

Nonetheless the same newspaper, which, it is clear from the preceding paragraph, certainly was not favorable to Mahler, acknowledged that from the very first rehearsals everyone concerned sensed that the young *Musikdirektor* had the makings of a virtuoso and possessed all the necessary qualifications for so considerable a task. Mahler was naturally delighted by the unexpected honor. He wrote to Epstein in March[22]: "Since this choice constitutes for a young man a vote of confidence that is extraordinary, coming, as it does, from a whole province (these are the Grand Musical Societies of Hesse and of a part of Hanover), I also allow myself the pardonable hope that the Viennese will get wind of this honor. Would you have the great kindness to make a point of spreading the news? Isn't it true that I am as brazen as ever?"

What was the reaction of the authorities at the Kassel Theater? There was considerable friction, as Mahler wrote to Löhr: "You will want to know whether this festival is making me happy. It's just as always when one expects fulfillment from others. Do you think that when two or three choruses are brought together under the pretext of producing art, the result can be very brilliant? Nowadays, it is fashionable to be festive in a musical and patriotic way. The selection of my person has provoked a formidable party struggle, and everything has threatened to collapse for that reason. They, particularly the musicians, cannot forgive me my youth. Our orchestra is on strike because the Herr Kapellmeister felt that he was disgraced, and the Intendant has had the effrontery to appeal to my generosity by asking me to withdraw. I naturally sent him packing, and now I am a dead man at the theater."[23] Even if this festival episode had not completely envenomed the relations between Mahler and the Kassel intendant Von Gilsa, the latter had certainly learned of the efforts that Mahler was making to find another post. It is understandable that he was annoyed with the little Austrian who, a year and a half after begging him for employment, was already searching for a more important post.

On March 16, Mahler announced to his impresario Gustav Löwy the happy outcome of his personal efforts.[24] Max Staegemann, director of the Leipzig Theater, had seen him conduct in Kassel, and had engaged him as of July 1886. Mahler was to spend one month "on trial" there during the summer of 1885 and was all the more delighted because his current work satisfied him less and less. He had to devote all his time to the imbecile members of the chorus and conducted only once every couple of weeks, which he considered "intolerable for a young man wanting to learn his profession." All he wanted was to leave Kassel as soon as possible, though the intendant had offered to keep him on as long as he wished. Mahler therefore asked Löwy to find him a temporary engagement for the following winter, while waiting for the start of his Leipzig contract.

Late in March, another incident brought him into conflict with the Kassel Theater. During a rehearsal of Schiller's play *Wilhelm Tell,* the producer, Wetzstein, decided to replace Reinecke's usual incidental music by music composed by Anselm Weber. This consisted of three arias, one of which, in Act I, was accompanied by an offstage clarinet accompaniment. Wetzstein claimed that he had shown this aria to Mahler and told him his presence would be necessary in the wings to indicate the tempo to the musicians.

On Wednesday, March 25, the day of the first rehearsal, Mahler was present, but the boy in charge of the score had forgotten to bring it, and the music was not rehearsed. Mahler seems to have decided, rather hastily, that his presence was no longer necessary, and on the day of the dress rehearsal he was not in the theater. The actor Ewald, forced to break off during the aria in question, blamed the clarinetist for his "absurd" tempo.

Wetzstein at once sent for Mahler and listed him for disciplinary action. On the day of the actual performance Mahler reached the theater late, after the aria in question had been sung, and Wetzstein again listed him for punishment. Mahler tried once more to justify himself in a letter to the intendant that is no more convincing than usual. He had not been notified in time; his "presence was almost never necessary for performances of this sort"; and furthermore the head producer had "given him to understand that his presence, as well as being unnecessary, would be insulting to the clarinetist." But all these explanations were judged insufficient, and disciplinary action was taken.

After this Mahler was more determined than ever to leave Kassel. On April 1 he officially requested to be released from his contract so that he could "spend a year nearer his home." Zulauf, substituting for the intendant, noted at the bottom of the letter that this decision depended upon a verbal agreement made by the intendant himself, for which reason a new request should be made in June. That same day Mahler wrote to Löhr that his only wish was to return to Vienna. "I am completely shattered. My heart is bleeding from many wounds."[25]

He had described his troubles to Löhr a few days earlier. "Lots of things have happened since I wrote you in Starnberg, and the worst was yet to happen. When we are together, you shall hear all about it. All that I can tell you for the moment is that I was close to the sweetest fulfillment, only to lose everything at one stroke; no one was to blame. For a long time I didn't know what to do, I had only one gloomy desire: to sleep without dreaming.

"With the coming of spring, I am calm again. From my window I see the town, the mountains, the woods, and the friendly Fulda, running peacefully through the landscape. When the sunlight plays on all this, then, as you know, one becomes relaxed again. That is what I feel today while sitting here at my writing table near the window, from time to time glancing serenely at those carefree abodes of tranquillity. Those around me who torture me unspeakably by the tumult of their occupations are all outside today. No distinct sound reaches me except now and then that of the bell that reminds me that people belong together."[26]

This is one of the last lyrical outbursts to be found in Mahler's letters, and it springs from his unhappy passion for Johanna Richter. "My Sphinx has not stopped staring at me with menacing questions. Otherwise I am treated partly as half mad—partly with well-intentioned pity, sometimes with malicious curiosity."[27] "In all probability, I shall leave here without having spoken a word of farewell to her."[28] We can only guess at the obstacles that stood in the way of this idyl and prevented Mahler from achieving the "sweet fulfillment" he seems to have desired so ardently, though perhaps more in a literary sense than in reality. At any rate Johanna can hardly be blamed for hesitating to bind her fate to that of this quick-tempered little *Kapellmeister,* who seemed to delight in creating both enemies and material difficulties for himself.

On April 19, Mahler conducted a revival of Marschner's *Ivanhoe* opera, *Der Templer und die Jüdin*. He was warmly congratulated for the training and precision of the chorus, but the opera itself was poorly received.[29] On April 20 and May 29, a "theatrical entertainment" entitled *Das Volkslied* was performed in Kassel for the benefit of the theater retirement fund. It was described as a "Poem with lieder, choirs, and tableaux vivants by C. H. Mosenthal. Folk song music orchestrated by Gustav Mahler. Arranged for the Kassel stage by Otto Ewald." This special performance, which consisted of eleven tableaux, cannot have required much work. Its principal interest was probably the opportunity it gave Mahler to study, and perhaps discover, folk songs that he could later use. He did, in fact, base some of his *Wunderhorn* lieder on authentic folk melodies.[30] Felix Weingartner, who had conducted a concert in Kassel the evening before, probably attended the April 20 performance. He had already met Mahler several times in one of the town's restaurants and "in the course of several interesting conversations" they had discovered that they held the same views on many artistic and intellectual subjects.[31]

The administration complained about Mahler more than ever in April. He was accused, probably with reason, of thinking only of his preparations for the Münden festival. Baron von Gilsa advised his Berlin superior to accept Mahler's resignation. "I take the liberty of informing you that this young man, who at the beginning of his engagement aroused the liveliest hopes, by making a contract with Leipzig, and at the same time hoping to shine as orchestral conductor at the festival, has gone to pieces completely, and appears constantly on the list of punishments for committing all sorts of irregularities. His position vis-à-vis chorus and orchestra therefore is completely compromised."[32]

On the very day that von Gilsa was complaining about Mahler in these terms, Mahler broke the rules again, being absent from the podium when he should have been conducting the performance. He was listed for disciplinary action by Meyer, the inspector. Mahler pointed out that, though not in the pit, he had nonetheless kept an eye on the performance from the auditorium, but he was still fined. On April 13, he learned that his contract would be canceled as of September 1, and he tried to bring this date forward to July 1. Von Gilsa wrote to the Berlin administration: "Since Mahler is no longer giving satisfaction, it is in the Theater's interest to let him go as soon as possible."

On April 23 he heard that his contract was canceled and he was free to leave on July 1. Not having heard from Neumann, he planned to go to Leipzig for a month. "What I shall do then is just as mysterious to me as what I shall do in fifty years. Here the spirits are more than heated: with cries of 'For Mahler' and 'For Treiber,' the two parties go into battle, and I receive the blows. I am also finished with the Herr Intendant already. Ever since I told him openly that my judgment in artistic matters is wholly different from his, he holds me to be a man who ignores the meaning of discipline, and considers me an outlaw. At the same time, I must work strenuously for the festival. Secretly I must run here and there to rehearse the various choruses. This is not without its difficulties, since I am often without a penny . . ."[33]

"The various threads of my life are more and more tangled—only Alexander's sword could now help. Although I wrote you some time ago that my relations with 'her' had entered upon a new and final phase, that was only the trick of a skillful theater director announcing a 'Final Performance,' who then—the next day—puts up an announcement of a very 'Last Performance.' That 'Final One' in fact, has been followed by a 'Very Last One,' but as only three weeks separate me even now from the eternal farewell, it is not probable that 'at popular request' an 'Ultimate and Last of All' will still take place. However, I cannot promise anything."[34]

A letter that Johanna sent to Mahler in Prague the following year seems to be, except for the various poems, the only surviving document that concerns this intense and painful episode. It begins with "My good friend" and ends with "unwavering friendship." About the move, Johanna wrote once more from the very place where they spent their last hours together in Kassel. "I had to admit honestly to myself," she says, "that when I received the letter expressing your impatience it gave me pleasure, since I had really assumed that you had already amply replaced, eclipsed, the past and what had been. I would like to hear more about your recent 'foolishness,' as you, my friend, call it; if I may know about it, I would be very interested . . ."[35]

In a friendly way Johanna asks Mahler for news of his family. She begs him not to hesitate to write to her, and never again to be afraid of bothering her.[36] Thus the two lovers had parted without quarrel and Johanna had forgiven Mahler their rupture, for which he was certainly responsible.

On May 28 it seemed that Mahler would be forced to spend the coming winter in Vienna, for his attempts to find a post—including Löwy's negotiations with the Graz Opera—had all failed.[37] The prospect of an idle winter would not have displeased Mahler, except that he was harried by financial worries. "The fact that I have been unable to save anything here causes me lots of anxiety, as you may imagine. It is only with considerable difficulty that I will be able to stay out of debtors' prison!" Only the famous festival, on which Mahler was counting to give new impetus to his career, kept his moral and material conditions from being unbearable during his final weeks in Kassel.

On June 6, at the archducal theater in Wiesbaden, the *tableaux vivants* from *Der Trompeter von Säkkingen* were presented, together with *Il Barbiere di Siviglia*, in aid of the theater's retirement fund. The local critics praised Mahler's music, written to accompany the poem and the *tableaux vivants*, "which did not at all limit the powerful effect on the spectator."[38] This was the first time that a work by Mahler had been performed in his absence.

News of this first success reached Mahler while he was busy with final preparations for the festival. Almost every day he took the train from town to town in order to rehearse the various choral societies.[39] One day, on his way to Münden, he got into a coach at the Kassel railroad station and sat there for about an hour, lost in his thoughts and studying the score. Suddenly becoming worried by the fact that the train was not moving, he looked out the window and discovered that his coach had been shunted onto a sidetrack and the train had left without him!

As the fateful date of June 29 approached, Mahler was increasingly busy, dividing his time between the Münden choir, the Kassel Oratorienverein, the Marburg Akademische Gesangsverein, and the Nordhausen Früh'sche Gesangsverein, which together made up the chorus of four hundred[40] required for the performance. The last pages of Mahler's dossier in the Kassel archives contain nothing but requests to the administration for leave of absence to rehearse the festival.

Early in June, Mahler sent Löhr some good news: his personal negotiations with Angelo Neumann, started the preceding winter, had been successful. He had been engaged by the Prague Theater as head *Kapellmeister,* and on August 1 was to conduct *Lohengrin,* his first Wagner opera! Later he was to be entrusted with the musical preparations for restagings of *Der Ring des Niebelungen, Tristan und Isolde,* and *Die Meistersinger!* He had to be in Prague for the first rehearsals on July 15. Neumann was to restore all its former glory to the Prague Opera, and Mahler would be conducting in front of a much larger public than before. Delighted by the possibilities this new job offered, he now regretted having signed a contract with Staegemann for the following year and took steps to find out if the Leipzig director would consider freeing him.

Unfortunately, there was a long-standing rivalry between Staegemann and Neumann, and the latter could hold out no hope to Mahler for the moment. Visualizing the time when he would have to give up the leading musical post in Prague and take second place in Leipzig, where he would be overshadowed by the somewhat ostentatious fame of Arthur Nikisch, Mahler bitterly regretted having committed himself too soon.

Encouraged by the thought of Prague, Mahler worked so feverishly to prepare the festival that his financial worries were forgotten. The concerts were to be held in the huge Münden regimental drill hall, a long, narrow building decorated for the occasion with bunting and banners. The last ordinary rehearsal was held on the oppressively hot afternoon of June 28, the day of the official opening of the festival. The next morning the dress rehearsal took place in front of a large audience, during a storm and to the accompaniment of thunder and lightning. The concert began at six o'clock that evening and, despite the usual cuts in the score, the performance of *Paulus* lasted from seven until nine-thirty.

The orchestra of eighty musicians consisted of various groups borrowed from the 83rd Infantry Regiment band and the Hofkapellen of Weimar, Meiningen, and Brunswick. The festival was made up of three performances; first *Paulus,* followed next day by a symphony concert led by a Marburg conductor named Freiberg, and a performance of chamber music.

Mahler had the place of honor. Three well-known soloists sang under his direction: the celebrated Viennese mezzo-soprano Rosa Papier,[41] the Dresden *Kammersänger* Paul Bulss,[42] who sang the leading role, and the tenor Heinrich Gudehus.[43] Mahler later recalled the pleasure of conducting 480 performers, and readily admitted that in order to be seen by everyone he had chosen a large stick instead of a conductor's baton.[44] He later attributed the enormous success of the concert to the pains he had taken to rehearse each of the choirs.

All contemporary accounts confirm that the festival was brilliantly successful. At least 1200 people crowded into the immense hall. Luckily the three soloists had powerful voices and the acoustics do not appear to have been unfavorable. All the singers were praised by the critics, except for Rosa Papier, who sang both the contralto and soprano roles. The *Hessiche Blätter* regretted that there had been no effort to differentiate these two parts. The critic does not seem to have known that she took over at the last minute from the intended soprano. The critic also had reservations about Papier's voice, which he thought more suitable for opera than for oratorio. The *Kasseler Journal,* however, praised her "temperament" and the fullness of her voice.

All the critics, including those who were unfavorable to Mahler, admitted that his performance had been accurate and that his talent and experience were obvious despite his age. The most interesting criticism, that in the *Kasseler Zeitung* of July 1, 1885, reproaches Mahler for his restlessness, "which did not assist the performers and considerably disturbed the audience." It also questioned the choice of certain cuts made in the score, especially that of the *"O Jesu Christe, wahres Licht."* According to this critic, Mahler had taken the fast choruses at breakneck speed, and the slow passages too slowly. Mahler's conducting was to be frequently criticized on both these points, as was his love of contrasts and effects in sound. In fact his choice of unusual tempos was due to a clearly defined personal inclination.

The *Kasseler Zeitung* and the *Kasseler Tageblatt*[45] could affirm as much as they pleased that though Mahler was gifted he was not yet "an efficient conductor" (*tüchtig*) and reproached him for "too much haste" and "excess of temperament." A great majority of the public gave him a long ovation, which showed that they disagreed. "For myself, everything came out for the best," Mahler wrote. "I have received for the most part sympathy and honors." He had good reason to feel proud. He had succeeded in overcoming considerable resistance and in making his authority felt under particularly difficult circumstances. News of his first success as a virtuoso conductor spread through all the German towns. Weingartner confirms this in his memoirs.[46] Also it was Rosa Papier's first contact with the man for whose appointment at the Vienna Opera she was later to intrigue. Thus this festival really marked the starting point in Mahler's conducting career. Thanks to its success, when, in October 1885, three months after the Münden festival concert, Hans von Bülow was looking for a conductor to take his place at the head of the Meininger Hofkapelle, despite the fact that he had treated Mahler in Kassel with such cold disdain, he listed him as one of the possible candidates, together with Weingartner, Nicodé, and Richard Strauss.[47]

The festival organizers and Mahler's admirers presented him with several gifts after the concert, among them a ring set with stones, a laurel crown, a gold watch, a souvenir album, but these honors, if they gratified Mahler's pride, did not fill his pockets. In order to settle some debts, he had had to pawn his old watch before the festival. Most of the Münden presentations probably met the same fate, so he could pay his journey back to Iglau. During his last days in Kassel, as well as somehow managing to settle his many debts and making all his preparations for leaving, he was also suffering from a sore throat, a seemingly mild infection from which he periodically suffered all his life.

On Monday, July 6, having finally put his affairs in order, Mahler shook off his Prussian "chains" with understandable relief. On the way to Iglau he spent a day in Prague with Neumann, and so had only three days with his family, from July 8, for he was expected in Prague on the twelfth for the rehearsals that preceded the opening of the theater. Luckily he had been able to cancel the one month's trial,[48] previously planned for Leipzig.

"In your school I learned what is most difficult: to obey in order to know how to command, to do my duty faithfully in order to know how to demand it from others. What trouble the rebellious pupil often gave you! You needed all your indulgence in order not to lose patience with me." Thus Mahler wrote the Intendant von Gilsa at the New Year, six months after leaving Kassel. Despite a wish to be agreeable to his former intendant—to whom he later several times applied for help—there is no reason to doubt Mahler's sincerity.

Kassel was a particularly stormy episode in his life. His interpretative talent was starting to reveal itself, while at the same time he was affronting the job of conducting. He was longing to prove himself, incapable of accepting discipline, driven on by his uncontrollable genius. He put his superiors in a difficult position by rebelling constantly. If it is true that one must learn "to obey in order to know how to command," the future director of the Vienna Hofoper had undoubtedly learned the hard but useful way in Kassel. And above all he had discovered to his cost that discipline is an integral part of all collective effort, even in the theatrical world.

"The call of love sounds very
hollow among these immobile rocks . . ."

# CHAPTER 10

*Mahler in Prague—First Big Theatrical Successes:*
The Ring, Don Giovanni, Fidelio—*The* Ninth Symphony—*Conflict with Neumann* (1885–86)

Despite unpleasant memories of his first stay with the Grünfelds, Mahler
was very fond of Prague all his life and always felt at home there. Therefore, it is easy to imagine his joy when he arrived on July 13, 1885, to take
up his position as *Kapellmeister* in the theater in which *Don Giovanni* had
had its premiere a hundred years before.

Capital of the kingdom of Bohemia and a masterpiece of baroque architecture, Prague at that time numbered about two hundred thousand
inhabitants in whose lives the theater played an essential part. Besides the
Deutsches Königliches Landestheater, which had been built in the fruit market square in 1781 and seated 1800 people, there was the much larger,
new Czech Theater, built between 1881 and 1883, which gave national
operas in Czech. Until Neumann opened the Neues Deutsches Theater three
years later, the mission of the Deutsches Landestheater[1] was to keep the
great German dramatic tradition alive for the large German population in
Prague.

Despite its brilliant past, the theater had recently gone downhill under
the direction of Edmund Kreibig, and its public had gradually deserted it.
Both artistically and financially it was a complete failure when, in 1884,
the intendant, Dr. Walbert, as a last resort appealed to Angelo Neumann,[2] hoping that, with his theatrical flair and experience, he would know
how to win back the public.

A good businessman, Neumann wished to take advantage of this situation
to recover a considerable outlay he had made some years earlier. Thus
his first condition was that the Prague Theater should buy the Bayreuth
"Nibelungen Fund"—that is, the scenery and costumes that he had had made

at great expense for his Wagnerian tours. The theatrical commission responsible for making this decision hesitated for some time, because of the debts left behind by the previous director and the large sums necessary to build the new German Theater. The condition was finally accepted in the hope that the money would soon be recovered.

Thus, in May, Neumann signed a ten-year contract that was to take effect from August 1. He reached Prague on June 1 and was at once given full authority to reorganize whatever was necessary. Since the theater was a private institution subsidized only by the city, he was his own master and could take what steps he wished to enlarge the chorus and orchestra and renew the scenery (he carried out all these reforms without increasing the price of the tickets).

Neumann was already famous at that time, partly because of the important part he had played in Wagner's life. Who else could have organized touring productions of the *Ring* in Germany, Belgium, Holland, France, England, Switzerland, Italy, Hungary, Austria, and Russia, all of them given with the Bayreuth scenery and costumes? With his legendary tenacity, energy, and courage, Neumann had gradually overcome the most insuperable difficulties, not the least of which had been the conservative resistance of all Europe to this "music of the future."

However, the long, tiring months of touring had begun to tell on the indomitable impresario. Declining a pressing invitation from Wagner, who was worried about the future of Bayreuth and his own financial situation and wanted Neumann to organize a "Wagner Theater" in Berlin, he had preferred to accept a less strenuous position in Bremen, where he spent two years. No one knew better than Neumann how to organize a theater, solve the most difficult financial and psychological problems, bring a dramatic work to life on stage, and discover new talent. He was the first, and doubtless the greatest, of the three impresarios (the other two were Staegemann and Pollini) for whom Mahler was to work for nine consecutive years, broken only by his stay in Budapest.

Neumann's energy and will power were almost as famous as his theatrical flair and business sense. An authoritarian who sometimes cared more about the end than the means,[3] he knew how to win obedience and respect, but many disliked him and only submitted unwillingly. Neumann knew this well, but, like Mahler later on, he never allowed it to influence a decision. However, there was one fundamental difference between them. Neumann was a man of the theater, a businessman, whereas all Mahler's energy was used to satisfy his artistic ideals.

Yet Mahler's relations with Neumann were mainly excellent, far better than those with his superiors in Kassel. Neumann had nothing in common with Baron von Gilsa: he was a fervent admirer of Richard Wagner and one of the best qualified at that time to teach Mahler Wagnerian interpretation and staging. Above all, he was also the first admirer of Gustav Mahler, the man who discovered his genius and revealed it to the world, and who gave to the young Mahler's lively, legitimate ambitions their first real satisfactions.

On the day of his arrival in Prague, Mahler was given the job of conducting some rehearsals of *Lohengrin* for Anton Seidl, conductor of the famous *Ring* tours and a disciple of Wagner.[4] The August 2 performance marked both the opening of the theater and the first day of Neumann's official appointment.[5] It was a great honor for Mahler to be *Kapellmeister* in such an important theater and to be on an equal footing with a conductor as famous as Seidl. How delighted he would have been if he had known that barely a month after his opening performance Seidl was to leave Prague for good!

Mahler, however, was not alone with Seidl at the German Theater: there was also Ludwig Slansky,[6] a Czech by birth and education. First violinist at the theater from 1859 on, he became chief conductor in 1871 and celebrated his one hundredth performance there in 1886. Slansky was not then fifty, but considered himself the representative of the old Prague tradition, in contrast to Neumann and his innovations. The orchestra worshiped him as a kind of household god, and the whole town admired his calm, slow interpretations of the Wagnerian dramas. Wagner had heard[7] that in Prague the overture to *Tannhäuser* lasted twenty minutes, that is eight minutes longer than when he conducted it himself in Dresden.

Slansky was a pleasant, routine conductor whose age made him the obvious successor to Seidl. But from the start Neumann made no attempt to hide his preference for Mahler and did all he could to bring him to the notice of the public.[8]

One thing of which Neumann had become convinced during his long career as singer and then impresario was that the future of Wagnerian music was in the hands of the conductors. He had realized this in Vienna when singing the Herald in *Lohengrin* under Wagner's direction, and had become even more certain of it when the Vienna Hofoper gave up the idea of staging *Tristan und Isolde,* after seventeen rehearsals, for lack of a competent conductor.

Since he no doubt already knew of Seidl's projected departure, Neumann was thinking about a replacement and therefore kept a close watch on the young Moravian about whom he knew so little.[9]

As soon as the first rehearsals of *Lohengrin* began, Neumann was impressed and charmed by Mahler's enthusiasm. One day, while Mahler was rehearsing the Act II *"Kirchengesang"* and Neumann was busy with the staging, he heard someone in the auditorium (probably Seidl) exclaim, "My God, I didn't think that was possible. To rehearse that way is admirable!"[10] Watching Mahler conduct, Neumann was immediately reminded of Bülow, who shared with Mahler the same fault, excessive mobility. Seidl and Neumann were both so delighted with the way that Mahler had prepared *Lohengrin* that the day after its first performance they decided to assign to him the rehearsals of Cherubini's *Der Wasserträger* (*Les Deux journées*). This was a great favor, for on August 17 a gala performance of this opera was given in the presence of the Kaiser on the occasion of his birthday.

Musical criticism in Prague was far from open-minded at that time; the critics were conservative, and their lack of culture led them to ignore the over-all impression and concentrate on the singers and on small details. The quality they appreciated most in a conductor was a respect for the traditions that Mahler so often deliberately ignored. For this reason, they criticized Mahler for unusual tempos and personal touches that they considered "arbitrary." The leader of the anti-Mahler faction was Karl Tobisch, a critic on the *Prager Tagblatt* who always enthusiastically praised Slansky's calm and hardly mentioned Mahler except to reproach him for his "excess of temperament."

The August 19 article by Tobisch about the first performance of *Der Wasserträger* does not mention Mahler, whose debut in the presence of the Emperor must certainly have made a stir in the Czech capital. Luckily for Mahler, Kulhanek, critic of *Bohemia,* was more objective. He praised the performance, "prepared enthusiastically by Herr Kapellmeister Mahler, who appeared on the podium for the first time," and took the opportunity of mentioning the young conductor's career, his work in Kassel, and the Münden festival. In the same article he announced Seidl's departure for America and stated that afterward Mahler and Slansky would share the operas between them.

The performance of *Der Wasserträger* brought Mahler into the limelight, and Neumann felt obliged to assign the next revival of *Don Giovanni* to his colleague. To his astonishment, Slansky visited him in his office a few days later and said, "Herr Direktor, do you really want to assign *Don Giovanni* to me? You have got the public used to coming to the theater again, do you want to put them off with a work that has never been a success here?" Neumann protested that it was inconceivable for *Don Giovanni* to be absent from the repertoire of the theater where it had first been performed, but Slansky insisted that the people of Prague did not like the opera, whereupon Neumann seized the opportunity and assigned the work to his young protégé.[11]

Mahler was delighted to conduct "this aristocrat among the operas,"[12] which Mozart himself had created in Prague, and his cup of happiness was full when, scarcely a month after his arrival, he was given, in addition to these two important first performances, the two principal new productions of the season—*Das Rheingold* and *Die Walküre,* which were to have their Prague premieres at the end of the year, with the Bayreuth scenery and costumes. The only dark cloud on the horizon was that he also had to conduct the opera by Viktor Nessler[13] based on the poem *Der Trompeter von Säkkingen* by Scheffel, which he knew so well from the *tableaux vivants* in Kassel.[14]

On September 6, Mahler wrote to his parents: "You cannot imagine the immense amount of work necessary to rehearse these two works [*Don Giovanni* and *Der Trompeter von Säkkingen*]! I have *truly* scarcely had enough time to eat and sleep." On *Don Giovanni* he worked very closely with Neumann, who was responsible for the staging, and the result of their collaboration won the approval of nearly all the critics. On September 6, when Mahler began his long, magnificent career as an interpreter of Mozart, Kulhanek wrote in *Bohemia:* "Herr Kapellmeister Mahler conducted with great attention and a profound knowledge of the score. Perhaps one could argue with his choice of certain tempos, but the ensemble made the best of impressions, and left us awaiting with pleasure the performances of the other Mozart operas."

The tempos, always the tempos! From then on, Mahler worked alone on most scores and had probably never heard them interpreted by well-known conductors. Already he was following his own personal ideas on interpretation, thus flying in the face of established tradition, which he was so often accused of despising and arbitrarily trampling underfoot by sheer perversity and caprice. The *Prager Tagblatt* also reproached Mahler for his fast, "agitated" tempos in *Don Giovanni,* and on September 27, referring to *Tannhäuser,* accused him of "willfully ignoring all that had been done before him." Neumann was taken to task for the same reason and was criticized for having grossly insulted Slansky and his admirers by assigning *Tannhäuser* to Mahler. Even Kulhanek was surprised by some of Mahler's tempos, so completely different from those of Seidl (whose interpretation of *Tannhäuser* Mahler had never heard).

From then on, however, Mahler's Mozart performances won the support of the majority and even pleased his enemies. The critics praised the singers' rapid and excellent diction in the recitatives, qualities that were clearly the result of Mahler's painstaking labors during the rehearsals. Only one of his innovations was received with critical reserve: the accompaniment of the *recitativo secco,* which Mahler and Neumann gave to the strings, whereas Slansky accompanied them on the piano.[15] In the celebrated Mozart performances in Budapest and Vienna, Mahler accompanied the recitatives at the piano himself, so this innovation was dropped later in his career. He also appears to have been the first conductor in Prague to replace the orchestra on the stage in the final scene.[16]

Mahler's spirits were naturally high during these first months. He was happy to do work that delighted him and found himself in a situation far beyond his wildest dreams: the orchestra, the chorus, the singers, and even the director, far from blaming him for his youth, treated him with great respect.[17]

As for the critics, Mahler had foreseen their opposition. The evening of the first *Don Giovanni,* he wrote to his parents: "Alas, alas! 'Tradition' has gone to the devil! By this word they designate established custom, that is to say the humdrum routine manner in which it is usual to present a work on the stage. I ignored everything and this evening I shall peacefully follow *my* own course."[18] It is interesting to see Mahler adopting so early a viewpoint that he kept all his life and that conditioned all his future interpretations and productions.

On September 12, Mahler conducted for the first time Nessler's *Der Trompeter von Säkkingen*. If we can believe a newspaper announcement, he was replacing Slanksy, "who was unable to appear."[19] The Prague critics recognized the weakness of this work, which Mahler considered "frightful," and the *Prager Tagblatt* made fun of Nessler's "popular quotations." The newspaper *Bohemia,* noticing that Wilhelm Jahn, director of the Vienna Hofoper, was present at the first performance, asked "whether he will give the Landknecht Werner [the hero of *Der Trompeter*] and his agreeable popular tunes access to the sumptuous Hofoper or if, on the contrary, such access will be forbidden to an insignificant and technically awkward score."[20]

Neumann had a special weakness for *Der Trompeter von Säkkingen,* probably because it was he who persuaded Nessler to give up orchestral conducting in order to compose. The public gave Nessler's work a much more favorable reception than the critics. As for Mahler, he was more and more exasperated by this feeble work, which he had to conduct twelve consecutive times, and one day amused himself by suppressing its principal leitmotiv. After the performance, Neumann innocently asked him what he had done to make the opera sound so unusually hollow. Naturally Mahler did not confess. "The work is so clumsy," he later told Natalie Bauer-Lechner, "that I might just as well have cut either the brasses or even all the strings from the score, as they constantly play exactly the same notes."[21]

After living for a time at the Blauer Stern Hotel, in September Mahler moved for a few months to a pension run by a singer named Zeckendorfer, with whom he was on friendly terms.[22] In 1925, Zeckendorfer's daughter recalled[23] some memories of this time. Mahler, it seems, was already most irascible and terrified the children of the house. He often rehearsed singers in his rooms, especially the sopranos Marie Rochelle and Betty Frank[24] (his first public performer), the mezzo-soprano Laure Hilgermann, the tenor Wallnöfer, and the bass Elmblad. Whenever Mahler was displeased, he would slam the piano shut furiously. These private rehearsals were probably for *Das Rheingold* and *Die Walküre,* which must have required particularly long and careful preparation for their Prague premieres. Zeckendorfer's daughter also remembered having seen Mahler laughing heartily from time to time, especially on the day when her younger sister, aged six, announced Wallnöfer's arrival by saying, "Herr Kapellmeister, *der Maikäfer* [the June bug] is here."

In October, Mahler was busier than ever. On the twenty-fifth he had to conduct *Die Meistersinger* for the first time, and it now seemed clear that Neumann was giving him all the new productions, while his colleague conducted the current repertoire. Slansky must have felt considerable bitterness at seeing his young associate constantly in the limelight, and in mid-

November he even went so far as to have his own departure for an engagement in Graz announced, but this rumor was later contradicted. As for
Mahler, for the moment, his relations with Neumann were excellent. He
often visited the director in his office to discuss theatrical matters, and
Neumann proposed an extension of his contract at a salary of at least 250
florins per month.[25] But before Mahler could accept this offer he had to
free himself from his firm contract signed with Staegemann. He spent
all October and November in fruitless negotiations, since the more successful
he was in Prague, the less Staegemann was inclined to release him from a
contract advantageous to the Leipzig Theater. It had been signed at a time
when Mahler was unknown. At the end of November, the Prague papers announced that Mahler had definitely failed and would be replaced the following year by Karl Muck, who was leaving Graz.

Besides the worrying prospect of having Nikisch as a rival, Mahler was
once more suffering from mysterious feelings of depression about which he
complained to Löhr. "I should love to begin my letter with sighs, as has
been my habit. . . . In spite of everything this period is so empty and dull
for me! I ardently wish I could pour out my whole heart to you. The call of
love sounds very hollow among these immobile rocks, and one ends up
afraid of the sound of one's own voice! I sometimes say to myself: if only
Fritz would arrive now, I could tell him everything as always and could
plunge into the sacred bath of friendship! What a lot of things have happened since we last saw one another. How much poorer are we both now!
If you remember the time when I returned from Olmütz to rehearse the
choruses for the Italian season, you will have a fairly good picture of my
present condition; with the sole difference that then I was younger and
richer in hope and not yet marked by worldly 'ways', a little like one who
does not feel the dust of travel because he sees a clear spring before him."[26]

Mahler was once more indulging in his literary excesses: his trouble may
have been only an access of indefinable *Sehnsucht,* understandable at the
age of twenty-five, but it seems likely, if not certain, that he was once more
in love. Again, the object of his affections was one of the opera singers,
Betty Frank, who was the first to sing his songs in public. No doubt this is
why he wrote: "I only commit one foolishness after another, and I have
just got myself into a situation, the consequences of which I shall feel for a
long time."[27]

Had Mahler been particularly careless during his affair with Betty Frank?
Emil Freund heard talk of the liaison in Iglau and wrote to warn him at the
start of 1886.

"I think there must be something to it, and am only surprised that it is
such common knowledge that it is even spoken about in Iglau! I, for my
part, am convinced that nobody can get the better of your sense, and that
you will not let yourself get carried away and in a weak moment make a
promise that you could either not keep at all, or fulfill only by endangering

your future happiness. However, there are people who do not have the same confidence; if your parents heard this rumor, they would certainly be worried.

"Please, don't take this situation too seriously, but don't take it too lightly either. . . ."[28]

Once more an unpublished document shows how stormy was Mahler's sentimental life: several times during his first years in the theater it threatened not only his peace but also his reputation and even his professional life.

It is easy to understand that Freund wished to spare Bernhard and Marie Mahler yet another worry, considering that they were both in deplorable health. Bernhard was suffering from a serious kidney infection and in the month of May 1886 took a cure at Karlsbad.[29] On his return to Iglau, because his feet were permanently swollen, he had to remain almost all the time in his room and "avoid all excitement and upset, which is difficult in business."[30] Marie Mahler found it more and more difficult to bear his irritability and his quick changes of mood, and she herself felt far better when he was away. Justi tried to please everyone and sometimes bore the brunt of her father's bad temper.[31] As with Gustav, one of Marie's greatest pleasures in life was to go for long walks, but she had to give them up owing to her attacks of asthma. One particularly bad attack forced her to get around only by pony and cart, which her husband had just bought. It also meant that she had to give up a long-awaited and ardently desired pleasure— that of going to Prague to hear her son conduct an opera.

The first uncut performance of *Die Meistersinger,* which had for four years been absent from the Prague repertoire, took place on October 25. It lasted four and a half hours and was a genuine triumph for Mahler. Though the *Prager Tagblatt* remained hostile, regretting the orchestra's "excessive violence," Kulhanek wrote of the performance: "Thanks to the unity created among all its elements and to the harmonious collaboration of all the performers, the performance itself was worthy of the German Opera. From the Kapellmeister to the last member of the chorus, everyone seemed stirred by the greatness of his individual task and tried to outdo the others in zeal both from the point of view of music and of production. First and foremost, let us praise the achievement of the orchestra under Mahler's direction. It seemed to be an organism apart, living a life of its own, separate from that of the equally independent and integrated one on the stage, though linked to the latter by close reciprocal interaction.

"The conducting, made possible only by an extreme tension and a prodigiously effective hand, was most satisfying. As the orchestra will become even more assured, the few passages that revealed either excess of agitation or excessive volume will no doubt find the plastic tranquillity that is theirs in succeeding performances."

Kulhanek concluded by noting that the chorus had been wholly involved in the action of the performance, and by praising the exemplary staging (no doubt prepared by Neumann) and in particular the casting[32] and the crowd scenes, which gave an impression of lively animation to the whole. Another critic, far from speaking of the "excessive volume" mentioned by Kulhanek and Tobisch, asserted that Mahler had conducted with commendable delicacy, that he and the singers had had to take five or six curtain calls, and that without doubt the evening had been a great personal success for Mahler.

Before the end of 1885, Mahler conducted four performances of *Die Meistersinger* and two of *Don Giovanni,* not counting the eternal *Trompeter.* Also, for the first time in his life he was entrusted with *Norma,* Bellini's masterpiece. Nonetheless Mahler's biggest task in the final months of 1885 was the preparation of the first Prague performances of *Das Rheingold* and *Die Walküre,* which were put on in Prague "with the original Bayreuth décors." The approach of these events created lively curiosity in the Czech capital, since up to then only orchestral excerpts from the *Ring* had been heard. The papers were filled with news of the preparations. Everyone was discussing Wagner. The most widely held and conservative opinion was that "it is possible to go along with him as far as *Lohengrin,* but that his other dramas, and in particular *Tristan,* are monstrous!" But the younger element in Prague, including Max Graf, the future critic of the *Neues Wiener Journal,*[33] was "already convinced that the *Ring* would be something new and splendid."

The day of the *Rheingold* premiere, "a queue formed from early morning outside the *Deutsches Landestheater.* Already the people were imagining the marvels of the production, the Rhine maidens, and the rainbow by means of which the gods reached Valhalla. After the performance everyone spoke of the young conductor who had played such an important part in the triumph. They praised the commanding and magic movements of his baton, the prodigious sounds he had obtained from the orchestra, and the rapier-like movements that he sometimes made in the direction of a player. It seems that this was the way that he indicated the entrance of the trumpet at the end of the Rhine maidens' trio."

However, the performances of the nineteenth and twentieth seems to have left the critics somewhat confused. Tobisch admits that "many things were clear for the first time" in *Die Walküre;* in his article he explains at length the technique of the leitmotiv and criticizes some production details, without saying a word about Mahler's conducting. Tobisch, who was leader of the opposition to Mahler, praises Neumann's participation, as did most of his colleagues, and congratulates him on his choice of singers, but he did not want to admit that Mahler was largely responsible for the success of the performance.

On the other hand, Kulhanek mentions the perfect orchestral performance. He was surprised by certain details of Neumann's staging, particularly the "gymnastic exercises" of the Rhine maidens and the rolling curtain that separated the two first scenes of *Das Rheingold.*[34] Finally, these performances, which had cost Mahler and Neumann so much effort and worry, created less of a sensation in Prague than had been expected. The two operas were given only five times each, on successive nights, in the 1885–86 season, always with Mahler conducting.

During the early months of 1886, probably to commemorate the hundred thirtieth anniversary of Mozart's birth, Mahler rehearsed two new Mozart productions: *Die Entführung aus dem Serail* (premiere on February 7) and *Così fan tutte* (April 11). The latter was billed to precede a ballet based on Weber's *Aufforderung zum Tanz*. This was the occasion for another barbed remark from Tobisch concerning Mahler. According to him, that evening was the first time he realized that the ease with which *Così fan tutte* seems to be performed (*sic*) is only apparent and that it was "not at all easy" to obtain the exactitude and precision necessary for the Mozart ensembles.

Around Christmas, Mahler appears to have believed that Neumann was going to assign *Tristan und Isolde* to him,[35] but in the end it was with this opera that Slansky celebrated his hundredth performance in the Prague Theater. But early in 1886, fate gave Mahler another chance to display his gifts as an orchestral virtuoso. On February 13, the third anniversary of Wagner's death was commemorated by a symphony concert at the theater. The program consisted of extracts from *Die Götterdämmerung* conducted by Slansky, two scenes from Parsifal (the *Verwandlungsmusik* and the *Liebesmahl* from the end of Act I)[36] with Mahler conducting, and Beethoven's *Ninth Symphony,* which Karl Muck came especially from Graz to conduct.[37] Tobisch took advantage of this event to praise Muck at Mahler's expense in a particularly subtle way. Muck, he said, had not put into his conducting that "exterior passion which others consider indispensable to demonstrate their enthusiasm." He did not deny Mahler's technique or his popularity with the public, but implied that this would not be enough if he were not supported with iron determination by Neumann. Tobisch did admire, however, Mahler's conducting of the *Parsifal* excerpts: "The public could experience the very original, profound effect of this music thanks to the orchestra, the singers, and, above all, Mahler."

When it was decided to repeat the concert a week later, on Sunday, February 21, 1886, at midday, for the benefit of the German *Schulpfennigverein,* Muck was not available, and Mahler conducted the entire program except for the *Götterdämmerung* excerpts. Whether he was notified eight days in advance, as Paul Stefan asserts,[38] or was given only two days' notice, because of an argument with Neumann, as Fritz Löhr states,[39] in either case it was a brilliant feat to conduct extracts from *Parsifal* and the *Ninth Symphony* from memory, after a single, brief rehearsal, during which he had only been able to work on the well-known double-bass recitative from the beginning of the Finale!

Since this second concert took place on Sunday at noon, the theater was less crowded than the week before. A special article in a local paper mentions Mahler's exploit,[40] and Professor Philipp Knoll, political leader of the

German colony in Prague, got all his colleagues at the university to sign a letter of thanks to Mahler.[41] After the concert, Kulhanek made an interesting remark about Mahler's conducting technique, saying that he sketched each nuance with his baton as medieval conductors "drew the melody in the air while directing church choirs." In his opinion, Mahler's interpretation compared favorably with Muck's. He had given each note its proper value, each color its degree of light or shade, and had obtained a skillful contrast between the first two movements by taking the Scherzo at a moderate tempo.

Shortly before this memorable event, Fritz Löhr had arrived in Prague to spend three weeks with Mahler, who had put him up in the small three-room apartment[42] in the house of a printer named Schulz, which, since the end of December, Mahler had shared with the Swedish bass Johannes Elmblad.[43] Mahler had just shaved off his beard, doubtless feeling that he needed no longer to conceal his youth. He was more careful of his appearance than in the past, and even occasionally made an effort to be elegant, but absentmindedness and his usual untidiness soon gained the upper hand.

Mahler's daily life was divided between his work at the theater and his hours of leisure at home, when he studied scores and was sometimes visited by colleagues. Day and night, the two friends would go for walks in Prague, to the Hradschin, the Belvedere, or even the old Jewish town, more picturesque and animated than in Vienna, for only poor people lived there. Mahler looked like a somber gnome beside Elmblad, a congenial blond giant whose wide blue eyes were as innocent as a child's. Elmblad had a simple nature and was filled with warmhearted affection for Mahler. Before the Wagnerian concert, Mahler ate some of his meals with the conductor Karl Muck, who was to take his place at the end of the season.

A small anonymous work entitled *Memoirs of a Prague Musician,* and without a doubt written by the son of the landlord of the Langegasse, Ernst Schulz, describes the house at No. 18.[44] It must have been an aristocratic building once, for the single floor was arranged in such a way that several independent rooms could easily be rented. Schulz was delighted to learn "that two gentlemen from the theater had been to see the vacant rooms," and was pleased when "the blond giant and the nervous, sprightly and shortsighted little man" appeared. Elmblad discussed terms and practical details with the landlady. He also asked her for permission to bring his own bed, all others being too short for him.

The room where the two musicians were to work was some distance from the others, and Mahler was rarely in it, since he spent most of his time at the theater. Only Elmblad studied his new roles in the house, accompanying himself with a few chords. The young Schulz was very anxious to show them his capacities as a pianist and purposely started to play an opera score when he heard the two musicians returning. They halted outside his door and Mahler gave a characteristic grunt. That very evening

Elmblad asked the young man to help him to rehearse the roles of Marcel, Daland, and King Mark.

The author discovered what it meant to work "with stage in mind" (*Bühnenmässig*); gradually he saw the musical phrasing and dramatic expression take on form, while the details acquired their real meaning. Mahler had a particularly forceful way of showing how the various passages should be sung: "Only to see him pacing up and down and explaining, showed at once his exceptional gifts of interpretation." When Elmblad was learning his roles by heart, Mahler drew his attention to the dramatic "moments." From the start he wished to unite the gesture to the musical phrase. For instance, in the first *Flying Dutchman* duet, for Daland and the Dutchman, Schulz was instructed to play the six orchestral beats that, after the reply of the hero "*Sie sei mein Weib,*"[45] express the surprise and satisfaction of Senta's father. Mahler insisted on a short, jerky interpretation of this passage. Beat by beat he mimed the gestures of fear, doubt, and then joy, which expressed the whole character of the eager old man. According to Schulz it was then easy to imagine the future conductor who was to revolutionize the routine production of opera performances.

One night, Mahler and Elmblad came back late from the theater. Awakened by the sound of the piano, their neighbor, full of curiosity, listened at the door: Mahler was playing a passage from the third act of *The Queen of Sheba,* by Goldmark,[46] but the young man could not hear what he was saying. Everything became clear, however, when Mahler repeated several times the passage in fourths, "*Errette mir den Freund vom Tod,*" for he wished to underline its resemblance to the start of Isolde's *Liebestod*. The next day the author started to play the two passages as soon as he heard Mahler come in, and Mahler patted him on the back with a laugh but without a word.

This anecdote shows that at this time Mahler's judgment of Goldmark's music was harsh, though it was highly thought of in Austria then. However, in Vienna he was obliged to conduct not only *The Queen of Sheba* but the world premiere of another of his works, *Die Kriegsgefangene.*

Schulz's description of Mahler at home is more human than that of many of his contemporaries. The way he laughed rarely but heartily, and sometimes paid a high price for his absent-mindedness: he recalls in particular the day Mahler lost his entire month's salary after having slipped it by mistake into a pocket with a hole in it. From then on Elmblad put Mahler's money aside for him and gave him small sums from time to time, as needed. Mahler's needs were few, though, for he did not drink or smoke and ate little. Only the plum or cherry dumplings (*Knödel*) that his landlady sometimes sent him really tempted him. Despite the presence of the young conductor, the children of the house did not give up their singing lessons. Sometimes in the evening they would practice for hours the famous round song *Bruder Martin* (the tune is that of *Frère Jacques*), which Schulz was later surprised to find in the *First Symphony*.

Two months after the Wagner memorial concert, Mahler conducted another benefit, this time in aid of needy law students. This concert took place
late on the morning of April 20, in the winter garden of the Grand Hotel,
and the program consisted of not less than twenty-eight pieces! Mahler
first conducted from memory the Mozart *Symphony in G minor,* then the
*Minuet in A* for strings by Boccherini, the Scherzo from Bruckner's *Third
Symphony,* and Wagner's *Kaisermarsch.* After this, he accompanied several
solists: the violonist Carl Halir in Raff's *Second Concerto,* the famous
Viennese singer Marie Renard[47] in Fidès's aria from Meyerbeer's *Le Prophète,* and his friend Elmblad in Swedish folk songs and an aria from
Haydn's *Die Schöpfung* (The Creation). This mammoth concert marked an
important date in Mahler's life, for it included the first public performance
of some of his own compositions. Betty Frank, the Prague opera singer, after
performing "with brio" an aria with vocalises from Peter von Winter's opera
*Das Unterbrochene Opferfest,* then sang three Mahler songs, among them
*"Hans und Grethe,"* which so pleased the audience that it was encored. Which
were the two other Mahler songs? Presumably they were chosen from among
those which he had composed two years earlier to texts by Leander and
Tirso de Molina, or perhaps they were two of the *Lieder eines fahrenden
Gesellen?* In any case, Mahler undoubtedly accompanied them on the piano,
since no orchestral manuscript exists for any songs up to this period. For
once the *Prager Tagblatt* was unsparing with its praise,[48] especially for the
"very original" songs by Mahler. It listed the program, and the only reservation
concerns the excessive length of the concert, which caused the audience to
become restive and to start to leave before the end. For the first time, Mahler's
conducting is described as "showing genius."

No doubt the unsigned article was not written by Tobisch, for it would
be surprising to find him using such a word in connection with Mahler. If the
article was by him, he made up for it some days later, when reviewing a
*Don Giovanni.* He deplored the "incidents that took place at the moment of
Zerlina's wedding and the delayed entrance of Elvira at the beginning of the
quartet." Certain faults, he considered, could be explained by the sudden
death of the producer, but Mahler was to blame for weaknesses in the
musical performance, including the lack of co-ordination between singers
and orchestra. He believed this was due to the orchestration of the *recitativo
secco,* and a similar "catastrophe" occurred in the ballroom scene: Zerlina's
cry, after the episode with various simultaneous dance rhythms, seemed to
him "a genuine SOS from the singer!" Was Tobisch once more pointing out
the disadvantages of Mahler's "agitation" on the podium? In any case his
hostilities did not lessen as the moment for Mahler's departure from Prague
approached.

Two months before, Mahler had been desperate at the idea of leaving
the Czech capital, but in February this was no longer the case, for a serious
conflict had broken out between him and his director at the time of the
Wagner concerts, and this darkened Mahler's last days in Prague.[49] The

trouble started during a rehearsal, since Bertha Milde, the ballet mistress, had a "very personal" conception of the tempo for the *Faust* ballet music. Certainly *Faust* (or *Margarethe,* as Gounod's work is called in German-speaking countries) was not one of Mahler's favorite operas. Nevertheless, he opposed Frau Milde and fought for the composer and the integrity of the text all the more energetically because in his heart of hearts he scorned ballet. According to the critic Julius Steinberg, Bertha Milde was an ex-dancer whose weight had forced her to change her profession, and the corps de ballet trained by her moved with a somewhat elephantine grace that suited her ample curves but was less compatible with the vivacious tempos of the young conductor from Bohemia. That day she indignantly refused to obey him and strode off to Neumann, to whom she entrusted the defense of out-raged Terpsichore. Neumann listened attentively to her complaints and sided with her all the more readily since she had a liaison with a highly placed official and wielded considerable influence. It is also possible that Mahler's newfound assurance and confidence annoyed him. So he declared bluntly, in front of all the theater personnel, that Frau Milde must have the final word where the ballet was concerned. Mahler objected and finally, after an exchange of angry words, Neumann sent him home.

Shaking with indignation, Mahler hurried to his friend and critic Julius Steinberg,[50] who had recommended him to Neumann and had considerable influence over him. Pushing aside Steinberg's daughter, who tried to stop him, he ran in and breathlessly explained what had happened. "Now what have you done?" exclaimed the critic, who knew his character well. "Only refused to do what that fat old Milde wanted!"[51] replied Mahler, who con-sidered himself affronted and wished to "set an example" by refusing to make the least gesture of reconciliation.

According to Steinberg, Neumann had mainly wished to teach Mahler a lesson, for Neumann's professional watchword was *"Kleinmachen"* (make small), and he wished to humiliate the young conductor who was paying less and less attention to his authority. Following Elmblad's advice, Stein-berg went to see Neumann to try and smooth things over. Steinberg reports Neumann as saying[52]: "A theater director must have principles and I was anxious to demonstrate mine and to prove that I stand by them. No one can accuse me of not having appreciated Mahler's exceptional talent. If he writes to me and apologizes for his rebellion against my authority, I will allow him to continue acquiring practical experience in his profession in my theater. My ballet mistress has had much more experience than he has: he must listen gladly to what she has to say and then comply with it. He did not obey, so I sent him packing. It is my right as employer. To refer to the composer and his tempos, as he has done with regard to *Faust,* is absurd. In Italy and Germany I have flayed and decapitated the *Ring.* I have offered its entrails cut into pieces as food to the public in concert halls, with the singers in dinner jackets and evening dresses. Richard Wagner considered that a necessary evil, and kept quiet. Now my ballet mistress has torn the insides out of *Faust*. Mahler must also agree to her wishes and serve those insides to the public prepared as well as possible. If he doesn't wish to do so, I will shake him off like a bug."

From a musical point of view, this speech of Neumann's shows that Mahler was in the right, but it also reveals the basic reasons for the conflict. Mahler complained that "a handful of mud" had been thrown in his face and the two points of view appear irreconcilable, but luckily a compromise was found by which Neumann agreed to publish a flattering letter about Mahler without referring to the conflict.[53] According to Löhr, who was in Prague at the time, this letter constituted "a most flattering apology"; Neumann congratulated his *Kapellmeister* and wished him (perhaps ironically) a future "rich in honors."[54] Still according to Löhr, it was partly to compensate Mahler for the blow to his pride that Neumann allowed him to conduct the *Ninth Symphony*.

On November 8, 1910, the *Neues Wiener Journal* published an article stating that Neumann had "dismissed" Mahler. Neumann corrected this in an open letter to the paper. Gustav Mahler had not been "driven from Prague" but had left on good terms with the director of the theater in order to fulfill a contract signed long before with Leipzig. Neumann also states that Mahler was in Prague in August 1889 to direct *Die Drei Pintos* when he received his Budapest appointment. When Mahler put on the first *Ring* dramas in Budapest in 1890, Neumann telegraphed his good wishes for success, and Mahler replied: *"Hab's ja bei Ihnen gelernt"* (I learned this in your school).

The incident involving Mahler, Neumann, and Fräulein Milde was written up humorously for a local paper[55]: "A ballet artist wished to free her light foot from the long-winded beat. She refused to subject her enchanting art to the baton, which lives in the depths of the orchestra. Because this priestess of Terpsichore naturally found a corrupt judge among men's law courts, she carried off the victory during the final rehearsals of *Faust,* and the *Kapellmeister* could only retreat. At this hour the lawyers of the opposing parties are studying the musical case, but the thorny problems of beating time and of measure[56] might be submitted to the courts if harmony cannot be restored quickly."

During these few months other, less serious incidents must have occurred between Mahler and Neumann, since none of the successive stages of Mahler's career passed without conflicts of this sort. He was too domineering and too fundamentally artistic to submit, even at twenty-five, to someone else's artistic will. Nonetheless, as the moment approached for him to leave his work in Prague, he grew more and more uneasy about his position in Leipzig, where he feared the rivalry of Nikisch.

On April 11, having read in a Berlin paper that the Hofkapellmeister Reiss in Wiesbaden was to retire, Mahler thought of applying for the post and, despite all the reasons his former chief, Von Gilsa, had to dislike him, he asked him to intervene in his favor with the Berlin management.[57]

In this letter Mahler casually refers to the "preparation" necessary to break his Staegemann contract and shows that he hopes Gilsa will help him over this also. In this respect, he was being overly naïve. One phrase written on the bottom of his letter by the Kassel theater intendant indicates that he has "answered" it and has "refused to intervene." Reiss's departure was in fact only hypothetical, there was already another candidate for the post, and Gilsa had met Staegemann, who was counting on Mahler.[58] Mahler's reply in fact shows that he was not very surprised by this refusal. He had hoped for a moment that, if he left Prague and Neumann, Staegeman would finally agree to release him. Now Mahler had no other choice but "to see what loyal determination and zeal" could accomplish in Leipzig.[59]

During Mahler's three final months in Prague, he still conducted four to six performances a month.[60] Besides the operas he had been conducting all year, he was assigned some new productions: Marschner's *Hans Heiling,* Lortzing's *Undine,* and Meyerbeer's *Le Prophète.* He spent June restaging two operas that he was to conduct for the first time: Gluck's *Iphigénie en Aulide* and Beethoven's *Fidelio.* The Gluck opera was given in Wagner's edition, and the *Prager Tagblatt* thought that the performance deserved high praise. Tobisch, not usually so kind, made up for it at the end of the article by reporting a "small incident" that had occurred at the start of the final scene.

When Mahler conducted *Fidelio* a week before leaving Prague, he adopted the custom, which persists to this day in many opera houses, of placing the *"Leonore" Overture No. 3* between the two acts (and not between the two scenes of the last act, as was later done in Vienna). Tobisch mentions Mahler only to condemn this initiative, which, he said, "destroyed the effect of the transition toward the darkness of the prison, so marvelously prepared by the composer with the *piano* conclusion of the first act."[61]

At the start of the season following Mahler's departure, Tobisch took advantage of a Wagnerian performance conducted by Slansky to note with satisfaction that the conductor had "tardily taken up again the place that belongs to him, an experienced conductor well versed in the Wagnerian works." Kulhanek bade Mahler a warmer farewell: after the *Fidelio,* he drew attention to the fact that Mahler had conducted both overtures from memory and said he had never demonstrated more clearly the extent of his knowledge both as musician and conductor.

After a final *Trompeter* (the twelfth!), Mahler left Prague on July 15 and went to Iglau for ten days of well-earned rest. As with Neumann the year before, he had suggested to Staegemann that he arrive in Leipzig before the opening of the season and the start of his contract—that is, prior to August 14.[62]

Before leaving Prague, Mahler wrote Staegemann, stating his views on some of the problems facing the director of the Leipzig Opera. He gave his frank opinion about a soprano whom Staegemann was considering engaging, and concerning the choice of repertoire made some suggestions that are interesting because they reveal something about his operatic taste at that time. He preferred Catalini's *Dejanice* to Ponchielli's *La Gioconda,* which always drew the crowds; a lifelong admirer of Czech and Slav music, he recommended operas by Smetana, Dvořák, and Glinka, which he had no doubt heard at the Czech theater in Prague and which he thought deserved to be known by a public as sophisticated as that of Leipzig. He considered that Smetana was a particularly authentic and original composer. Finally, he praised the works of Spontini, which he believed deserved revival in a theater that possessed the necessary singers.

Guided by one of the most theatrically experienced men of his day, Mahler had embarked on a new stage in his career in Prague. For the first time he had been given responsibilities that his talent deserved, and despite his youth was now considered one of the leading orchestral conductors of the day. For the first time, too, he had conducted the great works on which his whole career was to be based. He left behind him in Prague good friends and was always pleased to return to the city.[68] Several times he was on the point of accepting the offers of a new engagement made by Neumann. The reason why, in the end, he never returned was that Prague, after all, was only a provincial town as far as music was concerned, and he was famous enough to aspire to better things.

Although Mahler was violently attacked there, as everywhere else, by the press, he also met musicians who understood him and could appreciate his value, such as the critic of the *Prager Abendblatt,* who wrote on July 15, at the close of the season: "Herr Kapellmeister Mahler today completed his activities as a conductor in Prague. He has earned great credit by his determination to protect the integrity of the scores from the whims of singers and instrumentalists. The happiest memories of this young man will be kept alive in Prague. . . ."

"I cannot resign myself to being no more
than a pale moon revolving around the
sun of Nikisch . . ."

# CHAPTER 11

## *Mahler in Leipzig (I) — Nikisch's Rivalry and Illness (1886–87)*

At the provincial Kassel Opera, and also in Prague, where there had been
a renaissance in the German Opera House after a long period in eclipse,
Mahler's activities had been limited by many contingencies. In Leipzig, he
finally came into contact with a first-class opera in one of the most important
musical centers in Germany. The old Saxon city, which, including its suburbs,
then contained three hundred thousand inhabitants, had in fact inherited
a long and glorious musical tradition. Wagner was born there, and Bach
had died there after being for a long time the city's most famous church
musician. The most important music publishers, Peters, Breitkopf, Simrock,
and Hofmeister, were located there; so was the famous magazine *Neue
Zeitschrift für Musik,* founded by Robert Schumann in 1834, as were the
well-known Gewandhaus concerts, which became famous under the direction of Felix Mendelssohn (1835–43).

The Leipzig Neues Stadttheater, like the one in Prague, was run by a
private company who entrusted its management to a director. Angelo Neumann had held this post at the start of his career, and his reign had been especially brilliant. However, his contract had not been renewed, and it was
said that when he left Leipzig there was a deficit of sixty thousand marks.

In 1882, the directing committee of the theater replaced Neumann by
Max Staegemann,[1] a pleasant, cultured, courteous man with a weakness for
the fairer sex, particularly his prima donnas, and a reputation for having a
more civilized approach to his work than most managers.

The Neues Stadttheater had 1900 seats: it was one of the many luxurious
opera houses built in Europe during the second half of the nineteenth century to satisfy the increasingly widespread taste for opera, and in particular
for spectacular grand opera.

Staegemann also managed the old Lyric Theater, built in 1766, which usually only put on operettas. The orchestra, which Mahler called "one of the finest in the world,"[2] was made up of seventy-six regular musicians, as against forty-nine in Kassel and fifty-two in Prague. There was a chorus of seventy singers (instead of fifty-four in Prague), some of them in the international class. Also, the theater stayed open all the year, the repertoire was particularly large, and a different work was presented almost every evening. Besides Nikisch and Mahler, the opera employed two assistant conductors.

However, Mahler was only half pleased by this seemingly brilliant advancement, for it had one major drawback as far as he was concerned: instead of being the star, as he had been in Prague, he was now subordinate to Arthur Nikisch, who was not only his elder, but also one of the greatest conductors of the nineteenth-century German school. Born in Hungary in 1855, Nikisch had studied under Dessof and Hellmesberger of the Vienna Conservatory. He left in 1874 with first prizes for composition and violin, and was discovered in 1878 by Angelo Neumann, who engaged him as second *Kapellmeister* at the Leipzig Opera, together with Joseph Sucher and Arthur Seidl. When Staegemann took over in 1882, Nikisch was appointed first *Kapellmeister,* and had been in this post for four years when Mahler was appointed. He was thus Mahler's superior both by age and seniority, which was why Mahler was so uneasy at the idea of working with him.

After ten days' rest in Iglau, Mahler reached Leipzig on July 25, one week before his official engagement, in order to conduct the rehearsals of several operas that would be assigned to him during the first weeks of the season. These first weeks were to be particularly busy. For his first performance, on August 3, he rehearsed and conducted *Lohengrin,* and the following month he was entrusted with not only another *Lohengrin,* but also *Rienzi, Der Freischütz,* Halévy's *La Juive,* Meyerbeer's *Le Prophète, Les Huguenots,* and *Robert le Diable,* and finally *Die Zauberflöte.* He thus had no reason for the moment to complain of rivalry with Nikisch, who apparently reached Leipzig ten days later than Mahler and who in the whole of August conducted only *Norma.*

Writing to Justi at the end of August, Mahler told her that the orchestra was showing great respect for him, and that so far it seemed to have been freely acknowledged that he had equal rights with Nikisch and was quite independent of him. Furthermore, during the winter he was to share with his rival the conducting of the *Ring* cycle. He had been invited to dinner by the *Konzertmeister* of the orchestra, a "warmhearted Dutchman" named Petri,[3] who responded to the slightest indication of his baton. The conversation on this occasion was so agreeable that he had stayed until four o'clock in the morning. Everything then was much better than Mahler had expected, and the Leipzig air suited his health marvelously. He lunched every day in a restaurant at two o'clock and then went home to rest. Home was in lodgings on the Gottschedstrasse, near the Augustusplatz,[4] where his sympathetic landlord was so full of kindly attentions that almost every day Mahler showed his gratitude by sending him two balcony seats for the opera.

Mahler expressed more restrained optimism in a letter written to Löhr at the same time.[5] "I have quickly won a position here—but also an opposition!" In fact, in Leipzig as in Prague, the newspapers were far from unanimous in praise of his conducting, and Mahler sent his friend a number of articles in which the criticisms were contradictory and for the most part unfavorable.

At every stage in his career, Mahler seems to have engendered violent critical opposition, generally from one single man. In Prague, Tobisch had never forgiven him because Neumann preferred Mahler to Slansky. In Leipzig, this situation was repeated with Nikisch, who had, and quite rightly, won the admiration of the Leipzig critics. Thus for two years part of the press underrated Mahler's artistic successes, having immediately sensed that this reckless young man aspired to equal, and even to surpass, Nikisch.

Martin Krause,[6] chief critic of the *Leipziger Tageblatt,* one of the leading Leipzig papers, and a personal friend of Nikisch, became the chief spokesman of this anti-Mahler attitude, and several other critics followed suit. The first article on Mahler published in the *Tageblatt* dealt with the *Lohengrin* of August 3. It praised his energy and personality but pointed out "weaknesses" in the performance, lack of contact between singers and orchestra, and excessive rapidity of tempo.[7] Jean Schucht, critic of the *Neue Zeitschrift für Musik,* took the same view.

A few days later, Mahler conducted *Rienzi,* which was a triumphant success. In the *Leipziger Nachrichten,* Bernhard Vogel devoted the greater part of his article to the cast, and in particular the tenor, Schott, about whom he had reservations. "The work is difficult," he added, "for it requires an exceptionally large choir and orchestra and Herr Mahler conducted so ably, in most unfavorable circumstances, that his exceptional gifts as conductor appeared clearly. Not only did he have enough presence of mind to quickly gain control of the ragged ensembles, but his efforts to give full value to certain details and to use to the full *crescendo* and *decrescendo,* deserve the most enthusiastic approbation. And though in general his *tempi* were lively and animated he also gave full value to more solemn and reflective passages."[8]

Even the article in the *Tageblatt* appeared to make honorable amends for the reservations expressed in this last criticism; it praised the élan and fire of Mahler's conducting, his zeal and sureness of hand, and the perfect ensemble of the performance.[9] The article was not written by Krause, however, but by his assistant Schlemüller. On August 10, Krause again began to exercise his wit at Mahler's expense, saying that the conductor did not seem to understand sufficiently "the Leipzig tradition regarding the interpretation of *Le Prophète.*" He remarked on faults of timing between the orchestra, the soloists, and the chorus and mentioned "arbitrary nuances" that amounted to nothing but "seeking after effects."[10]

Martin Krause had expressed his opinion of Mahler only briefly and superficially when, on August 17, a *Tannhäuser* enraged him and resulted in a very long *Tageblatt* article.[11] Was it a bad performance? Certainly not. "Mahler is an extraordinarily gifted artist who does not have to conduct from memory to attract the attention of his listeners. Neither did he need to indicate to the musicians of the Leipzig orchestra, one of the best in the world, each entry by moving his head, his hand, and his foot" or to "move about so much on the podium." It was a fact that Nikisch conducted with extreme sureness and precision with almost invisible signals.

According to Krause, Mahler confused "the spirit of the theater" with that of a concert, rushing certain tempos so that, for example, the entrance procession into the Wartburg resembled a race and aroused hilarity in the auditorium. He further declared that Mahler did not place himself at the disposal of the work or relate his tempos to the demands of the stage.

Needless to say, this bitter attack exasperated Mahler. "This article is all the more interesting," he wrote to Löhr, for whom he had clipped it, "in that one sees a somber ignoramus pretend to side with me as a means of overthrowing me with more force later on. Anyone reading it will picture me as an elegant conductor of the Mendelssohnian school."[12] Mahler himself felt satisfied with the level of the performances. The first ones had been given with an invited celebrity, the tenor Anton Schott,[13] whose artistry and "energetic and authentic" personality enchanted Mahler. He was conscious of having already made a lasting impression on the Saxon city, particularly on the evening of the *Tannhäuser* decried by Krause, a performance that "lacked neither boldness nor élan."

Schott's visit having ended with the memorable evening of August 15, Mahler, who had spent some pleasant moments with him, consoled himself with the rehearsals of Halévy's *La Juive,* an opera for which he always felt a particular fondness.[14] After *Der Freischütz* on August 20, he was again attacked by Krause for his "often too agitated" tempos. The latter also accused him of adopting for the overture, as he had for *Tannhäuser,* a concert-hall style rather than one suited to opera.[15] For the second theme of the Allegro, especially, he had chosen a tempo that was different to that which the soprano later used in Agathe's famous aria. This in Krause's eyes, was an unpardonable fault. But Mahler did receive some praise for his interpretation of the opening adagio of the overture and for the very slow tempo in the peasant waltz.

Another article devoted to this concert particularly annoyed Mahler. It appeared anonymously in the *Leipziger Zeitung.* He sent it also to Löhr, after having furiously underlined a certain number of words and noted in the margin some exasperated comments. "Here is one small example. But in any case the public thought differently," he wrote on the top of the cutting. "This performance was in some ways *open to dispute*" (the emphasis is Mahler's), the critic stated, "because of Kapellmeister Mahler's *choice of tempo,* though he has made himself felt here as an energetic leader and has at once known how to affirm his independence. This is certainly not without importance, *considering the lively and immutable traditions* that have persisted in the orchestra for years, decades even, and it was easy to sense, as soon as Herr Mahler conducted his first work, that the orchestra did not always willingly *execute* the intentions of its new leader ["Quite false," comments Mahler in the margin].

"In such circumstances, if there is not complete unanimity, it is the orchestral musicians who are to blame, for they have not adopted their leader's conception. If, on the contrary, the orchestra follows its leader, as is always necessary, in the interests of the performance, it is the conductor who is entirely to blame for the eventual modifications that are contrary to established custom. The direction of yesterday's opera *naturally did not satisfy us,* and this is probably also true of *most of the audience* ["He means critics, for the public was fascinated," adds Mahler]. Herr Mahler, who knew how to *bring out* with care many new *effects* has however added *too many personal touches, in no way intended* by the composer ["In fact he took care to have the composer's nuances performed," notes Mahler]. This was not only surprising but extremely disagreeable, especially in an opera so close to the hearts of all Germans."

"The *most excessive slowness* of the introduction to the overture, the frequent *modifications of tempo* during the latter, were *arbitrary and violent, interrupting* the flow instead of aiding it. This example is sufficient. It must be admitted that the rest of the time Herr Mahler did his best to give *their full value to the nuances* ["Eh! Eh! At last," notes Mahler] and that he conducted the rest of the opera with circumspection, though the ensembles were *not always impeccable* ["quite irreproachable," corrects Mahler]." The critic ends by saying: "On the whole, the *performance was below average*" (to which Mahler proudly adds in the margin: "It was the best given here for several decades.").

In the *Leipziger Nachrichten* the critic Bernhard Vogel also expressed reservations, setting himself up as an enraged guardian of tradition.[16] Krause showed his hostility again after *Les Huguenots* on August 22, *Der fliegende Holländer* on August 25, and *Robert le Diable* on August 27. Mahler was an excellent conductor, but his conception did not always agree with that of the singers, he often lacked precision, and he did not always obtain a harmonious collaboration from all the performers. He was also criticized in the *Neue Zeitschrift für Musik* for his agitation on the podium and for his insistence on indicating all the entries, "which would seem more suitable during a rehearsal."[17]

At the end of the month Krause launched a final attack on Mahler after a performance of *Die Zauberflöte,* the overture having been conducted "too fast" in his opinion, whereas several other parts had been taken more slowly than was usual. Krause admitted, however, that the chorus *"O Isis und Osiris"* had been most effective. From then on, Krause's position was clear:

he praised Nikisch at Mahler's expense on every possible occasion; like the Prague critics, he never forgave him for flying in the face of tradition.

Compared to August, September proved comparatively calm. Nikisch conducted a large number of the operas, and Mahler was assigned to an unimportant new production, *Ramiro*, "a romantic opera in four acts" by Eugen Lindner. This little-known Leipzig composer, son of the first horn player in the opera orchestra, had already succeeded in having his opera staged in Weimar. The honor of having it presented in Leipzig was clearly an act of "directorial politics" by which Staegemann hoped to obtain from the city authorities an extension of his theater contract. All the critics mentioned the absurdity of the libretto, the lack of originality in the music, and the ineptness of the instrumentation, in contrast to which Nessler's *Der Trompeter von Säkkingen* seemed "masterly." The work was given three times without success, quickly nicknamed *"Blamiro"*[18] and immediately dropped from the repertoire.

Luckily, all Mahler's tasks that month were not so thankless. Apart from *Les Huguenots* and *L'Africaine*, Kreutzer's *Das Nachtlager von Granada*, and the inevitable *Trompeter* (which was unfortunately as popular in Leipzig as in Prague), he conducted *Der Freischütz* and *Oberon*, one of his greatest loves as an interpreter. The dramatic works of Weber, in fact, enjoyed great popularity in Leipzig, since their author had settled there toward the end of his life. During the succeeding months, Mahler was to conduct all of Weber's major operas except *Euryanthe*, which remained Nikisch's domain.

Staegemann welcomed all his colleagues with kindness, and his treatment of Mahler was no exception: almost immediately he was invited to the director's home in the Bismarckstrasse and spent many pleasant hours with this friendly family. "If you could see those magnificent organ pipes," he said, referring to Frau Staegemann and her numerous children, "topped by an exquisite 'vox coelesta,'" he wrote to Löhr, "you would understand why the words of gratitude would not come from my mouth, and why I have seemed cold and almost unfriendly each time." Mahler still was suffering from *Sehnsucht* and "homesickness" despite his delightful new friends.

As for the "vox coelesta" this no doubt referred to one of Staegemann's two elder daughters, the same siren who drove Mahler to "stop up his ears with cotton in the interests of his profession." There are two conflicting pieces of contemporary evidence on this subject. Max Steinitzer[19] is in favor of the younger Gretchen, whose charm he claims "refreshed" Mahler, and indeed all of Staegemann's guests. Another contemporary report claims that Mahler was interested in the eldest daughter, Hildegard, and this procured him numerous "advantages" from Staegemann.[20]

Mahler was not displeased to learn that the task of Karl Muck, his replacement in Prague—the "courageous duelist"—was no easier than his own had been, and that Muck had already received "many battle wounds." Neumann had sent Mahler the offer of a new engagement, suggesting a munificent salary of three thousand florins per year![21]

At the end of September, Mahler received bad news about his parents'
health. Bernhard's condition was worrying, and it was agreed that he should
go to Vienna, where Löhr would take him to consult a specialist. A letter
from Justi, dated September 29, informed Mahler, in a laconic message that
drove him mad with worry, that their mother was also ill. Mahler wrote to
ask for a detailed report on the state of her health, and the reply must have
reassured him, for his succeeding letters speak only of Bernhard's visit to
Vienna, which took place in mid-October. Mahler asked his friend Löhr
to let him know at once if the doctor found anything seriously wrong, but
to say nothing to his mother. The next letters tell us nothing of the diagnosis,
but Bernhard had probably developed diabetes, since from then on Mahler
regularly sent him saccharine—then a new commodity and probably still
difficult to obtain. Mahler took his parents' failing health very much to heart:
"You can imagine how much all this grieves me. I am unable to help my
people in any way, but must watch the waves breaking over them without
lifting a finger. How strange and alone I often feel! My entire life is one
immense homesickness."[22]

Meanwhile, in Leipzig, the rivalry with Nikisch, which had caused Mahler
so many sleepless nights, was proving to be much less hampering than he had
feared. Also, he was too intelligent and too honest to shut his ears to his
illustrious colleague's successes. "I often feel very happy about him, and
when I watch a performance by him, I am as confident as if I were conducting it myself. He cannot penetrate the profound or the sublime, but how
rarely can I myself express them! Most of the time I must content myself with
fighting outright vulgarity, letting the rest go as it will. I have no personal
contact with Nikisch. He is cold and distant to me—I don't know whether
from pride or from suspicion. Enough said! We pass each other in silence.
Other than that I am not deprived of admiration: sometimes it comes from
a particularly pleasant source."[23] Except for Bülow and Mengelberg, Mahler
never expressed such admiration for any other conductor. His objectivity is
all the more admirable since he had a thousand reasons to be wary of Nikisch's glory and talent.

During these years, Mahler's genius was developing with an impetuous
strength that made him more impatient and demanding of others and of himself each day. Certainly, experience had begun to teach him, as the letter
just quoted shows, that the sort of perfection conceived by his "idealism"
was a dream, and that as far as daily theatrical routine was concerned he
must limit himself to "correcting the worst faults." Yet this man, so passionately attached to artistic purity, was proud, for he knew that he was great
and suffered because this fact was not yet recognized.

One evening he dined in the company of a small group including the renowned Anton Rubinstein, at the home of Karl Reinecke,[24] conductor of the
Gewandhaus concerts, one of the musical glories of Leipzig. "Unhappily I
was completely unknown to him and could only 'look on rather than produce.' On such an occasion, it is very painful to be only one among many.

In such a case I keep silent so as not to be obtrusive . . . because I know
how annoying and ridiculous these anonymous admirers can be."[25] But
the very fact that he had been invited by Reinecke shows clearly that the
latter considered this young man of twenty-six a person of talent and importance.

In this letter, which throws light on a striking aspect of Mahler's character, he announces to Löhr that he has met "one of those creatures for whom
one commits follies." This was probably Marion von Weber, the wife of
Weber's grandson, a woman for whom Mahler soon conceived a violent passion. Was she also the "siren" met a short time before at Staegemann's? The
hypothesis is plausible, since the Webers were very close to the Staegemann
family. But if Mahler had met her first in the autumn of 1886, the evolution
of this infatuation was unusually slow, since it did not culminate until the
end of the following year.

In October, Mahler conducted ten performances, two of them new productions: Auber's *Le Maçon* (*Maurer und Schlosser*) and Marschner's *Der
Templer und die Jüdin,* two fairly unimportant works then popular in Germany.[26] In November he conducted a benefit performance of *Der fliegende
Holländer* for the theater's retirement fund. According to the *Musikalisches
Wochenblatt,* the orchestra was exemplary on that occasion "with some exceptions due to the conductor's conception." In addition to works in the current repertoire, Mahler rehearsed and conducted Mendelssohn's incidental
music for Shakespeare's *A Midsummer Night's Dream* while preparing a
revival of Gluck's *Armide.* At this time a serious conflict broke out between
him and Staegemann over an incident that hurt his artistic pride and ambition. This concerned the conducting of *Der Ring des Nibelungen,* which
Staegemann, after five years of effort, had just obtained the rights to perform.

Writing to Staegemann, Mahler said: "I ought now to pretend to be even
more surprised than you, but I know that such pretense would not be like
me. I ask you to deal as straightforwardly and frankly with me, as I expect
it from you.

"You know well that up to a certain point we had a tacit agreement that
I should share the conducting with my colleague whenever the *Nibelungen*
came to be given. There is evidence to prove that. You know too that it
would be impossible, with my nature and capacities, for me to remain in a
position in which I am excluded from tasks of this sort. I ask you to consider
also that even for financial reasons I should not be denied this exceptional
opportunity to win the public's confidence.

"I also permit myself to remind you that I have not proved myself unworthy of your confidence and kindness up to now, and you may be assured
that I shall strive to retain them always.

"I hope, furthermore, that this letter is not too unclear to you, and cordially ask you for the kind of reply that the kindness you have always shown
me entitles me to expect."[27]

A letter that Mahler wrote to Justi the preceding August confirms that Staegemann had in fact given Mahler to understand at that time that the direction of the *Ring* would be shared between Nikisch and himself. Why then did he change his mind? Doubtless because Nikisch, a renowned Wagnerian, insisted that his seniority gave him the right to conduct the entire cycle, since he was entitled to first choice in the repertoire. Doubtless, too, because it was normal to entrust the four consecutive evenings to one single conductor. What does seem surprising is that Staegemann was not completely frank with Mahler and that Mahler, at the age of twenty-six, dared to address Staegemann in such a tone.

Whatever the reasons, Mahler seems to have had no chance of winning this battle. On November 26, he read in the *Leipziger Tageblatt* that Nikisch would conduct the entire *Ring*. This time he wrote Staegemann a short, curt note, asking if the newspaper account expressed his intentions faithfully. The next day, he wrote to Staegemann "that it would be unjust on his part to render him responsible for this painful affair," for, from a directorial point of view, Staegemann was "wholly within his right, and could not have acted otherwise," but Mahler, to his great regret, felt obliged to resign. He was ready to make any sacrifice in order to regain his freedom: he left it up to Staegemann to fix the date of his departure.

At once Mahler began to make inquiries right and left in the hope of finding a new position. Writing to the intendant in Kassel, he confessed that after the important position he had held in Prague, he could not resign himself to being "no more than a pale moon revolving around the sun of Nikisch. . . . Everyone tells me: 'Patience! You will win in the end!' But you know, Herr Baron, that patience has never been my strong point!" Mahler knew that Staegemann would never let him leave to return to Prague, but he asked Gilsa about the situation in Wiesbaden and the possibility of succeeding Reiss. Had Gilsa any suggestion to make? Staegemann had done what he could for him but could not alter the situation. What "madness" it had been to sign a contract that could be automatically extended for three years at the end of the first three.[28] Considering how insubordinate he had been in Kassel, it is astonishing that Mahler should have turned to the baron for help.

By December the situation was less tense. Nikisch was thinking seriously of leaving Leipzig,[29] for he had received a splendid offer from the Budapest Opera. His departure would take care of everything, but if on the other hand Nikisch should remain, Mahler could be freed from his contract the following autumn and would thus be able to accept one of the two offers he had received: one was from Pollini, intendant of the Hamburg Theater (for the position that in fact he was to occupy five years later), the other, a very interesting one, from Neumann (in which case Mahler still feared that Staegemann would not free him). A third possibility would be to try for the position left vacant by Felix Mottl at the Karlsruhe Theater. He again wrote to Gilsa, asking for a recommendation to the Karlsruhe director,[30] for he felt that he had a "good chance" of being freed from his Leipzig contract. His decision in any case depended upon that of Nikisch; and this time he would only sign a one-year contract, for he had learned to his cost not to sign for any longer. Pollini gave him till January 18 to accept or reject the Hamburg offer, which carried an annual salary of six thousand marks, three months' holiday, and a repertoire including all Wagner's and Mozart's operas.

December was relatively calm at the theater. After the new production of *Armide*, Mahler conducted some repertoire works,[31] including a Weber cycle commemorating the hundredth anniversary of his birth; it consisted of *Preciosa, Abu Hassan, Der Freischütz,* and *Oberon* (Nikisch conducted *Silvana* and *Euryanthe*). The newspapers announced that Mahler had resigned, but that his resignation had not yet been accepted.

Although *Armide* was sung only once, the new production was praised warmly by Schucht, who was enthusiastic over "the variety of feelings suggested by this very simple string accompaniment" and by "the performance of the orchestral score, which included marvelous nuances."[32] At the same time, Nikisch was preparing a new production of *Das Rheingold,* which was to be given for the first time in January.

Mahler saw out the year in Leipzig, for his activities at the theater continued through the holidays. A letter that he sent to Löhr on December 26 reveals his state of mind: "I spent a sad Christmas yesterday. As usual I was all alone at home, and saw from my window the rows of surrounding houses, full of lights and Christmas trees. Then I pictured my poor joyless family waiting sadly in the dark, and all of you, my friends, so close to my heart and now so lost to me. After that—nothing—everything swam together before my eyes, and a veil of moisture, with some tears, hid the whole world in which I am condemned to wander without respite."[33]

During the performances of *Das Rheingold,* which put Nikisch in the limelight, two of Mahler's old Vienna friends, Heinrich Braun and Albert Spiegler, arrived in Leipzig, and Mahler went with them to Berlin for some days. Upon his return, he learned that Nikisch, rather than take over the responsibilities of the Budapest Theater, which needed to be completely renovated, had decided to remain where he was.[34] Staegemann no longer opposed Mahler's departure, so he would go to either Karlsruhe or Hamburg in the autumn. While waiting, Mahler moved to new lodgings (Gustav Adolph Strasse, 12) in the "artists quarter," very near the entrance to the Rosenthal and to the old Stadttheater. These lodgings, "almost too beautiful" for him, were on the street floor of a large house with a garden, and he had a huge room to work in. From now on he would be living more comfortably and would be able to entertain his friends. He had relatively little to do at the theater in January (six performances). The important event of the moment was the *Rheingold* performances with Nikisch.[35] The news from Iglau, unhappily, was no better: his parents were both ailing, with only the seventeen-year-old Justi to take care of them.

"Because of all this, I have naturally lost contact with myself, though I am still true to myself and am again on the point of committing 'blunders.' At times I feel such anguish that I should love to run away. I scarcely dare to think of home."[36] Any biographer of Mahler is unfortunately forced to guess at the different emotional crises through which he was passing. As far as Frau von Weber was concerned, he actually envisaged eloping with her,[37] but it is not sure that he had even met her in January. However, as we know that such emotions always reawakened his creative instinct, his relationship with her probably reached its peak at the end of the year, during the composition of his *First Symphony*. Given the fact that in his letters to Löhr all allusions of this sort refer to emotional questions, it is almost certain that the passage quoted above is an amorous confidence.

Early in February, an unexpected twist of fate gave Mahler the "occasion to shine," which up to then had been denied him in Leipzig. Nikisch suddenly fell gravely ill. On February 6, Mahler had to replace him without warning for *Il Barbiere di Siviglia,* and at the last moment he was entrusted with the final preparations and the conducting of a new production of *Die Walküre,* scheduled for the ninth. Luckily, he had already conducted this work in Prague, but the week leading up to the premiere must nevertheless have been one of feverish activity, as he was alone in the theater with the two assistants, Ewald and Porst, to whom he could not entrust "any essential task." The performance was a great success, for which Mahler's conducting, "full of nuances . . . was greatly responsible."[38] Schucht nevertheless criticized him for a certain lack of balance in the playing, the wind instruments having dominated the strings, and he noted that the ensemble of the Valkyries in the last act was not quite vigorous and precise enough. Nevertheless, the evening was a triumph for Mahler: every act ended in a storm of applause, and the fall of the curtain was followed by fifteen curtain calls, three of them for Mahler and Staegemann.

In the *Leipziger Nachrichten,* Bernhard Vogel congratulated Mahler for having proved again that he was "one of the great orchestral conductors of the world" even "if at times the fire of youth had carried him away." His choice of tempos was "perfectly assured" and "without useless haste" and he had made "the necessary modifications in the right places in the score."

Never did a colleague's sudden illness suit Mahler better than that of Nikisch[39]: he took advantage of the occasion to put into practice some of his theories about Wagnerian performance. In *Die Walküre* he cut out Fricka's chariot and rams. During Easter, he had the orchestra pit lowered, as in Bayreuth, and finally obtained some of the famous Wagnerian tenor tubas, which replaced to advantage the previously used trombones. In the *Neue Zeitschrift,* the critic Schucht praised most of Mahler's innovations but added that in his opinion the new position of the orchestra called for a reinforcement of the strings, particularly the violins and violas, and also the harps in the final episode of *Das Rheingold,* the Entry of the Gods into

Valhalla. Krause admitted that in the latter work Mahler had "performed his task with astonishing calm."[40]

Mahler's tasks during Nikisch's illness were not entirely Wagnerian—he also conducted almost all the grand operas (ten performances in February, seventeen in March, sixteen in April, and thirteen in May). Immediately after *Die Walküre*, he conducted *Così fan tutte, Carmen*, and Goetz's *Der Widerspenstigen Zähmung*, which were given during the visit of the celebrated prima donna Pauline Lucca.[41] She was over fifty and worried rather more about her appearance and the quality of her voice than about her technique. The critics, while recognizing the suppleness and beauty of her voice, deplored her inexact rhythms. "Mahler, who conducted the two performances, had occasion to display his skill, for it was thanks to him and to the presence of mind of the musicians that the worst was avoided in the scenes in which Frau Lucca sang."[42]

In March, Mahler conducted a revival of Boïeldieu's *Jean de Paris,* an "exquisitely humorous" work. The critics said that it had been conducted "skillfully" by Mahler, who had been acquitting himself of his duties "with intense artistic zeal" since Nikisch's illness.[43] That month, he conducted seventeen operas: *Der Freischütz, Die Zauberflöte, Der fliegende Holländer, Das Rheingold, Die Walküre, Lohengrin, Fidelio,* and *Le Nozze di Figaro,* as well as *Jean de Paris, Hans Heiling, Robert le Diable, L'Africaine,* and Edmund Kretschmer's *Heinrich der Löwe.* For the moment, Krause appeared to have been won over: he praised Mahler's clarity, style, and measured tempos in *Die Zauberflöte,* his calm and sureness of hand in *Robert le Diable* and *Das Rheingold.*

In April, Mahler prepared the premiere of Offenbach's *Les Contes d'Hoffmann* while still conducting all performances except that of *Der Trompeter von Säkkingen,* which he was happy to entrust to Porst.[44] He sent some of the criticisms to his parents to show them that "my situation is improving from day to day."[45] "I have clearly risen in the public esteem, and they often call for me by name at the close of the performances."[46]

On March 26, the anniversary of Beethoven's death, Mahler attracted special notice from the critics when he conducted *Fidelio* for the first time in Leipzig. Vogel had some reservations about the rapidity of certain tempos,[47] but was the first to express delight at the treatment of the *"Leonore" Overture No. 3,* which was soon to become one of Mahler's most celebrated interpretations. The opening Adagio, he wrote, had never before so gripped and held the audience. From then on Mahler always stated the first theme of the Allegro slowly and did not reach the main tempo until the forte repetition of the same theme.

Not surprisingly, Krause failed to share this enthusiasm: Mahler's tempos, much more rapid than those of Nikisch, "prevented the singers from making their text understandable," and lacked the necessary elasticity though Mahler had changed speed four times during the opening Adagio. Krause refused to credit Mahler with the least originality, accusing him of imitating Bülow[48] by working up slowly to the Allegro of the overture and even said that he had entirely misunderstood the nature of the work! Rocco's aria and the two prisoners' choruses were much too fast, in his opinion, and Mahler was wrong to resort always to subtle effects to heighten the impression produced by a work of art.

Krause's attitude is completely characteristic of the conservative critics who cannot resign themselves to seeing an art evolve and reflect the personality of an artist, however great he may be. At any rate, the opinion of the majority of the Leipzig public was completely different, especially that of the younger generation, whose admiration grew with each performance, for this section of the public had always reproached Reinecke and even Nikisch for their formalism. Later on the critic Steinitzer recalled his delight at Mahler's crescendos and ritenutos, in particular the magnificent effect he obtained in the first bars of the *"Leonore" Overture No. 3,* "with such strength and at the same time such simplicity. He slowed the *tempo* of each descending octave, thus creating an atmosphere full of eloquence and meaning, until he reached the F sharp, which stood out in majestic, tranquil dignity, like the waters above which hovers the Spirit of God."[49] In the Allegro, Mahler then obtained a pianissimo effect never before heard in Leipzig.

One month later, when Mahler again conducted *Fidelio* (May 1), Krause complained about his "excessive haste," but this time admitted that these were only the "little excesses of a fiery temperament"; he noted that the famous quartet in canon, taken half as fast as usual, had been most effective and that the tremendous crescendo obtained at the beginning of the Allegro in the *"Leonore" Overture No. 3* commanded admiration even from the unwilling. This time Mahler seems to have won the admiration of his worst enemy in Leipzig. He must have felt a pride that was all the more justified because Krause's prejudices had been evident from the beginning and because the critic must have felt some bitterness at seeing Nikisch's illness bring Mahler into the limelight.

The latter part of April was devoted above all to the preparation of the first performance of *Siegfried,* to follow the first two dramas of the *Ring.* Nikisch was still convalescing in Italy, and Mahler hoped for another occasion to display his capacities to the Leipzig public. He had decided to spare no pains to surpass himself that evening. "Thanks to the turn of events, I really am on the same level as Nikisch in every way, and now I can fight peacefully for the hegemony that ought to come to me, if only because of my physical superiority. I don't think that Nikisch will keep up the struggle very long. Sooner or later he will leave."[50] During a performance of *Fidelio* on April 29, Mahler was given a tremendous ovation after the playing of the *"Leonore" Overture No. 3,* and he expected *Siegfried* to "crown the edifice."[51]

Luckily this constant work kept Mahler from thinking too much about events in Iglau and the state of his parents' health. "My family is causing me, as it has for some time, great worry, and for this reason I have thrown myself into the work so willingly. I should not and cannot think about that too much, as I can be of no help. When, I wonder, will it improve?" On April 15, he suggested that his parents move into a small house that he would rent for them near Leipzig.[52] During these weeks of hard labor, Mahler was invited to the Staegemanns' constantly, spending "almost more time there than at home" and being treated like "a son."[53] His work left him no time for any other friendship at this point, but he tried his best to help his old friend, Rudolf Krzyzanowski, who, after having conducted in Laibach, Würzburg, and Hanover, was out of a job.

The premiere of *Siegfried* was set for Friday, May 13. The dress rehearsal took place on the preceding evening, and Staegemann, in the presence of the orchestra and singers, made a flattering little speech to Mahler. He thanked him for the great services he already rendered to the theater and in closing declared that he would do everything possible to "keep such extraordinary talent in Leipzig." According to Mahler, Nikisch, who should have returned already, had requested two additional weeks of vacation because "it would be painful for him to attend the premiere of *Siegfried* and see it conducted by someone other than himself."[54] Somewhat prematurely, since all depended on Nikisch's state of health, Mahler was assuming that he had "arrived" in Leipzig more rapidly than anyone else up to that time, and that press and public were "transformed in their attitude toward me."

Still, in expecting *Siegfried* to "crown the Leipzig edifice," Mahler had not been presumptuous: twelve curtain calls, a ten-minute ovation, and unanimous enthusiasm told him that victory was complete. Most of the critics praised him without reservations. Vogel named him as chiefly responsible for the success, due to his enthusiasm, his determination, his perseverance, the artistic insight and assurance with which he had assimilated and dominated the opera down to the final details. "Some people have thought it good—without, furthermore, quite understanding why—to keep on expressing reservations about the success achieved by Herr Mahler's magnificent talent as a conductor. One would think, yes insist, that they stop now," he wrote, no doubt with his colleague Krause in mind, adding that "not to grant his achievements the admiration they deserve would be a grave sin of omission," for which "one would be unable to escape the charge of injustice and dishonesty."

This article reflects the internal struggles then taking place in Leipzig musical circles between old and new, traditionalists and revolutionaries, the partisans of Nikisch and those of Mahler. But, once more, Krause admitted defeat, conceding that this Wagnerian performance was one of the best heard since Staegemann had taken over, adding that its clarity had been matchless and that perfect harmony had reigned among its constituent elements. Mahler's victory was complete, for Krause praised his choice of tempos even when they were contrary to tradition. Like Schucht,[55] Krause also praised the singers' excellent diction and the importance given to the text in the production. This concerned Mahler directly, since he had rehearsed each of the singers separately.

Nikisch returned from Italy several days after this essential date in Mahler's career, but Mahler now thought that he had no reason to fear him and had won the right to consider himself Nikisch's equal. He felt he could count on the support of Staegemann, with whom he was on excellent terms, since the director "clearly preferred him to Nikisch, whose resignation he would have accepted willingly."[56]

In May, besides three Wagnerian performances and those of works in the current repertoire, Mahler also conducted Mozart's *Don Giovanni* (a performance that again won praise from Krause) and Rossini's *Guillaume Tell* "with enthusiasm and absolute assurance,"[57] on the occasion of a guest appearance by the Dresden tenor Riese.

The critic of the *Musikalisches Wochenblatt* took advantage of Nikisch's first performance after his return (*Die Meistersinger* on May 22) to launch an indirect attack on Mahler. In Nikisch he praised "an artist not content with having unshakable confidence in his musical authority, but also knowing how to obtain, by his comportment, the complete compliance and friendship of the musicians." Which was the same as saying that Mahler exercised his authority only by tyrannical treatment of his colleagues.

The end of May and early June were devoted to rehearsals of *Die Götterdämmerung* conducted by Nikisch. Mahler had almost no work to do in the theater, and he spent his afternoons walking in the country. He had discussed his future in Leipzig at length with Staegemann, and they had finally decided that Mahler should remain there another year. "Even though Nikisch, because of his seniority, will continue to conduct most of the 'important operas,'" he wrote, "and that will surely end soon, my influence (on the director) in the matter is clearly greater than his. If nothing changes in the interval, I shall have to be considered the 'first' one day or another. A triumph over Nikisch will be of greater weight than the one I obtained over Slansky in Prague. Of Wagner's operas, I have definitely been assigned *Rienzi, Der fliegende Holländer, Tannhäuser, Lohengrin,* and *Siegfried,* and next season I shall also be given *Die Meistersinger.*"[58]

These were the works Mahler conducted during the cycle of Wagner's operas that were given between June 24 and July 10. Nikisch conducted most of the *Ring,* but Mahler retained *Siegfried,* since he had prepared the production. This division of labor naturally did not please everyone, as Nikisch had many supporters among the musicians and the critics. The critic of the *Musikalisches Wochenblatt* in particular said that the *Siegfried* evening had not been on the high level of the others, since Nikisch was a more reliable and polished conductor.[59]

A little before the Wagner cycle, a short article in the *Musikalisches Wochenblatt* stated that one of the prima donnas at the theater had left because of the "lack of consideration" on the part of the manager, the stage director and "recently Herr Kap. Mahler." This incident cannot surprise us,

for it was to be repeated a hundred times in Mahler's later career. He sometimes expressed his impatience and artistic demands with great force, above
all when he was dealing with mediocre artists.

In an article published at the time of Mahler's death, one of the members
of the opera orchestra admitted that Mahler seldom "minced his words"
when rehearsing the musicians, but he added "that he always aimed as high
as possible and for this reason insisted on the maximum effort from everyone." Others have spoken less kindly of Mahler's "inhuman" demands and
his fights with the stage director Goldberg and certain of the singers who
appreciated neither his character nor his methods.[60]

What was Mahler's daily life like during these two years in Leipzig, aside
from the many hours he spent in the theater? The critic Max Steinitzer,
the biographer of Richard Strauss, who was then one of Mahler's friends,
has described it briefly.[61] Often Mahler lunched with Steinitzer and the
singer Karl Perron in the Baarmann Restaurant in the Markplatz, the theater
café, or the French café on the Augustusplatz, where in the summer Mahler
liked to sit outdoors under the balcony. Steinitzer remembers Mahler smiling
at his garden gate calling his name as he had one day heard it pronounced
by a Czech—"Sdeinidhä," and talking in jest of inspiration: "Perhaps the
Devil[62] will call on us today." Among his friends were a chancellor of the
Austrian consulate named Grünberg, a lawyer called Freitag, a businessman
named Martini, and a musician with whom he kept in touch until Mahler's
death, Ferruccio Busoni.[63] He and Mahler did not know each other well,
but they undoubtedly had met, since they had both taken part in a concert
on May 30, 1887.[64]

Steinitzer has left us a significant portrait of Mahler's personality at this
time. "Among the many for whom man exists only as a form, the young
Mahler incarnated man as expression [*Ausdruck*]. He always tried to be
polite, but when someone addressed a banal phrase to him, though it may
have been appropriate his face expressed his true feeling too well. Before he
had had time to take hold of himself and be polite, one could read his
thoughts in his features.

"When, in Vienna later on, I read newspaper articles speaking of Mahler's authoritarianism, his despotism, even his satanism, I had to think of the
smiling affability, the humor, and the goodness of heart, which characterized
his relationship with musicians. Affectations, half measures, coquettishness
in artistic matters—these were so foreign and averse to his nature that one
guessed his reaction immediately, for he was incapable of hiding it."

At a reception one evening, in the presence of Reinecke and many other
musicians, a young man sat down at the piano to play one of his own works,
a sort of romance entitled *"Im stillen Tal,"* the insignificance of which
caused both indignation and embarrassment. To put an end to the icy silence
that followed, Mahler, unable to repress a smile, rushed up to the young
man and said, "Yes, that's it exactly! I know that valley. It's in Styria,
isn't it? Or at least I think that I know it. I thank you." The young man

blushed with pleasure while Mahler's friends were highly amused by his cleverness. The other guests were grateful to Mahler, as their host cared a great deal for politeness in society and would have blamed his guests if the young man's feelings had been really hurt. Reinecke, the oldest musician present, an extremely polite and affable man, was particularly pleased to be thus relieved of having to say something politely complimentary.

Steinitzer notes the astonishing resemblance between Mahler and Kapellmeister Kreisler in E. T. A. Hoffmann's *Kater Murr,* notably in his manner of appearing official yet at the same time direct and personal. During the same musical evening, a well-known artist thought to please Mahler by asking his opinion on a question of interpretation over which he disagreed with Wagner. Without even taking the time to smile politely, Mahler's expression darkened to reveal the force of his belief: "When Wagner has spoken, one can only keep silent."

On another occasion, Mahler was lunching at the Baarmann Restaurant with Steinitzer and the singer Perron when a delegation of students came up to ask for his co-operation and patronage for a new musical society with modern tendencies. Full of good will, Mahler listened seriously to a pompous preamble, studded with polite formulas. The leader of the delegation finally announced that they had decided to appeal to the two most important musicians in the city, that is, Reinecke and Mahler. The idea of wanting to enlist the help of the most hidebound conservative in Leipzig for this venture plunged Mahler into a state of such hilarity that all possibility of keeping a semblance of politeness was lost. Long after the pompous delegation had left, Mahler went on laughing until out of breath.

At the theater Mahler's demands had caused a considerable stir among the musicians and singers, especially during Nikisch's illness. "As if we had to wait for Mahler to come from Prague to find out what a *piano* is! As if nothing could be accomplished without these new crazes! If Nikisch had not returned quickly in good health, the whole orchestra would have fallen ill," muttered the musicians in cafés and theater corridors.

Nevertheless, Steinitzer states that Mahler often rehearsed, with the greatest care, certainly, but without losing his affability. During a rehearsal of *Siegfried,* he writes, the baritone Köhler several times missed his cue for the laugh of scorn and triumph that should be heard backstage on the last syllable of Siegfried's insulting phrase "Then feel my sword, disgusting babbler [*ekliger Schwätzer*]!" Mahler had Köhler advance to the front of the stage, and in his own clear baritone voice gave him the rhythm and the words as follows: "Then feel my sword, disgusting pig [*ekliges Schwein*]! Ha, ha, ha—ha, ha-ha!" He indicated the rhythm so precisely that, thanks to the elimination of one syllable (*Schwätzer—Schwein*), the singer did not make the mistake again.

Steinitzer then mentions some striking individualities in Mahler's conducting, in particular the introduction to the *"Leonore"* Overture and the fairly lively tempo of the Commendatore's death trio in *Don Giovanni.* Thanks to a continuous rallentando he managed to obtain an extraordinarily intense crescendo in this short piece, which continued right up to the final bars and ended in an immensely powerful and effective tempo adagio. When Mahler conducted, each bar brought new interest to the unprejudiced listener.

Steinitzer's comments already characterize Mahler's conducting as it was throughout all his life: fluctuating tempos, a wide range of dynamics, an expressive intensity almost unique for the period. Steinitzer also speaks, almost in the same words as Löhr, of Mahler's piano playing, which those in his small circle of close friends sometimes had occasion to hear. According to Steinitzer, it had the same plastic beauty as his conducting, and it aroused his listeners' admiration for even the most "thankless" pieces, such as the D Major Sonata by Schubert.[65]

Steinitzer ends one of his two Mahler articles with a particularly striking phrase: "Of all the men I have known, Mahler had the greatest power of expression."

# CHAPTER 12

*Mahler in Leipzig (II)* — Die drei Pintos *and the* First Symphony — *Marion von Weber* — Meeting with Strauss — *Departure from Leipzig* — Last Stay in Prague (1887–88)

During the 1886–87 season Mahler met at the Staegemanns' an officer who could not fail to attract his immediate attention. Baron Karl von Weber, a captain in the Saxon army, was in fact the grandson of Karl Maria von Weber, one of Mahler's favorite composers. Captain von Weber had in his possession many of his grandfather's unpublished manuscripts, including sketches for *Die drei Pintos,* an unfinished comic opera written shortly after *Der Freischütz.* Several people had already examined these fragments with the idea of completing the opera. The composer's widow, Caroline von Weber, had given them to Meyerbeer, who had promised to devote himself to the task after a revision of the text, which he thought unworthy of a great composer's music.[1] However, after long hesitation and more than ten years of correspondence with Caroline von Weber, Meyerbeer finally abandoned the project in 1852.

After the death of Caroline and Meyerbeer, the latter's son, Max Maria, had started negotiations with a Munich musician, Franz Lachner, on the subject of *Die drei Pintos,* but Lachner had also declared himself unable to solve the problems involved in finishing the work. The sketches, for the most part incomplete and undeciphered, still lay in the Weber family archives in 1887.

Karl von Weber's first meetings with Mahler must have shown him that the young conductor had the intelligence, musical skill, and understanding of Weber's style which would enable him to carry out the difficult task of completing *Die drei Pintos.* He suggested the project to Mahler, who at first refused, recalling the difficulties met by his predecessors. Of the seventeen numbers in the libretto, Weber had in fact sketched music for only seven, and most of his writing was illegible, no one as yet having been able to decipher his system of musical shorthand. As for the orchestration, there were only eighteen bars of introduction and the first choral ritornello.[2]

Karl von Weber had expected resistance on Mahler's part, but he nevertheless insisted on confiding the sketches to him and asked him at least to try to decipher them. Mahler kept them for several days, during which time he felt more and more attracted to the music of the fragments and tried vainly to discover the key to Weber's shorthand. One fine spring afternoon, as he arrived home from the theater, the bright sunlight that streamed through the windows and fell onto the yellowing pages suddenly revealed to him the secret of the great master's writing. In a flash Mahler realized how to complete one of the numbers, and then he deciphered them all. A week later all the sketches had been transcribed, and some even completed.

Mahler would rush to the Webers' home each day to play to them what he had just completed. When the whole original text had been transcribed, he played it to the Webers, and they became more and more enthusiastic about the treasures Mahler had thus brought to life. They decided to consult Staegemann, a true friend and able impresario, and to work out a plan of battle with him. Because of his profound admiration for Weber's genius, Mahler at first wished the score to be published just as it was, with a typographical style that would differentiate the original from his additions. That, in his view, was the best way to hallow the great master's memory. But Staegemann did not agree, nor did Captain von Weber or the Dresden critic Ludwig Hartmann, who had also been called in, and Staegemann urged Mahler to complete the opera so that it could be produced in Leipzig. Considerable material advantages could be expected from an event of such importance, not to mention the reflected glory for the co-authors and the theater. Mahler was finally won around; in his position he could not afford to miss such an opportunity: his parents' ill-health made the future of the Iglau business very uncertain, thus endangering the financial security of the whole family.

When Mahler left for a few days' vacation in Iglau in the middle of July 1887, he took with him the sketches of *Die drei Pintos* and other Weber manuscripts as well—those from which he intended to draw the music for the missing numbers, especially in the third act, for which Weber had not composed one single note. Mahler was firmly resolved to add to the score only the essential minimum of his own work. Captain von Weber, who had occasionally written plays, undertook to revise the libretto and cut its most glaring absurdities, assisted by Mahler, who drew on all his new-won theatrical experience.[3]

Mahler decided to take a vacation after this exhausting opera season before starting work on *Die drei Pintos*. He left Iglau about July 20, spent several days in Vienna and with Löhr in Perchtoldsdorf, where he received a long letter from Staegemann and another from Frau von Weber, with whom no doubt his relationship had already passed the limits of friendship. He then went on to Reichenhall, in the heart of the Bavarian Alps, close to Salzburg and the Austrian frontier, where he stayed for a while, going on several trips into the mountains, notably the classic excursion to the Thunsee, a limpid little lake hidden among meadows and pine trees.[4] From there he went to Innsbruck, where he met the Krzyzanowski brothers, and all three crossed the Alps on foot to the Starnbergersee, where he spent several more days at Heinrich's home before returning to Leipzig—either directly or via Iglau—early in August.

Upon his return Mahler's normal theatrical responsibilities[5] absorbed him much less than his work on *Die drei Pintos*. "Luckily everything goes ahead swiftly, and my work is making surprising progress," he wrote to his parents.[6] On August 28, Baron von Gilsa, the Kassel theater intendant, attended a large evening party at the Staegemanns' and Mahler played to the many guests all of *Die drei Pintos* that he had completed to date. Gilsa immediately decided to add *Die drei Pintos* to his Kassel repertoire in the coming season, and Mahler continued to work with more zeal than ever because of the interest he felt in this resurrection of a work of art. The critic Ludwig Hartmann, also present that evening, published in the *Leipziger Nachrichten* on September 1 a long article devoted to *Die drei Pintos*, in which he praised the subject—"excellent for a musical comedy"—and the beauty of the score. He spoke of Mahler's "Webermania" and stated that this reconstruction was a duty, because of the freshness, charm, and high level of the sketches.

In September, Mahler continued working hard on *Pintos* and in the theater only conducted Max Bruch's forgotten opera *Die Loreley, Der Freischütz,* and *Der Trompeter von Säkkingen*. Later that month he wrote proudly to his parents that the second act of *Die drei Pintos* was completely scored and that the whole work would be finished before the end of the month. On October 8, he sent a postcard announcing that he had sent the complete score to the copyist. It had been titanic and exhausting work, but the result was far better than he had dared to hope. As soon as the parts were ready, the rehearsals would begin, for the premiere had been set for December.

In October, Mahler's theatrical activities were reduced still more, as Staegemann granted him the necessary time to complete *Die drei Pintos*. He conducted only *Siegfried* (in a *Ring* cycle assigned to Nikisch), *Faust, La Fille du régiment, Die Loreley, Il Barbiere di Siviglia,*[7] *Armide,* and Weber's *Preciosa*. At the end of the month the Leipzig Theater gave the first performance in Germany of Tirso de Molina's *Don Juan,* and though the critics do not mention it, the lied sung by Fräulein Rothauser, playing "a coquettish fishwife," may have been Mahler's *"Phantasie,"* set to this Torso de Molina text.[8] In addition, this month had been chosen by destiny for one of the essential encounters in Mahler's life: it was then he first met the musician by whose side he was to fight for more than twenty years for "modern"—i.e., post-Wagernian—German music. This musician was his most famous contemporary, the Bavarian genius Richard Strauss, who visited

Leipzig to conduct, at the Gewandhaus on October 13, the first performance
of his own Symphony in F Minor.[9]

Though he had already had considerable success, at twenty-three Strauss
was far from being the strong musical personality we know today. Instead
of discovering his own style at once, as did Mahler in *Das klagende Lied*
and the *Lieder eines fahrenden Gesellen,* he began with works that reveal
sundry and strong influences, such as the *Burlesque,* and early *Symphony,*
and the *Horn Concerto,* which at once made him famous. Unlike Mahler,
he had already made his mark both as conductor and composer, thanks to
Bülow's support. When Strauss was only twenty-one Bülow had entrusted
him with the direction of the Meininger Hofkapelle Orchestra, when he himself gave it up to go to Hamburg.

These two completely dissimilar creators immediately sensed each other's
greatness. Without feeling any very great mutual attraction, they could not
help but remain in close contact until Mahler's death, writing together an
essential chapter in the history of music.

"Two weeks ago I had a quite nice success in Leipzig with my symphony,
troubled only slightly by the ill-will of some scribblers. But that is of no
importance! The public and especially the orchestra were very kind. I was
particularly pleased with the latter: the musicians mastered my symphony in
two short rehearsals and showed themselves remarkably intelligent as a
group. The woodwinds were not entirely to my taste, but the string quartet
proved excellent. The new concert hall completely delighted me. I have
made the acquaintance of a charming person, Gustav Mahler, who seemed
to me a remarkably intelligent musician and conductor, one of the few
modern conductors to understand 'modifications of tempo.' On every subject
he expressed excellent points of view, especially concerning Wagnerian tempos (unlike some of the accredited Wagner conductors of today).

"Mahler's arrangement of Weber's *Die drei Pintos* seems to me a masterpiece. I am absolutely enchanted by the first act, which Mahler played for
me. It is of an entirely different quality from *Sylvana!* It is true Weber, at
his most charming best! I think that you too will be delighted with it! One
delights in Weber's technical mastery; there is no trace of dilettantism such
as appears here and there in his other operas."[10]

Thus, in a letter dated October 29, 1887, Strauss told Bülow of his
meeting with Mahler. Did Bülow recall the letter he had received from
Mahler in Kassel? Was he at that time prejudiced against him for reasons
unknown to us, or did he really find Strauss's admiration for *Die drei
Pintos* unjustified? In a letter of March 23, 1888, he poured ice-cold water
over Strauss's enthusiasm. "I must tell you with complete frankness that for
some weeks I have been annoyed with you! I had to choose between two
possibilities: either you wanted to make fun of me or you showed complete
lack of judgment about *Die drei Pintos.* On your advice I sent for the piano
score (be it said in passing that it is of monstrous orthographic and 'syntactical' impurity), and with the best will in the world it is impossible for

me to find a praisable thing in it. Be it *Weberei* [weaving] or *Mahlerei* [painting], it's all the same to me—the whole thing is, *perbacco,* an infamous, old-fashioned bagatelle. I felt simply nauseated."[11]

Bülow thus sternly condemned both Weber and Mahler just a few days before the Hamburg premiere of *Die drei Pintos,* which he predicted would be a failure. A few lines later, however, he himself made one of those errors in judgment for which he was blaming Strauss, by praising highly *Quentin Durward,* a now completely forgotten opéra comique by the Belgian composer François Auguste Gevaert. The violence of his attack on *Die drei Pintos* is surprising, especially with regard to Mahler's "syntactical impurity." He accused Mahler in the same letter of having wanted "to prepare for the composer of *Der Freischütz* an apotheosis as a predecessor of Nessler"!

Strauss was shaken by Bülow's violence and apologized for having recommended so hastily a work of which he had heard only the first act. He somewhat hesitantly continued to admire Weber's sketches, but when he finally saw the other acts in Munich he found them mediocre and boring. In addition, he thought *Die drei Pintos* contained "gross errors" in instrumentation,[12] since Mahler "used the brasses too much and sometimes made them play too high."

"As for the 'orthographic' errors," he went on, "I noticed them too, and you are right. However, the worst fifths, those at the end of the C major trio of Act III, are Weber's. I myself have seen them in the sketches . . ." Thus we see that Bülow had innocently become one of the numerous critics who were to blame Mahler for Weber's "solecisms." Later Mahler modified the instrumentation somewhat, but it is not surprising that Strauss in 1888 was shocked at his using certain instruments in exceptionally high registers. Despite his skill at orchestration, Strauss was less daring than Mahler in this domain. Unfortunately none of Mahler's known letters contain a reference to his first meeting with Strauss. It would be interesting to have his impressions on it, as he nearly always gave them in writing after each of their later meetings.

In November, Cosima Wagner came to visit her famous husband's birthplace in order to hear the conductors and the singers at the Leipzig Opera. Mahler conducted *Tannhäuser* in her presence on November 13, and this no doubt was their first meeting.[13] Wagner's family was always more narrow-minded and conservative regarding Wagnerian interpretations than the master himself would probably have been. Though there is no record of Cosima's reaction to the production conducted by Mahler, we do know that she never asked him to conduct in Bayreuth, either for racial reasons or because she considered his conceptions too revolutionary.

In November, Mahler's only other opera was *Lohengrin,* but he also prepared a new production of Ludwig Spohr's *Jessonda,* which was to be sung in Leipzig for the first time on December 4, and also a Wagner concert to be conducted by Nikisch and himself. It had been decided that *Die drei Pintos* would be staged by Staegemann himself, and that the rehearsals would begin immediately after the concert. It was rumored that many important people in the musical world, in particular several intendants, would attend the premiere.[14]

Some days before the Wagner concert, Mahler was able to tell his parents of the biggest financial success of his career: the publisher C. F. Kahnt had offered twenty thousand marks for the rights to *Die drei Pintos*. Half of that amount would come to him at once, but the percentages to be paid by the various theaters staging the opera should bring him even more— easily forty or fifty thousand marks! A performance in Berlin had already been arranged, after Mahler had made a quick trip there to play the piano score before a large group of musicians, including Count Hochberg, intendant of the opera.[15]

The Wagner concert that took place at the opera on November 30 was divided into two sections. Nikisch conducted the symphony, some lieder (with Fanny Moran-Olden), and the *Faustouvertüre,* while Mahler, as in Prague, conducted the final scenes of Act I and Act III of *Parsifal* with the soloists and choruses of the Riedel-Verein and Lehrergesangverein. The *Musikalisches Wochenblatt* was particularly vicious toward Mahler in its review of this concert: not only his whole conception of the music, but also the preparation of the performance left much to be desired. The whole article, however, must be subject to suspicion, for it is clearly directed against Staegemann, accused by the writer of favoring Mahler at Nikisch's expense, of misunderstanding Nikisch's genius, and of withdrawing from him, for purely personal reasons, the direction of numerous operas that "he conducts in an unforgettable way" and that "belong to him by right."

The completion of *Die drei Pintos* was very advantageous to Mahler. Not only did it establish and extend his reputation, but it also, by forcing him to work at composition, very likely reawakened his creative urge, which had been dormant for three years. In fact, since he had left Kassel, the ups and downs of Mahler's career had given him little free time for composing. He had even had to give up his summer vacation three years running. In the autumn of 1887, when he was completing *Die drei Pintos,* Mahler accidentally came across Achim von Arnim's and Clemens Brentano's poetic anthology *Des Knaben Wunderhorn* at the Webers'. He discovered with delight a naïve medieval universe peopled by soldiers and children, animals and brightly colored saints. A universe filled with humanity, love, and sorrow, *Sehnsucht,* and eternal farewells, but filled also with a fresh humor that enchanted him. He had already touched on this universe three years earlier in the *Lieder eines fahrenden Gesellen,* and its colorful naïveté gave him the idea of a completely new kind of music, never before written. From then on, Mahler was never without this anthology, which was to be the chief source of his inspiration until 1900.

Toward the close of 1887, Mahler sketched out the first songs on texts from the *Wunderhorn*[16] and began both the *Titan* and the *Totenfeier.*[17] Urged on once more by his creative inspiration, Mahler composed whenever the opera allowed him a free moment. Steinitzer, who admired his manner of expressing himself and thought that Mahler had literary talent, advised him to become a writer rather than a composer, but Mahler only replied: "No hope of that, my dear Eckermann [Steinitzer had compared him to Goethe], I *must* compose." Steinitzer rapidly changed his mind when Mahler played for him the first sketches for his *First Symphony.*

To Steinitzer, and indeed to all Mahler's friends who knew him when he was in the throes of composition, Mahler seemed "drunk with the beauty of the world and with that of the sounds within him." Sometimes when Steinitzer arrived to take him to dinner, he could hardly drag him away from his work, and only on condition that they would not meet people whom he knew "capable of destroying his exalted creative mood." As before, the universe of his dreams and of his creation made him forget all worldly considerations. Steinitzer had to point out to him obstacles in the street, to keep him from walking into pedestrians or street lamps.

This new creative activity had undoubtedly been again brought about by a sentimental crisis. For how long had Mahler been in love with Marion von Weber? No doubt for several months, but this we can only guess. Mahler's work on *Die drei Pintos* had certainly brought the two closer together, for they saw each other almost every day.[18] But Marion was older than Mahler, with a husband and three children. And Mahler, until the premiere of *Die drei Pintos,* had not a penny except his salary from the opera. They undoubtedly feared that their guilty passion would be discovered and cause a scandal fatal for all three concerned. Captain von Weber himself became aware of the situation, since Steinitzer claims that "this sort of Wesendonck episode brought terrible suffering to three innocent people[19] toward the end of Mahler's stay" (in Leipzig).

According to the English composer Ethel Smyth, who was living in Leipzig at that time and who was a friend of the Webers, matters went much further than Mahler himself and his biographers have suggested: Marion was passionately in love, for "in spite of his ugliness he had demoniacal charm" and Karl closed his eyes as long as possible, fearing a scandal that would force him to leave the Army. Also according to Ethel Smyth, Mahler, "a tyrannical lover, never hesitated to compromise his mistresses. Things were getting critical, when one day, traveling to Dresden in the company of strangers, Weber suddenly burst out laughing, drew a revolver and began taking William Tell-like shots at the headrests between the seats. He was overpowered, the train brought to a standstill, they took him to the police station raving mad—thence to an asylum. Always considered rather queer in the Army, the Mahler business had broken down his brain. I afterwards heard he had lucid intervals, that his wife in an agony of remorse refused to see her lover again . . . and the rest is silence."

Even if Mahler's love life was more active than has been sometimes stated (for his first biographers were too much influenced by his wife's statements), it is not possible to say, as Ethel Smyth does, that his life was "full of incidents of this sort"; she had the impression that "none of the women who loved and were beloved by him could resist him."[20] Her evidence must be weighed against the personal and subjective attitude of the young English girl, especially when she suggests that Mahler's liaison with Marion von Weber was probably only "a mere passing fancy" for him. Certain passages in the *First Symphony* have a sorrowful and passionate ring that cannot be mistaken. In any case Mahler later spoke about Marion to Natalie, saying she was a "luminous being, entirely dedicated to Beauty and Good, and that she had given a new meaning [*Inhalt*] to his life."[21]

Mahler admitted that in a moment of madness he planned to run away with Marion. On the day agreed upon, he even spent an agonized hour waiting for her in the train, wondering what his moral and material future would be after he had carried off the wife of a man who had treated him so well. At the moment of the train's departure Frau Weber had still not arrived, so he got out onto the platform and went home, both disappointed and relieved. Incidentally, Ethel Smyth's description of Karl von Weber's madness is undoubtedly exaggerated, for he was still sane enough later that summer to recommend Mahler to the president of the Gewandhaus concerts, with a view to getting his *First Symphony* performed.

At the end of 1887, Mahler gave up his plan to spend his Christmas vacation in Iglau, the rehearsals of *Die drei Pintos* having begun. He conducted a few performances,[22] notably two Verdi operas, *Il Trovatore* and, for the first time, *Aïda*. He spent Christmas Eve in a happy, friendly group, first at the Webers' and then with them at the Staegemanns', where he received numerous presents: from the Webers "a little table with a cloth embroidered especially for him by Frau Weber, a large gold medallion, some handkerchiefs, and silk scarves among other things," and from the Staegemanns "an alarm clock, a typewriter, many Christmas cakes, books, framed photographs, pocketbooks, etc."

During the month of January Mahler met one of the most famous composers of the time, Piotr Ilich Tchaikovsky, who came to Leipzig on December 31 to conduct a concert of his work at the Gewandhaus.[23] According to the Russian musician's private diary on January 15, he heard the Petri Quartet giving a performance that consisted of a Haydn quartet, a Brahms sonata, and a Busoni quartet. Busoni seemed to Tchaikovsky "extraordinarily gifted" and, in the course of a meeting, he "made friends" with him. The same diary mentions, without any comment, a "meeting," which no doubt took place the same evening, with Gustav Mahler, who on January 26 was to conduct in his presence a performance of *Don Giovanni*.

Upon his return to Leipzig at the end of the month, Tchaikovsky heard on the twentieth the first performance of *Die drei Pintos*. He deemed the music "very nice" and termed the text "stupid" in a letter to his brother Modeste. This letter does not mention Mahler's work or his conducting; it even affirms that the *Meistersinger* was conducted on February 10 by Nikisch, though the papers of the time clearly state that Mahler was on the podium. It seems that the latter had not yet made so deep an impression on Tchaikovsky as he did four years later in Hamburg.

Rehearsals of *Die drei Pintos* went ahead, and Mahler wrote his parents that the manager of the German opera in New York, Edmund Stanton, had announced his arrival for the premiere of the opera, which he was thinking of adding to his repertoire. The co-authors had agreed with Staegemann that under no circumstances would they reveal which numbers were entirely Weber's and which had been composed or completed by Mahler: they had no wish to lighten the task of the critics! At the last moment Mahler added a new entr'acte to the score, which he considered one of the most successful numbers. It was placed between the first and second acts in the score.

In December, Mahler had started composing again, but this time not lieder. Gradually, larger projects were taking shape in his mind. He envisaged a long symphonic poem and a monumental funeral march that he entitled *Totenfeier* before he included it in his *Second Symphony* in 1894. The sketches of these two works are contemporary, for Mahler later told Natalie Bauer-Lechner that on January 21, 1888, he had a vision connected with the composition of the *Totenfeier*. His room was full of flowers from the premiere of *Die drei Pintos* the night before, and he suddenly saw himself lying dead in a bier surrounded by funeral wreaths; the hallucination persisted until Marion von Weber dissipated it by removing the flowers.[24] As for the *Titan,* the future *First Symphony,* he also worked on it during December.[25]

Mahler's creative efforts were unquestionably detrimental to his theatrical duties. In a letter that he sent on January 5 to Staegemann, he confesses— "so as to avoid adding to the misunderstanding that might jeopardize their very warm relations"—that he has not been attending to them as zealously as before, but asks permission to go on being negligent for another two months, after which, he promises, he will attend to them as enthusiastically as ever.

"I know perfectly well that I need not make excuses to you, as you will certainly look upon the cause of this negligence indulgently. You yourself, who from the beginning have encouraged this project with exemplary selflessness and energy, would be the first to make a sacrifice for its success by temporarily and partially relinquishing a force whose energy you have the right to demand wholly for your theater."[26]

Except for the fact that the premiere of *Die drei Pintos* was to occur three weeks later, one might think that it was for the completion of this work, "encouraged" by Staegemann, that Mahler was asking for some two months of peace and quiet. But as the project referred to was his composition of orchestral works that had no connection with the opera, one can only admire Staegemann's good will and forbearance in allowing Mahler to place his composing above his conductorial duties for such a length of time.

Mahler's temporary eclipse as a conductor naturally suited Nikisch, who could no longer complain that his colleague was entrusted with work that rightfully belonged to him; slowly he regained all the ground that he had lost earlier. Nonetheless, the premiere of *Die drei Pintos* alone was to bring Mahler more renown than he had gained in several years of conducting. It took place on Friday, January 20, 1888, before an especially large and brilliant audience, including five intendants: Baron von Bronsart (Weimar), Count Platen (Dresden), Count Hochberg (Berlin), Baron von Gilsa (Kassel), and Bernhard Pollini (Hamburg), as well as the conductors Schuch, Hermann Levi, and Fuchs, critics from all over Germany and—from Vienna—the celebrated Eduard Hanslick. It was a tremendous success. The two co-authors took many curtain calls, and Mahler was presented with several laurel wreaths, including one from Staegemann with a "marvelous" inscription and another sent by Heinrich Braun "from his Viennese friends."[27]

As was to be expected, the critics were far from being unanimous. Vogel in the *Leipziger Nachrichten,* for example, regretted the weakness of the libretto, but nevertheless stated that the occasion was "an important chapter in the history of the Leipzig Opera" and a glorious and memorable event in the life of Mahler, who had been acclaimed with boundless enthusiasm, applause, and cheers; many numbers had been encored. Mahler was pleased that two of the numbers most praised by the critics—the chorus of students (No. 1) and the "Ballad of the Cat Mansor"—were his own, "as were many other passages."[28] "How it amuses me," he wrote to his onetime teacher Heinrich Fischer, "to see some critics fall in the trap and praise *my* pieces. For 'business' reasons, I must say nothing for the moment. When it all comes out, certain of these gentlemen will tear out their hair because of their imprudence; and the world will be astonished and my friends will rejoice."[29]

The most certain proof of the success of *Die drei Pintos,* however, is the fact that it was sung fifteen times before the summer, not to mention the performances conducted by Nikisch after Mahler's departure or those given outside Leipzig. The first ten thousand marks were advanced to Mahler by the publisher before the premiere, and the Webers, fearing that he would squander this sum, opened an account for him in a bank and sent him the deposit slip. He immediately drew out one thousand marks and sent it to his parents, and he devoted another one thousand marks to paying his debts. But he firmly resolved to leave the rest in the bank and to add to it his future royalties, so his parents would be able to sell the Iglau business and live on this income. In July his salary at the opera was to be increased to four thousand marks, more than enough to cover his living expenses.[30]

A few days later Mahler's parents told him that they intended to invest the thousand marks he had sent them in their distillery, and he objected. He did not want to keep any of the income from *Die drei Pintos* for himself, but he did not want to see a single pfennig of it put into Bernhard's enterprises. The thousand marks were to be spent for their pleasure. They should give up the business and all its worries and come to live near him in Leipzig. Even if they wanted to hold onto the property so as to leave it to

Alois later, they must free themselves for the moment. "I hope, my dear Mother, that you will no longer accuse me of lack of delicacy, as I now count on your understanding," he said at the close of the letter.[31]

The success of *Die drei Pintos* continued. Mahler received offers from England, America, and Paris, where articles about him and *Die drei Pintos* had appeared.[32] The performances planned should bring him at least fifty thousand marks. In February, he conducted the opera four times and also conducted some repertoire Wagner—*Tannhäuser, Die Meistersinger, Rienzi,* and *Siegfried*. This was the first *Meistersinger* that he had conducted, and under the circumstances Vogel was not surprised that "he still has to acquire in this work the assurance that he brings to the other Wagnerian master-piece," though "new light had been cast on many details."[33] Martin Krause had resumed his constant and insidious attacks on Mahler. In *Faust,* the pre-ceding October, he reproached him for "adopting confusing *tempi*"; in a November *Lohengrin,* he had displayed "a strange artistic conception." He was too wrapped up in Weber in December "to have time to rehearse" *Il Barbiere di Sivigilia.* In *Don Giovanni,* in January 1888, his *tempi* were "un-certain." In *Tannhäuser,* early in February, he "showed only here and there his earlier qualities" of sureness, mastery, enthusiasm. Krause's hostility showed again after *Die Meistersinger.* Why had this work now been confided to Mahler? So as to take *Siegfried* away from him? That would justify the change. Luckily, Mahler had tried to imitate Nikisch, and there had been only a few imperfections in the performance. "The fact that this work has been entrusted to Herr Mahler ought to incite him from now on to devote more attention to the less important works."

Mahler was still devoting himself wholeheartedly to his "new work, a *big* symphony that should be completed next month."[34] The King and Queen of Saxony had been to *Die drei Pintos,* and had stayed until the end. The king had made a charming remark to General Tschirschky: "Now I am curious to discover in the *Pintos* what is *ge-malt* [painted] and what is *ge-webt* [woven]."[35] After the second act, he had sent for Mahler and conversed with him cordially throughout the intermission. Later the queen talked to him, just as he was about to start conducting again, and held up the curtain of the second act for ten minutes. She spoke of Iglau, which she knew well, and asked Mahler if his parents still lived there. The king, "who seemed to know a lot about music," had asked him which were his numbers and which Weber's. Mahler was somewhat naïvely proud of the fact that the king had seemed to prefer those which were his. "You would be astonished by their affability," he wrote to his parents. "It is much easier to deal with them than with the Mayor of Iglau. We chatted as if we were old friends."[36]

Some days later, the Prince of Coburg-Gotha also attended *Die drei Pintos* and chatted amiably with Mahler, who later joined Staegemann to accompany him to the railway station. During all this period, Mahler was reluctant to spend any time away from his worktable, not wishing to let the fires of inspiration die down. One night, having finished the first movement of the *Titan* toward midnight, he rushed to the Webers' home to play it for them. In the Introduction they stood on either side of him to help him play the numerous A's. "All three of us were happy and enthusiastic. I don't think that I ever experienced such a pleasant hour with my *First Symphony*. Later we all went out together, filled with happiness, to walk in the Rosenthal," he told Natalie Bauer-Lechner.

The second theme of the Finale was conceived at the Staegemanns' one evening. Mahler went into the next room to note down this long melody, which had come into his head suddenly. Then he went back to face the "slightly disapproving surprise" of the other guests and resume his interrupted conversation. On the days when he was completely free he started work the moment he awoke and did not leave his table until ten o'clock at night. He granted himself only two days of vacation at the end of February, joining the Webers on a short trip to Berlin, where they were all invited to the home of the poet Ernst von Wildenbruch and were "received everywhere with great friendliness." *Die drei Pintos* was to be performed in Munich and Hamburg in April, Dresden and Kassel in May, other cities in the autumn.[37]

Emperor Wilhelm I died on March 9, 1888, and the Leipzig Opera was closed for a ten-day period of mourning. Mahler took advantage of this and worked day and night to finish his symphony, his only relaxation being some walks in the Rosenthal.[38] On May 29 or 30 he wrote to his parents: "There! I have today finished my work and can say thank God that it has turned out well. I hope that I have taken a big step forward with it."[39] Simultaneously, he announced the news to Löhr: "There! My work is finished. I should love, now, to have you next to me at the piano and to be able to play it for you! You probably are the only one who in it will find nothing new about me; the others will find much to surprise them! These emotions became so powerful in me that they gushed forth like an impetuous torrent; you will hear it this summer. At a single blow, all the floodgates were opened within me! How this happened I'll tell you one day! . . . Spring won't let me stay in the house any longer! I must get out and breathe air deeply again. For six weeks I have scarcely left my worktable!"[40]

Mahler played the symphony twice more, to the Staegemanns and to the Webers; each time, he wrote his parents, it produced "the same profound impression on them." After the great success of *Die drei Pintos* he no longer worried about the future, for he had now become a "celebrity" and would be able to get his work played. What illusions he still held!

Frau von Weber still played an important part in his life, for he spoke of her to his parents as a sort of elder sister who spoiled him by bringing him fruit and sweets. She advised him to write an opera on an original idea of his, and Karl von Weber was to write the libretto.[41] Unfortunately the captain's rough outline contained too many secondary characters and transformed a "simple and original" intrigue into an overconventional opera libretto. This finally discouraged Mahler, who dropped the project, after having written several sketches. Only one musical fragment survives—a *Knaben Wunderhorn* song entitled *"Schildwache Nachtlied."*[42]

In April, his duties at the opera again kept Mahler busy, as he had to make up by increased zeal for the kindness that Staegemann had shown in allowing him the liberty needed for the completion of his work. He conducted a gala performance of *Die drei Pintos* to a full house, and it proved more successful than ever. He also prepared a new staging of Spontini's *Fernand Cortez* for presentation at the beginning of May. *Die drei Pintos* (3), *Der fliegende Holländer, Tannhäuser, Lohengrin, Il Barbiere di Siviglia, Così fan tutte* (on the occasion of guest appearance by Pauline Lucca), *Die Zauberflöte, Der Freischütz,* Lortzing's *Der Waffenschmied,* and *Le Prophète* made up his repertoire during the month, but clouds were gathering above his head in the theater.

The storm, one of the most violent in Mahler's career, broke early in May, just before he left for Dresden to attend the premiere of *Die drei Pintos* there. Unfortunately, we know neither its causes nor its details. There exists only the fragmentary draft of a first letter to Staegemann and the later, complete text of another, in which Mahler alludes to a dispute between himself and the chief stage manager, Albert Goldberg, probably during the rehearsals of Spontini's *Fernand Cortez.* Steinitzer says that Goldberg was excellent at his job, and he also had considerable influence on Staegemann.[43] For a long time there had been tension, and finally Goldberg had questioned Mahler's authority in front of the entire opera personnel in a manner that Mahler considered "incompatible with the authority needed by a conductor to carry out his duties." After this incident, Mahler sent Staegemann a first letter of resignation, which has not survived, then a second letter in which he tried to clear up a "misunderstanding" that had arisen between them. This second letter has also disappeared, but luckily an incomplete draft of it survives in the Rosé Collection.

From this fragment, it is difficult to make out the nature of the misunderstanding and the conflict that preceded it. "On my honor, I assure you that I consider it as little honorable as advantageous for me thus to retreat [as you have suggested I do].[44] My motto is 'forward,' never 'backward' . . . This is a poor moment for me to point out to you how much you wronged me in your last letter . . . All that remains for me to say to you is that if you agree to my request, I very willingly promise to avoid all professional contact with my former chief." These last words indicate that Staegeman had interpreted Mahler's intransigence in the conflict with Goldberg as a pretext for leaving Leipzig to take up the position offered him by Neumann, and he considered that a letter of apology or some other diplomatic step could easily put things right.

On May 4, in the middle of this crisis, Mahler still hoped that matters could be arranged, since he wrote to Albert Spiegler to congratulate him on his marriage and added: "Receive, in the calm of a port, the good wishes of someone who is buffeted by storms on the high seas. To be honest, my sails are already somewhat torn, but the helmsman is still unhurt! I am nearly safe and have been able to save some precious belongings from several shipwrecks."

On May 16, Mahler again wrote Staegemann a long letter,[45] which is to be found in Mahler's published correspondence. He insists that, having publicly been disavowed, he no longer had the necessary authority to carry out his duties. Before all the personnel of the theater, Goldberg had shouted at him, "Today you have conducted here for the last time!" Later that day, during a meeting with Mahler, Staegemann had said to him, "Whatever Goldberg does, I do—he is I." Thus Mahler assumed that Staegemann was agreeing to let him leave.

This conflict was certainly the gravest in which Mahler had been involved up to now. Considering the affection and admiration that Staegemann felt for him, the director would never have consented to his leaving had it been possible to do otherwise. What was the exact cause of this incident? Was it only a quarrel with Goldberg, or did it concern the division of the repertoire between Mahler and Nikisch? Certainly Mahler was longing to fly with his own wings and sooner or later would have had to leave a town where he had not succeeded in dethroning a powerful rival, and where the Weber scandal had certainly weakened his position. From then on he wanted to be his own master in a theater and could no longer bear a subordinate position.

Mahler was nevertheless completely sincere in assuring Staegemann that the Goldberg incident was in no way a "pretext for getting away." He did in fact leave Leipzig while still completely uncertain about his future, for he had not begun any negotiations since the preceding year and had only just started to seek a new position. His resignation was accepted officially on May 17, and Staegemann absolved him from conducting again at the opera. On June 1 the papers announced laconically that he had left "suddenly," in principle for family reasons and in fact because of a disciplinary break. His job was to be taken over by the new conductor who had been engaged in April, A. von Fielitz.[46]

The *Fernand Cortez* that was Mahler's swan song at the Leipzig Stadttheater was well received by the public. The *Neue Zeitschrift für Musik* thought that the carefully conducted performance had not been as elegant as could have been desired. Schuch complained that the orchestra "needed to familiarize itself with a musical language for which nothing is more unpleasant and detrimental than an indifferent performance."[47]

Immediately after Mahler's departure, Nikisch conducted a complete *Ring* cycle. The *Musikalisches Wochenblatt* avenged the humiliations that he had suffered at Mahler's hands by claiming that the performances given by his ex-colleague, despite their "perfect preparation," had given only a vague idea of the admirable poetry of the work (the critic, in his vengeful fury, forgot that, in the complete cycle of the preceding year, Mahler had conducted only *Siegfried*). According to this article, the difference was noticeable not only in the orchestral playing, but also in the singing: each singer recognized Nikisch's authority and was no longer "disturbed by Mahler's arbitrary changes of tempo." Luckily Mahler had left Leipzig by the time this article was published. Throughout his eventful life he was thus to encounter enraged "guardians of tradition" who preferred less adventurous conductors. Martin Krause, Mahler's sworn enemy, did not mention his departure in the *Leipziger Tageblatt,* except to say that he had been replaced by Herr von Fielitz.

On May 11, Mahler went with the Webers to Dresden for the first performance there of *Die drei Pintos,* staged by his friend Ueberhorst. He no doubt took advantage of this to play his *First Symphony* for Schuch and must have received some encouragement, since he announced to his parents that it would be played in Dresden for the first time on December 7.[48] The triumphal career of *Die drei Pintos* continued: performances were arranged for the start of the next season in Kassel, Brunswick, Breslau, Bremen, Frankfurt am Main, Nuremberg, and finally Vienna, where Mahler hoped to attend the premiere with his whole family.[49]

In the euphoria of *Die drei Pintos* and the feeling of security that Staegemann's friendship and admiration had brought him, Mahler had thought that his future in Leipzig was assured, and in March he had declined the offer of a position in Frankfurt am Main.[50] He thus left Leipzig about May 20, with no definite plans for the future but without much regret, after taking leave of his friends, especially the Staegemanns.[51] While waiting to hear from Frankfurt if his candidacy would be considered again, he went to Munich to see the intendant there, Karl von Perfall. There he received an offer from the Hanover Theater, and while waiting for answers to his various inquiries he went to spend a few days with Krzyzanowski in Starnberg.[52] Luckily he liked the atmosphere and the climate of the Bavarian capital, and twenty years later it did not displease him to recall his stay there, alone, without money and with no prospect of an engagement.[53] The impresario Hermann Wolff also offered him a series of concerts in Dresden, which he rejected "because he did not wish to be in a position of rivalry vis-à-vis Schuch."[54]

Having taken these final steps, Mahler went to Iglau to spend a few days with his parents, whom he had not seen for more than a year. No doubt he put a brave face on things, but his depressed state of mind shows in a letter to Steinitzer, who, knowing how worried he was, had written to console him and urge him to enjoy life during this enforced idleness. "Dear friend. You are right. If this goes on, I shall soon cease to be human. I am in the emotional state of the finale of my symphony.[55] How kind it is of you to think of me like this.

"I don't know what to do about the symphony. I should prefer not to have the first performance in a pub! First I'd like to try my luck elsewhere! Isn't there any hope of giving the first performance at Leipzig? Write me about this and tell me if anything can be done there. I shall take the necessary steps in Vienna this autumn. Steinitzer, things are bad with me. From here I shall return to Munich, where I shall wait for your letter at my Starnberg address. You won't be frightened off, will you? We'll find a way to keep in touch. For the moment, I am completely incapable of telling you anything about myself unless it be that I see no chance of finding an engagement anywhere, and I must confess to you in all honesty that this worries me terribly. I now need a very absorbing activity if I am not to perish! Write soon, I beg you, and remain the friend of a very confused Gustav Mahler."[56]

Mahler's only definite project for the moment was that of going to Prague to conduct rehearsals and the first performance there of *Die drei Pintos*. The intervening month of uncertainty weighed heavily on him. He knew that in the world of opera he had not acquired the best of reputations. Certainly he no longer needed to demonstrate his abilities, but the "affairs" that had multiplied over the years had set impresarios talking, and so had his liaison with Frau Weber: many of them would have nothing to do with this young man with the fierce eyes, dominating character, and radical conceptions. But he now enjoyed conducting too much to consider giving it up, and he could look forward to the future with confidence on the purely financial level, thanks to the success of *Die drei Pintos*. An article published in 1897 by Max Marschalk stated that Mahler had considered settling in Munich while waiting for a new position, and working there on an opera (which would have been either *Rübezahl* or the one he had planned with Karl von Weber).

Knowing that Mahler might find himself without employment, Angelo Neumann invited him to prepare and conduct the Prague production of *Die drei Pintos,* with which he would later tour Germany.[57] Steinberg, who had served as mediator and go-between during Mahler's and Neumann's 1886 quarrel,[58] was asked in April to make contact with Mahler, which he did in a particularly prudent and diplomatic way. Mahler answered his letter by quoting an old parable, that of the hungry messenger of Zybera (probably Cythera), who faced the Spartans, turned an empty sack upside down, and said, "There is nothing inside, put in something." He was given wheat, and told that he could have been even more laconic, since the empty sack made the reason for his visit clear. Neumann's "sack" was empty and obviously he must capitulate since his own was even emptier: the first storms had broken and he would in fact soon be without a job. As early as April 20 the *Prager Abendblatt* announced the projected performances.

In June, Mahler worked in Iglau on the *Totenfeier* before leaving to rehearse in Prague. After this the tour would start with performances in Berlin, and, in order to avoid sending the whole company for only one work, Neumann asked Mahler to conduct Cornelius' *Barbier von Bagdad* as well. He accepted gladly, for this was one of his favorite works.[59]

The dress rehearsal of *Die drei Pintos* took place on August 17 before an invited audience who gave Mahler an enthusiastic welcome. The following day his old enemy, Tobisch, praised him to the skies as the recreator of a work of art that he considered worthy of a place in the repertoire beside *Freischütz* and *Oberon,* while as an interpreter he had "given nobility and elegance" to the spirit of Weber's music. The first performance was scheduled for August 18 to celebrate the birthday of the Emperor Franz Josef on that day. No doubt Mahler's parents were already too weak to make the journey, for his family was represented by only Justi and Otto. The performance was even more successful than the day before, and news of Mahler's triumph immediately reached Bernhard and Marie Mahler. Indeed this was one of their last moments of real happiness.

The critics were unanimously enthusiastic. According to Tobisch, the first act deserved a place among the great works of art in the repertoire, even if the other acts were inferior. *Bohemia* considered that it was a long time since Prague had had such a unanimously acclaimed performance. The anonymous critic was enthusiastic over the "melodic treasures" of the score, in which he had noticed a hand other than Weber's, without being for a moment worried or shocked, for this "other face" pleased him as much as that of the original. The critic considered that this work was an excellent addition to the repertoire of the Prague Opera and that the admirable performance did it honor.[60]

In August, Mahler conducted five performances of *Pintos* (after this seven other performances were conducted by Slansky), and at the end of the month he started rehearsing *Der Barbier von Bagdad*. No doubt he had definite views on the staging of this fresh and lighthearted work, for, as two years before, he had a violent quarrel with Neumann during a rehearsal. Determined not to give in to a young man whose artistic and intellectual superiority he found unbearable, the latter at once left the stage, and an hour later, in the middle of rehearsals, Mahler received the following note: "You like Spartan conciseness. Put the enclosed fee into the empty sack. The rehearsal, and all the others for which I engaged you, is canceled, Adieu."[61]

After this particularly brutal and offensive dismissal,[62] Mahler went to Julius Steinberg's to announce the news; the latter reproached him for his intransigence, and Mahler replied that "art only gave itself completely to those who gave themselves completely to it and loved it more than they feared poverty and hunger."[63]

In the hope of getting Emil Claar, the Frankfurt Opera intendant, to take some interest in him, since no doubt he had not answered Mahler's previous letters, Mahler asked Steinberg, who knew him well, to write and intercede for him. On his way downstairs to post this letter, Mahler met the well-known Czech cellist David Popper,[64] who recognized him immediately, having been most impressed the evening before at *Die drei Pintos,* by Mahler's exploits as co-author and conductor. Popper asked Steinberg to arrange a meeting with the young man, who seemed to him to be "musical genius incarnate" and who in his eyes possessed "an artistic power that came from the magic garden of Armida."

The very next day Mahler was invited to lunch with Steinberg and Popper, who waited vainly for him for an hour.[65] Popper was about to leave when Steinberg sent one of the orchestral musicians to look for Mahler. He was found in his usual café, composing feverishly; he had completely forgotten the lunch appointment and was furious at being interrupted. According to Steinberg's daughter, it was already late in the afternoon when he finally arrived, his hair disheveled, and dying of hunger. While wolfing down his lunch, he carried on a lively and animated conversation with the cellist. The exchange of opinions and paradoxes at once showed how well the two men got on.

Together they evaluated contemporary musical production and, by the end of the evening, Popper took Steinberg aside and "while keeping one deeply admiring eye on Mahler's slim silhouette" said to him, "There is our next director of the Budapest Opera!" A few days later, Claar offered the young conductor a "guest engagement" and Steinberg hurriedly sent his letter on to Iglau, but events had moved fast and Mahler had already left for Vienna and Budapest.[66]

Mahler had in fact taken leave of his parents in the middle of September and left Iglau for Vienna, where Baron Franz von Beniczky, intendant of the Budapest Opera, had asked him to contact one of his collaborators. Thus Popper's mediation had been immediately effective: Mahler spent several days at the Höller Hotel and during the preliminary negotiations saw again some of his Viennese friends, Löhr, Dr. Bondy, and the Spieglers. He also probably took his brother Otto to Vienna with him, since Otto was about to start studying music at Mahler's expense.

Almost at once the negotiations took a favorable turn, and Intendant Beniczky invited Mahler to come to Budapest at once.[67] Before leaving, Mahler wrote to a friend in Dresden (no doubt the critic Ludwig Hartmann) to ask him if he "knew of the intentions" of the Munich intendant Perfall: he would have infinitely preferred a post in Germany to one in Budapest, however important. Considering the lamentable state of the Hungarian Opera and the urgent reforms that were needed, he feared he would no longer have any time to compose.[68] However, he was dazzled by the importance of the position that was being offered to him, and dropped vague hopes in favor of a brilliant reality.

Apart from *Die drei Pintos* and his future as a conductor, Mahler's chief concern that summer, while he was completing the *Totenfeier,* was to get his *First Symphony* performed.[69] As soon as he had finished the score, he wrote to Bülow on March 28, 1888, to ask if he might go and play it to him, for "before sending my work into the world, I greatly need to submit it to your judgment, immensely precious in my eyes."[70] Considering Bülow's attitude in Kassel and what he had just written about Mahler to Strauss, he almost certainly did not grant him the meeting in question; it is even surprising that Mahler thought of asking for it. Later, during his two visits to Munich in the month of June or July, Mahler tried to interest Hermann Levi in his work. He had made his acquaintance in Leipzig at the first performance of the *Pintos,*[71] but he did not manage to see him.

While *Die drei Pintos* was being rehearsed, Mahler went again to Dresden, this time to bring pressure to bear on Schuch. On August 20 and 23 the Prague newspapers announced that he would conduct his symphony at the Dresden Hofkapelle[72] and again in Prague the following year.[73] On September 11 Mahler went for the third time to Dresden for a performance of *Die drei Pintos,* given to a full house, and upon his return the *Prager Abendblatt* announced, at the same time as his departure from Prague, that his *Symphonic Poem* would be performed for the first time in Dresden on December 7 and that another "important work" (obviously the *Totenfeier*) would be given later. However, all these projects failed.

From Prague, Mahler wrote to Strauss and begged him to use his influence in Munich in order to get the work performed.[74] The letter to a friend in Dresden alludes to his "fatal mischance" in that town; no doubt this concerned the performance he desired so much. In Leipzig the only association that logically should have been interested in such a first performance was the Lisztverein, founded in 1885 as a reaction against the conservative Gewandhaus concerts and their conductor Reinecke. Unfortunately, the founder of the Verein was one of Mahler's bitterest enemies, the critic Krause, and its conductor was Nikisch, who had good reason not to like Mahler. So, following the advice of Karl von Weber, Mahler wrote on July 31 from Prague to Paul Bernhard Limburger, president of the Gewandhaus concerts, to "thank him for showing interest in his work," for "he need not tell him how much he would like his symphony to be performed by the institution which he headed and which is unique in the world both for its standing and artistic level."[75]

But all these efforts were useless, for the *First Symphony* was too "modern" and too revolutionary to attract the symphonic associations that were essentially conservative in outlook; despite *Die drei Pintos* its author was still almost unknown, at least as a composer. Successive disappointments were to convince him that he could only impose his own works progressively as his fame as an interpreter spread.

Nevertheless Mahler's two years in Leipzig established his career and reputation more firmly than all his previous engagements: not only had he acquired the technique and the rank of virtuoso conductor by competing with Nikisch on his own ground, but he had attracted the attention of the German musical world, and even of certain foreign countries, thanks to *Die drei Pintos.* This remarkable success put his name on the European musical map more surely than his successes as a conductor. Yet, despite the fame he had gained by finishing Weber's work, his nomination to Budapest caused great astonishment: it was indeed quite exceptional for a young man of twenty-eight to lead an institution as important as the Royal Budapest Opera.

# CHAPTER 13

*Mahler Director of the Royal Budapest Opera (I)*
*(1888–89)*

"The position offered me here is surprisingly good: it is so good that I feel some anguish about accepting it, and must consider it seriously. I would be director of the Royal Opera, with absolutely unlimited powers! All-powerful master of an institution as large as the Vienna Opera, and at the same time first conductor. I shall be responsible only to the minister, and thus absolutely free. Annual salary, 10,000 florins, plus a whole series of secondary revenues and *four months* of vacation! It is all simply incredible! At the same time, the responsibilities are immense, as I shall have at my disposition, with a single stroke of the pen, a treasury of one million florins! . . . I have been working without interruption for two days now with the officials and counselors so as to acquaint myself with the way things are done. I am altogether dizzy! . . ." This was the description of his future position that Mahler sent his parents after he visited the Hungarian capital for the first time in July 1888.

Mahler was only just twenty-eight, and indeed it was a dazzling offer, even when taking into account the rapid advancement of his theatrical career. What had induced Baron Beniczky, intendant of the two Hungarian theaters,[1] to confide the destiny of the national Hungarian opera to so young a man?

From January 26, 1886, to December 30, 1887, the two national playhouses—the opera and the legitimate theater—had been placed under the "impulsive and arbitrary" direction of Count Stefan Keglevitch, who had favored the theater and let the opera run downhill.[2] He soon turned out to be incapable of solving the complex problems connected with running an opera house. In fact, since the Ausgleich, the charter of 1867 in which Austria had accorded to Hungary at least a theoretical independence, there had been many fruitless attempts to satisfy the increasingly virulent Hungarian chauvinism by creating a national Magyar theater. But the public, eager for famous singers and Italian operas, had not responded, and the opera house suffered accordingly.

Keglevitch had gradually left all artistic initiative to the first conductor at the opera, Sándor Erkel, son of the then celebrated composer Ferenc Erkel, who had thus in fact been carrying out the duties of artistic director. He was a musician of talent and experience, but with a weak, fatalistic character; he let things slide, and, faced with the artistic and financial debacle, he proved absolutely incapable of imposing his authority or re-establishing the theater on a high artistic level. Because of this disorganization, the opera's "ensemble" of singers had deteriorated to such a point that most of them were not equipped to fill even secondary roles. This led to the financially disastrous expedient of constantly inviting outside singers; also, owing to lack of discipline, the orchestra was lamentable.

When Baron Beniczky, a cultured aristocrat without musical experience, replaced Keglevitch on January 13, 1888, he sent Parliament gloomy reports on the situation and was allowed to dismiss numerous performers and to diminish the number of "guest singers" and performances in order to have time to remedy the incredible disorder. The repertoire was nonexistent, and it had become difficult to give performances on set days, for the singers were always dropping out at the last moment.

Once the purely administrative problems had been solved, Beniczky decided to appoint a conductor capable of bringing back some prestige to the opera and who could also reorganize the theater, raise the artistic level of the performances, and win back the public. The empty or half-filled houses were in fact causing large annual deficits. He contacted various candidates, in particular Nikisch, before deciding on the Viennese Felix Mottl, who signed a tentative contract on June 5, 1888.

Three months later, on September 15, Mottl broke this engagement,[3] but Beniczky had no doubt foreseen this, since he had been in touch with Mahler since August, on Popper's recommendation.[4]

Mahler was probably in Iglau around September 20, when he received an official invitation from Beniczky, who was pressed for time and moved fast. As early as the twenty-fourth Mahler was in Vienna to meet his envoy; on the twenty-sixth he was in Budapest and two days later was formally engaged. From the time of his first contact with Mahler, Beniczky was struck by the young man's intelligence, enthusiasm, and knowledge of music. Further, he quickly sensed Mahler's latent capacities as an administrator. Thus he at once offered him the post, and the news of his nomination, kept secret for some days, was to burst like a bombshell.

The opera opened on September 1. On September 30 the journalist Ludwig Karpath, accidentally passing the stage door, noticed a small, clean-shaven man with a shock of black hair who entered without being stopped by the doorkeeper. When Karpath[5] asked the doorkeeper who this man was, he was told that the man was the new director: that very morning orders had been issued that he was to be allowed to come and go freely. Karpath rushed to his newspaper offices so they might be the first to publish a piece of news that was not officially announced for three more days.

Everyone in the Hungarian capital was astounded by this appointment, not only because Mahler was a Jew, but because he was twenty-eight and virtually unknown. On October 2 the press announced he had received a ten-year contract and an annual salary of ten thousand kronen; this was a considerable amount in those days and still further increased the general astonishment. On the same day it was announced that Erkel had been relieved of his administrative duties but would stay on as a conductor.

The Budapest Opera, built four years earlier, was one of the most modern theaters of its time. Equipped with all hydraulic stage machinery, it could seat 1200 people and was famous for its acoustics. The huge subsidy it received each year came in part from the Hungarian state, in part from the Emperor in person. Luckily for Mahler, Beniczky had no musical knowledge and was thus content to administer the opera's finances, leaving Mahler in full control of all artistic matters. Numerous problems faced the new director, putting his organizing abilities to the test at once. He not only had to re-establish discipline, but also had to reconstitute the repertoire (almost entirely Italian up to then), and to win back the public's interest without offending the Hungarians' anti-Austrian chauvinism. This last was so strong that German guest singers had to learn their roles in Italian instead of singing them in German. Mahler also had to discover some new Hungarian singers, without whom every new endeavor was doomed to fail.

Mahler was not welcomed in Budapest, because of his youth, his high salary, and his foreign origin; also because of the total freedom he was given, and because of his artistic conscience, which was, as we have seen, wholly demanding.[6] Many Hungarians also censured him for promising, in his first public statements, to create a Hungarian national opera, which neither Erkel nor his sons had managed to do. Thus automatically Mahler found that the entire Hungarian nationalist press treated him as an intruder and had firmly decided against being impressed by any of his deeds and exploits, however worthy. Political nuances were naturally reflected in the attitudes taken by the various papers, and this systematic opposition had certain paradoxical and even comic results. Maurus Vavrinecz, critic of the *Fővárosi Lapok,* the most unremittingly nationalistic anti-Mahlerian of all the Budapest papers, was a church musician who had so poor a command of Hungarian that he had to write his articles in German and then have them translated. Two other Hungarian papers—the *Zenelap* and the *Egyetértés*—adopted and retained the same hostile attitude.[7] But some were disarmed by Mahler's success and soon supported him. Among these were the *Pesti Napló* and the *Pesti Hirlap,* whose music critics were a father and son, both named Kornél Ábrányi.[8] Others were Béla Toth, also of the *Hirlap,* and Joseph Keszler, of the *Nemzet.* Also, the critics of the German-language papers, August Beer of the *Pester Lloyd* and Viktor von Herzfeld of the *Neues Pester Journal,* who had no nationalistic reasons for opposing Mahler, nearly always supported him during these difficult years.

Under these circumstances, Mahler's ability to nullify most of the opposition by his firm and able policy is not one of the least remarkable facts about his reign. His first action as director was extremely diplomatic. He announced to the newspapers that during the coming months he would learn Hungarian; to convince everyone of the seriousness of his intention, he added that his engagement should not be considered definitive for six months, at the end of which time he would know the language perfectly.[9]

The *Pester Lloyd* informs us that on the evening of September 30 Mahler left Budapest for the purpose of rejecting the contract offered to him by the Munich Opera.[10] Returning on October 3, Mahler at once took up his official functions. A letter that he wrote to the impresario Löwy on October 5 proves that he had for some time been negotiating for the engagement of a chief stage manager and some Wagnerian singers. He was particularly looking for a tenor and a dramatic soprano for the two principal roles in *Die Walküre,* as well as for coaches who spoke Hungarian.

On October 10, Beniczky officially introduced Mahler to the orchestra and the opera's singers.[11] Mahler made a speech, in which, while flattering Hungarian national pride, he made his motto clear to everyone: "Discipline, work. Work, discipline." He closed with these words: "Do not expect from me for the moment either promises or new decisions. I shall not even draw up a program. First we must get to know each other and, together, take the measure of our task."

As the only possible solution in a country governed by blind patriotism, he decided to institute Hungarian as the sole language at the opera—thus ending the earlier practices of singing a performance in two or three different languages simultaneously. On October 16, he engaged a Hungarian coach, Ernst Lanyi, and later a "diction master" who could also serve as his interpreter. For, despite his formal promises, he never could make up his mind to learn Hungarian. The actor Eduard Újházy was to superintend the singers and their diction and also to act as assistant for productions staged by Mahler himself.

"Neither a diplomat nor a society man—but a man sure of his purpose, lucid, and gifted with a strong will"—that was how Mahler appeared to the critic Viktor von Herzfeld when he interviewed the new director.[12] Mahler had expressed surprise to a journalist from the *Pesti Hirlap,* that, in a country "as rich as any other in beautiful voices," nobody had as yet tried to create a national opera or paid any attention to the operatic texts and the languages in which the operas were given." What could be more absurd than an opera in which a question asked in Italian was answered in Hungarian? In his opinion it would be better to do without the text altogether. It was necessary, then, at any price, to create in Budapest a national pool of singers rather than to teach this difficult language to foreign singers. But the public must moderate its passion for "stars"; the era of numerous guest singers must end, and new singers must be discovered with the help of Edmund von Mihalovics, director of the Musical Academy. In future no guest singer should give more than three performances. Mahler ended by mentioning a Hungarian singer, Fräulein Rothauser,[13] who had been most successful in Leipzig while still almost unknown in her own country.

The first press reactions to Mahler's work program were caustic. They would have attacked him bitterly if he had tried to create a German opera; now they made fun of him because he, a German, wished to create the Hungarian opera that they had all desired for years. The paper *Fővárosi Lapok* took the lead with a particularly mocking article. At the end of October another paper, the *Politisches Volksblatt,* called Mahler "a specialist in operatic maladies"; this aroused violent reaction on the part of the *Zenelap,* which commented that "on the contrary, the Opera ought to play the role of physician to Mahler, and prescribe an immediate and indispensable change of air." According to them, the *Volksblatt* had invented an imaginary orchestral rebellion so as to be able, later, to attribute to it the failure of the Wagnerian premieres.

None of this worried Mahler, who was deep in his preparations for *Das Rheingold* and *Die Walküre,* sparing no efforts to make the performances perfect and their success triumphant. He commissioned a Hungarian translation of the librettos,[14] and threw himself body and soul into his work. The intendant publicly gave him carte blanche, declaring that he too would obey the order: "work." Mahler was in the theater from morning to night; he listened to all suggestions and he engaged on the spot all the artists who seemed of interest.

On October 1 he declared that he would not conduct himself until the first Wagnerian performances, which, announced for December, had been postponed to January. He entrusted all performances up to then to Erkel and imposed an accelerated rhythm of work on the personnel of the opera, who up to then had led a largely contemplative life. His colleagues passed gradually from surprise to anger, then to indignation, and finally to consternation. But whether they liked it or not, they had to bow to demands that on a musical plane were without precedent in Budapest. They were all obliged to surpass themselves.

Mahler at once tried to extend the Budapest public's taste, then exclusively Italian. In order to do this, he therefore selected an opera unknown to himself, but close to the Italian tradition: Bizet's *Les Pêcheurs de perles.* This attempt failed, unfortunately. Neither the lovers of Italian opera nor the "moderns" were satisfied. Not at all discouraged, five days later, Mahler staged a new production of Donizetti's *La Fille du régiment* for the "guest appearance" of a young German coloratura soprano, Bianca Bianchi, who also appeared in two other Donizetti operas, *Lucia di Lammermoor* and *L'Elisir d'amore.*[15] The three Italian operas were well received by the public despite the fact that the supporting cast was Hungarian. Mahler did not conduct, but he had superintended the musical performance, the stage direction, and the singers' acting very closely. Gradually, he transformed the theatrical and orchestral forces into a supple instrument capable of expressing the spirit and not just the letter of the works performed.

On November 14, all the contract singers attended an audition organized by Mahler to complete the *Ring* cast. That same day he engaged a new stage manager, Koloman Alszeghy.[16] In November and December two further new presentations were Conradin Kreutzer's *Das Nachtlager von Granada,* an outmoded but always popular opera, and Josef Bayer's ballet *Die Puppenfee,* both of which were well received. These were concessions made by Mahler to public taste.

Thanks to them, after three months' administration he was able to bring the chronic deficit to an end. In December, Erkel also conducted *Lohengrin* with three specially engaged singers before a packed theater. He conducted again on December 17 a gala performance of *László Hunyadi* by his father Ferenc Erkel, the only Hungarian dramatic composer. Despite his seventy-eight years the latter took over the baton for the first act and at the end of the evening was presented with several laurel wreaths, one of which was from Mahler.[17]

The newspapers of November 15 announced that Mahler was rehearsing each of the singers individually for the *Ring.* The three months that he devoted to the preparation of these two performances seem miraculously short when one remembers that before his arrival neither the Hungarian translations nor the singers had been available. He wanted to prove to everyone that a Hungarian opera was not a Utopian dream; he also wanted to impose Wagner on Budapest, where only *Der fliegende Holländer, Tannhäuser,* and *Lohengrin* had been heard—apart from *Die Meistersinger,* which had been a complete failure. He lived in a small temporary room, working day and night amid mountains of scores. He demanded eighty orchestral rehearsals for *Die Walküre,* which was played uncut.

At the end of December, Mahler wrote to Staegemann: "I have terrible tenor troubles [*Tenornot*] and the most absurd difficulties of all sorts and kinds,[18] but I do not give in." At the same time he made many trips to hear singers: on November 4 he went to Frankfurt to hear the tenor Julius de Grach, whom he engaged; in Prague, through Steinberg, he engaged an excellent Hungarian dramatic soprano, Celia Radics.[19] He wrote to all his friends and acquaintances, asking them to let him know about any singers capable of singing in Hungarian, and carried on a correspondence with several impresarios, including Lewy, Fischhof,[20] and Wild.[21]

At the end of 1888, Mahler was particularly proud of having found, despite all the limitations imposed on him, some almost unknown Hungarian singers whom he nevertheless considered to be of the stuff *"Ring"* heroes are made of. In particular he had discovered a young singer named Arabella Szilágyi, who, after failing badly in the first performance of *Der Trompeter von Säkkingen,* had decided to abandon her operatic career and sing only secondary roles. Hearing her by chance one day, he immediately exclaimed: "Here is my Brünnhilde!"

After having announced mysteriously that he had found an excellent Brünnhilde, Mahler rehearsed the young soprano in secret for weeks.[22] For the other Valkyries, Mahler spent days listening to young students from the conservatory singing classes. For the roles of Wotan and Alberich, he selected two Hungarians—Ney and Takáts—who had not achieved the success they deserved. Working on the staging, he studied numerous aesthetic and historic treatises, especially the literary works on which Wagner had drawn.

At the same time, Mahler had to look after the opera administration, have translations made for every line of the documents submitted for his signature, and have the Hungarian version of the *Ring* altered whenever it displeased him. As in Leipzig, he had the orchestra pit lowered[23] and had a bridge thrown over the pit so that he could be everywhere at once—on the stage, in the hall, on the podium. Thin, pale, nervous, biting his upper lip, chewing his nails until his fingers bled, he would lead singers and chorus into place by the hand. They made fun of him behind his back, imitated him, mocked him. But his firmness and enthusiasm overcame all opposition, even that of the most obstinate.

An anecdote told by Ludwig Karpath clearly depicts the musicians' attitude toward Mahler. During the rehearsals, Mahler had trouble with the orchestra, in particular the percussion and the bassoons, whom he drove to despair.[24] One day he interrupted them to say, "Gentlemen, I ask you to pay particular attention to this passage. I have had to warn the orchestra here each time I have conducted the *Ring,* as it is easily bungled." During a rest period, one of the musicians buttonholed Karpath: "Do you see, he makes himself important. He is learning the score of the *Ring* while he rehearses it, as he has never conducted it before."[25] Karpath assured him that this was not true but the critic was considered as naïve by the musician. Mahler encountered hidden or overt resistance of this sort each day; each day he overcame it and won respect from everyone by his idealism and the magnetism of his baton.

During these absorbing preparations for the *Ring,* Mahler had only bad news from Iglau. Bernhard Mahler's condition was worsening. His irascibility and outbursts of bad temper were a severe trial to those near him. Justi, at twenty, had to run the household alone and was unequal to such heavy responsibility. Struggling with seemingly insoluble problems, she became discouraged. Her letters to her brother expressed her worries and her inner distress. Mahler replied in touching letters, exhorting her never to lose hope, at least not in front of their parents. He himself was kept in Budapest by the responsibilities of his position and furthermore did not dare to make an unannounced trip to Iglau, thus revealing his fears. He urged Justi to call the family doctor Schwarz to her assistance whenever necessary and not to allow Alois, the distillery bookkeeper, to neglect the business. He promised that if the situation became really desperate he would come himself.

*Die drei Pintos* was sung in Vienna for the first time on January 19, 1889, a great event for Mahler, who had once hoped that all his family could be present. The great critic Eduard Hanslick wrote a long, mainly favorable criticism, but the opera was only moderately successful and was sung only three times.[26] Mahler had no time to think about this failure or half success, being entirely absorbed in his preparations for the Wagner operas. On January 23, at ten in the morning, the dress rehearsal of *Die Walküre* took place before a large invited audience. It lasted until three that afternoon. Beer wrote: "One should not call a performance of this quality a rehearsal. An especially cordial and well-deserved ovation greeted the director at the beginning of the third act. Only his zeal, energy and circumspect artistry made it possible to prepare in so short a time the performance of two such important and difficult works."

The next morning, after the dress rehearsal of *Das Rheingold,* the same critic, in a second article, praised the staging, the costumes, the presentation of the fantastic elements, the swimming of the Rhine maidens, and—above all—the "unsurpassable" orchestral playing, a feast for the ears with its "discreet accompaniment, its varied shadings, its dynamics excellently achieved in each instrumental group."

On the evening of January 26, the moment awaited and feverishly prepared for during the last three months arrived. Before a crowded house, Mahler mounted the podium to conduct the first performance in Hungarian of the *Ring* Prologue. The first low E flats emerged from the depths of the orchestra, and the majestic fresco arose gradually from the bottom of the river when a cloud of smoke, followed by small flames, suddenly burst from the proscenium. The prompter's box was on fire and flames cast a ruddy glow over everything. Mahler went on conducting, until fully equipped firemen appeared on the stage, thirty people left the theater, and the agitation of the public forced him to stop.[27]

At the end of half an hour, the fire had been brought under control by hoses, the damage repaired as well as possible, and the performance could begin again. Despite this incident, and despite the public's complete ignorance of Wagner's art and thought, the performance was followed with mounting interest. According to Beer, under Mahler's conducting the orchestra at least showed its real worth. "With local and mainly unknown and unappreciated talents, Mahler offered us a performance in which everything was in its place and everyone collaborated harmoniously," Herzfeld wrote the next day. When the curtain finally fell, the audience sat motionless, as though by order, then burst suddenly into frenzied applause that lasted for several minutes, doubling in intensity when Mahler appeared on stage among the singers, to take three bows with them.

The next evening, with *Die Walküre,* success became triumph. Beer wrote: "The artistic victory was complete all along the line. The whole audience remained seated after the first act, frantically calling for Mahler. Gradually, the shouts came in unison: *'Éljen Mahler!'* [Viva Mahler!], until the hero of the evening appeared on stage to receive a laurel wreath sent by his admirers. Seven times in succession he was obliged to take a bow with the singers." The uncut performance had lasted from six forty-five until eleven o'clock, but the audience were not tired and repeated their ovation at the fall of the last curtain. "Yesterday was once again tremendous!" Mahler wrote to his parents. "All Budapest, the aristocrats, Parliament, etc., gave me a triumph. . . . It was real national enthusiasm such as is only possible in Hungary. Soon I shall tell you about it in person, as I must go on a short business trip for the Opera and shall spend two or three days with you in Iglau." The same day Mahler received from Beniczky an open letter of thanks congratulating him for "having achieved such flawless performances in so short a time and for having demonstrated that it was possible to obtain such artistic perfection with local singers."

The newspapers were unanimously enthusiastic. Some days later, Beer wrote a long article in which he rejoiced that this complete success had followed the failure of the Hungarian performance of *Die Meistersinger*. He recalled that a complete or partial closing of the opera had been considered, and hailed the "new spirit" that had taken hold of the musicians and singers, who now believed in themselves and knew their real capabilities. He praised in Mahler both the "experienced, profound musician who lived only for his art," the admirable leader whose baton magnetized the musicians, the clever organizer who was able to perceive each performer's talent and give it its proper place, and finally the teacher of diction and acting who saw to it that each phrase, each melodic line, each accent, had its meaning so that words, music, and action all contributed to the dramatic effect. Thanks to Mahler, a lot of previously hidden talent had been suddenly liberated and improved.

From the orchestral point of view, according to Beer, no comparable performance had been heard in Budapest since the visit of the Vienna Philharmonic. For the first time, Mahler had "tamed" the brasses, which formerly had made listeners grind their teeth, and had drawn from the orchestra sometimes powerful tutti that even at their height were never painful to the ear—sometimes eloquent, delicate murmurs, and sometimes electrifying crescendos. The clarity and precision of the rhythms had been unsurpassable, as had been the discretion of the accompaniments, thanks to which the singers had had no difficulty in making themselves heard. Never had the *Walkürenritt* (Ride of the Valkyries) been conducted with such realism: one thought to hear the neighing of the horses and see their wild flight through the air. Never had the magic fire music so vibrated, crackled, and roared, or the orchestra sighed so tenderly in the love scene.

As to the singers, Beer considered they had surpassed themselves, having learned, thanks to Mahler, to think about the text and its dramatic significance, and not only about the sound of their voices. If they occasionally had some difficulty in handling the excellent Hungarian translation, that was because they were not used to singing the language. Beer also praised the scenery and lighting and accepted without difficulty something that later shocked many Viennese critics: Mahler's suppression in the final act of the projection of the Valkyries mounted on their sky horses, replacing this by a scurry of clouds.[28]

This unprecedented triumph gave Mahler the chance to discover some of the most attractive traits in the Hungarian character: enthusiasm, generosity, and gratitude. Immediately after this he left Budapest for the "business trip" which he mentioned in the letter to his parents. He almost certainly went as far as Iglau, summoned by many urgent duties, not the least of which was to see for the last time his strong-willed father, whom he had revered more than loved, but from whom he had nonetheless inherited several basic traits of character.

Before Christmas, Mahler had written Staegemann complaining that he had not yet made any friends in Budapest. But now the two Wagnerian triumphs opened all doors and brought him the admiration of the best musicians in the city, among them Edmund von Mihalovics, Hans Kössler, Viktor von Herzfeld, and Jenő Hubay.[29] Other important Budapest personalities joined this friendly circle, notably two influential journalists, Max Falk and—above all—Siegmund Singer.[30] From then on, Mahler was loved, admired, and upheld at least by a minority, and this first step to fame silenced his enemies. Overjoyed by this triumph, Mahler immediately announced for the next season the Budapest premieres of *Siegfried* and *Die Götterdämmerung,* but he was never able to carry out this project.

From February 4 to 6, the opera was closed in mourning for the death of Crown Prince Rudolf at Mayerling. Mahler conducted *Die Walküre* again on the evening of February 17. There was no performance the next day, when he received a telegram from Iglau announcing his father's death. The following morning he left to attend the funeral, remaining in Iglau for several days to help solve the many problems raised by this loss and by his mother's ill-health.[31] Otto was sent to live with Poldi in Vienna and started studying at the conservatory. Alois was about to leave Iglau for his military service in Brünn. All the responsibilities would now fall more heavily than ever on the frail shoulders of Justi.

Upon his return to Budapest late in February, some voices from both the public and the press prophesied that this fervent Wagnerian would transform the Hungarian national theater into a branch of Bayreuth, and that they would see nothing but Elsas, Sentas, Brünnhildes, and Isoldes, though when he arrived Mahler had promised to include in the opera's repertoire "all styles except the boring style." Faithful to this principle, he immediately put into rehearsal a Hungarian opera by Ferenc Erkel, *György Brankovics,*[32] which he entrusted to Sándor Erkel, and Maillart's *Les Dragons de Villars,* which he conducted himself on March 31 with great success. The day after this premiere Mahler left on another "business trip."[33] It is possible, even probable, that he was arranging for the sale of his father's various businesses and the dividing up of his estate. He had realized that Alois was incapable of following in their father's footsteps, and he preferred to dispose of the capital belonging to his sisters and himself. We know also that he had no feeling for the family business, though it had enabled his father to bring up him and his brothers and sisters in relative comfort.

Mahler returned to Budapest on April 7, this time to prepare an opera much more important in his eyes than *Les Dragons de Villars*—*Le Nozze di Figaro,* which was performed with considerable success on April 27 before a packed house. Mahler had changed the former cast almost entirely, but August Beer nonetheless regretted the inadequacy of the singers, while acknowledging that the performance was far superior to all those which had been heard in Budapest since the opening of the new opera house. The orchestra had played with nuance and discretion, but in his opinion the happy rhythms of this opera buffa had been weighed down by the staging and acting despite a general air of good will.[34]

Herzfeld, on the other hand, was full of enthusiasm. "From the overture on, the work showed an entirely new conception—or, rather, the real conception of Mozart, thanks to a carefully shaded, vibrant performance, thanks also to the natural and measured changes of tempo. The violins have never sung so warmly and intimately, the woodwinds have never been so discreetly shaded nor have they fulfilled their essential role so well. It was really Mozart's spirit that lighted up the whole work, his blood flowing through the veins of the performance . . ."

During this first season, Mahler devoted himself above all to the reorganization of the opera, to revivals, and to musical preparations for first performances. He therefore conducted few repertoire works, and this earned him one of Beer's rare reproaches; according to him, Sándor Erkel's task had been too heavy. Mahler conducted during this season: *Die Walküre* (9), *Das Rheingold* (7), *Le Nozze di Figaro, Les Dragons de Villars, Il Barbiere di Siviglia,*[35] to mark the visit of the famous coloratura soprano Bianca Bianchi, and doubtless also *Der fliegende Holländer, Lohengrin,* and *Der Freischütz.*

At Easter, Fritz Löhr spent some time with Mahler at the Tiger Hotel.[36] He later described Mahler's daily life in Budapest, the walks they took along the Danube as far as Margarethe Island, and the afternoons when Mahler would play him sketches of his *Second Symphony* on the piano. Löhr also enumerated Mahler's friends: Mihalovics, Kössler, the singer Bianca Bianchi, the actor Újházy, Dr. Ebner and his family. On Holy Saturday, following Magyar custom, Mahler gave a lively, joyful dinner for some of his Hungarian friends.

Löhr also mentions the first "difficulties" that broke out at the opera and that Mahler rapidly resolved, for he never allowed capricious singers to interfere with his accomplishment of administrative tasks. The tenor Perotti was discharged because he refused to sing more than eight times a month;

Prevost, another tenor, met the same fate in April after a "conflict with the management,"[37] and Julius de Grach was engaged to replace him.

Beer, summing up at the end of the season, declared that for the first time in years, he could draw up a favorable balance for the opera season, which had finally rediscovered its moral credit and artistic level. The press and the public had unanimously agreed that Mahler possessed all the qualifications needed for a position of such responsibility. Certainly, he had been unable to solve one of the chief problems, that of the repertoire. He especially needed to cultivate French opera at the expense of old and "faded" Italian operas. But he had taught the orchestra not to cover the voices, and this allowed the singers to sing instead of shout. The relationship between conductor and singer, between singer and audience, had been entirely transformed. Nevertheless, the singers still needed to learn a good deal from the dramatic point of view, especially as regards their gestures, still too influenced by old-fashioned operatic convention. Beer had already understood that Mahler's ideal, like Wagner and all the great dramatic composers from Monteverdi on, was a complete unity of action and music. Toward that end, he was attempting to create an "ensemble" of singers both versatile and coherent. Like Beer, Herzfeld believed that Mahler had proved with brilliance that he was "the right man in the right place." Certainly the Hungarian press had already begun to speak of his "impatience" and "cruelty," accusations that were often to be repeated later. But these criticisms weighed little with Mahler in view of the gravity and vastness of his task. The final success of these reforms was to be compromised by the Hungarian national opera's insoluble problems, but this first year in Budapest was, even in the eyes of Mahler's enemies, a great success.

On May 10 and 11 sittings of the Hungarian Parliament were devoted to study of the opera's budget, for, in addition to the usual subsidy of 21,000 florins, the minister of the interior was asking for an additional 30,000 florins to pay the opera's outstanding debts. Some deputies criticized the intendant for not having kept his expenditures within the limits imposed by the annual subsidy. One of them, a Catholic priest named Komlóssy, launched into a long anti-Semitic diatribe. According to him, the opera employed no one but Jews and interested nobody but the Jewish bourgeoisie of Budapest; for this reason it had been dropped by the Hungarian aristocracy. This intervention was censured both by the Minister Baross and by the president of the chamber. But nonetheless it represented the virulent anti-Semitism of a large part of Hungarian society which was to become one of the principal sources of Mahler's difficulties.[38] This time, however, the debate ended favorably for Mahler, before whom "the entire [Hungarian] artistic world bows."

On May 20, a few days after the close of the regular season, Mahler conducted at the opera a performance of Schubert's *Der häusliche Krieg* given by a group of young singers who just had received first prizes at the conservatory. The purpose of the evening was doubtless to allow him to judge their merits and to select from among them those whom he would engage for the next season. Mihalovics later wrote him a letter thanking him for all he had done for the musical life of Hungary. During this first year Mahler had acquitted himself perfectly of his administrative duties, triumphing where many others would have failed. If the two other seasons under his direction ended less brilliantly, this was mainly because of forces outside his control—and also because the problems of running a theater are sufficiently difficult in themselves without having the prejudices, susceptibilities, and chauvinism of a whole nation added to them.

# CHAPTER 14

*Mahler Director of the Royal Budapest Opera (II) —*
*Physical Suffering and Family Tragedies — The Death*
*of Marie Mahler and Poldi — First Crisis at the Opera*
*— Journey to Italy (1889–90)*

The summer of 1889 was one of the unhappiest in Mahler's life. Material and moral problems added to his physical suffering and spoiled the few days' rest that he had hoped for after an exhausting operatic season. He left Budapest for Iglau on May 21. Now the head of the family was dead, the others were waiting for him impatiently, for their mother's health was worsening daily and many practical decisions had to be made. At the end of May he went to Vienna,[1] and on June 2 he was in Prague to hear the famous coloratura soprano Sigrid Arnoldson,[2] "the Swedish nightingale," in *Mignon,* after which he engaged her for Budapest the following season.

Mahler's activities from then on can be reconstructed by means of a note he sent to Fritz Löhr[3] and an exchange of letters between Henry Pierson, a Berlin Opera official, and the conductor Sándor Erkel.[4] After passing through Vienna again, Mahler spent some "agreeable moments" in Munich, no doubt with Heinrich Krzyzanowski, before undergoing an operation made necessary because of his worsening "subterranean troubles." The operation was particularly painful and afterward Mahler was "exhausted." In a letter written by Max Falk to Erkel in July, he says that "he cannot count on recovery for another two weeks."

Yet the next day Mahler was already in Salzburg,[5] went from there to Bayreuth for five days,[6] and then to Marienbad, where he took the waters and stayed with the intendant Beniczky. Yet a short time before, he had written to Erkel from the clinic: "I have just received your letter on my sick-bed. The gravity of the situation forces me to conquer all the resistance

springing from my weakness, in order to answer you, but I must express myself briefly. . . ."[7]

The grave situation was the projected departure of Sándor Erkel, who
had received, through Pierson acting for Count Hochberg, intendant of the
Berlin Opera, the offer of a post as conductor. Pierson had advised Erkel to
do all he could to free himself from his Budapest contract—to address
himself to the Emperor Franz Josef in person if necessary. Erkel had tried
to get Mihalovics and Max Falk to intervene in his favor, but his efforts
had proved unsuccessful. Everyone knew that the authorities would not deprive Mahler of his principal assistant at a moment when he himself was in
poor health.

Though we do not have Erkel's letter to Mahler, it is easy to guess the reasons for his request. Having been the director of the opera or at least the replacement for so long, he found it difficult to return to a subordinate position.
Mahler well understood Erkel's feelings, for he had experienced them himself in Leipzig. He told him that his hopes for a better financial position were
almost certainly unfounded, as his salary in Budapest was already 4,500
florins per year, with four months' vacation. Erkel was also necessary, even
indispensable, to both the opera and its director, and for Mahler to consent
to his leaving would be an unprofessional act. Mahler understood, however,
that Erkel's position had become difficult, even painful, and he declared
himself ready to make any concessions in order to "better" it. He would arrange for Erkel to be completely independent so that he should not feel himself relegated to the level of a second conductor. Mahler added that he himself would conduct much less often and would engage an assistant to help
him. "You will see—everything will arrange itself in time. Just as the most
terrible waves spend themselves, so the grass finally will grow over these
recent events, and soon you will find yourself as satisfied and peaceful as
your character allows you to be. We'll talk about all this in more detail after
my return to Budapest." Mahler ended by asking Erkel to withdraw his resignation.[8]

After leaving Marienbad, Mahler spent the beginning of August with his
mother in Iglau, as her health showed no improvement. With a heavy heart
he had to leave her and return to Budapest. Back in Vienna on August 18,[9]
he discovered another cause for worry. His sister Leopoldine had been suffering for some time from a mysterious neuralgia, news of which eventually
reached Iglau, and this added one more care to those already weighing on
Marie Mahler. In a letter written from Vienna to his mother late in August,
Mahler told her not to worry about Poldi: there was no danger, since the
doctor was convinced she was suffering from a purely nervous complaint. He
promised that if Poldi's condition did not improve rapidly he would return
to Vienna at the end of September and take her to a specialist. So as to free
Poldi from all responsibilities, he installed Otto for the winter in a room
rented in the Löhrs' house.[10]

It was no doubt at this time that he sent to Justi, from the Budapest Opera

House, Strauss's autograph, with a note "one of the most impressive new composers, who seems marked out for a great future." The note also asks: "Who is your doctor and what does he say?" No doubt this is in connection with Poldi.

Returning to Budapest, Mahler instituted a custom he was to follow throughout his years in Vienna, and during the early rehearsals lived on the outskirts of town, by the Schwabenberg. Before the opening of the season, he and the intendant welcomed Nasred-Din, the Shah of Persia, to the opera with a special ballet performance on August 27, which Mahler conducted. But his essential task during the first weeks was to prepare a new production of *Lohengrin*—to be given uncut for the first time in Budapest—which was to start the new season on September 15. On the eve of the opening, the intendant Beniczky was welcomed publicly to the opera by all the artists gathered on the stage, which was already set with the new scenery for Act II of *Lohengrin*. The entire artistic and technical personnel of the theater stood in a semicircle to welcome him; the brasses saluted him with a fanfare, and to everyone's surprise, Mahler made a short speech of welcome in Hungarian, without hesitation and "almost without accent."[11] This made a great impression, and Beniczky replied by acknowledging the titanic efforts that had been made, thanks to Mahler, in seventeen months. He added that the coming season would have to operate under the sign of austerity: the subsidy had been reduced by thirty-five thousand florins, and the number of guest stars would have to be even further curtailed.

Mahler had been worried and depressed when he conducted the rehearsals of *Lohengrin*. The news from Iglau was worse every day, and he expected at any moment a telegram informing him that his mother's condition was hopeless. At the same time, Poldi's health was not improving, and he himself was still suffering from the aftereffects of his operation and having to take morphine.

Despite Mahler's physical and mental torments, the September 15 performance of *Lohengrin* opened the season triumphantly. The theater was full, the enthusiasm great. Already, at the end of Act I, Mahler was shouted for but did not take a bow. Next day Beer did not share the unreserved enthusiasm expressed by Viktor von Herzfeld. According to Beer, the principal singers were not equal to their tasks and the uncut performance, lasting from six-thirty to eleven o'clock, had wearied the audience. Certainly the production had been perfectly rehearsed, but Mahler's detailed conducting had demanded excessive discretion from the orchestra, the choruses had lacked vigor and volume, and Bianca Bianchi, a light soprano of the Italian type, had too weak a voice for the role of Elsa.[12]

The same day, Beer criticized the repertoire announced by Mahler for the season: *Siegfried, Die Götterdämmerung, Die lustigen Weiber von Windsor,* and *Hans Heiling*—four German operas in succession were too much for a city in which the public's taste always had been cosmopolitan. So, on October 3, Mahler altered his program: he dropped the two last sections of the *Ring* and replaced them by French operas, Auber's *La Part du Diable,* *Mignon, Carmen,* operettas by Offenbach, and ballets. He even consented to make cuts in *Die Walküre.* On September 16, Beer also mentioned certain gaps in the ensemble of singers: the troupe lacked, for example, a good soprano, a dramatic and lyric tenor, and a baritone, without whom it was impossible to present much of the repertoire properly.

During a performance of *La Juive* on September 21, Mahler received a telegram announcing that his mother's condition was worsening.[13] He left Budapest for Iglau next morning and found his mother dying, while Justine, exhausted by long months at the bedsides of two invalids, seemed unlikely to survive her. However, when Marie Mahler's condition stabilized somewhat, her eldest son had to return to Budapest, taking Justine to Vienna on the way in order to have her examined by a doctor.[14] Poldi's neuralgia was much worse: she was suffering real martyrdom, but his duties in Budapest forced Gustav to leave her, too. He had scarcely reached Budapest when he learned that Poldi had died on September 27, barely three months after the first symptoms of her illness appeared.[15] No known letter from Mahler alludes to her death, but we know enough of his family feeling to guess at his state of mind, in the face of so much sorrow and unable to fulfill his normal role as head of the family.

While Mahler was facing tragedy in his family life, his professional life at the Budapest Opera was presenting him with new problems. Sándor Erkel continued to move heaven and earth to obtain his freedom. Pierson had asked the German ambassador in Vienna to intercede with the Emperor Franz Josef and had offered Erkel a two-year contract to start in April 1892. The negotiations were carried on in secret, but Mahler nevertheless heard about them. After the opening night, when Mahler conducted *Lohengrin,* Pierson hoped that its great success (*Lohengrin* had been previously conducted by Erkel), "Mahler's behavior and the tone of the newspaper criticisms would rob Erkel of any desire to keep his Budapest post."

On November 17 several Berlin and Vienna newspapers mentioned the offer made to Erkel. The *Hirlap* carried the news, adding that Erkel had asked to be released. Another letter from Pierson, written three months later, informs us of the failure of these plans "despite the wish expressed" by the Emperor Franz Josef. On May 6, 1890, Mahler himself wrote again to Erkel confirming that it was impossible to let him go, since Erkel's collaboration was vital to him: he was even ready to extend his contract by several years.

On October 9, just as Mahler was going on to conduct *Lohengrin,* he received a telegram saying that his mother's condition was very grave. If we are to believe what he later told Natalie, "his conscience would not let him abandon the performance, which he was to conduct; he concealed his sorrow deep within his heart, letting no one guess the blow that he had just received. Marie Mahler died on October 11, and it seems unlikely that her son was

with her: forced to remain in Budapest, no doubt because of opera commitments, he does not even seem to have attended her funeral.[16]

Mahler was obliged to appeal to Löhr to act on his behalf. After hesitating
for some time, he decided to leave young Emma with Otto in Vienna and
to take an apartment for himself in Budapest with Justi to keep house. Löhr
replaced Mahler as best he could. A few days after the funeral he took the
two sisters to Vienna and put the elder on a train for Budapest, where she
was to join her brother.[17] Ironically, in the midst of these family tragedies, Mahler was rehearsing one of his favorite works, which is also one of
the happiest in the German lyric repertoire—Nicolai's *Die lustigen Weiber
von Windsor*. After the first performances, the Hungarian newspapers spoke
mostly of the opera itself, less well known in Hungary than in Germany. They
say nothing about Mahler's interpretation of it except that it was "carefully
prepared."[18]

On October 1 the papers announced that Mahler would conduct the
Budapest Philharmonic in the first performance of one of his own still un-
titled "Symphonic Poems."[19] According to the *Pester Lloyd,* the rehearsals
had already begun. On October 13, Budapest heard three of Mahler's
lieder during an evening of chamber music given by the Krancsevics Quartet
and sung by Bianca Bianchi. Mahler himself played the piano accompaniment to his two *Leander Lieder* and one from the *Wunderhorn: "Scheiden
und Meiden,"* composed the preceding year. This last lied was enthusiastically received, and Beer judged that there was true originality in the three
songs. However, he felt that Mahler's musical style was not suited to the two
poems by Leander, for the *Volkstümlichkeit* (folkloric simplicity) worried
him in these "artistic" poems. Only *"Scheiden und Meiden"* received his
complete approval despite its "overartificial" conclusion.[20] The two
Ábrányis (in the *Hirlap* and the *Napló*) preferred the two *Leander Lieder,*
feeling that in *"Scheiden und Meiden"* Mahler had deviated too far from
the "popular" spirit of the text. Only Herzfeld was "entirely won over" by
the folkloric style of the *Wunderhorn* lied, considering that the alternation of
major and minor rendered the spirit of the text admirably.

For Mahler, the biggest event of November was the first performance of
his "Symphonic Poem," which was also the first public hearing of one of his
orchestral works. It formed the chief attraction of the Philharmonic Society's
second subscription concert. Löhr and Otto arrived from Vienna on the
morning of November 19, in time for the final rehearsal at eleven o'clock.
Afterward Mahler sent the following letter to the Philharmonic Society: "Still
full of the impression left with me by the dress rehearsal of today, I feel
bound to thank you and all the performers for the devotion and the really
artistic spirit with which you have helped me to bring my modest work to life.
The dress rehearsal of today has already convinced me that I shall never
again hear my work performed with such perfection. I am proud to lead your
great association, which is so zealously and disinterestedly devoted to the cult

of art, and I beg you to remain as kind to me in the future, as I am grateful and obliged to you now."[21]

On November 19 the *Pester Lloyd* published a long article by the Ábrányi son, who wrote at length on the difference between program music, pure music, and dramatic music. In his opinion, Mahler belongs to that class of creators whose entire personality is expressed in each of their works and whose originality appears everywhere. The impressions and passions they express create an atmosphere and a spiritual world that is completely personal, that "includes everything, from naïve illusion to doubt and skepticism." Though this does not result in "an absolute purification and liberation like that of Mozart," it also does not, like Schumann, succumb in the struggle with the large problems of humanity. He attains instead an "objective conception of the world which protects him against all of life's assaults." The "Symphonic Poem" might be called *Life,* illustrating as it does the life of one "who sees, who feels, who experiences, that life which throws earth's marvels into the paths of youth" and which, with "the first breath of autumn, takes back pitilessly everything that has been given earlier."

In the first part, the rosy clouds of youth and the feeling of spring; in the second, happy daydreams,[22] in the third a joyful wedding procession. But these fade away and, in the fourth, tragedy appears without warning. The funeral march represents the burial of all of the poet's illusions, inspired by the well-known "Hunter's Funeral." This bold, powerfully conceived movement is made up of two contrasting moods. The final section brings to man redemption and resignation, harmony of life, work and faith. Beaten to the ground, he rises again and wins the final victory. This philosophic resignation imposes its eternal verities and its conciliating harmony upon the end of the work. Clearly all these ideas were suggested to Ábrányi by Mahler himself.

On Wednesday, November 20, at seven-thirty, a large audience assembled in the spacious Vigadó (Redoutensaal) of the City Hall, drawn by the curiosity aroused in the capital by the young director of the opera. Mahler had divided his "Symphonic Poem" into the two following parts:

First part: 1. Introduction and Allegro commodo
2. Andante
3. Scherzo
Second part: Alla marcia funebre and Attacca: molto appassionato

The rest of the concert was conducted by Sándor Erkel.[23] The reaction of the audience was restrained, for a conservative public, devoted above all to Italian opera and unfamiliar with the German symphonic repertoire, was ill-prepared for such a work. Still, the first section, made up of the first three movements, was fairly well received. But after the Funeral March and the Finale, the disconcerted public gave only lukewarm applause, and there was even some booing.

There are many anecdotes about the famous "surprise" in the first movement of Tchaikovsky's *Symphonie pathétique*. The beginning of the Finale to Mahler's *First Symphony* is no less startling. An elegantly dressed lady sitting near Löhr during the first performance had dozed off during the pianissimo conclusion to the Funeral March. The violent, savage explosion of the Finale so surprised her that she leaped up from her seat, scattering on the floor everything that had been lying in her lap.[24]

In general the critics were not impressed by Mahler's composition. In a long, intelligent article Beer was almost the only one who recognized the merits of the work at once. He found, as in the lieder, a lively imagination and complete mastery of musical form. He also understood that the "Symphonic Poem" was a "youthful work," full of promise, the result of a talent in full evolution, in which everything expressed *Sturm und Drang,* a violent struggle to express art's highest values. Mahler's orchestral virtuosity, his sense of each instrument's color and expressiveness, showed not only profound knowledge of the scores of .Berlioz and Wagner, but also a personal, innate sense of orchestral coloring. Mahler managed great instrumental masses as ably as isolated instruments and mixtures of timbre, but *"this technical superiority easily leads him to choose rough sonorities, to exaggerate expression and sound effects."*[25]

Beer's most important critical errors were to mistake the "roughnesses" of Mahler's orchestral scoring for sins of youth and to believe, as did most of his colleagues, that Mahler's technical mastery was an obstacle rather than a means. He was disturbed by the combined presence in Mahler's music of both naïve, popular inspiration and supremely refined instrumental and musical techniques. Beer deplored "the absence of a fundamental poetic idea" that might have given the "Symphonic Poem" the unity it lacked. He even supposed that the program had been conceived after the composition, as he could discern no connection between the springlike atmosphere of the first three movements and that of the last two—the parody of the Funeral March and the drama of the Finale. However, he detailed the many striking beauties of the work despite much that was bizarre and despite the orgies of sound in the Finale.

Notwithstanding his admittedly shocked reaction to the "revolutionary" aspects of the works, Beer gave proof of greater intelligence and objectivity than the vast majority of his present and future colleagues. He could not fail to be amazed by some aspects of Mahler's aesthetic approach, particularly in the Funeral March, but his criticism reveals a remarkable insight into the real qualities and faults of the composition: it cannot be denied that the monumental pathos of the Finale is less controlled, less happily integrated into the symphonic form, than is that of the contemporary *Totenfeier.*

Viktor von Herzfeld, who was the critic of the *Neues Pester Journal* and also one of Mahler's closest friends, was unequivocal in his condemnation of the work:

". . . If Mahler's dazzling exploits as conductor had not revealed to us a refined musician endowed with exquisite taste and versed in all the most varied styles, listening to his symphony would not have told us so. Given the title "Symphonic Poem" and our talented conductor's confirmed penchant for the most advanced neoromanticism, we certainly should have expected extravagances of all sorts. But we had the right to hope that we should hear, at least in that direction, something interesting and significant. Instead, we have encountered music that, aside from some bizarrerie in the domains of melody, harmony and orchestration, never, even during its best moments, rises above the most mediocre level.

"The first movement begins with a long pedal in A held by all the strings, from the contrabasses to the violins, during which the winds here and there insert insignificant little motives. After this has been repeated to the point of satiety, one finally hears the main theme, not distinguished for either originality or refinement. The composer here, as in the succeeding movements, clearly has tried to imitate folklore (to be *volkstümlich*); most of the time this attempt has led him to be trivial. The development of the first movement is poverty-stricken, the harmony of a shocking simplicity approaching dearth.

"The two succeeding movements, andante and scherzo, are agreeable and pleasant, but they are anything but 'symphonic'. In the andante, for example, a few short polyphonic entries serve only to demonstrate the composer's complete lack of assurance in this realm. The fourth movement, *a la 'pompes funebres'* [sic], which elaborates a pitiful theme in canon in a very inadequate manner only to alternate it with one that is offensively trivial, is a complete disaster. The music is not humorous, only ridiculous. Most interesting of all, surely, is the last movement. After a deafening hubbub of painful dissonances, the woodwinds screech in an over-shrill register, and we finally hear an energetic and well-articulated theme, in which one even discovers a trace of genius. The whole movement is of monstruous tastelessness, but nevertheless something does emerge from it— a frightening storm, not only of wind and rain, but also of lightning and thunder. In a word, of all the movements, it is the only one that has a physiognomy, though not a very agreeable one. We have only one additional word to say, on the instrumentation. It goes without saying that a modern conductor like Mahler has a very complete—even a too complete—knowledge of all orchestral effects. There is scarcely a single phrase not decorated with brasses, triangles, cymbals, and the big drum, but with it there are subtle mixtures of timbres such as only a refined ear could invent.

"If we were to sum up all these notations in one general impression, we should have to state that not only Mahler the conductor belongs in the first rank of his profession, but he resembles the others in that he is nothing of a symphonist. All of our great conductors—Richter, Bülow, Mottl, Levi, Wüllner, etc.—either have themselves eventually recognized, or have proved, that they were not composers. Nor have their reputations suffered. This is

true of Mahler also. . . . When Erkel returned to the podium at the end of
the concert, the applause almost took on the character of a demonstration:
the public thus manifested its gratitude toward a conductor who does not
compose."

Most of the other Hungarian critics condemned Mahler's work without
reprieve. The *Pesti Napló* accused him of displaying an "unbridled and
unbounded personality" and a "gift of genius" that had not yet achieved
maturity. The "exaggerated and nervous" Finale seemed even more characteristic of Mahler's style than the other movements. The *Nemzet* dubbed
the work "Symphony on Organ Points" because of its length. The *Egyetértés*
noted that only Mahler's friends had applauded the "incomprehensible and
disagreeable cacophony," that "succession of formless, impersonal, atmospheric tableaux." The excess of publicity used to attract the attention of the
public had done this "boring hodgepodge," this "interminable series of organ
points and unbearable dissonances," a disservice. In the *Hirlap,* the younger
Ábrányi wrote that unhappily Mahler had buried the public's illusions
with his own, and that the detestable Finale should be suppressed and re-
written. In the *Fővárosi Lapok,* Vavrinecz spoke of Mahler's many *"Lieder,"*
which were "well known in Germany." He called Mahler's motives "not
very symphonic" and regretted that the early movements were weak and
that there was no logical development. Nonetheless, he recognized the rhythmic and harmonic qualities of the work, its polyphony, and, above all, its
masterly orchestration.

Finally the *Zenelap* reproached Mahler for not having helped the public
toward an understanding of his work by providing a commentary.[26] Most
of the audience had been initially interested in the symphony but had been
left completely in the dark. This critic also considered it "his duty" to distinguish between "the interesting" and "the beautiful." "Despite beauties of
detail" the incomplete motives seemed only "interesting," as did the pedal at
the beginning—the longest in all musical literature—and the instrumentation, which expresses every possible "atmosphere," and the vulgar anti-
musicality of the Funeral March, which the public had not understood at
all. The work, as a whole, took the listener from disappointment to disappointment. Despite the interesting and numerous melodic combinations and
modulations, Mahler was no "master of his art," but an able apprentice who
had not yet learned to dominate his overabundant inspiration and who
would have done better to study the old symphonic forms before breaking away from them.

To explain the total lack of comprehension that the *First Symphony* met
from the Hungarian public, Alexander Jemnitz[27] mentions that public's narrow limits of taste and knowledge. As far as instrumental and orchestral
music was concerned, Budapest knew the classic masters and the neoclassicism of Brahms, but was ignorant of most of the music that served as transition between the early romantics, that is to say Berlioz, the symphonic
poems of Liszt, the later works of Wagner, and Mahler. The following year,

the same public gave just as chilly a reception to the most inoffensive of Richard Strauss's tone poems, *Aus Italien*. Full of good intentions but led astray by what he had learned about the completing of *Die drei Pintos,* a Budapest critic named Josef Ságh carried absurdity to such lengths that he considered the direct influence of Weber could be discerned in the *First Symphony!*

The consensus of these critics justified Mahler's unhappy memories of the performance: "At Pest, where I conducted [it] for the first time, my friends avoided me in terror. Not a single one of them dared to speak to me about the work or its performance, and I wandered about like someone sick or outlawed."[28] Painful as such an admission must have been for Mahler, he was nonetheless forced to admit that he had not made contact with his public as he had dreamed of doing while composing his work. Certainly, Budapest was not the ideal place for such an experiment, but he was soon to discover that Germany was scarcely better.

The evening before the first performance of the *First Symphony,* Mahler conducted *La Juive*[29] at the opera. After his memorable and disappointing premiere, Mahler heeded the injunctions of the press and revived two French operas, *Carmen,* with Hermine Braga, a Hungarian singer from the Vienna Opera, and, at the end of November, Meyerbeer's *Les Huguenots*. His decision to cut the last act of this work led to violent criticism in the newspapers; Beer led the attack in the *Lloyd:* for him, the original denouement was indispensable and the opera as Mahler presented it was truncated, ending on a giant question mark. Mahler had only justified this cut by a brief communiqué to the press, which mentioned "artistic considerations." "An opera," Beer wrote, "is not an arbitrary succession of arias and ensembles; rather it is a drama set to music, subject to the same artistic laws as a spoken drama. . . . Even if part of the audience leaves the hall, as is often the case after the duet, even if only a dozen spectators remain, they are entitled to the authentic conclusion of the work. Why not perform *Carmen* without the act outside the bull ring, or *Die Walküre* without the magic fire?"

Visibly annoyed by this article, Mahler set out his point of view in an open letter to the *Pester Lloyd* next day. In *Les Huguenots,* he wrote, lack of unity is a major fault. Elsewhere in Europe it was cut down to half its original length. Thus, in the final act, usually only "the fusillade" was kept —the scene in which Raoul and Valentine die on stage.

"I shall not dwell on the fact," Mahler wrote, "that in the theatrical works we love and admire most, the actual ending of the drama—fusillade, hanging, drowning, etc.—generally takes place offstage, and that the spectators are invited to contribute to the drama by their imagination, each in his own way. Nor shall I deny that those among the spectators who have steady nerves and are not alarmed by a good fusillade prefer to see the drama culminate *ad oculos*. But, after an act containing great beauties and action of captivating realism, I believe that to raise the curtain again solely to present a frightening massacre lasting scarcely one minute—and that amid a terrifying uproar—is to commit an action offensive to all 'artistic sensibility.' "

Mahler felt that the sense of the drama had been respected despite the cut, as the audience already knows that no Huguenot will survive the night. On November 30, Beer replied, admitting that the libretto of *Les Huguenots* was not an ideal one, but saying that suppressing the denouement weakened it still further.

Apart from *Carmen* and *Les Huguenots,* the principal November events at the opera were performances of *Die Walküre, Das Rheingold,* and *Die lustigen Weiber von Windsor,* all conducted by Mahler, as well as a dozen other operas conducted by Erkel (the Budapest Opera gave an average of twenty performances per month). The new productions given at the end of the year—Auber's *La Part du Diable* (December 7) and Josef Bayer's ballet *Sonne und Erde*—were clearly Mahler's concessions to public taste. In December, Mahler conducted *Lohengrin, Die lustigen Weiber von Windsor,* and a concert of operatic arias given as a benefit for the Retirement Fund for Hungarian Journalists. During this performance Mahler's excessive movement on the podium led to his breaking a footlight.

On December 16, Mahler and Justi left Budapest for Vienna. Having installed his sister at the Löhrs', he went on to Iglau to complete the sale of his father's business. Some biographers have asserted that he asked his two brothers to join him in renouncing their shares of the inheritance in favor of their sisters, but there is no proof of this. Upon his return to Vienna, Mahler and his brothers and sisters spent their first Christmas since their parents' deaths with the Löhrs. Mahler then returned to Budapest for the last few days of the year. On January 3, 1890, he conducted another benefit concert at the opera. The program included the *"Leonore" Overture No. 3,* one of his virtuoso performances, which he interpreted, the *Pester Lloyd* said, with "great verve and remarkable rhythmic and dynamic subtleties."

There were no important new productions in January, except for Adam's *La Poupée de Nuremberg* and, on the nineteenth, *Mignon,* which marked the debut of both Sigrid Arnoldson, the "Swedish nightingale," and the mezzo-soprano Laura Hilgermann.[30] Brahms came to Budapest to attend an evening devoted to his chamber works, but Mahler seems not to have met him on this occasion, though they already had many mutual friends, including Kössler and Herzfeld. Mahler again conducted *Das Rheingold* and *Die Walküre* and another benefit concert, during which he was warmly applauded after each movement of Beethoven's *Fifth Symphony,* which he conducted from memory in an "energetic and poetic way." This was the first time Mahler conducted this work and Herzfeld has some interesting things to say about his interpretation. "Mahler approaches the performance of this symphony with a freedom that proves his familiarity with the composer's intentions. However indifferent to the usual routine, any return to the pure, the real, Beethoven must naturally struggle against prejudices deeply rooted in the orchestra and the public. . . ." Mahler had in fact already perfected his "version" of the symphony. He strengthened the wind section because "modern custom demands that today's orchestral strings be twice as numerous as they were in Beethoven's time." In the Finale, too, Mahler used "instruments of more penetrating sonority" such as the E flat clarinet, and in the opening movement he doubled the solo oboe, a doubling that Herzfeld criticized because the passage should have "the character of a solo and contrast strongly with the fortissimo *tutti* preceding it." However Herzfeld praised the slow tempo of the Scherzo,[31] which brought out many details, and, above all, "the clarity of the phrasing and the beauty of the sound both in its power and in its sweetness."

Other benefit concerts took place in March and April. Mahler at the piano accompanied the mezzo-soprano Laura Hilgermann in a selection of lieder by Schubert, Schumann, and Brahms. He conducted the orchestra on another occasion, when the evening was made up of arias from various operas. Between these two events he returned to Iglau,[32] having undertaken another trip on opera business.

Mahler devoted much of February to rehearsals of Marschner's *Der Templer und die Jüdin*, an opera that had never been given in Budapest, though it was popular in Germany. After its first performance, on March 8, Beer as well as the critics in the Hungarian papers, criticized the choice of the work, finding its music "flat, heavy, faded, and typically German." According to him, not one of the Budapest singers was really in command of his role, the vocal writing "in the old style" being particularly formidable. Although the auditorium was full, the atmosphere remained chilly, and even the best sections of the opera did not arouse the public from its apathy.[33]

Spring of 1890, in fact, marked the turning point in Mahler's Hungarian career. At Christmas 1889 he had still been able to write to Staegemann: "I am sending you some produce of this country, which will probably become my new homeland!"[34] Three months later he wrote differently to Löhr: "I am so restless and busy, I must swallow so much exasperation, that I cannot keep up the smallest correspondence."[35] What had happened in the interval? First, Mahler had begun to weary of never hearing German sung, of never having a moment to compose, and of spending too much time on so many unimportant details unrelated to art.[36] Also, he was suffering from the economies that had been imposed upon him that year, from the reduction in the number of premieres, the concessions demanded by the public's taste, and finally the mediocrity of the singers with whom he had to be content after having conducted performances of true international quality in Leipzig.

Despite his good intentions, Mahler found himself unable to adopt the local and national Hungarian point of view, and this was what finally led to his break with Hungary. He was unable to understand and assimilate the mentality of the country, with its limits, its prejudices, the pettiness and susceptibilities of a small nation. Irritated by the lack of ability of the local singers, he too often gave vent to exasperation during rehearsals. Numerous offended singers declared themselves ill at the last minute and found journalists ready to publish their grievances. Often they resigned, thus breaking up that very "ensemble" which Mahler had been trying to create. Then defections frequently made last-minute "invitations" necessary, thus compromising another of the essential aims, the linguistic uniformity of the performances. The opera again began to suffer from the evils that had menaced it before Mahler's arrival and the magnificent result of one year's work appeared threatened.

Mahler watched all this through embittered eyes. He began to weary of the systematic injustice of the Hungarian press, the personal attacks, calumnies, blame, and intrigue. At first, his administrative decisions had been beyond reproach, but a thousand rumors about his "rudeness, impatience, and cruelty" were now circulated. When it had become clear that he was still more unassailable as a conductor, the Hungarian-language press, ceasing suddenly to spread gossip about his impending resignation,[37] adopted a passive attitude of silence. Mahler was never even mentioned in the criticisms of the performances he conducted. The Hungarians, way behind the rest of Europe in many respects, were still far from understanding the importance of the conductor in the opera house.

In 1890, some aspects of Mahler's directorial policies were questionable, but he had been forced to adopt unsatisfactory solutions due to the difficulties he encountered. The nationalist press took advantage of this to attack him continually, yet it was hardly his fault if Hungarian singers were mediocre or if the scores submitted to him by young Hungarian composers were not worth performing. Almost every day he saw his own best intentions and happiest initiatives thus ridiculed and misinterpreted.

No one realized, for instance, that the "guest singers" were no part of his system, though they had been before his arrival. They were only an expedient for gaining time until local talent could be trained. Mahler himself grew impatient at the slowness of results obtained by his own efforts to perfect singers. He was furious when the press incessantly pointed out their lack of talent and at the same time reproached him unceasingly for the "guest singers." On the other hand he could not bring himself to put worthless operas into the repertoire just because they were Hungarian. That would have been against his conscience. Ferenc Erkel, the "nationalist" composer whose *György Brankovics* he revived during the 1888–89 season, was a talented composer entirely lacking in technique, and who spent his life hesitating between the style of *Tannhäuser* and that of *Rigoletto*.[38] Ödön (Edmund von) Mihalovics, director of the conservatory and Mahler's close friend, was a pale imitator of Wagner.[39] Jenö Sztojanovits, two of whose ballets Mahler had rehearsed and presented, wrote agreeable but mediocre music. As for the young Béla Szabados, whose ballet *Viora* was being given at the time of Mahler's departure the following year, he was a graceful imitator of Delibes.

An article in the *Zenelap* of January 30, 1890, noted that no Hungarian opera had been sung for more than a year, and blamed the press for not having protested sufficiently. In the absence of new operas, it was essential at least to go on presenting those of Ferenc Erkel. Mahler should also give the public an opportunity of judging the quality of operas by Mihalovics, Sárosi, György Császár, and Albert Franz Doppler. Everyone knew that Mahler spoke no Hungarian, but, worse still, he made no effort to favor Hungarian art, giving instead Offenbach operettas. He had also offered *Die Walküre* eleven times in thirteen months, and no one wanted to see it again. Even in Vienna, where the public was much more sophisticated, *Die Walküre* had never been sung more than four times in a season. The canceled performances, the once-only casts, the "experiences with debutant singers" should all stop. Mahler did not listen to or follow the wishes of the public and had in consequence lost its support.[40]

At the end of the 1889–90 season, the summing-up by August Beer in the *Pester Lloyd* was largely negative and reflected Mahler's difficulties and his discouragement. *Lohengrin* and *Die lustigen Weiber von Windsor* had started the season off well, but Auber's *La Part du Diable* and Marschner's *Der Templer und die Jüdin* had not brought enough new life to the small repertoire. The season had therefore turned out badly as regards both financial success and artistic achievement. For months on end, for example, only comic works and ballets had been presented, as though the public were to be served meals consisting entirely of desserts. True, the intendant Beniczky, a shrewd economist, had succeeded in banishing the demon of deficit from the opera. Now the only deficit that remained was an artistic one.

This summing-up continued with a list of the various singers at the opera: Bianchi was an excellent coloratura virtuoso, perfectly suited for soubrette and comic roles; Maleczky, a first-class versatile musician, an excellent actress, but with a voice showing signs of fatigue; Laura Hilgermann, the only new singer who had been constantly successful, deserved a firm engagement if she succeeded in freeing herself.[41] Arabella Szilágyi was the theater's best dramatic soprano, but her voice lacked fulness; the young Countess Vasquez was, for the moment, more promising than accomplished.

As for the men, Ney was excellent in bass comic roles, and Odry was almost as good; the young baritone Takáts, gifted with a fresh, metallic voice and good high notes, was only at his best in comic or semidramatic roles, and he needed to make great progress in diction. He could not really replace Bignio except in comic and semidramatic roles. If the voice of the tenor Prevost did not improve during the vacation period, he would be useless. And as for Broulik, a singer of fine taste and irreproachable technique, he was only suited to lyric roles.

Thus, according to Beer, the "ensemble" was still an incomplete, imperfect body. Only time, and the experience gained in the past year, would permit its complete formation. Above all, Mahler had been wrong to conduct only the new productions and to leave all the current repertoire to Sándor

Erkel. Since the departure of his brother Ladislaus, he had been alone in the theater,[42] overworked by almost daily rehearsals and performances, the result being that under his direction the orchestra played less and less well and that the soloists and choruses were constantly drowned out. If Mahler would agree to conduct some of the repertoire operas, he would give the public great pleasure, and this would also allow Erkel time to rehearse the orchestra more carefully.

In assessing this mainly negative report, we must keep in mind the fact that Beer had always judged Mahler objectively: his reservations were therefore probably justified. Perhaps he did not sufficiently take into account the economies forced on Mahler by the minister and the administration, or the difficulties inherent in his position as director of the Hungarian National Opera. And doubtless Mahler's poor physical and moral condition and the family troubles he had had at the beginning of the season influenced his work. He himself was certainly conscious of the flaws pointed out by Beer, and he showed, during the following season, that he knew how to profit from the bitter lesson.

During the month of May the opera sent Mahler to Northern Italy to hear new works and engage a tenor and a dramatic soprano. Having obtained complimentary tickets from the South Austrian Railway,[43] he decided to take Justi with him, for she had still not completely recovered from the sad events of the preceding year. Only a few brief letters addressed to Löhr give any indication of their itinerary.

Mahler was always more appreciative of the beauties of nature, music, and literature than those of the plastic arts. No doubt he was still too much attracted to the wild Alpine scenery to appreciate the classic, more controlled beauty of Italy. He does not, in any case, appear to have experienced the Mediterranean intoxication of the great German romantics, which is described so splendidly by Jean Paul in *Titan*, one of Mahler's favorite works.

The letters to Löhr give only a rough outline of their itinerary: Trieste, Venice, Milan, Lake Garda, Florence, Genoa. Not one description, not one anecdote, not one single impression of the journey appears in these dry missives. Mahler certainly went to operas and spoke with music publishers, for he returned from Italy with two new Italian operas that he conducted in Budapest the following winter: Alberto Franchetti's *Asrael* and Mascagni's *Cavalleria rusticana*. But none of his letters give us any information on this subject. We learn only that Justi was regaining her strength and her color under the Italian sun. Leaving early in May, brother and sister returned at the end of the month to spend the rest of their vacation with Otto and Emma in Hinterbrühl, six miles from Vienna, a small village situated in a fresh, wooded Wiener Wald valley, where the Löhrs had rented a spacious villa for the two families.[44]

Justi had not yet completely recovered, and upon his return Mahler sent her to take the waters in Franzensbad, Bohemia, while he himself went to Budapest for two days to give the intendant news of his journey and to complete plans for the coming season. He found Beniczky "agitated and nervous," and it took him two days to calm him and arrange all details of the *Spielplan*. He saw his Hungarian friends, lunched with the singers, walked to the Margarethe Island with Mihalovics, and had supper with Kössler. He also dined with Herzfeld, whose harsh article on the *First Symphony* he did not seem to resent, and then, without stopping in Vienna,[45] went directly back to Hinterbrühl, wanting to spend the rest of the summer there peacefully, and to compose again at last, after an almost complete two-year break.

"Am I, then, a wild animal, that
everyone stares at me, as though
I were in a zoo?"

# CHAPTER 15

*Mahler in Budapest (III) — Meeting with Brahms —
Cavalleria rusticana — Count Zichy — Farewell to Hungary (1890–91)*

In the whole of the Wiener Wald, few resorts are as fresh and attractive as
Hinterbrühl. Its villas and gardens are set on the shady side of a thickly
wooded valley, through which flows an idyllic stream, which could have inspired the Andante in Beethoven's *Pastoral Symphony*. In this peaceful and
poetic spot, Mahler at last spent a restful, studious summer. Freed from filial
obligations, he could finally enjoy a genuine vacation, conversing, reading,
walking in the surrounding forests, and visiting the nearby villages and ruined castles.

Certainly, since Vienna was so near, his privacy was often interrupted by
visits from friends, but it was not yet time for his great symphonic creations,
and he was happy in the peaceful family atmosphere of the villa that his
brothers and sisters shared with the Löhr family. He worked, composed,
and above all nursed his health, seriously affected during the past year. He
underwent a cure to improve his circulation,[1] rose at half-past five each
morning for a shower, then ate two breakfasts, separated by another shower
and followed by a cold-water massage. He dined at five P.M. and his evening meal consisted of a glass of milk or tea. Perhaps thanks to this strange
cure, his health improved rapidly. By the end of June he discontinued the
treatment, for "he had never felt better in years." However he continued to
rise at six and to go swimming with Otto, even when it rained. Almost at
once he composed a new lied from *Des Knaben Wunderhorn*.[2]

Justi was in Franzensbad for a month, and Mahler wrote her long friendly
letters, reminding her that her health depended upon her psychological balance,[3] and begging her to have confidence in herself and in him and not to
give way to the demons of worry and doubt. A second letter from Justi was

answered somewhat impatiently, Mahler assuring her that in the warm family atmosphere of Hinterbrühl she would recover quickly from the sadness of the preceding months.

On July 6, Mahler went to Vienna "on business," doubtless connected with the Budapest Opera. He met Justi there and sent her on to Hinterbrühl, while he visited Iglau for the last time to make final arrangements for selling the house and winding up his parents' estate. Apart from two other short visits to Vienna—including a disappointing evening at the theater that nonetheless afforded him the rare pleasure of hearing German spoken again on the stage—he spent the entire summer in the country wilderness of the Wiener Wald. From time to time, Budapest Opera personnel arrived to bring him their reports and receive instructions. His work that summer probably consisted of finishing the first lieder of the *Wunderhorn*.[4] He then devoted himself to studying the new operas *Asrael* and *Cavalleria rusticana*, which were to be staged during the coming season.

On August 22,[5] Mahler returned to Budapest, leaving Justi in Vienna, where she would now live with Emma and Otto in her care. Why did he not take her with him? "Because they had not yet learned to live together, despite their great mutual affection," asserts Natalie Bauer-Lechner.[6] But this decision may also have been purely practical, as Löhr's coming departure for Italy would leave no one to supervise the two youngest Mahlers. Mahler rented an apartment for them in Vienna, which, together with a housekeeper, a cook, and teachers for Emma and Otto, cost a considerable amount of money. From then on, his letters were filled with advice on how to live economically. The material needs of his brothers and sister became a daily source of worry to him, because of Justi's lack of experience. Indeed, she was never a good housekeeper.

On Mahler's return to Budapest, his first task, a real labor of love, was to prepare the new production of Mozart's *Don Giovanni*, which was to open the season on September 16. During the rehearsals a backstage conflict between Mahler and Countess Vasquez came to a head. She was to sing Elvira but refused to wear a certain velvet domino.[7] She was therefore replaced by Frau Maleczky. It was, according to Beer, one of the most memorable of Mahler's Budapest performances; he congratulated him on having "reestablished the classical tradition at last" and praised the "seriousness and passionate zeal" that he had devoted to the rehearsals. He said that the "precise and discreet" orchestra had admirably conveyed the psychological subtleties, with both sonorous beauty and exemplary polyphonic clarity. More faithful to the Mozartean tradition in Budapest than in Prague, Mahler had restored Mozart's recitativo secco,[8] which he himself accompanied at the pianino. He had selected a particularly "modern" way to stylize the production, changing sets without lowering the curtain, in order not to interrupt the action.[9] Also according to Beer, some of Mahler's tempos were too rapid and rendered the recitatives "unintelligible." He also considered that none of the singers except Arabella Szilágyi was as yet equal to his role.[10]

Herzfeld, on the other hand, made no reservations. He wrote that Mahler had turned his back on many customs in order to restore Mozartean truth. For the first time, for example, the Catalogue Aria ended in a lively andantino instead of a slow, sentimental adagio; for the first time, too, the hero sang *"La ci darem la mano"* as though he were a frivolously infatuated nobleman, not a tragic lover.

After this great success, Mahler once more experienced difficulties at the theater, which widened the gulf between the perfection he dreamed of and the reality in which he lived. The Hungarians' animosity toward him increased, and so did his bursts of ill-humor at the singers' lack of talent and enthusiasm.[11] The singers drew up, "often with reason, interminable lists of grievances, dismissals, and rudeness toward others."[12] They continued to show their disapproval by pretending sudden illness, which often made several changes of program necessary in one day. The audience sometimes learned only upon arrival at the theater the name of the opera they were about to hear. One day, the morning papers announced a last-minute performance of *Il Barbiere di Siviglia;* the evening papers, however, reported that this had been replaced by *Il Trovatore* because of the sudden indisposition of the prima donna. Later, at the theater itself, the audience was informed that the tenor had refused to sing, so the final program consisted of two ballets. Under these circumstances, Mahler did not dare to announce the program for more than two or three days in advance. As well as all this, the actor Eduard Újhazy, his assistant from the start, was dismissed, doubtless after a disagreement.[13]

All this seems to have discouraged Mahler, especially since the administrator, Beniczky, who had engaged and constantly supported him, was about to be replaced by Count Zichy, a mediocre composer, pupil of Liszt, and well-known one-armed pianist.[14] This haughty, arrogant aristocrat was an ardent nationalist and had—unlike Beniczky—many ideas about music which were often opposed to Mahler's. Zichy had examined the statutes of the opera and had decided to reform them. During their first meetings, he told Mahler he intended to assume most of the responsibilities of artistic director in person.

Foreseeing the consequences of this new nationalist crisis, Mahler, shortly after his return to Budapest, had begun to negotiate with the Dresden Opera and with Pollini, director of the Hamburg Opera, who renewed the offer he had made in Prague. Mahler, who now knew his own worth, wrote on September 26 to Pollini that he could not accept a salary of less than fourteen thousand marks per month.[15]

Projects for the 1890–91 season were discussed in another article by Beer. In June, Mahler had again announced that at last he would present *Siegfried* and *Die Götterdämmerung* in Hungarian, but once more this plan was dropped. But what really angered Beer was the publication of a list of guest stars for the season: Lilli Lehmann, Luise von Ehrenstein, Antonie Schläger, Marie Schröder-Hanfstängel, and Fanny Moran-Olden.[16] In trying to attract the public with sensational "guest appearances," Mahler, he believed was forgetting his most important promise, which had been to build up a resident company, and in consequence was running the risk of destroying everything so far accomplished. Beer wished that he would more often place at the service of the opera and the public his own great talent as a conductor: in fact only his presence on the podium could raise the artistic level of the performances.

When shortly afterward a rumor spread that Zichy's nomination would entail Mahler's departure, Beer defended Mahler. Much more than two years were required, he believed, to put back on its feet a theater that had been in such a bad way, and it would be unjust and absurd to let Mahler go.

After *Don Giovanni,* Mahler revived *Bánk-bán,* another work by Ferenc Erkel, which was again conducted by his son Sándor.[17] For a revival of *Un Ballo in maschera,* which Mahler himself conducted on October 16, the house was enthusiastic but only half full. Beer wrote that Mahler had proved his ability to "give distinction to Italian music as well as to German." Perhaps an Italian would have treated the rhythms more freely and would have "lingered more willingly over the organ points," but, taken all in all, the performance had been excellently prepared.[18]

The legendary susceptibility of the Hungarians quickly gave a tragi-comic aspect to an incident that occurred on stage during the dress rehearsal the day before this performance. The baritone Szendrői and the bass Takáts had been amusing themselves and the orchestral musicians by changing certain words in the text, thus giving them questionable implications. Szendrői also made "unseemly remarks" to the prompter and had addressed the stage director "in a voice so loud that it interfered with the rehearsal."[19] In a fury, Mahler called the singers sharply to order: "Gentlemen, I must ask you to behave on the stage in a dignified and proper manner, as artists and not as . . . [here some insults followed]." Offended, the two singers left the rehearsal.

Mahler went to the intendant that same day to tell him of the incident. A few hours later, the two delinquents also called to see him. Though admitting their guilt, they declared themselves offended, "not by Mahler's words, but by his tone of voice," and announced their intention of challenging him to a duel if he refused to apologize. Beniczky advised them to think the matter over calmly. When they returned without any change of mind, Beniczky said that there could be no question of an apology and that, in any case, he forbade the duel. He found it inadmissible that a conductor exercising his functions should be terrorized by his subordinates. If they wanted reparation, they must take the only way open to them: that of the law.

The same day, Mahler gave his version of the incident in the *Pester Lloyd.* He had acted in accordance with the duties of his profession, and he was not disposed to accord satisfaction (*ritterliche Genugtuung*) to the two singers, who had already sent their seconds to him. What would happen to theater discipline if each act of disobedience ended like this? In the end the affair more or less died down, and the two singers in question remained at the opera, but the incident helped to spread talk of Mahler's tyranny around Budapest—and at the same time made him better known than ever. Natalie Bauer-Lechner, who visited him shortly afterward, says that people "stopped in the street to gaze at him," for which reason he hesitated to go out, bitterly complaining to her: "Am I, then, a wild animal, that everyone stares at me, as though I were in a zoo?"[20]

In order to understand Natalie Bauer-Lechner's appearance on the scene, it is necessary to know that a year and a half earlier the South Austrian Railway had given Mahler free travel facilities, which had made possible his trip to Italy with Justi. One evening at Löhr's, he had offered to get free tickets to Budapest for all the guests present, praising the marvelous things that he would arrange for them to see and hear there. Natalie Bauer-Lechner, a young violinist whom Mahler had known since his conservatory days and who had always been extremely friendly toward him, wrote to him in the autumn of 1890, recalling his offer. She had just been through the sad crisis of a broken marriage and wanted to get away from Vienna for a few days.

Mahler replied in a friendly letter on October 14, suggesting that her visit should coincide with one of his periods of relative freedom, when he was not conducting at the opera. At such times he was busy with administrative duties only in the mornings and would be free to spend the afternoons and evenings with her. "I am curious," he wrote, "to find out if we shall be silent or if we shall talk."[21]

Mahler and Natalie talked, not only during her brief visit to Budapest, but for the next ten years. These friendly conversations were noted down by Natalie day after day; she left them to posterity in the form of the *Mahleriana,* the working title of Natalie's manuscript, of which only extracts have been published. She was to become a sort of Eckermann for Mahler and was an ideal eyewitness; a scrupulous, enthusiastic chronicler of his actions, gestures, and above all words. More than anyone else, it is she who thus immortalized many events, anecdotes, ideas, opinions, and impressions that otherwise would have been lost.

Natalie's blind admiration sometimes irritated Mahler, but he undoubtedly realized her value as a witness. He also felt a very real affection for her, without which he could not have spoken to her about so many of his deepest feelings and strongest impressions. Between them there sprang up a close friendship that both referred to as "camaraderie," but which in her case was quickly to become something more. From their first meeting in Budapest she proved to be warmly enthusiastic, receptive, and exceptionally understanding of all aspects of creative genius. It is true that she thought almost as highly of his childhood friend Siegfried Lipiner and his confused and indigestible literature as she did of Mahler and his symphonies, but then, so did Mahler.

Gallantly Mahler lent Natalie his lodgings, moving to a hotel for the duration of her stay. Arriving shortly after the incident of the averted duel, she came to the conclusion that it was Mahler's uncompromising, haughty attitude that had annoyed the two Hungarians more than the incident itself. But her concise, accurate account of this incident does not explain how they were calmed and persuaded by Mahler to return to the theater. As always, Mahler recovered from his theatrical difficulties by going on long, talk-filled country walks with her along the banks of the Danube.

In November, after Natalie had left, Mahler conducted the first performance of Franchetti's *Asrael*,[22] a "theatrical legend" with a thin, static libretto and music that lacked originality and force. Despite excellent staging and perfect musical performance, it did not hold the attention of the audience. Mahler was applauded after the first act, but the final curtain fell amid general indifference.[23]

The famous soprano Lilli Lehmann arrived in Budapest at the end of November for her guest appearances.[24] "It was then that Gustav Mahler entered my artistic life," she writes in her memoirs, "as director of the Hungarian National Opera. A self-willed and most intelligent newcomer. In a letter, he told me that my financial demands were too great for his budget, but added that nonetheless my visit appeared necessary in order to give his singers a good artistic example. What splendid days we spent there, in the centre of a small, select circle! Mahler, pursuing his aim with all the eagerness and idealism of youth; the great Hungarian actress Marie Jászay . . . who was simplicity itself, and who worked unceasingly at her parts. Also in the group were my dear friends from Bayreuth, Count Albert Apponyi and Professor Mihalovics . . . and my young niece. We met each other on every possible occasion.

"I sang all my parts in Italian except for Rachel in *La Juive,* which I sang in French, since they gave me the choice, without telling me that the Jew, Perrotti, had chosen Italian. All the others sang in Hungarian and one cannot imagine the linguistic confusion which reigned at these performances, during which foreigners had to sing without a prompter and had difficulty in remaining faithful to their chosen tongue. Young and full of fire, Mahler chose an ultra-rapid *tempo* for the short male trio in the first act of *Don Giovanni,*[25] claiming that Mozart had noted *alla breve,* though it is clear that this indicates a slower rather than a faster tempo. In the trio of masks he made the same mistake, but here I at once used my veto, for this time there is no *alla breve* indicated. I do not believe that he ever suffered from this 'speed madness' [*Allegrowahn*] again. When I spoke to Bülow of it, he was horrified and agreed entirely with me concerning the *alla breve.* I can still see Mahler kneeling before our stove and heating in a tin spoon a medicine he concocted for Hedwig [the great singer's niece] out of ingredients he brought with him and according to a time-honored recipe. Frau Jászay's maid often sewed on the buttons missing on his overcoat, which he had lost God knows where. We went for quick walks in the superb countryside surrounding Budapest and were as happy as kings. I considered Mahler a friend, I liked him, I respected his great talent, his incredible capacity for hard work, and his artistic integrity. I always took his side in the troubles which life brought him because of his great qualities, which were often misunderstood and ignored. I also understood his ambition, his steely enthusiasm, even his sudden attacks of nervousness. I knew that such attacks were only suffered by those unable to keep pace with their own great talent. I myself also once thought that a strong will was essential to fulfill one's potential, even at the cost of overtaxing his own energy."[26]

Thus began, in the most auspicious way, the collaboration between Mahler and Lilli Lehmann, which was to continue intermittently for almost twenty years. On December 5 she agreed to take part in a charity concert given in aid of a retirement fund for journalists and opera employees, and conducted by Mahler. She sang the Polonaise from *Mignon*. That same evening Mahler conducted (from memory as usual) a serious program that rather bewildered the mainly superficial audience, principally eager to hear Rudolf Raimann's operetta, last on the program. It consisted of the overture to *Oberon,* Mozart's *Symphony in G Minor,* and the overture to *Die Meistersinger*. Beer described the performances as "full of genius" despite some "eccentricities," such as "little crescendos" in the principal theme of the opening movement, abrupt accents, "like small exclamation marks," which interrupted the melodic continuity in the Andante, and the slow tempo of the middle section of the Finale.

Most of December was devoted to rehearsals of the "new Italian opera that has created a sensation in Rome," Mascagni's *Cavalleria rusticana*. But during this time the choice of repertoire gave Mahler serious problems: a first performance of *Les Contes d'Hoffmann* had to be postponed when the prima donna, Bianca Bianchi, fell ill.

In the middle of the month Brahms once again visited Budapest to conduct two of his works at a Philharmonic concert. On December 16, the eve of the concert, he went out walking with two Hungarian friends, Kössler and Herzfeld. They suggested going to hear *Don Giovanni,* which Mahler was conducting that evening with Lilli Lehmann as Donna Anna. Brahms made a wry face: he had never yet heard a good performance of *Don Giovanni* and preferred to read the score at home. He said that he would rather go to a café and drink a good Pilsen beer. His friends pretended to agree, but quietly directed his steps toward the theater. Reaching it, they suggested that since it was still too early to go to a café, they drop in for half an hour. Brahms agreed, after making sure that their box contained a sofa on which he could sleep comfortably.

So the two friends sat in the front of the box and Brahms stretched out behind them. During the overture, they heard approving grunts; then gradually Brahms became interested in the performance. His enthusiastic exclamations pleased Mahler's two admirers. Highly delighted, Brahms finally cried out, "Admirable! What a splendid fellow!" (*Teufels Kerl*). The two friends took him backstage during the intermission, where Brahms embraced Mahler and told him that never in his life had he heard so fine a performance of *Don Giovanni*.[27]

Mahler mentions this event in a letter to Justi: "Yesterday, *Don Giovanni*. Brahms and [Eugen] d'Albert attended the performance. Later I spent the evening with Brahms, and I had the great pleasure of seeing that he was absolutely delighted by my conducting: he spoke exactly as Goldmark spoke of *Lohengrin*. He told me that there were numerous things he had never noticed before, and that he had never heard Mozart played with so much style. Coming from Brahms, this really means something, as he is a die-hard member of the old school."[28]

Mahler also wrote to Löhr: "I lead an existence directed entirely toward others. Thus I have accomplished many useful things and have also experienced many joys. What will interest you is that Brahms heard me conducting *Don Giovanni* and since then he has become my most enthusiastic friend and protector. He commended me in what was, for him, a really incredible way, and has started a real friendship with me."[29] Brahms's admiration was not easy to win, and this meeting was to have many happy consequences.

The day after Christmas, Mahler achieved the most widely acclaimed success of his directorial career in Budapest. During his trip to Italy, he had discovered an opera composed by a young musician for a contest sponsored by the music publisher Sanzogno. It had been staged triumphantly in Rome on May 17, 1890: Pietro Mascagni's *Cavalleria rusticana*. The opera had not then been heard outside Italy, and Mahler had immediately signed a contract with the publisher. On December 26, 1890, he conducted *Cavalleria rusticana* in Budapest. Mahler's instinct had been correct: scene after scene was acclaimed, and the performance was several times halted by applause. Public and press alike acclaimed the new opera; the jealous, passionate Hungarians were a particularly good audience for this Sicilian "chivalry."

The next day, Beer dwelled at length on the qualities of the work, on the "new and promising talent" of the composer and his "astonishing technical mastery." In his opinion the performance, admirably rehearsed by Mahler, was perfect, and so was the casting.[30]

The orchestra, as was usual when he conducted, had performed exemplary feats, bringing out the "sound pattern of the various voices," "the vivacious rhythms and the brilliance of the colors." Arabella Szilágyi, in the role of Santuzza, had never sung or acted better.

Some days after this premiere, Mahler received a friendly letter from Mascagni, thanking him for the great effort he had made. Mahler's perhaps excessive admiration for him was based on the dramatic qualities of this work, and he was always indignant over the failure of Mascagni's later operas.

After the third *Cavalleria,* Mahler took a train to Vienna in order to spend the New Year with his brothers and sisters. Löhr was in Italy with his wife, so Otto and Emma were now living in a large apartment under Justi's ineffective guidance.

Lortzing's *Der Waffenschmied,* added to the repertoire in January, was another of Mahler's favorites.[31] The critics praised him for persuading the chorus to adopt a "conversational tone," but the public was too ignorant and inexperienced to appreciate such refinements. The first performance, on January 17, 1891, was warmly applauded, but the work scored only a *succès d'estime* and was performed only four times.[32] This unexpected setback was embarrassing to Mahler, since once again it drew attention to the inadequacy of the repertoire.

Five days after the first performance of *Der Waffenschmied,* on January 22, Beniczky retired, and Zichy's appointment was officially announced, bringing to an end one of the most harmonious collaborations in Mahler's life. For two years no dissension, no conflict, had shadowed even for a moment the relationship of these two men. Beniczky published on January 25 in the *Neues Pester Journal,* and on January 30 in the *Pester Lloyd,* articles in which he vigorously defended Mahler against all the press attacks, which, Beniczky said, could have been motivated only by "personal considerations." He listed the operas premiered or given new productions by Mahler (thirty-one in twenty months), and summed up the various stages of their work and their projects for the future. He recalled that everything had needed reorganizing, that some of the singers had been obliged to learn new roles, and that despite the reduction in the budget the performances had never been on such a high level. Finally, thanks to the money saved during the preceding years, there was a credit balance at his successor's disposition.

But these fine words counted for little in the face of the chill wind, or more precisely the whirlwind, that blew through the opera after the arrival of Count Zichy. The new intendant was a musician, determined to reinforce the national character of the opera and to assume the role of musical director. To do this, he had managed to get himself voted wider powers. Mahler, doubtless because he did not want to be held responsible for a possible rupture, at first appeared to be doing his best to please. In February, a series of interviews with Zichy led to a project for altering his contract, and Mahler accepted in principle the idea of staying on for another two years. However, if this alteration in his contract was not confirmed and ratified by the minister by May 15, he was to receive compensation of twenty-five thousand gulden.[33]

Zichy's appointment confirmed victory of the Hungarian nationalist faction. As early as 1889, in the course of a conversation with Wilhelm Kienzl,[34] Erkel had referred to Mahler as a "Germanist," whose influence could only be detrimental to Hungarian musical life. Right from the start Mahler sensed in Zichy a xenophobe, a haughty and self-satisfied aristocrat whose desire for power was so strong that any attempt at compromise was doomed to failure. The intendant's first announcements echoed those of Mahler two years earlier: first and foremost, an "ensemble," a reduction in the number of "invitations," linguistic unity, etc. And from now on Zichy had nearly all the powers that were once Mahler's: organization of the theater, choice of repertoire, engagement of singers without the approval of the director. Furthermore, he could now impose a veto on any of Mahler's decisions and could "exercise on his own responsibility his separate and combined powers in case of necessity," or, if he had sufficient reason, he could also ask for ministerial approval. This was equivalent to saying that the artistic director, who until then had had unlimited powers in the theater, would now become an assistant to whom the intendant might possibly delegate some authority. Furthermore, Mahler was directly attacked in the following paragraph: "It is no longer permitted to divulge, either orally, in writing, or through the press, the internal, private affairs of the two theaters. Anyone infringing this rule may be fined from 50 to 500 florins or, in serious cases, is liable to immediate dismissal." Mahler was thus deprived, not only of all initiative, but also of the right to express publicly the smallest grievance.

The fact that the minister agreed to sign this document clearly indicates that he had decided to get rid of Mahler, whose independent, authoritarian character was now well known. Mahler himself was ready to leave for Hamburg without regrets if he received reasonable compensation: this was his only concern during his negotiations with Zichy, who first proposed a sum of twenty thousand gulden, while making it embarrassingly clear that he would be obliged to "pay part of this out of his own pocket." He also insisted that Mahler's resignation should be, at least officially, for "personal reasons," while Mahler was adamant that the phrasing should read: "a change in circumstances," but this formula did not please the intendant, and their discussions were protracted.[35]

The February performances were especially poor, probably because the entire theater was waiting in suspense for an end to the conflict.

On March 1, Mahler conducted the first performance of *Loreley,* Mendelssohn's unfinished opera, Opus 98. The text had been altered somewhat, and the three existing sections were linked together and completed by the addition of an Ave Maria, a Vintage Chorus, and a Finale. The whole was preceded by the *Fingal's Cave* overture, which Herzfeld said had never been played in Budapest with such "ideal perfection."[36] On the evening of the first performance, the hall was far from full, which angered Mahler. He was enthusiastically applauded after the overture, but he decided to continue the performance without taking a bow. The applause went on so long, however, that in the end he was forced to do so. Mahler considered *Loreley*'s lack of success yet another condemnation of his management.

Nevertheless, on March 7, when Mahler took his place on the podium to conduct *Don Giovanni,* a noisy and enthusiastic ovation from the public clearly indicated its wish to see him remain at his post. The next day

Herzfeld wrote on the crisis at the opera that Zichy, in his view, should be more objective. There was no reason why his arrival should entail Mahler's departure, and on the other hand the fact that Zichy was a musician was not a sufficient reason for giving him unlimited powers. In fact, his influence at the opera could be dangerous: ". . . a child may sometimes be strangled by overeagerness or smothered by love."

Meanwhile, Zichy was doing all he could to annoy Mahler. He engaged singers and renewed the contracts of artists whom Mahler did not like, such as the Countess Vasquez. He added to the repertoire operas that Mahler had rejected; he increased the number of ballets.[37] Despite this the negotiations dragged on, for Mahler was determined not to leave until he got what he wanted. His relationship with Zichy worsened daily. There is a letter in existence asking an official from the Ministry of the Interior to send for Mahler and rebuke him for his "incorrect and undisciplined" conduct toward the intendant. Mahler was to be warned that if he continued disciplinary action would be taken.[38]

On March 15, Zichy summoned Mahler and announced curtly that he was prepared to pay compensation of twenty-five thousand florins.[39] "Can I draw it immediately?" Mahler asked with understandable suspicion. Zichy replied that he could, and telephoned the National Bank to give the order. Mahler went there at once, delighted to be free at last. Later, happening to meet Karpath at the Café Reutter, he joyfully announced the news of his immediate departure and of his new post in Hamburg.[40]

On March 16, Mahler conducted *Lohengrin* again. There was thunderous applause as the last note of the prelude died away, and cries of "Viva Mahler!" drowned the singers and the orchestra. The uproar subsided temporarily for Ney's monologue in the role of King Heinrich, but began again even louder a few moments later. Cries of "Viva Mahler!" "Viva Ney!" and "Down with Zichy!" lasted for several minutes. The singers were unnerved by this unexpected manifestation: the gloomy Ortrud "paled under her make-up" and Ney's voice "began to tremble."

After the quintet *"Mein Herr und Gott"* the applause began again and hundreds of voices shouted "Viva Mahler!" Zichy seated in the front of his box, "smiled ironically and shook his head with a disapproving air." The performance continued without incident until the moment when Lohengrin and Elsa are carried off on the shields. Then the audience once more applauded Mahler so enthusiastically that some of its members finally asked for silence. The tumult went on until a baritone named Veres, who was in the gallery and whose voice was particularly loud, thunderously called out for calm. A few seconds of complete silence were followed by laughter, then more applause and cries of "Viva Mahler!"

The ovation began again at the end of the last act and, fearing a repetition of this scene, Zichy decided that Mahler should not conduct a "farewell performance." Thus Mahler took his leave of Budapest in a dignified letter, the main passage of which read: "I have not been given the opportunity to say farewell from the post in which I have worked and fought for three years, nor to the Budapest public, which has so kindly appreciated my efforts, nor even to the artistic personnel of the Opera, which has supported me so faithfully and actively. . . . I leave conscious of having fulfilled my task faithfully and with the sincere hope that the Hungarian Opera may thrive and flourish."

There were many more or less fantastic rumors in Budapest concerning Mahler's departure. It was said, for example, that Count Zichy had sent Mahler the letter of dismissal in his dressing room during an intermission in the Szabados ballet *Viora*.[41] It was also said that the concierge of the opera, who hated Mahler, performed a dance of joy with one of the chorus members while Mahler was removing his possessions from his office, and it has even been added that, when Mahler walked out of the theater for the last time, this same man muttered through his teeth, but loudly enough for Mahler to hear him, "And now, clear out!"[42]

Beer's farewell article was most friendly in tone. "I will not discuss the circumstances under which Mahler's resignation was obtained, for this is no place for backstage gossip. It is enough to say that Mahler's departure was not brought about by any artistic limitations. On the contrary, everyone's opinion has always been favorable in this respect. We are not worried for this man. Many theaters would welcome a talent such as his. . . .[43] Few theatrical directors can ever have taken up their post under such difficult circumstances, and we will not easily forget what Mahler, in scarcely three years, has made of this deplorably neglected temple of the Muses. It must not be forgotten that he did not take over the direction of a well-run organization or of a theater in which the management was excellent whenever it was not bad, but that, on the contrary, he has had to build up everything from nothing."

Even an anti-Semitic, nationalistic Hungarian journalist named Eugen Rakosi regretted the departure of "this German Jew who alone has succeeded in transforming the polyglot Hungarian Opera into a coherent national institution."

Yet the majority of the Hungarian newspapers bade Mahler farewell without regrets. The *Egyetértés* considered that he had "failed entirely" as an administrator, and the *Hirlap* said that his post had become redundant since Zichy's nomination. As for the *Fővárosi Lapok,* it recalled Mahler's early promises, declaring that only one—the presentation of the *Ring*—had been fulfilled. The new intendant "could not accept the disorganization at the Opera," and Mahler had behaved with such "nervousness" that he had had to be called to order by the minister of the interior. The *Zenelap* went even further, referring to Mahler as "the source of all the trouble." Now that his post had been done away with and Zichy had taken over, the Hungarian National Opera would at last be directed "in a truly Hungarian way." It would be hard to find greater injustice and ingratitude.

Count Zichy also published in his memoirs a highly personal account of these events. According to him, the opera was in a very bad way upon his arrival, and discipline had completely disappeared. Mahler had been a mediocre administrator, singers had been "reduced to despair" by his "brusque ways," "nervousness," and "rudeness." "He broke batons into pieces as Don Juan broke women's hearts." Zichy continues, "When he conducted, he indicated the entrances (if he took the trouble to indicate them at all) as though lunging at the musicians with a sword. He spoke scathingly, and grimaced with anger."

Zichy admits Mahler's outstanding musical genius but affirms that he himself had considerable difficulty in calming the opera personnel, to whom he attributes the entire responsibility for Mahler's departure. Other contemporary sources present this whole affair in an entirely different light. But, of all the crises that marked Mahler's life, this was the one for which he was the least responsible. Zichy's power complex is incontestable, as is the change in the statutes. Under such conditions, who could blame Mahler for relinquishing his post?

How justified were Zichy's statements concerning the opera personnel's attitude toward Mahler? Undoubtedly tact was never Mahler's forte and he often lost patience with mediocre singers. It is also probable that by the autumn of 1890 he had realized how many insoluble difficulties stood in the way of ever creating a Hungarian national opera. Hungarians are well known for their violence and susceptibility. And even later on in Vienna, when years of experience had made him wiser, he still aroused much antipathy among his subordinates. .

Mahler's artistic fanaticism brought him particularly violent opposition in Hungary, but he also made many firm and faithful friends there: Mihalovics, Singer, Kössler, and a well-known political figure, Count Albert Apponyi.[44] In a letter of recommendation, sent to the Vienna Opera authorities in 1897, the count stated "that he is unequaled in his profession." The letter also mentions the "stupidity" and "despotism" of Zichy and the "unforgettable impression" that Mahler made in Budapest, where he had not only conducted the orchestra but had also supervised the attitudes, gestures, and movements of the actors on stage. Because of this, the performances he conducted were "perfect from every point of view."

If Mahler had not been nominated to Vienna in 1897, he might well have accepted the new offers he received from Budapest at that time: it seems that when, in March of that year, he conducted a concert in Budapest, he said, with tears in his eyes, that his years there were "the happiest period of my life."[45]

Mahler had left Hungary, however, in quite a different frame of mind, as the following phrase in a letter to Justi shows: "Hurrah! I am free. I obtained my release today under extremely favorable conditions. . . ." In fact he had just signed an excellent contract with the Hamburg Opera, and it was without regrets that he left the Hungarians with their susceptibility and chauvinism, their mediocre singers, and all the obstacles and limitations imposed upon him.

This first administrative venture was thus successful; where another might have failed Mahler had accomplished miracles on an artistic level. This is confirmed by both Brahms and Goldmark. When, in 1897, the intendant of the Vienna Opera recommended Mahler's nomination to the *Obersthofmeister,* he mentioned his direction of the Budapest Opera as having allowed him to prove "in a brilliant manner his genius and his enthusiasm both as a musician and a man of the theater." Indeed, Mahler abandoned the Hungarian capital with much less bitterness than his successor Nikisch, who could hardly be reproached for being a "stranger" or an "intruder" in Hungary.

On March 22, Mahler left Budapest with Justi, who had helped him with the move. On the way to Hamburg, he stopped in Vienna for two days with his brothers and sisters, but he had to give up the idea of similar halts in Dresden and Berlin in order to reach Hamburg by March 26, for he was due to conduct the first rehearsal there next day.[46] On the eve of his departure, a delegation of Hungarian admirers presented him with an impressive laurel wreath, as a token of their regret and gratitude. Three of Budapest's most outstanding citizens, Mihalovics, Count Albert Apponyi, and the important financier Moritz Wahrmann, opened a subscription list among opera patrons and presented Mahler with a silver baton and a vase with the inscription: "To Gustav Mahler, artist of genius, from his Budapest admirers."

At the railroad station, another delegation, headed by Count Géza Balogh, brought him a second wreath decorated with a tricolor ribbon, and the count made a farewell speech in German. Mahler replied, with more courtesy than sincerity, that he was leaving Hungary "with the happiest of memories," after having encountered among Hungarian audiences and musicians nothing but interest and understanding.

Despite the various difficulties that beset Mahler's stay in Budapest, it was there that he first made his mark as a musician of genius and a virtuoso conductor. Above all, it was thanks to Brahms that news of his artistic exploits spread through Germany. "Despite the discontent and the hostility that the young director immediately aroused, it was he who drew the crowds. His enemies could deny him everything except the profound musical sense with which he conducted and staged the productions. And sometimes they had to bow before his enthusiasm, his great competence, his zeal, his true musicianship and his self-sacrifice."[47]

Mahler's fanatic temperament aroused respect and fear rather than love in his subordinates. He himself spared no effort in serving the masters he loved, and one of his major faults was his lack of indulgence and his inability to understand and accept human weakness. Obsessed with the magnitude of his task as a re-creator,[48] filled with an almost religious fervor, he took no more notice of the hatred he aroused than a pilgrim climbing a holy mountain notices the sharp stones on which he treads.

"Let us see what
I will accomplish."

# CHAPTER 16

*Mahler in Hamburg (I) — The Hamburg Opera House
— First Triumphs — Hofrath Pollini — Scandinavian
Journey (March–August 1891)*

At first sight, Mahler's new post seemed less exalted than his previous one. He would no longer be responsible for a whole theater, but only for an orchestra and a group of singers. Nevertheless the position of first conductor at the Hamburg Opera was one of the most important in Germany.

Bernhard Baruch Pohl, who had Italianized his name to Pollini to facilitate his career, was one of the ablest and most unscrupulous impresarios of his time. He had been director of the Hamburg Opera since 1874, and, with an acute business sense, he had gathered together a group of first-class singers capable of satisfying an audience of bourgeois and financiers who were interested mainly in beautiful voices and vocal fireworks. If he had engaged Mahler and met all his demands, it was because he considered him a "star," a virtuoso capable of winning over the public and attracting it to the theater. Knowing how worried Mahler was at the thought of being completely under his orders, after having been his own master for so long, Pollini tried to allay his fears by holding out vain hopes of a totally imaginary position as director.[1]

Thus, though not yet thirty-one, Mahler became one of the most closely watched conductors in Germany. He had at his disposal in Hamburg artistic means infinitely superior to those in Budapest. Hamburg was then Germany's second city and had—together with the suburban Altona—almost one million inhabitants. The old and flourishing republic, its prosperity based on its long commercial traditions, was governed by an executive senate and consultative parliament and enjoyed almost complete political independence from Prussia. Except for Mendelssohn and Brahms, Hamburg had given birth to few musicians, but several important composers had worked there, among them Handel, Mattheson, and Philipp Emanuel Bach. There were several resident orchestras there. The opera house, built in 1827, and completely restored and modernized in 1874,[2] played a major part in the artistic life of the city, for the Hamburg citizens were enthusiastic theatergoers. In Altona a second theater, under the same direction, was reserved in principle for lighter works; nonetheless Mahler was to conduct important operas there almost every month.

Pollini's career strongly resembles that of Neumann. Born on December 16, 1838, in Cologne, he had, like Neumann, begun his stage career as a baritone in the city of his birth before going on to direct the Italian theater in St. Petersburg and Moscow. He then toured Central Europe with an Italian opera company before becoming head of the Hamburg Opera. There, Pollini demanded two and one half per cent of the profits for himself, and reorganized the theater in such a personal and autocratic way that the Hamburg press nicknamed the opera the Theater Monopollini or Polliniclinik (originally a joke made by Hans von Bülow).

Pollini is rightly considered as one of the first great modern theatrical managers. An infallible instinct guided him in his search for new works and previously unrecognized vocal talent; to find them, he undertook long yearly journeys. It was he, for example, who introduced the idea of special fees for guest appearances, and he was thus able to present to his audience such celebrities of the time as Gemma Bellincioni, Francesco d'Andrade, and Marcella Sembrich. He was not entirely devoid of artistic sense, but, primarily realistic, he considered art and artists mainly as merchandise: his directorial policy was based upon the law of supply and demand. He elaborated clever methods of gauging the public's taste and determining the importance and the market value of artists. He was rarely wrong about the public's taste and changes of opinion.

Pollini's system, which consisted of discovering singers, engaging them, and retaining them at any cost if they pleased the public, naturally had its drawbacks. He exploited his artists outrageously, making them sing almost every night, just as he later expected Mahler to conduct as many as 150 performances in a single season. Moreover, Pollini's direction was marred by negligence and serious omissions, since the orchestra and the choruses, as well as the staging and décor, were of secondary importance to him.

Four years before Mahler's arrival, Pollini had engaged Hans von Bülow to conduct a Mozart cycle and the first Hamburg performance of *Carmen*. The great musician had moved to Hamburg, dreaming of presenting opera cycles there each year. But his uncompromising idealism quickly clashed with Pollini's realism, and before long he withdrew, slamming the doors behind him, though he retained a certain influence inside the opera itself.

Mahler's material conditions in Hamburg were a little less favorable than those he had enjoyed in Budapest. His salary was only twelve thousand marks per year,[3] but it was free of tax deductions or payments to a pension fund. Pollini's rule was to favor mainly the star singers, the foundation stones of his "system." The orchestral musicians and members of the chorus, in particular, were getting starvation wages, and he had been exceptionally generous in granting Mahler such financial conditions.

In Hamburg, Mahler had at his disposal for the first time a group of first-class singers, and especially a Wagnerian "ensemble" of international repute that was then unequaled. In consequence, he was to experience unprecedented joys as an interpreter and musician, yet at the same time he suffered much frustration from a dramatic point of view, since such problems were always of secondary interest to Pollini.

Katharina Klafsky, the magnificent Hungarian dramatic soprano whose name topped the bill in many of Mahler's performances, had been in Hamburg for six years when he arrived.[4] Wife of the Wagnerian baritone Franz Greve, she was to sing Brünnhilde, Leonore, Isolde, and Elisabeth under his direction. The name of the contralto Ernestine Schumann-Heink, an artist whose deep and powerful voice was frequently praised for its bell-like quality, is also to be found in many Hamburg cast lists of the time. Under Mahler's baton, she sang not only Erda and Waltraute, but also Carmen, Amneris, and Azucena.[5] Their relationship was to be one of constant latent and then open hostility. She constantly offered active or passive resistance to Mahler's wishes, and often disregarded both good taste and common sense.[6] According to Mildenburg, Schumann-Heink nevertheless sang Mahler's lieder magnificently, surpassing herself whenever he was conducting. In spite of his dislike for the woman and the prima donna, too sure of herself and of her success to bow to his artistic demands, Mahler admired her talent. Much later he told his wife that one of the main causes of this hostility had been that Schumann-Heink, having tried in every possible way to seduce him, was furious at having failed and had spread all sorts of unpleasant rumors about him, including the statement that he was a homosexual.

Max Alvary, the heldentenor of the Hamburg Opera, was another celebrity.[7] In 1891 he had just returned from a trip to the United States, where, in spite of his rather mediocre voice and technique, he had been most successful thanks to his dramatic presence and superb costumes. Like Schumann-Heink, Alvary was stubborn, and Mahler, who hated certain aspects of his Wagnerian performances, even while respecting his artistic ability, had considerable difficulty in persuading him to respond to his demands. Knowing that he was the idol of a largely feminine audience, Alvary relied mainly on conventional attitudes and easy effects.

The Hamburg baritones were more obscure. Klafsky's husband, Franz Greve, a specialist in "black" roles, sang Hans Sachs, Telramund, the Holländer, Wolfram, Don Giovanni, and Pizarro for Mahler, before dying suddenly in 1892. Two other singers were the light soprano Maria Lissmann and her husband Friedrich, who sang Alberich, Hans Sachs, Telramund, and the Holländer under Mahler's direction. Finally there was Joseph Ritter, a lighter baritone, who left the Hamburg Opera six months after Mahler's arrival, but later they worked together again in Vienna.

The Hamburg Opera gave almost daily performances. During Mahler's first months there—from the end of March to the end of May—he conducted all of Wagner's major operas, which formed the lion's share of the huge repertoire (twenty performances out of thirty-five); the others were Weber's *Freischütz* and *Euryanthe,* Cherubini's *Fidelio* and *Der Wasserträger,* Mozart's *Don Giovanni* and *Die Zauberflöte,* and two Italian operas—*Cavalleria rusticana* and Franchetti's *Asrael.* The major drawback of such a vast repertoire was insufficient preparation for each work, and for Mahler this meant real suffering.

Upon his arrival on March 26, Mahler was wholly enthusiastic about Hamburg: "One cannot imagine how beautiful and animated the city is," he wrote to Justi. "The harbor is magnificent, much more impressive than Trieste or Genoa," he wrote on another occasion after watching the superb forest of masts in the docks.[8] Pollini, absent from the city at that time, had invited him to stay in his own villa while looking for lodgings, and Mahler was amazed by the comfort and luxury of his surroundings.[9] The town's climate struck Mahler as admirable, and his health, which had not been good during his last weeks in Budapest, improved considerably. For the time being he declared himself delighted by the variety of his theatrical activities, as well as by the richness of the repertoire. Things looked so good that he suggested Justi should join him at the end of the summer in order to arrange their lodgings and organize their life together.

As usual this euphoria did not last long, and Mahler soon found reasons to complain. First, the weather became suddenly worse, then there was the high cost of living in Hamburg, where it was impossible to find an apartment for less than a thousand marks a year, and, finally, his theatrical activity soon became "routine labor."

Pollini, upon his return, told Mahler that he would be named "director" of the opera in the autumn; a promise all the more surprising since it could never have been kept.[10] Until June, he was to be a "guest" conductor, and once each season he could conduct an evening performance for his own benefit in order to increase his income. His contract was signed for three years, and local newspapers flattered his vanity by referring to his "international celebrity."

Two days after his arrival, on Easter Sunday, March 29, 1891, Mahler made his debut at the opera, conducting *Tannhäuser.* Immediately afterward there was much talk of his "genius." Even the critics, more intelligent than those of Leipzig and Budapest, at once recognized his value:

"For a long time we have not heard a performance so perfect down to the smallest detail. . . . From the first note of the magnificently played overture to the last chord of the opera, one felt the leadership of a man with strong will and definite ideas; he has mastered his task completely, a second Bülow who—like him—knows how to transmit directly to the performers what he wants and feels, who leads the ensemble as if by invisible wires, who clearly expresses his least intentions, and who permits the soloists freedom of interpretation whenever possible, but knows how to impose his own will whenever it is necessary. . . . Especially as regards the freedom of tempo coupled with complete rhythmic control and the absence of arbitrary fluctuations does this interpretation seem so completely in the spirit of Wagner. A slight relaxation or tightening of the reins, an almost imperceptible hesitation over a melodic passage in the orchestra to give a deeper and more expressive effect, or a quickening of tempo for a more rhythmically animated line, together with strict observation of the composer's dynamic indications, all this gave the whole work a quality such as we have never heard before!"[11]

The author of this article in the *Fremdenblatt* was Carl Armbrust,[12] one of Hamburg's most influential critics, who remarked that the young conductor had been well rewarded for his efforts by the public's warm applause.

On the following day, in the *Correspondent,* Josef Sittard,[13] whose authority as a critic equaled Armbrust's, expressed the same enthusiasm: "Right from the first evening, and as so rarely happens, the audience was literally electrified by this conductor of genius!" After the performance, on April 1, of *Siegfried,*[14] the same critic spoke of Mahler's "genius" as a conductor, his "magic power," and "absolute possession of both the notes in the score, and the spirit of the work," thanks to which he had felt that he was hearing a completely new orchestra.[15]

Mahler had conducted these two performances at short notice, without a single rehearsal, and it was this fact that most impressed another Hamburg musician, much more famous and important than either Armbrust or Sittard, and one who had been anything but kind to Mahler in other circumstances: "Hamburg now has a new first-class opera conductor, Gustav Mahler (a serious, energetic Jew from Budapest), who, in my opinion, equals the greatest (Mottl, Richter, etc. . . . ). Recently I heard *Siegfried* conducted by him . . . and felt deep admiration for the way in which—without a single orchestral rehearsal!—he forced those rascals to dance to his tune. Despite my nervousness and other 'drawbacks,'[16] I succeeded in staying on to the last bar. The performance lasted for more than four hours, even though the Siegfried-Wotan scene had been reduced to the minimum."

This passage is taken from a letter that Hans von Bülow wrote to his daughter Daniela on April 24, 1891. It seems likely that Brahms, who was a close friend of Bülow, had mentioned Mahler to him after the famous performance of *Don Giovanni* in Budapest. The judgment seems of the utmost importance to us, because it came from one of the most illustrious and demanding of German musicians, a man who did not often grant his admiration and was not easily accessible to the young, as the Kassel incident proved in 1884.

This sudden and total conquest of Bülow opened an essential door in Mahler's career. It was wholly unexpected, since the great conductor had not only reacted negatively to Mahler's cry for help in Kassel, but he had later failed to answer another letter from Leipzig on March 26, 1888, in which

Mahler expressed his "need to submit his work to Bülow's invaluable judgment."[17]

Perhaps more famous today for his marital misfortunes than for his fabulous career as a performer, Hans von Bülow had settled in Hamburg in 1888. After having handed over the direction of the Meininger Orchestra to Richard Strauss in 1885, Bülow had taught for a time in Frankfurt and Berlin while still conducting concerts elsewhere. Engaged by the Berlin Opera, he had been summarily dismissed shortly afterward by Count Hochberg, and this was the main reason for his moving to Hamburg. After his break with Pollini, he agreed to conduct a series of subscription concerts organized by the Berlin impresario Wolff.[18] Bülow was then sixty. His musicality, his prodigious technique as a pianist and conductor, his astounding memory, his genius as an interpreter, most particularly of Beethoven, Brahms, and Wagner, were legendary at the time, even if his pioneering activities are somewhat forgotten today. By his mere presence in Hamburg and the concerts he gave there, Bülow had successfully aroused new enthusiasm among the city's music circles. Indeed, the admirable conductor of the premieres of *Die Meistersinger* and *Tristan und Isolde* was considered throughout Germany as a sort of musical pope. To him is attributed a real revolution in the technique of orchestral conducting and a break with certain of its best-established traditions.

Bülow's admiration was to help Mahler greatly with the public and the impresarios, not to mention the deep satisfaction to his pride. Now, as well as Brahms, another leader of German classical music had recognized him as a powerful new talent, and this was to bolster his courage during the daily battles with Pollini. From then on Mahler attended almost all of Bülow's concerts and was often his guest, as long as the older man's health allowed him to lead a normal life.

On March 30, Mahler conducted *Cavalleria rusticana,* the first performance of which he had given in Budapest three months earlier. Two days later it was the turn of *Siegfried,* and on April 2 he hoped to conduct *Fidelio* with the admirable Hamburg singers. Bad luck, though, was to postpone the performance. Max Alvary, due to sing his first Florestan, fell ill. Tenors were not lacking in Hamburg, and he was replaced without difficulty. But some hours later, Katharina Klafsky, a famous and magnificent Leonore, announced that she could not appear, and she too had to be replaced. At the last moment, Mathilde Brandt, her understudy, was also unable to sing. The performance had to be canceled, and Mahler conducted *Der Freischütz* instead.

The next day, Sittard in the *Correspondent* was ecstatic about the wonders that Mahler had accomplished, communicating his slightest wish to the performers without any previous rehearsal. He compared Mahler's conducting technique and profound knowledge of the opera with those of Wagner and Bülow, and congratulated him for having "demonstrated that he was as well versed in the classic spirit as in the modern." He detailed some of the special traits in his interpretation: the tranquil tempo of the German waltz, underlining its ländler character, and the fairly rapid coda in the second-act terzetto, thanks to which Mahler had obtained a magnificent dramatic crescendo.

Armbrust wrote an even more detailed review,[19] stating that all these new and surprising conceptions of Mahler's had such force and conviction "that they constitute the best proof of his genius."[20] The young conductor was much applauded that evening, and Pollini, back in Hamburg, witnessed his success, whereupon he made one of his "generous" gestures by increasing Mahler's yearly salary from twelve thousand to fourteen thousand marks.[21] To be sure, Pollini demanded a huge amount of work in return, but this gesture nevertheless established a cordial relationship between himself and his chief conductor. Mahler could no longer feel misunderstood or unappreciated, and a situation entirely different from that which had brought about the creation of his first compositions—newly acquired confidence in his destiny—was to encourage him to create his first mature works. The latter, in fact, did not spring from psychological crises, but from a knowledge of his triumphs as a conductor, thanks to which their performance and success seemed assured.

After *Tannhäuser*, *Siegfried*, and *Der Freischütz*, Mahler turned to *Die Meistersinger*. According to Sittard, his firm hand and great authority prevented the singers from indulging in their usual long-held notes and ritardandos. So fine a performance of Wagner's comedy had never been heard in Hamburg. A few days later, still according to Sittard, an entirely personal interpretation of *Die Zauberflöte* revealed Mahler's complete understanding of Mozart: right from the opening trio, "performed in a gracious *parlando* style," a kind of magic prevailed "comparable to the atmosphere of an Arabian Nights' tale." Ignoring the pathetic and dramatic tones adopted by so many of his colleagues, Mahler conferred a graceful, smiling character to the work; thus his interpretative genius restored for the first time the true values of a divine master. Under Mahler's baton, the orchestra had achieved the lightness and discretion of a chamber music ensemble capable of adapting itself and giving way to the voices; each instrument had preserved its individuality, while nuances and colors seemed to spring from the work itself.

Armbrust, equally enthusiastic, was amazed to find *Die Zauberflöte* revealed in a new light. He approved Mahler's insistence on mezza voce singing.[22]

By the end of April, *Fidelio* could at last be performed. This time Armbrust had some reservations about its interpretation: Mahler, once again, shed new light on the music and gave to each episode his personal imprint, but nearly all of the tempos had seemed too fast, especially those in the first act.[23] Even the famous quartet was too fast and its pianissimo so excessive that it blurred the polyphonic clarity. Yet the accompaniment of Leonore and Pizarro's big arias, the powerful crescendos, and the balance between instrumental and singing voices were incomparable, as was the interpretation of the *Fidelio* overture[24] and the great *"Leonore" No. 3* inserted between the two scenes of the last act.[25] "The performance of the great, the gigantic *'Leonore' Overture No. 3* was an accomplished masterpiece. . . . It was followed by enthusiastic, prolonged applause, which was wholly justified, as not even under Bülow's direction have we heard this great symphonic poem so magnificently rendered in every detail."

The city of Hamburg was thus giving Mahler a warm welcome. He was often invited out for dinner and got on well with the North Germans, with whom he shared many opinions and character traits. Even his search for winter lodgings had an unexpected consequence, a new friendship with Adele Marcus, a young artistically inclined widow. She had decided to spend a few months in Italy with her daughter, and was considering subletting her apartment during that period. Mahler was one of her first tenants, and an immediate attraction must have been felt, as he was to visit her frequently, whenever his theatrical occupations permitted it. Adele Marcus was six years older than Mahler. Her physical charm, her liveliness, and "finesse," her originality, as well as her taste for spiritual and artistic matters, qualified her as a friend and confidante of the "elite." She had already attracted a large number of admirers, whom she chose with great care, for she was in search of intellectual stimulation. Her financial situation enabled her to entertain frequently, and in her house Mahler was to meet many pleasant and cultivated people who provided him with a salutary change of scene. As with his other close friends, he advised Adele upon her choice of reading matter, invited her to the theater, and played chamber music in her home. His somewhat tyrannical friendship was soon to chase from her "salon" all the habitués whom he did not find worthy of her attention. From then on, Adele, accompanied by her mother, Helene Hertz, attended all Mahler's important performances. Their friendship appears to have existed entirely on a spiritual basis, and it seems quite certain that they were never bound by any other ties except those of an *amitié amoureuse,* often misinterpreted because of the unfortunate reputation as a Don Juan that Mahler had acquired.[26] That year Adele dropped her plans for an Italian trip, and in May, Mahler rented a large apartment on the upper floor of a villa near Pollini's, where his room looked out upon a restful perspective of gardens and fields. Despite his strenuous work at the theater, he was thinking of returning to composition: he asked Otto to send him his lieder manuscripts, even the incomplete ones. It was probably then that he discovered the joys of bicycling and practiced the sport regularly for relaxation in the company of one of Bruckner's former students, Zinne.[27] He also made plans for his family for the coming season: Justine would join him, leaving the two youngest members of the family with Löhr, on his return from Italy, unless Emma also were to come and cultivate her gift for painting at the excellent Hamburg school of design.

Fourteen performances were entrusted to Mahler in April, nineteen—including all of Wagner's big works except *Parsifal*—in May. Pollini seemed quite determined to take advantage of his new star. On May 18, Mahler conducted for the first time in his life *Tristan und Isolde,* that supreme work of art to which the memory of his interpretation remains indissolubly linked. The annual Wagner festival was followed by a benefit performance for Marie and Friedrich Lissmann, who sang the principal roles in Cherubini's *Der Wasserträger,* after which Mahler conducted the *"Leonore" Overture No. 3* and accompanied the singers at the piano in a few lieder.

Immediately after the seasonal closing of the opera, Mahler left Hamburg for Leipzig, where Pollini had asked him to hear some new singers. He may also have tried to arrange a performance of his *First Symphony.* On the way he stopped in Munich to visit Heinrich Krzyzanowski. He then spent several days in Vienna at the end of the first week in June, before finally settling down in a flat in Perchtoldsdorf with his brothers and sisters.[28] It was probably there that he completed the first *Wunderhorn* songs with piano accompaniment, which were published by Schott the following year.[29] He may also have sketched out, during that same month, some of the great orchestral songs that he was to compose during the winter. But the climate in Perchtoldsdorf, unfortunately even closer to Vienna than Hinterbrühl, did not suit Mahler, who was to complain later in a letter to his sister about this "impractical" summer. He decided that next year he would rent quiet and isolated quarters for a family vacation, for this constant wandering from place to place did not suit him.

Early in July, Mahler paid a diplomatic visit to Pollini, who was taking his annual cure in Bad Gastein in the Tyrolean Alps, about sixty miles south of Salzburg. There he met again the faithful Natalie, who, "tortured by terrible and painful conflicts of the soul," was happy to see him arrive unexpectedly. Most impressed with the grandeur of the mountain landscape, with its streams that seemed "to fall from the sky," Mahler went out each day, while Pollini played poker with Jauner and Schuch.[30] Mahler would call for Natalie in her small attic room, and together, fleeing the paths frequented by the visitors taking the cure, the esplanades, and the bath establishments, they would go on long walks in search of the calm beauties of the forest and the surrounding mountaintops.

One day Mahler was crossing the gardens of the thermal establishment, where the rich guests took their daily walks to the accompaniment of the local orchestra on a bandstand, playing extracts from Lortzing's *Undine.* He could not refrain from listening for a minute, and then attracted amazed attention by stamping his feet furiously and shouting, "Too fast, too fast, you fool!"[31]

Thanks to letters from Mahler to Justine, we can establish the schedule of this "wandering" summer. After leaving Perchtoldsdorf, he seems to have intended, as the year before, to take another cure in Marienbad. But after a few days he must have been reassured as to his health, and fled the "horror" of the great spa. He arrived in Eger, where the Krzyzanowskis lived, on July 25 and from there went on to nearby Bayreuth to attend three performances, one of *Tannhäuser* and two of *Parsifal.*

On July 30, Mahler left Bayreuth for a long six-hour excursion on foot across the Fichtelgebirge and all the way to Wunsiedel, the home town of Jean Paul. The next day he left for Eger, and from there went directly back to Hamburg. Since Löhr had postponed his return from Italy, Mahler dropped his plans for bringing his brothers and sisters to join him, for Otto could not be left alone. He therefore decided to sublet the villa he had rented earlier and selected more modest lodgings for himself alone. On August 3, he left for Kiel with the intention of embarking for an unknown destination, before ending his summer as planned in Sylt or Helgoland. On August 5, the weather being magnificent, he reserved a cabin on the Copenhagen boat for the following day. The same evening he arrived at Korsör, on the chief Danish island of Seeland.

In Copenhagen, Mahler visited the Thorwaldsen Museum and walked through the entire city. The next day he went along the Danish coast on foot and by boat, crossing forests in which he saw herds of wild animals. He visited Kronborg Castle at Elsinore and the battlements made famous by *Hamlet,* then crossed the Kattegat with a rough sea to Helsinborg in Sweden.

The next day he boarded a northbound boat, following the coast as far as Halmstad. The Swedish coast enchanted him, with its many rocks and cliffs, and its "lively and friendly" population. He was greatly impressed by the rocky, wooded mountains, fields, and valleys, around Göteborg, and he unexpectedly came upon a circular wooden arena set among the rocks, in which popular dances were held, probably reminding him of those in his native land.

On August 10, he left for the island of Marstrand, and later traveled by train for Moss in Norway, another superb coastal trip. At Moss, he was sickened by the penetrating smell of the fishing boats, which reminded him of Venice, and was so saddened by the smallness of the miserable, primitive houses that he decided to leave immediately for Oslo. Because of bad weather, he had to wait an hour and a half for the boat's arrival, and in the meantime, conversed by gestures with the local sailors. Out of politeness, the Norwegians spoke English, but Mahler, who did not speak this language, replied in Norwegian with the help of his Baedeker. The roaring of the waves and his linguistic performances exhausted him, but fortunately the steamer came to his rescue at eight-thirty and then set out into the black night. Mahler reached Oslo by midnight in a torrential rainstorm that continued all next day. Would he have enough money to stay on until the good weather returned, so he could visit the nearby countryside and then go home partly by land?

The weather having improved two days later, Mahler was able to see the complete panorama of Oslo from the peaks around the Norwegian capital. Returning to his hotel, he sat down one evening in the lobby to read his paper, when suddenly looking up, he saw Henrik Ibsen, one of his favorite writers, sitting nearby. Too deeply moved to utter a single word, he learned later from the hall porter that the famous writer lived in the hotel. Mahler's funds having run out, he had to give up his idea of visiting the interior of the country, and started back along the Norwegian coast. Nothing that Justi had ever seen, he wrote to her, could ever convey an idea of Norway—"not even the Alps and the southern countries."

The little port of Drammen on the same fjord delighted him because it was surrounded on all sides by forested mountains and divided by a river. He climbed for five hours through the forests, walking over alternately marshy and rocky ground to reach an isolated mountain lake. On the ship he took for Larvik, he spent the entire crossing on deck, in spite of wind and rain.

The sun was shining again when Mahler sailed to the southern tip of Norway, and this voyage among the "Schären" was for him the climax of the entire trip. On one side were rocks and "strange" cliffs, and islands sometimes bare, sometimes wooded, with houses or lighthouses. On the other side was a superb jagged coastline, alternating with the open sea. The wind blew violently when the boat, emerging from the inland sea, reached the famous Kattegat, and then began to roll badly. Happily, Mahler was not seasick and could distract himself by watching the other passengers. On the afterdeck a group of about fifteen men and women, whose manners and clothes seemed equally "ludicrous," extracted three guitars, a violin, and a trumpet from their luggage, and gravely began to tune up. Thanks to the insignia they wore on their shoulders, Mahler realized that they were members of the Salvation Army, which he had heard about but never seen before.

"They tuned up for almost an hour. Most of the passengers had gathered round expectantly—except for the seasick ones who were leaning over the bulwarks, for the ship rolled more and more. Finally they began to sing, the women screeching, the men in loud, husky voices. None of them knew the words or the music of their song very well, so that those who remembered most took the lead alternatively, in a sort of bizarre canon. Four women and one man formed the orchestra, and the violinist had a strange way of holding his bow by the middle. The song was laughable: a sort of complain based on a religious text. I understood only two words, 'Jesus Christ' and 'Portugal.'"

After this highly entertaining crossing Mahler reached Kristiansand toward evening, and at sunset could admire the impressive sight of a French fleet anchored in the bay. After scarcely two hours in Kristiansand, he took another ship to cross the dangerous Skagerrak, with another rough sea and a howling wind. Hardly had he arrived in Germany when he set out on another walk in the outskirts of Friedrichshafen (Frederikshavn).

"What a contrast to Norway! An endless heath, with here and there a small farmhouse, a windmill, a house, and, in the distance, the open sea. I walked and walked, until I suddenly found myself outside an attractive sort of park. I entered and discovered a cemetery in which I remained for a few minutes. The moment and the atmosphere made me think of the past. The end is always the same, whether in the Norwegian mountains or in the marshlands of Jutland." He spent the last days of his vacation on the islands of Sylt and Helgoland. Thus ended the one and only summer of his life during which he devoted most of his time to the peaceful pleasures of the tourist.[32] On August 21, he caught the boat for Hamburg.

During his Scandinavian trip Mahler had briefly noted down each day's impressions in his letters to Justine, thus providing us with a kind of journal. It reveals certain already known character traits, his romantic and slightly naïve love for nature and *"Volk."* On the other hand, certain episodes—the conversation with the Norwegian sailors, for instance, and the Salvation Army concert—give a far more human picture than most other contemporary accounts: he appears more observant, less wrapped up in himself, capable of looking about him and appreciating humorous situations.

Mahler's return to Hamburg and life in the opera house was accompanied by a series of problems. The crate sent from Budapest in early summer finally arrived but proved to contain only part of his possessions. The rest had probably been lost or shipped to Vienna by mistake. Also his clothes had not been cared for by a woman's hand for a long time. Most of his linen had been lost during the trip, and the rest was now unworthy of the first conductor of the Hamburg Opera. So much had to be replaced, including a suit. Having spent most of his money traveling, he had not a penny left to pay for all this or to meet the needs of his family in Vienna. Worse, he had not succeeded in subletting the villa that he had leased for two years, and in July the Iglau authorities had demanded payment of forty florins per month as a "military tax" (collected from all citizens not in military service and levied in proportion to their incomes). He had requested a reduction because he supported his family, adding that he had been unemployed for eight months (in reality it had been four) in 1888. The authorities, having questioned several theaters, had discovered the truth and were demanding payment of the tax.[33]

Mahler also had health problems: a "stomach catarrh," due to a "cold drink taken at Marienbad," obliged him to follow a very strict diet. After his vacation, during which he had been utterly alone, he experienced moments of exhaustion and discouragement, of *Sehnsucht,* such as he had experienced only rarely since his theatrical activities began to absorb all his energy.

"As far as my 'state of mind' is concerned," he wrote to Freund, "you will have a clear enough picture of it from my letters. I have suffered a great deal during the past weeks, and without any good reason. The past haunts me—all that I have lost—the present, with its solitude—and so many things. You know this state of mind of old; if such sadness could suddenly seize me among my friends, when I still had my youth, my freshness and my vitality, you can imagine how I spend the long afternoons and evenings here. Not a single being with whom I have anything in common—not even an experience or a hope once shared. During these past weeks, I have finished reading something remarkable, which doubtlessly will have a lasting influence on my life."[34] According to Freund this referred to Nietzsche, whose influence on

Mahler proved less profound than he had supposed, but which nevertheless inspired the fourth movement of his *Third Symphony*.

Mahler worried increasingly about the future of his brothers and sisters. Justi, on whose shoulders rested the whole responsibility for Otto's and Emma's education, was only twenty-two, and she went through moments of depression and doubts. He attempted to calm her with letters in which he expressed his total confidence, while at the same time admonishing her when she did not fulfill her responsibilities. One particular crisis had occurred early in April, after which Mahler extracted a secret promise from her; then, at the beginning of October, he was upset by something she wrote in one of the letters and he wrote back: "Your recent letters have told me a lot of things that pleased me. I can see that you are slowly developing into a more alert human being and starting to look around for yourself. But at the same time they have given me an insight into your way of life which does not satisfy me. Please try to be a little more explicit on this subject; it seems to me that your mutual relationships are very confused. Even if something bothers you, please trust me and tell me about it frankly.

"However, there is one thing I beg of you: don't ever imagine that you have any knowledge of human nature! The real deep-down truth is as follows: as long as you consider yourself to be different from others, it is all right. But if, believing this, you do not stop demanding from others what is possible only for yourself, everything will go wrong. Never forget that each human being represents a world of his own, of which we know a large part, but only to the extent that we carry this part within ourselves; the remainder will always be a secret. If one wishes to set up new laws, these will only be valid for that particular part of the others that we know, because it is within ourselves.

"But this might carry us too far! Please do not fight or mistrust each other. Enjoy what you have in common, don't blame what you cannot understand in someone else, and do not try to impose your laws on the 'whole of humanity.' To God you are, naturally, all alike! But in the eyes of men, each one remains an unknown world for his fellow-men, with that part in common to which comprehension is limited. Try to remain united thanks to this part and beware not to destroy this bond lightly! . . .

"But I have forgotten the most essential point of my sermon: what particularly exasperates us in others is ninety-nine per cent of the time that which we are ourselves capable of. This goes for mistakes common to men as a whole: we recognize our own world in others, and this reflected image infuriates us so much that we would like to break the mirror immediately."

From then on, the personalities and evolution of his brothers gave Mahler a foresight of pending catastrophe. Justi was by no means a pedagogue, and Löhr's generous idealism only equaled his lack of practical sense. Moreover Emma's Catholic governess and Justi's "Sunday teas" at which guests danced and made music—the whole way in which life was organized in the

Breitegasse apartment was unstable and unfavorable to work, since there was no authority.

From the other side of Europe, poor Mahler did his best to help Justine, who was too young and inexperienced to face the problems that concerned her brothers. He was willing to make all the necessary financial sacrifices so that they could lead an agreeable life after the difficult years in Iglau. Yet from time to time he secretly complained about the privations he had to impose upon himself: "I assure you that I shan't be able to stand this much longer; I have to restrict myself here again as much as I had during the Vienna period,"[35] he wrote to Löhr in 1891.

Mahler's principal worry was Otto and his studies. The boy was just beginning his fourth year at the Vienna Conservatory, and in spite of his many private tutors, his progress was most irregular. The time for his military service was approaching, and Mahler wanted him to obtain his diploma before then, but the level of his studies dropped even further during the winter 1891–92. Enrolled in Fuchs's composition class, he was not allowed to take part in the end-of-term competition "because of his too frequent absences." As for his classes of choral singing and the history of music, the records of the conservatory reveal that Otto did not even take the trouble to attend! He left the conservatory in April 1892 without a diploma and maybe even without the knowledge of his brother, to whom, until his tragic death, Otto was to be a source of endless trouble and anguish.

"I can no longer stand seeing these
gentlemen fall out of their chairs . . ."

# CHAPTER 17

*Mahler in Hamburg* (*II*) — *The* Wunderhorn Lieder —
*Bülow and the* Totenfeier — *The German Season in
London* (*1891–92*)

"It seems to be my fate always to live surrounded by struggles and adversity. But while keeping my head high and my heart true, I prefer this to being satisfied by mediocrity, with the gilded, detestable *via media*. Perhaps it is a happy stroke of destiny that prevents me from accepting life's yoke with resignation and satisfaction: I am still on my feet, and they will not defeat me for a long while!"

This passage from a letter written to Natalie Bauer-Lechner in the fall of 1891 shows to what extent the euphoria that had marked the beginning of Mahler's stay in Hamburg had vanished in spite of the many advantages his new position implied. "I can tell you that the orchestra here likes me very much, which has *never* happened before. It is so much more pleasant than in Budapest! This is equally true for the chorus, but the singers are divided: the majority detest me, but the minority, including the most important ones, are on my side."[1]

It had been easy to foresee from the start that Mahler's basic difficulties would spring from his disagreements with Pollini, who was not only perverse, cantankerous, and temperamental, but also a moneygrubber and a man of the theater whose financial realism was fundamentally opposed to Mahler's outlook on life: "I never talk with Pollini any more, not that anything has happened between us, and this is not very encouraging for the future," he wrote to Justine.

When writing to Natalie, whose feelings he had not the same reasons to spare, he gave an even darker picture of the situation: "With Pollini I have reached a point, that must be, ophthalmologically speaking, located between the eyes—the point where, by dint of seeing too much, one no longer sees at all; we simply do not see each other any longer. Since I am, for the time being, employed by him, I have to be constantly on my guard so as not to loose my sense of balance. I have to stare the beast straight in the eye, for I know that at my first moment of inattention it will leap on me. Naturally, this is no way to live, and you can well imagine that under such circumstances I worry a lot. But I beg of you, don't say *anything* to my sister! What would be gained by troubling her rare hours of happiness."[2]

In addition to his financial, professional, and family problems, Mahler was facing new housing difficulties. The lodgings he had reserved in August when he decided to leave the villa proved inconvenient. In September, when a premature cold spell set in, Mahler, returning weary from the opera house, had to light his own stove, which smoked constantly.[3] Having decided that he could no longer endure such discomfort, and that he must be taken care of and served, he finally moved to the Hotel Royal, a modest establishment where his material life would be easier.[4] But after two months he was driven away by the noise, after several sleepless nights due to slamming doors, neighbors dropping their shoes on the floor, and drunks falling in the stairway. Fortunately, the villa so thoughtlessly rented early that summer had finally been sublet. His health had also improved, after causing him considerable worry for several years. Following his doctor's advice, he got into the habit of taking a light meal every three and a half hours instead of his usual substantial meals, and his digestion benefited considerably.

The beginning of the season did not add any new work to Mahler's repertoire. For the opening of the opera on September 1, he conducted *Fidelio;* later he repeated most of the works given the preceding spring. He won one victory over Pollini of which he was particularly proud, conducting uncut performances of *Die Meistersinger* and *Tristan,* "this work which moves me more deeply than any other when I conduct."[5]

In November, Mahler prepared the revival of an opera of which his own judgment was more favorable than that of posterity. For him Anton Rubinstein's *The Demon* contained "marvelous beauties," but the public did not share this enthusiasm: it was performed only once.[6] The critic Armbrust found the music "too Russian" for his taste and deplored the rhythm of the declamation as well as the length of some of the ensembles. Mahler's conducting, both "tranquil, reflective, and impassioned," seemed to him the only reason for a limited success. A few days later—on November 27, Day of Penitence (*Busstag*) in Hamburg—the whole orchestra left with Mahler for Lübeck to give a concert at the Colosseum. It featured a Haydn symphony, the *"Leonore" Overture No. 3,* Mozart and Beethoven arias, and Wagnerian extracts.

At this time Mahler's increasing maturity and self-assurance reminded him of his apparently long-forgotten gift as a composer. On September 15, encouraged by Bülow's benevolent attitude, he wrote him the following note:

"Honored Master,

"With great regret I learned, when I tried to pay my respects to you, that you are not well. In the hope that your indisposition is now past, I beg you to be good enough to grant me a quarter of an hour of your precious time, for it is my dearest wish to show you one of my scores."

"In the event that you agree to this request, would you be good enough to tell the bearer of this note at what time and day it would be convenient for me to see you.

"With my deepest admiration, respectfully yours,

Gustav Mahler."[7]

Tired of seeing his compositions lying uselessly in dusty drawers, he hoped that Bülow would use his immense influence in their favor. He later gave the composer Josef Bohuslav Förster a complete account of this visit to Bülow, made toward the end of September:

Seeing Mahler arrive with his score under his arm, Bülow, after casting an apprehensive glance at it, asked him to sit down at the piano and play it, as thus "he would at least hear an authentic interpretation." After several minutes Mahler, looking up from the piano, saw Bülow standing near the window, holding his hands over his ears. Very embarrassed and aware of the older man's aches and pains, Mahler stopped playing, but Bülow asked him to continue. A few moments later, another worried glance told him that Bülow still had his hands over his ears. Until the end of the piece, Mahler wondered anxiously about this strange attitude. Bülow's nervousness and headaches being legendary, did he disapprove of the playing, find the fortes too violent, the attacks too brusque? Or was it the composition itself that he was condemning thus? The performance ended in deathly silence. Finally, Bülow exclaimed, "If what I have just heard is music, then I no longer understand anything about music!"[8]

"While I was playing my *Totenfeier* to Bülow," Mahler wrote to Löhr, "he was seized by a kind of nervous terror and reacted like a madman; he explained to me that in comparison to my work, *Tristan* seemed a Haydn symphony."[9] Replying a short time later to Strauss, who had asked him to send some of his works, he wrote: "As for my scores, dear friend, I am on the point of locking them away forever. You cannot imagine the *constant* rejections that I experience! In the long run, I can no longer stand seeing these gentlemen fall out of their chairs and explain to me that it would be incredibly presumptuous to perform them. This endless, useless peddling of them! A week ago, Bülow almost died while I was playing one of my works to him. You have never experienced anything like it, and you cannot understand that one finally loses faith. And, dear God, the world can get along without my works!"[10]

Mahler's disappointment was as great as the hopes he had cherished, for Bülow was not only a brilliant conductor and pianist and a superb interpreter of Beethoven and the classical repertoire, but also a conductor and music critic who had contributed more than anyone else to the propagation of the music of his time, including that of Liszt, Wagner, Bizet, and Bruckner.

The tragedy that had befallen him in Munich in 1866–67 had hurt him both in his love for his wife and in his friendship and admiration for Wagner. As he had admitted at the time, "the strings of my instrument are not just out of tune, they're broken." Nevertheless, he had put his genius as an interpreter and his fantastic memory in the service of both classics and contemporaries, tending to neglect Wagner not only for Mozart and Beethoven, but above all for Brahms. After leaving Meiningen,[11] where he had married the actress Marie Schauser in 1883, but where he was irked by the limits that provincial life imposed on his activities, he had settled in Hamburg. In 1887, following Bülow's quarrel with Pollini, Hermann Wolff, the great impresario, persuaded him to assume the directorship of both the Berlin Philharmonic Concerts and the Hamburg New Subscription Concerts, which he held until his death. He had always been intransigent and irritable, and the fact that he was in almost constant agony did not soften his character. Consequently, the atmosphere around Bülow was charged with electricity, and a storm could burst at any moment. All Germany knew about his clash with Count Hochberg, the intendant of the Berlin Opera, who in 1887 refused him access to the opera hall because of his repeated public criticism of the count's administration of the opera. On one occasion, after a poor performance of Meyerbeer's *Prophète* at the opera, he had even gone so far as to interrupt a concert and address the audience in the middle of a concert: "Ladies and gentlemen, we shall now play the march from *Le Prophète* not as the Hülsen circus plays it, but as the composer wrote it." (This was his sarcastic nickname for the Berlin Opera, after its superintendent, Hülsen.) In order to be avenged on Hochberg for having forbidden him to enter the opera, he played Beethoven's *"Danse russe"*[12] at a concert a few days later, a piece that in fact constituted a somewhat obscure allusion to the aria *"Se vuol ballare, Signor Contino"* (If Your Lordship wishes to dance) from the first act of *Le Nozze di Figaro*. The most surprising thing about the whole affair was that the public actually understood this subtle allusion and applauded him frantically.

Such occurrences were far from rare in the career of this great musician, whose eccentric behavior in public was often discussed in public and private. As a sort of aristocratic refinement, he always wore white gloves to conduct. Moreover, by glowering at the latecomers and refusing to begin the concert before they had reached their seats, he endeavored to educate the public and to instill it with respect for music. He was notorious for his sarcasms, his scathing irony, his icy humor, and his witticisms. During a rehearsal in which the Hamburg Singverein took part, he stopped the orchestra to make a remark to one of the musicians. The choristers started to chat and he bluntly shot out at them: "I wish to remind the ladies and gentlemen that the Capitol has already been saved." Another time, when the audience booed and hissed Liszt's symphonic poem *Die Ideale*, he called for silence and said, "Would those who are booing kindly leave the hall, for it is against the rules to boo here." The press stormed at him after every such incident, while his friends cautioned him against any fresh wrangle with the public, but the weight of his authority and the power of his genius silenced his adversaries every time.

One day, after bringing the house down with a superb performance of Beethoven's *Ninth Symphony,* he imperatively silenced the cheers and said, "Like you, I am overwhelmed. I am also deeply moved by your delight in this work of genius. I am complying with your heartfelt desire when I tell you that I shall perform it again right here and now." Part of the audience had started to applaud and others were on their way out when he spoke again, asking with exquisite politeness that everyone keep their seats, since all the exits had been locked carefully upon his orders.[13]

Although he frankly admitted his inability to understand Mahler the young and somewhat revolutionary composer, he was in no wise sparing of his admiration for Mahler the conductor, which he displayed in the same eccentric manner: "It is amusing," the latter wrote, "to see how, in his usual strange fashion, Bülow takes every opportunity of bringing me into the limelight in public as noticeably as possible. I sit in the front row and he always points out the most beautiful passages to me. As soon as he sees me, he bows ostentatiously. Sometimes he speaks to me from the podium. When he is conducting an unknown work, he hands me the score so I can follow it during the performance."[14]

One evening, after a performance by Mahler at the opera, Bülow, who was seated in the front row, went on applauding loudly, apparently not having noticed that the rest of the audience had left, and consequently obliging Mahler to return and bow to him alone. Bruno Walter tells of another day when Bülow, instead of responding to the applause that greeted his appearance, stepped down from the podium to offer his baton to Mahler. It seems that only Mahler's embarrassed refusal persuaded him to return to the podium.[15]

Mahler deeply admired Bülow and his symphonic interpretations. On March 28, 1892, the latter conducted Beethoven's *"Eroica"* in Berlin so superbly and so impressively that the public applauded even more wildly than usual. Whereupon, in a speech improvised with his customary brio he proceeded to dedicate his own performance to Chancellor Bismarck: "Beethoven's brother and the Beethoven of German politics," thereby proving once again his courage and independence for the famous chancellor had just been dismissed following a violent clash with the young Emperor Wilhelm II. He had hardly finished his speech before pandemonium broke loose in the hall, in the form of an exchange of frantic applause and furious booing between the chancellor's supporters and detractors. Irritated, Bülow took out his handkerchief and contemptuously dusted off his shoes.[16] He made the same speech in Hamburg on April 1, but here there was no uproar, for feelings did not run so high. Mahler attended the Hamburg concert, and, upon meeting a lady acquaintance who was as moved as he, said to her, "Never forget this evening! You have never heard anything like it before, and never will again: it is supreme perfection!"[17]

On November 30, 1891, Bülow conducted another concert in Hamburg[18] and made all sorts of jokes directly aimed at Mahler. Brahms happened to be in Hamburg, his native town, so he had the latter called to his box and asked him to attend the concert with him. He had already told all his friends and acquaintances about the famous performance of *Don Giovanni* in Budapest: "Musical circles here were greatly impressed," Mahler wrote to Justi, "and I hope to find myself referred to soon as 'our' Kapellmeister Mahler by the critics, etc. . . . which usually doesn't happen until one has spent twenty or thirty years in the city, and even less when one has achieved this in my usual manner, 'by storm.' I had supper with Brahms afterward at a restaurant. He is notorious for his 'irony' and it is really very unusual for him to take another person, particularly another musician, seriously and to show such heartfelt warmth. . . ."[19]

The first winter months of 1891–92, and especially December—a moment when activity at the Hamburg Opera slowed down—were for Mahler a period of reflection, concentration, and mental self-examination; at the time, he was obviously under the powerful influence of Nietzsche.[20] "I have read a lot this year," he wrote to Löhr, "and a lot of books have impressed me lastingly; they have developed and even transformed my view of the world and my conception of life. . . . Has it ever occurred to you that we have seen a new generation grow up—that the ideas for which we fought have now become commonplace—and that now we even have to fight the young in defense of what we have acquired? Think about it and you'll shake your head when looking at the good world around you, as I do, when I occasionally peer at it."

This period of transition was soon to bear fruit. Mahler's entire personality was taking a new turn. He had indeed won the struggle to assert his position as a conductor; he was no longer unknown. His first works had been composed amid storms of despair and passion, but he was now conscious of his strength, his fame, and the knowledge that he would be able to make himself heard. This fact was to play, from then on, a decisive part in his creative activity. He now composed with the certainty of having his works performed, unlike many other musicians who have found their *raison d'être* in the sole act of creating.

Poverty and the failure of his first creative efforts had forced him to become a conductor. This activity had for a long time absorbed him entirely, but now success had reawakened his creative instincts. This transitory period took place in a partly voluntary and wholly necessary solitude. "It really is strange that I am condemned to be alone everywhere; I accustom myself to this idea with as much pain as to that of attaching myself to someone."[21] "I am constantly invited to dinner, but most of the time I refuse."

Faced with new problems, Mahler re-examined every aspect of composition. About this time J. B. Förster saw him plunged into a study of the great contrapuntalists, and noticed on his piano the cantatas of Bach, "that Castalian spring by means of which I wash away the dust of the theater."[22]

December 1891 brought no new productions to the Hamburg Opera. On the fifth, Mahler conducted *Don Giovanni* for the centenary of Mozart's death and prepared two premieres for January, Goldmark's *Die Königin von Saba* and Tchaikovsky's *Eugene Onegin*. Toward the middle of the month he went to Vienna for a few days in order to take care of various family matters, in particular Otto and his army medical examination. Löhr had just returned from Italy, and Mahler again asked him to supervise Otto's studies—a useless request, since Löhr had no more authority over the boy than Justi.

Back in Hamburg around the middle of December, Mahler started rehearsing *Eugene Onegin*,[23] the premiere of which (the first in Germany) was set for January 19, 1892.

Tchaikovsky was to conduct; he reached Hamburg the day before the premiere and led the final rehearsal.[24] He returned to the opera house the same night, and Mahler's conducting of *Tannhäuser* filled him with admiration. The newspapers announced the next morning that, amazed by the exceptional care with which Mahler had rehearsed *Onegin*, Tchaikovsky had decided to let him conduct.[25]

In a letter to his nephew Bobyk, Tchaikovsky admitted that because of certain changes in the recitative he had lost the beat several times at the rehearsal. He added, "By the way, the local conductor is by no means the usual mediocrity, but a real genius dying to conduct the premiere." In the same letter, Tchaikovsky wrote of his disappointment with the stage direction, the costumes and the scenery, which was not surprising, considering the usual policies of Pollini. The evocation of Russian life and particularly the Mazurka in the third scene seemed absolute nonsense to him. Fortunately, Kathi Bettaque had sung Tatiana beautifully, and the orchestra, under Mahler's direction, had been "wonderful."

"I have been successful," Tchaikovsky wrote the following morning. "There was applause after every scene, even if it was not very loud. But then, that is not surprising, since *Onegin* includes no noisy effects."[26]

Mahler's fondness for Russian operas and particularly for Tchaikovsky is not disclosed in his correspondence of that time. In a letter written to Justi during the rehearsals of *Onegin*, he speaks of it as "mediocre rubbish" (*sehr mässiges Machwerk*). On the evening of the premiere, Mahler was invited by Pollini to a big supper, where he had a long conversation with the Russian composer, who recalled meeting him in Leipzig. Mahler described him to Justi as "an elderly gentleman, very likable, with elegant manners, who seems quite rich and reminds me somehow of Mihalovics."

The Hamburg critics underlined *Eugene Onegin*'s undeniable weaknesses —its lack of action and the faulty dramatic construction of the libretto.

Despite the quality of the music, Armbrust considered quite rightly that the opera appealed only to a limited audience.

In January the Vienna Philharmonic gave the first performance of Strauss's *Don Juan*. Mahler, having read a violent attack by Hanslick in a Vienna paper, wrote to Justi to ask what Otto had thought of the music. He later sent the enthusiastic reply on to Strauss to give him an idea of the "favorable impression his *Don Juan* had made on the young people of Vienna."

Toward the end of the month a messenger from Bülow arrived in haste to tell Mahler that Bülow's ill health would not permit him to conduct the next subscription concert. "Very happily I drew up a superb program," Mahler wrote to Justi. "Bülow had no sooner read it than he declared himself recovered!" Orders and counterorders followed before the concert, which Bülow finally conducted himself. Mahler nevertheless knew from then on that he must be prepared to replace Bülow at a moment's notice.

At the end of November, still under the painful influence of the scene at Bülow's, Mahler had written to Löhr: "You see, I myself have begun to think that my works are obtuse nonsense or . . . decide for yourself how to end the phrase. I can't stand all this any longer!"[27] but his creative instinct soon triumphed over all his doubts. Scarcely a month after writing those bitter words, Mahler, who had had the Arnim-Brentano anthology forwarded to him from Vienna, was back at work. "I now have the *Wunderhorn* in my hands. With that self-knowledge which is natural to creators, I can add that once again the result will be worth while!"[28]

In fact, in one month, Mahler composed five new songs on *Wunderhorn* texts: five lieder whose unusual character he tried to define in the title *Humoresken*. The accompaniments were immediately conceived for orchestra. On January 28, *"Der Schildwache Nachtlied,"* sketched out in 1888 in Leipzig as part of an opera, was completed.[29] On February 1 it was *"Verlor'ne Müh',"* followed at once by *"Wer hat dies Liedlein erdacht"* on February 6, *"Das himmlische Leben"*[30] on the tenth, and *"Trost im Unglück"* on the twenty-second.

Many years later Mahler was to tell Natalie that *Das himmlische Leben* had been the first to break forth from the creative source that had for so long remained dormant and stagnant in Budapest. He pointed out the hidden treasures of this apparently modest little song, which had given birth to "five pieces of the *Third* and *Fourth Symphonies.*"[31] *Das himmlische Leben*, in its orchestral form, was completed on February 12, two days after the sketch; the full score of *Trost im Unglück* is dated February 26, four days after the sketch. At the end of this song, Mahler wrote: "5 Humoresken completed." After four years of almost complete creative stagnation, these large vocal poems had poured out of him "like a mountain torrent"[32] in exactly the same way as *Das klagende Lied* in 1880, the *Lieder eines fahrenden Gesellen* in 1884, and the *First Symphony* in 1888. Mahler then began to sense that the "special" character of these lieder would allow him to integrate them into a symphonic structure. "I have found a good place for the *Wunderhorn,* and it is now part of my symphony, nothing less than the *Third.*"[33]

In April he wrote to Justi that the *Wunderhorn Lieder* were completed, and that the scores were already copied: "They are stranger still than the former ones, they are all 'humor,' in the best and truest sense of the word; something for which only a few exceptional men are created, and I will probably have to put them away with the others. It is really an exhilarating prospect for me to write a whole library for my drawers! As a matter of fact, I am in a very good mood, despite my recent attacks of biting insults; perhaps these very attacks are being transmuted into a symphony."

The three volumes of youthful lieder that Mahler had given to the publisher Schott had just been published and put on sale.[34] He wrote to Justi early in February to ask if she had seen them in the windows of music stores and whether any of them had already been sold. Having begun to compose again, Mahler was thinking of the coming summer, which he was determined to spend at last in a secluded, peaceful spot. Justine and Natalie were asked to prospect the Bavarian and Austrian Alps in search of this ideal location, which must be calm yet not too isolated, as otherwise "the first month everything is marvelous, the second, one wanders like a lost soul, and the third one flees in despair, preferring to breathe the heaviest and most poisonous town air just to find oneself among men again."[35] Mahler wanted a fairly large and comfortable house so that he could invite his friends, but there should be no piano in the neighborhood. Otto was to arrange to spend these three months in the country, as Mahler was unable to support two households simultaneously.

In Hamburg, Mahler had lived successively in Pollini's villa, the Hotel Streit, a modest private apartment, the small Hotel Royal, and had finally returned to the Streit. Early in 1892 he settled down in a rented apartment more expensive than the first but comfortable enough to spare him constant practical worries.[36] Always fearing the cold, Mahler found it warm enough, but this bachelor life, with no one to look after his clothes and his comfort, nevertheless started to weigh upon him. Once the lieder were completed, Hamburg life attracted him again. He had been invited several times to Bülow's for dinner, and the number of his acquaintances was increasing every day. They were more or less "the same as Bülow's," that is, to say, "the most important members of the local society" who "are not stuffed shirts." He had been asked to dinner "at the home of the most important man in Hamburg, Burgomaster Petersen, who had received him with great cordiality."[37] Unfortunately, the more Hamburg and its society pleased Mahler, the less happy he was at the opera: he felt that he would soon be "involved in a peculiar conflict there."

Invited to dine at the home of Anna Bernhardt, a prominent member of Hamburg society, a few days after the sudden death on May 12 of Franz Greve, Klafsky's husband, Mahler remained stubborn and unmoved by the other guests' sorrow. "What is so sad about it?" he was heard to say. "What is sad is the *Götterdämmerung* rehearsal I had today." The others then reminded him of Greve's kindness, only to hear him reply, "It always upsets me when people say about an imbecile that he is 'good.' Stupidity is a bad thing in itself!"

Mahler had undoubtedly suffered from Greve's stupidity at the opera, and it is likely that the "weepers" and their questionably sincere mourning had incited him to speak these words, clearly intended to shock. He was to be exasperated in the same way by the lamentations of the Hamburg bourgeoisie at the time of Bülow's death.

In March, while still working on the instrumentation of his *Humoresken,* Mahler conducted for his own benefit before a crowded auditorium. The *"Eroica" Symphony* was followed by a performance of *Fidelio,* after which he "received twenty-seven laurel wreaths, as well as innumerable bouquets, and various gifts."[38] His interpretation of the *"Eroica"* nonetheless aroused serious reservations, and from then on Josef Sittard never stopped criticizing his "scandalous" innovations and his scorn of traditions. He did not deny the technical quality of the performance and found nothing to criticize in the two first movements and the Finale, "despite some surprising changes in tempo." He protested mainly at the slowness of the Scherzo and Trio, "which seemed contrary to the spirit of the work," and at the acceleration in the final coda.

Mahler had too many worries at the opera to let himself be upset by the critics. Relations with Pollini were getting worse and worse. "He exasperates me so," he wrote to Justi, "that I cannot guarantee that one day or another I won't throw something at his head if some object happens to be lying handy. . . . Naturally, this worries me for many reasons. It is really impossible ever to be happy in this life! On the one hand I have a public that understands me perfectly and really adores me, and on the other I have an employer who is 'dumb as an ox.' "

Mahler felt that Pollini "watched with a certain jealousy as his popularity with the Hamburg public grew": "Strange as it may seem, he is beginning to be afraid of me and will no doubt do his best to disgust me of my post."[39] In another letter he tried to tone down his bitterness: "It is mostly a feeling I have that sooner or later things will come to a head. Hamburg is after all not a place in which it will ever be possible for me to be completely myself. Therefore, I consider this position solely as a stopgap on the way, but naturally I cannot deny that I am tired of this eternal wandering and I am yearning for a 'homeland.' Here again there is not a soul with whom I can share anything else but air and light. It is strange how strong my homesickness for Vienna is just now. For eight years, I haven't felt this. . . ."

Most of March had been spent at the opera rehearsing a work of the new French school, the first Mahler had had a chance to direct. Based on Zola's famous novel *Le Rêve,* the opera by Alfred Bruneau seemed to him "very difficult but most interesting," demanding all his attention, no doubt because of the totally new musical language. Bruneau, who was also the music critic of both *Le Figaro* and *Gil Blas,* attended the premiere on March 29.[40]

"I went to Hamburg, where Gustav Mahler rehearsed *Le Rêve* magnificently. Mahler is not content with composing the vast and flamboyant symphonies we all have applauded, he is a conductor of rare vivacity and intelligence. The ungainly motion of his long, unsteady legs,[41] the weird mobility of his skinny frame, his brusque commanding gestures, his clean-shaven face, his glasses quivering on his hooked nose, all made him resemble some Hoffmannesque doctor. He showed, while conducting, a communicative and irresistible faith not reserved solely for his own works, but from which his colleagues benefited greatly. . . . The performance was brilliant," continued Bruneau. "Gustav Mahler surpassed himself. The auditorium was filled with garrison officers, whose resplendent uniforms sparkled with gold and silver. It might have been a military gala."

The whole French colony turned up in force, and the first performance was a brilliant event, but the critics were uniformly hostile. They found the music "too light and transparent," calling it a sort of discreet, uniform "murmur" full of "harmonic monstrosities painful to the nervous system."[42] *Le Rêve* was performed only twice.

Since early 1892, Mahler had been negotiating, through Pollini, with Sir Augustus Harris, manager and director of Covent Garden, who was organizing a Wagnerian season in London that summer. Having failed to enlist the services of Hans Richter, who was engaged by the Vienna Opera all through June, Harris had contacted Mahler and had booked the best Hamburg singers as well as some Bayreuth stars. His proposed fee was modest but Mahler accepted it nevertheless, mainly "because of the honor."[43] "In case of success, German opera might prosper at Covent Garden annually."

Mahler spent much time with Pollini working out the details of this project, and in April he began to study English. He wrote several letters in that language, took lessons from Arnold Berliner, a young and intelligent physician he had met a few months earlier.[44] He went walking with him several times a week, conversing in English, and each day he filled his student's notebooks with words and phrases that might prove useful to him during rehearsals.

For the opera's annual Good Friday concert of sacred music, Mahler decided to direct at last one work by Bruckner and chose the *Te Deum.* The rapidity of certain tempos in the Mozart *Requiem,* which preceded it, again shocked Josef Sittard, who found such haste incompatible with the religious spirit of the work.[45]

At that time Bruckner was a relatively new musical figure in Hamburg, a city known for its conservative spirit. None of his works were known there but the *Seventh Symphony,* which had been played at a philharmonic concert six years before. The *Te Deum,* however, was greeted with unusual warmth by most of the critics. For once, Sittard showed himself capable of understanding a new idiom. He recognized in Bruckner a composer who was "in his way, a genius," and appreciated the beauty of the modulations and the intrumentation, the "periodic construction and harmonic richness of the work."[46]

Emil Krause was to make certain reservations in the *Fremdenblatt,* but Louis Bödecker, in the *Tageblatt,* expressed wholehearted enthusiasm: no new religious music had ever interested him so much.

Mahler wrote the good news to the old master: "Honored master and friend, at last I have the joy of telling you that I have conducted one of your works. Yesterday, Good Friday, I conducted your magnificent, powerful *Te Deum.* Both the public and the performers were moved deeply by the majesty of its architecture and the nobility of its ideas. At the end of the performance I witnessed what I consider to be the greatest triumph that a work can obtain: the public remained motionless, and it was only when the conductor and the performers began to leave the stage that the thunder of applause broke out.

"You would have been happy with the performance: rarely have I seen a group of performers work with so much enthusiasm. The reviews will not appear for several days because of the Easter holidays, but I shall not fail to send them to you. 'Bruckner' has now made his triumphal entry into Hamburg. I clasp your hand warmly, my noble friend, and am, in the real sense of the word, yours, Gustav Mahler."

At the same time, Bruckner received from Zinne, one of his disciples living in Hamburg, a letter confirming both the quality and the success of the performance and the admiration of his former pupil.[47] According to Zinne, the *Te Deum,* and especially the final chorus, electrified the public.[48] Mahler then showed his admiration for the *Te Deum* by crossing out on the score the words "for soli, chorus, organ and orchestra" and replacing them with "for the tongues of heaven-blessed angels, chastened hearts, and souls purified by fire"[49] and he wrote, in a letter to Justi: "Received a touching letter from Bruckner which reveals the poor man's complete frustration. It really is hard to have to wait seventy years to be 'played.' Unless the omens deceive, my fate will not be different from his."

Early in the spring news from Vienna and the Breitegasse (where the family apartment was located) became more alarming than ever. Almost every six weeks, Justi, using various excuses, asked for money in addition to the fixed sum Mahler was sending her regularly. Sometimes it was to pay Otto's teachers, sometimes to cover a debt. In order to convince Gustav of her good will, she told him of the small privations that she imposed upon herself in the spirit of economy, but this he did not appreciate. He wanted her to enjoy life, to take care of her health, and not to deprive herself for Otto's benefit. Other young men before him had acquired an education without spending fortunes. "Believe me, the teacher is a secondary question—it is the student who matters!" he wrote to her.

Just before leaving for London, Mahler wrote to Justi to remind her that his salary was not elastic: "The more one subtracts from it, the more it diminishes," he complained. Besides, he was sure that three people could live within the limits imposed by his monthly remittances, "Fritz does not seem to me to worry much about Otto. On that point too he is probably a fatalist! In truth, that is the point of view of all the people who are too lazy to follow an affair through to its conclusion. And it is characteristic of this fatalism that it exists usually at the expense of others and what they possess. As soon as those others aren't there, the fatalism disappears. . . . I am not myself a fatalist until something is completed. While it is unfinished, fatalism is nothing but cowardice and indignity. . . ."

Mahler seemed unaware of the fact that his brother had left the conservatory in April, and without a diploma. Alois too caused him endless worry: if only he could believe him, trust him, he could have recommended him to some of his friends among Hamburg's businessmen! But as a result of his constant lack of caution, Alois had just barely escaped being sent to debtor's prison.

The chamber-music concert given on April 19 in the Logenhaus Auditorium by two singers, Dorothea Schmidt and Richard Dannenberg, gave Mahler a chance to hear the first public performances of some of his lieder recently published by Schott. Accompanied at the piano by the critic Armbrust, Dannenberg sang *"Hans und Grete"* and two songs from the *Wunderhorn: "Aus! Aus!"* and *"Nicht wiedersehen."* Sittard, who had commented on the collection when it was published, made some rather vague reservations regarding these two songs. According to him, Mahler had not "listened to the advice of the musical ear" when writing chains of fifths in the bass.[50]

The *Fremdenblatt* was more favorable, speaking of Mahler's "original inventiveness" (rare praise from contemporary critics), the perfection of the declamation, and the quality of the themes, which disclosed "an experienced composer equipped to avoid anything commonplace."[51]

In April, Mahler conducted only a few performances at the opera, but as usual, starting May 8, Pollini entrusted to him a large section of the Wagner festival (all the major dramas except for *Rienzi*, the *Fliegende Holländer*, and *Lohengrin*).

The 1891–92 season was the least active of Mahler's Hamburg stay. He conducted only seventy-eight performances (Weber's operas were temporarily absent): *Fidelio, Don Giovanni,* and *Die Zauberflöte* each appeared six times on his list; *Eugene Onegin* and *Der widerspenstigen Zähmung* three times, *Wilhelm Tell* once, and finally four contemporary operas, *Le Rêve, Asrael, The Demon,* and *Die Königin von Saba.*

On May 26, the day after *Die Götterdämmerung*, which concluded the Wagner cycle, Mahler embarked at Cuxhaven for Southampton and reached London after an excellent crossing. The city's immediate impression upon him was comparable to what "one feels upon seeing the ocean for the first time." "The spectacle is so imposing that one suddenly understands what has happened to humanity." Mahler first lived in a hotel and then took lodgings in a private house "near the port"[52] where he had to "speak" English, since his hosts did not understand German.

Sir Augustus Harris, manager of Drury Lane Theater since 1879, and of Covent Garden since 1888, was, like Neumann, Staegemann, and Pollini, a man dedicated to the theater from birth. Son of a stage manager, brought up in the wings, he contributed more than anyone else to the development and formation of the English taste for opera, and particularly for the German repertoire. After having organized a German season at Drury Lane in 1882 with the help of Pollini, Harris had decided to give the English public another chance to discover Wagner's works. London had heard *Der Ring des Nibelungen* only once, when it was staged by Angelo Neumann at Covent Garden in 1882. Harris was now preparing Covent Garden, which had had electricity installed a few months earlier, for an early summer *Ring* cycle together with *Tristan und Isolde, Tannhäuser,* and *Fidelio.*

Most of the singers signed up by Harris and Pollini were from the Hamburg Opera: Klafsky, Bettaque, Schumann-Heink, Alvary, Landau, Lissmann, and Wiegand, plus a few Bayreuth stars: Rosa Sucher, Theodor Reichmann, and Grengg. The orchestra had been especially recruited in England and was strengthened by the "special instrumentalists (brought from Germany) necessary to play the complex works of Wagner."[53]

The performances were organized on a subscription basis at regular intervals. The *Ring,* for example, was to be given on four successive Wednesdays, but because of Alvary's vanity (he wished to make his London debut in his best role), the season opened with *Siegfried* on June 8, followed by *Fidelio, Tristan,* the *Ring* cycle, and two performances of *Tannhäuser.* To satisfy public demand, Harris also gave three performances of *Tristan,* one of *Fidelio,* and a *Ring* cycle at Drury Lane. Thus Mahler conducted eighteen performances in London between June 8 and July 23. The rehearsals turned out to be long and strenuous, for some of the singers had never worked under Mahler's direction, and he soon realized that the orchestra was mediocre.

Hermann Klein, critic of the *Sunday Times,* met Mahler immediately upon his arrival in London. Mahler's appearance and conducting immediately reminded him of Anton Seidl, who had conducted Neumann's London Wagner season; he found Mahler "not unworthy to be compared with him in termperamental qualities, well-balanced force, and rare concentration of energy." Klein reported that Mahler's determination to use the English language was a source of great amusement. Even with those who spoke German well, "he would rather spend five minutes in an effort to find the English word he wanted than resort to his mother tongue or allow anyone else to supply the equivalent. Consequently, a short chat with Mahler involved a liberal allowance of time. For the same reason, his orchestral rehearsals proved extremely lengthy and, to a spectator, vastly amusing." Klein was amazed to see that he knew almost all the Wagnerian scores by heart, and that he made each orchestral group rehearse the difficult passages separately.[54]

Hermann Klein describes his impressions during a rehearsal of *Tristan* to which Mahler had invited him: "And then it was that I began to realize the remarkable magnetic power and technical mastery of Mahler's conducting. He reminded me in many ways of Richter; he used the same strong, decisive beat; the same clear, unmistakable definition of time and rhythm. His men, whom he rehearsed first of all in sections, soon understood him without difficulty. Hence the unity of idea and expression existing between orchestra and singers that distinguished these performances of the *Ring* under Mahler as compared with any previously seen in London."[55]

To his remarks on Mahler as conductor, Klein added a physical description of the man: "Mahler was now in his thirty-second year. He was rather short, of thin, spare build, with a dark complexion and small piercing eyes that stared at you with a not unkindly expression through large gold spectacles. I found him extraordinarily modest for a musician of his rare gifts and established reputation. He would never consent to talk about himself or his compositions. Indeed the latter might have been non-existent for all that one ever heard about them; but his efforts to speak English, even with those who spoke German fluently, were untiring as well as amusing, though they tended to prolong conversation."[56]

The success of *Siegfried* at the opening night on June 8 was so great that Harris at once arranged for a second performance at Drury Lane five days later. Bernard Shaw, then a lively music critic, devoted a long article to the event which, as usual, is more amusing than instructive. "The performance was vigorous, complete, earnest—in short, all that was needed to make *Siegfried* enormously interesting to operatic starvelings like the Covent Garden's frequenters. The German orchestra is rough; but the men know the work, and are under perfect and willing discipline." Shaw seems unaware that the orchestra was in fact English, and went on to criticize its low "standard of tone quality." He considered the Covent Garden orchestra capable of a wider range of gradation from pianissimo to fortissimo.[57] "Mahler," he said, "knows the score thoroughly" and "sets the *tempi* with excellent judgment." The Hamburg scenery belonged, he added, to "the usual German type, majestic, but intensely prosaic."[58]

The success of that first performance, which lasted from eight o'clock until half-past twelve, was tremendous, "the gallery applauded wildly at the end of each act," according to Shaw, but London criticism was not very sophisticated at the time, and we learn little from the papers about Mahler's conducting, his style, technique, and Wagnerian conceptions. The critics noted, however, that "as is the German custom," he sat, or rather stood, not close to the stage, but among his musicians. This seems to imply that England still clung to the outdated custom of having the conductor of an opera orchestra stand with his back to his musicians.[59]

From London, Mahler sent several notes to Justi and to his new friend,

Arnold Berliner, with whom he had been taking English lessons. In his amusing English, he gives the latter some information about the Covent Garden season. Ever since the first performance, London had seemed to him a favorable terrain for German art. A week later *Tristan* was equally successful, and he found himself "acclaimed everywhere as one of the glories of the season."[60] Pollini was being especially accommodating, and Schumann-Heink, contrary to her usual attitude, bowed to all his demands.

After *Tristan,* given on June 15 at Covent Garden and June 18 at Drury Lane, Mahler conducted from June 22 to July 18 each of the four *Ring* dramas, first at one theater and then, after a five-day interval, at the other. When Sucher left for Bayreuth, Klafsky took over the role of Brünnhilde. In *Das Rheingold,* Shaw deplored the "defects of the orchestra" and poked fun at certain singers as well as at Lissmann's staging. He objected to the interruption of the performance by an interval, and to the "heaviness" of Grengg (Wotan); he also condemned Lissmann's "shouting and singing out of tune." Shaw's reprobation proved to be an exception among London critics, who otherwise unanimously praised Mahler.[61]

Doubtless Shaw found no cause for humor in *Die Walküre,* for his brief criticism merely takes exception to some cuts in the second act and the insufficiency of Reichmann (Wotan), who was then considered by the whole of Germany to be the greatest Wotan of his time.[62] Klafsky and Alvary were enormously successful in *Siegfried* and *Die Götterdämmerung.* The final *Ring* drama gave *The Times* the occasion to praise "Mahler's admirable conducting" while regretting the excision of the Norn scene.[63] In his last article on the German season Shaw praised some of the singers—Klafsky, Schumann-Heink, and Alvary—but never mentioned Mahler. He also remarked on the orchestra's "perfect knowledge of the work."

When Mahler conducted *Fidelio* at Drury Lane on July 2, it was, incredible as it may seem, the first time that Londoners had had the opportunity of hearing Beethoven's great opera in its original German version. Some aspects of Mahler's interpretation surprised and shocked the English critics, particularly the *"Leonore" Overture No. 3* placed at the beginning of the second act. ". . . we venture to say that the greatest of operatic preludes was very badly treated," the critic of the *Daily Telegraph* wrote. As in Hamburg, Mahler had adhered to the tradition of beginning the Allegro slowly and accelerating gradually until the forte restatement of the theme. At the beginning of the coda (presto) Mahler introduced a similar effect. The critic questioned his right to take such liberties and attacked interpreters who consider themselves "superior to the composers."[64]

Mahler remained undisturbed by these attacks, since the public clearly supported him and absolved him from his "blasphemy" by thunderous applause. "I had to take a curtain call after each act, and the entire hall shouted 'Mahler' until I reappeared."[65]

The French composer Paul Dukas attended this performance of *Fidelio* and later remembered "the incredible revelation of Beethoven's genius" which he experienced that evening. Thanks to a "conductor of genius" he felt as if he were "present at the creation of the masterpiece." Mahler's controversial interpretation of the *"Leonore" Overture No. 3* particularly aroused his admiration.[66]

Mahler's burden of work was undoubtedly exhausting during those six London weeks. He complained that with *Die Götterdämmerung* he had been faced with "the most incredible difficulties." The quality of the performances had deteriorated from day to day, though this did not lessen the public's enthusiasm. Before ending the season with two brilliant performances of *Tannhäuser*,[67] he managed to free himself of the obligation of conducting Nessler's ever popular *Trompeter von Säkkingen*. The *Morning Post* briefly announced: "Herr Mahler is evidently not in sympathy with this work, for he relinquished the baton to Herr Feld, his assistant."

On July 23, the day after the second *Tannhäuser* performance, a weary Mahler left London for Berchtesgaden, where his family was awaiting him. In a villa built on the side of the Salzberg, later notorious as the site of Hitler's hideout,[68] he could rest for a month and recover from a season that had been materially sucessful but artistically frustrating. He had undeniably obtained a considerable acclaim in London, and this is all the more remarkable since the English audiences were not yet fully aware of the importance of a conductor.

During the next few years in Hamburg, Mahler received further offers from Harris. No doubt deliberately, Mahler demanded such high fees that the negotiations always fell through. He was no longer willing to sacrifice his summer composition to such uncertain undertakings. The London season had not only shortened his vacation by two months, but, owing to its hasty and improvised preparation, it had brought him little artistic enjoyment.

"Fortunately, something always
remains to be harvested . . . so let
us not be idle . . ."

# CHAPTER 18

*Mahler in Hamburg (III) — Berchtesgaden and Stein-
bach — The Cholera Epidemic — The Second Symphony — New Family Problems (July 1892–August
1893)*

Since he did not arrive in Berchtesgaden until the end of July, Mahler had
only three weeks of freedom left, and this seemed too short a time to begin
composing. In fact, the long interruption of his creative work was starting to
obsess him, and he occasionally lost faith. Nevertheless, during this respite
which he called "his first vacation," he gave himself wholeheartedly to his
favorite sports: long walks and mountain climbing, both particularly tempting around Berchtesgaden, with its lovely landscapes. Wanting to share these
joys with some of his close friends, he managed to create a continuous
"coming and going" at the Villa Hechter all through the month of August.[1]
Thus his kindness triumphed over grave financial worries and the profound
desire for calm and isolation which in later years was to rule his summer life.
We can picture him, happily climbing the surrounding mountains and rowing energetically on alpine lakes.

Around mid-August, Mahler went to nearby Salzburg, and from there to
visit Löhr in Sankt Gilgen. After that he was to meet, in Salzburg, the well-
known singer Amalie Joachim, who wanted to work on some of his songs
with him, for she planned to sing them the following winter with the Berlin
Philharmonic.[2] Max Steinitzer, her accompanist and Mahler's friend ever
since Leipzig, had arranged this meeting and was to confirm the date. Still
without a word as to this date, Mahler told Justi to forward any telegram to
him urgently, and left for Sankt Gilgen, where two days later he received this
strange message: "Saturday bring also student Steinitzer will be sent immediately by messenger. Justine" (*Samstag fahren den Schüler auch mitbringen
Steinitzer wird sofort durch Boten geschickt. Justine*). After railing against

his sister's "muddled mind" Mahler, with Löhr's help, was finally able to decipher the actual text of the telegram: "Saturday bring also Wandering Student. Steinitzer. Sent immediately by messenger. Justine" (*Samstag fahrenden Schüler auch mitbringen. Steinitzer. Wird sofort durch Boten geschickt. Justine*). Amalie Joachim had told Steinitzer that she wanted to read the *Lieder eines fahrenden Gesellen* with Mahler, and Justine had sent the score to her brother by messenger. This bizarre deformation of the telegram long remained a Mahler household joke.

After taking Löhr and Steinitzer to Berchtesgaden for a few days, Mahler left for Hamburg. On August 26, he stopped in Munich to see the Krzyzanowskis, and on the twenty-seventh he was in Berlin. Just as he was about to leave for Hamburg, he met the baritone Theodor Bertram, who, "his teeth chattering with fright," told him how he and several other singers from the opera had fled from Hamburg because of the spreading cholera epidemic. At first localized around the harbor, the epidemic, which had broken out on August 16, had begun to spread across the city, arousing panic.

Having suffered from grave digestive disorders, Mahler, fearing contagion, decided to write to Berliner for details and to wait for the answer. A pessimistic telegram from Berliner informed him that the opera would remain closed for two more weeks, so Mahler returned to Munich to wait for the epidemic to end.[3] Terribly worried because she believed him to be in Hamburg, Justi had sent several messages to Kapellmeister Frank at the opera. Mahler wrote at once to reassure her: even if he were to return to Hamburg, the epidemic up to then had attacked only people who had been careless or lacked the financial means to take certain precautions. The cholera, brought by sea, had begun in the narrow, insalubrious streets of the old port, which was right across the other side of the city from the Bundesstrasse, where he lived.

Having spent several days with the Krzyzanowskis and having visited Pollini[4] without receiving any more reassuring news, Mahler decided to return to Berchtesgaden, after sending a telegram to Natalie Bauer-Lechner, inviting her there (she was then vacationing with Josephine Spiegler at Seis). In his room, a sort of ship's cabin perched right under the roof of the villa and furnished with ascetic simplicity,[5] he had long talks with Natalie and discussed in particular the interruption of his creative life. Frau Marcus and her daughter, Nina Hoffmann, and Frau Spiegler were also present and Mahler thus found himself among dear friends.

Although the Hamburg epidemic had not ended, Pollini decided to reopen the opera "to reassure the public," forcing his personnel to return upon threat of dismissal, though he himself remained prudently in isolation. After considerable hesitation, Mahler went as far as Munich with Justi and Natalie but stayed there a few days, awaiting better news. On September 20, he finally left for Hamburg, stopping in Berlin, where he found numerous friends and acquaintances also on their way back.

Immediately upon his arrival, he wrote to Justi to reassure her about the cholera. The critic Paul Mirsch had died only because he had foolishly eaten watermelon, but the epidemic was waning and the danger now was minimal.[6] He told her that his assistant, Feld, with whom he had traveled from Berlin to Hamburg, had been discharged upon arrival by Pollini because he had not returned on the day indicated. What Mahler's letter did not reveal, since he always wanted to spare Justi, was that he himself had been in a critical position upon his return.[7] In fact Pollini, having warned everyone to return at once and having threatened serious reprisals for disobedience, made no exception in Mahler's favor. Since Mahler had thought fit to defy him and stay away from Hamburg after the official opening of the opera, their first meeting was stormy: Pollini accused him of having broken his contract and tried to impose a fine of twelve thousand marks, almost a year's salary. This was a terrible blow to Mahler, who had only this money to support himself and who must have spent several anxious days.

This crisis was resolved by the intervention of a mutual friend, a disinterested and intelligent physician named Ludwig Seeligmann, but it was to poison the future relationship between Mahler and Pollini, who thereafter treated Mahler with more and more marked hostility. For the time being, Pollini was still firmly resolved to keep him at the opera, not yet having exploited fully his talent and his commercial value as a "star." Moreover, he did not seem to be retaliating in any way other than by overloading him with work, as witness the letter Mahler wrote to a *"Korrepetitor"* (chorusmaster) he hoped to have engaged in Hamburg to assist him.[8] As for Mahler, he had no other post in view and consequently wanted to remain in Hamburg at least until the expiration of his contract in January 1894.

Since the opening of the opera on September 15, eleven performances had been directed by the assistant conductor, Theodor Hentschel. While awaiting the outcome of his quarrel with Pollini, Mahler only conducted rehearsals and spent most of his free time either working or with Berliner. In his lodgings on the Bundesstrasse, where he had installed a magnificent Bechstein piano, he had got into the habit of having his housekeeper prepare his meals.

At last on October 5, he conducted for the first time that season: *Die Meistersinger,* then *Fidelio, Tannhäuser, Tristan,* and *Lohengrin,* while at the same time rehearsing the first Hamburg performance of Bizet's *Djamileh,* an opera he had discovered and recommended to Pollini. Contrary to expectation, the success of this premiere was considerable if judged by the number of performances.[9]

On October 25, 1892, Mahler received a letter from Bülow: "Esteemed Herr Kapellmeister, Numerous but by no means superficial attempts to penetrate the strange style of the songs (*Gesänge*) that you have been good enough to send me having proved vain, I find it impossible to assume the responsibility of conducting them at this November 7 concert, out of consideration for both the composer and the singer. Consequently, I have asked

Wolff, the organizer of the concerts, to ask you personally to be good enough
to rehearse and conduct the performance of your work."

This time Bülow had made the break between past and future definitive.
Mahler the composer had to abandon all hope of being "discovered" by one
of the brightest personalities of the preceding generation and thus of making a
brilliant entrance upon the German musical scene. "Isn't this another friendly
encouragement to the joys of creation?" he wrote to Justi after renouncing
the projected performance, which would never have been proposed had it not
been for the friendly insistence of Amalie Joachim. According to Marie von
Bülow, the great conductor's refusal was caused chiefly by his poor health
and the pain he was enduring.[10] Nonetheless, it is true that, after saying
farewell to his youth and the Wagnerian adventures, Bülow lost all curiosity
about new productions and was interested in Richard Strauss's first compositions only because of their relative conservatism.

Early in December several things happened at once. Bülow's health deteriorated; at the November 24 subscription concert he could hardly get
through Beethoven's *Ninth Symphony,* or the *"Eroica"* and Wagner's *Faust-
Ouvertüre* on December 5. He informed Mahler that he would probably
be unable to conduct on December 12 and asked him to take his place, from
then on, at rehearsals. Not knowing whether or not Bülow would be able
to conduct at the last moment, Mahler undertook the rehearsals. He then
learned that Amalie Joachim had decided to sing two of the *"Humoresken"*
with the Berlin Philharmonic on the day of the concert itself,[11] with neither
singer nor conductor having any clear idea of Mahler's intentions. He could
have gone to Berlin for a few hours at least if Hentschel, his chief assistant
at the opera, had not been taken ill suddenly, thus forcing Mahler to conduct
all performances during his absence.[12]

Throughout this busy week, until the last moment Mahler expected Bülow
to recover in time to conduct the concert, as he had the preceding February.
This time, however, Mahler would have had fewer regrets, since he could then
have attended the first performance of his lieder in Berlin. But fate decided
otherwise, and Mahler replaced Bülow to conduct the fifth subscription concert, the program of which included Mendelssohn's Overture to *A Midsummer Night's Dream,* Wagner's *Siegfried Idyll,* and Beethoven's *Fifth Symphony.*[13]

Once again this concert unleashed against Mahler the fury of the conservative critics, represented by Josef Sittard. This time he was accused of "imitating Bülow" and of taking liberties permissible only to a musician possessing the Master's "spirit, force of insight, and inflexible will." "Obliged to
protest against the mutilations that Mahler had inflicted," especially on the
two last movements of the Beethoven *Fifth,* Sittard asked: "What, then, will
be the result of this mania for original interpretations of what is written in the
score? . . . One has no right to indulge in subtleties with a work like the *Fifth
Symphony.* One has no right to smash into atoms the emanation of a great
spirit, or to dissolve the mighty torrent of tempestuous ideas by deviating

them into several secondary channels which finally disappear in motionless sands."

It is plain that Mahler, like his predecessor and model, Hans von Bülow, regarded tradition as the refuge of the lukewarm and mediocre and that to both conductors, "to interpret" a work meant "to re-create" it, to renew it at every performance. Bülow had never shrunk either from adopting slower tempos than his colleagues or from altering numerous details of classical scores in order to enhance their effect, and he always did so with the aim of doing full justice to the work and its composer's intentions. For instance, he did not hesitate to increase gradually the number of strings in a crescendo or to have one half of the basses play legato and the other non-staccato when he wanted to bring out the outline of a phrase. In the first movement of the *"Eroica"* he added the trumpets to the horn in the recapitulation of the main theme.[14] Mahler did the same and for the same purpose, but that which was granted his illustrious predecessor, because of his age, was not forgiven him and the critics were outraged.

In the *Fremdenblatt,* Emil Krause[15] adopted a similar attitude. He considered Mahler a Wagnerian conductor, theatrical rather than symphonic, who, misled by Bülow's example, had committed unforgivable extravagances. His conception of Beethoven was too subjective, too full of contrasts, nuances, and changes of tempo. Only Ferdinand Pfohl, in the *Nachrichten,* supported Mahler at this time.

Finally Louis Bödecker, Hamburg correspondent of the Leipzig *Musikalisches Wochenblatt,* joined those who considered that Mahler's slow tempos were at odds with Beethoven's markings.[16] These reviews are as many testimonies of Mahler's determined "modern" spirit. No criticism was ever to make him alter a single detail of these provocative interpretations.

On the day Mahler the interpreter was thus severely taken to task by the Hamburg critics, Mahler the composer was treated no better by the critics in Berlin. At the fifth Philharmonic concert Amalie Joachim—after the Brahms *Alto Rhapsody,* conducted by Raphael Maszkowski—sang two of the *Wunderhorn Leider: "Der Schildwache Nachtlied"* and *"Verlor'ne Müh'."*[17] The *Norddeutsche Allgemeine Zeitung* found the second "prettily orchestrated" but recherché. In the *Neue Berliner Musikzeitung,* Arno Kleffel expressed the opinion that "Mahler's songs did not reveal to the full Amalie Joachim's marvelous organ; I must confess," he adds, "that never have I heard anything so unsatisfactory, so distorted, so sad as these two songs. . . . A wasteland, nothing but mannered, insignificant phrases, not a single blossom or green leaf. And this is what Frau Joachim offers us? Who can solve this enigma? Judging by the depression that reigned afterward in the auditorium, it was easy to deduce that the public is unwilling to accept such tasteless gifts, even if offered by an artist as dear to its heart as Frau Joachim."

Mahler sent some of the criticisms to his brothers and sisters with a half-serious, half-humorous comment: "Now, dear children, to amuse you I send you, *primo,* the four articles by the Rhadamantheses of Hamburg about the concert, and *secondo,* the two little accounts by the Minoses of Berlin, the only ones that have reached me so far. As you will see, I have already found my *'Herzfeld.'* The other one at least admits that perhaps things should be examined a little more closely. Well, let's forget about it."

In a letter written at the same time to the composer Mihalovics, he freely expresses his bitterness: "Just imagine, I have been put in my place like a schoolboy, and in the most disagreeable way, by some of the critics who disapproved of my conception of the *Fifth Symphony.* I could not help remembering Pest where they understood me so well! . . ."[18] This proves how short the human memory can be: after having complained continuously and with good reason about the Hungarian critics, Mahler's only concern now is with the hostile Hamburg ones.

His theatrical activities, as usual in December, were less arduous, except during Hentschel's illness.[19] The trouble between Mahler and Pollini had died down after a "talk" that cleared away most of the causes of misunderstanding. Mahler congratulated himself for having been especially courageous on that occasion and for having settled matters at the risk of dismissal. Nevertheless, Pollini's demands continued to increase, and Mahler had hardly any time left for his own work. In January, for instance, he directed sixteen performances plus rehearsals, and consequently spent most of his time at the opera house. Having conducted *Le Nozze di Figaro* on December 24, he spent a happy and relaxed Christmas at the home of Frau Lazarus, a Viennese widow who was a close friend and ardent admirer of Bülow. On New Year's Eve, invited unexpectedly at the last moment to a party, Mahler felt alone among the noisy crowd. This feeling of solitude was slowly intensifying, for Hamburg society consisted mostly of businessmen who were not interested in artists. Besides, his position was less exalted than in Budapest, where secretaries of state would pay him formal visits because of his high administrative rank; at times his social standing as well as his own value seemed to have seriously decreased.

The first operatic event of 1893 was the German premiere of Tchaikovsky's last opera, *Iolanta,*[20] a one-act opera based upon a play by the Dane Henrik Hertz, *"King René's Daughter."* This new opera achieved only a *succès d'estime*[21]; however, Mascagni's *L'Amico Fritz* was far more successful on January 16. Mahler had conducted the rehearsals with tremendous enthusiasm: "I consider *L'Amico Fritz* a decisive advance on *Cavalleria,*" he wrote, "and I am fully convinced that once again those gentlemen, the orchestra conductors, have wrecked it by their conducting, for it is difficult to perform and full of great subtleties. With easily understandable sympathy for this unappreciated and abused composer, I dedicated all my energies to this work in order to impose it on that riffraff. . . . Between Mascagni and myself, there are a lot of affinities. In any case, this is the first time the work has succeeded, or rather the second, for the performance conducted by Mascagni at the Prater delighted the public. But his personality must have counted for something there, since he fascinates the Viennese."[22]

It is hard to discern the "affinities" that Mahler found between his music and Mascagni's, yet his efforts on the latter's behalf were not in vain: *L'Amico Fritz* was given ten times that season. The critics, however, found Mascagni's "passionately expressive" music lacking in originality and ill-suited to this long-static village idyll.[23]

Since the beginning of the season, new family problems had arisen: Alois had paid his debts only by borrowing more elsewhere and, as usual, he would take no advice. After deciding to enroll him in a business school in Hamburg, which would later enable him to find a job, Mahler learned in October that Alois was spitting blood and that the doctors had diagnosed tuberculosis. Since his lungs had been weak ever since childhood, this was most worrying. Justi watched over him day and night, and Mahler asked Freund to make sure that she did not wear herself out, but engaged a nurse.[24] Fortunately the illness soon took a turn for the better and at the beginning of November, at considerable expense, Mahler sent Alois with Justi to the southern Tyrol in order to convalesce.[25] Later a job would have to be found for him in a suitable climate such as Argentina or Egypt.

Mahler's letters also keep mentioning Otto's studies, his examination, and his military service. "His education in Vienna was ruined from the start, due to excessive spoiling by the young girls,[26] by Fritz, and then by Nina Hoffmann," Mahler was to write to Justi during the spring of 1893. He was distressed at the thought that Otto must give up his violin studies for three whole years of military service, a period that could have been reduced to one year if he had only volunteered. As always, Mahler asked Justi to watch over the young man, to make sure that he was working and not spending his nights out on the town. A certain "truth" about Otto had also been concealed from him and he had just learned it from Natalie (this could be that he had left the conservatory), who was supposed to supervise his violin studies but had succeeded no better than his former teachers. Otto, she confessed, neglected his studies because he would have to give them up anyway. Later, when he was discharged, he had already wasted a whole year. Did he, after leaving the conservatory in April, enter one of the numerous private music schools in Vienna, or had he decided to work on his own? Mahler probably did not know himself; he never ceased to worry: "I am really in a furiously bad temper. I mean inwardly, for I seem perfectly calm. Everything seems to cross me! I really deserve some consideration from you, for when one is obliged, as I am, to fight and bleed for every inch of ground, life is really no joke!"[27]

In the spring of 1893 Mahler finally lost patience with his brothers; Alois was running up new debts, even in Merano, and asking him for money under false pretenses. "Those gentlemen, my brothers, never cease causing me sorrow and worries," he wrote to Fritz Löhr's sister Ernestine in April. "I have nothing more to do with Alois: one cannot help him, and I do not

understand where he got his character. In all my life I have never seen anyone
so inconsistent, so thoughtless and, even less still, so deceitful! That is really
what makes the cup run over. When one simply cannot believe someone,
one loses interest. As for Otto, he is also boldly taking flight into the world,
as you doubtlessly know too! For him too there is no solution other than to
be taught by life itself. My sole consolation is that at last Justi's health
has improved. Everyone confirms this; it will finally turn out to be the only
comfort of this year, which, otherwise has not strewn many roses along my
path!"

Shortly after Alois returned from Merano, he sent Mahler a letter that
infuriated him: "I have written to this rascal in very strong terms. In the
face of such thoughtlessness, such falseness, indulgence would be a great
mistake. What will these two fellows do next to annoy me? . . . I am curious to see whether Alois will obey my order! If he does not, I shall take no
more interest in him! I am tired of thus being dragged up hill and down
dale hitched to the reins of those winged stallions, my noble brothers. I no
longer wish to follow their impetuous flights. *I am still young* and in no
mood to become a morose moralist. I still want to enjoy life and I am not
yet ready to groan beneath the cares of a bitter old man. God knows I
have my own flight to follow!

"I believe I made a serious mistake in being always so forgiving and
trusting toward these boys. . . . [Otto] must not imagine that I am going to
continue supporting him during [his military service] in the same way as before. I have done everything in my power to spare him, as well as myself,
this sacrifice. He wouldn't listen! Let *him* face the consequences! Perhaps the
only salvation for him is to find out for himself *what life* means and to be
obliged to *struggle* and *battle* on his own."[28]

Alois's reply did not change Mahler's mind. Denying that he had been
unstable or untruthful, he simply admitted to having "been foolish." He
had no more debts left, and the amount that he had requested for lessons
was in fact less than their cost. Besides, he would soon remove this burden
from his brother's shoulders, having been humiliated too often, despite his
total innocence. "My heart is so full of bitterness that I'd like to write
twenty pages, but prefer to keep silent," he concluded.

After years of advice, encouragement, battles, and financial sacrifices,
Mahler truly was growing weary. Happily Alois would soon be able to earn
his living, and Mahler sent him the address of a business employment
bureau.

In a letter dated February 13, Mahler complained of having to suspend
all personal work because "perpetual discussions and disturbances have destroyed the necessary atmosphere." What was he working on that winter?
Had he already started the sketches for his *Second Symphony,* or had he
been content to work the orchestration of the *Lieder eines fahrenden
Gesellen?* A letter of April 19, sent to a Hamburg critic, together with the
score of these four "Ballades with orchestra," contained an offer to play

them for him.[29] He also appears to have undertaken a revision of the score of *Titan,* the future *First Symphony,* for the first time and contemplated cutting out the Andante "Blumine," which he was to restore a few months later and keep until 1896.[30]

When Mahler wanted to work in peace, he used to lock himself into his study and gave orders to the little maid, Marie, not to disturb him under any circumstances. One day, instead of speaking to her of his "work," he told her that he was going to "compose." Shortly afterward his friend Frau Marcus called on him, and the girl thought that she was doing her duty when she said in a mysterious tone, "The gentleman cannot be seen. He is deposing!" No one knew exactly what she meant by the word, but from then on "to depose" took its place in the family vocabulary, being used for a quite different but nonetheless essential function in Mahler's life.

In the spring, Mahler added two more works to his operatic repertoire: they were presented first individually, and then together. They were Karl von Kaskel's insignificant, veristic *Hochzeitsmorgen* and Mascagni's *I Rantzau,* which somewhat dampened Mahler's enthusiasm for the young Italian composer. Everyone agreed that this third opera by the composer of *Cavalleria rusticana* showed signs of waning inspiration. *I Rantzau,* like *L'Amico Fritz,* was adapted from a novel by Erckmann-Chatrian and had little success in Hamburg. The tragedy of Pietro Mascagni's life was becoming apparent. *Cavalleria rusticana,* composed in 1889 for a prize contest, had brought him only the first-prize money, an amount utterly disproportionate to its worldwide triumph, and all his other works failed.

At the end of January, Mahler was invited to meet Anton Rubinstein at an elegant party, but the experience was frustrating since the great pianist only played whist, while "from the next room some of the guests watched admiringly, through a crack in the door, those large hands that could play the piano so marvelously." This was a great disappointment for Mahler, who, ever since his conservatory days had admired Rubinstein's playing of Beethoven.[31]

On March 20, after a concert in aid of a retirement fund, during which Mahler conducted Haydn's *Symphony in E Flat,* Sittard, "the doomsday judge," as Mahler called him, once more complained of his "too subtle" conceptions, which "often subordinate the sun of Haydn's genius to modern perception." He also criticized the "coldness" of his interpretation, his superfluous pauses and ritardandos, the excessive slowness of the adagio introduction, and the "overemphasis on details that destroys the whole character of the work."

After the religious concert, given as usual on Good Friday, when Mahler conducted before a small and unenthusiastic audience the world premiere of one of the works that Bruckner had just sent him, the *Mass No. 1 in D Minor,*[32] Sittard attacked his fast tempos. The work, he thought, lacked organic unity. Being made up of "episodes" and momentary impressions, it did not attain the level of the *Mass No. 3 in F Minor* despite its imposing orchestration. Sittard attacked Mahler for making his chorus and soloists sing while sitting down.[33]

Bruckner was deeply grateful to Mahler for having conducted another of his works: "Surrounded by an indifferent public and hostile critics (except for the *Fremdenblatt*) who perhaps will not understand my work for another few decades, it must be very difficult for you to offer these gentlemen something they know nothing about. Indeed, criticism is much more advanced here, with the exception of Hanslick, who has cost me at least 100,000 marks, and of one other, who is unimportant. I thank you very much again, noble hero . . . I embrace you in my thoughts and remain your . . . Bruckner."

On November 13, the tone of Bruckner's last letter to Mahler is even sadder: *"Omnes amici me dereliquerunt!* [All my friends have abandoned me!] With these words I have described the whole situation. Hans Richter calls me a musical madman because I have refused to make new cuts. Naturally, he will play none of my works, and now I am all alone." Mahler, who admired Bruckner as a man even more than a composer, was deeply upset by the old musician's unjust and cruel fate. After Bruckner's death, he became determined to do his utmost to make up for all this.

For his own annual benefit concert Mahler chose two works of Beethoven, the *Fifth Symphony,* followed by *Fidelio.* The hall was crowded, the concert most successful, and at the end of the evening Bülow sent him a laurel wreath inscribed "To the Pygmalion of the Hamburg Opera," which Mahler was to keep for the rest of his life.

Fortunately Sittard was out of town, and the article in which Armbrust defended Mahler's interpretation of the *Fifth Symphony* was clearly directed against the "doomsday judge." Why, he asked, should anyone consider arbitrary, or even criminal, in others the liberties accorded to Bülow? Mahler's interpretations did not differ essentially from the former's, and, as Anton Schindler had said, Beethoven himself took great liberties in performing his own works. One must either accept changes of tempo or reject them on principle but if one accepts them, how can one determine the permissible limits? It was impossible to deny Mahler's great assurance and his intensity of expression. Whatever one might think of his tempos, one could not deny the perfection of his performances or deny the effect produced by marvelous interpretations.

In May, Mahler brought Justine to Hamburg for the annual Wagner cycle, and, as in the preceding season, he conducted *Tannhäuser, Die Meistersinger, Lohengrin,* and the *Ring.* Before taking his leave of the city, he conducted a rather insignificant new production, Pier Antonio Tasca's *A Santa Lucia,* a "veristic" opera "of horrible realism" which was given only twice, with two well-known Italian singers, Gemma Bellincioni and her husband, the tenor Roberto Stagno.[34]

On his way to Austria, Mahler paused in Berlin to contact Hermann Wolff, organizer of the Bülow concerts, which he hoped to direct one day.

He arrived in Vienna on June 17[35] but spent only two days there, for he was eager to settle down for the summer and resume the composition of his great work.

During a tour of inspection they had undertaken the preceding spring, Justine and Natalie had toured all the green hills of the Salzkammergut and had chosen Steinbach, a small village located on the beautiful wooded lake of the Attersee. On the opposite shore two old socialist friends of Mahler's, Victor Adler and Engelbert Pernerstorfer, spent each summer with their families in the Nussdorf, and at the far end of the lake, in Unterach, the Austrian composer Ignaz Brüll invited many Viennese intellectuals to his house. Thus the Mahler family would not have to fear solitude. Steinbach was not a well-known resort, so it was possible to live there quietly for very little. The summer of 1893 was to have a special meaning in Mahler's life. For the first time he was to know the calm and studious life of a composer wholly devoted to his work. No more long journeys, no more guests, but the peace and quiet needed by the creator of vast projects.

In a small one-story inn on the shore of the Attersee, *Gasthof und Fleischhauerei zum Höllengebirge,* a few minutes' walk from the village, five rooms had been reserved for Mahler, Justine, Emma, Otto, and Natalie, who was to spend the summer with them; five scantily furnished rooms to which had been added some plain wooden tables and chairs made by the village carpenter and quickly covered with cretonne. The only cozy note was a sofa that could be moved from one room to another according to need. Mahler had a study with a grand piano, placed at his disposal by a manufacturer. A private kitchen and a spare room allowed the new *Gasthof* guests to feel themselves somewhat at home in this establishment, which usually lodged only passing tourists. The view from there was particularly picturesque—on one side, the village houses dominated by a church; on the other, the perspective of the lake looking toward the Schafberg, Unterach, Stockwinkel, and Nussdorf. In a large green field that extended onto a peninsula, Mahler was to build, the following year, his celebrated *"Häuschen."*

Just as he was getting ready to go to work, Mahler received from Hamburg a *Fremdenblatt* article announcing his departure for the United States, while in fact he had just refused an interesting offer from the Boston Symphony Orchestra.[36] Infuriated by this absurd statement, and doubtlessly worried about Pollini's reaction, he sent a telegram to Berliner asking him to publish an immediate denial in the Hamburg and Berlin newspapers.[37]

From the last week of June onward Mahler's days were organized around his creative activity. Rising around six-thirty, he worked through the morning until luncheon, usually at noon. At first he was punctual, but, gradually carried away by inspiration, he started to forget the time, and his brothers and sisters, dying of hunger, often had to wait until three o'clock before they could eat. Absorbed by his creative task, Mahler ate lightly to avoid the headaches and digestive ills to which he was prone, and he gave up all alcohol. He smoked cigarettes, and from time to time the cigars that his friend, the actor Carl Wagner, sent him annually at the time of his Hamburg Opera benefit. When Justi saw him, after luncheon, removing the gold paper from a cigar and placing it carefully before him on the table with a look of happy anticipation, she knew immediately that he was satisfied with his work.[38] The result of these three months of hard work was to be not only some new *Wunderhorn Lieder,* but also two, and possibly three, movements of the *Second Symphony.*

Five years had elapsed since Leipzig and the *Titan.* The *Totenfeier,* the monumental symphonic funeral march in which Mahler had tried in vain to interest Bülow, did not seem self-sufficient to him any longer. Great plans started to take shape in his mind. The symphony of the future should be written for the masses, for all Humanity—a sort of continuation of Beethoven's *Ninth.* All Mahler's efforts were at present aimed in this direction, as we can see from the letter he wrote in February to a young girl from Hamburg: "Dear Fräulein Tolney-Witt, even though I am not easily prevailed upon to start a correspondence, and even though my best friends have often complained about this matter, something makes me want to answer a question in your last letter.

"'Why does it require an apparatus as large as an orchestra to express a great thought?' I shall have to go quite a long way back to make you understand my point of view.

"You seem to have browsed through musical literature and I presume that even the earlier musicians as far back as Bach are not quite unknown to you. Haven't you been struck by two facts?

"First, that the farther back we go, the more primitive the indications given to the performer, i.e., the more do the composers leave the explanations of their thoughts to their interpreters. In Bach's musical scores, for instance, you will rarely find a designation of tempo or of the manner in which the work should be played—even the major differentiations like p or ff are missing. (And when such indications do exist, it is most likely that they were added by the editor, often quite incorrectly.)

"Second, the further music develops, the more complex the apparatus used by the composer to express his thoughts becomes. Just compare Haydn's orchestra in his symphonies (it was not even that used at the philharmonic concerts in the Redoutensaal because more than half the instruments were added later) with Beethoven's orchestra in the *Ninth,* not to mention Wagner and the more recent composers. Why is this so? Do you consider it accidental, an arbitrary extravagance, an impenetrable whim of the composer?

"I shall now try to explain my opinion on the matter. In its beginnings, music was merely 'chamber music,' meant to be listened to in a small space by a small audience (often consisting of the performers alone). The basic feelings that gave it birth simply reflected, according to the times, in a simple, naive and general manner, the adventures of the soul, happiness, sadness, etc. The *'Musicantes'* were sure of themselves; they were moving in a circle of familiar ideas and over ground formed by a clearly defined and well-established technique, always within certain set limits. That is why the composer gave no instructions; it was self-evident that everything would be seen, felt and heard in the right way. There was hardly any 'dilettantism' (a case like Frederick the Great remains almost unique). The rich and noble upper classes liked to listen to music in their salons for their pleasure, and this music was played by skilled and well-paid musicians. That is why their works were not mistreated by ignorance, the composer and the *'musicians'* being very often one and the same.

"In the church which, naturally, was music's chief domain, and was where this art originated, everything was strictly defined by the ritual. Briefly, the composers were not afraid of being misunderstood, and were satisfied with sketching notes for their own use—without giving much thought to the fact that others would have to interpret them, or might even misinterpret them.

"Then, maybe, as time went by, some composers had some unfortunate experiences and consequently tried to communicate their intentions to the musicians by decipherable signs. That is how, little by little, a vast system of written language was formed to indicate tempos or sound dynamics, as notes indicated musical pitch.

"Hand in hand with this went the acquisition of new emotional elements as subjects of expression through sound, i.e., the composer began to introduce into his work the constantly more complex and deeper facets of his emotional life. From then on, not only the basic feelings such as mere joy or sadness, etc., form the subjects of musical creation, but also transitions from one state to another, inner conflicts, surrounding nature and its effect upon us, humor and poetic thoughts.

"At this point, even the most complex signs were no longer sufficient. Instead of imposing upon one individual instrument a rich palette of colors (as Mr. August Beer would put it) the composer used a separate instrument for each separate color (the expression *'Klangfarbe'* still retains the true analogy). It was this need that gradually gave birth to the modern Wagnerian' orchestra.

"Third, I still have to mention the external necessity for enlargement of the musical apparatus: music became more and more a common good. Audiences and performances increased. The concert hall replaced the 'chamber' and instead of the church with its *new* instrument, the organ, there was the opera house. So you see, to sum things up: we moderns are in need of a large musical system to express *our* thoughts, whether large or small. On one hand because we are obliged, in order to protect ourselves against misinterpretation, to allot the many colors of our rainbow to various palettes; on the other hand because our eyes are learning to discern, in the rainbow, an increasing number of colors and more and more beautiful and delicate modulations.

Also because, in order to make ourselves heard by large audiences in huge theaters and concert halls, we are obliged to make a louder noise.

"Maybe, like many women who are rarely convinced, at best sometimes persuaded, you will reply: 'But then, was Bach inferior to Beethoven, or Wagner?' To which I shall reply, my little 'tormentor' (tormentor, indeed, for I have been struggling for almost an hour over this letter), you had better contact someone who can, in one glance, give you an over-all impression of the whole spiritual history of humanity. We are what we are, we 'moderns'! Even you are that way! Can I prove to you now, that you, little tormentor, require a much more complex apparatus for your daily life than the English Queen of the XVIIth century, who, from what I read recently, had a pound of bacon and a mug of beer for breakfast and spent the evenings in her apartments spinning by candlelight or doing something similar to escape boredom? What do you say to that? So, away with the piano! Away with the violin! They are all right for the 'chamber'! For moments when you, alone or with a good friend, want to recall the works of the great masters—like an echo—as a print can remind you of the richly colored paintings of a Raphael or a Boecklin. I hope that I have made myself clearly understood, in which case I shall not regret having devoted one hour of my life to you, who were kind enough to have trusted a stranger so charmingly.

"Since this epistle has become so long, I would also like to be sure that it was not written in vain. So please let me know if it has reached you.

"With my best wishes, Gustav Mahler."[39]

Here then, exposed in the clearest possible terms, are the aesthetic principles on which Mahler was to found his symphonic music, and in particular the two gigantic works he was about to compose. A posthumous homage must be rendered to Gisela Tolney-Witt, the now forgotten "little tormentor," for having asked her friendly question at the right moment. Thanks to her, Mahler places himself in historical perspective and reveals for the first time his conception of the orchestra, as the "modern" instrument par excellence.

New and unusual as the future works would be, they were still to be known as "symphonies." "I have already considered the problem of naming my symphony. I thought of searching for a title that would give some idea of the contents and define my aims in a few words. But 'symphony' is the only suitable description. Such titles as 'symphonic poems' are overworked and don't convey the right meaning. They call to mind Liszt's compositions, in which each movement describes something entirely different, with no deep relationship between them. My whole life is contained in my two symphonies. In them I have set down my experience and suffering, truth and poetry in words. To anyone who knows how to listen, my whole life will become clear, for my creative works and my existence are so closely interwoven that if my life flowed as peacefully as a stream through a meadow I believe I would no longer be able to compose anything."

Five years earlier, in Prague[40] and in Iglau, Mahler had composed the

*Totenfeier* and written on some loose sheets of paper a group of lyrical and lilting melodies in A flat.[41] He was to take these sketches up again in Steinbach, and, discovering their melodic value, decided to use them for an Andante in his new symphony. "The melody of this Andante gushes forth like a broad stream (in the manner of Schubert)," he told Natalie, who was playing her part of witness and confidante wonderfully that summer. "It constantly creates new branches with inexhaustible richness and regeneration." He set to work enthusiastically, and gradually the movement revealed itself full of "the most varied combinations." In scarcely a week, the complete sketch was finished. Not having composed such a vast symphonic structure for a long time, Mahler asked himself: "Who knows if this movement is going to be as good as I imagine at this moment? Perhaps everything seems quite different and better when one is working and everything seems to spring directly from the soul. . . . But what I wanted and what I visualized while composing has not always been realized. Many things often get lost. . . . It is easier to achieve a desired effect in short pieces. For instance, it seems to me that in *'Das himmlische Leben,'* I have realized the sketch perfectly, that I have even improved it. . . ."[42]

Establishing the order in which the various works were written that summer is difficult, because the only accurate dates we have are those of the autographed orchestra scores, and these were not necessarily completed in the same order as the sketches. According to Natalie, the Scherzo was written before the Andante,[43] while the orchestrations are dated respectively July 16 and 30, 1893. When, then, did Mahler compose the song *"Des Antonius von Padua Fischpredigt,"* which served as a model for the Scherzo? Its orchestration was completed only *after* he had finished the symphonic movement, that is to say on August 1. Certainly earlier, since Mahler himself declared to Natalie that he had *developed* the lied into a powerful symphonic movement "without even thinking about it or intending to do so." He was to compose two other *Wunderhorn* songs that summer: *"Das irdische Leben"* and *"Rheinlegendchen."* We know the exact circumstances of the composition of the latter,[44] but the other may well have been sketched earlier. It is difficult to believe that between June 21 and July 16 Mahler completed the whole sketch of the Andante, as well as the sketch and orchestration of the Scherzo, and the *"Fischpredigt,"* a sort of parergon[45] of the Scherzo.

"It is strange how one feels drawn forward," Mahler said while composing it, "without knowing at first where one is going, one gets farther and farther away from the original form, the real substance of which has been previously hidden just as a plant is completely enclosed in its seed. That is why, you see, I would have had difficulty in keeping myself within the well-defined limits imposed, for example, by an opera text (unless I had written it myself). . . ."[46] It's altogether different with lieder because there music can express much more than the immediate meaning of the words. The text merely suggests the buried riches that must be uncovered, the treasures that one must bring to light."

As always, when composing, Mahler lived in a kind of trance, lost in a mysterious world of his own creation. Even though the work flowed quickly from his pen, it seemed to spring from the very source of his emotional life, linked to the sufferings he had experienced—and still endured while creating. "I think it is thus for most men," he said to Natalie, "except perhaps for the greatest geniuses, whose names could be written on one fingernail. Artistic creation reminds me of the birth of a pearl, that treasure offered to the world only after having caused the oyster severe pain. Spiritual and physical birth have much in common: what struggles, what torture, what anguish accompany them—and what rejoicing too, if the infant be healthy and vigorous. Also the artist represents the feminine element opposing the genius that fertilizes him, giving himself entirely, carrying the seed in his innermost being, nourishing it as it comes to maturity, until the completed work can be born into the light."[47]

Mahler also compared the artist to a musical instrument played on by the spirit of the world, the source of all existence. Sometimes it is a splendid Stradivarius, whose tone astonishes and enchants the gods and the hands that made it. But most of the time "it is nothing more than a very ordinary violin trying to pass itself off as the treasure of an Italian master." Often he felt a kind of "mysterious, unknown force" dictating to him. One day he set aside a passage of his Scherzo which he had added on a loose sheet of paper, thinking it did not fit in. A few days later, glancing at it by chance, he discovered that, on the contrary, it was "the most important, the strongest passage."

"Creation, bringing a work into the world," thus appeared to him to be an "essentially mystical" act. "Sometimes, to one's own astonishment, inspiration coming from elsewhere may impel one to do something that later one no longer understands. I often feel like a blind hen discovering a grain of wheat. This mysterious unconscious force is the more remarkable in that it appears in individual passages, usually the most important and difficult, rather than in a whole movement or an entire piece. Most of the time, they are precisely the passages on which I have no inclination to work, those I would love to avoid, but which take possession of me and finally demand to be expressed."[48] Because creation was to him such a secret and mysterious action, Mahler could not bear to have anyone listening, or even nearby, while he was composing. The gross indiscretion of strangers' ears accidentally hearing a still-unborn work seemed to him like so many glances cast upon a child still in its mother's womb.[49]

During the weeks when he was composing the central movements of his *Second Symphony,* Mahler seemed "in an almost pathological state": he was nervous and strained, his face pale and drawn, but he would not allow himself even one moment of rest and calm. "Don't talk to me of not looking well," he said to Natalie, who must have got on his nerves. "Don't ever speak of this to me while I am working unless you want to make me terribly angry. While one has something to say, do you think that one can spare oneself? Even if it means devoting one's last breath and final drop of blood, one must express it." With regard to noise, or anything else that might interrupt or trouble his work, Mahler felt a fury that, ever since childhood, had made him dream of some secret punishment sent down from heaven upon those who despoil the silence. "One day humanity will become as sensitive to noise as it is to smells, and will finally promulgate laws and severe punishment for all those who offend the sense of hearing."[50]

Obsessed by a longing to be understood and listened to, Mahler was overwhelmed by doubt and anguish: "What terrible problems will the Scherzo, for instance, present to those who hear it. What will they say if they ever do hear it? Oh, that I could hear it once, to make sure I haven't lost myself and to discover whether that which to me is so profound and important is equally profound and important to others! Artists must rely on their fellowmen, at least a few of them. If my work does not transmit the message and awaken the same response that prompted me to create, then I have created in vain."[51]

Mahler also worried about not being able to verify his orchestration. Often, against his will, he orchestrated "too heavily," fearing that certain passages would be lost to the public because of too light a sonority. This lack of contact between his interior world and the outside world, between his work and the effect it would produce, made him suffer terribly. And yet, with his innate feeling for the orchestra, he already felt, while working, that the "seams," the stratagems made necessary by the inadequacies of the instruments, could be turned into a source of beauty by deft fingers, whereas a clumsy hand would try ineffectually to hide them. In the same way, an architect would arrange for openings and angles to be part of his building, while supports would become columns, pilasters or even elegant caryatids.[52]

Once Mahler finished the orchestral scores of the Andante and Scherzo of his *Second Symphony,* he turned again to the *Knaben Wunderhorn,* and on August 1 he completed the orchestration of the *"Fischpredigt."* While composing, he imagined eels, carps, and sharp-nosed pikes pushing their inexpressive faces out of the water and gazing at the saint with empty eyes before swimming away, not having understood a single word of his sermon. This image made him laugh aloud: he saw in it a delightful satire on human stupidity.[53] The contrast is striking between this mirth and the different programs of the Scherzo, which refer to it as a somber, grating episode. As always with Mahler, the ironic and the grotesque were allied to tragedy.

On August 10, having completed his day's work, Mahler explained to Natalie what he did when his inspiration dictated to him music that could not be used in the work he was composing. That very morning he had used in the *"Rheinlegendchen"* (temporarily entitled *"Tanzlegendchen"*) a melodic idea that had obsessed him three years before and that he had since forgotten. Leafing through the *Wunderhorn,* he had come across a poem whose subject and rhythm perfectly fitted this melody, though the poem was one he had never thought of setting to music, unlike many others chosen long ago.[54] With Mahler, the text of a song never took precedence over the musical form. Indeed, the opposite was often the case, as with *"Rheinlegendchen."*[55]

That August, Mahler also composed *"Das irdische Leben."* As for the *Wunderhorn Lied "Urlicht,"* a recently discovered letter from Mahler to his friend Hermann Behn has proved that it was composed before the rest of the symphony and that it originally had a piano accompaniment.[56] However, Mahler may have orchestrated it during the summer of 1893. In addition, he began to note down some sketches for the Finale, but they did not suit his purpose. "You can't imagine what tricks fate plays on one! Instead of the ideas in quadruple time, which I need for my Finale, I now have only ideas in triple time, which are of no use to me at all!"[57]

Despite the huge task Mahler had undertaken and partly accomplished, summer life in Steinbach included a few moments of relaxation. The afternoons were sometimes spent in walks and excursions. On July 7, Mahler's birthday, the whole family went in force to Moos, tucked away in the mountains about three or four hours' walk from Steinbach. They took with them a substantial picnic of chicken and birthday cake and spent some hours on the terrace of a small, isolated café, chatting peacefully and admiring the landscape. Each time Mahler completed a section of his work, he relaxed by organizing a long walk.

In mid-July, Fritz Löhr spent two weeks in Steinbach with his youngest sister. Mahler played the new *Wunderhorn Lieder* to him, as well as some movements from the *Second Symphony,* and read aloud passages from Goethe and his beloved *Don Quixote.* Conversation was lively, and one day, talking with Otto and Natalie about Beethoven, Mahler recalled with admiration the stupendous "progress," the transformation that he had brought about in music. "Only after comparing Mozart's *Symphony in G Minor* and the *Ninth,"* he said, "can one see how much he [Beethoven] has accomplished."[58] For Mahler the three great geniuses of Western Europe remained Shakespeare, Beethoven, and Wagner.

On another occasion they discussed the relative merits of Brahms and Bruckner. Otto expressed his preference for the latter, but Mahler did not agree. "To judge a composer's work, one must consider it as a whole, and then there can be no doubt that Brahms is the greater of the two" because "his works are perfectly unified and never obvious . . . their significance, on the contrary, appears richer and more profound as one plunges deeper into them. One must also remember his incredible productivity, an important element when considering an artist."[59] Mahler recognized Bruckner's "grandeur and his richness of inspiration" but deplored that they should constantly be undermined by his work's "lack of continuity." "Posterity, which respects only that which is perfect and complete, will probably like and understand Bruckner even less" than his contemporaries.

That same day, during a conversation about Liszt, Mahler insisted again on the necessity of judging a composer's work as a whole, and without considering the form as something separate from the material. To him the combination of these two elements determined value, durability, and vital force. Richard Strauss had expressed one day to Mahler his great admiration for Liszt, whom he formerly had scorned. Mahler had answered that Liszt's music reminded him of those thickly woven fabrics which soon begin to show the thread of the woof.[60]

Mahler's tone became passionate, as always, when the subject was Wagner. "Whenever I am in a bad mood, I suddenly think of Wagner, and cheer up again. That such a light could penetrate the world! What a spirit of fire, what a revolutionary, what a reformer of art without equal on earth! However, he was born when the circumstances were precisely right for the world to receive his message, and this is one of the essential prerequisites for the earth-shaking influence of such a genius. 'The essential is birth and the ray of light that touches the newly born,' as Hölderlin says.[61] How many great spirits may have come into the world at the wrong moment, were not recognized, and went for nothing! What a terrible role in posterity is that played by the *epigoni* born after great spirits such as Beethoven and Wagner! The harvest has been entirely brought in, and they are only a few little ears of corn to be gleaned here and there. Fortunately, something always remains to be harvested . . . so let us not be idle!"[62]

Finally, Mahler considered that one should not speak about "the fraternity of the Arts" for he believed they were neither fraternal nor equal. To him, the most important by far, the most "intimate" one [*des inneren Sinnes*] was music, followed by poetry, then a long way behind, "came painting and sculpture, drawing their very substance from the outside world." Right at the bottom of the list he placed architecture, "interested only in the harmony between dimensions and great masses." For him, "the great and true works of art were the ones that achieved union within the arts themselves," like those of Wagner. Goethe had already felt the imperfection of isolated arts, in particular with *Faust*, where certain passages cried out for music. Having reached the utmost limits of the universe of sound with the *Ninth*, Beethoven took a gigantic step forward by introducing the spoken word ". . . and with what incredible effect!" concluded Mahler, immediately adding, ". . . the degree to which the word sustains the sound can be measured when you pass from wordless music to text. It is like Antaeus feeling mother Earth beneath his feet and drawing from her all the gigantic force that allows him to vanquish with his bare hands the worst of enemies; that is, for the artist, matter itself. . . ."[63]

These conversations reveal Mahler's principal concern at that time. He was searching through "all Human Literature" to find the words, the texts to serve as a climax to the *Second Symphony*, to bring out its full meaning and make it a "total work of art" (*Gesamtkunstwerk*). The "harvest" of that summer had been abundant, but the completion of the *Second Symphony*

took place in an atmosphere of doubt and incertitude. The search for a text
worthy of this work and capable of giving it significance was fruitless for
some time, and only pure chance, or rather a stroke of inspiration, was to
bring the answer.

Since August was almost over, Mahler had to abandon his work, the Finale
of which was hardly sketched.[64] Having decided that Steinbach possessed
all the essential qualities for a holiday resort, he planned to have a little
cabin built on the lake shore not far from the inn, where he would be able to
concentrate and to enjoy the calm he needed for his work. A local architect
named Lesch was called upon immediately, and the site chosen with great
care. As soon as the cabin had been ordered, Mahler left from Hamburg,
stopping in Munich on the way to visit the Krzyzanowskis. His doubts and
hesitations were to continue until the following spring; nevertheless he felt,
as he was leaving Steinbach, the great satisfaction of having taken up again,
after a gap of five years, the interrupted thread of his symphonic creation.

"Since the world rejects me, I
shall return to the Venusberg."

# CHAPTER 19

*Mahler in Hamburg (IV) — J. B. Förster and* The
Bartered Bride *— Meetings with Richard Strauss — First
Performance of the* Humoresken *and* Titan *in Hamburg
and Weimar — Bülow's Funeral (September 1893–
June 1894)*

Back in Hamburg on August 26, Mahler started looking for new lodgings, for
that summer he had realized that it was the noise in the Bundesstrasse that
prevented him from doing any creative work. On August 28, he wrote to
Justi that he could hear a military band playing in the grounds of the nearby
zoo, to the accompaniment of roaring lions and bellowing African buffaloes.
"There aren't any rattlesnakes, or they would surely rattle as well. Outside
the window, a group of boys and girls shout all day long at the tops of their
voices, while on the second floor I can hear a woman doing vocal exercises
and someone playing the piano. . . . As for my work, I have no hope of
doing any and I realize now that during my two years here I have become
resigned to this, for otherwise I could not accept it all so calmly."

The first apartment Mahler visited did not offer the peace and quiet he desired; moreover the landlord wanted to be paid even during the summer
months when Mahler would be away. He visited some twenty other lodgings,
but the only one that pleased him was a two-room flat directly above Bülow's. Unfortunately the rent was ridiculously high.[1] Tormented by noise,
Mahler compared himself to a hunted deer, and he finally decided on a solution that he only put into effect the following year; that of renting an unfur-
nished apartment on a yearly basis, and bringing his own furniture from
Vienna. In the meantime he chose a small two-room apartment on the Fröbelstrasse, which overlooked a large, somewhat marshy field. It must have
been relatively calm, as during the winter and spring he was to do some important work there, in particular the revision of *Das klagende Lied.*

The last days of August were spent preparing a new production of *Der*

*Freischütz*[2] and rehearsing *Die Meistersinger* for the opening of the new season. A few days later, Tchaikovsky passed through Hamburg on his way back from New York, and Mahler conducted a performance of *Iolanta* in his presence. Afterward they spent another evening together at Pollini's.[3] For the time being the director was at his most charming. Mahler began to suspect that he was being friendly in order to persuade him to sign a new contract when the previous one expired in January 1894.

The revival of *Der Freischütz* on September 4 was a great success. Armbrust described the new production as "exemplary," comparing the "mastery performance" of the overture to those given by Bülow and Wagner. He also praised some tempos that were slower than usual.[4]

Natalie Bauer-Lechner writes of an event that can only have occurred at the start of the 1893–94 season, and that none of Mahler's biographers have mentioned.[5] The son of Mahler's landlady died suddenly and mysteriously. Almost simultaneously, the boy's grandmother became seriously ill, and the same night Mahler suffered pain and violent diarrhea. The next morning, a doctor diagnosed cholera and told him that there were still a few isolated cases in the town. He warned him that, if there was no improvement, the case must be reported to the health authorities and he would be sent to a hospital. He prescribed a remedy that was, it seems, contrary to both reason and custom.[6]

Justi was either in Hamburg or, which seems more likely, she hurried there when she learned of her brother's illness, and went to stay with Adele Marcus. Desperately worried, she spent every day at his bedside. She was thus able to convince the doctor that her brother should not go to a hospital, where there was great danger of infection, but rather to a private clinic where she could look after him herself. Half-drugged by the sedatives, Mahler did not have the strength to send her away in order to protect her. Panic-stricken to see his condition worsening, the unhappy girl decided to die with him, and secretly ate with the same spoon. It was a miracle that she escaped contagion. After hovering between life and death for several days, Gustav Mahler's strong constitution finally overcame the disease, which only left him with unpleasant memories and an added tendency toward intestinal troubles.

Upon recovery, he resumed work at the Hamburg Opera. According to the records, he was only absent for about ten days. A new opera by Alberto Franchetti, *Cristoforo Colombo,* was to be presented on October 5. Franchetti's *Asrael,* which had been only moderately successful in other parts of Germany, had been very much appreciated in Hamburg,[7] and Pollini had promised to stage his next opera, which he did more lavishly than usual. But despite the "magnificent" scenery, *Cristoforo Colombo* was not well received. Franchetti was criticized for his pompous, bombastic style, reminiscent of Wagner and nineteenth-century grand opera. The excessive length of the work had led to the suppression of its third and fourth acts, making the action almost unintelligible. Armbrust found nothing to praise but the "dramatic life" of the choral scenes.[8]

Lohse conducted the first Hamburg performance of Puccini's *Manon Lescaut,* and on October 22, Mahler led the yearly performance of Joseph Haydn's supreme masterpiece, *Die Schöpfung* (The Creation), in Altona.[9] Some days earlier (the eighteenth), in memory of Tchaikovsky, who had died on November 6, shortly after returning to Russia from Hamburg, Pollini had invited Mahler to conduct an evening of his music. The program included the Letter Scene from *Eugene Onegin, Iolanta,* and *Romeo and Juliet.* Writing of this symphonic poem, one of Tchaikovsky's best works, Emil Krause praised only "the original sound effects," having been unable to discern the least "melodic invention" in the music! Pollini had the bad taste to end the evening with a performance of *Pagliacci.*

After his unfortunate experience in Budapest, Mahler appears to have become resigned to "composing only for my own library." Indeed, the attitude of his contemporaries seemed to condemn him to such a fate. In the autumn of 1893, however, hoping that the Hamburg public would prove more enlightened, he decided to try again, and organized a "Popular Concert in Philharmonic Style." Only the name was "popular," in fact, as the program consisted mostly of first performances. The event took place on Friday, October 27, in the Ludwig Konzerthaus. The Laube Orchestra[10] and two well-known singers, Clementine Schuch-Prosska from Dresden[11] and Paul Bulss from Berlin,[12] took part.

The program was made up as follows:

### PART I

1. Overture to Egmont . . . . . . . . . . . . . . . . . . . . . . . Beethoven
2. Aria from *Hans Heiling* . . . . . . . . . . . . . . . . . . . . Marschner
3. Aria from *La Poupée de Nuremberg,*
   sung by Frau Schuch-Prosska . . . . . . . . . . . . . . . . . . . Adam
4. Overture, Fingal's Cave . . . . . . . . . . . . . . . . . . . Mendelssohn
5. a) "Das himmlische Leben"
   b) "Verlor'ne Müh' "
   c) "Wer hat dies Liedchen erdacht"
   Three *Humoresken* from *Des Knaben Wunderhorn*
   (Frau  Schuch-Prosska) . . . . . . . . . . . . . . . . . . . . . Mahler
6. a) "Der Schildwache Nachtlied"
   b) "Trost im Unglück"
   c) "Rheinlegendchen"
   from *Des Knaben Wunderhorn*
   (Paul  Bulss) . . . . . . . . . . . . . . . . . . . . . . . . . Mahler

### PART II

7. *Titan,* Tone Poem [*Tondichtung*] in Symphony form
   [manuscript] . . . . . . . . . . . . . . . . . . . . . . . . . . Mahler
[Followed by a list of movements and the "program" already referred to]

Preparations for this concert required considerable effort, especially since Laube's orchestra, "augmented for the occasion," was far from being the best in Hamburg. During rehearsals Mahler wrote to Richard Strauss, at that time conducting in Weimar, inviting him to attend. On the twenty-sixth he sent a note to the lawyer Hermann Behn,[13] a new friend who was to play a most important role in Mahler's life, informing him that there would be no dress rehearsal, because "up to the last moment I will have to work without interruption, as the music contains immense difficulties." He nevertheless expressed a hope that the performance would be adequate enough to reveal the work in its true light to those "capable of appreciating it."

A large audience filled the Konzerthaus on October 27 at 7:30 P.M., and Mahler's new works were more warmly received than in Budapest. The *Lieder* were loudly applauded, and so were the singers; *"Rheinlegendchen"* was even encored. At the end of the *Titan,* the applause was so enthusiastic that even Sittard was forced to admit that it easily drowned the boos of a few enemies. According to the *Fremdenblatt,* the orchestral musicians joined in the final ovation.

Not surprisingly however, the critics were still far from favorable. Like his predecessor on the *Hamburger Correspondent* twenty years before, who had covered a Wagner festival conducted by the composer himself, Joseph Sittard treated these exceptional works in a particularly hostile manner. He considered that the Konzerthaus concerts should give up experiments of this kind, as no composer, with the exception of Beethoven perhaps, deserved an entire evening to himself. After paying a few compliments to Mahler the conductor, he declared that he could not accept Mahler the creator, for his music was "the fruit of unrestrained subjectivity, with no substance and no aesthetic foundation." The "moderns" regrettably rated the "characteristic" higher than the "beautiful." "Imagination," that divine gift of poets and artists, which should unite and shape everything around a central idea, was lacking in Mahler, despite his technical prowess. His music had no soul; it was skillfully put together, but "even folk song succumbs when subjected to the deadly blight of reflection." The *Lieder* lacked a "naïve, touching expression," they were only laborious studies in instrumentation, and the words served solely as "pretexts for extravagances."[14] Mahler wove together "small, monotonous phrases" and tirelessly repeated the same motives in widely varied tonalities, but their "twisted" harmonies did not suffice to lend them interest.

While it was conceivable that these lieder might appeal to some listeners, Sittard felt that the same could not be said for Mahler's symphonic tone poem, a "mosaic" of small fragments that "aimlessly" followed one another and contained no single thought worth noting. The phrases were repeated endlessly instead of being developed, and these waves of brutal sound were "repellent to those with any sense of beauty." The introduction was "long and lacking in substance," and the best passage in the first movement was the kettledrum solo that came just before the sudden ending. "The Andante has no focal point, and for this reason lacks atmosphere." The Scherzo was original but vulgar; only the Trio, "based on a folk song,"[15] had some character. In conclusion Sittard made fun of the Marche Funèbre and its program, and saw nothing in the Finale "but an infernal unleashing of the elements, compared to which the Ride of the Valkyries is only a gentle breeze." Thus, more clearly than Hertzfeld in Budapest, the Hamburg critic here anticipated all the main critical leitmotivs with which his contemporaries were to reproach Mahler. In the *Hamburger Nachrichten,* Ferdinand Pfohl's judgment was less one-sided. Two conflicting forces could be discerned in Mahler's artistic personality, a Florestan and a Eusebius. His talent was unquestionable and his eloquence overpowering. While some Slavonic traits could be detected in his inspiration, his instrumentation was masterly, and his musical expression attained a high degree of dramatic intensity that captivated the listener. Of all the movements, the most original, according to Pfohl, was the Marche Funèbre, in which "the atmosphere is extraordinary from the very beginning." Admittedly Mahler's architecture was huge, he lacked any sense of measure, he "accumulates block after block," yet, while questioning some of the work's most characteristic parts, such as the Introduction and the sudden conclusion of the first movement,[16] while advising Mahler to lighten his instrumentation and shorten his Finale, Pfohl called this symphony "a work of genius," and one of the most important compositions of that time.

The anonymous critic of the *Fremdenblatt,* on the other hand, could not "follow Mahler in his absurd eccentricities" and regretted that the work did not contain "more substance and less art." However the *Lieder* had, he felt, "impressed the public deeply," since the "profound nature of the composer" expressed itself much more successfully in these "facetious" texts than in the great spiritual struggles. Finally Louis Bödecker, correspondent of the *Musikalisches Wochenblatt,* regretted the symphony's overlong passages and the harmonic and instrumental "strangeness" of the melodies, but admitted that "these works have generated great interest." Thus the critics were not unanimously hostile to Mahler and he had drawn attention to himself as a composer, not just as a "composing" conductor. It is worth noting that none of the critics speak of *"Kapellmeistermusik."* October 27, 1893, then, may be considered as the first important step along the hard road that was to lead Mahler to fame in a field that he considered far more important than interpretation.

Early in November, Mahler took advantage of a trip to Wiesbaden, where some songs of his were to be performed, by visiting Mainz and offering the music publisher Schott three of the new orchestral *Wunderhorn Lieder.* Although he was pleasantly surprised to find that three hundred copies of his earlier songs had already been sold and had earned him the sum of 120 marks in a year and a half, the meeting left him little hope for the future. A few days later he received a final refusal from the publishing house's director, Strecker. The Wiesbaden concert, on November 13, was conducted by the Konzertmeister Franz Nowak and included several orchestral pieces, with an interlude during which the baritone Paul Bulss once more sang the three *Wunderhorn Lieder*[17] that he had just performed for the first time in Hamburg. They were followed by the Prologue to *Pagliacci* and a few songs with piano accompaniment.[18] According to Mahler, although the orchestra played extremely well, the audience remained unmoved and the *Humoresken* obtained nothing more than a *succès d'estime*. Mahler took only two curtain calls.[19]

The lukewarm reception by the Wiesbaden critics reflected that of the public. While the Wiesbaden *Presse* stated that Mahler's *Lieder* were "warmly applauded," another critic[20] felt that the success had not been decisive, and saw nothing more than "interesting details" in these "fragmentary and disjointed" songs; he felt it was dangerous to center the interest upon the orchestra while using a "declamatory tone" for the voices. Finally the *Rheinischer Kurier* praised "the characteristic and striking instrumentation" though admitting that it sometimes threatened to cover the voices. According to the same paper, "there is something too deliberate in the means of expression" used in the *Nachtlied,* and the two other, less sophisticated *Humoresken* were better received by the public. Saddened by the indifference and general incomprehension of the public and musicians in Wiesbaden, Mahler took advantage of his only free day to walk along the Rhine from Mainz to Wiesbaden. The weather was splendid, and this was the only real pleasure he got out of his disappointing trip.

In December, Otto sent a registered letter to his brother declaring "in his usual arrogant way" that he had been "too deeply wounded" by him, and was no longer prepared to accept his money. Mahler's heart immediately softened and he wrote to Natalie, anxious about Otto's future and wondering how he could help him. He could not let him die of hunger and did not even wish him to live in poverty, so he entrusted him to Natalie's care and asked her to see to it that Alois, who had just begun to earn his own living, also had everything necessary for the winter months.

The tone of the letter sent to Justi, who was in Italy with Adele Marcus,[21] is quite different, for he considered her partially responsible for Otto's behavior, and in it he swears that he will not send him another pfennig unless he asks for it. Otto's pride was short-lived, however: a letter written on March 3 reveals that once again he was living comfortably on his eldest brother's monthly subsidy while waiting to take up a post in Leipzig which he had obtained on Mahler's recommendation.

Encouraged by the results of the concert on October 27, Mahler once again began to "work for himself" at the end of 1893. This time his task was not creative, but a revision of *Das klagende Lied.* He had found the score while leafing through some old manuscripts and had immediately realized that his first work contained something that was "already entirely original, although a little inflated [*schwülstig*] and overloaded [*überladen*]."[22] Of course he had already revised and considerably modified it, but "had not been able to take out all the decorations and superfluous ornaments," with which he himself had obscured the main lines. As with the *Titan* some months earlier, he intended to "prepare the score for a possible performance." This task was absorbing and meticulous, but after thirteen years Mahler was delighted to rediscover his work. "I see that the only progress I have made since then is technical," he wrote to Natalie. "But for the essentials, all the 'Mahler' whom you know was revealed at one single stroke. What surprises me most is that even in the instrumentation, nothing has to be altered, it is so characteristic and new; only some small details that I could not see at that time must be modified.

"In addition, I send you the poem so that you may know it too. Tell me what changes Trik [no doubt a mutual friend of Natalie and Mahler] wanted to introduce! I find nothing that could be changed, and I am certain that if Trik had found this text in an old collection of ballads like the *Knaben Wunderhorn,* such an idea would never have occurred to him. You will also see that at a time when I did not even suspect the existence of the *Wunderhorn,* I already lived completely in its spirit. Oh, dear God, if only I could have a little peace within my family! . . ."[23]

Eight days later Mahler told Justi that he was progressing with his work, making an "intelligent copy," an over-all "preparation, thanks to my experience as a conductor," as he found nothing to change in it. This work "has not ceased to astonish me since I have taken it up again. . . . I cannot understand how so strange and powerful a work could have come from the pen of a young man of twenty," he added, also predicting that he would probably never succeed in getting it performed. On January 4, another letter to Justi tells her that the work is completed: the score is already at the copyist's so that "it can be added to my library."

Mahler seemed to have been in better health that year. In the autumn, his hemorrhages had begun again, but he had managed to stop them, thanks to iron pills and the Swedish gymnastics that he practiced every morning. One major concern dominated all this period when his whole future was at stake: a year earlier, he had irrevocably decided to leave Hamburg when his contract expired at the beginning of 1894, but none of his attempts to find a new position had so far been successful. A letter written to Justi on December 5 shows that, among other possibilities, he had considered a post at the Vienna Opera, but there too without success.[24] "You can easily understand, after these Vienna episodes, that I am not in an optimistic mood."

Pollini was determined to keep Mahler in Hamburg at any price, and Mahler had decided, in view of this determination, to obtain certain concessions from him; in particular he was dying to conduct some concerts. Except for one occasion on which he had replaced the ailing Bülow, he had had to be satisfied with the Good Friday religious concerts and the Beethoven symphonies that he chose each year for his own benefit performance. He conducted the dramatic masterpieces of Mozart and Beetho-

ven at the opera every evening, so why should he be barred from tackling
their symphonies?[25] "On the stage, perfection can never be attained," he
told his friend the Czech composer Josef Förster, "for the theatrical machinery is too complex. You tighten up one little cog that brings it firmly
under control, and then another gives way suddenly at the most difficult
moment. A thousand seemingly minor factors play a destructive role on stage,
defeating everything that work, zeal and enthusiasm have succeeded in
creating. . . . I would rather be a concert conductor, for on the podium,
I could obtain infinitely better results."[26]

Bülow's condition was worsening daily. The two concerts he had conducted
in Berlin at the beginning of April had considerably taxed his strength, and
the second concert, which was given for the benefit of the Philharmonic
Orchestra's retirement fund and during which he sat down at the piano
and played the *Auf Wiedersehen* from the beginning of *Die Zauberflöte,*
had in fact constituted a farewell. On October 4 he rose once more from his
sickbed to attend the inauguration of the Bechstein Saal. By then, he was
being treated at the Pankow hospital, but nothing seemed to alleviate
either his violent neuralgia[27] or his fits of breathlessness and the excruciating
kidney pains from which he was also suffering. It thus seemed almost certain that he would be unable to conduct the subscription concerts again and
would name Mahler as his successor. On September 15, 1893, just before
leaving for Scheveningen, he wrote Mahler a letter expressing his "devoted
admiration" and expressed a wish to help him. Mahler at once forwarded
this letter to Justi, saying that "few men can boast of having received such
words from Bülow."[28] It seemed clear that he had a good chance of becoming Bülow's successor.

Mahler spent the Christmas vacation "largely alone," apart from a few
evenings with the Behns, or at Frau Lazarus'. Arnold Berliner, his most
faithful Hamburg friend, had gone to Breslau for the holidays, and Mahler
missed him; he was fond of him, despite the fact that he was "as unpleasant
and as fearfully pedantic as ever."[29] The last days of 1893 and the first of
1894 were devoted to rehearsing important new productions at the opera:
these were two of Mahler's favorite works, Verdi's *Falstaff* and Smetana's
*Bartered Bride.* Despite extremely cold weather, on January 2 *Falstaff*
was performed triumphantly, mainly thanks to Mahler: he had rehearsed
the opera with a care that equaled his devotion to the last of Verdi's
masterpieces.[30] The critics hailed the opera as a masterpiece and Armbrust placed it on a level with *Die Meistersinger* as one of the most important lyric creations of the nineteenth century. Immediately after this
brilliant premiere, Pollini's "forced labor" camp proved too much for another opera baritone, Friedrich Lissmann, who died suddenly of heart failure two days after singing Alberich in *Siegfried.*

The performance of *The Bartered Bride* finally enabled Mahler to express his admiration for his compatriot Bedřich Smetana. It also marked the
start of his long friendship and artistic collaboration with the singer Bertha

1. Gustav Mahler at the age of six.

2. Marie Mahler, nee Herrmann,
Mahler's mother.

3. Below: Bernhard Mahler and
Marie Mahler nee Bondy,
Mahler's father and
grandmother.

4. Mahler as a child.

5. Leopoldine and Justine
Mahler, Mahler's sisters.

6. Mahler's birthplace in Kalischt.

7. Entrance to Bernhard Mahler's house in Jihlava (Iglau) with author standing in doorway (1968).

8. The courtyard of Bernhard Mahler's house, where distillery was located.

9. Advertisement for Bernhard Mahler's distillery in the Iglau newspaper *Iglauer Sonntagsblatt*, 1866.

10. Hugo Wolf at the time he was a fellow-student with Gustav Mahler at the Vienna Conservatory.

11. Julius Epstein, Mahler's piano teacher at the Vienna Conservatory.

12. Heinrich Krzyzanowski, one of Mahler's first friends in Vienna. Picture taken at time when Krzyzanowski was in a mental institution.

13. Anton Bruckner.

Lauterer,[31] wife of the composer Josef Förster,[32] who was himself a great admirer of Smetana.[33] During a first brief stay in Hamburg, he had conceived an immense respect for Mahler when he heard him conduct *Die Meistersinger*. Some time after her engagement, Mahler asked Bertha Förster-Lauterer to learn the role of Eva in *Die Meistersinger*. She promptly studied it with her husband. During the first rehearsal, Mahler interrupted her in the middle of Act II to ask with whom she had prepared her part. Hearing that it was with Förster, Mahler said loudly, in the presence of the entire orchestra, "This is clearly the work of a musician," and asked the young woman to introduce her husband to him.[34]

Förster was delighted and a few days later called at the house on the corner of the Fröbelstrasse and the Welckerstrasse, where Mahler then lived. When he rang the third-floor bell, as he had been instructed, a pleasant woman opened the door and pointed to another at the end of a corridor, upon which he knocked several times without obtaining a reply. He finally plucked up his courage and entered, to find himself in a room containing only a bed, above which hung a dusty laurel wreath with the inscription "To the Pygmalion of the Hamburg Opera. Hans von Bülow." He then knocked on an inner door and after a friendly "Come in" found himself in Mahler's study. The two men were soon deep in a conversation that marked the beginning of a long friendship, though despite their equality of age, Mahler played the role of master, Förster that of disciple.

Studying Mahler's features, Förster was reminded of the Italian Renaissance. Like Savonarola or Malatesta, Mahler had a hook-nosed profile, tightly closed lips, a prominent chin, and high cheekbones. No less striking were his high forehead and sharp black eyes, which "glistened as though covered with dew" as they examined Förster with gentleness and warmth. The latter remembered his first impressions and later described the scene of the encounter, the narrow room that Mahler used as a study, with its two pianos, bookshelves, and writing desk. The grand piano, covered with scores, filled the center of the room while against one wall stood Mahler's favorite instrument, the upright piano, with the score of a Bach cantata open on the stand. On the walls hung some family portraits, a print of St. Anthony's Sermon to the Fish, a reproduction of Dürer's *Melancolia,* and another of Giorgione's famous *Concert.*

That day Mahler played selections from a Bach cantata for his new friend, growing enthusiastic over the melodic beauties and indignant at their neglect. "In this Castalian spring," he said, "I wash off the dust of the theater." He spoke of his idols, Beethoven and Wagner, and talked at length about Richard Strauss, whose new scores he studied with great care as soon as he received them. He considered Strauss to be Wagner's greatest successor. His orchestration, his inventiveness in the realm of sound, and his powerful creative talent deserved high praise. During these first meetings, Mahler did not mention a word about his own compositions. One evening, however, when it was already dark, he suddenly took a manuscript from a drawer and asked Förster: "Would you like to hear something?" They sat down at the piano and Förster was awed to discover the immense universe of Mahler's creation. The work (it was the *Totenfeier*) so moved him that afterward he was unable to utter a word. He merely took Mahler's hand and shook it hard. Delighted and surprised, Mahler told him of his recent experience with Bülow, and then spoke at length of his compositions and his work methods. He told him, among other things, that his mind almost never presented him with a simple melodic contour, but nearly always with a complete theme, often together with a secondary melody. He illustrated his point with extracts from his scores.[35]

Later, Mahler also told Förster of his main preoccupations, in particular his great desire to conduct concerts, and Förster witnessed the enormous enthusiasm and zeal that Mahler brought to rehearsals of *The Bartered Bride*. One evening Pollini invited to his house the stage director Jauner,[36] Bertha Förster-Lauterer, her husband, and the basso Hesch. They praised the work's lighthearted charm and beauty and placed it on a level with *Le Nozze di Figaro* and *Il Barbiere di Siviglia*. Hesch and Bertha Lauterer sang some excerpts, with Förster at the piano, and Mahler, who knew a little Czech,[37] made a few changes in Max Kalbeck's German translation of the libretto.

*The Bartered Bride* had so far been staged only in Berlin and Vienna, and in the latter city the few performances had been given by a Czech group during the world's fair. Opera administrators and many others interested in the theater flocked to Hamburg from all parts of Germany to attend the first performance on January 17, 1894. It was an immense success: Mahler never bettered it in Hamburg. All the critics praised the work itself, the masterly way in which he conducted it, and the wonderful harmony between the music and the subject matter: "an ideal comic opera," enthused Armbrust. It was given fourteen times before the summer recess and was performed again the following autumn—clear proof of its extraordinary success.[38]

Some time after this memorable performance, Mahler gave a dinner at the Hotel Streit, where he took all his meals, inviting the Försters, Berliner, and an old friend from Vienna, the actor Karl Wagner.[39] The dinner ended with a splendid plum pudding, and in this congenial atmosphere Mahler expressed his fervent wish—an apartment of his own at last in which he could receive his friends and play chamber music.

Meanwhile, throughout that winter and the spring, he wrote to Richard Strauss practically every day. The long and friendly relationship between the two musicians was settling into its definitive form, one of mutual respect and friendly assistance. Their projects that year were the performance of the *Titan* in Weimar and that of Strauss's first opera, *Guntram,* in Hamburg.[40] In the middle of January, Strauss visited Hamburg to conduct a subscription concert that included the performance of *Aus Italien*. He spent much time with Mahler in the home of their mutual friend Hermann

Behn, and later praised him highly in a letter to his father.[41] The two musicians parted, believing that they would meet again in less than a month, since Strauss was to conduct another subscription concert at the end of February. After his departure, Mahler wrote telling him of Hamburg's reactions to his music: the "little pond" had been much shaken by "the Strauss affair," and Mahler had often laughed at the astonished faces of the good citizens, but he was delighted by Pfohl's review.[42] Later Mahler wrote again, asking Strauss for the score of *Guntram* and repeating how moved he had been when he heard the opera on the piano.

Nor was Strauss inactive: he was doing his best to have the *Titan* included in the program of the annual festival of the "Allgemeiner Deutscher Musikverein" (he was one of its most important members), held in Weimar early in June. He would conduct the work himself if necessary, since Mahler might not have concluded the Hamburg season by then. But Strauss's next letter amazed Mahler, for it seemed that Pollini was once more indulging in "somber machinations." He had been particularly affable for some time, talking constantly of a new contract, into which Mahler had insisted on inserting certain conditions mentioned earlier. Yet Strauss, who was about to leave Weimar, wrote Mahler on February 3 to say that the Hamburg impresario had approached him regarding the possibility of an engagement there! "This news has deeply disturbed me," Mahler wrote in reply, "and I should like to discuss it frankly with Pollini, in order to clarify the situation. But I will do nothing without your permission. It may be nothing more than one of those sudden moves so dear to him, destined to curtail my present privileged position. Thus it would be in your interest also to bring matters into the open. . . ."[43] He is outwardly most polite to me," he added the next day, "so I cannot understand this business. He is extremely sly and God knows what he has in mind. At any rate, I do beg you, my dear friend, to think of your own interests only, as I think of mine, in this affair. That is the only way to act under such circumstances, otherwise one loses all judgment when dealing with people of his sort."

Pollini's behavior seemed even stranger to Mahler when he approached him on February 4, during the evening performance of *The Bartered Bride,* and said, "I have waited long enough. Tomorrow you must come to my office so that we can sign our contract!" Mahler stared at him in silent amazement: secretly he had "already prepared" his departure (at least, so he told Strauss). The next morning, when Mahler reached the theater, Felix Wolf, the office manager, handed him a contract already signed by Pollini, in which he agreed to all Mahler's demands. Mahler signed it, assuming that Pollini intended to divide the repertoire between Strauss and himself, "for, though it seems incredible, he sometimes has moments of great idealism. . . . You can imagine how delighted I would be!" wrote Mahler, with more courtesy than sincerity. "I know of no one else with whom I feel so much affinity, and for whom any petty inclinations on my part would be forgotten so completely. It is with the greatest pleasure that I would give up the *Nibelungen,* and we could work everything out together in the most friendly manner. I suggest, in order to save time, that you accept his proposals without any fuss (though naturally not letting him know that I have written to you)."

Thus Mahler was re-engaged by Pollini for five years and clearly wished at all costs to avoid making an enemy of Strauss (which would certainly have happened had Strauss gone to Hamburg). Even in Kassel and Leipzig, Mahler had discovered that he was totally incapable of playing second fiddle to a colleague, even for a short period of time. But his admiration for Strauss and his unsuccessful approaches to several theaters over the past months helped to overcome these misgivings.[44]

Strauss's role in this affair is far from clear, and Mahler had no illusions.[45] A letter he wrote to Justi clearly defines the nature of their relationship: "a friendship of reason" rather than a "chosen affinity." "I should be lying if I were to say that we have a lot in common. I am more and more aware of my total isolation from today's musicians. Our objectives are far apart. Everywhere I see only the old classical or the 'new German' trend. Scarcely has Wagner been recognized and understood than once more there appears a bigoted and sanctimonious priesthood that walls up real life everywhere and that feels impelled to reshape the art of yesterday—even when it has more grandeur and carries more weight than that of today—in order to create something new that responds to the demands of the moment. Strauss, in particular, is entirely priest or pope. Nevertheless, he is a nice fellow, as far as I can tell. Whether it is all genuine remains to be seen. All this is absolutely confidential, for he is 'my only friend among the gods,' and I really don't want to jeopardize my relationship with him.

"By the way, he had his eye on my position here. I would have been delighted to let him have it if only I could have found a small place somewhere else to give me refuge. With this in mind I tried everything, so as to have nothing with which to reproach myself, but it seems that my Judaism closes all doors before me. I received this reply from Munich (Possart), where I put forward my name through an agent: 'Although I am entirely convinced of Mahler's exceptional talents, I am unable to consider him!' From Berlin the same evasive reply. Since the world rejects me, I shall return to Venusberg! In fact, I am rather lucky, for, as you can judge by Strauss's attitude—my position here is not too bad."[46]

There is no need to stress the importance of this letter. When, three years later, Mahler once more tried to obtain a post at the Munich and Berlin operas, he met the same obstacles, and, until the last moment, he could not believe that his engagement at the Hofoper would materialize. In 1895 a conductor was needed for the Gesellschafts Konzerte in Vienna,[47] and Mahler, but the members of the committee first pretended never to have Ludwig Bösendorfer, the famous piano manufacturer, immediately suggested heard of him, and then answered that his name was "not very suitable."

In another letter, written to Löhr about the same time, Mahler seems to have lost faith[48]: "Some offers have reached me through various 'agents.' They propose that I should take Richter's place, but this is only so much talk. These gentlemen take such matters upon themselves without any sort of authorization. I think you are right to be apprehensive under the present circumstances. The fact that I am Jewish bars my access to all the court theaters. Neither Vienna, Berlin nor Dresden is open to me—the same wind blows everywhere. In my peculiar state of mind (which, taken as a whole, is not too gloomy), this does not bother me unduly. I must admit that today's artistic life no longer appeals to me much in any of its forms. In the last analysis there is always the same trickery and lying, all is rotten to the core. Even if I went to Vienna, how would I survive, with my way of seeing things? I would only have to try and explain to the famous Philharmonic— trained by the honest Hans Richter—my conception of a Beethoven sym- phony, in order to provoke a most distressing conflict. Haven't I experi- enced the same thing here, where, after all, thanks to the unreserved ad- miration of Brahms and Bülow, my position is no longer disputed?

"What storms I create every time I turn from traditional routine and try to do something new and personal! I have only one wish—to carry out my calling in some small town where there are no traditions, no guardians of the 'eternal canons of beauty,' and, if possible, no theater and no repertoire; someplace where I could give satisfaction to a small circle of simple, naïve people whom I could please at the same time as I satisfied myself. But as long as I must remain responsible for my noble brothers' impetuous actions and as long as my sisters are not independent, I must unfortunately continue to exercise a profitable and lucrative activity. . . .

"Do not think that I am in a 'bad mood'! On the contrary, I have acquired a kind of fatalism that has taught me to enjoy life and to look at it in all its forms with a certain 'interest.' This world pleases me a little more each day; I devour more and more books. They are, after all, the only friends I have at my disposal—and what friends! Dear God, what would I do without them? . . . They are always consoling and affectionate, my true brothers, my parents, and my beloved. . . ."

This letter sums up all Mahler's experiences during the years spent in Hamburg and the difficulties he encountered while accomplishing his "mis- sion." What great artist has not dreamed of a place where he might reign alone, protected from the crowds, surrounded by the chosen few who would help and support him? It is not surprising that Gustav Mahler should occasionally have grown weary of his destiny and dreamed of a better world.

The new contract brought with it a moment of relative calm after a long period of worry. Mahler was particularly happy to have won a victory over Pollini regarding the concerts, at the risk of being dismissed and finding himself jobless. The original agreement mentioned four concerts a year, or- ganized by Pollini in the Covent Garden hall, but Mahler had hardly signed the new contract when a representative of Hermann Wolff, the Berlin impresario, asked him to conduct the Bülow concerts, which the latter had had to abandon for reasons of health. Dismayed to find that Mahler was already engaged, the representative returned the following day and told Mahler that Wolff was prepared to meet all Pollini's demands in order to obtain his services; Wolff himself would visit Hamburg to discuss conditions with him. This worried Mahler, since the relationship between the two impresarios was strained, but Pollini finally agreed to "give him up" to Wolff for five hundred marks per concert. Mahler, who had vainly hoped for an offer from Wolff for so long, was furious to think that only a month earlier the transaction would have cost nothing. The final agreement was signed in March, granting Pollini not five hundred marks, but one quarter of the box-office takings.

Condemned to stay in Hamburg, Mahler started looking for a more suitable apartment, and even considered recalling Justi from Rome to help him with his search. In the meantime, he begged her to keep from their brothers the fact that he had signed a new contract; they would certainly start spending money thoughtlessly again if they knew of it. Mahler considered renting the first floor of a country house on the banks of the Alster, and later toyed with the idea of a whole house to himself, but in March he finally postponed the entire project until the autumn. He had not yet decided what to do about Emma, and hesitated between two solutions—either bringing her to Hamburg or sending her to live with Nina Hoffmann, where she could finish her studies and find a job in Vienna. The family situation was relatively quiet throughout the spring. Otto had finally been discharged by the recruiting board as unfit for service. Mahler introduced him to Staegemann before the summer, and the latter offered him an excellent temporary contract that ran until September 1, at which time he was to take up a three-year appointment as *chordirektor* and second conductor. His annual salary was to be gradually increased during the first years; 80 marks to begin with, then 120, then 200. Mahler also managed to obtain a temporary summer engagement for him at the Bremen Theater. "His debuts will be much easier than mine," he wrote to Justi, "but all to no purpose unless he himself shows some enthusiasm."

Mahler was working as hard as ever, and his circle of Hamburg friends was still small. Berliner was about to leave the city, and Mahler still could not make up his mind about him: "I experience more irritation than pleasure when we meet. Whenever I am in an exalted and excited mood, I receive the cold shower of his 'logic' and his 'justice,' so that I cannot truly regret his departure, now definitely fixed for this summer. His constant displays of friendship toward me in public annoy me. Nevertheless, I shall miss him, as the others understand me even less." A letter written in 1894 relates a characteristic episode in this stormy friendship: at the end of a violent discussion, Mahler, who supported Wagner's views on vivisection, became violently angry and deeply offended Berliner. The next morning he wrote to apologize, but added that Berliner had "an exceptional gift for making me lose my temper."[49]

At the Behns', where Mahler spent many evenings chatting or playing chamber music, he felt "completely at home," because there he had found "a small place that gives warmth in the winter and shade in the summer." They were staunch friends and had even commissioned a sculptor they knew to make a bust of Mahler, who wrote: "My contours seem better suited to the plastic art than to the art of sound." But in spite of Behn's unfailing kindness, he too often incurred Mahler's wrath.

During the first months of 1894 Mahler told Förster that the symphony, of which he knew only the first movement, also contained an Andante and a Scherzo that he wished him to hear. Afterward the two musicians discussed the structure of the work and the order of the movements, and Förster admitted that after such a powerful and emotional first movement, the composition of a Finale would be a formidable task.

In the meantime, Bülow's health had deteriorated. Richard Strauss had given him an enthusiastic account of Egypt and its climate—he had recently convalesced from a serious illness there—and the old man decided to go and warm himself in the Egyptian sun with his wife and Toni Petersen, the daughter of the Burgomaster of Hamburg. They arrived in Cairo on February 7, and he had a slight attack on the terrace of his hotel the following day. Four days later, death put an end to his long martyrdom.[50] As soon as the news reached Hamburg, it was decided to dedicate the ninth subscription concert (February 26) to his memory. The proper tone was set at once by an organ prelude played by the critic Carl Armbrust, followed by a quartet singing the chorale *"Wenn ich einmal muss scheiden"* from the *St. Matthew Passion.* Then Hermann Behn made a speech in which he praised the dead man, who had been a Hamburg citizen for seven years, and an "endless source of the noblest and purest artistic pleasures." During this concert, Julius Spengel also conducted the first two choruses from Brahms's *German Requiem.*

The year before, Bülow had conducted Beethoven's *"Eroica"* at his last concert, and Strauss had been invited to Hamburg to conduct it in memory of his friend and benefactor, but he refused at the last moment. Frau Stargardt, the daughter of the impresario Hermann Wolff, asserts that, in order to remain on good terms with Frau Cosima Wagner, who had invited him to take part in the Bayreuth Festival, he had refused to conduct Brahms's *Requiem,* which would have been an appropriate choice because of the deceased's admiration for Brahms. Instead, he proposed to give the *Héroïde funèbre* by Liszt, whom Bülow hated. Finally, after exchanging several telegrams with Fräulein Petersen,[51] he pleaded illness, and Mahler[52] was naturally chosen to replace him. He conducted the *"Eroica"* hidden behind a clump of green plants that surrounded a bust of the dead man. The audience refrained from clapping but Mahler considered that "the very quality of the silence and the sighing after each movement clearly indicated the power of the emotion produced." It had been a "victory on all fronts" for Mahler. This time Sittard considered his interpretation "entirely worthy of the departed Master."[53]

A month later, when Bülow's body had been brought back to Hamburg, a funeral ceremony took place at 9 A.M. on March 29 in the Michaeliskirche, one of the most famous buildings in the old city. Countless wreaths, "whole flower beds" buried the coffin, which stood before the altar on an enormous catafalque surrounded by thousands of candles. After a chorale from Bach's *St. Matthew Passion,* an extract from Brahms's *Requiem,* and a psalm read by the clergyman, the women and children of the choir sang another chorale, the well-known *"Auferstehn"* by Friedrich Klopstock,[54] bringing the entire ceremony to a rousing climax. Then came the funeral oration, and finally a chorale from Bach's *St. John Passion* brought the service to an end. The solemnity of the Klopstock chorale, together with the sound of the childish voices and the tolling of the bells, made an unforgettable impression on all those present. After leaving the church the funeral procession halted in front of the opera house while, from the terrace, Mahler conducted the Funeral March from *Die Götterdämmerung.*

Förster, who had been unable to speak to Mahler at the church, went to the Fröbelstrasse that same afternoon, eager to exchange impressions. Opening the door, he saw Mahler seated at his desk, his head bent low over the paper as he worked. Turning slowly, Mahler cried out, "Förster, I have it!" Some mysterious intuition told Förster what Mahler meant, and Förster began to recite, *"'Auferstehn, ja auferstehn . . .'"* (To be resurrected, yes, to be resurrected). Klopstock's poem, which they had both heard that morning, was in fact the basis of the Finale to the *Second Symphony:* Mahler had already noted down several preliminary sketches for the movement, and he completed it the following summer.

Autobiographical texts by Mahler are rare; a fact that gives particular value to the following one, taken from a letter written three years after the commemoration service at the Michaeliskirche: "The way in which I received inspiration for the Finale is deeply indicative of the essence of musical creation. For a long time I had been considering the idea of introducing a chorus into the last movement, and only the fear that this might be interpreted as a servile imitation of Beethoven made me hesitate so long. Then Bülow died, and I attended his funeral. The atmosphere in which I found myself and the thoughts I dedicated to the dead man were very much in the spirit of the work I was then carrying within me. All of a sudden the choir, accompanied by the organ, intoned Klopstock's chorale 'Auferstehn.' It was as if I had been struck by lightning; everything suddenly rose before me clearly! Such is the flash for which the creator waits, such is sacred inspiration!

"After that I had to create in sound what I had just experienced. Nonetheless, if I had not already been carrying the work within me, how could I have experienced this moment? Weren't thousands of other people with me

in the church? That's how it always is with me. I only compose when I
truly experience something [*erlebe*], and I only experience it when I
create!"[55] Once again, Gustav Mahler reveals himself to posterity as a
mystic, a seer, one of the elect who await the revelations of divine providence.
The magnificence of the Finale to the *Second Symphony* bears out the
statement in this letter.

Three of Bülow's friends, Fräulein Petersen, Frau Schiff, and Frau Lazarus, all of whom had accompanied him to Cairo, now became professional
mourners, and their concerted weeping exasperated Mahler. "I feel like climbing up walls or roaring with laughter," he wrote, thus probably expressing
a deep-seated personal reaction. "I have already done both and have had
more than enough of ceremonies and the cremation of Bülow. I have just
come back from the dress rehearsal! The weeping willows—alias the old
fools—are already swollen up with grief. They will shrink again once he is
buried. At present they are very angry with the weather because it does not
rain. . . . The great day has come at last. We shall be mourning from nine
A.M. till five P.M., at which time there will be a great funeral banquet at the
Behns'. My only hope is that the weepers will not have the idea of opening
a Bülow Museum (perhaps to display his chamber pots or his laundry lists).
How people flutter about a Bülow when he is dying or dead! As for the
young and the living, they are left alone to fend for themselves!"[56]

The first ceremony had in fact been followed by the second in the
Michaeliskirche, which had taken on particular significance in Mahler's life,
and then on the following day the cremation brought all Hamburg together
once more. The ceremony was held at Ohlsdorf, near Hamburg, in one of
the two crematories existing in Germany at that time, and was accompanied
by the choral transcription (with text of Hermann Behn) of the Dankgesang
from Beethoven's *Quartet No. 15*, Op. 132, followed by a eulogy and a
Schubert chorus. All Bülow's friends attended: Hermann Wolff and his wife,
the conductor Siegfried Ochs, Burgomaster Petersen and his daughter Toni,
the Behns and the Berlin poet Otto Ludwig. Frau Bülow's ostentatious
mourning caused even those most sincerely bereaved to smile. She had even
gone so far as to hang a black flag before the window of her husband's room.

Mahler finally grew weary of this succession of endless ceremonies. Only
a few years earlier, Bülow himself had expressed his disgust with the musical
world and his weariness of the eternal ingratitude of critics and musicians in
general,[57] and Mahler could not help thinking that he would rather have
been better treated during his life than mourned more hypocritically than
sincerely after his death.

Mahler's attitude toward Bülow before and after his death was undoubtedly
ambiguous, though he himself was not wholly aware of this. The psychologist
Theodor Reik has attempted a psychological explanation that is based on
indisputable facts.[58] He believes that the Michaeliskirche episode, which in
Mahler's mind took on the aspect of a mystical revelation, had in fact a
simple psychological explanation. The symphony's "subject" or "program"

deals with man's fundamental problem, which is the ultimate meaning of life and survival after death. Bülow's funeral reminded Mahler of the transitory nature of the human condition and of man's earthly creations. The *"Aufer-stehn"* chorale provided him with the answer; it was a mystical and mysterious sign, which brought peace and release from tension after months of soul-searching and worrying about his work.

Reik notes three essential stages in Förster's account:

1. The occasion, that is the funeral, which awakened in Mahler the emotions and basic ideas incorporated in the *Second Symphony*.
2. Surprise at hearing the choir of children singing *"Auferstehn!"*
3. The psychological element of "preparation."

Mahler spoke of "surprise" and "preparation," but the surprise was in fact the fulfillment of unconscious expectations, something that sometimes occurs when least expected, in a surprising yet liberating form. The episode would be easier to explain, according to Reik, if the central figure of the ceremony that day had admired Mahler as a composer. Before the "revelation" on the day of the funeral, had not Mahler been unconsciously reminded of the scene at Bülow's and the latter's condemnation of the *Totenfeier?* It is true Mahler later stated that he felt no anger or resentment, but the psychologist believes that these violent reactions were repressed, ignored, and driven underground. In fact Mahler's respect and admiration for the "master," for the great conductor and musician, his almost excessive humility,[59] and the gratitude he felt toward him, were incompatible with such reactions. Thus, according to Reik, sorrow and regret for Bülow's death coexisted with the memory of the earlier painful scene and reawakened Mahler's feelings at that time: rage, rebellion, a "death wish" and unconscious resentment that revealed itself as follows: "I will go on, and will succeed as a composer in spite of you." In the meantime, Mahler composed the other movements and added the *"Urlicht,"* but was unable to find a suitable text for the Finale.

The return of the "death wish" was accompanied by a certitude: Bülow was dead, and the fulfillment of the "desire" produced a moment of triumph, immediately repressed. The "death wish" was basically linked with the hope that the symphony would be completed and would turn out to be a masterpiece. When the children's choir intoned the famous chorale, the secret emotion was transferred to the words, and the long-sought-for solution sprang to Mahler's mind. The first words of the chorale do in fact express redemption: struggle is not vain, resurrection and salvation are assured. The unconscious satisfaction experienced because "his wish had the power to kill" had been, as it were, transposed to the chorale text, which contained verses that were perfectly suited to the Finale he was planning. Simplifying the thought process, Reik believed that Bülow's death "became not only the premise but the promise of Mahler's belief that his symphony would be successfully completed." Reik reconstructs the mental process in the following manner, which is the same for all obsessional thoughts: "As my unconscious wish that you who rejected me as a composer should die has been fulfilled, so my symphony will be finished, and will be a masterwork." Moreover Reik recalls that Mahler was attending a "funeral ceremony" and that the piece he had played to Bülow two years earlier bore the same title (*Totenfeier*), which makes the unconscious association of ideas all the more plausible. His attitude toward Nikisch's illness a few years earlier in Leipzig was also characterized by the same half-unconscious "satisfaction."

It is quite certain that Mahler had felt deeply resentful toward Bülow. His letters to Justi, and one sent to Strauss, which Reik never saw, fully prove this point. Mahler's resentment, then, was more conscious than Reik had believed, even if he was able to preserve intact his admiration for Bülow's artistic personality. Besides this, the revelation in the Michaeliskirche was that of the "Resurrection," and this image absorbed Mahler to such an extent that it was the basis of his biggest symphonic movement. Even if the flash of lightning, the unconscious point of departure for the Finale, originated in an unconscious "death wish," this feeling was rejected, transposed, sublimated into a message of hope, a transcendent vision and one of the most moving and stirring finales ever written.

In the spring of 1894, after Cosima Wagner decided to engage the tenor Birrenkoven for the role of Parsifal in Bayreuth, Mahler started rehearsing the part with him, and the tenor proved to be "far more intelligent and gifted" than he had expected. Birrenkoven conceived a great admiration for Mahler and was one of the few artists who respected him enough to obey him blindly. He even occasionally attended rehearsals that did not concern him, just out of interest. Mahler's first favorable impression did not last long however, for when he later suggested Birrenkoven to Strauss for the leading role in *Guntram,* he added that "his talent and reliability are beyond reproach, but his intelligence leaves much to be desired."

In January the famous actress Eleonora Duse visited Hamburg, where she was to give three performances at the Thaliastrasse Theater. Mahler attended all three and was deeply moved. On March 3 he included *Fidelio* and Beethoven's *Seventh Symphony* in the program of his annual benefit concert. At the end of the evening, the audience applauded him wildly while he was presented with a superb laurel wreath interwoven with gold, as well as many bouquets, one of which represented a podium made of lilies of the valley with a baton of violets. The Behns then gave a dinner in his honor. "Upon entering, everyone will be asked whether or not they admire my tempi," wrote Mahler, "and those who do not will not be allowed in. I find this a charming idea, and next year I intend to break off all relations with those who do not consider my tempi the only ones that lead to salvation."[60] These same tempos aroused Sittard's anger that very evening; he was "struck dumb with amazement" at "the arbitrary conception" of the *Seventh Symphony,* all the more so since Mahler had heard Bülow's interpretation of the work several times. He was also roused to indignation by several details in the first movement and by the slowness of the Scherzo.[61] Sittard nevertheless admitted that the interpretation, by and large, had been "entirely in the spirit of Beethoven" and that he had never heard the Finale played with such clarity and such enthralling enthusiasm.

A few days later, on March 13, Mahler conducted a brilliant cast in a charity performance of *Die Fledermaus,* by Johann Strauss, and then spent the Easter vacation alone, for Berliner was still with his parents in Breslau and Mahler no longer saw the "weeping willows," who exasperated him. In the meantime, an offer had arrived from Sir Augustus Harris in London for another German season in June. Mahler asked for a weekly salary of a thousand marks, plus living expenses, and Harris's refusal delighted him, as he would thus be able to devote the summer to completing his *Second Symphony*[62] in peace.

On May 10, Richard Strauss married the singer Pauline de Ahna; he had just been engaged by the Munich Opera. This kept his friendship with Mahler alive, for it would certainly not have survived rival activities in the same theater. Their exchange of letters continued during the spring, and Mahler kept Strauss advised of his efforts to persuade Pollini to stage *Guntram.* But however persuasively Mahler explained that Strauss was the rising star of German music and that his first dramatic work was "the most important since *Parsifal,"* Pollini refused to be convinced. Mahler preferred not to take extreme measures, for he knew that the impresario was capable of accepting and then of sabotaging the premiere. Nonetheless, he promised Strauss that he would try again when he found him in a better mood—always the best method with Pollini. Early in May, however, he had to tell Strauss that his latest attempts had also failed, but he suggested another project, which he in fact carried out—a concert performance of two extracts from *Guntram.*

The premiere of *Guntram* finally took place in Weimar on May 10, shortly before the festival of contemporary music that was to include the *Titan.* Mahler, to his great regret, could not attend it and had to confide to Strauss the task of conducting the first rehearsals of his symphonic poem. As always, he had carried out some important revisions in the orchestration after the Hamburg concert the previous October, wishing to make the sonority "clearer and more transparent." He sent the revised score to Strauss requesting that the winds and strings be rehearsed separately, as he himself had done in Hamburg. He planned to reach Weimar on May 29, two days before the concert.[63]

Thus, thanks to Strauss's influence and to that of the critic August Ferdinand Hermann Kretzschmar, the *Titan* had been included in the program of the thirtieth festival of the Allgemeiner Deutscher Musikverein.[64] Kretzschmar was probably the addressee of a letter that Mahler wrote two weeks before his arrival in Weimar, politely refusing to furnish any "analysis" of his symphonic poem. "In my opinion, such technical remarks," he added, "bewilder the public," which then tends to *read* rather than *listen.* "I naturally consider that the texture of motifs should be clear to each listener," he wrote, "but do you really think that quoting a few themes is sufficient to clarify a modern work? Acquaintance with, and understanding of, a musical work, must be acquired through *detailed* study, and the more profound the work, the longer and more difficult the process. What is important during a first hearing is to give oneself up entirely to the work, so as to be receptive to its human and poetic aspects. If one feels attracted to it, one sets oneself to studying it in detail!

"How can this be done, if one knows the *man,* who is always more profound and more complex than his work? Where is the 'program'? So, we diligently study the man; we tenderly and attentively pry into him. Of course, he evolves and is transformed, whereas his work remains the same— but comparisons are always lame!"[65] Although he refused to let anyone publish the briefest analysis of his work, Mahler kept the "program" of the preceding year. The first movement was still called *Aus der Tagen der Jugend* and bore the subtitle *Blumen Frucht und Dornenstück* (Flowers, Fruit, and Thorns), which was taken from Jean Paul's *Siebenkäs* and, according to Nodnagel,[66] added at the last moment.

On the morning of May 29, Mahler left Hamburg for Leipzig, where he met Otto, whom he had decided to take with him to the festival. As soon as they reached Weimar, he started to rehearse the *Titan,* which had already been prepared by Strauss. Apart from *Guntram* and Verdi's *Falstaff,* the main attraction of the festival was a new fairy-tale opera by Engelbert Humperdinck, *Hänsel und Gretel.*[67] Mahler met the composer and called his work "a masterpiece" and "a true enrichment of dramatic literature." He hoped for great things from the Weimar concert. He was deeply moved to be performed in the town made famous by Goethe, Schiller, and Liszt, and he also hoped to find greater understanding there, since the festival was one of modern music and the audience consisted mainly of musicians and critics. Soon, however, he discovered that the orchestra was exhausted after a long theatrical season, that it was ill-prepared, and that he had time for only one rehearsal.[68] Furthermore, the acoustics of the theater were "detestable"[69] and in his opinion the performance could only be "very mediocre."

Except for the *Titan* the concert was conducted by Eduard Lassen and started at 5 P.M. on June 3. The program was huge and varied: Liszt's *Weimars Volkslied* for male chorus, Rubinstein's *Cello Concerto in A Minor* (soloist: Julius Klengel), Wagner's *Wesendonck Lieder* (soloist: Rosa Sucher), and finally the *Titan,* which was received with rather weak applause and much booing.

In the second half, which started with *Des Sängers Fluch,* an orchestral ballad by Hans von Bülow played in his memory, Bernhard Stavenhagen's *Piano Concerto*[70] was warmly applauded by the public. Finally, about 9 P.M. Brünnhilde's Immolation from *Die Götterdämmerung* (soloist: Rosa Sucher) and Wagner's *Kaisermarsch* concluded this concert, which undoubtedly exhausted both performers and public. According to Carl Krebs,[71] despite the public's misgivings and Mahler's "bad reputation" as a composer, the conductor had immediately commanded attention: "When the little man with the ascetic face stepped onto the podium, raised his baton and cast a piercing glance over the orchestra, the musicians stiffened and one truly sensed the degree to which they were inwardly on guard and 'at attention.'" With his brisk and jerky gestures, Mahler was the living image of concentrated energy. Every single one of his nerves was taut and he managed to convey his every last emotion to the performers so that they carried out his wishes with divinatory insight.

"My symphony was received partly with furious opposition and partly with unbounded admiration," Mahler wrote to Berliner. "Opinions have clashed violently in the streets and drawing rooms in the nicest possible way! 'As long as the dogs bark, we know that we are galloping!' Naturally, I was again the best! (in my own view, at least, which was shared by only a tiny minority). In the end the orchestra was very pleased with the symphony and full of understanding toward my conducting technique, thanks to a barrel of beer. My brother was present—quite content over this half failure—as I am over this half success."[72] Otto had in fact declared before the concert that any work that won public applause must be worthless. He must have been delighted when he read the reviews: only the *Berliner Courier* (E.D.) was not entirely hostile. The anonymous critic mainly reproached Mahler for having taken his friends' advice and drawn up a program; in his opinion the music of the *Titan* was understandable without one. Mahler's "creative power" was great, his feelings were profound, and he had unusually strong powers of expression, though he sometimes lacked a sense of proportion. The "masterly way in which he painted orchestral atmosphere" was indisputable: he always expressed himself with eloquent originality and an "inexhaustable richness worthy of Jean Paul." His methods were new but showed no confusion. They sometimes surprised, but they achieved their aims. This unusually perceptive critic considered that Mahler had "still more to say." He was "one of those men who seem to have been chosen to enrich the kingdom of music by discovering new lands."

Otto Lessmann, a member of the Verein and the editor of the *Allgemeine Musik-Zeitung,* condemned *Titan* unconditionally. According to him, the work was given at the festival because Mahler was a Verein member and his symphony had not yet been performed (*sic*). In his opinion it was impossible to discover any similarity between the symphony and Jean Paul's novel that was supposed to have inspired it. There was "great disproportion between its form and its content," an "absence of well-constructed musical ideas," "unbelievably long tedious passages," "effects without causes," "search for novelty," and unpleasing "affectations," through all of which the composer groped blindly. Even Ernst Otto Nodnagel, who later became one of the most enthusiastic supporters of Mahler's music, wrote in the *Berliner Tageblatt* that the work contained a few attractive details, some strange and striking effects, but that it did not bear even the most superficial resemblance to its "confused and incomprehensible" program. To him the Finale appeared a "distinctly comic hubbub."[73] In the *Signale für die Musikalische Welt,* a critic spoke of the "total failure of this tiresome trash," and in the *Musikalisches Wochenblatt* and the *Neue Zeitschrift*[74] Max Hess declared the work stillborn, bewildering, for the movements were quite unconnected and bore no resemblance to their "program." The picturesque "classical" effects in the Introduction and the "Haydn-inspired" motifs of the first Allegro might lead the listener to believe that this is a satire on classical music, but in the Finale Mahler abandons this form of expression, "influenced by Bizet and the new French school," in favor of a "neo-German" style. At this point his inspiration deserts him and he "endlessly repeats the motifs of the first movement." The work was "interred to the accompaniment of boos and tentative applause."

According to a young journalist named Leonard Liebling,[75] who met Mahler at this time, the latter was particularly depressed by this failure. His career as a conductor seemed at a standstill, and both his own future and that of his compositions appeared bleak, at a time when so many great symphonic projects were forming in his mind. In a moment of despair he felt he would never be able to bridge the gap that separated his ideals from reality. He spoke of this anxiety to Strauss, who no doubt found it difficult to understand him. He himself never seems to have much difficulty in assuming a more pragmatic attitude.

A letter that Mahler wrote to Strauss from Steinbach a month later shows clearly that the latter had expressed some reservations about the *Titan,* and in particular had suggested a cut in the Finale. Mahler was not surprised by his remarks, for he already knew that Strauss had condemned the piece. In fact, he even wondered whether the latter's negative reaction had not influenced that of many other people. "Strauss is *not* above all suspicion," he wrote to Behn on June 15.[76] "It was his critic who wrote the *worst* article." Nevertheless, he did not betray any of these suspicions in his reply to Strauss: he merely thanked him for his frankness but added that he did not agree with him on this point.[77] He had already decided against making any changes, for, though he realized that he had not expressed all he had wished to say, he preferred to write another work, which would be better *in every way.* Mahler also took this opportunity of announcing that he had completed the Finale of the *Second Symphony.* From then on the *Titan* was an "abandoned, castoff skin"; "there is as much difference between these two works, which seven years separate, as there is between a man and a newborn baby."[78] This "castoff skin" is today one of the best-loved and most often performed of Mahler's works.

*"Mit Flügeln die ich mir errungen . . ."*
(With wings I have conquered . . .)


# CHAPTER 20


*Mahler in Hamburg (V) — Completion of the* Second
Symphony — *Bruno Walter — Mahler's Position in
Hamburg — The Subscription Concerts — Otto's Death*
(June 1894–May 1895)


After this new attempt to perform his own work had ended in another total
failure, Mahler was only too glad to leave Weimar with Otto on June 7,
and return to Steinbach, stopping in Munich and in Salzburg on the way.
Indeed this last failure seems to have strengthened rather than weakened
his creative urge, and he was eager to complete his *Second Symphony*. The
year before, after long talks with Lesch, the local architect, he had ordered
the famous *Häuschen* and requested that it be finished in time for the following summer.[1] Delighted that at last he had a quiet place to work, Mahler
wanted to sleep there on the night of his arrival, but finally abandoned this
idea, probably because of the lack of comfort and the unavoidable dampness.

The Steinbach *Häuschen*, where Mahler spent some of the greatest moments of his creative life, consisted of a single square room, lighted on three
sides by double windows, while the fourth side, facing the inn, had only a
glass door, with shutters from which a hail of insects dropped down onto the
heads of arriving visitors. There was a wood-shingle roof resting on a simple
frame. The cabin contained only a table, some chairs, a wood stove, and an
upright piano that Mahler rarely used for composing.[2] The cabin was at
once nicknamed the *"Schnützelputz-Häusel"* (Tiny House) after a *Wunderhorn* poem.[3] It stood on a small peninsula covered with mountain ashes
and bushes, which ran out into the lake. There was no path to encourage
strollers, and there was a magnificent view; one side faced the opposite
shore; the other, the Höllengebirge. Mahler at once resumed his "summer
composer's" life, getting up at six-thirty and going down to the *Häuschen*
for his breakfast. He would then spend all morning there, sometimes even

the whole day, with every window closed so as not to let in any outside noise. The "echoes of everyday reality" reached him in the form of a letter from Berliner, who sent him the most important articles the German press had devoted to the Weimar concert. "I've had great fun," he wrote to Berliner on June 15.[4] "You haven't yet read the most comical ones of the bunch that someone else has sent me. I've not yet seen the one in the *Frankfurter Zeitung*. Could you get it for me? The main thing is that I'm completely absorbed in my work. My little house (in the meadows) is brand new and an ideal resort: not a sound in the vicinity! I'm surrounded by nothing but flowers and birds which I see but don't hear."

Mahler had written to Justi early in May asking her not to invite Natalie to Steinbach, for he did not want to be "placed under surveillance." He added in another letter: "As for Natalie, I don't know what you're going to decide with her. Don't forget that even between the closest friends, those with whom one is on the best of terms, such subjects must be treated with the utmost tact. I should like your handling of this delicate matter to be irreproachable. You will see that this is best. I must confess to you that I am much opposed to Natalie's coming. Without mentioning a certain fact, and perhaps because of it, I cannot stand her constant mothering, advising, inspecting and spying. This year I would be fierce. Delay her arrival as long as you can, don't speak to her at all about her attitude toward me, but make her understand that I want no comment on what I am doing or not doing. I'd like it best if she did not come at all."[5]

The tremendous debt that posterity owes to Natalie Bauer-Lechner's gifts as a sympathetic witness and careful chronicler of Mahler's summer life should not blind us to her defects: she disturbed and exasperated him by her constant fussing. The reason why he so long accepted her somewhat possessive affection may have been partly because he sensed her usefulness as a biographer and partly because—as with Berliner—"In the final analysis, the others understand me even less." Mahler blamed Natalie most for the excessive and underlying intensity of her feelings toward him and for the hope he suspected her of cherishing that one day, moved by her silent devotion, he might marry her. Natalie nevertheless spent every summer until 1901 in his company. In 1894, however, she did not in the end visit Steinbach, which deprives us of her usual summer chronicle.

As soon as he arrived, Mahler asked Fritz Löhr to send him the complete work of Arnim and Brentano, together with Hölderlin's poems, and set to work. As before, he went on long walks after lunch, but always took his notebook along to jot down his musical ideas. One day, after much searching for the rhythm of a motif in the Finale, two crows flew by, and their cawing suggested to him the phrase he needed. He was restless and nervous as usual, and his sisters worried about his health. The war against noise started anew that summer but was made easier by the isolation of the *Häuschen*.

Thanks to intensive work, the sketch for the Finale, for which Mahler provided part of the text, was completed in less than three weeks. On

June 29, he wrote to Löhr: "I announce the happy birth of a healthy and vigorous last movement for the *Second*. Father and child are doing well, the latter not yet out of danger. At this holy christening he received the name of *'Lux lucet in tenebris.'* Silent sympathy is preferred to wreaths, which are gratefully declined. All other gifts, however, will be accepted."[6]

Later, on July 10, he wrote to Berliner: "Naturally, I am hard at work. The Finale is imposing and ends with a chorus for which I have written the text myself . . . the sketch is outlined down to the smallest detail and I am now writing the full score. It is a bold, powerfully constructed work. The final crescendo is gigantic."[7]

Early in July, Mahler went to Ischl to pay a second visit to Brahms. Once again he was received with great friendliness by the famous composer, and yet, later recalling his different contacts with him, Mahler was to make some disillusioned remarks. He regretted, among other things, that none of their meetings had provided the smallest exchange of enriching or stimulating ideas of an intellectual or professional kind. "It seemed that Brahms tried to spare himself the smallest intellectual effort, unless it concerned his own intense creative activity. It was as though he feared the least emotion of that kind, even if provoked by contact with a man of value. He gave the impression of trying to avoid any exchange of serious conversation. It was clear that he wanted to reserve his energies for his work, but the fact that he needed to do so was a very bad sign! He surrounded himself with all sorts of uninteresting musicians, critics, and socialites, who clustered round him like flies upon sugar. Naturally, he did not permit them to invade his privacy either, and not one of them could boast of having had any real contact with him, except for a few jokes and bons mots. Nevertheless, he was a kindly man, as could be seen when anyone was in need, for he was always ready to help and to comfort."[8]

Brahms was often ironic, and Mahler, in spite of his deep admiration, found it difficult to swallow his sarcastic remarks. The *Häuschen* in Steinbach, for instance, had been the subject of one of their talks and Brahms had nicknamed it the *"Wasserhäuschen"* because of its location: by extension, the symphony that Mahler was finishing became the *"Wassersymphonie."* "What do you mean by that?" Mahler asked him: "That it emerged from the floods, or that it is watered-down? All should not be dry!" he added, a veiled reference to certain of the old master's works. Brahms immediately became most affable again, "as he always did when somebody stood up to him," noted Mahler.[9] It is providential that Natalie noted down these remarks, for they reveal the gap that existed between the two men as human beings as well as creators, and help us to visualize their meetings, which Mahler rarely describes in his letters.[10]

One anecdote, often told by Mahler himself, has become famous: He was walking through the Ischl woods with Brahms, and the latter, "feeling sick and bad tempered," for once let himself be drawn into a musical discussion. He condemned contemporary composition with his usual pessimism, refusing to admit that any road might still remain open for their art. They were walking beside the Traun, and Mahler pointed toward the stream: "Master, look, the last wave is rolling by!" To which, it seems, Brahms replied, "May it flow toward the sea and not toward a swamp."[11]

At the end of July, Mahler was forced to interrupt his work on the Finale for a trip to Bayreuth, where Cosima Wagner had invited him.[12] This friendly gesture had seemed to announce a change in the Wagner family's attitude toward him. Frau Cosima's ambiguous attitude in fact stemmed from her anti-Semitism, which became even more violent after her husband's death. Indeed, she had even gone so far as to throw Levi out of Bayreuth in 1884, declaring him "morally unworthy and artistically incapable of conducting my husband's last masterpiece." And in order to "Christianize" Parsifal, she handed it over to an "Aryan" conductor, Felix Mottl, on whom, moreover she imposed an interpretation entirely different from that which the composer himself had approved at its first performance.[13]

Mahler's visit to the Wagnerian capital from July 28 to August 4 was "successful from every point of view." He visited Wahnfried almost every day and from the Wagner family's box watched performances of Parsifal, Lohengrin, and Tannhäuser (the last conducted by Richard Strauss).[14] He also met several old and new friends, including Reiff, Freund, the Behns and Nina Hoffmann, whom he went to see in Marienbad.

The critic Ludwig Karpath, faithful chronicler of many episodes in Mahler's life, also attended this festival. Having tea one day in a forest café, he noticed Mahler walking along, looking pensive. Mahler, having seen him, approached, offered him a cigarette, then disappeared without uttering a word. That same evening, they met again in the restaurant of the Hotel Sonne, and Mahler thanked Karpath for not having started a conversation: he had not wanted to pass by without greeting him that morning, but had been too absorbed in his thoughts to wish to interrupt them.

After leaving Bayreuth, Mahler met Otto at the Krzyzanowskis' on August 5. Total mystery surrounds the young man's activities during this summer. Staegemann had told Mahler in Hamburg early in May that Otto was popular at the Leipzig Opera because of his "reasonable, quiet and modest" nature.[15] Another letter to Justi makes it clear that Otto would have no vacation before leaving Leipzig for his new post in Bremen, and a postcard to Justi dated August 3 reveals a grudge against him: "As for Otto, think it over well and you will understand why I had him come." This is the last time Mahler mentions Otto in his correspondence. On a postcard written to Justi on August 25 from Bremen, Otto announced his arrival in that town "half mad" after a "dreadful" journey.[16]

Back in Steinbach, Mahler devoted his last two weeks to completing the score of the Finale of the Second Symphony, the orchestration of which had been well advanced before his departure for Bayreuth.[17] On August 20, already on his way to Hamburg, he stopped in Vienna, where he drew up a will at Emil Freund's. Then he went to Berlin in order to investigate the possibilities of an early performance of his new work.

Back in Hamburg, Mahler faced a particularly heavy season: in addition to his theatrical activities, the eight subscription concerts would demand considerable preparation. While waiting for Justi, who was soon to join him, he finally realized one of his oldest dreams by moving into a large apartment on the Parkallee. It was on the third floor, "so that nobody could dance or make music above his head." He was to live there with his sisters for almost two years, and life would be much pleasanter, for now he would be able to invite friends and arrange evenings of chamber music with musicians from the opera.[18] Two days after reaching Hamburg, he played the whole *Second Symphony* to Förster, who, deeply moved, paid him the greatest compliments by comparing his work to Beethoven's *Ninth Symphony*.[19]

The most important event in Mahler's life during this season appeared in the seemingly insignificant form of a new young *"Korrepetitor"* named Bruno Schlesinger, recently engaged by Pollini. This young musician, aged eighteen, had just arrived in the then famous musical city of Hamburg. He was eager to meet Mahler, for he had read, in June, the articles on the *Titan;* their very violence had attracted his attention: "Looking into the window of Bieber's piano store on Jungfernstieg," the young man later wrote, "my gaze was attracted to a photograph that struck me immediately as being that of a musician. A moment later I guessed it must be Mahler, for nobody but the composer of the *Titan Symphony* could look like that. . . . The following morning, leaving Pollini's office, where I had been to introduce myself, I immediately recognized him when I saw a lean, fidgety short man with an unusually high, straight brow, long, jet-black hair, deeply penetrating bespectacled eyes, and a characteristically 'spiritual' mouth. Pollini introduced us, and a brief conversation took place. Later on, Mahler's friendly and slightly amused account of it was to be laughingly repeated to me by his sisters. 'So you are the new coach,' Mahler said. 'Do you play the piano well?' 'Excellently,' I replied, because any false modesty seemed unworthy of a great man. 'Are you a good sight reader?' Mahler then asked. 'Oh yes, very good,' I said again truthfully. 'And do you know the regular repertoire operas?' 'I know them all quite well,' I replied, with such self-confidence that Mahler burst out laughing, patted me kindly on the back, and concluded the conversation by saying, 'Well, well . . . that certainly sounds most promising!' "[20]

A few days later, on September 15, 1894, young Bruno Schlesinger—who under the name Bruno Walter was to become one of the world's most famous conductors—made his Hamburg Opera debut on his nineteenth birthday, conducting Flotow's incidental music for Shakespeare's *Winter's Tale*.

Toward the end of September, Mahler was directing a piano rehearsal of Humperdinck's new work *Hänsel und Gretel* and the accompanist proved unequal to his task. Mahler saw young Schlesinger: "Would you risk ac-

companying an opera you do not know?" he asked him. The young man
having answered, "Why, of course!" Mahler dismissed the pianist and replaced him by Schlesinger. On another occasion, the often repeated echo
in the forest scene displeased Mahler, who turned to Schlesinger and said:
"I trust that you know what it's like in a forest! Go and rehearse the echo
for me."

Shortly afterward Bruno Walter was asked if he felt capable of acting as
"Korrepetitor." He accepted, and almost immediately took a chorus rehearsal
of Lohengrin, even though he had never before rehearsed a chorus. Like
Pollini, Mahler at once recognized the exceptional musicality of the young
man.

The eyewitness reports of this young musician, who arrived in Hamburg
with the freshness of youth, show us Mahler and the Hamburg Opera as
they were in 1894. Walter's first impression was that of a character from
Hoffmann's tales—incredibly fascinating, frightening, and satanic, with his
extraordinarily mobile face, the two deep furrows round his mouth, his intensity of speech and expression, his rapid changes of mood, and his sudden,
meditative silences. Sometimes Walter thought he was face to face with
Kapellmeister Kreisler himself; sometimes, when Mahler would walk away
at top speed with his strange, irregular gait, he reminded him of the archivist
Lindhorst of "Der goldne Topf," or sometimes of the ascetic, mystic monk
of Giorgione's admirable Concert, a print of which adorned Mahler's
study.[21]

Mahler's personality immediately had a determining influence upon the
younger man, altering his life completely. Mahler's slightest gesture expressed such will power that everyone immediately bowed to it. A born
ruler, he was deeply aware of the importance of his mission and had acquired
so much experience, such command of his art, that his authority had become unchallengeable. From then on, his harshness and impatience toward
lazy or untalented musicians was to be equaled only by the kindness and
confidence he showed toward those who understood his intentions and did
their best to execute them.

The general tendency of the period—and Walter recognized that it was
his own at the time—was to emphasize "feeling" first and foremost. Mahler, on the contrary, demanded from his singers an almost instrumental precision. This was, in his view, all the more necessary because, in the excitement of performance, they had a tendency to speed up the tempo or to hold
certain notes. This "precision" was the basic condition of any musical performance. To obtain it, he used all his authority, alternately terrifying and
encouraging the performers. Only now and then did he meet violent opposition from stars such as Alvary and Schumann-Heink.[22] But what most
aroused Walter's admiration, and which served as an example all his life,
was Mahler's utter disdain for routine. His state of perpetual "inspiration"
was the attitude of an artist never satisfied with himself or what he had accomplished, and who tried never to betray his highest aspirations.[23]

Having described Mahler's considerable influence over his entire destiny, Bruno Walter adds that this was never systematic or even conscious, for Mahler was by no means a pedagogue in the usual sense of the word: he was far too lively, impulsive, and self-centered. He exerted his deep influence through the strength of his personality, the intensity of his vision, the practical examples that he constantly gave, and by the fanatical zeal with which he corrected the smallest details. His was a hard school: indeed his example alternately stimulated and depressed the young man. But he was to receive magnificent encouragement: one day, returning from a performance of *Aïda,* Mahler said to Justi, "He is a born conductor."

Mahler's frustrations in Hamburg were many: the works that made up the vast repertoire were hardly ever rehearsed, and while he dreamed of uniting the opera's visual, dramatic, and musical elements, so that the spectators could "live" the drama and penetrate its inner meaning, Pollini paid attention only to the voices, caring nothing for staging, dramatic truth, or scenery. Consequently, in Hamburg, Mahler was never to conduct an "ensemble" such as the one he had created, in spite of all obstacles, in Budapest, but only a group of admirable soloists. As a result he never experienced one single complete artistic joy in all the time he spent there.

Not only did he have to face opposition from his stars, but also from the stage director Franz Bittong, a former actor who was stubbornly self-satisfied and deeply attached to his outmoded and conventional ideas.[24] Mahler was to complain many times about it; to Ferdinand Pfohl, the critic, he said, "Bittong is a blockhead. One cannot do anything with him!" He itemized, noted Bruno Walter, "with every nuance of feeling from a good-humored shake of his head to outbursts of acute despair, all the personal shortcomings and absurdities of the chief stage director, Bittong, whose constructive—or rather obstructive—co-operation had been bestowed upon him by an unkind fate."[25]

Bittong was a tall burly man who opposed the "dead weight of his inertia" to all of Mahler's artistic demands. He was too lazy to fight openly, but "the mere weight of his presence was equivalent to an inexorable refusal." When directing the chorus, that indispensable element of operatic life, Bittong merely showed each group its place, considering his task finished when he had given them some vague indications as to their roles; after saying, for example, to the good bourgeois ladies of Hamburg, that they "act like playful Spanish maidens" in Act I of *Carmen,* or telling solid Hamburg gentlemen "to cross the hall of the Wartburg with the courtly bearing of counts and princes" in Act II of *Tannhäuser.*

He never gave any precise directions, only calling out from time to time: "Some life, some life, ladies and gentlemen!" or inviting the members of the chorus to "take part in the action." The chorus would then overact, mimic the soloists, and make fun of them, before sinking back, after a few minutes, into their usual lethargy.

In order to enliven his performances at certain moments, Bittong had

formed the habit of snapping his fingers from the wings. But he often neglected to watch the action and sometimes snapped his fingers unintentionally, while telling some joke to a stagehand, thus causing an unexpected
burst of activity on stage. This happened one day in March 1895, during
a scene in Count Bolko von Hochberg's opera *Der Wärwolf*. The calm,
solemn, white-robed choristers impersonating angels suddenly began to flap
their wings and wave palm branches for no good reason—simply because
Bittong had snapped his fingers thoughtlessly. Such incidents, even if they
amused Mahler now and then, were nevertheless deeply depressing for a
man to whom the theater, like music, was sacred.

As for the stage settings, the situation in Hamburg was equally bad. Instead of trying to give each opera some sort of decorative style, Pollini had
his singers wear improvised costumes, and cared so little for the visual aspect that, out of economy, he often used old sets for a premiere, even
though they were seldom suitable. To evoke the splendors of Solomon's
court in Goldmark's *Die Königin von Saba,* for instance, he used Egyptian
décors from *Die Zauberflöte,* and seemed totally undisturbed by the absurdity
of the result. Mahler, who was to make the décors of the Vienna Opera
models for all of Europe, did not succeed in influencing him in the least.

Sometimes he was so deeply discouraged that he found it difficult to
proceed with a performance. At such times he would hide during the intervals in a storeroom, to get away from everything, and sometimes wept
bitterly as he considered the deplorable artistic standards of the opera.[26]
Even when the performance had been a good one, he felt lonely and misunderstood: "I worked with all my strength in Hamburg," he later told
Natalie, "and I prepared performances with the utmost care until they acquired complete unity. But with what aim? For what herd of sheep, who
listened vacantly and thoughtlessly, the music going in one ear and out the
other like the fish listening to St. Anthony's sermon! When I had prepared
an exemplary performance with all my soul and all my skill, as with the
Wagner cycle in the spring, when even that public sat in silence, often for
five hours at a time, the singers would take many curtain calls. Yet I myself
would leave the theater all alone, with no one to talk to in order to calm
my nervous tension, and I would eat a ham sandwich, all by myself, in some
café. I would have been utterly desperate over the uselessness of such effort
if I had not felt that perhaps its seeds would eventually bear fruit for someone somewhere; that, in itself, was sufficient!"[27]

All contemporary evidence agrees that Mahler had, to an unusual degree,
a keen understanding of the style and the inner meaning of the works confided to him. While acting as the conductor and mastermind of a performance, he knew how to establish the needed relationship between the
stage and the orchestra, the orchestral expression and the sung text, the
melody and the action. When the only effort asked of him was that of rehearsing the orchestra and singers, he did so with all his might. In spite of

the many limitations imposed on his activities during these six years, he never stopped demanding the utmost from himself and his collaborators.

Unfortunately, the poor quality of the orchestra imposed a permanent limitation on the quality of the performance. Mahler recognized the zeal and good will of the musicians, and he knew them to be capable of enthusiasm; he understood that their lack of brilliance, their mediocre sound quality, was in part due to their bad instruments, particularly the woodwinds. The orchestra included some first-class, scandalously underpaid musicians, but Mahler could not resign himself to such realities; he drove them all to surpass themselves, demanding interminable rehearsals even during the busiest periods of the season, trying to obtain precision and sonority of a standard unattainable from such an orchestra. The musicians bore his harshnesses and reproaches in silence out of respect for his phenomenal gifts, his technical mastery, and his miraculous ear. On one occasion, however, the atmosphere became menacing, as it had in Kassel, and Pfohl states that, to avoid reprisals by a musician who had been treated with particular severity, Mahler had to have police protection on his way home.[28]

Natalie asked him one day why the musicians were not grateful to him for forcing them to surpass themselves. "What a mistake!" he answered. "Do you really think they care about learning or getting ahead? For them art is only a cow to be milked. It affords them an ordinary life, which, however, they want to enjoy with as much comfort as possible. Some among them are better and more willing, but those require more patience than I am able to give them. When one of them doesn't immediately get something the way it is written, I could kill him on the spot; then I scream at him, and he becomes so completely flustered that he really hates me. In this manner I often demand more of them than they are actually able to achieve. No wonder they cannot forgive me that.

"The worst time is the end of the season, when everyone is weary and overworked. Musicians then are less able to concentrate and accomplish something. Therefore, I, who am just as tired as they, if not more so, must exert even greater energy and must be even more demanding, in order to achieve that same perfection without which I cannot be satisfied. Not very pleasant incidents take place then. I always win, but sometimes my anger almost kills me! And yet, I am much calmer than I was during the first years of my work."[29]

Mahler was aware of the financial difficulties of his musicians. Out of sheer humanity, he always tried to smooth their way. An official letter that he sent to the Hamburg burgomaster[30] contains some phrases praising Pollini and his "spirit of sacrifice" but brings to light one of the most flagrant abuses in his managing of the opera. When Pollini first arrived in Hamburg, he engaged the musicians by the year, which was the custom in all the large international opera houses. So as not to have to pay them during the three-month period when the opera was closed, he at first succeeded in finding temporary work for them. But competition from military bands had become stronger, and, no longer successful in "placing" his players in this way, he had brazenly changed their yearly contracts into nine-monthly arrangements without bothering about how they were to survive during the summer months.

"It is not a question of reproaching the director in the least," wrote Mahler, "for one could not expect an individual to support so many employees for such a long period without obtaining the smallest income from them." But that was in fact what the musicians rightly expected of Pollini; they could not save any money because of the starvation salaries that he paid them (from 130 to 150 marks per month). They were reduced to a miserable summer existence, playing in various cabarets. The best of them intended to leave the orchestra if the situation was not changed. The burgomaster cannot have failed to sense the severe condemnation of Pollini's management in this letter, despite Mahler's tact. But it was scarcely conceivable that the city could step in and act in the place of an individual in this matter, particularly an individual who assumed full responsibility for the opera's finances, and who certainly drew a considerable revenue from it.[31]

One of the best descriptions of Mahler's conducting in Hamburg is by the critic Ferdinand Pfohl.[32] According to him, Mahler's extreme mobility of the past had now disappeared and had been replaced by calm assurance. Pfohl stresses the economy of Mahler's gestures and their absolute precision. No rocking, no right-to-left swings of the pendulum; no dancing motion even at the most dramatic climax, no pose, no conspicuous gestures, no wasted energy; Mahler sustained the musical line with almost mathematical precision.[33] His fortissimos were never violent or shattering. He never "covered" the singers, even when they were singing piano or mezza voce; he never allowed the orchestral sound to become shrill or inexpressive. In a word, according to Pfohl, Mahler's conducting was the "triumph of a musical ear." One of his most characteristic gestures while conducting was his way of thrusting his baton toward musicians when he wished to indicate their entrances. At such moments, his face would become taut, his chin menacing, and his eyebrows would rise, so that the musicians were sometimes paralyzed with fear. Pfohl recalled an occasion when, in the mysterious *Todesverkündigung* of the second act of *Die Walküre*, he heard only the accompanying harmony, for Mahler had stared at the first tenor tuba with such intensity that the terrified player had been unable to produce a sound.

Pfohl thought Mahler a matchless coach for both singers and orchestra; none of his contemporaries possessed the same musical efficacy, the same technical knowledge and comprehension of the works played. No other conductor obtained performances so nearly perfect, so precise, so transparent, even in highly complex polyphonic passages. This was the main reason why the audiences spoke of genius; the performances were different from anything they had heard before. Even when Mahler erred, his errors were richer in significance and more attractive than the insipid truths of the "time beaters." He always sought above all the "cleanest phrasing," the most "careful punctuation," obtaining thus a "plastic" interpretation, in which caesuras and "breathing" played an essential part. The "principle of the upbeat" held the force of law for him, a fact that led Hans Richter to refer to this trait in his conducting as *"Zäsurenwahn"*—that is "pause madness."[34]

Mahler's uncompromising nature, as well as his devotion to the cause of music, makes it easy to understand that he always submitted with bad grace to the audiences' whims, and particularly to their encoring. Whenever he was forced to give in, he would complain afterward of the arrogance and ignorance of his public. Richard Specht attended an 1896 performance of *Die Walküre* conducted by Mahler. The slender, erect silhouette appeared on the podium, Mahler bowed toward the audience, and for a second it seemed that he had two huge sparkling eyes: it was his spectacles gleaming on his lean face. There were murmurs of "Ah, Mahler!" in the auditorium. He attracted the attention of the musicians by tapping his baton nervously on the podium, but the whispering still continued. There was a moment's pause, and then Mahler signaled to the strings to begin the stormy Prelude. At the end of the second measure, however, the hall was still not silent, so he stopped the orchestra, turned abruptly toward the audience, put his hand on the railing, and in dry tones said, "Go right ahead, I'm not in a hurry!" The gallery's loud applause was followed by deathly silence.[35]

During his long operatic career, Mahler was responsible for endless tension and quarreling, but his close friends knew an entirely different Mahler. Bruno Walter, who was very friendly with him in 1895, describes life in the Parkallee apartment, where Justi and Emma had joined him.[36] A cordial and typically Austrian gaiety reigned, a taste for good living that included the delicious cooking of Elise, a great specialist in desserts, whom Mahler had brought from Vienna, and who was expected to prepare a new one each day. Mahler would play his *Lieder* and his first symphonies for Walter, and often in the afternoon, they played four-hand pieces by Mozart, Schubert, and Schumann. Mahler especially liked Schubert's *Marches* and *Dances,* and he improvised texts for them in Viennese dialect which fitted the melodies so well that they almost seemed to have been composed for them. Sometimes they amused themselves by complicating their playing, and inverted the parts; the left hand of the first pianist would then play the top notes of the second, and vice-versa.[37]

Sometimes, also, Mahler had long conversations with Walter on literary and philosophical subjects such as the origin and destiny of man: these exchanges of ideas created the same impassioned, intense atmosphere as his theatrical rehearsals. Under his influence, the whole family had started reading Dostoyevsky, and even young Emma one day asked Walter suddenly, "Who is right, Alyosha or Ivan?" for she had just read *The Brothers Karamazov.* At that time, too, Mahler admired Nietzsche, whose *"Mitternachtsgedicht"* he was to incorporate into his *Third Symphony* the following year; he also admired Fechner and Schopenhauer, whose complete works he gave to Walter for Christmas, together with Albert Lange's *Geschichte des Materialismus,* "one of the most essential experiences of his life" and "a classical work dealing with the oldest malady of human thought."[38]

As always, Mahler's moods altered with astounding suddenness. After a long, serious philosophical discussion, he would abruptly break into gay, childlike laughter without apparent reason, as though it had been brought on by "a sudden inner spasm, or an attack of fierce and desperate pain."[39] Hoffmann's Kapellmeister Kreisler, and Mahler's own compositions, also often break into sudden and despairing laughter.

The extreme tension and concentration under which Mahler worked were equaled only by his absent-mindedness the rest of the time. During a rehearsal, for instance, a stage manager asked him for a moment's break. Impatient at first, Mahler gradually became lost in thoughts and totally unaware of his surroundings. Only finally when told that all were ready to resume work did he at last become conscious of the general astonished silence. He then tapped the podium several times with his baton, shouting, to everyone's amusement, *"Zahlen!"* (The bill!)

The first performance of *Hänsel und Gretel,* the rehearsals of which had brought together Mahler and Walter, took place on September 25, 1894. Some of the critics expressed reservations about Humperdinck's "orchestral orgies." Mahler himself, imbued with legends and fairy stories, found the music "beautifully fashioned" but regretted that Humperdinck had not succeeded in giving this work, which had so pleased him in Weimar, the unreal atmosphere of a fairy tale. Presented more than thirty times during the 1894–95 season and staged again early the next season, *Hänsel und Gretel* was nevertheless a considerable and lasting success with the public.[40] Armbrust found the music "highly significant" and "full of genius." On the other hand, he deplored the lack of originality and the exclusively lyrical character of Vilém Blodek's *Im Brunnen,* which vanished from the billboards after serving as a curtain raiser for this premiere of *Hänsel und Gretel.*

At that time Mahler increasingly felt the lack of feminine company; he needed a woman capable of understanding and sustaining him at moments of crisis. J. B. Förster heard him put his longing into words one day during the spring of 1894, when Mahler called on him and saw his wife, Bertha, an artist whom he admired wholeheartedly, fulfilling her modest role of housewife in Förster's home. "You must understand," explained Mahler, "that I could not bear the sight of an untidy woman with messy hair and neglected appearance. I must also admit that solitude is essential to me when I am composing; as a creative artist I require it without conditions. My wife would have to agree to my living apart from her, possibly several rooms away, and to my having a separate entrance. She would have to consent to sharing my company only at certain times, decided in advance, and then I would expect her to be perfectly groomed and well dressed. Finally, she should not take offense or interpret it as disinterest, coldness, or disdain if, at times, I had no wish to see her. In a work, she would need qualities that even the best and most devoted women do not possess."[41]

Thus it was a life of self-sacrifice that Mahler, due to the instinctive selfishness of his creative nature, envisaged for his future wife. Even though Förster replied that he would forget all that the day he fell in love, Mahler refused to believe him, adding that, certain of never finding a wife who matched his ideals, he had asked his sister Justi to keep house for him. It is strange to see how little the two women who were to play an essential role in his life resembled his feminine ideal of modesty and selflessness.

A month after the premiere of *Hänsel und Gretel,* Mahler conducted the first subscription concert, and it must have been a great day for him when, for the first time, he led a symphonic orchestra and turned to a repertoire that he had been studying passionately since the beginning of the season. Many times during the autumn Förster was to find him seated at his work-table, feverishly jotting down indications of all sorts and carefully revising the dynamic and expressive nuances of the score and instrumental parts. When asked the reason for this tremendous work, Mahler replied that he must "prepare everything in advance" in order to compensate for the small number of rehearsals.[42] In order to make himself understood, he showed Förster the start of the *"Leonore" Overture No. 3,* in which Beethoven had first written fortissimo for all instruments, from flutes to kettledrums, then piano and diminuendo, then again pianissimo for the bass-part, even though the latter had to contrast clearly with the restless f sharp of the strings, which execute a crescendo, followed by a decrescendo. The first difference between the nuances of the various instruments starts with the clarinets and the bass as they enter in A flat (second bar). Considering that double the number of strings were then in use, twenty-four violins instead of ten or twelve as in Beethoven's time, Mahler thought it necessary to balance, harmonize, and tone down, while accentuating certain "doublings" that, from his point of view, were not "modifications."

"Tempo," Mahler said, "is for me a matter of feeling. Of course there are many things that one can indicate or suggest. You know how meticulous I am in my work. I never trust the conductors or their capacities. Yet even if they follow every indication, all is lost if they make a mistake in the first tempo, since every change depends on this. The most precise indications by the composer usually result in something resembling the changes in organ registration: each register is suddenly replaced by another one, stronger or softer. This is exactly what happens with tempo changes, whereas the real art of conducting consists in transitions." According to Förster, this was, indeed, one of Mahler's major virtues as a performer. He was capable of "leaving the audience breathless, moving it to tears"—with the first bars of the *"Leonore" Overture* for instance. The listener got the impression he was descending a ghostlike staircase into the depths of the dungeon, right down to the famous low f sharp, while the moaning of the bass seemed to come straight from the mouth of the feverish Florestan.[43] Never before had

Förster been so moved by this music, nor heard such a perfectly controlled diminuendo, which seemed to be performed by one single, accomplished virtuoso.[44]

The subscription concert orchestra combined musicians from three different groups: the band of the 31st Regiment, the opera, and the Philharmonic. Again Mahler had to overcome tenacious resistance, particularly from two violinists, one named Marwege, whose indignation he had roused in December 1892 by his tempos and phrasing, and the other, Bignell, who, horrified by Mahler's "modern" spirit, "wore mourning for the classic principle."[45]

The eight concerts took place every second Monday at seven-thirty, and the first was held on October 22: two symphonies—Mozart's *G Minor* and Beethoven's *Seventh*—preceded and followed the appearances of two famous soloists, Ferruccio Busoni and Amalie Joachim. Frau Joachim sang nine folk-song arrangements by Brahms, with Mahler himself at the piano; Busoni played the solos in Weber's *Konzertstück* and also his own arrangement for piano and orchestra of Liszt's *Spanish Rhapsody*. Emil Krause warmly praised Mahler's interpretation of the Mozart for its "artistic truth," that of the Beethoven for its "impassioned eloquence."[46]

Sittard, pedantic as ever, discoursed at length about the style and expression of the Mozart symphony and criticized, as usual, certain aspects of Mahler's performance: too rapid tempos, excessive rhythmic energy, overweighted accents, suppressed repeats.[47] Sittard particularly objected to Mahler's "indifferent and slovenly (*saloppe*)" reading of the Andante. He was unsparing of praise for the soloists, for the arrangement of the *Spanish Rhapsody*, and for Busoni's performance of the solo part, saying that for such a pianist "nothing is impossible as far as technique is concerned."[48] Only Mahler's interpretation of Beethoven's *Seventh Symphony* was, for once, wholeheartedly approved by this "defender of tradition."

From then on, Sittard's attacks, and those of Emil Krause, succeeded one another as regularly as the concerts. On November 5, Sittard praised the performances of Berlioz's *Carnaval Romain* and the *Siegfried Idyll* but condemned Mahler for his "farfetched" and "tormented" conception of the great *C Major Symphony*, Schubert's *Ninth*. He disliked his tempo changes, which he considered "nervous and unnatural, calculated rather than spontaneous."[49] Krause in the *Fremdenblatt* expressed somewhat similar opinions, though less strongly. Mahler, he wrote, "lacks warmth," his execution is "too subjective," and his modifications of tempo finally "destroy the symphonic element." Besides, the orchestra, even while devoted to Mahler body and soul, was not first rate, particularly in the wind section.[50]

The next concert was given in November to a half-empty hall, despite the presence of two famous soloists: the American pianist Fannie Bloomfield Zeisler and an Italian singer by the name of Antonietta Palloni.[51] This time, Mahler had had the somewhat surprising idea of entrusting to the orchestral strings Schubert's *"Tod und das Mädchen"* quartet, "divine music" that he thus robbed, Sittard reproached him, "of its natural intimacy." Moreover Mahler's reading of Brahms's *Third Symphony* "lacked warmth" and made use of doubtful tempos.[52] Krause thought it an "almost total failure," really "astonishing," radically opposed to any previous interpretations. Incomprehensible diction in the Andante, excessive slowness in the Allegretto, excessive "agitation" in the Finale: Mahler really drove his "re-creation" too far.

The last concert of 1894 was partly dedicated on December 3 to the memory of Anton Rubinstein, who had died two weeks earlier. It attracted an even smaller audience. The opening movement of the *Ocean Symphony,* the ballet from the *Demon,* and three lieder by the Russian master[53] were, in Sittard's opinion, a controversial and too fragmentary choice. During the second half of the program, Mahler conducted Wagner's *Faustouvertüre,* at a "dragging pace" according to Krause, without "expressing its significance clearly," and "breaking it up into episodes" according to Sittard. Mahler's interpretation of Beethoven's *Pastoral Symphony* was to cause even more controversy: for Krause, it was, once again, a "re-creation of excessive subjectiveness," with "strange tempos, excessive contrasts," and scandalous retouching of the instrumentation. Apart from the Storm, he had found it "purely superficial as a whole."

Sittard believed that Mahler had "disfigured the symphony by the slowness of the Scherzo"[54] and "constant changes of tempo in the second movement." In a word, he would have none of Mahler's symphonic interpretations, which, "thank God, are unique of their kind in all Germany."

In every epoch it has been possible to distinguish, even in matters of interpretation, between "classics and romantics," "traditional and modern." Mahler was an ever-questing spirit. For him each score must be "lived," that is, "re-created" with all the necessary freedom, and this Sittard could not accept. America trembled for many years under the strictly rhythmical baton of a Toscanini, while in Europe Furtwängler was the incarnation of interpretative freedom and those essential values that we discern in Mahler's conducting and that awakened Sittard's wrath. The controversy will continue for as long as we have arts whose strength or weakness it is that they can be brought to life only through an interpreter. Should he attempt to render the work in its historical perspective and respect "tradition," which, like human memory, is self-destructive? Or should he try to "re-create"—that is to instill in the work his own life and personal conception, thus incurring the accusation of excessive subjectivity. The personal conceptions of a performer are today more widely accepted than they formerly were, mainly because "tradition" has been proved to be largely elusive and hypothetical as a concept. Few critics today would fail to agree with Pfohl, for whom "the worst evil is indifference," and the "errors" of a Mahler have more value than the lukewarm fidelity of the "time beaters."

The Andante of the *Pastoral Symphony,* which so exasperated Sittard, made a tremendous and unforgettable impression upon J. B. Förster, who wrote of "the peace and blissful wonder" he experienced during the scene by the brook, which "was all fragrance and song." He also described the "lyric wave" that emerged from the torrent and "rose little by little to the chord of the ninth and the dominant of the final cadence, the dynamic and emotional climax." Förster underlined all that he had found inimitable in Mahler's conducting, "the dynamics and the freedom of rhythm, all organically emanating from a completely personal and deeply individual conception that was mysterious, blessed and unique."[55]

During the autumn and early winter Mahler copied and corrected the score of his *Second Symphony,* in particular the Finale, which he completed on December 18. As always during the last month of the year, he had less work at the opera, while in November he had conducted, besides two subscription concerts, eighteen performances, an astonishing number when added to orchestral and theatrical rehearsals.

Pollini having decided to exploit the success of *The Bartered Bride,* the only important new productions that winter were two operas by Bedřich Smetana. On November 15, 1894, Mahler conducted a revival of *Two Widows,* an opera that Armbrust found "tearful and wearying."[56] This was followed two months later by *The Kiss.*[57] This time Armbrust deplored the lack of action and dramatic conflict but found the music a "string of pearls." Neither opera scored a success equal to that of *The Bartered Bride* the preceding year: *Two Widows* was performed only three times, *The Kiss,* six.

On March 3, Mahler conducted his own annual benefit: *Fidelio* and the *Pastoral Symphony.* Sittard did not review this concert, no doubt because he had criticized Mahler's conception of the symphony so savagely six months earlier. Armbrust, on the contrary, defended Mahler, stating that all interpretations are subjective and that one cannot condemn without taking this fact into consideration. Deeply impregnated with the spirit of the symphony, Mahler had brought it to life with matchless clarity and refinement of detail.[58] When a month later Mahler conducted as usual the Good Friday concert, this time composed of Haydn's *Die Schöpfung* and the Mozart *Requiem,* Sittard again criticized his rapid Mozart tempos.[59]

The last important new production of the season, *Der Wärwolf,* was a "romantic and legendary" opera written by Count Bolko von Hochberg, intendant of the Berlin Opera,[60] whose good graces Pollini wanted to assure. All his life Mahler was to devote himself body and soul to new works entrusted to him, sparing no effort to assure their success, even the mediocre ones. In this case, however, the score was so bad, the libretto so absurd, that he had difficulty in keeping a straight face during rehearsals, and made constant jokes and puns. When the chorus had to call several times "Oda!" —the name of the heroine—at a few moments' interval, Mahler gave the chorus its cue to re-enter by murmuring *"Entweder"* ("either"), thus considerably amusing the singer required to reply "Oda" (*oder,* that is, "or").

When Hochberg asked Mahler what he thought of *Der Wärwolf,* the only reply he could give—despite his desire to be polite—was: "This passage

here is better than that one," or "This episode is in C major, what a wonderful tonality!" or again "This passage unquestionably is in triple time." The
singers, equally eager to please the author and to be engaged in Berlin, tried
their hardest during the first performance on March 28, 1895, each one singing louder than the next. The performance suddenly resembled an absurd
parody, and Mahler was seized by such a spasm of laughter while conducting
that he had to hide his face behind a handkerchief. The critics considered it
their duty to condemn the "unoriginal" music, inspired by Weber and
Marschner, and the action, which "crawled" with improbabilities. Count
Hochberg's masterpiece disappeared forever from the repertoire after its
second performance.[61]

Mahler was to conduct a total of 134 performances at the opera during
the 1894–95 season, to which must be added two performances of Haydn's
*Die Schöpfung,* two concerts given to commemorate Bismarck's birthday,
and the subscription concerts. This was Mahler's busiest Hamburg season.
His repertoire included, as usual, all the Wagner operas except *Lohengrin,
Der fliegende Holländer, Rienzi,* and of course *Parsifal*[62]; *Der Freischütz*
(10 performances), *Die Zauberflöte* (6), *Don Giovanni* (3), *Fidelio* (9),
Méhul's *Joseph* (2), *Falstaff* (6), *Die Fledermaus* (4), *Faust* (1), *Mignon*
(2), *The Bartered Bride* (9), Smetana's *Two Widows* (3) and *The Kiss*
(6), *Hänsel und Gretel* (33), Blodek's *Im Brunnen* (1), *Der Wärwolf*
(2), and *Hans Heiling* (2).

Early in January 1895, Mahler and Strauss resumed their "friendly negotiations." At first, their object was to plan a Hamburg performance of
Strauss's version of Gluck's *Iphigénie en Aulide* (Pollini later abandoned
this project), as well as the performance by the Berlin Philharmonic of the
first three movements of Mahler's *Second Symphony.* Before sending the
score and parts to his famous colleague, Mahler wanted to check his instrumentation, so in January he held a private rehearsal of the three movements
with the opera orchestra in the small Covent Garden hall. It was attended by
a few carefully chosen guests, among them the actor Karl Wagner, the
lawyer Behn, the industrialist Wilhelm Berkan, and the Försters.[63]

Mahler had asked a member of the orchestra named Otto Weidich to sit
in the hall and take down corrections as the rehearsal progressed. At the beginning, it seemed to drag on forever, with Mahler constantly stopping the
orchestra. "Weidich, the cello in unison with the bassoon" or "Weidich, cut out
the oboe" or "Double the flutes," even "The harmony in the trombones."
During an intermission Mahler wrote most of these changes into the score.
Then he led an uninterrupted performance of the three movements, to the delight of his small audience.

Writing to Berliner with characteristic detachment, the creator of this
universe of sound that had thus for the first time been brought to life expressed
the pride he had felt: "The effect is one of incredible grandeur! If I were
to express all that I think of this great work, I would appear presumptuous.
But the *fundus instructus* of humanity will be enlarged by it—that is be-

yond a doubt. Everything seems to come from another world, and I don't think that anyone will be able to escape its power. One is thrown to the ground, stunned, and then borne up toward the heights on angels' wings."

Mahler's faithful friend Hermann Behn, himself a musician and composer, and one of Bruckner's students, was so impressed that he promised Mahler to make a two-piano version of it, "so that we will not be obliged to wait a year before hearing it again." Sometime later he and Mahler gave the first performance of this transcription at his home, in the presence of Frau Lazarus, the faithful friend and fervent admirer of Bülow.

After the rehearsal Mahler sent the amended score to Strauss, and their exchange of letters continued until the concert on March 4. Mahler asked for fifteen additional players and an extra rehearsal, all at his own expense. The weeks preceding the premiere were particularly busy, for not only did Mahler have to correct some more parts and conduct rehearsals in Hamburg, he also had to prepare Beethoven's *Ninth Symphony* for his final subscription concert. And, since Pollini arranged for him to conduct at the opera almost every evening, he was sometimes obliged to leave for Berlin in the middle of the night, after the performance, and to return the next afternoon so as to conduct again in the evening.[64]

The first incomplete performance of the *Second Symphony* took place on March 4, 1895, with Mahler conducting, in a half-empty hall. It was a considerable success.[65] There were four curtain calls after the Scherzo, according to Nodnagel,[66] who claimed that Strauss was quite astonished by the warmth of this reception, declaring that "this time he had been surprised by the Berlin public."[67] As always, the critics tried to minimize this success: the *Neue Berliner Musikzeitung* compared the hostile noise that had accompanied the applause after the first part to that of "cigarettes extinguished in water," but admitted that the second movement, an inoffensive "minuet in the old style," had been warmly applauded and that Mahler had been called back several times to take a bow. As for the third part, and the "aborted waltz,"[68] it had also been booed as well as applauded, for Mahler had "a taste for the bizarre," "lacked style," and "his polyphony was slovenly." Nevertheless, the critic recognized the originality of the inspiration and orchestration. Mahler's efforts "do not lack interest," he conceded, and "his musical pictures clearly carry seeds of the future within them."

In a sharper tone, the *Norddeutsche Allgemeine Zeitung* condemned the "strangeness" of the music, the "briefness" of the themes,[69] the "incomprehensible" form that seemed to ignore all existing canons, the gigantic orchestral forces, never heard before except in operas, his outbursts of violence that "tortured the ears," and the "nerve-racking" instrumentation. Why did Herr Mahler label *"Symphony"* a musical composition that had nothing in common with all the other works thus named? According to this critic, only the second movement had left "an agreeable impression."

The *Vossische Zeitung* credited Mahler with the virtue of "knowing at times how to orchestrate gracefully and delicately," but nevertheless claimed that the whole work had made a "disturbing rather than satisfying impression"; this music was incompatible with the "most elevated conception of the symphony" because it totally lacked certain essential qualities, such as "internal unity, noble and lofty ideas as well as interesting and well-devised development." This critic held that Mahler did not lack inventiveness but was incapable of "purifying" it. He also lacked taste, mistook "coarseness for power," and accumulated "theme upon theme, motif upon motif," all of which gave to his piece "a motley aspect injurious to the clarity of the form." The first movement struck this critic as full of "dry, laborious brooding and many orchestral effects offensive to the ear." The percussion was used "monstrously." The others were judged "fairly acceptable, having been written with more ease, though they sometimes bordered on banality."

Ludwig Bussler, in the *National Zeitung,* began by attacking the management of the Philharmonic for having presented "an incomplete work by a living composer," which "merits no particular attention, one way or the other," since it "showed no sign of artistic maturity." He thought Mahler did not lack invention, but his themes were unoriginal, he had no feeling for form, did not know how to develop, indulged in "ridiculous repetitions of minor motifs and searched in vain for an ending to his movements." According to the *Tägliche Rundschau* "the three endless movements seemed to be the product of a musical game or sport rather than of a creative spirit"; the only original and expressive one was the first, even though its development included some "disorderly noise." As for the others, with their "pretty contrasts" and "new combinations," they were nothing but "light and agreeable music."

The *Börsenzeitung* mentioned the date (February 8) written on the copy of the score, claiming that the third movement had just been composed. It had been a mistake to present it so soon, as the composer could have improved his work—for example the "exhausting" length of the first movement, its "noisy and bombastic pathos," and the "atrocious, tormenting dissonances, in which it was difficult to find even a small grain of music." The other movements were judged "more natural," their themes pleasant, though not profound, the instrumentation bizarre but relevant to the thought; in them, the laws of form and balance, "absolutely impossible to discern in the first movement, were more respected, or at least not utterly ignored."

In the face of the Berlin critics' unanimous disapproval, Mahler hoped for some support from his fellow musicians, and in particular from Strauss, which would indeed have been a consolation. Wilhelm Kienzl, the Austrian composer of *Der Evangelimann,* who attended the concert with Strauss and the conductor Karl Muck, claimed that at a "particularly dissonant" tutti fortissimo in the development Strauss had raised his eyes heavenward declaring "that there was no limit to musical expression," while Muck's face became distorted with disgust and he had muttered, between clenched teeth, *"Scheusslich!"* ("Atrocious!").[70] In fact, Strauss's reaction to all three move-

ments seems to have been rather negative, and Mahler was to lose all contact with him for almost two years. Indeed, when he sent him, early in 1897,
the orchestral score, together with Behn's piano reduction, Strauss acknowledged receipt in rather cool terms: The Finale "is really a gigantic undertaking," and the reduction is "a little masterpiece." "I was glad to hear
from you after such a long time. I thought that you had completely forgotten the first Mahler fan," he added, reminding Mahler of his efforts in 1894
to perform the *Titan* at the Weimar Festival and later the *Second Symphony*
in Berlin.[71]

For the time being Mahler's only consolation was an article written by
Oskar Eichberg in the *Börsen Courier,* stating that the orchestra had "played
lovingly" and that it was impossible to really judge the symphony without
knowing its Finale, which would necessarily be its climax. According to
Eichberg, Mahler clearly had something new and essential to say, which explained his meeting so much opposition. His instrumentation and its "richness in unprecedented colors" could be compared to that of Strauss, his thematic developments rested on new laws, the themes being modified as well
as worked out, thus losing their initial character. Eichberg found similarities
with *Parsifal* and Beethoven's *Ninth Symphony*—"similarities of atmosphere rather than direct reminiscences." Finally, Eichberg expressed the
hope of hearing the entire symphony soon and warmly praised Mahler's
conducting.

Deeply moved at being finally understood and encouraged by a critic,
Mahler wrote to Eichberg: "If you knew my *via dolorosa* as a composer, if
you knew the rebuffs, the frustrations, even the humiliations, that have
been my lot for ten years, if you could have seen how many works were
locked away in my drawer as soon as they were completed, or imagine the
lack of understanding with which I have been met when, despite all obstacles, I have succeeded in presenting my works to the public, then you would
be able to measure the extent of my gratitude. This explains, too, why I
hesitated so long before writing to you. Such gratitude, I feel, cannot be put
into words.

"I hope you will not think me presumptuous if I tell you that I am sustained by my confidence that one day everything may change for me, and
this because today I can point to one who, first and alone among the men of
his profession, has felt and understood the language I speak and the road
I follow; who has not only recognized it, but proclaimed and defended it
at a time when it still requires great courage to take arms against the flood
of enemies and detractors. Believe me, dear Herr Eichberg, I needed to experience such a moment in order to find the courage to persevere and continue to create. I am now thirty-four, and like Quintus Fixlein, I have already
written a small but complete library whose readers are only my closest
friends. Wings that are constantly bound must ultimately become paralyzed.
Now perhaps you understand why I am grateful to you."[72]

"How paralyzing this eternal tilting at windmills is," he wrote to Oscar

Bie, author of another favorable article, in the *Neue Deutsche Rundschau.* "A long time ago I stopped expecting comprehension from my 'fellow-workers.' I feel that I must not search for those who will one day understand me among those who 'make' music. My music is lived [*gelebt*], so how can it be understood by people who are not 'alive,' who haven't felt the slightest breeze from the raging gales of our great epoch?"[73]

The subscription concerts—and with them Sittard's attacks—had begun early in 1895. On January 21, Mahler conducted with great success a concert that included Beethoven's *"Leonore" Overture No. 3,* Mendelssohn's *Fingal's Cave,* and Schumann's *First Symphony,* but Sittard, the "Judge of Hades," had again condemned most of his tempos.[74] In the *Fremdenblatt,* Krause accused Mahler of "going contrary to the demands of nature," of searching for "novelty at any price," and of bogging down in mannerisms, "excessive slowness and exaggerated contrasts."[75]

The program of the next concert, on February 4, 1895, seems surprisingly long: the Berlioz *Symphonie fantastique,* the Grieg *Piano Concerto,* the Prelude to Strauss's *Guntram,* three piano solos played by Teresa Carreño,[76] and the Prelude to *Tristan und Isolde.* Sittard found the *Symphonie fantastique* "interesting, full of spirit," but also of "bizarrerie and ugliness." Mahler's "electrifying" interpretation had won him a noisy ovation and numerous curtain calls. Krause also went to war against Berlioz, noting that Mahler appeared to be in his element while conducting the *Fantastique,* since he could do "whatever he liked" with this music. Yet he had been unable to hide the weaknesses of this "mosaic work," this "suite of aphorisms," of "formless, shallow images" in which the themes "serve only as pretexts for sound effects."

Mahler had originally intended to conduct the two preludes from *Guntram* (to the first and last acts), but he had had to give up the second because of a misunderstanding or "negligence" on the part of the impresario Wolff. The work was highly successful and Mahler wrote to Strauss immediately after the concert to send him copies of the reviews. He now believed that Pollini would no longer hesitate to stage the opera. Krause certainly credited Strauss with an important place in the musical world as successor to Wagner, but Sittard found that he lacked originality and "imitated Wagner too willingly instead of letting his own nature have its head." "His rich, perhaps affected" harmony and his "marvelous sound combinations" were worthy of a master, but he lacked soul: "Only the intellect is stimulated, the heart is ignored."

During the second last subscription concert, Mahler for the first time conducted a Bruckner symphony. He had chosen one of the "easiest," the "Romantic" in E flat, which proved a great public success,[77] and about which Sittard wrote one of his strangest articles. He accused Bruckner of lining up with "unlimited subjectivity . . . small, ever-changing, jumpy motifs, without ever developing them . . . aphoristic fragments . . . new ideas constantly interrupted the flow" in a "more and more nervous way" (*sic*).

"Nervousness" and "pointillism" are indeed unexpected complaints against Bruckner's music, which cannot have sounded as modern to Sittard as that of Berlioz. Krause, favorable to Bruckner as a rule, this time accused him of having wanted, all his life, "to create novelty," and of modulating too often; he criticized his "lack of soul" and his "arbitrary, rhapsodic way of thinking."

In order to bring the concert season to a worthy conclusion, Mahler scheduled for March 11 Beethoven's *Ninth Symphony,* which he had not conducted since the memorable occasion in Prague eight years before. The new "alterations" that he introduced this time were the result of the long study of Beethoven literature that he had made early that winter. He had then read the writings of Beethoven's contemporaries and accounts of his concerts, in particular those by Schindler.[78] In the *Ninth Symphony,* Mahler went further than ever before. Basing his theory upon the fact that Beethoven, who had gone deaf, had been unable to "try out" his orchestration as had formerly been his custom, Mahler doubled some of the wind instruments, adding here and there a trombone, a piccolo, or an E flat clarinet—and even a new horn part in the D major passage of the Scherzo. (Sittard reported that he had even suppressed three measures and a repeat in this movement.)

His most daring initiative, which he was to drop later, was that of placing some of the wind instruments in the wings during the beginning of the alla marcia episode in the Finale which leads up to the entrance of the tenor. His aim was to obtain thus a gigantic crescendo, suggesting "the approach of a vast legion of enraptured, ecstatic beings, a jubilant hosanna on their lips, as on the first of all Palm Sundays."[79]

For this all-important concert, Mahler had a specially large podium built, from which he could see all the performers. Ordered at the last moment, it was ready only on the day of the concert itself. The carpenter, following Mahler's instructions too much to the letter, had made a shaky, narrow platform one flight high and perched on stilts. On the evening of the concert, when Mahler climbed the steps, he was seized by such vertigo that he almost fell. Only his will power kept him rooted to the fragile pedestal.[80] The concert ended with wild applause.

This time Mahler had really gone out of his way to shock the conservatives, yet criticisms were less severe than might have been expected. Sittard maliciously listed the "alterations" and once again regretted the "modifications of tempo." Probably aware that Mahler would not conduct these concerts in the future, he ended his final article of the season with some praise, thus appearing to make amends for his bitter attacks: Mahler was a conductor "of genius" who dominated his orchestra "like few others," and played "on it" like a virtuoso. Emil Krause, on the contrary, accused Mahler once again of following Bülow's example too closely and committing "extravagances . . . contrary to the essential principles" of the art, of taking impossible liberties and of committing unforgivable "lapses in taste."[81]

Thus the over-all result of these eight concerts was far from being wholly positive. Not only had some of the critics attacked Mahler constantly, but the public had also begun to stay away. Probably because the programs were "too modern," and Mahler's conceptions too subjective, it was slowly losing the habit, formed in Bülow's time, of attending the subscription concerts, preferring instead the Philharmonic concerts and their mediocre conductors. This betrayal hurt Mahler more deeply than the critics' attacks. One day, when Anna Bernhardt, the lady he had met at Bülow's last Hamburg concert, told him of the "immense prestige" that he enjoyed in Hamburg, he replied: "Yes, so I see it today! But I have no right to complain. When, in Vienna, Brahms was asked for his opinion of Hamburg's artistic life, he hesitated for a while, stroking his long beard, and then finally replied with conviction, 'The beefsteaks really are delicious there!' "[82]

Wolff, the impresario, later complained to Ferdinand Pfohl about this failure of the concerts, telling him that the deficit amounted to thirteen thousand marks. Under these circumstances, he gave up the idea of re-engaging Mahler for the following season. When a new conductor for the Philharmonic concerts was being sought sometime later, Mahler confided to Pfohl that he would accept this position for the modest salary of six thousand marks per year. Pfohl transmitted this offer to a particularly influential music-loving senator, but the latter's refusal was firm and definite. In his view, Mahler was a conductor for opera, not for concerts. The opinions of Krause and Sittard had taken on the force of law among the Hamburg public!

And yet Mahler was later to win a place among the most famous and admired concert conductors of his time! He hid his disappointment behind a bitter smile and a Latin quotation: *Mundus vult decipi*. But the wound hurt cruelly nevertheless. The enthusiasm with which he had approached this new task equaled the disappointment it brought him.[83]

If this bitter experience touched him somewhat less than might be imagined, it was because something far more terrible had just occurred: the suicide of his brother Otto, which took place on February 6, 1895, during a particularly busy musical season. What happened to Otto between the summer of 1894, when Staegemann engaged him for Leipzig, and the beginning of 1895? Mahler's known correspondence does not mention him once during these six months. Probably a certain feeling of shame and the desire to wipe out the memory of his violent and tragic death, about which strong prejudices then existed, induced the Mahlers, and in particular Justine, the scrupulous "archivist," to destroy everything concerning his suicide.

For the details of Otto's death, it is necessary to search in theatrical almanacs, Vienna police reports, and contemporary newspapers. In 1894, Otto had joined the Deutsche Bühnengenossenschaft, a sort of union of German musicians: his name appears in the records of the retirement fund of that institution, which also state that he held a post at the Leipzig Opera. Unfortunately, the Leipzig theatrical archives have been destroyed, and it is impossible to locate any trace of Otto there or to discover the reasons why he left Leipzig.

In view of his past, it is easy to imagine that his laziness and lack of self-discipline had put an end to his budding career, and that his natural pessimism had convinced him of his inability to provide for himself or adapt to society. The articles published at the time of his death[84] deplore the disappearance of "a gifted young musician who lived entirely for his art," whose "dreamy, negative" nature had not succeeded in "facing up to the difficulties of life." Some episodes of this "struggle" had "shaken him and made him melancholy"—in particular, if we can believe these newspaper accounts, a disappointment in love.

According to police reports, Otto had a room in Vienna (Margarethenstrasse 39), but on the other hand we know that he spent most of his time at the home of Nina Hoffmann-Matscheko (Theresianumgasse 6), an old friend of the Mahlers' with whom Emma had lived until the preceding summer. On February 6, whether he had been dismissed or had left the Leipzig Opera of his own free will, Otto was in Vienna. He spent most of the afternoon with Nina Hoffmann, whose bad health forced her to spend much time in bed. They often discussed Dostoyevsky's tragic sense of life, for Nina had translated his books into German. He pretended to leave her apartment, but at about four-thirty locked himself into an adjoining room, lay down on a divan, pulled out a revolver and put a bullet through his heart. The shot was heard instantly; the first people to enter the room found him covered with blood. When a doctor arrived, he could do nothing but certify the death. Besides his revolver, papers, clothes, and personal belongings, Otto left only seventy-seven kronen, barely enough to pay for his funeral. Since it was quite impossible for Mahler to find time to go to Vienna and attend to the customary formalities, he entrusted them to Emil Freund and an Iglau notary: their signatures appear on the official documents.

According to Bruno Walter, Otto left two symphonies, parts of which had been played and "ridiculed" by the public; also some lieder for orchestra and piano and an almost complete *Third Symphony*.[85] The silence surrounding this death reveals, not Mahler's indifference, but the gravity of his wound. He seems to have tried to erase even the memory of his unhappy brother, whom he never ceased to love in spite of his weaknesses, and about whom he most probably felt some guilt, as is only natural in such cases. Alma Mahler gives us a glimpse of his secret sorrow when she reveals that it was only thirty years later that she opened for the first time the trunk containing Otto's manuscripts and personal effects, among which she found the manuscript of Bruckner's *Third Symphony,* given to him by his elder brother. During the last sixteen years of his life, Mahler himself had lacked courage to open the trunk.[86]

One day in the Parkallee apartment, Mahler spoke of his childhood to Förster. Pointing toward one corner of his study, where a large easy chair covered with oilcloth and losing its stuffing, stood, he said, "My father used to work in that chair." Then, after a few minutes' silence, he added, "I also had a brother who was like me a musician and a composer. A man of great talent, far more gifted than I. He died very young . . . alas . . . alas! he killed himself in the prime of life."

"'Symphony'—to me this means
creating a world with all the
technical means available."

# CHAPTER 21

### Mahler in Hamburg (VI) — The Third Symphony — Premiere of the Second Symphony — Anna von Mildenburg (June 1895–February 1896)

The 1895–96 season ended with a new conflict between Mahler and Pollini over a concert that the latter was to organize for him at the opera. Several times Mahler had promised Strauss that he would conduct on this occasion the big tenor solo and the prelude to the last act of *Guntram,* which he had been forced to drop from the subscription concerts at the last moment. But Pollini refused to keep this promise, and this was probably the reason why, in May, Mahler sent him a letter of resignation that Pollini did not even bother to acknowledge.[1] The author of this letter—doubtless written in a moment of anger—soon regretted it, mainly because it was impossible to find another position quickly, so things continued more or less as before.

On May 31, 1895, after the Wagner festival was over, Mahler left for Steinbach, drawn there by a wish to get his new symphonic projects down on paper. "Others go to Spitzberg on vacation," he declared to Pfohl, "but I shall write a new symphony."[2] On the way he stopped first in Berlin to discuss arrangements for the first complete performance of his *Second Symphony,* and then in Vienna to call on the intendant of the opera, Josef Freiherr von Bezecny. He had heard a rumor that the aging director Jahn was ill and about to be replaced, and that the famous conductor Hans Richter was going to resign, since his time was increasingly taken up with concert tours. From then on, to leave Hamburg for Vienna was Mahler's dream, for his patience was exhausted and his nerves on edge. Unfortunately this first meeting with Bezecny had no immediate results.[3]

Mahler's mind was full of musical ideas, and he set to work as soon as he reached Steinbach on June 5.[4] The wild flowers in the meadow extending from the window of the Häuschen to the edge of the lake inspired him to compose a graceful, airy minuet that flowed easily from his pen. It was called *"Was mir die Blumen auf der Wiese erzählen"* (What the flowers of the meadow tell me).[5] "Those who do not know this place," Mahler told Natalie, "should almost be able to picture it from the music, for its charm is unique, the very place to offer such an inspiration."[6]

Almost at once Mahler began to work this musical idyl into a grandiose scheme for which he drew up two rather different "preliminary plans, while at the same time starting to note down the first outlines for the other movements."[7]

*Das glückliche Leben* [The happy life]

*Ein Sommernachtstraum* [A summer night's dream] (*Nicht nach Shakespeare. Anmerkung für Rezensenten und Shakespearekenner*) [Not after Shakespeare. Note for critics and Shakespeare experts]

1. *Was mir der Wald erzählt* [What the forest tells me]
2. *Was mir die Dämmerung erzählt* [What the twilight tells me]
3. *Was mir die Liebe erzählt* [What love tells me]
4. (*Was mir die Dämmerung erzählt*) [What the twilight tells me] (this movement was later cut out)
5. *Was mir der Kuckuck erzählt* [What the cuckoo tells me]
6. *Was mir das Kind erzählt* [What the child tells me]

*Ein Sommernachtstraum* [A summer night's dream]

1. *Der Sommer marschiert ein* (*Fanfare und lustiger Marsch*) (*Einleitung*) (*Nur Bläser mit konzertierenden Contrabässen*) [Summer marches in (Fanfare and gay march)] [Introduction] [For wind instruments with solo double basses]
2. *Was mir der Wald erzählt* (*1. Satz*) [1. Piece]
3. *Was mir die Liebe erzählt* (*Adagio*)
4. *Was mir die Dämmerung erzählt* (*Scherzo*) (*Nur Streicher*) [For strings]
5. *Was mir die Blumen auf der Wiese erzählen* (*Menuetto*)
6. *Was mir der Kuckuck erzählt* (*Scherzo*)
7. *Was mir das Kind erzählt*[8]

Mahler set to work the afternoon of his arrival, and the *Blumenstück* was completed within a few days, but not surprisingly its smiling face occasionally clouded over. "A stormy wind blows across the field," explained Mahler, "the leaves and flowers moan and cry out on their stems, begging the superior powers for deliverance." Once again Mahler closely blended joy and sorrow. At times, a kind of mysterious terror seized him, "greater than if he had been composing a tragic movement, for then he could defend himself with both gravity and humor." He no longer regarded the world, as in his first two symphonies, "from the point of view of struggling, suffering man," but "this time went to the very heart of existence, where one must feel every tremor of the world and of God."[9]

Mahler then composed a long movement, half parody, half dream; the kind of movement of which he alone had the secret. Its source was an old *Wunderhorn* song, *"Ablösung im Sommer."* This modest *Gesang,* scarcely three pages long in its original piano version, was changed into a symphonic movement lasting almost fifteen minutes and entitled *"Was mir die Tiere im Walde erzählen"* (What the animals in the forest tell me).

A huge symphonic structure was thus forming in Mahler's mind. For the next movement he drew inspiration from one of his most recent literary enthusiasms, Friedrich Nietzsche, using the great *"Mitternachtsgedicht"* from *Also sprach Zarathustra* as *"Was mir die Nacht erzählt"* (What the night tells me—Man). This poem forms the climax of Nietzsche's *Zarathustra.* It synthesizes the ideas underlying this great work. The hero sings of his disgust with contemporary man, his faith in the future of the human race, the hidden depths of the world, its deep woe, its joys that are deeper still, and its longing for eternity. He later compared this new piece to a "daydream" or a "gentle self-awareness" and remembered that its opening bars were the same as those of a short piece he had composed while he was still at school.[10] This somber and mysterious Nietzsche movement was to be followed by a fresh, cheerful sound picture taken from the *Wunderhorn, "Was mir die Morgenglocken erzählen"* (What the morning bells tell me), for a mixed choir of women and children; the outline for this was completed by June 24!

A long Adagio was also composed that summer. Mahler entitled it *"Was mir die Liebe erzählt"* (What love tells me—the angels). At the beginning of it he wrote: "Father, behold my wounds, do not let any creature be lost." Finally he decided to end his work on an idyllic note by using one of his favorite lieder, composed three years before in Hamburg—*"Das himmlische Leben"* (Heavenly life). This last piece was rechristened *"Was mir das Kind erzählt"* (What the child tells me). It was later cut out because of the already exceptional length of the symphony,[11] and five years later the same lied was used to conclude his *Fourth Symphony.* The title *"Was mir das Kind erzählt"* was then given to the fifth movement.

The whole conception of the *Third Symphony* thus evolved considerably during that summer, for Mahler first put the present third movement (Scherzo) at the beginning and changed the order of the others several times. In one of the "preliminary" programs the *Blumenstück* was the second-to-last movement, and the final Adagio (Love) was placed third.[12]

Natalie spent the whole summer in Steinbach with the Mahlers, and she kept as detailed a record of this important period as she did for the summers of 1893 and 1896. At first Mahler was delighted by the way his work was going; he announced that "with this symphony I will at last know success and earn money, since it is nothing but humor, gaiety, and an enormous laugh at the entire world!" But the next day he became more realistic and once even said, "I won't earn anything with the *Third,* for people will never understand and accept its gaiety. It hovers above that world of struggle and sorrow in the *First* and *Second,* and can be understood only as their consequence. That I call it a symphony is really incorrect, as it does not follow the usual form. The term 'symphony'—to me this means creating a world with all the technical means available. The constantly new and changing content determines its own form. In this sense, I must always be reminded that I create my own original means of expression, even if I am in perfect control of my technique, which I believe I am today."[13]

This important passage tells us more about Mahler's symphonic concepts than the many volumes of analysis that have been devoted to them. Faced by the immensity of his new project, he did experience, the following year, a moment of hesitation, when he considered calling the work *"Pan, a Symphonic poem,"* and congratulated himself on having freely introduced words into the *Second Symphony.* Already in 1895, he had begun to consider the first movement as a monumental gateway, an immense fresco, a double movement—an introduction followed by a stupendous march, the noisy procession of Dionysus, celebrating the arrival of summer. A "regimental band" would be needed to depict the tumult of this military parade, made up of a "whole rabble" (*Gesindel*), the like of which had never before been seen. "The summer is conceived as a conqueror advancing amidst all that grows and blooms, crawls and flies, hopes [*wähnen*] and desires [*sehnen*], and finally everything we know by instinct (Angels—Bell. Transcendental). Above all, Eternal Love spins a web of light like rays of sun converging to a single burning point. It is my most personal [*eigenartiges*] and richest work." After a violent struggle winter would be vanquished by this mighty throng, but the movement would be treated "in a humorous and even baroque style."[14] The entire work would bear a title taken from Nietzsche: *Die fröhliche Wissenschaft* (The gay science) and a subtitle: *"Ein Sommermorgentraum"* (A summer morning dream).[15]

For the time being, he had composed only a few sketches for this first piece, but he had already sent the "program" to his friends, to Löhr, to Berliner, to Behn,[16] and to Natalie, asking for their impressions as to whether it succeeded in "conveying its hearers in the direction that he meant them to take."

Upon his return to Hamburg, Mahler described the *Third Symphony* to Förster, likening it to a "gigantic hymn to the glory of every aspect of creation"; it was to evoke "the victorious appearance of Helios and the miracle of spring, thanks to which all things live, breathe, flower, sing and ripen, after which appear those imperfect beings who have participated in this miracle—the men."[17]

It seems unlikely that Mahler completed the outlines for all five movements before his early July visit to Brahms. Nevertheless, by the time of his departure at the end of August, he had not only completed them, but had also noted down some themes for the first movement and composed two more important *Wunderhorn* songs: *"Lied des Verfolgten im Turm"* (Song of the prisoner in the tower) and *"Wo die schönen Trompeten blasen"* (Where the beautiful trumpets sound). This was an astonishing output for two and a half months of work.

That summer, Mahler had really been favored by the gods. Directed by a will stronger than his own, he feared interruptions and noise more than ever. Those close to him had to wage pitiless war against everything that might disturb his work. Natalie and Justi promised candy and toys to the village children to prevent them from playing in the meadow or bathing in the lake near the famous cabin. All the animals, dogs, cats, chickens, and geese, were mercilessly driven away or shut up. Those which were noisy and edible were bought and eaten.

The same war was declared against the crows that regularly flew over the tiny peninsula. The children were paid to take away their nests, and a dead crow was hung up near the Häuschen as a warning. Mahler, who could not bear to see even a fly or a beetle needlessly killed, and who was a sworn enemy of hunting, which he considered a barbarous and horrible sport, agreed to all these Draconian measures in order to maintain the calm indispensable to his work. On the inland side of the Häuschen a hideous scarecrow with a straw body and a pumpkin head was stuck on a broomstick, dressed in a bathing suit of Justi's, a skirt of Emma's, and an immense hat belonging to Natalie.

Despite all these precautions, Mahler complained several times during the summer that he had been disturbed by a harvester whistling or sharpening his scythe nearby, or by peasants arguing in the garden of the inn. It was often necessary to use guile to make them understand what was expected of them, and to persuade them to be quiet by offering them beer. When all else failed, the others would be reduced to explain that "the gentleman was not quite right in the head." One day, an "actor-comedian" vacationing on the lake[18] who knew of Mahler's phobia, tried to play a practical joke by hiring a street musician to play a hurdy-gurdy near the Häuschen. Foreseeing her brother's fury, Justi had to pay dearly for the man's silence.[19]

During the first days of July, Mahler interrupted his work to pay his annual call on Brahms. The old master received him with all the warmth of which he was capable, and for once their conversation took a serious turn. Max Kalbeck, Brahms's biographer, says that at this time Brahms was considering writing a sort of "cantata-symphony," illuminated, like Mahler's *Second Symphony,* by an *"Urlicht* [primeval light] shining on eternal, happy life." This project finally took on a very different form in the *Vier ernste Gesänge,* but Mahler was nevertheless invited to send Brahms his symphony, which he did upon his return to Steinbach, using Kössler as his intermediary.[20] Brahms returned the score almost immediately. He was "astonished that he [Mahler] had not been better known than Bruckner and Richard Strauss for years . . ." Was this a criticism or a compliment? In any case, the phrase was wounding in its ambiguity.

Mahler took advantage of his trip to Ischl to take the waters for several days, after which he planned a long excursion from Ischl to the Aussee and Grundelsee, hoping to climb the Zwieselalm if the good weather lasted. Then he intended to meet Justi and Natalie in Ischl and return to Steinbach with them on foot. No doubt this plan was carried out, for a postcard dated July 3 confirms the rendezvous in Ischl.

That year Mahler's departure from Steinbach was advanced by a few days. He left about August 20 and spent three days in Berlin, settling the last details of a project particularly dear to him, the first complete performance of his *Second Symphony*. He had finally decided to organize it at his own expense, with the assistance of the impresario Wolff, "since I have, like the South Pole, remained unexplored for long enough." Back in Hamburg, Mahler moved for the fourth time, settling with his sisters in a suburban neighborhood whose name especially pleased him: Hoheluft (Air of the Heights).[21] This time they had the whole of a small house that was almost hidden by shrubbery, surrounded by trees, and overlooked fields and orchards. Mahler reserved for himself the whole upper floor: this consisted of a room for his piano, a study to write in, and a bedroom. Transportation to the city was almost as convenient as from the Parkallee, for an electric train passed quite close and went straight to the opera. No noisy disturbances were to be feared, as the Mahlers were alone in the house, and the suburb of Eppendorf, on the outskirts of the city, was almost in the country.

Despite his treatment in Ischl, Mahler was not in good health early that autumn. The hemorrhages had begun again more seriously, and he did not know how to stop them. Further he was submerged by work at the opera: the singer Katharina Klafsky had broken her contract and left for the United States with her husband, the conductor Otto Lohse. Mahler was therefore responsible for conducting almost the entire repertoire, since he could entrust only the lighter works to his assistant, Karl Pohlig. Not knowing that Pollini intended to give Lohse's post to Bruno Walter, Mahler was also disturbed to see that nothing was being done to find a replacement. Meanwhile, he conducted almost every day, giving no less than twenty-one performances in September! On the sixteenth he wrote to Berliner to borrow 170 marks, Pollini having played a "shabby trick" that had left him in financial difficulties. The bad impression made by Mahler's attempted resignation in May had no doubt not been forgiven or forgotten.

On September 12 Mahler took advantage of his first free evening to write to Behn, for he had received and corrected the proofs of his transcription of the *Second Symphony*.[22] That summer Pollini had made a decision that was to have many unexpected consequences for Mahler. Learning that Klafsky, his top dramatic soprano, was soon to leave, he had consulted one of his close friends, the Viennese contralto Rosa Papier, who had given up singing some years before in order to become a teacher,[23] asking for her advice regarding a possible replacement. She recommended one of her young pupils, a dramatic soprano gifted with a magnificent voice. Anna von Mildenburg, born in Vienna on November 29, 1872, was barely twenty-three when Rosa Papier brought her to Karlsbad during the summer of 1895 for an audition with the dreaded Pollini. She sang the main arias from *Oberon* and *Norma,* those of Donna Anna and the Queen of the Night, and, in conclusion, Ortrud's curse and the cry of Brünnhilde. The impression she made on Pollini was decisive. He engaged her on the spot and asked her to study first of all the roles of Brünnhilde, Leonore in *Fidelio,* and Elisabeth in *Tannhäuser.*

Upon her arrival in Hamburg, the young singer met all the opera personnel: singers, producers, assistant conductors, prompter, and dresser. Only one person was missing, the principal conductor, whom she had heard described as a tyrant and an unbearable pedant. When she ventured to say with a blush that she had nothing to fear from him, having studied her roles perfectly, she was told, "Yes, but you undoubtedly believe that an eighth note is an eighth note. Well, there is a world of difference between a Mahler eighth note and a normal eighth note."

One day Mildenburg was working on the role of Brünnhilde with an accompanist in a rehearsal room at the opera. She had just reached the passage in Act II, *"Vater, Vater, sage, was ist dir?"* when suddenly the door was flung open and she saw a small sunburned man, dressed in a summer suit, carrying a dark felt hat, and with a badly rolled umbrella under one arm, who looked at her coldly with clear gray-blue eyes.[24] Cutting short the polite greetings, he slammed the door, keeping his hand on the handle as if ready to flee, and called out, "Go on." A wink from the accompanist and an "M" formed by his lips told Mildenburg that this was the terrible *Kapellmeister.* Terrified, she shut her eyes, pressed her hands together, and tried to put into her submissive, entreating voice all the intense distress she felt at finding herself face to face with this new and terrifying theatrical experience.

Suddenly the little man frightened her by stamping his foot violently. His hat, followed by his umbrella, flew onto the piano. The accompanist was quickly dismissed with a "Thanks. I don't need you anymore," and his departure awaited in such glacial silence and such obvious impatience that the flustered man could not find his hat. "Start again at the beginning," Mahler called out, and all at once, in the presence of this man who had been described to her as a terrible despot, Mildenburg suddenly felt a profound confidence spring up within her, bringing with it calm and liberation. Everything about opera life had amazed and terrorized her, and now, suddenly, she found herself experiencing a new and not at all disagreeable sensation. She sang her cry, *"Ho-jo-to-ho,"* and then the episode that follows the departure of Fricka—all without the slightest comment from Mahler. Reaching the passage *"Sieh! Brünnhilde bittet,"* she broke down. Leaning against the small upright piano, she burst into tears.

Astonished, Mahler bit his lips and stared at her. Then he began to insult her. Finally, seeing her terrified expression, he suddenly started to laugh. His hands deep in his trouser pockets, he paced the room, then sat down again and calmly cleaned his glasses while reassuring the young girl. She had sung perfectly and had no reason to be upset. Seeing that, despite this, she had started to cry again, he added, "It is good that you should cry. One day, just like the others, you will be a victim of the routine of the theater, and you'll see that there no one cries!"

Delighted at having finally found an authentic talent and a truly artistic nature at the Hamburg Opera, Mahler set to work to orient and follow Mildenburg's progress step by step. Pollini regarded their incessant work together unfavorably: to him all that mattered was the possession of a beautiful voice, and he feared Mahler would exhaust the young girl with interminable rehearsals. Happily, Mildenburg understood immediately the value of their work. Mahler had started by telling her, "Exactitude is the soul of all artistic success." Faithful to this principle, she gradually learned under his aegis the value and significance of notes, studying one after another most of the Wagnerian roles, not to mention Rezia, Donna Anna, Norma, and Leonore.

In her memoirs, Mildenburg describes in detail Mahler's working methods at the Hamburg Opera. Before her debut in *Die Walküre* he called a general rehearsal with all the singers assembled around the piano. That day Mildenburg fully understood his extraordinarily powerful personality. Not one of those who had spoken contemptuously or angrily of his demands and his pedantry was able to resist him in his presence. As soon as he appeared, they became respectful and attentive, almost as though they were standing to attention. After a polite, brief greeting, Mahler shook hands with some of them, but passed Mildenburg rapidly with only a glance of somewhat amused sympathy. Then, after playing the first bars of Siegmund's entrance, he stopped suddenly, rose, took Förster-Lauterer by the hand, and led her over to Mildenburg. Without a word, he placed them together, realizing that the young girl needed some moral support among so many strangers.

During the rehearsals, which he accompanied from the orchestral score, Mahler rocked his chair dangerously back and forth. He played the piano without any pretension of being a pianist, passing rapidly over certain passages, but always emphasizing the notes that could help the singers or indicate their entrances. If by chance anyone sang a wrong note, he would hammer out the correct note on the piano, glaring furiously. If one of the singers did not know his part properly, Mahler became even more frightening. Without a word, with icy calm, he would rehearse the same passage twenty times, even after the unfortunate singer had sung it several times correctly. When a singer made an accidental mistake, Mahler would stare at him as if he had uncovered a shameful vice. Then, moved by the culprit's terrified expression, he would laugh, and all would be forgotten.

When a singer was prepared to make a real effort, Mahler nearly always relaxed and explained what he wanted in detail. Sometimes these bits of advice were interspersed with simple jokes, at which he laughed himself with childlike spontaneity. But he hated any show of hypersensitivity or susceptibility and ended by paying no attention whatever to manifestations of this kind; with or without tears, he always worked on to the end. From time to time he would express his anger in an especially violent way by swearing under his breath in sibilant, labored tones. He would brook no arguments or excuses. The best way to get along with him was to let him explain his point of view and then promise to do better next time.

For anyone with real artistic talent, this work was exhilarating, for he never stopped discovering, in every bar, something new and unexpected. He gave the impression that he himself was always searching for new truths, and discovering them constantly. For this reason, he sometimes seemed to contradict himself, changing his mind on questions of diction, tempo or dramatic action. But this was how he managed to inspire and carry with him those capable of following and understanding him.

The singers were divided into two groups: his friends and his enemies. One group believed implicitly in him; understanding him, they spontaneously recognized his greatness. The others hated him in silence: his personality was alien to them, even offended them. In the end, he always won them over, forcing them to change their minds and to conform to his slightest wishes, to think and feel as they had never believed that they could think and feel. They themselves did not even realize that it was because of him that they reached heights to which, on their own, they could never have aspired. What exasperated Mahler more than anything else was indifference; his own capacity for attention and participation was so great that others had to be constantly ready to listen, to follow, and to let themselves be dominated.

On the day of the dress rehearsal of *Die Walküre,* Pollini was there in the theater to hear Mildenburg's *"Ho-jo-to-ho."* A few minutes later she was waiting on top of some scaffolding for her second entrance cue, when she saw Pollini coming up the steps toward her. "No one can sing like you," he said, and slipped something into her hand. She later realized with amazement that it was a twenty-mark piece. The rehearsal proceeded without incident, for she knew her role so perfectly that she scarcely needed to watch Mahler. Later, Mahler lost his temper over Pollini's "tip." "Give it back to him at once," he cried, stamping his foot. But, after thinking it over, he dared not advise her to do so, for fear of hurting the redoubtable director's feelings.

Mildenburg had to postpone her debut for a few days because of a bad sore throat. Furious, Pollini did everything possible to persuade her to sing in spite of it. He argued with her each day, but despite the hail of cables and menacing letters, Mahler upheld the young singer in her decision, assuring her that Pollini had more need of her than she of him. To distract her during her illness, he sent her his two favorite books, *Don Quixote* and *Pickwick Papers.*

When Mildenburg finally recovered, Mahler entrusted the task of making her up—she was very inexperienced in such matters—to one of her colleagues. Before her first entrance in the second act, Mahler went to survey the result of these efforts. With his hands in his pockets, he murmured quietly and calmly, "It is abominable! Abominable!" After a second examination he suddenly cried, "Take all that off!" rubbing his own face as if the superfluous layer of paint was there. Then the warning signal sounded for the start of the act; it was too late to make the slightest change, and Mahler left, shrugging his shoulders in silent fury. Before disappearing, he turned violently back toward Mildenburg, literally transfixing her with his glance. "Will you promise me not to read a single newspaper tomorrow morning?" But the next day, it was he himself who joyfully read to her the many favorable reviews. In the *Fremdenblatt,* Armbrust said that he had been "astounded" by the young soprano's achievements. Certainly he considered that she had not yet reached absolute perfection: her voice still lacked evenness and had an excessive tendency toward sweetness and lyricism. But she had nevertheless established herself as a talented dramatic soprano, sensitive, musicianly, and remarkably assured for her young age.[25]

Thus Mildenburg began her brilliant career. During those first months, she was constantly directed and encouraged by Mahler, who gave her an almost hypnotic support. Still inexperienced, she followed his mysterious baton as it moved in the shadows, showing her the road to follow. At first, she contented herself, from the dramatic point of view, with some borrowed gestures, a few arm movements. Only little by little did she come to realize that she would not really be able to act until she was so sure of herself that she need not look at the conductor anymore. Unhappily, Pollini attached no importance to the dramatic aspect of opera, and Mahler was too busy to help her much at this point. She tired easily and he resorted to various stratagems to prevent her from straining her voice by singing too often; he also saw to it that between performances she always had two or three days' rest.

Pollini's strong dislike of Mahler and Mahler's low opinion of Pollini were now known to everyone, but the two men still had sufficient need of each other to keep up appearances. Unfortunately there were always well-meaning people who repeated to Pollini what Mahler had said about him. He had known for a long time, for example, that Mahler usually referred to his theater as the "jail" (*Zuchthaus*), but whenever he was reminded of it, he flew into a rage and for a time "punished" Mahler by assigning the big operas to young conductors who were careful to please him, while giving Mahler works he knew Mahler disliked.

Mahler did everything possible to conceal his own feelings. He tried to keep a straight face when Pollini made long speeches to him on Art, he forced himself to be as polite as possible toward Pollini's protégés, hiding his impatience and boredom when they appeared on stage, not collapsing with boredom onto a chair when they sang. But this self-control was exercised at the expense of his lips, which he sometimes bit until they bled, and of his nails, which were also bitten. Often, out of politeness, Mahler accompanied Pollini as he walked up and down outside the theater, a big cigar in his mouth; he would listen patiently to the director's interminable dissertations on the singers, on their best roles, and on their possible departures. Mahler was present out of courtesy, but most of the time he had not the slightest idea of what the director was saying, and answered briefly either, "Yes" or "Ah! Really?" while trying to get away each time they approached the theater entrance. But inevitably Pollini would begin his monologue again, saying affably, "Just a moment more. I've an idea . . ." It was by listening patiently to those outpourings that Mahler managed to obtain concessions, notably permission to conduct what he wanted and, in particular, Mildenburg's most important performances.

Mahler could not bear the least carelessness on the part of the singers, no matter how overworked they were. When he had some reproach to make, he would lay down his baton, streak across the orchestra pit, and climb the stairs to the stage four at a time to tell the culprit what he thought of him. While the singers were taking their bows after the acts, he would snatch a score from the hands of stage director or prompter, search for the passage that had caused his indignation, and feverishly scribble down remarks and nuances. He would then go off to remonstrate with the singer, but suddenly exclaim, upon noticing that the conversation was taking place in a cloud of dust raised by the changing scenery, "Why are you standing here in all this dust? Don't you know that dust is poison to singers? Get back to your dressing room!" Upon remembering that it was he himself who had started the discussion, he would burst out laughing.

Sometimes the singer, if he had a guilty conscience, had already retired to his dressing room by the time Mahler arrived. Then Mahler would scrawl a message in which angry exclamation marks indicated his disapproval and astonishment. One of the stagehands would be entrusted to deliver the note. These messages rarely surprised their recipients, for even while conducting Mahler had several ways of showing his disapproval of a tempo or phrasing. A question would take the form of a glance or a gesture; astonishment or incomprehension would be expressed by a movement of the shoulders or a menacing baton whistling through the air. Many singers understood this silent language and at once fell in with Mahler's wishes; others were shaken by it but could not instantly correct themselves. Discouraged, Mahler would finally make a gesture of resignation and gradually bow his head. Leaning back against the railing of the podium, he would beat time with the baton swinging negligently between his fingers, following the tempo that the singers had adopted against his wishes. In such a case, the singer could be certain of receiving a message in his dressing room at the end of the act.

Mahler also often terrorized the singers and musicians by thrusting his baton toward them as if he wished to cleave the culprit in two. He would then rivet the victim with a menacing glance, holding his eyes for a moment while still conducting with his free hand and indicating the other singers' entrances without even looking at them. His silent rage was frightening, and Mildenburg developed the habit of not looking at him at such moments. One day, in a coloratura aria, she repeated a passage, for she had not been able to reach the final bars. Imagining the expression that must be on Mahler's face, she looked away and entrusted her fate to the gods. Three times she went back to the start of the passage; three times Mahler followed her with the orchestra, before she finally reached the high C that ended the aria.

But Mahler also knew how to help the singers over difficulties. They only had to look at his lips as he enunciated the dangerous passages. In such cases, his gestures were so eloquent that the singer could not fail to get back onto the right track. When someone sang too high or too low, he raised or lowered his index finger unobtrusively as a signal to the guilty party. One day when he was conducting, Mildenburg saw him suddenly lower his head until his chin rested on his chest, while his shoulders started to shake with irrepressible laughter. He laughed so hard that the orchestra finally noticed, but he pulled himself together and re-established order by means of a few energetic gestures.

When Mahler was pleased, he knew how to congratulate as warmly as he had formerly blamed. His satisfaction became obvious while he was still conducting, but he never failed to seek out the singers later and express it in words. His praise gave great pleasure to even the most famous artists, who would then say that "despite his exorbitant demands and his injustice" he sometimes recognized their qualities.[26]

As examples of the extreme care with which Mahler worked on Mildenburg's roles, there exist some notes scrawled during performances: "About the last scene I'll speak to you!" he wrote to her after a performance of *Aïda*. "I am very pleased and satisfied! Only I can have noticed that you had trouble singing today, for we breathe in unison. The voice always sounded beautiful, the soft notes were marvelous, comportment and appearance excellent. You are retaining your high standard. Many passages were very successful, particularly *'uns ein neues Leben die Höchste.'* If the end of the aria did not work according to our plan, it was Schlesinger's fault, for he started with an overrapid tempo and rushed it so that you could not breathe properly. Otherwise, you would have had no trouble. Don't worry. From today on, I am sure that you will be able to do it. The first aria suffered a little because of your shyness, but despite that it was very beautiful. That you knelt down a second time in the next scene, at that place, was surely an oversight. Compared with those who have preceded you in the role, everything was marvelous."[27]

For Christmas, in order to help and guide Mildenburg in her Wagnerian studies, Mahler gave her a present of Wagner's complete literary works. Sometime later, after her debut as Ortrud, he sent her a message of congratulation dated the evening of the performance: "I am particularly delighted with one improvement: the clarity of the diction! One understood every word." The next morning he wrote again: "Today I was delighted. Your voice was superb, and everything sounded magnificent. Undoubtedly a great success with the public! Voice and comportment remarkable. Diction almost always clear, a great improvement. Unhappily, occasionally faulty: thus, as in *Tannhäuser,* you spoiled certain passages, particularly *'Zurück, Elsa.'* You did not retain much from our work, it was too superficial, and before the next *Lohengrin* we'll study it again with care. The scene with Elsa was excellent, but you sang too loudly, it was not the proper color, for Ortrud is all flattery, deceit, and false humility.

"Your appearance in the second act was superb in the first costume, much less so in the second because you held yourself badly. For heaven's sake, in such roles, let your beautiful bosom make its effect. Your ascension of the stairs ahead of Elsa was also wrong; the best moment was when you jumped up onto them; that was almost perfect. Vocally, the invocation to the gods was truly superb. If one person had started clapping, the entire audience would have applauded. On the whole, I am delighted to notice further progress. What a good omen for the year that starts today! Good night until we meet again."[28]

"Do you really think," Mahler later said to Justi and Natalie,[29] "that Mildenburg, for instance, who is now so admired and considered a truly classic actress, was born to it? You can't imagine how gauche and clumsy she was when she began! I not only taught her her musical part, I made her rehearse her gestures, her poses and her expression in front of a mirror. I demanded that her bearing be calm and controlled even in the street, that she always walk with neither an umbrella or a muff, empty-handed and at an even pace, and that she do gymnastics morning and evening. As soon as she knew her part inside out, I had a piano put on the stage and demonstrated to her precisely every step, every pose and every movement in relation to the music. I thus rehearsed every Wagnerian role with her from A to Z, and no one has ever been so zealous or so anxious to learn and understand. Our efforts were mainly devoted to making her rather heavy body light and agile. At first, she was so clumsy that she tripped over the train of her dress and we had to shorten it in front for fear she'd fall onstage. It was only when, on Justi's advice, she took to wearing long dresses at home that she got used to them in the theater. As often as possible, Justi sat in the front row when Mildenburg was singing and lowered her head every time the latter made an ill-timed gesture or a clumsy movement. Such was the meticulous care with which this exceptional artist was trained. The harder the work and the more self-sacrifice and professional conscientiousness were required of her, the greater became her mastery."

The exacting work that Mahler did with Mildenburg, the almost daily rehearsals, and their common study of the great masterpieces in the repertoire rapidly led to an attachment of an altogether closer nature. Mildenburg's comments on Mahler's work, character, and personality reveal the immense influence he already had upon her. In her eyes he immediately became the incarnation of music; he was the high priest, the initiator of a new cult that she wonderingly learned to worship. The fireworks of his intelligence, his knowledge, and his experience quickly dazzled her. The little notes he started sending to her while she was suffering from her sore throat became more personal in October. Soon, the first pangs of love brought anguish, crises, misunderstandings. Reading this abundant correspondence—about 180 letters and notes that Anna von Mildenburg faithfully preserved (now in the National Library in Vienna)—we can retrace the stages of a love affair that was one of the longest and most violent in Mahler's life.

United by their love for music, Gustav Mahler and Anna von Mildenburg nevertheless differed in too many ways for their liaison to be happy and harmonious. Mahler's letters are moving because they show him to us as tender and generous, sometimes also violent and jealous, and because they fully reveal his deep need to love. Contrary to what is often believed, he did not live only for his art. He had a deep nostalgia for the happiness that could spring from the union of two beings, from their understanding and love, and from the fact that their first concern is for each other's welfare.

But the obstacles were many. To begin with, for a year Mahler had been living with his two sisters, from whom he felt both morally and materially responsible. He believed that Justine, who had devoted herself for so long to the younger members of the family, and then to himself, had been sacrificed, and that her sacrifice demanded another in return. Again, art and music were a veritable religion for him, which meant that he could not give himself wholly to another person in the same way as those who had no "mission" to accomplish. Finally Mildenburg's character, oversensitive, easily offended, hot-tempered, possessive, passionate, demanding, gradually became another considerable obstacle. Mahler realized that marriage would only bring disaster to them both. A difficult situation resulted, since, because of Mildenburg's indiscretions, the entire opera knew of their relationship. For this reason Mahler went through many moments of anxiety and earned the quite absurd reputation of a Don Juan, which was to follow him even to Vienna. Crises and difficulties of all kinds marked this liaison, which should have been more carefully concealed from the eyes of a puritanical society! For example, Mahler forced himself to show a certain coldness toward Mildenburg when he met her at the theater, and this measure of elementary prudence hurt her feelings each time, thus becoming one of the many reasons for friction.

In reading Mahler's letters to Mildenburg, it is hard not to smile when one remembers the description of his dream woman which he gave to Förster two years earlier, for it would be difficult to picture any woman less like her than Anna von Mildenburg. A letter from Mahler that autumn bears witness to one of the first storms that broke over the heads of these passionate, emotional lovers:

"Your letter has upset me terribly! My God, Anna, what can I do? Have I offended you, if not, what has put you into such a state? I cannot understand it! It is perhaps that I didn't write anything about myself? Should I lie or make things still harder for you? Believe me, I don't think of myself, only of you. Tell me, Anna, what I can do to make things easier for you! Is it that you reproach yourself? Anna, believe me, please, you are without blame! Oh, my God, is it on my account? Do you feel sorry for me? Don't worry about me! You don't know me yet.

"Now, I tell you frankly, I am suffering to a degree I had not thought bearable. To lose the love of a being by whom one believed oneself loved, whose love was almost as precious as life—you can't imagine how terrible that is. I cannot *now* be a stranger to you, for otherwise I would not cause you all these torments. Don't you understand that? I cannot write or speak of myself! I cannot live with you and always thus conceal what is burning and aching within me. That would soon seem contemptible to you, Anna! Anna, better days will come. I cannot understand why you let yourself be so disheartened.

"Tell me, Anna, what I can do to make this easier for you? I shall do whatever you want! But don't lose courage! You are not guilty of anything, I swear it to you solemnly and earnestly! It isn't your fault! One cannot force oneself to love someone—I know that from my own experience. I am well and truly punished! Anna! I am desperately worried. Don't impose that on me too! I must drive myself terribly to make a living for my sisters and myself.

"If I pass near you and don't seem to notice you, don't take offense. Is *that* perhaps what has upset you? If I only knew! . . . I am completely at your disposal, Anna, for everything. Only a few lines, if you can, to give me peace of mind. I have such need of it! Anna, God bless you."[30]

But Mahler's liaison with Mildenburg did not bring only unhappiness; there were also moments of harmony. He at last experienced an emotional fulfillment that he had seldom known. The following letter was sent during his trip to Berlin, where he was to rehearse his *Second Symphony*.

"I do not write to you in order to be faithful to my promise, but to follow the urgent dictates of my heart. My whole being is so full of you, my love, my love! Don't you understand why I am so serious, so sad, when I look at you? Don't you know, yet, the deep sorrow that is bound to the happiness of abandoning oneself 'body and soul' to a being one loves? I feel as mysterious and melancholy as at the beginning of a new life. In this, we are probably very different, you are so young and inexperienced! Our future is still a dark region, everything undefined and undefinable. I will often look at you with sadness, but now you will know why! Oh, God, may the destiny that had brought me to you bring you happiness, and let the sorrow that the future may have in store for us fall only upon me!"

The only important Hamburg operatic event during the last months of 1895 was the first performance of Massenet's *Werther*. The composer at-

tended the rehearsals and, like Tchaikovsky and Bruneau, was won over
by Mahler's conducting. Many times he expressed his admiration, but Mahler could not bring himself to compliment him in return, as even the most
elementary politeness demanded. In fact, he thought Massenet's "affront to
Goethe's work" criminal and "worthy of forced labor." But as usual, he devoted himself entirely to the rehearsals of this new opera and did everything possible on its behalf.[31] He succeeded so well that he was almost
disappointed, and from then on he nicknamed the work *"Mein Aller-
werthester,"* (*Allerwertherster*—"My Most Esteemed"—that is, "My Behind"). After the October 10 premiere, Carl Armbrust, echoing the opinion
of the Hamburg audiences, judged *Werther* more favorably than Mahler.
"Characters of flesh and blood" had held his interest throughout, and he
believed that the work had more chance of lasting success than any of Massenet's others. Mahler's conducting was largely responsible for the success,
which the composer had not been present to acknowledge, having had to
return to Paris "for family reasons."

Two other important new productions were assigned to Mahler that autumn: Haydn's *The Apothecary* (or *Lo Speziale*), in which Schumann-
Heink was highly praised for a travesty role.[32] A month later an "anti-
German" French opera was presented for the first time: Alfred Bruneau's
*L'Attaque du Moulin,* with a libretto taken from the Zola short story. Armbrust acknowledged "all the French grace" that it contained, as well as a
simplicity that to him seemed almost labored, compared to the "atrocious
discords," "enormous difficulties," and "strange combinations of sound."
Once again Mahler had thrown himself heart and soul into the new work,
which had been given in a half-empty auditorium. After two performances,
Bruneau's opera was dropped from the repertoire.[33]

Rather than let his compositions, and particularly his new symphonic creations, lie idle in dusty drawers, Mahler had decided some months earlier
to arrange with the impresario Wolff a first complete performance of his
*Second Symphony* in Berlin at his own expense. He had met Wolff through
Bülow, but their relations had never been particularly cordial. Doubtless
the impresario had still not quite forgiven him for the considerable deficit
of the Hamburg Subscription Concerts. According to him, "Mahler followed
the composer's intentions almost to the point of pedantry, thus frequently
and severely trying the patience of both musicians and singers. The supreme
freedom with which Nikisch practiced his art was alien and even distasteful
to him . . ." Nevertheless, Wolff had "imperishable memories" of "his flash-
ing eyes."[34] Thus it was for practical reasons that Mahler asked Wolff to
organize the complete premiere of the *Second Symphony.* By September 12
he was still not sure of having a chorus since "Ochs won't swallow the bait
and Wolff will, as usual, not commit himself until the last moment."[35] The
numerous difficulties were gradually overcome, all the details of the performance were settled, and the date was set for December 13. Learning
that the director of the Berlin Stern'cher Gesangverein, Julius Gernsheim,

had agreed to rehearse the chorus, Mahler wrote to thank him and offered to visit him in order to play the work through on the piano.[36]

Mahler's letters to Mildenburg give a detailed account of the rehearsals and of the December 13 concert, at which she could not be present, since Pollini had refused to grant her the necessary leave of absence. On December 8, Mahler, having arrived in Berlin, describes his first day to Mildenburg:

"As you know, for my symphony I need the sounds of bells at the end of the last movement. I knew right away that only a bell founder could provide what I need. I finally located one, but to reach his foundry took almost half an hour by train, since he lives near the Grunewald. I left very early. Everything was marvelously covered with snow. The cold did me good since I had passed another almost sleepless night. When I reached Zehlendorf—that is the name of the village—I wandered through the pines and snow-covered firs, all very countrified, with a small church shining gaily in the winter sun, and I felt my spirits rise again. I realized how free and happy man feels as soon as he leaves the artificial bustle of the city and returns to the peace and quiet of nature. You too grew up in a small town, and ought to understand me!

"After a long search, I located the foundry. I was welcomed with great simplicity by an old man with a beautiful beard, white hair, and quiet, friendly eyes. Immediately I felt myself back with the 'Masters' of yesterday, everything seemed so charming and so beautiful. I talked with him, and, being of an impatient nature, I naturally found him garrulous. He showed me some magnificent bells, one of which, powerful and impressive, had been ordered by the Emperor of Germany for the new cathedral. The sound was truly powerful and mysterious; I should have liked something similar for my own work, but we have not yet reached the time when only the costliest and the best is good enough for a great work of art. So I looked for something more modest but still suitable, and then took my leave of the dear old man after two hours of conversation. The return journey was equally superb.

"Then to the Central Administration where I had to start my lobbying. Those faces! All these fleshless men! Every inch of their faces shows traces of that self-destructive egoism which tortures mankind! Always me, me, me, and never you, you, my brother!"

At the end of this letter, Mahler criticizes his earlier style of writing: "I recall with embarrassment that I formerly tried to write what are known as 'stylish letters.' It is clear that I had not yet found myself, and that my correspondent was for me only a pretext for expressing my thoughts . . . I beg of you! Never assume an inner or an outer pose, never a disguise."[37]

Upon his return from Zehlendorf, Mahler attended a dinner at which one of the other guests was the critic who had been hardest on him after the March concert. "When I saw that solemn, bovine face, I really felt like laughing. At first he wanted to impress me, but he quickly abandoned his attempts and gave himself up to the joy of stuffing himself—for the dinner was really excellent. His review of that ought to be really favorable!"

The rehearsals, as usual, were lengthy and thorough. Mahler had a percussionist beat his kettledrum so hard that the skin burst.[38] On December 9 he began drilling the "celestial phalanxes" for the first time. He explained to Mildenburg: "You will realize that this is no exaggeration when you hear this Finale." He then met his sisters, who arrived from Hamburg, and the day after took them to the second rehearsal, when he finally had the pleasure of hearing his Finale in its entirety. "Yesterday, for the first time, everything turned to sound!" he wrote to Mildenburg. "All was far beyond my hopes. The performers were so transported and enthusiastic that they themselves found the appropriate expression. If only you had been able to hear it! Such grandeur and power have never been attained before."[39]

Mahler invited to the concert a certain number of musicians and friends, in particular Richard Strauss, to whom he wrote: "I repeat, the three movements which you know are no more than the exposition of the work, and I think that it may be important for you to hear the end." He tried to persuade another of his colleagues, Engelbert Humperdinck, to come from Frankfurt for the concert: "You will undoubtedly wonder why I dare to hope that you are sufficiently interested in my work to go to the bother of taking such a long trip just to hear one among the innumerable orchestral premieres! On the other hand, I cannot yet say to you: this is not a small matter. It involves far more than just myself. I embark on this enterprise rather like a soldier who shoots arrows into the dark at an invisible target. By way of excuse, I can only tell you that I should love to count you, you above all, among my listeners! And I know that once you have heard this work you will know why I write to you."[40] Humperdinck at once answered that he would try to attend but did not dispose freely of his own time.[41]

The first hearing of the *Second Symphony* took place in Berlin on December 13, performed by the Berlin Philharmonic Orchestra,[42] the Stern Singakademie choir, the Sängerbund des Lehrerverein, and two soloists from the Hamburg Opera, Josephine von Artner and Hedwig Felden.[43] Mahler's two sisters, Frau Marcus and her mother, and the Behns, all of whom had attended the rehearsals, trembled as they entered the concert hall that evening, for none of them had forgotten the failure in Budapest and the two more recent performances in Hamburg and Berlin. Since the concert had been organized at Mahler's expense, and the box-office sales were almost nil, most of the tickets had been given away free at the last moment to musicians and students from the conservatory.

Already when arriving in Berlin, Mahler had suffered from a fearful headache.[44] "The very day on which he was to stake his whole future on one card," Bruno Walter wrote, "he was struck down by the most merciless of migraines, which left him incapable of movement, unable to take part in anything."[45] He mounted a high platform resembling the one he had had built for the *Ninth Symphony* the preceding spring, and Walter witnessed the moment when, deathly pale, he straightened up on this shaky structure and by a superhuman effort mastered his dizziness before starting to conduct.

The concert's success became more certain with each succeeding movement. The symphony gradually gripped its listeners, and, according to Justi,[46] at the end of the concert the most astonishing scenes took place: grown men wept and complete strangers kissed each other at the moment when the Bird of Death appears over the tombs; even Mahler had feared that this large audience would be unable to remain attentive, but there was deathly silence in the auditorium right up to the end. At the entry of the chorus, "the whole audience gasped." The effect was indescribable. All those who knew of Mahler's state before the concert were amazed to see how quickly he pulled himself together. At the start he had conducted rather stiffly, and once the concert was over he collapsed onto a divan, but half an hour later his migraine had vanished.[47]

Even if some details in this description are slightly exaggerated, the symphony undeniably produced a deep impression. A number of people in the audience gathered around the podium, the cheering went on so long that Mahler took "countless" curtain calls,[48] and even the singers and choristers joined in the enthusiastic final ovation. The many musicians who were present—Humperdinck, Nikisch, and Felix Weingartner—as well as some of the critics—became aware that evening of the emergence of a new creative talent, and this was of great importance to Mahler. From then on, a few admirers started to spread the word through Germany about this powerful, original, "modern" composer, worthy, in their eyes, to stand alongside Strauss in the ranks of the new school of music. Bruno Walter asserts that the concert of December 13, 1895, marked the real beginning of Mahler's career as a composer, and many others are of the same opinion.

Many of the critics who had heard the first movements the previous spring had considered it unnecessary to be present for the start of the concert. The adverse criticisms became more violent than ever. A critic named Krüger complained bitterly of the "cynical impudence of this brutal, ultramodern music maker."[49] The *Berliner Fremdenblatt* expressed amazement at Mahler's audacity in organizing the concert after the first movements' partial success, Mahler had had the courage to try again, and quoted ironically the contralto's words in *Urlicht*: "Mankind lies in greatest woe . . . I would fain to heaven go!" attributing them to the audience, exhausted by the noise that preceded them. Mahler's symphony was certainly unprecedented both for its length and for the number of performers it required—it was doubtless the "greatest" ever composed—but its construction was incomprehensible. Though impressed and "interested" by the instrumentation and by Mahler's strange and sometimes attractive effects, this critic believed that the tremendous forces brought into play were out of proportion to the musical quality of the themes.[50]

The *Vossische Zeitung* was no more favorable to Mahler. After describing his "intentions" and praising his exceptional talent, his lively, bold imagination, and his gift for harmonic as well as rhythmic invention and sound effects, the anonymous critic attacked the Finale for revealing "the most unpleasant aspect" of Mahler's nature, his lack of stylistic unity, his "taste for musical brutalities, for deafening discords, for violent instrumental contrasts, his contempt for the limitations of his art," and his lack of melodic personality, this last leading him to draw upon such varied sources as Meyerbeer, Verdi, Bizet, and the Wagner of *Parsifal*. According to this critic, the end of the symphony was wholly in "grand opera style."

Ludwig Bussler, in the *National Zeitung,* stigmatized the sonorous gigantism that affected the work, and also its "full opera orchestra," its "theatrical effects," and that "spirit of enterprise which, lacking elsewhere, has taken possession of the music."[51] All this, he suggested, was destined only to attract a crowd of idlers and curiosity seekers avid for distractions. They would, however, be disappointed, Mahler having used this immense power with great circumspection. The nuance piano dominated the work to such an extent that one wondered if it had been necessary to assemble such a phalanx. What really interested Mahler and his young colleagues, Bussler wrote, was musical color; they sought for novelty at any price. Unfortunately Mahler's ideas completely lacked originality, the development "benumbed the listener by its laborious uniformity." The ensemble "lacked style," the first movement was "Wagnerian," and the others "classic," though these last did have a certain charm, despite their similarity.[52]

The *Börsenzeitung* claimed that Mahler "had wanted to outdo Liszt and Berlioz in his use of the orchestra," and criticized "his taste for noise and for elaborate discords," the "bombast" of his language in the first interminable allegro. Mahler had "the makings of a great musician"; his determination and his titanic struggle inspired respect, but his budding talent ignored the elementary criteria of form and the beauty of sound. He astonished his listeners by his harmonic boldness, his juxtaposition of notes, his "completely impossible" combinations of chords, and "his cacophonies of the worst sort." This "program music without a program" was also lacking in clarity. His work was more promising for the future than satisfying in the present.

The spokesman of the *Musikverein* and Strauss's close friend, Otto Lessmann, also condemned the new work unconditionally and unhesitatingly in the monthly *Allegemeine Musik Zeitung:* the only qualities with which he credited Mahler were his serious approach to his art, his "bold combinations," and his new "sound effects," but he drew up a long list of his faults: atrocious dissonances, brutality, orchestral fracas, no logic, no central idea, no deep feeling, only a taste for the ugly and deformed. Mahler had gone further than any musician, any artist, ought to go, there were no connecting links between his movements, and only the central ones contained a few attractive passages. The musical confusion started with the *Urlicht;* the effect of the conclusion was "purely exterior"; only a public devoid of critical sense had been capable of applauding such a work. Despite Mahler's effort to do something original at any cost, there were no original ideas, so the only thing that one could admire was the technical mastery. His ambitions notwithstanding, Mahler "is not one of the elect who further their art," and, unlike Strauss, his excesses did not correspond to an inner necessity. They had nothing in common with the content of the work and were only there to "interest at any cost" and to "prove to the world what he is capable of doing."

As in March, Oskar Eichberg of the *Börsen Courier* was almost alone in recognizing that Mahler's novelty demanded from the listener both willingness and a certain preparation, but he emphasized that the work's content was as splendid as its form. He compared Mahler's technical mastery, particularly of orchestration, to that of Strauss. His combinations of motifs, his original conception of harmony, inseparable from the counterpoint, and his contrasts of tonality, surprising as they were, even shocking at times, always remained clear, so that one "followed the harmonic evolution with interest to the very end." Presented within a few weeks of each other, the premieres of this symphony and of Strauss's *Till Eulenspiegel* were the only worth-while new works of the season.

Among his new admirers, Mahler could not count another critic, Max Marschalk[53] of the *Vossische Zeitung*. They started a correspondence in which Mahler set down his main aesthetic beliefs, his ideas on "programs," symphonic form, and music in general. "I cannot help sighing deeply," he wrote to him after the concert, "when I see that the serried ranks of the daily papers are once again standing in the way of the unhappy children of my imagination, as always when they present themselves. Now I will probably have to wait a year before being able to make myself heard again."[54]

Humperdinck had finally made the trip from Frankfurt to Berlin to hear the new work, and he wrote Mahler a letter full of praise, which gave him all the more pleasure since he received it while in the state of mind that always followed the "increased love of life that comes after a first performance": "I have suffered so much from creating for so long without even arousing the least reaction," Mahler replied, "that obtaining your unreserved support touches me all the more.

"I beg you to believe a composer who, up to now, has felt only the thorns in his crown," he wrote to a new admirer, the music critic Annie Sommerfeld,[55] three months later. "Your few words made me intensely happy for they proved to me that someone else could understand and share [*miterleben*] my 'experience' [*erleben*] with me. It is probably the first time that someone who doesn't know me personally has cordially answered 'yes' to the question I so earnestly asked. For this is primarily the first revelation of the work of a new composer, or at any rate of a composer who formulates an old (but ever new) message in a new way. I failed to understand the deathlike silence that ensued and descended like a pall as soon as these powerful and passionate waves of sound subsided."

Upon his return to Hamburg, Mahler learned that the heart trouble that had been worrying Pollini for some time was causing great alarm. He rarely appeared at the opera now, and there was even a rumor that he would have to be temporarily replaced; meanwhile Bittong was making many decisions for him. This meant that Mahler's sphere of action at the opera was momentarily increased, but nothing could shake his firm resolution to leave Hamburg as soon as possible.

During the Christmas holidays Mahler divided his time between the peaceful family atmosphere of the Bismarckstrasse and his stormy liaison with Anna von Mildenburg, with whom he continued to work almost every day. He, who had complained of solitude and isolation on previous years, now found that every minute of his time was taken up. On December 18 he conducted *Oberon,* with Mildenburg singing her first Rezia, and on Christmas night she sang the Countess in *Le Nozze di Figaro.* Their working sessions were stormy at times, for Mahler told her in a short note dated January 24 that "the rehearsals in Room 9 are regarded with some suspicion, as it has been noticed, among other things, that the wall hangings, the piano scores and even the seats have suffered greatly."

Despite all this during that same January, Mahler once more revised the orchestration of the *Lieder eines fahrenden Gesellen,*[56] and in the spring he copied and corrected that of the *Third Symphony.*[57] He also conducted a new work at the opera, *Der Evangelimann,* a "popular" opera by the Austrian composer Wilhelm Kienzl,[58] which is still quite well known in Germany. Armbrust in the *Fremdenblatt* praised the composer's libretto and judged the score "agreeable, melodious, full of feeling," though excessively long.

On January 26, Mildenburg appeared for the first time in Bellini's *Norma,* meeting with great approval from both public and critics. Armbrust in the *Fremdenblatt* praised the agility of her vocalizing, her technical ability and musicianship, her noble, moving recitatives, and her poise onstage.[59] A month later she again sang Norma with Mahler conducting; he invited Justi and Natalie to this performance, since they had never heard Bellini's masterpiece, some passages of which "moved him to tears."[60] "How I should love to hear *Norma* for the first time, and hear it conducted by myself! I envy you!" he cried before they left. Later, however, he confessed to Natalie that, despite his deep love and admiration for *Norma,* it was both difficult and strange for him to conduct any opera in which the voice predominated throughout while the orchestra merely accompanied; he could always control the orchestral rendering, whereas he could not replace such mediocre singers as those, Mildenburg excepted, who had taken part in this performance.[61]

Among the operas of Smetana, his patriotic drama *Dalibor,* a fine but uneven work, was particularly close to Mahler's heart. For this reason he took special pains with its rehearsals in late January and early February. Armbrust considered Mahler mainly responsible for its very considerable success, and also praised highly the two chief protagonists, Birrenkoven and

Mildenburg. The latter's "sureness" and "warm expressiveness," as well as the splendor of her voice, made her an ideal heroine, even though her acting was somewhat unskilled. *Dalibor* was performed only four times: no doubt its dramatic flaws prevented it, in Hamburg as elsewhere, from winning a large public.[62] At the end of the month Mahler had to conduct another new work, an opera by a composer whose prolific output has not saved him from oblivon. This was *Sjula,* by Baron Karl von Kaskel[63]; it was warmly praised by the critics.

In mid-January Natalie, who was on tour with the Soldat-Roeger Quartet, spent several days in Hamburg. This visit gave Mahler so much pleasure that he had to reassure Anna, who became jealous of his old and faithful friend. It was then that Natalie met Bruno Walter. One evening at the Bismarckstrasse, he and Mahler played for her "in a wonderfully poetic manner" Schubert's *Variations for piano duet*[64]; later, at the Behns', they performed the two-piano transcription of the *Second Symphony*. Mahler also sang the *Lieder eines fahrenden Gesellen* for her, and Natalie never forgot the "feeling and character" his deep voice gave to them. He attended the January 22 concert given by the Soldat-Roeger Quartet and congratulated the four "valiant" artists warmly. He also arranged a private performance for them at the home of a rich Hamburg patron of the arts.

At the Parkallee, and later at the Bismarckstrasse, Mahler was in the habit of organizing evenings of chamber music in which musicians from the opera took part—the concertmaster, the violinist Mühlmann, the viola player Schloming, the elderly cellist Gowa, and occasionally a flutist or clarinetist. With Mahler at the piano, they played trios and quartets by Beethoven, Mozart, Schubert, Mendelssohn, and Schumann. Sometimes other musicians joined in to play quintets, sextets, and even Beethoven's *Septet.* Förster draws an admiring picture of Mahler's piano playing: the "vigorous, singing touch" and the "musical feeling and expression" that characterized it. These improvised concerts became a veritable rite during Mahler's last years in Hamburg, and Förster recalls, among other things, an unforgettable performance of Beethoven's *"Geister" Trio,* op. 70, no. 1, and the "magical atmosphere" of the well-known Largo, which plunged both listeners and performers into a mysterious ecstasy.[65] Mahler always spoke wonderingly of this movement, and its influence can be discerned from time to time in his own music.

During this visit Natalie was high in Mahler's favor, and he took her to a Philharmonic concert at which Joseph Joachim played the solo part in the Brahms *Violin Concerto.* The famous violinist appeared tired and played with a "certain indifference."[66] The concerto, thus interpreted, disappointed Mahler. He called it "antediluvian" and compared it to "the rope dance of Zarathustra, who commits suicide and is ready to be buried." On that particular day, too, he was in a very bad temper because Julius Barth, the uninspired conductor of the Philharmonic concerts, had given the *"Pastoral"* *Symphony*, which Mahler himself had conducted in the same hall the preceding year.

Natalie returned to Hamburg once more on February 16 to play again with her quartet, this time at the home of a wealthy Hamburg family named Ollendorf.[67] Mahler and Natalie went on long walks along the Alster as far as the harbor, where they both delighted in the constant movement of the ships, the tangled confusions of masts and sails, the old houses and dark, narrow streets of the port. Mahler talked of his childhood and gave Natalie the text of some poems he had written in Kassel. Even during the winter he never stopped taking physical exercise. He walked almost every day the whole way from the Bismarckstrasse to the opera, even when a storm raged over Hamburg and the isolated Hoheluft house was swept by a glacial north wind that shook the doors and windows.

Mahler took Natalie to visit Frau Lazarus and Behn, though the latter, despite his kindness and his admiration for Mahler, often irritated and annoyed him by his extreme self-satisfaction. Behn was so proud of having made transcriptions that he cared more for his own "complete piano arrangement" than for Mahler's work, though "the overloaded transcription was all but unplayable."[68] When Mahler became angry about such trifles, those closest to him feared that his lack of moderation and his excess of frankness would lose him yet another friend—sometimes, as in the case of Behn, an extremely powerful one. Natalie's warm friendship must have seemed particularly restful to Mahler that year. He regretted her departure and made her promise to be in Berlin a month later for the first performance of his revised *First Symphony* and the *Lieder eines fahrenden Gesellen*. And indeed, for this new and terrible struggle, he was to need the moral support of all his faithful friends.

"All that is not perfect down to the
smallest detail is doomed to perish . . ."

# CHAPTER 22

*Mahler in Hamburg (VII) — Emotional Storms — Failure in Berlin — The First Movement of the* Third *Symphony (February–July 1896)*

The first months of 1896 were among the stormiest in Mahler's emotional life. His correspondence with Anna von Mildenburg at that time reflects the sudden storms, followed by no less sudden periods of calm. Two letters written in February reveal a Mahler tortured by passion, on the verge of despair, and about to break off their relationship for good.

"How I have suffered, Anna! Dear God! Forgive me for everything! The monster of repentance holds me in its claws. If it lets me go for a moment, another, more terrible still, will come . . . the monster of jealousy. Forgive me what I do and what I am! Oh God, what have I done! Though God knows I could do nothing else. There is only one way out, and I will take it, but I need time, and until then you must forgive me! I am no longer in control. In my 'madness' I thought that tomorrow would not come! (But the worst was not yet over!) Dear God, I cannot be only a 'friend'; Anna, my darling, farewell. I have not said farewell! Farewell, Anna, farewell! If you need anything, write to me! If things get difficult (in the theater world this can happen overnight), write to me! If you have the slightest regard for me, write to me! If you need me, write to me! Oh, Anna, forgive everything and forgive me!"

This first letter was not posted until the day after it was written, together with another: "Anna, I cannot tell you what I have lived through during these last few days, and what I shall live through in the future! Anna, never before have I felt such a pure and sacred love for anyone—and you do not love me! Oh, God! How can I ever get over it? I wrote to you yesterday, but I kept the letter; you will get it today, and will be able to guess my feelings. The letter is at home, and I shall send it to you as soon as I get back there. Anna, I am not reproaching you! But what you done to me? You ask if I would prefer you to act coldly towards me, but how could you be colder than you are already? You consent to grant me your esteem and confidence. Don't you realize that these words pierce my heart like red-hot blades?[1] I must stay far away from you, since I no longer mean anything to you. This will be the death of me.

"Believe me, Anna, if you had asked me to die for you, I would have done so, but oh, God, how could you only pretend to love me? How could you do such a thing? Did I deserve it? Do you know the extent of the damage you have done? I have lost my faith! God help me—how can I go on living? Didn't you realize how sincerely and deeply I loved you? I kept my love for you intact and pure, before I even knew you! Anna! From today on, our paths divide. I must avoid you and keep out of your way! What little affection you still have for me cannot do you harm, so things will be easy for you. But you must know that for me our separation will be fatal. Oh, God, why did you pretend? Why did you make me blind? Why did you play with me, Anna? Don't try to answer this: I suffer day and night, unceasingly! Anna, I am in hell and without hope of redemption . . ."

So Mildenburg had feigned indifference and had spoken of parting. Perhaps she had wished to make Mahler more in love with her than ever, for she had no intention of breaking off their relationship. She was certainly successful, for Mahler's letters soon became more passionate than ever. Harmony had been re-established, and this crisis was never mentioned again in their correspondence. If, at that time, Mahler was more in love with Mildenburg than she with him, this situation changed later. From the summer of 1896 on, he obviously started to resist her attempts to dominate him, though he still assured her that his greatest wish was to be united to her forever.[2]

It would be unjust to consider only the negative aspects of this liaison, for it also had it moments of happiness. Most of Mahler's letters showed great affection and were frequently humorous: "So that my darling does not wait in vain tomorrow morning, I write again, just a few lines before going to bed. When my darling expresses even the slightest wish, even if I only read it in her sweet eyes, I no longer have a moment's peace, for this wish rings incessantly in my ears. So I write: 'Good morning, dear tormentor' [*Quälgeist*] (it's called 'sweet torture' isn't it!). Today I searched everywhere in vain, but my love was not to be found. Frau Förster was sitting up there, and she smiled to see me searching. So many thoughts came to my mind after I had left you; I'll tell them to you someday (not tomorrow, all the same!). All about 'being in love'! What I can tell you is that I have a better opinion of such a state than you. Why? Because I love you! You know the story of the man who set out into the world to discover Fear! Well, I have well and truly found it. Oh, how afraid I am! Now, from the middle of the night, I say good morning to you!

"I am at home. It is midnight, and my sister Justi has just left me to go to bed. I am in slippers because my shoes are soaking, but when I've finished this letter, I'll go out into the storm to post it so it will reach you in bed tomorrow morning and make you smile. You see, you wouldn't do that for such a small result. And I would do a great deal more to give you a little, a very little pleasure . . . Do you know one of the things I like so much about you? Your laugh! Don't you dare laugh when I am with you in public, for how could I stop myself from taking you in my arms and covering you with kisses! . . ."

Like many other lovers, Mahler sometimes invented pet names for his beloved, some of them extremely elaborate: "I smile a thousand smiles, my gently welcoming fir tree whose beautiful needles draw blood, and whose delicious perfume wakens the childhood tales slumbering in my soul . . . When will you wound me again? . . ." Sometimes the tone of his letters changes to that of wild passion: "I am at home and working, but I long to be at the theater, and it is difficult for me to resist! . . . My body burns, my blood is on fire. I have scarcely recovered from yesterday's heated battle; still full of daring, my eyes glint with the excitement of the struggle. Oh! How familiar all this is, how I understand my love when, caught between the two captivating goddesses 'past' and 'future' it forgets its friend, the present! How different things are with you, my fiery spirit, and with the others, the Philistines! They resolve themselves in the present, like 'vulgar' fractions (did you learn about them in arithmetic?), like donkeys coveting the nearest haystack, even when vast and aromatic fields of thistles and clover beckon in the distance! They would never understand if they saw how you sometimes treat me, my distracted darling! But I understand you, because I am the same. When you have a task to carry out, it weighs on your mind! I love you so much, Anna, just as you are!

"How adorable you were today, and yesterday too, when you made such an effort to be all love and kindness: how I laughed inwardly! Already I look forward to the time when I shall hold you in my arms again, safe from intrusion, without a thought for 'past' and 'future.' Then we will let the waves of 'present' break over our heads . . ." How different Mahler seems from his traditional image! As a lover, he is all impatience when his beloved ceases to enjoy a tête-à-tête and thinks only of the afternoon's rehearsal of the evening's performance; the same impatience makes him dash out in the middle of the night to post a letter in the rain.

Love did not, however, distract him from his other activities. Most of February 1896 was in fact taken up with preparations for a new event of extreme importance to his career as a composer: the first Berlin performance of the *Titan* (then simply entitled *Symphony in D Major* and minus the Andante), preceded by the *Lieder eines fahrenden Gesellen* and the *Totenfeier*.[3] The concert was organized by Wolff, with the participation of the Philharmonic Orchestra, and a great number of rehearsals had been planned, for Mahler wished to be sure that "this new attempt would not fail due to insufficient preparation." Wolff, who knew that the enterprise would earn him nothing, took very little trouble. In consequence Mahler himself had to deal with various practical problems in addition to the rehearsals.

Greatly worried as to the outcome of the evening, he spared no effort to make it a success, but these diplomatic chores exhausted and angered him.

Mahler had brought Weidich, his old Hamburg coypist, to Berlin, "so he could at last hear the music he had so often copied." Förster, the industrialist Berkan, Adele Marcus, and Frau Hertz were also present. So were the Behns, with whom Mahler and his sisters took most of their meals in their room at the Palace Hotel. Though grateful for their kindness, Mahler nonetheless continued to thunder against Behn's garrulity. "He never stops pontificating about my leitmotivs, although, in fact, he understands nothing about me or my music!" he exclaimed to Natalie.

The latter attended all the rehearsals. She was astonished by "the understanding that Mahler knew how to instill into his musicians" and "dazzled by the rhythmic independence of the voices and the individuality of the phrasing." The transparence of the polyphonic web conjured up for her a vision of "sunset, seen through branches so clear-cut that one could pick out each bough, leaf, and twig." When Mahler noticed a faulty nuance or note, he rehearsed the guilty player or players individually at first, then each of the sections—strings, wind, or percussion in turn—and finally the entire orchestra. One day, when a *piano* passage seemed to lack clarity, he stopped the orchestra and advised the musicians to make their entrance as if they were saying to the listener, "Look, here I am!" after which they could diminish the tone at once.

The worry and tension of the rehearsals drove Mahler into a hypersensitive state, "as though his deepest and most hidden feelings had been laid bare, exposed and bleeding in the light of day." On Sunday morning, the day before the concert, he went on a solitary walk in the direction of Schöneberg. As he was passing under the railway bridge that crossed the river, he saw an old man with an emaciated face stagger under a heavy burden and lean against a wall. The man was talking to himself and Mahler thought he was drunk, until he heard him murmur, "God help me!" and noticed that he was about to faint from exhaustion.

Mahler approached, lifted the burden, and helped the old man, who explained his troubles. He had been ill in the hospital for several months and had just been discharged as cured. No longer in possession of a livelihood or shelter, he was searching for some simple work that would enable him to keep alive. Deeply moved by this sad story, so much in variance with the lively, happy atmosphere of the Sunday morning, Mahler gave the old man all the money he had with him, returned to his hotel, and cried like a child while relating the incident to Natalie. This episode no doubt deepened his gloom. True, the prospects for the concert were far from good. The advance ticket sale had brought in only about fifty marks, whereas to organize the concert had cost several thousand. This time "my small Budapest capital will be reduced by some ten thousand florins," said Mahler, smiling sadly. A large number of tickets were given away free at the last moment; nevertheless the hall was half empty at concert time.[4] Mahler managed to calm his nerves before mounting the podium to conduct the first movement of the *Second* Symphony (still entitled *Totenfeier*), followed by the *Lieder* sung by the Dutch baritone Anton Sistermanns.[5] The *Totenfeier* was well received despite some booing, which started up again after the Funeral March of the *First Symphony*. The *Lieder* were warmly applauded. The audience wanted one of them encored, but the disheartened Mahler, realizing that the battle was already lost, replied to those offstage, who were urging him to grant the audience's request: "No, they haven't understood anything!"

The only consolation this depressing evening brought seems to have been the enthusiasm of Nikisch, Mahler's onetime rival, who, according to Natalie, raved about the "celestial melodies" and the gigantic strength in each note. He promised Mahler that he would soon conduct one of his works in Leipzig. After seeing him off at the railroad station, Mahler attended a supper given in his honor. The party included the impresario Wolff, a "soprano decked out like a clown," and the few critics who liked his work, but he was too depressed to derive any pleasure from their company, and, as soon as he could, returned to his hotel with Natalie. Some minutes after they had said good night on the hotel landing, she knocked on his door, entered hurriedly, and without saying a word kissed his hand. Greatly embarrassed, he exclaimed, "Natalie, what are you doing?" but his passionate and faithful admirer had already fled, slamming the door behind her.

In a letter he wrote to Frau Sommerfeld a few days later, to thank her for her laudatory article, he again expressed his disappointment. "You cannot imagine how much your words mean to me, nor how desperately I need a friendly word at a time when I'm fighting an exhausting battle against routine. I've been treading this path of sorrow for many years. And, were I not a 'blockhead,' did I not totally disregard the conclusive arguments of the honorable arbiters of art, did I not continue to hold my head high despite all the blows I receive, I would have only one desire left: to go and tend my garden in some corner of the earth and thank the Lord when it rained or when the sun shone. How long and thorny the way is! I've never realized so clearly that there are people who, like me, live only for enlightened *individuals*. And when the masses finally get around to accepting them, it is in blind response to the superior intelligence of these individuals, whose higher lucidity they vaguely apprehend. I thank you, individual, and beg you to remain my devoted and well-wishing friend!"

Unknown to Natalie, Mildenburg's silence also worried Mahler while he was in Berlin. Whereas she had written almost every day during his December absence, this time she sent only one or two postcards. In addition he had begun to foresee all that was finally going to separate them. It was her tactlessness and imprudence, thanks to which all Hamburg knew about their liaison, that pained him most, for it could not but jeopardize his position at the theater. Most of his closest friends were fully aware of what was going on, including Adele Marcus, in whom he often confided in times of crisis or when he was unhappy because of the young singer's feigned or genuine indifference. "What you say about Behn,"[6] he wrote, "has pleased me and almost completely reassured me regarding your attitude, which so recently distressed me. Thank God that in some things you too can be 'great' . . ."

Pollini's ill health and possible death (he suffered from a serious heart condition of which he was to die the following year) seemed to make Mahler's future in Hamburg problematic, and he called on the Berlin impresario Hugo Drencker to discuss his future. He also tried to arrange an "invitation" to the Berlin Opera for Mildenburg. Drencker confirmed that, if Pollini should die, Mahler's contract would automatically end, and Mahler instructed him to open negotiations with the Schwerin and Vienna operas. The day after the concert he learned that the Schwerin theater was unable to enagage a Jew and that "no position was available in Vienna." Seeing that all the doors were still closed to him, Mahler exclaimed bitterly, "Dear God, I could bear anything if only I were sure my works would live. But after yesterday's experience I have less hope than ever. Soon I'll have sacrificed my last pfennig in costly performances, and that will be the end of my symphonies, for no one else will want to play them!"[7] The industrialist Berkan had in fact agreed to bear part of the cost of the concert, but in the face of the general lack of understanding by the public and musicians, it was to be feared that he would not agree to repeat this gesture.

The Berlin critics' attitude was the same as ever. In the *Neueste Nachrichten,* Paul Moos proclaimed "either the work is of such genius that we are incapable of appreciating it, or it is completely pointless," and he opted for the second possibility.[8] The critics of the *Vossische Zeitung* and *Börsenzeitung* did not alter their earlier judgements. The former regretted that Mahler did not know how to "master his talent," the *Finale* of the *First Symphony* was "multicolored, interminable, slipshod, vulgar . . . a succession of odds and ends disguised in a charlatanesque ornamentation of instrumental effects."

The *Börsenzeitung* called the *Totenfeier* "a trial to the listeners' nerves," unintelligible both from the point of view of form and of conception. The German music magazines were no more favorable. The *Wochenblatt* noted with satisfaction that the public had been far cooler than in December. The *Lieder eines fahrenden Gesellen* had even made an "unfortunate impression," for the melodic line "does not sing," the declamation is absurd, and certain word repetitions are offensive, "as though the composer's text were too brief to justify the richness of his orchestral illustrations."

The *Neue Zeitschrift für Musik* said that Mahler had let himself be sidetracked in his search for "originality" and "strangeness," for new colors and unprecedented orchestral effects—with which he hoped to impress the public and "throw dust in its eyes." There was nothing in all this among these chaotic sounds to interest the serious musician.

When considered in historical perspective, it is now easy to understand why Mahler's art then seemed so scandalous and revolutionary. Yet after wasting so much time and money, and failing again so miserably, he was wounded to the quick, for he could not resign himself to composing only "for his library." As before, Oskar Eichberg in the *Börsen Courier* was the only critic who defended Mahler. He praised the *First Symphony*'s "exquisite grace and humor," and found it "much more agreeable, natural, and easy to understand" than the *Second*. The *Lieder* seemed to him no less admirable, and Mahler, he wrote, had "brilliantly strengthened the position he had won at the beginning of the winter."[9]

After the concert Mahler expressed his views about "programs," "titles," and symphonic music in general in a letter to the critic Max Marschalk. In calling his *First Symphony "Titan,"* he had "followed the advice of friends," and attempted to "facilitate the public's understanding of his work." Thus his added "titles and explanations" were afterthoughts. He had omitted them this time in the Berlin program because he found them "insufficiently exhaustive" and "not adequately characterized." He also considered that they "misled the public." "This happens with any program!" he concluded. "Even Beethoven's symphonies have their inner programs: the more one studies them, the further one goes along the road that leads to an understanding of their fundamental ideas and development. In the end it will be like that with my work one day."[10]

In another letter to Marschalk concerning the *First Symphony,* Mahler wrote: "I should like to stress that the symphony goes far beyond the love story on which it is based, or rather, which preceded it in the emotional life of its creator. The external event was only the occasion—so cannot be the subject of the work . . . We are faced with the essential question of knowing how, or even why, the contents of a musical work should be defined in words . . . Allow me to state briefly my point of view: I know, for my part, that as long as I am able to express my experience in words, I would never do so in music. My need to express myself musically, symphonically, begins only in the realm of obscure feelings, at the gate leading to the 'other world,' where things are no longer destroyed by time and space.

"Just as I find it trite to invent music to fit a program, in the same way I find it unsatisfactory and fruitless to try to invent a program for a musical work. The fact that the first impulse toward a musical creation has been a concrete, definable experience lived by its composer does not alter this at all. Here we have reached, and of this I am certain, the great fork where the two paths of symphonic and dramatic music diverge: that the two roads separate forever is visible to anyone who is acquainted with the nature of music.

"If you compare a Beethoven symphony and a work by Wagner, you will sense the essential difference immediately. Certainly, Wagner has appropriated the expressive means of symphonic music, in the same way that today the symphonist is entitled to take conscious advantage of the means of expression which music has acquired through Wagner's efforts. In that sense, all the arts are bound to each other and even to nature. There has not been enough reflection on this subject, because we have not yet seen it in its true perspective. I myself have not built this 'system' so as to organize my creation around it later: on the contrary, I have composed a few symphonies that were born amid veritable labor pains—and, after always encountering the same questions, the same misunderstandings, I have worked out this conception of things for myself.

"Nevertheless, it is useful at first, when my manner is still strange to a listener, for him to receive for his voyage some milestones and signposts— or let us better say, a star map, so that he can orient himself in the nocturnal sky with its shining worlds. But such an explanation will never offer more. Man must proceed from something known, otherwise he will get lost! . . ." Mahler's change of attitude clearly sprang from his recent contact with Richard Strauss and his realization of the fundamental difference between "program" and symphonic music.

Despite the strong position he was taking in the accompanying letter, Mahler sent Marschalk detailed programs for the *First* and *Second Symphonies.* But the following year he explained himself further to Anton Seidl: "It is strange how, in a certain sense, you help me to understand myself. You have perfectly defined my aims as opposed to those of Strauss. You are correct in thinking that in my music the program emerges only in the final conceptual analysis, whereas with Strauss, the program is assigned to the listener. I think that thus you touch upon the essential enigma of our epoch and at the same time set forth its alternative. When I conceive a large musical creation, I always reach a point at which I require the 'word' to carry my musical idea. It must have been like that for Beethoven with his *Ninth,* but his epoch could not furnish the texts he needed, for, in fact, Schiller's poem was incapable of formulating the grandiose, 'unheard-of' ideas that were in his mind . . ."[11]

Conscious of all that separated him from Strauss, Mahler nonetheless realized the advantages afforded to him by living at the same time as such a genius. "I shall never forget the truly generous way in which Strauss gave me my chance (to make my work known). Nobody should, in any case, think of me as a 'rival' (as so often happens). I repeat to you, I cannot envisage two such personalities 'detracting' from one another. Apart from the fact that my works would appear monstrous if Strauss's success had not prepared the ground, I am delighted to find among my contemporaries such a comrade in combat and creation. Schopenhauer used the image of two miners, each digging his tunnel from opposite sides of the mountain, who finally meet underground. This seems to me to describe perfectly my relation to Strauss. My struggle would appear solitary and desperate indeed if 'signs and miracles' of this sort did not enable me to foretell a future victory . . ."

All through the spring, Mahler continued writing to Marschalk. He wished to pay his debt of gratitude by giving him some advice on composition, for Marschalk had sent him several of his scores.[12] His aesthetic beliefs are well expressed in a letter of April 12: "Mood music is dangerous ground.

Believe me, for the present the situation has not changed: themes clear, plastic, and always easily recognizable when varied and transformed, and then amplification and execution based on the logical development of the essential ideas on one hand, and a forceful use of contrast between the juxtaposed motives on the other."[13]

Mahler returned to Hamburg the day after the Berlin concert, deeply shaken by its failure. He feigned unconcern when with his colleagues or with critics like Marschalk, but to those closest to him his attitude was one of sadness and discouragement. "You will see," he told Natalie, "that I shall not live to witness the victory of my works! Everything I write is too strange and too new, my listeners cannot find a way to approach me. What I wrote a long time ago at the conservatory, when I was still leaning on others, is all lost, or at least never played. What came later, beginning with *Das klagende Lied,* is already so Mahlerian, so sharply and completely set in my own style, that there is no longer any link . . . Nobody has any idea of what I am saying or of what I want to say, it seems foolish and unintelligible . . . I saw this clearly in Berlin during the first rehearsal of the first movement of the *Symphony in D:* to begin with the musicians did not understand it at all, so that I was faced with insurmountable difficulties. I felt like committing suicide at that moment, and I asked myself why I had to bear this suffering, all this fearful martyrdom! Not for myself alone, but for all those who have been and will be crucified for wishing to give the world the best of themselves, I feel the same immeasurable sorrow."[14] "I am trying very hard to make my way in the world," he wrote to Löhr. "I assure you that it is a struggle, a real one, in which one does not even notice that one is bleeding from a thousand wounds. During the intervals, one suddenly feels a dampness, and then perceives that one's blood is flowing. My 'successes' are even more of a sorrow to me because then misunderstanding starts before I have even had a chance to speak. I really suffer from homesickness. A calm little place in my own home—when shall I be able to obtain that? Not, I fear, before reaching the point where everything and all of us must end!"[15]

Despite these cruel disappointments, Mahler was not discouraged. The colossal *Third Symphony,* for which neither performers nor public as yet existed, was unceasingly in his mind. During the spring, he orchestrated the *"Blumenstück,"* which Nikisch had promised to conduct in the autumn (the orchestral score is dated April 11), and this was a source of great personal satisfaction. "You cannot imagine how it is going to sound," Mahler told Natalie. "It is the most carefree piece I have ever written. It is carefree as only flowers can be. Everything hovers in the air with grace and lightness, like flowers bending on their stems and being caressed by the wind. To my amazement I noticed today for the first time that the double basses play only pizzicato; they don't have a single bow stroke, and I don't use any deep and strong percussion. The violins, on the other hand, which have a solo, play animated, winged, and smiling motives. (While copying these successions of notes I hurt my hand because, unconsciously,

I observed the tempo and values of the notes, and wrote these innumerable groups at top speed.)"[16]

Mahler was still suffering from Mildenburg's indifference: "My dear, I should almost feel ashamed to torture you and myself over such a trifle (naturally there is a deeper reason behind it, if you could only understand it!). I beg of you, if only for this reason, to say yes. Or do you really want to humiliate me to the point of my 'crawling to the cross'? My sweet darling girl, I beg you to grant my request, even if you find it incomprehensible! I shall wait for you after the *Bettelstudent* near the post office, at the usual spot. I cannot go to bed in this state. I don't know what has happened to me, but I have such a desire to see you and hear you say yes you would think my life and your love depended upon it. Let me be mad just this once as well! I beg of you, my dearly beloved Anna! Grant me this! Can you really refuse me? Can you? Must I always approach you like a young man and humiliate myself? Anna, I beg of you, consent, for many reasons as well as to please me . . ." Again Mahler's deep devotion shines through these humble and tender words. They seem all the more touching since they come from a man well known for his iron will and "tyrannical nature."

Bruno Walter's imminent departure was another reason for Mahler's unhappiness, for he was fond of him and accustomed to his frequent calls at the Bismarckstrasse. He had been "sent from heaven the year before" and in a way had fulfilled the hopes Mahler had had for Otto, for he resembled him both physically and because of his prodigious musical gifts.[17] Nevertheless, Mahler advised Walter to leave the "Pollini jail" since the future seemed to hold nothing for him there. He had therefore recommended him to the director of the Breslau Opera, and Walter had been engaged there.[18] All the Mahlers were saddened by the imminent departure of the "only being with whom one could have a friendly relationship on the human and intellectual level."

At the Hamburg Opera, the repertoire included no significant new works that spring, unless one counts a new staging of Karl Millöcker's operetta *Der Bettelstudent,* presented in aid of the union of journalists and writers. Mahler certainly carried out such a thankless task—as Armbrust pointed out on this occasion—only because "the end justifies the means."[19] Also that year Mahler broke with a Hamburg tradition he himself had established, choosing for his own benefit concert *Die Walküre* rather than *Fidelio*. The next day Armbrust protested in the *Fremdenblatt* against the long cut in Act II, made probably because of the indisposition of the singer playing Wotan. Mahler was honored as usual with a fanfare and acclamations, and then showered with flowers and gifts.[20] Some days later, he once again conducted the annual Good Friday concert of sacred music, including the Mozart *Requiem,* Handel and Mendelssohn arias sung by Mildenburg, and for the first time in his career the final chorus of Bach's *St. Matthew Passion*. Natalie, who had returned to Hamburg for another week, was present.[21] Krause, as always, criticized Mahler's "subjective" conception of the *Requiem*.[22]

On April 15, for Bertha Förster-Lauterer's benefit performance, Mahler did Förster the honor of conducting the premiere of his *Third Symphony*. Entering the hall for the first rehearsal, Förster was welcomed by Mahler with a friendly smile. Mahler proceeded to sight-read the three first movements with infinite care, after which the members of the orchestra applauded the composer. Mahler shook Förster's hand, congratulated him, especially on the Scherzo, and then, after a short break, he sight-read the Finale and took his leave, stating that "the real work will start tomorrow!" The day of the premiere the public's reaction was reasonably favorable, but Krause, while recognizing the qualities of this work, suggested some cuts and instrumental revisions to the composer.[23]

During this spring Mahler was more concerned than ever about his future. His disgust with the Hamburg Opera grew stronger as his desire increased to find an artistic home. Refusing to be discouraged by the failure of his recent negotiations with the Vienna Opera, he again made contact, through Natalie and Mildenburg, with Rosa Papier.[24] Frau Papier-Paumgartner was a woman of energetic and stubborn character who, because of her affair with a high court official, the banker Wlassack, exercised considerable influence. Indeed, Hofrath Wlassack was practically replacing Bezecny, who was too busy to devote much time to the opera. On February 22, Mahler wrote to Frau Papier, reminding her of their meeting in Kassel twelve years before. He added: "You cannot imagine how happy I should be to work in my own country at last, after so many years of wandering! There are moments when I am so overwhelmed by homesickness that I need all my energy not to despair. I know very well that I have the reputation of a madman, but you know perfectly well what kind of people usually enjoy that epithet. Perhaps Bezecny[25] could confidentially inquire about me from my former chief, Baron Beniczky in Budapest. That would best show to what extent this 'madness' can be reconciled with the undoubted successes which the Budapest Opera enjoyed under my direction."[26]

In the same letter, Mahler promised Frau Papier never to mention her name and to let her act in complete anonymity. From then on, all his hopes rested on this eventuality, for in Hamburg matters were going from bad to worse. Pollini had expressly promised Mahler that he would organize some spring concerts for him, but this project, like so many others, had come to nothing. "With Pollini nothing can be done this year. He has been hovering between life and death for months, and I am now determined to leave Hamburg forever in September. I still don't know where I'll go . . ."[27]

That Pollini temporarily recovered made no difference, for, according to Pfohl, he could not even bring himself to meet Mahler, and only wondered what pretext he would use to oust him. "Everything Mahler does is grand, majestic, immense," he said at this time to the Prague critic Julius Steinberg,[28] "but do me a great favor, get rid of him for me! I no longer know which of us is in command!" He and Mahler had been "at daggers drawn"[29] for some time, and matters were bound to come to a head.

Thus the end of the 1895–96 season found Mahler in a state of uncertainty and anxiety. Exceptionally, he conducted a performance of *La Traviata* at the opera in May. The hall was crowded and the Hamburg public gave a warm welcome to an Italian prima donna guest star, Franceschina Prevosti. Bruno Walter, writing of this performance, called it one of the most perfect examples of a controlled use of rubato that he had ever known, free from any concession to the singers, solely dictated by "enthusiasm and passion."[30] Armbrust was impressed by the way in which Mahler had miraculously reconciled the prima donna's rather free interpretation with the more rhythmic and "conscientious" interpretation of the German singers.[31]

The annual Wagner festival was, as usual, entrusted mainly to Mahler. In May he conducted a total of twenty-one performances but nevertheless managed to work for himself as well. "I'm up to my eyes in my *Third,* at the moment," he wrote to Frau Sommerfeld in May.[32] "It's the best and most mature of my works. With it, I shall conclude my 'Passion Trilogy.' But, great heavens, what it has led me into!" Marschner's *Der Vampyr,* which was sung as a benefit for the box-office employees and which, in a letter to Mildenburg, he had called "repugnant," closed a season that had set him a really astounding schedule. He had in fact conducted the fantastic total of 138 performances. His repertoire included twenty-eight Wagner performances,[33] to which were added some revivals: *Norma* (3) *Carmen* (8), *Hänsel und Gretel* (16), *The Bartered Bride* (4), *Le Prophète* (1), *La Traviata* (1), *Der Vampyr* (1), not to mention the year's new productions: *Werther* (12), *L'Attaque du Moulin* (2), *Sjula* (2), *Der Evangelimann* (7), *Dalibor* (4), Haydn's *Lo Speziale* (9), *Der Bettelstudent* (10), *Die Fledermaus* (4). To this amazing seasonal list must be added the annual Good Friday concert and the annual performance of *Die Schöpfung* at Altona.

Leaving Hamburg on May 3, Mahler first broke his journey in Berlin to dine with Marschalk, and then in Leipzig, where he spent an afternoon in the country with Staegemann and succeeded in persuading the organizers of the Gewandhaus Concerts to perform a part of his *Second Symphony,* as Nikisch had suggested. The next day, in Dresden,[34] he was equally successful and was promised another performance of excerpts from the *Second Symphony* in the course of the season. He first played the symphony in its entirety on the piano for the organizers of the subscription concerts, and then again for Ernst von Schuch and the director of the opera.

Reaching Vienna on June 5, Mahler spent several days paying duty calls and taking all the steps advised by Rosa Papier and Hofrath Wlassack. He saw his old friends Löhr and the Spieglers and devoted much time to Mildenburg, for they were each to spend their summer vacations with their families, separated by the Alps; he in Steinbach, she in Malborghetto, in the Udine Province, Italy.

On the morning of the eleventh he left Vienna, determined to complete his *Third Symphony*. In Steinbach, where it rained unceasingly, Mahler found himself without a piano, for the one he rented from Vienna each year had not yet arrived. Actually, this bothered him less than formerly, for he had almost lost the habit of composing at the piano.[35]

A much more serious obstacle was revealed when, upon unpacking, he discovered that in his extreme haste to leave Hamburg he had left in his study the outline of the first movement of the *Third Symphony*. "Like an eagle deprived of its wings," he wandered aimlessly in and out of the Häuschen before finally deciding to telegraph Behn, asking him to go to the Bismarckstrasse at once, pick up the famous notes, and send them on. The faithful Behn was already in Timmendorf on the Baltic, but he replied at once, promising to take the necessary steps immediately.

While awaiting the sketches, which took more than a week to arrive, Mahler wandered around like a soul in torment, longing both for his work and the woman he still loved passionately, despite all the obstacles separating them. "I move about all day long," he wrote to Mildenburg, "as though deprived of my hands. I am not in the mood for anything, and I keep asking myself what I can do to see you again quickly. Both light and air fail me . . ."[36] "I drift around like a lost thing—what a difference between this year and last! Neither nature nor my work is able to replace your dearly cherished presence: each tree, each bird, and even your kittens—all these things make me feel more sharply the sorrow of our separation . . ."[37]

Mahler's impatience grew from day to day, for he feared that the sketches had been lost and that his summer's work would be entirely ruined by his forgetfulness. The rain persisted. He wrote to Anna every day of his love and his distress. He tried to work, but his thoughts were constantly drawn toward her. Sometimes he almost seemed glad that circumstances had brought him a "certain freedom," but quickly added: "Unhappily, I have come to like my slave's chains, and it seems to me a waste of time to want to change."

This desire for freedom must have worried Mildenburg, for a few days later he was reassuring her: "Can you believe, my dear, that I rejoice in my 'freedom' for a single instant? With what joy I would give it up forever in exchange for imprisonment in your arms, were it not that by doing so I would make another's life a prison. You see, my dear heart, it is always the same shadow that crosses the path of my wishes and my hopes. Perhaps you cannot understand this, since you have never found yourself in such a situation. I worry ceaselessly, but can see no solution. I know that by realizing my happiness, I would destroy forever that of another (you know of whom I speak). I always try to control myself when I am with you or writing to you because it upsets me too much to see you sad . . ."[38] "In every sense, I belong to you as much as it is in my power to give what is *mine* . . ."[39]

The other person, the "obstacle" to which Mahler alluded, was doubtless his sister Justi, to whom he still felt bound until her material existence could be assured by marriage. But was he entirely sincere when he reiterated that his happiness would be complete when he and Anna could belong entirely to one another and "would never part again"? It seems doubtful, particularly at this stage of their liaison.

Three days after reaching Steinbach, Mahler complained to Mildenburg that his "work still advances slowly," that his "thoughts don't want to obey" him. Nevertheless, he had composed a new *Wunderhorn Lied: "Lob der Kritik"* or *"Lob des hohen Verstandes,"* in which he took his revenge upon the critics. He described it to Natalie as "a very amusing lied . . . it concerns a wager between a nightingale and an old cuckoo, who ask a donkey to judge between them. He naturally, with an air of great importance, awards the prize to the cuckoo." "You will laugh when you hear it," he wrote to Mildenburg. "But of course it is my great work that obsesses me, and I'd dearly love to finish it this year . . ." To Natalie he also said of his lied: "Here it was essential not to spoil anything, but to render exactly what is in the poem, whereas often it is necessary to deepen and enlarge the text by means of sound."[40]

The sketches finally arrived on the morning of June 19, and by that time Mahler had decided that not only the circumstances but also the climate of Steinbach depressed him. He set to work but was still easily distracted, anxious, and prodigal with advice to Mildenburg, who was also depressed. "Dear heart, you should keep yourself busy. Not only does that drive whims away, but it is what makes a human being human. For myself, I know that when I am idle I bring no happiness either to others or to myself. I become argumentative, bad-tempered, egoistic, niggardly, and God knows what else, whereas I am an entirely different man as soon as I'm engaged in some activity that matches my strength. I become expansive, I feel well, I love life, and I want the best for other people. If I had to stop creating, I should be the unhappiest of men."[41]

As long as he had been unable to compose, Mahler had consoled himself by taking long walks. Once his sketches arrived, Natalie and Justi noticed that he was not satisfied with his work, since he was much more patient than usual with the outside world—and especially in regard to noise. Nonetheless, he worked every day and complained neither when things went wrong nor when the weather was bad. "Who knows if it is not all to the good? Perhaps just such an atmosphere is right for the immobility of the first movement, perhaps if everything had gone exactly as I wanted it to go I would suddenly have produced a flourishing summer, bursting with life, which would not have suited the spirit of my work, which would have negated the effect of the other movements and would have destroyed the general conception? So let us put up with the hardships inflicted by mysterious destiny, whose power over my life I understand better each day."

By comparing Mahler's almost daily letters to Mildenburg with the innumerable notes that Natalie made that summer, an important conclusion can be drawn regarding the relationship of Mahler and the young soprano. He, who never stopped talking about his work and describing his states of mind while composing, rarely mentioned these matters to her. A few passing references to the work that was absorbing him entirely and, at the end of the summer, the enclosed program of the symphony, which he had drafted the preceding year, were all that his letters contained. One must suppose that Mildenburg, absorbed by her art and by her own self, took only a superficial interest in her lover's work and was probably disconcerted by his musical style.

The first movement of the *Third Symphony* was originally to be divided into two distinct parts. Mahler at once became conscious of the exceptional nature of the powerful, mysterious D minor introduction. "My music is only the sound of nature [*Naturlaut*]," he wrote that year to the critic Richard Balka, who questioned him on his aesthetic beliefs. "I know of no other program. From time to time I give a few indications . . . Now it is the world, the whole of nature that awakens. I need say no more to you . . ."[42] None of the music in Mahler's other works has so passionately exalted this fierce, romantic love of nature as the first movement of the *Third Symphony*. "It is hardly music anymore, just the voice of nature: one shudders at this motionless, soulless material (I could have called this movement 'What the rocks tell me'), from which, little by little, life frees itself and finally conquers, developing and differentiating step by step: flowers, animals, men, right up to the kingdom of the spirit and that of the angels. In the introduction there is the scorched, brooding atmosphere of midday in summer, when all life is suspended and not a breath of wind stirs the vibrant, flamboyant air, drunk with sunshine. Life, the young prisoner of ever-motionless, inanimate nature, cries out in the distance and begs for freedom, until, in the first movement, which follows the introduction, this life breaks out victoriously."[43]

According to Mahler, to understand the first movement, one must "immerse oneself in nature, for music can capture its essence better than any art or any science. . . . I believe no artist suffers from the mystique of nature as much as the musician." There was a naïve, typically romantic and Rousseauist sentiment, a yearning for peace and simplicity in this nostalgic longing for a "return to nature." "That which nature has above art," he said later, "is that it yields itself such as it is, freely and openly, and requires no explanation."[44] He expressed the same yearning while reminiscing to a Prague journalist about his childhood in Iglau. One day, during a walk, a friend had suggested that the shepherd who had just crossed their path was undoubtedly thinking of the next village feast. Shocked at this idea that seemed to him excessively prosaic, Mahler had replied that "someone who dreams and meditates and lives in harmony with nature can't possibly have such sordid thoughts." Nevertheless, nature is not always idyllic in the *Third Symphony*. The creator of this new symphonic universe is sometimes seized with terror, when a superior force takes hold of him, that of the great god Pan, who, "hurtling down his unfathomable chasm, roams in regions far from the earth, leaving the destinies of men to vanish in the distance. . . . In the first movement, the southern storm blows wildly, as it has done here these last few days. Coming from warm, fertile lands, I am sure it carries more fertility within it than the easterly winds men so desire. In march tempo the movement never stops advancing; as it approaches, it becomes louder and louder, gathers strength and grows like an avalanche until its din breaks above our heads in powerful rejoicing . . . I would never have had the courage, I think, to finish this gigantic task if the other movements had not already been completed . . ."[45]

To describe the mobility and subtle variety of the themes in this first movement, Mahler used the image of water flowing over rapids, a river within which millions of drops are incessantly transformed. "Everything is carried away in an endless whirling torrent that scarcely touches the river bed, rising constantly higher as it boils up to the sky, encountering only the resistance of immobile matter, the stones and fallen rocks in the path of the stream, which slow or stop it occasionally."[46]

At first Mahler had intended to unify the separate movements thematically, but finally each of them developed individually. "However, at the end of the 'animal' movement, the heavy shadows of inanimate nature, inorganic and as yet undefined, fall once more. But this time, it is just a reversion to the more primitive animal forms of life before the powerful leap that leads on to the spirit, to the highest of earthly creatures—that is, man. Between the first movement and the last there is a link that will be scarcely noticeable to a listener: what in the one is muffled, stifled and rigid is developed in the second until it reaches the highest point of consciousness; the inarticulate sounds have become supremely articulate."

Mahler believed that the opening march was "the wildest thing he had written," but among the five succeeding movements,[47] three were "all humor" and only two—"Night" and "Love"[48]—were deeply serious. Unhappily, the chances were that the "humor" would be misunderstood. Mahler had realized this clearly the preceding year after playing the movements to a friend, who had judged the "Angel" movement "too light" after the deep shadows of the "Night." He did not understand then, and few people understand today, that the "humor" here represents the ultimate that cannot be expressed in any other terms.[49]

While composing the hymn to the glory of summer, Mahler had seemed a man possessed: "The flowers, the breezes, the sounds and the colors, all the life of summer, filled me," he said, "to the point at which I became conscious of it as of a person and thought that I could see its body and its face. The flowers, which musically are quickly described in repose, I observed shaken by wind and storm, then lulled by soft breezes, suffused and caressed by the sun's rays. Every form of the animal world appeared to me as distinct, characteristic, and alive, and humorous subjects were not lacking among them."[50]

The spirit and the essence of the new work were completely different from those of the first two symphonies: "The greatest problems of humanity, those which I have evoked and attempted to solve in the *Second* (why do we exist? Do we continue to exist after death?), can no longer touch me here. What, in fact, do they amount to in the face of the All-Powerful, of the Pan in whom everything lives and must live? Can a spirit that, as in this symphony, meditates on the eternal truths of creation and divinity die? Thus one becomes convinced that everything is blissfully created forever, human sorrow and misery have no further place here. Sublime gaiety reigns, an eternally sunny day—for the gods, naturally, not for men—for them all this is terrifying and monstrous, and eternally elusive."[51]

Though elated by these great thoughts, Mahler never stopped worrying about the future of his works. Compared to this new symphony, the *Second* seemed to him "child's play . . . A real terror seizes me when I see where I am heading and become aware of the road that lies ahead for music; when I understand that I have been chosen for the fearsome task of creating a work of this size. Today I suddenly thought about Christ, who, on the Mount of Olives, willingly drained his cup of sorrow to the dregs. When fate offers you this cup, you cannot refuse it, nor do you wish to refuse it, but you can sometimes be seized by mortal anguish when contemplating the future. Such are my feelings regarding this movement, and I know I will have to suffer on account of it; certainly I will not live to see it recognized and admired . . ."[52]

"Today I became horribly aware that the first movement will last half an hour, perhaps longer. What are people going to say to that? They won't leave a hair on my head. Nonetheless, I can answer for it. This work is truly concise, even brief, though it lasts two hours; brief because it is so diverse and naturally pleasant. They will say: How daring to present us with something like this! He is so obstinate, he has gone even further than in the *Second!* If they knew how little the force that drives me has to do with daring! What interior resistance I have to overcome in myself, in fact! How unhappy I am at having to take this road; but this work unconditionally demands it! I wanted, on the contrary, to rest after such a serious and heavy work as the *Second*, to rest with this work that today has outgrown me and sweeps me along. It is as though the torrent of creation has proved to be an irresistible force, after having been pent up for years; there is no escape!"[53]

While orchestrating his symphony, too, Mahler was disturbed to see the number of instruments constantly increasing: five trumpets, ten horns, six clarinets! He was confronted by a terrible dilemma: should he employ an "insufficient and outdated" orchestra—as Beethoven had done in his *Ninth Symphony*—or orchestrate as he wished and pass for a madman who could not restrain himself and did not deserve to be performed? Didn't Marschalk say, on hearing the *First Symphony,* "Either Mahler is a genius or he is mad," adding, "but I am certain of the answer: he is mad!"[54]

As he had done the year before, Mahler devoted the mornings to work, breaking off only to go on bicycle trips with Natalie. Often the rain lasted for several days, and then he asked himself, "Why do I always return, year after year, to the Salzkammergut?" But despite the bad weather he continued ranging over the mountainside, "splashing valiantly about in wind and rain."

Thanks to Natalie we know, down to the smallest detail, the chronology of the *Third Symphony*'s completion. Mahler devoted himself to it from the moment the famous sketches arrived—that is, from June 20. On the twenty-eighth, returning from the village, where she practiced her violin, Natalie met an excited, happy Justi who said, "Imagine, Gustav has finished the sketch of his first movement!" Natalie had still not recovered from her astonishment when Mahler called her to his room and told her delightedly how he had suddenly completed the outline, which he had believed would take him several more weeks. "I myself don't know how it happened. Naturally, I had already laid out the blocks, but how did I come to complete the whole edifice? No doubt it happened as with those jigsaw puzzles in which one vainly tries to decipher the picture until suddenly one key piece slips into place and the whole becomes clear! Nonetheless, this is only a skeleton, still lacking flesh and blood, and I still need four good weeks to add substance and life to it. But the essential is already there, and I can look forward more calmly and with great confidence to finishing the work." A little later he added, "To have finished such a sketch is like having a young girl's future assured!"[55]

A letter of June 29 to Mildenburg announces the same news more calmly. Mahler still hoped to finish the symphony in four weeks. "Nothing like my symphony will ever have been heard before! The whole of nature finds a voice in it and speaks of something deeply mysterious, something not even guessed at except perhaps in dreams! Believe me, certain passages give even me an uncanny feeling, as though I myself had not written them. If only I could succeed in completing it all as I now plan it![56] Then you would embrace a happy Gustl . . . Will you be jealous, then, of my symphony?"

Mildenburg was not as yet prepared to understand the reason for Mahler's silences. Now it was she who reproached him for his "indifference" and for his terseness. He replied, "You speak of a certain absent-mindedness in my letters; you have seen how, when I am with you, my thoughts are sometimes far away. However, as I told you, I am completing an important work. You must understand that it demands my whole attention and that for as long as I am absorbed in it I am dead to the outside world. Remember, too, that so insignificant a matter as a rehearsal at the Opera has been sufficient to distract you when you said good-by to me: I could have taken offense if I had not understood perfectly.

"Imagine a work of this size, which reflects all of creation; one is nothing but an instrument on which the universe plays. I have already explained this to you often, and you must accept it if you really understand me. All those who live with me have had to learn this. At such times I don't belong to myself. I cannot be otherwise; tell me if you can understand and accept this in me. This time, so many external factors are troubling me—physical ills and material cares—that the effort required to plunge my whole self into the flood of my art, into the atmosphere of this work that I must complete, is so immense that I am often in despair. The flood has begun to bear me along, and I beg you, my dear, to give me your support: help me to maintain my spiritual calm. When I have finished—then I hope you will have joy in me again, and I in you. Do you understand? Once and for all . . . ? The creator of such a work suffers from terrible birth pangs; before everything is ordered, constructed, and combined in his head, he must endure many moments of solitude and of absence, during which he is lost in himself and wholly cut off from the outside world."[57]

This letter was written shortly before the completion of the sketches for the first movement; with it he sent a program of the *Third Symphony,* in which this movement is still divided into two parts:
1. "What the rocks told me."
2. "Summer marches in!" (*Der Sommer marschiert ein*)

"Take careful note of this!" Mahler added. "The world also will have to take note, these are the first two movements of my work! . . ." The five movements that follow are those we know today. "My work is a gigantic musical poem; it includes all the phases of evolution and depicts its gradual rise: it begins at the heart of inanimate nature and progresses to the love of God! Men will take some time to crack these nuts which I have shaken off the tree . . ."[58] After completing the outline Mahler again wrote a long letter to Mildenburg, reaffirming his unhappiness at their separation and his wish to visit her. Unfortunately the trip was too costly because of his present high standard of living.[59] Also, he could not consider leaving his two sisters alone in Steinbach, where they were bored to death. Furthermore, he had received two insistent letters from Cosima Wagner, urging him to visit Bayreuth, and had promised to take Justi with him to show her "something of the world."

On June 30, as soon as his sketch was completed, Mahler took Natalie and his sisters to Unterach, at the far end of the lake, to lunch with the Austrian composer Ignaz Brüll. Brüll was an excellent pianist and he played the *Second Symphony* with Mahler on two pianos. "It made an instantaneous and deep impression on all the listeners—and there was quite a crowd." Brüll's sister, Hermine Schwartz, sang the *Urlicht* in her weak but expressive contralto.[60] As they were leaving, the Mahlers met the actor Karl Wagner on the pier. He was returning from a summer tour and "really looked marvelous" in his mountain costume. Mahler knew of Wagner's success with women, noted that Justi was not indifferent to the handsome actor, and invited him to dinner on his birthday a few days later in order to amuse his "two sparrows" (his sisters).

On July 6 he again wrote to Mildenburg: "I miss you so, my dear Anna, that if I did not have my work—your 'rival,' as you call it—I would undoubtedly succumb to melancholy [*Sehnsucht*]. Mankind will receive something beautiful in exchange. Summer is marching in, and it sings and rings in a way that you cannot even imagine! Everywhere, everything starts to grow, and then again, during a pause, there are mysterious, sorrowful sounds; inanimate nature, motionless and silent, is awaiting the advent of life. It is impossible to describe this in words . . ."[61] Orchestration was proving all the easier because in his outline Mahler had already noted down many instrumental details. Hadn't Weber gone even further in this respect when he orchestrated his works fully from the start!

On July 9, Mahler told Natalie, "The aspect of instrumentation in which I consider myself ahead of past and present composers can be summed up in a single word: clarity. Absolutely everything must be heard just as I myself heard it with my inner ear—that is my aim, and to reach it I use all the means at my disposal, without exception. Each instrument may be employed only in the right place and for its own qualities. I even go so far as to have the violins play on the E string in the singing, tender, exalted passages; while for more emotional and powerful episodes I use the G string.

"When I want to express something with passion, I almost never make use of the intermediate strings, which do not produce such a powerful sound: they are better suited to mysterious, veiled passages. It is unacceptable, in these matters, to form abstract ideas that do not correspond to reality. Naturally, I am often exasperated at having to work this out in such detail, for I rack my brains, I subtilize, I refine until I get just what I want. But then I tell myself that if my work is to endure, this effort is worthwhile, as the teeth of time, because of it, will have a harder task tearing it to pieces.

"At the beginning of my career, I lacked training and understanding, and I was much less careful. I paid dearly for it with my *First Symphony!* The results I obtained did not correspond to my intentions, and since they were neither so clear nor so finished as they could have been, later I had to revise the instrumentation completely. When the moderns claim that art is not essential in execution also, they talk nonsense. A far more incredible wealth of artistic means is required to carry a work from the sketch right through to the final details, than has ever been dreamed of by those gentlemen, the impotent realists. *All that is not perfect down to the smallest detail is doomed to perish even before it is born.*"[62]

A splendid profession of faith, and one too often forgotten by those who draw artificial boundaries between substance and form, inspiration and technique, creation and mere craftsmanship. "May heaven preserve me from losing this judgment if ever my works become weaker," he added. "As long as I work I shall want to destroy everything because of one detail, just the opposite of those who want to save Sodom and Gomorrah because of one just man. It is better to be carried off at the height of one's creative powers, while still hoping for even greater and higher achievements, and while no visible limitations restrain one's field of activity. Thus a mountain whose summit is hidden by clouds appears higher than the highest of all those mountains that rise unveiled above the earth. However, nature has set the ultimate boundaries to the growth of man's spirit and the field of his activity, and perhaps it is unrealistic not to acknowledge their existence."[63]

As usual, Mahler here shows extraordinary perception: if the glory of his work has not tarnished over the years, this is because the high quality of his craftsmanship sets off the great wealth of his musical imagination. Mahler created new forms, new techniques of development, new sonorities, and these purely technical innovations are inseparable from those which more frequently attract attention, that is, melodic, harmonic, and polyphonic invention.

In the third movement of the *Third Symphony* the flügelhorn was a "childhood memory" from the Iglau military band,[64] but Mahler feared that he would have difficulty in finding such an instrument. He was also disturbed when he recalled that Berlioz had used the E flat clarinet only sparingly, and in order to obtain a "vulgar" effect, whereas he himself used two E flat clarinets all through the symphony! But why should he worry when, in any case, it would be played only after his death?

On July 7 or 8, on an envelope that he had just received from Milden-burg, Mahler noticed three mysterious initials: P A N: the name of the Greek god after whom, for several weeks past, he had been thinking of naming his new symphony. He was about to accept this as a new sign from heaven, when he examined the envelope more carefully and noticed the number *30*, placed alongside the mysterious initials: *Post Amt Nummer 30*, Post Office Number 30.[65]

Mahler had worked so intensely over this period that he once more became nervous and irritable. Out walking, he would fall suddenly into a daydream and, taking his notebook from his pocket, would feverishly note down a theme or a new harmony. Natalie saw him covering innumerable pages with hundreds of variations, motifs, and modulations until at last he found exactly what he needed. From time to time he took day-long trips so that he could "return to work with a clearer mind and a surer judgment, as a painter draws back to examine his picture and add the final touches."

As for the *Second Symphony,* Mahler sometimes hastily jotted down a few bars with the intention of altering, developing, or even replacing them later on, only to perceive then that he had hit upon one of his best ideas and should not change a single note. One day a certain passage particularly troubled him, and that night, while he was asleep, he seemed to hear a voice ("That of Beethoven, or perhaps Wagner, with whom I now am in contact each night . . . not bad company, what's more!") saying to him, "Why not bring the horns in three bars later!" The next day he was astounded to discover that this was in fact the best and simplest way of over-coming his difficulty.[66]

Mahler's restlessness and his mental and physical tension were such that even the faithful and patient Natalie was happy to spend her days at a distance, practicing on her violin. The "perpetual ups and downs, like those of a ship tossed by the waves," to which he subjected his family and close friends were so stormy that they all needed to "rest and find themselves once more on terra firma." Justi, Emma, and Natalie were probably re-lieved to hear, early in the second week of July, that Mahler intended to follow his annual custom of taking several days off for a bicycle trip to Hallstadt, Mondsee, Salzburg, and finally Ischl, where he would pay his yearly visit to Brahms.

# CHAPTER 23

*Mahler in Hamburg (VIII) — Completion of the* Third
Symphony *— Setback in Leipzig and Success in Dresden
— The Call of the God of the Southern Regions (July
1896–January 1897)*

On July 14, 1896, after completing a large section of the orchestral outline
of the *Third Symphony*'s first movement, Mahler took advantage of the
belated return of the good weather to have a few days' rest and pay his
annual visit to Brahms. "I really could say, like Faust," he wrote to Mildenburg on the eve of his departure, "that from time to time I like to see the
old man. He is a solid, gnarled and ancient tree, which bears sweet, ripe
fruit, and I enjoy the luxuriant foliage. Of course, we don't have much in
common, and our friendship exists only because I, a young artist of the
future, gladly show him the consideration and respect due to an aged and
revered master, revealing only that side of my character which I think he
finds agreeable."[1]

Mahler expected to be away from Steinbach for about five days, so just
before his departure he entrusted to Justi a small suitcase containing all his
manuscripts; he never stopped worrying about them all the time he was
away. The day after his departure, he wrote a letter urging her to watch
over the suitcase faithfully, to take it with her wherever she went, and to
write him each day assuring him of its safety. He left for Ischl on the morning of Saturday, July 11, and called on Brahms before lunch.

As always, Mahler received a warm welcome in the little house at the end
of the Salzburgstrasse, but Brahms had recently been deeply affected by the
death of his friend Clara Schumann. She had been buried in Bonn, instead
of Frankfurt, and Brahms had not been notified of this change. As a result,
he had only arrived in time to throw a few handfuls of earth on top of her
coffin as it was lowered into Robert Schumann's grave. Also, for the first
time in his life, the old man was ill; he was suffering from the cancer of the

liver which was soon to cause his death. "Gloomy and hating life," he spent most of his time sitting under a tree in his garden. Nevertheless, he was as usual quite friendly toward Mahler and questioned him about his work. But Mahler felt that he must not overstay his welcome and soon took his leave. No doubt sensing that this meeting would be their last, he turned back after he had left the house and saw the old master take his frugal lunch, a sausage and a slice of bread, from a stove. This simple gesture seemed to symbolize all the loneliness of old age, and Mahler, remembering the great man's genius and fame, was vividly reminded that "all is vanity."[2]

In one of Mahler's letters to Mildenburg he wrote that "for the first time Brahms took an interest in my work and asked me to send him the score that is to be published next winter."[3] A mistake or forgetfulness? Natalie's carefully kept notes reveal that the first three movements had already been sent to Brahms the preceding summer and that Mahler had received an enigmatic and disappointing reply.[4] So in 1896 he can only have sent the Finale, and according to Richard Specht it was then that Brahms noticed the resemblance between the opening measures of his own *German Requiem* and those of the *Resurrection* theme. He found the Scherzo "touched with genius" (*ein ans Geniale streifendes Stück*)[5] and added that "up to now, I had the impression that Richard Strauss was the leader of the rebels, but I now consider Mahler the king of the revolutionaries."[6]

Mahler's own attitude toward Brahms's music was undoubtedly influenced by his early passion for Wagner. Yet he was too honest and objective a musician not to recognize its greatness, despite occasional hard judgments.[7] He never saw Brahms alive again, but he was soon to benefit from the master's early recognition of his talent as a conductor.

Mahler remounted his bicycle and pedaled on to Hallstadt, where he stopped for the night, enchanted with the "celestial" lakeside landscape. Returning to Ischl next day, he met Löwe, the director of the Breslau Theater, who had followed his advice and engaged Bruno Walter. He spoke to Löwe warmly and at length about the young man before taking the train to Salzburg on Monday morning. There he met Siegmund Singer, an old friend from Budapest, who agreed to intercede for him in Vienna. After this, he returned by train and bicycle to Ischl, by way of Sankt Gilgen and Mondsee. This otherwise relaxing trip was unfortunately marred by violent and constant headaches.

On the homeward journey, Mahler called on his old friend, the Hungarian composer Mihalovics, who was staying in Aussee[8] and who also promised to support his candidacy for the Vienna Opera post. Mahler returned to Steinbach on July 16 to complete the score of his *Third Symphony* and to greet Bruno Walter, to whom he had written on July 2: "Dear friend, Just a few words in reply to your greetings and to invite you to join us here about July 16, if you have not already made other vacation plans unknown to me. You must already know, through my sisters, that I have not been idle and that I hope to have the *Third* happily completed soon. I am busy with the orchestral score, having almost entirely finished the first sketch. I think that the heads of the honorable critics, appointed or self-appointed, will again spin, whereas friends will find the excursions that I have prepared for them wholesome fun. The whole thing is unfortunately once again corrupted by my notorious sense of humor, 'and I have on many occasions indulged my fancy for barren noise.' Often, too, the musicians will play 'without the least consideration for what their neighbors are doing' and my 'barren and brutal nature will thus be exposed to the light of day.' That I cannot do without 'triviality' is now a well-known fact. But this time I have exceeded all bounds. 'Occasionally it is like being in a café or a stable.' So come quickly and be well prepared. Perhaps your taste, which has possibly been purified by Berlin, will become corrupted!"[9]

The weather was beautiful when Bruno Walter reached Steinbach on July 17. On the landing stage was a delighted Mahler, who insisted upon carrying Walter's suitcase. On the way to the hotel, Mahler noticed the young man looking up at the Höllengebirge, the great rock face that dominates the Attersee. "There's no need to look at that," he said, "for it's all in my music"[10] (das habe ich schon alles wegkomponiert). Then he began to tell Walter about the Third Symphony, on which, as before, he worked every morning from six o'clock. Immersed in his composition, he refused to play a single note to Walter before it was complete. Nonetheless he was at times gay and relaxed, especially in the evenings when he read aloud from his beloved Don Quixote, torn as so often between laughter and "compassion for the idealism and purity of Cervantes' hero."

For several days he played constantly with two kittens, taking them about with him everywhere in his pockets and watching their games with delight, until one day he found them in a barn eating a bird. After that he completely lost interest in them. He was then still watching with endless wonder all the forms of animal life that had inspired his Tierstück. He confided to Walter that sometimes in the evening he was greatly moved to hear the deep lowing of the herds, which "expressed the animals' very soul."

During Walter's visit Mahler took him to dine at the Berghof with Ignaz Brüll, whose opera Das goldene Kreuz (The Golden Cross) the young man had conducted in Hamburg. There they met Richard Specht, the future biographer of Brahms, Mahler, and Strauss, and some other young writers, including Hugo von Hofmannsthal, the most promising Austrian poet of the time.[11] Again Mahler played the Second Symphony, arranged for two pianos.[12]

All this time he continued to work on the Third Symphony, while reading Carlyle's "History of Frederick the Great" and reflecting upon "how much of himself and his life unconsciously went into his work." Was not the warlike spirit of the book to be found in his summer procession? "The victorious columns of troops that instantly overthrow the enemy rabble are just like the Prussian armies. And what about the role played by both Prussian and Austrian military bands? . . ."[13]

His work was progressing rapidly. "I feel," he told Natalie that same day, "like someone who has undertaken a long swim (as we did last year). At first, the distance seems interminable; there is nothing but water to be seen and we appear to make no progress. Having reached the halfway mark, the destination still seems remote and unattainable! Then the goal draws closer and suddenly, in a couple of strokes, we have arrived!"[14] He still worried about the gigantic orchestral forces required to perform the first movement and its unaccustomed length, though in his opinion there was not one superfluous bar. "When you consider how much happens in it, it seems concise, even though it equals a long symphony in length! There are so many forces at work! First the secret growth of nature, awakening from her slumber, throwing off her chains; then the approach of summer with her followers; what life, what innumerable sounds! Then the battle against hostile forces . . . it is a gigantic fresco, in contrast to the painted miniatures of the other movements. You cannot imagine the effort required to construct such a long movement, to support and control the whole edifice. And yet I needed this foundation, this colossal base on which to build the pyramid which, in the other movements, gradually tapers off, becoming progressively more transparent and more delicate!"

The next day Mahler was even happier: only sixteen bars to polish, and everything would be complete! Examining the symphony as a whole, he suddenly realized that, unintentionally, he had used the classic musical forms created by Mozart and Haydn and later expanded by Beethoven. Though the movements and the links between them were different and each one of them was more varied and complex than their model, they still followed the same familiar patterns—Adagio, Rondo, Minuet, Allegro—with the same construction, and the same bar structure, which must correspond to some "eternal law." That day, July 27, Mahler prayed "that nothing happens to me today, as no one but myself could complete those sixteen bars, that gigantic fanfare which heralds the arrival of Pan and his magic procession." Scarcely an hour later, he decided to go swimming and as usual ran down the steps to the lake four at a time. Such was his haste that he missed a step, lost his balance, and sprained his left foot so badly that he fainted. As soon as he recovered consciousness, he hobbled off in search of help—and finally collapsed in Justi's room, exhausted by pain and shock. She doused him with water, gave him "wine soup" to drink, and nursed him so well that after lunch he slept for a couple of hours and then felt sufficiently recovered to take his swim.[15]

The next day Mahler returned to his work, completing the movement—the longest he had ever composed—in less than six weeks. During the winter he was to alter a few details, but the essence of the work, which had to be conceived quickly so that the symphony "could emerge as a coherent whole," had been created. He was satisfied with it all, except for the opening of the first movement, which he intended to alter. Everyone was astonished to see him so happy, as he was usually morose and restless at such times, fearing that his work was a failure and regretting the loss of "his reason for living." The next day only Bruno Walter was permitted to hear Mahler play over the first movement. The young musician thought it better than any of his previous works and they discussed the composition together. At that time, Mahler already considered Walter as his only important disciple, at least according to Natalie. That evening she found in her bedroom the sketches for the first movement, with this dedication: "July 28, 1896, a strange event has occurred: I have been able to give to my friend Natalie the seed of a tree which, nevertheless, has grown with all the force of life, and bears branches, leaves, and fruit."[16] Yet Mahler's good humor did not last for long: soon he regretted the loss of the "daily companion" who had filled his life. He did not even smoke the one cigar that he allowed himself each day.

When an excursion to Berchtesgaden was called off two days later because of bad weather, he once more revised the opening of the first movement "in the manner of an architect who must establish the right proportions between the various sections of his building." He doubled its length by slowing the tempo, thus giving it "the necessary size and importance." The next day he also changed the closing bars of the Adagio, which did not seem "simple" enough, giving it its present stupendous ending with the great D major chords. "In the Adagio," he explained, "everything is resolved in the calm of existence. The Ixion's wheel of appearances finally stops turning. In the quick movements—Minuet and Allegro—and even in the Andante of my *Second,* everything is flux, change, movement. Thus, without at the moment knowing why, and contrary to custom, I have ended my *Second* and my *Third* with Adagios, the superior rather than inferior form of music."[17]

The form that Mahler gave to his *Third Symphony* during those last days of July was not changed again, yet none of his other works underwent so many alterations in the order and number of the movements. Eight different programs marked the stages of this evolution, six of them dating from the summer of 1895, only two from 1896.[18] The finished work was an imposing fresco dedicated to the glory of creation, starting with inanimate nature and progressing step by step to its highest form, that is to say, God. The following is the final program, sent to Marschalk on August 6, 1896, after Mahler had completed the symphony[19]:

A MIDSUMMER MORNING DREAM

1st part:    Introduction: Pan's awakening
             No. 1: Summer marches in (procession of Bacchus)

2nd part:    No. 2: What the flowers of the field tell me
             No. 3: What the animals of the forest tell me
             No. 4: What man tells me
             No. 5: What the angels tell me
             No. 6: What love tells me

On the morning of August 1, the weather having finally improved and Bruno Walter having left, Mahler decided to go on an excursion. At dawn he and Natalie set out on their bicycles for Berchtesgaden, to visit their old friend Siegfried Lipiner, who was spending the summer there with his wife. Lipiner played almost as important a part in Natalie's life as Mahler did, and she must have been overjoyed to find herself in the company of her two idols. Lipiner spent much time talking to them of his literary projects, few of which he realized: a trilogy entitled *Christus,* composed of *Mary Magdalen, Judas Iscariot,* and *Paul in Rome,* to be preceded by a prologue entitled *Adam.* After lunch the friends started to walk to Achauer Weiher but were caught in a sudden downpour. Clementine Lipiner and Natalie took refuge in a café, and from there watched Mahler and Lipiner, deep in conversation, gesticulating excitedly with their one free hand, while the other held their umbrellas in the pouring rain. Rooted to the spot, Mahler listened, pawing the ground "like a wild boar," as he always did when deeply interested. This strange discussion in the rain aroused the curiosity of the other people in the café, who pressed against the window to get a closer look. Clementine and Natalie felt so embarrassed that they abandoned their shelter and, despite the downpour, headed the two men for home.[20]

Returning from Berchtesgaden, Mahler passed through Ischl and Aussee, arriving in Steinbach on August 5, and from there, a few days later, he went on to Bayreuth. At first his reception by the Wagner family struck him as very cold; indeed, he wondered if someone had prejudiced them against him. Among others he suspected Schumann-Heink, who had been suspiciously friendly when they met accidentally on the street. But happily this unfortunate first impression soon vanished. Mahler attended the third complete *Ring* cycle[21] conducted by Felix Mottl that summer, and Frau Cosima bade him a "warm and friendly farewell" on August 20.

Six months later Mahler learned that, for reasons that were above all racial, Frau Cosima had favored Mottl as a candidate and had done everything possible to stop his own nomination to Vienna.[22]

As usual, Mahler spent the final week in Steinbach in a state of deep depression. "How strange it feels," he wrote to Mildenburg, "to set aside such a task when, for two years, it has given meaning to my life! Can you understand? It always seems to me that when I express such a thought, it really hurts you. Is that so?"[23] He also realized that he was leaving Steinbach forever, and though he had complained often about its climate and the "unbearable noise," at the last minute he was reluctant to abandon a place so rich in memories. He tried to book the usual apartment there for the following year, but unfortunately new owners had taken over the inn. They were careless in their work, and their financial demands were out of all proportion to the comfort of the accommodation. On the last day, going up the familiar road toward the village, Mahler turned around, and, taking one final look at the Häuschen, in which, for four years, he had fought, suffered, and created two great symphonies, he burst into tears.

On his way back to Hamburg, Mahler stopped in Vienna to continue his discussions with the opera authorities. Hofrath Wlassack, who at first told Rosa Papier that Mahler's nomination was impossible because of his race, had later exerted all his diplomacy and power in his favor. Nothing, however, had been as yet fixed, and Mahler decided to try his luck in Munich as well, for he had heard that Hermann Levi needed an assistant there. He called on a journalist friend, who telephoned in his presence to Ernst von Possart, the opera intendant. After a moment's hesitation, Possart replied that he had already heard of Mahler and had considered his candidacy, and he advised the journalist to consult his superior, the Intendant General von Perfall. But when the latter saw a photograph of Mahler, he apparently declared that it was impossible for him to engage anyone with such pronounced Jewish features immediately after Levi.[24]

On his return to Hamburg, Mahler found himself in a more difficult situation than ever. Rudolf Krzyzanowski, his childhood friend, had just been engaged by Pollini, and Katharina Klafsky had returned from America with her husband, the conductor Otto Lohse. Several times Pollini had expressed in public his intention to "get rid of him," while for his part Mahler had for several years refused all offers, since Pollini had always asserted that he would never release him![25]

"I dread to return to Hamburg," Mahler had written to Mildenburg before leaving Steinbach. "How is the situation going to develop? I don't think that Pollini knows himself, but the sparks will fly when our varying interests clash. Will he succeed in frightening me away? If he does, I have absolutely no idea what I would do, for at present I don't see a single post available that I could accept."

Mahler had nonetheless firmly resolved to "be sensible" and not to abandon his post until he had found a suitable position, even if this required superhuman self-control. His future with Mildenburg was another serious problem. The many letters that he had sent her from Steinbach revealed no signs of growing coldness; on the contrary, they were filled with affection and tenderness. Nevertheless, the two had countless small misunderstandings, for she was passionate and possessive, and numerous difficulties still stood in their way. Mahler considered Justi the chief obstacle to marriage: "She likes you very much," he wrote to Mildenburg on June 12, "and seems to know how things stand between us. Oh, dear God, maybe everything will still come out all right in the end! I did not realize how much I love you and how I find in your love everything I need for my happiness . . ." The letters that he wrote to Cosima Wagner about her at the end of 1896 and the beginning of 1897 clearly show how concerned he still was about her health and her career.

Mildenburg, subject to fits of depression, tended to read the worst into everything that Mahler wrote to her. She had morbid whims (*Grillen*), and his letters that summer often attempted to cheer her up. She could not understand how he could devote himself so wholeheartedly to his work, and this was always one of the chief sources of discord between them. "If God wills it, I'll be with you one week after you receive this letter," Mahler had written at the end of the summer. "What is it, then, that you have noticed in me, as you say so frequently? I have often explained it to you; after all both of us have always had the deepest concern for the future. My heart can only be heavy, for obstacles to our union loom up on all sides. Don't forget that it is harder for me than for you, because it is up to me to remove them. A question often tortures me: What will come of all this? I suppose this is what you often read between the lines of my letters. But you never seemed very concerned when I spoke to you about it."[26]

Worried and anxious about his career, clinging to the only hope that could resolve everything—his nomination to Vienna—Mahler started the new season by rehearsing the opening opera, *Tannhäuser,* which was to mark Mildenburg's first appearance as Venus. Pfohl's review of that evening in the *Hamburger Nachrichten* listed the worrying symptoms already noted at the opera during the preceding season. "A creaking, as of rotten beams," he wrote, "foretold disaster . . . The first menacing symptoms of decay" were discernible in the imperfect performance by the ragged ensemble, in which "stammering beginners performed alongside the brilliantly talented," not to mention the many ill-inspired guest appearances "which had caused much coming and going, worthy of Hamburg's harbor, but not its opera."

The *Tannhäuser* cast for September 1 was almost entirely new.[27] Back from America, Klafsky once more sang one of her best parts, to the delight of her many admirers, while Mildenburg, Pfohl said, performed her new role with an astounding authority. Leopold Demuth, making his debut as Wolfram, also won Pfohl's admiration for his voice rather than for his dramatic performance. Mahler's "commanding hand" had guided the whole, but Pfohl pointed out numerous orchestral deficiencies.

Pollini's new policy, intended to drive Mahler out by inflicting all sorts of humiliations upon him, first showed itself on September 4, when he entrusted the direction of *Tristan* (*Tristan* and *Fidelio* were Mahler's favorite operas) to Rudolf Krzyzanowski, whose wife, Ida Doxat, was making her debut as Isolde.[28] In a rather lukewarm article, Pfohl praised the new conductor's "precision" and again remarked on the many weaknesses in the orchestral performance, blaming them not on the conductor but on the theater's "system," which resulted in "the most exhausted" orchestra in the world. The *Fremdenblatt*[29] was equally reserved in its praise of both Krzyzanowski, "a careful conductor rather than a virtuoso," and the new Isolde.

Some days later, Mahler conducted *Le Nozze di Figaro* with an excellent cast, and Pfohl again had reservations both regarding the slowness of the tempos and the insufficient preparation.[30] On September 11, Mahler again directed Klafsky in one of her most celebrated roles, Leonore in *Fidelio,* and on the twenty-ninth[31] she died in her sleep of a "brain disease" that seems more likely to have been a heart attack. An immense crowd of weeping admirers followed the singer's funeral procession. She was buried in the costume she had worn in the final act of *Tannhäuser*.

Toward the end of September, Mahler conducted *Fidelio* in the little Altona Theater. J. B. Förster and Natalie have both left accounts of this performance, which they found memorable despite the small orchestra and the lack of rehearsals. In their presence Mahler hotly defended his insertion of the *"Leonore" No. 1*[32] overture between the two scenes of the final act. Did not this "summary," this "condensation" of the opera, lead perfectly into the final exultation? As the three of them walked back to Hamburg, Mahler told Natalie of his bitterness concerning his unhappy theatrical experiences. "During the performances, I am disgusted with life and feel a rage building up inside me that is gradually destroying me. The idea of not being able to impose my will, of allowing these sins against music to be committed, and even of being obliged to participate in them, sometimes upset me so much that I could put a bullet through my head. Don't be surprised if, by the end of the winter, I have become an out and out neurotic!"

Each of this particular evening's two observers relates his personal memories without mentioning the other's presence. What Förster remembered most clearly was Mildenburg's interpretation of the title role. He soon forgot the smallness of the theater and the orchestra and was carried along by the drama. Later, while walking with Mahler through the narrow streets of Altona, he confessed his own love for *Fidelio*. "You place *Fidelio* ahead of everything, even the works of Wagner?" Mahler asked. "Yes, ahead of everything," replied Förster. Mahler embraced him and said, "We think alike. We'll always remain friends."

Two days later, a performance of *Don Giovanni*, given without a single rehearsal and with mediocre singers, again plunged Mahler into a state of depression, for it had been impossible for him "to bring out a single one of the finer points of that divine work." It seemed to him that bad luck always dogged this masterpiece, whereas *Figaro*, despite the failure of its first performance, had been born under a lucky star.

After a performance of *Carmen*, Natalie asked Mahler why "one does not grow weary sooner of so spicy a dish." Mahler answered that the only reason was the "absolute perfection" of Bizet's score. When conducting it, he said, he always experienced a profound happiness, finding new qualities in it each time. These remarks led him to formulate one of his basic aesthetic principles: each orchestral part should sound as though written for a human voice. The greater the orchestral means employed, the less he felt that exceptions to this rule were admissible. "Even the bassoon, the bass tuba, and the kettledrum," he said, "should sing." Infractions of this rule were permissible only with instruments playing natural harmonics and that had obvious lacks and limitations.[33]

About this time, Förster asked Mahler to lend him a score of *Die Meistersinger,* so that he could study its polyphony and instrumentation. Mahler replied that this great opera was, in his opinion, "badly orchestrated" and that he preferred to send him *Carmen,* in which "not a single superfluous note is to be found." Förster at once realized how Bizet's masterly economy invariably produced the desired effect without a single unnecessary doubling, and Mahler, who was then deeply concerned with such problems, summed up his orchestral aesthetics as follows:

"The fortes and fortissimos are easily obtained. Beauty and fullness of tone can be achieved by having the whole orchestra play with high clarinets and a carefully selected number of piccolos. But that is only a dynamic effect that increases with the number of performers and instruments. It is in delicate shadings, in untried combinations of colors that one finds virgin fields when searching for new effects, harmonics and complementary notes that organ builders have exploited for a long time. They serve the composers of today and will continue to do so in the future, leading to unknown combinations of sound. That is where the future of music resides, not in the experimental tone-painting of the impressionists." Thus, Mahler was sometimes aware that he was breaking new ground for those who would come after him.[34]

The summer weather continued, and Mahler and Natalie cycled or walked through the wooded fields that bordered the Bismarckstrasse. Cattle grazed there, and Justi and Emma nicknamed one grass-banked, winding path "The Avenue of Sighs" because Mahler often strolled there, a prey to intense homesickness, while awaiting the "call of the God of the southern regions" from Vienna. When in Hamburg, he rose each morning at seven, even when he had conducted the night before and gone late to bed. A cold shower preceded his breakfast, which he took alone in his room as soon as he was dressed. During the winter, these early morning hours were in fact the only ones that he could devote to his own work. While drinking his coffee and smoking, he read Goethe, Nietzsche, or the *Wunderhorn,* having banished all newspapers from his rooms. Then he set to work, which that winter meant copying and perfecting the first movement of the *Third Symphony.* After that, at about ten-thirty, he set out on foot for the opera. There and back meant a walk of an hour and a half each day.

On arriving home, Mahler whistled the opening bars of Beethoven's *Eighth Symphony,* a signal for the cook to serve up the soup. When the family budget allowed, he often brought a friend home to lunch with him. At the beginning of October, Ignaz Brüll, in Hamburg to attend rehearsals of his opera *Gloria,* was a frequent guest. Later it was Karl Goldmark, present for those of *Das Heimchen am Herd.* Mahler's daily siesta was often interrupted by calls from composers or singers. Almost every day he visited his copyist Weidich and then took another walk if he was free that evening. If it was a theater evening, he would reach the opera at about six

14. Mahler, 1878.

15. Mahler, 1881.

16. Mahler, 1883.

17. Mahler, 1884.

18. The first theater in which Mahler conducted at Bad Hall.

19. The Kassel Theater, where Mahler conducted, 1883–85.

20. The Alt Market Theater in Prague, where Mahler conducted, 1885–86.

21. Betty Frank, singer at Prague and one of Mahler's first loves.

22. Richard Strauss in his youth.

# Königl. Deutsches Landestheater.

## Sonntag, den 21. Februar 1886
### um 12 Uhr Mittags

zum Besten des deutschen Schulpfennig-Vereines.

# Grosse Musik-Aufführung.

### Orchester-Aufstellung auf der Bühne.

Das Orchester ist auf **85 Mann** verstärkt durch die Mitwirkung hervorragender Künstler.

Kunst-Freunde und Schüler des Conservatoriums.

### I. Abtheilung.

1. Duett: **Götterdämmerung**

(Brünnhilde und Siegfried)

Richard Wagner.

**Brünnhilde — Marie Rochelle. Siegfried — Adolf Wallnöfer.**

Das Orchester des königl. deutschen Landestheaters. — Dirigent: LUDWIG SLANSKY.

2. Verwandlungsmusik, grosse Chor- und Schlussscene des I. Actes

# Parsifal

Richard Wagner.

Chorpart: Deutscher Männer-Gesangverein, Gesangverein Sct. Veit.

Chordirigent: Musikdirector FRIEDRICH HESSLER.

Das Orchester des königl. deutschen Landestheaters. Dirigent: GUSTAV MAHLER.

### II. Abtheilung.

# NEUNTE SYMPHONIE

für Soli, Chor und grosses Orchester

Ludwig van Beethoven.

Chorpart: Deutscher Männergesang-Verein, Gesangverein Sct. Veit.

Chordirigent: Musikdirector FRIEDRICH HESSLER.

Das Orchester des königl. deutschen Landestheaters. Dirigent: Gustav Mahler.

Die Soli gesungen von Betty Frank, Laura Hilgermann, Adolf Wallnöfer, Johannes Elmblad.

**Der Chor besteht aus 200 Mitwirkenden (100 Damen und 100 Herren.)**

Zwischen der 1. und 2. Abtheilung findet eine längere Pause statt.

Anfang 12 Uhr. | Ende halb 3 Uhr.

Preise der Plätze

## Königl. Deutsches Landestheater.

Montag, den 22. Februar 1886. | 59. Abonnements-Vorstellung. (3. Serie weiss.)

# FAUST und MARGARETHE.

Romantische Oper in 4 Aufzügen von J. Barbier und M. Carrée. Musik von Ch. Gounod.

23. Program of first important concert Mahler conducted in Prague.

24. Karl von Weber.

25. Marion von Weber.

26. Angelo Neumann, director of the
Prague Theater, 1885.

27. Max Staegemann, director of the
Leipzig Theater, 1886.

28. Bernhard Pollini, director of the Hamburg Opera.

29. Gustav Löwy, Mahler's first impresario.

o'clock, and almost always returned home in a furious temper, complaining
of that "Augean stable that even a Hercules would not know how to clean."

Most of the people who knew Mahler have mentioned his untidy appearance, his total lack of elegance, and the disorder of his clothes and his
hair, which particularly struck Natalie during this visit to Hamburg.[35] If
we are to believe her, his clothes were often soiled or creased. His socks
had a habit of hanging down over his boots, and if he left the house in the
morning without inspection by some female eye, white traces of his toothpaste
and shaving soap were often to be seen around his mouth or on his cheeks
when he returned. Sometimes he also forgot to comb his hair and went about
all day with it sticking up on end, but this was usually when he was traveling, for at home he washed from head to foot, his hair included, every day.

The condition of Mahler's room also left much to be desired. When he
went out in the morning, it looked as though it had been ravaged by bar-
barian hordes: the bed in disorder, the bolster and covers on the floor, and
the sheet rolled in a ball in a corner of the bed. Comb, toothbrush, handkerchiefs and soaps, nightshirt and undergarments were strewn about the
floor or on the bed. Envelopes and scraps of paper everywhere, even in
the basin. When anyone criticized him for this, Mahler always answered,
"I cannot conform to aesthetics in my daily life. This is a question of personality and temperament, and if I weren't the way I am, I shouldn't
write my symphonies."

Like Bruno Walter, Natalie dwells at length on Mahler's absent-mindedness and abrupt changes of mood. One day he went to fetch her from the
home of a Hamburg friend. He seemed in excellent spirits when he arrived
there; gay and relaxed, he tore through the house like a whirlwind. But a
moment later, he sank into silence and did not open his mouth again until
they left the house. The rapidity of these changes was such that he almost
never remained the same for an hour at a time; his ever-changing point
of view constantly saw in a different light the objects and the people who surrounded him. But despite these changes, these "variations," he always returned
with remarkable constancy to those whom he had chosen for his friends, "as
the pointer of a pair of scales always returns to the center," and one could rely
upon him to a much greater extent than on most other people.[36]

His forgetfulness, his "absences," caused by a deep inner absorption in his
thoughts, diminished with the years. But Natalie relates that when Mahler
was a young man he once stirred his coffee with a cigarette and then instead
of smoke puffed a stream of liquid onto his landlady's table. One evening in
Budapest, he took Justi to have coffee at the Stadtwäldchen, one of the city's
most elegant cafés. They sat at a table on the highest terrace in order
to enjoy the view, and Mahler, used to frequenting more modest establishments, provoked a small scandal by wiping the cutlery and china before
using them, and rinsing out his glass. His attention taken up by the conversation, he tossed the water over the balustrade, onto an elegant group on

the lower terrace. He apologized profusely, and, his absent-mindedness being legendary, he was forgiven without difficulty. But a few minutes later he asked Justi to pour him out another glass of water, and, before she could stop him, he repeated his gesture. This time, mirth spread through the whole café, and one waiter laughed so hard that he had to put down his tray for fear of dropping it. Horribly embarrassed, Justi made her brother leave, and neither of them ever dared set foot in the Stadtwäldchen again.[37]

Like most of Mahler's other contemporaries, Natalie has described his curious gait, which sometimes drew jeers from children in the street. Each of his steps breathed impatience, which showed in the way he raised each leg and then struck the ground "like a horse or a blind man," and also in his habit of seizing his interlocutor's hand or clothes, thus forcing him to remain beside him while he himself stood, excited by the conversation. He "never took two successive steps alike" and constantly changed his gait; it was impossible to walk in step with him. When he rowed, his strokes were even less regular, sometimes rapid, sometimes slow, but he flew into a rage if by any chance his rowing partner criticized him.

Of less than middle height, slender and weak in appearance, Mahler had in fact exceptional strength and suppleness. He was an enthusiastic sportsman, swimmer, bicycle rider, and mountain climber, but he does not seem to have ever practiced gymnastics. Natalie tells us that he hammered the piano "like a giant" and in Budapest he frequently carried his sister Justi—heavier than himself and dressed in a fur coat—up to the third floor, to save her strength at a time when she was exhausted by the illness and death of their parents.

Mahler's age could not be determined from his face alone, for he sometimes looked young, and sometimes mature. Within a few days, a few hours even, his appearance, like his state of mind, could change from the best to the worst; only his liveliness, his spiritual intensity, never left him. When he was in a good mood, he seemed incredibly young, partly because, unlike many of his contemporaries, he wore no beard. He was often taken for an actor, a fact that annoyed his friends, for his face never had the "rather empty look of many theatrical people," but on the contrary was open and expressive, reflecting his mind and his whole self. When he was advised to grow a beard again, he replied that he had not shaved it off out of vanity or because of a whim, but because he conducted not only with his eyes and his fingers, but also with his mouth and his lips, seeking to transmit sounds to the singers and musicians by his facial expression.

Mahler's small dark eyes shone with a burning intensity and could terrify musicians and singers even through the spectacles or pince-nez that myopia forced him to wear constantly. Deep thought had modeled furrows and wrinkles on his high and powerful forehead. His temples were traversed by two small blue veins nicknamed the "lightning veins" because they revealed his inner storms, swelling up menacingly whenever he became angry. At such times, his face was terrifying, for every feature seemed to contract, glow, and sparkle, while each strand of jet-black hair appeared to stand on end.

Mahler's head had one characteristic trait that was revealed whenever he was photographed in profile: the back of his skull descended to his neck in a straight line.[38] His nose was slender yet domineering. His firm, energetic mouth disclosed teeth that were uneven but pearly white and very strong. His thin, fine-drawn lips, with their half-scornful, half-sorrowful expression, were not unlike those of Beethoven, whose life mask hung in Mahler's study. The harshness, severity, and austerity of this mouth disappeared as soon as Mahler laughed; indeed, his happy, deep, childlike laughter was so infectious that sometimes you only had to hear it through a wall and you would be laughing too.

It was in Hamburg, in the autumn of 1896, that Natalie heard for the first time the big opening movement of the *Third Symphony,* and once again Mahler explained, "Zeus overthrowing Kronos, the superior form casting down the inferior—that is what is expressed in this movement. I see more and more that my conception of nature here is basically Greek." A moment later, he compared artistic creation to Jacob's struggle for God's blessing: "God does not wish to bless me either; I have to wrest a blessing from him by the terrifying struggles to which I must submit while creating my work."[39]

The same day, Mahler let Natalie go alone to a party at the home of the industrialist Berkan, since he was suffering from one of his migraines. Natalie described to her host, a good friend and fervent admirer of Mahler, the terrible anxiety that he felt for his precious manuscripts and how this restricted the diffusion of his music. Berkan was so moved that he promised that he and Behn would meet the expenses of Hofmeister's publication of the *Second Symphony* and would later see about the *Third.*[40]

At the theater, Pollini continued to assign to Krzyzanowski the best operas. After *Tristan* he gave him *Die Meistersinger* and *Die Zauberflöte,* while Mahler conducted uninteresting new productions, such as Brüll's *Gloria,* based on a "frivolous and not very attractive subject," according to Krause, better suited to a "passionate Italian" than to a "lyrical German." Brüll's opera was followed by another "popular" work, *Runenzauber,* by Emil Hartmann, a Danish organist-composer who lived in Hamburg. Both operas were only moderately successful, though the "two composers had been well served by the performance."[41] *Gloria* was withdrawn immediately and *Runenzauber* repeated only twice. Ten days later Mahler conducted a third new work, this time with real success. It was Karl Goldmark's *Das Heimchen am Herd,* a "gay opera" based on Dickens' *The Cricket on the Hearth.* The *Fremdenblatt* critic spoke of the "genius" of the composer and the opera was sung over twenty times during the season.[42] This must only have exasperated Mahler more, since he hated Goldmark's music.

In November, as usual, Mahler conducted the annual performance of Haydn's *Die Schöpfung* in Altona. Pfohl was somewhat shocked by the "new, very modern" recitatives that Mahler had introduced, and found that they considerably changed the color of the work. Nonetheless, Krause, who for years had been criticizing Mahler's "subjectivity" now blamed him for demanding from his soloists "absolute fidelity to the text" in place of the total liberty that "the interpreters of an earlier generation had allowed." However, he recognized the wonders wrought by Mahler with only one rehearsal, thanks to his "despotic conducting," his energy, and his "authoritative glances."

Of all the successes achieved up to this time by Mahler the composer, the most unanimous and undisputed was that of the *Blumenstück* from the *Third Symphony,* given for the first time in a packed Berlin concert hall on November 9, by the Philharmonic Orchestra under the direction of Mahler's onetime rival, Arthur Nikisch.[43] Shortly before the concert, Mahler had written to the music critic Annie Sommerfeld: "The piece to be performed is the smallest and the most 'inarticulate' (it symbolizes that moment in evolution when the creation still cannot speak a word or make a sound). But a beggar such as I, who is turned away from every door, must be content with a stove, though he begs for bread."[44] Having arrived on the morning of the concert, Mahler rehearsed the orchestra once: Paul Bekker[45] has described a long session that was interrupted so many times for petty details it seemed they would never reach the end. Finally Konzertmeister Breuer informed Mahler that the orchestra had to stop at noon, for it had another rehearsal after lunch. When the time was up, Breuer got to his feet and announced that the rehearsal was over. A few moments later the composer found himself deserted by all but the boy whose job it was to collect the scores.

After the performance the applause was so warm and prolonged that Mahler had to rise from his seat, cross the hall, and bow several times after shaking Nikisch's hand. The Berlin critics were clearly astonished at having so few reservations to formulate. The *Vossische Zeitung* judged the piece "poetically felt" but "less original in its ideas than in its instrumental setting." Apart from "a passage in which the piccolo's piping was accompanied by a cymbal stroke," the *Blumenstück* gave no indication of the "composer's taste for extravagances."

In the *National Zeitung,* Ludwig Bussler, usually so severe, declared that Mahler "had rediscovered a secret lost to many of his contemporaries, that of continuously developing a simple and not very original theme, in a somewhat *altfränkisch* (old Franconian) style," and "of making happy use of musical color and modern harmony without necessarily forgetting about rhythm, that powerful, reliable element with which many present-day composers have lost touch." The critic of the *Börsenzeitung* also declared himself "pleasantly surprised" by this piece, which he found "tenderly poetic and melodically attractive . . . discreet and natural . . . with Oriental overtones" like "a tale from the Arabian Nights." Oskar Eichberg, Mahler's warmest supporter, expressed a wish to hear the symphony in its entirety.

The Berlin Philharmonic played the *Blumenstück* again a month later in

Hamburg, this time under the direction of Felix Weingartner. The piece was encored and the critical acclaim was as enthusiastic as in Berlin. For once the "Infernal Judges" had really enjoyed Mahler's music.[46] Even Sittard considered the Minuet "exquisite," its inspiration original and pleasant, its instrumentation "witty." It was "pure music" in an original language. The "variations" contained "marvelous, warm and deeply felt" passages; the piece had a "playful" and "at times even impertinent and unbridled" style, as at the start of the second theme; a string of diverting ideas "were linked together with happy effect . . . The flowers have absorbed so many dewdrops that they become drunk and, beneath the smiling rays of sun, perform a wild dance that reaches its climax at the beginning of the third theme, when the gaiety grows even wilder . . . The piece pleased everyone, and we look forward to hearing it again," Sittard concluded.

In the *Fremdenblatt*, Krause expressed a belief that Mahler's earlier failures had been undeserved, for a close study of the score of the *Second Symphony* had convinced him of the work's beauty. Its "tonal experiments" were often daring, but they remained "subordinate to the whole," which was a mass of splendid color. In his opinion, the *Blumenstück* was full of poetry, expressed a great warmth of feeling, and Hamburg should have an opportunity of hearing the whole symphony. As for Pfohl, he considered the movement "a rare and precious jewel [*Cabinetstück*] full of magic color; a happy and exotic dream; its flowers were blossoms from the south . . ."

Three days after this unanimous and unexpected success, Mahler left for Leipzig, where he had been invited to conduct a Lisztverein concert. The program had been changed at the last moment. Nikisch had promised to conduct at the Gewandhaus the first three movements of the *Second Symphony*, but after an exchange of letters he had decided to give only the *Blumenstück*, which he had already conducted in Berlin, plus the choral section from the *Third Symphony*.[47] So, at the last moment, Mahler was able to replace the *Symphonie fantastique* and Beethoven's *Fifth* in his own program by the first movements of his *Second Symphony*. Reaching Leipzig on December 11, after a journey that had seemed interminable, he thought it necessary to assure himself of the good will of the city's chief personalities, and, starting immediately, he paid twenty-four calls, chiefly on critics and the local correspondents of various German periodicals.

The next morning, the first rehearsal for the concert was "as always, the least agreeable!" Mahler complained to Justi of the "stupidity" and "rudeness" of the orchestral musicians, who applauded him after the rehearsal, but whose mediocre standards hardly surpassed that of Hamburg. Nevertheless, his general impression was good, and he had been told that the entire symphony would be presented the following year. The second rehearsal, however, was even more disappointing. "I was in a mad rage and would have loved to throw my baton at those people's heads. It is a cabaret orchestra, tired and sullen. But never mind. I'll find some way of inducing them to play. I had to make a tremendous effort not to show how upset I was."

Between rehearsals, Mahler continued his courtesy calls. He lunched with the great pianist Teresa Carreño, who complained to him bitterly about her ex-husband, Eugène d'Albert, and about marriage in general; he also dined with the ex-wife of the cellist David Popper, who spoke to him in similar terms of her former husband.[48]

The Lisztverein's[49] fifth concert, on December 14, lasted almost three hours. The vast Albert Hall of the Crystal Palace was crowded, and the program was one of those incongruous assortments then so popular. The two movements of Mahler's symphony were followed by six of Hugo Wolf's lieder sung by Carl Lang.[50] The Russian virtuoso Wassily Sapelnikov, the concert's "chief attraction" according to the *Neue Zeitschrift,* then played Schumann's *Piano Concerto,* followed by Liszt's B minor *Sonata,* and as encores one of his *Hungarian Rhapsodies* and the Chopin *Berceuse.* This strange potpourri ended with the *Coriolan Overture* conducted by Mahler. The first movement of the *Second Symphony* was applauded by some and booed by others; only the Andante was, as usual, entirely successful.

Of all the Leipzig critics, only the *Leipziger Zeitung* and the *General-Anzeiger* were favorable to Mahler. The first acknowledged only the "great enthusiasm" that was responsible for creating such a work, and the "astounding boldness" with which Mahler turned his ideas into music. The critic spoke of orchestral mastery, subtle mingling of colors, "surprising and original effects . . ." However, he preferred the simplicity of the Andante to the complexity of the Maestoso and regretted that "such a rich talent should lose its way in a flight of Icarus . . . often going beyond the limits of musical beauty" and breaking new ground over which it is difficult to follow him.

In the *Anzeiger,* Edmund Winterfeldt compared the "brutal effect" of the first movement to the "immense rocky landscape of the far north, surrounded by impenetrable night," a "powerful but frozen" picture, the "angry cry of a heart trodden underfoot." It was impossible to remain indifferent in the face of such art, or to forget it, and the hostility it provoked could only "strengthen the courage of its creator." Was Wagner not also considered a heretic? So long as the art is authentic, everyone must practice it as they think fit.[51]

In the *Leipziger Tageblatt,* Schlemüller[52] on the contrary considered that, despite the program notes (written by Marschalk), the first movement was "almost incomprehensible." To him it seemed that Mahler, despite his "great ability," had aimed only at a superficial effect and that his inspiration came from others. The "almost vulgar" simplicity of the Andante did not match the false grandeur of the opening movement. As for Bernhard Vogel, he declared that this "gracious but cosmopolitan serenade" contained traces of Rossini, Saint-Saëns, and Massenet. According to him, Mahler took far too long to present what little came from his own heart,[53] but borrowed from other composers[54] in the Maestoso, which seemed an "interminable paraphrase of musical ideas whose power has long since been recognized." Most of these ideas were "more convincing in their original, modest form than in Mahler's incredibly emphatic orchestration." The conductor Mahler was also blamed in the same article for the many "liberties" he had taken with the *Coriolan Overture*.

Finally the critic of the *Neue Zeitschrift für Musik* accused Mahler of borrowing his themes from *Der fliegende Holländer*, "which seemed to materialize now and then" in the first movement. The excessive length of the work and "the bizarre treatment" of its themes would prevent it from having any lasting success." So the "Infernal Judges" of Leipzig had run true to form, and it is easy to understand why Mahler said that in Leipzig "the orchestra is inferior to all the critics and the criticism inferior to all the orchestras."[55] Once more his efforts had failed.

Mahler's break with Pollini was to become complete upon his return to Hamburg. "You cannot imagine how this ground burns my feet!" he wrote to Karl Goldmark. "I feel deeply humiliated both as a man and as an artist; I cannot stand it any longer without losing all my self-respect."[56] In December, Mahler complained to the director of the way that Bittong drew up the schedule of rehearsals without ever consulting him, despite the fact that a stage director had none of the musical experience required to make such decisions alone. Although Mahler had pointed out the need to plan ensemble rehearsals for Cherubini's *Les Deux journées*, the stage director had arranged for them to take place at times when some of the singers were busy elsewhere. Furthermore individual rehearsals were unnecessary for this opera, since all the singers knew their roles perfectly. Bittong had replied to Mahler's objections with his usual stubborn insolence, saying that he was acting "according to the director's wishes."

At the end of the year, Mahler's overtures to the Vienna Opera became more pressing than ever, for the situation there had evolved somewhat favorably. Wilhelm Jahn's departure seemed almost inevitable, since he had gone very nearly blind. Rosa Papier advised Mahler that for the moment he should apply for a position as conductor. Before Christmas, he got in touch with everyone likely to be of help in overcoming the various obstacles. On December 21, Lipiner, then librarian in the Parliament, wrote to Intendant Bezecny to refute the main official objections: Mahler's "irritable character" rarely revealed itself. It was but one aspect of his "profound, intense" nature. Only laziness and idleness angered him, all his efforts were directed toward maximal achievement. Theatrical performers needed a firm hand on the reins and he had all the qualities needed to make a good conductor and director. Further, in the last few years he had made great progress as regards patience and self-control.

On the same day, Mahler wrote to Mihalovics: "In Vienna the problem of a conductor-director is acute. At the moment I am high on the list of candidates, but two factors are against me, it seems: my 'madness,' which my enemies mention whenever they want to put difficulties in my path, and the fact that I was born a Jew; as regards this point, I must tell you, in case you don't know it yet, that I was converted to Catholicism very shortly after I left Budapest."[57]

Mihalovics knew of Mahler's planned conversion, since on December 8 he had already mentioned it to the intendant in a letter describing Mahler as "one of the best and noblest beings I have ever met, on both the human and artistic levels." At the end of December, Mahler went to work again on Mihalovics, and also wrote to Count Apponyi, asking him to intervene in his favor with the Lord Chamberlain (*Obersthofmeister*), Prince Liechtenstein, on whom all important decisions regarding the opera and the Burgtheater depended. "After my endless artistic adventures, I really am very excited by the idea of at last finding an activity that will be worthy of me and will set me free forever from the miserable theatrical junk."[58] Mahler wished to win the support of Prince Liechtenstein by all possible means. With this aim in view, he asked Mihalovics, Max Falk, Goldmark,[59] and even Nina Hoffmann, who knew one of the prince's sisters, Countess Kinsky, to intervene on his behalf.

On December 21, Mahler again reminded Bezecny and Wlassack of his candidacy, promising to devote all his energies to the Vienna Opera if he were honored with an engagement. He begged them to consider him and help him. He had been in exile too long and was eager to return to his native land, to put into practice both his natural talent and his fifteen years of theatrical experience. He reminded them of his success in Budapest, underlined the fact that he had been converted, and attacked the "good friends" who had spread rumors of his "excitability" and "eccentricity."

On January 10, 1897, Count Apponyi wrote Bezecny the most enthusiastic letter of recommendation that he had so far received concerning Mahler. Mahler was warmly remembered in Budapest. Brahms and Goldmark could testify that they "had never met so complete an artist and that his character deserved as much praise as his artistic personality." Beniczky, the former intendant of the Budapest Opera, intervened at the same time to reassure Bezecny as to Mahler's "excitability," which had "no other cause but his profession," to assure him that Mahler possessed excellent judgment on the practical, financial level and that his integrity, combined with his other qualities, largely compensated for whatever "weaknesses" he might have.[60]

In January, Mahler was told that "under the present circumstances, it is impossible to engage a Jew for Vienna." Nevertheless, he decided that whatever happened he would leave Hamburg at the end of the season, even if he had to make a living in Berlin by lecturing and giving lessons.[61] "A few days ago," he wrote to Berliner, "urged on by the irresistible pressure of circumstances, I tendered my resignation, which has been accepted.[62] Despite negotiations with Munich and even Budapest, I can find no other employment. Everywhere, things fall through at the last moment on account of my race!"[63]

Mahler was being overpessimistic: the Vienna Opera authorities were now well disposed toward him. Only one obstacle remained. Despite his age and his nearly total blindness, Wilhelm Jahn was still director of the Vienna Opera; his consent to Mahler's appointment would be necessary even after Bezecny proposed it. With the help of Rosa Papier and Bezecny, by the end of December Wlassack had devised a plan: since Jahn had to go to Dresden in January to attend the premiere of August Bungert's new opera *Odysseus' Heimkehr,* Mahler must find some excuse to meet him there and inquire if there were not a post available for a conductor at the Vienna Opera. Wlassack would then suggest engaging Mahler, and Jahn would thus be forced to give his consent.

The excellent pretext for Mahler's trip to Dresden was an incomplete performance of his *Second Symphony,* which Ernst von Schuch had been planning for some time. He wrote to Mahler on January 10: "Dear friend, now that I am deep in the score, I regret still more that I cannot give the entire *Second Symphony;* the present solution is just a patched-up one, unworthy of a master. I hope that you will not consider this as mere flattery, for it is a heartfelt conviction. But unhappily nothing can be changed now. As you suggested to me by telegram, then, I shall give the three movements. As for the *Blumenstück,* I regret it, but it seems to me that its inclusion would give us too much music in triple time. The movement is spellbinding . . . Is the movement in C minor in three-eighth time slow enough for me to beat it in threes? I am delighted with the music and by your coming visit, and I promise you that next time I shall give the complete work. With all the profound respect due to a Master . . ."[64]

Mahler had in fact first advised Schuch to give, in addition to the *Blumenstück*, the Andante and Scherzo of the *Second Symphony,* followed by the *Urlicht*. This collection of "raisins from various cakes" was to be included in the program of the Dresdner Hofkapelle fourth subscription concert on January 15, but at the last moment the *Blumenstück* was dropped by Schuch.[65] Reaching Dresden on the morning of the fifteenth, Mahler attended the final rehearsal and found the performance thoroughly satisfactory. The invited public applauded warmly, and so, next day, did the audience; among those present were King Albert of Saxony and the Heir Apparent. Both men asked the intendant of the opera to congratulate Mahler, who was all the more pleased because this gave him some hope of an engagement in Dresden if things went badly in Vienna. The piano soloist for this concert, Otto Neitzel, met Mahler for the first time on this occasion and described him as "a supernatural apparition," a sort of Dr. Miracle. He had heard much about him, as being a "strange and quite remarkable case," a composer whose works were almost never played, for public and critics alike considered him a man of the theater, a "banal successor to Schubert, who dressed in Meyerbeerian clothing."[66]

Schuch had no doubt accustomed the Dresden public and critics to modern music, for the press was far more favorable to Mahler than in Leipzig and

Berlin. The *Anzeiger* congratulated him for having included this work in the program despite Mahler's repeated failures in Berlin, for "these three movements reveal a composer who uses counterpoint with ease and mastery," an "orchestrator of genius," altogether a man who "knows how to express himself with originality." There was no "system" in the work, which was neither classical nor "program" music. "It is wholly Mahler, who is a real personality [*Charakterkopf*] among present-day composers." The "reminiscences" always took on a personal aspect and Mahler composed as he should compose, without worrying about the general public or caring for what already existed. "All great artists draw on the past in their own way," this particularly open-minded critic continued. "With or without a program, the composer wants us to listen to his tone poem as pure music, and this is possible thanks to the expressive quality of his themes and the clarity of his construction."[67]

The *Dresdner Journal* found Mahler's melodies "expressive and agreeable," his rhythms "animated," his harmony "unaffected," and his instrumentation "colorful, harmonious [*klangvoll*] and sober [*massvoll*] in its frequent combination of solo instruments." He nonetheless felt that at times the means employed exceeded the quality of the ideas in the first movement. The *Nachrichten* also hailed the *Second Symphony* as an "exceptionally important work . . . romantic and tragic," firmly constructed, full of atmosphere and melodic originality, the effect of which was powerful and convincing. Most of the critics expressed a wish to hear the complete work soon. They do not seem to have been disturbed by the introduction of the voice. The correspondent of the *Musikalisches Wochenblatt* went so far as to say that it was a "clever transfusion of new blood into the old and solid classic form." Perhaps such innovations ran the risk of blowing "the symphonic style to bits," but in any case Mahler's melodic invention was most "attractive." His polyphony seemed "masterly," even if his "ultramodern sensibility leads him to develop the use of voices infinitely and to build a complex network of structures that sometimes weigh on the heart."

This concert, and that of the Leipzig Lisztverein, brought Mahler a new friend and supporter, the Leipzig critic Arthur Seidl,[68] who praised him highly in two articles, one of which was published in the anti-Semitic paper, *Deutsche Wacht*. Ignoring that Seidl worked for such a paper, Mahler had called on him in Dresden the previous December. When he became familiar with Mahler's music, Seidl developed a deep and sincere admiration for him.[69] In January Mahler sent him the two-piano score of the *Second Symphony*[70] and rejoiced at having found a new "adept," "one of those men who form 'my public' and for whom I write my music . . . My only pleasure as a creator," he added, "is when sometimes I find an admirer who is not 'outside time and space.' "

Another letter from Mahler, dated February 17, contains the well-known description of the genesis of the *Second Symphony* Finale, as well as a statement that includes some of his essential ideas on artistic creation: "What

is a musician? This is almost impossible to put into words. It would be easier
to define the traits that distinguish him from other people. However he himself could never explain what those distinctions are. The same is true of his
aims; he reaches them like a sleepwalker, oblivious of his path. (It may
lead him to the edge of a treacherous abyss.) He heads toward the distant
lights, be they the eternally shining stars or enticing will-o'-the-wisps . . ."

First in Berlin and Hamburg, now in Dresden, Mahler had finally experienced the success he had dreamed about. Not as yet for a complete
work, but at last it seemed that the public had begun to accept and understand
his own personal style without forever accusing him of "banality" and
"eclecticism." As can be seen from a short sentence in a letter he wrote to
Frau Sommerfeld after the Dresden concert, he was both delighted and
amazed by this unexpected success.[71]

The meeting with Wilhelm Jahn took place as planned in Dresden. Mahler
spoke to him "frankly and at length,"[72] and Jahn assured him that for the
time being he was not considering resignation but was awaiting the result of
his forthcoming operation for a cataract before deciding whether or not he
should engage an assistant. If he should decide to do so, he promised to
bear Mahler in mind. The general impression this conversation made on
Mahler was excellent,[73] but nonetheless he continued to seek all possible
support among his friends and acquaintances. Several people had in fact
told him that if he were not a Jew his nomination would already be an accomplished fact. In Mottl he had a powerful rival who enjoyed the protection
of Princess Metternich, but Mahler knew that he himself had the support
of Prince Liechtenstein, who had replied to one of his supporters who mentioned his Jewish origin: "Happily, we in Austria have not yet reached the
point where the anti-Semites can dictate our decisions to us."

Although Mahler was not aware of it, he had another distinguished admirer whose influence over the opera's affairs was greater than that of Princess
Metternich. Though he did not know Mahler, Eduard Hanslick favored his
nomination, not only because of his friendship with Brahms, but also because Hanslick was a sworn enemy of Mottl, who had insulted him un-
forgivably at the time of the Wagnerian controversy in Vienna.[74] Karpath
states that, when Hanslick was consulted by Bezecny about a successor to
Jahn, Hanslick replied, "I'd be agreeable to any good musician except
Mottl.[75]

"The reason for my letter is not a personal concern; it is one of interest to
all friends of the opera," Hanslick wrote to Bezecny on March 27. "I have
just learned that Jahn's resignation is said to be an accomplished fact; that
would be a disaster. The only candidates mentioned to succeed him are
Mottl and Mahler. In my modest opinion, it might be a disaster if Mottl
were to become director. It is known from his activity in Karlsruhe that he
loves and conducts only the works of Wagner and his horrible German and
French epigoni. Furthermore, the fact that he insists on employing his wife
as prima donna, though she is nothing of the kind, is cause for apprehension.

To judge by what Mahler has accomplished in Prague and Hamburg, he on the contrary would give our opera new life without violating its classical tradition.

"I hope Your Excellency will pardon me if, for once, I am unfaithful to my principle never to give advice that is not asked for, and if I speak freely and sincerely of something that is very important to me, I can assure you, furthermore, that I speak in the name of the best and most serious friends of art and connoisseurs of music . . ."[76] Thus Hanslick supported Mahler wholeheartedly, and his authority was considerable in a city where, for fifty years, he had exercised the profession of music critic with a keen and perceptive intelligence. His letter played a large part in channeling the current that slowly but surely carried Mahler to the post of director of the Vienna Opera.

"Is it my fault if they . . .
would prefer me to be the
opposite of what I am?"

# CHAPTER 24

*Mahler in Hamburg (IX) — Third Setback in Berlin —
First International Tour — Departure from Hamburg
(January–April 1897)*

While continuing to think about his future, and doing everything possible
to get the Vienna appointment, Mahler was still first *Kapellmeister* of the
Hamburg Opera. On January 5, 1897, he conducted a new production of
Cherubini's *Les Deux journées,* known in Germany as *Der Wasserträger.*[1]
This opera had been one of his first big theatrical successes; he had conducted
it at his Prague debut in 1885 in the presence of the Emperor Franz
Josef.[2]

Despite critical praise, the opera was sung only three times, but exactly
a month later Mahler's last important assignment—the Hamburg premiere of
Umberto Giordano's *Andrea Chénier*—was far better received. This opera,
which pioneered *verismo,* was the composer's third. It had been triumphantly
acclaimed at its premiere in Milan the preceding year, thus putting Giordano's name on the musical map of Europe. Always on the lookout for new
hits, Pollini soon bought the performing rights from Giordano, and the
opera's success in Hamburg was to be almost as great as in Milan. The
*Fremdenblatt* noted that the music "does not seek to distract the listener's
attention from a particularly attractive plot," and added that *Andrea Chénier*
had everything to please the public. The opera was conducted six times by
Mahler before his March tour, later performances being led by Krzyzanowski.[3]

On February 1 the Hamburg Theater celebrated the centenary of Schubert's birth with a concert. After the *Unfinished Symphony,* Mahler was
applauded enthusiastically, but by a rather small audience.[4] Then he accompanied a series of lieder sung by Mildenburg, Schumann-Heink, Birrenkoven, and Demuth.[5]

On January 20 and 21, Nikisch finally kept his promise and conducted the *Blumenstück*[6] at the Leipzig Gewandhaus: as in Berlin and in Hamburg, it was highly praised. The following day he wrote Mahler to tell him about the success of Wednesday afternoon's final rehearsal, attended mainly by students and musicians. The orchestra had greatly enjoyed playing the piece and even the more conservative Thursday evening audience had applauded warmly. This success, Nikisch said, had effaced once and for all the bad impression left by the Lisztverein concert: "Prejudice has been overcome, the way is open. Now, on to further victories!"[7]

The *Leipziger Nachrichten* critic, the most hostile after the December concert, had, according to Nikisch, been "enchanted" and had expressed a wish to hear the entire symphony. In reporting this, Nikisch was improving on the truth: all that Bernhard Vogel had in fact written was that "after this handsome success, perhaps the management will have the courage to present the complete work." The article was nonetheless flattering: "Mahler has broken the chains of the imitator, found his own personality, and fulfilled our highest hopes." Thanks to its inspiration, form, wit and brevity the new piece had been highly successful. The *Leipziger Zeitung* thought that Nikisch had conducted this "elegant idyl with extreme delicacy and unsurpassed beauty of sound," but in the *Tageblatt*, Schlemüller repeated his earlier opinion: the piece, "richer in superficial decoration than in ideas . . . frequently recalled Schubert and the Wagner of Parsifal," to say nothing of its "harsh passages that would be unforgivable even in Bach."[8]

A major event in Mahler's career as a virtuoso conductor was his first international concert tour in March 1897. After having agreed, some time before, to conduct in Moscow and in Budapest, he was invited in February by Franz Kaim, founder of the orchestra of that name, to give a third concert in Munich at the end of the month.[9] Since there was a chance that he might be appointed conductor of this orchestra if he did not get the Vienna post, he had obtained from Pollini an extension of his leave of absence. On his way to Moscow, Mahler stopped in Berlin to attend the first performance of three movements of his *Third Symphony,* which Felix Weingartner conducted at a Königliche Kapelle concert.[10] After the first complete performance of the *Second Symphony* in Berlin in December 1895, Weingartner had claimed to find in it "a more authentic sense of music than in Strauss's symphonic poems," and a certain sympathy had sprung up between the two men, partly because they both felt equally unhappy and misunderstood, Mahler in Hamburg and Weingartner in Berlin.

According to Mahler's letters to Weingartner, it was Behn who first suggested to the latter that he should conduct the *Third Symphony,* for the success of the *Blumenstück* had not induced Wolff to risk a complete performance.[11] "I know of no one to whom I would entrust my work with more joy and confidence," Mahler wrote to his colleague on November 14. "Let me say plainly that it is at your disposal whenever you wish . . . I must admit that sometimes, in my wildest dreams, I have imagined my work being brought to life by the Berliner Hofkapelle, which has become the best orchestra in Germany under your leadership. But I always feared to waste the time and patience of the busiest conductor in Europe and never dared to contact you; perhaps I also felt that a refusal coming from you would be more painful than from anyone else.

"Your letter has filled me with such joy that I can hardly put it into words," Mahler wrote five days later. "My dear Weingartner, I will never forget this! What a difference between your answer and the embarrassed letters to which I am accustomed! Each time I beg for bread, and I am offered stones. This time, I did not ask for anything and I receive manna from heaven! And just think! It is what I have always secretly hoped for!"

Mahler promised to play his work to Weingartner as soon as possible, and agreed to go through the selected movements with the Hamburg orchestra in order to correct the orchestral parts. He also felt obliged to express an interest in Weingartner's own works. Not only did he travel to Bremen to attend a performance of his symphonic poem *King Lear,* but he started pulling wires to induce the Hamburg Opera to stage his opera *Genesius.*[12] With characteristic egocentrism, when Weingartner later wrote his memoirs, he devoted more space to Mahler's admiration for his work than to his personality or the subjects of their conversations.[13] He claims to have been immediately won over by Mahler's "enthusiasm for art" and his "fiery spirit," though he regretted the "almost unbearable banality of his music" and the alterations he made in the orchestration of classical works. Weingartner's judgment was not so harsh in 1896 when he immediately accepted Behn's suggestion that he should perform the three instrumental movements of Mahler's "new symphony" at a concert of the Berlin Königliche Kapelle. Mahler naturally hoped that this partial first performance would later lead to a complete one.

At this time, symphonic life in Berlin was mainly divided between two orchestras and two rival conductors, Nikisch at the Philharmonic and Weingartner at the Königliche Kapelle. Unfortunately for Mahler the public of the latter was considered rather reactionary and "accessible to modern works only when they belong to the virtuoso category," as did Rimski-Korsakov's *Scheherazade,* Tchaikovsky's *Pathétique,* and Strauss's *Till Eulenspiegel.*[14] Weingartner thus showed courage in conducting during this season both Strauss's *Zarathustra* and, shortly afterwards, Mahler's symphonic movements.

After leaving Hamburg on the sixth, Mahler was present at the final rehearsals and heard for the first time the *Tierstück* (No. 3) and the closing Adagio (No. 6), preceded by the already popular *Blumenstück* (No. 2). Weingartner had paved the way for the first performance by a lecture[15] that was shortly to be published as a booklet, together with other texts by himself. In it he regretted the great length of Mahler's works as well as the considerable instrumental means needed to perform them, but he considered their author to be someone who possessed a "strength and depth of character which enable him to express himself in his own way, and to say what he has to say without thinking of success or how to be performed." He admired his long melodies,[16] the "entirely musical character of his works" and their relationship to those of his "mentor Bruckner . . ." One may find in his work "much that is bizarre . . . excessive," he added; "one may even find that he lacks critical judgment in his choice of themes. But everything he writes nevertheless bears the imprint of a rich imagination and a flamboyant, almost fantastic enthusiasm." According to Weingartner, "history shows that the admiration and enthusiasm aroused by works have often been revealed in inverse proportion to their real value."

This courageous if reserved eulogy would have delighted Mahler, if only Weingartner's lectures had not been so obviously designed to boost his own works. Mahler was fully conscious of this fact, as is shown in a letter he wrote to Behn two years earlier (September 12, 1895), after receiving from Weingartner a pamphlet discussing "the lessons of regeneration, etc.": "I've never read anything so childish, so immature and at the same time so pretentious. How far will the sacred cows of fashion go? A good whip is needed!"

For the time being Mahler had to humor Weingartner if only because of his good intentions. Arriving at the Berlin Habsburger Hof Hotel on March 7, Mahler spent the first day in that city as he had done in Leipzig some months before, making "diplomatic visits."[17] After this he dined with Weingartner, and it was probably then that an incident occurred that the conductor mentions in his memoirs. It seems that Mahler asked him during dinner if the Königliche Kapelle orchestra had eight horns. When Weingartner replied that it had ten, Mahler said, "Then I am going to add two parts. Why should those horn players spend the evening drinking in a café instead of playing my work?" In Weingartner's opinion Mahler made this remark in all seriousness, but it was obviously a joke, for the *Third Symphony* calls for eight horns, and Mahler certainly did not change his orchestration for the occasion.[18]

The final rehearsal on March 8 satisfied the composer, the conductor, and the musicians, who applauded Mahler. He considered this a good omen for the orchestra's eighth subscription concert the following day. The first half of the program was made up of the overture to *Euryanthe* and the three Mahler movements; after the intermission three pieces from Mendelssohn's incidental music for *A Midsummer Night's Dream* were followed by the Overture to *Rienzi*. The hall was full and the *Blumenstück* was enthusiastically received. Mahler then took a first bow. But after the *Tierstück* there was some booing as well as clapping, and after the Finale all hell broke loose, the boos almost drowning the applause.[19]

"Yesterday I was engaged in two battles (final rehearsal and concert)," Mahler wrote to Mildenburg, "but alas I must confess that the enemy won. The applause was very warm, but the opposition was powerful too: booing and clapping. Finally Weingartner came to fetch me after all and I took a bow. Then the audience really went wild. The press is going to tear me to shreds."[20] Mahler's two sisters, who had accompanied him to Berlin, were much more upset than he was. Absorbed in his preparations for departure and his projects for the future, he was less disappointed than the year before. The next day he could find only one newspaper at the railroad station before boarding the train for Moscow, and his worst fears were confirmed: "I can tell that I'm going to be so battered and pulled to pieces that no tailor will be able to "iron me out . . . Last evening I had to listen to so much nonsense from both friends and enemies that I became completely dazed . . ."[21]

In the Berlin *Neueste Nachrichten* Paul Moos surpassed himself and his article deserves to be quoted at length: "So as to be sure of my facts and not unjust to the *Hamburg Kapellmeister,* I twice subjected myself to listening to his work; painful as it was for me, I attended both the final rehearsal and the concert. Had I retained the smallest spark of hope that anything good still might come from Mahler, it would now be extinguished forever. I have nothing to add to the opinion that I formulated earlier, not a word to retract. Of course, Mahler is the hero of a tragicomedy, but he is beginning to be frightening because, with the assistance of his fellow conductors, he is becoming firmly entrenched in the concert halls. Thanks to Arthur Nikisch, we already know the second movement of his famous symphony. It continues to be a piece skillfully made up out of a thousand reminiscences; it does not contain one original poetic idea. Nevertheless, this second movement is so good-mannered, it is so thoroughly saccharine, that at least the easily corrupted ladies take pleasure in it and find pretexts for applause.

"The third movement is a very wicked fellow, in which Mahler allows the animals of the forest to speak. The composer adds a program here that affords a glimpse into the depths of his soul. He who is tormented by such strange notions is certainly no ordinary man. In this third movement, the animals are roving the forest, happy and carefree, when man appears and walks calmly by. At once, a sudden terror grips the animals, because 'they guess the peril that man represents for their lives.' So much for the program.[22] The music is even worse; here and there it apparently tries to be humorous and to depict the language of the animals. The donkey brays 'hee haw' on various instruments (see *A Midsummer Night's Dream*); there is bleating, whistling, crying, screaming, groaning and raving. After having abused the orchestra thus, Mahler introduces, in the form of a weak, uninteresting melody, 'Man'—obviously some sentimental fellow who is a worthy counterpart of the Mahlerian animal world. The worst is not that a *Kapellmeister* lacking imagination should write bad music, but that his lucubrations should be presented in all seriousness to a serious public in the course of a serious concert. That is what is so worrying: have we then reached this point? Richard Wagner would turn in his grave at such goings on. True, one section of the audience honored the *Tierstück* with its applause, but another group—the larger, I believe—showed its disapproval by means of energetic booing.

"The final movement, *'Was mir die Liebe erzählt,'* was also booed. Mahler has had the audacity to give this piece the 'exergue': 'Father, behold my wounds; no creature should be lost.' After that, his music must seem blasphemous; it is so verbose, superficial, theatrical, unreal, that the composer should be denied the right to suggest any relationship whatever between those grave words and his thoughts, thereby giving the latter a semblance of profundity. Without wishing it or even realizing it, Mahler is a musical comedian, a practical joker of the worst kind, a man who imitates and pretends feelings. And this is the 'artist' to whom Felix Weingartner accords his support, whom he judges worthy of attention as a symphonist? Bad, very bad! . . ."

The *Börsenzeitung* critic also expressed his thorough disapproval at great length. The *Blumenstück* had been less effective than under Nikisch, for Weingartner had "accentuated the harmonic asperities," and the Scherzo was an "insignificant game," affected and insincere.[23] Only the "varied and colored instrumentation" deserved praise. The Finale's religious and mystic "airs," copied from *Parsifal,* were particularly ill-suited to Mahler, for inspiration was what he lacked and the main theme was "a formless tapeworm that twisted and wriggled through the whole piece, merely passing from one instrument to another." This music was "vain affection, tiresome and soporific; the content was in painful contrast to its pretentious form."

Even Oskar Eichberg, until then the most ardent Mahler supporter in the Berlin press, was disconcerted by the Finale, which he found too much like *Parsifal,* too drawn out and too uniform. He felt that its length prejudiced the symphony as a whole, as did the post horn solo, and the whole of the Scherzo, which he considered "deviated too far from the symphonic genre." Eichberg reminded his readers, however, of the number of bad works that had never been booed, whereas here the booing had started even before the last chord was over. This he considered a kind of success, since nothing is worse than indifference.

Some critics, however, dared to raise their voices in defense of Mahler. Otto Nodnagel of the *Musikalisches Wochenblatt,* in particular, stigmatized the baseness of his colleagues' methods and the perfidiousness of their insinuations.[24] In his opinion, Mahler was going his own way, in a direction different from that of any other musician of his time. Although his "programs" were sometimes awkward, his music stood on its own feet, and the *Second Symphony* was obviously a masterpiece. The *Blumenstück* was "delicate, graceful, exquisite," and the *Tierstück* a "humoresque for orchestra . . . full of insolent humor," only slightly weakened by the sentimentality of the Trio. As for the last movement, although its sonority was somewhat monotonous, it sprang from the depths of the soul and set the orchestra singing.[25]

Unaware of most of these furious attacks, but perfectly conscious of having failed yet again, Mahler took the train for Moscow on the evening of March 10, suffering from a terrible migraine that had not completely left him all the time he was in Berlin, and that was to last throughout the journey.

When he reached his destination on March 12, after two days and two nights on the train, he was met at the station by an employee of the Philharmonic Orchestra, who recognized him thanks to a photograph. Despite Mahler's ignorance of Russian, he made an effort to talk with the man, using what little Czech he knew, as a sleigh bore them to the Hotel Continental. His first impression of Moscow was excellent. He was immediately charmed by the silence, due to the way the sleighs slid over the snow, but he was thankful he had brought a fur coat with him, as such vehicles were for the most part open, and the temperature was well below freezing. Moscow struck him as "imposing and majestic" and he appreciated the purity of the air, which, after two days of virtual fasting, at once relieved his migraine and digestive troubles.

The first two days strengthened this original impression of euphoria. Mahler was enchanted by everything—the life, the people, the air, the food, and particularly the sleighs! These could be rented for only half a rouble (one mark) per hour, so he could afford to drive through the entire city and observe the Muscovites, who seemed to "spend all their time strolling about. . . . The people have an almost Mediterranean vivacity, but are incredibly bigoted," he wrote to Justi. "Every two steps there is a holy image or a church before which each passer-by stops, beats his breast and makes the sign of the Cross in the Russian manner . . . It is most amusing to watch the people in the street! Every third building is a church with twenty cupolas. Everyone who passes makes the sign of the Cross twenty times before each cupola. You can imagine all the hand waving and bowing!"[26] As a devoted admirer of Russian literature, Mahler imagined that he already understood this race as portrayed by Tolstoy and Dostoyevsky. The weather remained superb, but since the temperature was rising slowly, the snow was melting and the sleigh rides were becoming bumpy. As was the custom in Russia, whenever Mahler returned to his room he found a samovar of boiling tea that greatly eased his digestion.

After a few days his enthusiasm as usual started to wane. He was exasperated at not understanding what was being said to him and at not being able to talk with the people he met. The thing he disliked most was having to go about all day unable to say a word, "something that does not suit me at all." He finally rejoiced that he was not obliged to live in Russia and even tired of the food, except for the caviar he ate morning and evening. In the end he lived on nothing but apples and decided to take a big basket of them along on his return journey. He remained delighted, however, by the wonderful smell of wood smoke that hung everywhere.

Fortunately, from an artistic point of view, everything was going well. The excellent orchestra treated him with respect and even affection. But after the first rehearsal, Mahler realized that the musicians were overworked and lacked discipline. As a result he often could not be too demanding. The results he obtained satisfied him, however, for he wrote to Justi: "I see more and more what I could achieve with a good orchestra if I had the time to train it properly." On the day of the concert Nikisch arrived for rehearsals of his own forthcoming concerts, and Mahler had the pleasure of speaking German again with him.

The concert on March 15, the eighth concert of the Imperial Russian Music Society,[27] began with two works that Mahler particularly liked: Beethoven's *Fifth Symphony* and Wagner's *Siegfried Idyll*. Two soloists then performed: a soprano, Maria Antonova, who sang the waltz from Gounod's *Romeo and Juliet* and an unidentified encore, and a pianist, Viktor Staub, who played the Schumann *Concerto* as well as Liszt's *Eleventh Rhapsody*, the Chopin *A Flat Polonaise,* and a Moszkowski *Waltz*. After this potpourri Mahler closed the concert with the *Rienzi Overture*. The Russian public appears to have been as uneducated as it was impolite: its main interest was in the soloists, and many people only arrived after the Beethoven and left again before the pianist's last encore. The Moscow critics were somewhat disconcerted by Mahler's conducting: a short article in the *Russkoye Viedomosti* states that his manner on the podium was strongly influenced by his theatrical activities, that his technique was irreproachable, as was his faithfulness to each detail of the score, but that "this scrupulous exactitude . . . excluded all passion and was incapable of moving the listener." In agreement with his Hamburg colleagues, the critic of *Russkoye Slovo* reproached Mahler for the paradoxical slowness of his tempos in the Beethoven symphony, "as though the Philharmonic Orchestra were not able to play this piece at its normal speed." Like Karl Muck, who had been in Moscow the preceding year, Mahler was a pedant and a Wagnerite—apparently a very damning epithet for this critic, who judged the *Rienzi Overture* most severely and claimed that the *Siegfried Idyll* had bored the Moscow public to tears.

These wholly negative reactions show how backward the Russian public and the critics were at that time. In his correspondence an amateur musicologist named Lipaeff[28] also reproached Mahler for his "excessive originality" and accused him of drawing out the Scherzo and the Finale of the *Fifth Symphony* to a point where they were unrecognizable. "Of course," he added, "this young conductor does know how to get anything he wants from an orchestra," but the interpretation of the *Siegfried Idyll* seemed "too studied," even though the *Rienzi Overture* was "full of fire." On the whole Mahler's visit was much less successful than those of Nikisch, who had become an idol in Russia and returned there every year. Mahler only complained, however, of the public, whom he found "too Asiatic . . . too undisciplined and not very attentive."[29]

After a postconcert supper with Nikisch, Mahler left Moscow without any real regrets, for he had given up hope of establishing any contact with the Russians. Those he had met did not speak German, which shows he had not been received by anyone in Moscow society, where that language was spoken fluently. This time he was only a young conductor from Hamburg, whereas he was later to return in all the glory of his position as director of the Vienna Opera.

His return journey seemed even longer and more tiresome than the outward one. Somewhere between Moscow and Warsaw the train suddenly halted right in the middle of the country until a wrecked freight car could be removed from the track. Despite the fatigue of the long journey, Mahler reached Berlin in reasonably good form on the afternoon of March 18 and dined with Marschalk, who had been so shaken by the failure of the March 9 performance—and so "strongly influenced" by his colleagues—that he "could no longer formulate a personal opinion." But Mahler felt that he had completely talked him around during the course of the evening. He wrote a long letter to Justi before taking the train for Munich. She too had been crushed by the Berlin setback and had not dared to send him a single press clipping.

"You seem either to have taken this matter more to heart than I had anticipated, or you imagine me crushed by it. Well then, let me assure you that it does not worry me in the least. It cannot be otherwise. Remember that all the performers, all those who know the work well, are filled with enthusiasm. Any listener who puts his nose into it for the first time gets a shock; my friends are disconcerted; my enemies are exasperated! That's just fine! I look upon these three movements as an advance guard, since I intend to present the complete work. Then you'll see something! I speak in earnest when I tell you that all this is excellent. It would take too long to explain why. Understand only that this failure gives me back my *freedom,* lets me do as I wish; otherwise I might have succumbed to the weakness of trying to please the public. We'll talk about it later. So don't worry . . . Not even Wagner, perhaps, could boast of such a collection of stylistic extravagances. Now there can be no more doubt about it: either I am a barefaced dilettante without talent or I am someone so original that people don't know how to come to grips with me. Is it my fault if they are afraid of me and would prefer me to be the opposite of what I am?"[30] "In ten years these gentlemen and I will discuss this matter again," Mahler remarked in a letter to Mildenburg. About the same time he wrote to Weingartner: "Considering the Berlin critics—those dying ducks in a thunderstorm—and their flashes of genius, it is only too clear to me that the 'metropolis' of German thought is stony ground in which the 'New Spirit' [*neuen Geistes*] is hardly likely to flourish. No doubt this will gradually be understood. In any case, I consider it an honor now, to share *your* fate, in such contrast to our colleagues."[31] This last phrase is not devoid of irony; nonetheless it is quite obvious that the "boundless ineptitudes" of the Berlin critics wounded Mahler to the quick. Once more he realized that they had "not even understood the surface values, the main lines" of his work. "They have devoured the *Blumenstück,* as donkeys eat hay, without even guessing at its real meaning and true form."[32]

In a combative rather than depressed state of mind Mahler departed for Munich, where he was to conduct the Kaim Orchestra.[33] There, as was his custom, he began to pay "calls." The Bavarian capital was exceptionally important in his eyes because he might be offered the post of director of this orchestra, left vacant by the departure of Hermann Zumpe. He had always felt a particular affection for Munich and had recently tried in vain to be named conductor at the opera.[34]

Mahler was hardly settled into the Hotel Marienbad before he read an article by the Berlin correspondent of the *Allgemeine Zeitung,* in which he was once more torn to pieces: "an excellent introduction" to the Bavarian capital. "I am enormously amused! This makes things perfect and smooths my path, as you can imagine," he wrote to Justi. Luckily he had just received great encouragement from another source. He had seen Strauss again and played on the piano for him the last movement of his *Second Symphony.* Strauss had praised it enthusiastically and had told Mahler that in his opinion he had found the way most suited to him and that now victory could only be a matter of time.

The program of the Kaim Concert at first included the Berlioz *Symphonie fantastique* and the *Blumenstück,* but the latter was dropped because the score did not arrive in time for rehearsals. Mahler then had to resign himself to giving only two movements of the *Symphonie fantastique,* replacing the others with Beethoven's *Fifth Symphony,* because the number of rehearsals and orchestral musicians available were insufficient for a complete performance of the Berlioz. Despite these disappointments he was immediately won over by the orchestra, made up largely of young, enthusiastic musicians with excellent instruments, who at once took a liking to him and tried to play exactly as he wished.

The rehearsals, however, induced in him some bitter reflections on the bad habits of contemporary instrumentalists: "They are incapable of paying attention to the indications and thereby sin against the sacred laws of dynamics and the inner, secret rhythm. As soon as they read 'crescendo,' they at once accelerate and play forte, just as when they read 'diminuendo,' they suddenly lower the volume and reduce the tempo. The other nuances— mezzo forte, fortissimo, etc.—are unknown to them, to say nothing of sforzandos and forte-pianos. If one asks them to play something that is not written, as is frequently the case if one is accompanying singers in opera, when they have to observe the slightest indications by a singer, then they are lost. Nevertheless, they got used to me quickly, and it was a pleasure to make music with them."[35]

After the final rehearsal the public applauded enthusiastically and the orchestra joined in. Kaim himself seemed enchanted and "paid court" to Mahler, who was overjoyed to discover that he had real admirers in Munich, people who had bought and sung his songs. When he made his entrance for the concert on the evening of March 24, he was happily surprised: the hall was full, the orchestra again applauded ("That never happened before") and he saw a famous colleague, Hermann Levi, the old Munich conductor, in the auditorium. The program finally consisted of the overture to *Die Meistersinger,* the second and third movements from the *Symphonie fantas-*

*tique,* and the Beethoven *Fifth.* At the end of the evening the orchestra again took part in the ovation; this time, however, there were also some demonstrations of hostility. Mahler left Munich the next morning in a rather optimistic state of mind, but without having had time to read the newspapers.

Unfortunately the *Allgemeine Zeitung,* the most important Munich newspaper, confirmed his worst fears. All the epithets of a Sittard or a Krause were to be found in the unsigned article! Mahler was described as a "new style" podium virtuoso who had no place in the highest category of those who "promise happiness." He had adopted, in the Beethoven *Fifth,* new tempos and phrasings, because he wanted to be different from his predecessors. This wish to be different was incompatible with a "strict" conception of Beethoven and resulted in an interpretation that was too fast and over-elaborate in the first Allegro, languid and anemic in the Scherzo, "dry and boring."

The same critic admitted that the Andante had some "beautifully poetic" qualities, but found Mahler's instrumental alterations to the Finale more serious than all his earlier errors. Although in the Berlioz *"Scène au bal"* and *"Scène aux champs"* Mahler had shown himself to be an excellent conductor of "modern" music, it would be necessary—if he were to be offered the leadership of the Kaim Concerts—to hire an associate conductor for the classics. But the critic thought it preferable to select someone like Hermann Zumpe,[36] equally at ease in both fields.

While the *Bayerische Kurier* saw in Mahler a "clever, intelligent and thoroughly modern" conductor, "worthy of leading a fine orchestra," the *Sammler* praised the "solidity of his sense of rhythm" and "his desire to bring out all the details of the score," but considered that he worried too much about precision and worked over "the rhythmic and dynamic beauties" of the score until he lost "the over-all line and atmosphere." Finally the *Münchener Post* recognized Mahler's "overpowering will," energy, character, and great and pure feeling for music, but deplored his "virtuoso temperament," which caused him to give his own "mediocre feelings and love of violent effects precedence over the objective contents of the work of art." The orchestra had followed him throughout the concert with exemplary unanimity, zeal, and even reckless abandon, but the performances had been "stormy, uneven and more dramatic than symphonic." Mahler was more interested in small, witty details than in the works' great, expressive moments. His conception of Beethoven made him a daring innovator who turned his back on historical tradition. His performance of the Berlioz had been a real "declaration of faith."

Mahler realized that once again his conception of Beethoven had met with nothing but incomprehension and disapproval and that the Munich public considered him "extremely anticlassical." "I should have pleased them by interpreting Beethoven in their dispirited, senseless manner and then they would have spared me," he concluded bitterly. "But at least in music I want to keep my hands clean; in life, as it is, I am obliged to make too many compromises."[37]

Once more Mahler had shocked and displeased, and for that reason the post of conductor of the Kaim Concerts was not offered to him. Fortunately the situation in Vienna was to develop so swiftly in his favor that he had no time to regret Munich. He had accepted an engagement to conduct in Budapest after the Munich concert, and this gave him a chance to visit Vienna, where he found Natalie Bauer-Lechner and Frau Papier waiting for him at the station with the latest news. After settling into the Hotel Höller, he dined with them and next morning went to see Jahn. As planned, Wlassack had again intervened on Mahler's behalf, and Jahn had been obliged to give his consent to his possible engagement. The old director received him graciously and assured him that as long as he remained director Mahler would not be forgotten, but he added that no decision would be taken before September, when his own cataract operation was due to take place.

Mahler's nomination was part of a large program of reforms involving the two Viennese national theaters—the opera and the Burgtheater. At the instigation of his treasurer general Wetschel,[38] the lord chamberlain, Prince Liechtenstein, had decided to dismiss both Wilhelm Jahn and Burckhard, director of the Burgtheater,[39] as well as the intendant, Freiherr von Bezecny, who no longer wished to retain his post after the departure of the two officials whom he had personally named. Sensing that a wind of change was blowing, Jahn had handed in his resignation in January,[40] hoping that it would be refused. The intendant had not replied to Jahn's letter, and Prince Liechtenstein had later reproached him bitterly for not accepting the resignation. Jahn finally decided to favor Mahler's nomination, for he did not know what was going on behind the scenes, and he thus hoped to keep his own post a little longer. All the hesitations and delays that so worried Mahler sprang from the fact that Bezecny knew that soon he would no longer be intendant and was therefore unwilling to make any important decisions.[41]

After his visit to Jahn, Mahler went to see Wlassack and Bezecny, and during the two days he spent in Vienna he also renewed contact with some old friends, including Brüll, Fritz Löhr, and the Hoffmans. No one in Vienna believed he could be nominated, since his race was considered an insurmountable obstacle, and as a result there was no time for an opposition to form. This was in fact the principal reason for his success. The most varied and absurd rumors filled Vienna: even Bezecny's departure was widely attributed to a reason far from the truth: the opera's annual deficit under his management.[42]

Mahler left Vienna on March 28 for Budapest, where he stayed at the Hotel Reine d'Angleterre. He was permitted three short rehearsals for a Philharmonic concert to be given for the benefit of a newly formed Syndicate of Journalists. The program once more included Beethoven's *Fifth Symphony*, preceded by the *Rienzi* and *Tannhäuser Overtures*, the *Blumenstück*, Weber's *Invitation to the Dance*, orchestrated by Weingartner,[43] and two arias from *Fidelio* sung by Sophie Sedlmair, a soprano from the Vienna Opera. Mahler was greeted with open arms by his Hungarian friends, who were so happy to see him again that they competed for the pleasure of his company. At the supper given in his honor after the concert, he gallantly declared that on crossing the Danube en route to Budapest he had 'felt that he was returning to his native land."

The success of the concert was considerable. When he appeared onstage, he was greeted by an ovation. This was repeated at the end of the evening, when two immense laurel wreaths were presented to him. The *Blumenstück* was particularly well received—and this small, unexpected triumph helped to make up for the unhappy 1889 concert. Beer described it as a "bright, pleasant spring picture of simple design and delicate shading." He found the instrumentation "piquant" and "somewhat exotic," but the whole was "decorative" and, he thought, "too elegant for a big, serious symphony." Rather incongruously he compared it to a Delibes ballet. He warmly praised Mahler's interpretation of the Beethoven *Fifth*, full of life, "directed by an energetic, yet sensitive hand."

Herzfeld was even more enthusiastic in the *Neues Pester Journal*. He, who had condemned Mahler's *First Symphony* with such violence, marveled at the *Blumenstück,* the "musical symbolism" of which made him think of contemporary literary and pictorial symbolism rather than the programs of Strauss. "Mahler's orchestra coos and caresses, whispers and rustles, buzzes and chuckles until it lulls the listener into the indescribable enchantment of a fresh spring day."

After the concert a huge supper for two hundred people was given in the ballroom of the Redoubt in honor of the "illustrious musician." Some divas from the opera, among them Szilágyi, Maleczky, and Diósy, attended this festive occasion, which was accompanied by speeches and toasts. Hungary thus tardily made up to the courageous ex-director of the Budapest Opera for the way it had treated him six years earlier.

Returning to Vienna on April 1, Mahler found that Jahn's departure had already been announced in the newspapers. No doubt in order to favor Mahler's nomination, Hanslick had published in the *Neue Freie Presse* on March 27 a violent attack on Jahn, the departing director, emphasizing the poverty of the repertoire and the defects in the "ensemble" of singers.[44]

Mahler once more began to pay visits and got in touch with Ludwig Karpath, a newspaperman he had known in Budapest. A born intriguer, Karpath knew every detail of the negotiations,[45] which he had sworn to keep secret. Two days later Mahler left Vienna for Hamburg. On April 4 he saw Bezecny and agreed in writing to accept a possible offer of a one-year contract with the Vienna Opera as of June 1, with an annual salary of five thousand florins (the final offer to reach him before April 14). The day before, Johannes Brahms, one of his most illustrious supporters, had died in Vienna after a long, painful illness, but Mahler was unable to attend the funeral, which took place on April 6, because a hail of telegrams demanded his immediate return to Hamburg.

On the evening of April 6, Mahler was to have conducted *Andrea Chénier* in Hamburg, but this performance was given by Krzyzanowski, for Mahler was still on the train, where he met Weingartner, who had been conducting the Berlin Philharmonic in Vienna. Before Mahler's departure the intendant had sent the lord chamberlain an official letter in which, "given the frequent absences of Kapellmeister Fuchs and the present illness of Director Jahn," he recommended hiring Mahler as a conductor. Jahn added a footnote to this letter, stating that he had no objection to this engagement, should "the General Administration deem it necessary." Nevertheless, on April 7, the *Neue Freie Presse* announced that Jahn was about to take a leave of absence to go to Karlsbad for a health cure, and that the two principal candidates for the post of director were still Schuch and the director of the Czech Theater in Prague, Schubert. The news finally broke on the evening of April 8. A laconic communiqué in the *Wiener Abendpost,* the official government newspaper, announced that "Herr Gustav Mahler has been engaged as *Kapellmeister* at the Opera." The astounded editors of the chief newspapers searched everywhere for Mahler in order to interview him, only to learn that he had left two days before.[46] They were thus obliged to publish the facts alone, pointing out the secrecy that had surrounded the negotiations. The *Neue Freie Presse* raised the essential question, "Will Mahler be just another conductor, together with Fuchs, Richter, and Hellmesberger, or is he intended to fill a different position?"

On April 9, Mahler wrote to Regierungsrath Wlassack to thank him and ask for his support "in the struggle ahead of me." He had found himself in a somewhat similar situation in Budapest, but then he had been in complete control, whereas in Vienna he was going to have to face numerous difficulties. This letter was in fact a roundabout way of asking Wlassack not to relax his efforts to have him named director of the opera. Since Pollini was still absent from Hamburg, Mahler was not yet able to say when he could start his work in Vienna. For his debut he suggested that he should conduct a Wagner opera or *Fidelio,* which would satisfy both the Wagnerians and the classicists. The first thing to do, in his opinion, was to draw up the plans for the coming season and remedy the disastrous poverty of the repertoire. "I shall be Jahn's successor," Mahler wrote on April 12 to Behn, "and I have already been named conductor in an important capacity [*leitende*]. Now I have to get the agreement of my torturer Pollini, but he will not raise any objections." Mahler's contract was ratified by the administration on April 15, but in the meantime he had telegraphed on the twelfth to announce that he would be free on the twenty-sixth. On April 10 the intendant's resignation was announced, and Mahler immediately feared that the anti-Semitic press would infer from this that his nomination had been the cause of the crisis (the truth was exactly the opposite), so he wrote to Karpath and Rosa Papier on April 11 to ask for their advice as to the attitude he should adopt in this "comedy of intrigues."[47] Happily his fears were unfounded: his enemies did not foresee his future nomination as director; if they had, Karpath believed that they would certainly have prevented it.

Also on April 10 one of the two anti-Semitic papers, the *Deutsche Zeitung,* had recognized the need to engage a new conductor because of Jahn's poor health, Richter's frequent absences, and Fuchs's absorption in his duties as director of the conservatory. It was true that in Budapest Mahler had proved himself to be a musician and a man of the theater, but Vienna did not lack "young musicians just as gifted as Mahler," men whose names had a "good ring" to them. "Whether Mahler could accomplish something here, should he really be called upon to head the institution, would depend upon his attitude toward his colleagues. To act without asking for Richter's advice would be most unfortunate; but it does seem as though, by making decisions behind his back, someone is trying to push the greatest German conductor to the point where he will lose the last vestige of interest that he may still have in the Hofoper. And if this should happen, farewell, Hofoper, despite Mahler, Jahn and company!" The article ended with an attack on the "frightening Jewification of art in Vienna." Was a Jew capable of defending "our great music . . . our German opera," even if, like Mahler, "he had just been baptized three weeks before?"[48] The appointment—and here the critic of the anti-Semitic paper was totally ill-informed—was the last mocking gesture made by Jahn's outgoing administration.[49]

On April 15, Mahler read in the Munich *Allgemeine Zeitung* an article that once more aroused his anxiety: it attributed to him a "declaration of principle," projects for reorganization, dismissals and new engagements. Would not this story turn the entire staff of the opera against him before his arrival? "Heavens," he wrote, "what a nest of hornets I have stirred up! . . . But I shall do what is right, without fearing anyone, and if I don't please these gentlemen, so much the worse for them! What a rabble! Both my friends and enemies!!"[50] "I had no idea that the administrative crisis would break out so soon," he wrote to Weingartner,[51] "and I am far from pleased! My head spins in this journalistic whirlwind. I must now seize the bull by the horns, but—between ourselves—I am not in the best of tempers, for I will now have to deal with a complete stranger—the new intendant!"

The last weeks in Hamburg drove Mahler "almost mad." He was so relieved, however, to escape from Pollini's prison (*Zuchthaus*) that he scarcely noticed how tired he was. He again conducted the annual Good Friday concert, made up of the Mozart *Requiem* and the Bruckner *Te Deum,* as well as some classical arias.[52]

Mahler was to conduct three more times in Hamburg—two performances of *Carmen* and one of *Das Heimchen am Herd,* before his farewell benefit evening on April 24, for which, as usual, he chose *Fidelio.* When he mounted the podium, he was greeted by a triple fanfare from the orchestra.[53] The *"Eroica" Symphony* and the *"Leonore" Overture No. 3* were then wildly applauded by an enthusiastic audience, and many spectators waved their handkerchiefs. No doubt Mahler "wished them to regret his departure," for he surpassed himself. Only some "arbitrarily" performed passages and the insufficient force of the orchestral strings seemed open to dispute, according to the Hamburg correspondent of the *Neues Wiener Tagblatt*. Mildenburg had been "impressive" in *Fidelio,* though her portrayal of *Leonore* was not yet completely mature. At the close of the evening Mahler received from Pollini, the members of the orchestra, and the public a mountain of wreaths and flowers, in front of which he bowed some sixty times. He then expressed his thanks to all those who had supported him, and who now "overwhelmed him in this manner."

Except for Pollini, certain critics, and the failure of the subscription concerts, Hamburg had given Mahler little to complain about, for it had fully recognized his genius as an interpreter, at least in the opera house.[54]

All Mahler had to do now was to say good-by to Mildenburg. How had their affair progressed during this last winter? Six months earlier, during his last stay in Bayreuth, he had spoken of the young singer to Cosima Wagner and had strongly recommended that she be engaged for the 1897 festival. Frau Wagner had later written asking for more detailed information, and Mahler's next letter, dated October 24, 1896, was entirely about Mildenburg: "She has aroused the highest hopes," he wrote, "her voice is of exceptional beauty and power, she is tall, her face can express everything from the childish to the demoniac, she has immense dramatic talent and treats her work seriously and with great enthusiasm—in short after only a year of theatrical activity she is more than worthy to appear on the Bayreuth stage." But would Pollini allow her to accept a summer engagement, while her contract with him still had three and a half more years to run? That was the problem, for this "young genius" was "a prisoner" of theatrical routine, subjected to all the evils of the profession, constantly obliged to sing new roles after only one or two rehearsals. If Frau Wagner hired her, Mahler agreed to coach her fully in her roles.

It is clear from another letter, written by Mahler in December, that Cosima had asked Mildenburg to audition for the role of Kundry.[55] It is quite obvious from these letters that Mahler still took a warm, artistic, and personal interest in the girl's future. His relationship with her still seems to have been fairly close throughout the winter. Although his letters are fewer than in the preceding year, they are affectionate and trusting. When she reached Bayreuth at the end of February, Mildenburg found the following note: "My dear good Anna! I salute you in Bayreuth! Soon you will find yourself in a place where one of the most magnificent spirits that ever existed among men once ruled. This awareness should enable you to overcome any timidity you may feel upon approaching its present inhabitants. Always remember: he would be pleased with you, for he sees into your heart and knows all your abilities and your aspirations. Few have started out better prepared than yourself. You can be sure of that!"[56]

To encourage her, Mahler also told the young woman of the failure of her rival, Ida Doxat, who "sang off pitch from beginning to end" in *Aïda*. The tone of the letter is affectionate and more humorous than usual: "You ask me if I miss you. How wicked of you! Can you doubt it? Do you think it is any different for me than for you? When one is accustomed to such a sweet 'tormentor,' when the time comes when one used to go to that horrible boardinghouse in Magdalenstrasse, then enter a certain beloved room, take that usually unruly little head in my hands and cover it with . . . then of course one misses many things! Just wait: when you come back, I shall show you what I mean!"

Later, when speaking of Mildenburg to his wife, Mahler tried to minimize everything concerning this affair, in order to avoid her retrospective jealousy. Alma's statements on this subject cannot therefore be trusted. Despite what Mahler later told her, there was no brutal leave-taking before his departure from Hamburg, even though Mildenburg had tried to trap him by asking a Dominican monk, a certain Father Ottmar, to her home in order to celebrate her marriage to Mahler. The latter acted as any man might do in such a situation: he took advantage of his departure to end their relationship without violence: "I cannot say farewell to you and I am heartbroken. Yes, I know we both feel the same way. When you read these lines, I shall be on my way to Vienna and I shall write to you in detail as soon as I arrive. *Au revoir,* my darling, my dear little Anna! . . . May this forthcoming separation, which we must accept, be only physical! The tie that we have formed must never be broken: I am yours, my dear, and I shall remain faithful to you! I beg you, my Anna, to live as though you always felt my eyes upon you and never to do anything important without first asking me about it! . . ."

The words are less passionate, the tone less sincere than in the past. The real break took place later, when Mahler learned that Mildenburg had been engaged by the Vienna Opera without his knowledge. This liaison, which brought him more trouble than happiness, had nevertheless been his longest, most intense affair.[57] Mildenburg had considerable influence on his future, and she indirectly contributed to his Vienna nomination. Her influence was also determinative in another major event of his life, one that always remained veiled, for Mahler never alluded to it later: his conversion. To the Hungarian composer Mihalovics and to the journalist Karpath[58] he declared that he had been converted long before there was any question of the Vienna Opera. Yet his baptism took place on February 23, 1897, in the Kleine Michaeliskirche in the Sankt Angar district of Hamburg,[59] when his negotiations with the Vienna Opera had nearly succeeded. It is therefore clear that he embraced the Catholic religion because he knew that his native Judaism would prove an insurmountable obstacle to his appointment. Rosa Papier and Regierungsrath Wlassack had convinced him of the absolute necessity of this conversion and probably even advised him to lie about the date, for the first secret opera reports already give his religion as Christian.[60]

Mahler concealed the truth even from Karpath, to whom, however, he gave the reason for his conversion: "to escape from Pollini's *inferno.*" But he added: "I do not hide the truth from you when I say that this action, which I took from an instinct of self-preservation and which I was fully disposed to take, cost me a great deal.[61]

Mahler's attitude toward Jews and Judaism was already complex. Though he had been brought up in an Orthodox Jewish family, nothing proves that as an adult he practiced the religion of his forebears or that he ever belonged to a Jewish "community." He was often ill at ease among other Jews, if he became aware of their too sharply marked Hebraic characteristics,[62] and, as his own marriage was to prove, he always hoped to see the two "races"—Christian and Jewish—mix.[63] He considered himself above all Austrian and Viennese and only became really conscious of his origins between 1894 and 1897, when his race appeared to be an insurmountable obstacle to his career. But he never liked to hear this subject treated lightly, nor would he listen to any of the "Jewish stories" so common in Central Europe.

However wary one must be regarding arbitrary generalizations, some facets of Mahler's character appear deeply Jewish. For too long Christian civilizations have been ignorant or have pretended to be ignorant of the spiritual tradition of Judaism, the cradle of Christian thought.[64] It cannot be denied that Wagner was both the inspirer and the spokesman of German anti-Semitism at the end of the nineteenth century; for him Judaism meant the lowest form of materialism. A violent polemicist, he was ready to judge according to his own personal experience[65]; it was enough for him that Mendelssohn had conducted his music badly or that Meyerbeer had been more successful than himself for him to consider all Jews to be materialists who therefore deserved what they got.

The trouble was that Wagner's ideas were shared, consciously or unconsciously, by a large number of Germans and Austrians. Mahler's fierce idealism, his artistic fanaticism, his unending devotion to "causes"—and he suffered the frequently disastrous consequences of these qualities every day of his life—were the exact antithesis of the "materialism" so decried by Wagner. So, unable to make such a charge against Mahler, some of his contemporaries associated his "Judaism" with the "banality" of his music and compared him unfavorably to Richard Strauss, the Germanic superhero, heir to the pure, immortal "Aryan" tradition. In fact, the "impurity" of Mahler's style was typical of the period rather than of the man, and Strauss's music is just as "impure" as Mahler's; yet such was then the prevalent opinion. Further, it is hardly logical to condemn Mahler's "blending of styles" (one of the principal causes of his present popularity) and the "quotations" he introduced into the "noble" genre of the symphony and not to address the same reproach to Strauss, whose operatic heroines all dance the Viennese waltz—even Elektra, that terrifying spirit of destiny and revenge.

Mahler's personality, like that of all great men, was rich in contradictions, but the mixture of optimism and pessimism that characterized him is, according to André Siegfried, one of the essential traits to be found in the children of Israel. The long wait for the Saviour and their unshakable belief in the coming of the Messiah are, in fact, fundamental. "In the manner of the Puritans, who inherited this tradition from them, the Jew is metaphysically an optimist. In his eyes, the Kingdom of God must be realized on earth for and by the Chosen People . . ." Among both Puritans and Jews a dangerous deviation often sidetracks "this ardor toward money and the accomplishments of this world . . ." This is what leads to such a respect for success and prosperity and, as a result, "the next life fades into the background and all energy is channeled toward success in this one."[66] Mahler was indeed ambitious, but only in so far as he needed to exercise an activity worthy of him. He had all the qualities necessary for managing a theater, but, unlike Strauss, money and the financial management of his career were always of secondary importance.

Alongside this instinctive and metaphysical optimism, there exists among Jews, still according to Siegfried, a deep, centuries-old sadness, a tragic sense of man's destiny, well expressed in the great verses from the Psalms: "As for man, his days are as grass: as a flower of the field, so he flourisheth. For the wind passeth over it, and it is gone; and the place thereof shall know it no more."[67] Though Mahler has often been accused of self-pitying sentimentality, his sadness is of the same metaphysical and ancestral, rather than subjective and introspective, form. Thus his art is not truly pessimistic, since man's salvation and eternal life are never in doubt. Mahler is a poet of suffering, but he does not revel in it. He accepts it as an inescapable reality, but he also transcends it. Finally, true to romantic tradition, he considers it a purifying force that lifts man high above the absurdity of everyday life.

Restlessness and a striving, questing spirit are, in André Siegfried's opinion, the other fundamental characteristics of the Jewish people: "If one looks more closely, the striving seems even more fundamental than the fulfillment that, to a certain degree, limits its absolute, divine character . . . Minds that can be described as 'finite' take pleasure in possession, but 'infinite' minds take more pleasure in striving, confident of ultimate success; preferring to pursue the hare rather than to catch it!"[68] In this sense Mahler was essentially an 'infinite' spirit; he never stopped searching for new ways of improving and perfecting every detail of his compositions and interpretations; he was never satisfied with the present and often seemed to change his mind, for, to a person enamored of truth, beauty is always new and accomplishment always betrays the ideal image. This was why Mahler hated traditions, habits, everything that is comfortable and established, everything that blunts the senses and tarnishes inspiration, everything that does not well forth from an almost supernatural source.

In his wife's words Mahler was *"ein Christgläubiger Jude"* (a Jew who believed in Christ), and the *Second Symphony,* which he wrote prior to his conversion, does indeed reveal his taste for the Christian mystique. The very concept for the Resurrection, around which this work was constructed, is not a fundamentally Jewish idea. It was widespread in the Jewish community at the time of Christ, but it was a "deviation from the original thought" of

Judaism, made "at the cost of weakening the intransigent claim for earthly justice."[69] If the *Third Symphony*'s glorification of nature and of life seems pantheistic, almost pagan even, the *Second* is obviously closer to Christian thought. Like many great men, Mahler was little concerned with orthodoxy and religious pratice. During his instruction in Catholicism he never ceased putting embarrassing questions to his catechist, with "the pride of an Old Testament adept."[70] In one of his programs for the *Second Symphony*, describing the moment when the risen dead come before their Creator, according to Mahler there will be "neither justice, nor sinners, nor judges, nor great nor small, nor punishment, nor reward: a feeling of universal love will fill us with blissful awareness of existing."[71]

. Thus, despite his deep and ardent mysticism, Mahler never practiced Catholicism, yet he execrated atheism as much as materialism. Nourished during his formative years by the great German philosophers, and moved by a profound Dostoyevsky-like pity for man's suffering, he always "believed" and, while composing, never ceased to express his faith and compassion for the ills of humanity. "We shall all return," he told Specht[72] in 1895, "and only the certainty of this gives meaning to our life. It is immaterial whether or not we remember our previous incarnations. This does not depend upon the individual, his memory, or his willingness, but upon the great progression toward perfection, upon the purification that sweeps through each incarnation. That is why I must live ethically, in order to spare my future 'ego' some part of the road and thus render its existence easier. Therein my moral duty resides, whether or not my future 'ego' knows of it or thanks me for it."[73]

"Every injustice done to me is an injustice toward the whole universe and must pain the Almighty spirit [*Weltgeist*] (or whatever else one may call the 'essence' of the universe)," Mahler told Specht on another occasion. "If I hurt my little finger, I feel pain not only in my little finger, but the functions of *my* body are impeded. It is the same in the larger sense; even though I cannot consider myself as the little finger of the cosmos. Goethe spoke *infinitely* of this. What I want to say, I naturally can only express in music. I am a musician and nothing else. That is what has been given to me, and it is on this alone that I have accounts to render." Here we come to the very essence of Mahler's thought. He whose life is ruled by such a philosophy can elude no problems and always prefers dangerous, difficult solutions—which to him appear the most positive ones. He will never lose sight of his mission on earth and will constantly aim higher. Forced to be ever bolder, often despite himself, he will be exposed to the disdain and hostility of his contemporaries and accused of desecrating tradition.

According to Alma Mahler, he always liked visiting Catholic churches and loved both the incense and the Gregorian plain song. It is hard to appraise, on the basis of such superficial details, the faith that conditioned his entire personality and life as well as his art. If he had not so firmly believed in some supreme and mysterious order, Mahler would have felt useless, a squanderer of nothingness. Joy and hope rather than fear conditioned his faith: he never stopped believing in the miracle of life and the grandeur of man's destiny. The essence of his spirituality and his amazement when faced with atheism and materialism are reflected in the following passage from a letter he wrote to the Viennese critic Max Kalbeck[74]: "I cannot understand that you, with your musician's and poet's soul, find it impossible to believe in anything that elates you when you experience music. What is it, then, that makes you so light and so free? Is the world less enigmatic if you construe it materialistically? Is it an explanation to consider it as the play of mechanical forces? What are those forces? And who 'plays' them? You believe in the 'conservation of force' and the indestructibility of matter! Well, isn't that immortality? Put the problem in any form you wish, you will always reach the point at which your 'wisdom' turns 'to dreams' . . ."[75]

"A homeland! A homeland at last!"

# CHAPTER 25

*Vienna and Viennese Music — Conditions at the Opera*
*(May–July 1897)*

Much has been written about Vienna, yet no one has been wholly successful in explaining the legendary charm that has endeared the city to the hearts of so many artists; so far no one has clearly defined the magnetic forces that have attracted so many composers and for so long made it the musical capital of Europe. Geographically speaking, Vienna is undoubtedly the center, the pivot, of Europe. It is the ideal meeting place for north and south, for east and west, for such different ethnic groups as Italians and Slavs, Germans and Turks, Magyars and Bohemians, all of whom have blended together to form one single and exceptionally vigorous culture. In 1900 Vienna was already a cosmopolitan city and an imperial capital, while Germany had only just emerged from the long Middle Ages to achieve unification. Vienna was both loved and hated, but its magic name was never mentioned without admiration and a touch of envy. Gustav Mahler, a provincial boy with a simple family background, had discovered this enchanting world at the age of fifteen and had never completely recovered from the shock of revelation; so it is easy to imagine his secret triumph when he arrived in 1897 to take up a key position in the capital of German music.

Much of the irresistible attraction of Vienna springs from its miraculous setting among some of the most bewitching landscapes in the world. Lying just south of the Danube, whose banks (not particularly picturesque at this point) it disdains, the city stretches across a plain whose borders rise toward the south and west. The suburbs spread gradually up these gentle slopes, as urban Vienna blends into the foothills of the Wienerwald, thickly covered woodlands in which the clear green of deciduous trees contrasts with the deeper green of conifers. The Viennese forest extends to the west of the capital as far as the Danube, dominating it at Kahlenberg and Leopoldsberg. Outside the gates of the city, for as far as the eye can see, lies such a calm, contrast-filled and friendly landscape that no one who has ever seen it can call it to mind without emotion. The architecture of the villages, with their long, low, freshly whitewashed houses, their colored roofs, latticed windows, flower-filled gardens, and climbing vines, carries visitors several centuries back into the peaceful past.

To the west of the town, on the slopes of Heiligenstadt, Grinzing, and Nussdorf, the visitor can follow in the footsteps of Schubert and Beethoven, whose houses still exist, while in the rural creeper-covered taverns the passer-by can pause in the shade to taste the fresh-pressed wine, the *Heuriger*. All the inhabitants of Vienna go there to escape from the urban bustle and to enjoy the popular orchestras, made up of zithers, clarinets, accordions, and violins—the famous *Schrammel-Musik*.[1]

At the end of the nineteenth century, Vienna was an imposing metropolis of two million inhabitants, and the decadence of the empire was hidden beneath a luxurious exterior. While Germany, for so long divided into tiny provinces, had no capital worthy of the name, Vienna was a universal cosmopolitan and European city in which Slavs, Germans, Hungarians, Spaniards, Italians, Frenchmen, and Flemings lived in peaceful cohabitation. This mixture of races, and the welcome that Vienna extended to foreigners, attracted these different elements, and they in turn gave the city its own physiognomy, its atmosphere, and its role as the capital of Central Europe. Vienna was a catalyst, a melting pot in which the most varied elements, cultures, and geniuses were blended and fused.

As an imperial capital, Vienna offered artists a field of activity infinitely richer and more varied than any of the German cities; this was why so many German musicians, among them Beethoven and Brahms, had settled there. Life in the hospitable, luxurious, and sensual city was elegant and cultured, while in the German principalities it remained narrow, provincial, and crude. In Vienna the artistic talents were cultivated with care; so was the art of knowing how to please and the art of conversation, combined with good taste, moderation, tolerance, and courtesy.

Viennese politeness was legendary. Titles such as *Herr Doktor, Herr Professor, Herr Kammersänger* (chamber singer), *Herr Opernsänger* (opera singer), *Herr Hofrath* (court counselor), *Herr Regierungsrath* (government counselor), and special forms of greetings like *Euer Gnaden* (Your Grace) and *Gnädiger Herr* (gracious sir) were characteristic of Austrian good manners. Nonetheless, the amiable character, the permissive morality, the conciliating disposition hid passions that could become violent, and even dangerous, as the success of the Nazi ideology in Vienna was to prove. Yet courtesy was law and tolerance was considered a moral obligation, even between deadly enemies; they insulted one another in writing but were courteous when they met.

One of the most striking aspects of Viennese life was that of the coffeehouse, a type of democratic club accessible to all for the modest price of a cup of coffee, where one could spend hours conversing, writing, or playing cards. A large portion of the bourgeoisie and officialdom spent part of

each day there discussing events, exchanging ideas and impressions, and
—above all—engaging in intrigue, for this was one of the most striking,
though not one of the most appealing, sides of Viennese life. Regular cus-
tomers had their own tables, their letters were sent direct to the café of their
choice, and they never failed to find Viennese and foreign newspapers
awaiting them punctually. If someone wanted, for example, to meet such-
and-such a journalist, businessman, or musician, it was enough to go on any
day at a specified hour—generally during the evening—to the café that he
favored. Nobody was surprised to receive an important visit in a café. Some
Viennese would frequent the same establishment all their lives, and every
day the waiters would prepare the same blend of coffee and hand them their
newspapers, their correspondence, and their messages. Most political decisions, even some of historic importance, were made in cafés.

When Mahler reached Vienna, the Emperor Franz Josef was sixty-seven
years old and had reigned for almost fifty years. The unity of the empire
depended, in principle, on reactionary political philosophy and the state
religion, Catholicism. The very fact that the Emperor had nonetheless placed
a Bohemian Jew at the head of the principal cultural establishment of the
empire reveals an astonishingly liberal state of mind. Thanks to the absence
of anti-Semitism among the Habsburgs, and Franz Josef in particular, an
especially happy symbiosis was established in Vienna between the Austrians
and the Jews, who played an essential part in the city's life. The Jewish
bourgeoisie had taken over from the aristocracy as patrons of the arts and
artists.[2] They had become part of the spirit of Vienna, and at the end of the
nineteenth century were to produce a whole series of creative talent, including
Mahler, Schoenberg, Goldmark, Hofmannsthal, Schnitzler, and Max Reinhardt. In a city whose principal quality had always been that of harmoniz-
ing and uniting the most varied ideological, ethnic, and linguistic groups, the
Jews lived and worked in peace, feeling themselves free from all restraint
and prejudice.

Unfortunately, it cannot be said that anti-Semitism was unknown to the
Viennese; it occurred even during Mahler's stay there, and in a particularly
unpleasant way. The financial crisis in 1873 had sparked off the first wave,
with the Christian Socialists waxing indignant over the large areas of land
belonging to "cosmopolitan financiers" rather than to "national families."
And when anti-Semitism was finally organized into a party that became the
forerunner of Nazism, its supporters immediately suggested replacing the
Christian calendar by one that dated from the Battle of the Forest of Teuto-
burg. The *Deutsche Zeitung* and the *Deutsches Volksblatt* never stopped
attacking Mahler in ways and in terms that were already typical of Nazi
anti-Semitism.[3]

In 1879 the Minister Taafe restricted Jewish freedom and limited Jewish
access to schools and universities. In 1895 one of the leaders of the Anti-
Semitic Party, Carl Lueger, was elected Mayor of Vienna and became
very popular because of his physique and great talent as a speaker. Lueger

was to head the city's affairs right up to World War I, and he knew how to exploit to his own ends the discontent of the embittered middle classes, as did Hitler later. It is his sad privilege to have discovered the political expediency of the word "anti-Semitism"; by offering a scapegoat to the middle classes, he channeled their hatred away from the large landowners and the still-feudal aristocracy. Nonetheless he displayed a remarkable sense of justice in his handling of the city's affairs; during his administration the Jews held the same rights and positions as before. According to Stefan Zweig, in spite of the virulence of some extremists, the "good Jewish bourgeoisie," which had brought so many essential qualities to Viennese culture, led a peaceful, quiet, and usually happy life.

About 1750 the exploits of Frederick the Great at the head of the Prussian armies had started to bring about the political decline of Austria and at the same time had led to the rise of the newly formed Prussia to a dominant position within Germany.[4] This Austrian decline was partly concealed by the prosperity of Vienna and the brilliance of its culture, particularly daz-zling in the field of music. At the turn of the nineteenth century, as the political difficulties became insoluble for a government that lacked both effi-ciency and vitality, the dominant Viennese characteristics were a sort of pessimism, a hedonism, and an amused, blasé, and often morbid skepticism. The Austrian state of mind was well summed up at the end of World War I, when it was said that, for the Germans, the situation was "serious but not desperate," while for the Austrians it was "desperate but not serious."

In Vienna, where tolerance and politeness were considered essential, youth was suspect. Respectability was epitomized by "serious, ponderous, slow-moving men": "My father, my uncles, my professors, the salesmen in the shops," wrote Zweig, "and the musicians behind the podium were all portly and imposing men of forty." Beards and gray hair were considered the attributes of dignity, and any manifestation of high spirit was considered unseemly. The bourgeois society above all appreciated moderation and calm, and no one ever gave the impression of being in a hurry. "For all posts which called for a sense of responsibility, age was considered one of the essential qualifications." Vienna, unlike Berlin, a newer capital, worshiped its past and considered anything new with prudence and reserve if not hos-tility. The Vienna-born Max Reinhardt would have taken at least twenty years to achieve, in his native town, the rank that he obtained in Berlin after only two. So most of the Viennese reacted with a mixture of surprise and indignation to the nomination of a thirty-eight-year-old Jew to head their opera, and this conservatism was to be a terrible obstacle for Mahler.

The essential problem for Viennese artists, then, was to reconcile their cosmopolitan tendencies, their easy life, and the destructive cynicism of a people conscious of its political decline with the passion, the stubbornness and the intransigence essential for any important artistic work. This political decline of Vienna and the Austrian Empire increased the Viennese taste for culture in general and for music in particular. Since the Austrian monarchy had abandoned most of its political ambitions and lost face on the battlefields, the patriotic pride of the Emperor's subjects took the form of a strong determination to conquer artistic supremacy. Military and political affairs no longer played a preponderant part either in the life of individuals or of society. The average Viennese citizen, on opening his paper, would not look first for the account of the parliamentary sessions or the reports on world affairs, but for the theater news.

The president of the City Council or the richest banker in the capital might well walk down the street without being noticed, but all the salesgirls and coach drivers would immediately recognize a famous actor from the Burgtheater or a prima donna from the opera. In the schools the pupils boasted of such encounters with pride: these well-known personalities were in a sense the collective property of the Viennese, and this fanatical cult for the fine arts was common to almost all classes of society. The citizens greatly valued concert halls, theaters, and other places devoted to the arts. When, for example, the Rosé Quartet gave a concert to mark the closing of the Bösendorfer Saal, the audience was still in their seats, sobbing bitterly, an hour after the end of the concert, remaining even after the lights had been turned out.

Wherever one went in Vienna, people were ready to discuss the Burgtheater or the opera; portraits of leading actors decorated all the shopwindows, and the day before important premieres at the opera young college students would play truant and queue for hours to obtain standing room. Stefan Zweig tells us that he showered a boy in a lower class with presents because, as the nephew of the lighting inspector at the opera, he could smuggle Zweig onstage during rehearsals. There he would "tremble like Virgil when he rose up into the sacred spheres of Paradise." This universal Viennese love of spectacle has often been mocked, for it even extended to funerals, marriages, and other manifestations of public life. But such theatromania led to the amazing quality of the lyrical and theatrical performances: the audiences were so well informed that they noticed the least fault, missed entrance, and smallest cut. Thus the artists were constantly obliged to give of their best; there was no margin for error.

Music and opera had been at the center of Viennese artistic life for two centuries, and the violence of the passions roused by Mahler during his years there would have been unthinkable elsewhere. Indeed, music still has real power in Austria, and national vanity is particularly susceptible on this point; the Austrians are justifiably proud of their artists and their musical life. For ten years Mahler's prestige and fame were to be measured against those of the Vienna Opera. Attacked, insulted, incessantly vilified, he nonetheless became one of Austria's national glories, one of the most outstanding personalities in musical Europe.

The Vienna Opera, the Hofoperntheater, was constructed between 1861 and 1869, in neo-Renaissance style, on the Ring, the site of the ancient ramparts. It was built at the same time as the Paris Opéra, which it matched in grandeur and in the magnificence of its ornamentation, if not in its site. Built in eight of the most troubled years in Austrian history[5] by Eduard van der Nüll and August Siccard von Siccardsburg, the opera cost in all six million gulden.[6] Even before it was completed, scandalous rumors were circulating in Vienna: the building was sinking, there were fatal errors in its conception, and improvised couplets were sung in the streets at the expense of the two architects, predicting the most dishonorable of failures. This is a typical example of Viennese ingratitude, for once the edifice was completed it was found that, apart from a few minor errors inevitable in a project of such importance, the building was a success and the theater acoustics almost the best in Europe. The two architects did not witness their triumph; deeply affected by the campaign against him, Van de Nüll hanged himself in 1868, and his colleague Siccard von Siccardsburg died the same year of heart disease.

The 1945 bombardments left only the walls and the main staircase of the original building, but at least its exterior has been preserved. In Mahler's time, the huge auditorium provided seats for 2500 people and standing room for 500 more. The extensive, recently electrified stage machinery necessitated fifty permanent stagehands and a dozen electricians. For big productions, sometimes as many as thirty-five additional stagehands were employed. The annual subsidy granted by the Emperor rose during the final years of Mahler's reign to 600,000 kronen, enough to cover the deficit. Many spectators bought annual season tickets for all performances except court galas,[7] but there were also tickets for half or a quarter of the season, which ran from August 1 to June 15 and included more than three hundred performances.

Apart from the opera, the most famous musical institution in Vienna was the Philharmonic Orchestra. Its musicians were those of the opera, but they formed an independent democracy, elected their own leader each year, and gave eight subscription concerts, and one benefit concert, every second Sunday morning in the Musikvereinsaal, a hall that seated 1500 people.[8] Another symphonic association, the Konzertverein, gave popular concerts and twelve symphonic subscription concerts in the same hall.

Besides the opera, two theaters—the Volksoper, in principle reserved for operettas, and the Theater an der Wien—held performances of lyric works, and four choral societies regularly took part in orchestral concerts[9]: the Akademischer Gesangverein, the choir of the Gesellschaft der Musikfreunde,[10] the Singakademie, and the Männersingverein. Vienna thus had an exceptionally active musical life, which also included numerous recitals as well as concerts of chamber music and touring German orchestras.

The internal and administrative structure of the Vienna Opera was complex. Its administration, like that of the Burgtheater (the Viennese equivalent of the Comédie Française), and indeed all the artistic affairs of the empire, was in the hands of Prince Rudolf Liechtenstein, the Lord Chamberlain (*Erster Obersthofmeister*), a high official and administrative dignitary who did not concern himself closely with theater affairs. While he occupied this post, and during all of Mahler's time there—that is to say, up to 1908 —the opera was in fact administered by Liechtenstein's assistant and future successor, Prince Alfred Montenuovo, a grandson of the Empress Marie Louise and Count Neipperg.[11] It was to him that Mahler had to justify his theatrical activities, for the Emperor almost never interfered. Elegant and aristocratic, with a gray beard and mustache, Montenuovo was as well known for his cold, determined character as for his unswerving convictions. His stubbornness was as famous as his lasting resentment, which even death did not dispel, as he proved by his behavior on the very day of the funeral of his enemy, the heir apparent, after the assassination at Sarajevo. This rather stiff but extremely dignified and exacting bureaucrat deeply admired Mahler and protected him to the very end from all the intrigues and "scandals," and even against the administrators of the opera. He believed in both Mahler's artistic genius and his moral integrity, and it was with regret that he saw him leave ten years later.

Prince Montenuovo had his office at the Oberste Hoftheaterdirektion in the Imperial Palace, and his office manager was the famous Franz Freiherr von Wetschel, who had been criticized for his excessive interference in opera affairs at the end of Jahn's reign. Wetschel's authority was in fact much diminished after Mahler took over. The intermediary post between the Oberste Hoftheaterdirektion and the artistic direction was held by the theater intendant, Baron August von Plappart. His office was some distance from the opera, in the Bräunerstrasse, and he was concerned almost exclusively with technical and financial matters. Eduard Wlassack, Rosa Papier's friend and Mahler's patron, was the administration's "director of the chancellery." He had hoped that Mahler's appointment would enable him to keep control of the opera's affairs, but Mahler did not consider himself responsible to anyone but Prince Montenuovo. A conflict broke out almost immediately, but Mahler resisted either actively or passively all of Plappart's and Wlassack's efforts to interfere. Wlassack's attitude reminded him of "those princes who elect one of their number Emperor, and then all try to reign together." He added, "I am the Emperor, and I am determined to reign." Wlassack was finally forced to give way, but the struggle was long and bitter, and Mahler found him a dangerous enemy.

Later Mahler was to control an army of opera musicians, technicians, and several producers, but when he arrived on April 27, 1897, he was still only a conductor and shared performances with the director Wilhelm Jahn, with Johann Nepomuk Fuchs—the brother of his former harmony professor—with Joseph Hellmesberger, who was mainly responsible for ballet performances, and, above all, with Hans Richter,[12] Wagner's protégé from early youth. Richter had conducted many Bayreuth premieres in the presence of the Master, as well as several first performances in Vienna. His many supporters considered it scandalous that he should not have been made Jahn's successor, though he had no administrative talent and already spent a great deal of his time in England. Richter had not been consulted about Mahler's engagement, and frowned upon the arrival at the Vienna Opera of a colleague twenty years his junior, who, like himself, specialized in conducting Wagner and who was well known for his exacting character and his "modern" ideas. Richter himself embodied tradition, with all that implies of self-indulgence and inflexibility.

Foreseeing the difficulties that this collaboration would entail, Mahler had written to Richter before leaving Hamburg: "Since my earliest youth, you have been my model, and through all the difficulties and troubles of theatrical life I have tried to emulate you. With what rapture did I listen and watch when, as a young man, I attended performances you conducted at the opera and in the Musikverein hall! Later, when I myself took that frail wooden baton in my hand, the memory of your exploits always guided me. When doubtful about something, I always asked myself: 'What would Hans Richter do?'

"Until my dying day, I shall be proud to express the unwavering admiration that I feel for you. This is what impels me to write to you today, for, since I have been accorded the honor of working near you—within your sight, so to speak—I finally have the opportunity of expressing to you all I have felt for so long. I can imagine no greater joy than pleasing you, and should I fail in this, I beg you to give me the benefit of your masterly advice. I am completely at your disposal! It would be a great pleasure to me if I could relieve you of any task unworthy of you or that might in any way be disagreeable to you! I beg you to have confidence in me; I will do all I can to deserve it."[13]

The admiration expressed in this letter was only partly sincere, for Mahler was in the habit of referring to Richter as "honest Hans" in his letters, considering him too faithful to tradition. However, his intentions were commendable, as he wished to live in harmony with his famous senior. Mahler's efforts, however, were unsuccessful: his personality as an interpreter was too different from Richter's and he could "learn" nothing from him. Richter's reply to this letter was reserved and arrogant. Mahler would find him "a colleague full of good will" once Richter was "convinced that Mahler's contribution would be of use to the opera and dedicated to the highest values of art." In fact, Richter was no more capable of appreciating Mahler's art than Mahler was capable of appreciating his. Their generations were irremediably opposed, though there was never any open clash.

For the time being, though, Mahler's nomination to the post of director was far from settled and there remained many difficulties to be overcome: "It's true I must be prepared for a fight, but I would like to be the referee,"[14] wrote Mahler before leaving Hamburg, and he added: "My appointment to Vienna has, for the moment, brought into my life nothing but extraordinary apprehension and anticipation of numerous struggles. I'll have to wait a while before I'll know if this is a suitable post for me. In any case, I must be prepared for a year of bitter opposition from all those who don't

want to follow me or can't follow me (the two usually coincide). Hans
Richter, in particular, will do everything possible to make hell as hot as possible for me. But—*Vederemo!* My life here was not a bed of roses, and especially of late, I have had to put up with many affronts. A new chapter is
beginning, but I am returning home, and I shall do everything possible to
put an end to my wanderings for good . . ."[15] "What gives me the greatest
happiness," he wrote in another letter, "is not the fact that I have secured
a seemingly most important post, but rather that I have a homeland, a homeland at last, that is if the gods will only guide me! For I must be ready for
a terrible struggle."[16]

On April 26, the day after his farewell Hamburg performance, Mahler
departed, leaving Justi with the job of completing the move. Upon his arrival
in Vienna he settled into the Hotel Bristol[17] and on the same day called
upon Bezecny and Wlassack: "Everything has gone much less badly than I
feared," he wrote to Justi. The Viennese were in fact at their most charming, and several papers had already sent reporters to interview him. His first
meal was at a supper party given in his honor by Rosa Papier. Mahler's
initial week in Vienna was entirely spent in making official requests and
personal calls. Like all the singers who were newly engaged by the Vienna
Opera, Mahler called on every important critic, in order not to neglect any
possibility of ensuring his success.[18] Jahn was still away, but he summoned
Mahler upon his return to Vienna, on May 2, a Sunday morning. Mahler
had to wait some time, for Richter had preceded him in Jahn's office. The
old man received him very pleasantly and introduced him to his nephew
Chordirektor Hubert Wondra, now the opera's artistic secretary. He suggested that he make his debut with Mozart's *Don Giovanni.* "What could
give me greater pleasure than *Don Giovanni?*" Mahler wrote to Justi. Later
in the week it was decided that he would conduct *Tannhäuser,* and at one
time there was also talk of *Hans Heiling,* before they finally decided on
*Lohengrin.*

Since Pollini was in Vienna and staying in Mahler's hotel, they met in the
hall. A "touching meeting," Mahler wrote ironically to Mildenburg. The
Austrian author Hermann Bahr happened to be talking to the director of
the Hamburg Opera at the time when Mahler appeared. He never forgot
his entrance, "like a gust of wind suddenly opening a window, like water
gushing from a pipe . . . like some element." Mahler disappeared a few
moments later, and "the wind dropped, the fountain ran dry." "A strange
man for a conductor, don't you think?" said Pollini, while Bahr tried to recall the memory that Mahler's sudden apparition had stirred. All of a sudden he knew; Mahler had reminded him of Hugo Wolf, though the two
men were as dissimilar as possible. Wolf had often made Bahr think of a
handsome prince who had been changed into an animal. Now here was
Mahler, another animal, this time stray and half wild. Both seemed marked
in the same way; perhaps they lay under the same enchantment. Their ar-

tistic genius was stronger than their personal characteristics: man and music were inseparable, the man was music and the music was man.[19]

The day after his arrival, Mahler once more saw Jahn, who asked him to leave immediately for Venice, in order to attend the world premiere of Leoncavallo's *La Bohème,* which he wished to produce the following season. Before leaving Vienna on May 4, Mahler had his first meeting with Prince Liechtenstein, the lord chamberlain, who received him for half an hour with "extraordinary politeness." Mahler was favorably impressed by this first meeting.[20] Jahn was also extremely kind; Richter began to "show himself as being human," and only Johann Fuchs seemed irreconcilable, doubtless because "he lived in the well-founded fear of henceforth having to limit his gymnastics on the podium." Worn out from walking up and down so many stairs, dazed from the effort of being charming to so many people, Mahler left for Venice on the evening of May 4 in a most optimistic state of mind. His career seemed assured, and he would probably be made director in the autumn. Vienna, with her most enticing smile, had welcomed the prodigal son's return.

At the Hotel Britannia in Venice, Mahler met Pollini, and together they went first to the Teatro La Fenice on May 6 and then to the San Benedetto Theater on May 7 to see the two operas based on Murger's *Scènes de la vie de Bohème.* Violent controversy had raged around the two works in Italy; the whole thing had started one day when Puccini met Leoncavallo by chance in a café and announced that he was at work with his librettist on a *"Bohème."* Leoncavallo had furiously reminded him that he himself had suggested this subject sometime earlier and had decided to work on it only after Puccini had refused to consider it. Puccini denied this hotly and replied, "In that case, there will be two *Bohèmes!"* The next day the paper *Il Secolo* announced Leoncavallo's coming opera, and that same evening the *Corriere della Serra* announced Puccini's. The conflict opposed the two chief Milan publishers, Ricordi and Sanzogno, and Puccini won the first round by finishing his opera well before his rival. His *Bohème* was presented for the first time in Turin on February 1, 1896, whereas Leoncavallo's was only staged a year later in Venice, which was when Mahler saw it.

In a letter addressed to Jahn on the day of his return, Mahler states that Puccini's work was by far the better. The music was both new and easy to understand; the orchestration was "very effective"; the voices were admirably treated; the libretto was interesting and ably conceived. As for the "perils inherent in the subject," Mahler thought that a "certain decency [*sic*] of diction, added to the charm of the music, would enable them to be overcome." Some of the more "shocking" aspects could in any case be toned down. "However, I cannot speak in similar terms of Leoncavallo's work," he continued. "The music is without originality, and poor in inspiration, in spite of all the technical refinements. The text of the first two acts is boring; the third sentimental in the worst sense of the word, and even

lewd. It is mainly for this last reason that a performance in our Royal
Theater seems to me impossible," he added. "Given the sterility of contemporary operatic creation, I should like to intercede for the acceptance
and presentation of Puccini's opera at the Hofoper, if such performance
would not involve insurmountable difficulties."[21]

Posterity has confirmed Mahler's judgment, since Leoncavallo's *La Bohème* has long since disappeared from repertoires, whereas Puccini's has
lost none of its charm and popularity. But Mahler's efforts were in vain
because Jahn was on excellent terms with the composer of *Pagliacci*, and
had already committed himself. The Vienna Opera was therefore one of the
few that chose Leoncavallo's *Bohème* rather than Puccini's. It was the fact
that Jahn was about to leave that prompted Mahler's suggestion, for he
knew he would inherit his unfortunate choice. As in Italy, Puccini finally
won the race between the two composers; his opera was staged at the
Theater an der Wien in September 1897, for the smaller theater, generally
reserved for less important works, was able to put on a production much
more quickly than the huge Hofoper. When Mahler became director, he had
to respect Jahn's commitments and therefore unwillingly presented Leoncavallo's *La Bohème* the following February (see Chapter 27).[22]

Back in Vienna on May 7,[23] Mahler set about preparing for Monday,
May 11, the day of his debut at the Vienna Opera. To his delight *Lohengrin*
had finally been chosen instead of *Tannhäuser*. On May 8, the day after
his return from Venice, wishing to get the feel of the auditorium, he went
with Natalie to a performance of *Die Meistersinger* conducted by Richter,
on whom he passed the following unkind judgment: "I enjoyed the performance very much at first. He conducted Act I like a master, Act II like
a schoolmaster, and Act III like a master cobbler."[24]

On the morning of May 10, Jahn officially introduced Mahler to the orchestra, making a brief speech in which he declared that "he has been engaged to help me and take some of the weight off the shoulders of the conductors." Mahler replied in a speech he had prepared with great care,
speaking with assurance despite his nervousness. He said how conscious he
was of the honor of working with "such glorious collaborators." This diplomacy was received somewhat coolly, however, doubtless because the
listeners had already heard of his "tyranny," and his "exorbitant demands."[25] He then started rehearsing the Prelude to *Lohengrin* and immediately regained his peace of mind; he "discussed each point in detail
and went through everything from A to Z." For the rest of the work he
had to make do with rehearsing a few isolated passages with some of the
singers, particularly the baritone Benedikt Felix, whom he forced to sing
the Herald in stricter time.

Mahler had expected difficulties and serious resistance from the orchestra:
instead he was delighted by the result of their work: "In a single rehearsal
I accomplished more with them than in years with others. It is true that the
auditorium of the opera idealizes the tone quite incredibly just as defective

acoustics elsewhere can give an astonishing crudity and grossness to any sound."[26] But most credit must go "to the inborn Austrian musicality, the élan, the warmth, and the intrinsic natural feeling each brings to the task."

Two days before Mahler's debut Viktor von Herzfeld published in the *Neue Musikalische Presse* an enthusiastic article introducing the new Hofoper conductor and describing him as "a musician through and through . . . an impetuous character tempered by a keen intellect . . . dramatic to his fingertips," irreproachable except for an "excess of nuances," but it was impossible not to admire both the way he could simultaneously control both stage and orchestra and his uncommon knack of blending the visual and aural worlds. In Budapest, Herzfeld recalled, *Die Walküre, Lohengrin, Don Giovanni,* and *Le Nozze di Figaro* had been performed at the opera with rare perfection by a man who possessed all the qualities of a conductor and a stage director, and who was in addition inspired by the most idealistic motives.

Although Mahler's debut had been announced only a few days before, the atmosphere in the auditorium was electric on the evening of May 11, 1897. All Mahler's champions were present: Wlassack in his box, Karpath with Rosa Papier in the stalls, Natalie and the Spieglers in the circle—all of them strained and anxious. Apart from them, almost no one in the auditorium knew Mahler. At the end of the Prelude, the "sublime slowness," the "nuances and subtle gradations" of his interpretation were striking enough to earn a first round of warm applause, which Mahler acknowledged several times. It was at once clear that the battle had been won. Soloists, chorus, and orchestra surpassed themselves, and during the performance the atmosphere was tense both onstage and in the auditorium. According to Natalie, the audience applauded each time Mahler's tempos differed from the customary ones; after the prelude to Act III and at the end of the performance the enthusiasm was at its height. A crowd of young people, probably students from the conservatory, gathered outside the stage door to acclaim Mahler, and their enthusiasm pleased him even more than the unanimous approval of the critics. "They feel what I felt at their age," Mahler remarked later. "After longing to hear works that I knew only from the score, the performance was always a cruel disappointment, because usually only a fraction of what was actually written was brought out. When one finally hears everything, when the effect sometimes even surpasses what one has imagined, then one's joy and gratitude toward the man who has made this possible are boundless."

After the performance, Mahler had supper at the Grand Hotel with old friends, among them Albert Spiegler and his wife, Professor Grün, later a first violinist at the opera, and Karpath, whom he questioned as to the reactions of the critics, in particular Richard Heuberger[27] of the *Neue Freie Presse* and Max Kalbeck[28] of the *Neues Wiener Tagblatt.* Karpath gave him wholly favorable replies, for the enthusiasm had been unanimous. The next day's articles proved him right. Ludwig Speidel's particularly pleased Mahler. The critic of the *Fremdenblatt* began by comparing his conducting to his physical appearance, "full of energy and noble understanding," with gestures that "characterize and embody the spiritual contents of the work." Speidel continued: "Mahler entered fully into the dreamlike music of the Prelude, and it was only at the climax, with the wind fortissimo, that he suddenly took the entire orchestra in hand; with an abrupt, energetic gesture, he lunged toward the trombonists as though with a foil. The effect was magical . . . He noticed everything. He was in close and constant touch with the chorus, the orchestra and each individual; not one performer missed his smallest gesture . . . Nothing could show more consideration for the ailing director of the opera nor be of more active support for him than the placing of such an artist at his side. Herr Mahler will certainly have a good artistic influence on the opera, provided he is given a free hand."

In the *Neues Wiener Tagblatt*, Max Kalbeck, one of the city's most influential critics, at once ranked Mahler among "the elect." His conducting was a deathblow to "routine" and proved that he was "capable of far more than directing a Wagner opera." He had given *Lohengrin* a completely new aspect, and, though certain details had been surprising, on the whole it made a "highly significant and artistically agreeable" impression. The Prelude had never been conducted so slowly, but the result had been entirely satisfactory. As for the vivacity and rhythmic energy of the dialogue, usually dull and long drawn out due to the singers' bad habits, they "seemed to have been set free," and the chorus was greatly improved, Kalbeck wrote. "Wagner's dramatic crescendos, with their long-awaited climaxes, were wholly effective," and the audience had accepted Mahler's innovations with surprising willingness.

In the *Wiener Abendpost*, Robert Hirschfeld[29] drew the following portrait of "the conductor, so recently appointed and already such a talking point." He was "all life and movement . . . Even his profile seems to radiate energy, will power, and a desire to forge ahead." Hirschfeld described the light movements of Mahler's baton: "He not only indicated the rhythms, he brought each measure to life; and he knew how to obtain all he wanted." For the orchestra, Mahler was often "content to jerk his upper body, or turn significantly his head," but he "never took his eyes off the singers, imposed his will on everything taking place onstage, conducted, enlivened, attenuated and suppressed individual voices in the ensembles. In this manner, the vast onstage organism remained in a constant state of tension and animation . . . He has eyes for everything but the score, which he knows completely. His glance, therefore, can even linger on the chorus, and enter into a visual dialogue with its leaders, when necessary. His movements are as clear and distinct as his artistic intentions: not a single finger movement is without meaning; there is no motion without inner motivation." From the Prelude on, the audience seemed won over, and warmly applauded the Act III Prelude. The choral performance seemed "transfigured," though certain piano passages suffered because of the present stage positioning of the chorus.[30]

In the *Neue Freie Presse,* Richard Heuberger, who was gradually taking over from Hanslick, was equally enthusiastic. "Mahler is not only extremely self-assured and full of temperament, he is an excellent dramatic conductor and has a sense of the theater: his attention does not stop at the footlights— in fact, it really begins there. He gives the correct rhythm to the chorus and the soloists, which is most essential to a meaningful interpretation. It is already clear that Mahler prefers the fluid tempos that Richard Wagner loved. He will not tolerate any dragging or distortion. From the orchestra he obtains extreme discretion in accompaniment, but also great power when it is required for dramatic effect. It was a joy to watch our Philharmonic players attentive to its new conductor's smallest batting of an eyelid, and to see them convert his clear and eloquent signals and gestures into sound."[31]

Finally, an anonymous critic in the *Neue Musikalische Presse* praised the total victory that Mahler had won, thanks to his "spiritual force," his "unusual energy," and his "artistic and human personality . . . Just as complete works of art [*Gesamtkunstwerke*] exist, so Mahler is a complete orchestral conductor [*Gesamtdirigent*]. His concern is for the orchestra, the singers and the chorus alike. His glance, his will, his gestures command and unite the ensemble of performers. He thereby achieves not a sum of parts but a unified whole . . . A small gesture with his head or his left hand, a slight movement of his body, indicates a detail, while a firmer gesture underlines the essentials, the principal voice, which must be brought to the fore. His gestures are subtly graded: each signal is of such eloquence, each intention so easily grasped, that singers and orchestra follow him easily and joyfully, as if they had been used to him for years." The same writer then praised the "clear and controlled" performance of the Prelude and the "magic sound" of many passages, such as the Act II choruses and the appearance of the swan. A "virile and noble" artist, Mahler brought to his work a dedicated earnestness. Certain people wished to "make life difficult" for him at the opera, but all secret and unofficial opposition must surely give way before such a performance.

The most surprising of all these laudatory articles was undoubtedly that in the anti-Semitic paper, *Deutsche Zeitung,* whose critic, Theodor Helm, asserted that "Mahler has done well," that he was a "musician of wit and character," that he knew the work "thoroughly," that he had put an end to the singers' shameful abuses and made them keep in time, and that, exactly like Wagner on March 2, 1876, he had conducted the Prelude "with unusual slowness," but every note seemed to sing.[32] "Everything was admirably precise, clear, and artistically beautiful, in particular the choruses." Entirely won over, Theodor Helm, in spite of his paper's bias, made only one small reservation: he claimed that the choruses sang better under Richter. His remarks so closely resemble those in an anonymous letter addressed to Mahler the day after this debut that it seems almost certain Helm was the

writer. The author of this letter claims never to have heard anything like
this *Lohengrin* since Wagner's death. The tempos, the nuances, and the
rhythmic stresses had seemed, in the real sense of the word, "Wagnerian."
"This was how the Master interpreted his work, this was how it was played
under his direction; unfortunately since then all has been forgotten."[33]
"Your conducting is truly Wagnerian, since you know how to modify the
tempo in the spirit of the Master,"[34] concluded this anonymous musician,
who considered that "since Wagner and Bülow, no orchestral exploit has
been comparable to yours."

Immediately after this debut Mahler wrote to Justi, who was still in
Hamburg, and sent her the most important press cuttings. He was delighted
by their unanimity. "The anti-Semitic papers are either silent or favorable,"
he wrote with truth. "The orchestral musicians, etc., etc., are quite won
over." In the same letter he reproaches Justi for complaining about his silence. He can hardly find the time to breathe. While waiting for a permanent place to live, he had taken a small furnished flat,[35] after giving up the
idea of an apartment in the Brülls' house, "because of the anti-Semites."
The family cook, Elise, was to come to Vienna since she could sleep in the
"well-lighted" kitchen while waiting for him to find permanent quarters. His
chief occupation for the moment was still "a constant succession of congratulations, visitors, etc.," but "thank God, my worries are over! All
Vienna welcomes me with real enthusiasm . . . I am almost certain to be
appointed director soon."[36]

Mahler's euphoria increased during the succeeding days: Jahn had assigned to him *Die Walküre, Siegfried, Le Nozze di Figaro,* and *Die Zauberflöte,* and the importance of these operas showed that he wished Mahler to
be on an equal footing with his colleagues. For *Die Walküre* on May 26 he
was even allowed to rehearse the singers as he pleased. "Before the vacation, I hope to be firmly entrenched here," he told Justi. "Only when you
come to live here will you realize how much more humanely I am treated,"
he wrote in another letter.

In these early days, Mahler wished to avoid hurting Mildenburg's feelings
and lessened the pain of separation by writing to her constantly, despite his
many other occupations. He assured her again that "sooner or later everything will come right for us." Mildenburg had received a contract offer from
America which he advised her to refuse, for he feared she would tire her
voice by singing too much and thought the proposed salary unworthy of
her.[37] When Justi heard of the advice her brother had given Mildenburg,
she supposed that he had opposed the project so as not to prolong their separation. "Natalie is a fool and so are you," Mahler wrote to her. "I never
even thought of that. I advised her not to go to America because she could
easily lose her voice there. Under no circumstances will she come here.
Those are only the schemes of Papier and Natalie, etc. . . . I have had
enough of their constant gossiping, and now have other things to worry

about." In another letter: "I hope your vertigo is cured," he wrote to Justi on May 25. "It is an illness often found in sheep."

It seems that, before leaving Hamburg, Mahler promised Justi that he would not marry Mildenburg. His reserve can be sensed beneath the affectionate tone of his letters, and it was with considerable uneasiness that he learned shortly afterward that in fact the engagement of Mildenburg in Vienna was being seriously considered.

On May 18, during a short trip to Dresden, where he had gone to attend the premiere of an opera by Anton Rückauf,[38] *Die Rosenthalerin,* Mahler caught a cold. He returned to Vienna still suffering from it, and the infection gradually settled in his throat, forcing him to stay in bed for several days. He got up to conduct rehearsals of *Die Walküre,* but the performance finally had to be canceled at the eleventh hour because the Sieglinde, Luise von Ehrenstein, was taken ill. Mahler then devoted himself to preparing two of his other Vienna "debuts": *Der fliegende Holländer* and *Die Zauberflöte.* During a rehearsal of the latter, he realized that he could not obtain a sufficiently quiet effect from the cellos, for the strings were as numerous as for a Wagner opera. Amid general applause, he at once sent away about half the orchestra. "What success!" he said, smiling. "But, gentlemen, don't imagine that I'm trying to please you! It is my conviction that so large an orchestra can only destroy the delicacy and magic of the Mozartean work."[39]

Mahler was already full of grandiose projects, in particular a revival of *Der Freischütz* with new tempos and simplified staging. A year later he faithfully carried out this project, but, as this passage in Natalie's memoirs proves, from the moment of his arrival in Vienna he was envisaging new experiences and already foresaw some essential elements of his operatic reform: "Existing décors and costumes should go to the devil." He planned to guide the public's taste in another direction; one in which imagination "must play an essential role."[40]

During rehearsals of *Die Zauberflöte* and *Die Walküre,* Mahler's persistent cold developed into a serious sore throat. No sooner did this seem better than an abscess appeared. On May 21[41] he took to his bed, getting up only to attend rehearsals. Exhausted and feverish, he could scarcely utter a word, and until the very last moment he was not sure if he would be able to conduct the performance of *Die Zauberflöte* on May 29. Natalie, who took great care of him in Justi's absence,[42] brought him by carriage to the opera and was relieved to see that, when he started to conduct and the music gradually took possession of him, he began to forget his illness. On the way home, Mahler proudly pointed out to Natalie that his tempo in the Overture has been almost twice as slow as usual, thanks to which he had been able to accent each eighth note in the theme, thus giving it an altogether different character. He added that the performances he conducted were often shorter than the others, even though he always gave the melodic elements their full value, without ever hurrying. The difference in a Wagner opera could be as great as half an hour, he said, because "most conductors don't know how to distinguish the essential from the subordinate and give the same importance to all passages, instead of just lightly passing over those that are secondary."[43]

The success of *Die Zauberflöte* almost equaled that of *Lohengrin*. In the *Neues Wiener Tagblatt*, Karpath wrote that "a spirit breathed through the performance, one that has been absent for a long time: the spirit of Mozart." He also praised Mahler's purity of style; he is "as sensitive to Mozart as to Wagner." All impression of routine had been banished from the stage, and everyone had made an effort to "sing in style." Theodor Helm was equally enthusiastic in the *Deutsche Zeitung:* in his opinion ten rehearsals at least must have preceded the performance, and the new conductor had a miraculous influence over the singers' diction and phrasing. The ensemble was admirably "Mozartean" in style, though "perhaps overly subtle."[44]

The excitement and pleasure of performing had enabled Mahler to forget the state of his health, but next morning he suddenly felt worse and the doctor found a second abscess forming in his throat.[45] A specialist was summoned, and he decided to lance it immediately. The pain was so great after the operation that Mahler could not eat or even swallow: that evening he received an injection of morphine.

After spending three days in bed, Mahler considered himself sufficiently recovered to conduct a third performance on June 5. This was *Der fliegende Holländer,* on which he also managed to impose his personality, despite the insufficient preparation. "I have succeeded here," he told Natalie, "because of my inner drive [*Furor*], which in my view is indispensable to any true conductor. It enables him to wrest from even the most mediocre orchestras, choruses, and singers, a realization of his own inner image of the work. This is the reason why I fly into such a rage when they play or sing badly or out of time . . . If a woman of whom I was attracted sang a single false note or unmusical phrase, all my affection for her would vanish instantly, and might even turn to hatred. Inversely, a beautiful voice or some other manifestation of musical talent has bewitched me many times."[46]

After this performance of *Der fliegende Holländer,* Theodor Helm, critic of the *Deutsche Zeitung,* once more expressed unreserved enthusiasm. He compared the "freshness and decisiveness" of the Overture and of the choral passages to Fuchs's "superficial and purely conventional" interpretation. The audience, moreover, had clearly sensed the difference, for the Overture had been enthusiastically applauded, something that had never happened before. Urged on by an enthusiasm and love for his profession infinitely greater than his predecessor's, Mahler had a beneficial influence over the soloists.

Heuberger admired the firm hand "that orders and purifies all" and the "conductor who penetrates to the very heart of the work of art." He particularly remarked upon the improvement in the chorus, which, after a long eclipse, had come out into the light.[47] In his opinion "the only really important innovation during the past season is 'Gustav Mahler.'"

Feeling himself unanimously supported like this by the Viennese press was some consolation to Mahler, for he heard no more talk of his appointment as director. Jahn appeared to consider him as an indispensable assistant and as a means of hanging onto his own position. But if Mahler did not get the post of director, he would be content to continue as conductor, provided they gave him a long contract and sufficient remuneration. At the same time he thought he might be able to take over the direction of the Gesellschaft concerts.

After *Der fliegende Holländer,* Mahler should have remained in bed for almost a week. He had a high fever and felt very weak. On June 6, however, he conducted *Lohengrin* again, and this time Justi, who had joined him in Vienna, was in the audience. But it was to be feared that the abscesses would recur; a physician warned him of the possibility of chronic "nasal catarrh" and prescribed daily throat painting, a later operation to remove his tonsils,[48] and several days' complete rest. Mahler finally asked for a leave of absence before the end of the season, for the heat in Vienna was increasing daily and he had been advised to rest and convalesce in the mountains. Natalie and Justi had already rented a small house in Kitzbühel, about 2600 feet above sea level, so Justi, Emma, and Elise, the cook, left on June 11, and Mahler joined them three days later. The Villa Hohenegg was "the most attractive yet of all our summer places." The view was superb and the climate excellent. Mahler was already considering constructing a *Häuschen* and a house there when three days later an epidemic of scarlet fever broke out in the village. As none of the three Mahlers had ever had this dangerous disease, they decided to abandon this paradise, especially since Mahler was still very weak. So they had to bundle up the scarcely unpacked luggage and seek a vacation spot elsewhere. They stopped briefly at Innsbruck[49] before finding in Steinach am Brenner a most attractive house that was unfortunately rented to a Munich family from July 1.[50] During the last ten days of June, Mahler's health gradually improved, thanks to the fresh air and the daily throat paintings administered by Justi.

"We live entirely cut off from the world," Mahler wrote to Rosa Papier. "Our little house is completely isolated and peaceful, on the edge of a forest, and surrounded by meadows. Only Johann and Nandl come every day to bring us the mail, spinach, chickens, etc. The marvelous air and the refreshing calm have already half made me into a Hercules (the other half, unhappily, is decidedly absent). We take walks across the hills and in the forests around us, and from time to time we bathe in the nearby Schwarzsee. When it is too hot, we sleep or read. Such is the faithful description of life as I do not ever remember having lived it before. When, by chance, I have twinges of conscience, I quickly remind myself that I am a convalescent; a dignified state that I have only known for the last two weeks; so then I sink back into a *dolce far niente.*"[51]

Mahler and his sisters, however, had scarcely time to appreciate a comfort that seemed like paradise after the uncomfortable inn in Steinach, before they had to make way for the Munich tenants. Moving up toward the

Brenner Pass, they selected a much less pleasant residence in Gries. But it turned out to be too uncomfortable, and once more they had to leave. This time they went a long way on foot and by bicycle, reaching Ridnautal, near Sterzing,[52] on the Italian side of the Alps. In this high altitude, Mahler was delighted to find both rain and cold, after the canicular heat of the preceding days. Contrary to expectation, all this bustle and constant moving had no ill-effects. It kept him occupied and brought him into close contact with nature, an experience he had not known for several years. The incessant moving about also kept him from thinking too much about his creative work, a thought that descended like a black cloud over the idle, sunny holidays whenever he forgot that he was convalescing.

One day, as Mahler and Natalie were bicycling down from Gries to Innsbruck, he began to zigzag across the road impatiently. At that spot the road ran beside a deep ravine that had been formed by a torrent. As they reached a corner, a moment's distraction or a rut in the road made Mahler swerve, and his bicycle ran over the edge of the ravine. He tried in vain to hold it back, then had the presence of mind to catch hold of a bush providentially growing on the downward slope. By great good luck he and the bicycle remained there, suspended over the void, and, apart from a few scratches on his hands, he came out of the adventure unscathed.

Mahler was always delighted to go climbing,[53] and invariably he descended with a feeling of regret. "It's the same when I compose," he explained to Natalie. "When I have taken flight (as, for example, in the Finale of the *Second*), when I have reached a summit, I leave it with great reluctance, unless it is to reach for another, even higher one, unattainable during the first ascent."

Every time that Mahler found a quiet, picturesque spot on one of his walks, his imagination built a *Häuschen* there, and some distance away, out of earshot, a house. At the end of one excursion he discovered in Vahrn, near Brixen (nowadays Bressanone), a villa whose "Mediterranean gaiety" enchanted him. He decided to finish his vacation there and spent long and unusually idle hours contemplating the landscape. "It's a magnificent scene, mysterious and promising," he would exclaim ecstatically, "like a joyful future stretched before us. It is so beautiful that I believe I could create here!" So, after all his long exploratory trips, it was finally in Vahrn that Mahler decided to spend the following summer. There he rented the Villa Artmann, in which, by an irony of fate, he was to spend one of the most gloomy and unproductive summers of his whole life.

"I am hitting my head against the
walls, but the walls are giving
way . . ."

# CHAPTER 26

*Mahler in Vienna (II) — Substitute Director — Open-
ing of the New Season — The Opera under Jahn (July–
September 1897)*

During Mahler's summer of convalescence, which brought him so many
hopes and fears, he once more had to face a problem that he had thought
solved before he left Hamburg. If he had not broken completely with Mildenburg then, this was probably in order not to hurt the young singer's feelings, and perhaps also to avoid antagonizing her onetime singing teacher,
Rosa Papier, for it was mainly thanks to the latter's efforts on his behalf that
Mahler had received the Vienna appointment.[1] His first Vienna letters to
Mildenburg were friendly and even somewhat paternal in tone. After refusing the offers from America, she sang that summer in Bayreuth, and
Mahler still gave her much advice. From time to time he even allowed himself a touch of irony. "It seems that my star is in the ascendant again in
Hamburg: it appears that Fräulein Sachs is now thinking of having me appointed conductor of the Philharmonic. If things go on like this even Marwege may finally consider me a tolerable conductor . . . As for that goose
Artner, ignore her. I am delighted they once more find so many good things
to say about me. I've heard this from several sources. What a pack of
scoundrels! I can't tell you how disgusted I am when I think about them. I
beg you, steer clear of them."[2]

Toward the end of June the trouble started: Mahler received a telegram
from Mildenburg asking him not to read the registered letter that he was
about to receive. What it contained is open to speculation. At any rate, the
young singer had doubtless become aware of the change in the tone of Mahler's letters during the past few months. Rosa Papier had strongly urged
him to beware of renewing their liaison, and though this intrusion into his
private life annoyed him intensely, he well knew it was sound advice.

Early in July, Mildenburg's engagement in Vienna, which until then had seemed uncertain, was confirmed by the administration, and a Vienna paper immediately announced that it was Mahler himself who had arranged to have his "girl friend" hired. However, it seems doubtful that he had intervened in her favor as strongly as he later asserted; it is far more likely that his sole aim had been to please Rosa Papier, since Mildenburg was, after all, her best pupil, and the only one who had succeeded. In a letter dated July 9, Mahler advised Mildenburg not to discuss her expectations with anyone. He had told Bezecny and Wlassack how talented she was, and they planned to ask Pollini to free her for the autumn of 1898. In Venice, Pollini had given him to understand that he might consent, because the Emperor of Austria had just granted him one of his highest decorations. Mahler felt confident that Anna's certain success in Bayreuth would "force her enemies and those who envy her to lay down their arms," but he preferred to cancel his proposed visit there in order not to provoke fresh gossip. Finally, he urged Mildenburg not to drop her negotiations with Berlin, since nothing was as yet decided in Vienna.

Her engagement was evidently going to be ratified sooner than he expected, for he wrote to her again at the end of July, before leaving the Tyrol. "I feel obliged to speak frankly and to ask you an important question that, despite my desire not to upset you at such an important moment,[3] I cannot put off any longer. I have prepared the ground for you in Vienna to such an extent that, with Pollini's consent, they will soon be sending you an offer of engagement. If you accept, it is essential (I now perceive clearly) that we restrict our personal relations to an absolute minimum, in order not to make life intolerable for one another again.

"The entire opera personnel is on the alert because of the gossip from Hamburg, and the news of your engagement will burst like a bomb. If, therefore, we were to give the slightest reason for further gossip, *my own position* would rapidly become untenable and I'd have to pack my bags again, as I did in Hamburg. You too would suffer once more, even though your job would not be in danger. I therefore ask you now, dear Anna, whether you feel strong enough to accept an engagement that would mean our working together here in Vienna and yet avoiding all personal contact and preferential treatment, at least for the first year? I trust you realize that this will be just as hard for me as for you and that these words are dictated solely by dire necessity. The stakes are too high, and I cannot— nor have I the right—to leave either of us with the slightest illusion.

"I beg you, my dear Anna, however busy you may be, to give me a brief, if necessary, but frank and sincere answer! You will soon receive the offer. The difficulties with Pollini will be smoothed out without your having to intervene. But now that the whole matter is almost settled, I am beginning to get cold feet, and I ask myself, as I am asking you, just *what* we are taking upon ourselves? Please, answer me at once, for so much depends on your reply. I fear we may be imposing an unbearable ordeal upon ourselves and, if you feel the same way, I beg you quite simply to refuse the offer and accept the one you will shortly receive from Berlin. Whatever happens, it can only benefit you to have been solicited by the Vienna Opera, and that is why I have let matters go this far without telling you. I beg you to answer me quickly and candidly, even if only in a few lines. I'll give you further details as soon as I receive your letter . . ."

Mahler's firmness on this occasion was due to the fact that "the worries and humiliations of the last months in Hamburg are still very fresh in my memory."[4] Although Mildenburg's answer has disappeared, there is no doubt that she accepted Mahler's conditions without admitting to herself the break between them. Later, in fact, she was to complain that he "had erected an impenetrable wall between them from the very first day she entered his office in Vienna."[5] The firm letter that Rosa Papier wrote to her in September strikingly reveals Anna's behavior and character:

"Mahler has just left me. It has now been decided that you are to sing as a guest star in December, with a view to a contract. Mahler said he would write to you today . . . I beg you to be reasonable and not to claim that Mahler compromised you. It was your fault if he stayed with you until late at night and it was you who chose to advertise the whole affair in your usual way. Now you must simply put up with the consequences of your foolhardiness. What is so disastrous? What have you got to complain about? He did not dishonor you, thank God, and for the two of you to marry would be calamitous, absurd, idiotic, sheer folly! Since marriage is out of the question, why continue your liaison? If you were to see one another as often as you did in Hamburg, and if you were to dominate him as you did there, you would both lose your jobs. Don't you realize that the poor man is suffering as a result of his foolishness? Don't you understand that, like all men, he is weak?"[6]

This letter is of particular interest because none of Mahler's surviving letters to Anna contain any reproach, and none of their contemporaries have left any account either of Anna's character or the nature of their liaison. Her love for Mahler had led her to try and overcome his reticence by publicizing their relationship. Knowing this makes it easier to understand his attitude.

Before closing this important chapter in Mahler's life, it must be added that Mildenburg was especially sensitive to male admiration. It would perhaps be discourteous to draw a list of the many "admirers" of this great artist, who was as passionate as she was fickle. The list is long and Mahler was undoubtedly right to decide against a marriage whose consequences would have been tragic for them both.[7]

During his summer of rest and convalescence, Mahler never lost track of what was happening at the opera, where the situation developed rapidly during his absence. He studied scores[8] and revised the plans for the coming season. Early in the summer, the news from Vienna had not been reassuring: a cable from Rosa Papier informed him that "the director is staying on," and Mahler wrote to Wlassack immediately for details.[9] The latter replied that "everything seems to be settled—both Bezecny and Jahn are remaining!"

"No one knows what will happen later on," Mahler wrote to Mildenburg, "or when and on what terms my contract will be extended . . . Richter is, and remains, first conductor. I shall be anxious to see how things develop. My contract expires in a year's time, and I don't know if or how they will be prepared to renew it." He nevertheless went out of his way to be diplomatic. "If things go on like this," he wrote to Adele Marcus, "even Marwege may finally consider me a tolerable conductor . . . What do you think of my 'popularity' and of this favorable wind blowing? At present, I have only three enemies in Vienna: Jahn, Richter and Fuchs! Everyone else thinks I'm a charming person and a delightful companion! Grrr! . . . What a surprise is in store for them!"

"With determination and iron self-control," he wrote to Rose Papier on July 2, "both of which I promise you I possess, it is possible to overcome all difficulties . . . I wish things would start moving again. This idleness is getting me down! If only the situation would clarify. If only the pudding would finally jell! If my hands were not tied, I could accomplish so much, but I fear they'll remain tied as long as Wilhelm [Jahn] hangs onto his sinecure. What does Wlassack think?"[10]

Mahler was unaware that matters were evolving favorably. On July 13, Intendant Bezecny officially informed the opera personnel that "when the season reopens on August 1, and for the duration of Director Wilhelm Jahn's leave, that is, for as long as he is unable to direct the affairs of the opera, his responsibilities will be taken over by Kapellmeister Mahler."[11]

Mahler was on a long bicycle trip in the Pustertal and had therefore not seen the newspapers for several days. Upon his return to Vahrn on July 23, he got the news in a letter from Jahn, "whose shaky signature resembled that of a blind man." A few hours later he also received a letter from Wlassack, telling him to go at once to Jahn in Trofaiach, Styria, and ask for instructions. Mahler answered immediately: "This is Wlassack, all over! Like a bolt of lighting, like a sudden explosion, just when I thought I was farther than ever from my goal! I have already telegraphed you, both in Vienna and in the Semmering, and hope to hear from you soon."

Mahler wrote to Rosa Papier on July 26: "I was all the more astonished to learn that Wlassack had obtained my appointment as 'substitute,' as I'm living in the mountains and never see a newspaper; my friends' congratulations came as something of a surprise, for I had no inkling the Vienna papers had already announced the news. It was a bolt from the blue which, I think, several people may have a hard time getting over."[12] Mahler scarcely had time to enjoy this good news while making preparations for a hurried departure. Only a week remained before the reopening of the opera, and he had to visit in turn Jahn, Wlassack, and Hanslick in Ischl.

As he was boarding the Vienna train at Vahrn, the sight of some workmen throwing the final spadefuls of earth onto a grave moved him strangely. "How long will it be before they'll be throwing it on us?" he said to Natalie. "It is a sobering thought, amid all the storms of life; but as long as we are alive, we must believe in life, and cannot escape it. We are completely at the mercy of the raging elements." And indeed the Vienna Opera was soon to demand all Mahler's energy, causing him momentarily to lose "his own direction."

Having left Vahrn on the evening of July 26, Mahler reached Vienna the next day and left again immediately for the Semmering, where he met Wlassack on the morning of July 28. At first the latter was "somewhat reserved" because he had not yet forgiven Mahler for not calling upon him as soon as he arrived in Vienna, but gradually the atmosphere became friendlier: "How was I to know it was so important to him?" Mahler wrote to Rosa Papier from Vienna on July 31. "Surely today is just as good! Anyway he'll be back tomorrow and we can start working together." On the advice of Wlassack and Heuberger, Hanslick's replacement on the *Neue Freie Presse,* Mahler then went to Ischl to see Hanslick and thank him for his strong support. "I cannot do less," he wrote to Rosa Papier, "for everyone says he has paid me an exceptional honor, and that I would be committing a crime of *lèse-majesté* if I didn't go."[13] Unfortunately his journey to Ischl was fruitless, since Hanslick was away that day.

On the evening of July 29, Mahler was received by Jahn in his Trofaiach villa in Styria. He spent the whole of the next day there, "overwhelmed" by the kindness of the old director, who "seemed to be afraid of me." "I would love to know just how much his kindness and friendship are worth," he wrote after this visit. "In any case, I feel it's a good sign that he went to such trouble to be pleasant. He himself officially announced to me that I can make my own decisions in the future; however, he then presented me with the complete program for August (I don't know if he was entitled to do so). Although I'm not entirely in agreement (it does not suit me at all to have so many Wagnerian works this month, with all the difficulties this entails), I am quite happy to start with it, since I am still so ignorant of conditions with regard to the personnel."[14]

Nevertheless, the visit made an unpleasant impression on Mahler, for he sensed that his host was completely in the dark regarding the decisions that had been reached concerning him. "I must admit that I almost felt guilty at the thought that my appointment will shorten and embitter the little time that he still has left to live."[15] "The poor man doesn't seem to have the slightest suspicion that I shall soon be appointed in his place," Mahler said to Karpath a few days later. "I must admit that, from a purely humane point of view, I feel terribly sorry for him. But such feelings are of no importance, for if I do not replace him, someone else will, and I naturally prefer to be the chosen one. Jahn's fate is sealed: when he returns to Vienna early in September, he will be officially asked to hand in his resignation."[16]

Mahler thus returned to Vienna with a secret sense of triumph. But first he spent a little time in Pötzleinsdorf, where the Spieglers were on vacation.

But the weather was wretched and the local "society" difficult to bear, so he returned to the city and started living in hotels again while waiting for his new apartment. "Full of kind attentions," Jahn placed an office at his disposal, and its door was constantly opening to admit opera employees wishing to consult Mahler about their work. He began to realize that "the job of substitute director is no bed of roses."[17] It was literally raining difficulties, not only because opera discipline was slack, but also because torrential rain had flooded most of the railway lines, which meant that many of the opera's employees had been unable to report for duty. The *Lohengrin,* announced for the reopening on August 1, was almost canceled because of the absence of some singers, but at the last minute everything was arranged. During the performance, according to the *Neue Freie Presse,* Mahler again showed his "brilliant qualities as a conductor." Two days later, *Guillaume Tell* had to be replaced at the eleventh hour by *Faust,* which Mahler conducted without a single rehearsal.[18] In addition to the administrative tasks that took up so much of his time, he also had to conduct almost every evening in early August, because Fuchs was on holiday and Richter was stranded by the floods at Hainfeld, in Lower Austria. Mahler telegraphed Richter, asking him to come to his aid as quickly as possible, but Richter, who thought he detected some implication of blame in this telegram, answered that he "knew his duty" and that his delay was due to circumstances beyond his control. He finally reached Vienna on August 5 or 6, and Mahler saw him at once, so that they could divide the season's programs between them. Their meeting was friendlier than Mahler had anticipated, and in particular Richter agreed to hand over to him the *Ring* cycle productions of *Das Rheingold* and *Die Walküre,* scheduled for late in August.

Shortly after returning to Vienna, Mahler again saw Prince Liechtenstein. During their half-hour conversation, Liechtenstein confirmed that Jahn would be retired upon his return. In the middle of August, during the rehearsals of the *Ring,* Max Kalbeck, critic of the *Neues Wiener Tagblatt,* wrote from Vienna to his assistant Karpath, giving him news of the Vienna Opera, which he said was unrecognizable: work went on there all day long, and, "unlike in the past, special attention is paid to the classics." Jahn was on leave until September 15, but he had announced his intention of returning on September 1. Kalbeck now considered it impossible for Mahler to relinquish his functions; it would be "like trying to stop the locomotive of an express train." In addition, all the opera personnel were enthusiastically in favor of Mahler, especially after a performance of *Le Nozze di Figaro* on August 14.[19]

This performance of Mozart's work delighted not only the members of the opera but also Vienna's most eminent critic, Hanslick.[20] "While it is true that a performance of *Figaro* suffices to transform an ordinary day into a holiday," he wrote, "this is doubly true when the spectator knows that the conductor will protect him against any musical atmospherics. Herr Mahler is such a conductor. He had delved deeply into Mozart's masterpiece, both dramatically and musically, thereby undertaking a renovation that is not yet complete, but that has been started with intelligence and success. First and foremost, he has succeeded in forcing the singers to respect the text. In a theater, no actor, whether great or small, could permit himself the slightest modification of our poets' masterworks, yet, at the opera, this has been a daily occurrence. It is in this august institution, home of our greatest singers, that the most criminal offences have been committed. How many times have we heard Fräulein X or Herr Y 'improve' Beethoven, Mozart or Wagner?

"How Herr Mahler has resolutely put a stop to all such goings on. With the exception of one passage in the aria *'Deh vieni, non tardar,'* the whole conformed exactly to the score. The audience's attentiveness and vigorous applause should convince the singers that neither their absurd cadences nor their misplaced 'auxiliary notes' will win them artistic success and success in general, but rather fidelity, both in word and deed, to the work they are interpreting. Our heartfelt thanks to Herr Mahler, for having thus courageously and unexpectedly given our excellent artists good reason to be pleased with themselves."[21]

After a second performance of *Figaro,* Hirschfeld, in the *Wiener Abendpost,* judged that "Mozart's spirit pervades Mahler's conducting," for "he knows how to render the melodic line as light as a feather, so that it rises from the orchestra like perfume from flowers. The ensembles, such as the duet preceding the first *finale,* floated airily on wings of gossamer, while the *finale* itself was lovingly nuanced and each voice individualized with infinite care. . . . In the past, *Figaro* has always been a last-minute opera, performed only in case of necessity; this version of Mozart is new to the Hofoper . . . Mahler has managed to unite the singers, some of whom are technically below standard, into a pleasing ensemble which makes one forget the dimensions of the hall. He keys everything to Mozart's *fortes* and *pianos* in an interpretation which has its own dynamics, its own color."

The critic Max Graf, who had watched Mahler conduct this opera in Prague, later dwelled on the sobriety of his conducting compared to his former impetuosity. "He now seems to control both his nerves and the orchestra," he is a "musical thinker" rather than the "ecstatic conductor" he was to become in the last Vienna years.

Before and after this memorable *Figaro,* Mahler conducted *Der fliegende Holländer, Die lustigen Weiber von Windsor, Le Prophète, Der Freischütz,* and *Don Giovanni,* and also prepared the complete *Ring* cycle for the end of the month. After an interval of fifteen years, he renewed his friendship with Hugo Wolf, who wrote to his friend Hugo Faisst on August 10: "I shall henceforth be a frequent visitor at the opera. Since Mahler is on the podium, I dare to enter those *'unheiligen Hallen'* again . . .[22] Thanks to him—he is temporarily replacing the director—I can get a box or orchestra stalls whenever I want, without paying a penny—a great advantage. They'll be giving *Der Corregidor*[23] at the end of January or in February . . ." Writing to another friend, Oskar Grohe, on August 25, 1897, Wolf said: "There are many interesting things I'd like to tell you about Mahler, with

whom I am on friendly terms, but I'll follow your example and remain silent."
Wolf's silence is regrettable, since it would be fascinating to know the details
of their reconciliation.

Before August 24, the date set for the beginning of the Wagner cycle,
Justi returned to Vienna, where she met Frau Marcus and her daughter, who
had come to see Mahler conduct. He had moved into the new apartment in
the Bartensteinstrasse on August 11, which he appreciated all the more because he had not felt "at home" anywhere since leaving Hamburg six months
before. However, completely wrapped up in administration and reform, he
had not a moment he could call his own.[24] When Natalie Bauer-Lechner
reached Vienna, she found him deep in the final preparations for the *Ring,*
which was to be given in four evening performances, with a one-day interval between *Die Walküre* and *Siegfried.* He was working like a man possessed; each day he was at the opera from nine to two o'clock, and on many
evenings he also had to conduct. His intitial euphoria had already begun to
wear off. The orchestra, which had pleased him so much at first, now no
longer satisfied him: the "eternal portamentos, the decrescendos of sound
in mid-bow," favored by the Vienna string section, was intolerable to him.
The musicians appeared quite unable to sustain a note without diminishing or swelling it. "Instead of piano, which should be their usual conversational tone," they always played forte and would only consent from time to
time to produce a real pianissimo. "I can't manage to hold them back," he
complained. "My gestures are not sufficient. If one of the strings has a solo
part, the player thinks it is solely in order to give him a chance to show off
loudly. Even their rhythm is sloppy. But in time I'll change all this."[25]

On the day of *Das Rheingold,* Mahler was as happy and impatient "as
a child on Christmas morning" and could scarcely wait for the evening to
arrive. He had obtained permission to have the work performed for the first
time without an intermission, as Wagner had wished, and even though he
had been able to have only one orchestral rehearsal, which he had devoted
almost entirely to passages usually cut, he gave the opera an entirely new
appearance that evening. All the performers had felt his musical will power
and had been infused with the spirit of the work. Every note and word could
be read on his lips; indeed he almost indicated facial expressions and movements too as he conducted![26]

The concertmaster Rosé had assured Mahler that *Die Walküre* would be
the more successful of the two: the musicians knew it better and would be
more sure of themselves; but Rosé was wrong. "The dust of negligence
and mistakes lies thick over the whole work; much more so than in *Das
Rheingold,* which they have played less often, so that the faults are not as
deeply ingrained as yet!" In the last act Mahler indicated an entrance to the
kettledrummer, with whom he had carefully rehearsed the passage on account of a long trill; hearing nothing, he glanced angrily in the musician's direction and saw with astonishment that the man was a replacement and had
missed his entrance in consequence. After the performance, he demanded

to know the reason for this incident and was told that, because the kettle-drummer lived in suburban Brunn, he had to leave the opera before the end of the evening so as not to miss the last train.[27] Outraged, Mahler sent the man a telegram at midnight, summoning him to his office at seven o'clock the next morning. He hoped to give him a sleepless night and thus discourage him from repeating the incident. He gave the musician the choice of abandoning either the opera or his home in Brunn, but doubtless finally granted him an allowance to help him to move,[28] for it was then that he learned that some of the musicians earned no more than sixty gulden a month, a sum on which it was impossible to live in Vienna, even as a bachelor.[29] Mahler decided to obtain a salary increase for them, compensating for it by economizing in other fields. In this way, he hoped to do away with the system of replacements in the orchestra.

Mahler had taken great care with the staging of the opening of the last act of *Die Walküre,* but he was dissatisfied with the Valkyries, who were mediocre solo and choral singers. "One day, I will only employ first-class singers and then I'll finally be able to revitalize the scene." At the end of the cycle, Hugo Wolf told Natalie that "for the first time, I have heard the *Ring* as I have always dreamed of hearing it while reading the score."[30]

Despite the admiration that he had aroused, Mahler was far from satisfied with the results of his work. "What a tragedy," he once said, "that the greatest composers should have written their works for such a pigsty as the theater, the very nature of which precludes perfection." Nonetheless, Natalie recalled some sections of this *Ring* with emotion: the "magic of nature" in the *Siegfried* "Forest Murmurs," the splendor of Brünnhilde's awakening, and finally the burning passion of the final love scene, given for the first time in its uncut version. "That cut was shameful," Mahler exclaimed in this respect, "for it more or less turned Brünnhilde into a harlot who resisted Siegfried's solicitations for only a moment before throwing herself into his arms. The whole transition, in which she tells him everything she is obliged to renounce, and all the intermediate steps that prepare for the great final crescendo were missing!"

The following evening, in *Die Götterdämmerung,* Mahler restored to the drama the essential Brünnhilde-Waltraute scene, but he had to resign himself to keeping the cut in the Norn scene, as he did not have the necessary singers.[31] The success of *Die Götterdämmerung* was particularly striking; many enthusiasts shouted, "Mahler!" at the end of the performance, and a group of young people and conservatory students gathered to acclaim him as he left the opera.

The first uncut presentation of the *Ring* was to mark the final break between the old and new generations regarding Wagnerian interpretation. Certain of Mahler's tempos, especially at the end of the third act of *Die Walküre,* were in fact livelier than Richter's. When the critic Max Graf pointed this out, Mahler replied that "Richter has no idea of tempo and has certainly forgotten Wagner's." As for Richter, he told Graf that Mahler's rendering of the "Magic Fire Spell" had struck him as good, but he added that Mahler had not known how to get the most from the transfiguration and the tragic resignation scenes at the end of the third act.

These *Ring* performances, on which Mahler had expended so much time and effort, were less talked of in the press than the earlier performances. The *Neue Freie Presse* merely stated, after *Die Walküre*, that Mahler "conducted with great seriousness and tremendous enthusiasm," adding that all but one of the passages previously deleted had been restored. In the anti-Semitic *Deutsche Zeitung*, Theodor Helm, whose admiration for Mahler had probably rendered him suspect, had been replaced by his colleague Albert Leitich, who championed Richter. The effects obtained by Richter in *Das Rheingold* were "greater and more profound," whereas Mahler "attenuates certain passages to the work's detriment."[32] The latter was certainly justified in "restraining the orchestra," but it would have been still better had he sunk it into the pit. However, he had failed (*versungen und vertan*) with *Die Walküre,* for the singing was off key and his Magic Fire had not been nearly as good as Richter's. "The notes but not the meaning" had been rendered, and the end of the first act had been too rushed. In his opinion *Siegfried* had been the best performance of the cycle, except for the "Forest Murmurs." The Act III "Fire Music" and the final duet, finally performed uncut, struck him as "acceptable, because here Mahler followed Richter's tradition . . ." As for his rendering of *Die Götterdämmerung,* Leitich states that it lacked "the elementary force of destiny."

Mahler's position at the opera grew rapidly stronger, and there was already much talk of his replacing Jahn. The latter, no doubt having heard of Mahler's triumphs, returned to Vienna on September 1, two weeks earlier than planned, though his vision had not been much improved by his recent operation.[33] On August 10, Prince Liechtenstein had instructed Bezecny to obtain Jahn's resignation. "Perhaps this is the final station of the Cross before the directorship," wrote Mahler, who knew of this development. "I have already borne the full weight of the cross, though I haven't as yet had to drudge as I did in Budapest. My position is still uncontested, but once I have my appointment in my pocket, I'll be prepared to resign at any moment. For the time being, of course, I haven't the slightest reason to do so. Even Richter has acknowledged my authority, and, since I granted him six weeks' leave, he considers me an acceptable 'representative of the directoral dignity.' "[34]

Mahler suffered from doubts and anxiety right up to the moment of his appointment. Hearing of a violent scene between Jahn and Wlassack on the day of their first meeting after Jahn's return, he once more felt remorseful. "My heart bleeds, I feel so terribly sorry for that sick old man," he said to Karpath. "But Wlassack tells me we must put an end to it . . . What else can we do?" Karpath asked him if Jahn was irrevocably condemned. "I am absolutely certain of it," replied Mahler, "even though I haven't exerted any pressure, the administration has decided to end this awkward situation."[35] After this conversation Karpath announced briefly in the *Neues Wiener Tagblatt* that Jahn was about to retire because of his failing eyesight. On the same day, Wlassack, realizing that Jahn was determined to hold onto his position, insisted that he ask to be retired. Jahn again refused and left Wlassack's office extremely upset. He finally capitulated the next day.

Toward the end of August, Bezecny and Wlassack wrote to the lord chamberlain suggesting that, over and above the decoration and the increase in his pension (it had been raised to six thousand florins) the Emperor should confer on Jahn the title of *Hofrath*. For Jahn's successor, the two officials recommended "Kapellmeister Gustav Mahler, a young Christian Austrian of 37, who, in his previous posts as Director of the Royal Budapest Opera and leading conductor at the Hamburg Opera, as well as more recently during his brief spell as conductor and substitute director here, has given proof of his genius and his zeal as a musician and man of the theater." He has "known how to attract the attention and admiration of a public dedicated to art, as well as how to gain the devotion of the artists he directs and with whom he has, in fact, weathered a bad storm." Furthermore, "the integrity of his character" was well known and the "artistic direction of the opera could be safely placed in his hands, with every hope of success." The financial aspects would be left to the administration, and this clause in Mahler's contract was to cause him a host of problems. He would receive a salary of six thousand florins, a supplement of two thousand florins as conductor, and an expense allowance of two thousand florins.[36]

Mahler would be payed an indemnity of two thousand florins for lodgings (the administration suggested that the lodgings previously occupied by the director should be handed over to them); this would raise his income to a total of twelve thousand florins per year, a sum inferior to that which Jahn had been receiving latterly.

Knowing that the Emperor would be reluctant to grant Jahn the title of *Hofrath*, which was given to only the highest officials,[37] Prince Liechtenstein suggested that he merely decorate the retiring conductor. However, the matter hung fire for a few days, and although the prince had assured him there was no cause for alarm, Mahler wondered anxiously about the reasons for the delay and feared some eleventh-hour obstacle. He finally discovered, at the beginning of October, that the Emperor had merely been trying to decide what final honor to confer upon Jahn; in the end he made him a Commander of the Imperial Order. The same decree, dated October 8 and signed by the lord chamberlain on the fifteenth, appointed Mahler director of the opera.

Thus, from October 8, 1897, Mahler took over the direction of one of the most illustrious musical institutions in the world. Considering the fundamental incompatibility between his personality and the free and easy ways of the Viennese, it was not hard to foresee the many conflicts that were to arise during the next ten years. Vienna was the capital of pleasure, a city that prided itself on not taking anything too seriously, and in which art was too often considered as an amusing pastime,[38] whereas Mahler worshiped art with mystic fervor. He may have been Viennese at heart and by adoption, but he never became Viennese in character. Of all the great German-speaking musical centers, Vienna was the one in which tension and energy were at their weakest, so Mahler's fanaticism was certain to clash with the most deep-rooted Viennese instincts: hedonism, indolence, and unreasoning devotion to tradition, which were to "eat into him like acid." But, having at last become master of the opera's destiny, he put his nose to the grindstone and demanded that his subordinates do likewise.

The intensity with which he worked struck the Viennese as insane. Neither the orchestra nor the singers nor the public nor the critics were given time to breathe, but Mahler himself derived great satisfaction from all this frantic activity. What to another might have seemed forced labor or torture was to him a kind of liberation. His superhuman and too-long-repressed energy enabled him to realize his dream of dramatic harmony (*Gesamtkunstwerk*) in the theater. It was impossible for him to rest or spare himself. He was often exhausted but never relaxed. His inner fire burned at maximum intensity; it sometimes terrified, but it also encouraged and purified those who dared to approach its flames.

The force that enabled Mahler to resist his numerous enemies sprang, above all, from his absolute integrity and from the fact that he was always ready to resign his position as director rather than make artistic concessions. Having nothing more to gain on the material plane, his only aim was to realize his dreams of perfection, and to this end he was prepared to devote every last ounce of his strength. "I am up to my eyes in activity, as only a theater director can be. What a terrible, consuming existence!" he wrote to Marschalk. "All my senses and feelings are turned toward the outside. I get farther and farther away from myself. How will it end? I send you greetings! Remember me with the thoughts usually dedicated to the dead!"[39]

The situation at the opera was far from brilliant, and it had become steadily worse during the preceding years because of Jahn's illness, even though he had started out as a good musician and an excellent theatrical director. Born, like Mahler, in Moravia, Jahn was entirely different from him: he was a heavily built and phlegmatic Viennese bourgeois, whose benevolent face, pointed beard, and honest and still-youthful eyes, peering from behind thick lenses, gave him the air of a schoolmaster. He was an effective and brilliant conductor, and Vienna particularly appreciated what it called his "French" sensitivity and the refinements of his "realistic" stage productions. Even after he had become very fat, Jahn frequently laid down his baton to climb onto the stage and indicate a gesture or a pose. He was particularly keen on precision, liveliness, delicacy, and melodic continuity; he brought out details with the soul of a miniaturist, without ever being either pedantic or Teutonic, and triumphed above all in lighter works, thanks to a kind of sparkling grace that was all his own.[40]

Despite his taste for realism and for French and Italian operas, he had accorded Wagner a large place in the repertoire. Yet he had only once given an uncut *Meistersinger* and had never understood Wagner's mature masterpieces, which he generally assigned to Hans Richter, together with the operas of Mozart and Gluck. Unlike Pollini, however, he was an extremely cultivated and artistic man, and, while sharing Pollini's love of beautiful voices, he took much more interest in the sound of the orchestra, the costumes, and the direction of performances. Nevertheless, he was an epicurean, a man incapable of fighting a battle or taking a risk, above all that of being unpopular, and whereas Mahler constantly strove to surpass himself and elevate his fellow men, Jahn was content to offer refined entertainment to an elite of cultivated aristocrats.[41] Jahn's greatest successes as producer and conductor were *Manon, Werther, Cavalleria rusticana, Pagliacci, Hänsel und Gretel, The Bartered Bride, Otello,* Goldmark's *Das Heimchen am Herd,* Nessler's *Der Trompeter von Säkkingen,* Wilhelm Kienzl's *Der Evangelimann,* Berlioz's *Béatrice et Bénédict,* Wagner's *Tannhäuser* and Liszt's *Die Legende von der heiligen Elisabeth.* Although none of these works figured among those Mahler most esteemed and admired, Jahn, within his natural limitations, knew how to attain perfection. Gifted with much common sense, like Pollini, Jahn never lost sight of either the box office takings or the public's taste, and he had permitted enormous cuts in Wagner's operas, which still attracted only small audiences. Deferred until 1883, the first Vienna performance of *Tristan und Isolde,* with Richter conducting, had aroused surprise rather than admiration, and a great deal remained to be accomplished in this field.

Hans Richter, the chief orchestral conductor, was entirely devoted to Wagner and had exercised a happy influence during Jahn's reign. Yet he too preferred an easy life and had readily accepted the shortened versions of Wagner's works, though he made up for this in Bayreuth and each year vainly attempted to replace at least some of the cuts. Jahn believed that under no circumstances should the performances cease to give pleasure. Even in its abridged version, even with Winkelmann and Materna, *Tristan* usually only half-filled the opera and most of the audience left *Die Meistersinger* after the quintet. Nevertheless many Viennese felt that to appoint Mahler to a post that was Richter's by right had been an inconsiderate act, even though Richter had neither the desire to fill it nor the temperament of a director.[42]

The ensemble of singers formed by Jahn reflected the spirit of his regime, but Mahler gradually made changes in accordance with his own. Some of the survivors from the great days—the tenor Herman Winkelmann[43] and the baritone Theodor Reichmann[44]—had retained their popularity, if not quite all their former vocal powers. The top gallery at the Vienna Opera had its favorite singers among these old-timers, and when Winkelmann and Reich-

mann sang together in *Tannhäuser,* the applause turned into a competition
between the fans who shouted, "Winkel" and those who shouted, "Reich."

The other singers from Jahn's era were less illustrious. The coloratura
sopranos Irene Abendroth and Emmy Teleky, the light soprano Ellen Forster, the dramatic soprano Sophie Sedlmair, the American contralto Edyth
Walker, the tenor Andreas Dippel,[45] the baritones Josef Ritter and Franz
Neidel, and the bass Franz von Reichenberg were good singers, but most of
them left the opera after a time, unable to conform to Mahler's severe discipline. Two of them had already met him: the baritone Karl Grengg, in
London in 1892, and the Czech bass Wilhelm Hesch, in *The Bartered Bride*
in Hamburg. The lyric tenor Fritz Schrödter had been with the opera for
more than ten years and was exceedingly popular with the public.

Over this cohort reigned two stars especially beloved by the Viennese:
the soprano Marie Renard and the tenor Ernest Van Dyck. The former[46]
represented a type very much in fashion, the "charming young girl," the
lovelorn heroine who was sometimes a countess, sometimes a laundress.
She was a real prima donna, for whom nothing mattered except her pianissimos, her trills, and her roulades, and who made little effort to fit in with
an ensemble. The Belgian tenor Ernest Van Dyck[47] had gained recognition
thanks to his exceptional voice and despite his odd appearance: he had a
round body, a tiny head, and a circular mouth and eyes. He too was a
virtuoso singer, blending "Flemish violence" with "Parisian culture," but his
dramatic pretensions often made him look ridiculous. His acting was artificial in the extreme; for example he would suggest delight by leaping grotesquely about the stage. His best Wagnerian role was Loge, but most of
his other performances were "perfumed" and affected.[48] Both he and die
Renard constantly played on their popularity to reject Mahler's authority.
After two years he got rid of them, and thereafter he avoided engaging stars
who thought more of their popularity than of their artistic duties.

Under Jahn's directorship, the smaller roles were generally very badly
sung; this, together with the chorus's lack of discipline, was one of the principal weaknesses of his "system." In the end the public was applauding the
vocal feats rather than the performance. Everyone hoped for some improvement but without believing that such a thing was really possible. They
thought that, in the theatrical world of pleasure and illusion, nothing but the
relative and the ephemeral could be successful. The regular public did not
want to have their habits changed, and altogether Vienna was unprepared
for the surprises Mahler had in store.

The latter part of Jahn's directorship had been particularly disastrous.
Even the essential qualities of his direction had begun to fade. The ensemble
of singers no longer matched the requirements of the repertoire, and new
singers constantly had to be brought in from the provinces. Even the best
artists had their off moments, all the more noticeable because the chorus
was poor and even the orchestra was far from always being at its best. Jahn
was especially criticized for having made his nephew Chordirektor Hubert

Wondra, and for giving him an important part to play in the administration of the opera. The performances had become increasingly tawdry and dated, and most of the singers were no longer talented enough to attract the public. The stars often feigned illness at the last moment if they considered their stage partners unworthy of them, or they demanded and obtained leaves of absence in mid-season. All these difficulties sprang mainly from Jahn's lack of authority, from his ill-health, and from the incompetence of his subordinates, especially Wondra.[49]

The attacks published during the last months of Jahn's regime show how lax it had become. The last singers he had engaged,[50] the paucity of the repertoire, the new productions he had chosen,[51] the last-minute cancellations of performances, and the power he had delegated to his nephew had turned most of the critics against him. The *Deutsche Zeitung* had been particularly severe regarding undue interference in the opera's affairs by Wetschel, the administrative treasurer, an able financier, who was accused of totally lacking both artistic and theatrical experience. In the paper's opinion, the productions were extremely second-rate, scarcely worthy of a provincial theater. Stoll, an "incompetent and lazy" producer, Gaul (the designer), and Hassreiter (the ballet master) "form an iron band that stifles all artistic life at the Hofoper." The "few people with talent" choke in its "lazy and fusty atmosphere," and "the air needs to be thoroughly purified."

Despite the constant virulent reproaches made to Jahn by the anti-Semitic papers, they were naturally displeased to learn that Mahler would replace him. From September 12 on they attacked him for being "non-German" and condemned his program, "which places German works last" and ignored "great masterpieces like Wolf's *Der Corregidor* and Cornelius's *Der Cid.*" On the whole, however, their attacks were less violent than might have been expected.

The moment he arrived, Mahler set to work to carry out his program of reforms, endeavoring first and foremost to restore law and order. On October 11 he addressed the following circular to the members of the opera:

"With the aim of bringing to an end the deplorable abuses of the claque, the director of the theater has taken numerous measures that would have effectively abolished this practice, had not some members of the opera, in the most undignified manner, secretly sidestepped the regulations on the pretext of defending their own interests . . . After private conversations with them, I am happy to say that they are now as determined as I am to do away with this custom, which brings discredit to the opera and prevents us from attaining our artistic goals. I therefore take the liberty of demanding a solemn promise that henceforth you will all abstain from any contact with the claque, and will cease all payments and distribution of free tickets, so that we may put an end to a practice incompatible with the dignity of our institution. For my part, I promise you that I shall not only do everything in my power to support you in this endeavor, but that also, in our common interest, I will use all the means at my disposal to ensure that our mutual agreement is respected."

Of all Mahler's reforms, this was one of the most difficult to carry out, and he never succeeded completely, despite the detectives he placed in the gallery to watch the suspects. His wishes were respected for a few months, and then the singers, deciding that they were not receiving enough applause, reverted to paying the claque in secret. However, the abuses of the system never became quite so blatant as before.[52]

A still more revolutionary reform consisted of forbidding latecomers access to the auditorium during the overtures (except for the boxes and standing room), for latecomers were especially noisy in Vienna, and the overtures were always accompanied by an incessant coming and going that distracted the audience's attention.[53] For the Wagner operas, Mahler decided that no one should be allowed in during the whole of the first act. With *Das Rheingold* this was tantamount to keeping latecomers out entirely. Wlassack at once asserted that such a measure was inconceivable in Vienna, because those who arrived late were often important government officials, but Mahler stuck to his guns. A few incidents gave him the chance to prove his determination. The president of the Länderbank, a man named Palmer, who often played whist with the Emperor, occupied a seat on the end of a row and near an exit, which meant he could come and go without disturbing anyone. He applied directly to Mahler for permission to take his seat after the start of the performance, but Mahler replied that the new rule admitted no exceptions. One day, as he was conducting, he saw an usher show a spectator to his seat after the curtain had risen. The next day he summoned the culprit and threatened him with dismissal if such a thing occurred again. To the usher's claim that the latecomer had struck him and opened the door by force, Mahler replied that he doubted a man of the usher's strength would let himself be struck with impunity; then, leaping from his chair and shaking his fist, he shouted, "The blow you received was in the shape of a florin slipped into your hand, and if this happens again I'll dismiss you."

Some of the courtiers complained to the Emperor, who was astonished at such intransigence but upheld Mahler, even though such severity was hard for Franz Josef to understand, for he regarded the theater as a place for people to enjoy themselves. However, he had appointed the director personally and he must be obeyed. He forbade the high officials of his household and even his own family to interfere in opera affairs in future, and through Prince Liechtenstein he instructed Mahler to ignore any suggestions they might make. From then on even the highest in the realm had to arrive on time, and this first tentative "scandal" failed.[54]

With the Emperor behind him, Mahler's attitude toward the Court and the aristocracy could afford to be proud and reserved. Innumerable stories of his behavior naturally went the rounds, in particular one about a singer named Mitzi Günther, who presented herself to him armed with a recom-

mendation from the heir apparent, Franz Ferdinand. Mahler simply tore
up the letter of introduction, saying, "Well, then, sing!"

Another time, a Swedish singer named Anita Karin, having found a powerful friend at Court in the person of the Archduchess Maria Theresa, complained to her that Mahler had declined to extend her contract, caused her
to refuse another engagement, and broken his promises. He "juggles with
destinies," she said. The Emperor, quickly informed of this "abuse," summoned Mahler to his villa in Ischl in midsummer. The latter had to appear
in court dress at midday, and the Emperor demanded to know why he did
not wish to re-engage Frau Karin. However, before Mahler had finished
giving his reasons, Franz Josef, bewildered, interrupted him: "That's all
right, you know more about it than I do."[55] Later on, explaining his refusal
to engage a singer recommended by the Emperor, Mahler said to Prince
Montenuovo: "Your Highness, I am fully aware that your wishes and those
of His Majesty must be respected at the opera and that is why I am waiting
for a written order to engage the lady." The Emperor, having come to respect Mahler's judgment and integrity, did not attempt to make him change
his mind.

Still another time Prince Liechtenstein urged Mahler to put on an opera
written by his old enemy, Count Zichy, a composer of mediocre talent who
had many supporters at the imperial Court; he assured Mahler that this
gesture would strengthen his position at the opera. "I am subject only to
His Majesty the Emperor," Mahler replied, "and if he orders me to produce
the opera, I'll give it. One has only to look at Zichy to see that he's no
composer." "But supposing he has composed an opera worthy of Beethoven?" asked the prince. "That's not entirely impossible," said Mahler, "yet
it is hardly likely that a chestnut tree will ever produce oranges." Matters
did not stop there, for an elderly lady-in-waiting to the Empress Elisabeth,
Countess Staray, pleaded Zichy's cause before the Emperor, asserting that
he had been Mahler's "benefactor" in Budapest.[56] Nevertheless Mahler
still refused to give in, explaining to Karpath that "I am in no way seeking
revenge; I have played through Zichy's opera painstakingly and had every
intention of producing it had it been even halfway passable. If the Emperor
insists that it be performed, the posters will read '*Auf allerhöchsten Befehl*'
[By Royal Command]."[57]

Having won respect for his integrity and force of character, Mahler saw
no point in frequenting Viennese society, and he was not forgiven for this
disdainful attitude, particularly since personal contacts were an essential
part of any career in Vienna. While he was still substitute director, he heard
that there had been disparaging talk about him in the salon of the Countess
Anastasia Kielmannsegg, wife of an important official, who entertained the
cream of the Viennese aristocracy and bourgeoisie. Since his appointment
was still pending, Mahler was disturbed by these intrigues, and, at Karpath's
instigation, the singer Luise von Ehrenstein decided to help Mahler by making some inquiries of the lady in question, who was an old friend of hers,[58]

in order to learn what was going on. Having discovered that the Countess Kielmannsegg felt no animosity toward Mahler and had taken no part in her guests' inoffensive gossip, Luise rushed to Mahler's office at the opera to reassure him personally. This, however, was a great mistake; he was so displeased by the idea that someone might think he had requested this service of a member of the opera that he answered her brusquely, showed her unceremoniously to the door and never forgave her for having put him in an awkward situation. Thereafter, without ever actually being impolite, he was so thoroughly inconsiderate that she soon left the opera.[59] Mahler later rebuked Karpath for having interfered in the matter and, from the moment of his official appointment, stopped worrying about the gossip in the Viennese salons. It was in this way that so many legends sprang up around him, sometimes depicting him as a tyrant, a devil, a monster, and a dangerous revolutionary.

Mahler's last important innovation at the opera was the abolition of complementary tickets, which forced the newspapers to pay for their critics' seats. At the same time, he began to change the repertoire; in his first year of office there were ten times as many Mozart operas and the total number of Wagner performances exceeded by twenty those of the preceding year. The day-to-day opera activity was already completely changed, and work went on uninterruptedly, for he had only one aim, which he was to pursue throughout his whole ten years in Vienna: "To ensure that each performance is better than the last," whether it be *Cavalleria rusticana* or *Die Meistersinger*.[60] It was a Utopian aim for a repertory opera company, but the desire to achieve it never left him. In order to avoid last-minute cancellations, he endeavored to have two complete casts for each opera, which, as far as productions were concerned, meant a considerable amount of extra work. Nevertheless, as in Budapest, he had only one motto: "work." "Has Deckner told you of my *artistic demands?*" he wrote to the baritone Demuth in December. "It is necessary, though I know you were acquainted with them in Hamburg and that you didn't like them. My insistence on them here has benefited everyone and I expect new members to comply with them willingly. Dear Demuth, do you remember all I mean by 'accuracy'? Are you both able and willing to submit to my artistic demands, not just passively as in Hamburg, but actively, by accepting my artistic program wholeheartedly? I beg you to give me a frank and clear answer to this question without trying to evade the issue. We must be in complete agreement on this point if we are to sign a contract that could commit us to a lifetime of artistic collaboration."

In November 1897, Mahler wrote in the same vein to a soprano who, having been invited to take part in some performances at the Vienna Opera, had asked to sing the role of Pamina in *Die Zauberflöte,* which he had recently restaged. Mahler replied, saying he did not feel that Fräulein Mackrott would have time to learn to "interpret" this role as he wished during her short stay, and therefore suggested she should choose another role, for he would no longer agree to let anyone sing his new productions without conforming to all his requirements.[61]

A final anecdote illustrates Mahler at work during these first few months. While rehearsing the revival of *Die Zauberflöte,* he made the soprano Elizza repeat the words *"Die monster"* so many times that finally, shaking with rage, she screamed them at Mahler himself. Mahler smiled at her and said, "That would suit you down to the ground, wouldn't it, Fräulein Elizza?" From then on the legend of a tyrannical and ruthless Mahler spread through Vienna, but the delight of the public and the enthusiasm of the press were still too unanimous for this hostility to break out into the open. As he remarked one day to the intendant, "I am hitting my head against the walls, but the walls are giving way . . ."

"... a real labor of Sisyphus! A task
that will take all my strength ..."

# CHAPTER 27

*Mahler in Vienna (III) — Official Appointment — First
Productions — Conflicts with Leoncavallo (September
1897–February 1898)*

Even before his appointment as director of the Vienna Opera, Mahler restaged some repertoire operas. On September 11 the revival of Lortzing's
*Zar und Zimmermann,* which had not been given for almost ten years, was
well received by a capacity audience and warmly praised by the critics.
Heuberger especially admired the complete unity of the forces involved,
which all worked together toward the perfection of the whole, and the purity
and beauty of the orchestral sound and the choral singing, which had at last
become an integral part of the action. "We were expecting a carpenter
[*Zimmermann*] and a czar [*Zar*] arrived," he concluded. The *Neues Wiener Tagblatt* congratulated Mahler both for selecting an unjustly neglected
opera and for the efforts he had made to guarantee its success. This critic
found particularly noteworthy the discreet accompaniments[1] and Mahler's
incomparable talent as a miniaturist: like a subtle engraver he had brought
out the smallest details, especially in the ensembles—"always one of Lortzing's strong points."[2]

Shortly afterward Mahler repaired yet another injustice by giving the first
Vienna performance of Smetana's *Dalibor,* on October 4, the Emperor's
birthday. Mahler had prepared this new production with great care and had
exchanged a series of letters and telegrams with Schubert, the director of the
Czech National Theater in Prague, on the subject of scenery and costumes.[3]
Unfortunately the work has dramatic and musical flaws, and during the
rehearsals Mahler made many alterations in the written indications on the
score and even some in the orchestration. He also cut the conclusion—the
victory of the royal troops, followed by the battle that ends in Dalibor's
death—which he replaced by some twenty bars, diminuendo, following
Milada's funeral chant. The opera thus ended "on a note of tender emotion"

that he considered far more suitable than the short battle scene of the original.

After rehearsals began, Mahler dropped one of the changes he had planned. At the close of the second act Milada disappears with her torch, leaving the hero in the darkness of his prison cell. Dalibor's solitude is suggested by powerful chords that suddenly interrupt the tender, expressive melody of the love duet.[4] During rehearsals, Mahler suddenly realized the dramatic value of these chords, which had earlier seemed devoid of musical logic; this discovery struck him as a characteristic example of the difference between "pure" and dramatic music.

The entire performance of *Dalibor* bore Mahler's mark: he had supervised and checked every detail, not only of the musical performance, but also of the scenery, costumes, and lighting. Despite the deficiencies of the ensemble of singers bequeathed to him by Jahn, each individual fitted in perfectly, the chorus played an active and essential part in the drama, and the orchestra, which had been particularly attentive during rehearsals, surpassed itself. Thanks to all this the opera was a genuine if unexpected success: it was performed thirteen times that season and repeated early in the next.[5] The critics, however, were rather lukewarm in their praise. Heuberger pointed out the weaknesses of the work, the musical value of which he thought far outweighed its dramatic effectiveness. He admitted that it contained "real gems," and congratulated Mahler on the improvements he had made in the score. Helm enthusiastically applauded the choice of *Dalibor*, although, to his mind, this opera would never become "a complete, coherent, captivating whole, both dramatically and musically," on a German stage, because of the flaws in the libretto and the music's lack of stylistic unity.

In a long article Hanslick also criticized the "insignificant and awkward" libretto,[6] as well as the first act's dramatic similarity to *Lohengrin,* and the second act's debt to *Fidelio.* Smetana's music he found "excellent," though less inventive and less attractive than that of his light operas. Nevertheless he considered *Dalibor* "a welcome addition to the repertoire" and an "entirely original" work, the success of which stemmed largely from the excellent performance. Mahler shared with Jahn the exceptional virtue of caring as much about the staging as about the music. He had rehearsed *Dalibor* with "intelligent insight and minute care" and had emphasized all its good points. According to Hanslick, this young, ambitious, and experienced musician was undoubtedly the man to "breathe new life into our Vienna Opera, which has been slumbering wearily for some time."[7]

Some years later, when reviving *Dalibor,* Mahler exclaimed, "You can't imagine how furious I became again today over the imperfections in this work by a profoundly gifted artist; he was defeated by his lack of professional ability and by his Czech origins, which barred his way, cutting him off from the rest of European culture. Outside Vienna, this opera is no longer performed, though it contains delightful passages; even here it is difficult to keep it in the repertoire, for the public cannot be induced to like it. Whenever I conduct it, I am always in a rage, I would like to cut a passage here, change the orchestration there, and sometimes even entirely recompose a passage, for, despite its beauty, the whole thing is clumsy."[8]

On the evening of October 9, Natalie, on her way to meet Mahler under the arcade of the opera, where he had just conducted *Zar und Zimmermann,* saw him at a distance, already calling out to her: "My appointment is official!" The next evening he was to conduct *Dalibor* and knew that the audience would acclaim him when he went to the podium. He therefore dashed out with the speed of lightning and raised his baton without even sitting down. During the short pause between the end of the overture and the rise of the curtain, he kept his arms raised to prevent any applause, and at the end of the performance, despite frantic clapping and cries of "Mahler," he refused to appear onstage with the singers.[9]

The Vienna papers were almost unanimous in singing Mahler's praises at the time of his appointment—even the anti-Semitic press, who announced it a day late. He was happy, above all, because his future was now secure: appointed by the Emperor and without a contract, he could leave only by resigning to claim his pension. This comforting thought, and the prospect of the operatic work he would be able to accomplish, were marred only by a single worry: the many activities that would now fill his life would surely prevent him from composing. "You will see," he wrote to Natalie, "I won't be able to stand these horrible conditions, even until the time when I could ask for my pension with a clear conscience: I wish I could just run away from it all. If only there were some point to the whole thing; if at least, as happens in Bayreuth, I could achieve the flawless productions of a certain number of works (only ten times more!) and could then present them in a real festival, how gladly I'd do it! But with the situation in our theater, where there must be daily performances, where I encounter incredible disorganization and deeply rooted mismanagement everywhere, where, at the very moment of performance, at the height of the battle, I sometimes long to destroy everything and start all over again, where I have to be content with a repertoire that places the vulgar alongside the sublime, where the apathy and stupidity of the performers and audiences loom before me like a wall, then my task becomes a real labor of Sisyphus! A task that will take all my strength, even my life, but that cannot lead either to perfection or success! The worst of it is that, harried by a thousand different worries, I never have a moment to be myself!"[10]

"I am writing in haste," Mahler wrote to Weingartner about the same time, "just to thank you for your kind words. You are the only one of my colleagues capable of understanding me when I say that this position, this office, this honor for which I am so envied, is just a source of *worry.* So you see I am far from 'basking in my own glory.' Fate has forced me to accept that which I have fought against so strongly—the *direction* of a theater. This will certainly put an end to my 'creations' for a long time to come. I don't need to tell you what *this* means to me. Nothing can replace this loss! I am about to be officially named director, and when this happens, my life will take on—for many years—a new and most unwelcome aspect. That day, which will bring me congratulations from all and sundry, will in fact be a day of mourning.

"I can hear you asking 'So why not *refuse?*' But believe me, I have been vainly seeking a position as conductor for years, and—strange as it sounds— I am compelled to accept this one or die of hunger. I simply *had* to unburden myself of these regrets to someone, and you, my dear Weingartner, are the only one to whom I feel I can talk. I will never forget your kindness as a colleague, nor your deep and genuine understanding of my problems at a time when everyone else humiliated and misunderstood me!"[11]

Completely absorbed by his operatic activities, Mahler soon realized that he would have to shelve his own creative work, and when someone asked him about the performance of his symphonies, he replied, "Right now, I don't care whether my works become known a few years sooner or later. At the present moment I understand myself so little that I often think I'm not the same man as before." However, this period of tension and feverish activity also brought moments of intense satisfaction, particularly when Mahler succeeded in giving a first-rate performance, recognized the progress achieved by the orchestra, and appreciated the efforts the musicians had made to satisfy him. Nor was it unimportant that his enthusiastic nature could now operate free of all restraint: he was his own master and the means at his disposal were superior to those in most of the other European opera houses. Astonished by the admiration and understanding he met at every turn, Mahler sometimes felt he was living in a dream, a fairy tale to which he gave himself up entirely, probably realizing that his euphoria would not last.

During the first weeks of his temporary directorship, Mahler apparently promised his old conservatory friend Hugo Wolf that, should his appointment become official, he would produce Wolf's first opera, *Der Corregidor.*[12] On September 19, after the performances of the *Ring,* which he much admired, Wolf—emaciated, his eyes gleaming with excitement—visited Mahler in his office and happened to see on his desk the score of Anton Rubinstein's *The Demon.*[13] Wolf made some disparaging remarks about the score and the libretto of this opera, which Mahler had admired ever since he had conducted it in Hamburg. A discussion followed, concerning the dramatic qualities of the libretto, and Mahler doubtless became violent and bitter, as sometimes happened when he felt himself attacked: he ended by reminding Wolf of the weaknesses in *Der Corregidor,* and in particular of the dramatic weakness that made its performance increasingly problematical. When the discussion became too heated, Mahler secretly rang for his usher; this was a signal for the man to enter and announce that the intendant wished to see Mahler. Thus Wolf, his heart filled with bitterness and rage, was obliged to leave. In his already-deranged mind, the incident took on catastrophic proportions. Obsessed by the idea that Mahler was not worthy to direct the opera, he began to take this desire for a reality. Ringing the door-bell of Mahler's apartment in the Bartensteinstrasse, he told the cook Elise that he himself was the new opera director.[14] When she slammed the door in his face, he ran off to announce the "news" to some of his acquaintances. The next day, while visiting friends, he drew from his pocket "with diabolical glee" a speech to the opera personnel in which he announced Mahler's dismissal. It finally became clear that a curtain had dropped between him and reality, and soon it was necessary to put him into an asylum. To persuade him to leave his apartment, the doctors told him that he was being taken to Mahler's home.[15]

After *Zar und Zimmermann* and *Dalibor,* Mahler restaged *Die Zauberflöte*. He wished to restore to this work, of which he was particularly fond, its fairy-tale atmosphere, and in the scene where Tamino plays the flute he had all kinds of animals come on stage: a lion first appeared, then two lionesses lay down at Tamino's feet; next a tiger emerged from a thicket, then some birds flew in, a rabbit leaped onto the stage and pricked up its ears ("How I do it is my secret!" Mahler said), a huge serpent coiled itself up in a corner and finally a crocodile climbed out of the Nile. "You can imagine what an effect of childlike simplicity is created," Mahler wrote to Natalie, "when Tamino cries out that all creatures come to him except his Pamina. But at the sound of Papageno's chimes the whole group instantly takes flight. I hope people will understand, and will not consider this a violation of 'classic' Mozart. I express nothing that is not in the text and have only brought some life to the dreadful boredom of the usual staging."[16]

Mahler made other changes in the traditional staging: the three temples with their inscriptions; Tamino's flute and Papageno's glockenspiel placed in the wings rather than in the orchestra; the restoration of the fanfares at the beginning of the second act, accompanying the procession of priests, who entered two by two, holding hands.[17] All the critics mentioned these "new ideas." Yet they conformed exactly to Schikaneder's stage directions, which Mahler was also following when he made the three genii arrive in aerial chariots covered with roses and drawn by doves. One of the girls complained of dizziness and refused to get into the flying machine, but, since she was not a good singer in any case, Mahler threatened to take the role away from her unless she overcame her vertigo. From then on the three singers arrived like celestial voyagers, flying down from the upper reaches of the flies.

Mahler also restored the original text in all its earthy simplicity, for he believed that it had been "overrefined and rendered insipid."[18] This new version of *Die Zauberflöte* played with considerable success to a packed theater: the orchestra performed with sensitivity and delicacy in chamber-music style, and the stage production enchanted even the most captious Mozart lovers. Laughter rippled through the theater when the animals appeared, and Mahler himself often chuckled with childish pleasure during the performance. He planned to make further changes later, such as having the three genii sung by boys, and changing the traditional conception of the Queen of the Night, "who should be a creature of supernatural cast," a "gigantic goddess-mother capable of carrying all the characters in her nocturnal womb." For this role he wanted a woman of regal stature, like Mildenburg, who would emerge from the night (and not, as was customary, from a grotto), with her hair blowing free and her black mantle billowing in the wind.[19]

The Vienna critics greeted the new *Zauberflöte* with delight. None was more enthusiastic than Theodor Helm: he did not make one single reservation, except to express a fear that "certain details of the staging might distract attention from the music." In his opinion, the almost too faithful restoration of the original text had given the action a logic it had previously seemed to lack. Thanks to the clarity of the singers' diction, the reduced size of the orchestra, and the new cast changes, certain passages had "become unrecognizable." "What simple joy and happiness Schikaneder would have felt at seeing this!" he added after another performance.

Heuberger rejoiced that the Hofoper could now offer its audience a "new attraction" that, "like all those of the new regime," was of the highest quality. The new staging had generated a "healthy excitement." Each role had been "rethought," the acting of the singers had been completely transformed: Mahler had demanded and obtained from them absolute fidelity to the musical text. In the *Neues Wiener Tagblatt,* Kalbeck expressed his delight at the "renaissance" inaugurated by Mahler, who thus restored to Mozart his place as "the greatest musical dramatist." Once again the new director had "tried to render the soul of a masterpiece by reconstructing its body," so that, "astonished and delighted, the listener heard the voice of the score reborn, as though emerging from a youthful dream, thanks to the extraordinary subtleness of the nuances and the quality of the casting."[20]

Mahler's influence was starting to make itself felt everywhere. He was already enlarging the repertoire and devoting more time to "quality" operas. Massenet, Mascagni, and Meyerbeer slowly disappeared, and ballet was given only one night a week. The rather facile successes of the preceding regime were gradually replaced by the great masterpieces and many more uncut Wagnerian performances. Mahler dreamed of building up a "treasury of exemplary performances" on which he could draw at need, and in which no jewel would be neglected, even "if it did not appeal to the public": he would merely let more time elapse between performances, in order to stimulate the interest of the public and performers.

Vienna never admired Mahler more than at this moment. The Emperor in person received him in audience and congratulated him on having become master of the situation in so short a time, and Prince Liechtenstein was delighted by Mahler's indubitable triumph. All Vienna discussed his exploits, and even the conservatives said, with satisfaction, "Something is always happening at the opera, even if one doesn't always approve."

At the beginning of November, Mahler prepared another first Vienna performance; a work that, like *Dalibor,* he already knew: *Eugene Onegin.* This aroused great interest, since Tchaikovsky was already popular in the Vienna concert halls, and the press emphasized the exceptional nature of the work. "The libretto is not a play nor the music an opera," Kalbeck wrote. The same critic reproached Tchaikovsky for his abuse of the conversational and monologue style, "too rarely interrupted by a passionate outburst." He also regretted that the orchestra provided only a "gray and brown sound background" that "accompanies rather than underlines or comments." Nonetheless, the composer's dramatic genius was, in his view, indisputable.[21]

Hanslick and Heuberger both welcomed these "lyric scenes" all the more warmly since they considered them an antidote to the "harsh and violent work of the Italian moderns." The former hoped that this opera, "perhaps too delicate for the stage," would be given a place in the repertoire, for he admired "the feeling for form," "the great force of truth," the originality of the inspiration and the instrumentation. Hanslick chiefly deplored the dramatic weakness of the work despite its charm, musical quality, and wonderful orchestration. Thanks to Mahler, who was responsible for both the orchestra and the staging, the production had nevertheless awakened a high degree of "interest and comprehension."[22]

On October 24, before restaging *Der fliegende Holländer,* a task that was to take up much of Mahler's time, for it was to be his first new production, he conducted *Tristan und Isolde* for the first time in Vienna, replacing all the passages previously cut[23] except for the beginning of the love duet. The performance began at six-thirty and ended much later than usual, but the capacity audience showed no signs of boredom.

Max Kalbeck, a staunch anti-Wagnerian, found this respect for the text somewhat excessive. On the other hand, though Mahler's rapid tempos were in conformity with the score, they prevented the singers from "making themselves understood, drowned as they were by the 'surging tides' of the orchestra." After all, "Wagner himself had made exactness on their part an illusion, for his demands on them were superhuman . . . In general, it should not matter whether or not they sing on pitch. . . . The composer's style does not allow for an allegro; he needs six hours where another would be content with half that time." This opinion indicates the state of mind prevailing among the city's conservative elements.

Although he preferred Richter's "more powerful" interpretation, Hirschfeld nevertheless noted with pleasure that even the public in the boxes had remained until the last note died away, and admitted that he had been "constantly enthralled," for "the singing on stage resembled that formerly heard only in the orchestra."[24] He considered Mahler a past master in the art of husbanding his strength and reserving it for climaxes; the result was irresistible. The same critic emphasized the improvements in the staging: in the first act the ship's crew no longer witnessed the lovers' embrace, for the pair were immediately separated by the women; from then on they only held hands and gazed ecstatically at one another. Despite the age and ugliness of the scenery, the finales of the other acts were also "visually beautiful, poetic and full of meaning." Similar praise is to be found in an article by Helm, who judged the over-all effect much more impressive than usual, thanks to this "restoration."[25] "It seems to me," Helm concluded, "that Wagner's all-powerful instrumental language has never been rendered in a more stirring and enthusiastic way."[26] The compliment meant all the more since it came from a confirmed Wagnerite who considered Richter the supreme interpreter and guardian of tradition.

Four days after this first *Tristan,* Mahler conducted an uncut performance of *Tannhäuser,* before a very large and appreciative audience.[27] Helm again lauded Mahler, despite his paper's policy, and praised his "energetic conducting," though he did express some reservations concerning tempos.[28] For *Der fliegende Holländer,* Mahler at first had only planned to improve the current staging, but one thing led to another and in the end he altered everything, recasting the roles, doing away with the remaining cuts, and transforming the staging, the costumes, and the lighting, while still respecting the limitations imposed by time and money. Mahler was starting to give the full measure of his talent as a director and obtained the most astonishing scenic effects in next to no time. For Act II he reduced the size of the stage by half (as he had done earlier for the letter scene in *Eugene Onegin*), decreased the number of spinning women by two-thirds, and grouped them around the fire. Through the window the small harbor and its boats could be seen. Simple dresses replaced the low-cut "theatrical" peasant gowns. Wigs, "as natural as possible," had been prepared by the designer Gaul, but Mahler eliminated half of them at the last minute because they were all alike. For this scene the spinners' movements and gestures had been carefully rehearsed to make them more lifelike and to convey their feelings: at first fear, when the women think that Senta has gone mad, then a sudden burst of laughter when she begins to stare fixedly at the portrait of the Dutchman.

According to Natalie, Mahler had taken particular care over the laughter; in an effort to avoid the typical "opera laugh" he made the singers breathe in on the first *"Ha-ha"* and out on the second. At the start of Senta's ballad two of the younger women began to laugh, an old woman scolded them, then gradually the song attracted the spinners' attention, and they gathered around Senta, staring at the portrait, which suddenly seemed to come to life. When they realized that she was speaking to it as though it were alive, they became frightened and tried to bring her back to reality. After their departure, while Erik described his dream, Senta remained with her eyes closed, as though hypnotized, leaning on the back of her chair. For Mahler the most important moment of the opera was the entrance of Daland with the Dutchman, and he directed it so well that the entire audience "froze in terror" at Senta's cry. The two protagonists then stood motionless, as though rooted to the ground, staring at each other; every eye was drawn to these two people, "whose feet hardly seemed to touch the floor." Reichmann brought to the Dutchman a melancholy and demonic splendor: he really seemed to have come from another world. Mahler had intervened vigorously during rehearsals to stop him from moving unduly. All else having failed, he finally had his arms and legs tied, and thus succeeded in obtaining slow, trancelike movements from him, though not without bitter opposition from the famous singer. He also had a line painted on the floor beyond which Reichmann was not allowed to step. He wished the action at this point to appear suspended, all appearance of life having left the enraptured Dutchman. Neither of the protagonists seemed to hear what Daland was saying as he moved from one to the other. When he finally left them alone, the Dutchman did not dare to step forward. At the end of the scene Daland reappeared just as they were finally about to fall into each other's arms; this created a far more dramatic effect than when the two sang the entire duet locked in an interminable embrace.

Having staged this scene with so much care, Mahler grew violently angry during the first performance, when Winkelmann's admirers, sitting with his son, started to applaud the tenor warmly after Erik's exit. "I conduct the whole work, from the very first note, as a colossal build-up to the Dutchman's entrance, and those good-for-nothings ruin it. With one stroke, they break my spell over the audience, and I have to start all over again. In my rage I felt like striking Winkelmann, who allows and even encourages, these shameless practices." Mahler later said that when the curtain fell he rushed backstage and gave the tenor "the strongest scolding he had ever received."[29]

In the last act Mahler made a special effort to show the contrast between the day-to-day lives of the port's inhabitants and the grim, shadowy existence of the Dutchman's crew. The fishermen and their women arrived gaily to offer the sailors baskets of food, but the latter totally ignored their calls. The fisherfolk ended by eating and drinking the provisions, and the scene closed with a happy dance, staged with great care by Mahler. Then, since the ship's crew remained silent, the women returned home. The Dutchman witnessed the big scene between Erik and Senta, cursed the latter with terrible violence as she clung to his knees, and then tore himself away from her to give the signal for departure, a strident whistle that finally awakened the crew from its magic sleep. Will-o'-the-wisps danced above the heads of the phantom sailors, the blood-red sails unfurled and billowed in the wind, and all the gay lights of the port went out simultaneously. A dark, stormy night fell as the ship left port, and the first flush of redeeming dawn appeared as Senta threw herself into the sea. The moment when the shipwrecked vessel sails up into the sky was also entirely "restaged in a more poetic way" by Mahler.

For this new production of Der fliegende Holländer, Mahler used one of the earliest versions of the score; Wagner had later lightened the orchestration, first for Dresden and again for Zurich. In the second version, presented in Dresden, he had in particular reduced the trombone and percussion parts. When Richter heard that Mahler was going back to the original version, he made no secret of his disapproval. Mahler replied, "If Wagner were alive today, he would approve of what I am doing."[30] The day after this revival the newspapers noted its exceptional success: not one member of the audience arrived late, Kalbeck remarked. Reichmann had "surpassed himself," and Mahler and the singers had been "overwhelmed by the applause." Helm particularly praised the restoration of the cuts (the opera lasted half an hour longer than usual) and Mahler's conducting, "full of intelligence and life."

"I no longer know whether I'm on my head or my heels, and must ask you to be patient for a while," Mahler wrote to a friend at the end of 1897. "Harassed and exhausted I come home to eat and to snatch some rest, then return to the hurly-burly!"[31]

To Behn, always interested in his composing activities, Mahler also confessed that his job "took up all his time and energy." At the opera "everything goes better than I had imagined, and yet worse, for I have not even a moment to think about working."[32] "The awful galley of the opera is crushing my soul," he wrote in a third letter,[33] which expressed his anxiety at feeling so cut off from his own works. His life differed greatly from that of the average Viennese, both because of the intensity with which he worked and because he did not regularly frequent any of the salons. He did not even have time to go to the cafés, but sometimes dined with his sisters at the Spatenbräu bar,[34] at the Leidinger restaurant in the Kärntnerstrasse, or, occasionally, after galas or premieres, at the Hotel Imperial with old friends like Koessler and Guido Adler, who constantly quarreled on his account, because Koessler reproached Adler for not being sufficiently shocked by Mahler's "modern" ideas.[35]

Mildenburg had been invited to sing at the Vienna Opera in December, and on October 1, Mahler sent her a tentative contract that was to be ratified at the end of her visit. Mahler asked Pollini to grant her two weeks' leave of absence instead of only one, but since Pollini refused, Mildenburg finally sang only three guest performances. Mahler continued to write her letters full of friendly advice, particularly regarding the best way to handle the crafty Pollini.

After the outspoken reproaches in Rosa Papier's letter, Mildenburg accused Mahler of "indiscretion" regarding their personal affairs.[36] "What she means by 'former rights,'" he replied, "I don't understand, as I have never divulged any of our secrets, which concern only ourselves. No doubt she is simply fishing for information and I advise you not to swallow the bait. As regards your letter, in which you say I treated you badly, it is true that I enlightened her as to the nature of our relationship, as she had completely misinterpreted your remark. I haven't committed the least indiscretion, so you have nothing to worry about . . . I am so looking forward to your guest appearances here. You can be certain that I'll do everything I can to help you. Come, then, without bitterness, so that you can grow and prosper here, and won't have to give up my guidance and my personal concern for your artistic well-being. I hope things will go well for you here; after that life of servitude in Hamburg you will find this a new world."[37]

Mildenburg's guest performances finally started on December 8 with *Die Walküre,* which Richter conducted, and continued with *Lohengrin* on December 14 and *Fidelio* on December 17. The planned week was thus somewhat extended,[38] and the young artist's success was considerable. In a particularly enthusiastic article, Kalbeck wrote that few debuts had ever been so impatiently awaited, or had fulfilled their promise so well. Mildenburg had brought a "kind of marvelous jubilation" to Brünnhilde's cry, and the audience had immediately burst into applause. Her acting and the expressive force of her singing had gone from strength to strength. "It is evident that she has something to say," he added: "she combines the freshness and vocal powers of youth with all the advantages of a first-rate musical education."

While they were both in Hamburg, Mildenburg had had in Mahler an "excellent teacher and promoter of vocal talent," who "had taken a student and molded her into a professional artist" by giving her an admirable precise sense of rhythm, an exemplary style, and diction "almost worthy of Bayreuth." Gustav Schönaich in the *Wiener Allgemeine Zeitung* emphasized her dramatic temperament and her intelligent acting; he said that her engagement would fill an important gap in the Vienna ensemble, which lacked a dramatic soprano.[39] This already considerable success was to be surpassed by Mildenburg's first Ortrud in *Lohengrin* on December 14, when the freshness and range of her voice and the "lively energy" of her acting, "even more natural" than on the day of her debut, were noted by Hirschfeld in the *Abendpost.*[40]

The note that Mahler sent to Mildenburg after she left Vienna reflects the state of their relationship: "I understand everything perfectly and only wanted to make the moment of our farewell easier for you (it is always so terrible for both of us). There you have the reason for my 'smile,' dear Anna, and you must undertand it, as I always understand your melancholy moods. Further, let me tell you for the future: I shall never again 'interpret' anything you do or say, and you can count on my consideration and indulgence. Naturally, should you feel you want to write to me about something, do so without hesitation and straight from the heart. If, however, it is some formal request with which I must deal in my official capacity, then please send me a formal letter that I can put into the files. Let me say again that you have been highly successful and can count on a brilliant future here. 'For the rest, trust yourself to Hans Sachs.' Come to live here confidently . . . you will be well looked after. As one of 'my' ensemble, your life will be as pleasant as in your father's or your brother's home—or even more so!"[41]

On October 31, Mahler conducted a well-sung benefit for the opera's retirement fund. Johann Strauss's *Die Fledermaus* was given to a packed house and in the presence of the aged Waltz King himself. The latter sent Mahler a telegram the next day to thank him for the extreme care with

which he had rehearsed his "old *Fledermaus*" and for the performance itself, which he had found "exemplary, thanks to your genius as a conductor."
The press once again drew attention to the extraordinary quality of the
performance, which was even "overly subtle" according to some critics.[42]
Heuberger remarked that, as "an accomplished man of the theater," Mahler
had brought out innumerable nuances and previously unremarked orchestral details. Kalbeck asserted that Mahler had touched the hearts of many
Viennese and had won over "not only the public in general, but also the
most demanding musicians." Strauss himself must have found in the score
many forgotten qualities that had been buried beneath the dust of routine.

Once again Mahler had given striking proof of his professional conscientiousness, for he was far from sharing the admiration of the Viennese for
Johann Strauss: "I don't consider waltzes negligible," he told Natalie Bauer-
Lechner in 1899. "I accept them for what they are. Nonetheless, like popular
songs, I can't admire them as works of art. However moving, their too
short melodies, always divided into the same eight-bar periods, and without
the slightest attempt at development, cannot be accepted as 'compositions.'
Compare them to Schubert's *Moments Musicaux,* for example, works of art
with delineation, development and content in each measure. Strauss is a
poor fellow; with all his melodies and ideas going to waste he reminds me of
a man who has to pawn his few possessions in order to keep going, and soon
has nothing left, whereas another (the real composer) finds large bills
and small change in his pocket whenever he needs them."[43]

In 1898, Guido Adler, the musicologist from Iglau whom Mahler had
known since their conservatory days, left Prague for Vienna, to become
history of music professor at the university, a post just vacated by Hanslick.
Some years previously Adler had had the idea of starting a new edition,
subsidized by the government, of old Austrian music. He named it *Denkmäler der Tonkunst in Österreich* (Musical Monuments of Austria). No
doubt in order to obtain the backing of the imperial court, in 1892–93 he
had produced a trial publication consisting of the works of the three emperors, Ferdinand III, Leopold I, and Joseph II, and the preparations for
this project had brought him into contact with a great many influential people, aristocrats, and officials. Hanslick and Brahms had both backed him
and, no doubt to replace the latter, in 1898 he arranged for Mahler to be
elected to the board of the *Denkmäler.*[44]

It was also thanks to Adler that Mahler received a sum of three thousand
guilders from the Society for the Encouragement of German Science, Art,
and Literature in Bohemia, as a subsidy for the publication of his *First* and
*Third Symphonies* by Waldheim Eberle in Vienna. This rather unusual firm
also reprinted the *Second Symphony,* and Mahler wrote to Behn on January
21, 1898, asking for the piano transcription. "From now on, naturally, all
subventions to Hofmeister must stop," he added. "This [Waldheim
Eberle] firm does things in style: they have already printed all Bruckner
and want to engrave everything of mine, both the piano scores and the or-

chestral parts. The firm of Eberle only engraves; they are printers in the style of Röder, with plenty of capital (a corporation) and were created to promote Austrian works; they also secure the most suitable publisher: my work will probably go to Doblinger. Advertising and distribution will be done on a large scale."[45]

Mahler's relief upon receiving this good news can be judged by the way he worried over his precious manuscripts; until then he had possessed only the original and one copy of each. Because of this he had hardly ever dared to let them out of his possession, so their chances of becoming known had been almost nonexistent. He had no illusions, however, and knew that he owed this honor chiefly to his present position: "It has always been thus," he wrote. "Things are given only to the rich, whereas the little the poor have is taken away from them!"[46] A few weeks later a particularly enterprising conductor was planning to give a performance of one of Mahler's symphonies without the composer being present—the first time this had happened. The Belgian composer-conductor Sylvain Dupuis[47] had founded the Nouveaux Concerts in Liège in 1888—an annual series of four evening performances given by some of the best-known soloists and mainly devoted to contemporary works.[48] Both Vincent d'Indy and Richard Strauss had been to Liège to conduct whole evenings of their music. The courageous Dupuis programed the *Second Symphony* for March 6, 1898.[49] It was so successful that he wrote to Mahler to give him the news and to inform him that he was going to perform it again.

"My dear and honored colleague," Mahler replied on March 15, 1898, "Allow me to express my deep gratitude for the great joy you have given me by accepting my work and presenting it in a performance that—according to all the critics—was brilliant. I apologize for not expressing myself in your own beautiful language, which I understand but cannot write. I scarcely need to tell you how much I should have liked to be present. This is the first time that someone other than myself has cared for one of my spiritual children and has adopted it so completely. It is also the first time that it has won so complete a victory, to judge from the articles I have before me. I owe this to your energy and to your artistic skill, which I can measure more easily than anyone else, since I well know the great difficulties of approach and performance presented by my work . . . ."[50]

After spending Christmas with his sisters in the mountains some sixty miles south of Vienna,[51] Mahler returned to face 1898, his first complete year at the Vienna Opera. His initial important production was to be the Vienna premiere of Bizet's *Djamileh,* an opera unknown in Austria but which he had already presented to the Hamburg public. He devoted himself to this task with as much enthusiasm as energy, for he felt the "svelte, aristocratic music" and the "psychological realism" compensated for the banality of the libretto. In order to strengthen the dramatic effect, he slightly altered the sequence of events and "took the greatest care with each sound, each word, each movement, even the heroine's dance" performed by Marie

Renard.[52] He thus "created the magic atmosphere of an Oriental tale" without undue expense, for he made use of scenery borrowed from former productions yet succeeded in giving the whole performance an impression of freshness.

Bruno Walter[53] arrived from Pressburg to attend the first night of *Djamileh,* and he marveled at the quality of the musical interpretation, which he later discussed with Mahler during a supper at the Spieglers'. Some of the tempos had surprised him, one in particular, by their slowness. "I took that passage faster, even in the final rehearsal," Mahler told him, "but in the presence of the audience I am always quite certain how something should be. To obtain what one wants from the orchestra, one can only indicate the beat, or rather its essence," he added, reminding Walter of the maxim quoted a thousand times by Wagner: "The essential thing in music is clarity."[54]

According to Hanslick, *Djamileh* was an opera for connoisseurs rather than for the general public, but it had received "a friendly welcome" thanks to the "gentle nuances" of its "exquisite" score, its unity of style, its "brilliant technique," its "characteristic touches," its "charming melodies," and its "delightful orchestral sound," rather than for any striking tunes or dramatic effects. Helm felt that Bizet had managed, better than anyone else, to express in music "the tender poetry of the East," and Kalbeck thought the "atmosphere and musical poetry" of the first scene had been "unforgettable, magical . . . like the infinite variety of colors and sounds perceived in a dream." In his opinion, Mahler was largely responsible for this achievement (*Djamileh* was given eight times during the season).[55] Mahler's stage direction, even more than his musical interpretation, had made a success of this opera, no more likely to appeal to the public than *Dalibor* or *Eugene Onegin.*

Nonetheless, the state of the opera and the day-to-day standard of the performances were still far from satisfactory to Mahler. On the evening of January 30, *Don Giovanni* was scheduled, with Richter conducting and Lilli Lehmann as guest artist in the role of Donna Anna. The performance was almost canceled because Fanny Mora, the Donna Elvira, was taken ill at the last minute. To save the performance, Mahler was obliged to turn the role over to a singer formerly from the Dresden Opera, despite her fears and hesitations and despite Richter's opposition. He was beginning to realize that getting replacements was one of the basic problems of Austrian opera, for Vienna was the only musical center of importance, whereas all over Germany there were opera houses within two hours' traveling distance of each other, making it possible to get last-minute replacements by telephone.

Justi and Nina Spiegler were present that evening in Mahler's box. He listened to every note, followed every movement, watched everyone: not even the smallest detail escaped his notice. He was constantly springing to his feet and rushing to the telephone that linked his box to the wings:

"What's that costume Dippel [Don Ottavio] has on?" he asked the designer Gaul. "He looks like an undertaker, not a Spanish nobleman!" During the ballroom scene, in which the musicians forming the three small orchestras appear onstage in costume, Mahler again hurried to the telephone. "How can the viola player come on wearing a pince-nez? Let him wear spectacles if he can't see well, but not a pince-nez!" Turning to Nina, he added: "If I let that pass, they would soon come on in *Fidelio* wearing monocles!" A moment later one of the stage musicians played a wrong note: "Who is that clarinetist onstage?" he asked, determined to summon the man to his office the next day.

In the cemetery scene, he seized the telephone again: "Is that a marble statue? It looks as though it were made of pasteboard! The face is abominable. Don't ever let it appear again!" At the start of the final storm, Mahler complained about the electrician's efforts: "The lightning is laughable! Has the electrician gone out of his mind?" In the closing scene[56] an incident almost turned the dramatic conclusion of the opera into a farce: Reichmann was wandering round the stage looking for the trap door through which he was supposed to disappear, while a stagehand hesitated to set in motion the collapse of the scenery for fear of hurting him. In desperation, Richter held the final chord, the astonished audience waited, and Mahler, not understanding what had happened, shouted down the telephone, "Dear God, isn't that set ever going to fall?"[57]

At that time the series of reforms planned by the lord chamberlain had not yet been carried out, and Intendant Bezecny was still in his post.[58] It was undoubtedly thanks to Prince Liechtenstein's insistence that Bezecny finally resigned at the end of January 1898. In a farewell letter to the members of the opera, Bezecny congratulated himself for having "had the idea" of proposing Mahler for director. His successor, Freiherr von Plappart von Leenheer, was officially named on February 15 and introduced to the opera personnel on February 20. The journalists, who visited the opera every week to discuss past and future events, were seated in the second row of the stalls on the day of this presentation, and Richter, who was seated nearby, whispered to one of his friends, "This gives the imbeciles something to write about." One of the journalists overheard the remark and found it insulting; two hours later a press delegation called in Mahler and demanded that Richter apologize. Mahler replied that he would look into the matter, and with Richter's approval he wrote to Karl Rolleder, publisher of the *Deutsche Zeitung* and dean of the journalists, explaining that Richter's remark had not been intended to offend anyone. This closed the incident.[59]

At the time of Plappart's appointment, the *Dienst-Instruktion* promulgated in 1885 for the intendant of the theaters[60] was modified, and most of the intendant's powers were severely limited, undoubtedly because of the deficit incurred during the preceding years. Henceforth nearly all important decisions, such as the instructions to the directors of the opera and the Burgtheater, the hiring of artists, and the drawing up of contracts, had to be ratified by the lord chamberlain. All negotiations prior to engagements were the responsibility of the two directors; the intendant had to be consulted only after the preliminary "invitation." Furthermore, four times a year Plappart had to submit to his superior an over-all schedule of engagements and a report on the singers and their salaries, as well as a proposed budget, thus enabling the lord chamberlain to control all expenses and bills.

This curtailing of the intendant's powers was lucky for Mahler, as both Plappart and his subordinate Wlassack rapidly became his deadly enemies, but thanks to the new *Dienst-Instruktion,* he was much less dependent on them than upon their superiors. If the previous arrangement had continued, his situation might well have become rapidly untenable, since the intendant would have been in a position to oppose all his initiatives. One of the first conflicts arose over the guest appearance of a star singer. Plappart objected to the engagement, asking Mahler "to bear in mind the opera's finances." With some haughtiness Mahler replied: "Your Excellency, that is not the right approach. An imperial institution such as the Hofoper should feel honored to spend money in this way; it could not be put to better use. Nevertheless, I shall do my best to take your request into consideration."

Thus, despite the change of intendants, Mahler's authority was extended during his second year as director, and this notwithstanding the periodic "scandals" caused by certain singers. Once, when Mahler had a difference of opinion with the ballet master, Prince Liechtenstein suggested to him amiably, affectionately even, that he should not play into the hands of his enemies so easily. Mahler replied that, on the contrary, such periodic storms were necessary to ensure discipline. "The establishment of order necessitates the greatest severity," he added. "Each scandal, then, has a meaning and a beneficial effect: you should summon me only when there are fewer than two 'scandals' a week."[61]

The last weeks of February 1898 were particularly busy at the opera, for Mahler had inherited from Jahn an especially dull task,[62] that of producing Leoncavallo's *La Bohème,* the dramatic and musical weaknesses of which he had been aware ever since seeing it in Venice. The composer, who had heard from Jahn about Mahler's lukewarm opinion of his opera, had been in correspondence with the intendant from early September 1897 on, to complain about the postponement of the first performance, originally planned for November 19. Mahler had explained the delay: the tenor Van Dyck had invoked a clause in his contract which enabled him to refuse the part of Marcello, and for the moment Vienna had no other singer available for the role.

Leoncavallo was not satisfied with this explanation. He wrote again to the intendant on September 18, in ludicrous French, protesting that Van Dyck's refusal did not justify the postponement or cancellation of the premiere, which was damaging to his reputation: "Ah, I already perceive the changes due to the absence of good Maître Jahn. Nothing like this would ever have happened when he was director, especially after the problems raised by the

*Médicis*.[63] When one has Schrödter available (whom I myself suggested for the role, because I know his voice and his physique would be more suitable), and when one has the nerve to tell me that because Mr. Van Dyck does not wish to sing, *one can no longer give the opera,* it is like saying that the Vienna Opera will be closed when Van Dyck stops singing!! What nonsense! It seems that my enemies lack inventiveness for their pretexts. And believe me, this is a pretext. As to the value of the work, come here on the 24th or 25th (I will telegraph you the exact date) for the premiere. Deign to honor the performance with your presence, and you will see the work that Mr. Mahler is treating so badly. If you cannot come, send Maître Richter, or someone else in whom you have confidence (but not one of Mr. Mahler's friends), and you will learn what my theatrical work is like. I have written to Mr. Mahler, asking for Schrödter as tenor, and saying that I do not accept the postponement."

Leoncavallo finally asked Bezecny to "prevent this infamy" and offered to go to Vienna and plead his cause before Archduke Eugen.[64] Mahler was not a man to be intimidated by such maneuvers; Leoncavallo had threatened to "take the necessary steps if he [Mahler] did not conform to his wishes," and, exasperated, Mahler had answered that such "shameful" threats were of slight importance compared to the interests of the opera. The premier had been and would remain scheduled for the end of February. Mahler later devoted as much time and care to the preparation of this opera, which he scorned, as he would have if it had been a masterpiece.

Leoncavallo reached Vienna in mid-February 1898 and learned that Van Dyck had decided to "fall ill," hoping to postpone for three days the first performance, scheduled for February 23. Having resisted the pressures brought to bear by Leoncavallo, Mahler was determined not to submit to those of a singer. Since his arrival in Vienna, he had insisted that two complete casts be assigned to each new opera; if Van Dyck did not sing on the twenty-third his role would be taken at the premiere by Andreas Dippel.

Having earlier insisted that his opera be given with or without Van Dyck, Leoncavallo now decided that Van Dyck was absolutely indispensable to its success.[65] "Dear Master," he wrote on February 17, after the penultimate rehearsal, "I am certain that, due to your great artistic conscientiousness and competence, you have already realized, after today's *most unfortunate rehearsal, that it is absolutely impossible to give the premiere next Wednesday!* The artists' hesitations and the uncertainty of some members of the orchestra, the lack of ensemble and precision in the chorus, the *absolute need* to polish the *mise en scène* further, prompt me to ask you at once to postpone the premiere until Saturday . . . I must tell you that *I cannot give up* Mr. Van Dyck in the role of Marcello for the first performance. His collaboration is too essential for such an important premiere; this point is capital. Moreover you yourself told me three months ago that Mr. Van Dyck was *indispensable and that without him you would not give my opera! . . ."* Leoncavallo concluded his letter with another threat: he hoped he would "not be obliged to take further steps."

"Dear Sir, I consider your criticism of the *hesitations* of the *soloists* and the *orchestra* a personal insult," Mahler wrote back the same day. "During today's rehearsal, Frau Saville and Herr Felix were in fact uncertain of their roles. You know, however, that neither of them is to sing on the evening of the premiere! The other soloists can be relied upon, and no one in the world except yourself would dream of doubting the orchestra's ability to perform its task perfectly! Furthermore, in the interests of my own reputation I cannot risk an inferior performance. I only mention this in passing. Let us discuss the matter again after tomorrow's rehearsal, when the premiere soloists are to sing.

"Moreover, whatever date I set for the premiere, I cannot be sure Mr. Van Dyck will be present; I know this from experience. An opera house as important as ours cannot depend upon the caprices or health of a singer. That is why I have prepared two casts, so as not to be embarrassed by possible cancellations. The premiere must be perfect; on that point we are in agreement. However the decision lies with me alone, and I shall make it tomorrow after the rehearsal. Should you again criticize our work, rather than run the risk of alarming public opinion, I will postpone the premiere (and entrust it to another conductor).[66] I shall not modify the schedule except in a case of *force majeure! Au revoir* until tomorrow's rehearsal."

That evening Leoncavallo wrote again just before midnight, pulling in his horns a little: though he claimed the right to "make a few comments," he nevertheless felt that the most important thing was for Mahler to conduct the premiere, for he was "the principal artist, the life and soul of the work!" However Van Dyck had given him his word of honor he would sing, and in view of this he was sure Mahler would agree to grant him the two extra days of work, since he had not had the stage rehearsals he had asked for. "You pointed out wittily the other day *that I ought to know my Bohème well.* May I remind you that I am also *the author of my libretto,* and consequently know what I can ask of my artists."

The next day, February 19, Leoncavallo arrived at the opera house, accompanied by a compatriot whose task was to tell him, in Italian, what was happening. They took their places in the stalls, ready to watch the rehearsal. As soon as Mahler appeared on the podium, he informed the orchestra and singers of the exchange of letters the previous day ("his tone was agitated," according to Leoncavallo): "Herr Leoncavallo believes that additional rehearsals of his opera are necessary if everything is to go smoothly. I don't agree. I am delighted that he is present now and that his Italian friend can translate everything to him, so that he may know what is being said. I consider his doubts superfluous: an elite of artists are gathered here onstage and in the orchestra pit; they will give his work the best possible performance, certainly better than he could get anywhere else. As director and conductor I can guarantee this and I believe I am qualified to judge. Now that we have double casts I cannot allow a single singer to make difficulties for me. Ladies and gentlemen, let us begin the rehearsal and show Herr Leoncavallo what the Vienna Opera is capable of achieving."

Mahler was about to give the signal to begin, when Leoncavallo approached the orchestra pit and, to everyone's astonishment, began, in French, to speak: of course he had the highest regard for the Vienna Opera, "whose artists are far better suited than anyone else to bear my opera to triumph," but, while considering his work "with modesty," he nonetheless thought that he "could judge the stage production and the voices" and believed it was absolutely imperative that Van Dyck sing the premiere. Mahler himself had in fact once stated that he would not give the opera without Van Dyck.

"Since Leoncavallo has overcome his scruples and admitted that the Vienna Opera company is capable of performing his opera, I consider the matter closed," Mahler answered in German. "Oh no," Leoncavallo shouted, "permit me to add a few more words." Exasperated, Mahler replied that "there will be no more talk here. Let us have silence and start to rehearse!" Leoncavallo put on his hat and left the auditorium in a rage.

The rehearsal was interrupted in the middle of Act I by Stoll, the stage director, who entered, accompanied by a lawyer, and handed Mahler a letter from Leoncavallo. Mahler refused to accept it, declaring that he had no time to read while conducting, and his reply was accompanied by "such energetic gestures" that the letter was knocked from Stoll's hands. Mahler then resumed conducting despite the lawyer's protest,[67] and at the end of the first act he congratulated the singers and the orchestra, saying, "do not let yourselves be disconcerted," for everything had gone perfectly.

Leoncavallo's letter, written in German, accused Mahler of conduct "to which I am not accustomed," and once again praised the Viennese artists, whom their director had misinformed regarding the contents of his first letter. Leoncavallo continued to maintain that Van Dyck must sing the premiere, after two additional rehearsals. "If you refuse to agree to my wishes, which are artistically justified," he went on, "and persist in giving my work in this unprepared, imperfect manner, you will expose your own reputation, as well as that of your institution, to a fiasco. Should this be the case, I withdraw my opera. I protest against its performance, and I shall never again set foot on your stage. The public will then be able to judge how you treat a composer who flatters himself that he has already given to the Vienna Opera a not unsuccessful work."[68]

Mahler refused to give in, and for the two days preceding the premiere Leoncavallo aired his grievances to the newspapers, moved heaven and earth to get his own way, and even drew the Italian ambassador, Count Nigra, into the battle. Mahler's superiors, however, backed him and advised him to stand firm. During a final meeting with Leoncavallo, the latter refused to attend the dress rehearsal next day. This took place with Dippel in the role of Marcello and proceeded without incident. Finally realizing that the premiere would indeed take place as scheduled, Leoncavallo tried to persuade Van Dyck to sing, even though the famous tenor had threatened to resign if Mahler performed the opera before his "complete recovery."[69] Mahler merely gave Van Dyck an ultimatum: either he must change his mind before noon on the day of the premiere, or Dippel would sing in his place.

On the day of the performance, Van Dyck sent Mahler a doctor's certificate from one Professor Chiari, stating that he was suffering from a cough and serious catarrh. Mahler did not reply; at noon he turned the role over to Dippel, and stuck to this decision despite desperate last-minute attempts by Van Dyck to get him to change his mind. In the end Leoncavallo attended the premiere and not only declared himself satisfied but finally admitted that Dippel's personality suited the role of Marcello better than Van Dyck's. The theater was full, for the newspapers had kept their readers informed about all the various stages of the conflict. Mahler dashed to the podium with the speed of lightning but was unable to prevent immediate, thunderous applause. Without turning to acknowledge it, he at once began the overture, but this did not prevent the same outburst of clapping at the beginning of Act II. Throughout the performance the keen antagonism between Mahler's and Leoncavallo's supporters was very obvious.

The Viennese critics were severe: Kalbeck considered the second act merely a "useless variation" of the first and wrote that the whole opera "lacked original ideas." Modern verists, he thought, were mistaken in seeking the truth without bothering about the dramatic construction, which was defective in Leoncavallo's work, since at the end the emphasis suddenly shifted from Musetta to Mimi. "One cannot celebrate thus in a single day both Shrove Tuesday and Ash Wednesday," Kalbeck concluded. Heuberger criticized the length of the exposition, which was clearly inferior to Puccini's. He considered the music of the last two acts clumsy, and the orchestration threatened to drown the singers' voices.[70]

Hanslick thought that Puccini had "more musical talent and feeling for reality" than Leoncavallo, who moved heaven and earth to plunge the spectator into an atmosphere of wild gaiety, but "laughter is something that must come naturally . . . The characters onstage constantly voiced the 'ha-has' called for by the libretto, but the public did not utter a sound." The slightest sign of any wit had to be accompanied by trombones; a chorus of violins, cellos, and horns had emphasized each line of "comic dialogue"; the whole effect was one of "brutal, pretentious hubbub." Hanslick's conclusion was "no creative force, no personality, no sense of beauty—a caricature of Italian music," a criticism no more severe than that of posterity, which has quite forgotten Leoncavallo's *Bohème*.[71]

The opera was in fact successful enough for Mahler later to regret having gone to so much trouble to "throw dust in the eyes of the Viennese public." After having worked for almost a year to improve the public's taste and raise the opera's artistic level, he had then "corrupted it against his will," thanks to a magnificent performance of "rubbish." He was, however, pleased by his victories over Leoncavallo and Van Dyck, for which he was warmly congratulated by Prince Liechtenstein. Despite his opera's success, Leoncavallo continued to complain (particularly to Karpath) about its "tepid" reception, which he attributed to Mahler's alterations.[72] He was convinced that Mahler had not done his best for the opera; at the end of March he appealed to Mahler's "loyalty" and asked that the role of Marcello be assigned to Schrödter during Dippel's leave of absence. Mahler replied that Schrödter would need two months to learn the part and that Dippel would be back on April 10. The success of this *La Bohème* having fallen off considerably, it was dropped after the sixth performance; Mahler had nevertheless carried out his obligations with exceptional loyalty, despite the mediocre quality of the work and despite a composer who had done everything possible to anger and discourage him.

"I can make the whole opera dance
on my fingertip, but I derive
no satisfaction from it . . ."

# CHAPTER 28

## Mahler in Vienna (IV) — First Philharmonic Concerts — First Battles at the Opera — The Ring and Der Freischütz (March–December 1898)

Late in 1897, Guido Adler had suggested to Mahler that he might obtain for him a grant from the Gesellschaft zur Förderung deutscher Wissenschaft, Kunst und Literatur in Böhmen (Society for the Encouragement of German Science, Art, and Literature in Bohemia) for the publication of his *First* and *Third Symphonies* and the orchestral parts of the *Second Symphony*.[1]

Adler's first contact with the society was undoubtedly successful, and he soon followed it up by sending a detailed official report and a longer *Referat* covering Mahler's life and achievements, with special reference to performances and publications of his works up to the *Third Symphony*.[2] "I personally value him greatly—as a good friend and as an artist. He always keeps the artistic ideal in view," Adler added as a postscript to the report. In the *Referat,* Adler speaks of Mahler and Strauss as "standing side by side, and, to speak frankly, also in the vanguard of the most modern movement in music." Adler also analyzes the symphonies and their general structure enthusiastically, although making a few reservations such as the *"unerhörten Kakophonien"* (unprecedented cacophonies) of the third movement of the *Third Symphony,*[3] and Mahler's refusal to accept the boundary that had defined up to then the canons of pure beauty. Adler nevertheless suggested that posterity might think otherwise.

It is greatly to his credit that, despite his conservative outlook and a profession that forced him to live mainly in the past, he made such great efforts on Mahler's behalf. In the *Referat* he estimated the cost of publishing the symphonies at twelve hundred gulden. Two grants of three thousand gulden were requested from the society, one immediately, the other in January 1899. The importance of this publication can hardly be overestimated, for, from then on, Mahler began to gain widespread recognition as a composer. Adler cannot be blamed for one minor inaccuracy. The two symphonies had already been, or were just about to be, published. It seems certain that the printer Eberle and the publisher Weinberger had been persuaded to issue the scores only after Adler's assurance that the subsidy would be granted.

Mahler's guest appearance with the Prague Philharmonic Orchestra, recently placed under the direction of Angelo Neumann, was certainly not due to chance, but had probably been suggested by the Society for the Encouragement of German Science, Art, and Literature in Bohemia. The performance was due to take place on March 3, 1898, at the German Opera House in aid of the theater's pension fund.[4] Mahler was warmly welcomed to the Czech capital, and the *First Symphony* won its first decisive success that evening. Each movement was enthusiastically applauded, and during the final ovation Mahler was presented with a laurel wreath and palm. The rehearsals had been conducted by Franz Schalk. In one of the notes that he wrote to Guido Adler, Mahler suggested bringing the mezzo-soprano Edyth Walker with him to Prague to sing the solo from his *Second Symphony* to a Philharmonic committee as a gesture of thanks, but the next note indicates that this project did not materialize. Mahler also asked his friend "not to count on him for any dinners or receptions," as he expected to be too busy paying visits and correcting the parts of his *First Symphony*. After the concert he took Justi to a supper that Neumann gave in his honor and to which the principal artistic figures of the city had been invited, including the director of the conservatory, Mahler's onetime rival, the conductor Ludwig Slansky, Guido Adler and Lipiner, as well as the members of the opera and the theater, the most influential journalists, and many important officials.[5] One of the opera directors, Richard Tauber,[6] made a speech in his honor, in the course of which he read the letter that Mahler had sent to Neumann from Kassel in December 1884, and enthusiastically praised his work in Prague.

Before the concert the *Prager Abendblatt* published an article on the *First Symphony* which referred to the Magyar "burning tears" and the Slav motifs in the third movement. Misinformed about the date of composition, the writer believed it to be "a reminiscence of the period when Mahler was conducting in Budapest." The *Bohemia* was the only paper to publish a proper account of the concert itself, and it also mentioned the battles that had raged around the work. Even Mahler's enemies, it said, must detect his "rich and abundant imagination" and the "fiery exaltation" of an author who "cares little about the possibilities of performance and the chances of success with the general public." Nor could these enemies deny the captivating beauty of certain details and the "startling new effects of instrumentation." Mahler undoubtedly belonged to the "modern school of outdoor painting," but he had not yet freed himself from "the style of his master, Bruckner." The paper also deserves merit for praising the parodic Funeral March, though it regretted that the Finale failed to provide either "a sense of purity or any true artistic enjoyment."

On the same evening as this Prague concert, Ferdinand Löwe, another of Bruckner's pupils, conducted Munich's Kaim Orchestra in the Vienna premiere of the Andante from the *Second Symphony*. The piece was, as usual, well received. Helm found it difficult to judge the short, "melodious and ably orchestrated" extract, but considered its "studied naïveté" and "reminiscences" unattractive. Heuberger on the other hand praised its "charming sound" and its resemblance to a "graceful ländler."[7] Kalbeck felt a "clear influence" of Beethoven and Brahms in this piece, which he found "harmonious, melodious, lilting and dancelike; it honors the composer's talent and confirms his technical mastery."

In the middle of April, Mahler went to Budapest, where he attended a performance of the ballet *Die Rothen Schuhe,* by Raoul Mader, a *korrepetitor* at the Hofoper, who was no doubt hoping to have his work performed there.[8] He also revisited the Hungarian Opera after six years of absence and was received by the director. On his return to Vienna he met Bruno Walter, who had come to spend ten days with him,[9] and played for him the revised score of *Das klagende Lied.* Walter urged him not to put off the publication of this work any longer. Consequently Mahler completed the last and definitive version of the score that spring.[10]

The only important operatic event in the spring of 1898 was a new production of *Aïda,* greeted with the same unanimous enthusiasm as its predecessors. Though he had reservations about some of the tempos,[11] Helm again declared his admiration for Mahler's magnificent achievement. He praised the marvelous pianissimos in the Prelude, as well as the clarity and grandiose effect of the second Finale, which had been much applauded. Heuberger also admired the "prodigious majesty" of the triumphal scene, for which Mahler used the slow, majestic tempo he also applied to the priests' chorus and the women's chorus in Act II. He felt that the whole interpretation showed genius, and that the orchestra had never played such a lively and eloquent role in the dramatic action.[12]

During the early months of 1898 Mahler's popularity in Vienna constantly increased, while his efficiency as a director became continually more apparent to his superiors. In spite of this he began to realize the drawbacks of his post and the amount of time and effort he was obliged to devote to administrative tasks; "You cannot imagine," he told Natalie and Justi, "how bored I am already with running this opera, in spite of all the work it involves! Perhaps it's because nothing presents me with the slightest difficulty. I can make the whole opera dance on my fingertip, but I derive no satisfaction from it, unlike the intense joy I feel when I am composing. I feel at present like a traveling salesman who, while going about his own business must, as a sideline, also work for others; only in my case, the sideline has become my main job, so that I no longer have the opportunity of time for the supreme task with which the Lord has entrusted me . . . I find it repugnant to live in the midst of all this splendor. How people admire me and grovel to me! How I'd love to tell them how miserably modest I feel, and that, in my job here, I want nothing but to do my duty!"

After the first thrill of triumph that he felt on his appointment, Mahler, who knew nothing of the intoxication of power, began to suffer from not having the time to compose. His anxiety was further aggravated by ill-health, which soon obliged him to undergo an operation. Some of his reforms, too, took longer to accomplish than he had foreseen: Reichmann, Winkelmann, Van Dyck, and Renard were not prepared to surrender overnight to a young tyrant's demands[13]: they would pay lip service to his orders, while secretly taking every opportunity of challenging his authority. There was a world of difference between the easygoing comfort of opera life that had previously been the rule and the incessant work that was now expected from everyone; especially since the stars felt that in the past they had already more than satisfied the public's wishes. Mahler's main preoccupation during the early months of 1898 was to discover those artists who could adapt themselves to his rhythm, and to replace the others. Fortunately some great singers were intelligent enough to understand him and polish their performances under his direction. Reichmann was a man of exceptional merit and integrity with an amazingly expressive voice, but his musicianship and sense of rhythm had their shortcomings: Mahler found his acting mannered and blamed him for the way in which he angled for the limelight and held certain notes to draw applause. Reichmann had other faults, which were due to his age, but they were amply compensated by his artistry: he frequently sang out of tune and sometimes missed his high notes. Their relationship was stormy from the first. After long years of Richter's quiet authority, Reichmann expected every conductor to follow him and conform to his will. He was thus unable to adjust to the presence at the opera of a nervous, tyrannical revolutionary who disturbed and altered everything to suit his whims. He was not prepared to accept such behavior, and once even swore to "spring at his throat." He was unable, for instance, to understand Mahler's efforts to do away with the claque. During a performance of *Tannhäuser* at the end of 1898, some members of the audience tried to applaud Reichmann's aria in the second act, but the others, who were aware of the new ruling, whistled as the applause started. Reichmann took this as a personal insult, threw down his lyre, and sang the rest of the act "with great indifference." The same thing happened again in the last act, and this time he not only threw his instrument down again noisily, but shouted "unrepeatable" insults at the hecklers.[14]

Despite all this, Reichmann, who was one of the most celebrated Hans Sachs in the history of opera, and who had sung the role for years to everyone's satisfaction,[15] altered many aspects of his well-known performance under Mahler's influence. Mahler made him work at every detail and attempted to force him to respect the note values printed in the score: in the *Schusterlied,* Reichmann never knew exactly when to strike the hammer

30. The Leipzig Opera.

# Freitag, 20. Januar 1888.

# Neues Leipziger Stadt-Theater.

**Anfang 7 Uhr.**  19. Abonnements-Vorstellung (3. Serie, weiß). **Anfang 7 Uhr.**

## Zum ersten Male:

# Die drei Pinto's.

### Komische Oper in 3 Aufzügen von C. M. von Weber.

Unter Zugrundelegung des gleichnamigen Textbuches von Th. Hell, der hinterlassenen Entwürfe und ausgewählter Manuscripte des Componisten ausgeführt:

der dramatische Theil von **Carl von Weber**, der musikalische von **Gustav Mahler**.

### Regie: Director Max Staegemann. — Direction Kapellmeister Mahler.

#### Personen:

| | |
|---|---|
| Don Pantaleone Roiz de Pacheco, | Herr Köhler. |
| Don Gomez Freiros, Edelleute zu Madrid | Herr Hübner. |
| Donna Clarissa, Don Pantaleone's Tochter | Fr. Baumann. |
| Laura, Clarissen's Zofe | Frl. Artner. |
| Don Gaston Viratos, ehemals Student zu Salamanca | Herr Hedmondt. |
| Don Pinto de Fonseca, ein junger Landedelmann aus Castilla | Herr Grengg. |
| Der Wirth der Dorfschänke zu Penaranda | Herr Proft. |
| Inez, dessen Tochter | Frl. Rothauser. |
| Ambrosio, Don Gaston's Diener | Herr Schelper. |
| Ein Student | Herr Marion. |
| Der Haushofmeister Don Pantaleone's | Herr Tietz. |

Studenten von Salamanca. Dienerschaft im Hause Don Pantaleone's. Knechte und Mägde in der Dorfschänke zu Penaranda.

Ort der Handlung: 1. Aufzug: In der Dorfschänke zu Penaranda, halbwegs zwischen Salamanca und Madrid. 2. und 3. Aufzug: Im Hause Don Pantaleone's zu Madrid.

Die neue Decoration des 1. Aufzuges ist von Herrn Hoftheatermaler Kautsky in Wien angefertigt.

Nach jedem Akt findet eine längere Pause statt.

Krank: Frl. Göhrs.

Der Text ist an der Kasse und bei den Logenschließern für 50 Pfennige zu haben.

## Opern-Preise:

| | Mrk. Pfg. | | Mrk. Pfg. | | Mrk. Pfg. |
|---|---|---|---|---|---|
| Parterre | 1 50 | Mittel-Balkon, Hinter-Reihen | 3 — | Logen des I. Ranges: Ein einzelner Platz | 2 60 |
| I. Parquet | 4 — | Seiten-Balkon | 4 — | II. Rang, Mittelplatz, Sperrsitz | 1 80 |
| II. Parquet | 3 — | Balkon-Logen: Ein einzelner Platz | 3 40 | Seitenplatz | 1 25 |
| Parterre-Logen: Ein einzelner Platz | 3 — | Proscenium-Logen im I. Range: | | Stehplatz | 1 — |
| Proscenium-Logen im Parterre u. Balkon: | | Ein einzelner Platz | 3 — | III. Rang, Mittelplatz | 75 |
| Ein einzelner Platz | 5 — | Amphitheater, Sperrsitz | 3 — | Seiten- und Stehplatz | — |
| Mittel-Balkon, Vorder-Reihen | 5 — | Stehplatz | 1 50 | Proscenium-Logen im III. Range | 1 — |
| Mittel-Reihen | 4 — | | | | |

### Einlaß 1/2 7 Uhr. Anfang 7 Uhr. Ende 1/2 10 Uhr.

Der **Billet-Verkauf** für den laufenden Tag findet an der Tages-Kasse von 10 Uhr Vormittags bis 3 Uhr Nachmittags, der Vor-Verkauf für den nachfolgenden Tag (mit Aufgeld von 30 Pfennig) von 1 bis 3 Uhr Nachmittags statt. — Sonn- und Festtags wird die Tages-Kasse erst um 10½ Uhr geöffnet.
**Garderobe-Abonnements-Bücher**, 25 Billets enthaltend, werden an der Tages-Kasse à 4 Mark verkauft.

## Repertoire:

| Neues Theater. | Altes Theater. |
|---|---|
| **Sonnabend, 21. Januar** 20. Abonnements-Vorstellung (4. Serie, gelb): **Ein toller Einfall.** Hierauf: **Zehn Mädchen u. kein Mann.** (Anfang 1/2 7 Uhr.) | **Der Sonnwendhof.** (Anfang 7 Uhr.) |

Druck von G. Reusche in Leipzig.

**Die Direction des Stadt-Theaters.**

32. Program of the first performance of Mahler's *Symphonic Poem* in Budapest (*First Symphony*).

OPPOSITE:
31. Poster for the premiere of Weber's *Die drei Pintos,* completed by Mahler.

# MAGY. KIR.  OPERAHÁZ.

Évi bérlet 73. szám.  Havi bérlet 13. szám.

## Budapest, csütörtökön, 1889. április 18-án:

**Bianchi Bianca** kisasszony csász. és kir. kamara-énekesnő fölléptével

# A SEVILLAI BORBÉLY.

Vig opera 2 felvonásban. Zenéjét szerzette Rossini.

### Személyek:

| | | | |
|---|---|---|---|
| Gróf Almaviva | — Pauli | Bertha, Rosina nevelője | — Doppler J. |
| Bartolo, orvos | — Hegedüs | Őrtiszt | — Váradi |
| Rosina, gyámleánya | — Bianchi Bianca k. a. | Fiorillo, Almaviva inasa | — Stoll |
| Bazilio, zenemester | — Odry | Jegyző | — Vincze |
| Figaro, borbély | — Takács | Örök. Zenészek Inasok. | |

A második felvonásban, az énekleczke alkalmával: »Magán-dal«, Donizetti LINDA czimü operájából énekli BIANCHI BIANCA k. a.

### Az opera után: Harmadszor:

# UJ ROMEO.

Eredeti ballet 1 felvonásban. Irták STEIGER LAJOS és SZTOJANOVITS JENŐ. Betanította MAZZANTINI LAJOS balletmester.

### Személyek:

| | | | |
|---|---|---|---|
| Stella, a párisi opera első tánczosnője | Müller Kati | Marco, India-utazó | — Pini H. |
| Lisbeth ) | — Zsuzsanits E. | Milo | — Mazzantini L. |
| Susanne ) Stella barátnői | — Maruzzi F. | Prudhomme | — Vincze |
| Adrienne ) | — Kürthi H. | Prudhommné | — Hansné I. |
| Guy ) | — Zolnai | | |
| Gontran ) Stella udvarlói | — Forrai | Álarczosok, báli vendégek, a… | |
| Gaston ) | — Juhász | Szinhely: Párisi kerti… | |

### Előforduló tánczok:

1. **Legyezőtáncz és csoportozatok.** Előadja: az összes tánczszemélyzet. 2. **Stella-keringő.** Tánczolja Müller K., Zsuzsanits E., Maruzzi F., Kürthi H. — 3. **Indusnők táncza.** Előadják: Monori T., Schleiche A., Ramberger L. és a tánczkar. — 4 **Négyes-táncz.** Előadják: Müller K., Zsuzsanits E., Maruzzi F., Kürthi H. — 5. **Tánczleczke és Gavotte.** Előadják: Mazzantini L. és Pini H. — 6. **Legyező-lassú.** Tánczolja: Müller K., Mazzantini L. és az összes tánczkar. — 7. **Pezsgő-polka.** Előadja: az összes tánczszemélyzet. — 8. **Szerelmi jelenet.** Előadják: Müller K., Maruzzi F., Zsuzsanits E., Kürthi H., Pini H. és a tánczszemélyzet. — 9. **Nagy keringő-egyveleg.** Tánczolják: Müller K., Maruzzi F, Zsuzsanits E. Kürthi H., Pini H., és az összes tánczszemélyzet. — 10. **Gallop és zárjelenet.**

Az uj jelmezek a m. kir. operaház szabómühelyében készültek Caffi Péter jelmezszabó vezetése alatt, az uj diszlet festették Spanraft és Hirsch, a m. kir. operaház diszletfestői.

## Kezdete 7 órakor, vége 10 után.

☞ Az opera szövege az esteli pénztáraknál, páholy-, földszinti támlásszék- és III. em. zártszéknyitóknál 25 krért kapható. ☜

### Rendes helyárak:

| Páholy: | Támlásszék: | II. em. körszék | III. emeleti erkély- és zártszék: | |
|---|---|---|---|---|
| Földszinti . . 12 frt | | | Erkélyszék az I. sor 1 frt 50 | Zártszék az I. sorb. — frt 80 |
| I. emeleti . . 12 frt | Az I—X. sorb. 3 frt | Az I. sorban 2 frt — | " a II.—V. . 1 frt — | " a II. — frt 60 |
| II. emeleti 11. sz. 10 frt | A XI—XIX. 2 frt | A II. . 1 . 50 | " a VI—VIII. . 1 frt 80 | " a III—IV. — frt 40 |
| II. , 1—5. , 8 frt | | A III. . 1 . — | | |

Jegyet válthatni d. e. 10 órától 1-ig és d. u. 3—5-ig a hajós-utczai nappali pénztárnál. Esteli pénztárnyitás 6½ órakor.

Kéretik a t. cz. szinházlátogató közönség, hogy a nézőtéren a férfiak felöltő, bot és esernyő, a hölgyek pedig kalap nélkül sziveskedjenek megjelenni. A ruhatárban a felöltőért 10 kr., kalapért, pálczáért, esernyőért 5 kr. fizetendő.

## Holnap, pénteken 1889. április 19. és szombaton 1889. április 20-án:

# Az operaház zárva.

### MŰSOR:

Vasárnap, 21-én: **Babatündér és Villars dragonyosai.** Bianchi Bianca k. a. fölléptével. Bérletszünet IV. sz. Rendes árak. (Kezdete 6½ órakor.) — Hétfőn, 22-én: **Babatündér, Jó ójt Pantalon ur és Uj Romeo.** Havi bérlet 14. szám. Rendes árak. (Kezdete 6½ órakor.)

☞ A műsoron levő előadásra elő lehet jegyezni, az elővételi ár lefizetése mellett, a jobboldali (hajós-utczai) nappali pénztárnál, 12—1 óra közt Az előjegyzett jegyek az előadást megelőző napon 12—1 óra közt ugyanott adatnak ki. Az operaház szinlapjaira előfizethetni a pénztárnál. Előfizetési ár, házhozhordással: egy hóra 1 frt.

Budapest, 1889. Nyomatott Müller Károlynál (ezelőtt Münster Károly) 11. ker., Főherczeg Albrecht-ut 3—5. szám.

33. Poster for the performance of Rossini's *Barber of Seville* conducted by Mahler at the Budapest Opera.

34. *The Huntsman's Funeral,* an etching by Moritz von Schwind which was the inspiration for the Funeral March in the *First Symphony.*

35. Count Bela Zichy, director of the Budapest Opera.

36. Mahler in Hamburg, 1896.

37. Hans von Bülow.

38 & 39. Ernestine Schumann-Heink and Max Alvary, singers at the Hamburg Opera.

blows and had to have a prompter in the wings to give him his cues. Reichmann's diary[16] shows his exasperation, he refers to Mahler as a "little Kobold," and is indignant that this "Jewish monkey" should try to teach him, the famous *Kammersänger,* his job. He changed his tone after the first performance of the new production, in which he obtained a great personal success: Mahler then became a god to be worshiped because, thanks to him, Reichmann was singing better than ever; he had not thought it possible to achieve such a triumph, so he must forgive and forget everything![17]

If an artist like Reichmann was occasionally able to see in Mahler the instrument and servant of a cause, there were others who considered him nothing but a tyrant—an implacable despot. He took Draconian measures to combat the stars' displays of temperament; he would sometimes engage minor singers for important parts; thanks to him they would sometimes enjoy a moment of glory, only to accuse him of having ruined their careers when they relapsed into their usual mediocrity. In Vienna, more even than in Hamburg, he imposed a new concept of work which included the musical expression, the posture, the acting, and the diction of the singers. Whenever he had a moment he would hurry to the rooms in which the soloists and chorus were rehearsing. If the accompanists failed to satisfy him, he would interrupt to demonstrate what he wanted. As he could hardly treat conductors in the same way, he constantly summoned the singers to his office after rehearsals, to work on the passages that had displeased him.[18]

Mahler not only had music in his blood, but the theater as well, and he expected every performance to be a theatrical and musical rebirth of the work in question. He considered the appearance, personality, and dramatic ability of the singers as much as their voices when he was distributing parts. Sometimes he made mistakes and entrusted dramatic parts to lyric tenors, heroic roles to Italian tenors, and even bass parts to baritones.[19]

As in Hamburg, his temper sometimes made him merciless. When his face was distorted by rage it took on a "demonic" expression, often referred to by his enemies. At the same time he would bite his nails, and his usually calm brown eyes would flash green fire. His full, almost feminine lips would be contorted into a perfidious smile, with the right-hand corner of his mouth drawn down so that his expression was both threatening and terrifying. It was not only hostility and opposition that aroused his anger, but mediocrity, incompetence, and lack of self-confidence as well. Some artists froze in his presence and afterward wished him dead for the way in which he had humiliated them. This was dangerous, for the singers in Vienna had power that was unheard of elsewhere; most of them had contacts with journalists who asked for nothing better than an "affäre" or "scandal." Mahler's demands and his perfectionist ideals meant nothing to most of his colleagues, who thought only of their careers; he, on the other hand, was perfectly prepared to regard them as instruments in the service of a cause and he discarded anything that hindered the realization of his ideals. He was accused of "ruining voices," of wounding sensibilities to the quick, of "exhausting his collaborators," and of "working them till they dropped."

Just as he was beginning to realize the extent of the task ahead of him and the time it would take, the anti-Semitic press attack began. In April the satirical paper *Kikeriki* published an article entitled "Get rid of Mahler, the executioner of Art," in which he was accused of leading the opera to ruin; placed at its head thanks to "the intrigues of an old singer and her lover," he was torturing his subordinates, tyrannizing the public, removing Italian opera from the repertory, dismissing and disgracing well-known singers, etc. But for the time being these criticisms carried little weight in the face of his overwhelming success. The balance sheet of his first year at the opera was magnificent, Wagner took first place with sixty-two performances of nine works, that is, twenty more than the year before. In an article published at the end of the season, Richard Heuberger[20] expressed satisfaction not only with the number of performances but also because they were uncut versions that had played to full houses. He also mentioned that no conductor's repetoire was fixed in advance and that great freedom of choice was allowed. Richter had not been obliged to conduct more frequently than he wished and thus had not, as in previous years, shown signs of exhaustion due to overwork.[21]

The idea that Mahler and Richter should conduct certain works alternatively had been a great success, as it had aroused healthy controversy among the public. Gluck and Weber were in temporary eclipse, but *Zar und Zimmermann* and *The Magic Flute* had been performed frequently and were always well received.[22] Thus Heuberger's summing-up was optimistic. He believed that Mahler had been right to cut the number of evenings devoted to Meyerbeer to seven. Among the new additions to the repertory, only Leoncavallo's *La Bohème* seemed unworthy of the Vienna Opera.

In poor health for some time, Mahler had to take a leave of absence from the opera on June 6 to enter the Rudolphinerhaus clinic in Döbling for an operation to stop hemorrhages from which he was suffering more and more frequently. He stayed there a week and then left to convalesce in Vahrn: he had rented a villa there the year before and in it passed a summer clouded by continual pain.

In Natalie's manuscript, which has been carefully censored by outside hands, there is a reference to "painful circumstances" in Mahler's personal life, which prevented him from enjoying the freedom of nature; was it perhaps the revelation of Justi's romance with Arnold Rosé which angered him? He himself was to say the following year that his troubles had been purely physical.[23]

On June 2, Emma married the cellist Eduard Rosé, and they were soon going to leave for the United States, where he had been engaged by the Boston Symphony. Eduard's brother, Arnold, who was *Konzertmeister* of the Philharmonic Orchestra, spent the summer in Vahrn with the Mahlers, probably at Justi's suggestion, as there seems no doubt that she was already greatly attracted to him. According to Alma Mahler, whose statements about her sister-in-law are open to doubt, Justi and Arnold "arranged" Emma's marriage so that they could see each other oftener. Arnold Rosé was the founder and first violin of the well-known quartet, and Mahler and he played together on several occasions; this gave Mahler the chance to get to know Brahms's sonatas for piano and clarinet, which he had previously examined and judged too hastily.[24]

Although she had not given up bombarding Mahler with suggestions and advice, Natalie spent at least part of the summer in Vahrn.[25] On July 14 she took all the occupants of the Villa Kaley off to look for a path that she had known as a child and that led into the mountains as far as the Schalderertal. From the first summit they gazed at the view of Vahrn, Brixen, the monastery of Neustift, and the castle of Bedeneck, right across the snow-capped crest of the Brenner and the savage peaks of the Dolomites in the distance. Mahler was so enthusiastic that he decided to take the same walk almost every day. He was still in pain as a result of his operation,[26] but he bore it "heroically." He composed nothing except three new lieder for the *Wunderhorn,* "just to prove I can still do it."[27] According to Natalie, one of them expressed the "violent anger and fury that, for a number of reasons, have been his constant frame of mind this year." One evening he happened to read in a Berlin paper that a professor in a German university disapproved of women studying medicine. He flew into a rage at this idea and exclaimed that "this Tcherman" (*dieser Teutsche*) is certainly an ox; his ideal woman must be a cow and can continue to be one!"

He returned to Vienna on August 2[28] and began preparing the new season. During the first month he left most of the conducting to Richter and Hellmesberger, conducting only *Lohengrin* on the fifteenth and *Tannhäuser* on the twenty-fifth. On the twenty-sixth Richter, who was not feeling well, relinquished his baton, and Mahler conducted an uncut performance of *Die Meistersinger*[29] before a house packed in spite of the torrid heat. Paradoxically, the anti-Semitic *Deutsche Zeitung* was the only paper to report this event; Leitich admired Mahler's energetic rendering of the two finales and the "dreamy poetry" of the prelude to Act III. According to him, the slow tempos brought out the strength and brilliance of the opera.

The assassination of the Empress Elisabeth in Geneva on September 10 delayed the opening of Mahler's entirely revised production of the *Ring* for ten days. His enthusiasm for this renaissance was all the greater since he now had two new Wagnerian singers; Mildenburg, who had just arrived in Vienna with a permanent engagement, and Erik Schmedes.[30] In spite of his pain, which was no less than during the summer,[31] he spent all his waking moments thinking up improvements, "like an inveterate gambler whose days and nights are devoted to running through cards and calculating the odds."[32] He recast the parts many times in his head and mulled over every problem in the hope of improving some new detail. In *Das Rheingold* he cast Sedlmair as Fricka, Schmedes as Froh, and Demuth as Donner. All three far surpassed their predecessors as "they have not been ruined by earlier wrong interpretations." Mahler admired Josef Ritter's Alberich so much that "although he has almost lost his voice he would be worth his salary even if he only sang four times a year!" Grengg and Reichenberg, as the two giants, were another improvement of the previous cast, thanks to their "cyclopean strength," their "rugged appearance," and their perfect diction. The Magic Storm was a success, thanks to Demuth, but Mahler was still dissatisfied with the reaction of the gods at the moment of Fasolt's murder. Although *Das Rheingold* was less popular than the three other dramas in the *Ring* cycle, it played to a full house. The *Neue Freie Presse* praised most of Mahler's changes and especially that of the main set. This showed only part of Valhalla, leaving the rest to that essential collaborator in any theatrical performance—the audience's imagination. Mahler was also praised for casting important singers in secondary parts and for infusing "a little Mahlerian nervousness" into the dwarfs of the Nibelheim episode.[33]

In *Die Walküre,* Sofie Sedlmair was cast as Sieglinde for the first time, and Natalie felt that she brought a "magical tenderness" to the part. As Brünnhilde, Mildenburg was a "true goddess." Mahler was delighted with her performance, which he had built up from scratch, but he found Reichmann, whose interpretation he had been unable to alter, a "languid and feeble" Wotan. The orchestra was just as unsatisfactory as in *Das Rheingold.* "Too much negligence and error, accumulated here over the years, lies like a curse upon the orchestra as the dragon Fafner lies upon the gold."[34]

In *Siegfried,* a guest tenor, Julius Spielmann, who was an intelligent and gifted artist, nevertheless introduced some "unforgivable clowning" to the role of Mime: "He tries to be funnier than funny, thereby turning a characterization into a caricature. In this way, he destroys the role and cuts his own throat," said Mahler, "and I'm going to fire him immediately. He's already ruined by the sloppy habits of the theater routine. The worst thing about his performance is his Jewish jargon. No doubt, with Mime, Wagner intended to ridicule the Jews (with all their characteristic traits—petty intelligence and greed—the jargon is textually and musically so cleverly suggested) but for God's sake, it must not be exaggerated and overdone, as Spielmann does it, and in Vienna at that, at the 'K.K. Hofoper.' This would be sheer folly, and create a welcome scandal for the Viennese. I know of only one Mime," he concluded, "and that is myself . . . you wouldn't believe what there is in that part nor what I could make of it!"[35]

Mahler was little better pleased with Erik Schmedes' Siegfried that evening. His heroic appearance and his personality were perfectly suited to the part, but his acting was "more affected and unnatural" than the season before, while his musical interpretation was "more inaccurate and careless."

Mahler was so angry with him that he didn't look at him once during the performance and wouldn't speak to him afterward. He also refused to take him to supper and reprimanded him severely the following day. Demuth, on the other hand, delighted him as Wanderer, because "his somewhat in-

dolent temperament was well suited to the calm and disillusioned God."
Mildenburg was the one who pleased him most that evening, for "the divine
expression" that she brought to the awakening of love and life was the
crowning glory of the opera."[36]

In *Die Götterdämmerung,* Mahler conducted the Norn scene for the first
time in Vienna. Natalie considered that he conveyed its "mystic significance"
so powerfully to eye and ear that the spectator received "a terrifying impression of Genesis and the Last Judgement." Thanks to Mildenburg, the
Waltraute scene, which had previously been cut, was the success of the
evening. Schmedes had corrected his recent faults, and the two heroes
"seemed to dominate the drama like a pair of demigods." Compared to the
year before, the chorus and orchestra seemed revived and transformed. With
the very modest means at his disposal, Mahler had eradicated all the absurdities in the staging and created an atmosphere heavy with foreboding.
In the final tableau he cut out the vision of the gods and suggested the burning of Valhalla by a sort of tremendous aurora borealis, the first step toward
a reform particularly dear to his heart—the abolition of realism. In *Die
Götterdämmerung* even the orchestra pleased him, particularly in the Funeral March, and he was especially delighted at having obtained this improvement fairly easily, particularly after his inconclusive and endless struggles of the year before.

According to the *Neue Freie Presse,* "an unprecedented tension" had held
the audience spellbound from 7 P.M. until 11:45. Most of the singers
had adopted a new conversational style, a *Sprechgesang* infinitely preferable
to the shrill cries of earlier performances. Reichenberg, in particular, distinguished himself by lowering the volume of his voice for the first time,
while Mildenburg's vocal splendor and dramatic fire brought back "the
era of the opera's glory." The orchestra's performance was admirable, "un-
recognisable," and Mahler could only be criticized for a few moments of
excessive haste, notably the Funeral March and the final scene. Vienna "has
rarely seen such a performance, and this evening the Hofoper was transformed into Festspielhaus."[37]

After some hesitation Mahler suppressed the thread in the Norn scene,
using real thread for rehearsals only and then removing it at the last moment.
Consequently the Norns only seemed to be casting their thread into the air
and catching it, and few noticed its absence. He nonetheless received a letter
of protest from Cosima Wagner, to which he replied that he had taken this
step "at the dictates of his conscience as an artist and man of the theater."
Schönaich, the critic, who dined frequently with Mahler and Natalie, brought
the matter up again on behalf of the Wagner family. "Spare yourself this
trouble, I beg you!" replied Mahler. "You must concede that I too understand something of these problems and don't let myself get carried away
by my own ideas—I abandon nineteen out of twenty of them every day.
At Bayreuth, I have never yet seen this scene done successfully; it was
managed so badly, the last time, that the Norns dropped the thread and

had to rise to pick it up. If they can't manage it in Bayreuth, where no pains are spared over rehearsals, it seems clear that it is impossible. I am certain that Wagner would have been much more tolerant than his descendants, and would have agreed with my choice of the lesser of two evils."[38]

The *Ring* brought Mahler into conflict with the administration over the electricians' and stagehands' wages. Their work on it had been especially tiring, and because of the long rehearsals most of them had not been able to get home to eat; Mahler felt that, as their pay was so low (from thirty-five to a maximum of fifty florins a month for a job with no fixed hours), they should be given a bonus of two florins each to encourage their enthusiasm and good will.[39] But Intendant Plappart wrote him on September 26, refusing this request, "although the production has been unusually successful." According to him, expenses of this kind "can only be entertained in the case of spectacular ballets, which make much greater demands on the men." Mahler finally paid the ninety-four gulden out of his own pocket, though he pretended to his friends that he had won his point.[40] He thought that the position of the stagehands and technicians should be looked into immediately and that improvements should be made; he was ashamed that he had done nothing about these unfortunate men sooner; he hardly knew them and only saw them coming on stage from time to time like "avenging angels." After a long struggle and after first raising the orchestral salaries, he obtained a general salary increase for the technical staff around 1900.

In August, Richter asked for and obtained a leave of absence from the opera on the grounds of fatigue and "pains in his arms." In fact, he had decided to leave Vienna, where all the talk was of Mahler, and go to England, where he had received attractive offers for a series of concerts. He informed the Philharmonic Committee on September 23, before their annual election, that there was no question of his resuming the direction of their concerts. The musicians were surprised by this unexpected announcement and forced to look around for a replacement.[41] Mahler was the man of the moment, very much in the public eye. He seemed the ideal successor to Richter. In spite of a few protests about his character, his "excesses," and his revolutionary ideas, he was elected unanimously. On the evening of September 23 a delegation came from the orchestra to make him an official offer to direct the Philharmonic concerts.[42] Though this was the realization of his fondest dreams, Mahler hesitated, thinking of the extra work it would involve. But not for long. He felt that he had almost unlimited reserves of energy, and besides he had been assured that there was no question of Richter changing his mind, as he had done once before. This new event not only made Mahler the uncontested king of music in Vienna,[43] but gave him the satisfaction of having an orchestra at his disposal which he could mold as he wished.

The Philharmonic subscription concerts took place every second Sunday at twelve-thirty. There were eight in the series, plus a few special concerts—the Gesellschaft and the Nicolaï Concerts. The psychological climate of this new collaboration between Mahler and the orchestra was clear from the first rehearsal. In the welcoming speech to Mahler, Joseph Helmsky, the horn player, spoke mainly of the loss that the orchestra had suffered by Richter's departure. Mahler replied, "First I must express my regret at losing a colleague as valuable as Hans Richter. I didn't take seriously his decision to leave the Philharmonic Concerts, in which he has won so many well-deserved triumphs. I therefore hesitated until the last moment before responding to your appeal, and accepted only when I realized that the circumstances that led to Richter's decisions could not be reversed. Now that I find myself at the head of your admirable association, I would like to express the joy I feel at the idea of making music with you outside the theater."

This democratic group of Viennese *bons vivants* had been attached to Richter by bonds of affection, but with Mahler it was a marriage of reason, since the peace and quiet of an easy life counted for more in their eyes than "artistic truth." Richter's placid and debonair character, and his attitude toward his art, had suited them perfectly. "He sometimes suffered from an excess of confidence, both in his talent and his craft," wrote Kalbeck of Richter, "but he was never guilty of bad taste or complacency."[44] Neither was his conducting personal or subjective. A pure, thorough knowledge of music guided his acts and his interpretations, whereas with Mahler, all spiritual, moral, and artistic problems were indissolubly bound to the problems of his profession. He was far more demanding than Richter. His "modern" approach was as much that of a philosopher or a writer as that of a musician. He caused shock and surprise when he insisted on getting to the heart of things, on re-examining every question. A number of experiences had convinced him that the value of tradition was relative. In February he had given Natalie some striking examples of tempo errors in Mozart, Wagner, and *Fidelio.*

Sometimes the choice of a tempo should depend upon an "unconscious reminiscence" on the part of a composer. One day, when the critic Gustav Schönaich blamed him for an overrapid tempo in the prelude to the third act of *Lohengrin,* affirming that Wagner himself conducted it more slowly, Mahler replied that, in his opinion, the piece in question was a reminiscence of a Beethoven theme

and stated that when composers introduced such "recollections" into their work, the "copy" almost never altered the tempo of the "original."[45]

In the hands of bad singers and musicians, Mahler considered that works sometimes became unrecognizable. "The worst of it is," he had added, "that this kind of superficial performance becomes the tradition. Then, when someone comes along who wants to blow the pale embers of the work into a living flame, he is accused of being a heretic and an innovator. This is exactly what has happened to Wagner. Except here at the opera, where I am understood and approved, I am submerged with invective and obloquy wherever I conduct."[46] It was a fact that the modern trend of Mahler's interpretations had displeased and shocked public and critics everywhere, and his anxiety on this subject was particularly justified in Vienna, where the tradition of the Philharmonic Orchestra was staunchly conservative. Even Brahms, who was Viennese by adoption, had never figured in its programs as often as he had in those of other German orchestras. The routine that Richter had adopted was only rarely disturbed by "invitations" to conductors like Bülow, Strauss, Nikisch, or Weingartner.

Two days before the first concert some of the musicians[47] showed their hostility in the particularly unpleasant form of an anonymous article (the initials E. Th. preserve the writer's anonymity) in the *Deutsche Zeitung*. Helm had warned Mahler about it but was unfortunately unable to prevent its appearance. The author of "The Jewish Gentleman at the Vienna Opera" claimed that he was "not concerned about Mahler's results[48] but about the methods by which they were obtained. . . . If we view matters from this angle, his work cannot fail to appear in quite a different light from that which is commonly assumed," said the anonymous writer. Though the uncut productions were a happy innovation, Mahler distracted the orchestra and the singers by his excessive movements on the podium, which were responsible for "many false notes": absolute disaster would occur if musicians were to place all their confidence in his baton. "What Mr. Mahler does at times cannot be called conducting. It is more like the gesticulations of a dervish, and when the *Kapellmeister* has St. Vitus's dance, it's really very difficult to keep time. His left hand often doesn't know what the right one is doing; this may be all very well for 'charity,' but it's extremely harmful when conducting an orchestra[49] . . . His left often marks the 'Bohemian circle' with convulsive jerks, scrabbles for hidden treasures, shudders and shakes, clutches, searches, smothers, battles through the waves, strangles infants, thrashes, slaps; in a word it is often in a state of delirium tremens, but it does not conduct[50] . . . Mahler's conducting is affected; it is meant to impress the public, but not at all intended for the performers, whom it confuses, rather than helps . . . Mahler wants to leave the stamp of his personality everywhere, and the result is a series of caricatures.[51]

"All men of taste, musicians or laymen, understand Mahler's intentions and are annoyed by them. Nevertheless, his pretensions grew with his success. In the orchestra, there are some lackeys who want to earn the good graces of their all-powerful chief at all costs. With or without previous prompting, one of the members even proposed that Mahler's Great Symphony for chorus and orchestra be given at a Philharmonic concert! But the orchestra rebelled; in view of the colossal efforts the musicians are obliged to make to fulfill their director's demands at the opera alone, they prefer to perform a symphony by Beethoven the Small rather than one by Mahler the Great."

The article ends with an attack on Arnold Rosé, who had become "head of all the *Kapellmeister*." The "talented brother-in-law" is contrasted with his "untalented" brother, "who is in America." The anonymous author also accused Mahler of trying to "improve Beethoven,"[52] claiming that the latter "had not succeeded in carrying out all his intentions . . ." Beethoven's talent for orchestration must have been very imperfect," he goes on, "for he failed to use an E flat clarinet in the *Coriolan Overture*. How lucky you are, Beethoven, to have found an epigone to immortalize your work; without him, *Coriolan* would have been eternally deprived of the E flat clarinet. If Mr. Mahler wants to make corrections he should tackle the works of Mendelssohn and Rubinstein, though the Jews would probably not stand for that. But let him leave our Beethoven in peace, since he already impresses and pleases us, even without an E flat clarinet and without Mahler! . . . Yes, Mr. Mahler has E flat clarinets on the brain. Not content with adding one to the *Eroica,* he has also reinforced the trombones and double basses and it is even said that he will send his brother-in-law to Jericho to rediscover Joshua's trumpets, because Aryan trumpets are not loud enough for him. Perhaps there he will find a means of obtaining the trumpets of Israel for the opera, the selfsame trumpets that the entire Jewish press have been blasting in praise of 'Mr. Director,' with such deafening noise that the walls of Vienna are beginning to crack! The orchestra is preparing to hold the forthcoming rehearsals of the *Eroica* on the Steinfeld,[53] so that Mahler can engage the field artillery with some cannons to reinforce the kettledrums."

From the same source, we learn that Mahler had apparently acquired the nickname of "Duty Sergeant" (*Korporal vom Tag*) due to his tone of voice when addressing the members of the orchestra. "Nobody, from the most insignificant employee and stagehand right up to—but excluding—his brother-in-law, is completely free from feelings of anti-Semitism toward the director; even the Jewish members of the orchestra, except of course for the talented brother-in-law, have become anti-Semites; they are willing enough to work . . . but no one will stand for the militaristic tone of his commands. They preferred their duty well enough under Richter and Jahn, and are ready to continue, but they have the right to be treated as artists and civilized human beings, instead of being beaten into submission. Resistance is smoldering, even the most cowardly and submissive musicians will finally join the majority, and one of these days Mahler will find himself without an orchestra. Then we'll see how, with only his brother-in-law to help, he will manage to put on *Tristan.* He will have no choice but to engage the *Přelouver Stadtkapelle* . . . or he could perform *Tristan* with a harmonica and his two brothers-in-law, the gifted one as well as the American. The ensemble would be marvelous, provided he adds an E flat clarinet!

"If they fail to say amen to all the dictates of Mahler's caprices and whims, the older members of the orchestra can only expect to be treated like the director's porters. The number of musicians who have been pensioned off places a heavy strain on the opera's pension fund and endangers its availability in the future. The chorus alone has found the decisive tone and manner needed to combat this Jewish audacity. They have committed themselves upon their honor to deal jointly and as one man with the Duty Sergeant, and have obliged him to capitulate. Musicians too should insist on being treated, not only as human beings, but also as artists. Their unity would force Mahler to change his attitude, because it is conceivable to have the opera without Mahler, but not without the orchestra."

This article, inspired by a spirit of pettiness, intrigue, and jealousy, to say nothing of racism, shows that it did not take long for resentment and hatred to threaten Mahler once more. It was written while the rehearsals for the first Philharmonic concert were taking place, and the details of orchestral "retouching" had been supplied by a member of the orchestra who also sent, both to the intendant and to various newspapers, anonymous letters signed: "A musician who wants to hear authentic, unadulterated Beethoven." In a letter to the intendant dated November 23, Mahler wrote that it was inadmissible for a member of his orchestra to conspire against him. Having obtained the original of one of the letters, he had it analyzed by a graphologist, who "confirmed his suspicions" and identified the writer.[54] Nevertheless he decided not to inflict any sanctions[55]; he only wanted to know who he was, because this sort of attack "turns against its author anyway, and discredits him." Mahler's integrity made his position invulnerable, and in any case the article's anti-Semitism was too virulent to convince anybody.

The first concert took place on November 6. Mahler conducted the *Coriolan Overture,* Mozart's *Symphony in G Minor,* and Beethoven's *"Eroica" Symphony*. The public, to show that they missed Richter, gave him a cool reception when he walked to the podium.[56] "The blond giant who, till then, had faced the orchestra, solid and unshakable, was replaced" wrote Kalbeck, "by a slender, nervous, incredibly supple silhouette that jumped lightly up onto the podium. We were already acquainted with that silhouette's almost diabolical powers of suggestion, and we now realized that his spell would be as powerful in the concert hall as in the theater." The audience gradually thawed, and Mahler was loudly applauded after the *"Eroica"* brought the concert to an end. He conducted everything from memory; his calm and his economy of gesture were remarkable "since he had been able to work out every tiny detail in rehearsal. There was never time for perfection at the opera, and he had often been obliged to improvise and bring out new subtleties during the performance."

Mahler placed the *Coriolan Overture* among the most concise and rich (in substance) of Beethoven's works; it was also one of the most neglected. He identified with it more than any other piece of music because of its "ever-growing intensity of expression, in which harshness and violence alternate with tenderness and expressiveness." He saw "the whole destiny of

Coriolanus" embodied in the first five notes.[57] The last thing Richter conducted at the Philharmonic was the *"Eroica,"* and Mahler's inclusion of it in his opening concert was a sign of his determination to impose his new conceptions. As at the opera, where he had closed the auditorium to latecomers, his steely gaze here prevented some hungry music lovers from leaving to lunch after the Scherzo. "From the impetuous orchestra's unison and the pizzicati right through to the end, the Finale was one of the great moments of the concert." A few months earlier Mahler had in fact expressed some particularly original ideas concerning this Finale. After the impetuous opening passage, he felt that the pizzicato motif on the basses was mistakenly considered to be the main theme and was usually played too fast in consequence. On the contrary, "Beethoven is trying, meditatively, humorously, to walk, and gradually succeeds." For this same reason, the end, like an answer, should be imperceptibly faster. Above all this, the themes branch out against a moving background that directs and accompanies the whole. The themes should sing and flourish and should never be destroyed by too fast a tempo.[58]

The next day Hanslick's article in the *Neue Freie Presse* shows that Mahler's admirers were not recruited exclusively from the ranks of the young revolutionaries. Although he regretted Richter's departure, he thought that the "Philharmonic could not have found a 'more highly esteemed or better conductor' than Mahler," and noted that "this conviction seems shared by the public, since the entire series was sold out immediately after the first tentative announcement of Mahler's appointment." In his eyes it went without saying that this magnificent "vote of confidence" was "more than justified by Mahler's performance on the preceding day." During three long rehearsals Mahler had made the orchestra rehearse the music "which, for years now, our excellent musicians have so thoroughly had in their heads and at their fingertips that they could almost play it in their sleep." But Mahler wanted them to remain wide awake and play with all the enthusiasm and strength of life. This was why each of these masterpieces had seemed new. "This is not the proper place" Hanslick went on, "to enumerate the new musical details that sparkled like diamonds, without detracting from the unity of form and mood." Also according to Hanslick, "Mahler's main efforts consisted in tuning each piece to a dominating idea and preserving its character and style. This was clearest in the Mozart symphony, which some people might have liked to hear performed with livelier colors and more energetic accents. Nevertheless, it was thus and not otherwise that Mahler wished to present this faultless music, coming as it did between Beethoven's two volcanoes. The *Coriolan Overture* and the *"Eroica"* had produced an indescribable impression. Such clarity and transparency had almost never been heard before, even in the most complex polyphonies with, at the same time, such power and grandeur in the total effect. The public, used to the best, had given free rein to its enthusiasm after each piece of the *"Eroica"* and had untiringly recalled the man in command over and over again. All's well that starts well!"

Though Hanslick accepted and approved the "novelty" of Mahler's interpretations, his colleagues were all more reserved. Kalbeck found the contrast between the two themes in *Coriolan* overemphasized and thought that as a whole it lacked "sober defiance and angry grandeur." On the other hand, Mahler had approached the "personal, subjective and passionate" Mozart symphony "thinking he could transmit the classic spirit with coldness in guise of objectivity."[59] He had accelerated the tempo and used ritardandos too freely. Neither had he brought out the true value of the composer's nuances. In the *"Eroica,"* he had shown "strategic vision," and his imperious and calm approach had mastered and clarified the most complex polyphony, thanks to a moderate tempo. Kalbeck ended by comparing Mahler to Bülow: "May he adopt all that unforgettable master's qualities and avoid his faults."

In the *Abendpost,* Hirschfeld pointed out the difference between dramatic and symphonic conducting, and admitted that Mahler had shown a perfect acquaintance with the symphonic repertory. Nevertheless he took issue on his "strange, elegant, almost indifferent" reading of Mozart. Even so, the performance had contained much exquisite detail,[60] and he did not think that most of the liberties, which had shocked the conservatives, had harmed the work. The performance of *Coriolan* was "animated, dramatic," its line "never broken by pretty details"; the rendering of the symphony was "a protest against its title—'*Eroica,*'" for the pathos of Beethoven, which Richter had so often evoked, was missing. However clear, however interesting this performance had been, however noble and powerful the Funeral March, Mahler had failed "to plumb the innermost depths of feeling."

In his article one can feel Helm's extreme embarrassment at the conflict between his personal feelings and the policy of the *Deutsche Zeitung,* which was violently hostile to Mahler. He hardly mentioned the instrumental "retouching" and considered that, when conducting, Mahler had overcome his nervousness. As with Bülow, Mahler's concern is mainly for the "interesting and surprising detail,"[61] but "his rendering did not achieve the imposing majesty of Richter's." *Coriolan* had "authentic drama" despite the slow tempo. The opening of the *"Eroica"* had been "curiously deprived of expression," and "credit was mainly due to our Philharmonic for the effect of the magnificent crescendi" which received the lion's share of the applause (the Viennese public retained the barbarous custom of applauding between movements). The extremely dramatic version of the Funeral March was the high spot of the concert. Sometime later, writing in the *Musikalisches Wochenblatt,* where he was more at liberty to say what he thought, Helm approved the freedom of Mahler's conducting, which he contrasted with the "metronomic rigor" of the classical conductors, and praised him as a wholehearted and fervent adept of Wagner's doctrines.

At the second Philharmonic concert on November 20, Mahler played the

*Oberon Overture,* Schubert's *Unfinished Symphony,* and Berlioz's *Symphonie fantastique.* Weber's overture, "all sparkle and fire," was loudly applauded, but in spite of its "divine tenderness" and orchestral legato, his interpretation of Schubert was less warmly received. This time, Mahler had attacked the "exaggerated sentimentality dear to the Viennese, their everlasting abandon [*ewig Loslegen*], which completely falsified not only the spirit but the structure of a work." The Austrian public was still uneasy about the *Fantastique,* more than sixty years after its first performance. Part of the audience left the hall after the third and fourth movements, thereby sending Mahler into a fearful rage, because "though this work is not perhaps one of the highest artistic achievement," it contained, in his opinion, such "inspiration and originality [*Geist und Eigenart*] that it fully deserved a hearing." He was even more indignant and exasperated by the attitude of the critics. "There is always something new to be learned from conducting a work like this, yet critics have the effrontery to condemn it irrevocably after a single hearing."[62]

"Mahler led his troops more independently than ever," wrote Kalbeck, "and the public is more deeply convinced of his Philharmonic mission than it was before. He can control himself and therefore he can control others. When he errs it is by conviction rather than through weakness." He seemed "as blissful as a violinist who finally has a Stradivarius in his hands," a position that might have made others lose their heads. His interpreter's temperament brought him closer to the romantic than to the classical school, and "Wagner would not have conducted the *Unfinished Symphony* and the *Oberon Overture* any differently."[63] He ceaselessly imagined a "hidden program" and under his baton works were transformed into "colorful pictures" and "dreams of magic light." The *Symphonie fantastique,* which was "impossible to understand without a program" and "all the more laughable the more the composer tries to be serious," aroused Kalbeck's ire. Having come to "the end of his musical gifts," Berlioz had, "in one perilous bound, left the confines of music, and others who did not even have his spirit and temperament had followed him to the limits of art." Hanslick was just as severe. He thought it would have been better to suppress Berlioz's Finale, even though a "sensible and impulsive" conductor "brought it back to life with a blend of consciousness and genius which made it interesting and effective, if not beautiful." Finally, in the *Musikalisches Wochenblatt,* Helm expressed reserve about Mahler's tempos and his "somewhat unnatural" reading of the *Unfinished,* but he could not conceive of anything more "fascinating" than his interpretation of the *Fantastique.*

Mahler had a very special attitude toward concert programs. When there was a long, serious piece to conduct, he preferred to place it at the start of the evening, so the audience could concentrate better. Because of this he began the Philharmonic concert of December 4 with Brahms's *Second Symphony,* followed by Dvořák's new symphonic poem, *Heldenlied,* which was still in manuscript form,[64] *Variations on the Austrian Anthem* from

Haydn's *Emperor Quartet* to celebrate the Kaiser's fiftieth coronation anniversary, and Mendelssohn's overture to *A Midsummer Night's Dream.* Dvořák was present and took a bow after his piece had been played. Hanslick, writing the next day, praised its instrumentation and the "contrapuntal work." He then went on to congratulate Mahler for conducting the Brahms symphony with "care and love," thus showing his affection for a work by a composer whose "engagement in Vienna he had recommended in vain for years." The *Deutsche Zeitung* agreed that Mahler had "shown his esteem" for Brahms, but felt that Weingartner had conducted the *Second Symphony* in a more "poetic" manner, three years earlier. The writer did however admit that in the Finale Mahler had been unequaled; he had understood, for once, that it was possible to conduct "with calm and energy at the same time." Hirschfeld, on the contrary, thought that this same work "never received a more poetic interpretation." Mahler had followed Brahms's instructions (moderato, tranquillo) to the letter and had thereby created a "purer and more personal atmosphere" than Weingartner. Hirschfeld also defended Dvořák's work against the indifference of the public and the hostility of his colleagues. Lastly Kalbeck, who was a passionate admirer of Brahms, and also his biographer, warmly applauded the "marvelous clarity, without a trace of pedantry," of this interpretation, in which Mahler "has respected the composer's slightest indications and has known how to transmit them to the performers easily, and by subtlest means." Kalbeck nevertheless disapproved of Mahler's interpretation of the first movement, "too fast and too pathetic in tone," but noted that the last three had "enraptured the general public and connoisseurs alike."

In the last concert of the year, given on December 18, Mahler conducted the first Vienna performance of Bizet's symphonic suite *Roma,* followed by the *Siegfried Idyll* and Beethoven's *Eighth Symphony.* Hirschfeld praised "the charm, tenderness and delicacy" of *Roma,* the "warm and penetrating" interpretation of *Siegfried,* and the "profound seriousness and true artistic feeling" that had revealed many aspects of the *Eighth Symphony* "hidden in earlier performances." The *Neues Wiener Tagblatt*'s anonymous critic particularly applauded the varied and moderate tempos, especially in the Finale of the Beethoven symphony. Helm wrote that "Mahler laid bare his heart" in his "noble and deeply felt" interpretation of the *Siegfried Idyll,* while the correspondent of the *Neue Zeitschrift,* on the other hand, accused him of "dissection" and claimed that he had given the public an "anatomical plate" of Siegfried, while in the Beethoven symphony he had managed to achieve "the very opposite of the composer's intentions. The only surprise of the concert was the public's patience."

The first important event of the opera season was the revival of *La Dame blanche,* by Boieldieu, on October 4, to celebrate the Emperor's birthday. Mahler devoted a great deal of time to rehearsing this opera, and the effort was not wasted, for, as Hanslick said, the style of romantic opera had been lost, and the musicians and singers contaminated by "highly declamatory" music (a clear allusion to Wagnerian drama). Mahler's masterly conducting restored to Boieldieu's music its true worth. He had lavished the same care and enthusiasm on the staging as he had devoted to the *Ring*. He had known how to express "the pure happiness" of its tranquil joy and gaiety by means of a "continuous mezza-voce." According to the *Abendpost* this time, he had thus proved that "his modern spirit" did not impose the feeling of the music on the listener, but gently led his sensitivity toward it. An achievement as successful as this made one forget all the difficulties that had to be surmounted in order to attain it.[65]

Kalbeck applauded a "valiant artistic deed," thanks to which this eternally youthful "Lady" (*Dame*), like *Der Freischütz* and *The Barber of Seville,* "has preserved her popular national character" and has been "reborn in all her pristine clarity." He criticized only the size of the stage and the auditorium, which, favoring the singers at the expense of the music, did the work a disservice.

The preparations for the revival of *Der Freischütz,* on October 22, demanded an even greater effort from Mahler, for this was to be one of the first important steps in his theatrical reform. He spent no less than an hour and a half rehearsing the overture alone, to the fury of the musicians. The original production had abounded in ludicrous details. Hanslick listed some examples from the *Wolfschlucht* scene; Samiel's red costume; the cascade that drowned both orchestra and singers; the devils waltzing in the background; the "terrifying" creatures crawling around the fire; the riders in the "infernal hunt" descending from the wings on horseback and brandishing rockets beneath the actors' noses; objects that resembled sealing-wax sticks, which were meant to represent a "chaos of smoke and sparks," coming and going onstage. At a time when realism still held undisputed sway in the theater, Mahler discarded all these wax and cardboard forms and suggested ghostly happenings by an interplay of light and shade. In his production the *Wolfschlucht* became a little ravine framed by two huge rocks, and simple smoke clouds took the place of the projected images, the black boars and the flaming wheels of the fantastic hunt.

As soon as he had reached Vienna, even before his appointment to the opera, Mahler had expressed revolutionary ideas about performing *Der Freischütz.* "If you heard me conducting *Freischütz,*" he told Natalie, "you wouldn't recognize it. My tempos are entirely different from the usual ones, yet quite correct; in this way I manage to bring out all sorts of details that one usually never notices. The second Finale is always played fast and loud —while I see it as slow and quiet, a magnificent effect. The music should fall like a breath of wind from the sky, like the silent recognition of original sin. The prayer that follows must be imposing and strong, thus forming an eloquent contrast. The interpretation of Weber always gives rise to serious misunderstandings. If I become director, I shall restage *Freischütz,* and then you'll see something! Not a single one of the soloists will keep his role, because when casting one must take the man's character and appearance into account, not only his voice. If I don't have just the right singer for each part, I will cast the whole thing with guest artists rather than use someone unsuitable."

A year later Mahler kept his word; he presented the opera in its original form, three acts instead of four, for the first time in Vienna. The final trio of the *Wolfschlucht* scene was played in front of a curtain, with a short pause afterward to finish changing the scenery. He hesitated for a long time before casting Kaspar, as he considered neither of the opera's basses suitable; Reichenberg was too debonair and Hesch ridiculous because of his Czech accent. In the end Mahler chose a baritone, Josef Ritter,[66] who managed, thanks to his intelligence and artistry and in spite of his vocal weakness, to bring out the demonic character of the part. His aria had to be transposed, and, apart from Kalbeck, most of the Viennese critics were incensed by this daring innovation.

Hanslick found the *Wolfschlucht*[67] too bare and bleak but considered the staging in general excellent. Hirschfeld blamed Mahler for trying to impose "dramatic logic" on the opera, for losing its "childlike magic," its make-believe ghosts, its good old Singspiel naïveté, and for turning it into a "music drama—an opera for the educated."[68] Like his colleagues, Kalbeck criticized the bareness of the sets, but unlike Hirschfeld, he praised Mahler for trying to give back to the work "its simplicity and its legendary character" by stripping it of the refinements and splendors of *opera seria*. Kalbeck considered the "marvelously staged" Finale in the last act the crowning moment of the performance. Schrödter and Forster sang "in a much more natural and feeling manner than before."

Besides the new productions, Mahler spent much time improving the ones he could not restage completely. On October 29 he gave Vienna its first uncut performance of *Tristan*.[69] It was received quite well, though the theater was not full. Just over two months later, on January 7, the opera's fiftieth performance in Vienna played to a full house. By now Mahler had stopped presenting extracts from the *Ring;* instead, the complete uncut cycle was given several times a year.[70] On November 4, after a performance of *Don Giovanni,* Kalbeck noted that in spite of "some mistakes and inadequacies, the masterful touch of the new conductor was noticeable, even after only one rehearsal . . . How much deep-rooted prejudice and inherited errors still weigh down this work!" he added. "Fortunately the will to correct everything and also the strength to persevere are present too." Anything was better than the "routine of sleek smoothness that characterized *Don Giovanni* in the past."[71]

There was only one important new production in view at the start of the season, *Donna Diana,* a comic opera by the Viennese composer Emil Nikolaus von Reznicek.[72] The summer before, Mahler had summoned him by telegram and spent long hours with him, discussing the work and its production.[73] At that time Reznicek was conductor of the Mannheim Theater orchestra, and Mahler also mentioned the possibility of an engagement in

Vienna. One day the two musicians took a cab together outside the opera, and Mahler told his companion that the cabdriver hated him and took every opportunity of showing his dislike, although he always tipped him generously. Reznicek was astonished, as he had not observed the slightest sign of hostility, but Mahler was insistent. Perhaps the enmity with which he had been surrounded for years and the uninterrupted flow of insults from the press were starting to have an unfortunate effect on his character.

Reznicek was dazzled and delighted by the trouble Mahler took to satisfy him during rehearsals, turning constantly to ask for his advice. In all his career, he had never met such a scrupulous conductor and had never heard his work so perfectly interpreted. He said that the performance was superior to any he could have given himself. Sometime after the rehearsals started, Mahler wrote to him suggesting a minor alteration in the last scene, based on Moreto's comedy. "I beg you, my friend, compose these four lines[74] as effectively as possible and send them to me as soon as you can. There's no other way of doing it! And it would be a great mistake not to. Forgive my haste! And let me have the pleasure of an affirmative reply by return mail." Before the dress rehearsal Mahler warned Reznicek that the invited audience was always lukewarm, and suggested he should congratulate the prima donna, Marie Renard, as soon as the curtain fell. Just as Reznicek was carrying out this advice, he heard Mahler whisper in his ear, "More, more compliments!" During the dress rehearsal some applause broke out after an orchestral interlude, but Mahler turned to quell it with an angry gesture. Later he explained to Reznicek that he had done this as a favor to him. "The interlude is followed by Floretta's lied. Once the rule against applauding had been broken, they would also have clapped this piece and then Perin's lied; in consequence the heroine's great aria would have fallen flat, because of its place at the end of the act and because of its serious character. And if this had happened, the prima donna would have canceled her performance tomorrow."[75]

The day before the opening, Reznicek was astonished to receive a visit from the leader of the claque, for Mahler had assured him that he had completely stamped out this questionable practice. He mentioned this to the old man, who replied with a smile, "Yes, it's true, Mr. Mahler doesn't know what's necessary in the theater. All the same, he can't do anything without me, and Mr. Director will leave one day, but I'll still be here!"

In spite of Mahler's efforts *Donna Diana* was not a great success. Hirschfeld accused Reznicek's score of "passivity," "reserve," and lack of character. The music "does not accompany the events, it drags after them," and in any case it seemed a stranger to the action. Mahler was really the "star" of the production, for he had given it unity by a magnificent performance and admirable sound effects. Kalbeck placed the main responsibility for failure on the libretto and condemned the style of the music and the vocal score, as did Helm, who described it in the *Musikalisches Wochenblatt,* as "perpetuum mobile in 3/16 time"(!). Hanslick regretted the stilted vocal declamation and the poverty of the libretto; "only the orchestra and the ballet dancers have rewarding tasks to perform in *Donna Diana*." Because of the "both superb and exasperating virtuosity" of the instrumentation, the voices were always being covered and the ear never had a moment's rest. Posterity has judged *Donna Diana* in the same way. Only a few orchestral fragments have survived in the repertoires of German orchestras; the rest of the work has been completely forgotten.[76]

The imminent departure of Fuchs and Richter was a new worry for Mahler. His first idea had been to replace one of them by Bruno Walter, who received the following offer on the eve of his departure to take up an appointment in Riga: "I wish to know if you are able and willing to respond to my appeal to join the Vienna Opera. If the answer is yes, I will send you a contract that would begin to take effect on the expiration of your present engagement, and we'll see how we can get you out of your Riga obligation then. I'd like it best if you could start with us next autumn, as soon as you are free."[77]

At this period of his life Walter was still unsure of himself. He felt the "need for more self-confidence, before exposing himself to Mahler's powerful influence." His reply was hesitant and embarrassed. This disappointed Mahler, who had expected immediate acceptance. "What are all these evasions in your letter?" he wrote. "When I make an offer, I know what I'm doing. I need an aide-de-camp to carry my field marshal's baton in his bag (now I am conducting everything and I'm exhausted). What does it matter to you or to the public to know who you will succeed? Furthermore, you won't be any more accomplished two years from now, or ten. If one amounts to anything at all, one is always learning. You yourself could not tell me where, today, you could learn more than you could here with me. So accept bravely, and, for the rest, rely on me and on your own ambitions. I am very anxious to have you before 1900, since I shall be dead by then if things go on like this! Let me ask you again to explain yourself by return post, and without evasions! You will receive a starting salary of five thousand florins."[78]

However, Walter persisted in his refusal, and he spent two years in Riga, as planned. And in the end, Mahler did not have to make an immediate decision, as Richter finally agreed to stay on in Vienna. Taking Mahler's subsequent silence as a sign of disapproval, Walter wrote him a friendly letter sometime later and received the following reply: "You have misinterpreted my silence completely. As you well know, I was always the laziest of correspondents, but nowadays, every line is a sacrifice for me! I forgave you a long time ago, if there was anything to forgive. Now I never give the matter a thought. In any case, the position here has changed and for the time being nothing is available. So let's forget about it and remain friends! . . ." Thus Walter continued his apprenticeship far from his master, and three years later, when he felt strong enough to resist the Mahlerian fire, he did not hesitate to accept the offer when it was renewed.

"I cannot hold my own and maintain
my honor in this cesspool."

# CHAPTER 29

*Mahler in Vienna (V) — New Anti-Semitic Campaign
— Second Philharmonic Season — The* Second *Symphony in Vienna (January–May 1899)*

Viennese anti-Semitic tendencies, which had been expressed so violently at
the time of the first Philharmonic concert, appeared again early in 1899 in
the form of one of the "scandals" that unhappily seem to have been a Viennese speciality. The Court was in mourning because of the death of the
Empress Elisabeth, and the big charity ball given each year at the town hall
was consequently replaced by a special Philharmonic concert, scheduled for
February 1. Mayor Lueger invited Felix Mottl to conduct it, regardless of
the fact that this was an affront to Mahler.

There were, however, many Mahler supporters among the Philharmonic
players; their committee invoked a clause in the new regulations which
stated that the orchestra could be conducted only by its titular chief, and on
December 31 the committee sent an official letter to the mayor demanding
that Mahler be invited to conduct. Mahler made no attempt to influence this
decision, but despite this, anti-Semitic journalists got hold of the story and
asserted that the orchestra had been "compelled and forced" by him to take
this action under threat of dismissal. Their "indignation" was all the greater
because the concert was for charity and because Mottl was a Viennese musician who had risen from the ranks of the orchestra itself. Anyone else,
they said—someone like Richter, for example—would have stood aside in
such a situation. Mahler, however, had proved that he was incapable of a
generous gesture, so anxious was he to monopolize the musical life of Vienna. If he was as great as his supporters claimed, why did he fear Mottl's
competition? Feelings of solidarity and loyalty should have inspired his
course of action, instead of which he had let himself be guided by his Jewish hatred for non-Jews, thus revealing the baseness of his soul.[1] Further,
the Philharmonic had often invited "guest" conductors such as Siegfried

Wagner and Humperdinck, but apparently it could no longer be conducted by just anyone, because it now had a Jewish leader.[2]

The fifth Philharmonic concert, on January 15, promised to be particularly stormy. Not only was it expected that the audience, roused by the affair of the charity concert, would stage a demonstration, but also Mahler had conceived the especially daring idea of having the Beethoven *Quartet in F Minor,* op. 95, played by the orchestral strings. According to Hanslick, he justified this action by saying: "Chamber music is written for a small room. It is really only enjoyed by the performers. Once it is transferred to the concert hall, its intimacy is lost; but more still is lost: in a large space the four voices are weakened and do not reach the listener with the strength and intensity intended by the composer. I give them this strength by reinforcing each voice. Don't we do the same in the orchestral movements of Haydn and in the Mozart overtures? Does this alter the character of those works? Certainly not. The sound volume of a work must be adapted to the dimensions of the hall in which it is to be given, and I would give the *Nibelungen* in a small theater with a reduced orchestra, just as in an enormous theater I would reinforce its original instrumentation."[3] Beethoven's last quartets, which "in their very conception have a different dimension," he then told Natalie, "simply demand a string orchestra. As an example, from all of them I have selected the greatest and the most difficult, the Quartet in C sharp minor, and I should like to reproduce Wagner's text for it as proof that these works can only be played in this manner. For the musicians, naturally this poses technical and interpretation problems that are even more difficult than those of the most difficult symphony; but such work will greatly benefit them and me and only by doing this can I lead them to the highest achievements. The style for this type of work has yet to be created. Not a note of the composition is to be changed. At first I had thought of adding double basses, but dropped the idea, for the whole thing is completely solid and inviolable in its construction. You will see what an unsuspected effect the result will have!"[4]

Before the concert started, Mahler said to Hanslick in vengeful tones, "Of course, I am prepared for a battle today, for you'll see that all the Philistines will rise up as one man against this performance of the quartet, instead of being curious and pleased at hearing it like this for once."[5] In fact Mahler's enemies were in a strong position and did not hesitate to take advantage of it. Right from the start of the concert, some booing was heard as well as applause, thus showing the city of Vienna's mixed reactions. According to Natalie, the violence and conciseness of the first movement of the quartet passed "like a storm," while in the expressive passages Mahler obtained a "discreet piano" and "a magical sound not possible with a string quartet." However, "the Lilliputians in the concert hall refused to accept this offering from two giants, one dead and one alive."[6]

The end of the first movement was received in deathly silence, then applause broke out, mixed with some vigorous boos from, among others, two young men seated in the front row. Mahler sent one of the orchestral musicians to ask them to leave the hall. If they did not, he would have the whole row cleared. They stopped booing but sent him word that "despite their admiration for him, they could not accept this orchestral rendering of a quartet." After the Finale, the audience's reaction was even cooler, and this still further increased Mahler's anger.

Schumann's *First Symphony,* on the other hand, was applauded warmly. Mahler had painstakingly annotated and revised all the orchestral parts, suppressing "everything the composer had tried to put in but that was not realizable." From the beginning the trumpets, "which seemed capable of making the walls of Jericho fall," sounded out with maximum strength and radiance but without violence or harshness. Mahler explained to Natalie that he had obtained this result "because I always give precedence to the principal voices, which are often drowned out if the instrumentation or performance is at fault." "When the secondary voices dominate, the sonority is vulgar. They should never be louder than the principal ones," he had stated a few months earlier, "for then the melody, the clarity and the musical logic are all destroyed. Because the deeper instruments are stronger, ninety times out of a hundred the accompaniment drowns out the melodic line."[7] He had taken even more trouble than usual with this Schumann symphony, which was so often badly played, and had left nothing intact from the previous performances. The concert ended with Tchaikovsky's noisy *1812 Overture.* This Viennese first performance was warmly applauded. Lunching with Rosé and Natalie after the concert, Mahler spoke about Schumann's "marvelous" symphonies. He was astonished that Wagner had not understood and admired them. Perhaps he had heard a bad "incomprehensible" performance that had given him the wrong impression. In any case, he had caused a lot of harm by influencing his sheeplike disciples, who thus felt free to despise Shumann. Arnold Rosé told him that most of the critics "deplored" his rendering of the Beethoven quartet. Mahler replied that, even if it was only out of stubbornness, he intended to carry on with this enterprise and that he was going to schedule Beethoven's *Quartet in C Sharp Minor*[8] for the final Philharmonic concert.

Hanslick alone courageously declared that he was not prepared to "refuse for pedantic reasons a new impression, an unusual pleasure."[9] In his view the experiment could be considered largely successful, thanks to the quality of the orchestra. Mahler had in fact made no changes in the text. Other works such as the Schubert and Mendelssohn octets demanded the same sort of strengthening, and an exception was not likely to become the rule. In the *Deutsche Zeitung,* Helm deserves even more praise for considering the trial performance with a certain objectivity. But in his opinion it was an unfortunate experience, for the "chaste," intimate character of the quartet had disappeared.[10] Kalbeck also condemned Mahler's "arbitrary act." He considered that a string quartet was the uniting of four individual personalities, of four voices, and it was unnatural to double them. Especially since the orchestral conductor was condemned to be nothing more than the "fifth wheel of the carriage." Instead of the "delicate polyphony of four good 'friends' . . . there was only an army exercising in rhythm." The intermediate instruments had been drowned out throughout, and the over-all effect was regrettably uniform and monotonous. The Schumann symphony, interpreted with genius, had luckily won forgiveness for the "sin against Beethoven." Finally, Hirschfeld condemned the uniformity and lack of harmonic balance in this "transcription" as well as the "absence of all emotion." He was dazzled by the Schumann interpretation, but, like most of his colleagues, he considered "antimusical" the racket made by Tchaikovsky's *1812 Overture*.

Two days later Mahler conducted at the opera the first important new work of 1899: the world premiere of Karl Goldmark's *Die Kriegsgefangene*,[11] an opera based—like Gluck's two *Iphigénies*, Berlioz's *Les Troyens*, August Bungert's *Die Homerische Welt*, and Chabrier's *Briséis*—on a story from Homer. The action takes place in Achilles' tent and centers around the burial of Patroclus and Achilles' anger with Briseis, a slave captured during the Trojan War, because she has treated Hector's corpse with honor. During a long scene with Priam, Achilles finally consents to the burial of Hector, and the work ends with a long love duet with Briseis. Hanslick judged this static libretto severely and also condemned Goldmark's "Wagnerian" style, his "tiresome and boring" music, and his "long, monotonous declamations, sustained by constant orchestral polyphony," which he compared to a "gray sea." He considered that the opera had been received well entirely thanks to Mahler's magnificent performance and the excellent cast.[12] Kalbeck carefully avoided expressing his opinion of an opera he clearly disliked: he merely found its good qualities "not very obvious," noted that the orchestral performance had been perfect, and mentioned that the initial tepid audience response had grown progressively more enthusiastic. But the *Allgemeine Zeitung*[13] said that the Viennese public had been disappointed in this new opera by the composer of *Die Königin von Saba,* finding it lacked depth, body, power, and grandeur.

Mahler himself got no pleasure from this performance, for he despised both Goldmark and his work: *"Das Heimchen am Herd* first opened my eyes to the banality of his music, its weakness and its sentimentality," he had said a year before. *"Merlin* also deeply disappointed me and I never liked the overture to *Sakuntala.* The only exception is *Die Königin von Saba,* for I must admit that the first two acts enchant me, especially the scene in the temple. The music of the Ark of the Covenant is really great, there is something of the spirit of the Old Testament in its power and splendor. The rest of Goldmark's music is superficial; the orchestral and instrumental points are useless. Brahms was of the same opinion. Indeed, one evening in Hamburg, when we were returning together from a performance of the *Sakuntala* overture, he was even harsher in his judgment. He was so annoyed and irritated by Goldmark and his music that day that even I thought he went too far!"[14]

Mahler's position at the opera had a favorable influence on his career as a composer, but though he was performed frequently, his works were not always well received. In December, Schuch gave the first Dresden performance of the recently re-edited *First Symphony*[15] in the presence of the King of Saxony.[16] It was received with weak applause and vigorous boos and the next day was torn to pieces by the press. Albert Fuchs, in the *Dresdner Zeitung,* considered it "the dullest work that the new epoch has so far produced in the realm of symphonic composition." He deplored the "apathetic calm" of the first movement and its lack of inspiration as well as the banality of the Trio and "Frère Jacques."[17] Only the melancholy theme of the central passage of the Funeral March had given momentary pleasure, but the "kettledrum orgies," the "Wagnerian reminiscences," and the "choral finale *à la Rubinstein"* were not enough to make the Finale interesting. This critic thought it regrettable to use orchestral forces of such quality for so thankless a task.

The *Second Symphony,* on the other hand, had been so well received the year before in Liège that Mahler had agreed to go there and conduct another performance, for he wished to "make contact with the first town to welcome one of his spiritual children."[18]

The day after the premiere of *Die Kriegsgefangene,* Mahler left for Liège, where he arrived on the morning of January 20, feeling rested and ready for anything. Dupuis and his wife—"a pleasant young couple"—went to so much trouble to make him comfortable that he was finally embarrassed by their efforts and decided to accept no further invitations of this sort when on tour, except from very close friends, for he found that excessive consideration and attention were tiring when he was trying to work.

The town of Liège did not impress Mahler, and neither did Sylvain Dupuis's orchestra, which he judged "mediocre and badly behaved" (*Ruppig*). However, he realized that after the Vienna orchestra, whatever he might say of it, every orchestra in the world must seem poor by comparison. He also found that the necessary supplementary instruments had not arrived— bass tubas, contrabassoons, and five-stringed double basses. He made a final effort to obtain them, and when this failed, he had to alter the orchestration of some passages at the last moment.[19] By good fortune the chorus master was competent and obviously full of good intentions, but the sopranos and contraltos exasperated Mahler by singing off key. He swore to himself a hundred times not to become involved in adventures of this sort again, for "the misery of life such as I have described it in the first movements is never-ending here." Despite all this, despite the "very French" soloists,[20] the concert promised to be successful. On Sunday, January 22, the *Second Symphony* headed the program[21] of the third of that year's "Nouveaux Concerts."

Despite the poor quality of the performance, Mahler's work made a deep impression. "Aware of the importance of the event," wrote the *Gazette de Liège*, "the public listened with great attention that gradually changed to growing enthusiasm." "A great, unqualified success," the same paper states. Mahler was called six times to take a bow and was presented with a "monumental wreath of real laurel leaves, sent from Vienna by his admirers." The *Gazette* also considered this symphony the most masterly work of its kind since Mendelssohn, "a composition of genius that does honor to the German school." Its qualities had seemed even more striking than on its first hearing, the year before.

"In this colossal and impressive work," the critic added, "the subjugating music passes like an autumnal squall." Impossible not to be "electrified by the Allegro maestoso," conquered by the good humor of the Scherzo or the emotion of the Andante,[22] and "filled with admiration for the gigantic Finale." Having exhausted his epithets, the critic finally exclaims: "Masterpiece, masterpiece, masterpiece!" Mahler's admirable conducting was "original and impulsive," underlining the "flexibility of the beat, the accentuation of the rhythms, and the great importance given to tone."

"I am just back from Liège, where my II (in C minor), which you know from Berlin, has been performed for the second time and wildly applauded," Mahler wrote to Frau Sommerfeld, in Hamburg.[23] As soon as he returned, he had to start rehearsing the sixth Philharmonic concert (January 29), the program of which included the first Vienna performance of Liszt's *Festklänge*, followed by Mendelssohn's *"Fingal's Cave,"* a *Rigaudon* from Rameau's *Dardanus,* and the *Symphony in F Major* by Hermann Götz, composer of *Der wiederspänstigen Zähmung.*[24] Hanslick, who was an enemy of Liszt, deplored the *Festklänge*'s melodic line, the "sound effects," and the orgies of "Turkish music." Its success, in his opinion, was due to the magnificent performance. As for the symphony by Götz, Hanslick could hear nothing in it but a "work by an experienced Kapellmeister," lacking all originality. The critic of the *Neues Wiener Tagblatt* also judged it severely, and said of the *Festklänge* that it would have been better for them to remain unknown rather than to "reveal all their poverty." He also considered that Mahler had "destroyed" Mendelssohn's overture by "excess of delicacy" and "countless changes of tempo."

In the middle of February, Mahler agreed to replace Strauss at a Philharmonic concert of contemporary music and thus gave the first Vienna performance of the two preludes to the first and third acts of *Guntram.*[25] On this occasion Mahler was pleased to renew his acquaintance with Humperdinck, who had been present in 1895 for the first performance of the *Second Symphony,* and with Wilhelm Kienzl, with whom he went for walks in the countryside around Vienna.[26]

A week later, the penultimate Philharmonic concert gave Mahler an opportunity of realizing an old ambition—that of performing a Bruckner symphony with the glorious Vienna orchestra. After considerable thought, he decided to give the first complete performance of the *Sixth*[27] ever heard in

Vienna together with three numbers from Beethoven's *Egmont* music and Schubert's *Rosamunde Overture*. Placed at the beginning of the program, the work was very well received, but some Bruckner supporters reproached Mahler for cuts (in particular the third thematic group) and for altering the instrumentation.[28]

A few days later Mahler left for Frankfurt-am-Main to conduct his *First Symphony* in the final subscription concert on March 8.[29] This time the orchestra was better than in Liège and the musicians "increasingly enthusiastic as they got to know the work." Mahler was "more encouraged by this growing professional admiration than worried by the lukewarm reactions of the laymen."[30] According to the *Allgemeine Zeitung*, the orchestra applauded his first appearance on stage with an enthusiasm strangely in contrast to the "bitter disappointment" of the audience. "Astonished silence, and polite, rather than enthusiastic, applause," was Mahler's impression. He added that he took only two curtain calls.[31]

According to the *Frankfurter Zeitung*, Mahler was wrong to supply his listeners with program notes, and, despite his "vivacity of feeling," despite his "originality and inventive force," he was also wrong to aim for "something new at any price." Also, he too often gave way "to his taste for refinement and baroque instrumentation." Finally the *Allgemeine Musik Zeitung* unfavorably compared his aims and his technical genius with "his weak inventiveness and his hollow, swollen, showpiece."

After his return to Vienna, Mahler forced himself to undertake a task that must have seemed to him a diplomatic necessity. A young priest, Don Lorenzo Perosi,[32] had just been named director of music for the Sistine Chapel. Despite his music's lack of character, Perosi was at that time considered a "new Palestrina" and, to the accompaniment of noisy publicity orchestrated by the Catholic Church, was conducting his music everywhere and being hailed as a renovator of religious music.

*La Risurrezione di Lazzaro* had been heard in Vienna for the first time in 1898, conducted by the composer. Now, due to the influence of some of the strongest Catholic members of the Imperial Court, such as the Archduchess Josefa, two more charity performances of the oratorio had been organized for March 13 and 14, 1899, with soloists imported from Italy. Once more Mahler devoted himself wholeheartedly to a thankless task and, according to Robert Hirschfeld, managed to "bathe the work in a gentle, noble light," a "consecrated halo." It is easy to understand how Mahler must have felt, when conducting this unsatisfactory work, when one reads Hanslick's comments on the score's "heartbreaking poverty" and on its "lack of invention and lyricism." Only a really devout believer, he said, could "escape from being bored to death by this music." The *Neue Freie Presse* spoke mostly of the "admirable" performance. Kalbeck considered that Perosi had an "unexceptional, attractive talent that lacked personality." It did, however, "have a semblance of originality." Theodor Helm registered great disappointment over the "operatic" style of the arias and the "absence of style" of the rest.[33]

Less than a week after the Perosi oratorio Mahler conducted, on February 26, the eighth and final Philharmonic concert; it was a Beethoven festival that included the overture to *Fidelio*, the *Fifth Piano Concerto* (with Busoni as soloist), and the *Seventh Symphony*. In Hamburg he had foreseen that, if he were to try to impose his Beethovian conceptions upon the Vienna Philharmonic, "as trained by Richter," he would one day encounter insurmountable difficulties. His versions, his stormy, dynamic, impassioned "modern" interpretations, and his instrumental alterations did in fact scandalize the Viennese. But for the moment he was still *persona grata* and this Beethoven festival was one of his rare, almost unanimous triumphs. Mahler considered that the *Seventh* was one of the least popular of Beethoven's symphonies, because "it suffers more than the others from bad performances," especially the Finale, in which the numerous unexpected touches called for "a free and animated interpretation that is expressed by holding back here, forging ahead there and broadly lingering elsewhere."[34] This movement should plunge the audience into a "real Dionysian intoxication." To Natalie he said: "You should have heard the force unchained there, but it did not sound out of proportion, as the principal voice stayed predominant and every passage, line and ornament came through as clear and bright as possible. In order to obtain this result, it is necessary that each musician give his all, he must give even more than he has to give, he must surpass himself. I force them to do this, because all of them think that I'll leap upon and tear to shreds anyone who doesn't carry out my intentions. With this extreme tension of all our being and all their faculties, the impossible can be achieved."

Mahler's accompaniment and Busoni's solo playing in the E flat concerto "had equal claim to greatness" according to the critics, who give an impression of unanimity, without one discordant note. Nevertheless, Richter accosted Busoni in London sometime later and said that he had heard that "Mahler had given him a lesson" during the rehearsal. "It's the limit," he added. "He cannot bear soloists because he lacks technique and is unable to conduct a score while reading it at sight, which a conductor should be able to do as easily as a pianist."[35]

Richter was about to leave Vienna, and it was with growing exasperation that he viewed Mahler's total success and increasing popularity as a virtuoso director who conducted from memory. During his fifteen years of constant work in theaters, Mahler had acquired substantial, reliable, and irreproachable knowledge of his profession. It was impossible to accuse him of "lack of technique." Further, Busoni had known Mahler since his Leipzig days. They had played together in a Hamburg concert in 1894; then again, only a month before, in Liège; their relationship had always been cordial. The way that Busoni, when writing to his wife, states that Richter "got this off his chest," clearly indicates that he did not agree with him.

Another anecdote, no doubt somewhat garbled, is related by Otto Klemperer: arriving in Vienna on the morning of the first rehearsal, Busoni found an urgent message from Mahler waiting at his hotel: he wanted to see him at once at the opera. Busoni hurried there without even taking the time to shave or breakfast. After a long wait, he was astonished to see Mahler burst from his office and run over to him, holding out his hand: "You agree, don't you, my dear Busoni, the Finale must not be too fast!" After a quick "Good-by" he disappeared again, but not before whistling for him the main theme of the movement. Mahler clearly feared that the famous pianist's virtuosity might lead to some excess of speed. The fact that he could treat Busoni in such an offhand manner proves that they got on well together. For once, this Beethoven concert was well received by the critics.

Mahler, waiving his performance fee, had agreed to conduct, for the Nicolaï Concert, to be given on April 9, the first Vienna performance of his own *Second Symphony,* and this project stirred up a lot of trouble in the ranks of the orchestra. Two cellists named Kretschmann and Sulzer spread a rumor that the work had been badly received everywhere, and it was at their instigation that another article appeared in the *Deutsche Zeitung,* in which Mahler was accused of having made orchestration "mistakes that one learns to avoid during one's first year at the conservatory," of reducing the sum due to the Philharmonic retirement fund by demanding supplementary musicians, and of "torturing" the first trumpeter all winter and then replacing him by another musician, whom he had already insulted during a rehearsal.[36]

Mahler did not reply to this article, despite the disgust he felt at the ingratitude of those for whom, a year before, he had obtained a salary increase of thirty thousand florins[37] at the opera, not to mention the substantial amounts that he had earned for them by packing the Philharmonic concerts all year. The increase in the box-office receipts had greatly exceeded the cost of the first performance of his *Second Symphony,*[38] but the cabal that had been formed inside the orchestra hoped to bring about his departure or at least the cancellation of the project.

During the first rehearsal, which Justi and Natalie watched, hidden in the Musikverein's box, the musicians were, as always, suspicious, astonished, even hostile, for the work was "entirely strange" to them. But they were gradually won over.

Mahler conducted these rehearsals with "lightning speed and intensity." He "stamped with his feet when he was not satisfied, slashed the air with his baton whenever he heard a wrong note, shouted and raged when a musician would not admit to a mistake he had made, but calmed down as soon as he confessed it." As always, he rehearsed the various instrumental groups separately in awkward passages and paid special attention to the percussion section, which had a particularly difficult part to play. He kept insisting that the kettledrummers play faster and louder, until it was feared that the membranes might split, as had happened in Berlin. But Mahler continued to ask for more sound, until in the end it was the exasperated musician's drumstick that broke. The man finally struck with all his strength and then asked derisively, "Is that loud enough?" "Even louder!" Mahler shouted, while the unfortunate musician hammered violently on the drum, his face screwed up with effort, as though to say, "The devil himself could do no better." Then Mahler shouted, "Bravo! Very good! Now, louder still!"[39]

In one week, with four rehearsals, Mahler obtained an excellent performance, thanks to the fact that he had trained the musicians thoroughly and had taught them to understand exactly what he wanted. However, he complained bitterly about the Singverein, saying that the standard had dropped since it had been taken over by mediocre men like Gericke and Perger. When not accompanied, the singers, despite their willingness and enthusiasm, went out of tune, and the result was far inferior to that in Berlin.

According to Natalie, who hadn't heard the Berlin performance, it seemed that the music "spread out"—up, down, and indeed in all directions. Yet these rich and varied harmonious effects were so well adapted to the text, so completely "determined" by it, that they went unnoticed.

Despite the deeply conservative attitude of the Viennese, Mahler's personality aroused such interest that the hall was full to overflowing on April 9th. The first movement was applauded, but as usual, the second was more unanimously appreciated. The cellos, carefully rehearsed by Mahler, interpreted their song "with quiet control, neither dragging nor lacking restraint."[40] The public was disconcerted by the terrifying humor of the Scherzo and amazed by its brusque, unexpected conclusion, which was followed by deathly silence and finally some timid applause.[41]

Sung "simply and movingly" by Marcelle Pregi, whom Mahler "never expected to hear bettered,"[42] the Urlicht was so loudly applauded that Mahler decided to encore it in order to respect his own indications concerning the uninterrupted performance of the last two movements. In the Finale the "Grosse Appell" (Judgment Day trumpet call)—in which a small orchestra, placed in the wings, is interrupted by "commonplace and terrible earthly noises"—was less effective than in Berlin, because of the hall's acoustics and the Musikverein's wheezy organ, which was incapable of suggesting "an ascension to the upper regions, far above the crumbling walls of the terrestrial dome." Most of the listeners were awed by the power of this movement, and Mahler's enemies "did not express their disapproval as noisily and angrily" as before, his position now being more firmly assured. After the concert a long ovation brought him forward many times to acknowledge the applause.[43]

After this somewhat unexpected triumph, Mahler was particularly happy and confident, not only because at last he had resumed contact with his own work, but also because in his heart of hearts he had been dreaming of success as a composer in Vienna since the age of nineteen, when he had completed *Das klagende Lied.* The same evening he discussed his work at length with Natalie, but the next morning he had a rude awakening when he read the first criticisms, which were full of bitterness, accusing him of "shooting sparrows with cannon balls."

In the *Deutsche Zeitung,* Maximilian Muntz claimed that Mahler had, "with his clique, reached and passed the peak of arrogance and antiartistic activity." Not content with the "previously described preparation of the symphony," he had "assured and planned its success at the performance," as otherwise, despite its "purely superficial" effects and the "ear-tickling" of the middle movements, even an "almost wholly Jewish audience" would not have shown such enthusiasm or "defied all the rules of decency." A public that, both from laziness and prejudice, fled from Liszt, Bruckner, and Richard Strauss, young students who shouted for "their Mahler" at the tops of their voices, was not capable of finding the smallest trace of music in Mahler's cacophonies. Amid this "shameless enthusiasm on the part of young Israel," the boos from those who had been justly indignant over this scandalous success and the insignificance of the music had "clearly revealed that Mahler's star has begun its decline." Muntz returned to the attack the next day, resisting the temptation to "employ against him all the insults and outrages that his clique proffered against Bruckner, Liszt, and Strauss." He must, however, use their favorite expression, "pompous impotence." Nobody, Muntz wrote, "could discern in all this hubbub "a work of art, to say nothing of a symphony." He called the two middle movements "banal musical buffooneries" that only "tickled the auditory nerve." The whole composition was a slap in the face to the fundamental rules of a work of art. It revealed "the composer's intention to create a great work, his consciousness of his own inability to carry it out, and his desire to hide this inability with clever tricks. The contrast between the hugeness of the means employed and the smallness of the ideas," the "calculated and deliberate deceiving of the listener," the "pompous sham, is comparable to that of Meyerbeer." Mahler was the "incarnation of Jewish musical decadence, ignoring all measure, all regard, all restraint in the pursuit of his goal." His behavior toward the orchestra clearly demonstrated that he considered it a horse he was "ready to ride to a standstill in order to reach his personal ends."

The liberal *Neue freie Presse,* which was owned by Jews, naturally took a more lenient, if not particularly sympathetic, line. In an unsigned article (no doubt by Heuberger) the writer likened the *Second Symphony* to a "piece of imaginary theater." The Andante evoked the serenades of Robert Fuchs (one of Mahler's teachers), the Scherzo recalled Bizet, Wagner, and Berlioz, but the great paroxysms of the Finale "lost all concept of harmony and counterpoint." The same effect, the writer considered, could have been obtained "without a score if all the musicians had been simultaneously permitted to rage at will and fortissimo on their instruments." Nevertheless, the general effect had been "favorable, even overpowering." Mahler was undeniably a very talented composer, gifted with an audacious imagination and a strong and well-defined personality, even if his work was not entirely "well rounded or above criticism in all its parts." He deserved all the public's attention, and his success had been considerable, despite a "factious opposition." In the *Neues Wiener Tagblatt,* Karpath asserted that this work, which was fascinating from its first note to its last, was undeniably a symphony, conceived along polyphonic lines; its orchestration was magical and it was directly descended from Beethoven, Schubert, and Wagner. Mahler was an artist of genius, who must continue composing at all costs. It would not be long before people began to admire what at present astonished them.

After this second performance, Mahler began to regret a serious defect in the work which had not hitherto struck him: the excessive contrast between the dancing rhythm of the Andante and the dramatic ending of the first movement. He remembered that he had conceived the two movements separately in Leipzig, not intending to use them in the same symphony: it would have probably been better to start the Andante with the impressive singing sound of the cellos, but by now he was no longer close enough to his work to be able to envisage such a change.

Five months later he heard a private performance of a two-piano, eight-hand transcription of the *Second Symphony,* played by four excellent musicians who were all enthusiastic about the work, which they had heard Mahler conduct. This was Mahler's last chance to make a few disillusioned remarks: tempos, phrasing, expression all seemed to him so false that the result was chaos: "and all this was conducted and rehearsed by someone who believed he was following 'traditional' lines![44] At least this shows us what traditions are: they are nonexistent! Everything is left to individual initiative, and if no genius presents himself, the works are lost. I understand perfectly why Brahms let people play his works however they liked. He knew it was useless to say anything. This is a deeply saddening experience and a situation to which it is difficult to become resigned."[45]

Mahler's delight at the public's reaction to the concert was followed by equal disappointment at the reaction of the critics and "professionals," even those who were his friends. One of them, Eusebius Mandyczewski, said for instance that the symphony showed talent but lacked "unity in the developments and true thematic progression." "As though it were possible to form the slightest judgment on a single hearing," bellowed an exasperated Mahler. "These gentlemen always attribute all the responsibility for their disappointment to the artists and the works of art, not willing to admit that their lack of judgment and their understanding alone are at fault." After having condemned the symphony roundly, the Viennese critics continue to "greet me warmly in cafés and restaurants, constantly trying to meet me" he said to Natalie. One day, in a fit of perverse humor, he told some of them that for his *Third Symphony,* in order to obtain the right empty, mournful sounds, he needed human skulls. He added that to achieve the particularly tense atmosphere required for this work, he would satisfy his own blood-thirsty instincts by having some exceptionally careless musicians killed off before the concert and would use their skins for the drums—unless the critics would offer him their own, which would be every bit as good as oxhides.[46] It is easy to imagine his listeners' reactions!

During the Philharmonic concert season Mahler was more active than ever at the opera. February saw the first performance there of two shorter works, Haydn's *Der Apotheker* (*Lo Speziale*) and Lortzing's *Die Opernprobe* (*The Opera Rehearsal*). Haydn's little comedy, taken from a story by Carlo Goldoni, had been translated and "adapted" by the critic Robert Hirsch-feld[47] and had been given once by Mahler in Hamburg. Again he accompanied the recitatives himself on the piano and replaced the lost overture by the London *Symphony in D Major* (No. 104), which, according to Hanslick, he performed "in an unforgettable manner, perhaps never equaled anywhere in the world."

The story of the old apothecary Sempronio, in love with his pretty niece, who loses her to a young suitor after being tricked many times, was in the *commedia dell' arte* tradition, and Hanslick thought the music "disarming in its naïveté." The ensembles in this little masterpiece seemed "full of invention," and the whole revival had been a delight, thanks to the perfect direction and casting.[48] Helm found it "too pure and too light" for the vast opera house, but Hirschfeld congratulated Mahler for devoting all his art and all his efforts to "making the enjoyment of Haydn's work as easy and agreeable to us as possible." He too was delighted with the freshness and vivacity of the ensembles, performed so delightfully that they seemed improvised in the best *opera buffa* style.

*Die Opernprobe,* based on an old French play by Raymond Poisson called *L'Impromptu de Champagne,* was the swan song of Albert Lortzing, a dramatic composer who died in poverty at fifty.[49] *Die Opernprobe* had just been republished in 1899 and Hanslick praised its freshness while admitting that it was not on a level with *Der Waffenschmied* or *Zar und Zimmermann.* The libretto, like all those by Lortzing, was delightful, one of the rare German comic operas worthy of revival, and Hirschfeld also marveled at Mahler's "matchless sense of style," which had given the score its real values, while avoiding two hidden dangers, an "excess of old-fashioned stiffness" and an "easy, very sophisticated modern attitude."

The only important new production in the 1898–99 season presented to the Viennese public a new operatic composer who bore an illustrious name, since he was the only son of the composer of the *Ring*. Richard Wagner had encouraged him to take up architecture, but Siegfried, who was only fourteen when his father died, had later studied music under such celebrated teachers as Richter and Humperdinck and finally decided to write operas. His first, *Der Bärenhäuter* (*The Sluggard*), performed in Munich on January 22, 1899, had won considerable success, which it would be unfair to attribute entirely to its composer's name. The original libretto ("There

are obligations one cannot escape when one bears the name of Wagner,"
Hanslick remarked ironically) concerns the adventures of a young soldier
named Hans Kraft, who descends into hell and is employed there to heat
up Satan's caldrons. He is saved by St. Peter, who wins his soul at dice.
The devil takes his revenge by turning the soldier into a dirty, lice-ridden
vagabond who can be redeemed only by the love of a young girl. The
Wagnerian influence is easy to detect in this libretto; the idea of redemption
by love, the legendary subject borrowed from the world of the sagas, the
journey into hell, and so on. Siegfried Wagner, having studied music rather
too late, lacked technical skill as well as originality. Nonetheless in this
"musical drama" he was intelligent enough to turn to folklore for his inspiration, in order to escape, as much as possible, the influence of his great
father.

That *Der Bärenhäuter* was a real success, both with the Viennese public
and the critics, can be measured by the fact that it was performed eighteen
times in 1898 alone. Mahler deserves all the more credit for having performed so conscientiously a work whose weaknesses he knew only too
well.[50]

In Mahler's estimation the quality of the work was insufficient to interest
the intelligentsia; neither was it likely to appeal to the general public, who
were impressed by Mascagni and Leoncavallo. The first act dominated the
work to such an extent that the rest hardly seemed to have been written by
the same man. "The melodies have no sooner begun than they are over," but
the opera as a whole had a certain charm and an incontestable gracefulness
that might be due to the fact that Siegfried "was born on Sunday, a lucky
omen." Mahler had made certain cuts in the score which he considered
largely responsible for the success in Vienna, since everywhere else the work
had been a failure or near failure. Cosima Wagner, who now spent more
time furthering her son's music than she did the works of her great husband,
wrote to Mahler to protest at these "inadmissible" cuts, and Mahler felt a
mixture of utter amazement and exasperation when he realized "that she
rated her son's works as high as her husband's." He did not give way, however, but expressed his opinions to Siegfried with complete frankness, telling
him that the last act was mediocre and carelessly written and that he would
have to be a "base flatterer" to say otherwise. No one could ignore the fact
that he was completely opposed to cutting, since he had replaced all those
cuts formerly made in the works of Richard Wagner! This convinced Siegfried
that Mahler would not give in, and their conversation ended in an atmosphere
of tension. However, a short but cordial letter sent by Mahler some months
later[51] proves that the friendly relationship between himself and Wagner's son
was not permanently damaged by this conflict.

If, then, Mahler cut the work, it was in order to increase its dramatic effect. But Frau Wagner, firmly convinced of her son's great talent and faithful to the family's anti-Semitic tradition, at once spread a completely differ-

ent version of the affair, which shows to what extent she misjudged Mahler's character in particular and that of the Jews in general. "My son is at present in Vienna, to direct the *Bärenhäuter,*" she wrote from Wahnfried on March 12, 1899, to one of her friends,[52] "and has written to tell me how kind all the opera staff have been to him. The director, Mahler, has done all in his power to understand the work and to rehearse it, but has decided, for some mysterious reasons—or perhaps one which it is only too easy to explain—to make some quite incomprehensible cuts; for example, all of Luisel's prayer, which must be considered as the heart of the work, as well as all other parts where there is an atmosphere of 'communion!' In front of everyone, my son asked him quite calmly: 'Is it all the religious parts which you dislike?' But showing great patience, he has managed to get most of the important passages replaced. This incident is all the more interesting since I am just reading a book: *Chamberlain's XIX century,* in which the author explains that what distinguishes the Semites from the Germans is that the latter have a strong penchant for religion, which the Semites lack completely . . ."

After the first performance of the *Bärenhäuter,* Hanslick pitied Siegfried for being Wagner's son and admitted that he had been agreeably surprised by the opera, particularly the second act. In the first and the last, it seemed to him that the young composer had been too willing to imitate his father's style. Hanslick wrote that Mahler's exemplary performance had contributed greatly to the work's success.[53]

One April evening, a few days after the first Vienna performance of his *Second Symphony,* Mahler felt very feverish, and the next morning he awoke with influenza and had to remain in bed all day. A doctor was sent for, who forbade him to conduct *Der Bärenhäuter* that evening. Mahler spent the entire day dozing, which was so unlike him that the whole family was worried. That evening Justi was chatting with Natalie in the next room when he called to them to announce that he no longer had a temperature and wanted to eat. They talked with him till midnight and then left him with some food beside his bed. The rapidity of this recovery was considered by the family as more proof of Mahler's solid constitution, and he caused great astonishment at the opera the next day when he arrived in excellent health, although the newspapers were already full of news about his illness.

Once the Philharmonic season was over, Mahler began to set aside some time each day for his personal work. In May he revised for the last time the scores of the *Third Symphony* and *Das klagende Lied.* During his previous revision of the cantata in Hamburg in 1893, he had done away with the off-stage orchestra in the second half, hoping to make the piece "easier to perform." Now, as he revised it again, he realized that this cut had been prejudicial to the music, and he restored his original version.[54] As Bruckner had said to Behn in the past, "Now I'll have no further need of the Schalks,"[55] Mahler would have liked to have no further need of the Philharmonic! But a "trial" performance would have been of great help to him in order to "check" his orchestration. Unfortunately the hostility and passive resistance of various musicians made this impossible. Mahler was sad and bitter about this, for he should have been able to request such a service from his colleagues, to whom he devoted so much of his time.[56]

On May 9 the dress rehearsal of Daniel Auber's *Fra Diavolo,* which Mahler had restaged completely, was marked by an accident that affected him deeply. The baritone Neidel forgot that a cut had been made in the dialogue preceding the second act finale, and, too far downstage, he was struck by the descending iron curtain. He reeled under the blow and fell unconscious. Dr. Boer, the opera doctor, was called immediately, and Mahler, full of worry and remorse, as though "he himself had brought about this misfortune," suspended the rehearsal. During the preceding scene, the young singer Michalek had had to undress, at least symbolically, and some of the orchestral musicians had stood up in order to be able to see her. This had exasperated Mahler, who ordered them back to their scores and continued conducting in a fury, without once glancing toward the stage, while wondering how he could avoid performing this "nonetheless exquisite and in no sense frivolous" opera. It was at this point that the accident occurred, and he feared that he had caused it by his "angry conducting." The unfortunate singer was at once carried to his dressing room, where he remained unconscious for some time. Mahler stayed by his side, refusing to go home until the doctor had reassured him regarding Neidel's condition.

Neidel was forced by the accident into retirement and six years later sued the Vienna Opera. In his opinion Mahler was mainly responsible for this accident and his "cerebral hemorrhage," having ordered the curtain down too soon. His career had been interrupted by the accident, and later he had had a nervous breakdown. He claimed fifty thousand crowns in compensation and reminded the court that Mahler had given him eight thousand for his medical expenses. Called as a witness, the latter declared that, far from being an admission of responsibility, this payment had been a simple "act of humanity." He was able to prove to the judges that Neidel had crossed both the limiting lines drawn onstage,[57] the first of which it was forbidden to go beyond. Infraction of this rule called for disciplinary action. The baritone having neither the character nor the natural enthusiasm that could have resulted in his crossing over the line by mistake, it seemed more likely that he had attempted to show off so as to obtain the renewal of his contract and should have been punished severely. Neidel had been neither cut nor bruised, but only suffered from "nervous shock." As to the curtain, it was he himself who gave the signal for it to be lowered, with a prearranged stage gesture. Since Neidel's responsibility was thus proved, he did not win his case,[58] but many of Mahler's enemies considered this as yet another proof of his "cruelty."

After attending a poor performance of *Le Prophète* on May 7, 1899, conducted by Fuchs, Mahler was again seized by pessimism regarding his work: "I feel like a procurer who has to supply the public with a prostitute to its humor and taste," he said to Natalie. "If she does not please and finds no taker, I am not entitled to my pay and must sustain the loss of putting something else on sale. It is the most demanding profession imaginable, and after such an evening, I feel as though I am personally guilty."

The friends whom he met at a café after this performance put all the blame onto Meyerbeer, whom they condemned utterly, but Mahler defended the composer, explaining that, despite his love and enthusiasm for Wagner, this did not mean that he had ceased to appreciate artists "smaller, less gifted and less productive, which would be like throwing the baby out with the bath water . . ."[59] About the same time, a performance at the Burgtheater[60] caused Mahler to compare its purity with his own "inartistic activity" at the opera. "You'll see," he said, "one fine day I'll suddenly take leave from here. I cannot hold my own and maintain my honor in this cesspool." Shortly before this he declared to Reznicek, "My position could change from one day to the next, for I am quite determined to hand in my resignation if necessary! Even if they chase me away, I will have done them good!" This pessimism sprang from the long months of overwork and from the many "inartistic" aspects of his position as director. But it was also the result of the merciless battle he was fighting against the opera administrators.

"A simple test, to find out whether
the spring had dried up completely."

# CHAPTER 30

*Mahler in Vienna (VI) — War with the Administration
— Difficulties with the Singers — Aussee, the* Fourth
Symphony (*May–December 1899*)

Hofrath Wlassack, *Kanzleidirektor* and mainspring of the administration,[1]
who had played an essential part in Mahler's appointment, quickly
realized that his "protégé" was an "ungrateful wretch." From the moment
Intendant Plappart, who had also become Mahler's sworn enemy, was appointed, no opportunity was lost to let Mahler feel the weight of administrative authority by means of daily interference, pestering and knuckle-
rapping. When, in the autumn of 1898, Mahler drew up his yearly list of
contract singers, giving both their current and their "ideal" salaries, the sum
total of his recommended increases came to sixty thousand florins (twenty-
five thousand florins for the men, and thirty-five thousand for the women).
His request was refused; Plappart, on the contrary, suggested a further
saving[2] by dismissing several older singers and again urged the strictest
economy, as Mahler's expenditures had already exceeded his budget. True,
performances had drawn larger audiences than in previous years and profits
had been greater, but this was secondary; given the size of the deficit, it
had to be reduced.

In December, the intendant icily reminded Mahler that on several occasions he had asked him to prepare a *Dienst-Instruktion* (a handbook of
opera regulations) along the lines of that drawn up by the Burgtheater director. In it Mahler would of course attribute to himself the rights already
accorded to him in the decree appointing him, but Plappart also suggested
modifications. In particular he wanted to force Mahler to draw up a general program for the season in advance and to seek his written agreement
for all decisions.

In short, Mahler had been wielding complete executive power,[3] even
though he had had to get the intendant's consent to all important decisions.

Whereas now Plappart wanted Mahler to request written assent for *all* decisions, Mahler still claimed the right to make them himself "in emergencies," though he was prepared to ask for the intendant's consent afterward as a matter of form. Mahler won this first round, for the changes proposed by the intendant do not appear in the final version of Mahler's *Dienst-Instruktion*. This preliminary clash is of great importance because most of the disagreements that flared up later stemmed from it.

Plappart then expressed his lack of confidence in Mahler's handling of finances, in an official letter written shortly afterward to the lord chamberlain, accompanied by a second, confidential letter. The official letter, unlike the confidential one, was meant to be passed on to Mahler. In it he recommended the appointment of an official responsible for supervising expenditures and financial projects for all new productions. This suggestion seemed "vague and not very effective" to Prince Liechtenstein, who feared that it would be "open to various interpretations," and Mahler prevailed again, for his *Dienst-Instruktion,* signed by the interested parties on February 10, did not limit his previous powers.[4]

Almost before this battle ended, another had begun regarding two of Mahler's "victims," the stage director Albert Stritt and the soprano Frances Saville. The former, hired in 1898, claimed that he had received from Mahler "an assurance that during the term of his one-year contract he would continue to supervise the staging of operas on which he had worked." But, returning from a leave of absence in January, he learned from an opera employee that "he had been relieved of his duties." Stritt claimed that he had been forbidden access to the stage, but Mahler asserted in his letter to the grand master of the Court that he had never given such an order. Stritt felt that he had done nothing to deserve this "disgrace" and could not continue to accept a salary that he had not earned: he therefore protested violently to the intendant, reminding him that at the start Mahler had been satisfied with his work. And hadn't Mahler once asserted that he "simply needed an inspector, not a creative artist, as stage director"?

At the end of February, Mahler received a short, curt note from the intendant demanding an "immediate" explanation. As exasperated "as if they had prescribed to him in advance a tempo" for an opera, he replied just as curtly that he had had to "give up using Stritt as stage manager, the latter having proved himself incapable of carrying out his wishes."[5] In fact, this new official interference was all the less welcome because Mahler had already spoken to the intendant about Stritt, who had been seen several times in Plappart's office and obviously had been urged by him to formulate his complaints officially.

On February 28, Mahler justified his decision to the intendant at greater length. A singer could be evaluated rapidly by the conductor and the public, but the more complex activities of a stage manager could be judged only after some time had elapsed. When a candidate seemed to have the required qualifications but was working elsewhere, the only solution was to

offer him a temporary contract, to observe him at work, and to let him go
if he was unsuitable. Mahler himself had had to carry out duties normally
incumbent on Stritt, and "it is not really possible to have a clear idea of
what that involves unless one has done it."[6]

"It is the right and duty of a director to really *dispose* of all the forces
under his command. Even the malicious, as long as they respect the truth,
cannot deny that my actions here at the opera have been guided only by
objective considerations; furthermore, it should be obvious by now that I
have the knowledge required to judge the artists and performance. To
come back to the central question, I feel obliged to point out that complaints like these of Herr Stritt's will not be tolerated in the future. To compel me incessantly to interrupt important work to attend 'immediately'[7] to
incidents of this kind, is to hamper me in the execution of my duties, and
thus harm the Royal Opera. Surely the administration does not mean to
add to my many and often unavoidable problems and difficulties, nor to
waste on trivial matters a large proportion of my time, my energy, and my
strength, which are entirely taken up, often to the furthest limits of my
physical endurance, with grave and serious problems."

This was the equivalent of telling the intendant in no uncertain terms to
mind his own business, of accusing him of spite, and of reproaching him
haughtily for stirring up unnecessary trouble.

As for Frances Saville, whether Mahler had conceived for her one of
those "infatuations" for which he was often criticized, or whether he had
engaged her reluctantly, as Karpath claimed,[8] she had won the public's
favor. Feeling that she was not being treated properly by the director, she
had defied his authority on several occasions. Mahler had then expressed
his displeasure by reducing her performances to a minimum, which drove
the young prima donna to seek engagements abroad to make up for the
financial loss that she suffered in Vienna.

At the beginning of 1899, Saville was on unpaid leave of absence in the
United States. In order to accept a new series of concerts, she requested,
upon her return in March, an immediate, paid, one-month leave of absence.
Mahler refused, and this privilege was granted behind his back by the intendant,[9] who did not even inform Mahler of his decision. This time, Mahler had every right to be angry. He wrote to the intendant and sent a copy
of his letter to the lord chamberlain. According to Mahler, Plappart, in
doing this, had wasted opera funds and flagrantly violated the director's
rights as set forth in the *Dienst-Instruktion*.

It was the director's responsibility to decide both the dates of the singers'
leaves of absence and their schedule of performances, as well as the payment of indemnities.[10] Saville's unexpected absence could in fact cause
serious difficulties with the repertoire, which had been arranged on the understanding that she would be in Vienna.

Two days later the intendant defended himself in an angry letter to the
lord chamberlain. Mahler himself had complained that he couldn't find

roles that suited Saville, and the extension of her leave had made no difference to the repertoire. Furthermore, he had refused to concern himself with
the Stritt affair and regarded it as an "insignificant matter." Both the tone
and content of Mahler's letter were "unacceptable" and contrary to operatic
procedure. Another official letter refutes Mahler's point by point, accusing
him of losing interest in his protégés, of getting rid of them by humiliating
them in every conceivable way, and of wasting money with his changes of
mind. Plappart explained in his letter that he had granted Saville leave of
absence because she had already cost the opera a great deal of money.
For the one-year period of her engagement, December 8, 1897, to December
7, 1898, she had been paid a high salary, but had sung only twenty times
instead of the sixty-four stipulated in her contract.

In Stritt's case the whole dispute concerned an indemnity of five hundred
gulden which the intendant had granted without Mahler's knowledge. Mahler had criticized Plappart for not consulting him and for wasting money.[11]
The lord chamberlain decided that Mahler had been wrong about Stritt
and right about Saville, and privately informed the intendant that in his
opinion, "by studying in advance the interests of the singer and the opera,"
he could easily have foreseen and avoided this "discord."

In an official letter destined to be read by Mahler, Liechtenstein agreed
that the tone and content of Mahler's letter were "contrary to operatic procedure" and accused him of inconsistency: by protesting the indemnity
granted to Stritt, Mahler was defending his alleged rights by claiming that the
intendant had not acted in the best interests of the opera, whereas by no
longer using Saville, it was *he* who was open to this charge. The appropriate
procedure in this case apparently did not apply to himself: despite Mahler's
"artistic ambitions and the success he had achieved," Liechtenstein felt he
must insist that Mahler respect procedure in the future, because "only those
who know how to obey can govern properly."

Stung to the quick by this criticism and not realizing that the lord chamberlain considered him in the right regarding Saville, Mahler, with the
help of his old friend Siegfried Lipiner, drew up a long report in which he
"defended his honor," gave his version of the facts, and tried to show how
the administration endlessly placed all sorts of obstacles in his path. He admitted to being wrong in the case of Stritt but pointed out that he had informed the intendant verbally of his intentions and that the latter had encouraged Stritt by saying, "We'll see whether Mahler or I will be the
stronger." The "urgent" note from the intendant had exasperated him because the members of the opera would be encouraged to defy the director
with the intendant's blessing. Any trace of discipline would then disappear.
In the Stritt affair, he had realized that Plappart was trying to force his
hand, but he had nonetheless preferred not to keep a collaborator whose
work would ultimately "damage the opera." He himself must be allowed
to *propose* any measures that concerned the personnel. The intendant had
usurped his rights in this respect, as well as concealing his intentions from

Mahler: as he was director and because of his long theatrical experience, it was imperative that he have "the next-to-last word" in cases of this kind.[12] He had been rebuked for the tone of his letter, but the truth of the matter was that he had no time for paraphrases or for conventional formulas. His "harsh objectivity [*herbe Sachlichkeit*] was in no sense a lack of respect but the way he felt he should express himself under the circumstances." After the Saville affair any singer might decide to follow her lead and oppose the director. Each day new incidents proved to him that he, and he alone, was capable of making all decisions regarding repertoire and singers.

Mahler then recalled the many reforms that he had tried to impose in the interests of the opera, and for which he needed the lord chamberlain's support. There were many interlocking cogs in the immense, complex, theatrical machine, and seemingly unrelated circumstances did in effect depend on one another. One ill-considered action could be the cause of many more, and therefore no detail could be overlooked. The public, the artists, and the director himself were human beings, and subtle psychological reactions were triggered between them, sometimes for mysterious reasons. Mahler gave many examples to support this assertion. For instance, before his arrival, the singers had received a supplementary "performance fee" even when they canceled appearances. Mahler had abolished this privilege, which only encouraged illnesses and cancellations and had caused the opera a considerable financial loss. Since this reform each singer thought himself an "exception" to the rule; each one was secretly jealous of or hated his neighbor, either believing himself unjustly treated or specially protected; each believed that he could defy the director with impunity. Fresh cancellations would lead to a general demoralization: the regulations must apply to everyone, or they would be worse than useless. To alleviate these "sanctions," Mahler tried to take into consideration illnesses and unavoidable accidents and softened the blow by having the artist in question sing oftener. One of the women singers, furious at losing her "activity pay" for the second time, had recently complained to the intendant, who had advised her to "write him a letter." Fortunately, she had not dared to do so but had repeated this reply to Mahler, who wondered if the intendant understood the possible consequence of his act. The very next day the singer could have reported sick, to the serious detriment of the opera.

Mahler next, in the most interesting passage in the letter, drew up a long list of the obstacles that the intendant had put in his path. When he had suggested giving Weber's *Oberon,* Plappart had merely replied that he "was not in favor of it." When he spoke of *Rienzi,* which he thought could be a great success if it were completely restaged, he was refused again.[13] If he took new initiatives, must he always expect new difficulties, and how would he surmount them? While working on a production, he sometimes needed to have a new expenditure approved. To get what he wanted, must he resort to stratagems, express artistic beliefs different from his own to make them persuasive? Even a talented actor would find this difficult, and for Mahler it was impossible. One of the particularities of his position as theater director was that he was unable to write "progress reports" on the most important aspects of his activity: the conditions of his profession required him to work on a purely individual basis; he was often unable to explain and justify his ideas, feelings, and personal convictions. He alone was responsible for everything that took place inside the theater, and at least he should have the rights attached to such a responsibility.

When, for example, he was strongly convinced that painted furniture would damage the general effect of a performance, and when he was refused necessary credits, how could he convince his superiors that he was right? When the intendant told him that "settings that have been considered usable for years cannot suddenly be judged unusable," what could he do, as it was a question of artistic opinion? All improvements could be vetoed if one thought that what had been good enough before would still suffice.

Mahler then called his reader's attention to one of the basic truths of opera: it is impossible to achieve success in purely musical terms. The charm of a setting, its novelty, the harmony and vivacity of a tableau, a judicious collaboration between action and music, all had a tangible effect on the box office. By systematically refusing, the administration could economize slightly, but in the long run this could cause the opera an incalculable loss, as innumerable small details contribute to the theatrical effectiveness of a work. In *Djamileh,* the gilt trellis that cut off one side of the stage created an air of intimacy, as did the carpet unrolled in front of the heroine for her dance; and again, in *Dalibor,* the barrier that prevented the chorus from swarming over the stage focused the audience's attention on the central action.

Such seemingly unimportant details could make all the difference to the success of a performance. It was sometimes only during final rehearsals, when he saw the work as a whole, that Mahler became aware of the need for small expenses of this sort, and he found it agonizing to meet with last-minute refusals. On the eve of the revival of *Der Freischütz,* he had noticed that Agathe's and Aennchen's costumes were ridiculous—the first had a dress buttoned up to the chin, and the second a ball gown. Pressed for time, and having received no answer to a request addressed to the administration, he had ordered two new costumes without realizing the indignation that this decision would arouse.[14] Yet surely this had been the right thing to do, even if he had gone about it in the wrong way? In addition, the preceding November, after the scandalous article in the *Deutsche Zeitung,* he had paid an expert graphologist out of his own pocket in order to unmask the culprit. When a second opinion was considered necessary, he had asked the intendant to refund him the expert's fee of forty gulden, since the matter was official. The intendant's agreement had once more been accompanied by severe criticism.[15] After several such incidents he could not help wondering whether the opera's interests would not be better served if the administration stopped placing obstacles in his path and stopped endlessly obliging him to give up his work to concern himself with trivia. The time and energy of its director were part of the opera's capital. Should they be wasted?

Although he had already shown, in Budapest, his dislike of useless expenditure, he nevertheless thought it indispensable to reward suitably exceptional efforts made by the opera's technical staff. The simultaneous productions of *Der Apotheker* and *Die Opernprobe* had cost the opera almost nothing (exactly fifty-eight gulden) but had required extensive preparation. Wasn't he right to recompense the stagehands? After the *Ring* the administration had thanked them for the success of the performances by refusing to pay for the men's midday meals (though the performances' success and even the singers' safety depended upon the stagehands). Yet there was only one *Tetralogy*, whereas the year before, during rehearsals of the ballet *Tanzmärchen*, four hundred gulden in "meal allowances" had been paid to the technical personnel. He had paid the men out of his own pocket after the *Ring* because he had considered it absolutely necessary.

In the realm of stage décors Mahler believed that he had already shown how much he was against any kind of extravagance. He was in fact deeply opposed to it but felt that he must take into consideration the taste of the public, as long as there was no artistic reason for not doing so. He had been refused ten thousand gulden to present Giordano's *Andrea Chénier*, though this amount would have been easily recovered by the opera's certain success. Mahler did not envisage building extravagant sets, he only wished to re-create the historic atmosphere on which it was impossible to economize. In any case, this money would have been spent more wisely than the 7500 gulden allotted in 1896 to Messager's *Le Chevalier d'Harmental*. However, thanks to savings made at the start of the season, 20,000 gulden out of the opera's 24,000-gulden subsidy remained to be used that autumn.[16]

Once again, Mahler requested that he participate in the preparation of the first budget, as he alone knew all the practical details of running the theater.[17] He wondered if the administration could not make an effort to back him up in his work, since "the pride, the vanity, and the laziness of the singers" occupied a great deal of his time, not to mention that taken up by rehearsals, by preparing new works for performance, by perfecting the stagings, and by searching for possible new productions. One day he would be interrupted by a singer determined to have a new costume, the next by another "driven half mad" by a critic's insignificant phrase; a third would threaten to leave the opera on the pretext that her rival had been given the best roles; on other occasions an unexpected cancellation would require a last-minute program change. All this was naturally part of the daily battle fought by opera directors, but the intendant appeared to forget it when he needlessly placed further responsibilities on Mahler's shoulders.

Although the lord chamberlain's reply is not in the opera archives, Mahler clearly won the day.[18] This clash was yet another episode in the series begun in Prague with Neumann, and continued in Leipzig and Hamburg with Staegemann and Pollini, but this time Mahler had proved himself: he was the right man in the right place and the Imperial Court would support him throughout. The intendant's bias against him is beyond a doubt: certain passages in the report are utterly convincing in this respect. The lord chamberlain probably urged Mahler to be more patient and discussed matters with him more frequently in order to minimize future disagreements.

During these depressing struggles Mahler thought nostalgically of nature and the solitude of the countryside where he would take up his composing again during the summer—the only activity that gave him unalloyed pleasure. For this purpose he rented a house in Upper Austria, but before taking refuge there he had to go to Prague. After his success there the previous year Neumann had invited him to the annual Wagner festival, where he was to conduct Beethoven's *Ninth Symphony,* preceded, as thirteen years before, by excerpts from *Parsifal* (conducted by Josef Stransky, Josef Manas and Desider Markus). Wanting to make alterations in the score in his usual way, Mahler searched for clean orchestral parts and discovered to his amazement that Richter had failed to add most of Wagner's alterations to the Philharmonic score. In Prague, where Mahler arrived several days before the performance, Josef Stransky, who had met him the previous year, was surprised to see that the famous director of the Vienna Opera, before whom everyone trembled, was trembling himself while ascending the stairs to Neumann's office, just as he had at the age of twenty-four, the first time he visited him as a young conductor.

At the first rehearsal he rehearsed only the cellos and double basses, making them work on the long recitativo of the Finale[19] for three hours. The Czech chorus, whose women's section particularly pleased Mahler, worked under him with admirable zeal and proved themselves far superior to their Viennese counterparts. Unfortunately the orchestra lacked "precision and experience," and, despite all his efforts, he could not elicit a performance of the hoped-for quality. After the concert, a packed hall applauded rapturously, and Mahler was particularly susceptible to praise from the critic Richard Batka, a fervent admirer of Richard Strauss, who now took up Mahler's cause and promised to see that the *Second Symphony* was performed in Prague.[20] The reviews disappointingly do not discuss his interpretation of the *Ninth Symphony;* most of the articles list important people in the audience and describe the banquet following the concert, which Mahler did not attend, since he had to leave at once for Vienna.

On June 3, the day of the Prague concert, Johann Strauss, the Waltz King, died in Vienna. Three days later, before going on vacation, Mahler attended his funeral. Studying the faces around him during the ceremony and the funeral procession, he reflected bitterly that they expressed nothing but indifference and stupidity; not one of them appeared to be really moved or concerned. Some were thinking of their own affairs, others were discussing copyright or the dead man's will. At the church, the pastor Zimmermann made an unctuous speech that totally failed to create the appropriate atmosphere, and the Männergesangverein added to Mahler's uneasiness with an *a cappella* chorale during which the voices gradually dropped, ending a tone and a half lower than they had begun.

With a feeling of great relief, Mahler left Vienna a few days later with Justi and Natalie for Laussa, a small village off the beaten track in Upper Austria,[21] where he counted on finding the peace and quiet for which he longed. Scarcely had they arrived with their bags, trunks, piano, books, music, food, and clothing necessary for a summer spent alone in the heart of nature, when all three learned with consternation that the ground floor of the house containing all the comfortable rooms was locked, the owners reserving it for themselves. Only a small, uncomfortable, poorly furnished apartment was left for them. Was this sharp practice or a misunderstanding? In any case, there was no question of staying in Laussa under such conditions, and all three set out with their belongings in search of another summer retreat—at a time when most of them had long since been rented. Mahler was longing to get to work, and he sent off frantic telegrams in all directions. Ten days of his hard-won vacation passed in this wearying search. As always when he was not working, Mahler relaxed in spite of everything, and little by little his physical tension subsided.

In Aussee, a small watering place in the Salzkammergut known for its salt baths, the travelers thought that they had finally found a haven of tranquillity, and the Villa Seri, situated a half-hour walk above the town, seemed perfectly suited to Mahler's needs. Unhappily, he soon found out that from it he could hear the municipal orchestra, which played on a bandstand in the center of the thermal establishment each day to the people taking the cure. In despair, he complained bitterly of "his mood being completely shattered" and feared "that these six weeks, the only important ones in the whole year," were lost. "I can't even enjoy a vacation like anyone else," he continued, "or wait for the Holy Ghost to visit me, for the end of vacation is always hanging over my head like the sword of Damocles. It is torture for me to do something when I'm not completely in the mood and when I feel that the result will not be entirely right. What a poor devil the musician is! A scholar or poet can prepare himself by studies, the painter by the contemplation of nature—thus they put themselves into the proper frame of mind, whereas I have nothing but this sheet of blank paper before me and I must be able to smell [sic] what is going to be on it."[22]

The weather was cold and rainy, as it often is in the Salzkammergut.[23] But gradually Mahler emerged from his depression and began to think about a new composition. As usual, he chose to work in a small, dingy, isolated room under the eaves, where he talked one afternoon with Natalie. She asked him if he intended to finish the lied outlined the year before in Vahrn.[24] "The life of a baby born in the sixth or maybe even the fifth month can perhaps be saved," he said, "but not that of an embryo, which needs a longer period in the protective maternal womb in order to reach maturity." Feeling the effects of some medicine taken that morning, Mahler then broke off to make a hasty departure. A little while later he returned, as cheerful "as the *Malade imaginaire*," bringing with him the complete sketch of *Revelge*, a new *Wunderhorn* lied that he had just jotted down in his notebook. Later on it often amused Mahler to remind his friends of the place where he had composed this lied, which he considered the most beautiful and the most successful of his *Humoresken*, perhaps even "the most important of all his lieder."

No doubt it was then that Mahler thought of Carl Löwe, the author of the well-known *Ballades*. "He would understand my *Humoresken*, for he is really the inventor of the form, even though he has not achieved great heights with it. Into the bargain, he has been content to use the piano only, but a vast composition, which really plumbs the depths, cannot do without an orchestra. Neither has he managed to liberate himself completely from older forms; he repeats his stanzas literally, when the contrary is necessary—I even believe that this is an essential principle, valid for all music—to always move forward as a poem does and to compose without literal reprises [*Durchkomponieren*] . . . you will never find a reprise at the start of a new stanza in my work, precisely because the basic law of music is eternal transformation, perpetual development, just as, in the universe, one particular place will change and renovate itself endlessly. Naturally such development must progress and really move forward, otherwise it is valueless."[25]

During the rest of June, Mahler continued to work in spite of "odious interruptions and the hubbub of the band, which plays serenades, funeral marches and wedding marches every day from eleven o'clock, and on Sunday from eight in the morning." His room was very cold and damp, it never stopped raining, and despite it all he orchestrated *Revelge*, which was finished at the end of the month.

Long before, he had decided to set this poem to music, but the inspiration never came until that famous afternoon: the first movement of the *Third Symphony* now seemed to have been only a "simple rhythmic study" for this lied, which he could never have composed without it. It is comparable to "feeling a tree that carries on its cut surface the traces of its entire life and development . . . You will be amazed at the eerie, mystical qualities of this poem; though it is drawn in mere outline, it is still crystal clear: the drummer at the head of his troop passes his beloved's house, then falls on the field of battle. He begs his comrades not to leave him wounded, but no one hears him because they all have been 'mowed down like grass.' Finally, he gets to his feet and, 'so as not to lose heart,' starts beating the drum again to lead his side to victory; the soldiers then march back through the streets of the town, and their limbs stand 'like tombstones' before the beloved's windows. About this poem Goethe wrote: 'Invaluable for him who has sufficient imagination'!"[26]

Until July 8 the weather was glacial. Although the house was heated every day, Mahler felt cold; this interfered with his work, and he lost the healthy look he had acquired during the first week of his vacation. He nevertheless completed the orchestration of *Revelge,* constantly fearful of interruptions that might delay this almost mechanical task, and on the seventh, his birthday, he played his new work to Justi, Natalie, and Arnold Rosé, who, moved and deeply impressed, at once understood the greatness of its "naïve simplicity" and its "perfect mastery of form." Once again a poem from the *Wunderhorn* had enabled Mahler to "create a world," whereas a more perfect text would only have limited him.

Despite his worries and the endless interruptions, Mahler found time to delve into his favorite authors. He read Goethe's correspondence with Schiller, his *Conversations with Eckermann,* his writings on aesthetics,[27] and *Elective Affinities;* his friend Siegfried Lipiner's *Adam;* Euripides' *The Bacchantes;* and Paul Sébastien's *François d'Assise.* He was also delighted by a small volume of Schubert's works which Dr. Stöger had sent him, and reread these scores with great joy even during the evening meal. (Mahler would have liked to see the whole literature of music available in miniature scores that he could carry with him on vacation.) He also sight-read works by Handel and Bach, and with his future brother-in-law, Arnold Rosé, played transcriptions of Brahms's *Clarinet Quintet* and *Clarinet Sonatas,* which he had discovered with delight the year before.[28] Remembering how he had "changed his mind" about the Brahms pieces, he felt he could no longer be indignant at the foolishness and lack of judgment of the musical public, since even professionals were capable of such mistakes. Although his vacation was almost over, Mahler seemed at ease and happy, for the household was peaceful, "partly due to the absence of Emma," whose "disturbing presence" had sometimes weighed on him.[29] But Aussee provided every annoyance imaginable. He ran into many acquaintances there, and, even more often, strangers recognized him, followed him, called to him, or stared at him openmouthed "as though he were public property." He did not feel safe even in the villa, where he received anonymous cards and letters, often from female admirers who wanted an autograph or a picture of him, and there were sometimes shouts of "Long live Mahler!" from tourists in carriages or on bicycles. Sometimes while out walking he would hear whispers of "It's Mahler"—to which he sometimes replied crossly, "Do you want an autograph?" "All that I ask," he would groan, "is that they don't look at me through opera glasses." Day by day he became more misanthropic at each contact with these aimlessly wandering idlers, who gave him an impression of boredom and emptiness.

As in previous years at the same period, Mahler went for long walks: on July 22, after climbing the Pfeiferalm by way of a picturesque trail, he began thinking aloud to Natalie, as he often did. "Music should always express yearning, a yearning beyond the things of this world. Even as a child, it was something mysterious and exalting for me; though at that time my fancy also added trifles that were not there at all." Inevitably he returned to his chief preoccupation, the interruption of his creative work. "During these three summers, I have felt like a swimmer who takes a few strokes just to convince himself that he still knows how to swim. It could also be a test to find out whether the spring has dried up completely; there is a trickle in mine, but not more."[30]

And in fact it was out of the question for Mahler to undertake any other important work after finishing *Revelge*. He did manage to correct the proofs of the *Third Symphony* and the *Klagende Lied,* and was pleased to see that Josef von Wöss's piano[31] transcription of the latter work was "clear and easy to play and nevertheless complete." He went over the second and third movements of the *Third Symphony* with Arnold Rosé in order to mark the bowings, which he did not want to leave to the musicians. To achieve perfect unity, he insisted that the phrase marks must be identical in all the parts. Everything about this work seemed so strange and new that he was struck by it, particularly the Scherzo, "the most farcical and at the same time the most tragic musical passage that ever existed, as only music can make the mystical leap from one to the other. It is as if all nature is making faces and sticking out its tongue; its crazy humor inspires fear rather than laughter. The next passage—'The Night'—comes like the awakening from a nightmare, or like the gentle dawn of self-awareness."

After these various tasks were finished, the inhabitants of the Villa Seri noticed, around mid-July, that Mahler's absences were becoming longer and more frequent. They soon guessed that, despite all he had said, he had begun working again, but this time he was composing more than a lied. Only ten days of vacation remained, but, determined to accomplish the impossible, he went on working despite all obstacles and began to take solitary walks or drop behind his companions to jot down a melodic idea, something "he had not done since *Das klagende Lied*."[32] Even during these walks he could not escape the *"Kuhgäste,"*[33] the idiotic tourists who made him long for a solitary *Häuschen*. He even came to envy Beethoven's deafness, despite the great pain and sorrow that it had caused him[34]: at least it had had the merit of isolating Beethoven from the "empty" and destructive restlessness of the world and of closing him up forever in his own creation.

Fearing lapses of memory, Mahler carried a notebook everywhere, ready to change some detail instantaneously, so as to be able to simply write in the correction on his return. He complained at this time of his faulty memory, because he forgot most of the stories he was told: "I feel like someone whose digestion is too good, and whose system either rejects food or immediately transforms and assimilates it: absorbed or not, the food disappears right away." From then on, composition appears to be "a game of construction, in which one is always building a new edifice with the same stones. From childhood, the only time one gathers and assimilates, the stones are all there, waiting to be used."[35]

On July 21, Siegfried Lipiner visited Aussee to read his "symphonic drama," *Hippolytos*. Mahler had already heard it and spent the afternoon working, leaving Lipiner an audience consisting of Justi, Natalie, and Arnold Rosé. Later Mahler recalled the anguish of those last vacation days when he set to work each morning, his project rising before his eyes like a tower that he had scarcely begun to build, and he asked himself, "Will I be able to cling to it and make it my own during the few remaining days? How long till that damned band starts again?" This idea threw him into such agitation and anguish that he began to suffer from attacks of dizziness. A few days before his departure he, Justi, and Rosé climbed the Sattel, a small mountain from which they intended to make their way down to Alt-Aussee. While walking along peacefully behind his companions, the ground suddenly seemed to disappear beneath Mahler's feet, and he almost lost consciousness, he who had never had dizzy spells. Justi saw that he was deathly pale, and ran to take his arm. As the inevitable day of departure drew nearer, the physical manifestations of his suffering increased, and he had to give up his work. "I have never had trouble finishing an entirely sketched composition, although my imagination often deserts me during the first draft. This time, however, ideas poured out so abundantly that I scarcely knew where to begin and was almost at a loss to fit everything in. And on that frightening 'wrong note' the holidays ended, leaving me haunted by the fear that this atrocious vertigo will take hold of me whenever I want to work again. Now that I am going to have a *Häuschen,* and peace, all that does me good, the Creator may well be lacking."[36] It is strangely disturbing to realize that this composition that tormented Mahler has such an atmosphere of well-being, of naïveté, and of love of life, and that in the midst of a creative output predominantly tragic in mood, the *Fourth Symphony* (with the partial exception of the Adagio) should provide a carefree interlude, a sort of lyric intermezzo.

At the end of July, Mahler left with Natalie and Rosé for Ischl, where he was to visit Prince Liechtenstein and meet Lipiner, whom he then accompanied to Sankt Wolfgang, near Salzburg. The two friends spent July 30 together there, happy and relaxed, talking about old days, and Mahler related several amusing episodes about his life in Hamburg and Budapest.[37] Two days later he had to return to Vienna, where new difficulties at the opera awaited him. In Aussee, he had received an extremely unpleasant letter from the intendant accusing him of having behaved in an "incredible" way "contrary to the principles that he should observe," and criticizing him for granting the bass Hesch a prolongation of his leave of absence.[38]

This letter was doubtless the reason for Mahler's call on Prince Liechtenstein, before answering these charges in a letter that reveals his indignation. In it he reminded the intendant that he had entreated Hesch never to fail him at the last minute as the other opera basses (Grengg and Reichenberg) often did, and that by co-operating Hesch had overworked himself; his doctor had certified that he could not resume work at the beginning of the next opera season without gravely endangering his health. Mahler had therefore promised him that at the beginning of August he would be granted leave to take a cure at Karlsbad. It also seemed to Mahler an excellent occasion to present a new bass named Moritz Frauscher without causing unnecessary rivalry. The intendant had never before blamed him for granting leave for rest or convalescence, because he had always been very severe in all other cases. Questions of humanity apart, the interests of the opera required the singers to be in perfect health and to perform under the best possible conditions. Furthermore, this convalescence would also give Hesch an opportunity to recover from a recent personal sorrow, his wife's death. (Hesch had begun to experience the first symptoms of the cancer that eventually killed him, and was shortly to have the first of several operations.)

In conclusion, Mahler again demanded full authority in all matters concerning opera personnel, since he did his best to avoid making administrative mistakes, adding that "a theater cannot be run as strictly as a business office."[39] Although he never gave leave to singers solely to permit them to accept "invitations" elsewhere, he would continue to grant leave for health reasons, and he had given the administration sufficient proof of his firmness in this matter.

Upon his return on August 1, Mahler was confronted with one of those problems he knew were "inherent in a director's work": the tenor Fritz Schrödter refused the role of Eisenstein in *Die Fledermaus,* alleging that it was beneath his dignity: "An operetta is simply a small and gay opera," Mahler wrote him, "and many classical works come under this heading. The fact that mediocre compositions have been given this title recently makes no difference. Johann Strauss's work surpasses them in every way, notably in its excellent musical diction, and that is why the administration has not hesitated to include it in the repertoire. You yourself, dear Herr Schrödter, have often sung works that are far below the level of *Die Fledermaus—Am Wörther See,* for example." Schrödter was therefore obliged to sing the part, but as he had a particularly full season, he could alternate the role with one of his colleagues without receiving the supplementary pay he claimed. An appeal to the intendant would not change this decision.

In a note dated the end of September, the administration reproached Mahler for having "set a bad precedent" in permitting Selma Kurz to repeat the last stanza of *"Je suis Titania"* in *Mignon,* and of again giving way to the audience the next day by encoring the duet sung by Hesch and Schrödter in *The Bartered Bride.*[40] This time, Mahler's reply was heavily ironic: "I must call your attention to the fact that it is absolutely impossible to ask, from the podium, during a performance, for the authorities' consent to an encore. A work of art depends, and always will depend, upon the inspiration of the moment; under no circumstances can it be subject to any control other than the good taste and good will of the performers. Of course, in keeping with my obligations, I will try to prevent a repetition of this kind of thing. May I add, however, that under conditions such as prevailed during the last two performances, where I was confronted with a spontaneous demand by the audience, it is almost a physical impossibility to resist this demand. Furthermore, I should like to remind you that there are several precedents for this . . . when the administration did not seem to find it necessary to hold the director accountable."

In August, to escape the city heat, Mahler spent two days in the mountains of the Semmering and Hochschneeberg but returned to Vienna when it began to rain. After a brief visit to Dresden at the end of the month to see Rubinstein's *The Demon,* which he was soon to conduct at the Hofoper, he joined Justi and Natalie in Maiernigg, on the Wörthersee. The recent Laussa adventure and the disastrous Aussee summer had convinced him that calm and seclusion were indispensable to his creative activities. He had considered renting a house on a long-term basis, or building one in Carinthia or southern Tyrol,[41] where the climate is much better than in the Salzkammergut. House-hunting was the order of the day, and for this purpose Justi had joined Natalie in Aussee; the two had then set off on an exploratory bicycle trip.

On August 18, Mahler's two emissaries had arrived in Maria Wörth, on the Wörthersee.[42] There, before boarding the little steamer for Maiernigg, they met Anna von Mildenburg, who came from this province of Austria and offered to accompany them on their search. Almost at once she introduced them to a talented amateur architect named Alfred Theuer, who promised to build a house for them quickly and for a reasonable price. Installed in a small hotel, the Schwarzenfels, the two friends began visiting possible sites and comparing their respective advantages of silence and isolation.

Summoned by telegram, Mahler joined the search, which was unsuccessful for some time. He was picturing himself back in Vienna without having made a decision, when he finally found the ideal spot: a wooded piece of land on the shores of the lake, far from any houses, and with, some distance away, where the ground rose up to a real primeval forest, a well-isolated, ideal site for his *Häuschen.* Before knowing if the land was for sale, they started poring over plans, and Mahler gave Theuer his instructions. The architect promised to remain in Maiernigg until the end of October to make sure that the *Häuschen* would be ready for the following year.

The beauty of the Wörthersee was unrivaled when Mahler returned on September 10 to sign the purchase deed and the architect's contract. The little church of Maria Wörth was mirrored in the lake at the end of a narrow peninsula, around which small sailboats and white swans drifted. Only Lake Maggiore has a landscape of comparable beauty. Mahler bustled around constantly, examining the ground and discussing every detail of the house. All the necessary decisions had been taken before he returned to Vienna, and for the following summer, he rented the Villa Antonia, a twenty-minute walk from the site of the *Häuschen.* Now he could look forward to his next vacation with confidence; here, in this tranquil spot, he would finish his *Fourth Symphony* without difficulty.

Despite his conflicts with the intendant and the singers, Mahler was particularly happy that autumn, for his opera reforms were beginning to make themselves felt. The ensemble had never been better: he had just engaged the excellent mezzo-soprano Laura Hilgermann, who had sung for him in Budapest and whose personality was admirably suited to "naïve and sentimental roles."[43] On September 3, Selma Kurz, a lyric-coloratura soprano, won considerable praise in *Mignon,* and Mahler at once realized that she had all the qualities he wanted for a coloratura soprano.[44] Also during the autumn he succeeded in having the opera vacations extended to August 15, a change especially important to him because it would give him two more weeks for composing each year.[45]

The first two events of the season could be regarded as concessions made by Mahler to public taste. In April, Donizetti's *La Fille du régiment* had been highly successful with a "guest singer" named Hedwig Schacko. Mahler therefore decided to present the opera again in September with Margarete Michalek, whom Heuberger felt was not up to the part. The latter tells us that Mahler took great pains over this revival, but the hall was not full. Hanslick found this short Donizetti opera soothing to the nerves, after the "dramatic and musical poison" of "verismo." For Hirschfeld, the new version had finally been organized and developed "around the strengths and weaknesses of Michalek"; the sound was finely disciplined, and an enthusiastic audience had mainly applauded the singers' efforts,[46] because Donizetti's score, illuminated by Mahler's interpretation, "revealed its unworthiness."

The revival of *Fra·Diavolo,* which had been postponed for some time because of Neidel's accident, took place on September 29. According to Hirschfeld, the performance was a success, thanks to "the universality of Mahler's genius," which could deal equally well with "the anguish of the Norn scene, the pure gold of *Die Zauberflöte,* the ardor of the Italians, and the grace of the French." He found the casting and the freshness and charm of the direction irreproachable. Karpath compared his "miraculous renaissance" of *Fra Diavolo* to that of *Zar und Zimmermann* in 1897; Mahler "knew how to revive the living, waken the sleeping, brighten the tarnished."[47]

Always on the lookout for an assistant conductor capable of replacing Fuchs, Mahler had hired, the previous spring, one of Bruckner's former disciples, Ferdinand Löwe, who had been highly successful as director of the Kaim Orchestra. Löwe had no theatrical experience, but his debut in *Hänsel und Gretel* had shown great promise: Mahler let him conduct two rehearsals, and some days later he entrusted *Lohengrin* to him. This time his rehearsal and the results were deplorable: "Since the singers and the conductor did not know the other's tempos," Löwe could not hold them together, and the young conductor left the Hofoper with an indemnity of five thousand gulden and the title of *Hofopernkapellmeister.*[48]

Richter had asked for his annual leave in order to conduct in England. Fuchs was ill, Hellmesberger was also on leave, and Chordirektor Luze had only a very limited repertoire, so Mahler was again conducting nearly every day. The guest conductors he invited disappointed both himself and the public: Paul Prill from Nuremberg, Josef Göllrich from Düsseldorf, and Ludwig Rottenberg from Frankfurt. Mahler had met Rottenberg the previous year in Frankfurt, where they had both conducted at the same concert, and they had met again in Aussee. Mahler assigned *Tristan* and *Don Giovanni* to him, and admitted that Rottenberg conducted these operas "conscientiously and with exactness, better than all the others." Despite this he did not think that Rottenberg had brought out "the true and living spirit of the work, that spirit which I feel so clearly and deeply in my own soul . . . I must get used to this," he said. "A work remains a book with seven seals," hermetically closed until the day when a creator arrives and succeeds in opening it. "How painful it is," he added, "to see works buried alive this way, and how frightening the growing isolation of which I become increasingly conscious. It would be best to cut oneself off from the world, for it is vain to hope for understanding. I am filled with distaste, not only for opera, but for concerts as well. The only thing that I cannot and will not give up is my creative work. But it is not for the outside world that I persevere; it will be the last to understand and accept it. I have barred the way too thoroughly for that: I create for myself alone."[49]

As always when he voiced such thoughts, Mahler was furiously active in the world that he despised and repudiated. Fuchs had died on October 4, and he had to replace him. He had corresponded the preceding May with a pupil of Humperdinck named Leo Blech, whom he agreed to meet in Frankfurt. Blech sent him many letters proclaiming his admiration and devotion, but Mahler finally decided against engaging him, fearing that he would be accused of filling the opera with Jews.

None of the guest conductors mentioned earlier having had the success expected of them, he eventually decided to hire Franz Schalk, the younger of two brothers, friends and disciples of Bruckner, whom Mahler had met at the conservatory. He was not particularly impressed either by the man or by the musician, but Schalk's Viennese origin and his conservatory training were strongly in his favor. In November, Schalk agreed to replace Fuchs if he were offered at least the same salary as that which he was receiving at the Berlin Opera, which he badly wanted to leave. He appeared as guest conductor in February 1900, and was engaged shortly afterwards.[50]

In the meantime, Mahler, on October 9, assigned the direction of the revival of *Lucia di Lammermoor* to Karl Luze, a former member of the opera chorus who had become his assistant and who apparently did very badly. Mahler's enemies, notably the correspondent of the *Neue Zeitschrift für Musik,* waxed indignant over Luze's "incompetence," the poor casting,[51] and the "unfortunate choice" of "the admirable Saville" for the title role, following a series of falls from grace suffered by Van Dyck, Dippel, and, most recently, Luise von Ehrenstein.[52]

Despite its dramatic flaws, Rubinstein's *The Demon* still had a special appeal for Mahler, who personally rehearsed and conducted its first Vienna performance on October 23. The story, adapted from Lermontov, is not good theater material: a young woman struggles with the devil, who, out of love for her, arranges her fiancé's death. The last-act appearance of the tempter in the convent where the heroine has taken refuge, and her subsequent redemption, did not hold the attention of the audience, according to Hanslick, and basically the whole opera was nothing but an interminable duet.[53] Mahler had made a number of cuts in the score of *The Demon* which lightened it and gave it a faster pace.

Hanslick, like the Hamburg critics, was delighted by Mildenburg's performance, the ease of her runs, her trills, the chromatic scales that she unleashed with such amazing sureness and agility in the upper registers. This proves that she had not yet lost the vocal brilliance of her early days. As for Reichmann, a specialist in diabolical roles such as the Dutchman, the Vampire, and Hans Heiling, according to Hanslick he had added a new and magnificent characterization to this somber collection.

Other critics, including Helm, wondered why Mahler bothered to revive such an old work after Rubinstein's successive opera failures. According to Helm, the audience was left uncertain as to whether the hero was a ghost or a real person. The music didn't clarify things, because Rubinstein was unable to characterize his dramatis personae or to suggest an atmosphere of evil. The work oscillated incessantly between oratorio and opera, and the melodic invention was not sufficient to hold the interest. Mahler labored over the production, galvanizing all the forces at his command, "as if he were dealing with a superb tragedy rather than a dramatically stillborn work." Why had he not chosen "a great German work" instead?

For Hirschfeld, who deplored the "old-fashioned romanticism" of the libretto, the hero was "an underworld neurotic," and Rubinstein's music an "Oriental bazaar of musical attractions" that illustrated none of the libretto situations. Finally Schönaich ascribed the success solely to the performance, which surpassed everything Mahler had done previously. Thus the critics unanimously condemned the choice of this opera.

During the rehearsals, Mahler, as always, took great pains to bring the opera to life, and he clashed with the baritone Reichmann over his interpretation of the main role. The great baritone had appeared to be convinced by Mahler's arguments, but at the third performance, on October 29, he again went his own way instead of following Mahler's instructions, and managed to avoid him after the performance, hoping to escape the inevitable scene. Mahler expressed his great annoyance to his chief assistant, Luze, who overenthusiastically carried out his job of go-between, so that Mahler received a letter from Reichmann on November 1, full of exclamation marks and underlined words. Far from acting in bad faith, he had tried to follow Mahler's advice during the rehearsals and the first two performances, Reichmann insisted, but "I would risk my health and my voice if I did not free myself from Mahler's tyrannical yoke and follow my own instincts.

"Your haste, your eternal agitation on the podium," Reichmann wrote, "can confuse people calmer and less devoted to their art than I. Once on the stage, an artist has to risk his own reputation and it is too much to ask that he do only as *you see fit*. I have proved that I am someone in my own right, and people ought to have some faith in my judgment. I am always grateful for good advice from an artist of your caliber but I will not be tyrannized! I wanted to make an exception in your case, but this proved impossible for me. All my colleagues agree with me that your demands are excessive; furthermore, despite the great respect that we feel for you, I have often been the only one to stand up for you, pointing out that you mean well and that you are a great artist.

"You demand the impossible by insisting that we *conform completely to your wishes* in tempo, gestures, and expression. I have been singing for thirty years in the theater, and have the right to my own beliefs and opinions. Your interpretation of the role of the Demon is completely wrong; you have taken away all its musical charm. Last Sunday's success was much greater than usual. Above all, my nerves do not permit my being tyrannized in this way. You threaten to *take Hans Sachs away from me!* If that's what you want, do it, although this is a role I am so sure of that you and I could not disagree about it. I have sung the part everywhere with great conductors and always to our mutual joy. You say that you are afraid you might become angry again, but that does not bother me, even if you intend to make me the victim of your world-famous despotism . . . Do you really believe that you could boycott me?

"No, certainly not! It is shameful to exaggerate this affair, and you are absolutely wrong to consider your opinion the only valid one. My own artistic reputation is too great to be damaged by this. I will spare no effort to protect myself from your harassment. Thank goodness I have plenty of friends among the public here, and I don't believe they will allow you to sacrifice a Reichmann to your whims. I will only say, in closing, that I don't understand how you can reach the point of persecuting me with deadly hatred, just because I dared for once to be myself; your way of doing things lacks dignity and cannot succeed."

In his reply Mahler apologized for being brief, because, "on the one hand, I do not have the time, and on the other, my arguments will not have the desired effect . . . Not one word I spoke should have permitted Luze to reach such conclusions." There would have been no misunderstanding in the first place if Reichmann had answered the message sent to him by Wondra, and had come in person to straighten things out, instead of invoking a clause in his contract which allowed him to refuse. If the singer had heard Mahler's words repeated and twisted by a third party, it was his own fault. In any case, Mahler had no intention of boycotting him or of "persecuting you with deadly hatred," or of taking the part of Sachs away from him, for it was one of his best roles and one of the "great achievements of the German stage." He intended, on the contrary, to do his best to make Reichmann happy at the Vienna Opera.

A number of later letters show that this crisis did not last long. Nevertheless, Demuth was given the role of Sachs in the revival of *Die Meistersinger,* for Mahler refused to accord anyone the exclusive rights to a part, and the new baritone must be able to replace the older singer when he retired. Demuth had sung the role in Bayreuth the preceding summer, and Mahler made only minor suggestions to deepen and sharpen his interpretation. *Die Meistersinger* was to be given uncut[54] for the first time in Vienna, and Mahler devoted almost all of November to it, congratulating himself on the fact that "my fear that I might weary of this work after hearing it too often has fortunately proved groundless." He had not conducted it for two years, which was in fact sufficient "to make it as meaningful to me, even more so, than before." "I tell you, what a work this is!" he concluded. "If German art were to disappear completely, one could reconstruct it from *Die Meistersinger.* Everything else seems empty and superfluous in comparison." Mahler's creative enthusiasm was such that, when he devoted himself to a work, he forgot all the others and found the one at hand superior to everything that had gone before.

During the final week Mahler conducted three orchestral rehearsals and three complete stage rehearsals of the opera. The performance on November 27 lasted almost five hours, including the intermissions, and the theater was full. Not a single member of the audience arrived late or left before the final chord. In record time Mahler succeeded in transforming everything: he even reduced the stage area for Sachs's workshop, despite the opposition of the intendant, who felt that no changes were necessary in so "popular" an opera.

Before the curtain rose the audience was as expectant "as for a premiere," according to the *Neues Wiener Tagblatt.*[55] Loud applause greeted the Prelude but was mixed with booing, which came from a group of young anti-Semites in the balcony who were doubtless Reichmann supporters. The other members of the audience then doubled their applause, so that after five minutes the tumult threatened to ruin the atmosphere. Mahler cut the applause short by starting the first act, but he could not do the same thing at the beginning of Act III without spoiling the sublime Prelude, and this time he had to let the opposing sides confront each other at length: each time he raised his arms, the noise increased. Resigned, he sat down and leaned forward as though the whole thing had nothing to do with him, as if he was "bowing before the storm."

Among the particularly successful moments of this performance, Natalie mentions Walther's reply, *"Fanget an,"*[56] in the first act, which seemed "the divine birth of creative genius" and received vigorous applause. The Finale of the second act, according to Natalie, "was perfection and clarity itself, both scenically and musically, and contrasted with the disorganized uproar preceding it." Selma Kurz was an exquisite Eva, fresh and youthful,[57] and

Sachs's *"Wahn"* monologue, simply and feelingly sung by Demuth, made a deep impression. Mahler was extremely unhappy over Benedikt Felix's Beckmesser and felt, as he did about the character of Mime, that he himself "was the only person capable of playing the role well." As he left the opera house after the performance, a young admirer who had been waiting outside the door ran toward him and to Mahler's astonishment kissed his hand.

One of the most interesting eyewitness accounts of this new staging of *Die Meistersinger* comes from Reichmann himself. Sometime later the writer Felix Salten discovered the private diaries kept by the famous baritone. In a naïve, childish hand page after page has been covered with expressions of rage, furious interjections, threats against Mahler, all interspersed with exclamation marks that show the extent of his agitation: Mahler is a tyrant prepared to profane *Die Meistersinger;* he shows no pity but tries to "violate my real nature" and to "get his hands on the very roots of my art" by "ignoring my greatest natural gifts" in order to "drag from me oversubtle and elaborate effect." The whole diary is filled with similar explosions of anger; Mahler is referred to as a "little Jewish dwarf" who shamelessly forces him to start again from scratch, who dares to treat him like a beginner, he, the famous *Kammersänger*. In any case, he will not accept such treatment any longer, but "at the first opportunity, I'll spring at his throat."

A few pages farther on, after Reichmann had been acclaimed in *Die Meistersinger* even more enthusiastically than usual, the tone changes to a hymn of delight and gratitude: "Thanks be to God and . . . to Mahler! . . . It is true, he drove me crazy, it is true he lacked respect toward me, but all is forgiven and forgotten, for he has forced me to surpass myself. Never, but never, have I sung the role better: I didn't believe it possible that I could be so effective, never have I been so acclaimed! Yes, I must kneel at Mahler's feet, and apologize in front of everyone!"[58]

Reichmann was not the only one to surpass himself: the day after the performance, the *Neues Wiener Tagblatt* considered that the whole work had been not only revived "but brought to life as its composer had intended and wished!" Mahler had given its comic tone back to it; he had clarified the "richly interlaced polyphony" and emphasized the relationship between the various motifs; he had created new ties between stage and orchestra, and had carried out all his intentions perfectly. Winkelmann and Schrödter were admirable in the roles of Walther and David, the orchestra and chorus had surpassed themselves, and the audience's enthusiasm had taken on "a Mediterranean quality." The *Neue Freie Presse* contested the wisdom of replacing the cuts and thought that excessive zeal had been expended on this revival, for the artists had shown "constraint."[59] Mahler's tempos had been "inhumanly strict,"[60] forcing the singers to carry on a sort of conversation. The critic admitted, however, that the rest of the performance had been exemplary, particularly the orchestra, the chorus, and the staging, notably the animated, realistic movements of the crowd.

In Speidel's eyes, Mahler had a superhuman ability to get the most from the means at his disposal: even in Bayreuth a performance of comparable quality had never been heard; such "perfect harmony between stage and orchestra, between eye and ear," right up to the tremendous second-act Finale, in which singers and members of the stage crowd seemed to have been individually rehearsed. Everything was lively, harmonious, and effective, the chorus seemed to be singing an entirely new score, and the soloists, even those who, like Winkelmann and Schrödter, had sung their parts a hundred times, appeared fresh to their roles.

In a long article, Hirschfeld also found this performance "worthy of Bayreuth": for the first time *Die Meistersinger* had been treated as the light, gay comedy it really was, and the conversation was sparkling. Instead of burdening the production, the orchestra had been its moving force; it had never drowned the singers, so that each word and all the most subtle relations between the motifs were easily perceived. The first dialogue between Walther and Eva had seemed an easy, rapid improvisation, "suitable to a first meeting." Each apprentice had been given a character and personality. During Walther's song, the growing agitation of the guild of mastersingers had been marvelously portrayed, "each voice within the group keeping its own character and value." The whole performance seemed far superior to the usual conception of "a good staging," and even Bayreuth could not surpass an achievement of this order.

On November 19, a week before the opening of *Die Meistersinger,* the *Deutsche Zeitung* had attacked Mahler with the same violence as before: an "unprejudiced" (!) author explained "the damage that he did to the musical life of Vienna," the "incredible brutalities" suffered by the members of the Philharmonic orchestra, as well as the "violence" done to works in the classical repertoire. Despite the orchestra's "unequaled hatred" for him, Mahler had succeeded in being re-elected director,[61] thanks to his "well-organized clique," and he kept his position at the opera only because of the "systematic adulation" of the Jewish press. But his latest undertakings had gone too far, and their results had done "incalculable harm to the opera." From the beginning Mahler's role had been "extremely easy" because reforms had been essential after the complete stagnation of Jahn's regime: Mahler would not have kept his post for more than six weeks if he had not carried them out. He had not yet presented a single new work of quality, not even that work of genius by the greatest living German composer, *Der Corregidor,*[62] but had undertaken an "organized exploitation" of the Wagnerian dramas, so that his famous "indisputable successes" were actually the least that could be expected. No one escaped his "brutal tyranny," he "wounds, offends, humiliates, and drives the best singers from the opera, thereby threatening it with ruin." For several months Mahler had prevented Gertrud Forster from singing and had assigned all her roles to Michalek, his "favorite." Also, some time ago he had taken *Manon, Werther,* and *Mignon* out of the repertoire in order to deprive Marie Renard of her best roles.[63] As for Winkelmann, he had just humiliated him by lowering his salary in his new contract; he had done the same thing to Neidel, who, hearing the news before he had recovered from his accident in May, had had a "nervous breakdown."

Mahler's tyranny did not stop with the singers. Hellmesberger had just learned that his new contract contained an "incredible clause," namely that he "could no longer conduct operas," he who had saved so many performances by replacing an indisposed conductor at the last moment."[64] Schrödter, Sedlmair, and Felix served as his whipping boys almost daily, and two members of the orchestra had just been dismissed by Mahler for having "once played wrong notes" and for "working against him." Wishing to remain "objective," the anonymous author refrained from listing Mahler's many other misdeeds and revealing what means he had used to get the post of director. He only wanted to show that Mahler was doing serious harm to the musical life of Vienna.

It was in this climate of hatred, carefully fostered by the anti-Semitic press, that Mahler was to undertake his second season of Philharmonic concerts, during which time he was to stand out, even more than during the preceding year, as a dangerous innovator by attacking the most deeply established traditions of Viennese music.

"Even if people censure me, they should do so 'hat in hand.'"

# CHAPTER 31

## *Mahler in Vienna (VII) — Fresh Anti-Semitic Attacks — Richter's Departure — Beethoven's* Ninth *Symphony — Hirschfeld's Declaration of War (December 1899– April 1900)*

As was its custom every year, the Vienna Philharmonic Orchestra met on August 25, 1899, to elect a conductor. Of the eighty-four musicians present, sixty-one voted for Mahler.[1] Because he had not been unanimously elected, Mahler at first declined, insisting that, "as director, I must be above parties and cannot head an organization divided into factions."[2] Thereupon, the press began to be concerned about the orchestra's fate were it to be left in the hands of "guest conductors." Many journalists felt that the orchestra was wrong to resent the work Mahler demanded of them. As one put it, "a conductor who managed to win over the minority might indeed make life easier for the orchestra by cutting down on first performances and re-hearsals, yet the public would be the loser."[3]

According to the September 9 issue of the *Neue Freie Presse,* Mahler sought nothing less than an overwhelming vote of confidence; should he turn down the second offer about to be made, then Mottl would be elected instead, or, at worst, the orchestra would make do with guest conductors. At the meeting on September 16, ninety out of ninety-six musicians voted by a show of hands for Mahler. Moreover, the committee set out to counter-act "the trouble caused by a few isolated individuals." That same day, it was announced that Mahler would resume his role as conductor and that he would take the orchestra to Paris the following June.

The November 5 program of the season's first Philharmonic concert con-sisted of Weber's *Euryanthe Overture,* Mozart's *"Jupiter" Symphony,* and Beethoven's *Fifth Symphony.* While rehearsing the Beethoven, Mahler was overcome by doubts about the interpretation of the opening bars, the famous "Knocking of Destiny." He recalled that the Hamburg critics had reproached him for unduly lengthening the theme's pauses. He was convinced that their duration should be in direct proportion to that of the bar (thus equaling two bars [two-four time] or four bars [four-four time]). He did not find Beethoven's meaning in the score clear[4] and could not believe that a musician of Beethoven's stature could have made a mistake, especially as the bulk of his work was "clarity, luminosity and accuracy itself"[5] and each of his textual notations was indispensable.

In every performance of the *Fifth Symphony* he had heard, Mahler had noted the imprecise rendering of the three introductory "knocks"; sometimes there seemed to be four notes, and sometimes five. He felt the problem to be almost insoluble for a conductor who had not completely solved the problem of the beat. "If Beethoven had emphasized each of these hammer strokes with the kettledrums, the rigorous tempo would have been easier to maintain, because the orchestra would be obliged to play in perfect unison,"[6] he concluded.

The rehearsals of the *Fifth Symphony* did not increase his popularity with the orchestra. He was frustrated by "the musicians' style and bad phrasing" and, despite all his good intentions, lost his temper at the outset, shouting, "Gentlemen, this must not be massacred! [*heruntergespült*]."[7] As if this were not enough, he almost demolished the podium by stamping his feet and broke his baton while interrupting the orchestra to modify a phrase.

Mahler felt that Beethoven's powerful first movement should be accompanied by "frenzy and stormy restlessness." To him the first notes resembled "a violent assault, stemmed by a giant's fist descending on the pauses." He thought the famous sentence attributed to Beethoven—"Destiny knocking at the door"—a pale and insufficient description of the movement's meaning, for, as far as he was concerned, the first notes cried out, "Here I am!"[8] When the musicians became furious and resentful, he snapped, "Gentlemen, if you will save your rage for the performance, we shall at least play the beginning correctly."[9]

In the second movement, Mahler attempted to lighten the theme, thus creating the grace and elegance it required.[10] To the devoted Natalie he explained that "the greatest artist is also invariably the most delicate; this is as true of Beethoven as of others: naturally, because the intensity of the whole man, the depth of his feeling and perception are all-pervasive. Of all Beethoven's symphonies," he added, "only the *First, Second* and *Fourth* are still well performed by contemporary conductors and orchestras, all the others are beyond them. Only Wagner, before me, was faithful to Beethoven's spirit. One could say that he discovered all Beethoven's symphonies. If I succeed, it's because I frighten each musician into abandoning his little ego and soaring beyond himself."[11]

When he had conducted Beethoven's *Ninth Symphony* in Prague the year before, Mahler had been particularly pleased that the critic Richard Batka had compared his interpretation with Wagner's, showing, by reference to contemporary reports, the degree to which Mahler's renditions had resembled his predecessor's. "Our aims were always identical and almost always achieved in the same way. Sometimes, we achieved the same result by completely different methods, but our intentions never conflicted. There are great violinists and great singers, in short, great interpreters, but there are not many great conductors and even fewer great composers. Indeed, only those who themselves create can really interpret and usually they lack the necessary experience to conduct; fortunately for them, most are lucky enough to know nothing about this profession!"

Mahler's fresh interpretation of Beethoven created a sensation, for he had again changed the instrumentation of a passage in the Finale. The news had been carefully spread by his enemies in the orchestra.[12] According to Ludwig Karpath, the public waited impatiently for the "scandalous" passage and was disappointed to discover that the modification was almost unnoticeable. Some of the critics cried sacrilege, but others, the *Neue Freie Presse,* for example, merely emphasized the concert's extraordinary success. So many people had been turned away for lack of seats that the committee decided to give a second performance three days later. This repeat performance took place on November 8 at 7:30 P.M. and attracted an even larger audience, which was an exceptional occurrence in the history of Viennese music. Mahler's conception of Beethoven, his changes in the instrumentation and his tempos were sharply criticized by the Viennese press. Robert Hirschfeld hailed Mahler's version of the *Fifth Symphony* as "moving by its very novelty," for the conductor sees in Beethoven a "mighty prophet of the new style in music rather than a product of the classical tradition." According to Hirschfeld, Mahler developed the first movement entirely on the basis of the opening notes, which he did not interpret evenly but rather as "a chaos of bowing produced by the ominous resonance of the violins." Throughout the movement he sustained a "dramatic and awesome tension" that held the audience spellbound until the last note. For the Andante con moto he adopted a very moderate tempo, perhaps even too moderate; yet it lent the Scherzo an aura of mystery, which artfully paved the way for the triumphal explosion of the Finale.

Hirschfeld approved of most of Mahler's instrumental modifications,[13] except for his audacious doubling of the bassoons in the Finale, which he regarded as "intolerable and contrary to the nature of Beethoven's music." Schönaich was also opposed to it and indeed to Mahler's whole interpretation of Beethoven, which he found "surprising and unusual," as much in the rapidity of the first movement as in the slowness of the others. Nevertheless, he conceded that the "triumphal jubilation" of the Finale, with its "proud and blinding brilliance," was "eminently typical of Beethoven." In another article in the *Wiener Tagblatt,* the same critic, in a more liberal mood, declared that it was ridiculous to be put off by changes of tempo, even if they were contrary to tradition, and to refuse to recognize Mahler's feeling for Beethoven's "grand style"; his powerful accentuation, his imposing crescendos and the radiance of the final hymn to victory indeed revealed "a magnificently talented conductor, who is entirely familiar with the work."

The Philharmonic had not played Mozart's *"Jupiter"* *Symphony* for ten years. Hirschfeld thought Mahler's interpretation of it was as "incontestable and irreproachable" as his interpretations of *Die Zauberflöte* and *Le Nozze di Figaro.* "In works in which there is no conflict, but only absolute perfection" Mahler ceased to express his own personality and revealed instead a Mozart "pure and unadulterated, bathed in gentle light and completely devoid of modernism." The performance of the complex polyphony of the Finale was exemplary with its "imperceptible slackening of certain lines, which constitutes a summit in the art of conducting and of orchestral technique." It was impossible to lay down any standard for "this impressionistic style of conducting," which spontaneously graduated coloring and chiaroscuro or modified the slightest rhythmic inflections. Even if one could not always accept Mahler's very personal artistic concepts of a work, it was nevertheless "rewarding to endeavor to discover the merits of each." In any case, the orchestra followed its conductor implicitly, and the violins, in particular, played "as one man."

Helm followed the usual line of the *Deutsche Zeitung,* mocking the "snobs" who had subscribed to the concerts of the Philharmonic even before the programs had been announced. At the opening concert, the selections were played with the highest degree of virtuosity, but Mahler's interpretations were "as personal as usual,"[14] which showed that he had paid no attention to previous criticism.

The second concert, on November 19, included only two works: Beethoven's *Second Symphony* and the first of Strauss's symphonic poems, *Aus Italien.* Mahler had first heard the Strauss piece in 1890 in Budapest and had been so struck by its last two movements that he had written to Strauss expressing his admiration and asking him to send more of his scores. The theme of the Finale had immediately caught his attention; he had regarded it as supreme proof of Strauss's genius until he discovered that the melody was none other than *"Funiculì, funiculà."* He finally decided that, had he been born a German in the land of symphonic music, the author of the melody could perhaps have been a great musician.[15] It was a sobering thought that great melodies could even be created, accidentally, as it were, by mediocre musicians. "Melodic invention is one of the surest signs of a divine gift. If one possesses it, then, like a gambler, all one has to do is to gamble a great deal and one day one might hit the jackpot. Nevertheless, all assumptions of this nature are totally vain, for if one is not born with this gift, one will never acquire it by chance."[16]

Addressing his musicians on the subject of the last movement of Beethoven's *Second Symphony,* Mahler summed up one of the main points of his concept of interpretation:

"Take a good look at this passage; where do you find any of the 'monumental calm' or 'fervor' that is presumed, rightly or wrongly, to pervade

Beethoven's music? Here, you will find only grace and humor, there, only reserve and tenderness. But suddenly one comes across an ardent passage, an unparalleled crescendo or a superb burst of feeling, which must be approached in quite a different spirit: one must sweep the audience off its feet by the sheer intensity, warmth and grandeur of one's playing."[17]

The first performance in Vienna of Strauss's *Aus Italien* did not alter Hanslick's opinion of the composer. While admiring its instrumentation and some of its melodic ideas, he discerned in it "nothing new, nothing significant," nothing that "leaves a lasting impression." The piece, in his view, failed to render the atmosphere of Italy, and the manner in which *"Funiculì, funiculà"* was introduced into the Finale seemed to him "entirely gratuitous." An artist and composer "full of temperament and poetic ideas and clever in the choice of his effects," Strauss was nevertheless no great composer, he said, and the public's applause had been, above all, for the performance.

The third concert of the season included Brahms's *Third Symphony,* a work for which Mahler had the greatest enthusiasm. True, its orchestration lacked brilliance and the conductor longed to re-edit it but dared not, lest he shock the critics. Doubtless it was out of sheer "anti-Wagnerism" that Brahms had deprived himself of "such a wealth of modern orchestral means," which he had nevertheless used in his chamber music. In order to supplement the violins, Mahler thought of making the second violins play together with the first in the most important passages. In his view Brahms's music had only one limitation, that of "never bursting its bonds and soaring above things human to a supernatural world of light and liberty. Brahms treats everything in a very fervent and personal manner, but he always remains a prisoner of this earthly life, never lifting his eyes to what may be above and beyond; it is for this reason that his works never achieve the greatest, the ultimate effect."[18]

Yet Mahler had deep admiration for Brahms, and he was not just paying off a debt of gratitude by including his works in the Philharmonic concerts. However, just as when he had gone to visit the aging composer at Ischl, he still felt very conscious of the abyss that separated the two of them as creators. "I was again dumfounded," he said while studying the score of another of Brahms's symphonies[19] the following winter, "to see what a puritan Brahms is. Everything resembling ornamentation, embellishment or fantasy is strictly excluded from his works, leaving nothing but a pure and austere play of sounds, albeit wonderfully imaginative and artistic. The only thing that seems to matter to him is to express himself as a great artist and a great man. I've often wondered whether my style and mode of musical expression, which differ so radically from his, are perhaps nothing more than a hodgepodge of 'Catholic' mysticism." Mahler's interpretation of Brahms was a success with the Viennese critics. Hirschfeld praised it to the skies, with the exception of the third movement, in which he found the tempo too slow and "contrary to the vivacity and grace sought by the composer."

Mahler had also long sought to pay tribute to Anton Dvořák, one of the greatest composers of the time. He had written to Dvořák the year before to ask if the latter would entrust him with some new symphonic work, and it was with some reluctance that he finally accepted *Die Waldtaube,* because he hated descriptive music.[20] "This sort of trash gives the public an aversion to all so-called 'program music,' because it doesn't see the difference between such works and compositions that have nothing in common with them, except that they are based on a text and have titles or some definite subject matter, such as Beethoven's *Ninth Symphony* or his *Pastoral Symphony,* or even my own *Third Symphony* if I had left in the titles." Conducting *Zur Weihe des Hauses* after *Die Waldtaube,* Mahler felt like the giant Antaeus finding the ground under his feet again: "Here I have no doubts about the interpretation, whereas with the others I find myself groping and searching and wondering whether I'm being faithful to them. With Beethoven and Wagner, I feel sure of myself: there's only one way to play their works. They're like lofty mountains towering above the vanity and inanity of this world and in this way they surpass all others. However, their brilliance should not so blind us that we scorn all others who have also created beauty in their own way."

Mahler quite deliberately took the risk of finally alienating all the conservatives in Vienna by playing Beethoven's *"Pastoral"* Symphony at the last Philharmonic concert of the season, a symphony with which he had caused a scandal in Hamburg some years earlier. Of all Beethoven's works, this was perhaps his favorite. "In order to understand it, one must have a *feeling for nature,* which most people lack. From the very start of the piece, one must be able to share Beethoven's somewhat naïve thoughts on the subject: the pleasure of breathing fresh air and admiring the sunlight breaking through a forest, or the open sky above an open field. In particular, no one seems able to render the scene by the brook, which is taken either too fast (in four beats), or too slowly (in twelve beats). The former is usually the case, because of Beethoven's joke at the end of it: surprised by the rain, the nature lovers run for shelter and the tempo accelerates. This is why most unthinking people play the whole movement too fast, whereas most of it should flow as tranquilly as the stream itself, in keeping with the uniform and continuous flow of the accompaniment, which must be monotonous in the extreme. However, the theme running parallel to this monotonous accompaniment is of such beauty and spontaneity that only those totally lacking in humor and sensitivity could find it boring." Even Bülow, who far outshone all other conductors in intelligence, failed to render it correctly, and this was precisely because, as Frau von Bülow had confirmed, he had no feeling for nature.[21]

As in Hamburg, the critics were astonished by Mahler's moderate tempo for this andante. Hirschfeld, in particular, called it incompatible with the indication "molto moto," which Mahler considered meaningless. In the same way that one frequently finds the abbreviation "all'o" for "allegro," he surmised that "moto" was probably an abbreviation for "moderato." This explanation had in fact been suggested to him by the violinist Sulzer, according to whom the indication was in any case incorrect and should have read "molto mosso." The term does not occur in any of Beethoven's other works. Mahler justified his tempo for the Andante by saying that "unless and until a conductor feels the musical and artistic need for this tempo and can justify it to his orchestra's satisfaction, this absurd indication will continue to be followed to the letter."

Only two passages—two bars of the slow movement and four of the Finale—seemed to Mahler to express Beethoven's "subjective feeling" and "passionate emotion." Elsewhere, nature spoke for itself; therefore, the conducting of the whole piece should emphasize, and be centered around, these two passages. "How then should one conduct the Scene by the Brook?" he asked some years later.[22] "Twelve-eight time is too slow, and four-four too rapid!" To which he then replied, "With a feeling for nature!"

At the same concert, the violinist Marie Soldat-Roeger, who led the string quartet of which Natalie Bauer-Lechner was a member, played the Brahms *Violin Concerto*. Her teacher, the famous Joseph Joachim, who was in Vienna with his quartet, asked Mahler's permission to attend the final rehearsal in order to hear his former pupil. At first Mahler hesitated, for he had never forgiven Joachim for his public condemnation of Wagner's music, but Natalie finally persuaded him to let Joachim attend by reminding him of the latter's encouragement of young performers and composers. In fact, he gave in readily after hearing a private recital by the Joachim Quartet in the house of Karl Wittgenstein, the famous businessman and music lover who had been a close friend of Brahms. This concert had so delighted him that, at the rehearsal, he not only asked his musicians to rise in the violinist's honor, but also made him a short and exceedingly warm speech of welcome.

Mahler was still *persona grata* in Vienna, and his revolutionary conception of the *"Pastoral" Symphony* was far better received than it had been in Hamburg. Even Theodor Helm, who called the revival of the overture to Spohr's *Jessonda* "unnecessary" but praised the interpretation of the Brahms *Concerto,* reluctantly conceded his enthusiasm for that of the *"Pastoral,"* in which, he was pleased to note, Mahler had emphasized the storm, a storm that "broke precisely as that divine music requires." He found the "Scene by the Brook" "marvelously phrased" and, despite the somewhat excessively slow tempo of both the latter and the Scherzo, pronounced the whole performance "captivating."

Hirschfeld called Mahler's interpretation "a true miracle of sound." The conductor was not content merely to conduct, he "molded and painted, bringing nature itself to life in all its varied aspects" and transported the audience "on the wings of poetry." Despite its strikingly slow tempo, he had never found the Andante so enchanting, nor the singing of the birds so natural. "It is no longer a mere artifice; it is the twilight echo in the soul of a man who has become impervious to material sounds. It speaks, with the simplicity of nature, of lost happiness. One cannot smile, for one is on the verge of tears and one's heart seems to stop beating."

Exhausted by the Philharmonic concerts, Mahler seized the occasion of the off-peak season at the opera to escape from Vienna and spend New Year's Day with Justi and Natalie at Rodaun, a little village a few kilometers to the southwest on the road to Mödling. At first glance the place so enchanted him that he decided to spend all his future free time there. However, the very evening of his arrival, realizing that the little inn where he was staying was somewhat noisy, he wanted to leave immediately, and it was only with the greatest difficulty that Justi and Natalie persuaded him to remain overnight.

In the course of the same evening, he received a visit from his publisher, Josef Stritzko, who was the director of the Waldheim-Eberle firm, and had a long talk with him on the *Denkmäler der Tonkunst in Oesterreich,* then in process of publication. Mahler told him bluntly that the collection contained only "mediocrities of the last century" on which he considered it a shame to spend so much money. Thanks to Guido Adler, he himself was a member of the committee that selected the works to be published and he had attended one of its first sessions with Bezecny, Wilhelm Ritter von Hartl, and Adler. However, the lengthy discussion of points that could have been dealt with in a few words had made him so impatient that he pleaded a rehearsal as an excuse to walk out in the middle of the meeting, vowing to himself as he went that he would never attend another.

The year 1900 was not only Mahler's fortieth but also that of his breakthrough at the opera: the departure of Richter and the principal stars of Jahn's day, Marie Renard and Ernest Van Dyck, marked the end of the old regime and enabled him firmly to establish his own methods. It was also the year that a new press campaign was launched against him. On January 6 the *Deutsches Volksblatt,* not content with casting aspersions on Mahler's character, questioning his competence as a conductor, condemning his administration of the opera and reproaching him with "betrayal" of the classic masters, also brought far more serious accusations against him. In an article purportedly written in Budapest on January 3, a certain Béla Inden said: "The recent news that the present director of the Hofoper is about to be offered a new four-year contract[23] has caused a certain amount of astonishment among art lovers here, since, considering the said gentleman's past exploits, with which everyone in Budapest is familiar, one would sooner have expected precisely the opposite. Herr Mahler must be an exceedingly lucky person, for the circumstances surrounding his departure from the Royal Hungarian Opera were such that people in the know doubted that he would succeed in getting himself re-employed as a conductor by even a modest provincial theater. It is not his musical talents that are at issue, but matters reflecting on his honor. That Herr Mahler all too frequently blew his own trumpet in order to take the credit for the merits of others was pardonable in view of his notorious vanity; that he set up a pasha's regime and obliged every male and female member of the Budapest Opera to pay homage to him could be overlooked on account of the loose morals of Hungarian society[24]; that he was presumptuous could be attributed to his Semitic origins; and that he even had himself baptized in order to advance his career was also understandable because of his race. However, the ugly rumors concerning his traffic in percentages, author's royalties and commissions were never denied and eventually led, let us say, to his resignation.

"When he left the Royal Hungarian Opera to reappear as a star at the foremost artistic institution of the Empire, Hungarians merely smiled pityingly at the thought that a man who had retired so dishonorably from an official post in Budapest should subsequently be called to an office in the imperial city, which put him in direct contact with the highest authorities. Although it seemed most unlikely, we could only suppose that the Court officials and the administration of the Imperial Opera were uninformed as to Herr Mahler's activities in Budapest. We presumed, however, that they would soon be apprised of the facts and predicted that the gentleman in question would therefore not occupy his present position for long . . . Thanks mainly to the influence of a certain nobleman[25] who wishes to spare him, the circumstances of his dismissal have so far been hushed up. Nevertheless, there are still innumerable witnesses of his 'exploits' in the Hungarian capital who, should it be necessary, could reveal the truth about a man who has attained such giddying eminence solely because he has powerful protectors. If the rumor that he is to be kept on as director of the Vienna Opera (where he has already done so much harm) should prove true, then many hitherto sealed mouths will doubtless soon open. For any cultivated person, however chauvinistic he may be, considers art an international sanctuary, the guardianship of which should be entrusted only to those whose hands have been purified and sanctified by true genius."

Mahler's enemies had gone too far this time. Their calumny was the more odious for being vague and insidious—quite apart from the fact that it was totally unfounded. Mouthpiece of the municipality of Vienna, the *Deutsches Volksblatt*[26] was an important newspaper, and Mahler feared that some people might believe its slanderous allegations. He went to see Prince Montenuovo about the advisability of publishing a denial. Aristocrat that he was, Montenuovo forbade him to enter into any sort of discussion with his slanderers. Not at all reassured, Mahler went to see Karpath and asked him to consult Apponyi. The latter also refused to intervene in any way,[27] and a surprised and saddened Mahler concluded that this must be due to his own refusal to present Mihalovics's operas in Vienna. However, the letters of recommendation written to the authorities of the Vienna Opera by his friends in Budapest, and even by the administrator of the

Budapest Opera, Beniczky, amply proved the absurdity of the *Volksblatt*'s accusations.

Four days after the *Deutsches Volksblatt,* the *Deutsche Zeitung* also set out to prove that Mahler was leading the opera down the road to ruin. Despite the obvious harm it was suffering under his directorship, the *Oberst-hofmeisters* seemed inclined to wink at his activities instead of "removing this harmful man." The only reason why the whole city of Vienna had not yet turned against him was because it remained ignorant of many of his transgressions within the four walls of the opera, and also because the press had adopted a shamefully partisan attitude toward him. "Contrary to the wishes of all impartial people in Vienna, despite the warnings of all the musicians concerned (some of them world-renowned), despite the many serious accusations brought by an oppressed, disconcerted and discontented personnel, despite the failures manifest in a deplorable repertoire and an even more deplorable box office, and notwithstanding the extraordinary rumors concerning his resignation from the Budapest Opera, the two *OBersthofmeisters,* and Prince Liechtenstein in particular, quite simply keep Gustav Mahler on."

The *Deutsche Zeitung* went on to say that it was the *Obersthofmeister* who was to blame for this disgraceful state of affairs, since he had chosen as administrator a mere civil servant who knew nothing about the theater and could be of no help in important matters. "This fault on the part of the *Obersthofmeisters* is the more regrettable as the discipline throughout the opera is deteriorating dangerously because of it; the *Obersthofmeisters* regard Mahler's stern discipline as a virtue, without realizing that, imposed by this parvenu, it becomes injustice, brutality and tyranny . . .

"Since the administrator is incapable of performing his duties, the *Oberst-hofmeister* has become the director's immediate superior; and Prince Liechtenstein, who was formerly Master of the Horse, knows less than nothing about running a theater and is quite unaware of the measures that should be taken against 'the Mahler scandal.' Instead of always seeking information from Mahler, he might occasionally consult reliable people. He thus bears the full responsibility for the decline of the opera. Concerning Mahler, we have nothing further to say, but Prince Liechtenstein should make some inquiries and then act quickly, before it is too late!"

During the first months of 1900, these two anti-Semitic papers continued to launch the most varied and libelous attacks on Mahler. At Marie Renard's farewell performance, on January 29, he was "the only person at the opera who did not join in the demonstration, quite simply because he is the cause of this irreplaceable artist's departure." During the applause[28] he "stood in the front of his box for a few moments, looking pale and drawn" and biting his lips with ill-disguised agitation as he contemplated Renard's triumph. Unfortunately, he had already left by the time somebody in the audience shouted out, "Away with Mahler, let us keep Renard."

Ten days later the *Deutsches Volksblatt* reproduced a passage from the

*Neues Wiener Journal,* according to which Mahler was supposed to have stuck his tongue out at Demuth, because the latter had made a mistake during a performance of *Die Meistersinger*. Frau Förster, who was singing Eva, had been so taken aback that she had sung off beat. "Only servants behave in this vulgar manner" was the concluding comment of the anonymous author. In the middle of February, the *Deutsche Zeitung* wrote of an "uneven and disorderly" performance of *Zar und Zimmermann,* in which Naval had been replaced at the last minute (on February 9) by Stoll, a singer "recently relegated to the background because of his incompetence." The Emperor had left the hall after the second act, but had returned two days later to hear *Fra Diavolo,* which Mahler had only decided to conduct at the last moment upon hearing that His Majesty would be present. His "nervous and spasmodic vibrations" had caused such confusion that he had been obliged to stop the singers in the middle of an ensemble and make them begin it again, a very rare occurrence at the opera. The Emperor had obviously come away with "no very favorable impression of his talents!"

Since the anti-Semitic press had considered such minor incidents justification for such violent attacks, Richter's departure provided them with an even better occasion. Having signed a new five-year contract with the opera, which doubled his salary, Richter wrote to Mahler on February 25 to ask that his contract be annulled, because "my health and, above all, my nerves make it impossible for me to carry out my duties in the manner expected of me." In recent years the mere business of conducting an entire concert had required every ounce of energy he possessed.

Having been a conductor since 1859, first in theaters and, since 1868,[29] at the Vienna Opera, he considered that "these 'war years' have counted double" because of the numerous new works he had conducted. "My life in the theater has been one long struggle against incomprehension, incompetence and vulgarity, all too rarely compensated by the joy of achieving artistic success or of having had devoted and selfless collaborators. Moreover, even this joy has invariably been short-lived, for the Viennese press has never lost time in poisoning it with its spiteful and offensive criticisms. It is not my intention to rake up old grievances; I merely wished to explain why I am fed up with the theater!"

As a reward for his services, Richter asked only that he be released from his obligations, which he nevertheless agreed to fulfill until the end of May. He also sent Mahler a personal letter in which he stressed "the excessive nervous tension of life in the theater, tension that is becoming dangerous both for me and for my family." He frankly admitted to having signed the new contract only because he knew of "no better way of finding a suitable job elsewhere." No one could consider him capable of facing another five years of theatrical activity, since he hated the theater and in future wanted to conduct only concerts. Mahler would surely understand his position and, "out of the kindness of his heart," obtain his release from a post "for which I am no longer strong enough and in which I no longer take any pleasure."

These two letters put Mahler in an extremely awkward position: in order to persuade Richter to remain, he had gone to a great deal of trouble to have his salary raised from six thousand to twelve thousand gulden, only to learn that he had signed the contract solely for the sake of being in a solid position to discuss terms with the Manchester Concert Society,[30] which was in fact offering him five times the salary he was getting in Vienna. Mahler knew that the newspapers would blame him for Richter's departure. "I do not deny that I did oust him," he told Karpath later. "It was not out of ill-will, but simply because of my success. I would never have been able to undermine his position if he had remained in Vienna and taken the trouble to interpret Wagner to perfection."[31]

Realizing that there was nothing more he could do to prevent Richter from leaving, he instructed Karpath to draw up a statement for the *Wiener Abendpost* mentioning Richter's two letters and his appeal to Mahler's "kindness of heart." The following day he sent Richter a letter saying that he would agree to cancel his contract, since he realized that it would be pointless to try to keep him against his will. Expressing his "surprise and dismay," he wrote: "You told me, when you signed the contract, that you looked forward to continuing your artistic activity with me and said that you would devote yourself to furthering the interests of our institution. Having received such an assurance from you, your present decision was the last thing I expected. Not only will it be difficult for me to find a suitable person to replace you, but my own work load will be considerably increased." He ended his letter by extending his "warmest and most sincere thanks" and saying that he would always remember Richter with emotion and gratitude.[32]

Despite his well-intentioned efforts[33] Mahler had in fact rendered Richter's position at the Vienna Opera untenable. By his reforms, his demands for a hitherto unheard-of fidelity, and his introduction of uncut performances of Wagner[34] (which earned him the reputation of being Wagner's "savior"), he had drawn the public's attention to himself. There was simply not enough room for two artists of such stature in one theater. Richter deeply resented the fact that the Viennese press forgot his own glorious past and extolled Mahler as "the man of the day."

As the latter had foreseen, the *Deutsches Volksblatt* described Richter's departure as "a new success of the Mahlerian epoch" and accused the "young director" of having "disgusted and ousted a brilliant and *ipso facto* dangerous rival." After replacing Marie Renard by a Jewess, Selma Kurz, he was now replacing Richter by a half-Jew, Franz Schalk.[35] And the only reason he got away with it was because the Emperor appointed as *Obersthofmeister* a Master of the Horse who knew more about equines than art.

The *Deutsche Zeitung* accused Mahler of having "rid" himself, by his innumerable underhanded provocations, of "the most celebrated *Kapellmeister* of the day," thereby depriving Viennese musical life of its leader; and all because he was jealous of his art, his authority, and his very presence. "The manner in which Richter was made to lose interest in his own work in Vienna constitutes one of the ugliest chapters in Viennese musical history." Out of sheer duplicity Mahler extolled him, but the Jewish press immediately began to refer to him in the past tense, as though everything had been mediocre and insignificant until the coming of the Messiah. The supreme authority at the opera would have to answer to the Viennese public "for the loss suffered by the Hofoper."

On March 18 the *Deutsche Zeitung* published an "Open Letter to Gustav Mahler," in which an anonymous journalist attacked Mahler's administration and, above all, his repertoire. He claimed that he had at first been delighted to see him throw off the inertia of the Jahn era and breathe new life into Mozart, Auber and Boïeldieu. However, instead of Handel and Gluck, Berlioz's operas, Cornelius' *Der Barbier von Bagdad* or Wolf's *Der Corregidor,* Vienna had been given no more than a few Jewish works like *The Demon* and *Die Kriegsgefangene,* or such mediocrities as Siegfried Wagner's *Der Bärenhäuter* and Reznicek's *Donna Diana.*

"As conductor of the Philharmonic, you have not only neglected Liszt and Bruckner, you have massacred them. As for Beethoven's *Ninth,* you have merely used it to show off! And do you know why, Herr Mahler? Because the man is too great for you; because taste, routine and a sense of history are not sufficient for such tasks and you become paralyzed when confronted with the 'really great.' We suspected as much when we heard you conduct Wagner; your performances of Beethoven and Bruckner have entirely confirmed our suspicions. Anyone else would long since have been dismissed," the anonymous author continued. "Your arrogance and childish ambition have obviously gone to your head: you have endeavored to command attention as a creator, but the sound and fury of your grand symphonies merely reveal your inner emptiness. Disregarding one of your own rules, you have given lieder of a popular nature at the Philharmonic concerts.[36] Forgive us, O hallowed masters of the German lied, that we even call them lieder!

"You have installed yourself like a satrap in Vienna's musical life; you hate and fear those whose importance you cannot deny and, by force or cunning, remove those who do not please you. Your ruthlessness, which we were prepared to put up with because we believed you to be dedicated to a sacred cause, turns out to be merely despicable, since it serves your own unsacred person. By throwing out Marie Renard, Hans Richter and Ferdinand Löwe, you have deprived the opera of a wealth of talent. Richter publicly admitted that he was fed up with being thwarted and crossed at every turn. You finally cast aside all disguise and showed your true colors, which frightened us. One wonders whether someone as tyrannical as you can tolerate the competition of any important artist. Are you planning to take over the whole opera and fill all the posts with your own creatures, as you are already attempting to do at the Philharmonic? Are you or are you not intending to create a conductorship for Marie Gutheil-Schoder's husband and relegate Hellmesberger to the Burgtheater?

"Since we can expect nothing more from you, we have quite simply decided to turn our backs on you. However, there still remains a faint ray of hope, which you yourself, by your very excesses, have kept alive: we all know that the folly and tyranny of dictators lead, if not to their death, at least to their downfall."

One can only wonder whether any other city in the world has ever heaped such insults and injury on its great men. Fortunately, Mahler's energy, idealism, and determination gave him superhuman strength; besides which, his work left him little time for despondency, and the year 1900 was one of the busiest of his career. After a single performance of *La Traviata,* conducted by Richter on January 19, in honor of the famous Australian soprano Nellie Melba (an evening which "gave me no great thrill, since I would have preferred to listen to a clarinet"), Mahler himself conducted the first new work of the season on January 22. This was the opera *Es war einmal,* by Alexander von Zemlinsky,[37] teacher and future brother-in-law of Arnold Schönberg and, together with him, the moving spirit of the young Viennese school of music.

Zemlinsky was not yet thirty and still virtually unknown when he sent Mahler the score of *Es war einmal,* his second opera, based on one of Andersen's fairy tales.[38] Although "terribly simplified and flat," it reminded the conductor of his own *Rübezahl,* and, at the end of six weeks, he invited Zemlinsky to come and play it to him on the piano.[39] He was immediately struck both by the young man's "incredible technique" and by the lack of originality of his music, which was "so full of resemblances and plagiarisms" that "Zemlinsky must have a very bad memory if he was not able to avoid them."[40] Despite this, he decided to stage the work and managed to overcome all resistance to the project. (The story is that of a cold princess wooed by a young prince disguised as a gypsy. In exchange for a kiss, he presents her with wonderful gifts, which cause her to be disowned by her father, the King. She then marries the young man, who succeeds in transforming her into a warm and loving human being.) With the help of Lipiner, he slightly abridged and modified the libretto, and his final version and ultimate presentation of the opera were, as usual, superb. Performed twelve times during the season, *Es war einmal* was an undisputed success, and Mahler himself was delighted to have discovered a new talent.

Hanslick, in his review of the opera, deplored the influence of Wagner on young composers, who "elaborate modest themes to excess." While praising Zemlinsky's talent and sound technique, he nevertheless found his music "too artistic and too subtle" for the simplicity of the libretto, the vocal parts too declamatory and not sufficiently melodious, and the orchestration too sumptuous. In a more indulgent mood, Heuberger paid tribute to Zemlinsky's "dramatic talent" and, while criticizing his lack of creativity, admired his musical, dramatic and orchestral virtuosity and gift for "illustration." The only thing wrong with his music, Heuberger felt, was that it illustrated "the visible rather than the invisible and described actions rather than feelings."

The anti-Semitic press and the correspondent of the *Neue Zeitschrift* in particular[41] used *Es war einmal* as an excuse to attack Mahler, declaring that he was interested in Zemlinsky only because of his Slavic name, since the composer had neither creative talent nor dramatic gifts, but merely a sense of orchestration.

During the first half of February, Mahler staged a revival of *Tristan und Isolde,* which was to be a tremendous success, for Winkelmann was in particularly good voice that evening and Mildenburg was making her first appearance in Vienna as Isolde.[42] The *Deutsches Volksblatt,* while regretting that Mahler had not let Schalk conduct, in order to "give him the chance to distinguish himself," acknowledged that, of all Wagner's works, *Tristan* was the most suited to Mahler's "non-German" temperament, whereas the "typically German" quality of *Die Meistersinger* and the *Ring* remained alien to him. The paper also praised Mildenburg's magnificent mastery of the part, in which she showed "brilliant strength, fiery temperament, exceptional intelligence and a noble and powerful voice," and compared her to Amalie Materna and Lilli Lehmann, the two greatest interpreters of the part. Some slight signs of vocal fatigue, due to her long rehearsals with Mahler, had passed almost unnoticed, the paper said.

Hirschfeld was critical of Mildenburg's Isolde, which he called a "fury of gigantic stature and strength . . . Her ample garment blew about her in wildly curving baroque lines, hate seething in, and exploding from, its every fold. True, it is her sheer ineptitude that makes her such a fury, since it is far easier to rant and rave than to develop a character in all its psychological nuances." Kalbeck agreed that Mildenburg was a "goddess of fate and a prophetess rather than a woman in love and more infuriated than impassioned," but he praised her grandeur and nobility. Her portrayal of Isolde was indeed to become one of the glories of the Vienna Opera.

After *Dalibor* and *Eugene Onegin,* Mahler decided to present a work he had already conducted in Hamburg, Tchaikovsky's *Iolanta,* a one-act opera based on the play *King René's Daughter,* by the Danish author Henrik Hertz. According to Hanslick, the heroine of the story, a blind princess whose sight is restored by love, is more of "a musical spirit than a dramatic character," and this "pale blue" idyl is eminently suited to what Alfred Kauders called "Tchaikovsky's feminine musical soul." Mahler prepared the performance with his usual meticulous attention to detail. In order that Selma Kurz, who sang the princess, should learn to move like a blind person, he blindfolded her during rehearsals. The premiere had to be put off until March 22 because Naval fell ill, and was then almost interrupted in the middle because he had a relapse and lost his voice at the crucial moment of his duet with the heroine. Only the presence of mind of the tenor Pacal, who was singing a small part that evening, saved the day.[43] Even so, because of the change of tenor, the curtain had to be lowered before the final scene, thus marring the success of the premiere. Despite Mahler's conducting, the audience showed more interest than enthusiasm. "The refined product of a great artist rather than a masterpiece or an effective stage piece," said Hanslick, who, because of a few "frankly trite" scenes, found Tchaikovsky's last opera inferior to *Eugene Onegin.*

Alfred Kauders, who had replaced Speidel on the staff of the *Fremdenblatt,* was of the opinion that modern opera "numbers few works of such engaging melodiousness, such harmonious form, such rich themes and such general charm" as *Iolanta,* and he felt that it should remain in the repertoire as "the testament of a great and noble artist."[44]

Since Hellmesberger was ill, Richter was on tour and Schalk had not yet arrived,[45] Mahler was obliged to conduct an exceptionally large number of performances in early 1900. Anyone else would have been completely exhausted by such a frenzy of activity, but Mahler's energy was apparently limitless. However, he continued to complain that opera was nothing but "shameful prostitution," a "blast furnace that reduces the noblest material to dirt," and added that his rehearsals of the Philharmonic concerts constituted his "only moments of happiness."[46]

The first of these concerts took place on January 14, when Mahler conducted the first performance in Vienna of a group of his own lieder. He had debated the choice at length with his family, with the Spieglers, with Lipiner and with Arnold Rosé, for they all had their favorites. He finally chose the second and fourth songs from the *Lieder eines fahrenden Gesellen* and three songs from *Des Knaben Wunderhorn: Das irdische Leben, Wo die schönen Trompeten blasen,* and *Wer hat dies Liedlein erdacht.* Since Michalek was ill (a very bad cold, according to Natalie), he decided to try out a relative newcomer at the opera, Selma Kurz, who had conquered Vienna by the beauty and agility of her voice. According to Natalie, he gave Kurz the lieder without telling her who had composed them, and she was so enthusiastic that he asked her to perform them in place of Michalek. She sang them by heart and Mahler was instantly amazed at the quality of her voice, which he found even better adapted to concert singing than to the stage, particularly admiring "the incomparable softness [*Weichheit*]" of her personality, her legato, and her vocal control in pianissimo singing.

The very tone of these remarks, as recorded by Natalie, reveals an enthusiasm that was not merely artistic. Mahler himself admitted that he was unable to hear a beautiful female voice without falling slightly in love with the singer. Selma Kurz had a soft and supple voice, which she used with great art; moreover, she was very beautiful and Mahler fell for this combination of charms. A few short notes from Mahler to Kurz are the only remaining testimony of this doubtless short-lived affair.[47] The first of these indicates that, in March 1900, while they were rehearsing *Iolanta,* he took her to one of his new friends, the invalid artist Henriette Mankie-wicz, to be made up. Another note, written at about the same time, asked her to come to his office so that they could arrange to meet somewhere. A third fondly reproached her for having "slipped away after rehearsals" before he had had time to speak to her, while still another referred to *Tannhäuser,* of which Kurz was studying the leading part. Judging from the contents of the last two notes, the lovers' relations were no longer as warm as before, but these few lines, mostly dashed off in between rehearsals, reveal no more than that. His misadventures with Mildenburg in Hamburg had made Mahler wary. Besides, with so many enemies in Vienna ready to seize any and every occasion to create a fresh "scandal," he thought it prudent to proceed with caution. Selma Kurz must have destroyed some of the letters he wrote to her, for Mahler was a profuse letter writer when in love and there must have been many more.

It may be of interest to note that, early in 1900, Mahler had engaged Marie Gutheil-Schoder at the Hofoper, a singer who met his dramatic requirements far better than did Selma Kurz; moreover, with her performance of *Carmen* in May 1900, the new singer fascinated him as an artist and probably also as a woman. However, this does not alter the fact that he was enraptured at hearing Kurz sing his lieder in January and, indeed, her rendition was a great success. The last song was encored, and Natalie somewhat too hastily assumed that "the public has finally ceased to approach his works with mistrust."[48]

The very same day, upon reading the newspapers, Mahler and his friends realized they had been mistaken. Max Kalbeck, an archconservative among the Viennese critics, was the only one who had recognized the "intensely personal" beauty of the songs, with which Mahler had created "a new musical form": the orchestral lied. "Far more than merely interesting or experimental," these pieces were "the precious realizations of a fertile imagination, masterpieces, models of their kind." Mahler had "entered into the soul" of the popular lied and "assimilated its secrets." Thanks to his exceptionally discreet use of the orchestra, "these songs, true children of nature, display their exquisite orchestral raiment with such modesty and spontaneity that one would think they had been born in it."[49]

As was to be expected, the anti-Semitic papers blasted Mahler. The *Deutsches Volksblatt* acknowledged that his orchestration was excellent, but declared that it was no great merit in someone of his profession. On the other hand, it questioned his "musical illustration" and "declamatory style"[50] and was indignant that these lieder were praised and applauded whereas Richard Strauss's were so frequently condemned.[51]

In the *Deutsche Zeitung,* Theodor Helm noted that Mahler had "broken his own rules" by introducing a soloist at the Philharmonic, and that merely for his own glory, although he had not yet conducted a single work by either Bruckner or Liszt during the season. His lieder were "subtly orchestrated in the manner of the Secession, yet their melodic invention was anything but original," and they did not begin to take the place of an important orchestral work. Helm also complained of Mahler's "errors of diction" and his laborious "striving for a naïve and popular tone."

In the *Wochenblatt,* Helm was less severe: he pointed out, but this time without condemning it, the contrast between the "popular" style of the lieder and the subtlety of their orchestration. As to the correspondent of the *Neue Zeitschrift,* he found the four lieder formless, "unsingable," and totally lacking in any sort of charm.[52]

Hanslick, who was always extremely favorably disposed toward Mahler, showed some embarrassment. The conductor of the Philharmonic had undoubtedly proved his modesty by so long withholding from the Viennese public "works that have achieved great success elsewhere." The composer of these melodies was against the traditional and customary, he was "what the French would call a *'chercheur,'* without attributing any pejorative sense to the word." His songs were a sort of cross between lieder and dramatic arias, and the only genuine precedents that could be found for them were Berlioz's great orchestral songs. Although a "modern," Mahler had endeavored to "run to the other extreme" by adopting the naïveté, the sentimentality, and the simple, concise, and somewhat clumsy language of the *Volkslied.* Unfortunately the texts were not at all his genre and simply did not lend themselves to an accompaniment that, with all its exuberance and sudden modulations, was far too rich and too subtle for them. However, he had carried off his "daring undertaking" with great sensitivity and masterly technique," and the future might well belong to the musical "Secession" represented by Mahler, Strauss, and Wolf.[53]

While paying tribute to Mahler's "stupendous technical skill," Hirschfeld also objected to the orchestra's trespassing on the domain of the lied. To him the striving to find exactly the right tone and color for every word, which led to a constant changing of atmosphere, was another "manifestation of modern individualism." Mahler's music, he said, was very personal and enthralled both one's intellect and one's emotions. However, there were moments when the shifting and complex voices of the orchestra tended to submerge the song and one heard the incidental rather than the essential.[54]

The *Neue Musikalische Presse* accused Mahler of "composing solely with his intelligence," and Schönaich went even further, declaring that the lieder contained no trace of either the *Knabe* or the *Wunderhorn.* Once again, the majority of the critics were hostile to Mahler. What exasperated him most of all was that they always condemned him for the apparent contrast between the simplicity of a folk song and the complexity of his orchestration: "as though a folk song could have nothing profound to express, as though it were not possible to say everything in a few simple words, merely by suggestion and allusion, as though, in its endeavor to convey the hidden message in such a text, the music didn't need to be far richer than that accompanying the fully elaborated text of an artistic song." Kalbeck's approval surprised him far more than Heuberger's hostility, for the latter, "having composed bad operettas, is angry with me for refusing to perform them."

Mahler had begun the concert with Schumann's *Fourth Symphony*. Its "Beethovian" beauty filled him with admiration, and he had spent long hours revising its orchestration in order to bring out "all the latent treasures of the work, which the composer's imagination but dimly perceived." Since a few of the critics wrote that for the first time Schumann had seemed to them a good orchestrator,[55] he felt that he had been successful. Hirschfeld said that Mahler had "illuminated every detail of the work and expressed the quintessence of the romantic spirit." He particularly admired the way in which he had managed the transition between the first two and the last two movements, and declared that in Mahler's hands the Philharmonic became "an instrument that responded to the merest touch, a keyboard with an unlimited range of orchestral colors, which obeyed his slightest wish."

A month after the first Viennese performance of Mahler's lieder, Selma Kurz sang three others during a concert by the Rosé Quartet in the main auditorium of the Musikverein: *Hans und Grete, Erinnerung,* and *Scheiden und Meiden.* The audience was so enthusiastic that it encored the last two, and Kalbeck's criticism was once again extremely laudatory. Unlike his colleagues, he felt that the "popular" style came entirely naturally to Mahler and even praised the poem of *Hans und Grete.* A recital given on February 15 in the Kleine Musikvereinsaal by Eugen Gura, a Bohemian baritone who had left the stage to give recitals mainly of Löwe and Wolf lieder, also included three of Mahler's songs: *"Wo die schönen Trompeten blasen,"* the last of the *Lieder eines fahrenden Gesellen* and *"Selbstgefühl"* from the early *Wunderhorn Lieder.*

At the sixth Philharmonic concert on January 28, Mahler conducted Bruckner's *Romantic Symphony,* Mendelssohn's overture *Meeresstille und glückliche Fahrt,* and Wagner's *Kaisermarsch.*[56] Although he had made a few cuts in the second and fourth movements of Bruckner's symphony, he wondered at the last moment whether he had been right to include it in the program of the Philharmonic concerts, where there was no place for anything but masterpieces. "One really cannot expect the public to listen to musical junk and the worst kind of absurdities, even though they may frequently contain divine ideas and themes."

As a Bruckner expert, Helm reproached Mahler with having "torn the poetic and musical form of the work to shreds" with his cuts, which were the more damnable as the symphony had always been given in its entirety before. The interpretation had been weak and arbitrary, but then "one could hardly expect Mahler to possess true German spirit."

Hirschfeld, on the other hand, who did not share Helm's wholehearted admiration for Bruckner, found Mahler's version and interpretation a complete success. In fact, Mahler had toned down the "bizarre cesuras" that "disrupted the continuity" and, in short, served Bruckner with love and understanding where others "followed him to the letter, but to his detriment."

The annual Nicolaï Concerts for the benefit of the Philharmonic Retire-ment Fund traditionally included an important work for chorus and orches-tra. Having given the first performance in Vienna of his own *Second Sym-phony* the previous year, Mahler decided that, at the 1900 concert, to be given on February 18, he would conduct the greatest masterpiece of all, Beethoven's *Ninth Symphony*. He had already prepared a singularly bold version of this in Hamburg, adding his own modifications to those of Wag-ner. The hall was packed, Mahler's success surpassed any he had ever achieved in Vienna, and the chorus joined in the lengthy final ovation. Moreover, the tickets were sold so rapidly that the concert had to be re-peated on February 22. Having been told about Mahler's tempos and mod-ifications, Prince Liechtenstein said to him afterward: "A very beautiful performance, Herr Mahler, quite magnificent, and what a success! How-ever, I have heard other tempos!" "Oh really, so Your Highness has heard this work before?" was Mahler's calm reply.[57]

The critics who had thus far been relatively courteous as far as Mahler was concerned, suddenly lashed out at him. Only Kalbeck defended him and his "version," in an article that was at once moderate and authorita-tive.[58] The faithful performance of a piece of music is, after all, merely "a question of confidence"; and when a conductor gave so clear, expressive and convincing a rendering of a monumental work without missing a single detail, he deserved the confidence of the public, even if it did not always share his views.

The other critics proved less broad-minded. Heuberger decried this "ob-jectionable practice of repainting classical works," as sheer "aberration" and "barbarism." Contrary to the clearly expressed wishes of the composer, Mahler had altered not only the sound of certain passages, but also their very meaning. His over-all tempos had been too slow and his accelerandos too frequent.

A brilliant polemicist, Hirschfeld assumed a virulently hostile attitude. Concerning Mahler's interpretation of the *Ninth Symphony,* he wrote: "Each note is lighted from within, the darkest pathways are illuminated, nothing is left to the imagination; the voices that murmur in the shadows are exposed to the glare of the sun, the airy lines are weighed down, every nervous fiber of the melody is detached and isolated from the sound fabric as if with a scalpel. Great surges of sound or subtle nuances draw attention to every minute detail of the *melos;* a ritardando or an accelerando alerts the audience to what is coming, for fear it should miss anything. This *Ninth Symphony* is a triumph of lucidity . . . With it, Mahler has asserted himself as a modernist, at least in so far as this modern age impels the ship of art toward the reefs of science . . . Instead of silencing him, the grandeur of the *Ninth Symphony* aroused his intellect . . . and he has scaled its heights with clever interpretations and pretty details . . .

"The diminuendo of the horn in the D major melody of the Trio in the Scherzo is superb but does not appear in the score; the rendering of the majestic final melody, where it is taken up by the basses, was admirable, but, as always, the simplest rendering would have been the most effective . . . Instead of trying to understand Beethoven, Mahler should simply believe in him, as Richter did. The pathos of *Eroica,* the Funeral March from *Götterdämmerung,* and the *Ninth Symphony* are alien to him, for neither nervousness nor intellect has any place in the overwhelming and awe-inspiring peace of solemn feeling."[59]

In view of the opposition of certain members of the orchestra and the almost unanimous condemnation of the critics, Mahler, for the second performance of the concert, on February 22, had the following text (whose ponderous style betrays Lipiner's collaboration) distributed at the entrance of the hall:

"In as much as, on account of certain utterances voiced abroad, the belief might spread among a portion of the public that, on the part of the conductor of today's performance, arbitrary alterations of details in Beethoven's works, and in particular in his *Ninth Symphony,* have been undertaken; it seems imperative not to withhold a few explanatory observations on this subject.

"Due to his auditory ailment, which led to total deafness, Beethoven lost his indispensable and intimate contact with reality and the world of physical sound at the very period of his creative activity in which the prodigious increase in his powers of imagination impelled him to discover new means of expression and to achieve a hitherto unsuspectedly vigorous mode of orchestration. This fact is as well known as the fact that the quality of the brasses of his time quite simply rendered them incapable of producing certain sequences of notes required for the development of a melody. Since time has corrected the defect of these instruments, it would seem a crime not to use them in such a way as to perform Beethoven's works as perfectly as possible.

"Richard Wagner, who, throughout his life, fought passionately, both in word and in deed, to rescue the interpretation of Beethoven's works from a neglect that was becoming intolerable, explained in his *Concerning the Execution of the Ninth Symphony* how this symphony should be performed in order to conform as nearly as possible to the intentions of its creator. And all conductors since then have followed the same path. Because of his deep conviction, confirmed by his experience with this work, the conductor öf today's concert has followed precisely the same course, without, as far as the essential is concerned, trespassing beyond the limits set by Wagner.

"There has, of course, been no question of any instrumental modifications, alterations or even 'improvement' of Beethoven's work. The long-observed custom of multiplying the strings has—and that likewise long since— also resulted in an increase in the number of wind instruments. This in no way implies that the latter instruments have been given any new orchestral role; on the contrary, their number was raised exclusively for the purpose of amplifying the sound. On this point, as on every other concerning the interpretation of the work, both in its entirety and in detail, the conductor can demonstrate, score in hand (and the more one goes into details, the more convincingly), that, far from following any arbitrary purpose or course, but also without allowing himself to be led astray by 'tradition,' he was constantly and solely concerned with carrying out Beethoven's wishes in their minutest detail, and with ensuring that nothing the master intended should be sacrificed or drowned out amid the general confusion of sound."

Far from calming the tempest or winning over his enemies, Mahler's text merely intensified the controversy, and the press reacted even more violently than it had four days earlier. Heuberger, in the *Neue Freie Presse,* wrote that "one goes to a concert to hear music, not to read a treatise on aesthetics."

In almost identical terms, Helm condemned both Mahler's attitude and his attempts to justify it, while Hirschfeld, under the pseudonym of "King-Fu," wrote with biting irony: "Herr Direktor Mahler has . . . written a speech and distributed it to the assembled public. We now possess one of his writings; a decree, a summons, formally dated and signed Gustav Mahler, and one surmises that it constitutes the first of his complete works. Its style and tone are a happy mixture of official gravity and benevolence. The occasion, a performance of the *Ninth Symphony* conducted by Gustav Mahler, was unquestionably greater than this shadow it has cast. We censured it, not so much for the instrumental tricks in which Herr Mahler indulged yet again, but because the powerful work did not produce the powerful effect expected. Others were more severe: they took note of each new trumpet, each new horn, and debited it. This was too much for Herr Mahler: he had to refute the 'utterances voiced abroad.' At the second performance of the symphony, every concertgoer was handed a leaflet containing the latest decree . . .

"Beethoven was stone deaf. Herr Mahler sorely bewails the fact, but one would think that, precisely because of his deafness, the great man desired dense rather than sparse orchestration. Herr Mahler denies this and maintains that we should compensate the imperfection of the instruments of Beethoven's time. He then sets out to prove that he undertook no instrumental modifications, but that they were both necessary and inevitable! Herr Mahler is not obliged to be acquainted with the laws of logic and is therefore no more obliged to apply them. Herr Mahler is not obliged to write intelligible German, but neither is he obliged to demonstrate this fact to the public . . ."[60]

By thus furnishing the critics with an all too easy weapon against himself, Mahler had provoked the first salvos of a press campaign that was henceforth to continue uninterrupted. Although he termed the vituperation of someone like Hirschfeld "absurd," there is no doubt that he was often hurt by it and found it exceedingly hard to take, especially as he would have been happy to have Hirschfeld on his side. "Hirschfeld's attacks are so absurd," he said to Karpath, "that they no longer interest me. It's his tone that I find outrageous. Even if people censure me, they should do so 'hat in hand.' He adds nothing to his glory by treating me so uncivilly. In any case, he may do his worst, for I shall go my own sweet way whether he likes it or not."[61]

Considering that, as far as his style was concerned, Hirschfeld was one of the most brilliant of the Viennese critics, one wonders what could possibly have been the reason for his antagonism and injustice. Some writers, and notably Paul Stefan, attributed it to the fact that Mozart's opera *Zaïde*, which he edited and completed, was a flop; however, the opera was only performed in 1902, whereas Hirschfeld's hostility became apparent as from 1900.[62] It seems more likely, as Karpath suggested, that he would have liked to establish personal relations with Mahler and was offended that the latter held him at arm's length. In fact, when he first took on the directorship of the Vienna Opera, Mahler had rather enjoyed Hirschfeld's company and his lively wit. Later on, however, he began to see him for the vain, intolerant, irascible, and embittered man he was, "exasperated by success" and "jealously and malevolently opposed to anything young and new."

In any case, Mahler's enemies had found in Hirschfeld a leader and an eloquent spokesman, who would stop at neither injustice nor abuse in his campaign of systematic disparagement.

"All I ask of Providence is a secluded spot where, for a few weeks of every year, I can be entirely my own master."

# CHAPTER 32

*Mahler in Vienna (VIII) — Engagement of Gutheil-Schoder — Paris — Maiernigg — Completion of the* Fourth Symphony (*April–August 1900*)

After the uproar over the *Ninth Symphony*, the two final Philharmonic concerts took place in an atmosphere of relative calm. The seventh concert, on March 19, included Haydn's E flat major *"Drumroll" Symphony*, Weber's *Konzertstück* (Liszt's version), with Ferruccio Busoni as piano soloist, Liszt's *Mephisto Waltz*, which was one of the Philharmonic's best pieces, and Karl Goldmark's *Frühlingsouvertüre*. According to the *Neue Freie Presse*, the Haydn Symphony was a tremendous success, although certain details, and particularly the somewhat overly emotional interpretation of the introduction, were "not in keeping with Haydn's style."

During rehearsals for the last concert, on April 1, Mahler became steadily more delighted that he had included Brahms's *Variations on a Theme of Haydn* in the program, since the composer "shows an unparalleled musical mastery in this piece. He takes the seed out of its matrix and conducts it through all the stages of development to its highest degree of perfection. In fact, he has no rivals in this field, not even Beethoven, whose albeit admirable *Variations* are of a totally different nature. Carried away by his own soaring imagination and flights of fancy, Beethoven is incapable of sticking to the details of the theme. The Andante of my own *Second Symphony* and the *Blumenstück* from the *Third* are also variations, but they are just as far removed as Beethoven's from Brahms's rigorous style and constant elaboration of the same theme. Rather than a continual development of the same sequence of notes,[1] mine are decorative variations, arabesques, and garlands woven around the theme. Brahms's variations are like an enchanted stream, with banks so sure that its waters never overflow, even in the sharpest bends, whereas Schubert (whose *Symphony in C Major* is also in the program) is something else again. His music is like a rushing river flowing freely and indomitably, a river one cannot tame but from which one can take long drafts."[2]

Despite the enthusiasm with which it had been rehearsed, the concert received a bad press. Even Kalbeck was hostile: "our dull and cloudy spring weather pervaded the hall; the nightingales in Schubert's *Symphony* remained silent, the anemones and violets in Brahms's *Variations* hung their heads and the radiant sun in the *Leonora Overture* never emerged from the clouds." The audience's applause was conventional and polite rather than enthusiastic. Specifying his objections, Kalbeck said that Mahler had again overstepped the bounds of the permissible. "Were it not for the fact that one must make allowances for human failings, we would find it incomprehensible that so intelligent, so sensitive and so rigorously idealistic an artist could follow a course directly opposed to the aims which he pursues. In his attempts to avoid the Scylla of the routine and obvious, he falls into the Charybdis of the strange and unusual and thinks to save himself from misunderstandings by emphasizing every point on which he differs from general opinion. As a result, he disintegrates the work of art. Someone should remind him that such an excess of nuances is just as objectionable as total uniformity and monotony, for it leaves nothing to the audience's imagination and either exasperates or bores them. Thus the interpreter destroys their artistic enjoyment by drawing their attention to himself rather than to the work he is interpreting. Doubtless nothing could be more painful to Herr Mahler than to be taken for a vain virtuoso; yet none of Schubert's works has quite the spirit [*Geist*] which his *C major Symphony* appeared to be endowed with last night."

After the final concert, Hirschfeld pronounced a less negative verdict on the season as a whole than one might have expected: "Mahler's interpretations are very meaningful [*sinnig*] and very personal [*eigen*], but also exceedingly wayward [*eigensinnig*]. With his infectious enthusiasm, he immediately fires both orchestra and audience and rouses the tired spirit from its lethargy. With such a conductor, one does not merely hear the music, one is privileged to share in his most intimate reactions to it. Even those who would resist are carried away in spite of themselves. Thus their leader constantly spurs the musicians of the Philharmonic on to further glories . . ."

Helm, in the *Wochenblatt,* complained of Mahler's tendency to sacrifice the whole for the details, his excessive preoccupation with problems of accentuation and the fact that he was apt to turn andantes into adagios and allegros into prestos and to underline with sforzandos certain details that could more easily have been emphasized in some other way. We listen to his interpretations with the greatest interest, but not without a secret fear of being suddenly "upset, even offended, by some arbitrary modification of a traditional interpretation." Moreover, we deplore the fact that he does not prepare his programs in advance so that they form an ensemble or a cycle and that he "always gives himself the leading part."

Despite the critics' severity, the Philharmonic concerts had attracted larger audiences than ever before, the financial returns surpassed those of any previous season, and, on May 30, Mahler was unanimously re-elected director of the orchestra for the following season.

While Mahler was spending his Easter holidays in Venice, Richard Strauss conducted a Philharmonic concert in Berlin at which the soprano Emilie Herzog[3] sang three of Mahler's *Wunderhorn Lieder*. These were given a far better reception than the orchestral works Mahler himself had conducted in the Prussian capital. The public encored *"Rheinlegendchen,"* but the critics had their usual reservations. Otto Lessmann, in the *Allgemeine Musik Zeitung,* felt that the lieder did not fit in with the rest of the concert and that, without "their elegantly elaborated instrumental adornment," they would lose much of their charm.

As usual, it was Mahler's *Volkstümlichkeit* that aroused disapproval. According to the *Vossische Zeitung,* it is "neither clear nor pure and sometimes borders on vulgarity"; the *Börsenzeitung* called it "affected simplicity" and said that the contrast between "the style of the texts and the refinement of the orchestration" was intolerable; the *Börsen Courier* said that Mahler "has done better" and that, despite "his enchanting orchestration," his efforts to adopt a "popular" style were in vain.

"Your *Lieder,* which Frau Herzog sang beautifully," Strauss wrote to Mahler in April, "delighted both me and the public. Needless to say, as far as our lofty critics were concerned, they were not important enough, for any work that isn't tinged with boredom is automatically regarded as 'insufficiently stylish' for a concert. That reminds me, has your *Third Symphony* been published yet? I'd like to conduct your *Was die Blumen erzählen* in Paris next winter! . . .[4] by way of an introduction! . . . It goes without saying that I only presented your *Lieder* so as to be sure that you'd accept my ballet!"

In this same letter, Strauss also asked Mahler to conduct at the Vienna Opera the ballet he was composing, a somewhat daring work that "differs from the usual set pieces," and demanded "a simple yea or nay and, if your answer is in the negative, kindly refrain from wrapping it in the usual formulas and excuses of which I have had my fill."

Mahler wrote back saying he would accept the ballet sight unseen, provided Strauss sent him the scenario by return of post so that he could draw up a rough estimate for the décor and costumes. "But why the devil did you have to add such a postscript?" he went on. "You must indeed have had some pretty bad experiences to try on the *Manus lavat*[5] game with me, even as a joke. Believe me, I'm happy anytime I can pay your work the homage it deserves. Naturally, I have to proceed with caution in my efforts to educate the Viennese, since, for decades now, they've been methodically brutalized.

"You will doubtless have noted that I'm not vain and that I'm used to forgoing at least the outward joys of a creator. All I ask of Providence is a secluded spot where, for a few weeks of every year, I can be entirely my own master and, in addition, at least to have heard *one* good performance of my works. My sincerest thanks for including my trifles in your concert. I read and understood.[6] It's always the same old story! Please don't take it amiss if I ask you not to perform the movements of my symphonies separately; it's merely because I fear it would give rise to a host of misunderstandings. However, I shall be delighted to send you my *Third Symphony* (though I don't expect you to perform it, for I'm fully aware that it presents formidable difficulties: it lasts two hours) . . ."

On the evening of April 7, Mahler and Natalie boarded the train for Venice, where Justi was to join them with Selma Kurz, in whom he was evidently still interested. The holiday began most unpromisingly, for the incessant rain had caused a landslide in the mountains which delayed the train. Nevertheless, when the passengers were told they would have to wait several hours for another train to arrive from the opposite direction, Mahler returned to his berth and slept peacefully while his fellow travelers fidgeted restlessly and bumped into one another in the dark. And when everyone was finally asked to change trains, bag and baggage, in the pouring rain, he roared with laughter at the sight of a canary being laboriously carried in its cage, along with a thousand other pieces of luggage, since the bird could have flown over the landslide with the greatest of ease.

Having missed their connection and lost half a day, the travelers stopped at Klagenfurt, where Mahler began to feel a bit more at home at the thought of the *Häuschen* that he was having built there. At the Kaiser von Oesterreich Hotel, where he met some old acquaintances, he made an effort to be friendly and considerate to all in order to build up "the best possible reputation for myself as a homeowner" and also in the hope that "here, people will be pleasant and open and treat me like a human being rather than the knave the Viennese critics consider me."

The unceasing rain turned to snow in the Alpine passes as Mahler sat chattering gaily to Natalie in their compartment and laughing over the incredible stupidity of his childhood friend Guido Adler, whom he had just seen in Vienna. Partly for fun and partly out of irritation, he had nicknamed him "Science," an epithet that the musicologist had good-humoredly accepted. Contrary to Adler, Mahler considered art and science as totally irreconcilable and incompatible as the two faces of Janus. "What a lot of nonsense he's started proclaiming again about 'heresies' [*Irrlehren*] in Wagner's writings and the abasement of the chorus in his works. Had he felt either the desire or the need to do so, Wagner would have been quite capable of using the chorus to the utmost effect. Adler also has a singularly naïve conception of the nature of Mozart's polyphonic composition. He says he envies him his ability to hear each voice separately at the same time as all the others, even in the most complex polyphony. That, however, is an impossibility and a complete fallacy. I'm quite convinced that even the greatest musical genius is incapable of composing like that. One simply can't hear each voice separately for more than a second at a time, any more than one can follow a precise point in the ocean, for one's eye rapidly becomes distracted and ends up by seeing nothing but the mass of water. The rainbow, with its billions of constantly changing and blending drops, provides an even better example. One sees merely the magnificent whole, without being able to distinguish a single one of its components or even its colors. Besides, could anything be more pointless than this endeavor to analyze and break up that which necessarily forms a perfect whole? Just when one thinks one has fully grasped and defined it, one has in fact dismembered and destroyed it.[7] The composer strives to give the impression of an indivisible and unfathomable whole, of an inexhaustible and divine abundance. Thus, waves, rainbows or polyphonic compositions must all be approached in the same way. Any attempt scientifically to explain that which produces this impression is nothing but an exercise in futility, for the final, artistic effect of the whole is all that matters.

"Adler, in his folly or ignorance, fancies that when Mozart was obliged to compose the overture to *Don Giovanni* in one night and had no time to make a rough draft of it, he wrote each part separately while constantly hearing the whole in his mind's ear, a feat that would call for quasi-supernatural powers of imagination. To him, all the great composers of the past were magicians and no amount of explaining on the part of a musician more intelligent than he will make him understand them as they really were. My efforts met with a skeptical smile. I told him that, if Mozart really composed that overture in one night, he doubtless went about it in the same way as I did when I had to compose a scherzo in one night for an exam at the conservatory. Since I hadn't the time to write a complete score, I spread out all the parts in front of me and wrote the pieces as a whole rather than, as our Guido imagines, writing each part separately, for that would have been impossible."

Mahler and Natalie finally reached Venice the following night under a leaden sky. They were therefore immensely surprised and delighted to wake up to beautiful weather the next morning. Because of the many and various noises in the old city, Mahler could not sleep a wink. In fact, he changed lodgings three times without ever finding the desired quiet. The day after their arrival, he and Natalie went for a long walk along the embankment opposite the Giudecca, a neighborhood entirely free of the tourists who infested the center of the city. The beauty of the spot so moved him that he decided to go there every day, and it was during one of these walks that an incident occurred that particularly amused him in view of a similar misadventure he had recently had in Vienna. Being suddenly caught short, he looked around for some place to relieve himself and managed to find a privy in the courtyard of a private house. However, the janitress saw him and came rushing out in fury to upbraid him and hurl insults down the street after him as he departed. Mahler could not help wondering whether she would have preferred him to use the street!

On another walk along the Giudecca Canal, he was again caught short and, with Natalie acting as interpreter, asked a beggar to direct him to the required spot. The latter, with a broad grin, led him to a private house, where he was most courteously received by the lady of the house and ceremoniously installed in her drawing room with a chamber pot. Exceedingly embarrassed, he asked whether there were not some more private place, but his hostess was so insistent that he finally accepted her unusual hospitality and performed amid the baskets of oranges and vases of flowers adorning her drawing room. Later on he presented her with a bunch of violets in token of gratitude.

According to Natalie, it was on this trip that, for the first time in his life, Mahler took an interest in the visual arts and diligently visited all the monuments of Venetian painting and architecture. She felt that his former indifference was due solely to a lack in his education and that the discovery of this branch of the arts would enrich his own work. Mahler himself had long been resigned to this trait in his nature. "To me, such theorizing is as pointless as that of people who wonder what sort of a life they would have led if they'd made a different marriage. The children of the union exist. One loves them and can't imagine them as being any different from what they are. Therefore there's no point in discussing the matter any further."[8] Lipiner had already attempted to educate him three years before by giving him a collection of photographs, engravings, and colored reproductions accompanied by a multitude of explanations. Mahler had taken no interest in these lessons, maintaining that his lack of visual curiosity was common to all musicians and that visual beauty, particularly in nature, merely made him more introspective. While he was busy transforming everything into sound, any external object that attracted his attention also distracted it, and, for that very reason, he scorned elegant and even comfortable furnishings, contenting himself, as at Steinbach, with a table, a chair, a piano, and a few prints stuck on the wall. Later on, he admitted that Lipiner had picked a particularly inopportune moment, when he had been unusually busy at the opera.

A few months before his trip to Venice, however, Mahler had made the acquaintance of the painter Henriette Mankiewicz, who, stricken with a chronic disease that rendered her virtually an invalid, bore her sufferings "with angelic fortitude." He often went to see her, and the two of them frequently discussed the stage sets at the opera as well as painting in general.[9]

Upon his return from Venice, Mahler's time was more than ever taken up by his activities at the opera, where he still had little or no help. Richter had left, and Schalk, although he had already conducted at the Hofoper, had not yet been officially installed. Thus Mahler himself was obliged to conduct the two complete *Ring* cycles given before and after the Easter holidays.[10] Some of the critics objected to the length of these complete performances, which ended so late that there was no more public transport, and also to his attempts to simplify and stylize the staging. The *Musikalische Presse* felt that he was demanding too much of the audience to expect it to imagine the bridge leading to Walhalla at the end of *Das Rheingold*.[11] On the other hand, "his conducting constantly created new miracles of sound and shading. The pianissimos were ineffably delicate, the fortissimos magnificently exuberant, and stage and orchestra were in perfect unison. Each instrument spoke, each phrase had plastic beauty and each drumbeat significance. Moreover, the immense crescendo, which mounted steadily from the beginning of Act III of *Die Götterdämmerung* and reached its climax with the death of Siegfried, was sublime."

At the end of the season, Mahler, for the third time, invited Lilli Lehmann to give a series of guest performances.[12] The prima donna's ingenuous vanity is touchingly expressed in the letters she wrote to him beforehand, such as that dated March 6: "I sang *Norma* for the third time yesterday, and very well . . ." or that dated March 13: "You can hardly imagine the stupendous reception I was given here [in Paris]; not only was I recalled three times after the aria from *Armida,* but I also had to repeat the Schubert lieder . . . and took four curtain calls after the final scene of *Götterdämmerung*. It was truly magnificent . . ." or again, that dated April 6: "I've just sung Valentine [in *Les Huguenots*] in Wiesbaden *very well!*" and in a postscript added the same day: "This time you must make me an honorary member of the opera [*Ehrenmitglied*]. I've been waiting for that for so long."[13]

For a short season of Italian opera in May, Mahler had sent for a complete troupe to come from Italy, together with two celebrated stars, the soprano Gemma Bellincioni and the tenor Fernando de Lucia. The chief attraction of this season, which was conducted by Schalk, was the Vienna premiere of Umberto Giordano's *Fedora*. Giordano himself came to attend the rehearsals, and he and Mahler had several friendly chats. Among other things, they discussed Verdi, whom Mahler greatly admired for his earnestness, his simplicity, and his modesty. Giordano told him that the old maestro hated having people talk to him about his own work, whereas he was very happy to discuss that of others, and particularly of Puccini and himself, but he had never been interested in either Mascagni or Leoncavallo. He had devoted the greater part of his fortune to building a home for aged musicians and continued to compose regularly, for he felt that a composer should never lose a single day but constantly exercise his pen, even if he later destroyed what he had written.

Verdi at that time occupied a large place in Mahler's thoughts. The preceding autumn, in the course of a conversation with Natalie, he had rejoiced at the fact that, in his latest works, the great Italian had learned to channel the gigantic flow of his inspiration; instead of "pouring out his individual ideas without lingering over them, he now develops and expands them logically."[14] With his profoundly German ideas, Mahler contrasted Verdi in this respect to the majority of the other composers, such as Lortzing and even Weber, whose inventiveness was not so abundant. Only such "giants" as Beethoven and Wagner soared above everybody else, and of course Mozart, who, as a "first-rate genius" and a "renovator of music and of opera in the highest sense," also belonged in the category of superior composers, for his brilliant creative talent went hand in hand with a supreme formal beauty carried to incomparable heights of insight and perfection.

Giordano's vivacity and "sunny charm" enchanted Mahler, and *Fedora* increased his admiration for his talent, which he compared to that of the young Verdi. He had let Schalk conduct because *Fedora* "doesn't mean that much to me," but Giordano was bitterly disappointed, since Schalk had not the "temperament" of Mahler, whom he had just heard conduct *Der fliegende Holländer.* As far as Mahler's entourage was concerned, *Fedora* provided yet another example of the degree to which his judgment as an interpreter was indulgent. He himself acknowledged this but felt that it was neither weakness nor bias, but the indulgence of an interpreter and theater director who sought to re-create a work, to experience it in his imagination and identify himself with it as though it were his own. He readily admitted, however, that, were he a critic and obliged to judge "from the stalls," his opinion might well be entirely different.[15]

In the case of *Fedora,* the judgment of both the public and the press was in fact less favorable than Mahler's. Although the hall was packed, the applause was subdued. Most of the critics pronounced la Bellincioni ("the Duse of Italian opera") "unconvincing as a woman of the world, but impressive as an impassioned tragedienne." In fact, she was then reaching the end of her career and beginning to lose her voice, so that the expressive force and realism of her acting did not always compensate for her vocal weakness.

The Italian season, which included three performances of *Fedora* followed by *La Traviata* and *Rigoletto,* was a financial failure, because the prices of the tickets had been doubled at a time when, the season being virtually over, the public was already dwindling. The Italians had promised to give other works, but they had neglected to learn certain essential parts and some of them had to leave to fulfill engagements elsewhere. The end of their stay was further marred by painful discussions concerning their fees, a few of the singers having sought to back up their demands with lies. Thus, it was without regret that Mahler took leave of these Mediterraneans, whom he had welcomed with open arms so short a time before.

During May he immersed himself in Tolstoy's *Resurrection,* which upset him so much that he became depressed and irritable, because "I'm quite unable to reconcile the meaning of my own life with the truth as revealed by this book, which has caused the scales to fall from my eyes."

On one of his free evenings he took Natalie and Nina Spiegler to a performance of *Le Misanthrope* at the Burgtheater and became incensed at the rapid tempo of the actors in the first scenes. He himself was always at pains to present each new element in a musical performance clearly and firmly so that the audience would remember it when they heard it again. And in order to prove the absurdity of so rapid and light an exposition, he grabbed Nina Spiegler's opera glasses when she was not looking, tossed them up in the air and then asked her to identify them as they flew.

Another evening, during a discussion of the situation at the opera, he remarked to his intimates that he was finally on the point of overcoming the last pockets of opinionated resistance he had encountered during his first years. "It's strange," he added, "that the person who's been able thus to command and compel obedience should himself be the most disobedient and inflexible of men!" Yet few people knew better than he how to obey when it was worth while, for instance when some exterior force left him no peace until he had brought a particular work to life in the way in which its creator had desired, or when he spent sleepless nights on account of a sixteenth note.[16]

The most important event of the end of the season was a new production of *Carmen,* which marked the first appearance after her engagement of a new singer, Marie Gutheil-Schoder,[17] a first-rate dramatic talent and, in Mahler's own words, a "musical genius." Born of poor parents in Weimar, she had studied under an unknown teacher and "in truth, was completely self-taught." Mahler had become interested in her merely from hearsay[18] after a recent guest appearance she had made in Berlin. She was then painfully earning five thousand marks a year at the Weimar Opera, but, in the few letters they exchanged, Mahler immediately recognized a genuine personality. He therefore invited her to the Vienna Opera, where she made her debut in February 1900 in *Pagliacci.* Gutheil-Schoder recalls that first evening in her memoirs. Mahler called on her in her dressing room before the performance and was appalled by the red wig in which she proposed to sing Nedda. Her only answer was to dismiss him with the plea that he reserve judgment. Later on, she decided that it was the ingenuousness of this reaction which had enabled her to establish harmonious relations with the imperious genius who was to fascinate her for the next seven years.

The *Deutsches Volksblatt* immediately spoke of Gutheil-Schoder as a possible successor to Marie Renard, but advised against engaging this "remarkable actress" because of "her extremely ordinary voice and by no means outstanding vocal talents." What Vienna needs is an "exceptional singer," not a "decadent actress." Continuing in this polemic vein, the paper accused Schalk of having performed such acrobatics that "it could have been Mahler we were watching," and wondered whether "Gutheil-Schoder and Schalk are not of the same race as the director . . ."[19]

Heuberger, on the other hand, hailed this young "guest" as "one of the most interesting discoveries of recent years." Despite the harshness of her voice, her acting talent was worthy of the stage, for she knew how to create a character by her least gesture and movement. She sang the *Ballatella* lying on her back and she entirely altered her interpretation for the *commedia dell' arte* of the second act, while emphasizing each appearance of the real person behind the "part" with a subtlety extremely rare at the opera.

Two days later, after Maillart's *Les Dragons de Villars,* the second opera in which Gutheil-Schoder sang, Hirschfeld wondered whether, with her "lack of vocal grace and mellowness," she would ever be able to make a name for herself in a city that particularly loved vocal beauty. Helm added that her voice was small and lacked charm, but that Vienna had never seen Nedda played so "naturally and convincingly." This young soprano, with her "frizzed and ill-combed" hair, "lived" the character from beginning to end.[20]

In May, Gutheil-Schoder scored another success in *Carmen,* a part that, according to Helm, "seemed written for her," such was her capacity to identify herself with the character and "suddenly to jump from mirth to raging passion and from bitter contempt to total indifference." Her performance was questionable only in passages in which she was required merely to sing "calmly but lyrically," for in these she was distinctly inferior to Marie Renard, who had preceded her in this sensational part.[21]

Gutheil-Schoder's success in Vienna was such that it attracted the attention of several impresarios, and as a result Mahler had to tempt her with the considerable salary of sixteen thousand gulden a year in order to keep her. Having engaged her, he decided to revive *Carmen,* since he had long been looking for a singer capable of both singing and acting this title role. He replaced the spoken dialogue with recitative, assigned the children's chorus in Act I to real children, and directed the choruses of soldiers and cigarette girls to perfection. He had the singers of the quintet sit around a table rather than stand downstage. He had the rocky chaos of the third act entirely remodeled, and, in short, meticulously revised every dramatic and musical aspect of the production. His admiration for Gutheil-Schoder grew with each of her expressive words, gestures, and notes and with each eloquent motion of her flexible body. She brought so much personality to her part that there was practically nothing he had to teach her. The slightest indication, the briefest word sufficed to make her understand and even surpass his wishes. "It's always in women," he said, "that I find the best and the greatest. Schoder and Mildenburg tower above all the others, proving that there's no cause for despair and that character and talent still exist on the stage alongside all the affectation and dishonesty . . . Gutheil-Schoder is another example of the enigma of personality, which is the sum of all that one is. With her mediocre voice and its even disagreeable middle register, she might appear totally insignificant. Yet each sound she utters has 'soul' [*Seele*], each gesture and attitude is a revelation of the character she's playing. She understands its very essence and brings out all its aspects as only a creative genius can do."[22]

To Mahler, the great moments of the lyric theater were never exclusively vocal. They occurred when a singer succeeded in "re-creating a role, in breathing life into it. Where that is the case, it doesn't matter if there's an occasional rough spot."[23] This declaration of principles, or exposition of new standards of beauty in the lyric theater, was not without precedent. During the period generally regarded as "the golden age" of singing, such a prima donna as the celebrated Wilhelmine Schröder-Devrient, whom Wagner so admired, moved the audience by her emotional diction, her stage presence, and her histrionic skill rather than by her purely vocal talents. However, such ladies constituted glorious exceptions, whereas Gutheil-Schoder conformed more nearly even than Mildenburg to Mahler's criteria of theatrical art. Hard-working, endowed with a feeling for beauty and a subtle sense of artistry, she managed to adapt to a variety of styles and apparently even to remain expressive in coloratura singing. She rapidly became an eminent interpreter of Mozart, proving a memorable Pamina, Elvira, Susanna, and Cherubino, thanks to her consummate skill in vocal color, while her prodigious dramatic qualities made her a fabulous Elektra and her musicianship the chosen creator of Schönberg's *Erwartung* and *Second Quartet*. To those who heard her sing the title role in *Carmen* and Gluck's *Iphigénie en Tauride,* or Frau Fluth in *Die lustigen Weiber von Windsor,* she remained unforgettable. Though less intelligent than was usually supposed, she had immediately recognized the limitations of her voice and realized that she would have to find other means to command attention. Thus it was that she sought, and achieved, a thrilling unity of music, gesture, and text. At first, the novelty of her art disconcerted the public and aroused violent hostility on the part of certain critics. Nevertheless, Mahler came to regard her as an indispensable collaborator, for she managed to grasp, to carry out and even to transfigure his innermost intentions.

After the new production of *Carmen,* Heuberger congratulated Mahler on having engaged Gutheil-Schoder, who might make mistakes as a "repertory singer" but whose gifts were "supremely unusual, captivating and brilliant." The anonymous critic of the *Extrablatt* described her as "a living paradox, a great singer with a little voice," who in *Carmen* "turned into a slender, supple, lively and passionate Spanish gypsy" even though her voice weakened in the last act. Like his colleagues, Karpath congratulated Mahler on having both improved the production of Bizet's gem and replaced the dialogue with recitative and said that, in addition to the fact that Gutheil-Schoder's voice seemed to have improved since February, she had thrown "new light on certain aspects of the part."[24] Later, however, many critics protested about this new engagement and denounced the vocal limitations of Gutheil-Schoder. The critic Max Graf saw Mahler seated one day in the Imperial Café, a huge pile of newspapers on the table in front of him, distressed by the realization that not one Vienna critic had found anything to admire in her performance as Eva in *Die Meistersinger*.[25]

During this 1899–1900 season, Mahler finally obtained not only an increase in the stagehands' salaries, for which he had long been fighting, but also the dismissal of the chief stage designer, Franz Gaul, whose overriding influence he had gradually managed to undermine. Gaul had held this position since 1867, and his predilection for ballet had contributed not a little to their strained relations. Mahler finally persuaded the administration not to renew his contract, and Gaul was retired and replaced by Heinrich Leffler, who was a far more gifted painter.[26]

It was as conductor of the Philharmonic concerts that Mahler set out for Paris early in June 1902. In addition to the provincial villages, glass buildings, and other innumerable attractions that drew a constant flow of visitors from all parts of the world to the International Exposition, someone had had the odd idea of inviting the Philharmonic Orchestra of Vienna to come and give three concerts in Paris. Contrary to the Männergesangverein, which had also been invited but which traveled frequently, thanks to a special fund provided by the contributing members of its committee, this was the Philharmonic's first trip abroad since its founding. The twofold visit was patronized and encouraged by Princess Pauline Metternich-Sandor, whose husband had been Austrian ambassador to Paris under Napoleon III and who had already played an important part in the disastrous premiere of *Tannhäuser* at the Paris Opéra in 1861.

In organizing this trip, the committee of the Philharmonic counted on no more than a *succès d'estime* and thought it had provided for all possible emergencies by setting up a guarantee fund of twenty thousand crowns, underwritten by a few rich Viennese, to cover the musicians' travel and living expenses. Mahler had vehemently opposed the undertaking, feeling that the heat of June and the atmosphere of the International Exposition would be anything but propitious to serious music[27]; besides which, having just ended an exhausting season, he yearned for the peace and quiet of his *Häuschen*. However, when he realized that the musicians regarded his objections as unfriendly, he finally agreed to go.

The departure took place on the evening of June 15. Thanks to Princess Metternich, who had gone to stay with her friend Countess de Pourtalès in Paris three weeks before in order to publicize the concerts,[28] Mahler was graciously welcomed by the Austro-Hungarian ambassador, Count Wolkenstein. The Viennese newspapers commissioned several of their correspondents to accompany the orchestra and write detailed reports of the whole trip and the Parisian public's reaction to the Austrian musicians.

Mahler had hardly stepped off the train before he noticed enormous posters announcing concerts "under the direction of M. Gustav Malheur, Director of the Imperial and Royal Court Opera." "What a fine start!" he exclaimed. To his relief, he discovered that the programs had not yet been printed, so that there was still time to correct the Malheur spelling mistake. Other circumstances, however, immediately inspired him with more serious misgivings. The preparations and publicity for the concerts had been practically nonexistent. One short column had been printed in *Le Figaro,* whereas a genuine publicity campaign was what was needed to fill, four times over, halls as large as the Châtelet and, above all, the immense Trocadéro. At the last moment, a large number of free tickets had to be handed out to members of the Austrian colony, but many seats remained empty notwithstanding.

Mahler at once set out to discover Paris, which made a great impression on him, to the extent that he wrote to Justi that "the difference between this city and Vienna is as great as that between Vienna and Iglau." His apartment at the embassy was peaceful and isolated, and he had renewed his acquaintance with such Viennese friends as Count and Countess Kielmannsegg. During the first days of his stay he took long walks through the outskirts of Paris with either an Austrian friend named Mandl or Arnold Rosé, made excursions to Saint-Germain and Versailles, and even went on a long walk across fields and woods to Marly. He devoted his first evenings to visiting the exposition, which he praised to Justi with his usual brevity by saying that "its illuminations evoke the Arabian Nights."[29]

The first concert took place (at 2:30) on the broiling hot afternoon of June 18 in the Théâtre du Châtelet. The meager audience included such celebrities as the minister of national education, the writers Anatole France and Catulle Mendès, Calmette, the director of *Le Figaro,* the composers Saint-Saëns and Alfred Bruneau, Countess de Pourtalès, the singer Victor Maurel,[30] the deputy Jules Roche, the industrialist Krupp, Georges Clemenceau and his brother-in-law, Jacques Maire, as well as Colonel Picquart, a famous Dreyfusard and great music lover who was to become one of Mahler's best friends. The fact that the hall was half empty was not considered overly disastrous, since it was felt not only that the French wanted to be certain, before attending a concert, that the event would be worth while, but also that the press notices would attract larger crowds to the succeeding concerts.

The afternoon was a tremendous success. An atmosphere of euphoria reigned in the hall, in which most of the Paris Austrian colony had gathered. The Viennese correspondents wrote that the overture to *Die Meistersinger* had been extremely impressive because of the exceptional sonority of the orchestra, the brilliance of the strings, and the power of the brasses, whereas Mozart's *Symphony in G Minor* had in contrast been "as simple and transparent as only Mahler could make it." In the *"Leonore" Overture No. 3,* the pianissimo of the first theme of the Allegro had had a phantasmagorical effect as it gradually mounted in a crescendo to a grandiose forte. The audience had been enraptured and had applauded wildly. The tension had increased during the second half of the concert, made up of the overture to *Oberon* and Beethoven's *Fifth Symphony.* Mahler's "version" of the Beethoven had been received with some surprise, but its force had overcome all hesitations and the whole concert had ended in a genuine triumph for the conductor. Throughout the afternoon, the attentiveness of the audience was such that Mahler felt confident that the Trocadéro concerts would attract a considerably larger public.

The chief interest of the articles published in the Paris press lies in the fact that they give an appraisal other than Viennese of the Philharmonic and Mahler's interpretations. The most picturesque, if not the most instructive, was that published in *Comoedia* by the facetious journalist Willy, alias the "Ouvreuse." "Yesterday, at the Châtelet," he wrote, "the Philharmonic Society of Vienna (of which all the artists, according to the program, are members of the Imperial and Royal Court Opera), gave its first concert. Large audience, enthusiastic reception, very finished performance. Rather too finished: by his abuse of nuances, his strenuous search for contrasts and his exaggerated polish, a conductor as meticulous as M. Mahler ends up by upsetting his audience who, bewildered by this excess of arabesques, loses track of the general outline of the work thus handled. . . ." In another article, Willy, in the same breezy vein, declared Mahler "overly dexterous" and found "too much skill, too many tricks" in the Beethoven symphony.

The other French critics were fortunately more enlightening as far as Mahler and the concert were concerned. Pierre Lalo, in *Le Temps,* emphasized "the qualities of this orchestra," which clearly distinguished it from most French orchestras. He particularly praised the strings, for "the precision and vigor of their attack, their velvety richness, their powerful or delicate sound and their consummate virtuosity," which was far superior to anything that Paris had ever heard. He preferred the French woodwinds to the "heavier and harsher Viennese instruments."

As far as Mahler's interpretations were concerned, Pierre Lalo found his overture to *Die Meistersinger* very different from Richter's and declared that he had had "some difficulty in discerning the advantages of the change." Mahler's Beethoven he found "supremely unusual, supremely personal and also supremely questionable." His tempos, and particularly the slowness of the opening theme, had been most unusual, and yet it had been this very slowness ("which is becoming more and more customary in Germany") that had given the piece "all its meaning and tragic power." Nevertheless, the Scherzo had seemed "excessively dragged out" and the Finale, with its "constant changes" of tempo, "sacrificed some of its unity and grandeur to these convulsions."

His conclusion was that the defects of German conductors were the opposite of those of French conductors: "whereas we give no thought to the scores of the masters, our neighbors give them far too much. They discover some intention in every note, emphasize every detail and end up by overcomplicating the structure and destroying the plan of a composition . . ." He also regretted that Mahler, "one of the most distinguished composers of the German school," had not included one of his own works in the program.

Mahler's Mozart seems to have particularly bewildered French critics like Gaston Salvayre (*Gil Blas*) and Alfred Bruneau (*Le Figaro*), who compared

it to "those wonderfully fragile and faded miniatures of the past." After this
"exquisite" performance, Bruneau went on, the *"Leonore" Overture No. 3,* "the
major work of the program, both aroused and deserved the greatest and most
wholehearted admiration; its poetry, its vehemence, its sovereign splendor
were expressed in an entirely novel and absolutely superb manner and the
whole constituted a genuine revelation."

In an interview published on June 21 in *Le Soir,* Mahler very tactfully
said that he was delighted with his Parisian success and enthusiastic over
both old and modern French music.[31] The following day this same paper
published an article by a critic named Lomagne, who said he was an
"unconditional admirer" of the Philharmonic's performances, which were
"masterly, flawless, absolutely remarkable for their smoothness, their homo-
geneity, their disciplined power and the delicacy and subtlety of their gradations." Oscar Berggruen, in *Le Ménestrel,* admired Mahler's program,
"thought up with infinite subtlety so as to bring out all the qualities of the
orchestra," as well as the manner in which, in the prelude to *Die Meistersinger,* he had followed "its firm structure, despite the rich and sparkling
colors woven into the polyphonic texture of the piece, which is as amusing
and brilliant as an old gold-threaded Flemish tapestry." From then on the
orchestra "had conquered, together with its conductor, whose gestures are
totally and forcefully sober and who rarely uses his left hand, which remains almost constantly on his hip."

Although, according to Berggruen, the public had been disconcerted by
Mahler's slow tempo and pianissimo in the opening passages of the *"Leonore" Overture,* "his brio and fire thereafter worked wonders and literally
transported it." In the Mozart symphony, "the amateurs were enraptured
by the delicious languor of the strings," while the "grandiose and Promethean
cast" of Beethoven's C minor symphony had been superbly rendered. In
short, despite the sharpness with which it separated each phrase, the audience had admired not only the beauty and power of the orchestra but also
its unity and harmony, and had wholeheartedly accepted several tempos
that differed from those at the conservatory.

Thus in general the reactions of both the public and the press were favorable. On the evening of the nineteenth, also at the Châtelet, the Männergesangverein gave a choral concert under the baton of Richard von
Perger, with the famous tenor Winkelmann as soloist and with Mahler conducting the *Freischütz Overture.* Thanks, no doubt, to the patriotism of
members of the Austrian colony, the audience was much larger than that
of the preceding day.[32] The second half of the concert was to open with
the *Freischütz Overture,* but at the moment when he should have made his
appearance, the president of the Männergesangverein, Franz Schneiderhan,
came out to announce in French that Mahler was indisposed and had asked
for a few moments' grace, during which Perger would conduct Wagner's
*Das Liebesmahl der Apostel.* Overcome either by exhaustion or by the heat,
Mahler had in fact felt sick on reaching the theater[33] and, stretched out on

40. Amalie Joachim, who sang the world premiere of two *Wunderhorn Lieder* in Berlin.

41. Natalie Bauer-Lechner, Mahler's close friend and confidante.

42 & 43. The Steinbach Häuschen where Mahler composed the *Second* and *Third Symphonies*.

44. Program of a Bruckner concert conducted by
Mahler in Hamburg.

**Montag den 12. December 1892, Abends 7¹/₂ Uhr sehr präcise.**

# V. Philharmonisches Concert.

*Dirigent: Raphael Maszkowski*

Mitwirkende: Amalie Joachim, Joseph Slivinski
und der Sängerbund Berliner Lehrerverein.

✦ ✳ ✦

## PROGRAMM.

1. Zweite Sinfonie C dur, Op. 42 (Ocean) . *Rubinstein.*
   1. Moderato assai. — 2. Andante. — 3. Allegro.
   — 4. Adagio. — Allegro con fuoco.

2. Concerto pour le piano avec accompagne-
   ment d'orchestre. Op. 23 . . . . . . *Tschaikowsky.*
   1. Allegro non troppo e molto maestoso. — Allegro
   con spirito. 2. Andantino semplice. — Allegro
   vivace assai 3. Allegro con fuoco. —

3. Rhapsodie (Fragment aus Goethe's Harz-
   reise im Winter) für eine Altstimme,
   Männerchor und Orchester . . . . . *Brahms.*

4. Klaviersoli:
   a) Nocturne . . . . . . . . . *Paderewski.*
   b) Etude F moll . . . . . . . . *Liszt.*

5. Lieder mit Orchester-Begleitung aus
   „Balladen und Humoresken" nach „des
   Knaben Wunderhorn" . . . . . . *Mahler.*
   a) No. 1. Der Schildwache Nachtlied.
   b) No. IV. Verlorne Mühe.

6. Grosse Ouverture zu „Leonore" No. 3 C dur  *Beethoven.*

### Concertflügel Bechstein.

➤ ✳ ◄

## II. Cyclus der Philharmonischen Concerte (1893).

*Dirigent:* **Dr. Hans von Bülow.**

*Solisten:*

| | | | |
|---|---|---|---|
| 9. Januar: | **Theresa d'Albert-Carreño.** | 27. Februar: | **Eugen d'Albert.** |
| 23. „ | **Jean Gérardy** (Cello). | 13. März: | { **Hugo Becker** |
| 6. Februar: | **J. Krasselt** (Violine). | | { **Hans von Bülow.** |

45. Program of a Berlin concert.

Concerthaus Hamburg

(Gebr. Ludwig).

Freitag, den 27. October 1893,

Abends 7½ Uhr präcise:

# Erstes populäres Concert

im philharmonischen Styl,

unter Leitung

des Herrn Capellmeisters **Gustav Mahler** vom hiesigen Stadttheater,

mit gütiger Bewilligung des Herrn Directors Hofrath Pollini,

unter Mitwirkung der

Kgl. Kammersängerin Frau **Clementine Schuch-Prosska** aus Dresden

und des

Kgl. Kammersängers Herrn **Paul Bulss** aus Berlin.

☞ Während der Dauer der Musikstücke bleiben die Saalthüren geschlossen.

46 & 47. Program of Mahler's "popular concert" in Hamburg.

# PROGRAMM.

## I. Abtheilung.

1. **Ouverture** zu „Egmont"................................................. *Beethoven.*
2. **Arie** aus „Hans Heiling"................................................ *Marschner.*
   Gesungen von Herrn Bulss.
3. **Arie** aus: „Die Nürnberger Puppe" ................................ *Adam.*
   Gesungen von Frau Schuch-Prosska.
4. **Ouverture** zu den „Hebriden" (Fingalshöhle) ..................... *Mendelssohn.*
5a. **„Das himmlische Leben",**
   b. **„Verlorene Mühe",** ⎫ drei Humoresken aus: „Des Knaben Wunderhorn" . . *Mahler.*
   c. **„Wer hat dies Liedchen erdacht",** ⎭
   Gesungen von Frau Schuch-Prosska.
6a. **„Der Schildwache Nachtlied"** (eine Scene aus ⎫
   dem Lagerleben der Landsknechte),
   b. **„Trost im Unglück"** (aus dem Leben der ⎬ aus: „Des Knaben Wunderhorn" . . *Mahler.*
   Landsknechte),
   c. **„Rheinlegendchen",** ⎭
   Gesungen von Herrn Bulss.

### Pause von 10 Minuten.

## II. Abtheilung.

7. **„Titan",** eine Tondichtung in Symphonieform (Manuscript)........... *Mahler.*

### 1. Theil.

„Aus den Tagen der Jugend", Blumen-, Frucht- und Dornstücke.

I. **„Frühling und kein Ende"** (Einleitung und Allegro comodo).
   Die Einleitung stellt das Erwachen der Natur aus langem Winterschlafe dar.

II. **„Blumine"** (Andante).

III. **„Mit vollen Segeln"** (Scherzo).

### 2. Theil.

„Commedia humana".

IV. **„Gestrandet!"** (ein Todtenmarsch in „Callot's Manier").
   Zur Erklärung dieses Satzes diene Folgendes: Die äussere Anregung zu diesem Musikstück erhielt
   der Autor durch das in Oesterreich allen Kindern wohlbekannte parodistische Bild: „Des Jägers Leichenbegängniss", aus einem alten Kindermärchenbuch: Die Thiere des Waldes geleiten den Sarg des gestorbenen
   Jägers zu Grabe; Hasen tragen das Fähnlein, voran eine Capelle von böhmischen Musikanten, begleitet von
   musicirenden Katzen, Unken, Krähen etc., und Hirsche, Rehe, Füchse und andere vierbeinige und gefiederte
   Thiere des Waldes geleiten in possirlichen Stellungen den Zug. An dieser Stelle ist dieses Stück als Ausdruck
   einer bald ironisch lustigen, bald unheimlich brütenden Stimmung gedacht, auf welche dann sogleich

V. **„Dall' Inferno"** (Allegro furioso)
   folgt, als der plötzliche Ausbruch der Verzweiflung eines im Tiefsten verwundeten Herzens.

---

Am Freitag, den 10. November 1893, Abends 8 Uhr präcise:

## Zweites populäres Concert im philharmonischen Styl

unter Leitung des Componisten und Capellmeisters Herrn Jean Louis Nicodé aus Dresden.

1. **Ouverture** „Le carneval romain"....................................... *Berlioz.*
2. **Adagio (Cis-moll)** aus der 7. Symphonie ............................. *Bruckner.*
3. **Siegfried-Idyll**....................................................... *Wagner.*
4. **Das Meer,** I. Satz, aus der Symphonie-Ode „Das Meer".................. *Nicodé.*
5. **Symphonie C-moll**..................................................... *Brahms.*

48. Anna von Mildenburg, the great soprano with whom Mahler had an affair in Hamburg.

the concierge's bed, took about twenty minutes to recover. After the *Lie-besmahl*, Schneiderhan addressed a few words of thanks to the audience and, just as people were beginning to think that Mahler would be replaced by his brother-in-law, Rosé, he appeared, looking very pale, and was greeted by thunderous applause that redoubled at the end of the *Freischütz Over-ture*, which, according to Willy,[34] was "brilliantly played."

Completely taken up by receptions and rehearsals, Mahler had little time to see much of Paris itself, but, in any case, the hectic atmosphere of the exposition marred the city's charm for him. He never even got to the Louvre and, despite his desire to avoid receptions, had to attend a huge banquet given by President Loubet at the Hôtel Continental. During his stay he made a new friend in Colonel Picquart, who had taken a much-publicized stand on the Dreyfus trial the year before and whose "forceful personality and integrity" immediately attracted him. Picquart, together with Paul Clemenceau, was to become one of his most faithful friends and fervent admirers.

As far as the biggest operatic hits in Paris were concerned, Mahler felt there was no point in his going to hear Charpentier's *Louise*, since he had already studied its score,[35] but he did go to the Opéra Comique to hear Erlanger's *Le Juif polonais*, which he had discussed with Lilli Lehmann by letter the previous spring. According to Karpath, who accompanied him, it immediately aroused his interest, possibly because the bell effects in it re-minded him of those in his own *Fourth Symphony*.[36] In any case, he pre-sented the work to the Viennese six years later.

The concert given by the Männergesangverein drew a larger audience than that given by the Philharmonic at the Châtelet, but merely because the committee had again resorted to handing out complimentary tickets. More-over, since the sale of tickets for the final concerts, which were to take place in the immense auditorium of the Trocadéro, was also negligible, some-thing had to be done to remedy the situation, for the guarantee fund was almost exhausted, and it was quite obvious that there was not going to be enough money left to pay for the return journey. Mahler and Arnold Rosé discussed matters with Karpath one evening at the Café Poucet. In the middle of the conversation, Mahler suddenly blurted out in a loud voice, "And I tell you, there's no art but German art!" This outburst having at-tracted the attention of the entire café, Karpath and Rosé hurriedly paid the bill and hustled him out.

The situation was becoming increasingly serious, for the musicians were beginning to be anxious and to inveigh against the members of the com-mittee who had dragged them into this adventure. The members, in dismay, appealed to Princess Metternich for help, but she replied that there was nothing she could do. Learning that the head of the Rothschild Bank, Baron Albert, was in Paris, Mahler asked her to appeal to him, but this she re-fused to do, since she was obliged to ask him for so much money each year for her good works that she felt sure she would meet with a refusal to which she did not wish to expose herself. So, on the day of the final concert, Mahler himself went to see the great financier. The latter immediately offered to advance him the four thousand crowns he contributed annually to the Philharmonic Orchestra, but Mahler was forced to tell him that what they needed was twenty thousand francs in order to be able to pay their journey home. Rothschild was a cold man and little interested in music. He made it quite clear that he felt he had done his patriotic duty by giving four thousand crowns and asked who on earth had encouraged the orchestra to undertake so foolhardy a venture. Mahler in turn pointed out that this was no time for futile arguments and said that, if Baron Albert found it impossible to pay the sum, he would be obliged to pay it himself, which would mean the sacrifice of all his savings. He finally extorted from Rothschild the promise that his secretary would deliver the sum at the Trocadéro that afternoon. While the musicians were tuning up before the concert, the secretary of the committee, Simandl, announced that, thanks to Mahler's intervention, Baron Albert had put up the money for their return journey. They all cheered Mahler and invited him to dine with them that evening.

Meanwhile, the enthusiastic articles in the French press had fortunately borne fruit and more people came to the final concerts. A Parisian impresario even offered the committee an advance of twenty thousand francs for five more concerts. The Viennese, however, decided to refuse, since they were tired of both the stifling atmosphere of the exposition and the atrocious hall of the Trocadéro, in which the last two concerts took place. With its grubby flags, its Oriental decoration, its 4500 seats, and its abominable acoustics, it was an appalling setting for music. Mahler had tried to improve it by changing the placing of the orchestra, but, even so, most of the nuances and subtleties of his interpretations were lost because the strings were almost inaudible and the brasses, according to Oscar Berggruen, were disproportionally loud.

The program of the concert of June 20, which included Beethoven's *Egmont Overture,* the *Prelude* and *Liebestod* from *Tristan und Isolde,* and Beethoven's *Romance,* played by Arnold Rosé, ended with Berlioz's *Symphonie fantastique* as a tribute to France. The overture was warmly applauded, and the excerpts from *Tristan* were given an enthusiastic hearing. As for the *Symphonie fantastique,* despite the fact that it was the war horse of Parisian orchestras, Mahler's interpretation of it was considered "brilliant," and he was recalled no less than twelve times by an ecstatic audience, while someone presented him with a laurel wreath on behalf of the Société Maternelle, for whose benefit he had conducted the evening before.

For its final concert the following day, the Philharmonic treated the Parisians to two Viennese works they had not yet heard, Karl Goldmark's overture *Im Frühling* and the Scherzo from Bruckner's *Romantic Symphony.* Oscar Berggruen, in *Le Ménestrel,* had warm praise for both, and particularly for the latter, which had manifested "the joyful serenity of Haydn" combined "with all the orchestral refinements of Berlioz and Wagner." In addition to these two pieces, the program consisted of Beethoven's *"Eroica"* *Symphony,* Schubert's *Unfinished Symphony,* and the Overture to *Tannhäuser,* which the audience applauded with shouts of "Hurrah for the orchestra! Hurrah for Mahler! *Au revoir!"*[37] Berggruen deplored the fact that the wretched acoustics had not only prevented the ten double basses from "delivering their beautiful phrases with the desired intensity" at the beginning of the *Unfinished Symphony,* but also rendered the distinctive accompaniment of the violins practically inaudible above the brasses playing the pilgrims' theme in the Overture to *Tannhäuser.*

Although it had drawn an audience of about four thousand people, including such musicians as Charles de Curzon, Emile Paladilhe, Saint-Saëns, Gustave Charpentier, and Charles Malherbe, and although almost all the best seats had been sold, this third and last concert was virtually ignored by the press, which had only been really interested in the first concert. Willy again accused Mahler of being "too slick" and too cold and of having "conducted Wagner as though he had never heard his prodigious predecessor, Hans Richter." The prelude from *Tristan* had been "distressing because of a certain inexplicable and to be quite honest, even rather unintelligent coldness here and there, alternating with superbly rendered passages." *L'Ouvreuse* peevishly complained that Mahler had "illuminated that which should remain obscure," in other words, that he had "shown his suspenders . . . As for the *Eroica,* thus chopped up it was unacceptable. True, there was a large audience in the hall, but Beethoven was absent." In Willy's opinion, it was too easy "to have eight horns blow certain themes written for one or two." Instead of being "a gay sylvan fanfare, the Trio of the Scherzo sniveled gloomily." Willy did admit, however, that his disappointment had been largely due to the acoustics of the Trocadéro, for "even God's musicians, the angels, archangels *ac beata seraphim,* would be incapable of producing any effect there." He concluded with a final tribute to the "Kappellmeister, who sometimes beats time, frequently beats the nuance, but never beats about the bush" (translator's note: an untranslatable French pun: *qui bat parfois la mesure, souvent la nuance et jamais la campagne; battre la campagne,* meaning both to wander [in one's mind] and to scour the countryside).

At Karpath's instigation, Catulle Mendès, one of the leading critics of the time, summed up his impression of the concerts in the following letter to the editor in chief of the *Neues Wiener Tagblatt,* published on June 22.[38] "With its strikingly perfect discipline and its rare, alternately powerful or delicate, sonorous opulence, M. Mahler's orchestra won us over immediately. The strings vibrate in glorious unison, whether their tones be thrillingly strident or languishing; the woodwinds, of which there seem to me to be a greater number than in most orchestras, achieve exceptional accuracy in their plaintive tone, as though only one man gradated their sonority, while the brasses, when required to do so, crash and glitter like thunder and lightning.

"As to the spirit in which the works were performed, and which was that of the 'Kapellmeister,' many people found it truly inspiring, whereas others were surprised, particularly in Mozart's *Symphony in G Minor,* by certain *rallentandi,* a somewhat excessively subtle gradation and the overly harsh contrast between *pianissimi* and *fortissimi* . . .

"There is no one to equal Gustav Mahler in the simplicity of his deportment and the sobriety of his gestures, which can suddenly become magnificently impetuous. Everything about him reveals a headstrong and highly strung personality, while his approach to a work and manner of conducting are at once stately and familiar. His interpretation of the overture to *Die Meistersinger* showed fine feeling, both for the structure of the principal themes and in the way he emphasized them (even Richter could not have done better); that of *Der Freischütz* was infinitely poetic and that of *Oberon* ineffably dainty, airy and, one might almost say, fairylike."

All things considered, the four concerts gave Mahler precious little satisfaction. Although the takings of the last one amounted to twelve thousand francs, which fortunately reduced the deficit, he came away with the impression that Paris, like Vienna, considered his interpretations of Beethoven "anticlassical." He commented bitterly on the subject, noting that his interpretations of classical works "shock both public and musicians as much as do my own compositions. Everyone talks about 'subtle nuances' and 'arbitrary alterations' because the difference between the real work, in the way I present it, and the cold and empty performance to which they're accustomed, is like the difference between a tree in bloom and the bare branches of a tree in winter."[39] Such were the grievances he aired to Natalie upon his arrival at Maiernigg. Karpath quoted others in the *Neues Wiener Tagblatt;* according to him, Mahler deplored the fact that the French press had said so little about the concerts and that what it did say was thoroughly superficial.[40] He and his musicians had not felt at home amid the tumult of the exposition, but they had at least been gratified by "the enthusiasm of the true friends of art."

On the eve of their departure from Paris, Mahler dined with the musicians of the orchestra at the Buffet Rapp, where they were all staying. They cheered him loudly on his arrival, and the evening constituted one of the few relaxed and pleasant moments of his three years' work with them, as also one of the rare satisfactions of the trip, which had won him nothing but the hearts and admiration of a few French music lovers. Having thus spent ten days of his impatiently awaited and hard-won holidays working in Paris, he joyfully and eagerly set out for home and an immense happiness denied him for four years: a *Häuschen* isolated in the woods, in which he fervently hoped to finish his *Fourth Symphony.*

He reached Maiernigg on June 23 and immediately dashed off to the *Häuschen,* situated some twenty minutes' walk away from the Villa Antonia, which he had rented for the summer. He threaded his way along a narrow footpath that twisted and turned through "all the marvels and terrors of the forest" and, as he closed the *Häuschen*'s two latticed doors behind him, finally savored a far greater "peace, security and Dionysiac wonder" than in his beloved little cabin at Steinbach, for here he was going to be able to work with the window open and breathe the pure forest air, instead of having to seal everything hermetically to keep out the noise.

He was so delighted he at once decided to have his breakfast there every day, come rain or shine, and brushed aside all Justi's objections to the inaccessibility of the place. Despite this delight, and contrary to his habit, he found it difficult to reimmerse himself in his work, which had been interrupted in such painful circumstances. He kept remembering his anguish of the preceding autumn, when he had feared that by the time he had a *Häuschen* he might have nothing more to write. However, this period of temporary sterility, such as he had experienced on other occasions,[41] was probably largely due to physical exhaustion and perhaps also to the fact that he may have found it more difficult to resume half-finished works than to begin an entirely new work.

After about ten days Natalie and Justi, noticing that he had become more silent and remained in his *Häuschen* for up to eight or ten hours at a stretch, concluded that he had begun composing again. This was indeed the case and, although July 7 marked his fortieth birthday, he decided to put off its celebration for a month in the hope that by then his work would be almost completed. Returning from Klagenfurt with Natalie on his birthday, he sadly reflected that Mozart and Schubert had composed legion works and died before they had even reached forty! "The time I've lost! Until I went to Steinbach, I didn't know how to provide myself, during the little time at my disposal, with the peace and solitude I need. And to think that I almost gave up composing for that reason! Now, during these few short weeks, I have to work every moment of the day, even when I'm weary and out of sorts, merely in order to get finished. And my work must inevitably suffer from the strain."[42]

Despite his hard work, Mahler occasionally found time for an excursion, such as that of July 12, when he bicycled to Viktring. Along the way, he noticed a beetle and carefully avoided it because he was "becoming increasingly conscious of the individuality" of such an insect "whose life must be respected just as the life of men, which appears to hang on the protection of higher beings, including Earth, who is certainly one of them."[43] During his holiday he also perused Schubert's chamber music. This time, however, the majority of his great predecessor's works failed to please him; he only found four of the twelve entirely satisfactory and, likewise, only eighty of Schubert's eight hundred lieder "consummately beautiful." Admittedly, that was more than enough, but he wished that Schubert had composed fewer lesser works that enabled certain people to deny his talent. He decided that this inequality stemmed from the fact that Schubert's technique was weak in comparison to his intense feelings and fertile imagination. In particular, the organization of his development was too simple, the sequences moved through various keys without any true thematic elaboration, so that, in certain cases, one could leave out half of a piece without damaging the whole.

In this connection, Mahler formulated an aesthetic rule that was increasingly to govern his later works: "Every repetition is in itself a lie. Like life, a work of art must constantly progress on pain of becoming insincere and histrionic. Yet Schubert's melody, like that of Beethoven and Wagner, belongs to eternity; therefore, the formalism that constituted the solid and logical base of Mozart's and Haydn's works was of no help to him. And the reason why, shortly before his death, Schubert wanted to take up counterpoint was because he realized what he lacked . . ." Mahler was particularly well able to appreciate this, since he also lacked a thorough grounding in counterpoint. His intelligence usually helped him to overcome this lacuna, but at the cost of double the effort.[44]

As well as perusing Schubert, Mahler began to reread E. T. A. Hoffmann, who, in his opinion, "wrote more intelligently about music than anyone else" and, with incomparable shrewdness, found the words that best suited it. On the other hand, he considered Hoffmann's music more or less negligible, including his opera *Undine,* which he found clumsy and defective; one could see what he had intended and one was bound to admire the quality of his imagination, but his technique was definitely too coarse. Mahler in turn felt incapable of expressing his feelings in poetry, because his literary endowments were defective and clumsy in comparison to his musical skill.

His work and the brevity of his holiday notwithstanding, he even managed to devour the dramas of his friend Siegfried Lipiner, to whom he wrote three long letters full of comments, counsel, and encouragement, particularly after reading *Hippolytos,* which Lipiner had most recently sent him. Judging by these letters, his profound and even fanatical admiration for Lipiner's prolix writing had not diminished.[45]

When he finally began composing again, Mahler realized that a "second me" had been active during the long sleep of the conscious "me," pursuing and maturing the latter's work. He was amazed to discover that the *Fourth Symphony* was far nearer completion than when he had abandoned it the preceding year at Aussee, even though he had never had it consciously in mind. Perhaps his thoughts had flown to it during the many sad and troubled moments of the past year; or perhaps the "unconscious me," refusing to have anything to do with his surface life, had retired into the innermost recess of his soul, there to lead a purer and loftier life. Most people, he decided, never discover this "second me" because they "flee it and kill it by social contact. They don't realize that their salvation lies in solitude, where it instantly appears and goes to work."[46]

Despite its total isolation and the happiness he found in it, his *Häuschen* did not afford Mahler the peace and quiet he both desired and needed. It was in vain that he put up scarecrows and fired off blank shots, the birds still bothered him[47]; the barking of the architect Theuer's dog bothered him, and the barrel organs and military bands on the lake bothered him. Now and again, as at Steinbach, the summer visitors paid wandering musicians to go and disturb him, for they had soon discovered his phobia about noise and the precautions he took to prevent it. His idiosyncrasy and "semimadness" became the joke of the neighborhood. "A creator is like a fly out of season and, like the fly, droops his wings," Mahler moaned, as he again bewailed the barbarity surrounding a man and which he cannot escape, because it never occurs to most of his fellow men to respect his freedom, preoccupied as they are with satisfying their own childish whims, like tearing apart flowers and killing animals. He began to envy the deaf and the blind who were cut off from this miserable world, and to understand why a musician could go so far as to deprive himself of hearing as Democritus had blinded himself.

Completely absorbed in his work, he at last began to talk about his *Fourth Symphony,* of which he had composed "about half of each movement" the year before. "You can imagine what I felt like," he said to Natalie, "when I had to interrupt my work and leave Aussee, for I was sure it would be quite impossible to take it up again. And indeed it has meant a gigantic effort. I made a package of all the sketches, which are undecipherable by anyone but me, put it in the bottom drawer of my desk and haven't been able to think of it since without experiencing the most excruciating anguish."[48]

The *Fourth Symphony* was to be in G major and was to last forty-five minutes, that is, as long as only the first movement of the *Third.* He had first conceived it as "a symphonic humoresque" but later developed it into a symphony of normal length rather than of double or triple the normal length like his earlier symphonies, which he had in fact initially intended to be of the usual dimensions. *"Das himmlische Leben,"* the lied originally destined for his *Third Symphony,* was to form its Finale, and he had already named it the "tapering spire of the edifice."[49] "What I had in mind," he said, "was extremely hard to achieve; the uniform blue of the sky being much more difficult to render than all its changing and contrasting hues. Well, that's the general atmosphere of the piece. Occasionally, however, it darkens and becomes phantasmagorical and terrifying: not that the sky becomes overcast, for the sun continues to shine eternally, but that one suddenly takes fright; just as on the most beautiful day in a sunlit forest, one can be seized with terror or panic. Mysterious, intricate and sinister, the Scherzo will make your hair stand on end, but it will be followed by the Adagio, which puts everything right again and shows that no harm was intended." He added that only the Scherzo recalled one of his earlier works, that of the *Second Symphony,* but that he had "introduced new elements into the old framework."

Despite its uniformity the work was tremendously lively from beginning to end. In fact, Mahler thought he had never before made quite as much use of polyphony. "The thousand little pieces of mosaic that make up the picture are shaken up and it becomes unrecognizable, as in a kaleidoscope, as though a rainbow suddenly disintegrated into millions of dancing drops so that the whole edifice seems to vacilliate and dissolve." This was especially true of the Andante, which he regarded as the best movement and in which he had composed his "first real and fully developed variations . . . A divinely joyful and profoundly sad melody pervades it throughout, so that you'll at once laugh and cry . . . This movement also contains the features of St. Ursula," one of the saints of the *Himmlische Leben,* of whose legend he was totally ignorant. St. Ursula's smile, which the Andante purported to express, had become identified here and there with "my mother's infinitely sad face, as though she were laughing through her tears, for she too, in spite of her immense sufferings, always lovingly resolved and pardoned all things." Contrary to what he had done with his *Third Symphony,* Mahler would not hear of giving any titles to his new work, even though he had "devised some marvelous ones," for he had no wish to "divulge them to stupid critics and audiences who would again misunderstand and distort them in the worst possible way."

In the slow movement, which he called alternately Andante and Adagio, he felt he had achieved "the most complex mixtures of colors ever produced." The decrescendo at the end, "music of the spheres" (*sphärisch*), had an "almost religious and Catholic atmosphere . . . Neither in this movement nor anywhere else in the symphony, in keeping with its subject, will there be a single fortissimo and those who accuse me of always having recourse to grandiose means will be astonished: in the entire *Fourth,* there are no trombones." In fact, he could have done with them in a few bars at the end of the Adagio, but decided it was not worth while for so few notes.

More than ever before, Mahler did not search for originality, either in his style or his instrumentation, and, if he sometimes achieved it, it was certainly unintentionally: "At one time I liked all that was striking in my works," he had declared the previous summer to Natalie. "Everything that broke away, even if only in appearance, from tradition. In the same way, a young man eagerly draws attention to himself by the way he dresses; but later on, when he no longer thinks about being different from others, he has in truth become more deeply, more essentially different than ever. Today I am quite content to pour my message [*meinen Inhalt giessen*] into traditional molds; I carefully avoid all unnecessary innovations. At one time I used to force myself to end in A flat minor a piece that began in D. Today, on the other hand, I go to a great deal of trouble to end in the original key."[50] Going over his first movement again, Mahler noticed two reminiscences that he had let creep in, the first from one of Brahms's symphonies, and which Brahms himself had "purloined from Weber," and the second from one of Beethoven's piano concertos.[51]

Despite its apparent unconventionality this movement was constructed "in accordance with the academic rules of form." Moreover, the entire work was "artistically the most finished" he had yet composed. In any case, he felt that he had at last reached the peak of his technical skill and would henceforth be able to compose exactly what he wanted to.

During a bicycle ride with Natalie, he again talked about the first movement, which "begins as if it didn't know how to count up to three, but then it suddenly starts to multiply on a grand scale and ends up by calculating in dizzying millions." He called the short fanfare of the development a "little summons" (*kleiner Appell*), in contrast to the "great summons" in the Finale of the *Second Symphony*. "Just when the confusion is at its height and the stampeding of the initially disciplined troops has surpassed all limits, a command from the general instantly restores law and order."[52]

Mahler realized that his *Fourth Symphony* was closely related to his first three, and, as it were, completed them so that the four together formed a veritable tetralogy. The affinity between the *Fourth* and *Third* was particularly marked, since the two had themes in common, an occurrence so odd and unusual that he himself was disturbed by it. Wonderstruck at the world of sound in which he was now living more happily than ever, he told Natalie yet again that music seemed to him to be vastly superior to poetry because it could say everything. Thanks to a modulation or an interrupted cadence, it was able to express and elucidate that which could be neither described nor even hinted at in the other arts. "Our modern Impressionist poets would love to be able to express a given atmosphere or impression, but, aside from the fact that they're bunglers, they'll never be able to do so with mere words."[53]

As the month of July flowed past, he derived increasing pleasure from the climate, atmosphere, and scenery of Maiernigg. The house was growing steadily down by the lake, and he had been making secret wagers as to which would be completed first, it or the symphony. At the beginning of the summer, he had despairingly noted the rapidity with which the work on the house was progressing, but he had soon caught up with it, and the symphony was now nearing completion, whereas the house would not be ready until the end of the summer.[54] For the first time, he had not worn himself out by "ceaseless combat with adverse spirits who absorb more nervous energy than my work," nor had he ever enjoyed composing as much as he did here.

His many walks through the "mysterious labyrinths of the forest bordering the lake, which lure one into the unknown," constituted almost his only moments of rest and relaxation. He had feared he would be bored at Maiernigg because its few good roads were crowded with people. However, he discovered that there were numerous footpaths unknown to the *Maiernigg Kuh-Gästen* (a play on the words *Kur-Gästen*—guests taking the cure; *Kuh*—cow), where one could roam without meeting a soul. Moreover, he felt as though this wonderful world of mountains and forests was his "private property" where he was free to seek rest and inspiration. He often went down to the lake to inspect the work on his house and spent long hours watching the workmen or revising its design.

Nevertheless, he continued to be haunted by the fear that his holiday would come to an end before he had finished his work. Thus, when Lipiner sent him another new play, called *Adam,* which he was afraid he would not have time to read (or perhaps he was beginning to be aware of the literary faults of his childhood friend), he began to inveigh against the "damned opera" and the slavery that every fiber of his being resisted, especially when he thought of it at Maiernigg, in the "pure kingdom of my own activity." Ideas came so spontaneously when he could work for himself that even an entire year hardly seemed long enough to take advantage of them.

In between the various stages of composition, he undertook a few lengthier excursions. On July 15 he went on a solitary tour of the valley of Ampezzo, precisely in order to get away from his work and be able "to judge it from a distance." On the way he was stopped by the police, who, seeing him with a two-day beard, an open shirt, no jacket, no suspenders, and no belt, mistook him for a vagrant. He returned, a sunburned tramp, on July 19 and gleefully recounted the incident.

He had walked and bicycled for four days without addressing a word to anyone. Several Viennese had recognized him but had fortunately not dared to speak to him, for "I looked so furious whenever someone came up to me that they went away immediately and left me in peace."[55]

As always, nature was to Mahler a "profound and impenetrable" reality that "people always regard as something superficial. This is only true of its external aspects, but they who have not trembled in the face of its eternal and divine mystery can neither understand nor penetrate it; the most they can do is guess at it. In fact there's a story in the *Edda* which offers a good example of what I mean; the one in which the giants pour the sea into the drinking horn of the biggest drinker of them all, who has boasted that he can drain any amount. He drinks and drinks until he's exhausted and then suddenly realizes he's been had and throws his horn away. The sea is of course infinite and every work of art must contain a trace of this infinity if it's to be an image of nature. That which moves in a work of art is precisely that which is mysterious and unfathomable. Any work of art that can be taken in at a glance loses its magic and its power of attraction, in the same way as the most beautiful of parks seems boring once one knows all its paths."

A few days after his return from Ampezzo, Mahler told his family he had had to alter a certain passage in his symphony for reasons of musical logic and that, having altered it, he had, to his amazement, found himself in a new region as though, in the middle of a walk through the flowering Fields of Elysium, he had suddenly been transported to the icy gloom of Tartarus. There were times when his music seemed to contain, as it were, emanations from a mysterious world; this time, it was the at once magnificent and terrifying forest that had inspired him and insinuated itself into his symphony. "I'm coming increasingly to realize," he concluded, "that it's not man who composes but man who is being composed [*man wird komponiert*]."⁵⁶

Toward the end of July, when his symphony was almost finished, he remembered how, only a month before, he had laboriously toiled and moiled, fearing all the while that his work would reflect his mental distress, until it had dawned on him that he had never, since Steinbach days, worked with so much joy and exhilaration. Perhaps after all, he reflected, it was not necessary that a work "should gush forth spontaneously from a mood like lava erupting from a volcano." Sound technique, "that true art which is always at the disposal of him who possesses it and which overcomes all difficulties, including his own discomfort," should be able to take the place of inspiration.

When, on August 5, he announced the completion of his symphony, he as usual did so sadly, for he suddenly felt "empty and depressed because life has lost all meaning." Fortunately Wondra, one of the chief officials at the Vienna Opera, arrived to discuss the repertoire of the coming season with him, and they took long walks together. During one of these the sound of a barrel organ, which delighted Wondra, upset Mahler considerably. However, when a second barrel organ struck up and threatened to drown out the first, he began to enjoy himself, whereas Wondra became exasperated. A military band soon joined in the fun, whereat Wondra covered up his ears in despair while Mahler stood listening in ecstasy, as though rooted to the spot.

Recounting this incident to Rosé, Mahler added that his reaction should not surprise anyone who liked his symphonies. Thereafter, he often returned to the same spot to hear distant melodies, military bands, and male choruses mingle with the noise of merry-go-rounds, shooting booths, and puppet shows, which came across the lake with prodigious clarity. "There's polyphony for you!" he exclaimed, as he evoked childhood memories of the forest of Iglau.⁵⁷ "It's precisely thus that themes should come from different directions, with distinct rhythms and melodies, in music, except that in the latter the artist must adapt, order, and unite them into a harmonious whole."

Before returning to Vienna, Mahler wanted to free himself of his companions, and so, on August 10, he decided, map in hand, to bicycle to Velden via the Loiblpass. Having started out on the wrong road, he noticed, just as he thought he was about to reach his goal, that he still had almost a thousand meters to climb before reaching the road down to Velden on the other side of the pass. Worn out, he paid a young boy a florin to push his bicycle to the top of the pass while he took a short cut. Just before reaching the top, he took the wrong way again and, rather than retrace his steps, scrabbled up a rocky slope and landed in a, fortunately dry, discharge ditch whose entirely smooth and almost vertical masonry walls offered no hold. In the end, he discovered a section of the wall that had begun to crumble and, grabbing hold of some ferns which he feared might give way under his weight, he painfully hoisted himself up onto the road. When the boy, who had been waiting a long time for him, saw him appear from the wrong direction, soaked in sweat and with his hands and feet torn by the rocks and brambles, he stared in amazement as though he were seeing an apparition. And in fact it took over a week for the cuts and scratches to heal.

Such excursions worried Justi, not only because of her brother's imprudence and absent-mindedness, but also because he always lost practically everything he took with him, this time his bicycle bag containing his linen and all his belongings. Moreover, people took advantage of him and caused him to spend all the money he had with him so that he invariably returned penniless. Yet these solitary expeditions were a source of infinite pleasure and relaxation to the unhappy composer chained to a civil servant's office and obliged, year after year, to face a new season as exhausting as the one before.

"The spirit . . . can assert
itself only through the medium of
clear form."

# CHAPTER 33

*Mahler in Vienna (IX)—Quarrel with the Bühnen-
verein—Triumph of the* Second Symphony *in Munich
—Failure of the* First *in Vienna—Beginning of the
Third Season of the Philharmonic (August–December
1900)*

The manuscript of the *Fourth Symphony* ends with the words: "The third
movement, and with it the entire symphony, completed on Sunday August 6, at Maiernigg."[1] Mahler in fact put some finishing touches to the
orchestration and recopied the score during the winter, but the bulk of his
work was indeed completed. And, although he felt somewhat depressed at
having thus lost his *raison de vivre,* he was nevertheless happy and relieved
at having found his bearings as a composer again after four years of silence.
Thanks to the extra two weeks' holiday he had obtained for the opera the
year before, he only returned to Vienna on August 15, leaving Natalie and
Justi to supervise the work on the house for another six weeks.

During the first weeks of the season, he devoted all his energies to a new
production of Mozart's *Così fan tutte,* which he had been contemplating for
three years. Indeed, in 1897, he had corresponded with Hermann Levi, a
friend of Wagner's who had conducted the premiere of *Parsifal* and was
then conductor at the Munich Opera, on Levi's new version of *Così fan
tutte.* The opera had practically disappeared from the repertoire during the
nineteenth century, because Lorenzo da Ponte's pessimistic and frivolous humor shocked the moralistic bourgeois sentiments of the romantic era. Various people had attempted to correct the "platitude" of the original text and
align it with current taste. In Ludwig Schneider's "version," performed in
Vienna ten years before, the two heroines, let in on the plot by Despina
from the start, played the entire opera as a joke. In another, given at Stutt-

gart in 1858, the laws of morality were met in a slightly different way, namely by having them courted by their own fiancés.

In his letters to Mahler, Levi had advised him, in order to maintain the continuity of the performance, to have the sets brought in from the wings, as was done during the baroque period. However, Mahler was evidently dissatisfied with this solution, for, upon hearing, after Levi's death, of the revolving stage, a revolutionary procedure invented by Moritz Lautenschläger for plays by Goethe and Shakespeare and later taken over by the Bavarian Opera for *Così fan tutte,* he went to Munich in September 1900 and immediately decided to adopt it for the Vienna production, the premiere of which was to be given on October 4 in honor of the Emperor's birthday.

Levi's version had the singular merit of remaining almost wholly faithful to the original, and his German translation was, moreover, of a high literary standard. Mahler cut a few arias in the second act in order to speed up the action, restored the *recitativi secchi,* which he himself accompanied at the keyboard,[2] and reduced the size of the orchestra. He also introduced the Finale of a *Divertimento* (K. 287) at the beginning of the second act (which normally begins with a recitative) and, as Wagner had done in his version of Gluck's *Iphigénie en Aulide,* added a few melodies during the scene changes.

The large revolving stage—about fifty feet in diameter, eighty-five in circumference, and divided into six sections—worked to perfection[3] and, for once, both public and press were unanimous in their praise of the entire performance.[4] However, Vienna was not yet ready to appreciate *Così;* it left the repertoire after seven performances and was not revived again until 1906.

The only "novelty" presented at the end of the year 1900 was the Austrian composer Joseph Reiter's[5] one-act opera *Der Bundschuh.* Reiter had made his debut as a lyric composer with this "national" opera, which was first performed at Troppau in 1894, and it was out of diplomatic necessity and as a concession to Germanic nationalism that Mahler was obliged to give it its Vienna premiere. Max Morold's libretto dealt with a particularly "German" episode of the sixteenth-century Peasants' War, the love affair of a young Evangelistic peasant, Hans Fuchs, and a young chatelaine, Ehrengard, and their death as a result of the struggle between their respective classes. Although Reiter's music seems to have been about as insubstantial as the libretto.[6] Mahler, as always, threw himself heart and soul into the undertaking, witness the letter he wrote to Reiter during the final rehearsals[7] to draw his attention to the musical and stage directions that were incompatible with dramatic verisimilitude. He also suggested making a few slight changes in the text, for instance, *"Wehrlos' Weib"* (defenseless woman) instead of *"Zartes Weib"* (tender woman), since it would be more in keeping with Mildenburg's "powerful physique," but ended his letter with the words: "I trust that I have convinced you as to these points; however, out of respect for the author's wishes, I am prepared to bow to them if you insist."

*Der Bundschuh* was no great success and was performed only five times. However, there is no doubt that the production was first rate, as both the composer and the librettist wrote to Mahler the day after the premiere to express their delight and their gratitude for "the perfection of every touch and every dramatic and musical detail, as well as the excellence of the casting down to the smallest roles."

The critics were generally unenthusiastic.[8] Kalbeck called the opera "a belated offshoot of the sanguinary tradition of Italian drama," despite the "intensely patriotic spirit" manifest in the subject and its treatment. He found its dramatic qualities meager, its orchestration too heavy, and the composer's predilection for "folklorism" excessive.

In the autumn of 1900, Mahler had urgently to solve a major problem that had been hanging over him for several years, that of finally finding assistant conductors who could take over some of his responsibilities. True, Franz Schalk had replaced Richter in May,[9] and, even though he was not consistently inspired, Mahler could confidently entrust him with part of the repertory, but Fuchs had still not been replaced, and his own work load thus remained crushing. In a letter written in September, Leo Blech assured him that, this time, no contract in the world would prevent him from complying with his request and promised to do his best to free himself from his five-year contract with Neumann at the Prague Opera. Considering the latter's high regard for Mahler, he felt sure he would succeed. Blech went on to complain of the all too numerous "deficiencies" he saw around him that "drain the energies that I would prefer to devote to more noble ends . . . Every artistic success is a bitter struggle from which I almost always emerge victorious, but it's a Pyrrhic victory," he added.

It was a letter that so closely resembled those Mahler himself had written when he was young that it could not fail to move him. Moreover, Humperdinck having warmly recommended Blech, Mahler wrote to propose "that you replace X at the Hofoper. Tell me quite plainly whether or not you are able and willing to be and become the man I need. Without vulgar conceit and bearing in mind the brilliant future awaiting you here, give me a yea and the job is yours. You will start with a salary of 20,000 florins which will gradually increase with time."

Neumann did not consent to part with his closest collaborator, and Blech's contract evidently proved indissoluble, for Mahler again offered the post to Bruno Walter, begging him to consider the "brilliant future" that was in store for him in Vienna and ending with the urgent request that he "reply as quickly as possible, since I myself have to find a solution sooner than I'd expected."[10] This time Walter overcame his scruples and doubts. He tore off to Vienna the moment he was released from his Berlin contract, and made his debut at the Hofoper in the autumn of 1901.

Toward the end of October, it was rumored that Intendant Plappart was about to resign. The *Neues Wiener Tagblatt* of November 3, while admitting that there had already been talk of this resignation twice before, asserted that this latest rumor came from the most reliable sources. Moreover, since Prince Montenuovo had virtually taken over the administration of the opera, the role of the intendant had in any case been reduced to a bare minimum, the paper said. At all events, Mahler was undoubtedly thankful, for he was once more at loggerheads with the intendant as the result of a much bigger bone of contention between the directors of the Vienna and Munich Operas and the Deutscher Bühnenverein (Association of German Theaters), whose president was none other than Count Hochberg, composer of the immortal *Wärwolf*.

The intendance of the Munich theater had complained to the Bühnenverein about offers made to Munich actors by Paul Schlenther, the director of the Burgtheater in Vienna. A few months later, Mahler had made a proposition to a singer at the Munich Opera, Josef Geis, and had even sent him a contract, which was "to become effective upon the arrival of the singer in Vienna, in the event that he has legally succeeded in freeing himself from his present obligations." However, one of the fundamental rules of the Deutscher Bühnenverein stipulated that its agents and impresarios would automatically be excluded from the Verein if they endeavored, with tempting offers, to entice singers from a member theater. As a result of Mahler's offer, the Munich intendant, Ernst von Possart, had been obliged to raise Geis's salary in order to keep him and had complained about it to Hochberg. The latter had in turn written to Prince Montenuovo to denounce this procedure and demand that the Vienna Opera apologize to the Munich Opera.

Hochberg's letter had hardly reached Vienna before a Munich paper reported that, while in Munich to conduct his *Second Symphony,* Mahler had made similar offers to several other singers at the opera.[11] Possart had run into him in the foyer of the Munich Opera and had informed him of his intention to submit the case to the Bühnenverein. Mahler had retorted that if the Bühnenverein censured him, he and Schlenther, his colleague at the Burgtheater, would quit the association and thus be free to engage whomsoever they pleased.

Such a decision was in no wise within Mahler's competence, and Plappart consequently summoned him to explain his conduct. Mahler did so in a long letter stating that he had sent Geis the draft contract because the latter had not only expressed his desire to be engaged in Vienna, but also felt certain he would obtain the annulment of his Munich contract. However, Geis had used the offer merely as a means to put pressure on Possart, who had promptly confiscated the contract in order to send it to Count Hochberg, a proceeding which had "dumfounded" Mahler.

As to his encounter with Possart, he added, it had indeed taken place at the end of October. Knowing nothing of the precious rule, he was unaware of having committed the slightest infraction, especially as the draft stipulated as a preliminary condition the "legal" dissolution of the singer's Munich contract. Besides which, rival theaters constantly tried to allure members of the Vienna Opera by far less fair means. However, when he had said that it might eventually be a good thing if the Vienna Opera left the Bühnenverein, Possart had replied that he had frequently thought of doing so himself. Both had been expressing purely personal opinions, and he failed to understand why this private conversation had been reported in a newspaper. In fact, Mahler undoubtedly realized that, furious at having had to increase Geis's salary, Possart had deliberately done him another ill turn.

Obliged to support his director, Plappart answered Hochberg that the rule in question was designed to protect the little theaters rather than the royal theaters, but that he would nevertheless instruct his two directors to see to it that such an incident did not recur. He subsequently sent both Mahler and Schlenther a stiff note reminding them of the numerous complaints recently lodged by the Bühnenverein and demanding that they henceforth refrain from offering contracts without his agreement. He specified, however, that he was not referring to "preliminary discussions" but to definite offers, for which the rules required them to obtain beforehand the written permission of the intendant. Once more, the censure was clear, even though the infraction had been purely formal. Nevertheless, the contents and tone of this letter show that Mahler had won his case in his clash with the intendant two years earlier. Indeed, but for this, his "breech of discipline" would have been taken much more seriously. Hochberg continued to press for an indemnification from the Hofoper, but this was refused.

Now that he was free in Vienna to control every theatrical and musical detail of the performances, Mahler was able to carry out the reforms he considered essential. He coached the new singers in order to break them of the habit of overgesticulating and thus reducing the significance and expressiveness of their acting, especially as most of their gesticulations were entirely superfluous. "When a character says 'you,' he extends his arm and points pathetically to the character he's addressing, and when he speaks of his 'heart,' he places his hand over it. The women think to impress by constantly raising their hands to their faces . . . To put a stop to this, I forbid them to use their arms or their hands during rehearsals until they've learned to express the dramatic and musical content of their parts without gesticulating. At the same time, I drill them in the musical substance of their parts and, when they've become thoroughly familiar with them and begun, as it were, to live them, I allow them, nay I order them, to re-create the whole thing themselves with the maximum artistic freedom. The final result is therefore never as crude and inappropriate or as careless from a rhythmic point of view as if I had not trained them properly from the beginning."[12]

Mahler had advised the stage director Stoll, who taught at the conservatory, when working with a pupil, to tie his arms together. To him this was essential, since "natural" gestures were always ridiculous. No singer, even one thoroughly versed in his part, was capable of finding the correct gestures by himself. "Unless every motion is stylized and translated into art, unless every step and expression is sublimated, the whole performance becomes puerile. A singer must not be permitted to remain himself and to impose his own personality at the expense of the character he's playing and the drama as a whole . . . Considering that everything, even the cobbler's trade, has to be painstakingly learned, why should an actor be capable of creating a musical and dramatic role spontaneously and without any guidance? The answer is that he's not and that, like everyone else, he has to work long and hard at it."

As an example, Mahler cited Mildenburg, who had been so awkward and clumsy to begin with and then blossomed into the "most admirable and truly classic" of actresses. She was often compared to Duse, her regal bearing, noble femininity, and imposing proportions creating a stir at her every entrance. Moreover, her musical talents matched her dramatic qualities. According to the critic Erwin Stein,[13] her voice was, at that time, one of the most magnificent one could hear anywhere and her range such that she could sing both soprano and mezzo roles (*e.g.,* Amneris). Unfortunately, it soon began to show signs of fatigue, and she frequently embarrassed Mahler by canceling her performances at the last moment. Her top notes were already beginning to be less smooth, but she managed to fill every word with drama and significance. In the role of Brünnhilde, her face reflected each of the character's emotions, particularly in the great final scene with Wotan. Her contemporaries described her in *Fidelio* as "animated at the outset by unshakable determination" and then, conversely, after Florestan's release, "tender and devout in the face of her own destiny" and constantly genuine in all her attitudes and expressions. She had come to sense Mahler's every wish so absolutely that he hardly needed to look at her during performances, a fact that particularly pleased him, for he felt that the conductor's baton was there to guide only "beginners or people devoid of musical sense," whereas true artists should sense his wishes without having to look at him. She and Mahler continued to be bound by a common intent and a deep artistic understanding, even though the nature of their personal relations had changed. On the occasions when he wanted her to look at him, which were almost always during an ensemble, he told her so beforehand.

Within this "ensemble" he was gradually building up at the Hofoper, Mahler tried to convert the jealousy so prevalent at the opera into healthy rivalry. When, on his advice, Selma Kurz was learning the role of Sieglinde, he asked Mildenburg not only to coach her, but also to sing the entire role for her as he had taught it to her years before. Each gesture and each movement was so entrancing that he himself was moved. "She now is," he said to his intimates, "that which I imagined she'd become when she arrived in Hamburg barely out of the conservatory. However imperfect she may have been then, her dramatic and musical genius already illuminated everything she did. For the '*Todesverkündigung*' in *Die Walküre,* she found a tone at once so modest and so majestic that she moved me more deeply than all the others I'd ever seen or heard."

After an initial period of resistance due to her exceedingly forceful personality and innate talent, and once she had realized how much she could still learn from him, Gutheil-Schoder had also adopted Mahler's conceptions. She was so gifted that one had only to give her a hint or show her something once for her to take advantage of it instantly. During his many years of theatrical experience, Mahler had acquired the conviction that the way in which words were expressed was of prime importance in the interpretation of a role, and that therefore a musical and dramatic character ought always to be built upon the basis of words. In his view, no matter how beautifully a phrase was sung, if the singer failed to bring out the full meaning of its words, it would not produce the desired effect, even though the audience might not always recognize the cause of its disappointment. If, for instance, instead of singing *Mutter* (mother), a singer became carried away by the music and broke up the word into *Mut-ter,* both its meaning and dramatic effect would be lost, even though his voice might be divine. Short vowels, he felt, should always remain as short as the corresponding note; otherwise the word and its sound, which should be as inseparable as the body and the soul, would become disunited. When correctly pronounced, words should, as it were, create their own music. Thus he often judged a singer by his "r."

While filling the opera with exceptionally talented but still relatively docile artists like Mildenburg and Gutheil-Schoder, Mahler continued to wrestle with others who, like Reichmann, considered themselves stars. One day he rushed backstage between the second and third acts of *Lohengrin*[14] to tell the latter that "your rhythm is impossible," but Reichmann, unperturbed, replied that "my rhythm is of no importance; my fans are only interested in my voice . . ."

Van Dyck having left the opera some months after Marie Renard, Mahler came to loggerheads with the tenor Franz Naval, who had taken over some of Van Dyck's roles.[15] Naval finally handed in his resignation, which Mahler, in order not to appear to be giving in to him, pretended to be loath to accept. According to Karpath, Naval left numerous admirers in Vienna, and his departure was considered fresh proof of Mahler's tyranny. With the new singers he had engaged, Mahler was extremely demanding, to the point of checking even their personal habits and way of life. For instance, he discovered that Schmedes[16] often sat up drinking and smoking in a certain café until late at night, so he went there one evening to remind him that he had to sing Siegfried the following evening and needed a good night's sleep.[17] Schmedes also rode and often caught cold during his equestrian excursions, so Mahler slyly suggested to him that he ride onto the stage in *Rienzi.* Terrified by the noise of the orchestra, the horse almost charged the walk-ons, and this narrow escape persuaded the great tenor to give up his perilous sport. Unfortunately, however, after selling his horse, Schmedes bought himself a bicycle and then an open car and Mahler concluded that "one must be frivolous to spend one's money on such crazy things instead of taking out a life insurance policy." Although he was at any rate partially successful on this score, Mahler found it a great deal harder to dissuade Schmedes from spending his evenings in the café, even before important performances. On the eve of a performance of *Siegfried,* he was particularly upset to find him there puffing away on a big cigar. All other arguments having failed, he finally resorted to telling him how disappointed his admirers would be when they learned that Leo Slezak had replaced him in one of his finest roles. Inflated like a balloon and grinning from ear to ear, Schmedes left the café and surpassed himself the following evening.[18]

After a long period during which he had prepared and conducted all the important performances singlehanded, Mahler entrusted the baton to Franz Schalk for the first time on October 26 for a revival of Verdi's *Il Trovatore,* which he had endeavored to reinvigorate by "sweeping away all the routine and indifference" with which it had all too often been performed. The tenseness of the audience was such that evening that several critics compared the atmosphere to that of a premiere. Moreover, Mahler had indulged in a particularly risky experiment by assigning the role of Leonora to Selma Kurz, who was far from possessing the vocal volume needed for it.[19]

On October 15, accompanied by Justi and Natalie, Mahler took the train for Munich, where the newly founded Hugo Wolf Verein[20] had decided to include his *Second Symphony* in its inaugural concert. Delighted at this fresh opportunity to conduct and hear his own work, he left Schalk to conduct the fourth performance of *Così fan tutte,* asking the critic Max Graf to cable him a report on it, and threw himself heart and soul into preparing the performance. He balked at nothing, not even financial sacrifice, in order to make the concert a success, despite the fact that he was apprehensive of the reactions of a press and public that had never heard any of his works before. At the last moment, the intendant of the Munich Opera, Ernst von Possart, still rankled by the Bühnenverein affair,[21] refused to allow one of his sopranos to take part in the concert, although she had already learned her part. Moreover, after the penultimate rehearsal, Mahler had to dismiss another soprano whose vocal ability was inadequate. Fortunately, however, the wife of the conductor of the Verein, Agnes Stavenhagen, offered to replace her and, after rehearsing the part once with Mahler at the piano, sang it to perfection. Elise Feinhals, the contralto, had a very lovely voice but lacked emotion and sensitivity. "For this part," Mahler said disappointedly, "I need the voice and naïve expression of a child, as I myself, when I hear the tinkling of a small bell, imagine the souls in heaven obliged to start everything afresh, like a small child in a dolls' world."

The Munich chorus also caused Mahler problems. Although inferior to those in Berlin, the female voices were nonetheless superior to those in Vienna, and the choristers plunged enthusiastically into the task. The tenors were unfortunately too few, changed at each rehearsal, and sang one of the passages *a cappella* so badly during the dress rehearsal that Mahler interrupted it with a despairing "Oh! This will never do!" For a moment, he considered canceling the whole concert so as not to compromise the success of his work, but finally collected himself and announced, calmly and confidently, that he had thought of a solution to the problem and would tell them about it after the rehearsal. He had in fact decided to have the passage in question played by the clarinets, which, being near the tenors, would help them to sing in tune. Nevertheless, it was but a makeshift solution and one to which he resorted only with great reluctance. He made the tenors rehearse for another three and a half hours the following morning and was obliged to pay for both this extra rehearsal and that which he had demanded of the Scherzo at least partially out of his own pocket.

Since the Munich orchestra was no match for the Vienna Philharmonic, Mahler foresaw a performance inferior to that of the preceding year, but looked forward confidently to the Finale, which, in Vienna, had been spoiled by the mediocrity of the chorus and the asthmatic sound of the Musikverein organ. "The statue may lack a 'little toe' or the 'tip of a thumb' this time, but not, as in Vienna, its head." One of the Munich orchestra's drawbacks was its shortage of strings, only twelve each of first and second violins, whereas Mahler dreamed of having his symphony performed by thirty violins, eighteen cellos, and sixteen double basses: "When that happens, people will be amazed to see how much it magnifies the effect!"

Despite everything Munich was immensely impressed by the *Second Symphony*. The public had been looking forward to the concert as a major event in contemporary music[22] and, as from the dress rehearsal on Friday morning, greeted the famous director of the Vienna Opera with warm applause. Thus it was an eminently favorably predisposed audience, including such celebrated musicians as Felix Weingartner, Eugen d'Albert, and the former intendant of the Munich Opera, Baron von Perfall, that packed the hall on the evening of October 20. As usual, it was disconcerted by the first movement but vigorously applauded the second. Its enthusiasm constantly increased throughout the final movements, which Mahler conducted without a pause, and at the moment of the "bird of death," one could have heard a pin drop in the hall. The chorus chimed in without rising (it rose only for the last verse), and the audience shuddered as one man. During the Finale, which attained an exceptional amplitude, Mahler found himself thinking for the first time that "these great waves of sound would stun the audience if the crescendo were less gradual and if the outburst were not deeply motivated and essential to the full satisfaction of the ear! If one were to tell the audience that the worst explosions in the first movement were but mild in comparison to that of the Finale, they would fear for their eardrums!" In a work like this, the building up and gradation of effects was all-important; for instance, he could have had the organ and the chorus enter sooner but had preferred to save them for the climax.

According to the *Bayerische Kurier,* the sudden dead silence that followed upon the last note was abundant proof of the audience's state of tension; it was immediately succeeded by "unparalleled jubilation," and it seemed as though the ovation would never end. A large number of people crowded around the podium, while others waved their handkerchiefs from their seats.

Having gathered together a group of friends at the Park Hotel after the concert, Mahler showed his good humor by monopolizing most of the conversation. He held forth at length on the subject of program music and recalled the misunderstandings that his "own programs" had caused between himself and the critic Arthur Seidl, who had just published his letter of 1897.[23] He had been most disagreeably surprised suddenly to come across it again in print, for he was afraid it would cause him to be regarded as an enthusiast of program music, whereas he was harshly critical of composers of such music, who, in his opinion, "commit one of the biggest musical and artistic errors and are not artists. It's a totally different matter when a master's work becomes so alive and transparent that one can't help reading some action or event into it, or when a composer tries, as I've always done, to explain his work to himself by some mental picture, or indeed, when his message takes on a sublimity and form such that he can no longer be content with mere sound and seeks a more forceful means of expression by resorting to the human voice and the poetic word, as Beethoven did in his *Ninth* and I did in my own *Symphony in C Minor.* This has nothing to do with picking a particular episode and illustrating it step by step like a program, which is the wrong way to compose."

Mahler had refused to allow the old program of his *Second Symphony* to be distributed for the Munich concert, even though the text had already been printed. "Music must speak for itself and the most sublime and universal message it conveys is contained in the words of the conclusion. The deeper meaning of a work, its message, will only emerge gradually, more often than not after the composer's death . . . The most important thing is that it remain music and solely music!" In the end, he regretted having exaggerated his admiration for Strauss in his letter to Seidl. "There you see," he said to Natalie, "the price one pays when one's not completely sincere and makes a small concession out of friendship! They've taken me at my word and now consider me an ardent advocate of Strauss and that program music which I've had to fight fiercely and openly." (Mahler's opinion of Strauss changed radically when he heard *Salome.*)

After the Munich concert Guido Adler brought up the strangely contrasting reactions, at either the Berlin or the Vienna performance,[24] of three prominent figures, Strauss, Karl Muck, and Wilhelm Kienzl, to a passage in the first movement. Muck could not stop laughing, Kienzl had been deeply moved, and Strauss had exclaimed that a new star had risen for him, adding, as Mahler often did when speaking of him, that he had benefited greatly from his colleague's work and that the main difference between them was that he used "cacophony" unnecessarily and merely for the "fun of offending," whereas Mahler's use of it was justified by the strict laws of polyphony.[25] Mahler himself confirmed that he was always careful to try to avoid harsh sounds and to remove them from his own works, "as I did in a passage in my *Second Symphony,* whereas Strauss contrives gratuitous dissonances solely in order to show off and to startle people."

After this third hearing of his big symphony Mahler again had doubts about the excessively marked contrasts between the first two movements. He had thought of remedying this by placing the Scherzo after the first movement, except that then the contrast between the Andante and the following *Urlicht* would not have been strong enough, since their tonality was insufficiently contrasting. Such a "dissonance" would have been impossible in the *Third* and *Fourth Symphonies,* for which he had begun by drawing up a plan and determining the order of the movements before drafting them in their final tonalities.[26]

For the first time in Mahler's career, the critics did not immediately destroy the pleasure he derived from his success. Even the article in the *Allgemeine Zeitung,* which was one of the least enthusiastic, acknowledged that the *Second Symphony* was a "very distinguished and undeniably interesting" work and compared it to Strauss's symphonic poem *Also sprach Zarathustra,* in as much as it also portrayed "the human being grappling with the concept of immortality" through "earthly suffering, joy and passion." The two subtitles of the Finale, *Der Rufer in der Wüste* (The Call in the Desert) and *Der grosse Appell* (The Great Summons), proved that this was a program symphony and belonged to the school of Bruckner. Its religious atmosphere, choruses, and abundance of brasses likewise confirmed this, even though Mahler's aims were totally different. However, despite his profound knowledge of all the "secrets of musical technique" and superior mastery of form, he lacked Bruckner's "noble faculty for transforming themes and rendering them expressive." The critic nevertheless admired the first movement, which, with "two poor themes" and "grammatical clarity," expressed the very depths of sorrow; the transparence of the Andante; "the cry of despair in the form of a stylized waltz" of the "berliozissimo" Scherzo; the simple and profoundly touching pathos of the *Urlicht,* and, finally, the Finale, which he found captivating in spite of its slightly "affected" ending. "Thunderstruck, petrified and enraptured," the audience had applauded interminably, he said.

*Der Sammler* regretted the excessive publicity surrounding Mahler, since it aroused the "distrust of reasonable people." Defining his music as "lived" rather than "manufactured," it implicitly condemned all other composers. Incomprehensible without a program, the *Second Symphony* showed more striving for grandeur than "demonic impulse," it said; the first movement stood out above all the others, and particularly above the Andante, which lacked melodic distinction, and the Scherzo, which was "unimaginative and vulgar" and full of "musical and instrumental tricks of doubtful effect."

Fortunately this severity turned out to be the exception. The *Bayerische Kurier* reported that Mahler's "sweeping victory" had "established the *Wolf-verein*." The anonymous critic preferred the first and final movements to those in between, which contained "too many '*Pikanteries*' and humorous affectations," as well as some "intolerable cacophony and dissonances." Nonetheless, this same critic did Mahler the uncommon honor of praising "the rare originality" of his thematic imagination and instrumentation and also congratulated him on never being boring and on keeping the audience on tenterhooks thanks to his matchless subtlety. Even Strauss, he said, did not hold the public breathless to such a degree. However, the reason why, according to the *Bayerische Kurier,* this great work had been so enthusiastically received was because it followed the great symphonic poems of Strauss in the line of Berlioz, Liszt, Bruckner, and Wagner, composers of whom Mahler had made a particularly thorough study. More specifically, this critic admired the magnificent pathos of the first movement and the Viennese charm and originality of the second, while pronouncing the *Urlicht* "a gem of poetry and lyric and religious feeling." As for the lofty and introspective Finale, and especially the entrance of the chorus, which was "unique in modern music," it revealed Mahler as a "symphonic dramatist."

A month later, Rudolf Louis, one of the most distinguished Munich critics, finally discussed the triumphal success of the concert in the review *Kunstwart.* A convinced anti-Semite, he held that Mahler had no "powerful and personal" imagination, but was an eclectic whose themes were almost all borrowed. His dynamic and fiery temperament rendered his musical language captivating and compelled the audience, at least during the performance, to "surrender unconditionally to the composer," even though, upon recovering its judgment, it was finally left with the embarrassing impression of having been fooled and "overwhelmed rather than convinced." Nevertheless, Mahler was neither a poseur nor a charlatan, and there could be no doubt as to the seriousness of his intentions. As a craftsman, Strauss was his only peer. With almost unparalleled audacity, he disregarded all the traditional rules of music, but for all that there was something disturbing, "unattractive," and, to a certain extent, even not very lofty about his work. He described immortality without suggesting the beyond, the world to come of Christian theology, that is the negation of time, for he had "no sense of eternity." While refusing to admit to any anti-Semitic tendencies, Louis regarded this a "specifically Jewish" element in Mahler's work, which he was therefore unable to accept wholeheartedly.[27]

Other critics had, however, tried to see further ahead and on a higher plane, in particular Arthur Seidl, who, in magazine articles published at that time, discerned two principal streams in German music, one from the north and the other from the south. Thus he opposed Bach to Handel, Beethoven to Cherubini, Schumann to Mendelssohn, Wagner to Liszt, Brahms to Bruckner, Strauss to Mahler, and smiled at the "astonishment of the musical astronomers at the sudden appearance of this bright new star in the artistic sky." With a moderation and lucidity rare in those days, Seidl considered that "it is not possible to reproach Mahler for having wished to compose [tondichten] before he knew how to build vast architectural constructions," and that "it is too soon to make any precise judgment, or to be able to evaluate the over-all development of technique, ideas and new forms of expression."[28]

On the whole, the reactions of the Munich press had thus been extremely favorable, and those of the German magazines and periodicals were even more so, their enthusiastic accounts spreading the news of Mahler's triumph everywhere. According to the correspondent of the *Zeitschrift für Musik,* Paula Reber, no one who met Mahler for five minutes could deny the "religious seriousness" with which he regarded his art. Although the opening of the *Second Symphony* was perhaps a joke, be it good or poor, a sort of mixture of Richard and Siegfried Wagner with a few bars of a funeral march by Chopin and Beethoven thrown in, Mahler had nevertheless shown that he knew the meaning of the term allegro maestoso. The other movements were excellent, notably the Finale, the "absolutely captivating, enthralling, indescribable, supernatural, impressive and powerful beauty" of which was impossible to imagine without having heard it. The *Hugo Wolf Verein* could not have made a happier choice.[29]

Thus, for once, Mahler had no reason to complain of either the public or the critics, of whom he wrote to Justi that "those gentlemen are already changing their tune."[30] Back in Vienna, he found everyone talking about his success. He gathered a selection of the Munich articles to send to Justi, who was staying with Emma in Weimar, together with the gratifying news that Munich had decided to give his *Second Symphony* again, two weeks later, under the baton of Stavenhagen.[31]

How different was to be Vienna's reaction to the *First Symphony,* which was performed at the second Philharmonic concert on November 19! After some hesitation, on account of the strict rules of the Philharmonic, Mahler allowed Justi and Natalie to attend the rehearsals of this concert, which was to begin with Beethoven's overture to *Die Geschöpfe des Prometheus* and Schumann's overture to *Manfred.* He had carefully revised the orchestration of the latter, for "Schumann's indications are, as almost always, contrary to his intentions." The beauty of these works, he felt, could not but set off his own work and enhance its effect.

As from the opening bars of the *First Symphony,* the strange A pedal plunged the audience into a mixture of boredom and uneasiness. A number of people, and especially those in the pit and the boxes who attended concerts only because it was the thing to do, "began to laugh, cough or clear their throats in the face of this weird and incomprehensible music." On the other hand, a lot of young people, students or pupils of the conservatory, followed the performance with great interest and, as from the end of the first movement, their enthusiasm contrasted with the disapproval of the rest of the audience.[32]

The second movement was, as usual, warmly applauded, but the Funeral March dumfounded the audience and provoked derisive laughter, and only the absence of a pause between the last two movements prevented the majority of them from leaving. However, the stormy Finale gradually calmed them down and ended amid a "mysterious silence." Thereupon, the first timid "Bravo!" was greeted by violent hissing that momentarily drowned out the applause and, just as in Weimar six years before, pandemonium broke loose. Mahler had fled at the first catcall but was prevailed upon to return to thank his young admirers.

For Mahler's friends the concert was torture, because "we heard it with the audience's ears, so that the pleasure we had derived from it during the rehearsals was gone[33] and we dreaded all the passages that we foresaw would arouse the audience's indignation." As from the end of the introduction, Mahler himself had sensed the hostility and, anxious to get through the symphony as quickly as possible, had accelerated most of the tempos. Once his "martyrdom" was over, he went home with some friends but, contrary to what they expected, did not seem in the least downhearted. "After this," he exclaimed, "there's no danger that I shall now compose to order or seek to curry favor with the public. The *First Symphony* is and will always remain my child of sorrow!"

As to the Viennese critics, they reacted even more negatively than they had to the *Second Symphony*. "One of us must be crazy, and it isn't I!" Hanslick's article began. However, after recovering from the terrors of the Finale, he had wondered whether it was not, after all, he who was crazy; albeit he continued to feel that the *First Symphony* was "alien to music." Admittedly, he said, a more thorough knowledge of the score might perhaps have helped him to a better understanding of its significance, but only on condition that a program had been available to explain the connecting link between its different movements. He wondered about the reason for the sudden "end of the world" after the Funeral March, in the form of a students' round, and, in his perplexity, he was obliged to confine himself to admiring Mahler's "legion witty details and stupendous orchestral technique." Theodor Helm, in the *Deutsche Zeitung,* quoted the program published in Weimar and recalled that this "crude din deliberately presented as a parody of the excess of the new German school had been indignantly rejected." Contrary to a well-established custom, Mahler had forbidden the publication of even a thematic analysis in Vienna, doubtless fearing that his "quotations" from Beethoven, Wagner, and Bruckner, Mendelssohn, Weber, etc., might thus be revealed[34]; according to Helm, this hypermodern work jumped, without any sort of transition, from pastoral innocence to savage bedlam and, caught between Mahler's "clique" of young admirers and his enemies, the majority of the audience had hesitated, smiled, and feared the effects on its eardrums of the explosions and "grotesque cacophony" of the Finale. With or without a program, the symphony was both a "stylistic absurdity" and a "total failure," and Mahler should never have been allowed to inflict it on the Philharmonic while Vienna continued to be deprived of so many estimable works.

Even Gustav Schönaich, who until then had shown considerable fairness in his estimation of Mahler and had found his *Second Symphony* "pleasing and intensely personal," had perceived no link between the movements and declared the "entire picture" unintelligible. "Is it a weasel, a cloud or a camel?" he asked, paraphrasing Shakespeare (*Hamlet,* Act III, Scene 2). The melodious passages had irritated him as much as the dissonances, for both were equally unjustified. Mahler had already become a master of orchestration sixteen years before, but his personality had still not asserted itself. Recalling that Wagner had feared that Berlioz would end up being "buried beneath his own orchestral machinery," Schönaich remarked that Mahler had also succumbed to the hazardous joys of using a hitherto unprecedented orchestral language and that, unbeknown to him, "the glittering outer garment has taken the place of the thought." Moreover, his humor merely grated, for "Callot's manner" was unsuited to music. With its lack of unity, the whole symphony, and particularly its catastrophic fourth movement, was thoroughly exasperating, and Mahler should never have compromised his reputation as a composer by conducting it.

It was, above all, the ironic and burlesque tendencies of the *First Symphony* which attracted the attention of Hirschfeld and Kalbeck, who dwelled at length on them. The former pretended to believe that Mahler had not intended anyone to take him seriously. In his opinion, it was quite normal that such a versatile artist should have wanted to compose a "satire on the symphony," parodying "inspiration" and making fun of those who "fill up sheets of music paper before deciding upon the final form of a theme." He had therefore lined up a host of reminiscences and, in his third movement, ridiculed heroic funeral marches. In such a context, one could not take anything seriously, even the attractive melody of the Finale. With its formless themes, the first movement had "no organic development," and even the crescendos were quite unwarranted; the whole was arranged like a "shopwindow," with burlesque counterpoints added to totally unrelated themes and countermelodies. Hirschfeld also jeered at Mahler's "absurd" efforts to use the fourth motif, which appeared over and over again, to suggest the cuckoo, whereas the latter sings only minor thirds.

In the Finale, with its clamor of vulgar themes, Hirschfeld saw only a "satire on the overweening conceit of powerful modern geniuses." Even Mahler's orchestration was caricaturish, for it aspired only to having the instruments play in an unnatural manner and in unaccustomed registers. The harmonics of the Introduction suggested no more than the creakings of a door and could hardly have constituted a more effective mockery of the "modern search for originality." Although certain passages of the symphony were "marvelous and intoxicating," the piece as a whole proved that the "physical or material" aspect of a work and a composer's craftsmanship were of little importance in comparison to its purely intellectual content.

Whereas Hirschfeld, with his now usual malevolence, had pretended to believe that Mahler was joking, Max Kalbeck genuinely credited him with the noblest intentions. Mahler's sarcasm seemed to him to be of a "tragic nature," and he felt that there could be no doubt about his sincerity. In an article headed "Gustav Mahler's Sinfonia Ironica" he nevertheless admitted that he could neither accept nor understand Mahler's standard of beauty. In his opinion the work was a total failure. Nevertheless, the regenerator of the Vienna Opera deserved more respect than the public had shown him. In any case, Mahler need not feel offended, for Brahms's *Fourth Symphony* had been no better received.

Clearly, his symphony had not surmounted the ordeal of being deprived of either a commentary or a program. Despite the beauty of certain details, it was the work of a young man still imbued with the extravaganzas of Berlioz and Liszt, but in no wise a "masterpiece of pure music." As far as Kalbeck was concerned, only two genres were open to symphonic music, the idyllic and the heroic, both of which had been perfectly represented in Beethoven's *"Pastoral"* and *"Eroica" Symphonies*. Mahler had endeavored to unite them with the help of an element alien to pure music, namely irony. This latter, however, had no place in music, except in combination with the word, for "the noblest of the arts," that of sound, could not "say the opposite of that which it means." The "solvent harshness of irony" alone sufficed to explain the fragmentary character of the first and last movements of the *First Symphony*, for Mahler had not managed to protect its broad and stately form from this rupture. Drawn from Callot and Hoffmann, he went on, Mahler's tragicomic effects were incomprehensible without a program. Moreover, his fertile imagination had led him to create legion small motifs that might have formed the substance of a new Scherzo or Adagio. Far from being worthless, the first movement and the Finale contained many excellent inventions. However, the composer's efforts to depict the crises and convulsions of the human soul were merely an indiscretion of youth, just as his fondness for popular songs partially explained the lack of thematic development indispensable to any symphony worthy the name. As to his orchestration, it was incomparable and deserved a thorough study. In short, the symphony was a veritable summary of the laws of art, its effects having been prepared with supreme skill "for the greater enjoyment and, also, terror of the audience."

The Viennese critics had never before been so unanimous in their condemnation of Mahler. On the evening of the concert, he dined at Frau Mankiewicz's with Justi, Natalie, and Rosé and presented his hostess with one of his scores signed *"Der ausgepfiffene Gustav Mahler"* (The booed Gustav Mahler). That afternoon he had heard Liszt's *Die Legende von der heiligen Elisabeth,*[35] a work for which he had such a fondness that he attended every performance of it. Its "religious tranquillity" had seemed like a "balm and a veritable blessing" after his own tortured and impassioned work. "This work needs the support of the stage," he later said of the Liszt oratorio.[36] "The music alone would be meaningless, it is much too flabby and deliquescent, too atmospheric, even if it is the most wonderful atmosphere imaginable. It can rightly be called a real aryan work."

Yet the charm of Liszt's *Elisabeth* did not soothe Mahler for long, and he vented his resentment against Vienna, which had once more received his music so badly and from which he would even have liked to escape for a while. He felt particularly bitter about the attitude of the orchestra, "which is able to understand my work better than anyone else, but nevertheless deserted me at the end of the concert. The musicians positively rejoiced at the fiasco and averted their faces to hide the malice that flowed in their eyes, whereas those in Berlin and elsewhere always stood by me and my work, which they applauded with their bows."

A few days later, as he faced the orchestra for the rehearsals of the next concert, he unintentionally and unpremeditatedly "unburdened himself in an improvised speech: 'I did not act like a man offended and wounded in his pride, but like a general abandoned and sacrificed by his troops.'" No artistic work was possible, he said, unless a general and his troops settled their differences, otherwise the bond between them would break. He had often shown his devotion to them, not only as their lord and master, but also as a man, and had proved it by intervening in their behalf and looking after their interests. They, on the other hand, had lost no opportunity to show him how much they disliked him. By their sometimes equivocal and sometimes hostile attitude, they had constantly done their best to disillusion him. The behavior of the audience after the performance of his *First Symphony* had again shaken their confidence in him, whereas he was always the last to be surprised or angry when people failed to enjoy one of his works at first hearing. They had let themselves be influenced by the audience, and this he had found all the more regrettable as the work had stunned and bewildered them only at the first rehearsal. Later on, they had come to like it and even acknowledged as much, but had forgotten all that the moment they saw the audience and the critics turn against him.

Pointing a vengeful finger at the violinist Theobald Kretschmann, Mahler reproached him with having asked, as everyone knew, at a recent session of the Philharmonic committee, "Who gave Herr Mahler the right to include his symphony in the program?" "The answer," he shouted, "since I've no desire to hide it from you, is that I and I alone *assumed* the right. The right to draw up the programs entirely in accordance with my own wishes is one that I reserve in all circumstances. If that's not compatible with the democratic constitution of your association, which I find extremely congenial in other respects, tell me so frankly and I'll leave at once."

Beneath the stunned and leaden silence in which his speech was received,

Mahler sensed the musicians' suppressed irritation. He began to rehearse with the humiliating thought that "my *Fischpredigt* wasn't to their liking and has achieved nothing." No doubt he cursed himself afterward for having thus futilely unburdened his heart to men who feared but did not like him and who were later to be only too ready to forget all that they owed him.

At the first Philharmonic concert of the 1900–01 season, which had taken place on November 9, two weeks before the Vienna premiere of his *First Symphony,* Mahler had conducted Berlioz's *Rob Roy Overture,* an early work and new to Vienna, which the critics damned. Helm called it an "interesting curiosity," Hanslick "the barren and clumsy work of a dilettante," and Kalbeck felt that Berlioz would have done better to destroy it. Once again, the highlight of the concert was Beethoven's *"Eroica" Symphony,* and Mahler had decided to prevent the Viennese from leaving at the beginning of the Finale by sustaining the fermata preceding the entrance of the main theme. His furious glances, and the mutterings of the rest of the audience, forced those who had stood up to sit down again.[37]

Ever faithful to his homeland, Mahler included two works by Smetana in the program of the third Philharmonic concert, *Vltava* and the prelude to *Libuše.* He thought it a pity that the latter opera was not up to the standard of its prelude, and resolved to revise it someday, as he had *Dalibor,* so that it would be able to hold the stage.[38] Unlike Mahler, Kalbeck felt that the prelude to *Libuše* cut a sorry figure at the concert and contained "too much din and not enough symphonic development," an opinion that Hanslick shared. *Vltava,* on the other hand, won everyone's approval. Hanslick found Smetana's talent not only "genuine and brilliant" in this piece, but also entirely original despite the influence of Liszt, while Kalbeck praised the warmth of the melodies and the beauty of the music.

Although the critics' hostility usually left him cold, Mahler was extremely upset that his rendering of the second *Leonore Overture*[39] and of Beethoven in general had again provoked their anger. The previous neglect of this overture seemed to him to be thoroughly unjust, and he had devoted "as much time to it as I usually devote to re-creating a symphony, in order that it should be both what I wish it to be and what it is." Hanslick reproached him with his "inaudible pianissimos" and long oratorical pauses,"[40] which he considered overly subtle, and all the critics again condemned his "disregard of the main outline" (*grosser Zusammenhang*) of the work. Mahler in turn was annoyed with them for "not realizing the importance of clarity and accuracy, in art just as much as in science, and the value of every detail, however small . . . The spirit, which can only assert itself through the medium of clear form, remains, like all that is of spiritual and incommensurable essence, forever hidden in the re-creator himself. The only thing they notice about him is his lucidity and intelligence; they will never perceive his genius."

This same concert had been exceptional for the presence of a soloist, the pianist Carl Friedberg,[41] who played Bach's *Concerto in D Minor* and the Vienna premiere of César Franck's *Variations symphoniques*. Kalbeck summarily dismissed Bach's concerto "as an arrangement of a lost violin concerto" and said that he supposed the soloist "bore this cross in order to obtain forgiveness for his sins as a virtuoso as well as for those of other pianists," a judgment that, coming from the pen of so conservative a critic, was somewhat surprising to say the least. Hanslick added that the concerto was marred by the surfeit of strings in the orchestra. Franck's *Variations symphoniques* were given a good reception. Helm considered them "very interesting" and, like Hanslick, preferred them to *Les Béatitudes*. The latter called them not only "extremely interesting and ambitious," but also "beautifully written and orchestrated."

To commemorate the one hundred thirtieth anniversary of the Master's birth, Mahler, on December 16, conducted a Beethoven festival concert that included the *Coriolan Overture* and the *First* and *Fourth Symphonies*. During the rehearsals he was entranced with the beauty of the *First Symphony,* in which he saw a "supremely accomplished Haydn," and envied Beethoven for having been able thus to adopt a style familiar to his contemporaries to whom "his future, fully formed personality would have seemed incomprehensible and mad and, indeed, did seem so when he produced his *Fourth Symphony."*[42]

Toward the end of 1900, Mahler's health began to give cause for alarm. The nervous energy he expended on operas and concerts brought back his headaches and stomach-aches and caused a recurrence of his "subterranean troubles." Although these danger signals should have made him wary, he not only insisted upon conducting the entire *Ring* cycle himself before Christmas (and considering the inauspicious moment at which it was given, *i.e.,* at the beginning of the holidays, when, as a rule, the Viennese public had neither the money nor the time to attend, it was a great success), but he also steadfastly refused to take the holiday that his health demanded after Christmas. Furthermore, he set himself to finish his *Fourth Symphony,* which he wanted to hand over to his publisher at the beginning of the new year, and even gave up the excursions he had planned. However, he was soon to regret having thus presumed upon his strength.

"It's not just a question of
conquering a summit previously
unknown, but of tracing, step by step,
a new pathway to it . . ."

# CHAPTER 34

*Mahler in Vienna* (X) — *Premiere of* Das klagende Lied
— *Illness and Operation* — *Resignation from the Philhar-
monic* — *The* Fifth Symphony *and the* Rückert Lieder
(*January–September 1901*)

During the Christmas holidays, Mahler continued to work two hours each
morning and evening on his *Fourth Symphony* in order to be able to hand
it over to his publisher at the beginning of the new year, together with
*Revelge,* since it was to have its premiere in Munich the following November. "With great difficulty" he "restored the original version of the Scherzo
as I drafted it a year and a half ago at Aussee with the intention of turning
it into a more extensive movement ending in a tarantella," for, as always,
"this first draft seems [to me] to be the only one that's effective and right."
Struck, as he resumed his work, by the relatively modest means he had
used in this symphony as compared to those in his preceding symphonies, he
likened the sound of the Scherzo to "a spider's web, or one of those woolen
shawls whose threads are so fine that one can fold them into a nutshell or
unfold them ad infinitum." He also decided to have the solo violin tuned
higher than usual, so that "it will have a harsh and shrill sound, as though
death were playing it," and to "alter the disposition of the various instrumental voices," for during the interval between Aussee and Maiernigg
everything had grown and swollen "like tumors on a limb."

He remembered the trouble he had had the preceding year with the
orchestration of "so simple and elementary" a theme as that of the first
movement, in fact, infinitely more trouble than with the most complex
polyphony because "I've never been able to think of music otherwise than
in terms of polyphony." With the apparent inconsistency that was typical
of him, he concluded that his difficulties doubtless arose from his "weakness

in counterpoint," as a result of which he lacked the sense of the "pure phrase" (*reiner Satz*) natural to those familiar with this discipline. He also emphasized the "modest" entrance of this theme, describing it as being "like dewdrops gleaming on a flower before sunrise, which burst into a thousand lights and colors with the first ray of sunshine and sparkle like a sea of radiance."

During the first weeks of 1901, Mahler threw himself into the production of *Rienzi,* working as though he were reviving one of the greatest masterpieces of the repertory. Indeed, he felt that the first of Wagner's works had been unjustly neglected and that, although it belonged in the domain of grand opera rather than in that of music drama, it was nevertheless "powerful and effective enough to deserve such an effort." He reduced its length to three and a half hours, which was quite sufficient for its substance and, after carefully studying Wagner's own cuts and his "Bayreuth version," decided that it was "inadequate . . . contrary to the musical sense," and prepared a version of his own. He hoped that *Rienzi* would thus finally be a huge success, but had few illusions on the subject: "certain badly performed works invariably draw a crowd, whereas others, which are unquestionably masterpieces, often fail to attract the public, even when staged to perfection." Carried away by his enthusiasm for this labor of re-creation, he dumfounded one of the Viennese critics by asking "whether he didn't agree that *Rienzi* was Wagner's most beautiful opera and the greatest musical drama ever composed."[1] The critic in question was probably Schönaich for, according to Max Graf, the latter had long since noticed this peculiar trait in Mahler's character. "I'll tell you what your enthusiasm reminds me of," Schönaich said to Mahler one day in the Café Impérial, *"foie gras."* Mahler having demanded an explanation, Schönaich had replied, "Because geese are stuffed until they develop a liver disease. With them, this results in a succulent *foie gras* and with you in a marvelous performance." Thereafter, when preparing a new production that required a great deal of effort, Mahler would often announce, "The *foie gras* will soon be ready," and later on, when the critics began to attack each of his innovations, *"Die Herren Vorgesetzten* once again consider it a liver disease . . . In our opinion the *foie gras* is excellent!"[2]

Casting *Rienzi* had presented knotty problems, especially because of the high tessitura of the two principal roles. In order to facilitate the task of the two leads, Winkelmann (who was replaced by Schmedes at the first performance) and Mildenburg, Mahler gave some of their high notes to the tenor Franz Pacal and the soprano Elise Elizza, whom he hid among the choristers. At the same time, he prepared alternative casts so that the opera would have a longer run. A few days before the premiere, which was to take place on January 21, he was prostrated by a frightful sore throat and a high fever and, to his immense regret, had to entrust the final rehearsals to one of his assistants. Even on his sickbed, he demanded detailed progress reports by telephone and continued to dispense orders and instructions. On the day of the premiere, although his tonsils were still swollen, he insisted upon conducting the performance himself despite the protests of Justi and Natalie. The entire day was fraught with difficulties of every kind and description. Winkelmann fell ill toward the end of the morning, and Schmedes, who was his understudy, declared that he had caught cold as he left the steam bath where they had gone to fetch him. His cold was in fact only stage fright, and he burst into tears when told that he must sing. Informed of Schmedes' breakdown while taking half an hour's rest in the middle of this exhausting day, Mahler immediately wrote him a long letter, thanks to which "he not only sang, but sang very well." Meanwhile, Mildenburg, who was overworked, developed a fever that may also have been no more than a fit of nerves; fortunately, she recovered at the last moment, but Jenny Pohlner had to take over the part of the Messenger of Peace from Michalek, who dropped out at zero hour. Although the task of preparing an alternative cast had demanded a considerable amount of extra effort and filled the rehearsal rooms from morning to evening during the final weeks, Mahler was glad that he had undertaken it. His influence was manifest throughout the performance: the singers and the chorus acted "with complete naturalness," and the costumes and sets, for which he had had an uphill struggle to obtain the necessary funds, largely contributed to the success of the evening, which was considerable from the end of the overture on.

Far from rejoicing at such a revival, the majority of the critics devoted the greater part of their articles to enumerating the flaws in this "early work," which Wagner himself had disowned and which they declared unworthy of so much effort. Some objected to the removal of the cuts, others to the casting of certain parts, and poor Schmedes was particularly badly treated. "What a bunch of idiots!" Mahler exclaimed. "As if they had any right to judge Wagner and the manner in which he talked about his early works toward the end of his life! When a great man, one of the Blessed, a creator, is about to depart this life, he begins to regard his body as a mere 'corpse' or slough and it was thus that Wagner regarded his early works. How dare these abject human insects, who neither see nor produce anything, venture to repeat his words?" The censure of the critics notwithstanding, Mahler reasserted his admiration for a work that, despite its inadequacies and imperfections, heralded Wagner's future greatness. Moreover, he was confident that the derogatory comments of the press would do it no harm, and he was right, for *Rienzi* (which had its Vienna premiere that year) was performed eight times in 1901 and several times each season up until 1918.

The Viennese press was indeed almost unanimously opposed to this revival. Hanslick wondered why Mahler had gone to so much trouble "considering that the 1871 performances proved that *Rienzi* was of no more than biographical interest." No living opera director would have agreed to give it if he had not known its composer's name. Mahler had been the life and soul of the performance, sparing no pains to ensure its success, and the gigantic efforts had "seemed to multiply his strength tenfold . . . If Wagner had attended this performance," Hanslick concluded, "how he would have rejoiced . . . no, how irritated he would have been, he who strove for thirty years to live down the mistake and excess of *Rienzi.*"[3]

During the rehearsals of *Rienzi,* Mahler had joyfully resumed his activities with the Philharmonic. At the first concert of 1901, on January 13, he conducted Mendelssohn's *Scottish Symphony*[4] and the Vienna premiere of Tchaikovsky's *Manfred Symphony,* a work that so delighted him that he even went so far as to note every metronomic marking and its alterations in the course of the movements.[5] Weber's Chinese overture, *Turandot,* was also on the program, but he dropped it at the last moment for fear that it would unduly prolong the concert.

Though still not fully recovered from his attack of quinsy, Mahler conducted Beethoven's *Ninth Symphony,* for the third time in Vienna, at the Nicolai Concert of January 27. The public having once again fought for tickets, both the final rehearsal and the concert itself were played to full houses. The atmosphere was electric throughout the performance, which ended in a triumph. For all that, the anonymous correspondent of the *Neue Zeitschrift* asserted that "by altering the performance of the work in a manner alien to that of the composer," Mahler had left the public "cold and hostile," and the other critics declared that they could in no wise reverse their earlier verdict: Mahler had not conducted Beethoven, but rather "his own version" of Beethoven, a version lacking in Olympian calm and majesty. This, at any rate, was how Mahler himself summed up the critics' comments, adding that their judgment was based above all on his rendition of the Adagio, which, in his opinion, demanded the sort of physical calm needed "to describe large circles with a spoon brimful of liquid without spilling a single drop." According to Hirschfeld, his interpretation was a "curiosity" that "moved farther away from Beethoven as it drew nearer to Mahler." It lingered over details and seemed as impervious to the greatness of the *Ninth* as to the pathos of the *"Eroica."* Kalbeck found the "coarseness, harshness and inequalities" in Mahler's interpretation more glaring than ever and felt that they had "chilled" the audience. He also said that the first movement should have been more majestic, the Adagio section of the slow movement faster, and the Andante slower. As for Heuberger, he accused Mahler of having conducted a "transcription of Beethoven," even though he had not put his own name beside the composer's on the program. Such a powerful poem gained nothing from being touched up, since by modifying the coloring of a work one inevitably modified its essence.[6]

Always heatedly challenged as an interpreter, Mahler was also to be questioned as a composer two weeks later, for the Viennese publisher Josef Weinberger had just published the "child of sorrow" of his twentieth year, *Das klagende Lied,* which was to be given its first performance on February 17, 1901, during a "special concert" of the Wiener Singakademie. Since the piece presented considerable difficulties, Mahler having composed it at a time "when I naïvely thought that the whole world would accept it and play it immediately," it required numerous rehearsals. The Singakademie was far from being a good chorus, and Mahler had to contend not only with strictly musical obstacles, but also with the laziness and virulent anti-Semitism of its members and particularly the men, most of whom arrived late for the first rehearsal. Although he wondered at first whether he would not have done better to give the work with the opera chorus, he was finally won over by the zeal and musical talent of the women singers, thanks to whom the rehearsals became a source of both personal and artistic joy, as well as by the fact that almost all the singers turned up on time for the second rehearsal and did their very best to please him.

Like both Justi and Natalie, Mahler was struck by the surprising originality of this youthful work, which "sprang from my brain as fully equipped and finished as Minerva from that of Zeus" and was "far more daring than its successors." The memory of the difficulties and torments he had suffered as a composer of twenty led him to take a pessimistic view of Vienna's musical life, which he felt ought to be subsidized and controlled by the state, so insufficient was the number of concert halls and conservatories. Owing to the price of the tickets, the few concerts given were heard by only some ten thousand people, and the creation of a new orchestra,[7] which would provide music for other classes of society, was therefore a cause for rejoicing. The opera was the only exception, the state actually having taken it over. There, all works of any consequence were almost certain to be performed at least a dozen times, whereas the composers of pure music had the greatest difficulty in obtaining so much as a hearing.

Justi and Natalie persuaded Mahler to let them attend the first orchestral rehearsals of *Das klagende Lied,* and they were enchanted with it. If not packed, the hall was well filled for both the final rehearsal and the concert, and each was a tremendous success; Mahler and his soloists had to return to the podium several times to acknowledge the applause. As usual, the critics unanimously attacked this "eccentric work of youth," and their fury and indignation exceeded all limits.

Five days later Hirschfeld devoted an article, one of his longest ever, to *Das klagende Lied,* which he found "shocking and subversive." Everything in the work, its very length, its subject, the dividing up of the episodes, the parceling out of the text between different voices, its "harmonic overanimation," the use of the orchestra offstage, the "effects that become an end in themselves," its operatic style, its affected simplicity, the dissonances caused by the intermittent superimposing of the chorus on the orchestra and the great melodic leaps in the vocal parts, in short, all these "anomalies" gave Hirschfeld the opportunity to attack the composer and his work. "Today, Mahler conducts his youthful follies but no longer composes them. After nineteen years of experience and contact with masterpieces, he has discovered the value in art of economy of means. He knows that each art form has its own laws, which were not laid down arbitrarily but evolved naturally, and that the ultimate consequence of this development is called style. In art, there is only one crime and that is a very serious one, the crime of going against style . . ." As far as Hirschfeld was concerned, the choral writing of *Das klagende Lied* was a "crime against the nature of the voice."

"Today, Herr Direktor Mahler himself smiles at the dilettantism of his early vocal writing. Youth lacks maturity and aesthetic maturity always comes later than intellectual maturity. Yet there are people who do not realize this elementary fact and rely entirely on their 'I'; blinded by self-glorification and self-adoration, they will never reach aesthetic maturity but continue, throughout their lives, to create curiosities and anomalies . . . Gustav Mahler is well aware of the dangers of individualism, which tends to deny style, development and perfection; he knows that, in art as in life, it is the opinion of the majority rather than the opinion of the individual which lays down the rules and regulations. A man who clings to his own ideas in the center of the vicious circle of his abnormalities doubtless reasons as follows: I do not acknowledge the criticism of those whom I displease. Do as I do: we live for ourselves, let us not bother about others. I am proud of having ideas other than those of the majority, the common herd. It fails to understand my forward-looking ideas; they are beautiful and I pity all those who have others and are incapable of recognizing the beauty of mine!

"It would be a waste of time to take the trouble to refute such arguments," Hirschfeld concluded. "Gustav Mahler composed *Das klagende Lied* when he was nineteen; today, he would not dare to uphold its merits before the majority of reasonable people. I note that he conducts it notwithstanding. He wants to prove that, at nineteen, he had more orchestral effects in his head than most musicians of that age. As I have already said, the demonstration has cost a lot of money; it has also been successful."

Kalbeck also disliked both the work and its style, in which he too discerned a "sharp contrast between form and content, subject matter and presentation . . . Who has ever seen a nightingale two meters tall?" he wondered. Mahler had sought to "make a songbird out of an ostrich"; his piece was neither an oratorio nor even a symphonic poem but, doubtless, in the final analysis, a "symphonic poem with a program set to music. Here, the music has been made the servant, nay the slave of poetry . . . At first, the orchestra appears to introduce, accompany and sustain the singing, but the instruments soon assume a threatening attitude toward the voice and its uncertainties. They reveal their true intentions and force it to go along with them. The voice realizes all too late that it has fallen into the hands of thieves and murderers. Subjected to the most frightful tortures, it is obliged to surrender all its goods to satisfy the insatiable greed of its torturers and finally falls half dead by the wayside." Kalbeck called Mahler's failure "comic were it not tragic." Though interesting to a musician, his techniques "contain germs fatal to music."

According to Heuberger, in the *Neue Freie Presse*, *Das klagende Lied* contained only "a few rare moments of touching and authentic music, some remarkable and vividly defined moods . . . original but terribly labored harmonies and orchestral experiments that reveal an unquiet spirit and a veritable cult of the ugly." Mahler created "a flood of ugliness . . . atrociously mangled the voice and unnaturally dislocated melody, rhythm and harmony."

In the *Deutsche Zeitung,* Theodore Helm revealed the close relations between Mahler, "his brother-in-law, the impresario and music merchant Alexander Rosé," and Friedrich Ehrbar, the director of the Singakademie,[8] which had made the performance of *Das klagende Lied* possible. Moreover, he said, in view of the fact that the work had been announced with much fanfare and well in advance as "sensational," that it had required a veritable army of performers, that the composer had conducted it in person, and that it had lured all his "faithful," it could hardly have failed to rouse the interest and enthusiasm of the public, even if it had been twice as wretched (*kläglich*). Despite a few "interesting" passages, it could not "satisfy" anyone, owing to the disproportion between its subject and its means, its arbitrary use of solo voices, and the difficulty of its vocal writing. Mildenburg's soprano part was "particularly inhuman and murderous for the voice," even though her bravura piece had earned her tremendous applause. The work possessed no originality whatsoever for it recalled the "ancient synagogal chants," Mahler's childhood memories, interspersed with reminiscences of Wagner and Bruckner.[9] Helm concluded that *Das klagende Lied* was altogether "an insignificant trifle."[10] Despite this unanimous condemnation on the part of the critics, Mahler and Ehrbar planned a repeat performance of the work in March, with the same performers, since they felt confident that the public would not be overly influenced by the attitudes of the press.

The sixth Philharmonic concert, on February 24, went off relatively smoothly, even though it was the first time in two years that Mahler had conducted one of Bruckner's symphonies, on this occasion the *Fifth,* in Vienna, and he had made a few cuts in it which caused him to be accused by such fervent Brucknerians as Helm of an "outrageous lack of regard" for his former master and of having "smashed the statue with an impious hand, leaving only its torso intact."[11]

In fact, it distressed Mahler that so many of Bruckner's passages and themes, "of a Beethovian grandeur, are not carried through, developed and integrated" into the whole. By shortening the first movement, he had sought "merely to eliminate that which is empty and irrelevant," for its general effect was that of "a collection of cabbages and beets" devoid of any logical structure, "a sort of fabric that someone has woven with old threads chosen at random and coarsely knotted, without bothering about whether or not they blend in and without noticing that they destroy the unity and beauty of the ensemble." While he preferred the Scherzo, and above all the Trio, to the rest of the symphony, Mahler nevertheless felt that "Bruckner will never enter the repertoire and that the only way to promote his cause is to abridge him." In any case, he himself had "done my best thus to keep alive" the three symphonies he had conducted.[12]

These remarks, which reflect Mahler's deep-rooted and ultimate convictions with regard to Bruckner's music, may be compared with two other passages in Natalie's unpublished manuscript. One day in January 1900, as they were passing the monument to Bruckner in the Stadtpark in Vienna, Natalie told Mahler that two small boys, upon seeing this tiny bust dwarfed between the two immense figures crowning it with laurels, had exclaimed, "The man's too small for all that fuss!"—a remark that had neatly summed up the disproportion in his work.[13] The anecdote, moreover, is an excellent illustration of Mahler's admiration for, as well as his exasperation with, Bruckner's music. He returned to the charge a year later after having reread Bruckner's *First Symphony:* "It has left me the worst possible impression! Without any transition, the most magnificent neighbors with the most mediocre. After a superb beginning, a whole lot of confused and disordered nonsense, as clumsy from a contrapuntal as from a musical point of view, follows by way of development. At the end of this desert [*Wüste*], the beautiful theme returns (unchanged!), followed anew by the most appalling of wildernesses [*ärgste Wüstenei*]. As for the grandiose conclusion, it bears no relation, either profound or superficial, to the rest."[14]

Such, needless to say, was not the opinion of the Viennese Brucknerians, who taxed Mahler with having "torn" the first movement of the *Fifth Symphony* to shreds and, in so doing, having justified those who complained of the master's "lack of logic and clarity." In fact, like the majority of his contemporaries, the correspondent of the *Neue Zeitschrift* admitted that Bruckner had been incapable of expressing his thoughts on a large scale and that, because of his lack of any "sense of form," his music was made up of a succession of "little phrases." Helm nevertheless berated Mahler for having "violated" Bruckner's tempos by accelerating them beyond all reason in order to reach the Finale, the only movement he had conducted with "unparalleled power, dash, virtuosity, beauty of sound and intelligence." Whereas the "snobs" among the Philharmonic public had perhaps applauded the work thus abridged more warmly, he added, "the connoisseurs were filled with boundless fury and bitterness at such a shameful mutilation of an immortal creation." Hirschfeld and Kalbeck, on the other hand, congratulated Mahler on his judicious cuts and his dazzling performance of the Bruckner work. The rest of the program consisted of Weber's little Chinese overture to *Turandot* and the first performance of Dvořák's *Serenade* for wind instruments, op. 44. According to Helm, Mahler had undoubtedly chosen the former, which was based on an "authentic" Chinese theme mentioned by Jean-Jacques Rousseau, for its exotic orchestration. As to the *Serenade,* in Mahler's view, it not only contained "far more music" than Dvořák's big orchestral works, but also revealed the essence of his musical soul, whereas "when he strives for grandeur, he is often empty and bombastic."

During the winter Mahler had overtaxed his health by not taking any rest, even after his serious attack of quinsy in January. On February 24, after conducting the sixth Philharmonic concert in the afternoon, he conducted the hundredth anniversary performance of *Die Zauberflöte* in the evening. A ravishing young Viennese girl in the audience, who was later to play a major part in his life, upon seeing "that Lucifer-like face, those pale cheeks, those eyes like burning coals," declared to her companions, "with deep compassion," that "no one can go on like that."[15] And indeed, that same night, Mahler's "subterranean troubles" caused a sudden and violent hemorrhage. He waited some time before calling Justi and might well have died had she not telephoned immediately to a Dr. Singer. The latter's iced water did not help, and they were obliged to summon a surgeon, who, upon his arrival, told them they had taken a terrible risk by not sending for him earlier. However, with immediate and radical measures, he managed to stop the hemorrhage, which had been caused by a hemorrhoid located particularly high up in the intestinal tube.

The following morning, Mahler was extremely weak and admitted that the anxiety of the two doctors had made him think his last hour had come, for, while administrating their painful treatment, they had constantly taken his pulse and "listened to his heart," which fortunately "was solidly installed in his breast and determined not to give up so soon." Hovering on the border line between life and death, he had wondered whether it would not be better to have done with it at once, "since everyone must come to that in the end." Besides, the prospect of dying did not frighten him in the least, provided his affairs were in order, and to return to life again had seemed almost painful. The surgeon told him that, although his own fears had been somewhat exaggerated, he would nevertheless have to undergo a third, difficult but unavoidable operation, for he would not survive another such violent hemorrhage.[16]

The same day, Mahler had the score of his *Fourth Symphony* brought to him in bed, the copyist having just finished the first two movements of it. He noticed that the Scherzo had been labeled as the third movement, and was horrified to think that "if I had died last night, the entire structure and significance of the work would have been destroyed by this reversal of the movements, since the Adagio is supposed to serve as the basis of and transition to the Finale." Another passage, where he had written a second version alongside the first with the intention of choosing between the two later on, also upset him. After his death the publisher would doubtless have printed them one after the other and "only a musician like Bruno Walter would have the sense to strike out this nonsensical repetition." Even then, people would probably not believe him; the Philistines would call him an assassin and accuse him, because he had the cheek to be still alive, of correcting "a classic work." With grim humor he pictured those who then seemed ready to lynch him calling him "our Master . . . a classic . . . an immortal" once he was dead. He even drafted the obituary notice that would doubtless appear in the newspapers: "Gustav Mahler has finally met the fate that his many crimes deserved."

Mahler recovered so rapidly that Hohenegg, the surgeon, decided to operate on him a week later. The Emperor urged Hohenegg to devote the best of himself and his science to the director of the opera, and Mahler was happy to note that, despite all the hatred and scorn with which he had lately become surrounded, there were still many people who desired his recovery. Prince Montenuovo, in particular, called on him several times and told him not to worry about anything, since he would deal directly with his subordinates and take all the necessary decisions with them, so that the intendance would have no opportunity either to undermine him or to do him an ill turn in his absence.

On March 2 the prince sent him word of an increase in his salary. He was henceforth to receive seven thousand instead of six thousand florins, plus a further eleven thousand instead of six thousand in various other emoluments,[17] and the pension to which he was entitled after ten years of service was also to be increased.[18] The news came as a relief, for he had already begun to worry about the cost of his illness; moreover, such a token of confidence on the part of his superiors proved that he was not universally hated and opposed.

Expertly performed on June 4 by Hohenegg, the operation dispelled all anxiety for Mahler's health, but, since the deterioration of the lining of the intestinal tube was even worse than he had feared, Hohenegg nevertheless prescribed a long period of convalescence. Mahler was put into a nursing home on the outskirts of Vienna and forbidden to work more than a few hours a day. Natalie having gone to see him one evening to beguile his loneliness, he talked to her about Beethoven's quartets, which he said were "far more polyphonic than his symphonies," and told her that his own *Fourth Symphony* was conceived like a quartet, with as many as six and ten separate voices. He feared that "by paying too much attention to the trees, people will lose sight of the forest" and that this eminently cheerful work, which was easier to play and shorter than its forerunners, would fall flat.

Three years earlier he had quoted Bach to her as the supreme example of polyphony, adding that he regarded Beethoven as "the founder and creator of modern polyphony" and that "Wagner used genuine polyphony only in *Tristan* and *Die Meistersinger,* for the themes of the *Ring,* for instance, are built almost entirely on chords." Obsessed by this problem, Mahler constantly aimed at having his own themes "develop freely, side by side, each with its own impetus and purpose, so that people will always be able to distinguish them one from the other." Indeed he had expressed a strikingly original conception of polyphony only the summer before, at Maiernigg, while listening with Wondra to the noises coming across the Wörthersee.[19]

During the long hours of peacefulness he plunged once more into the volumes of the *Bachgesellschaft*. "Bach often reminds me," he said to Natalie one day, "of those stone figures recumbent on their ashes and that always move me because they suggest the continuation of life beyond the limits of existence. Their very raison d'être seems to be their profound faith in and desire for eternal life. Bach, too, has something so petrified about him that only a small minority are capable of reviving him. This is why one hears so many bad performances of his works, performances in which nothing conjures up the great cantor at his clavier, raising his hands to the keys to demonstrate his art [*vormusizieren*]. Instead of the true Bach, his interpreters give the public nothing but a wretched skeleton. The chords that were intended to give it its marvelous fullness of body are quite simply missing, as though Bach had noted a figured bass without rhyme or reason. And yet what a magnificently exuberant tumult[20] these chords produce. It's thus that not only the violin sonatas, which it's quite absurd to entrust to one small violinist,[21] but also all the cantatas should be played and you'd be amazed at the sound they'd make!"

One day he played through Bach's cantata *Ich sündiger Mensch*,[22] which to him was not only "one of the most beautiful and perhaps even *the* most beautiful of his works," but also the one that opened up the widest perspectives. He went into ecstasies over "this miraculous freedom of Bach's, to which probably no other musician has ever attained and which is based on his unparalleled skill and command of technique . . . In Bach," he exclaimed, "all the vital cells of music are united as the world is in God; there's never been any polyphony greater than this!" Two years before he had expressed the desire to perform the *St. Matthew Passion* for the benefit of the opera's retirement fund and to enhance its polyphony by placing the orchestras and choruses on both sides of the stage. He had contemplated adding a third chorus, consisting of the public, to represent the congregation of the faithful and, of course, one of children, which he had planned to place "as high up as possible, around the organ, so that their voices will seem to come from heaven." He would thus have succeeded in creating the impression of an exchange of questions and answers, which was clearly what Bach had sought to achieve.[23]

During Mahler's convalescence, the opera continued to run "like clockwork, its by now well-oiled wheels turning to perfection." From his bed he supervised the rehearsals of Ludwig Thuille's *Lobetanz,* the premiere of which was conducted by Schalk on March 18 and achieved only moderate success.[24] *Lobetanz* was sung only six times, but Mahler attributed its failure at least partially to his own absence, for "the lemonade was too watered down and seemed insipid," whereas his presence on the podium would have added "a little pure lemon that might have made it more tasty."

On March 20 he and Justi set off by train for Abbazia, a famous beach in the Istrian Peninsula, now called Opatija, where he had rented a four-room apartment on the top floor of the Villa Jeannette for the Easter holidays. As usual, he picked an attic room for himself, which had a view over the whole countryside. Arnold Rosé, on his return from a tour of Italy with his quartet, and the ever-faithful Natalie joined them shortly after their arrival. The four of them spent their evenings on the vast terrace-roof of the villa, from which they had a panorama of the island-studded sea. Mahler was in such good humor that nothing bothered him. He devoted several hours a day to completing the revision of his *Fourth Symphony*, recopying the Adagio and altering certain orchestral details of the Finale, in which he had decided to use the full orchestra he had chosen for the lied. "I'm living here, as it were, in the atmosphere of my *Fourth*," he wrote to Guido Adler. "I'm preparing it for publication and expect to have it ready tomorrow or the day after . . . With its mixture of malice, profound mysticism and delicious absurdities," the text of the Finale, which he had set to music nine years before, continued to delight him. "One would think one were seeing the side of the moon that remains forever hidden from us," he said of it one evening as he watched the moon rise, luminous, behind the mountains and bathe the sea and the coast in a flood of silvery light. Waxing dreamy at this magnificent sight, he mused on the ever new difficulties with which he had to cope every time he was composing a new work. "It's not just a question of conquering a summit previously unknown, but of tracing, step by step, a new pathway to it, whereas the audience and the 'judges' come rushing in all of a sudden and want to see everything immediately, without realizing that their shortsightedness prevents them from seeing anything more than the nearest bush. It's as though they saw garbage in a landscape and were therefore unable to perceive the beauty and divine liberty of nature. They then utter harsh criticism, nothing satisfies them, everything must be otherwise; although it might never even have occurred to them beforehand that such a path was possible, they are determined to make us responsible for the fact that nature is thus and not otherwise."

During his first years as a composer, Mahler had been impatient for his works to be played and become widely known, but soon his attitude changed. The first sign of evolution can be sensed in the reply he gave (no doubt upon his return from Abbazia) to Justi and Natalie when they were urging him to make some effort to get his works known: "They will do all that is necessary themselves; today or tomorrow, what does it matter? Must one be present, when one becomes immortal?"[25]

During a walk in the moonlight, Mahler told Natalie about a dream he had had at the age of eight and which, because it had seemed so symbolic of his wandering destiny, he had never forgotten.[26] He also recalled an equally painful dream he had had in 1891, when he had gone to Gastein to see Pollini and Natalie had joined him.[27] He had found himself amid a throng of people in a vast and brilliantly lighted hall just at the moment when the last guest arrived, a very tall man of somewhat stiff bearing, magnificently attired and with the air of a *bon vivant*. Suddenly realizing that this figure was none other than Death, he had tried to flee, but, unbeknown to anyone, the stranger, as though by means of some magnetic power, had lured him into a curtained-off corner, seized his arm in an iron grip, and ordered him to follow him. Only waking had broken Death's fearful hold over him. The dream may have been a foreboding on Mahler's part of his premature death. At all events, it was doubtless because he had just narrowly escaped dying that he remembered it at this particular time.

These long rambles in the moonlight, these confidences so precisely noted down, and these long talks on artistic and musical subjects reveal the close intimacy between Mahler and Natalie at that time. Although she still frequently irritated him, he nevertheless appreciated her enthusiasm, her steadfast loyalty, and her modest and self-effacing attitude as a witness of his life and work. At Abbazia, according to her,[28] "Justi and Rosé, Gustav and I, according to our physical strength or innermost bents, gave ourselves up 'two by two' to the joys of nature." These words betray her secret and long-cherished hope of one day seeing her friendship with Mahler crowned by marriage. He finally discovered it the day he found out a family intrigue and the nature of the bond between Justi and Arnold Rosé. It seems that Natalie had threatened to let the cat out of the bag if Justi refused to facilitate her intimate walks with him. According to Alma Mahler, he was furious about his sister's "treason," but it must nevertheless be most emphatically stressed that his letters to Justi reveal no trace of even a passing falling-out between them. Be that as it may, although she did her best to hide the fact, Natalie was bitterly disappointed when she learned of Mahler's engagement.

The original version of Alma Mahler's manuscript contains a cruel anecdote concerning Natalie, the details of which, however, are unreliable, for Alma Mahler long remained jealous of all those who had played an important part in her husband's life before she entered it. According to her, at the end of the summer of 1901, after Mahler's return to Vienna, Natalie was supposed to have stayed on at Maiernigg with Justi to tidy up the house, but had actually had an urgent telegram sent to her from Vienna in order to have an excuse for joining him. Upon her return, she had implored him to marry her and had even tried to kiss him, but he had repulsed her with the words: "I can't love you, I can only love a beautiful woman," to which she had replied, "But I *am* beautiful. Ask Henriette Mankiewicz!" Brokenhearted at this rebuff and the announcement of Mahler's engagement three months later, she apparently became enamored of a painter, with whom she hastened to "flaunt her liaison." Mahler perhaps showed that he had been fonder of her than he had owned by remarking later that "she could have waited out a year's separation."

The holiday in Abbazia did Mahler a world of good and his health "improved hourly . . . I'm so busy eating, sleeping and going for walks that I've hardly a minute to spare," he wrote. "I've finally realized that the hidden cause of all my ills was that which the doctors have just discovered. But for my hemorrhage, they might never have discovered it . . . As for Vienna, these last weeks have taught me a lesson and I hope I shall never again allow myself to become swamped by such a whirlwind of minor activities. In future, I'll leave the piloting and steering entirely to others. I must in any case find or train a few more trustworthy sailors."[29]

After having put on over thirteen pounds and recovered his strength, Mahler returned to Vienna on April 6. Two Philharmonic concerts had taken place since his operation, the first under the baton of Hellmesberger and the second under that of Schalk. Many critics had sung the praises of these conductors, who belonged to a good solid "classical tradition." All Mahler's enemies, who by then constituted the majority of the press, declared that they had heard nothing so admirable since Richter's departure. Hirschfeld rejoiced above all that Hellmesberger was "without willfulness," a merit that he felt made up for his "lack of individuality . . . To be sure, he does not present all of Beethoven, but neither does he try to present anything other or more than Beethoven. The audience would rather complete the picture in its imagination than have to remove extraneous elements from it. A portrait from which a few of the sitter's features are missing will always seem a better likeness and more successful than even the cleverest of images or reproductions containing the slightest foreign element. I am both willing and able to hear more than is offered me with my inner ear, but I cannot, even with the utmost good will, cut out anything that I actually hear . . . An atmosphere of profound peace pervaded the hall, every personal element, in so far as it did not come from Beethoven, seemed to have been erased, and we all experienced perfect happiness, as though we had left our nerves behind in the cloakroom."

Max Graf in the *Neues Wiener Journal,* was delighted to rediscover "good old musical blood" and a tradition and soundness of craftsmanship in Hellmesberger that fully made up for his "lack of initiative." The correspondent of the *Neue Zeitschrift für Musik* dwelled on the interminable applause of an audience "delighted finally to hear Beethoven's works performed as he had intended them to be," while Helm exulted at having rediscovered a conductor "who does not impose his own personality at the expense of the work" and is not possessed of "the devil of always doing better." Though titular critic of an anti-Semitic paper, Helm was alone in admitting, in the *Wochenblatt,* that the subscriptions had fallen off as soon as it had become known that the Philharmonic concerts would be conducted by Hellmesberger.

The critics showed the same enthusiasm two weeks later, after the final concert of the season conducted by Schalk. "The best part of it all," according to Max Graf, "is that, for the first time since Richter's departure, people were delighted to hear a conductor who, in all objectivity, gave free rein to the innate genius of the orchestra." It would indeed be hard to utter more specious praise!

Mahler undoubtedly felt considerable bitterness at seeing these two mediocre conductors lauded to the skies at his expense. At all events, the advice of his doctors and his acute awareness of the deep-rooted personal and artistic misunderstanding between himself and his musicians strengthened his resolve not to renew his candidacy for the conductorship of the Philharmonic. Thus, when a delegation of the orchestra headed by the horn player Wipperich came to ask him not to withdraw, he replied that he would stand again only if he were unanimously re-elected, well knowing that nobody could possibly guarantee him any such thing, no conductor, not even Richter, ever having been unanimously elected.[30] He therefore wrote the following letter to the committee on April 1: "Dear Sirs, I much regret to have to inform you that, owing to my ill health and the exhausting labor that my position demands, it will henceforth he impossible for me to assume the conductorship of the Philharmonic concerts. I ask you to convey my decision to the honorable members of your corporation and to be good enough to express my sincere gratitude to them for the confidence they have hitherto reposed in me. I need hardly add that, in future as in the past, one of my most cherished duties will be to encourage and assist the Philharmonic and its conductor in every way possible and on occasion, if my strength permits, to conduct its concerts myself."[31]

Relieved to be free at last of his powerful grasp, the musicians promptly elected one of the most mediocre of the Viennese conductors to replace Mahler, Josef Hellmesberger,[32] who was as dumfounded by this unexpected honor as by the laurel wreath presented to him after the first concert of the 1901–02 season. Though not a bad musician, he had neither the stature nor the versatility to attract the public, so that both the artistic level of the concerts and their success slowly declined. Under Mahler, the requests for subscriptions had become so numerous that the committee had been able to raise the price of the tickets and the musicians' individual income, which had amounted to about 300 florins per concert in Richter's time, rose to 350. Under Hellmesberger, it dropped to 300 again and then to only 200 during his last season.[33] Although their financial loss was thus quite substantial, most of the musicians were glad to see Mahler go, since they accumulated grievances against him daily at the opera,[34] and most of them had never accepted his more "scandalous" initiatives and his scorn for sacrosanct "tradition." The cellist Theobald Kretschmann was one of Mahler's sworn enemies, but it seems clear that here he was expressing the general opinion of the orchestra's musicians: "Mahler tried, with unflagging zeal, to throw new light onto a work through its performance, but too often this just interfered with [störte] its over-all line by introducing too many analytical refinements. In his enthusiasm and eagerness he went so far as to alter the instrumentation; he himself even claimed to be a symphonist. Only time will tell whether all this has done art a service, for opinions were violently divided on the subject."[35]

Kretschmann also reproached Mahler for his "delight in shocking people by doing just the opposite of what all the other conductors did," particularly with Wagner, whose tradition only Richter effectively represented. Had not one of his Vienna friends exclaimed, after hearing Mahler conduct at the opera, "I no longer recognize my *Meistersinger!* O Holy Hans Richter!" According to him Hellmesberger had immediately won over the orchestra and confirmed his "early exploits" by conducting Beethoven's *Ninth Symphony* "entirely in the spirit of Richter . . ."

Thus, even when they did not consider, like the anti-Semites, that Mahler relied, in his interpretations of the repertoire works of art, on his "pure intelligence," and his "rabbinical logic," instead of on a "natural and lively feeling," and that, "incapable of handling the whole, he concentrated on highlighting details in a completely arbitrary way," "thus disfiguring and falsifying the great German works of art,"[36] it is nonetheless true that the majority of the Philharmonic musicians saw Mahler go without regret. However, thanks above all to his conducting technique and also to his previously unheard of demands in matters of sound and precision, he had a lasting and determining influence on the style, tradition, and destiny of the orchestra. There can be no doubt but that he was deeply hurt by the attitude of the musicians, especially as he felt that he had given them the best of himself and done far more for them than his predecessors; besides getting them a raise in salary at the opera, he had succeeded in having them named *Hofmusiker,* a title on which they set great store. Apart from this, he regretted giving up the only one of his activities he considered "purely artistic" because it had nothing to do with the theater. He was henceforth to devote himself exclusively to the latter and, most fortunately, to find immense satisfaction in a new and crucial aspect of his theatrical activity.

Meanwhile, there still remained many difficulties to be ironed out at the opera, not the least of which were the vanity of the stars and their jealousy. He had already had a hard time smoothing the ruffled feathers of Reichmann two years earlier and, on January 28, 1901, this same star wrote to inform him of his "amazement and indignation" because he had entrusted a forthcoming performance of *Die Meistersinger* to "another singer . . . You assured me, both viva voce and in writing, that my incarnation of Hans Sachs was one of the most accomplished performances of the German stage and now, for no reason at all, you refuse to give to me this very part??? I greatly admire your art and have made every effort not to upset you and to be at your disposal at all times, so that you should not find yourself in difficulty *because of me.* Yet you reward me with this uncalled-for slight, as though you wished to prove to me that I am nothing but a poor devil of a subordinate who does not deserve any consideration! No Sir, if this is how you treat me, I shall move heaven and earth to escape you and to resign from an institution that shows so little respect and gratitude."

The fact of the matter was that, eaten up by jealousy of his younger rival, the baritone Demuth, who, though both theatrically and artistically his inferior, still had all the vocal freshness and ease in his high register, which Reichmann had lost, the latter could not tolerate Demuth's repeatedly singing one of his own best roles. Mahler answered him immediately: "I have just received your letter (at home and in the middle of my lunch, for which I well deserve an hour of leisure and peace). I have already told you how much I admire your interpretation of Hans Sachs. I now tell you so again and shall go on telling you so as often as you wish. However, I have never told you that I would grant you the monopoly of either this or any other part, nor shall I ever do so for, in an institution like the Vienna Opera, so important a part cannot belong to any one person. I have decided to assign it to Herr Demuth this time, after a long interval, in order that he should not forget it and also in order to be able, in case of emergency (which, please God, will not arise), to count on him to replace you.

"Aside from this, it just so happens that *Der fliegende Holländer* is coming up and that this is another of your most masterly interpretations. Today, you will sing Wolfram and I therefore see no reason why you should feel sorry for yourself. I feel obliged to tell you quite frankly and in all friendship that I consider this pettifoggery unworthy both of you and of me. If anyone has reason to complain of me and my attitude, it is not you. I have never at any time been lacking in respect or regard for you and you should not degrade yourself by constantly complaining, like a mere beginner, because someone else has sung one of your parts.

"Our artistic relations are based on mutual esteem and, at least as far as I am concerned, on friendship. You should therefore refrain from giving way to passing ill-humor and (forgive me the harsh words), out of entirely misplaced vanity, constantly destroying our good relations by your exorbitant demands. Do remember that you and I are here to serve the opera, the opera is not, as you sometimes seem to think, here to serve us. I trust you will realize that it is only out of respect for so valuable a member of this same opera as you are that I am answering your letter so patiently and at such length, but do not presume to bend the bow too far! You have already suffered the unfortunate consequences of so doing and I would be very sorry to see a man whom I sincerely respect, both as a human being and an artist, re-embark upon such a disastrous course. I am in considerable pain and you have most frivolously deprived me of the little time I had to rest today. I do not think it was very fair of you. Your faithful admirer, Gustav Mahler."

Things did not stop there, however, for the great but aging baritone had become morbidly touchy. Another exchange of letters reveals the wealth of patience Mahler had to expend on him in May. On the seventh Reichmann frankly admitted that he had been at great pains to sing the role of the Dutchman through to the end the day before simply because he knew Demuth was ready to replace him, but that he had momentarily lost his voice as a result. He was well aware, he said, of Mahler's "partiality" for "a certain gentleman" to whom he was about to assign the new productions of *Don Giovanni* and *Le Nozze di Figaro,* as well as a performance, to be given in the presence of the Emperor, of a new and unabridged production of *Tannhäuser*. "I hope that you will now prove to me that I still find some favor in your eyes," he added, "otherwise I shall be deeply offended, since my admiration and respect for your art are boundless."

Ten days later Reichmann lost his voice again, this time "as a result of singing Telramund before I was completely recovered from an attack of catarrh . . . I am distraught beyond words," he wrote, "for I am not, thank God, prone to such accidents." He begged Mahler not to reduce his pay because of his forced absence, especially as he would already have recovered if he had not sung this role. "My nerves are strained to the breaking point and my life is that of a martyr," he ended. Ten days after that, he nevertheless implored Mahler not to send him on holiday but to let him sing the final *Die Meistersinger* of the season. "Could you not curb your enthusiasm for certain persons?"[37] he continued. "You can be enchanted by them without being unjust to me, for there is no reason why you should thus prematurely take my rôles away from me and assign them to others . . . While I am still in full possession of my vocal means, I shall not let anyone oust me . . . When you first arrived . . . I refused to take part in any sort of opposition to you. Just think back to the early days . . . I do not look for gratitude, but neither do I expect to be repaid with ingratitude. For a long time now, you have been persecuting me and saying that you cannot work with me because I do not submit to discipline. How rarely you have let me sing of late! You promised me the Templar but I get nothing, always nothing! . . ."

According to Ludwig Karpath, Reichmann became so exasperated that he finally wrote and told Mahler that he refused ever to sing under his baton again! He doubtless imagined that Mahler would let one of his assistants conduct the performances in which he was singing, but Mahler, with good-humored sarcasm, replied that, "in future, he would automatically exempt him from singing any of the works he was conducting." Since Mahler's repertoire included most of the works in which Reichmann achieved his biggest successes, the latter had to give in.[38]

The same trouble arose a few months later with the great Danish tenor Erik Schmedes, who felt the same jealousy toward his young Czech colleague, Leo Slezak.[39] Recommended to Mahler by Reichmann, Slezak later admitted that he had felt some anxiety at the idea of joining the Vienna Opera company, where several other tenors would be in competition with him (as well as Schmedes, there were also Winkelmann, Van Dyck, and Fritz Schrödter). However, on January 23, 1901, he made a sensational debut in *Guillaume Tell*.[40] Mahler was as deeply impressed as was the Viennese audience by the brilliance and flexibility of his voice, equally well suited to lyric as to dramatic roles, and he ratified Slezak's contract in his dressing room during the performance.

By the end of summer, Schmedes, already very jealous of his young rival, was nonetheless forced to step down in his favor, and he suffered accordingly. He complained to Mahler, in a letter of November 5, that Slezak was singing all the parts, whereas he himself had not had the chance to learn any new ones. He had always presumed that his rival would be assigned the light and lyric roles and that he would keep the heroic roles, such as *Tannhäuser*. "My young colleague Slezak sings legion parts, whereas I am given none . . . In order that you should be good to me again, I repeat to you, Herr Direktor, that I can accomplish anything so long as you look after my interests and treat me kindly . . ."

Yet another "problem" was the tenor Pacal, who, having received a marvelous offer from the Frankfurt Opera the year before, had agreed to remain in Vienna only on the strength of certain promises Mahler had made him. Later on he said that Mahler had not only denied having made them, declaring he had no recollection of them, but had also added that "if you dare speak to me like that, I shall have nothing more to do with you." Thereafter, according to Pacal, he had "ruined my career" by describing him to the whole opera as a "man without talent" who "should be kicked out of the theater." Pacal therefore wrote to the intendant and the lord chamberlain to air his grievances.

The most important event of the latter part of the 1901 season was the new production of *Tannhäuser,* which Mahler prepared with such loving care that some of the newspapers made fun of him for spending unnecessary time and effort on trifles. The *Fremdenblatt,* in its *"Aus der Theaterwelt"* column, claimed that he had insisted upon ordering every detail of the Venusberg scene himself and had even demanded an extra rehearsal of it, during which he had tried in vain to "make the dogs bark fortissimo" when the Landgraf blew his horn. This same paper added that he had used no less than twelve horns in this scene.

For this new production, which constituted a further step in his reform of the staging of Wagner's operas, Mahler restored the original Dresden version in its entirety.[41] Unfortunately the intendance imposed the strictest economy on him, so that Schönaich deplored, above all, the "ridiculous garments" of the pilgrims, which he found painfully shabby in comparison to the magnificent entry of the royal retinue in Goldmark's *Die Königin von Saba,* another opera that had recently been restaged. Nevertheless, he acknowledged the merits of several of the reforms, especially of those of the Venusberg scene and the final scene, which had previously been neglected, and he said that, thanks to the "miraculous" precision of every last sixteenth note, the entire performance had revealed the hand of Gustav Mahler. However, he disapproved of certain of his "dragged-out and contorted" tempos, asserting that they were contrary to the composer's metronomic indications and out of keeping with his style.[42] Even though Wagner had fought for slowness, he had never advocated such excesses as "turn reason into folly and blessings into curses," Schönaich said.[43]

Kauders and Heuberger resolutely defended Mahler and his conception of *Tannhäuser.* Kauders pronounced it a "miracle of the art of interpretation" and full of "delicate nuances of expression and surprising, novel and subtle dynamic nuances," while Heuberger detected Mahler's influence in every last detail of the score, the singing and playing of the actors, the movements of the crowd and the "grandiose style" of the whole performance.

Two other events of lesser importance completed the season at the opera. One was a splendid revival of Karl Goldmark's most famous opera, *Die Königin von Saba,* with sumptuous scenery and costumes on which the anti-Semitic press accused Mahler of having spent ten thousand kronen. As always, he had endeavored to harmonize the various elements of the performance and to revitalize the music, which he found somewhat uninspiring.[44] The performance was a great success, but the *Deutsche Zeitung* reproached Mahler with serving up the inferior work of a Jew, who was nothing but a poor imitator of Wagner and Meyerbeer, and with neglecting such German composers as Weber, Cornelius, and Hugo Wolf. Never, Leitich wrote, had the weaknesses of Goldmark's opera been so glaring, despite Mahler's "improvements" and the lavishness of the production.[45] The other event was a new production of Flotow's *Martha*,[46] an opera Mahler had frequently but reluctantly conducted in his youth and to which he resigned himself only in order to please the general public. He took this opportunity to introduce a young conductor whom the anti-Semitic papers promptly attacked because he was Jewish and, according to them, lacked technique. A protégé of Richard Strauss, who had recommended him to Mahler, Gustav Brecher,[47] they specified, had not managed "to give the desirable precision to the ensembles." The *Neue Freie Presse*, on the other hand, found them "faultless" and "superior to the rest of the performance" and congratulated Mahler on having had the new conductor make his debut with *Martha* rather than with something like *Lohengrin*.

For once, Mahler agreed with his adversaries. In a letter he wrote to Strauss in August, he called Brecher a "charming and likable boy" but regretted that he had "far too little routine and experience" for the Vienna Opera, and promised to find him a temporary job in the provinces for a couple of seasons. It was then that he decided to write again to his favorite and most zealous disciple, Bruno Walter, to offer him the post he had intended for Brecher.[48]

The building of his new house at Maiernigg had been nearing completion when Mahler had left there at the end of the preceding summer. During the winter, he had constantly urged Theuer, the architect, to do everything possible to finish the job before the following summer so that he would finally, and for the first time in his life, be able to experience the tranquil joy of a proprietor. Thus it was full of happy anticipation that he took the train to Klagenfurt at the beginning of June. Justi had gone ahead to put everything in order at the Villa Mahler and make it look lived in.

Ideally situated between the forest and the lake, the house, which still stands today exactly as Mahler built it, was a rather graceless mass of wood and masonry of a style popular around 1900, a sort of cross between a villa and a chalet with a veranda on the ground floor, an open terrace on the second floor, and a balcony on the top floor. All the rooms had a panoramic view over the lake, Justi's room and the living room opening onto the veranda and the dining room and guest room onto the terrace. Mahler's quarters, which were as usual up on the top floor under the roof, consisted of a large room opening onto the balcony, which he furnished with a huge table so that he could use it as both bedroom and study, and a small dressing room and washroom. Standing on his balcony and looking out over the Wörthersee on the day he arrived, he exclaimed, "It's too beautiful, one shouldn't allow oneself such a thing." Deep down inside his puritanical soul, he felt as though, after having so long fled luxury, pleasures, and in general everything that could contribute to making his life pleasanter and more beautiful, he were there merely by some irony of fate. He often smiled to himself during the summer as he pondered the novelty of so sweet and harmonious an existence. However, the things that pleased him most were the garden and a piece of forest land he owned and through which he had stepped paths built, together with a "shore walk" on the embankment below the house that became his favorite place for strolling after dinner. During one of his first exploratory walks, he was delighted to discover a spring close by his property which would supply the house with drinking water. He hastened to buy the additional piece of land, had the flow of water measured, and took a passionate interest in the tapping process, which necessitated the digging of several channels.

Having had a small boathouse to hold two boats built on the lakeshore and, on either side of it, two bathing huts with flat roofs for sunbathing, he went there daily, for he had become one of the first advocates of the "new method" of alternate swimming and sunbathing. He also got into the habit of plunging into the lake first thing every morning.

In September 1900, Natalie, who had stayed on alone at Maiernigg, had written Mahler several letters informing him of the progress of the building and telling him about her difficulties in finding a direct route between the new house and the *Häuschen*. Nevertheless, a steep pathway, which became dangerously slippery when it rained, had finally been plotted out and built, and, from the moment he arrived, Mahler retired to the *Häuschen* for several hours a day, while complaining of his usual difficulties in resuming his composing. Before this began to take up all his time, he devoted a lot of it to reading. An article by Hermann Kretzschmar[49] particularly interested him because it scientifically substantiated the principles of the interpretation of early music at which he himself had arrived by instinct, "like a wizard surveying a terrain with his wand for running water," whereas science arrived at the same result "with the help of a barometer and a hygrometer, just as one uses a pig to find truffles and thereby humidity."

As from 1901, polyphony played an ever-increasing part in Mahler's music. It is therefore interesting to learn from Natalie that he regularly received and carefully perused the volumes of the Bachgesellschaft. Both the polyphonic works and the harmonizations of chorales fascinated him, and he was again surprised to note the little importance people attached to originality of themes in Bach's time. "In those days, art was the manner in which one decorated or varied themes and subjects that were common to all composers since the time of the Greeks." Bach's place in musical history seemed to him to be unchallenged. "His miraculous polyphony was unparalleled in his time and will remain so throughout time," he exclaimed after reading, *inter alia,* his *Third Motet.* "The way the eight voices are led along in a polyphony which he alone masters is unbelievable! I only manage to read them rather slowly (they're impossible to play on the piano), but I'd love to perform them someday and I must, the world would be amazed. Wondrous to relate, Bach teaches me something every day (but then, of course, I'm nothing but a child sitting at his feet), for my method of composing is innately 'Bachic!' If only I had the time to devote myself entirely to his teachings, the greatest of them all! Just think what it would do for me, I hardly dare think of it myself! However, it's to him that I shall devote my future time, when it finally belongs entirely to me! . . . It's only now that I realize, in quite a different way, that I ought to give up the opera in order to be able to work."[50] Mahler promised himself that when that time came he would read numerous scores by the masters, and above all those he did not yet know. Why, he wondered, were there so many complete editions of classic writers, but not of classic composers whom every musician ought to know? Even among Beethoven's works, there were still some, such as the *First Mass,* which he himself did not know.

In his view, reading scores was a must for every musician. While talking to Natalie a few weeks earlier about a blind musician,[51] he had said that a man deprived of his sight was predestined to become a musician, but that he must have possessed it at some point, for hearing a pianistic reading or a bad performance could in no wise replace the perusal of a score. Likewise, he felt that it would be impossible to compose without writing down all the various possibilities in turn and that no one could replace the composer himself in this task. He thus concluded that he would have to give up composing if he ever lost his sight, whereas he would undoubtedly be able to continue even if he became deaf.

During this peaceful summer, he reread the songs of Schumann, "the second greatest composer of this kind of music after Schubert," a musician who "surpassed all others in his mastery of form and created the most accomplished and complete lieder." By constantly remaining within the limits of the genre, which he had never sought to exceed, Schumann had always maintained a restraint in his emotion, an authenticity in his lyricism, and a depth in his melancholy which Mahler found particularly enchanting in the lesser known songs, such as the *Frauenliebe und Leben.* Whereas in his youth such reading matter had depressed him and hampered him in his work, because it gave him the discouraging feeling that he would never be able to equal the masters, it now afforded him immense joy. Conversely, feeble and inadequate works were beginning to depress him, for he perceived their limitations and "smelled the odor of mortality" they emitted, an odor that was "absolutely intolerable in art."

At the beginning of the holidays, Mahler organized musical evenings on the top floor of the house with Natalie and Rosé, he himself using an unfortunately rather poor piano he had hired in Klagenfurt. He had them play the duos for violin by Spohr, whose charm and skillful instrumental writing he admired, and he and Rosé played transcriptions of Brahms's clarinet sonatas, which he wondered he could ever have misjudged.

After one of these musical evenings, he and Natalie went for a walk along the lakeshore and the new pathway to the spring, and he again went into ecstasies over the beauty of the place: "You see," he said, "that which one desires in one's youth one attains to later on. Would you ever have believed that we would be able to call so heavenly a place 'ours'?"[52] When they got back to the house, they went up to Mahler's balcony to watch the scores of lights along the shore turning into millions of sparks in the calm waters of the lake.

Hardly had they parted to go to bed before Mahler heard a cry scarcely louder than a groan coming from the shore. He dashed out onto the balcony, shouting, "Who's there?" but, receiving no answer and hearing nothing more, he went back to bed. A few minutes later wailings and gurglings sent him flying down the stairs and out to the lake. In the water close by the little landing stage, he descried a drunkard who seemed about to drown. With great difficulty, he pulled him out, laid him down unconscious on the bank, and then ran to call the others. They all bustled about reviving him, comforting him, feeding him, and even finding dry clothes for him, and within an hour he had recovered and gone on his way, but he never told them his name or how he had come to fall into the lake, and the Mahlers never heard of him again.

During July, Mahler composed a few lieder. The first sketch of *Blicke mir nicht,* the first song for which he had given up *Des Knaben Wunderhorn* in favor of the romantic miniaturist Friedrich Rückert, is dated the twelfth. Apart from this, a few other *"Rückert Lieder"* and a last *Wunderhorn Lied,* *"Tamboursg'sell,"* he did not get down to composing anything else of importance during the first month of his holiday. However, no sooner had he decided to allow himself two weeks of complete rest than he plunged head to foot into what was doubtless a larger project, and that despite the noise of hammering and sawing that reached him from the villa.

Having finally acquired the habit of jotting down all his musical ideas in notebooks, he regretted not having done so much earlier, because in the event that his abundant flow of inspiration should one day run dry, he would be able to fall back on that which he had stocked up over the years. "What an expenditure of superhuman effort," he exclaimed, "to have to create everything on the instant, when one has neither set by nor 'harvested' anything (in the literal sense of the word)." If, on the other hand, he let nothing go to waste during the summer but collected everything and set it aside, then at some future date he would only have to take out his notebook in order to find all that he needed. It was thus that Beethoven, toward the end of his life, had unearthed and used themes he had noted down years before.

In August, Mahler brought up the subject of these notebooks again, stating that he did not on any account want them to survive his death and that he would destroy everything he himself had not finished, for "such fragments only lead to misunderstandings." Beethoven's notebooks had revealed nothing except that he apparently worked on several different projects at once, whereas he was, in fact, constantly jotting down themes for future use. Musicologists had underlined the "progress accomplished" in the final version, but no one knew what he might have done with his first inspiration, nor indeed what any other idea might have become in his hands.

Although Mahler continued to say nothing whatever about his activity, none of his family doubted but that it was an extensive project he was working on. During another walk with Natalie in early August, he began to speak of Brahms, of Steinbach, and of Ischl. "They were the most blissful days of my life, those of my honeymoon with my muse! Since then, our marriage has produced one child after another, as though that were quite normal, and it hardly even occurs to us to thank one another for this happiness. My present creative work is that of an adult, a man of ripe experience. Although I no longer attain my former heights of enthusiasm, I now feel that I'm in full possession of my powers and technique, that I'm master of my means of expression and capable of carrying out anything I put my hand to."

At the beginning of August, Justi and Rosé departed with Albi Adler (a childhood friend of the Mahlers from Iglau) and Dr. Boer, the physician of the Vienna Opera, to Heiligenblut, where Justi was to take a cure prescribed for her after her operation of the previous year. Left alone with Natalie for a few days, Mahler reveled in the complete peace and quiet "that I so badly need and is so seldom granted me." From time to time, however, and despite his isolation, intruders would come and disturb him. On July 25 a boat approached the house and, amid catcalls, shouts, and the noise of clashing oars, a whole group of young people carried on a quasi-confidential conversation: "Do tell me what you've got against Mahler. What's he done to you? . . . He wrote a bad symphony (the *First*) and the *Klagende Lied*"—and the uproar continued louder than ever. The following day, he was gazing at the lake from his balcony, when some young girls spied him from a motorboat and began to yell, "Mahler! Look there! Bravo! Bravo!" He beat a hasty retreat into his room, for such an ovation was just as distressing to him as the shouts of the day before, but he could not help smiling to himself as he thought of the contrast between the two scenes.

Throughout the summer, Mahler seemed calm and relaxed. As usual, he made a few excursions, but they were less successful than those of the previous year, for the weather was poor. One day, he raced up to the Drei Bärenhütte in pelting rain and came back soaked and with his shoes full of water.[53] However, despite such mishaps and all the disturbances, he remained unusually serene. Whereas he had made war on the birds the summer before, and especially on those nesting in the roof of his *Häuschen,* he was now on excellent terms with them and enjoyed listening to their vocalizations. He called them "the first composers" and sometimes had the feeling he would be quite unable to equal them. "Already as a child," he said, "I used to listen to these songs that start off like conscious melody and rhythm and then degenerate into inarticulate chirping, as though some four-footed creature suddenly sat up on its hind legs and then fell back into its natural position."[54]

Owing to one of those contradictions so typical of him, Mahler often made war on animals when they disturbed him, but nevertheless observed them with a kind of romantic wonder. Two years earlier, while on a visit to Sankt Wolfgang,[55] he had been amused to see a small dachshund, who had seemed to be enjoying his caresses, suddenly become fascinated with the smell of cooking and forget him completely. This immediate, total, and absolute truthfulness of animals, for whom life is a perpetual present, never failed to delight and stimulate him; "Indeed, I often find the basic themes and rhythms of my art in nature."

During the signally sterile summer of 1897, he had talked about nature's influence on his work and of the importance he attached, for instance, to the squawking of hens, peacocks, or crows. At Steinach am Brenner, the latter's strange modulations had made him "desperately sad," whereas at Steinbach, two years before, these same cries had made such an impression on him that he had introduced them into the Finale of his *Second Symphony;* albeit he stressed that, when he had introduced bird song into his work, he had not tried to imitate reality but to stylize it. For example, in his *First Symphony,* he had suggested a cuckoo's cry by a third rather than a fourth. He had cared little whether or not it was lifelike, yet everyone had recognized this "call of spring" in the first movement. He listened just as attentively to the thundering of a waterfall, the bells of a herd of cattle, and even the modulated creakings of a door. "It's in nature," he explained, "that we find our initial themes and rhythms; she offers them to us very succinctly in the sounds made by each different animal. Man, the artist, derives his forms and subject matter from the world around him, to which he naturally lends a totally different and much wider meaning, either because he's in a state of blissful harmony with nature or because he's in painful or negative and hostile conflict with her or, again, because he's trying to rid himself of her by laughing at her from the top of his ivory tower. Such are the sources, in the most restrictive sense of the word, of an artist's style, which is sometimes noble and sublime, sometimes sentimental and tragic and sometimes satirical and humorous."[56]

The Mahler of 1897 was still the composer of the *Wunderhorn* and the *Third Symphony,* obsessed by the beauty of nature and moved by its tragic dissonances. The Mahler of 1901 could listen to the birds more serenely, and during these exceptionally happy days ideas for his new symphony flowed abundantly. He finally broached the subject with Natalie at the beginning of August, when he was in the middle of the Scherzo: "both the construction and the ordering of the details and proportions [*Verhältnisse*] of which demand great artistic mastery because its apparent confusion must, as in a Gothic cathedral, be resolved into supreme order and harmony." On August 5 he again talked to his faithful confidante about this particular movement, feeling that it was perhaps the grandest he had ever composed. "You wouldn't believe the trouble it's giving me, the obstacles and thorns it's strewing in my way, largely because of the simplicity of its themes, which are almost all based on tonic and dominant chords. No one else would dare do such a thing today. The progression of the chords presents formidable difficulties, above all on account of my principle of avoiding repetitions and

always letting things develop themselves. The individual voices are so difficult to play that only soloists will be able to manage them. So well do I know
the orchestra and the instruments that I've indulged in the boldest passages
and melodic movements [*Passagen und Bewegungen*]."[57] Having used a
theme by Thomas Koschat, *"An dem blauen See,"* in the second movement,[58] Mahler was thankful to have taken it from this mediocre composer
rather than from Beethoven, who "was able to develop all of his themes himself."[59]

He had already begun to realize that his Scherzo was entirely different
from anything he had ever composed before. "It's so thoroughly kneaded
that there's not a single grain in it which isn't blended and transformed.
Each note is endowed with supreme life and everything in it revolves as
though in a whirlwind or the tail of a comet. Neither romantic nor mystical
elements belong in it, it's merely the expression of an unparalleled power,
that of man in the full light of day who has reached the climax of his life.
The entire work will be orchestrated in the same vein, no harps or English
horns. The human voice has absolutely no place in it. It doesn't need words
for everything is expressed in terms of pure music. It will be a symphony
in four movements,[60] in accordance with the rules, each one of them independent, complete in itself, and linked to the others solely by affinity or
mood."

In late July and early August, while working on his Scherzo, Mahler also
composed and orchestrated seven lieder. On August 10 he invited Natalie
to the *Häuschen* to play them for her. Only *"Der Tamboursg'sell"* was
based on a poem from the *Wunderhorn,* and the musical idea for it had
come to him one day as he was leaving the table. He had hastily jotted
down the first notes of the melody and then installed himself near the
spring to complete it. Having done so, he had been surprised to note that
what he had written was not a symphonic motive but that of a lied and had
remembered *"Der Tamboursg'sell."* Recalling its opening words, he had
realized that they fitted the music so perfectly that the latter seemed to
have been created for them. Thereafter, he had compared the whole text
with the music and had found that the two fitted one another from start to
finish.[61]

Like the *"Tamboursg'sell,"* the three *Kindertotenlieder* composed during
this peaceful summer were all mournful. Indeed, the day he first played
them to Natalie, Mahler himself confessed that "it hurt me to write them
and I grieve for the world which will one day have to hear them, so sad is their
content."[62]

The powerful major conclusion of *"Um Mitternacht"*[63] reminded Natalie of the end of the *Second Symphony,* while the text of *Blicke mir nicht
in die Lider* seemed to her "so typical of him that he could have written it
himself." This notwithstanding, he surmised that, since it was the least important of the lieder he had composed during the summer, it would undoubtedly be "the most successful." During his last few days in Maiernigg,

Mahler resumed work on another *Rückert Lied* he had started at the beginning of the holidays and then dropped for his symphony, *"Ich bin der Welt abhanden gekommen."* "It's I myself," he said to Natalie as he stressed its intimate and personal nature and tried to define its mood of complete but restrained fulfillment, "the feeling that fills one and rises to the tip of one's tongue but goes no further," whereas *"Ich atmet'"* described "the way one feels in the presence of a beloved being of whom one is completely sure without a single word needing to be spoken."

Thus of all Mahler's summer holidays, none was as fruitful as that of 1901, which saw the completion of two movements of the *Fifth Symphony* and seven lieder that are reckoned among his greatest achievements in this field. His first stay in his new house had in no wise justified his chronic anxieties about sterility, and it was with the usual gloom at the prospect of having to wait another whole year before resuming his work that he left it to return to Vienna.[64] "All things considered, I can be quite satisfied with what I've accomplished this summer," he wrote to Nanna Spiegler just before leaving Maiernigg.[65] "Of course, it's the same old story, too much haste and too little time! And I always have to leave when I'm right in the middle of something. But my mind is now at rest on that score, for I've finally come to realize that a creator can interrupt his labor without injuring his child and resume it at an opportune moment, a bit like hens, perhaps, who sit conscientiously on their eggs and then suddenly get off them to go and eat."

Although one of the major problems of Mahler's creative life, that of the interruptions necessitated by his activity as a conductor and administrator, thus seemed to have been solved, he nevertheless had no great illusions as to either the fate of his works or their reception by the public. "I've read almost nothing this summer because I've been too busy with my creative activities. The situation hasn't changed for ten years now and there'll soon be no other solution left to me than to follow Quintus Fixlein's example and write my library myself. As a result, somebody will one day put up a plaque on my Häuschen in the forest, 'G.M., a man of great fame in his time, sat here every morning.' Please do not make a mistake and put up the plaque on the little hut next door, where such a token of respect would doubtless be more appropriate but quite incomprehensible to anyone but Natalie and myself. How lucky mothers are not to have to interrupt their labor and perhaps even their children."[66]

"It should be one's constant
and sole endeavor to see
everything afresh and create it
anew."

# CHAPTER 35

*Mahler in Vienna (XI) — Correspondence with Strauss
— Arrival of Bruno Walter — Die* lustigen Weiber von
Windsor *and* Les Contes d'Hoffmann — *Premiere of the*
Fourth Symphony *(September–December 1901)*

Among Mahler's projects for the new season, the one closest to his heart
was the first performance in Vienna of *Feuersnot,* Richard Strauss's second
opera. The latter had come to Vienna with the Kaim Orchestra in January
to conduct a concert of his own works, of which Mahler had enjoyed the
charm of the lieder and the humor of *Till Eulenspiegel* far more than the
"platitudes" of *Ein Heldenleben.* Strauss and his wife had dined with him,
and Strauss had played through *Feuersnot* on the piano after dinner. Both
the work and its composer having made an extremely favorable impression
on him (according to Natalie, he had found Strauss "modest, likable, not
particularly profound [*bedeutend*], but hard-working and decent [*tüchtig
und ehrlich*]," Mahler had decided then and there to give the opera in
Vienna and accordingly wrote to Strauss in March: "I'm very sorry indeed that you won't let Vienna give the premiere of your opera, even
though I don't crave 'first performances' since I'm not overly concerned
about what *die Herren Journalisten* consider an 'event' in our institution. If
I like a work, I accept it and give it as soon as possible. As far as your
opera is concerned, however, the situation is slightly different, for it must
be given a model performance. We, and I say this without boasting, can
produce it with more loving care than anyone else and, most important, we
can take our time over it. I must therefore, and above all in the interest of
your work, refuse any sort of 'race' against other theaters, unless, having
duly considered the matter, you still insist upon a time limit, in which
case I'll do everything I can to satisfy you. (Between you and me, this

latter consideration seems to me to be by far the most important and I therefore trust you'll permit me to join with you in this aim)."[1]

The two musicians exchanged numerous letters during the summer because the Viennese censor had raised objections to *Feuersnot,* and Mahler was therefore unable to set a date for its premiere. Not having heard from Strauss for some time, he wrote to inform him of this obstacle before leaving Maiernigg: "Our very moral intendant, who manages to be on just as good terms with the graces and the Nine Muses as with our patron saints, is plotting to prevent the performance; all my arguments and allusions to mere human comprehension have so far been of no avail."

At the same time, and in return, Strauss was doing his best to promote Mahler's works. On March 14 he had conducted the *Lieder eines fahrenden Gesellen* in Prague with a baritone named Runold.[2] In January, Mahler had given him the score of his *Third Symphony* (completed six years before but never performed in its entirety), to which, according to Natalie, he had added the ambiguous inscription: *"Mein lieber Strauss, was nimmst du dir daraus?"*[3] Strauss immediately considered giving the first performance of it at one of the six Novitäten Konzerte he was to conduct in Berlin during the winter.[4] However, when Max Schillings told him that the *Fourth Symphony* required only modest orchestral means, he wrote to Mahler on July 3 to suggest that he give that instead, since he was neither sure that he would have sufficient time to rehearse the *Third* nor that the stage of the Kroll Theater, where the concerts were to take place, was big enough to hold such a large number of performers. Mahler replied that "I haven't yet completed the orchestration" and that "I don't want to give the Berlin public, which doesn't know me and has been prejudiced against me by a shortsighted press, the premiere of a new work that, because it's the first that is more or less easy to perform, might, if it were received in a kindly and unbiased fashion, win for me the only reward I expect for my creative activity, that of being heard and understood." He added that he had in any case promised its premiere to Munich, "where the Kaim Orchestra and the Odeon are having such a tug-of-war over it that I'm finding it hard to try to choose between them" and he would therefore rather Strauss "didn't include the *Fourth* in your projects." He also laid down three conditions for the possible performance of the *Third:* that both the orchestra and the acoustics be first rate and that, because it lasted two hours, it be the only work on the program. He apologized for "being so difficult in return for all your kindness," but nevertheless pleaded in favor of either the *Third Symphony* or, if Strauss had a good chorus at his disposal, *Das klagende Lied.*

In this letter, written in midsummer, Mahler again mentioned the fuss the Viennese censorship was making about *Feuersnot.* Strauss promptly replied: "You are and will always remain a stubborn old so-and-so, but never mind." He suggested that, instead of in Berlin, he give the *Third Symphony* at the festival of contemporary music to be held the following year in Krefeld, where he (Strauss) was cock of the walk. He had not con-

sidered performing the *Fourth Symphony* "for the glory of a first performance," but merely in case he were unable to give the *Third* in accordance
with Mahler's conditions. As far as the Berlin concert on November 18 was
concerned, he would attempt to attract the public by preceding the *Third
Symphony* with Liszt's symphonic poem *Tasso* and the Love Scene from
*Feuersnot,* adding that he preferred not to attempt *Das klagende Lied,* since
he was not sure enough of his chorus.[5]

Once again, Mahler raised objections. Strauss's program was unthinkable,
he wrote, for there would have to be a ten-minute intermission after the
first movement of the *Third Symphony,* with the result that the concert
would last over three hours and the audience would be worn out long before it was over. He asked Strauss to give either some lieder or, if the
concert were to take place in the Philharmonic Hall, which had an excellent
organ, the *Second Symphony* rather than the *Third.* He said he would also
agree to a performance of his *Fourth Symphony* provided it took place after
that in Munich, failing which he suggested the *First,* unless Strauss regarded as an insurmountable obstacle the fact that it had been a complete
flop in Berlin a few years earlier. Strauss's patience was obviously unlimited, for he was not put off by any of these complaints. He finally included the *Fourth Symphony* in the program of the concert of November 18,[6] and postponed the performance of the *Third* until the following
Allgemeiner Deutscher Musikverein festival to be held at Krefeld in June
1902.

It is strange to note the impatience with which the first performances of
Mahler's symphonies were awaited, considering the reception they later received from both press and public. Sometime later this same Strauss was to
write to the director of another Berlin concert association,[7] refusing him
permission to invite Mahler to conduct his new symphony: "You know that I
can only give new works . . . Mahler's *Fourth* is my principal attraction
[*Hauptzugstück*] . . . Your concerts are not, like mine, made up exclusively of first performances. Why don't you invite Mahler to conduct his
*First* or *Second Symphony* in December? It would not hurt the Berlin public to hear these difficult works again. Unfortunately I cannot relinquish the
*Fourth:* this is not a personal decision; I am speaking for our whole organization. So why don't you perform the *Second,* or the excellent *Klagende
Lied!*"

Even the Vienna Philharmonic sent several delegations to Mahler, asking
him to entrust them with the first performance of the *Fourth.* He told them
to take the matter up directly with Weingartner. But at the end of the summer he advised the latter to refuse out of hand, for he was anxious that the
first performance should take place in Munich.[8] A little later Mahler again
wrote to the head of the Kaim Orchestra: "May I ask you a direct question,
and beg you to give me a frank answer? Do you have any objection to my
conducting the first performance myself? I hope you understand why I am
asking this? You know that there is no one in the world to whom I would

entrust my work with more pleasure and confidence than yourself! But the fact that I have never heard this work, that I am anxious about the rehearsals because of the unusual orchestration, and that I am not sure if I have really succeeded in expressing what I intended, all make me wish to be on the podium for the first performance, for I am the only one who knows my score by heart . . . I am not used to listening from the hall and making 'apoplectic' changes. Up to now, I have always been able to go over my scores at least once with my own orchestra, and this gave me a certain sense of security. I have almost always had to make essential changes (during rehearsal)."[9]

Mahler succeeded in prolonging his summer holiday until roughly a fortnight after the beginning of the new season at the opera,[10] leaving Maiernigg on a gloriously moonlit but bitterly cold night. Natalie accompanied him to the station in Klagenfurt, and they had to huddle close to one another in the car in order to keep warm. Natalie's manuscript confirms that she herself was back in Vienna three days later, and it was doubtless then that, according to Alma Mahler, she tried to persuade Mahler to marry her.

No sooner had he returned to Vienna than he replunged into his theatrical activities. During the first week or so he lunched at the Imperial Hotel with Rosé and Dr. Boer every day and went for walks in the environs of Vienna. A delegation from the Philharmonic, headed by Franz Simandl, called on him, doubtless in a last attempt to persuade him to resume the direction of the concerts, for, in a letter to Justi, he referred to "poor Hellmesberger, who is still waiting for an official honor." On August 29 he attended a performance of *Faust,* with Katharina Fleischer-Edel of the Hamburg Opera as Marguerite and the newly engaged baritone Theodor Bertram as Mephistopheles. Once again he was exasperated not only by the platitude of Gounod's opera but also, as always when he emerged from "the pure and authentic world of my composing," by the Vienna Opera as a whole. "I can no longer feel the same affinity with this mire for I've lost touch with it; I now soar above it and it's become completely alien to me. My world is elsewhere and this one has ceased to concern me any longer. How I sympathize with Wagner's fury, he whose supreme task was carried out in the theater, at having to plow up the ground and alter the soil before he could build his work on it."

After a performance of *Der fliegende Holländer* on September 4, Mahler again returned from the opera dismayed, and he told Natalie that, although he had made quite a hit, Bertram had been thoroughly disappointing as far as he was concerned.[11] He had not been any more successful than his predecessors at "giving the impression of centuries-old suffering." Schalk, moreover, had not helped matters with his "restless tempos," which should, on the contrary, have been infinitely smooth "like the long waves of the ever-rolling sea and the long shadows that this elemental work casts." He admitted, however, that he himself would have difficulty in making Wagner's intentions clear and in rendering the eternal Wanderer's sort of "petrified calm" without a singer possessed of the necessary grandeur and power. Even Reichmann had completely forgotten the strict instructions he had given him when he restaged the opera in 1897.[12]

Mahler certainly admired Bertram in many respects for, in a letter written to Strauss in August, he spoke highly of his acting and even more highly of his voice, whose "high register is as beautiful as its low," and suggested him for the leading role in *Feuersnot* in preference to Demuth, who, despite his vocal superiority, "hasn't a particle of genius." However, the baritone must have got wind of the reservations Mahler had made about him, for a letter he wrote him on September 6 breathes wounded pride. It starts out with his refusal to sing a role in *Lohengrin* (probably the Herald) he considered "secondary and unworthy of my reputation" and continues: "Would you kindly let me know in advance the days of the month on which my presence will not be required, so that I can at least arrange to earn elsewhere the money I need to feed my family . . . Should it be impossible for you to give me leave to do this, I shall be obliged, much to my regret, to hand in my resignation. When I signed my contract, you treated me, even in artistic matters, in an entirely different manner, but now you criticize and challenge me in every respect for the quality of my voice, which, only yesterday, you judged so superb. As I have already told you, I only signed the contract in order to be able to work with a person of superior talents who would understand me and because, in my view, there is no greater name in opera than that of Vienna." Bertram was obviously mortally offended, but Mahler could just as obviously not allow him to "earn money elsewhere." He therefore accepted his resignation, so that his engagement at the Vienna Opera lasted only from September 1 to 19.

A performance of *Tannhäuser* which he himself conducted early in September disappointed Mahler just as much as had those of *Faust* and *Der fliegende Holländer*. The orchestra seemed to have gone downhill since he had stopped conducting it so frequently, and traces of the sloppiness he had worked so hard to eliminate were beginning to reappear. "What a vain labor of Sisyphus one carries on in this infamous place where one can't achieve anything wholly beautiful or absolutely pure," he moaned. A few days later, immersed in the "sacred bath" of nature in the Wienerwald, he added: "And it's for that that I wear myself to the bone, to that that I'm obliged to devote all my time and my entire being! Could anything be more repulsive than the incredible vanity and emptiness of theatrical life in which no one thinks of anything but his or her interests and not a soul considers for one second either the work of art or its creator!" He barely preferred Vienna to Hamburg, where "I used to go and hide in a box room, from which I could neither hear nor see anything, to weep during the intervals."

As a compensation for these disappointments, two happy events were about to occur in the new season. At the end of August he was visited by two very good friends from Hamburg, the composer Josef Förster and his wife, Bertha Förster-Lauterer, who hoped he would engage her at the Hofoper. He found her "just as good as before as far as her voice is concerned," whereas she "was not in full possession of her means" in Hamburg, and invited her to sing the title role in *Mignon* and Sieglinde in *Die Walküre* in September. Delighted to see her again, he explained to Natalie the "difference between intelligent and unintelligent singers. The former always manage to communicate the substance and soul of their part by singing in accordance with the text, whereas the latter don't articulate and the text thus loses both its meaning and significance. They treat it as though it were unable to share, either intensely or superficially, in the words and action of the opera. Such artists can, in a pinch, make good violinists, but they'll never be either good singers or good actors."

An even greater joy to Mahler was the arrival of his closest associate in Hamburg, his favorite disciple and one of his dearest friends, Bruno Walter. The twenty-four-year-old conductor was thrilled with both Vienna and the opera, especially after hearing his master and friend conduct *Tristan und Isolde* on September 20. "To hear this work conducted by Mahler is more than one can bear," he exclaimed. "I always have the feeling I might die in the middle of *Tristan* if I were to listen intently every second of the time and I sometimes wonder if that isn't what one *should* do."

Walter bears witness that Mahler's popularity was then at its height; his worst enemies were obliged to take notice of him, and he was so famous in Vienna that even the taxi drivers cried, "Long live Mahler!" whenever they saw him. With Walter's youthful enthusiasm for everything, he was eminently disposed to submit himself anew to Mahler's influence.

He made his debut at the opera with *Aïda* on September 27. Mahler followed the performance from his box, "every tempo and every musical intonation filling me with serene satisfaction," which he frequently expressed out loud. He looked forward to being able to entrust the most difficult works to Walter with complete confidence, whereas when his other assistants conducted, "I'm in constant agony, as it were, musically seasick."

Unfortunately, Mahler's satisfaction was not shared by the Vienna critics who, only too happy to find an excuse to renew their attacks, hastened to detect signs of a "slavish imitation" of Mahler in Walter and declared that "the Vienna Opera is not a school for budding conductors." In the *Deutsche Zeitung*, Theodor Helm called him "an executor of Mahler's intentions" and accused him of imitating "even his hand movements and the nervous contractions at the corners of his mouth." Max Graf, while acknowledging his control of both stage and orchestra, also stigmatized Walter's "servile imitating" of Mahler, from his "slight, angular gestures, looks of ecstasy and nervous agitation to his sword strokes toward the instruments," and pronounced him nothing but a bundle of "affectation, fabrication and inauthenticity."[13]

Despite the critics' disapproval, Mahler stuck to his guns and assigned

Walter such operas as *L'Africaine, Tannhäuser* and *Der fliegende Holländer,* as well as *Die Meistersinger,* which soon became exclusively his province, when Mahler did not conduct it himself, and eventually even *Fidelio* and *Die Zauberflöte.* He later engaged an Italian conductor for the Italian operas but, in the meantime, entrusted most of them to Walter too. However, before finally achieving his first undisputed success the following year, Walter was obliged to fight a grim battle. Although, like Mahler before him, he grew a small beard to hide his youth, he later complained of having been called a "beginner." After a performance of *Tannhäuser,* the critics unanimously issued "a public protest against his holding so important a post." For the first time in his life, he was insulted, humiliated, and declared "incapable of conducting even a military band." In despair, he went to see Mahler, who described to him in detail the complexities and intrigues of Vienna's artistic life, stressing the pleasure the Viennese papers took in dragging artists in the mud and explaining that, since they had not managed to find anything with which to reproach him for several months, the arrival of a young conductor known to be his protégé had provided them with an opportunity that was too good to be missed.[14]

In addition to the increasingly frequent and violent attacks of the press, Walter became aware of distinct hostility on the part of the opera personnel and finally began to have doubts about the very quality of his conducting technique, in which he thought he perceived serious flaws. He therefore considered leaving Vienna at the end of the season for Cologne, where he had been offered the position of first conductor on extremely favorable terms.[15] He had just recently got married, and his wife decided to go and consult Mahler without telling him. Mahler said he was afraid her husband had lost the battle and could no longer be a success in Vienna. He regretfully advised his accepting the position in Cologne but emphasized that Walter was in no wise responsible for his failure. Encouraged by this answer, the young conductor decided to continue the struggle and, "in the first place, to regain his self-confidence." Aware that his beat lacked precision, he applied himself to improving it by keeping a constant watch on himself and exercising all his self-critical faculties. He thus won "the essential battle, that against his own uncertainty."

The critic Richard Specht, who heard some of Bruno Walter's early performances in Vienna, confirms that he was still immature and too frequently imitated Mahler both on and off the podium. Like him, he walked with a jerky stride, like him, he shouted, laid down the law, preached and stormed rather than spoke, like him, he bit his lips and chewed his nails. He went into contortions on the podium, he expressed and lived the music with his body, and his conducting was agitated, uneven, nervous, and impulsive. He made a cult of stormy vehemence, fervor, and passion at all costs and tended to overemphasize certain episodes and minor passages. In time, however, he calmed down, his technique matured, and the real Walter, who was more easygoing and romantic, less harsh and eloquent than Mahler, finally came to the fore and asserted his innate sense of drama, his zeal and enthusiasm, and his love of beautiful orchestral sound and ability to obtain it.

Whatever his faults may have been at the time, Mahler far preferred Walter's intensity to Schalk's prosaicism. With his broad tempos and the veil that seemed to settle over the orchestra when he conducted, Schalk gave the impression of being so preoccupied with the letter of the score as not always to notice the weaknesses and deficiencies in the performance. He was not without a sense of beauty, and he abhorred sentimentality as much as coarseness, but he lived in a sort of ivory tower. Taste rather than fervor dominated both his life and his art, so that he never saw eye to eye with Mahler, whom he only really came to understand and appreciate after the latter's death. Mahler did his best never to favor Walter at Schalk's expense and never to forget his prerogative, but could not constrain himself so far as to conceal his preference.[16]

After one of his evening performances during this disastrous first season in Vienna, Walter had the pleasant surprise of receiving a note in a familiar hand which read: "Bravo! Very beautiful! Supremely majestic expression and well-controlled tempos. A great pleasure. Mahler." This warm praise from so venerated a source was worth more to him than a wealth of critical acclaim.

Walter was not the only artist who infuriated the press at the beginning of the new season, for Mahler took it into his head to assign the role of Venus in *Tannhäuser* to Gutheil-Schoder.[17] Hirschfeld seized this opportunity to attack his entire administration. In equivocal tones he praised the "reassuring soundness" of his artistic ideas and deplored the fact that "his evil genius so frequently causes him to stray from the straight and narrow and the realm of art." His quirks and shortcomings, he said, should have been kept out of public life and would have been if he had had a variety of passions on which to exercise his demon, but he unfortunately had only one, art, with the result that "his personal feelings constantly intrude on it." He always let himself be guided by his personal likes and dislikes, and the more one criticized one of his protégés, the more he upheld him. Thus the favors heaped on first Spielmann and then Michalek had been multiplied on account of the critics' protests. He seemed impelled to choose tempos different from those of other conductors, whereas his natural tendency would probably have been the right one.

Alluding to Gustav Brecher and Walter, Hirschfeld complained that, by continually bringing in debutant conductors, doubtless in the hope of finding some who were docile, Mahler had turned the Hofoper into a sort of school or testing ground, nay a laboratory. In this laboratory, moreover, great singers were sometimes allotted tiny parts and vice versa, and certain performances stood out one evening on account of some new detail that was discarded the following day. "One day, the Landgrave of Thuringia is given a horn, the next a pack of hunting dogs and thereafter a poor old horse dragged out of well-earned retirement," he said, referring to the new production of *Tannhäuser* of the preceding May. Consequently "strange objects lie abandoned in the corners of this laboratory: castoff tempos, dust-ridden favorites and moth-eaten ensembles whose holes have to be patched up by people like Pacal and Elizza. Only Mahler's masterly hand can lend a semblance of order and harmony to all these conflicting elements which include the good and the mediocre, the splendid or the outmoded. He takes especial pride in his unceasing experiments, whereas other people aspire to continuity and stability. His latest experiment has been Gutheil-Schoder, who alone constitutes a permanent challenge to the wishes of the public and the amateurs. With her, Mahler has realized the impossible: our Despina and Cherubino have been introduced into Wagner's Hörselberg as Venus. One fine day, however, Frau Gutheil-Schoder will come in an eighth note too late and immediately fall into dire disgrace with the director, a mishap that will finally enable her to mature calmly and steadily in accordance with her true nature. For the time being, she continues to enjoy his dangerous favor and is therefore obliged constantly to jump from one role to another and dare the indescribable."

While acknowledging the young singer's musical instinct and her artistic intelligence, Hirschfeld nonetheless pointed out the limitations of her "brittle" (*spröde*) voice and said that she had neither the vocal amplitude for nor the vaguest affinity with the role of Venus, for it was hard to imagine this personage as "a calm and calculating intelligence," that is to say, a complete contradiction to the "pleasures of the Venusberg . . . Out of love for his Goddess of Pure Reason, Mahler toned down the music and reduced it to an academic discourse as from the prelude. Frau Gutheil-Schoder asked her question uncertainly and prepared her movements and poses with the thoughtful care of a window dresser. Despite a debilitated and enfeebled orchestra, she produced only sounding cramps rather than song. She fought not with Tannhäuser but with her part, so that the hero could not but regard the episode as a passing fancy and joyfully return to the warmth of human passion. Thus both the music and the basic meaning of the drama were totally distorted and perverted. The aesthetic restraint of the Venusberg music may be original and the notion of a chaste Venusberg is doubtless a modern interpretation evolved during a nebulous philosophical discussion around a café table, but we protest against this violation of Wagner's intentions . . . Since Gustav Mahler makes bold to be so personal and so arbitrary," Hirschfeld concluded, "we must simply close our eyes to the brilliant artist we so admire and insist upon his deplorable obstinacy, obstinacy that is detrimental to the development of the very Hofoper which had begun to reflourish under his direction."

This mistake in the casting of *Tannhäuser* also angered Theodor Helm, a Wagnerite of the old school, who declared he had attended a "parody of the Venusberg scene . . . Gutheil-Schoder sang Venus, or rather uttered a series of piercing, meaningless and totally incoherent sounds instead of words, as though she were strangling with asthma. Still less did she portray

Venus: we saw a small, slender figure, female, naturally, and dressed in a pink tunic, who waved her scraggy arms and rapacious fingers dangerously around Tannhäuser's face, so that he involuntarily shielded himself from this living specter . . . Such was Gutheil-Schoder's Venus, a figure out of Holbein's *Dance of Death,* a Dutch vision of St. Anthony rather than the goddess of love . . ." Helm felt it his duty "stoutly to defend a great work of art from such blasphemy and such an insult," adding that Gutheil-Schoder had been ill-advised to subject her voice to such "tortures" and Mahler equally ill-advised to abuse Wagner as he did Beethoven, by altering his orchestration. This critic then quoted Richter's comments on the orchestration of *Tannhäuser* and his criticisms of Mahler's modifications.[18]

In the autumn of 1900, Mahler had intended to restage one of the most popular masterpieces of the German *Singspiel,* but had come up against the opposition of the intendant, who found his planned production "too expensive" for Nicolai's *Die lustigen Weiber von Windsor.* In a long letter to the lord chamberlain Mahler had explained that he could only justify his requests with purely aesthetic and subjective considerations and was therefore unable to furnish more precise arguments. It would not be a question of renewing all the costumes but only of refurbishing those of the chorus, above all for the fairyland of the last act, when the latter had to be on stage with the ballet. It would be impossible to paint new scenery on the old canvases because the opera no longer possessed any that were clean enough, and, try as he might, the painter would not be able to recondition them in time. Not only could the estimate not be lowered, but also any delay would have adverse effects on the opera's finances by increasing the projected expenditure.[19]

Despite these unanswerable arguments, the intendant must have held out, for Mahler had to wait a whole year before giving *Die lustigen Weiber,* the new production of which was finally presented on October 4, 1901, in honor of the Emperor's birthday. Thanks to the beauty of the score and the charm and humor of the text, which he felt stuck very closely to the Shakespearean original, Mahler thoroughly enjoyed the rehearsals, which "amused the performers quite as much as the performance amused the public." As always, he expended as much time and care on it as he would have devoted to a serious opera, and Gutheil-Schoder, in her memoirs, tells of a striking detail he introduced into this new production. She was playing Frau Fluth, who, in Scene 2, which takes place in Frau Fluth's room, pretends to cry because her husband is jealous and has just made a scene. He then goes up to her and says, "I have learned from a letter that Sir John Falstaff was with you!" Whereupon, instead of letting her leap up immediately in amazement, Mahler made her remain immobile for a whole bar, which not only created considerable suspense but also heightened the comic effect of her subsequent shriek. In addition to ordering all the theatrical details, Mahler restored the full text of the opera, cut out all the interpolations, and worked over the singers' every word, note, and movement. Gutheil-Schoder cherished the memory of these rehearsals to her dying day, while Mahler in turn was constantly enchanted by her "genius" and the eagerness with which she carried out his slightest wish. To him, such artists were "the reward for the stupidity, the resistance and the lack of talent I have hitherto encountered." As for the revolving stage, he felt it was as "admirably suited to this Shakespearean fantasy" as to Così fan tutte.

The revival of Die lustigen Weiber was greeted with an enthusiasm both worthy of the occasion and shared, for once, by the majority of the critics. Kalbeck pronounced the performance "full of genius." Mahler had discovered "the opera's tender soul" in the nocturne in the third act and emphasized the fantastic element, thanks largely to the revolving stage, which set the work in a sort of dreamland. Everyone had fallen under the sway of this "modern magician" and the performers had succeeded in maintaining the illusion, especially Gutheil-Schoder, the "fairy of this poetic and musical dream."

Opinions were again violently contrasted on Gutheil-Schoder's performance. Heuberger found her "an artist and a virtuoso in both singing and acting and one of the few singers who possesses a genuine sense of humor, which she combines with the noblest and most sublime stage art." He wished that her entire performance could be filmed and thus preserved for posterity. Hirschfeld, on the other hand, accused the young soprano of "trumpeting Nicolaian parodies" in the audience's ears and very nearly piercing them with her shrieks, while, in her attempt to be funny, she "coiled herself inside out with snakelike movements and grimaces instead of humor."[20]

A month later Gutheil-Schoder starred in another important new production, that of Offenbach's Les Contes d'Hoffmann, which had not been performed in Vienna since the fire at the Ringtheater on December 8, 1881.[21] With this opera, Mahler hoped to achieve a financial success comparable to that of Cavalleria rusticana and Pagliacci and thus be able to stage works by Mozart and Wagner. While not indifferent to Offenbach's music, since he had conducted his operettas at the start of his career, that which appealed to him most about Les Contes was the fact that it recaptured some of the romantic genius of an author who had so moved and influenced him in his youth. Intending to perform it a large number of times, he simultaneously rehearsed alternate casts, a procedure that was not without creating serious problems,[22] mainly because he had insisted that the singers attend all the rehearsals, including those in which they were not taking part, so that they would become familiar with the staging. For example, the tenor Naval wrote to excuse himself for not having attended one in which his rival, Schrödter, was taking part. "I am not exaggerating when I say that it is torture to me to listen to him, for nothing could be more painful than two artists comparing themselves with one another during their respective performances. Every artist, you will grant as much, must create in isolation, without seeing or hearing how another develops the same theme for fear of involuntarily adopting certain gestures of his interpretation and being accused of plagiarism, which is to be avoided at all costs. On the other hand, an artist obviously benefits greatly from the advice of a genuine master and I mean, in this case, yours. However, such a master never makes the same suggestions to two different artists, for their personalities are not the same and each must be guided in accordance with his own."[23]

The reactions of both the public and the press were exceptionally favorable. Kalbeck declared that he had attended one of the most brilliant premieres the Hofoper had ever given, remarking that the public had even encored the intermezzo between the second and third acts (the reprise of the celebrated Barcarolle). Hanslick dwelled at greater length on both the opera and its performance, pointing out that never before had the same opera been presented two evenings in succession with different casts.

As for Theodor Helm, he praised the opera's "pretty lyricism" and subsequently emphasized its huge financial success in the *Musikalisches Wochenblatt*. Indeed, *Les Contes d'Hoffmann* was performed sixteen times between November 11 and the end of the year, thirty times in 1902, and remained in the repertory for twenty-five years. Mahler even ended up by complaining of its popularity, for he rapidly wearied of having to conduct it so frequently.

Be that as it may, this triumph enabled him to form new projects, and he went through the entire repertoire in order to make his choice. Of all the German operatic composers, Mozart was, in his view, the most "certain of his goal and the most accomplished." And had he been compelled to set another composer alongside Mozart and Wagner, he would not have chosen Weber, because he died too young and his last two works, *Euryanthe* and *Oberon,* were unfortunately not consummate masterpieces. If one took into account not only music but also text and action, then Lortzing was probably the third glory of the German lyric theater, and that despite the fact that he had also died too young and not been able to put in enough work on his operas.[24] As usual, Mahler set *Fidelio* in a class apart and perhaps even above all other operas, for "in each of the fields in which he exerted himself, Beethoven always succeeded in creating the supreme."

With the arrival of Bruno Walter, Mahler had not only acquired a conductor worthy of his confidence and anxious to comply with his wishes, but also regained a staunch and faithful friend who was one of the people with whom he most enjoyed conversing. Over dinner one evening in late September, he discussed the problems of conducting and interpretation with Walter and Lipiner. "I've come to the conclusion that the nuances noted in a score usually exceed the composer's intentions," he said. "The forte being too loud, the piano too soft, the largo too slow, the presto too fast and the crescendos, diminuendos and accelerandos exaggerated. As for me, how sober and restrained my conducting has become compared to what it once was! When one sees the extent to which everything is exaggerated and deformed in one's own music, one begins to realize what others suffer. In fact, one is almost tempted not to give any indications of either tempo, nuance or expression but to let each interpreter express one's work in accordance with his own personal conception of it." Playing the four-hand arrangement of his recently completed *Fourth Symphony* with Joseph von Wöss, he let him take the initiative in order to see what he would make of the nuances and, when Wöss faltered and overemphasized one of them, he simply erased it from the score.[25]

During another conversation with Walter a few days later, the latter said that there were certain passages that seemed to him to present no problem of interpretation because "they can only be thus and not otherwise." Mahler advised him to beware of opinions and prejudices of this sort, founded sometimes on chance and sometimes on early impressions or tenacious memories. "It should be one's constant and sole endeavor to see everything afresh and create it anew," he concluded. It was with this same idea in mind that he had once told the *Kapellmeister* of the Frankfurt theater, Ludwig Rottenberg, who had looked him up in Aussee, that "one should know a work by heart before learning it by heart," in other words, one should be entirely familiar with its form and content before learning its notes, for one could thus form a far clearer and more spontaneous mental picture of the whole. It had in fact happened that this resolutely objective attitude had revealed the true spirit of a work to him and made it easier for him to determine its structure.

Early in October, Mahler discussed Beethoven's *Missa Solemnis* with Lipiner, Walter and Natalie. "Probably none of you have ever heard it, for the academic performances of it are singularly intolerable and if any work needs to be very freely interpreted, that one does. I'd love to be able to give it just once, but it would be impossible in Vienna, where, I'm ashamed to say, there's no chorus, whereas one would need a gigantic mass of singers, a veritable sea of voices." Lipiner having asked if it were true that Beethoven's vocal writing was poor, he replied, "If the singers lack enthusiasm, yes, but if the conductor succeeds in communicating a bit of the divine spark to them, the result is phenomenal, witness the passage *Ahnest Du den Schöpfer, Welt?* from the *Ninth Symphony*. You can't imagine how jubilant it sounded when I conducted it, yet it's usually atrociously tortured because the singers want to spare themselves instead of giving everything they've got to it. It's the same thing with the *Missa Solemnis*. I didn't understand it myself to begin with, the Credo least of all; because the tempo indicated was presto, I played it too rapidly (this will always be the case). But one day I forgot the indication and played it to myself in accordance with the meaning of the work as a whole[26] and, for the first time, saw it before me as it ought to be. Beethoven proclaimed the Credo in a strange way, with a sort of rage: 'I believe because it's absurd to believe,' whereas Bach did so quite differently, with confidence and trust."[27]

For Mahler, the big event of the autumn was to be the first performance of his *Fourth Symphony,* which was to take place in Munich on November 25, and he considered it all the more important as no new symphonic work of his had been performed since the creation of his *Second Symphony* in 1895. The Munich premiere was to be followed by several other performances, for Weingartner had included the new work in the program of the

Kaim Orchestra's tour, and Strauss had invited Mahler to conduct it himself in Berlin. Before handing over the final version of the score to his publisher, Mahler wanted to hear and check his orchestration. He therefore arranged a reading rehearsal with the Philharmonic on October 12, which also served as a first rehearsal for the Vienna premiere to be given in January. The session promised to be difficult from the opening bar, for the novelty and complexity of the work considerably upset the somewhat hidebound and traditional musicians, and Mahler immediately sensed their hostility in their behavior and the looks on their faces. "And it's on this heap of dead wreckage," he exclaimed, "that I must build a whole flourishing world!"

The violins and cellos played the opening cantabile theme "in a far too massive [*massig*] and heavy manner" and subsequently failed to give the "dithyrambic crescendo" of the same theme its "exultant power and dash." This initial theme, which the audience would undoubtedly find "too simple and old-fashioned . . . gradually turns into six or seven different themes, all of which are elaborated in the development."[28] Mahler felt that any work worthy of being called a symphony ought to have such "richness of substance" and "genuinely organic development . . . It must have something cosmic and inexhaustible like the world and life itself in order to merit this title. Its structure should be such that nothing inorganic, no chance patchings or mendings can impair it.[29] The gaiety of the first movements is that of a strange superior world that tends to bewilder and terrify us. In the last movement, a child explains the meaning of it all, even though he still belongs in a doll's world [*Puppenstand*] that nevertheless transcends ours."

During the rehearsal Mahler asked the first violinist to tune his instrument one tone higher than usual for the Scherzo and to accentuate the harsh and strident sound thus obtained. He even considered[30] assigning this part to a viola and having the concertmaster play it. Moreover, because the strings, and particularly the cellos, overemphasized them, he erased certain crescendo and diminuendo indications from the beginning of the Adagio. "The orchestration of this symphony is in no wise aimed at creating sound effects, but rather at clearly expressing what I have to say. In this respect, no one has taught me more than Verdi, who has opened up an entirely new road in this field."[31] He also cut out a few notes from a passage of variations because they not only thickened its sound and blurred its outline but also seemed unnecessary, its harmony being quite adequately suggested by the part writing, "which, like the work of a miniaturist, consists in the intertwining of tangent and intersecting lines."

In the hope of avoiding possible exaggerations, Mahler had become more wary than ever in his choice of indications of tempo. Instead of ritardando, he wrote simply *nicht eilen* ("do not hurry") and, conversely, for a slight increase of speed, *nicht schleppen* ("do not drag"). "Such are the tricks to which musicians like to be treated," he remarked.[32] Correcting the score of the *Fourth Symphony* one evening ten days later, he discovered a faulty chord progression. "There was something coarse about this passage, which

bothered me every time I heard it, but I didn't realize what it was. A composer who finds a fault of this nature in one of his scores must feel a bit the same way as a member of the highest aristocracy who suddenly discovers a swineherd in his family tree." In this connection, he and Walter discussed the "hidden octaves" the latter said he had found, for instance, in Bach's and Schumann's music. "It's only in Beethoven," Mahler said, "that I've never found any. The fact that one comes across a multitude of such mistakes in some composer's music doesn't mean that they're any more excusable. And when one composes only one work each year, they positively shouldn't occur."

Though full of gaiety and sunlight, the *Fourth Symphony* had cost Mahler more toil and anguish than the monumental symphonies that had preceded it, and, notwithstanding he was apprehensive of the reactions of its first audience, he secretly hoped that its modest dimensions and the clarity of its style would finally win him the approval of both the public and the musicians. Indeed, it was because he had achieved his first total success in Munich the year before that he had decided to give this premiere to the Kaim Orchestra,[33] and he prepared it at length in an exchange of letters with the orchestra's principal conductor, Felix Weingartner, whom he had already asked that summer for permission to conduct the world premiere of the work himself. Weingartner had intended to include a Brahms symphony in the same program, but Mahler no doubt made him change his mind, by begging him to replace it by works that were easier to understand and perform. Not only were four full rehearsals scarcely enough for him to rehearse the *Fourth,* but he wanted the public to be fresh and receptive when they heard it. He was also against another vocal work preceding his symphony, for he wanted the appearance of the soprano to come as a complete surprise before the Finale. "These are naturally all secondary considerations, only valid for the first performance. I have every confidence in you and your artistic judgment for all the others."[34] The Munich concert was first planned for November 18, but at the end of October Mahler sent Weingartner a telegram asking him to postpone it for a week, because of "insurmountable difficulties." In fact the first performance of *Les Contes d'Hoffmann* was scheduled for November 11, and Mahler anticipated having to conduct the work several times in the following week in order to take advantage of its sure success. After the performance of *Les Contes d'Hoffmann* on November 20, Mahler left Vienna by the night train with Bruno Walter, Natalie, and Justi. The following morning in Munich, after the first rehearsal, he realized that his task was going to be herculean, in fact comparable to that of "a sculptor obliged to fashion a statue out of a coarse block of stone," for the musicians, though full of enthusiasm, were young and inexperienced. Moreover, their lack of polish made him more than ever aware of the subtleties and difficulties of the work, especially after the happy-go-lucky of the *Second,* which they had managed fairly easily the year before. Unfortunately, the best one among them, the first cellist, had to leave Munich on the day of the concert because his father died,[35] and Mahler soon realized that neither the performance as a whole nor above all the quality of the sound that he had worked so hard over, mixing the timbres and using certain instruments in unusual ways, would fully satisfy him.[36]

As always upon his arrival in a new town, he made several courtesy calls in between rehearsals. Coming home one day, a friend of his, the critic Arthur Seidl, found his cook greatly perturbed. In her racy Bavarian dialect she told him that a fierce-looking gentleman dressed all in black had arrived at the house and was in Herr Seidl's room. He seemed worried about something and she had never been so frightened, wondering if he might not perhaps be a thief or a murderer, for he had darted about the house and insisted upon going into Herr Seidl's room, where he was now sitting at the desk writing something. Needless to say, the strange gentleman in question was Mahler, who, thinking he had mistaken the time, was writing to Seidl to ask for another appointment.

With the *Fourth Symphony,* which was shorter than its predecessors and required no more than a normal-sized orchestra, Mahler had obviously hoped to be the more readily understood, as he had renounced the titanism of his earlier symphonies. However, just as Wagner, who, with *Tristan und Isolde,* had attempted to create an Italian-style and therefore more "popular" opera than the *Ring* but in fact ended up by asserting his own style and musical personality more strongly than ever, so Mahler had merely expressed himself more personally than ever in this new symphony. Indeed, his "simplicity" was to disconcert the public far more than the "titanic" style and dimensions of his previous works. William Ritter, a young French-Swiss musician[37] living in Munich, who had never heard any of Mahler's works but was intrigued by what he had heard about his *Second Symphony,* attended one of the final rehearsals, of which he wrote the following account. Weingartner was rehearsing his part of the concert "when Mahler and his friends, one of whom is Klaus Pringsheim, enter and seat themselves in the first row of the red plush stalls. A thin little man with spectacles, swarthy, frizzy-haired, yellow, with a very pointed head, dressed all in black, in a frock coat, looking like a clergyman, very absorbed. Weingartner finishes and leaves the podium. Mahler strides straight up and immediately inspires us with confidence. Great calm, absolute simplicity, the man is sure of himself and totally without charlatanism. One couldn't have said as much of Weingartner at that time. The orchestra hasn't turned a hair but we sense that certain passivity of musicians who have no intention of committing themselves: 'We'll play what's put before us but we won't answer for it.' And Weingartner has prudently slipped away . . . There's something afoot . . . We feel it right away . . . The symphony obviously presents some pitfall.

"It begins . . . We get it instantly . . . It couldn't be more odd . . . A bell . . . of horse or mule, yes . . . Emma Bovary would immediately have imagined a steep path in the Sierra . . . *tras los montes.* A bell accompanied by two staccato flutes, while a clarinet in A slowly begins a ceremonious figure

. . . And suddenly the first theme . . . But such that, since Haydn—only with what spices!—no symphony has had one as graceful, as enticing, as melodious and as prolonged . . . It's at once childish and, upon my word, not half malicious . . . and, above all, nothing less than innocent . . . Just like the theater when the ingénue is played by the most corrupt member of the troupe. We're at once bewitched and flabbergasted, won over and horrified. Besides, we are of those who are still not too accustomed to hearing closed notes on the horns. But now the orchestra starts up its clownery, emitting sounds that surprise even after Strauss's *Till Eulenspiegel* and Dukas' *Apprenti-Sorcier*. We don't know what to think. 'What unseemly music!' says one of us . . . Finally the first movement ends. We've never been so non-plused—it's painfully obvious we're resisting our pleasure! Is this really serious music? And the public, which is fairly large, seems just as much put out. I'm sitting next to the poet Wolfskehl, a friend of Stefan George. Be he never such a modernist, he seems as dumfounded as we are, he agrees with us: 'Nothing but Viennese corruption, carnival, *G'schnas,* just the stuff for Ronacher's (the big Viennese cabaret).' The second movement seems more serious, but so gloomy after the turbulence and humor of the first! Then the third, a heart-rending funeral march shortly mixed with a sort of gaiety, which we can make nothing of. And suddenly, as rondo finale, *Des Knaben Wunderhorn*. What does it actually amount to? And where are we in relation to the noble world of great music ranging from Bach's Passions to the austere, Promethean and magnificent symphonies of such as Beethoven, Brahms and Bruckner? It's as though we'd gone from Bayreuth to a sort of *Überbrettl* [variety theater].

"And the audience around us is just as bewildered as we are! But being German and not thinking for a moment that the Kaim Orchestra and a di-rector of the Vienna Opera would make fun of it, it's reacting less than we are . . . And in the evening, having ruminated our impressions during the afternoon, we booed our heads off, as they boo only in Paris or in Italy! The which, as always happens, served merely to renew the strength of the partisans who opposed us at all costs. The audience, moreover, had been pretty much hand-picked . . . All of Munich's Jewry was there . . . Hearing us booing in this way, a viper-eyed woman, whom I still see before me, copiously insulted us . . . The following day, the Vienna papers an-nounced that the success of this premiere of the *Fourth* in Munich had been *stürmig* [stormy]. But Mahler, as far as we were concerned, was henceforth . . . a sort of Raskol of German musical orthodoxy."[38]

William Ritter's colorful style vividly recreates the atmosphere in the hall and the reactions of the audience to this "scandalous" work. He left the rehearsal "disgusted, declaring to whosoever would listen that I would never have believed anyone capable of writing such dishonest music," that "I felt as though I had been reveling in an unavowable way in a sort of musical Black Mass" and that "indeed, Satan and all his pomps and works have never chosen a better home in an orchestra."

Although in a less baroque style, Natalie also describes the amazement at the simplicity of the first theme on the part of an audience who expected an "aggressive" and grandiose work from Mahler. Thereafter, unable to follow the complexity of events in the development, the audience, in which there were many musicians, including Max von Schillings, Ludwig Thuille, Max Reger, Siegmund von Hausegger, and Felix von Rath, went from astonishment to consternation, and, at the end of the movement, a great many boos were to be heard amid the applause. The Scherzo baffled it still more, so that Mahler's young admirers were no longer able to drown out the hooting. Fortunately, however, Margarete Michalek, an attractive young singer newly engaged at the Hofoper, whose almost childlike freshness was perfectly suited to the lied, saved the day: her very youth and charm calmed "the flood of opposition and exasperation" and "poured oil on the troubled waters."[39]

Fully aware of the audience's mood, Mahler let Michalek take several bows before reappearing himself. He sent her into the wings and fulfilled this obligation "in a manner more infuriated than friendly." After the final rehearsal several of the musicians had told him "that they hadn't been able to make head or tail of the work but would do their best to change their minds the following day." However, when not a single one of them, except for Weingartner, came to say "anything sensible that might please him," he realized that the *Fourth* had lost him all the admirers that the *Second* had won for him the year before.

Ritter also describes the storm raised in the peaceful Bavarian capital by "this symphony, generally taken to be humorous and paradoxical," which he had found "infernal." "The first movement could be Daniel in the lions' den, Orpheus butchered by the Maenads, genius delivered to the beasts! It's nothing but acrobatics and the performance of a lady in tights in a menagerie. 'It's a menagerie' was the first impression and the cry of dismay of one of us upon hearing these comic sounds that try their strength and assert themselves one after the other in this first movement, a movement ideally pretty, fresh and graceful in its piano version, which lulls any suspicion that prodigious and clownish things might be going on in the orchestra. It's the continual head down, legs up of Salome's dance on the door of Rouen Cathedral. And one fancies the astonishment with which old Haydn, himself a lover of jokes and musical 'quips,' would have listened to this fearsome revival of the childish symphony in which he imitated the squawking of fowl and the squeals of animals . . . The plain fact is (and it's as typical as our regrettable hoots in Munich!) that, throughout the performance, one row of people after the other got the giggles. At a certain moment, a voice shouted out '*grossartig*' [magnificent] and the owner of it burst out laughing. An absolutely delicious waltz melody, though played very simply by an ordinary violin, enters in the midst of these croakings—the symphony begins with a sort of chorus of nasal and caricatured toad bells doubtless inspired by the environment!"

The same Ritter truculently enumerates Mahler's surprising "sound effects," the muted trumpets, harp harmonics, and "dividing up" of the instruments, as well as the constant changes of tempo, and describes his indignation at the second movement, which "now dies so gently of consumption, now works itself up into paroxysms of frenzy." As to Michalek's entry after the Scherzo, "It was not oil poured on troubled waters but fuel added to the fire . . . With the most complete lack of chivalry, we became enraged at this 'expedient to silence us' and our animosity redoubled."

It would be impossible, Ritter continues, "to convey the sensation of madness (there's no other word for it) that such a symphony arouses! It's no consolation to me to think that the feeling of revulsion that rose in my soul upon hearing this work was shared by a good half of the calm and serious Germany that applauds absolutely safe, not to say totally reliable musicians . . . That which blinded my friends and me was everything about it that seemed to us to be merely vulgar self-advertisement; the way in which it constantly appealed to the lowest instincts of the crowd and so expertly caressed, aroused and then incited the sensuality latent in each one of us to indulge itself; it was the breeze of contagious madness that made one shriek with laughter; the constant overloading and the perversion of an alluring melody with every possible large or small sound effect; the way it swung from the sublime to the ridiculous, in an apparent effort to please everyone from the aristocrat down to the peasant; the way in which its Jewish and Nietzschean spirit defied our Christian spirit with its sacrilegious buffoonery and the fact that it exasperated our loyalty to the past by crushing all our artistic principles to a pulp."

As far as these young music lovers were concerned, Mahler had "multiplied a hundredfold the sarcasm of Heine and his caricaturish parody of the greatest and most sacred things in the most idolized art" and introduced "jugglers into the temple and the circus into the cathedral," with the result that they had "perceived nothing of the symphony except the absolutely desperate sublimity of its third movement," which they had considered "profanation" upon seeing it "revert to delirium." Although they had "taken the boards for the show and the painted clowns of the parade and the backdrop coarsely daubed with wild beasts for the drama" and had regarded Mahler as "one of the most dangerous adversaries of our aesthetic faith and our national aesthetics," they had nevertheless recognized "the musical giant behind the grimaces and the thoroughbred beneath the grotesque trappings."

Ritter's verbal extravaganzas describe and explain his contemporaries' reactions to perfection. As far as he himself was concerned, the impression Mahler's music had made on him was too strong to be entirely negative: he "couldn't sleep anymore" because of it; he and his friends were "indelibly marked" by it and already beginning to hear a still small voice deep down inside them murmuring, "You rebel against this music. You reject it with all your wisdom, all your experience and all your convictions . . . but you're fighting against your own pleasure . . . you're trying to be virtuous . . . at bottom . . . there's nothing you like better. You're defeated. Whether you will or no, you admire it! It was bound to happen that you, an anti-Semite, should be bowled over by admiration for something Jewish! . . ."[40]

More deeply disturbed than he would admit, even to himself, Ritter wrote Mahler a letter whose frankness evidently pleased the composer, for he sent him the still-unpublished proofs of the orchestral and four-hand piano scores of the *Fourth Symphony* almost by return post. Thus the young people who had so booed its premiere began to "finger" the disparaged work and ended up by "conceding its mastery and veiling their faces."

The Munich journalists, however, were far from possessing the same broad-mindedness and lost no time in reflecting the general disappointment. Only the *Allgemeine Zeitung* showed some degree of moderation, declaring that the boos had not drowned out the applause and that the work was "not readily accessible and, in any case, impossible to judge after only one hearing." The first movement, it said, recalled the Andante of the *Second Symphony,* "mellifluous, exquisitely transparent and felicitously modeled themes with pleasant rhythms that Mahler, with admirable contrapuntal skill, weaves into a filigree of the highest quality. The individual instruments are almost constantly treated as soloists, chamber music on a grand scale and sometimes even relaxed drawing-room music. Meanwhile, amusing but subtle and technically ultrarefined chatter on the part of the orchestra, which babbles, cackles, squeaks, burlesques, roars and creaks in every corner; an endeavor to translate into music and cacophony St. Anthony as painted by Breughel or Callot. The second movement is too much like the first and therein lies its weakness. A contrast, a change of mood, is needed. It too, contains a few rather tasteless orchestral jokes: a cohort of Kobolds at large torments the audience and, without actually smacking it, pierces and tickles its ears, tears out its hair and repeatedly flicks it on the nose. And then, quite suddenly, an exquisite melody reappears, a melody brimming with charm and roguishness, a genuine melody, sound, well modeled, radiating Viennese gaiety and spirit, a cross between a ländler and a sentimental and parodic couplet . . .

"The theme of the slow movement is long drawn out and has little or no character, while its development contains totally vacuous passages . . . As for the *Volkstümlichkeit* of the Finale, it is highly questionable and totally inappropriate as a symphonic finale . . ." Summing up the symphony, this critic referred to the caricatural passages of *Die Meistersinger,* such as Walter's *Diese Meister* or Beckmesser's appearance on the platform in the last act, and declared that "the grotesquely comic means something in the theater, but in the symphony it must at least be justified by a precise program on pain of degenerating into a hodgepodge of instrumental dissonances and jokes devoid of artistic maturity. In my view, the musical and spiritual content of the work is insignificant in comparison with its pretensions, which try both the patience of the audience and the quality of the orchestra. It assumes the most imposing symphonic airs but the audience does not know whether it should take the composer seriously or whether it is being dazzled with the derisive fireworks of a cheap serial. This sort of thing trespasses against the Holy Spirit of music, a veracious spirit that, even in humor, tolerates no inauthenticity."

After recalling the controversy stirred up by Mahler and his symphonies, the anonymous critic of the *Münchener Zeitung* launched into a lengthy analysis of his own disappointment. Although he had not been entirely convinced of the genuineness of the artistic emotions Mahler had expressed in his *Second Symphony*, mainly because of the vastness of the means he had employed and his supreme technical subtlety, he could not understand why he had subsequently presented such a totally different work whose content was "neither sufficiently clear nor sufficiently important to hold the audience's interest," such a "succession of disjointed and heterogeneous atmospheres and expressions mixed with instrumental quirks and affectations." Was Mahler merely indulging in tasteless jokes at the expense of his audience?

The *Bayerischer Kurier* also failed to understand why the "brilliant," composer of the *Second Symphony* had produced a work like this. People had looked forward to something "powerful and transcendental," or at least to "dazzling effects and tragic pathos" from him and instead he had come up with this "tame humoresque loaded with orchestral mannerisms and of a protean style that ranges between Mozart, Richard Strauss and Koschat." This "restless and nervous" work, full of "incredible cacophony," had remained incomprehensible; it conjured up visions of "a man so haunted by painful and disagreeable hallucinations that he cannot sleep." Only the two final movements had aroused a certain amount of interest, this paper said. As for the critic of *Der Sammler*, "simplicity verging on affectation," saucy orchestration, "clownish pranks," and a "cats' chorus" were all that he could see in the *Fourth Symphony*.

A more moderate critic in the *Kleine Journal* nevertheless objected to the "nervousness" of the work, its lack of stylistic unity, and its "many reminiscences" of Wagner and popular gypsy music. In his view, Mahler was "making a mistake in using only superlatives and in constantly maintaining his expression at a paroxysmal level of intensity . . . Despite the subtlety and complexity of the counterpoint and the meticulously devised harmony, no passage gives the impression of being powerful and profound in its orchestral expression; the whole thing is transparent, sensitive, almost hysterical." Despite his authority, Mahler was a decadent. Whatever the opinion of the conservative public, however, the Finale was "quite simply a work of genius . . . All honor to the young who have the courage to express their opinion in defiance of the majority," this honest and open-minded critic concluded. Mahler's one and only genuine defender was the critic of the *Münchener Post*, who proclaimed the new work a "great step forward on the road to artistic clarity," the expression of a genuine and powerful personality who succeeds in "gilding the miseries of life with Dionysiac gaiety" and "a treasury of striking [*sinnfällige*], original [*urwüchsig*] and joyfully welling melodies."

Unfortunately, this approval was not only unique in the Munich press but also in the music periodicals, all of which condemned the *Fourth Symphony* irrevocably. Karl Potgiesser, in the *Allgemeine Musik-Zeitung,* declared it vastly inferior to the *Second* despite its interesting and occasionally even fascinating orchestration, incomprehensible without a program, and unlikely to satisfy anyone with its totally unoriginal themes and constant references to popular Viennese and Styrian music. Theodor Kreyer, in *Die Musik,* said that "the bad seed perceptible in parts of the *Second Symphony* had become immense spiky thistles in the *Fourth.*"[41] According to him, its "false images" had neither originality nor personal inspiration, not one genuine emotion or true color. It was nothing but "technique, calculation, vanity, a morbid and insipid supermusic, a shapeless stylistic monstrosity that collapses under the weight of a surfeit of witty details."

Only a chosen few tried to rise above the melee and to understand Mahler's unique position in the historic and artistic context of his time. Arthur Seidl wrote[42] that most musicians in Munich were expecting another *Second Symphony* and did not go to the trouble of studying the score or trying to make something of the work. He himself had changed his opinion between the rehearsals and the concert. In the absence of any commentary, everyone found it incomprehensible. "One ends up wondering," wrote Seidl, "whether texts and 'programs' have not made audiences so deaf they can no longer react spontaneously or make an effort to understand a work . . . Mahler is a real 'God Seeker.' His most secret inner being contemplates the immensity of nature with a really religious fervor; he is inexorably drawn toward the enigma of existence. I thus disagree entirely with the widespread opinion that holds that, as a musician, he is content to exercise his biting irony and his misplaced skepticism at the expense of celestial joys . . . (I wish to God that others had the same serious, almost sacred approach to their work!) . . . The truth is quite different: it is the critics who consider him with an ironic eye and find only affectation in his music; it is they who are stubborn and who cannot find the key to his naïve and childlike fairy-tale world!" Although wrong in supposing that the famous "reminiscences" from Haydn, Mozart, Schubert, Bruckner, etc., are "deliberate and intentional," Seidl proves in this article that he was one of the few receptive minds who considered Mahler as something more than a charlatan and a symbol of the musical decadence of his time.

The late composer Ernest Bloch, who was ill in Munich at the time of the first performance of the *Fourth Symphony,* has related how, the following day, one of his friends burst into his bedroom to speak of the "musical Voltaire," the "skeptic," the "ironist," whose "icy sarcasm" had pierced him through.[43]

But, of all Mahler's contemporaries, it was doubtless William Ritter who best defined the sources of his art and expressed the strange, simultaneous terror and fascination experienced by many of Mahler's most staunch supporters. "From Nietzsche he has acquired an impassioned and sarcastic vehemence that encourages him to risk all in order to assert his passions, his enthusiasms, his monumental, sidesplitting humor, and no doubt his utter contempt for humanity. What he has to say comes from Nietzsche; the art of saying it, from Bruckner; and the way he says it, from Vienna and his race.

"Perhaps this Jewish heritage is in fact responsible for his nervous predisposition toward an often epileptical musical form of expression, and for his stubborn tenacity to fixed beliefs, whether ridiculous or sublime; for his indomitable urge to impose, at any price, his most exorbitant demands, as well as his need for beauty; his wish to prove the opposition wrong by any means, to force hate, to disgorge admiration, and for the power with which he exploits luxury, opulence and the odd and unexpected to the full; then there is his harmonious control and infallible balance in composition, which conjures up the perfect balance of a *credit* and *debit* account, and evokes expert banking operations; and finally there is that very special note of concupiscence whose affiliations with the *Song of Songs* and, at a later date, the banks of the blue Danube are evident. It is indeed Vienna that he has to thank for such a plethora of fresh and youthful riches; the guileless sensuality of the melodic lines which even the king of waltz himself, Johann Strauss, only possessed to a lesser degree; the continuous musical curtsies, the melodic spasms, the dancing, swooning rhythms, the languishing inflections of desire, which give his work so disquieting and troubled a character (*morally*, for the physical clarity is absolute). This strange, solemn and yet fun-loving city has certainly also influenced him by its secessionist aberrations and the extreme bad taste fomented by its carnival of many races; and he also owes to it—to his old Austrian background—some adorably old-fashioned and sentimental touches. Finally, in these composite surroundings, where East meets West and North meets South, where Slavism becomes Germanism and Italianism Magyarism, the whole raised by a Jewish yeast, it is easy to imagine what eccentricities can cross the mind of a musician of genius who has in his thrall the gayest opera house in the world."

Ritter goes on to describe certain of the public's reactions to Mahler's Vienna themes: "And when some of them appear, moist and persuasive, tantalizing and seductive, then you should see the lewd glances in the concert hall, the salacious dribble running from certain old men's lips, and above all the ugly, whoring laugh of certain respectable women! And what glances are then exchanged or averted! It would be enough to put one off Mahler for life if the antidote did not immediately appear in the form of the dismay of both fools and cods, the turkey-cock anger of the critics and the modest blushes of the hypocrites. Mr. Mahler has all the necessary talent to write the symphony-ballet and the symphony-panorama about which we dream." Perhaps his study of the sources of Mahler's art, and of the troubled Viennese atmosphere that fostered it, prevented Ritter from understanding how much more important his works are as promises for the future than insults to the past. And yet Ritter's subconscious and almost surrealist approach led him to a deep understanding of them. With his flamboyant style and unbridled imagination, the young Neuchâtel art critic was more penetrating and clear-sighted than almost every professional musician of this time.

Weingartner had consented to let Mahler conduct the world premiere of the *Fourth Symphony,* but he himself conducted it on the Kaim Orchestra's tour, which included Nuremberg, Frankfurt-am-Main, Karlsruhe, and Stuttgart. Everywhere except in Stuttgart public and press were unanimously uncomprehending, exasperated, and disdainful. According to Nuremberg's *General-anzeiger,* only the erroneous report of a success in Munich had prompted the applause of "a few gregarious people who have no opinions of their own." The only praiseworthy thing about this pure *Kapellmeistermusik* was its orchestration. The first movement was a hodgepodge of a hackneyed sentimental ditty interlaced with "some classical embellishments" and "strange Secessionist contortions" and "an outmoded and droned type of Turkish music" mixed with "Scottish bagpipe squealings" and a potpourri of "Gypsy, Russian, Bohemian and Hungarian" melodies; in short, a "thoroughly international piece." The return of the German melody would have been a consolation if it had not been previously "translated into so many different languages" and preceded by such "musical vaudeville." After playing the "fearful musical sinner" with his "international yodelings" in the Scherzo, Mahler had proceeded to "murmur sweet nothings" (*Dideldumdei*) in the Adagio. And the interminable final lied adorned with melismata that had followed this "third act of a comedy rather than a symphony" had conjured up a "young girl wearing her grandmother's pleated bonnet." After the frills and furbelows of this "Vaudeville-Symphony" the pure music of Brahms had finally afforded the audience unadulterated enjoyment.

The following day, Henriette Mankiewicz attended the concert in Frankfurt, where the public's reaction was such that she preferred to say nothing to Mahler about it. The majority of the audience seemed to think the whole thing was a joke and a scandalous hoax. The *Musikalisches Wochenblatt* compared the "angry and violent" hissing to "the sound of an autumn wind blowing through the dead leaves and dried twigs of a forest." The *Frankfurter Zeitung* had prepared the ground by publishing a review of the Munich performance which called the symphony an "immense disappointment," accused Mahler of having striven after "cacophony at any price," alleged that he had reached "a dead end in his symphonic development" and suffered a "drying up of his melodic spring," and reproached him with propounding disconcerting and even insoluble riddles by juxtaposing a burlesque and caricatural style to the folkloric simplicity of Schubert and Viennese songs. "Worldly tumult smothers the melody of the heart, the coarse noises of this lower world drown out the serene beauty and destroy the daydream of the ideal artist. Unless he is able to save his soul from despair by escaping into romantic fantasies of a blissful and sparkling paradise, the creator's childlike innocence will inevitably turn into a grimace of disgust and tedium." Having patterned himself after Callot and Hoffmann, Berlioz, and Liszt, Mahler, the review concluded, had composed "program music without a program, literary music that satisfies none of the basic demands of music, namely, feeling, imagination, atmosphere."

Two days later, this paper's own music critic took the same view after the Frankfurt performance. He said that the approving smiles of the many people in the audience who had enjoyed the popular Viennese melodies had rapidly frozen on their faces at the sound of the atrociously and deliberately false notes and "effects murderous to the ears," which exceeded anything of this kind anyone had ever heard. The composer's talent was manifest solely in the orchestration of the symphony, which had worn the audience to a frazzle. According to *Die Musik,* the Frankfurt public had condemned it utterly on account of its "ill-fermented ideological content, its reckless and cacophonous developments and its, as always, willful incomprehension of Beethoven's *Ninth.*" As to the *Musikalisches Wochenblatt,* it claimed that the public's negative reactions were fully justified and that it had realized it was being made fun of, since the work was incomprehensible and its music "insipid, humorless, tiresome, painful and built on vulgar themes that, thanks to all sorts of devices, dragged on and on."[44]

At Karlsruhe, third stop on the tour, after beginning the concert with Berlioz's *Roi Lear Overture* in an almost empty hall, Weingartner had someone announce that he was not feeling well and needed a short rest. When he returned to the podium half an hour later, he conducted only the final lied of Mahler's *Fourth Symphony.* Adam Heid, in the *Badische Landeszeitung,* surmised that the many performances of this "cacophonous *Fourth* have overstrained his nerves" and added that, despite its "deliberate simplicity," the piece was "complicated and incomprehensible." The *Karlsruher Zeitung* criticized the choice of text, and the correspondent of *Die Musik* insinuated that Weingartner had not had the courage to conduct the whole work.[45]

The only town in which the symphony was given a favorable reception was Stuttgart, where, according to the *Schwäbischer Merkur,* its expected failure did not materialize. Mahler could be classed, this paper said, "above the composers of simple talent" and, even though his aims were not very clear, he was one of the "new stars that are steadily rising and in no danger of falling back into the night." In spite of its oddities, the work gave an impression of unity. Rather than the musical "thunder and lightning" that everyone expected, it was a touching idyl, a "wreath of good-humored melodies and folk dances." The critic of the *Neues Tagblatt,* however, condemned the symphony for its "vulgar passages, its sentimentality and its affectation" and said that he hoped he would "never again encounter this Mahlerian tone painting, either on earth or in heaven." Thus this unfortunate tour had produced nothing but negative results, and Weingartner despaired of ever getting the public to accept any of Mahler's works, and even their personal relationship suffered. After a final letter sent by Mahler early in 1902, they did not communicate again until 1907, when Weingartner took Mahler's place at the Vienna Opera.[46]

Mahler himself, exasperated by the insults of the Munich critics who had beaten the *Fourth* to death in the name of the *Second*" and refused to admit that he had any imagination or originality, declared that, "corrupted by program music, they're incapable of appreciating any work from a purely musical point of view." He felt that it had all begun with Liszt and Berlioz, "who at least had talent and who, with their 'programs,' arrived at new means of expression . . . Since they've now become universally accepted, what further purpose do such crutches serve?"

Having been informed of the total failure of the tour, it was with a heavy heart that Mahler, two weeks after the Munich concert, set out for Berlin, where the critics had always been particularly hard on him. The concert at which Strauss had invited him to conduct the *Fourth Symphony* was the third in the series given by the Tonkünstler Orchester and was to take place at the opera. Together with the orchestral material for the symphony, Mahler had sent Strauss a letter[47] telling him that he would only arrive in time for the last three rehearsals of it, since he had not yet decided whether or not he would in fact conduct it himself. The young Czech soprano Emmy Destinn was apparently supposed to sing the Finale, for Mahler later wrote to Strauss again asking for confirmation of her participation.[48] However, either because she was not free on the appointed day or because Mahler's music did not appeal to her, it was not Destinn who sang the Berlin premiere but Thila Plaichinger, a very mediocre soprano who had recently joined the Berlin Opera.

On his way to Berlin, Mahler spent the day of December 10 in Dresden to rehearse the two ladies engaged to sing in his *Second Symphony* under Ernst von Schuch's baton and was so reassured by the latter's enthusiasm that he conceived high hopes for the success of this concert. He was just as happy about the first Berlin rehearsal of the *Fourth Symphony* the following morning, and he and Strauss agreed that he would conduct the premiere himself. In the afternoon of the same day, he set out for Weimar to see the conductor of the Weimar Opera, Rudolf Krzyzanowski, and put in a good word for his brother-in-law, the cellist Eduard Rosé, who had solicited a post at the opera. During a walk to the Belvedere with Krzyzanowski, the latter proved as "kind and trusting as always" and promised to hasten Eduard's appointment. Having found, moreover, that the "friendliest relations" had been established between Emma and the Krzyzanowski family, Mahler left Weimar again with a load off his mind.[49]

On his return to Berlin, he renewed his friendship with Arnold Berliner, one of his oldest and most faithful and devoted friends. Their relations had become somewhat chilly over the years, but Mahler had written to him three months earlier to say that "my feelings for you haven't changed a bit and I still think with the same warmth of our former relations . . . In fact, the only cause of our separation has been . . . our separation, at any rate I can't recall any other . . . Unfortunately, it's impossible for me to keep up my friendships from such a distance for I simply haven't the time. However, I'd like nothing better than to renew ours and bring it up to date—and my forthcoming trip to Berlin will give me the chance to do just that."[50]

In a letter he wrote to Mildenburg during the final rehearsals of the *Fourth Symphony,* Mahler called the Berlin orchestra *sehr ruppig* (very clumsy) and said that he appreciated its behavior far more than its professional qualities. The concert, which was given on December 16 and, apart from Mahler's symphony, conducted by Strauss, consisted of Liszt's poem *Les Préludes,* Mahler's *Fourth Symphony,* three of Friedrich Rösch's *Mörike-Lieder*[51] with orchestral accompaniment and the Love Scene from *Feuersnot.* The audience's disappointment with the first movements of the symphony was even more virulently displayed than in Munich and, although the Adagio was a great success, the Finale, in which the soprano proved unequal to her task, raised a storm of boos that persisted amid and finally drowned out the applause. Mahler deduced that Berlin's musical circles were as hostile to him as ever, and the reviews proved him right the following day.

Indeed, the Berlin press took a malicious delight in tearing the new work to shreds. The *Börsenzeitung* branded Mahler a "member of the extreme left" and an "ultra" of the new German school and said that, compared to the "bombastic pathos" of the gigantic and pretentious *Second Symphony,* the new work was "an idyl about Arcadian shepherds or a musical illustration of Watteauesque rococo . . . In this work, Herr Mahler has tried to be as simple and naïve as possible. The trouble is that one cannot believe in this naïveté because it does not suit his face . . . It smacks of a raillery, a deliberate fraud perpetrated at the expense of the audience and only the dazzling orchestration and the use of all the newest techniques remind one that this is a contemporary work. Does Herr Mahler aim to be the composer of tomorrow? Perhaps this sweet and simple style, this conscious leaning [*Anlehnen*] toward the old and the very old, this formlessness and these gigantic sophisms [*Trugschlüsse*] are a sign of ultranovelty and hypermodernism." With its "affected and vulgar" simplicity, the Finale was nothing but a caricature of that of Beethoven's *Ninth Symphony,* for Herr Mahler, needless to say, was "incapable of translating such superb poetry into music," this critic scoffed, and then proceeded to express unconvincing praise for the excerpt from *Feuersnot.*

Leopold Schmidt, in the *Berliner Tageblatt,* declared that he could give no more than his own personal impressions of this *"Second [sic] Symphony,"* which, like all the new works presented at the Strauss concert, had been applauded indiscriminately by a group of "radical progressives." With its "odd humor," the Finale outshone the other movements, but its relationship to them remained mysterious. Mahler's technique was unquestionably stunning, but "it is devoutly to be hoped that the time when people were more interested in *how* a work was composed than in *that which* it expressed is definitively past . . ."

The *Vossische Zeitung* regretted finding no trace in the *Fourth Symphony* of the "striving for power and the struggle with his genius" that had marked the *Second*. Unsatisfactory either as pure music or as "program music," of scant inspiration and weak construction, the work wore out the audience by its excessive length and insoluble riddles. The paper wondered how a "clever" musician like Mahler could have failed to perceive the absence of style in this interminable symphony, in this "idyl that bores and anesthetizes with its lack of contrasts" and that consisted of nothing but "witty and artful details without any genuine melody or any climax in the crescendos."

Ferocious as these articles were, none were quite as bitingly sarcastic as that signed by Karl Krebs and published in *Der Tag:* "Gustav Mahler's so-called *Symphony No. 4,* which Richard Strauss presented at his third subscription concert, is nothing but a silly joke in poor taste, a really silly joke. I fancy the conception and carrying-out of this pasticcio as follows: Herr Mahler finally realized that he lacked the essential faculties for composing, since, at best, his musical invention produced only reminiscences of peasant songs, Viennese dances or Hungarian ditties; having realized as much, he decided to abandon composition but, before taking leave of it, he wanted to wreak vengeance on his contemporaries by making fools of them. Thus he said to himself: 'I'll see just how much the public can be made to swallow without perceiving that it's being ridiculed.' So he took the ingredients at his disposal, a little 'Viennesishness,' a little 'Hungarianishness' and a lot of boredom, and wrote four movements, the third of which has something almost heroic about it, so unbelievable, so monumental and boundless as the desert is the emptiness that pervades it. He then treated himself to another good joke; rightly surmising that all the boredom he had concocted would send his audience to sleep, he proceeded to have the entire orchestra shriek fortissimo in order to terrify and startle even the most inveterate sleepers out of their sleep. Yes, that is Herr Mahler! Onto this bric-a-brac he glued a few instrumental effects, such as a squealing flute, a howling trumpet and a clinking harp, to hold the whole thing together and finally forced a soprano voice to sing an old street refrain in the Hungarian potpourri of the last movement. Thereupon he examined his opus, found that it served his purpose perfectly and handed it over to Richard Strauss. The latter also looked it over and said: 'Ah! What a marvelous joke, we'll make real fools of the public with this!' And indeed, the public noticed absolutely nothing, it applauded very prettily and so much so that it silenced the few people who, since they are not altogether lacking in artistic receptivity, had hooted. Dear Public, you truly deserve 'composers' like Gustav Mahler . . ."[52]

Even Oskar Eichberg, who had been one of Mahler's friends and supporters when the latter made his debut in Berlin, wondered if he had not set out deliberately to flout the public with themes that were "really only fit for children's songs" and contrasted oddly with the subtlety of the orchestral trimmings. However, he preferred to reserve judgment concerning the symphony as a whole, of which he had sincerely admired only the orchestration.

Among the correspondents of the various musical reviews, one declared that, "if such is the future of the symphony, then this is the end of all musical logic," since even the "glorious and solemn" Adagio ended in a farce,[53] while others made unfavorable comparisons between the *Second Symphony* and the "oddities, curiosities, absurdities and eccentricities of the *Fourth*," which, chameleon-like, "constantly switches, too rapidly and without transition, from beautiful to ugly, from genuine to artificial and from naïve to sophisticated."[54]

In the face of this barrage of disparagement, Mahler's only consolation was the enthusiasm shown by Strauss, who had attended all the rehearsals and become "more and more" interested in the work. After hearing the Adagio, he had said that he himself would have been "quite incapable of writing such a piece" and on the subject of a particularly dissonant passage in the Scherzo, had laughingly remarked, "There you've depicted a brush with your critics." In fact, he had even gone so far as to tell Mahler that "I've studied the score of your *Second Symphony* very thoroughly and benefited from certain of the lessons it contains."[55]

Although this latest meeting of Mahler and Strauss in December 1901 had been friendlier than usual, the views they had exchanged during a long night's discussion had been as far apart as ever. Strauss had probably considered the *Fourth Symphony* inferior to the *Second,* while Mahler, still unaware that Strauss was about to become one of the greatest dramatic composers of all time, had "tried to point out to him that he had come to a dead end," but, "unfortunately, he [Strauss] couldn't quite follow me," as he wrote in one of his letters. "He's a charming young chap and I'm touched by the way he behaves toward me and yet I can't be anything to him because I already see beyond him, while he sees only the pedestal as far as I'm concerned . . ."[56]

On his way back from Berlin, Mahler stopped a second time in Dresden, where, thanks to Schuch's intelligence and courage, a lot of modern music was played and where people were exceptionally well disposed toward him. At the request of the King of Saxony, he had drawn up a "program" of the *Second Symphony,* a program "intended to be read by someone rather naïve and superficial . . ."[57] Whereas the *First Symphony* had caused amazement in Dresden, the *Second* was warmly applauded by an audience that tried to force Mahler to take a bow, while he, "hidden in among it in an orchestra seat, was happy as a faun not to be recognized," at least so Heinrich Platzvecker of the *Dresdner Zeitung* said.

Unfortunately, the critics in no wise shared the public's enthusiasm. The same Heinrich Platzvecker declared that, for want of a thematic analysis, he was unable to make head or tail of these "heavenly lengths." In his opinion, the *Second Symphony* betrayed many influences. Despite the beauty of certain details, "the whole is unfortunately marred by dissonances that change as constantly as the patterns in a kaleidoscope, by 'noises' and by its interminable length . . ."

Hermann Starcke of the *Dresdner Nachrichten* claimed that the work had aroused only "profound indifference" in Dresden and that the applause had been intended solely for the performers. Nor was this to be wondered at, for the symphony consisted of nothing but "a play of characterless, aimless and shapeless sounds, an endless conglomeration of odds and ends collected here and there and sham sentiments . . . It subjects the audience to both mental and physical torture by exhausting it and imposing superhuman endurance on it." As a symptom of "the incredible confusion and virtuosic decadence" of modern music, it belongs in the "abnormal babies department of an anatomical museum of music."[58]

This time, all Germany seemed in league against Mahler and his symphonies. Even in Graz, a "superhuman" symphony like the *Second* had been expected, and the *First,* under the baton of the local conductor Martin Spörr, appeared only a pale joke, too caricatural and eclectic to be of interest. Most of the listeners were perplexed by what they heard, and the light applause that followed the first movements had changed to energetic booing by the time the Finale ended.[59]

Back in Vienna, Mahler must have wondered whether it was worth while continuing to travel and conduct his music, considering that it universally and invariably met with nothing but hostility and incomprehension. His disappointment may be measured by the high hopes with which he had set out, and, in the circumstances, it was miraculous that he retained any at all. Fortunately, however, his personal life was about to enter upon a new stage and a major event was to take his mind off the animosity and contempt that he encountered on all sides.

"... *one* voice that drowns out
everything else and that will
never again fall silent in my
heart ..."

# CHAPTER 36

*Mahler in Vienna (XII) — Mahler in Love — Alma
Schindler — Engagement (December 1901–January
1902)*

The stormy concerts in Munich and Berlin made Mahler aware more
acutely than ever of his loneliness and isolation as a composer and of the
obstacles he still had to surmount in order to be heard and understood.
Moreover, the fact that people applauded his *Second Symphony* and
booed his *Fourth*—which he had thought was more readily understandable
—meant virtually nothing as far as he was concerned. "If, one day," he
wrote, "one of my works should finally come to be understood, (I've already
been fighting against shallowness and incomprehension and experiencing all
the disappointments, nay misery of a pioneer for fifteen years), and particularly in Vienna, where, after all, people have an instinctive conception
of my personality, this should no more bother you or make you distrust my
work than does the incomprehension and hostility. The important thing is
never to let oneself be guided by the opinion of one's contemporaries and,
in both one's life and one's work, to continue steadfastly on one's way
without letting oneself be either defeated by failure or diverted by applause.
The fact is that I think some of the seeds I've sown are now beginning to
come up. Be this as it may, I'm immensely happy that this should happen
at this precise moment and that you, my dearest beloved, will no longer
feel all the thorns, even though I shall never spare you them where it's a
matter of remaining true to myself and, from now on, also to you, for
you and I will henceforth be but one. We will thus help and encourage one
another to remain constantly and proudly indifferent to all outside things,
for that is the high honor to which we aspire!"[1]

Thus Mahler, as a human being if not as a composer, no longer felt alone.

For the first time in five years,[2] a note of passion and tenderness appears in his correspondence. To whom were these words of endearment addressed? It had all begun the year before in Paris, where he had met Sophie Zseps, a young Viennese woman married to Paul Clemenceau. She had asked him to telephone, as soon as he got back to Vienna, to her sister Berta Zuckerkandl, who was married to a well-known anatomist and who entertained intellectuals and artists in her salon every Sunday. Mahler had taken an immediate liking to the Zuckerkandls and accepted an invitation to dine with them on November 7, 1901,[3] in order to see Sophie Clemenceau, who had returned to Vienna on a visit. He was seated beside her, with the distinguished painter Gustav Klimt and the ex-director of the Burgtheater, Max Burckhard,[4] opposite him and, between them, a fair-haired girl whose spectacular beauty and "harsh [*herb*] and nervous" tone of voice had already attracted his attention earlier in the evening. She was carrying on an animated conversation, punctuated by peals of laughter, with her two neighbors, and Mahler, becoming more and more intrigued, finally asked: "May I not laugh with you?" He had hardly made the request when another guest arrived and apologetically explained that he had just come from a concert by the great Czech violinist Jan Kubelik. However, Mahler was delighted when the young lady later confided to him that she was not in the least interested in virtuosos.

The conversation then drifted on to the decadence of Vienna's artistic life and to that of the Viennese ballet in particular. Mahler told how an archduke had asked him to engage a singer who, though young and pretty, had no talent, so that, when the somewhat abashed court chamberlain had come to ask him for his reply, he had said merely, "Tell His Highness that I threw his letter into the waste paper basket." Burckhard remarked that the fact that the archduke had not pressed the matter showed the degree to which at least one situation in Vienna had changed since he had been director of the Burgtheater and an archduchess had had the audacity to have a play banned because it featured an illegitimate child. "Why did the public accept such a thing? Why didn't it demand the dismissal of a director who allowed himself to be treated like that?" the young beauty chipped in. "Only youth could ask such a question," Mahler exclaimed, "for it knows nothing of cowardice and compromise." Thereupon he relapsed into his usual silence and became engrossed in choosing an apple for his dessert.[5]

After dinner, the guests split up into groups and Mahler managed to join the girl in one discussing physical beauty and its relative criteria. He said that, in his view, Socrates had been a handsome man and the young stranger said she thought Alexander von Zemlinsky was handsome too, even though he was considered one of the ugliest men in Vienna, because of the intelligence that shone in his eyes. Mahler thought this was going too far and merely shrugged his shoulders. A few moments later, Frau Zuckerkandl noticed a heated argument going on and came over to the group. Alma

Schindler, for it was she, was flushed with anger and her eyes were blazing, while Mahler, just as angry as she, was hopping from one leg to the other or simply standing on one like a wader. The cause of the argument was Zemlinsky's ballet *Das Goldene Herz* (The Golden Heart). "You have no right to keep a score that's been submitted to you for a whole year," Alma protested, "especially when it's been sent in by a real musician like Zemlinsky. You could at least have answered him." "But the story is just a lot of nonsense," Mahler growled, "and nobody can make head or tail of it. How can you who are interested in music and who are, I believe, studying it, possibly defend such trash?" "In the first place, it's not trash and you've probably not even taken the trouble to look it over. And secondly, even if it is bad music, that's no excuse for being so rude!" Mahler bit his lips, but held out his hand, saying, "Let's make peace! I don't promise to put on the ballet, of course, but, since you support your professor so courageously and express your opinion so frankly, you force my respect and I do promise to send for Zemlinsky not later than tomorrow." Alma then offered to give him a detailed explanation of the complex symbolism of Hofmannsthal's libretto of *Das Goldene Herz*. "I can't wait to hear your explanation," he replied, whereat she, sensing the sarcasm in his voice, insisted that he first explain the synopsis of *Die Braut von Korea* (*The Korean Bride*), a particularly absurd ballet by Joseph Bayr, which drew large crowds to the opera. Enchanted by this counterattack, he grinned broadly, began inquiring about her studies, and finally asked her to show him some of her latest compositions one day.

Meanwhile, the groups were gradually thinning out as the guests began to leave and Mahler remained alone with Alma, separated from the others, according to her, "by that space created around themselves by two people who have found one another." She promised she would bring him "something good" as soon as possible. He merely smiled, "as if to say that, in that case, he would have to wait a long time" and, filled with remorse at having lost her temper with a man she admired and worshiped, she finally wandered away. Sophie Clemenceau and Berta Zuckerkandl came over, and Mahler invited them and their fiery young guest to the dress rehearsal of the *Tales of Hoffmann* the following morning. "It's a work of which I'm very fond," he explained. "All through his life, Offenbach strove to escape from operetta and create an opera. He succeeded in doing so only in his old age, when he was at death's door. Such is the fate of every one of us: we don't fulfill our dreams until we're about to die." He took leave of Frau Zuckerkandl, frankly admitting that he had never felt so at ease in society. Alma then came to say good-by to him, but without having definitely accepted his invitation. Hearing that she lived at the Hohe Warte,[6] he offered to walk her home, but she turned down his offer because it was so late. He tried once more to make her promise to come and see him at the opera. "Yes, yes, provided I've done some good work," she replied. "Word of honor?" (*Ein Mann, ein Wort*) he called after her. When he had left,

Alma again apologized for having lost her temper, but Berta only smiled slyly. She later claimed that, since Klimt had been in love with Alma when she was sixteen and Burckhard was in love with her at the time, she had jokingly remarked to the young girl, "This evening, I invited your past [pointing to Klimt], your present [pointing to Burckhard], and, who knows, perhaps your future!"

This account clearly shows that, despite her twenty-three years, Alma Schindler had immediately bewitched the celebrated director of the opera, not only with her beauty, but also with her fiery temperament, alert mind, and quick wit. A powerful intellect if ever there was one, an exceptionally cultured and open-minded musician, Mahler had nevertheless remained marked by the provincial bourgeois origins that had long kept him apart from artistic circles. Although literature and music had provided an escape from the mediocrity of his early life, he had never felt entirely at home in the world of the arts. Alma, on the other hand, was born in Vienna as the daughter and stepdaughter of painters, and all the Muses seemed to have gathered around her cradle. Her father, Jakob Emil, was the most celebrated landscape painter of the Austrian Empire.[7] Her great-uncle, Alexander Schindler, had written novels under an aristocratic pseudonym and also played an important part as a liberal member of Parliament. In his youth, Jakob Emil and another famous painter, Hans Makart, had shared a studio where the two of them had given "Renaissance parties" at which Liszt would play the whole night long under garlands of roses for guests in sumptuous fancy dress, while velvet-liveried pages served them a profusion of the most exquisite wines. In 1879, after marrying Anna Bergen, an amateur singer and the daughter of a Hamburg brewer, he had moved into Plankenberg, a small, reputedly haunted baroque château in the suburbs of Vienna. It was here, in surroundings as idyllic and poetic as her father's water colors, that Alma had spent her childhood.[8]

The portrait she has left us of Jakob Emil is uniformly laudatory. He was exceedingly handsome, he had "aristocratic tastes," he was a close friend of Archduke Johannes Orth, he adored music, he had a fine tenor voice and enjoyed singing Schumann's lieder. His conversation was enthralling in the highest degree and, from her earliest childhood, Alma had spent hours listening to him and watching him paint. She was only just eight years old when he told her Goethe's story of *Faust* and gave her the book, urging her to read it and keep it carefully, for "it's the most beautiful book in the world." As a child, she often had fanciful dreams in which she pictured herself entertaining famous men[9] in vast Italian gardens, dressed in long velvet robes and floating around in gondolas.

Anna Schindler tried to exercise a moderating influence over her daughter, but only succeeded in inspiring Alma with profound contempt for her. Moreover, the frequent and violent quarrels between her parents merely strengthened young Alma's passionate love for her father. When she was ten years old, her parents took her with them on a long trip through Dalmatia, the crown prince having commissioned Schindler to do a series of drawings and water colors of the prominent towns on the coast. The trip ended with a long stay on Corfu, which Alma never forgot, for it was there that she began studying music and composition.

In 1892, the year of the cholera epidemic in Hamburg, Schindler was seized by violent intestinal pains just as the family was about to leave for Sylt on the North Sea. The doctors made a mistake in their diagnosis, and the trip, undertaken with acute appendicitis, was fatal to him. A few days later, at Sylt, Anna Schindler informed her two daughters that he had died. Alma, who was only just fourteen, immediately realized that she had lost not only her father but also "my guide whom I had always done everything I could to please and whose look of understanding had been the only thing that satisfied all my vanity and ambition."

Two years later, unknown to her mother, who, according to Alma, took very little notice of her, she became passionately fond of reading and more and more of an "introvert." She was then studying counterpoint with a blind organist and, just as Mahler had done in his youth, was devouring mountains of scores. Moreover, in her zeal for Wagner, she irreparably ruined the pretty voice with which nature had endowed her by singing all the Wagnerian roles one after the other. Eager for knowledge, she began to look about her for men who could direct her reading. Thus each stage of her intellectual development turned into an emotional crisis. Max Burckhard, the director of the Burgtheater, a generous and cultivated man who had introduced Ibsen and Hauptmann to the Viennese, sent her two huge linen baskets containing a complete classical library as a Christmas present. At seventeen, she was still "totally immature," though fascinated by Burckhard's "forceful virility," which, however, "became repulsive to me" when he later began to court her.

She was eighteen when her mother married Schindler's leading pupil, Karl Moll, who, as far as she was concerned, was an "eternal student," an artist who had wasted the little talent he possessed by constantly changing masters. Indeed, this marriage only increased her scorn for her mother, for she could not understand how, after having once possessed a "complete clock," one could be content with just a "pendulum." According to her, moreover, Moll's efforts to educate his stepdaughter incurred "nothing but hatred on my part."[10] In reaction to the academism of Viennese art, Moll and some of his friends had recently formed a movement, the *"Sezession,"* composed of painters, sculptors, and architects who met regularly at his house. The leader, or at any rate the dominant personality of the group, was the renowned painter Gustav Klimt. He in turn undertook to educate Alma in the plastic arts, but he too fell in love with his pupil and followed her all through Italy when she was on a trip with her family. This time, however, the very violence of Klimt's passion appealed to her. Anna Moll, who happened to learn from her daughter's diary that Klimt had kissed her, put an immediate stop to the nascent idyl, for which Alma was later to reproach her bitterly.

Meanwhile, Alma consoled herself by devoting all her time and energy to the study of composition, becoming a pupil of Alexander von Zemlinsky, an incomparable teacher and one of the most outstanding Viennese musicians of his time.[11] Before or after her lessons, master and pupil would spend hours playing through scores (including one day that of *Tristan und Isolde*). Although, according to Alma, he was a "small, repugnant, chinless, toothless and unwashed gnome," she nevertheless became irresistibly attracted to him, too. Indeed, by her own admission, "the hideous Turkish drawing-room" of the friends with whom she was then living in Vienna almost "witnessed my fall" and only her "old-fashioned upbringing" and her "mother's daily sermons" prevented her from giving herself to him.

At the time of the production of *Es war einmal,* Zemlinsky had told his pupil of Mahler's superhuman efforts on behalf of his opera, including his painstaking revision of both text and music. The two had even "drunk to the only man of whom one can speak no ill." For all that, Vienna fairly buzzed with slanderous rumors of Mahler's exploits as a Don Juan and of the favors he bestowed on the female singers with whom he became enamored. Though "strangely fascinated" by Mahler the conductor, Alma had nevertheless left the hall "full of anger and bitterness" after hearing his *First Symphony* the year before. "For six months now, I've been doing my utmost not to meet him," she told the Zuckerkandls when they ran into her on the Ring and invited her to dine at their house with him. This, in spite of the fact that Justi had telephoned that very day to ask that no other guests be invited, since Mahler could not bear strangers.

A week later, Berta Zuckerkandl invited Alma again. Mahler had excused himself at the last moment the week before but had promised to come this time in order to see Sophie Clemenceau. However, the fact that two of Alma's best friends, Klimt and Burckhard, were also going to be there, finally persuaded her to accept the invitation, and we already know the result. She left the party thoroughly out of sorts, feeling she had not been herself and had "created misunderstandings." Because of her shyness, she tended either to remain silent or to "pour out all I think in such a way that I appear to be brazen and forward," yet it was precisely this that had captivated Mahler and several others before him. He, on the other hand, pontificated that evening whenever he opened his mouth, prefacing all his remarks with "Yes, but I tell you . . . !" as though there had been a crowd assembled to listen to him. Alma presumed that this grandiloquence must be due to the loneliness of a man who wielded too dictatorial a power over others, but she was fascinated in spite of herself. "I must confess I liked him enormously," she wrote in her diary. "To be sure, he's frightfully nervous. He bounced around the room like a wild beast. The fellow's pure oxygen: one gets burnt when one comes close to him . . ."

The morning after the party, Berta Zuckerkandl and Sophie Clemenceau took Alma to the opera, where they found Mahler impatiently awaiting them outside his office. He helped the young girl off with her coat, which he kept on his arm, but quite forgot to render the same service to the two ladies. Then, with a clumsy gesture, he invited them all into his office, where the two sisters engaged him in conversation while Alma, "incapable of making small talk," leafed through a pile of scores on the piano. Mahler repeatedly threw her imploring glances, but she, "with the typical unconcern of youth, wasn't even thinking about him or what was going on in his mind." Although she had not yet discovered "the only thing about him that could impress me," the grandeur of his personality, she nonetheless felt "a mysterious respect" for him. Finally, he plucked up his courage and said:

"Fräulein Schindler, did you sleep well?"

"Exceedingly well, thank you, why?"

"I didn't sleep a wink all night!"

Thereupon, he escorted his guests to the hall and, on taking leave of Alma, reminded her of her promise to come and see him. The rehearsal of *Les Contes d'Hoffmann* proceeded without a hitch. Mahler interrupted it only once at the beginning of the second act, when Gutheil-Schoder (as Giulietta) came on stage in a gown split up to her waist on one side. Shocked at this "lack of taste," he sent her packing then and there, demanding that she have it sewn up immediately. While the dressmaker was busy, he inveighed in an undertone against the singer who had "dared to appear on stage in such a costume." It was then that Alma realized that "the theater was sacred to him."

The next morning she received the following anonymous poem:

| | |
|---|---|
| *Das kam so über Nacht!* | It happened overnight. |
| *Hätt' ich's doch nicht gedacht,* | I would never have believed it, |
| *Dass Contrapunkt und Formenlehre* | That counterpoint and the study of form |
| *Mir noch einmal das Herz beschwere.* | Would once more oppress my heart. |
| | |
| *So über eine Nacht* | Thus, in just one night |
| *Gewann es Uebermacht!* | They gained the upper hand! |
| *Und alle Stimmen führen nur* | And all the voices lead ever more |
| *Mehr homophon zu einer Spur!* | Homophonically in only one direction. |
| | |
| *Das kam so über Nacht* | It happened overnight |
| *—Ich habe sie durchwacht—* | —I spent it wide awake— |
| *Dass ich, wenn's klopft, im Augenblick* | That, when there's a knock |
| *Die Augen nach der Türe schick'!* | My eyes immediately fly toward the door! |
| | |
| *Ich hör's: ein Mann—ein Wort!* | I hear: "Word of honor"! |
| *Es tönt mir immerfort—* | It rings in my ears constantly |
| *Ein Canon jeder Art:* | Like every sort of cannon: |
| *Ich blick' zur Tür—und wart'!* | I glance at the door and wait! |

The author of the poem had deliberately given himself away by his transparent allusions, and in her book Alma affirms that she guessed at once who he was. She nevertheless showed the poem to her mother, who, "convinced that a man like Mahler would never send poems to unknown young girls," concluded that the whole thing was a hoax. Thus Alma herself long remained in doubt. Meanwhile, however, thanks to Burckhard, she was not unaware that she had made quite an impression on Mahler, for the two men had left the Zuckerkandls' house together, and Burckhard, in answer to Mahler's questions, had said, "Fräulein Schindler is a bright and interesting young lady." Mahler had then observed that "I didn't like her to begin with, because she seemed to be nothing but a doll. It's not every day one meets such a pretty young thing who's actually busying herself with something serious," after which he had plied Burckhard with further questions, which the latter refused to answer, saying merely that, "Those who are acquainted with Fräulein Schindler know what she is. The others have no right to know."

Alma in turn thought constantly of Mahler but bitterly reproached herself for doing so because, as her diary reveals, her affair with Zemlinsky was a great deal more serious than she was later to admit in her two books. She was, or at any rate thought she was, deeply in love with him and even wanted to have a child by him. ". . . Whether, if he doesn't give himself to me entirely," she wrote two days after the party at the Zuckerkandls', "my nerves would suffer terribly; or whether, if he were to give all of himself, the result would be disaster? Both are equally dangerous! And I long so madly for his embraces. I shall never be able to forget how his touch stirred me to the depths of my soul—such a blaze—and such a feeling of ecstasy filled my being—Yes, one can be completely happy—supreme happiness does exist. I experienced it in the arms of my beloved. But for a tiny detail,[12] I would have been a god—And once again, everything about him is sacred to me, I want to kneel down in front of him and kiss his open thighs [*Schoss*]—kiss everything, everything! Amen!"

On November 11, Alma attended the premiere of *Les Contes d'Hoffmann*, and her diary shows that her thoughts were running increasingly on Mahler. On the eighteenth she went to the opera again, with her mother this time, to hear Gluck's *Orfeo ed Euridice*, which Walter was conducting. After a while, she got bored and her eyes wandered up to the director's box. At first, Mahler did not recognize her, but then "he started to flirt with me in a way I never would have believed so serious a man could."

During the intermission she and her mother were strolling through the foyer, when he suddenly appeared in front of them and, after having been introduced to Frau Moll, invited them into his office for a cup of tea. Having taken an instant liking to Frau Moll,[13] he was at his most "affable and charming," and the conversation immediately flowed, while Alma, doubtless feeling a little left out, seated herself at the piano. Mahler was about to leave for Munich to conduct the premiere of his *Fourth Symphony*.

# ✳ Philharmonie. ✳

Montag, den 4. März 1895, Abends 7½ Uhr sehr präcise.

# IX. Philharmonisches Concert.

Dirigent:

### Hofkapellmeister **Rich. Strauss.**

Solist: **J o s e f  H o f m a n n** (Klavier).

## PROGRAMM.

1. Ouverture: „Die Hebriden," op. 26 . . *F. Mendelssohn.*

2. Concert für Klavier mit Begleitung des
   Orchesters No. 4, C-moll, op. 44 . . *C. Saint-Saëns.*
   Allegro moderato ed Andante. — Allegro
   vivace, Andante ed Allegro finale.

3. 3 Sätze a. d. Symphonie No. 2 (z. 1. Mal) *G. Mahler.*
   I. Allegro maëstoso. ⎫ Diese 3 Sätze bilden
   II. Andante con moto. ⎬ den 1. Theil
   III. (Scherzo) Allegro commodo. ⎭ der Symphonie.
   (Unter Leitung des Componisten).

4. Klavier-Soli:
   a) Nocturne, C-moll . . . . . . . *F. Chopin.*
   b) Rhapsodie No. 6 . . . . . . . *F. Liszt.*

5. Ouverture zu: „Oberon" . . . . . . *C. M. v. Weber.*

**Concertflügel: BECHSTEIN.**

◄••►

### X. (letztes) Philharmonisches Concert: Montag, 18. März 1895.
Dirigent: Hofkapellmeister **Rich. Strauss.**
Unter Mitwirkung des Philharmonischen Chors (**S. Ochs**).

**Rich. Strauss:** Vorspiel zum II. Act, Friedenserzählung, Vorspiel zum I. Act,
Schluss des III. Act aus der Oper: „Guntram". — **Beethoven:** IX. Symphonie
(mit Chor).

49. Program of the Berlin concert that included the incomplete premiere of the
*Second Symphony*.

50. Program of the Berlin concert with premiere of the *Lieder eines fahrenden Gesellen*.

Da in Folge gewisser öffentlich gefallener Aeusserungen bei einem Theil des Publikums die Meinung entstehen könnte, als wären seitens des Dirigenten der heutigen Aufführung an den Werken Beethoven's, und insbesondere an der Neunten Symphonie, willkürliche Umgestaltungen in irgend welchen Einzelnheiten vorgenommen worden, so scheint es geboten, mit einer aufklärenden Bemerkung über diesen Punkt nicht zurückzuhalten.

Beethoven hatte durch sein in völlige Taubheit ausgeartetes Gehörleiden den unerlässlichen innigen Contact mit der Realität, mit der physisch tönenden Welt gerade in jener Epoche seines Schaffens verloren, in welcher ihn die gewaltigste Steigerung seiner Conceptionen zur Auffindung neuer Ausdrucksmittel und zu einer bis dahin ungeahnten Drastik in der Behandlung des Orchesters hindrängte. Ebenso bekannt wie diese Thatsache, ist die andere, dass die Beschaffenheit der damaligen Blechinstrumente gewisse zur Bildung der Melodie nöthige Tonfolgen schlechterdings ausschloss. Gerade dieser Mangel hat mit der Zeit eine Vervollkommnung jener Instrumente herbeigeführt, welche nunmehr nicht zu möglichst vollendeter Ausführung der Werke Beethoven's auszunützen, geradezu als Frevel erschiene.

Richard Wagner, der sein ganzes Leben hindurch in Wort und That leidenschaftlich bemüht war, den Vortrag Beethoven'scher Werke einer nachgerade unerträglich gewordenen Verwahrlosung zu entreissen, hat in seinem Aufsatze „Zum Vortrag der Neunten Symphonie Beethoven's" (Ges. Schriften, Bd. 9) jenen Weg zu einer den Intentionen ihres Schöpfers möglichst entsprechenden Ausführung dieser Symphonie gewiesen, auf dem ihm alle neueren Dirigenten gefolgt sind. Auch der Leiter des heutigen Concertes hat dies in vollster, aus eigenem Durchleben des Werkes gewonnener und gefestigter Ueberzeugung gethan, ohne im Wesentlichen über die von Wagner angedeuteten Grenzen hinauszugehen.

Von einer Uminstrumentirung, Aenderung, oder gar „Verbesserung" des Beethoven'schen Werkes kann natürlich absolut nicht die Rede sein. Die längst geübte Vervielfachung der Streichinstrumente hat — und zwar ebenfalls schon seit Langem — auch eine Vermehrung der Bläser zur Folge gehabt, die ausschliesslich der Klangverstärkung dienen sollen, keineswegs aber eine neue orchestrale Rolle zugetheilt erhielten. In diesem, wie in jedem Punkte, der die Interpretation des Werkes im Ganzen wie im Einzelnen betrifft, kann an der Hand der Partitur (und zwar je mehr in's Detail eingehend, desto zwingender) der Nachweis geführt werden, dass es dem Dirigenten überall nur darum zu thun war, fern von Willkür und Absichtlichkeit, aber auch von keiner „Tradition" beirrt, den Willen Beethoven's bis in's scheinbar Geringfügigste nachzufühlen und in der Ausführung auch nicht das Kleinste von dem, was der Meister gewollt hat, zu opfern, oder in einem verwirrenden Tongewühle untergehen zu lassen.

Wien, im Februar 1900.

Gustav Mahler.

Buchdruckerei: Wien, I. Dorotheergasse 7.

51. Public explanation by Mahler of his instrumental alterations of Beethoven's *Ninth Symphony*.

52. Mahler in Vienna, 1899.

53. Caricatures of Mahler by Otto Böhler.

54. Mahler with his sister, Justine.

55. Mahler in Vienna at the time of his marriage.

but he accepted Frau Moll's invitation to visit them at the Hohe Warte as soon as he got back, and Alma promised to change the time of her counterpoint lesson that day. As she and her mother were leaving, she jokingly asked him if he would agree to engage her at the opera as a conductor, to which he replied in the affirmative, saying he did not doubt that her conducting would please him. "Your judgment would not be objective," she retorted. "Is any judgment ever objective?" he concluded. That evening, they parted like a pair of lovers, "convinced that something important and wonderful had entered their lives."

After the performance, Alma and her mother joined Burckhard and Moll for supper, and Moll, on being told about their encounter, upbraided his wife for having allowed her daughter to enter the office of that "roué," that "rake." From then on, according to Alma, he did his level best to break up her budding affair by pointing out the disadvantages of marrying a man like Mahler: his age, his debts, his ill health, his "shaky" position at the opera, etc.; he even went so far as to remark, "He's not good-looking and his work can't be worth much." As for Burckhard, he was quite jealous. When he asked Alma what her answer would be if Mahler asked her to marry him and she replied, "I would accept," he burst out, "But it would be a sin for so lovely a creature of such good family as you! Don't go and throw yourself away on this rachitic and degenerate Jew.[14] Think of your children! Besides which, fire and water can, at a pinch, get along together, but not fire and fire. He'll trample you underfoot and you'll end up by being miserable." Alma was in no wise convinced. On the contrary, she could hardly wait for Mahler to return, and confided to her diary on November 20: "I ought to be ashamed of myself—but Mahler's image lives within me. I'll tear out this poisonous weed. Another's place. My poor, poor Alex! If only the poem had been from him, if only. I could hate myself!" "I was so far away from my Gustav, so infinitely far"—she wrote two days later, "I've sent Alex a fateful letter. What will come of it? He'll write me a sarcastic and really angry letter and never come back again. Oh, what I'm losing! Such a marvelous teacher! I've certainly miscalculated this time. Whatever happens, I must bear the consequences!"

Mahler presumably did not go to the Hohe Warte on Saturday, November 23, for Alma's diary does not mention him that day. On Wednesday the twenty-seventh, she was working out figured basses with Robert Gound, when the maid came running in, almost speechless with excitement, to make the startling announcement that "Gustav Mahler is here!" A few moments later, he entered her room for the first time. Since the Molls had only just moved into No. 8 Steinfeldgasse at the Hohe Warte, Alma's books were still all piled on the floor, and he started to go through them, commenting on each one. Coming upon the complete works of Nietzsche, he suddenly got angry and wanted her to throw them in the fire then and there. "In so far as your abhorrence is justified," she replied, "you'll have no difficulty in convincing me but, in the meantime, it would seem to me to be more reasonable to leave Nietzsche unread in my library than to burn him and regret it afterwards." Annoyed at being thus put in his place, Mahler suggested that they take a walk. As they were going downstairs, they met Frau Moll, who invited him to stay for dinner, adding, "We're having *Paprikahändl* [chicken with paprika sauce] and . . . Burckhard." "I don't much care for either," he remarked archly, but accepted all the same.

"Side by side, at once close and yet strangers," Mahler and Alma, their feet crunching on the fresh snow, set out for Döbling, where he wanted to telephone Justi and tell her he would not be back for dinner. His shoelaces kept coming undone, and Alma was strangely moved by the childish awkwardness with which he invariably chose the highest and most uncomfortable footrests to do them up again. Upon reaching Döbling, he realized he had forgotten his home telephone number and had to call the opera. When he finally got through to Justi, he merely said he would not be home for dinner, without giving any explanation, a thing that, according to Alma, had never occurred in all the nine years they had lived together.

As they wandered back up the hill to the Hohe Warte, he finally voiced the thoughts that were absorbing him: "It's not easy to marry a man like me! I am and must remain entirely free and can't allow myself to be bound by any material things. Moreover, I could lose my position at the opera at any moment." The realization that he was thus "dictating his will and rule of life" to her, without so much as asking her opinion, almost took Alma's breath away. However, the remarks he was making seemed self-evident to her, for, being the daughter of an artist, she had always lived among artists and therefore shared his views on the life of an artist. Apart from this brief exchange, they walked in silence, admiring the reflection of the street lamps on the snow. Mahler appeared to have calmed down and, when they got back to the house, he went up to Alma's room with her and kissed her for the first time. Thereupon, he began to talk about marriage "as though it were a simple and obvious thing, as though it had all been settled by the few words he'd uttered along the way—so why wait?"

When they went down to dinner half an hour later, Burckhard and a young architect who had also fallen under Alma's spell had already arrived. Mahler enchanted everyone with his wit and charm. He strongly defended Schiller against Alma's indifference, quoting a large number of his poems by heart. His defense was so convincing that, "after allowing him to kiss me without really wanting him to and after letting him set the date of our marriage," she had no doubt that "both these decisions are right and for the best and I can no longer live without him . . . He's the only man who can give meaning to my life, for he far surpasses all the men I've ever met."

The following morning, Mahler sent her his lieder, and she and Zemlinsky discussed them, "he with intense scorn, I coldly. Indeed, they're not him—such labored naïveté and simplicity for someone who is, if anything, a highly complex person. I'd so much like to tell him so, but am afraid of offending him." Not daring to admit that she found them "inauthentic," she finally wrote: "Dear Herr Direktor, Many many thanks! I don't want to write anything about the lieder—There's something I must tell you—and ask you. How I look forward to Monday! I'd very much like you to read what Maeterlinck wrote on 'Silence'—I was so strongly reminded of it during our first beautiful walk together. It was singularly beautiful and glorious. You'll have to get used to my writing gradually—so this must suffice as a beginning. I shake your hand most warmly and send you my kindest regards—until Monday! Alma Schindler."[15]

In the letter accompanying his lieder, Mahler had written: "Yesterday was very pleasant and happy, despite all the uneasiness; I felt it on my way home, after L[16] had left me and I was alone. All the love and loveliness continued to reverberate softly within me, even in my dreams." Alma, on the other hand, was in the depths of distress: "Alex was here and a trifle angry with me—but otherwise as sweet as ever. I had the feeling that I belong to him . . . Conflicting emotions are at war inside me. Here Alex, here Mahler—Mahler I trust absolutely." Two days later, on Monday, December 2, after Mahler's second visit to the Hohe Warte, she wrote: "He told me that he loves me—we kissed—he played his things for me—my senses remain numb . . . his caresses are sweet and nice. If only I knew—him or him—I must gradually put Alex out of my mind. I'm overwhelmed with remorse; if only all that hadn't happened—I would have become engaged today. But I couldn't return his caresses—someone stood between us . . . I told him so without mentioning the name—I had to tell him so! . . . Had he but come three years earlier. A mouth undefiled! . . . I'm in a terrible dilemma," she added the following day. "I keep saying softly to myself 'my beloved' and each time I add Alex! Can I really love Mahler as much as he deserves and it lies within my power to love someone. Will I ever understand his art—and he mine!? Mahler only said, 'That must be taken seriously. It's something I hadn't expected!' How shall I tell Alex that! I'm on 'Du' terms with Mahler—he told me how much he loves me and I wasn't able to say anything in return. Do I really love him? I've no idea—sometimes I think quite simply 'no.' So many things about him annoy me: his smell—the way he sings—something in the way he speaks! And desire? How passionately I burned with desire for Alex—at first . . . Every minute—every second—and now—yes, I desire, but no longer with the same passion! Perhaps I can't love that way a second time. He [Mahler] is a stranger to me, our tastes are diametrically opposed. He said to me, 'Alma, think it over very carefully—if you have any reason to be disappointed in me, say so immediately. Today, I can still get over it—although it will be hard—but in four months' time, it may no longer be possible.'

"And I don't know what's going on inside me—whether I love him or whether I don't love him—whether it's the director—the superb conductor—or the man . . . if, when I remove the one, something remains for the other and for his art, which is so far removed from me. In a word, I don't believe in him as a composer, and I should bind myself to him . . . The fact is he's closer to me from afar that at close quarters. I'm afraid . . . And if I now say 'no'—a dream of many years gone up in smoke! We kissed but without hugging one another. Although his hands are expressive, I don't love them as much as Alex's. Habit can do a lot of things—and so can time . . . but patience is not my Mahler's forte. What to do? And supposing Alex becomes great and mighty? . . . I've written to him—I've no idea what's going on inside me—This morning, I played some of the first act![17] It's so near to my heart! There's one thing that torments me: whether or not Mahler will encourage me to work—whether or not he'll support my art—whether he'll love it as Alex does—for *he* loves it for itself."

On Wednesday, December 4, Mahler sent Alma tickets for *Les Contes d'Hoffmann,* which he was conducting that evening, and also announced that he would be leaving for Berlin on the following Monday. "Since I'll have to stay away for about ten days, I'm very miserable and fear I fought my fight against the clay idols[18] quite in vain yesterday. Only the wounds I received in the process will remain. However, neither was it at all nice of you to resign yourself patiently and submissively to fate and just let me remain in exile for a whole week. Hero was quite different: she said 'come tomorrow.' So I shall not swim across the Hellespont but like a modern Leander, steam by fast train and sleeper, via Berlin, to Döbling and arrive in a completely 'decadent' state after all the strain and insomnia. Pyrrhus, the conqueror conquered."

At the end of each act of *Les Contes d'Hoffmann,* Mahler turned around to throw a loving glance at Alma. "If only he were Alex," she noted in her diary that night. "Oh, if only I'd already told Alex—I'm constantly thinking of t'other. Mahler [probably a slip of the pen for the young architect] sat in our row—oh God! If he doesn't come to us again before he leaves, I'll go to him."

The following day, Mahler wrote her another letter in which he talked about Hoffmann, one of his favorite authors, and Offenbach's opera, which he loved, "although Hoffmann's spirit is all but gone from it and only the phlegm remains.[19] It's only with the greatest inner repugnance that I manage to get to the end of the first two acts. But yesterday it was a pleasure—because it was for you! The third act is more felicitous; at least it contains the material with which one can, by using one's own inventive powers, re-create the demoniac traits of the original! . . . In just a few days," he concluded, "it's already become such a pleasant habit to chat with you—to fight for my cause or even to hold my tongue, that I cherish and express but one fervent wish before I leave: that you be and remain a loving comrade [*Kamerad*] to me and that you make a small effort so that I may be the same to you. Remember our beloved Evchen and Hans Sachs! Good-by!"

"I keep thinking of him more and more," Alma wrote in her diary after reading this letter. "His dear, dear smile. I've actually kissed this man, or rather he's kissed me. I'm beginning to think that I really do love him. Alex weighs on me like lead. I really do want him now . . . If I can just see Mahler before he leaves . . . In the evening, this letter—I could cry my eyes out! I have the feeling I've lost him—and yet I've already possessed him in spirit. How lucky I've been! I'm miserable. I must see him—before he leaves—I've got to see him. He doesn't want me, he's abandoning me—that last sentence, that terrible last sentence! I realize now how much I love him—I suddenly feel so empty. I must go to him tomorrow. My longing knows no bounds. Evchen and Hans Sachs—an idle subterfuge—it's just not possible!"

The last sentence in Mahler's letter continued to haunt and torment her throughout the following day: ". . . Evchen and Hans Sachs, I was not prepared for that." On Saturday, he could resist no longer and went to see her. "We kissed one another over and over again," she wrote. "I feel all warm inside when I'm in his arms. If he'll just go on loving me, but I think he's temperamental, frightfully temperamental. He tried to convert me to his way of thinking. I shan't see him for the next 10 days—he leaves for Berlin on Monday. I don't know what else to write, except that my heart has chosen him in preference to Alex. I've never watched the hands of the clock so closely as today. I wasn't able to do any work at all, for sheer longing . . . I keep seeing Gustav's eyes before me—so kind and so dear to me—and ceaselessly questioning—and his beautiful hands somewhat spoiled by biting his nails. He'll write to me from Berlin. I've never in my life met anyone who was more foreign to me than he—so foreign and yet so close! I really can't explain it—perhaps it's precisely this that attracts me to him. But he must leave me the way I am—I'm already conscious of the changes that are coming over me because of him. He takes a lot from me but he gives a lot. If things go on like this, he'll make another, a new person of me. A better person? I don't know, I don't know at all—my future is more than ever just one big question mark. It's all in his hands now. He told me everything today, all his faults and I some of mine. He guessed Alexeus' name and was appalled—he couldn't understand it. So that's it for both—and without a glance into the unknowable 'tomorrow.' At least we had today and that was beautiful, really beautiful. He's the purest person I've ever met—because Mahler, thank God, has had few affairs—nothing more than routine [. . . *nur mit Routine was geschehen*]."

On Sunday, December 8, Mahler sent Alma the score of *Das klagende Lied* together with the following letter: "Here is a 'Tale' from my youth! You gave me real joy yesterday. You both listened to me and answered me so sweetly. Alas, such an afternoon is dreadfully short and the coda of evening is almost mournful." He was going to give *Die Zauberflöte* for her that evening. "Today brings me the evening during which we shall be together and united in the deepest sense of the word. I'll think of you through every bar and conduct just for you. It will be like yesterday at the piano when I talked to you so frankly and straight from my heart. Every so often, I'll have that suspicious look that so frequently surprises you. It isn't suspicion, nor what one usually calls such, but questioning, of both you and the future. My dearest, do learn to answer! This is indeed very difficult, for one must have tested and learned to know oneself. Nevertheless, it's still more difficult to question! This can be learned only through the closest and most intimate relationship with another person. My dearest, my love, learn to question! You seemed to me to be so entirely different and so much more mature yesterday. I sense that these last few days have opened up and revealed a host of things to you. What will it be like by the time I get back? I'll then ask you again whether you love me, even more than yesterday, whether you know me and whether you recognize me. Adieu for now, my love, my comrade!"[20]

Alma recorded her reactions to this letter late that same night. "I feel as though all were chaos inside me—everything's upside down and something new is starting. A new philosophy, a new creed . . . I'm quite incapable of doing any work—I can't think why. Alex had already given me everything —I already had a lot myself and had picked up a lot. Now I'll have to discard a lot in order to be able to accept new things, better things. This afternoon, he sent me *Das klagende Lied*. Today was wonderful. Inspired melodics [*"Melodik ein beselten Leben"*; Alma probably meant *"Melodik eines beseelten Lebens"*], but the development is good and effective. I can imagine that several passages must produce an absolutely enthralling effect."

During the "divine" (*himmlisch*) performance of *Die Zauberflöte* that Mahler privately dedicated to her, Alma suddenly recognized the "genuine grandeur and beauty of this work. Then I looked at Gustav and couldn't help smiling blissfully. At the end of both acts, and particularly after the last, he gave me the most tenderly loving look—a thread was spun from him to me. Later on, we drove past him—he was walking with his sister and the Lechner-Bauer [*sic*] woman and didn't see me. My dearest Gustav, think, please think of me!"

The following morning, Alma was finally sure she was in love! "I . . . pace up and down in my room, now over to his photograph, now back again to his last letter." In the afternoon, Mahler sent her a box of almond toffees (*Kugler*) and still another letter. "How happy I'd be to receive a line from you upon my arrival at the Palace Hotel in Berlin. It would be like a little bit of home in that strange lodging, for, from now on, home is the place where I know you are. The least sign of your beloved life will make me forget for a few moments the agony of being parted from you. Write to me about *Die Zauberflöte,* too, I can well imagine that a thing like that is not yet within your grasp, since you're still too much all that yourself. This was also long the case with me as far as the works you call 'naïve' are concerned. Nevertheless, everything you tell me about yourself is adorable and precious to me, even the most insignificant things. Please don't go to any trouble over your letters: just put down the words that come into your head. Always imagine, when you're writing to me, that I'm sitting beside you and that you're chatting about everything under the sun. I'd always like to know all about your life—*in detail!* Just one thing, my Alma: please write legibly!"[21]

Before his departure, Mahler had told Justi everything and they had talked "until late in the night." "She understands everything and will be a faithful friend to us," he wrote to Alma, asking her to give him an exact account of the meeting he had arranged between them. According to Alma, however, he had said nothing to Justi at first, "for fear of the dire effects of her jealousy." One day, as he and Justi were walking on the Ring together, they had met Karl Moll, whom he had already introduced to her. Justi had exclaimed, "What a nice chap, that Moll," and Mahler had rashly replied, "Yes, but wait till you meet her mother!" In fact, Justi had already begun to suspect that her brother's absences were due to a woman, and had thus discovered the truth.[22] Nevertheless, Alma Mahler's assertions, and especially those concerning her sister-in-law, are highly unreliable.

"It's too cruel that I have to go away again at this precise moment," Mahler complained in his last letter written from Vienna. "I'm so unhappy about it and yet it's almost as though a voice of the Master, (I'm using this word in order not to say 'God,' since we haven't discussed that subject fully enough and I couldn't bear a 'word' to come between us) calls out: 'Be courageous, be forbearing, be patient!' You see, my dearest, we shall need this throughout our lives and, indeed, this Master also appears in thunder, for he must always remain intelligible to us. Oh God, there's so much noise going on around me, I can't write anymore! I can't even hear my own thoughts anymore—only the *one* voice that drowns out everything else and that will never again fall silent in my heart, a voice that repeats but one sentence, one sound: 'I love you, my Alma!'" Mahler also wrote to Frau Moll the day he left to express his regret at having to tear himself away for a whole fortnight "from a family with whom I've already come to feel so close and so at home."

He had hardly arrived in Berlin before he sat down to write to Alma again. "I'm conducting my symphony myself in Berlin. Oh, if only you could be here! However, whereas others must needs gain the key to my personality from my work, you, you, my Alma, starting from your knowledge of me, from the all-embracing present, and made perceptive by love, will learn everything about me—you will become me and I you. Astronomers are obliged to identify stars by their rays (and still grope around in darkness because their procedure—it's called spectral analysis—enables them to discover only the matter related to the earth; that which is peculiar to the stars will remain forever inscrutable)—but what could the rays possibly be to him who inhabits the star itself. True, the comparison is not entirely apt, but it does most nearly convey what I feel at this moment and what makes me so calm and so happy.

"What will it be like once you share everything with me and I everything with you—when this violent and consuming desire mixed with so much fear and anxiety is assuaged and, even when parted, we shall know everything about one another and be able to love and permeate one another without misgivings! (Not that I'd give up *anything* that's allotted to me on account of you, not even the apprehension and the pain—don't misunderstand what I've just said) . . . If notes and sound waves had as much force as my longing for you, you would perforce hear them ringing all this afternoon. Everything that lives in me must belong and be dedicated to you, my beloved Alma!—Your G."

Alma in turn felt calmer and more confident after Mahler's departure. "I feel I'm becoming a better person—he's uplifting me. My longing for him won't cease." Nevertheless, the very day Mahler left, she received a "handsome, rich, cultured and musical" young man who had long been courting her and to whom, curiously enough, she frequently refers in her diary as "Mahler." They played several piano duets together and he finally asked her again what her "intentions" were concerning him. "I couldn't do otherwise than tell him the truth—hard as it was for me," she wrote in her diary that evening. "He stood before me pale and trembling and said: 'Fräulein, if you say "no," I shall kill myself.' I was filled with pity. I like him so much—as a friend—and am convinced I'm not mistaken???—Shall I take him as a friend?!! But there are things that are beyond our control. My love and longing for you are boundless, Gustav, my dearest, my beloved . . . I desire only one thing, I dream of only one thing, to belong to you alone." Doubtless out of jealousy, the young man told her that a doctor friend of his had said that "Gustav has an incurable disease, his strength is visibly diminishing. Oh God, I'll guard him as if he were my child—he mustn't be destroyed because of me. I'll curb my desire and my passion—my strength and youth shall make him well again, my beloved master . . . So much has happened within me in this past fortnight!!! How old I've become!"

Alma finally met Justi at the Zuckerkandls' two days after Mahler's departure: "There's one thing I like very much about her—I recognize him in her . . . I'm going to see her on Saturday." Justi in turn wrote Mahler a letter full of "warmth and gaiety," mostly about Alma. "If things will just turn out, for you as for me, the way they appear to be turning out at this moment!" he replied, clearly alluding to Justi's marriage plans with Rosé, as well as to his own. "I beg of you really and truly to love Alma, it would make me twice as happy again. Yet she's still so young and my courage continually fails me when I think of the difference in our ages. If you can, keep calm and consider, or at least help me to consider. It's no small matter and the desire must not engender the thought."

Mahler had no illusions about the difficulties that this marriage would present. He begged Justi to help Alma to understand "my life and my personality" and even invited her to join him in Dresden. The trip would be his birthday present to her, she would be able to hear his *Second Symphony* and the two of them would be able to discuss their future. Fortunately, Alma's last letter had "removed all my doubts about the warmth of her heart and her essential honesty . . . There's only one thing that worries me: whether a man who's reached the threshold of old age has the right to tie his extreme maturity to so much youth and freshness, to chain spring to autumn, missing out summer? I know I have much to give, but one cannot buy youth at any price. If Beethoven, Wagner and Goethe came to life again today, her young heart would kneel down before them and worship them. Flowers can only grow and bloom in spring, that's the big problem as far as I'm concerned. For the time being, of course, all is well, but what will happen when winter follows my fruitful autumn? Do you see what I mean?"

During Mahler's absence, Alma and Justi became friends. Alma duly went to the Auenbruggergasse on December 14 and saw Mahler's room, his bed, his desk, and his books. While she was there, a letter arrived for Justi in which Mahler had enclosed the program of the *Second Symphony* to be given to Alma. Although Justi was "exceedingly sweet and kind to me . . . she watches me like a lynx . . . There are several things about her that annoy me. If she continues to watch me with such inquisitiveness, things could become dangerous for me. If, for instance, she should discover that I'm heartless and loveless—things which I only whisper to my diary—that I'm incapable of any warm feelings, that it's all nothing but calculation, cold, clearheaded calculation. All nonsense, for he's a sick man and has a precarious position; he's Jewish, already middle-aged and deeply in debt as a composer. So where's the calculation? Is it just stupidity then? No, there's something that draws me to him, no doubt about it! But if Justi conspires against me and he falls out of love with me, I won't die. I love him and I shall stick with him! . . . I'm terribly uneasy. I have a nasty feeling Justi is poisoning him against me. I'm filled with inexplicable anxiety."

Justi, too, was worried. Despite her youth, Alma had already acquired a solid reputation as a flirt. She was considered frivolous and capricious and took an all too obvious pleasure in her powers of charming the opposite sex. Mahler suspected as much, and she, moreover, had not entirely concealed this aspect of her personality from him. Indeed, in one of her letters, she had told him about the musical young man who had threatened to commit suicide for love of her, and he had chided her by return of post. "So a handsome, young, rich, cultured and musical gentleman gave you such a difficult afternoon? Almschi, Almschi, do stop and think it over again! God knows what an exchange you'd be making. I don't possess half these fine qualities! He stood before you pale and trembling—and is even prepared to kill himself! Such a thing never occurs to me! How I'd like to give your pretty locks a little shake! And anyway, as you well know, quite simply curled, you would please me a great deal more.

"If only I weren't constantly surrounded by a whole escort of people here, who don't leave me alone for one second! I have so much to say to you! . . . Oh, Almschi (is that how it's spelled?) if you would only write more clearly! Believe me, I'd gladly spend hours deciphering these precious hieroglyphs, but the thing that torments me is that the immediacy of the message is lost when, instead of feeling as if I were listening to your voice and feeling you near me, I'm constantly interrupted and so distressingly disturbed by having to stop every second to unravel and decipher. Besides, it frequently happens that there are several words I simply can't make out despite all my efforts. My beloved girl, do take the trouble to write clearly!"[23]

In this same letter, Mahler went on to talk about his material success as a composer. ". . . I've caught myself (at least lately, since my thoughts have become bound up with you) in a completely commonplace ambition that is almost unworthy of someone like me! I would suddenly like to win success, recognition and whatever else all these insignificant and, literally speaking, *meaningless* things are called! I'd like to be a credit to *you!* Don't misunderstand what I mean by ambition! I've had ambition for years, but have not aspired to the honor my neighbors and contemporaries can bestow on me. On the other hand, I've always striven to be understood and appreciated by my equals, even if I were not to meet them in my lifetime (and, indeed, they are only to be found beyond time and space), and that will continue to be my highest aim in life. Toward this end, you will have to help me, my beloved. And you know that, in order to gain this reward, this crown of laurels, one must forgo the acclaim of the masses, nay, even that of the elite (which isn't always able to follow either). How gladly I've borne the slaps of the Philistines and the scorn and hatred of the ignorant [*Unmündigen*] up to now! Oh yes, I'm, unfortunately, all too well aware that the little respect I have won is perhaps due only to a misunderstanding, or, in any case, a vague intuition of something higher but inaccessible. Needless to say, I'm not referring to my activities as a 'director' or a conductor, for these are, after all, and in the fullest sense of the words, only abilities and merits of an inferior kind. I beg you to write to me on this subject and tell me whether you understand me and also whether you are willing to go along with me. Alma! Would you be able to bear all the adversity with me, even to the point of wearing the robe of ignominy, and joyfully take up such a cross? . . .

"I no longer imagined it possible that once in my life I could meet with such happiness, to be loved as I love. Every single time a female being has crossed my path, I've had to recognize, in agony, that dreams of happiness are shattered by the inadequate reality. I blamed myself for it and became completely resigned to it. Young as you are, Alma, you well know what has happened to you and will be able to understand my feelings when, with all the emotions of my heart and my being, I now not only feel, but may also say, with supreme tenderness and bliss, that I'm in love for the first time! I still can't rid myself of the fear and dread that so beautiful and sweet a dream may vanish, and can hardly wait for the moment when I shall inhale from your mouth and your life's breath the certainty and fullest awareness that the ship of my life has found shelter in its home port from the stormy seas. I realize that we first came truly close to one another the last time we were together and that, although apparently separated, we've now become truly united for the first time . . .

"Just as everything that I am is henceforth yours, so I encompass all that is you with my whole soul. Oh God, today, from sheer anxious suspense and longing for you, my life, I'm talking away like Walther von Stolzing and forgetting the other half, poor old Hans Sachs, who, after all, is far more deserving of your love. You see, my sweet, I'm sometimes almost sad that one cannot deserve or win the highest rewards. You've given me so much, my Alma! You've so prettily declared what you'd like to be to me. When I think of what I want and ought to be to you, I become almost solemn. I've so deep and strong an awareness of my duties—which are also my supreme happiness—that I wouldn't dare make you any vows or promises for fear of tempting fate! I think you feel as I do about it: that which fills us and renders us so united is a power above and beyond us; to venerate it in silence will be our religion! If, at such a moment, I utter the name of God to you, you will understand that, through the almighty passion of yours and my love, this power embraces us both and pervades us as *one* being.

"What I find so infinitely sweet about you is that you're so genuine, so truly modest. I don't believe you're capable of grandiloquence. That is, in fact, the one sin against the Holy Ghost, a lie, because one thus lies to oneself! Do you remember our first conversation in the presence of Burckhard? Everything I said was directed solely to you that evening. God had already willed then that we should become *one*—only we didn't know it—but *I* had already received the baptism of fire! Oh, Alma, my dearest, my dearly beloved, I'd like thus to talk to you constantly about my innermost self and can't get around to telling you what's happening on the outside! Yet that, too, I must do! We must indeed share everything."[24]

After the final rehearsal of the *Fourth Symphony* on December 15, Mahler wrote again to his fiancée in the lounge of his hotel, amid the "noise and confusion of the bellboys and guests." He expressed his admiration for Friedrich Hölderlin, "one of my favorites both as a poet and as a human being. Indeed he is one of the truly great . . ." and complained once more about their separation. "Heavens! When I imagine myself back in that room, under that roof, I become so impatient and wild that I could get up and run away!"

Mahler's reply to her letter about the "pale young man" annoyed Alma, for she sensed the reproach behind the teasing. "How deeply you cheered and strengthened me!" he wrote on December 16. "How vividly I realize that love has made you perceptive and that 'everything became clear to you!' From the tone of my letter, you recognized, with incredible sensitivity, that your letter, to which this was the reply, had—how should I put it—slightly vexed me. I may well have misread you, but there's one thing you've misunderstood: I have never in any way, shape or manner considered that you are faced with a *choice*. The passage that begins—I remember it perfectly—'Almschi, Almschi!' was written in a bantering tone that you hadn't heard from me before. Had I spoken to you thus, I would have laughed and tweaked your ear as I did so. I only wanted to pull your leg.

You see, my beloved girl, I was so longing for a few words from you at that moment, and then along came this enumeration of the young man's accomplishments and, above all, I didn't understand how such a thing could affect a person so. Isn't that just a dissipation of the most intimate part of oneself? At that moment, the difference in our ages, which (since we began corresponding) I'd not felt anymore and was immensely happy that I hadn't, suddenly weighed on me anew. However, I made every effort to get over it immediately and this, my Alma, must be our strenuous endeavor throughout our lives, never to let *susceptibility* get the better of us. But I had to be frank and write it out of my soul . . . we'll soon come face to face at last and learn to know one another . . . Before that, it was all really only a sort of 'conversation' between us—the social barriers, etc., were removed by this letter in which, for the first time, my beloved, you struck the note that will determine our lives and our love . . ."25

Before returning to Vienna, Mahler asked Alma to tell her mother everything. "As you know, I wanted to talk to her myself to begin with—but that was when I (and above all you) was still undecided.—At that time, it would have been more of a consultation with her, since she knows you so well. But now that everything's already so definite and indissoluble between us, I wouldn't know what to say to her other than 'Give me what belongs to me. Allow me to breathe and to live'—for your love has become as much a condition of my existence as the beating of my pulse and my heart. And it seems to me to be ever more significant for, and fundamental to, our whole future that, precisely during our 'exalted period' [*hohe Zeit*] (which is in fact the true *wedding* [*Hochzeit*], whereby souls intermingle after having 'recognized' one another) we have been not physically but only spiritually united and have grown together so closely. We could not have told one another so much nor have understood all this so fully in a month of Sundays as we have in these two interminably long weeks. I'm so blissfully aware that, in this short time, we've ripened under a star more powerful than the radiant sun above, for the latter requires an entire summer, whereas our whole beings have bloomed in two weeks. This would certainly not have been so if I hadn't had to go away at the very moment when, in the literal sense of the words, you opened up and gave yourself to me . . . My—I cannot find a word. They're all so insipid and so worn out by stupidity and weakness. You know, my only treasure, what it means when I say 'My dearest beloved! My Alma!' May God bless and preserve you! Oh that I may become a blessing to your life just as your life is, from now on, the earthly kingdom in which I take root and hope to continue to grow."

Three days before his return, Mahler wrote from Dresden to tell his fiancée about his visit to Strauss.26 He enclosed another copy of the program of the *Second Symphony,* "intended only for someone rather naïve and superficial," and bitterly lamented the fact that she could not hear the *Second Symphony* before the *Fourth,* which would be "completely alien" to her on account of its "humor" and "naïveté." He told her that she had become the focal point of his whole existence and that he thought constantly of "the details of our future life."

During Mahler's absence, Alma had in no wise given up flirting, witness the entry in her diary on December 12. "In the evening, *Die Meistersinger:* Winkelman, Gutheil-Schoder, Schrödter, Hesch, Hilgermann . . . Across the aisle, but in the same row, sat young Dr. Adler, whom I find exceedingly attractive, and I more than flirted with him. We ended by smiling at one another. I suddenly noticed to my horror that Mahler [*sic;* she undoubtedly meant her suicidal young suitor] was sitting next to him and had probably been watching the whole maneuver. I was ashamed, quite simply ashamed. Then I noticed that M. was looking away, so I quickly glanced in Adler's direction and we gazed longingly at one another—he's got long, beautiful hands—not caring about who might be watching us. There's something extraordinarily sensual in gazing that way and the man's an Adonis, with eyes as black as night and . . . in short, a face that I find most attractive. It has breeding, which is more than one can say for Mahler's [*sic;* here again, she probably meant the same young man]. Nevertheless, I naturally remain faithful to Gustav in spirit. These brash looks didn't come from my heart."

That same day, Alma had finally resolved to "make a clean breast of it" to Zemlinsky. "I've written to Alex; he'll be furious and never forgive me. I wrote: 'Alex! You're staying away because you know about everything. You know about all that's happened. You even know my unsuspected thoughts. These last weeks have been torture for me. You know how much I loved you. You filled my life entirely. This love has ended as suddenly as it began, it's been supplanted—and now I'm in love again with renewed intensity! I'd like to go down on my knees to beg your forgiveness for the pain that I've caused you. There are things that are beyond our power to control —perhaps you can explain them. You who know me much better than I know myself. I shall never forget the blissful hours I spent thanks to you— please don't you forget them either. If you're the man I take you to be, you'll come on Monday, give me your hand and the first kiss of friendship. Be nice, Alex, we can mean so much to each other, if you're willing, and remain faithful friends forever. But above all, please answer me at once and say exactly what you feel—Mama won't read the letter. Forgive me, I don't know myself anymore. Alma."

"My poor Alex," she wrote in her diary four days later, "he's terribly angry, refuses to write and quite rightly hates me. I could weep at the thought of the pain I'm causing him—the poor, poor fellow! I loved him so much. Afternoon—I'd just got up, because I'm, inexplicably, so exhausted, when I suddenly had a premonition that something was about to happen. I went to the door and . . . Alex was coming up the stairs—I was speechless. He came into the room, paler than usual and rather subdued. I went to him, drew his head onto my breast and kissed his hair—I felt so strange. Only then did we sit down beside each other—we, who had wrestled with one another in the fiercest frenzies of passion—to talk about what was on our minds; he was a bit sarcastic, as usual, but touchingly kind. My eyes were filled with tears the whole time, but my senses were numb. A beautiful, beautiful feeling was buried today. Gustav, you'll have to do a lot to compensate me for it. Although it was I who told him that I didn't love him anymore and he should by rights have been the one to feel humiliated, yet it was I who had a strange sensation . . . He seemed so dignified and so pure, so vastly superior to me! Had he but uttered an angry or accusing word, I would never have felt this way. I revere you, Alex, as only one human being can revere another . . .

"My poor Alex, his face betrayed his suffering. You noble, noble person!" —"I'm physically ill from all the emotional turmoil of the last weeks," she added later that day. The following day, she received another letter from Mahler. "He's a darling, darling man. I'm already looking forward to his return so much. How kindly and lovingly he writes. And Alex?—if only I knew how he was feeling—poor thing. But one thing was curious: I was and remained quite calm yesterday, I looked at him and suddenly realized with a shudder how ugly he is, how overpoweringly he smells, etc.—Midsummer Night's Dream!—things that I hadn't noticed at all before. It's strange, all the same!—I shall never forget these last weeks."

Mahler had been surprised and shocked by several things Alma had written in her letters. One day, for instance, she excused herself for writing "more briefly than usual," explaining that she was expecting Zemlinsky, who "knows everything and yet still continues to give me lessons," thus showing "fortitude and magnanimity" in the way in which he was overcoming his grief. Another time, she told Mahler about an afternoon she had spent with Justi "without talking lovingly of me and about me." She even described a conversation with Burckhard, who had said that two people with personalities as strong as hers and Mahler's could never be happy together, for one of them would eventually have to "give way."[27]

These things exasperated Mahler, who, feeling that they revealed serious misunderstandings that should be cleared up immediately, wrote a last letter to Alma just before he left Dresden.

My dearest Almschi!

It's with a somewhat heavy heart that I'm writing to you today, my beloved Alma, for I know I must hurt you and yet I can't do otherwise. I've got to tell you the feelings that your letter of yesterday aroused in me, for they're so basic to our relationship that they must be clarified and thoroughly discussed once and for all if we're to be happy together.

Admittedly, I only read between the lines (for once again, my Almschi, it was only with the greatest difficulty that I managed to read the lines themselves). There seems to me to be a glaring contradiction between this letter and those which I've been receiving from you since the evening of *Die Zauberflöte*. You wrote then: "I want to become the sort of person you *wish* and *need!*" These words made me immensely happy and blissfully confident. Now, perhaps without realizing it, you take them back. Let me begin by going through your letter point by point. First, your conversation with Burckhard—what do you understand by a personality [*Individualität*]? Do you consider yourself a personality? You remember I once told you that every human being has something indefinably personal that cannot be attributed to either heredity or environment. It's this that somehow makes a person peculiarly what he or she is and, in this sense, every human being is an individual [*Individuum*]. But what you and Burckhard mean is something quite different. A human being can only acquire the sort of personality you mean after a long experience of struggle and suffering and thanks to an inherent and powerfully developed disposition. Such a personality is very rare. Besides, you couldn't possibly already be the sort of person who's found a rational ground for her existence within herself and who, in all circumstances, maintains and develops her own individual and immutable nature and preserves it from all that's alien and negative, for everything in you is as yet unformed, unspoken and undeveloped. Although you're an adorable, infinitely adorable and enchanting young girl with an upright soul and a richly talented, frank and already self-assured person, you're still not a personality. That which you are to me, Alma, that which you could perhaps be or become—the dearest and most sublime object of my life, the loyal and courageous companion who understands and promotes me, my stronghold invulnerable to enemies from both within and without, my peace, my heaven in which I can constantly immerse myself, find myself again and rebuild myself—is so unutterably exalted and beautiful, so much and so great, in a word, my wife. But even this will not make you a personality in the sense in which the word is applied to those supreme beings who not only shape their own existence but also that of humanity and who alone deserve to be called personalities. I can tell you one thing, however, and that is that in order to be or to become such a personality, it's no use whatsoever just to desire or to wish it. Goldmark once told me with pride that he deliberately avoided listening to, or looking at, any new music in order not to lose his personality. And that to me, my little Alma, was proof of his total lack of personality! It's just as though one were to avoid eating beef at all costs in order not to turn into a bull. You must realize, my Alma, that everything you absorb can only be nourishment to you and will determine your inner growth either favorably or unfavorably. The important thing is that this nourishment should agree with you, be beneficial to you and that your organism should be able to digest it. Not one of the Burckhards, Zemlinskys, etc., is a *personality*. Each one of them has his own peculiarity—such as an eccentric address, illegible handwriting, etc.—which, because inwardly lacking self-confidence, he defends, by constantly remaining on his guard against his "nourishment" for fear of becoming unoriginal. A true personality, on the other hand, is like a robust organism that, with unconscious sureness, seeks out and digests the nourishment appropriate to it and vig-

orously rejects that which is unsuitable. Happy he whose early development is not impeded or even completely upset by harmful things. Perhaps
an initially healthy organism lays the foundation for its own ultimate
weakness and sickliness by absorbing the unsuitable and noxious.

Now, after this somewhat lengthy introduction, I finally come to you!
My Alma, look! Your entire youth, and therefore your entire life, has been
constantly threatened, escorted, directed (while you always thought you
were independent) and abused by these highly confused companions who
spend their time groping around in the dark and on false trails, drowning
out their inner beings with loud shouting and continually mistaking the
shell for the nut. They've constantly flattered you, not because you enriched their lives with your own but because you exchanged big-sounding
words with them (genuine opposition makes them uncomfortable, for
they only like grandiloquent words—I'm referring more to people like
Burckhard than to Zemlinsky, whom I don't know but imagine to be rather
better, although he's undoubtedly confused and insecure too), because you
all intoxicated each other with verbosity (you think yourselves "enlightened," but you merely drew your curtains so that you could worship your
beloved gaslight as though it were the sun) and because you're beautiful
and attractive to men who, without realizing it, instinctively pay homage to
charm. Just imagine if you were ugly, my Alma. You've become (and
however harsh I sound you'll nevertheless forgive me because of my real
and already eternally inexhaustible love for you) vain about that which
these people think they see in you and wish to see in you (i.e., you would
really like to be that which you appear to them to be) but which, thank
God, and as you yourself said in your sweet letter, is only the superficial
part of you. Since these people also flatter each other all the time and instinctively oppose a superior being because he disconcerts them and makes
demands on them that they cannot live up to, they find you, on account of
your charms, an exceptionally attractive and, due to your lack of pertinent
argument, a most *comfortable* opponent. Thus all of you have spent your
time running around in circles and presuming to settle the affairs of humanity between you—"that which you don't touch on is far removed
from you." And even you, my Almschi, are not completely without the *arrogance* that invariably inhabits people who regard their own insignificant
and exceedingly limited thought processes as the sole task of intellectuals.
Some of your remarks (and I've no intention of taking you to task for them,
for I know full well that they're only a façon de parler [*sic:* manner of
speaking]—even though that, too, comes from an acquired way of thinking) such as that "we don't *agree* on several things, ideas, etc." prove it, as
do many others! My little Alma, we must agree in *our love* and in our
hearts! But in our ideas? My Alma! What are your ideas? Schopenhauer's
chapter on women, the whole deceitful and viciously shameless immoral-
ity of Nietzsche's superiority of an élite, the turbid meanderings of Maeterlinck's drunken mind, Birbaum and company's public house humor, etc.,

etc.? These, *thank God,* are not your ideas but theirs! That this wonderful and supremely incomprehensible world is nothing more than the humorless joke of some thoroughly musty and obtuse "natural force" that is totally unconscious of either itself or us (and therefore not even on a level with man, for whom all of you have so little regard), a bubble that will one day burst; that this miraculous heart that so inexplicably fills me with bliss or grief is only a lump of flesh with two valves, my brain merely a mass of very cleverly "twisted" jelly interwoven with fibers and filaments filled with blood, etc., etc. is certainly not your idea but that of everybody who, in truth, comes by it very easily now that the great scientists (exclusively great men who, moreover, didn't regard life as a mathematical exercise) have discovered it, thanks to the labors they performed so diligently, *silently* and without bragging. So here am I, poor fellow, who couldn't sleep at night for joy at having found her, her who, *from the start,* was intimately at one with him in everything, who, as a woman, belonged wholly to him and had become an integral part of him; who had even written to him that she felt she could do nothing better than embrace and enter into his world; who, through her faith in him, no longer searches but has become convinced that his creed is hers, because she loves him, etc., etc.

Again I wonder what this obsession is that has fixed itself in that little head I love so indescribably dearly, that you must be and remain yourself—and what will become of this obsession when once our passion is sated (and that will be very soon) and we have to begin, not merely residing, but living together and loving one another in companionship? This brings me to the point that is the real heart and core of all my anxieties, fears and misgivings, the real reason why every detail that points to it has acquired such significance: you write *"you* and *my music"*—*Forgive me, but this has to be discussed too!* In this matter, my Alma, it's absolutely imperative that we understand one another clearly at *once,* before we see each other again! Unfortunately, I have to begin with you and am, indeed, in the strange position of having, in a sense, to set *my* music against yours, of having to put it into the proper perspective and defend it against you, who don't really know it and in any case don't yet understand it. You won't think me vain, will you, Alma? Believe me, this is the first time in my life that I'm talking about it to someone who doesn't have the right approach to it. Would it be possible for you, from now on, to regard *my* music as *yours?* I prefer not to discuss "your" music in detail just now—I'll revert to it later. In general, however—how do you picture the married life of a husband and wife who are both composers? Have you any idea how ridiculous and, in time, how degrading for both of us such a peculiarly competitive relationship would inevitably become? What will happen if, just when you're "in the mood," you're obliged to attend to the house or to something I might happen to need, since, as you wrote, you ought to relieve me of the menial details of life? Don't misunderstand me and start imagining that I hold the bourgeois view of the relationship between husband and wife, which regards the latter as a sort of plaything for her husband and, at the same time, as his housekeeper. Surely you would never suspect me of feeling and thinking that way, would you? But one thing is certain and that is that you must become "what I need" if we are to be happy together, i.e., my wife, not my colleague. Would it mean the destruction of your life and would you feel you were having to forgo an indispensable highlight of your existence if you were to give up *your* music entirely in order to possess and also to be mine instead?

This point *must* be settled between us before we can even contemplate a union for life. For instance, what do you mean by "I haven't done any work since! . . . Now I'm going to get down to work," etc., etc.—What sort of work? Composing? For your own pleasure or in order to enrich humanity's heritage? You write "I feel that I now have nothing better to do than to submerge myself in you, I play your songs, read your letters, etc." I understood and imbibed this like a promise of eternal bliss. But the fact that, precisely during this period (which I've called our true *"Hoch-Zeit"* [exalted period]), your conscience should be bothering you because you're not working on theory or counterpoint is incomprehensible to me! As I've already said, I'm not talking about your compositions, which in any case I don't know yet, but only about the nature of your relationship to me, which must perforce shape our future. I must go now—to *work* (you see, *I really* must, for a whole company of 300 people is waiting for me). I'll continue this letter—perhaps the most important I'll ever have to write to you—this afternoon.

There, the rehearsal's over and here I am again, pretty tired and also really rather depressed. I have read through what I wrote this morning, but it was written in such haste, since it must be in your hands tomorrow, that I fear it's become quite illegible; so don't fling my own reproaches back at me, for it's only due to the haste that my profession imposes on me. You, however, have only *one* profession from now on: *to make me happy!* Do you understand what I mean, Alma? I'm quite aware that you must be happy with me in order to be able to make me happy, but the roles in this play, which could as easily turn out to be a comedy as a tragedy (and either would be wrong), must be correctly assigned. The role of "composer," the "worker's" role, falls to me—yours is that of the loving companion and understanding partner! Are you satisfied with it? I'm asking a great deal, a very great deal—and I can and may do so because I know what I have to give and will give in exchange.

I simply cannot understand the heartless way in which you treat Zemlinsky. Were you in love with him? Then how can you now demand that he play the unhappy role of continuing to be your teacher? You consider it manly and noble of him that, with suffering written on his face, he sits facing you, meek and silent and, as it were, "obeys orders"?! You were in love with him and can endure this? And what sort of a face should I put on if I were sitting there too—and you ought to be thinking of me as sitting

there too! Is your life not subject to other forces of nature now—hasn't its
course been altered too much for you to be willing and able gradually to resume your former activities, theory (nature of the violin? was what I read
but couldn't understand), Philharmonic concerts conducted by Hellmesberger (!) etc.? How were you able to "make conversation" with my sister
whose heart was wide open to you and who was only too anxious to give
you the whole of it? Could you really spend a whole afternoon with her
without talking lovingly of me and about me? Almschi, Almschi—it's all
quite incomprehensible to me! What sort of conversations are these that can
still come between us—what third party (4. *Fall*)[28] is still imminent?! What
is this defiance, this pride? Toward me who trustingly gave my whole heart
and, from the first moment, dedicated my whole life to you—(though I also
know certain pretty, rich, cultivated, young, etc., girls and women). I beg
you, Almschi, read my letter carefully. There must never be any question of
a passing flirtation between us. Before we talk to each other again, things
must be absolutely clear between us. You've got to know *what* I desire and
expect from you, what I can offer you and what *you must be to me*. You
must *"renounce"* (as you wrote) all *superficiality,* all *convention,* all vanity and delusion (as far as personality and work are concerned). You must
give yourself to me *unconditionally,* shape your future life, in every detail,
entirely in accordance with my needs and desire nothing in return save my
*love!* What this last is, Alma, I can't tell you—I've talked of it too much
already. I can tell you one thing more, however: I am prepared to sacrifice
both my life and my happiness for the one I love as much as I would love
you if you were to become my wife.

I had to unburden myself in this unrestrained and almost (it must
seem immodest to you) immoderate manner today. And, Alma, I must
have your answer to this letter before I come to see you on Saturday. You
will have these lines by tomorrow, Friday, so you can and, if you're what
I hope you are, indeed will *have to* answer me immediately and get your
letter to me by Saturday afternoon. Better still, I'll send a servant to pick
it up at your apartment on Saturday morning. Almschi, beloved, be strict
with yourself—and (sweet and beautiful though I otherwise find it) don't
be swayed by your love for me. Imagine that you're writing to a stranger
who has to report to me. Tell me everything you have to tell me quite
ruthlessly and bear in mind that to part now would be infinitely preferable
to a continued self-deception for, as I know myself, that would end in a
disaster for both of us.

What a terrible moment I'm causing you—I do realize it, Alma—but you
will appreciate that I myself am suffering just as much, even though
this is poor consolation. Although I'm aware that you don't yet know
Him, I pray God that He may guide your hand, my beloved, so that it
may write the truth and not be moved by infatuation—for this is a crucial
moment that will decide the fate of two lives for eternity! God bless you,
my dearest, my love, whatever you may have to tell me. I won't write

tomorrow but will wait for your letter on Saturday and, as I've said, I'll
send a servant to get it, so have it ready.

A thousand loving kisses, my Alma, and I beg you: be truthful!

Your Gustav.[29]

One wonders what to make of such a letter, which points up Mahler's
self-centeredness as much as his love for Alma. In his desire for total honesty,
he goes straight to the point and cares little about hurting his fiancée's
feelings. For instance, he doesn't hesitate to write: "Just imagine if you
were ugly," thereby implying that "people find you witty only because you're
beautiful." Though passionately in love and therefore weak and vulnerable,
Mahler nevertheless attempts to remain lucid and is constantly questioning
himself, fearful of his infatuation. One can hardly imagine a woman less
likely to bow to his demands than Alma. Flirtatious and selfish, capricious
and vain, she was momentarily captivated by the depth, the purity, and the
strength she thought she could see in Mahler. After receiving his letter, she
wrote in her diary: "Friday, December 20 . . . Back home to this letter. My
heart stood still—Give up my music—relinquish that for which I've lived until now? My first thought was to call the whole thing off . . . But then I
burst into tears because I realized that I love him. Almost unconsciously I
put on my coat and, still crying, drove out to meet Siegfried! I told Pollack
about it and he was furious—he'd never have believed it possible. I feel as
though my heart had been torn from my breast by an icy hand. Mama and
I talked about him until deep into the night. She read the letter—! I was
so distraught. I find it so inconsiderate and clumsy of him—it could have
come out by itself—very gently—but this way it will forever remain a thorn
in my side . . .

"Saturday, December 21. I forced myself to sleep soundly the whole night,
read through his letter first thing this morning and suddenly felt warm all
over. How would it be if, *out of love for him, I were to give up*—that which
has been! I must now admit that hardly any music interests me apart from
his. Yes, he's right—I must live entirely for him, in order that he may be
happy. I now feel in a strange way that I deeply and truly love him. For
how long? I don't know, but that's already a great deal—a great deal. I long
for him more than I can say."

By advising her daughter to break with Mahler, it seems that Anna Moll
in fact pushed her into acceding to his wishes, since Alma had consulted
her mother only in order to test her loyalty. After she had written to Mahler
to give him the required promise, Alma's heart "trembled in expectation"
throughout the morning. While she was out on an errand in Döbling, she
ran into Mahler's servant, who was on his way to pick up her answer and
bring her another letter, which, in her excitement, she read on the spot. "A
thousand fondest regards from the same air you breathe, my homeland!
I'd hardly entered my room (how lovely that you already know it!) before I
saw the sweet and familiar lines from your hand and, not without emotion,
read the tender words that must have been written before my letter of yester-

day. The latter has weighed heavily on my soul these past two days, as I thought of the impression it would make on you at first. I hope for you as well as for myself that you read only my love and loyalty in it and appreciated their strength and depth. You did understand, didn't you, how adamant and implacably truthful I can be when I'm in love. Everything must be clear between us before we embrace one another—for this afternoon I'll no longer have the serenity and self-control to tell you and ask you about all that. Never have I more ardently desired or more fearfully awaited a letter from you than that which my servant will shortly bring me. What will you say to me! But make no mistake, even that which you say is still not final, only that which you are! The passion that has now quite literally enthralled us must be mastered for this present moment (and this can be done only if we're apart—that's precisely why I've been writing for as long as possible), so that we may be able to tie the knot that must bind us together indissolubly until our last breath, with inward reassurance and loving confidence . . ."

After receiving Alma's letter, which was the greatest proof of love she could possibly have given him, Mahler went to the Hohe Warte that afternoon looking calmer and more cheerful. However, although the clouds were thus momentarily dispersed, Alma later maintained that the wound inflicted by this ban on her composing long continued to fester and never completely healed. "How lovely it was yesterday!" she wrote in her diary the following day. "My longing for him is indescribable. Everything about him is dear and familiar to me, his breath so pure . . . I feel that I could live for him . . . If —then we'd get married in spring—that's what I've been thinking . . . Oh— just to bear his child—provided he's strong enough. He so desperately hopes so. Nothing, nothing, nothing more than to be his." She went to see Justi in the afternoon and she and Mahler kissed each other when his sister was out of the room and held hands in the car on the way back to the Hohe Warte.

Moll had had a "kind and serious" talk with her that same morning. "He nevertheless remonstrated with me. He's right. On the one hand, he felt he he could be glad because he thinks that Gustav can't much longer . . . [sentence unfinished] but he's wrong as far as I'm concerned. Have I no heart?! ["too much," she added later in the margin] yet I have such affection for him. And I also have the feeling that he uplifts me, whereas my association with Burckhard aggravates my frivolity. I feel ashamed of my vulgarity when Gustav's listening and, furthermore, I'm almost incapable of saying everything I think. Is one happier with a frivolous and unscrupulous life or when one has woven oneself such a beautiful and sublime conception of the world? Freer in the first case—happier??? One becomes a better and more noble person. Isn't that just another obstacle in the way of freedom? Yes, yes, a thousand times yes, and I tell you, one must be pitiless! He's right: we're suited to each other like fire and water—both mentally and physically! Yes, that's for sure! But is it really necessary for one of us to give way? Couldn't two radically different views with the help of love be made into one beautiful one? I know everything—he's a sick man, my poor darling, he weighs 63 kilos—far too little—I'll coddle him as though he were a child. I love him with infinite affection. It's sweet that he can't pronounce his R's and curious that he wishes I were called Marie[30] because he loves the strong R in the middle of the name—curious and . . . ! I'm so afraid that he'll get ill; I don't know how to explain it—I can just see him lying in his blood." Alma here reveals the hidden motivation of her feminine psychology. She loves Mahler not only because he is, as she herself puts it, "great and important," but also because he appears to her to be weak and defenseless and because with him she hopes to escape from herself and her "vulgarity."

A few days later, Mahler took her the score of his *Fourth Symphony*. She could not understand it at all and admitted, with somewhat excessive candor, that "in this type of thing, I prefer Haydn." He merely smiled and predicted that she would change her mind one day. While they were playing the work as a piano duet, she forgot a sixteenth note and he laughingly said, ". . . but I'll make you a present of it—I'll even make you a present of a quaver—in fact, I'll give you the whole piece." Afterward they joined Frau Moll, to whom Mahler happily declared, "Mama, after playing the piano with your daughter, I again ask you for her hand."

On December 23, Mahler went with Justi to the Hohe Warte, where he and Alma were to celebrate their engagement officially together with Karl and Anna Moll. "From now on," Alma wrote, "he alone must fill my heart, only he. I never again want to look at any other man. I want to give everything, everything to him, to my husband! We're already so close that I can't imagine we could be any closer. Whereas I was madly, passionately in love with Alex Z., I'm now filled with the most sacred feelings. I once told Z. I wanted to become the mother of his children, but I wasn't really sincere. I thought then that I was incapable of feeling anything so deep and so beautiful—today, I didn't say it but I feel it. When we sit snuggling up to one another like that, it's as though he were my body—not the slightest bit strange—so unimaginably precious to me . . ." Although she lived in "fear of the gods who can't tolerate any pure joy," she was nevertheless prepared to give up everything for Mahler since "I already belong to him, to him and to Justi whom I love because she's his flesh and blood. Justi told Mama that Gustav had asked '. . . Isn't it a crime for me, Autumn, to chain Spring to my side? She misses out Summer.' No, my Gustav, no!"

From then on, Mahler went to the Hohe Warte almost every day, often staying until late at night. And sometimes, when he missed the last streetcar, he cheerfully walked all the way home, even though it meant crossing the entire city. One day, he and Alma resumed a discussion on the subject of religion, which they had begun during one of their first meetings. The daughter of freethinkers, she violently opposed the traditional beliefs, while he in turn was angered by her indifference and "found myself in the curious position of a Jew upholding Christ to a Gentile."

One evening, at a dinner party given by the singing teacher Gustav Geiringer, Alma met the critic Ludwig Karpath, who, according to her, was discussing Mahler with the composer Adalbert von Goldschmidt. Furious at having had the score of his latest work returned to him by the director of the opera, Goldschmidt launched into a violent tirade against Mahler: "He's not even a man, he's a gnome and his music's not music . . ." Karpath warmly defended Mahler, declaring that he was "in a position to know him since it was thanks to me that the Hofoper engaged him!" The following day, Mahler asked Alma about the party and she, knowing nothing about Karpath except that he was Goldmark's nephew, innocently repeated what he had said, whereupon Mahler flew into a towering rage. The day after that, the critic of the *Neues Wiener Tagblatt* called on him to inquire about the opera's forthcoming projects and Mahler reproached him for having publicly defended the contralto Edyth Walker, "who's no longer suited to my ensemble." Karpath replied that his opinion was shared by the Viennese public, whereat Mahler suddenly leaped from his chair and shouted, "I think I know better than you and your colleagues whether or not I can use a singer! As a result of your attacks, the prince has forced me to re-engage her. Don't forget the respect you owe me as director of the opera —and I'm not talking about myself as a composer. For a while, I thought you understood my work, but I see now that I was wrong. Anyhow, I couldn't care less what you and your colleagues write about me as a composer, but," he added, shaking his fist at Karpath, "if you try to undermine my authority as director of the opera, I'll show you!" Then, quite suddenly, he sat down again, asked Karpath to do likewise, and finally came to the point. He accused the critic of having lied by declaring in public that Mahler owed his position as director of the opera to him. Karpath admitted to having touched on the subject two days earlier but said that it had been in private and with a young girl whom he had just met.[31] Moreover, he had merely said that he had not been "uninvolved" (*unbeteiligt*) in Mahler's appointment. The young girl had plied him with numerous questions, but the conversation had gone no further. Mahler then calmed down and explained with a smile that the conversation had been reported to him quite differently. Karpath was upset that he, a "fanatic of the truth," should have been thus slandered, but, before they parted, Mahler assured him that he bore him no grudge.[32] Karpath finally understood the situation when Mahler's engagement was officially announced at the end of December, and he promptly wrote to Alma to accuse her of indiscretion. She affirms that this incident was the cause of the breakup between Mahler and Karpath, but in fact this only occurred three years later, after the premiere of the *Wunderhorn Lieder*. Be that as it may, it served to open Alma's eyes to Mahler's touchiness and prompted her to be more cautious from then on.

When Mahler went to the Hohe Warte on the day before Christmas, he found his fiancée excitedly making all sorts of preparations that seemed to him somewhat "excessive" and "superficial," but he nevertheless spent a long time with her. "We felt our blood racing, listened to our hearts beating and were happy . . . I wish I already belonged to him," she noted. Burckhard, Kolo Moser, and Zemlinsky dined at the Hohe Warte that evening; Mahler went home to be with Justi, but had a letter delivered to his fiancée. "The first Christmas Eve on which I send you my good wishes, and also the last, for from now on, my beloved girl, we shall spend it together. What will it be like, Alma, when soon, I hope, united, we shall no longer have need of any go-between?! When I sit here in my room, I can already picture you running the house by my side. My—Our happiness seems like a fruit that—having ripened quickly in the warm sun of a love that is perhaps untried but nevertheless happy and confident in the future—will fall from the tree straight into our laps. This day, which united us and all men, even before we knew about one another, in joyful and childlike faith, and which should always remain a symbol to us so that, even though united and happy in our love, we may leave room in our hearts for the rest of mankind—because an immense and superhuman love, which we can only call divine, has tied a knot around us that binds us indissolubly to all living beings.

"On this day, which belongs to children, in whom the seeds of both earthly and divine love take root exactly as the Sower casts them, I bless you, my dearest Life. May my life become a blessing to yours, so that, above and beyond our earthly love and through its essence, which must be sacred, you may come to know the divine love, and be able 'silently to revere the unfathomable'! (Essentially, the only thing that matters is that we cannot be completely happy as long as there are others who are unhappy). You must clearly understand, my Alma, that I'm unable to say anything else to you today—perhaps nothing will enable you to appreciate the boundlessness and sanctity of my love for you more fully than the fact that—now that I'm so close to the fulfillment of my sovereign wish and am so intensely happy—I would like to transport us both beyond ourselves into those regions where we shall experience a breath of the eternal and divine—It's *thus* that I'd like to be yours and you must be mine!"

On Christmas afternoon, Mahler invited Alma to the Auenbruggergasse. "I sat on his lap the whole time—I love him so unutterably. We kissed each other so much. He had to conduct *Tannhäuser*. I stayed behind with Justi. I like her." On Boxing Day, Mahler lunched at the Hohe Warte, and afterward Alma and her mother drove him home. On December 27, as a result of an indiscretion, the news of Mahler's engagement burst on Vienna like a bombshell. All the newspapers raved about Alma's youth, beauty, and musical talents, and she received a shower of letters, bouquets, and telegrams. The following evening, she went to dinner at the Auenbruggergasse, hoping to calm Mahler, who was exasperated by all the publicity. "Drank a glass of friendship with Arnold Rosé, but otherwise spent most of the time alone with Gustav in his room. We stood for a long time in a dark passage and were happy. My one and only wish is to make him happy. He deserves to be." On the evening of December 29, Mahler conducted *Les Contes d'Hoffmann* and, for the first time, Alma sat in his box. However, she was so embarrassed by all the opera glasses trained on her that she did not hear a note of the music and finally moved to the back of the box, where an ingratiating Mildenburg came to call on her. Mahler received more prolonged applause than usual and had to take several curtain calls at the end of the performance. After supper at Hartmann's Restaurant with the Molls, Justi, and Arnold Rosé, he and Alma went for a walk together and decided to get married in the middle of February.

According to Alma, Mahler had never had any sexual experiences (or so, at any rate, he had apparently told her) and he was extremely worried about the consummation of their marriage. She admits that she failed to understand his fears, but the two of them nevertheless decided that they would have their first experience together as soon as possible. According to Alma's diary, Mahler was not very well at the time, and she feared that her continued refusal of herself would be bad for his mental and physical health. "December 30. Rendez-vous with Gustav . . . We halfway united today . . . an emotion more pure and sacred than I'd ever have imagined possible . . . No one knows how unspeakably intense is my desire. And yet—I can't imagine giving myself to him before the time is ripe. The feeling of wrongdoing and shame would debase the whole gloriously sacred mystery . . . we could hardly tear ourselves away from one another. Why these frightful conventions? Why can't I just move in with him?—Without any blessing. Oh! We're consumed with desire, it's sapping all our strength. He bared his chest and I put my hand on his heart—I feel as though his body were mine . . . I had my hair loose—he likes it that way . . . Oh, to have a child with him! His mind, my looks. If only I were already his!"

On the afternoon of New Year's Day, the two of them were alone in Mahler's room, and, after an exchange of caresses, the supreme moment seemed to have come when "suddenly he lost all his strength and lay limp on my breast, almost crying with shame. I comforted him, even though I was desperately miserable myself. We went home depressed and shattered. He became somewhat more cheerful, but I was suddenly overcome and couldn't help crying—sobbing my heart out—on his chest . . . I can't describe how much the whole thing has frustrated me. First the mental torment, then, with the goal in sight, no satisfaction. And hence, his anguish, his unparalleled anguish! My beloved." However, the simple words "Joy beyond all joy" (*Wonne über Wonne*) entered on January 4 would seem to indicate that all obstacles had been overcome. A few days later, Alma noted that "My poor Gustav is undergoing medical treatment—an inflamed swelling—ice packs, sitz-baths, etc., etc.—Was it due to my prolonged resistance? How he must suffer!" Nevertheless, she soon became pregnant and, according to her memoirs, this pregnancy before their marriage was a source of "dreadful torment" to both of them. Indeed, they were obliged to acknowledge "the hidden truth that exists behind the laws of bourgeois morality."

Since Mahler and Alma had arranged to get married in the middle of February, it was decided that Arnold and Justi would get married on the same day; Alma could thus move immediately into her sister-in-law's room. Over the years, her feelings for the latter gradually changed from friendliness and affection to violent hatred. Her memoirs, written many years later, reveal this animosity, which renders many of her assertions doubtful. If she is to be believed, Mahler's anger when he discovered the intimate relationship between his sister and Arnold Rosé was such that he did not speak to her for several weeks. Moreover, his "fury" at her "treason" to a certain extent influenced his own decision to get married. However, none of his letters confirm this; on the contrary, they contain frequent references to Rosé and even suggest that Mahler was well aware of his sister's feelings toward him. Having overcome her initial distrust, Justi, for her part, became very fond of Alma and did her best to allay her brother's qualms about his marriage. Moreover, Mahler's own daughter has stated that Justi, who was warmhearted and impulsive if not always lucid, felt great affection for Alma at first and that this affection was reciprocated for several years. In December, when Justi told Mahler that she was looking for a flat for Arnold and herself, he replied that her search was premature: "I still have to think things over a great deal. The dear little thing [Alma] is beginning to get quite anxious herself; she's in a situation that's entirely new to her and I have to keep my eyes open for both of us. She still has to mature a lot—I've just realized it again—before she can contemplate taking such an important step. As far as you're concerned, you're of course entirely free to make your own decisions. Come what may, we shall remain united for life. I want to see you happy and I'll give you all the help you need so that you'll be able to make the right decision." Thus, if Mahler and his sister did have any rows on the subject of Rosé, they took place before he met Alma, for their letters of 1901 show nothing but affection and harmony. Besides, Mahler by this time was already very close to his future brother-in-law.

As for Mahler's friends, it was with some concern that they viewed his forthcoming marriage to so lovely and so lively a young girl who, moreover, moved in a social circle entirely different from their own. Everything about her shocked and irritated them, she later reported: her clothes, her hair style, her behavior in public, and the freedom of her language. She in turn immediately dismissed them as provincial, narrow-minded, and petty, objected to the fact that they seemed to treat Mahler as though he were their property, and felt that they were friends whom "Mahler has been dragging behind him like chains ever since his youth."

However, both parties merely eyed each other somewhat suspiciously until they were officially introduced at a dinner that Mahler gave at the Auenbruggergasse on January 5. He had invited Lipiner and his wife, Nanna Spiegler (Lipiner's first wife), and her husband Albert, Mildenburg, Kolo

Moser, the Molls, Justi and Arnold Rosé. Alma later recalled the "bogus formality" of the party, at which, feeling she was being inspected with malevolence on all sides, she did her best to shock and offend everybody. Indeed, she had tartly declared, even before the party, that "I don't enjoy the company of old ladies one little bit." Throughout the evening, she spoke to no one but her mother and her fiancé and, on the rare occasions when she joined in the general conversation, it was merely to add insult to injury. On the subject of the courts and magistrates, she referred to the judges as "powdered old crones"; of Plato's *Banquet,* she said that it had "tickled her pink" and about a painting by Guido Reni, of which Lipiner was particularly fond, she asked with cruelly contrived ingenuousness, "What on earth does it represent?" The last straw came when Mildenburg asked her what she thought of Mahler's music and she replied, "I know very little of it and the little I do know I don't like." The whole company gaped in consternation, Frau Moll blushed with shame, and only Mahler burst out laughing. In fact, he appeared to take great delight in his fiancée's caustic remarks and kept having long whispered conversations with her, to the exclusion of the rest of the guests. However, sensing the horror this last sally had caused, he found some excuse to take Alma off to his room. "It was ghastly in there," he said. "We'll be better off alone here for a few moments." She complained of the "examination" to which she was being subjected, particularly by Lipiner. His "haughty" tone and his way of addressing her as *"Mädchen,"* made her call him "the most sterile person I've ever met." How dared he insist that she admire Plato and Guido Reni, who were of no interest to her whatsoever. The absence of the fiancés having become somewhat prolonged, Justi went along to call them to order, and had to do so again fifteen minutes later. When they did finally return to the drawing room, Mahler made Alma sit between himself and Anna Moll on the sofa, and there, apart from exchanging a few absent-minded words with Mildenburg, she steadfastly continued to ignore the rest of the guests.

They voiced their indignation the following day, in the form of a letter from Lipiner, to which Mahler replied, attempting to minimize the incident. Alma, he said, was young, shy, and embarrassed by these strangers whose distrustful looks and obvious misgivings had driven her to distraction. They should be more tolerant and forgive her because of her youth and inexperience. Far from being pacified, however, Lipiner wrote a second letter, which is still in existence and which clearly reveals just how badly Mahler and Alma had behaved. He reproached Mahler for his "contempt for his fellow-men" (*Menschenverachtung*), his "profound, lasting and everlasting coldness," and the self-centeredness that made him underestimate the wounds he inflicted on the grounds that he himself had already forgotten them. "At heart," he continued, "you don't consider anyone a *person;* we're all just *objects* to you. For no reason at all, you throw people away—you usually pick them up again—but not always—and everything's supposed to be all right again. You make no exceptions for anyone . . ." As for Alma, Lipiner had "done" with her from the evening of the party. Perhaps "she *alone*" would satisfy Gustav's requirements. In that case, he could live with her in splendid isolation, undisturbed by "troublesome, useless people." Rather than a "shy and timid young girl," she was all "unnaturalness, superficiality and heartlessness [*Lieblosigkeit*]," and her behavior could not have been more affected (*unwahr*) and foolish (*unklug*). Moreover, her remarks were those of an "unpleasantly impudent, opinionated and hypercritical" creature who, "from the start, is loath to associate with people to whom she's obliged to show *respect*, who, straight away, finds it disagreeable that people 'judge' her—and who expresses her annoyance in ugly and extravagant language." Lipiner wondered what ties there could possibly be between her and Gustav and whether the latter was not deluded by the words he senselessly provoked her to utter.

A breakup between Mahler and his friends thus seemed inevitable. Alma affirms that they "swore to ruin me and launched a violent campaign against me." According to her, moreover, Mildenburg, who had become Lipiner's mistress, was only pretending to be resigned to Mahler's indifference and his firm resolve never to renew his affair with her. Since her arrival in Vienna, their relations had frequently been strained, and he had undoubtedly had to exercise a great deal of self-control on numerous occasions, as witness, for instance, the letter he wrote to her shortly before his engagement was announced. "My very dear Anna, how could you have done such a thing to me and run away like that? I had something very urgent to write and was sure you'd wait for me! I did so want to have a little chat with you. You will come back *soon,* won't you? . . ." "I'll come and see you soon, not just for a quarter of an hour but for a whole afternoon," he added a few days later. "You hope the new events won't cast any gloom over my life. I leave that to God, but there's one thing I hope (and I know I've not misunderstood you): that they don't and won't cast any over *your* world. In any case, all that is in God's hands, but also in *ours,* for we already know each other in God. Your Gustav . . ."

Alma recounts that, after the official announcement of the engagement, Mildenburg called on Mahler in his office, made a scene, and even pretended to faint, but Mahler, who was well acquainted with her theatrical wiles, "forced her to walk out into the street with him, where she came to her senses." On the same occasion, she apparently also tried to persuade him to go back to addressing her with the familiar *Du,* but he replied that he would have to consult his fiancée about it. She then changed her tactics and pretended interest in Alma, with the result that Mahler promised they would both call on her. Like many other men in his situation, he had lied to his fiancée, claiming that he had never actually had an affair with Mildenburg. Be that as it may, he did indeed take his fiancée one afternoon to Hietzing, where the famous singer occupied a "gloomy hotel room." Mildenburg installed Alma in a corner with a score and then made some feeble excuse to drag Mahler off into another room, where their conversation rapidly turned into a heated argument.

Meanwhile, Alma studied the "atrocious" engravings by Stratz adorning the piano score of *Tristan und Isolde*. She and Mahler then proceeded to quarrel about them on the way home because he admired them, but, as Alma puts it, "the quarrel had nothing to do with either Stratz or his insignificant engravings." In point of fact, two conflicting influences were at war inside Mahler; that of his friends, Lipiner in particular, and that of Alma, daughter and stepdaughter of painters, who "refused to put up with their contempt and arrogance." They had thought they could "use me and my twenty years as a docile instrument to prolong and consolidate their power over Mahler," she wrote. And, when they realized they had been mistaken, they did their utmost to prove to him her lack of maturity in every possible way.

Alma maintains that they made their final attempt to discredit her in January, on the occasion of the second performance of *Das klagende Lied*, which Mahler was conducting, by hastening to tell him that she had "flirted" with other people in the hall all through the first half of the concert. Her version is that she had not been "flirting" but merely waving to an old friend, the president of the Gesellschaft der Musikfreunde, because she had been "so happy to see a friendly face in that hall where I knew I was being closely watched." On the same occasion, Mildenburg, though prostrate on her dressing room sofa after feigning another swoon, made the "sacrifice" of singing the formidable soprano part, and Mahler's friends also hastened to magnify her heroism and the sufferings she had endured. Consequently, he was "cold and reserved" toward his fiancée after the concert, but a long talk soon cleared up the misunderstanding between them, and, according to Alma, it was then that Justi realized that "we had found one another for good."

The following passage from a letter Hermann Behn wrote to his former mistress Mildenburg on November 26, 1902, typifies the attitude of Mahler's friends toward his marriage: "I simply can't picture Gustav's marriage! Why did he get married and why did he marry that woman? . . ."[33] Having heard that Alma did not like her husband's music, he added: "That, at least, is what I am told. . . . Is it true? It would be really tragic!"[34]

As a direct result of this new development in Mahler's life, Natalie Bauer-Lechner's manuscript ends abruptly in January 1902,[35] just at the time of the Vienna premiere of the *Fourth Symphony*. Its concluding sentence, concerning her feelings about Mahler's marriage, speaks for itself: "Mahler became engaged to Alma Schindler six weeks ago. If I were to discuss this event, I would find myself in the position of a doctor obliged to treat, unto life or death, the person he loved most in the world. May the outcome of this rest with the Supreme and Eternal Master!"

The dignity of this conclusion does Natalie credit. Although she, like many women whose love is not requited, was often tiresome, she was nevertheless a most loyal and devoted friend and an invaluable biographer. Mahler's alienation from her seems to have been total and complete, for her letters to Mildenburg never mention him again. Deprived of two of the essential reasons for her existence—Mahler and the diary in which she had meticulously noted his every word—she continued her activities with the Soldat-Roeger Quartet and finally became destitute.[36] She died in poverty on May 8, 1921, almost exactly ten years after the man she had so passionately admired and loved. The grossly abridged version of her *Mahleriana,* edited by E. J. Kilian, was published by Tal & Company in 1923. Most regrettably, various unknown persons have torn up numerous pages of her original manuscript, which doubtless contained a wealth of further information about the psychological atmosphere that prevailed in the Mahler family.

Mahler himself, whom happiness should have made relaxed and gay, was, according to Alma, "filled with anxiety and torment" throughout his engagement. Whereas she ascribes this to his lack of sexual experience, it seems more likely that he was fearful of taking on the responsibility of so young and lovely a creature, for he knew that she was expressing only one side of her nature by this marriage. "Which is the real me?" she wondered in her diary. "Won't I make him and myself unhappy if I lie—but am I lying? This pervasive feeling of ecstasy when he looks at me with rapture— is that also a lie? No, no. I must get to know the other me, who has dominated up to now—it must step aside. I must do everything I can to become a human being, let everything possible happen to me." Two weeks later, she noted: "For a while, I've been genuinely happy . . . but things are no longer what they were. He wants me to be different, totally different; I want to be too—and can even manage to be as long as I'm with him—but when I'm alone my second vain and bad me reappears and demands to express itself. And I give in: my eyes radiate frivolity, my lips lie—? lie unceasingly—and he feels it, knows it. I've just at this moment realized it— I must go to him. Yesterday afternoon . . . he begged me to say something and I couldn't find a single warm word, not one. I wept—that was how it ended . . . Spent the evening with Pollack. We talked a lot about Gustav. I unburdened myself somewhat of all the rancor weighing on my soul. Everything that was raging inside me had to come out. If the moment arrives and I do become his in time, then I must bestir myself energetically right now in order to make sure of the place that's being sacrificed to me—artistically, that is [*So muss ich mich schon jetzt gehörig rühren, um mir den Platz zu sichern, der mir geopfert. Nämlich künstlerisch*]. The plain fact is that he thinks nothing of my art but highly of his own, while I think nothing of his but highly of mine!—that's the way it is!" On January 5, however, she wrote: "He sent me his *Fifth Symphony* yesterday. We played it through together today; I found it thrilling and liked it enormously. Now he's continually talking about preserving his art, but I can't do that. With Zemlinsky, it would have been possible because I shared his feelings for his art—he's a genius. But Gustav is so poor, so frightfully poor. If he only knew how poor he is, he would hide his face in shame. And I'll always have to lie . . . to lie constantly, throughout my life—with him, that's just possible—but with Justi, that female! I have the feeling she's checking on me the whole time— but I must be free, absolutely free!"

On reading these lines, who can avoid being appalled by the dangers to which marriage was about to expose these two people so singularly unsuited to each other. On the one hand, Mahler: a great man, if ever there was one, passionately in love but as overbearing as he was demanding, a prisoner of himself and his ideals, a fanatic who was totally unable either to understand or to tolerate the weaknesses of others. On the other hand, Alma: pulled this way and that by the impetuous and often contradictory currents of her capricious temperament; flirtatious, conceited, flighty, and frivolous certainly, but also attractive, warmhearted, witty, spontaneous, extremely musical, a woman simultaneously capable of the most fabulous generosity and the most sordid meanness, of the most absolute honesty and the most devious duplicity.

Indeed, the whole drama unfolded not between herself and Mahler but between the different characters that lurked within this multifaceted woman. Her friends could only wonder whether she would ever succeed in overcoming the many inclinations and desires within herself that, as she well knew, her life with Mahler could not possibly satisfy. To be sure, the frankness and lucidity she shows in revealing the innermost aspects of her nature in her diary do her credit. Although, more often than not, she preferred to embellish certain truths for posterity in the books she published, she was at least absolutely honest with herself. Moreover, all those who knew her and who have read the original versions of her various writings know that, when she put pen to paper, she was almost invariably her own worst enemy. No doubt she was aware of the risks she was taking by marrying a man of such stature and, whatever sufferings and strife their union was to engender, it cannot be denied that Alma completely transformed and enriched Mahler's life and gave him a new incentive to live, to strive, and, of course, to create. She cared little about dignity, moderation, conventions, and objectivity, but had the presence and majesty of a goddess and men longed to lay offerings at her feet. She was to be Mahler's goal, his "haven," a new and essential reason for his existence. It goes without saying that he had divined and foreseen at least some of the difficulties and conflicts that were to arise, but he did not hesitate to face up to them, for he did not underestimate either the vital power of his love or the unique qualities of the magnificent creature fate had placed in his path.

# APPENDIX 1

## *The Children of Simon Mahler*

Bernhard (August 2, 1827–February 18, 1889), Gustav's father, (the only one of Simon's children not inscribed on this register).

–Josef (born 1830, died after 1880). He married, on May 26, 1857, Barbara Feder, widow of Hermann Neumann, a native of Benesov, from whom he inherited a flour and food business in Kalischt.[1] He later moved to Deutsch-Brod, where he doubtless died (six children).

–Hermann (May 7, 1832, presumably died before 1868[2]).

–Markus (October 2, 1833, presumably died before 1868).

–Philipp (December 15, 1834, died after 1868). He married a girl named Josefa and ran a food business in Deutsch-Brod (ten children).

–David (born before February 18, 1838[3]). He married Franziska Bermann of Ledec and ran a food business in Kalischt. He moved to Iglau after Bernhard, in October 1862, where he ran a dry goods shop, a tavern, then a flour business, then a perfumery (eight children).

–Barbara (born before August 16, 1840[4]). She married Wilhelm Pik, with whom she ran a toy shop in Iglau.

–Sophie (February 17, 1843, certainly died before 1868).

# APPENDIX 2

## *The Children of Abraham Hermann*

– Franziska (born before April 25, 1835, died July 7, 1838).
– Maria (born March 2, 1837, died October 11, 1889), married Bernhard Mahler.
– Anna (born before October 8, 1838–??), married in 1857 to Ignaz Frank, landowner in Pawlowic. She was very probably the mother of Gustav Frank, the only one of his cousins whom Mahler was to see often later in Vienna and St. Petersburg.
– Rosalia (born before February 3, 1841–??), married in 1859 to Nathan Kern, a Ledec merchant.
– Antonia (born before April 14, 1843–??).
– Johanna (born before February 26, 1845–August 10, 1846).
– Barbara (born January 25, 1847–??).

# APPENDIX 3

## Mahler's Works

I have attempted to assemble as concisely as possible all the available information concerning the composition, the different versions, the form, and the first performances of Mahler's works. The following complete catalogue is chronological, and, except for the compositions that have been lost, the reader will find in it the essential information about each work. A more detailed history and analysis follow the catalogue. Since the symphonies and most of the lieder have already been analyzed by many authors, I have restricted my analyses of them to a structural minimum.

## CATALOGUE

(The dates given for Mss. are those on which the sketch or orchestration of the work was finished. First performances were accompanied or conducted by Mahler unless otherwise stated. References to various sources are given only when former biographers have disagreed about the date of a work or its existence.)

### UNFINISHED, DESTROYED, OR LOST WORKS

THEATRICAL WORKS—OPERAS

*HERZOG ERNST VON SCHWABEN* (before 1875), undoubtedly incomplete (Libretto by Josef Steiner, after Uhland [?]) (MBR, No. 1; GAM, 97; cf. Ch. III)

*DIE ARGONAUTEN* (1879–80), incomplete (Libretto by Mahler, after Grillparzer [?] in *Stabreimen*) (NBL, 39; GAM, 97; PSM, 28; cf. Ch. V)

*RUEBEZAHL* (1880–90), unfinished fairy-tale opera in five acts (Libretto by Mahler. A copy of this, lacking Act III and a fragment of Act V, was in the possession of Alma Mahler. No known copy of revised libretto of 1882 is in existence.) (AMM, 83; GAM, 98; PSM, 34; RSM 1, 17; NBLS, VII.93 and

22.I.00; NBL, 104; MBR No. 15; Br. an Krisper I.83; an Spiegler VI.80; an Justi IX.90; cf. Ch. V)

*UNNAMED OPERA PROJECT* (1887–88) (Libretto by Karl von Weber based on an idea by Mahler) (NBL, 162; cf. Ch. XII)

INCIDENTAL WORKS

*VORSPIEL MIT CHOR* for the actor Karl Häser's jubilee in Kassel. 1st perf. Kassel Theater 2.XI.83

*DER TROMPETER VON SAEKKINGEN*, incidental music to *tableaux vivants* on the poem by Joseph Viktor von Scheffel. 1st perf. Kassel Theater 23.VI.84
  a) *Ein Ständchen im Rhein*
  b) *Die erste Begegnung*
  c) *Das Maifest am Bergsee*
  d) *Trompeten-Unterricht in der Geissblattlaube*
  e) *Der Ueberfall im Schlossgarten*
  f) *Liebesglück*
  g) *Wiedersehen in Rom*

*DAS VOLKSLIED*, "Poem with lieder, choruses, and *tableaux vivants*," by H. S. Mosenthal. 1st perf. Kassel Theater 20.V.85
  a) *Altgermanischer Bardengesang*
  b) *Provençalischer Minnehof*
  c) *Aennchen von Tharau*
  d) *Neapolitanische Improvisation*
  e) *Heimweh: "Herz, Herz, warum so traurig"*
  f) *Gaudeamus Igitur*
  g) *Die Loreley*
  h) *O du himmelblauer See*
  i) *Abschied von der Heimath: "Es ist bestimmt in Gottes Rath"*
  j) *Heil dir im Siegerkranz*
  k) *Das Volkslied: Apotheose*

ORCHESTRAL WORKS

*SYMPHONY* (No. 1) (1876–78). Entered in a conservatory competition. (NBL, 1; cf. Ch. III)

*SYMPHONY* (No. 2), A minor (1876–78?), three movements in ms. (NBL, 39; cf. Ch. III)

*NORDISCHE SYMPHONIE* (or SUITE) (1878–82?) (Br. an Krisper 14.XII.79; GAM, 98; PSM, 28; cf. Ch. V)

*FOUR SYMPHONIES* ("Dresden") (1878–88?). Examined by Willem Mengelberg and Max von Schillings in Baroness von Weber's library in Dresden around 1937 (One or two of these works probably identical with those already mentioned above) (*Musical America* 10.IV.38)

CHAMBER MUSIC

*POLKA MIT EINEM TRAUERMARSCH ALS EINLEITUNG* (for piano?) (ca. 1867) (NBLS VII.93; cf. Ch. II)

*PIANO PIECES* (Before 1875) "Wagnerian" in style, probably not written down. Played by Mahler to Julius Epstein in Baden: IX.75

*PIANO SUITE* (1875–78?) won a prize at the conservatory (NBL, 1)

*NOCTURNE* for cello (and piano?) (1876–78) (NBLS VII–VIII.93)

*SONATA FOR PIANO AND VIOLIN* (1876). 1st perf. 31.VII.76 Iglau (NBL, 39; 39; 66; PS1, 14; GA, GAM, 97; cf. Ch. III)

*LIED* (ca. 1867), poem by Gotthold Lessing *Die Türken haben schöne Töchter* (NBLS, VII.93; cf. Ch. II)

*LIED*, composed for a competition at the conservatory (BMG, 62; cf. Ch. IV)

*LIEDER* (1875–80), of which two fragments have survived: see FRAGMEN-TARY WORKS C and D (NBL, 39; cf. Ch. III)

*STRING QUARTET* (?) (ca. 1880), composed in one night (AMM, 82; cf. Ch. IV)

*PIANO QUARTET* (No. 2?) (1878). 1st perf. at Theodor Billroth's. Ms. sent to Russia for a composition competition and lost. This work may be either the A minor piano quartet, of which the first movement has survived (see FRAGMENTARY WORKS), or the quintet of 1878 (NBL, 39; cf. Ch. III)

*PIANO QUINTET* (1876), first movement received a prize at the Vienna Conservatory VII.76. 1st public perf. 12.IX.76 Iglau (NBL, 39)

*PIANO QUINTET* (1878), probably unfinished. Scherzo received a prize and was performed at the conservatory 11.VII.78. (This may be the quintet mentioned in NBL, 39, or even the piano quartet listed above.)

## FRAGMENTARY WORKS

A) *PIANO QUARTET* (1876): 1st movement, A minor (*Nicht zu schnell; Entschlossen*). 1st perf. (?) 12.II.64 New York/Peter Serkin-Galimir Quartet

B) *PIANO QUARTET* (1876): Scherzo, G minor (approx. 30 bars)

C) *LIED* (undated), D minor, poem by Heine, *Es fiel ein Reif in der Frühlings-nacht* (approx. 22 bars)

D) *LIED* (undated), C major with many modulations, poem by Heine, *Im wunderschönen Monat Mai* (18 bars)

E) Fragment of a transcription (or original version) for piano duet of the *First Symphony* Scherzo (approx. same period as the preceding fragments). A major. Prima: 22 bars; Seconda: 30 bars

## FINISHED WORKS

1) *3 LIEDER* (1880) for tenor and piano, poems by Mahler, dedicated to Josephine Poisl. 1st perf. 30.IX.34 Radio Brno/Zdenek Knittl, tenor; Alfred Rosé, piano. Unpublished (A. Rosé Collection)
   a) *"Im Lenz"* (19.II.80)
   b) *"Winterlied"* (27.II.80)
   c) *"Maitanz im Grünen"* (3.III.80)

2) *DAS KLAGENDE LIED*, original vers. (1880) for soprano, alto, 2 tenors, baritone, bass, solo, chorus, and orchestra (XII.93). Poem by Mahler. Rev. V 1899. Ed. 1900/IX.02 Weinberger
   a) *"Waldmärchen"* (cut in 1893 vers.) for soprano, alto, tenor, bass. 1st perf. 25.XI.34 Radio Brno

    b) *"Der Spielmann"* (Sketch 21.III.80). 1st perf. 17.II.01 Vienna

    c) *"Hochzeitstück"* (Sketch III.80). 1st perf. 17.II.01 Vienna

3) *5 LIEDER* (1880–83) forming Vol. I of the *Lieder und Gesänge* named after
GM's death *Lieder aus der Jugendzeit,* poems by Leander, Mahler, and Tirso
de Molina, entitled, in the only known manuscript *5 Gedichte komponiert
von Gustav Mahler.* Ed. II.92 Schott

    a) *"Früehlingsmorgen"* (Richard Leander). 1st perf. 20.IV.86 Prague

    b) *"Erinnerung"* (Leander). 1st perf. 13.XI.89 Budapest

    c) *"Hans und Grethe"* (Mahler) (identical with 1c). 1st perf. 20.IV.86
       Prague

    d) *"Serenade aus* Don Juan" (Tirso de Molina and Mahler)

    e) *"Phantasie aus* Don Juan" (Tirso de Molina and Mahler)

4) *4 LIEDER EINES FAHRENDEN GESELLEN,* poems by Mahler. 1st vers.
Voice and piano (XII.84); orchestra 1893 (?) and I/VI.96. 1st perf. 16.III.96
Berlin. Ed. XII.97 Weinberger (piano). 1912 Weinberger (orchestra)

    a) *"Wenn mein Schatz Hochzeit macht"*

    b) *"Ging' heut' morgens übers Feld."* 1st. perf. with piano. 20.IV.86 Prague

    c) *"Ich hab' ein glühend'Messer"*

    d) *"Die zwei blauen Augen"*

5) *FIRST SYMPHONY,* D major (1885?–88) Sketch: "Symphony I" (1885)
(GAM, 99). 1st perf.: "Symphonic Poem in two parts" 20.XI.89 Budapest.
1st rev. without b) I.93. 2nd rev. with b) 16.VIII.93: "Symphony ("Titan")
in 5 movements (2 parts)." 2nd perf.: "Titan, Tone-poem in the form of
a symphony" 27.X.93 Hamburg. 3rd perf. 3.VI.94 Weimar. Final rev.
without b) 1896. 4th perf. "Symphony in D major" 16.III.96 Berlin. Last
rev. 1906–07. Ed. II.99 Weinberger; V.06 Universal Edition

    a) Langsam. Schleppend; Immer sehr gemächlich

    b) Andante alegretto *(sic)* "Blumine" (16.VIII.93 renovatum) ed. Presser
       1968 (later suppressed)

    c) Kräftig bewegt, doch nicht zu schnell (27.I.93 renovatum)

    d) Feierlich und gemessen, ohne zu schleppen

    e) Stürmisch bewegt; Energisch (19.I.93 renovatum)

6) *9 WUNDERHORN LIEDER* with piano (1888–91) forming the 2nd and
3rd vols. of the *Lieder und Gesänge* named after GM's death *Lieder aus der
Jugendzeit.* Ed. II.92 Schott

    a) *"Um schlimme Kinder artig zu machen."* 1st perf. 14.XII.07 Berlin

    b) *"Ich ging mit Lust"*

    c) *"Aus! Aus!"* 1st perf. 29.IV.92 Hamburg

    d) *"Starke Einbildungskraft"*

    e) *"Zu Strassburg auf der Schanz' "*

    f) *"Ablösung im Sommer."* 1st perf. 14.XII.07 Berlin

    g) *"Scheiden und Meiden."* 1st perf. 13.XI.89 Budapest

    h) *"Nicht Wiedersehen!"* 1st perf. 29.IV.92 Hamburg

    i) *"Selbstgefühl"*

7) *10 WUNDERHORN LIEDER* with orchestra (1892–96) a), b), c), and 10d
named in 1892 *5 Humoresken)* Ed. 1899–00 Weinberger

    a) *"Der Schildwache Nachtlied"* (1888–28.I.92). 1st perf. 12.XII.92 Ber-
       lin/Raphael Maszkowski

b) *"Verlor'ne Müh'"* (1.II.92). 1st perf. 12.XII.92 Berlin/Raphael Masz-kowski

c) *"Trost im Unglück"* (22.II.92). 1st perf. 27.X.93 Hamburg

d) *"Wer hat dies Liedlein erdacht?"* (6.II.92). 1st perf. 27.X.93 Hamburg

e) *"Das irdische Leben"* (1893: NBL, 10). 1st perf. 14.I.00 Vienna

f) *"Des Antonius von Padua Fischpredigt"* (1.VIII.93). 1st perf. 29.I.05 Vienna

g) *"Rheinlegendchen"* (9.VIII.93). 1st perf. 27.X.93 Hamburg

h) *"Lied des Verfolgten im Turm"* (1895). 1st perf. 29.I.05 Vienna

i) *"Wo die schönen Trompeten blasen"* (1895). 1st perf. 14.I.00 Vienna

j) *"Lob des hohen Verstandes"* (21.VI.96)

k) *"Es sungen drei Engel"* (Sketch summer 1895). (Cf. 9e)

l) *"Urlicht"* (1892). (Cf. 8d)

8) *SECOND SYMPHONY*, C minor (1888–94) with soprano, alto solo, and mixed chorus, 1st perf. a), b), and c) 4.III.95 Berlin. 1st complete perf. 13.XII.95 Berlin. Ed. XII.95 Hofmeister (2 pianos); 1897 Hofmeister; IV.06 Universal Edition

a) Allegro maestoso (mit durchaus ernstem und feierlichem Ausdruck). 1st vers. Sketch 8.VIII.88; Orc. 10.IX.88: *"Totenfeier."* Final vers. 29.IV.94 renovatum

b) Andante moderato (Sehr gemächlich) (1888–30.VII.93)

c) In ruhig fliessender Bewegung (16.VII.93)

d) *"Urlicht,"* alto solo, from *Des Knaben Wunderhorn* (1892–94) (Sehr feierlich, aber schlicht)

e) Im Tempo des Scherzo. Wild herausfahrend; Kräftig; Langsam; Mis-terioso, poem by Friedrich Klopstock extended by Mahler (Sketch 29.VI.94; Orc. 18.XII.94)

9) *THIRD SYMPHONY*, D minor (1895–96) with alto solo, women's and children's choruses. 1st perf. b) 9.XI.96 Berlin/Nikisch. 4th perf. b) 31.II.97 Budapest. 1st perf. b), c), f) 9.III.97 Berlin/Weingartner. 1st complete perf. 9.VI.02 Krefeld. Rev. summer V.99. Ed. VII.02 Weinberger; I.06 Universal Edition

a) Kräftig. Entschieden (Sketch 28.VI.96; Orc. 17.X.96)

b) Tempo di Menuetto (sehr mässig) (Sketch VI.95; Orc. 11.IV.96)

c) Comodo. Scherzando. Ohne Hast (Sketch VI.95; Orc. 25.IV.96)

d) Sehr langsam. Misterioso, alto solo *"O Mensch!"* poem by Nietzsche (Sketch summer 95)

e) Lustig im Tempo und keck im Ausdruck, alto solo, women's and children's choruses. *"Es sungen drei Engel,"* from *Des Knaben Wun-derhorn* (Sketch 24.VI.95; Orc. Sketch 11.VIII.95; Orc. ?.V.96)

f) Langsam. Ruhevoll. Empfunden (Sketch summer 95; Orc. 22.XI.96)

10) *FOURTH SYMPHONY*, G major (1899–1900) with soprano solo. 1st perf. 25.XI.01 Munich. Rev. 1902. Last rev. VII.10. Ed. I.02 Doblinger; I.06 Universal Edition

a) Bedächtig, nicht eilen (1899–00)

b) In gemächlicher Bewegung, ohne Hast (Sketch 1899–00; Orc. 5.I.01)

c) Ruhevoll (Poco adagio) (Sketch 1899–00; Orc. 6.VIII.00)

d) Sehr behaglich, soprano solo *"Wir geniessen die Himmlischen Freuden"* from *Des Knaben Wunderhorn* (10.II.92; Orc. 12.III.92; 1st perf. (separate) 27.X.93 Hamburg; Rev. 1900)

(Information on the following works will be found in Volume II.)

11) *7 LIEDER* named after GM's death *"Aus letzter Zeit"*

 A) *2 WUNDERHORN LIEDER* with orchestra (1899–1901). Ed. VIII.05 Kahnt

   a) *"Revelge"* (VI/VII.99) (NBLS). 1st perf. 29.I.05 Vienna

   b) *"Der Tamboursg'sell"* (summer 1901) (NBL, 166). 1st perf. 29.I.05 Vienna

 B) *4 RUECKERT LIEDER* with orchestra (1901). 1st perf. 29.I.05 Vienna. Ed. VII.05 Kahnt

   a) *"Blicke mir nicht in die Lieder!"* (14.VI.01)

   b) *"Ich atmet' einen Linden Duft"* (summer 1901) (NBL, 166)

   c) *"Ich bin der Welt abhanden gekommen"* (summer 1901) (NBL, 166)

   d) *"Um Mitternacht"* (summer 1901) (NBLS)

 C) *1 RUECKERT LIED* with piano. Ed. VII.05 Kahnt (piano); Orc. M. Puttmann (1900) (?)

   *"Liebst du um Schönheit"* (VIII.02) (AMT)

12) *FIFTH SYMPHONY,* C sharp minor (1901–02) Orc. 1903. Rev. 1904. 1st perf. 19.X.04 Cologne. Ed. IX.04 Peters

1st part:   a) Trauermarsch (In gemessenem Schritt. Streng. Wie ein Kondukt)

           b) Stürmisch bewegt mit grösster Vehemenz

2nd part:   c) Scherzo (Kräftig, nicht zu schnell)

3rd part:   d) Adagietto (Sehr langsam)

           e) Rondo-Finale (Allegro)

13) *5 KINDERTOTENLIEDER* (1901–04), poems by Friedrich Rückert. 1st perf. 29.I.05 Vienna. Ed. VIII.05 Kahnt

   a) *"Nun will die Sonn' so hell aufgeh'n"* (summer 1901) (NBL, 166)

   b) *"Nun seh' ich wohl, warum so dunkle Flammen"* (summer 1901) (NBL, 166)

   c) *"Wenn dein Mütterlein"* (summer 1901) (NBL, 166. Sketch in NBL collection)

   d) *"Oft denk' ich, sie sind nur ausgegangen"* (summer 1904) (AMM, 91)

   e) *"In diesem Wetter"* (summer 1904)

14) *SIXTH SYMPHONY,* A minor (1903–04). 1st perf. 27.V.06 Essen. Rev. summer 1906 and early 1907. Ed. III.06 Kahnt

| | 2nd Ed. | Final vers. (?) |
|---|---|---|
| a) Allegro energico, ma non troppo (Sketch summer 1904) | | |
| b) Scherzo (Wuchtig) (Sketch summer 1903) | b) Andante | b) Scherzo |
| c) Andante moderato (Sketch summer 1903) | c) Scherzo | c) Andante |
| d) Finale (Allegro moderato) (Sketch summer 1904); Orc. 1.V.05 | | |

15) *SEVENTH SYMPHONY,* B minor (1904–05). 1st perf. 19.IX.08 Prague. Ed. XII.09 Bote und Bock

   a) Langsam; Allegro risoluto ma non troppo (Sketch VII.05)

   b) Nachtmusik (Allegro moderato) (Sketch summer 1904)

   c) Schattenhaft (fliessend, aber nicht schnell) (Sketch summer 1905)

    d) Nachtmusik (Andante amoroso) (Sketch summer 1904)

    e) Rondo-Finale (Allegro ordinario) (Sketch summer 1905)

16) *EIGHTH SYMPHONY*, E flat major (1906) with 3 sopranos, 2 altos, tenor, baritone, bass solos, children's and double mixed choruses. 1st perf. 12.IX.10 Munich. Ed. II.11 Universal Edition

    a) Hymnus *"Veni Creator spiritus"* (Sketch VII/VIII.06)

    b) Final scene from Goethe's *Faust* (Sketch VII/VIII.06)

17) *DAS LIED VON DER ERDE* (1908) "A symphony for tenor and alto (or baritone) and orchestra," poems from the Chinese by Hans Bethge. 1st perf. 20.XI.11 Munich. B. Walter

    a) *"Das Trinklied vom Jammer der Erde"* (Sketch 14.VIII.08)

    b) *"Der Einsame im Herbst"* (Sketch VII.08)

    c) *"Von der Jugend"* (Sketch 1.VIII.08)

    d) *"Von der Schönheit"* (Sketch 21.VIII.08)

    e) *"Der Trunkene im Frühling"*

    f) *"Der Abschied"* (Sketch 1.IX.08)

18) *NINTH SYMPHONY*, D major (1909). 1st. perf. 26.VI.12 Vienna. B. Walter. Ed. VII.12 Universal Edition

    a) Andante comodo

    b) Im Tempo eines gemächlichen Ländlers

    c) Rondo-Burleske (Allegro assai. Sehr trotzig)

    d) Adagio (sehr langsam; molto adagio)

19) *TENTH SYMPHONY*, F sharp (1910), unfinished. 1st perf. a) and c) 12.X.24 Vienna. F. Schalk. Ed. FS 1924 Zsolnay. Ed. a) and c) 1951 AMP. Performing vers. by Deryck Cooke 1963: 1st perf. incomplete 19.XII.60 BBC London, Berthold Goldschmidt. 1st perf. complete 13.VIII.64 BBC London, Berthold Goldschmidt. Ed. Schott.

    a) Andante; Adagio

    b) Scherzo (Schnelle Vierteln)

    c) Purgatorio (Allegretto moderato. Nicht zu schnell)

    d) (Scherzo II) *"Der Teufel tanzt es mit mir"*

    e) Finale (Einleitung; Allegro moderato)

## UNFINISHED WORKS COMPLETED BY MAHLER

*DIE DREI PINTOS*, opera in three acts by Karl Maria von Weber (1887–88) (Libretto rev. by Karl von Weber and Mahler). 1st perf. Leipzig Theater 20.I.88. Ed. 1888 (?) Kahnt

## TRANSCRIPTIONS

BRUCKNER: *SYMPHONY No. 3* (Piano-four-hand transcription in collaboration with Rudolf Krzyzanowski) (1878). Ed. Bussjäger & Rättig 1878

J. S. BACH: *SUITE AUS SEINEN ORCHESTERWERKEN* (1909) Ed. II.11 Schirmer

    a) Overture (from Suite No. 2)

    b) Rondeau (*id.*)

    c) Badinerie (*id.*)

    d) Air (from Suite No. 3)

    e) Gavottes 1 and 2 (from Suite No. 4)

## REVISED WORKS

ORCHESTRATION

BEETHOVEN: *SYMPHONIES Nos. 5 to 9*
OVERTURES: *CORIOLAN, EGMONT, DIE WEIHE DES HAUSES, "LEONORE"* No. 2
SCHUMANN: *SYMPHONIES Nos. 1 to 4*
*MANFRED OVERTURE*
BRUCKNER: *SYMPHONY No. 5* (abridged version)

SCENIC VERSIONS

MOZART: *LE NOZZE DI FIGARO* (new recitative for the judgment scene), Ed. Peters
WEBER: *EURYANTHE* (alterations to libretto and several passages in the score), Universal Edition
*OBERON "Neue Bühneneinrichtung"* ("Melodramas" added), Universal Edition

# DETAILED HISTORY AND ANALYSIS

## UNFINISHED, DESTROYED, OR LOST WORKS

### THEATRICAL WORKS—OPERAS

*HERZOG ERNST VON SCHWABEN*. (See Chapter III.) Mahler was working on this first operatic project in Iglau before he left for Vienna in 1875, and
he played excerpts from it to Gustav Schwarz at Morawan. The story was
probably drawn from Ludwig Uhland's (1787–1862) famous verse drama of the
same name. The author of the libretto was Mahler's childhood friend Josef
Steiner, to whom he wrote in 1879 the longest, most "literary" of his early letters
(see Chapter V). Both Gustav's dead brother Ernst and the hero of this early
opera are referred to in this letter as "ghosts of my youth." Although Guido
Adler assigns a later date (1877–79) to *Ernst von Schwaben*, it is almost certain
that Mahler abandoned it when he reached the conservatory and started to
acquire the techniques that he had previously lacked.

*DIE ARGONAUTEN*. (See Chapter V.) Mahler's libretto was probably based on
the second play of the trilogy *Das goldene Vliess* (1818–21), by the great Austrian poet Franz Grillparzer. According to Guido Adler, it was written, like
Wagner's texts, in *Stabreimen* (alliterative verse), and some of the music was
composed in 1880. Mahler's 1896 statement to Natalie suggests that only the Prelude was partly committed to paper, and this at an earlier date than that given by
Guido Adler. (I cannot accept Donald Mitchell's interpretation of this passage;
according to him the Prelude was composed "after the opera." I do not believe
that the score was ever completed, or even consisted of more than a few fragments.)

*RUEBEZAHL*. Natalie's unpublished manuscript corroborates AMM's account
of the origin of this project, which eventually led to a break between Mahler
and Hugo Wolf. A newly discovered letter from Mahler to Albert Spiegler[1]
proves that Mahler worked on *Rübezahl* during the winter of 1879–80; therefore
the break must have occurred at about that time (see Chapter V).

The hero of a well-known East German legend, Rübezahl is a mythical
mountain spirit from the Silesian Riesengebirge who assumes various shapes to
defend Good against Evil and take revenge on those who have made fun of him.
He appears in several stories by Hoffmann and Grimm. At one time Weber
considered a serious opera on this theme, and it was actually set to music by
Josef Schuster (1789), Wilhelm Würfel (1824), Flotow (1853), and Hans Sommer (1904). Mahler probably knew the opera by Flotow, a very popular composer
at that time.

Although NBLS clearly states that Mahler broke with Wolf over the
*Rübezahl* libretto, it no less clearly affirms that he showed the completed text
to him and to other friends. "It only partly met with their approval. I cannot
quite recall what they said about it. As far as I remember today, it contained
many crude and unfinished passages that I would have smoothed and transformed
when setting them to music. Someone who could sense when a text is really
meant for music, and only needs sound to come to life, might have found some

good things, even in its imperfect form . . . But I could not complete it today. I have come too far from the frame of mind I was in then . . ."[2] In 1896, Mahler considered showing his libretto to the Berlin critic-composer Max Marschalk, but he soon gave up the idea.[3] In 1908 he heard by chance that his sister Justine had kept a copy of the text and had shown it to his collaborator, the painter and set designer Alfred Roller. According to Alma Mahler, he flew into a rage and insisted that his sister send it to him immediately in Hamburg, where he was about to embark for America. Alma Mahler claims that he threw the manuscript into the Atlantic, yet a copy remained in her collection until she died. There is in existence a letter from Mahler to Justi, written after the Roller incident, in which he reproaches her for having sent him some other juvenilia instead of *Rübezahl*.[4]

Mahler told Natalie that he was working on the score of *Rübezahl* before he left for Laibach in 1881,[5] and he complained in a Kassel letter that he did not have enough time to give to it.[6] In January 1883, he still hoped to complete the first act shortly, and wrote to Anton Krisper that the libretto had been given a "completely new twist." He had still not abandoned the project in 1890, for in September of that year he wrote to Justi saying that he had left the text in Hinterbrühl and requesting her to send it to him in Budapest.

ANALYSIS OF THE LIBRETTO

The opera originally began with a Prologue, which no longer exists but is mentioned several times in the libretto. Its function was to present the main characters: the King, his daughter Emma, her companions, and her beloved Ratibor, as well as the King of the Mountain Spirits, Rübezahl.

Act I, set in the royal palace of a mythical country, opens with the arrival of three Greek princes who have come to ask for the hand of the Princess. She rejects these grotesque suitors (whose entrance was accompanied by a march that was praised by Paul Stefan (PSM, 39) for its "mad humor"), and an uproar is then heard coming from the palace gates. It is caused by Rübezahl, who, in human form, with his red beard and magic cudgel (*Keule*), bursts in after casting a spell on all those who attempt to prevent him. Soon he flies away again, carrying Emma off with him.

Act II takes place in Rübezahl's underworld kingdom. Emma bewails her sad fate, and the enamored spirit attempts to console her, first with kind words, then with a magic wand and a basketful of beets (*Rübe* in German), which can be changed into anyone she wants as a companion to share her solitude. Rübezahl's magic succeeds, and Emma's five companions materialize to tell her of Ratibor's despair. She then changes another beet into a hawk, which she entrusts with a message of distress to the young man: Let him come and save her!

Act IV follows the second in the manuscript, although there seems to be no break in the action. Emma's companions have quickly changed into odious old women, thus revealing their illusory nature. They dance and sing for her a lied that must have been *Hans und Grethe*, as the two first lines of the poem are nearly identical (this assumption is confirmed by PSM, 34):

*Ringel, ringel Reih'n!*
*Wer fröhlich ist, der schlinge sich ein!*

Left alone with Rübezahl, Emma sends him away to gather flowers and promptly dispatches a new messenger—this time a white hawk—to Ratibor. When Rübezahl returns, she sends him off again to count all the sugar beets in his kingdom (*Rübe*—beet or any other root vegetable; *zählen*—to count) and then uses the magic wand to conjure up a winged steed on whose back she flies off to her fiancé.

Act V is set in an idyllic Riesengebirge landscape. Ratibor sings of the return of spring, accompanied by cowbells and a shepherd's pipe. (According to Richard Specht's 1905 booklet, some themes from *Rübezahl* were used in the *First Symphony*.[7] If this is the case, the beginning of the last act could have become the introduction to the first movement of the symphony.) In Ratibor's solo, which follows, several lines evoke other Mahler texts. *"Der Lenz ist da, der Lenz ist kommen"* recalls a line from the poem *Vergessene Liebe* (sent to Anton Krisper on March 3, 1880): *"Kam der Lenz gezogen und Blumen blühn ja überall,"* or another one from the letter accompanying it: *"Der Frühling ist über Nacht gekommen . . ."* It is also reminiscent of the verses Mahler added to Hans Bethge's poem *Der Abschied*, at the end of *Das Lied von der Erde: "Die Liebe Erde überall blüht auf im Lenz."* Further on, in the following stanza:

*Im Busch seh' ich ihr Haar nur wehen,*
*Am Himmel ihre blauen Augen steh'n,*
*Und mag ich träumen oder wachen,*
*Nun klingt immer ihr silber Lachen!*

Further similarities with lines from the *Lieder eines fahrenden Gesellen* Nos. 3 and 4 are also evident.

No sooner has the hawk delivered its message than Emma appears on her white charger to sing a lengthy love duet with Ratibor (strong Wagnerian influences, particularly from the Tristan and Siegfried love duets, are apparent in Mahler's text). The King arrives with his suite and orders a wedding feast. (Two pages from the manuscript are missing here. They presumably included a change of scene for the marriage, following Emma's dialogue with her father and her narration of preceding events, which are now to be found at the end of the libretto.)

During the festivities there is a sudden storm, and Rübezahl appears in his true form, as King of the Mountain Spirits, surrounded by his elves. "Man's heart is small and narrow," he sings. "Immortality, virtue I wanted to give thee! Thou chosest man's pitiful fate. Go hence! Be happy in thy wretchedness!" After Rübezahl's departure the bridal procession walks up to the castle in brilliant moonlight, accompanied by singing peasants and village musicians with their instruments. (The dead Huntsman in the third movement of the *First Symphony* is accompanied to his grave in the same way by animals performing on various wind instruments; also a group of village musicians perform in *Das klagende Lied's* Hochzeitstück. The words of the Bridal Chorus, *"Du Spielmann mein,"* are also to be found in *Das klagende Lied*.) A mourning chorus of elves is heard backstage, singing of their king's homecoming and his suffering through Man's ingratitude. In the sad elfin chorus that ends the opera the last lines strangely anticipate *Das Lied von der Erde*:

Man's heart is dark and small
The spirit is clear as sunlight
And full of eternal life.

Before judging this libretto one must bear in mind that the version that has
survived is most probably the original 1879–80 one, and not the 1882 revision
that Mahler alludes to in his letter to Krisper. This undoubtedly accounts for
many of the weaknesses and gaucheries of a nineteen-year-old's text. Yet it is
easy to understand why Mahler considered his libretto so well suited for musical
adaption. Many episodes—Rübezahl's entrance and that of the suitors, Emma's
lament, her young companions' transformation into old hags, the bird messenger's solo, the contrast between man's earthly joy and the mourning of the
spirits at the end—provided excellent material for musical illustration. Many
passages were in any case eminently well suited to Mahler's "Callot style," as
exemplified by the *First Symphony*. Yet it certainly required a musician of genius
to bring a semblance of life to such conventional situations and stereotyped
characters. The most surprising fact, then, is that Mahler should have considered
setting such a libretto to music, even after he had acquired a certain amount of
theatrical experience.

Furthermore, charming as it is, and well suited to the folklike character of his
first songs, the naïve style of Mahler's early years was wholly inadequate for
opera. Besides, the Wagnerian influences (Lohengrin—the demigod in love with a
mortal—Tristan in the love duet, Siegfried in the singing bird, even the names of
Emma's playmates: Brinnhild, Edelgard, Irmentraut, Adelheit, and Kunigund, to
cite only a few) are all too obvious in the text and strangely ill-matched to
the Hoffmannesque humor of the rest. Much as one longs to have heard the
completed fragments of the score, it is unlikely that they would have added a
great deal to Mahler's stature as a composer. Furthermore, the best of them were
undoubtedly incorporated in various later works.

*UNNAMED OPERA PROJECT* (1888). According to Natalie Bauer-Lechner's
detailed account of one of her conversations with Mahler, it was Marion
Mathilde von Weber's "wish and impulse" that led him to conceive the following plot after the successful premiere of *Die drei Pintos*. As he remembered it in
1901: "A soldier is saved on the way to the gallows because he has awakened a
young girl's compassion: following a medieval custom, she obtains his pardon
by publicly declaring her intention to marry him. The funeral march is then
transformed into a bridal procession, which accompanies the pair to their home.
Although quickly falling in love with the girl, the proud and obstinate young
man cannot overcome the feeling of shame which torments him, because he owes
his pardon solely to her pity. His inner conflict becomes so unbearable that he
eventually refuses her hand and prefers to die. However the last act ends happily, thanks to the girl's entreaties and faithfulness."[8]

It is easy to understand why Mahler's imagination was fired by this idea, and
why he found the soldier's unswerving character, his dilemma, and desperate
decision an interesting subject. The death march and the mourning chorus, which
changes into a bridal procession, are of particular musical interest: all Mahler's
opera projects contain some such episode, in which joy and sorrow mingle or
alternate. One is reminded of Mahler's childhood "Polka with an introduction in

the form of a funeral march" and of innumerable similar episodes in his mature works.

The plot as devised by Mahler was obviously too thin for a full-length opera, and Karl von Weber, who was entrusted with the task of writing a libretto, altered the story by adding an important secondary character, one of the soldier's former sweethearts. As a result, Mahler claimed that Karl had ruined his idea, and soon gave it up. Only one of the musical numbers has survived, in the form of the orchestral lied *"Der Schildwache Nachtlied."*[9] It is based on a *Knaben Wunderhorn* poem, for Mahler discovered the anthology that played such an important part in his creative life while working on this libretto with Weber's grandson. In a short biography published during Mahler's lifetime and based on material that he probably provided personally, Max Marschalk writes that, upon leaving Leipzig, Mahler considered settling in Munich to "finish an opera based on his own libretto." He was undoubtedly referring to the project begun with Weber.

According to a very reliable source,[10] Mahler did not give up the idea of writing an opera after 1888 and was still discussing another such project with his childhood friend, the lawyer Emil Freund, as late as 1901.

## INCIDENTAL WORKS

One of Mahler's tasks at the Kassel Theater was to compose music for benefit performances. He did so on three occasions, only one of which inspired an important and original work.

*VORSPIEL MIT CHOR* (Prelude with Chorus). November 2, 1883, was the fiftieth anniversary of actor Karl Häser's first stage appearance; Mahler's *Vorspiel* preceded lieder by Häser himself, who was an amateur composer. Mahler probably destroyed the score, but the vocal and instrumental parts, handwritten by a copyist, survived in the archives of the Kassel Theater until it was bombed in 1944.

*DER TROMPETER VON SAEKKINGEN.* For a single gala performance (June 23, 1884) Mahler composed, in the space of a few days, incidental music for a series of seven *tableaux vivants* based on Joseph Viktor von Scheffel's (1826–86) then very popular narrative poem. Some confusion may have arisen from the fact that Mahler later reluctantly conducted Nessler's opera by the same name in Prague and Leipzig. This opera was first performed in Leipzig on May 4, 1884, at which time Mahler was working on his own *Trompeter* score.

After the *tableaux vivants* the fourth act of *Les Huguenots* and the last act of *Il Trovatore* were performed. Eighteen actors and many walk-ons appeared in the *tableaux,* which were linked together by extracts from Scheffel's poem recited by an actor named Thies. They were performed again in 1885 in Mannheim and Karlsruhe, although the projected Wiesbaden performance mentioned by Mahler[11] does not seem to have materialized.

Mahler himself became satiated with the score and made his friend, the Leipzig music critic Max Steinitzer, promise to destroy the piano transcription he had made of the first number. The original orchestral score probably belonged to the Kassel Theater and was destroyed with it in 1944. Mahler's *Trompeter* music was based on a single theme, the trumpet serenade, treated in turn as a march, an adagio for the love scene, and spirited battle music. The *Kasseler Zeitung's* June 25 review of the performance emphasizes the virtuosity required of the solo trumpet, as well as Mahler's great "technical knowledge" and gifts as an orchestrator.

Until recently only one theme, Werner's serenade, was known from the *Trompeter* music. It was quoted by Max Steinitzer in a magazine article and runs as follows:

When the unknown slow movement (*"Blumine"*) of the *First Symphony* recently came to light, it was discovered that its main theme was the very melody quoted above, also entrusted to a trumpet. Mahler told Steinitzer how exasperated he was with its "sentimentality."[12] This proves that the former owner of the *"Blumine"* score is wrong to claim it was an "ardent declaration of love" for Johanna Richter, Mahler's Kassel sweetheart. Such declarations are to be found in the *Lieder eines fahrenden Gesellen* and other contemporary poems written for the young singer, rather than in the sugary *"Blumine,"* which Mahler later eliminated from the *First Symphony* (see below).

*DAS VOLKSLIED.* H. S. Mosenthal, the author of this *"Gedichte mit Liedern, Chören und lebenden Bildern"* (Poem with Lieder, Choruses, and Tableaux Vivants), was none other than Otto Nicolaï's librettist for *Die lustigen Weiber.* The music was announced as a selection "from existing *Volkslieder,* orchestrated by G. Mahler" and "arranged for the Kassel Royal Theater by Otto Ewald." *Das Volkslied* was first performed on April 20, 1885, at a Theater Pension Fund benefit, and was preceded by a "farce," *Der Jüngste Lieutenant,* by E. Jacobson.

The task of arranging these folk songs, hastily composed between frustrating rehearsals and mediocre performances at the Kassel Theater, was no doubt unrewarding for Mahler, except that it provided an opportunity to study their style and structure, which later strongly influenced his own *Wunderhorn Lieder.*

ORCHESTRAL WORKS

*SYMPHONY* (No. 1) was composed, according to Natalie Bauer-Lechner, for a competition at the conservatory and refused by Hellmesberger because of the many mistakes in the orchestral parts. This anecdote has survived in several different versions. Richard Specht[13] claims that Mahler's fellow students deliberately wrote in the mistakes and that the work rehearsed was a quintet (probably the one performed at the conservatory and in Iglau in 1876). Bruckner related the same anecdote but spoke of a "Sonata Andante."[14] Yet Natalie was a member of the conservatory orchestra, and it is unlikely that her memory played her false. Thus there is every reason to believe her version of this episode. In a letter written jointly with his cousin, Gustav Frank, on September 19, 1877 (or 1878?), to Frank's parents in Ledetsch, Mahler informs them that "one of my works is likely to be performed soon at a conservatory concert, and this keeps me very busy."

*SYMPHONY* (No. 2) in A minor. On June 21, 1896, Mahler said to Natalie: "Three movements exist. The fourth was complete, but only in my head—or rather on the piano on which, at that time, I still composed everything (something one should not do and which even I gave up doing later)." This A minor symphony is doubtless not the same work as the above Symphony No. 1, and the same passage in Natalie's recollections even mentions "two symphonies" *before* the A minor. The *Nordische* and the A minor symphony were probably among the "Four Symphonies" discovered by Mengelberg and Schillings in Baroness von Weber's library (see below).

*NORDISCHE SYMPHONIE* (or SUITE). This work is mentioned by nearly all the early biographical sources, but they disagree as to its date. Guido Adler suggests 1882, while Paul Stefan lists it among the conservatory works. The following passage from Mahler's letter of December 14, 1879, to Anton Krisper proves that work on it was already in progress at that time: "Also, there is a new shadow looming in the background of my visions, but I must first wait for its representative. When he appears, I will tell you more about him. I can only surmise that he is a very ancient Nordic king who will rouse me from my resting place with his heroes and his carousing. I have also taken a sip from Hippocrene —my heart is now so full of inspiration that it wells up into my mouth."

It appears from one of Natalie's letters to Mahler in the summer of 1897[15] that Mahler took up and abandoned this work several times and finally "lost contact" (*ganze Partien abhanden gekommen sind*) with it. The *Nordische Symphonie* is thought to have been one of the works Mahler gave Marion von Weber when he left Leipzig, yet the Dresden scores were reportedly complete, and the above passage in Natalie's letter suggests that this work remained unfinished.

*FOUR SYMPHONIES* ("Dresden"). On March 25, 1938, Paul Stefan, who was then living in Zurich, sent *Musical America* in New York a report concerning "Four unknown early Mahler Symphonies," which had been discovered and recently re-examined by one of Mahler's closest friends and greatest interpreters, Willem Mengelberg. Presumably for reasons of his own, the Dutch conductor made a fairly vague statement to Stefan, who wrote: "It does not seem at all improbable that archives, which Mengelberg specifically designates, should include Mahler manuscripts." Stefan believed that the Baroness von Weber, whom Mengelberg met in Dresden, was Marion Mathilde, Mahler's close friend and mistress; yet when she died in 1931 her library became the property of her daughter Katharina Mathilde Maria (1878–1946). Stefan claimed that the Dutch conductor, together with Max von Schilling, once spent a whole night playing these scores through on the piano and that they both were "profoundly moved by the musical content of the unknown works."

The story as it stands is not altogether convincing. First of all, if Mengelberg's discovery was actually "recent" (1938), the baroness was obviously Marion's daughter rather than Mahler's old friend. Furthermore, it is surprising that Schillings, who was a staunch Nazi, should have devoted so much time to Mahler, a Jewish composer for whom he had little admiration. A possible explanation of both these mysteries is that the playing through of the scores took place before 1931, *i.e.*, before Marion's death and before the advent of Nazism. There remains one unanswered question: how four early complete scores of such quality could have survived, especially from a period during which Mahler himself has confessed to having left most of his works unfinished. The three early scores that have been discovered to date (*Poisl Lieder*, *"Blumine,"* and *Waldmärchen*) have confirmed the unerring self-critical sense that led him to suppress them. All that is presently known of the Weber manuscripts is that most of the library was destroyed by fire during the Allied bombing of Dresden in 1944, and that whatever remained was later sent to the Deutscher Staats-bibliothek in Berlin, where no trace of a Mahler manuscript is now to be found.

## CHAMBER MUSIC

*POLKA MIT EINEM TRAUERMARSCH ALS EINLEITUNG.* This polka is mentioned by NBLS as one of the works that Mahler composed as a child. He made an ink spot on the manuscript while copying it for his parents (see Chapter II). It was undoubtedly for solo piano, like all his other childhood compositions.

*PIANO PIECES.* Mahler played some of these pieces for Epstein when his father took him to see the famous teacher in Baden in September 1875. Despite their "Wagnerian style"—a great fault in the old man's view—they must have been of some quality, for they led him to proclaim young Gustav "a born musician."

*PIANO SUITE.* According to Natalie, this suite was composed in great haste for a competition, to replace the symphony that Hellmesberger refused to perform. It received a prize, Mahler said, "because it was superficial and far weaker [than the symphony], while my better works always displeased the honorable members of the juries." Like several others that Mahler claimed to have received, no trace remains in the conservatory archives of this particular prize.

*NOCTURNE.* For cello (and piano?). This work is mentioned by NBLS without any other details.

*SONATA FOR PIANO AND VIOLIN.* Most early biographical sources mention this work. Paul Stefan even states that "it enjoyed a certain popularity among Mahler's friends." Natalie's claim that it was rehearsed in the Musikverein building is not implausible, as Mahler actually performed it in public (probably for the first time) at the Hotel Czap in Iglau on July 31,[16] with a fellow student and compatriot, Richard Schraml, and again on September 12 with another, August Siebert. Mahler told Natalie that the sonata "had received a prize" and that it was not entirely written out, but the conservatory archives have no record of it. "I was too involved then," he said to Natalie in 1896, "and my mind was still too restless and unsettled. I jumped from sketch to sketch, and worked out the whole composition, mostly in my head. Of course I knew every note so well that I could play it at will . . . until one day I found I had forgotten it!" To which may be added the passage from Natalie's unpublished manuscript[17] in which Mahler recalls Krzyzanowski's and his other conservatory schoolmates' prediction that he would never finish a single composition because at that time he had never actually written more than two or three movements of anything. "It was not only because I was anxious to begin something new," he said, "but because, while still involved in the work, I had already outgrown it and was no longer content with it . . . But who of course could have known then that it wasn't lack of a creative urge, of strength or perseverance [which hampered me]?"

*LIED.* Based on a poem by Gotthold Lessing, *"Die Türken haben schöne Töchter."* Mahler mentioned this song to Natalie in 1893; he probably composed it in his early childhood, although he could still remember every word of the poem twenty-five years later.

*LIED.* This song was composed for a competition at the conservatory. A young musician named Ludwig, who later became a piano teacher at the conservatory, won the first prize, while Mahler's entry won nothing, according to Ludwig Karpath, who recounts Mahler's much later meeting with Ludwig (see Chapter IV). If Mahler's lied at all resembled the lieder fragments surviving from that period it is not surprising that it shocked the jury.

*LIEDER.* Composed at the conservatory; Mahler's judgment of these is harsh: "My lieder of that period were most unsatisfactory, because my imagination was then too wild and uncontrolled, and the hardest task of all, that which requires the greatest skill, is to pour a rich substance into a small mold."

*STRING QUARTET.* The existence of this work, mentioned only once in Alma Mahler's book, is extremely hypothetical: "Mahler composed a quartet movement for a competition while the other two [Wolf and R. Krzyzanowski] spent the night on a bench in the Ringstrasse." Could the anecdote in fact refer to one of the movements of the Piano Quartet?

*PIANO QUARTET* (No. 2?). (For No. 1, see below, FRAGMENTARY WORKS.) Mahler himself called this "the best" of his juvenilia and claimed to have composed it "at the end of his conservatory studies." "It was very well received. Graedener[18] kept it for some time, and he liked it so much that he had it performed at Billroth's.[19] I later sent it to Russia for a competition and it was lost." There seems to be such endless confusion in contemporary sources between piano quartets and quintets (see below) that this most successful of Mahler's early chamber works could possibly be the quintet, the Scherzo of which received a first prize for composition at the conservatory in 1878.

*PIANO QUINTET* (No. 1) (1876). The announcement of a concert that took place at the Hotel Czap in Iglau on September 12, 1876, lists twice: "Quartet for piano, two violins and alto" under Mahler's and Krzyzanowski's names. A criticism published on September 17 clearly refers to two quintets and adds that Mahler's has just earned him a first prize for composition at the conservatory. The archives there confirm that on July 1 a first prize ("for excellence") was awarded to the first movement of Mahler's quintet. Despite Donald Mitchell's conjectures, there seems no doubt that this piano quintet was entirely different from the 1876 quartet (see FRAGMENTARY WORKS). This quintet is probably the one that Mahler mentioned to Natalie as not being entirely written out.

*PIANO QUINTET* (No. 2?) (1878). The Scherzo earned Mahler a first prize for composition on July 2, 1878, and he performed it in public on July 18 with a string quartet of conservatory students.

## FRAGMENTARY WORKS

All the fragments listed in my catalogue under this heading were contained in a folder belonging to Alma Mahler and inscribed in her hand: *"Frühe Kompositionen."* This folder vanished from her collection at the time of her death.

A) *PIANO QUARTET.* The title page of the quartet movement reads as follows: *"Clavier Quartet; Erster Satz; Gustav Mahler; 1876."* The stamp of the music-publishing firm of Theodor Rättig appears below the title, which seems to indicate that Mahler submitted it to him for examination in 1878, when Rättig published the four-hand arrangement of Bruckner's *Third Symphony.* As with many other early manuscripts, Mahler has let his pen wander in the margins and on the title page, which, like the sketches of *Das klagende Lied,* are covered with doodles and elaborate arabesques.

The very fact that the Scherzo sketches were in the same folder seems to prove that they were both part of the same work, yet it is strange indeed for a conservatory student to compose a G minor scherzo for an A minor work! The writing is clear, except for the last three pages, when the young composer was undoubtedly pressed for time. The only notation for the last bars of the pianist's left hand is a tonic tremolo over which *"Orgelpunkt ——"* has been hastily scribbled.

Mahler's models for this student work were Schumann and Brahms, which is hardly surprising, for Julius Epstein, his piano teacher at the conservatory, was a well-known interpreter of Brahms, and Franz Krenn a very "classical-minded" composition teacher. The style is not particularly original, but the writing is skillful, and while the themes themselves are not always very distinguished, a certain amount of invention and craftsmanship is displayed in the development. The two first subjects (A: *nicht zu schnell,* and B: *Entschlossen,* 4/4) defy all the rules in as much as they are in the same key. They are nevertheless strongly contrasted. The first is somber and ominous, the second rhapsodic and chromatic. They are followed by a very simple concluding theme (C), which undergoes many modulations. Anticipated in augmented note values earlier in the exposition, it is somewhat primitive and self-conscious in its "learned" imitations between the instruments.

Theme A is by far the most expressive and successful of the three, but it is also used too extensively throughout the movement. It is restated in unorthodox fashion in the main key of the movement at the start of the development, which later adheres strictly to the rules. Motives A and C are combined and tiresomely repeated in various keys throughout the eighty-five-bar elaboration, which shows more skill than inspiration. The only original feature in the recapitulation is that B and C now reappear in inverted sequence. C is then transposed into F sharp minor, varied and combined with a new version of A for the cello. Although it has already been used very extensively in the development and the recapitulation, the main theme again provides the entire substance of the coda, where it is expanded into a little cadenza *"ungemein rubato und leidenschaftlich"* [rubato and passionate throughout] for first violin.

The musical writing is skillful enough throughout, at least for a fifteen- or sixteen-year-old composer, but it is a little too "learned" and self-conscious. Remaining faithful to Brahms and Schumann, the instrumental style shows little originality. Busy, sometimes even concerto-like, the piano part bristles with arpeggios, octaves, and repeated chords.

B) *PIANO QUARTET*. Scherzo, G minor, 6/8 (no tempo indication). An energetic theme, again very reminiscent of Schumann and Brahms, is stated by the first violin over a sixteenth-note ostinato, which starts on the viola and is taken up by the piano in the fourth bar. The various instrumental parts are nearly complete in the first eleven bars. The sixteen following bars are only sketched in roughly, particularly for the piano. The fragment shows no more originality of musical and instrumental style than the A minor first movement.

C) *LIED FRAGMENT*. In D minor, the lied is based on a poem by Heine, *Es fiel ein Reif im Frühlingsnacht*. Jack Diether has recently traced the original folk poem to a lower Rhenisch folk song, of which two versions have been published in the Erk-Böhme *Deutscher Liederschatz*.[20] According to Diether, Mahler himself provided a new ending to the poem, as he often did later on, describing the two intertwining blue flowers that have grown on the grave of the ill-fated young lovers, symbolizing their union in death. The choice of the poem is easily explained: "three times without a country" himself, Mahler always favored descriptions of lost souls and suffering wanderers.

Unlike the other Heine fragment, *Es fiel ein Reif* begins in an intimate atmosphere of Schumannesque simplicity with a short prelude in descending thirds. At first the vocal line does not contradict this simplicity and the dotted march rhythm in the fourth bar is as Mahlerian as anything in these early fragments. The same march rhythm pervades the whole song, but Mahler soon embarks on a series of modulations, and even he himself does not seem to know where they are leading him. C minor, E major (?), F major, D flat major (?), C major, C sharp major, F sharp major . . . The fragment terminates abruptly with a cadence in this last key. It fully justifies Mahler's remark to Natalie that his imagination was too "wild and uncontrolled" at the time and that he did not yet have the strict self-discipline necessary to handle small forms. Lacking this discipline, the song wanders aimlessly from one key to another and never achieves any kind of unity, a quality in his mature songs, regardless of how free their treatment appears to be. Jack Diether has also underlined a remote similarity between an ascending phrase in *Es fiel ein Reif* and another in *Waldmärchen*, yet it is more remarkable still that so little in these two fragments should resemble any other known Mahler song.

D) *LIED FRAGMENT,* C major, on a poem by Heine, *Im wunderschönen Monat Mai.* To have chosen the text of one of Schumann's most famous lieder (the first song in the *Dichterliebe*) is in itself surprising. If the two fragments were more orthodox, one could suppose they had been composed for a competition prescribing Heine texts. At approximately the same time (1876–77) Wolf composed some songs that were based on Heine poems and that Mahler undoubtedly knew.

The charming and simple poem has been set to music by Mahler in the most extravagant way, with morbid syncopations, chromatic post-Wagnerian harmonies, anguished tremolos, constant changes in rhythm and harmony, and even a short recitative-like cadenza in the accompaniment. Again, Mahler's treatment lacks any kind of unity, strength of purpose, or unifying structure. Starting with the short piano prelude, which boldly modulates from D flat to C major in less than two bars and settles heavily in the latter key with a textbook cadence, Mahler seems to have no idea where he is going. Not only does he fail to impose a coherent structure on the song, but the elation he no doubt felt at his newly acquired harmonic techniques has led him to display them unnecessarily in a strange combination of wild daring and servile devotion to conservatory rules. Donald Mitchell has rightly pointed out the languid character of the music, but its morbid and sensuous Wagnerian harmonies of altered chords and yearning suspensions are even more surprising since they have so little to do with the text.

The little solo recitative in the accompaniment may conceivably anticipate the flexible arabesques that adorn the principal melodies in Mahler's last works, from the *Eighth Symphony* on. However, given the unsure style and hasty workmanship of these fragments, it would be unfair to take them too seriously. It is doubtful that Mahler devoted more than a few hours to each, abandoning them when he felt that they were leading nowhere. If they served any useful purpose, these songs may have convinced him that such "free" treatment was utterly unsuited to song writing, which requires the most subtle and controlled workmanship.

E) *PIANO FOUR-HAND FRAGMENT* of the Scherzo of the *FIRST SYMPHONY.* (*Fröhlich bewegt;* 3/4; A major). Was this a transcription or the original version of the movement? The *"Ringel, ringel Reih'n"* motive from *Hans und Grethe* (or *Maitanz im Grünen*), which opens the Scherzo, suggests a later date than that of the song, which is 1880, even though the fragment was found among Alma Mahler's *"Frühe Kompositionen"* folder. Guido Adler claims that Mahler sketched a "Symphony No. 1" in 1885, but the existence of an earlier scherzo is of course possible, as this fragment seems to prove. Except for a few small details, the fragment is identical to the beginning of the present Scherzo. *"Fröhlich bewegt"* was of course later changed to *"Kräftig bewegt."*

One other fragment from an early work has survived in a mature one, the first bars of the Nietzsche lied from the *Third Symphony "O Mensch."* Mahler claimed to have composed them for an unspecified work while still at the Iglau Gymnasium, "but thereafter," he said to Natalie in 1899, "[the music] became quite trivial."[21]

## FINISHED WORKS

1) 3 LIEDER for tenor and piano. The manuscript of these songs is in the Rosé
Collection. The title page reads as follows:

JOSEPHINEN ZUGEEIGNET
5 LIEDER
(Für Tenorstimme)
von
GUSTAV MAHLER

1. Im Lenz                    4.
2. Winterlied                 5.
3. Maitanz im Grünen

The last two songs were probably never composed, possibly because the break
with Josephine and the Poisl family occurred soon after *"Maitanz im Grünen"*
was finished in Vienna. Mahler, who was then busy with the *Klagende Lied*,
may then have abandoned the idea of completing the cycle, which he had
probably intended as an Easter present for the young girl. The manuscript is very
clear: it is obviously a clean copy of the original sketches.

a) *"IM LENZ."* The first song is dated February 19, 1880, and is based on the
following poem:

*Sag' an, du Träumer am lichten Tag,*
*Was willst du heut' mit dem Bangen?*
*Du wandelst so stumm durch Lenz und Hag,*
*Als wärst du von Blindheit befangen.*

*"Ich bin nicht blind und sehe doch nicht,*
*Mir ist nicht dunkel und ist nicht licht,*
*Könnt' lachen und könnte weinen,*
*Doch sagen könnt' ich es Keinem."*

*O sieht dich die Sonne so freundlich an,*
*Was sollen dir Schmerz und Reue!*
*Wirf ab deine Last, du trauriger Mann,*
*Und freu'dich an Sonne und Bläue.*

*"Mich freut keine Sonne, mich freut kein Blau*
*Und hab' doch den Frühling so gerne,*
*Ach, die ich allein nur am liebsten erschau,*
*Die weilt schon lang in der Ferne."*

O tell me, dreamer in midday's light
The cause of thy boundless terrors,
Of the silent wandering through vernal groves
As though struck with blindness.

"I am not blind and yet I see not
I see no darkness and yet no light,
So close to laughter, so close to tears
That my lips can utter no word!"

Does the Sun's friendly smile not cheer thee?
Let thy sorrow be, regret no more!
Cast away thy burden, thou sorrowful man,
And rejoice in the sun and the sky

"No sun can warm me, no sky cheer me,
Yet Spring does fill my heart with joy
Ah! she alone who delights my eye
Tarries so long and so far from here."

The poem is of course a secret message to Josephine, who was then in Iglau, and who, at her parents' request, had stopped writing to the despairing Mahler. The style and content of the poem, the contrast between nature's beauty and man's sorrow, are of course typically romantic and can also be found in the *Lieder eines fahrenden Gesellen,* which Mahler wrote four years later under similar circumstances.

KEY: F major/D flat. TEMPO: *Sehr lebhaft; Noch einmal so langsam.*

TIME SIGNATURE: 4/4. Although not the longest (fifty-three bars), *"Im Lenz"* has by far the strangest modulations of the two "art songs" of the group (No. 3, *"Maitanz,"* or *"Hans und Grethe"* as it was later called, is not a lied but a folk-style *Gesang*). As in the early song fragments, the key changes constantly, from F major to A minor, and back again to F, then to A flat major/minor (*Noch einmal so langsam*), F minor, C major (*Wie im Anfang*). But strangest of all is the key structure of the last stanza, which is a varied and shortened restatement of the second. Starting from C, Mahler seems to be aiming for C sharp. But just as one expects the song to close in this key, there is an enharmonic modulation to D flat and an unexpected conclusion on an A flat major chord, clearly a dominant, because of the preceding G flat in the bass.

The two main tempos characterize the poem's two protagonists, the "questioner" and the "daydreamer." On the upbeat, a fast piano scale (forte-pianissimo) gives the initial impetus to an accompaniment of repeated chords in triplets. The voice enters at the end of the first bar with a melody that is neither very Mahlerian nor particularly appealing. When, after thirteen bars, the tempo slows down and the "daydreamer" speaks, Mahler quotes an entire passage from the *Klagende Lied,* starting *"O Wunder, was da nun begann,"* which he transposes from D flat to A flat major.

The soprano entry in the eighth bar (No. 22 in the Universal Edition score) is
transposed down one octave to suit the vocal range of a tenor, but aside from this
the two passages are identical. In February–March 1880, Mahler was hard at work
on the *Klagende Lied*. Momentarily setting this aside, he probably adapted from it
a passage that more or less fitted the words of his poem, perhaps in the interest
of speed. The song as a whole cannot be called a success. Although related to
the one borrowed from the *Klagende Lied*, the main theme is not of the same
quality. In addition, the four sections are too short and too strongly contrasted
to make a satisfactory whole.

b) *"WINTERLIED"* (February 27, 1880). Luckily this second song is quite another matter. Longer (seventy-four bars), more substantial, it is much more carefully worked out, although the poem is even more naïve and folklike:

| | |
|---|---|
| *Über Berg und Tal* | Through hill and vale |
| *Mit lautem Schall* | The echoes everywhere |
| *Tönet ein Liedchen.* | Loudly repeat my song |
| *Durch Schnee und Eis* | Through snow and ice |
| *Dringt es so heiss* | Making its way |
| *Bis zu dem Hüttchen.* | To the warm cottage |
| *Wo das Feuer brummt,* | Where the fire hisses |
| *Wo das Rädchen summt* | And the spinning wheel hums |
| *Im traulichen Stübchen.* | In warm and cozy rooms |
| *Um den Tisch herum* | Around the big table |
| *Sitzen sie stumm.* | They are seated in silence. |
| *Hörst du mich, Liebchen?* | Does my sweetheart hear me? |
| | |
| *Im kalten Schnee,* | In ice and snow |
| *Sieh' wie ich steh',* | See where I stand |
| *Sing' zu dir Mädchen!* | Singing to thee, my love! |
| *Hat denn mein Lied* | Was it my song |
| *So dich erglüht* | Which reddened thy cheek, |
| *Oder das Rädchen?* | Or the spinning wheel? |
| *O liebliche Zeit* | O sweet, happy times |
| *Wie bist du so weit* | So far away and now lost |
| *O selige Stunden . . .* | Sweet hours of bliss . . . |
| *Ach nur ein Blick,* | In a fleeting instant, |
| *War unser Glück* | Our joy was over |
| *Ewig verschwunden.* | And lost forever. |

Once again, the poem is autobiographical and intended as a message of love for Josephine, far away in Iglau while Gustav was pining in Vienna. However, the poem must have been hastily composed, for it is unskillful in form and somewhat incoherent. In the first stanza, the "little song" makes its way "through hill and vale" to the beloved's cottage, while in the second, the absent lover is already standing under her window. At the end of the first stanza, who are "they" who sit around the table in silence? The girl's family no doubt, but their appearance is puzzling, to say the least. While the winter landscape is cheerful enough, with the snow, the firelit rooms, the spinning wheel, and the rosy-cheeked sweetheart, the melancholy evocation of the past comes as a complete surprise at the end. Luckily Mahler the composer far surpasses Mahler the poet.
TEMPO: *Leicht bewegt* (gently animated), *Durchaus im gleichen Zeitmass* (always at the same tempo), *Ernst doch ruhig* (serious but calm).
TIME SIGNATURE: 6/8 changing here and there to 9/8, until the second stanza, which remains in 9/8 until the piano coda.
KEY: rather than modulating constantly, as in the early song fragments and in *"Im Lenz"*, Mahler seems to have his tonalities better organized. After an A major beginning, he modulates to C major and minor, then to E flat, and later embarks on a series of expressive modulations, a kind of development section that well suits the serious and melancholy last lines. Several keys are touched

upon: E flat, C minor, E flat minor, G flat major, and D flat, until Mahler finally settles in F minor and concludes with a coda, in the same key but in major, based on the opening section.

This time Mahler observed one of the basic rules of lieder composition, devising a (five-bar) melody that the piano states in sixths at the very beginning. This melody and its opening motif recur many times and serve as a unifying principle. Its gently rocking motion gives it a lullaby character, yet the part writing and the appoggiatura on a raised supratonic chord keeps it far removed from the style of the folk song. It is perhaps closer to Mendelssohn than to Schumann or Brahms, particularly in the continuous sixteenth-note motion that is established in the bass at the end of the first section (*"zu dem Hüttchen"*) and suggests both the fire's hiss and the spinning wheel's hum. Yet, in the same passage, the three marchlike pizzicato dominant-tonic motifs in the bass assert Mahler's personality more clearly than any other feature of this song. Even more Mahlerian is the corresponding passage at the end of the following section (*"Hörst du mich, Liebchen?"*), where a similar pattern in the bass accompanies a typical major-minor transition to the middle section, *Ernst doch ruhig.* This section is entirely based on a new motif, stated just a few bars earlier and later interspersed with reminders of the first. The intimate atmosphere, the expressive modulations, and the seventh chords are all very reminiscent of Schumann, yet the episode has a charm all its own. After a long descent on an F minor diminished seventh chord, Mahler returns to the original motif. This is developed into a lovely sixteen-bar piano coda, in which the syncopation, the part writing, the subtle rhythmic changes from 6/8 to 3/4 display a degree of craftsmanship far superior to any of his previous known works. *"Maitanz im Grünen"* was of course to confirm this growing mastery, but in quite another realm, that of the little folk-style *Gesang,* as opposed to the Schumann-Brahms type of art song represented by the two other lieder.

c) *"MAITANZ IM GRÜNEN"* (March 1880). This song is the original version of Mahler's earliest published lied, *Hans und Grethe,* No. 3 (or c) in the first book of *Lieder und Gesänge* (Schott, 1892). Paul Stefan has traced its origin to a chorus in *Rübezahl,* but the surviving libretto includes a quintet sung to the same words by Emma's five companions at the beginning of Act IV. The original *Rübezahl* libretto was undoubtedly written several months before *"Maitanz,"* but Mahler may have composed the two versions of the music, the song and the quintet, almost simultaneously, as he did when he borrowed from *Das klagende Lied* for the first of these songs and later on with *"Des Antonius"* and the Scherzo of the *Second Symphony.*

There are only slight differences between the published and unpublished versions of the song. *"Maitanz"* is in D major, while *"Hans und Grethe"* is in F in the original ms. copy that Mahler made for his sister, simply because the high C in the final version would be dangerously high for a tenor (the published song has an optional one octave lower). The tempo marking for *"Maitanz"* is *"Lustig und keck. In Zeitmass eines Ländlers"* [Gay and pert. In ländler rhythm], while in *"Hans"* it reads *"Im gemächlichen Walzertempo"* [in measured waltz tempo]. Textual differences are slight. Mahler has added a small asymmetric touch by cutting out the dominant upbeat before the first bar, the accompaniment has been altered slightly here and there, with occasional note doublings or added voices, but it is generally simpler and lighter in the later version. Like the two other Poisl songs, *"Maitanz"* has a pianissimo close, which in the original version was marked *"murmelnd"* [murmuring], *"sich verlierend"* [gradually vanishing], and finally *"wie aus der Ferne"* [as from a distance].

In 1900, Mahler told Natalie that *"Hans und Grethe"* was the first of his songs that he found worthy of publication,[22] and it is indeed a little gem. Number one in a series of folklike lieder and scherzos in the form of ländler, it is the source of two important motifs in the Scherzo of the *First Symphony*. Mahler later recalled having written both the text and music of the second stanza one evening before going to bed. He then woke up in the middle of the night, the first and last stanzas suddenly clear in his mind, and he wrote them down as well. The next morning he was so pleased with the result that he "did not find a single note to change." There is one major inaccuracy in this story: *"Hans und Grethe"* contains two, rather than three, stanzas, but this is not the first time Mahler's memory played a trick on him. It proves in any case (unless the incident refers to the composition of another song) that the lied preceded the *Rübezahl* quintet.

Although Mahler himself was no doubt responsible for calling the song *"Volkslied"* in the first edition, the poem and the music are undoubtedly his own, although both are obviously inspired by the genuine folk style. Only here and there does Mahler introduce a discreet "artistic" touch: a five-bar phrase, the "echo" effects in the accompaniment at the beginning of the second stanza, the brief diminuendo postlude, and the short modulation to the key of the flatted mediant (A flat in the F major version) at the end of the first page.

*"Maitanz"* (or *"Hans und Grethe"*) is a strophic *Tanzlied* of the simplest kind, with a characteristic tonic pedal running through most of the song and a held fifth, which creates a drone-bass effect. There is practically no difference between the two stanzas. The octave portamento upbeat, in which the inexperienced singer "searches" for the right high note, is typical of "folk" singing. The heavily accented first beats, the harsh and "clumsy" dissonances, the wide melodic leaps all combine to create a musical idiom that, although strongly influenced by folk music, is thoroughly new and original. Particularly Mahlerian are the dominant-tonic intervals in the bass and small gruppetto-like figures such as the *"schlinge sich"* in the first line. These motifs return to their starting point, as does the main theme of the first of the *Gesellen Lieder* and *"O Wunder"* from *Das klagende Lied* (see above, 1A). Consequently this unassuming little *Gesang* is far more important in Mahler's work than its naïve folk-style character suggests. Like its contemporary, the more ambitious *Das klagende Lied*, it is the origin of a whole new world of sound.

2) *DAS KLAGENDE LIED* for solo voices, mixed chorus, and orchestra. The complete poem, dated March 18, 1878, was inserted by Mahler in the three-movement orchestral score, which belonged until recently to Alfred Rosé.[23] The composition proper, a task he later described to Natalie as "herculean toil," seems to have lasted about two years.[24] Mahler worked on the score when he returned from Hall. He then finished the final part and polished the last details of the score, which was ready in November 1880.[25]

THE MANUSCRIPTS. There are five different manuscripts of *Das klagende Lied*: 1) A short sketch of *Der Spielmann*, Part 1 in the final version (from now on it will be alluded to by this title, although Mahler later eliminated it), dated March 21, 1880, on the last page.[26] Some sections, such as the orchestral prelude, are sketched in detail, with certain orchestral indications, whereas others provide only the bare essentials of the vocal parts and the accompaniment is written in a kind of musical stenography. Some of the most subtle features of the orchestration already exist in this sketch. Mahler's haste becomes discernible toward the end, where the manuscript is just barely decipherable. The coda is much shorter and less elaborate than the version we know.

2) A complete orchestral sketch of *Hochzeitstück*, dated October–November 1880, which used to belong to Alma Mahler. Under "Part 3" a 4 is still clearly legible, which means that Mahler at one time thought of composing an additional part.

3) A manuscript orchestral score of *Der Spielmann*, which is complete, except for the thirty-one bars of the prelude (in the Vienna Stadtbibliothek). This is probably the first orchestral score. The margins are filled with doodles and calligraphic names—friends of Mahler's (Kralik, Steiner), cities (Teplitz), etc. Differences between this orchestral sketch and the final version are slight.

4) A complete orchestral score of the original three-part version in a copyist's hand, but with many annotations by Mahler. This undoubtedly dates from the same year, and it is this copy that Mahler used when he revised the work in Hamburg. (This is the ms. that now belongs to the Yale University Library, Osborn Collection.)

5) A complete orchestral autograph of the final version in two parts, probably dating from 1898. (This manuscript formerly belonged to Alma Mahler.)

REVISIONS. Two unpublished letters from the Rosé Collection have finally revealed the correct date of the first revision, about which early biographical sources and Mahler's own statements often differ. Guido Adler places it in 1898, just before the 1899 publication,[27] and claims that the orchestration was revised after 1900. Yet Paul Decsey and Natalie clearly state that *Das klagende Lied* was first revised in Hamburg and that in 1898[28] Mahler restored certain elements of the original version, such as the offstage orchestra in *Hochzeitstück*. Consequently, there were at one time three different versions of the work, but only the first and last have survived.

An examination of the 1880 score of *Das klagende Lied* reveals a startling and previously unknown fact: although Mahler's inexperience as an orchestrator is occasionally revealed by some minor detail, the score as a whole differs very little from the published version. Consequently, at nineteen Mahler already possessed a fantastic command of the orchestra and an uncanny instinct for "new," striking, diversified, and highly contrasted orchestral sounds. Such knowledge and such precocious mastery are astounding in a young boy who had thus far conducted only operettas in the little wooden theater of a provincial spa.

Here are, in brief, the principal deductions that can be made from a study of the score:

1) Mahler's primary task in revising the score was to eliminate a few unnecessary doublings and many "romantic" tempo indications, such as *"Mit höllischer Wildheit"* (With hellish fury); to clarify a few passages; to decrease the number of soloists, and revise some instrumental details (one of these afterthoughts was to suppress the tam-tam). Only one passage was substantially

altered, that which prepares the first entry of the chorus in *Der Spielmann* (between Figures 14 and 15 in the orchestral score).

2) The score bears many later penciled annotations in Mahler's hand. These were no doubt made during the earliest revision. Even the first, previously unknown part is partially annotated, which proves that he did not immediately eliminate it.

3) Paul Decsey informs us that "In Hamburg, Mahler revised the score with the eyes of a conductor, simplified it and gave it its present form. If he had not been active in the theatre, he might have made a stage work out of it, but as a man of the theatre, symphonic art was more his domain."[29] The first part of this statement, obviously based on Mahler's own words, is substantiated by three letters to Justi. On December 5, 1892, Mahler wrote: "I am at present preparing *Das klagende Lied*, as I did *Titan*, so that the score may be ready for an eventual performance. You cannot imagine how time-consuming this is!" "I am now immersed in *Das klagende Lied*," he wrote again on the seventeenth, "and my task consists of making an 'intelligent copy' of the score, and perfecting every detail thanks to my experience as a conductor. Because I cannot find any major changes to make, you can imagine how amazed I am by this composition since I started working on it! It is so original and powerful that I can't understand how a young man of 20–21 could have penned it. The nuts that my tree produced at that time are perhaps the hardest to crack of all those I have offered to the world. God only knows if I will ever manage to have it performed! . . ."

4) The poem *Ballade vom Blonden und Braunen Reitersman,* which Mahler sent to Krisper in 1880,[30] is practically identical with the *Waldmärchen* poem.

THE POEM. Donald Mitchell's recent research has brought to light some new information concerning the literary sources of Mahler's text, which had previously been incompletely or inaccurately reported. Hans Holländer claims that, when Mahler was a child, one of the kitchen maids in the Mahler household sang a *"Ballade vom Brudermord."*[31] Ernst Otto Nodnagel suggests as a source Grimm's *Joringe und Joringel,* and Bruno Walter Grimm's *Der singende Knochen* [The Singing Bone]. Even Donald Mitchell devotes little space to what was probably Mahler's first and main source, Martin Greif's "poem" *Das klagende Lied*,[32] which was "performed" by the drama pupils at the Vienna Conservatory on May 3, 1876, while Mahler was studying there. Martin Greif was the pen name of Friedrich Hermann Frey, an obscure Bavarian poet, author of verse dramas and patriotic poems, who was born in Speyer on June 18, 1839, lived in Vienna and Munich, and died in Kufstein on April 1, 1911. Of his works, only *Das klagende Lied*,[33] a five-page narrative poem or ballad, seems to have achieved a certain renown. It was revised by the author several times and set to music by various composers. The final version supposedly dates from 1869, yet Greif wrote another still later in Vienna.[34] The dramatic version performed at the Vienna Conservatory, probably in Mahler's presence, has not survived. Although it may well have provided the inspiration for the project, Greif's long-winded poem was in fact scarcely utilized by Mahler in his own text. True to Wagnerian tradition, he made a thorough and scholarly study of the poem's literary sources, as he also did for *Rübezahl,* and thus found a wide range of inspiration in the rich world of folk legend.

The title *Das klagende Lied* appears for the first time in a tale by Ludwig

Bechstein (1801–60), one of the many romantic writers to assemble an anthology of folk legends. Bechstein himself knew that the tale resembled two Grimm stories, *Der singende Knochen* and *Von dem Machandelboom*, the first of which particularly influenced Mahler. Divided into three episodes, Mahler's text can be summarized as follows:

a) *WALDMÄRCHEN* (Forest Legend). A proud young queen promises her hand to whoever is brave enough to search the forest for a certain red flower. Two brothers, one good and one evil, engage in the quest. The good brother finds the flower, sticks it in his hat, and lies down to sleep under a willow tree. The evil brother finds him, murders him in his sleep and snatches the flower. The body of the young man remains under the tree, where it is slowly buried under leaves and flowers.

b) *DER SPIELMANN* (The Minstrel). A traveling minstrel happens to pick up a bone that glistens among the dead leaves. He carves a flute out of it and starts playing. To his amazement, the flute assumes the dead brother's "plaintive" (*klagende*) voice and intones the story of the murder.

c) *HOCHZEITSTÜCK* (Wedding Piece). The inhabitants of the royal castle are rejoicing in honor of the queen's wedding. With his magic flute, the minstrel comes to the castle gates and once again recounts the murder. The guilty king in turn seizes the instrument and plays. The flute repeats its accusation, the queen faints, the guests flee, and the walls of the castle crumble to the ground.

In Bechstein's tale, the only source for Greif's poem, the rivals are brother and sister, and the succession to the crown is at stake. The princess is murdered by her younger brother. Later, a young shepherd minstrel carves a flute, whose song accuses the murderer in a child's voice. A wandering knight then takes the flute and plays it for the queen mother, who is still in mourning for her child. To avenge her daughter, the queen herself then plays the flute before the whole court. The tale ends as in Mahler's version.

Mahler's idea of replacing the brother and sister with two brothers comes from Grimm's *Der singende Knochen*. His story is simpler, more naïve perhaps than Bechstein's, but also more logical (the quests in medieval poems are generally pursued by two knights, rather than by a boy and a girl) and more effective. The guilt-ridden pair of the *Hochzeitstück*, a Hamlet-like situation, may also have aroused the imagination of the composer, an ardent admirer of Shakespeare since childhood. Not only is this version more dramatic, but the contrast between the bridal rejoicing and the secret tragedy in the royal palace provided the composer with superb musical possibilities, comparable to the Finale of *Rübezahl*.

Mahler's literary style is of course closely modeled on romantic ballads of medieval inspiration. Generally speaking, his libretto supports the score effectively, despite its many naïvetés and obvious weaknesses, such as the rhetorical questions: "Why is the bridegroom so pale and silent?" or again: "Why did you deal a deathblow to my young life?" Whatever the qualities of this text, it is not surprising that Franz Liszt should have thought little of its "artlessness" and decreed that "the poem was not such as to guarantee the success of the work."[35]

GENERAL STRUCTURE. Most of Mahler's biographers have claimed that *Das klagende Lied* was originally conceived for the stage.[36] Mahler himself once confirmed this, telling Paul Decsey that he originally thought of it as a *Mär-chenspiel* (fairy-tale opera).[37] Many features in the work as it now stands are clearly of theatrical origin—for instance the style of the two preludes, the optional child's voice for the flute narrative, the dramatic wedding feast, the offstage orchestra, the division of the original score into three parts—yet Mahler obviously abandoned this original plan in the initial stages, even before he wrote his 1878 poem, which does not fulfill any of the requirements of an opera libretto. Fritz Egon Pamer has pointed out its resemblance to folk ballads in that it lacks unity of place, the settings are not even specified, except for the forest in the newly discovered first part. The characters are not individualized by a particular voice and the soloists have no defined roles. The voices are generally used only for purely musical reasons. The half-epic, half-dramatic style, with narrative solos and choral commentary, is that of Martin Greif's poem[38] and also that of the folk ballad. *Das klagende Lied* is therefore a cantata, but a Wagnerian *"durchkomponiert"* cantata, lacking clear-cut recitatives, arias, and choruses.

*WALDMÄRCHEN.* KEY: A minor, with many modulations, ending in F sharp minor.
TIME SIGNATURE: 4/4 changing several times to alla breve.
TEMPO: *Langsam und träumerisch* (slow and dreamy)—*Lebhafter* (faster); ritenuto; *Immer im gemächlichen Zeitmass* (always in moderate tempo); *Zurückhaltend,* etc.

The manuscript score of the original first part of *Das klagende Lied* (written out by a copyist) has seventy pages of full score, as opposed to forty-four for *Der Spielmann* and sixty for *Hochzeitstück.* In style and workmanship this first piece is somewhat less polished than the others. Mahler was probably working on it when he sent the text to Krisper in the early months of 1880, but perhaps it was sketched earlier if, as Mahler later told Decsey, he worked on the whole score for two years. He seems to have changed his mind several times concerning the soloists: in the 1880 score (from here on referred to as "OR"), the word "tenor" is sometimes crossed out and replaced by "baritone," and there are occasionally two tenor parts, raising the number of soloists to six. One of Mahler's decisions in 1893 was to suppress the baritone part, which was quite important in *Der Spielmann.*

The complete original score of *Das klagende Lied,* and in particular the *Waldmärchen,* has been analyzed in detail by Jack Diether,[39] who points out all the thematic relationships between the various parts. Now that *Waldmärchen* has been found, performed, and recorded, the question that inevitably comes to mind is: why did Mahler suppress it in 1893, and why did he maintain his decision in 1898? Jack Diether has offered a possible explanation, based on psychological insights, an explanation that had already been suggested by Donald Mitchell some years ago, based on Mahler's alteration of the Bechstein story. From Grimm's *Singende Knochen,* which has little to do with the Bechstein tale, in that it deals with an old king, a boar hunt, and three princes, Mahler borrowed the idea of changing the brother and sister into two brothers.

Using methods of contemporary psychoanalysis, Diether draws a parallel between the brothers' relationship and Mahler's own feelings toward his brother Ernst, whose death in 1874 deeply affected him. Ernst was ten months younger than Gustav, and psychiatrists are aware of the jealousy that older children sometimes feel toward their juniors, whom they fear will deprive them of their parents' affection. Theodor Reik has already suggested that conscious or unconscious memories of his brother's death may have motivated Mahler to set the *Kindertotenlieder* to music; one of Rückert's children, whose death is the subject of these poems, was also named Ernst. If Mahler had had suppressed feelings of remorse after Ernst's death, he might have unconsciously chosen the murder of one brother by another as a subject. This would explain why he altered the Bechstein story.[40] Twelve years later, while revising the score, Mahler might, for the very same reasons, have suppressed *Waldmärchen*, which contains the murder scene. Furthermore, Diether suggests that a connection can be made between this deletion and Otto's suicide in 1895, but such a theory is untenable since the revision took place two years earlier.[41]

There is in my opinion a strong argument against attributing *Waldmärchen*'s suppression to Mahler's unconscious feelings of remorse: the entire work, not just the first part, is concerned with the good brother's murder by the evil one; the story is repeated three times by the flute's accusing voice. Why would Mahler's guilt feelings lead him to suppress just the first part of the story, the only one, as a matter of fact, in which the words "murder" or "death" are not uttered?

From the "dramatic" point of view, Diether claims that *Waldmärchen*'s absence weakens the original plot by introducing it through a "secondary" character, the minstrel. But can the minstrel really be considered a secondary character? The central action starts with the discovery of the flute, and everything preceding it can be considered a prologue. Jack Diether has given other and more persuasive reasons for restoring *Waldmärchen* to its former place. Speaking of the symphonic construction of the whole work, he points out the use of a number of key motifs that provide a common musical substance for the three parts and the flashbacks in the two remaining parts, which are identifiable as such only when *Waldmärchen* has also been performed. In his view, therefore, not only is the whole "arch-like structure" emphasized when the work is heard in its totality, but it provides a "richer musical experience," as well as becomes a "more viable and moving musico-dramatic one." With its A minor ending recalling a beginning in the same key, it comes full circle rather than half-circle as before.

Diether's detailed analysis need not be quoted here, for anyone acquainted with the final version will immediately notice that *Waldmärchen* uses the same thematic material. Rather than finding this a strong argument in favor of the restoration, I personally believe that it explains precisely why Mahler excluded the earlier first part from his final version. To explain *Waldmärchen*'s suppression, Professor Alfred Rosé, the former owner of the first manuscript score, has advanced the thesis that the length and "extravagance" of the original work seemed to preclude any concert performance. It does in fact increase the total length of the work by twenty-five or thirty minutes. Yet length in itself was never, in Mahler's style, an insurmountable barrier. In 1898, when he revised *Das klagende Lied* for the last time, he had already managed to perform and publish the longer *Second Symphony*. Yet, like every great composer, he knew that a work lacking contrasts can *seem* longer than it is. Except for the murder at the end, the events depicted in *Waldmärchen* are all of an idyllic nature. Therefore, the music is lyrical and pastoral and contains little material that is neither developed nor restated more concisely later on. Now dramatic intensity is generally one of Mahler's greatest qualities as a composer. It is fully evident in the second and third parts, where the scenes are violent and colorful and the forces of revenge and destiny are powerfully evoked. However, this intensity all springs from the conclusion of the first part, *i.e.*, the murder. Thus the newly discovered music, lovely as it is, is essentially dreamy, static, and somewhat spineless. In my view, two motifs are seriously overused in it: the horn fanfare in the seventh bar and the descending scale that recurs between each section. Furthermore the powerful, original, concise, dramatic *Spielmann* Prelude provides the work with a much stronger and more characteristic opening than the drawn-out "forest murmurs" and distant horn fanfares in the much longer *Waldmärchen* Prelude.

Although Jack Diether has accurately pointed out the thematic relationship between the three parts, in my opinion he gives too much emphasis to their thematic logic. Mahler was not yet the powerful musical mind and the great symphonist that he was to become later. His thematic elaboration is not so inevitable or so thoroughly based on the laws of an obvious (or hidden) musical logic, precluding literal restatements. His style is still free and modeled on textual requirements, adapted from the Wagnerian theater; the motifs appear and reappear more or less like characters on the stage. Some of them were originally meant to be heard as flashbacks, but this seems like a weak argument compared to one at least of the unhappy results of restoring: that of telling at great length the simple story of the murder, which will be later retold three times in the "flute songs" and thus weakening the general effect of the work.

Thus there is no doubt in my mind that Mahler made the cut for purely musical reasons. He had strong feelings about key relationships and the contrasts required to avoid monotony within a given work. He often regretted not having established such contrasts between the first movements of the *Second Symphony,* and admitted to Natalie that he cut the *First Symphony's* Andante largely out of such considerations. I personally believe that his reasons for eliminating *Waldmärchen* were even more fundamental. A reference, in an 1899 conversation, to the "present first part" proves that he was still very much aware of the former one but did not consider restating it. *Waldmärchen* certainly deserves to be performed occasionally, because it contains some lovely music and also some that anticipates later Mahlerian works. Yet he left it out of the final 1898 version, and his decision should not be reversed, if only because his judgment of his own work has invariably proved so excellent.

THE FINAL VERSION

The former titles were probably discarded by Mahler in 1893 and the work entitled in its final version:

DAS KLAGENDE LIED (in 2 Abteilungen) [in two parts]

PART I (formerly called *DER SPIELMANN*).
KEY: C minor, with many modulations.
TIME SIGNATURE: Alla breve (with several changes).
TEMPO MARKING: *Sehr Gehalten* (Very moderate) (OR: *Mit sehr geheimnis-vollen Ausdruck* [With very mysterious feeling]). The Chorale melody (thirteen bars after Figure 4) is marked "Religioso."

The Prelude is conceived as a genuine opera overture, and it reveals the miraculous mastery of form that Mahler had attained by the age of nineteen. As has already been noted, he later made only slight changes in the orchestration. A small but typical alteration occurs in the instrumental accompaniment to the first contralto narration. The words *"biem Weidenbaum"* were originally accompanied in unison by the horn, which Mahler later replaced by a flute playing in its lowest register. Only years of orchestral experience could have suggested such a bold choice. The original score reveals one important afterthought, dating from 1893. After the alto solo has described the carving of the flute, the short orchestral interlude based on the first theme ends with bare octaves in the low brass and strings. After a short rest, the G flat suddenly descends to F with tremendous dramatic effect. This new transition to the pianissimo chorus is infinitely more effective than the suppressed passage: a short tenor solo *"O Spielmann,"* supported by a long kettledrum roll, a sequence of sudden modulations and the recurrence of a passage from *Waldmärchen,* with horn calls, bird trills, and a triangle imitating "distant bells." Thus the B flat minor (instead of G sharp minor in OR) unexpected entrance of the chorus in the new version has a magical effect and prefigures the choral entry in the *Second Symphony* Finale.

Mahler changed his mind several times about the use of a child's voice in the "flute songs." In the first sketch his intention was to double the alto solo with a child's voice offstage. In the 1880 version, the first and last "songs" are entrusted to a child and the second (page 89 in the Universal Edition pocket score) combines a child's voice with the soprano solo (replacing the alto voice that he had also considered). Still hesitating in the final version, Mahler noted for the first flute song: "To be sung when possible by a child." Nevertheless he himself does not seem to have used a child in the 1901 and 1902 performances. He wrote instead in 1902 to an unnamed alto (either Hermine Kittel or Edyth Walker, both of whom participated in that year's performance) asking her "to accept this very small part because it is all-important for me that the 'child's voice' be different from that of the narrating contralto."[42] The last flute song in *Hochzeitstück* is now entrusted to a soprano, the only important solo assigned to that voice. This was probably suggested by the Bechstein tale, in which, at this climactic moment, the young sister's voice speaks through the flute.

PART II (formerly called *HOCHZEITSTUECK*)
KEY: B flat, ending in A minor.
TIME SIGNATURE: 6/8, later alla breve alternating with 4/4 and a few more 6/8 passages.
TEMPO MARKING: *Heftig bewegt* (Lively, agitated) (OR: *Mit höllischer Wildheit* [With hellish frenzy]), later *Viel langsamer, langsam, Sehr gemessen, Sehr langsam und schleppend* (Much slower, slow, very moderate, very slow and drawn out).

The beginning is undoubtedly the most theatrical music known to have been written by Mahler. How well it would serve to start the third act of an opera, and what an opera it could have been! The influences of Weber and the young Wagner are of course obvious, but the liveliness, brilliance, and originality of the music are far more striking still. The minor horn fanfare (on the third page of the orchestral score) comes from *Waldmärchen;* its effect is in my opinion greatly heightened when it is heard as a new theme rather than a flash-back.

The offstage orchestra and separated instrumental groups are originally theatrical devices required by the stage action. One of the earliest, most famous, and effective examples is that of the trumpets in *Fidelio* (and the *"Leonore" Overture No. 3*). In *Das klagende Lied,* Mahler placed offstage a small wind band composed of "military" instruments, two flutes (if possible in D flat), piccolo, two oboes, two clarinets (one in E flat), four horns, two B flat trumpets (if possible flügelhorns), triangle, kettledrums, and cymbals. On the first page of OR he carefully explained his intentions: "In this piece, a small wind band should be placed offstage to suggest the sounds from the wedding, sometimes clearly brought by the wind and sometimes blown away. It is indicated in the score as ORCHESTRA B . . ." Further on, when the small orchestra starts to play, he adds: "When possible, double the instruments. The nuance markings should be observed in performance; the distance [*Entfernung*] should be so calculated that a forte reaches the listeners as a pianissimo and a fortissimo as a piano. The change-over from one orchestra to the other should be extremely precise, even when it is sudden."

When Mahler prepared the final version of *Das klagende Lied* in 1898, he remembered having eliminated the offstage orchestra in his earlier 1893 revision, fearing that the additional instruments would create one more obstacle to its performance. He then entrusted the "Orchestra B" music to the regular orchestra.[43] However, in 1898 he decided that the work's effect was thus weakened, and he restored the original distant band. The choice of "vulgar" instruments such as the E flat clarinet, the flügelhorn, and D flat flutes, is of course as important as the village band's "repertory," stylized folk music, which for the first time breaks into the sacred domain of art. The similarity between the band's second tune and that which is played by a similar group in the *First Symphony*'s "Huntsman's Funeral" has often been pointed out.

There are only a few slight differences between the 1880 and the 1898 version of *Hochzeitstück:* again there are some instrumental alterations, a line added here and there in the chorus part and a few markings eliminated that Mahler had finally found unnecessary or too romantic: for instance *"majestoso"* (*sic*) two bars after 51; *"Pause, lang und schauerlich* (Long and terrifying pause) just before 53; and *"Wild bewegt"* (With wild frenziedness) three bars after 68. There is a suggested cut at the end of the piece (from third bar after 78 to seventh after 82) which luckily Mahler did not in the end make, for it would have done away with one of the finest choral passages. The alternation between the two orchestras is a source of fascinating new sound effects: it is one of the first conscious uses of space in music. During its third intervention at a climactic moment (one bar after 69), the wind group plays a major-minor version of its original tune, thus the village musicians seem to be participating in the tragic events within the castle. The tenor solo's last intervention (*"Die Lichter verloschen"*) again quotes from *Waldmärchen* a theme that is no less effective for being heard for the first time.

Today, more than ever, it is clear that *Das klagende Lied* marks an important date in the history of music. For the first time, Mahler had discovered, in this work, the essential traits of his musical style, as well as his ardent nostalgia for the "lost paradise" of medieval Germany. The models for his cantata are easy to find in such works as Schumann's big choral ballads, *Der Königsohn,* Op. 116, and *Des Sängers Fluch,* Op. 139 (the first of these has wide melodic vocal leaps comparable to Mahler's *"Dess' muss ich ewig klagen!"*). Yet Mahler's characteristic style is everywhere present in *Das klagende Lied,* in the fanfares, the marches, the bass dominant-tonic ostinatos, the "open air" music, the chorale tunes, the major-minor alternations, the dotted rhythms, etc. Furthermore, speaking in more general terms, other Mahlerian features can be found in it, such as the combination of the macabre and the ironic, the "novelesque" style and dimensions (which Theodor Wiesengrund Adorno was the first to point out), the utter naïveté, combined with absolute sophistication, and finally the "evolutive" development, precluding literal restatement, which remains one of his most important innovations.

Mahler once said that all the "building bricks," all the material that an artist uses in his lifetime, are acquired by him during his youth. Similarly, Pierre Boulez[44] finds in *Das klagende Lied* the "one and only source" of Mahler's creative power, adding that all he did later was to elaborate upon this fundamental idea. In this respect the importance of *Das klagende Lied* can hardly be overestimated.

### 3) *5 LIEDER* for voice and piano (1880–83)

Guido Adler established a myth that was prolonged by several later biographers, *i.e.,* that Mahler's first book of *Lieder und Gesänge* was issued by Schott in 1885, seven years before the others. The printing plates themselves prove that all three were printed within a few weeks of each other early in 1892. They were all reviewed in the monthly Hofmeister report of printed music,[45] and the Stanford Library has a copy of Volume I inscribed in Mahler's hand: February 8, 1892. Unfortunately, the lieder are undated, and the only known manuscript to date is the copy made by Mahler for his sister Justine, probably later. According to Guido Adler, who may well have asked Mahler himself, they were composed in Vienna and Iglau "in and around 1883," after Mahler left Laibach (April 1, 1882) and before he started his work in Olmütz (January 1883). Adler's date is consistent with other known facts, for after this last date, Mahler had little free time. He was too busy to compose in Olmütz, even more so in Kassel, and between these two engagements, most of his two months' freedom were devoted to Merelli's Italian opera stagione.

Contrary to the works that precede and follow them in Mahler's production, these four songs (discounting *"Hans und Grethe,"* which is identical with the 1880 *"Maitanz"*) were not composed in a moment of crisis. Nor are they as intense and charged with autobiographical meaning as most of Mahler's other early works. Judging by the musical style and the workmanship, it would be logical to assign an earlier date to the *Tirso de Molina Lieder* than to the *Leander Lieder,* which they follow in both the Schott edition and the Rosé manuscript.

### a) *"FRÜEHLINGSMORGEN"* (Spring Morning)

Richard Leander was the pen name of a physician named Richard von Volkmann, the author of a small volume of verse published in Leipzig in 1878 and entitled simply *Gedichte.*[46] The two poems set to music by Mahler come from the *Kleine Lieder* (Nos. 9 and 19), dated 1854–56, without any further title. The reasons for Mahler's choice are easy to discern. *Früehlingsmorgen* is naïve and folklike and resembles the *Wunderhorn* and Mahler's own early poems, whereas *Erinnerung* is refined and intimate like Heine or Mahler's favorite romantic poet, Friedrich Rückert. Mahler often declared himself loath to set great poems to music, because they were already self-sufficient.

KEY: F major[47] (same as "low" version published by Schott)

TIME SIGNATURE: 6/8 with two 3/8 bars.

TEMPO: *Gemächlich, leicht bewegt* (Measured, gently animated). The title is Mahler's, but the original text is followed much more closely than is usual in his songs. The only differences are:

| | | |
|---|---|---|
| line 1: | or: *An die Scheiben* | M: *An das Fenster* |
| line 10: | or: *Und dein fleissig Lieb'* | M: *Und dein munteres Lieb'* |
| last line: | | M: *Steh'auf* (repeated from the beginning) |

FORM: Strophic *"durchkomponiert"*: the two stanzas are closely connected thematically, but the second quickly modulates to the flattened submediant key and from then on the music is different. As is often the case in Mahler's lieder, the accompanying figure in broken chords is used as a unifying element. The final diminuendo coda is based on the first bars of the prelude. Melodically speaking, the ninth in the pianist's right hand, based on the superposition of two fifths, is particularly striking. There is a gentle suggestion of ländler rhythm, which, together with the naïve mood, the "bird trills," and the fourth and fifth motifs, creates a typically Mahlerian climate. The workmanship is very skillful throughout: Mahler has come a long way in three years, since *"Im Lenz"* and *"Winterlied."*

### b) *"ERINNERUNG"*

KEY: G minor, ending in A minor (as in the high voice edition).

TIME SIGNATURE: 3/4.

TEMPO: *Langsam und sehnsüchtig* [Slow and nostalgic].

TEXT: There are no changes except for the placing of one word.

FORM: Simple three-part da capo, a form rarely used by Mahler. The second stanza is a kind of development section, with free modulations and a new melody connected to the earlier one by the same common accompaniment figure. It is followed by a long and intensely expressive chromatic descent, starting with the voice, later pursued by the accompaniment in a succession of two five-bar periods. The last stanza is a shortened restatement of the first, with the two earlier phrases inverted.

Schumann and Brahms are clearly Mahler's models for this song, which is probably the most Brahmsian of all his compositions. The poem must have awakened emotional memories, for the music is much more dramatic and expressive than the text. Although the chromaticism and the successive sevenths chords are exceptional in Mahler's work, the song is not unworthy of his pen and prefigures the masterpiece he wrote in 1901 in the same introspective vein: *"Ich bin der Welt."*

### c) *"HANS UND GRETHE"* (See above 1c.)

### d) *"SERENADE AUS DON JUAN"*

KEY: D flat (D in the high, and C in the low voice edition).

TIME SIGNATURE: 3/4.

TEMPO: *Leicht fliessend* [Smoothly flowing].

TEXT: The Spanish monk Fray Gabriel Téllez (1571?–1648?) wrote, under his pen name Tirso de Molina, about four hundred plays, some one hundred of which have survived. *El burlador de Sevilla o el convidado de piedra,* from which Mahler borrowed the poems for two songs, was the first to dramatize the famous Don Juan legend. In Laibach, Olmütz, and Kassel, Mahler was often called upon to conduct incidental music for various plays. Were these two songs at some time or other meant for the stage? The "wind" accompaniment suggested for *"Serenade,"* and the harp effects in *"Phantasie,"* would seem to suggest it. The Tirso play was in fact performed, probably for the first time in Germany, on October 28, 1887, in Leipzig, to celebrate the hundredth anniversary of Mozart's opera. Strangely enough, Mahler was no doubt present, for he was then conductor of the Leipzig Opera. It is nevertheless practically certain that his *Tirso Lieder* had been composed earlier. The translation Mahler used was not the first one, by C. A. Dohrn,[48] but a later version by Ludwig Braunfels.[49] The serenade is sung in the play's closing scene by one of Don Juan's servants, just before the famous invitation to supper. Mahler used Braunfels' translation verbatim.

FORM: The two Tirso de Molina songs are simple *Gesänge* rather than fullfledged lieder or art songs. *"Serenade"* is a simple three-part strophic song, with a free modulating middle stanza based on earlier material. The last stanza repeats the first, with a few small expressive alterations. The characteristic appoggiaturas and the subtle phrase construction are truly Mahlerian, yet, despite its splendid workmanship and a remote resemblance to one of Mahler's last and loveliest songs, *"Liebst du um Schönheit,"* it is perhaps the least original of all his lieder.

e) *"PHANTASIE AUS DON JUAN."* This song precedes *"Serenade"* in the Rosé manuscript, as it does in the play.
KEY: B minor (as in the high voice edition).
TIME SIGNATURE: 4/4.
TEMPO: *Träumerisch* [Dreamy]; *Etwas Langsamer* [Somewhat slower].
TEXT: Like *Serenade,* this poem is called *"Gesang"* in the play (Act I, Scene 21). It occurs in the scene in which the hero seduces a young fishing girl. Mahler has used the one stanza verbatim, but added another of his own:

> *Die Winde streifen so kühl umher,*
> *Erzählen leis' eine alte Mär'!*
> *Die See erglühet im Abendrot,*
> *Die Fischerin fühlt nicht Liebesnot*
> *Im Herzen, im Herzen!*

> The winds blow so freshly all around,
> They softly tell an old fairy tale!
> The sea glows red in the evening light,
> The fishermaid feels no love's torment
> In her heart, in her heart!

FORM: Together with *"Hans und Grethe,"* *"Phantasie"* is the simplest of all Mahler's songs. Only a few additional notes in the accompaniment, mainly octave doublings, differentiate the two otherwise identical stanzas. Although the song is obviously written in folk style, nonetheless the outline of its melody, the march rhythm, the fifth and fourth intervals in the voice, and the little melismas at the end of the two stanzas give it a typically Mahlerian flavor. Centered on the dominant, the melody has a modal, folklike character: Mahler is quickly discovering the style of his future *Wunderhorn Lieder*.

4) *4 LIEDER EINES FAHRENDEN GESELLEN* with Orchestra (1884)

The poem and the music for these songs were written (with piano) between Christmas, 1884, and January 1, 1885. Neither Liszt's songs, nor Berlioz's *Nuits d'été*, nor Mahler's other orchestral songs were conceived as true cycles, and the *Gesellen Lieder* are probably the first orchestral lieder cycle in musical history. The original autograph of the two last poems (formerly in Alma Mahler's collection) are dated December 15 and 19, 1884. Consequently the earlier date suggested by Paul Stefan and Guido Adler, and by Mahler himself in the 1897 first edition with piano, is obviously wrong. The cycle cannot even be considered to have been sketched earlier, for Mahler wrote in a letter to Löhr on January 1, 1885: "I have written a cycle of lieder that are all dedicated to her." There is no reason to believe that the two first poems were written before the others, or that the cycle was sketched earlier.

In the same letter Mahler speaks of "a cycle—six for the moment," yet there are only four songs. Did he destroy two, did he publish them elsewhere, or did he simply write the poems without setting them to music? The last assumption is the most plausible, for in 1896 Mahler gave Natalie the text of two further poems dated from December 1884: *"Die Sonne spinnt"* and *"Die Nacht blickt mild,"* admitting that "he had not set them to music." Before deciding that the cycle was to have an orchestral accompaniment and that each song was to exceed the normal length, it is understandable that Mahler should have considered writing more than four. He may well have realized later that he would not improve the cycle by adding to it.

An even more difficult problem is that of the original accompaniment to the cycle. Natalie claims to have seen Mahler "orchestrate" the cycle in Hamburg early in 1896, before the March 16 Berlin premiere. The earliest known orchestral manuscript, given by Mahler to Hermann Behn, is dated December 1895 and is now in the Mengelberg Foundation in Amsterdam. However, he wrote to a Hamburg critic on April 19, 1893, obviously enclosing the score of a *"Cycle of Gesänge* consisting of 4 ballads with orchestral accompaniment," called *Geschichte eines fahrenden Gesellen* (Story of a Traveling Wayfarer): "I would be particularly happy if I could have a chance to play this work to you myself, because my own personal interpretation would not be superfluous for a work of such unusual character."[50]

The autograph in the Rosé Collection is entitled:

Geschichte von einem "fahrenden Gesellen" in 4 Gesängen
für eine tiefe Stimme mit Begleitung des Orchesters
von Gustav Mahler
Clavierauszug zu 2 Händen
Lieder des fahrenden Gesellen—ein Cyclus

(Story of a *"fahrenden Gesellen"* in 4 songs for a low voice with orchestral accompaniment by G.M. Piano 2-hand version. Songs of the *fahrenden Gesellen* —a Cycle.)[51]

It has a richer and more elaborate piano accompaniment than the published 1897 version and it can therefore be considered either the original piano accompaniment or a transcription of an early orchestral version. Yet, according to Professor Rosé, this is not an original autograph, but a manuscript copy made by Mahler for his sister, who was particularly fond of these songs. Until the original 1884 manuscript comes to light,[52] one cannot be sure that Mahler actually wrote the songs with orchestral accompaniment. It seems likely that, after having composed the five *Humoresken* (*i.e.*, the first orchestral *Wunderhorn Lieder*) in 1892, he orchestrated the *Gesellen Lieder* shortly after. His intention must have been strengthened by the fact that he had already orchestrated most of the second lied and half of the fourth in the second and third movements of the *First Symphony* and knew how much better the songs would sound with orchestral accompaniment. Nevertheless the orchestration of the whole cycle was undoubtedly made long after the composition was completed, and 1884 cannot be cited.

When the *Lieder eines fahrenden Gesellen* were published, Mahler did not reveal the poet's name, possibly because the first poem was not entirely his own. However, the letter to Löhr quoted above proves not only that he was the author but that he had written them as passionate love messages to Johanna Richter. As early as 1921, the musicologist Siegfried Günther noticed a striking similarity between *Wenn mein Schatz Hochzeit macht* and two poems from *Des Knaben Wunderhorn* (see below). Fritz Egon Pamer later suggested that Mahler had consciously or unconsciously quoted from poems he had known in his youth or had read in a newspaper or an anthology (other than the *Wunderhorn*, which he discovered in Karl von Weber's library in Leipzig four years later). In any case these poems prove beyond a doubt that Mahler was already thoroughly acquainted with German folk poetry, of which he had made a thorough stylistic study.

Like the earlier Poisl lieder, these songs are built around a theme dear to the romantic imagination: a man deceived and ill-treated by fate wanders aimlessly in search of peace. Mahler himself often felt an exile among his fellow men. The contrast between nature's beauty and man's sorrow is another well-loved romantic theme. The cycle uses a few musical leitmotivs, small recurring figures like the gruppetto (see below), the descending and ascending fourth, and the ascending sixth. The prevalence of march rhythms is also typical of *"Wanderlieder,"* the model of which is found in the first song of Schubert's *Winterreise*.

### a) "WENN MEIN SCHATZ HOCHZEIT MACHT"

MANUSCRIPT: two complete autographs of the cycle are in existence: one, for piano and voice ( in the Rosé Collection), probably dating from the early nineties; one for voice and orchestra dated December 1895 (Mengelberg Stiftung, Amsterdam).

KEY: D minor, B flat, ending in G minor.

TIME SIGNATURE: 2/4, 6/8, 2/4 (several important rhythmic differences exist between the piano and orchestral versions).

TEMPO: *Leise und traurig bis zum Schluss* [Slow and sad until the end]; *Sanft Bewegt* (Gently animated) for middle section. (In the Weinberger piano score: Allegro—Langsam—Andante, Allegro, etc.; Moderato for middle 6/8 section.)

TEXT: The *Wunderhorn* text quoted below[53] has no title in the Arnim-Brentano anthology. It is made up of two different folk poems, one called *Horch, was kommt draussen rein* and another, from Posen, *Ach, Blümlein*. Mahler has used the *Wunderhorn* text practically word for word, adding several verses of his own.

| WUNDERHORN | MAHLER |
|---|---|
| *Wann mein Schatz Hochzeit macht,* | *Wenn mein Schatz Hochzeit macht,* |
| | *Fröhliche Hochzeit macht,* |
| *Hab' ich einen traurigen Tag,* | *Hab' ich meinen traurigen Tag!* |
| *Geh' ich in mein Kämmerlein,* | *Geh' ich in mein Kämmerlein, dunkles* |
| | *Kämmerlein* |
| *Wein' um meinen Schatz.* | *Weine, wein' um meinen Schatz,* |
| | *Um meinen lieben Schatz!* |
| *Blümlein blau, verdorre nicht!* | *Blümlein blau! Blümlein blau!* |
| | *Verdorre nicht, verdorre nicht!* |
| | *Vöglein süss! Vöglein süss!* |
| *Du stehst auf grüner Haide;* | *Du singst auf grüner Heide!* |
| | *Ach! Wie ist die Welt so schön!* |
| | *Ziküth! Ziküth!* |
| | *Singet nicht! Blühet nicht!* |
| | *Lenz ist ja vorbei!* |
| | *Alles Singen ist nun aus!* |
| *Des Abends, wenn ich schlafen geh',* | *Des Abends, wenn ich schlafen geh',* |
| *So denk' ich an das Lieben.* | *Denk ich an mein Leide! An mein* |
| | *Leide!* |

Except for a few word repetitions to strengthen the folklike character, and Mahler's addition of the bird, the two poems are identical.

FORM: The last stanza is a da capo restatement of the first (without the "inserts" in fast tempo), and the middle stanza, in the submediant key, is a kind of development, with a new melody and free modulations. The "bird" passage, with its trills and sixteenth-note motifs, is a fine and typical example of Mahler's consummate mastery of form and technique. As always, the musical structure takes precedence over everything else, even the natural rhythms and accents of the text. Even the "illustrative" effects are integrated, as in the middle section where the "bird" figures alternate with the principal motifs of the song. (Similarly, in the Introduction of the *First Symphony*, the cuckoo sings in fourths rather than in nature's thirds—later, the main theme of the first movement starts with a fourth.)

Connoisseurs of Czech music have singled out this first song as the most typical example of the influence of Bohemian music on Mahler. The principal figure, a well-known baroque ornament called "gruppetto," is a Bohemian melisma frequently used by Dvořák and Janáček. It is repeated no less than twenty-three times throughout the song. Likewise, the alternating binary and ternary rhythms of fast and slow tempos have been traced to the Bohemian *Furiant*. It is interesting to note in the first line an important difference between the 1897 piano edition and the later orchestral one. In the former Mahler clearly expresses his rhythmic intentions: the quick bars should be of unequal length (four eighth notes, then three, and so on), whereas in the orchestral score published later (as in the original 1895 one), he specifies that they should be of equal length whether they are divided into two or three quarter notes.

For the alternation of slow and fast tempos Fritz Egon Pamer found the following psychological explanation: the *"Gesell"* quickly flees from memories of his unfaithful beloved, but now and then sad thoughts obsess him and bring him to a standstill. The contrast in the orchestration between wind instruments (for the quick interruptions) and the strings (for the accompaniment to the voice) heightens the musical and dramatic effect. More intense and expressive still is the da capo last stanza, in which most of the quick interpolations are done away with.

### b) "GING HEUT' MORGENS ÜBERS FELD"

KEY: D major, B major, F sharp (in Rosé OR: D flat).

TIME SIGNATURE: Alla breve.

TEMPO: *In gemächlicher Bewegung; Langsam; noch langsamer; Tempo I.* (Weinberger: *Gemächlich; Allmählich in ein sehr gemächliches Tempo einlenken* [Gradually leading into a very moderate tempo]; *Noch etwas langsamer* [A little slower still]; *Sehr leise und langsam* [Very soft and slow].)

ORCHESTRATION:

There is one slight change in the published version; Mahler introduces a short glockenspiel part (after Figure 11 in the Philharmonia Miniature score). The spareness of the instrumental texture is striking throughout, particularly in the beginning, which is exquisitely scored for piccolo, flutes, and harp, an instrument used extensively throughout, sometimes even melodically.

FORM: Free strophic. The second stanza is a subtle variation of the first, while the third is based on the same material, with the tempo changed to *Langsam*. Only in the third, more intense and "subjective" stanza does Mahler introduce new melodic material, after two seemingly unsuccessful sequential attempts to reintroduce the first theme. As Fritz Egon Pamer has pointed out, Mahler thus retains the general aspect of the strophic lied, indispensable for such a simple folklike text, while at the same time borrowing a freer and subtler method from the *"durchkomponiert"* art song.

This song was used by Mahler as a basis for the first movement of the *First Symphony*. The "happy" recurrence of the song's nostalgic motif deserves attention (*"Guten Tag"* at Figure 16). Mahler's codas are always miracles of musical invention and poetry, but this one surpasses many of the others and shows the incredible mastery that he already possessed at twenty-four.

### c) *ICH HAB' EIN GLÜHEND MESSER*

KEY: D minor, G minor, E flat minor (B minor in Rosé OR).

TIME SIGNATURE: 9/8 changing into 4/4 at the end.

TEMPO: *Stürmisch, wild* (Stormy, fierce); *molto ritardando; più lento ancora; Poco, puis molto stringendo; Wieder zurückhaltend;* etc. (Weinberger: *Schnell und wild* [Fast and fierce]; *sehr schnell; langsamer; sehr schnell,* etc.).

While Mahler usually translated into German his Italian tempo markings, sometimes found in the earlier version, here, for once, he had done the opposite. Strangely enough, the markings in the 1895 orchestral score are closer to the published orchestral version than to the 1897 piano transcription, onto which he must have transcribed them from an earlier version.

TEXT: There is a slight difference between the final text and that in the Rosé autograph, which has *Todtenbahr* rather than *Schwarzen Bahr* (Philharmonia pocket score: three bars after 25).

FORM: *"Durchkomponiert"* art song: the contents of the poem determine the form rather than the reverse. Of the four songs, this is the most dramatic and declamatory, the least folklike. There are no divisions between stanzas, only two separate sections separated by a long orchestral interlude. For once the declamation of the text is of central interest. The short phrases separated by rests suggest the *Gesell*'s intense despair, culminating toward the end in an upward leap of a sixth and a long descent into the lower register, followed by a strange, eerie triplet coda. The only moment of relief is provided by the meditative middle section *"Wenn ich in den Himmel,"* in which the descending minor second *"O Weh'!"* recurs constantly like a refrain. At least two of Mahler's rare chromatic passages are found in this song. They are well suited to its despairing character.

#### d) *DIE ZWEI BLAUEN AUGEN*

KEY: E minor, C major, F major, F minor, same as in Rosé autograph. The contrast between the beginning in E minor and the E flat minor ending of the preceding lied is startling.

TIME SIGNATURE: 4/4 (with three 5/4 bars).

TEMPO: *Mit geheimnisvoll schwermütigen Ausdruck. Ohne Sentimentalität* (With mysterious mournful expression. Without sentimentality) (Weinberger: same indication in small print with *"durchaus"* [throughout] added and *"nicht schleppen"* [without slowing down] at the end) (1895 orchestral manuscript: same marking, preceded with *"Im Tempo des Trauermarsches"*).

This is the first of Mahler's lieder to really exploit the rhythm that he preferred to all others: the march. It is a leaden, relentless, and grief-laden march, with first beats heavily accented. The predominant mood is no longer frenzied anguish and revolt, as in the preceding song, but somber at first, resigned and meditative at the end.

FORM: Strophic *"durchkomponiert."* There is practically no da capo. The second stanza is closely related to the first but ends differently. Using the same motifs, the third stanza freely develops and extends them. The fourth (F major), quoted in the Trio of the "Funeral March" in the *First Symphony,* is entirely different and introduces a new lyrical and serene atmosphere. Only the final bars restate the main theme of the first stanza. Fritz Pamer has pointed out that the 5/4 bars are psychologically motivated: The wanderer interrupts his sad march for a moment, as the peasant singing at his work holds a note and briefly changes rhythm. (Such effects are frequently found in folk songs.) Thus here again, art and folk elements are blended in an original way. As in the first song, the melodies often return to the first note, as if unable to proceed. The extreme economy of the scoring, a small ensemble of flutes, clarinets, English horn, and harp, greatly heightens the emotional intensity. The two unexpected changes of key, from E minor to C and from C to F, are typically Mahlerian and exceptionally beautiful. The last transition, with its harp triplets, has a direct parallel in the last movement of *Das Lied von der Erde.*

One final point should be made: despite the minor quotation of the first theme at the end and the low register of the voice, *"Die zwei blauen Augen"*—and indeed the whole *Gesellen* cycle—closes in an atmosphere of serene and hopeful resignation, as do the *Kindertotenlieder* and *Das Lied.* As a matter of fact, it is interesting to note the great similarity of atmosphere between the conclusion of this latter work, written nearly twenty-five years later, and that of the 1884 *Gesellen Lieder.*

The importance of this cycle in Mahler's work and in the history of music is great, as is its expressive beauty and superb craftsmanship. Its very conception, the length of each song, the diversity of the various episodes were all new to song composition, as was also the orchestral accompaniment. For the first time, Mahler also employed a new procedure adapted from opera: "progressive" tonalities. No longer wildly experimental, as in the early songs, it had become a real system that he was later to adopt for most of the symphonies. The very fact that Mahler transposed two of the four songs from the earlier Rosé autograph version proves how carefully he established the key progression in the whole *Gesellen* cycle. It can be interpreted as a refusal to reverse the course of time and return to the starting point, just as, in life, past events do not recur. Such a device is far more significant than at first appears, for it anticipates Mahler's "novelesque" symphonic technique, so brilliantly analyzed by Theodor Wiesengrund Adorno.

## 5) *FIRST SYMPHONY*, D Major (1885–88)

### COMPOSITION AND DIFFERENT VERSIONS

Both Natalie Bauer-Lechner (on the title page of the folder in which she assembled all the material pertaining to this symphony) and Guido Adler (in his list of Mahler's works) claim that "Symphony No. 1" was sketched in 1885 (probably in Kassel). As the four-hand fragment suggests, the Scherzo may have been started even earlier (see above: FRAGMENTARY WORKS). According to the account of his conversation with Natalie, the composition took place in February and March 1888, immediately after the premiere of *Die drei Pintos*, and Mahler's correspondence corroborates this date. In his letters he sometimes alludes to a "symphonic work" and sometimes to a "symphony." Still according to Natalie's title page, Mahler finished the scoring in Budapest in 1888. At the first performance, in November 1889, the work was entitled "Symphonic poems in two parts." No "program" or analysis was provided, and the two "parts" were designated as follows:

1st Part: Introduction and Allegro Comodo 2. Andante 3. Scherzo

2nd Part: A la pompes funebres [*sic*], attaca. 5. Molto appasionato [*sic*]. Nevertheless, Mahler gave some "clues" to certain journalists, because Kornel Ábrányi, in an article that appeared in the *Pester Lloyd* before the performance, describes the first movement as "spring sounds," the second as a "serenade" evoking love's rapture, the third as a "bridal procession expressing boundless joy and delight," the fourth as a funeral march inspired by the "Huntsman's Funeral" and representing the burial of the symphonic hero's illusions. The Finale was "the victory of the hero who has been beaten to the ground, but who rises anew and triumphs because he has succeeded in creating his own inner world, which neither life nor death can take away from him . . . In the course of this transfiguration, the memory of lost illusions, contained in all the previous themes, returns, as if the sun were suddenly emerging after a stormy night." The manuscript of this first version is inaccessible at present and indeed may have been destroyed, although the late president of the Australian Mahler Society, Dr. R. L. Ernst, claimed that a copy remained in Budapest.[54]

In January 1893, in Hamburg, Mahler recopied and revised the entire manuscript, which he now entitled:

*SYMPHONIE ("Titan")*
*in 5 Sätzen (2 Abteilungen)*
*von*
*GUSTAV MAHLER*

I TEIL: *"Aus den Tagen der Jugend"* [From the days of youth]
1. *"Frühling und kein Ende"* [Spring without an end]
2. *"Blumine"*
3. *"Mit vollen Segeln"* [Under full sail]

II TEIL: *"Commedia humana"* [Human comedy]
4. *"Todtenmarsch in Callots Manier"* [Funeral march in Callot's manner]
5. *"Dall' Inferno al Paradiso"* [From Hell to Heaven]

This title page (which was later crossed out) was certainly written during the summer of 1893, for it includes the slow movement that Mahler recopied and reinstated at that time. Part of a deleted page having luckily remained in the ms., one important alteration in the Finale can still be noted (see below).

Sold in 1959 by Sotheby's in London, the 1893 manuscript is now part of the Osborn Collection at the Yale Library.[55] Its former owner was John C. Perrin, the son of an American sales executive who lived in Brussels and was married to Jenny Feld (see above Chapter VI). Jenny's father, a Budapest insurance broker, had sent his three children to Vienna in 1878, and the two girls had been Mahler's pupils. The younger of the two, it seems, had a pretty soprano voice, and, later in Budapest, Mahler occasionally accompanied her (although no trace of any public concert remains in the Budapest newspapers). Until now, there has been no reason to doubt Mr. Perrin's story. But a real problem arises regarding his claim that the gift was made in 1891, when Mahler left Budapest, and that Jenny returned the score twice to him for revisions, once in 1893, when he chose a Steinway piano for her in Hamburg, and once again in 1897. As the manuscript is dated 1893, it obviously could not have been given to her in 1891. Mahler probably had at least one copy made after the 1893 concert and was thus able to part with the original. The rest of Mr. Perrin's story, concerning the previously unknown Andante movement, is, in my opinion, even more doubtful (see below). The score was extensively revised by Mahler at a later date. The orchestral texture was considerably lightened and clarified, with many held notes and unnecessary doublings suppressed. The original orchestration is far less refined than the one we know.

## PROGRAMS

On October 27, 1893, Mahler conducted the symphony for the second time in Hamburg (see Chapter 19) with a new title and a new "program":

*TITAN, eine Tondichtung in Symphonieform* [A tone poem in the form of a symphony]
I TEIL [1st Part]
*"Aus den Tagen der Jugend," Blumen-, Frucht- und Dornstücke.* [From the days of youth, flower, fruit, and thorn pieces[56]]
1. *"Frühling und keine Ende"* (*Einleitung und Allegro Comodo*). [Endless Spring

(Introduction and Allegro Comodo)]. *Die Einleitung stellt das Erwachen der Natur aus langem Winterschlafe dar.* [The Introduction depicts the awakening of Nature from its long winter sleep.]

*II. "Blumine" (Andante)* [57]

*III. "Mit vollen Segeln" (Scherzo)* [Under full sail]

II Teil [2nd Part]

*"Commedia humana"*

*IV. "Gestrandet!"* [Stranded] (*ein Todtenmarsch in "Callots Manier." Zur Erklärung dieses Satzes diene Folgendes: Die Äussere Anregung zu diesem Musikstück erhielt der Autor durch das in Österreich allen Kindern wohlbekannte parodistische Bild: "Des Jägers Leichenbegängniss," aus einem alten Kindermärchenbuch: Die Thiere des Waldes geleiten den Sarg des gestorbenen Jägers zu Grabe; Hasen tragen das Fähnlein, voran eine Kapelle von böhmischen Musikanten, begleitet von musicirenden Katzen, Unken, Krähen, etc., und Hirsche, Rehe, Füchse und andere vierbeinige und gefiederte Thiere des Waldes geleiten in possirlichen Stellungen den Zug. An dieser Stelle ist dieses Stück als Ausdruck einer bald ironisch lustigen, bald unheimlich brütenden Stimmung gedacht, auf welche dann sogleich . . .*

[For this movement, the following explanation will help: the basic inspiration for it was found by the author in a humorous engraving, well known to all Austrian children: "The Huntsman's Funeral," from an old book of fairy tales. The forest animals accompany the dead hunter's coffin to the grave. Hares carry the banner, in front of them march a group of Bohemian musicians, accompanied by singing cats, toads, crows, etc. Stags, deer, foxes, and other four-legged and feathered animals follow the funeral procession in all kinds of farcical positions. The mood expressed is sometimes ironic and merry, sometimes gloomy and uncanny, then suddenly . . .]

*V. "Dall' Inferno" (Allegro Furioso)*

*folgt, als der plötzliche Ausbruch der Verzweiflung eines im Tiefsten verwundeten Herzens* [follows, like the last despairing cry of a deeply wounded heart].

The very length of the "program" for the "Funeral March" proves that this, the most "modern" of the five movements, had met with considerable incomprehension, and that Mahler was making a desperate effort to explain the piece's uncanny atmosphere and "scandalous" mixture of styles. When Mahler conducted the *First Symphony* the following year at the Tonkünstlerfest des Allgemeinen, Deutschen Musikverein, the same program and the same titles were used. He himself admitted that his "programs" were only meant to facilitate the listener's access to his music, yet he also admitted that they were often devised after the music. In a letter written to Max Marschalk in 1896,[58] he briefly summarized his earlier "program" for the *First Symphony*. Two features were constant, for, as long as he considered it necessary to publish one: The "Awakening of Spring" for the Introduction, and the "Huntsman's Funeral" for the march. It seems fair to assume that Mahler had both in mind when he composed the relevant music.

Around 1900, Mahler became suspicious of the explanatory virtues of his "programs," conscious of the enormous gap that separated him from the composers of "program" music, headed by Richard Strauss. After that he made it a rule to renounce "programs." Nevertheless, when the *First Symphony* was performed in Vienna in November 1900, he allowed, or perhaps even induced, Natalie to send to Ludwig Karpath, the *Neues Wiener Tagblatt* critic, the following text, which is nothing if not another program: "Mahler originally called his *First*: 'Titan,' but he has since rejected this, together with all other titles and inscriptions, which, like all 'programs,' are always misinterpreted. He dislikes and discards them as being 'antiartistic' and 'antimusical' despite their author's intentions. The titles appeared to relate Mahler's *'Titan'* to Jean Paul's novel, although he did not have this in mind, but imagined rather a strong heroic man, his life and sufferings, his battles and defeat at the hands of Fate. In Mahler's own words: 'The real, the climactic denouement comes only in the *Second Symphony!'* The *First* was conceived and composed from the standpoint of a defenseless young man, who easily falls prey to any attackers. In the first movement, the listener is seized by a dionysiac feeling of jubilation, which is neither disturbed nor interrupted. Here, as later, Gustav never ceases to repeat that it is quite unnecessary to have this 'Titan' in mind, this young *'Feuergeist'* [fire spirit] in whom the world is reflected, but that all can be understood and enjoyed in purely musical terms. The first sound, the long-held A harmonics, sets the scene in the midst of nature, in a forest where the sunlight of a lovely day sparkles and shimmers. 'The listeners will certainly not understand the end of this movement,' Mahler continues. 'It will not be successful, yet I could easily have made it more "effective." My hero bursts out laughing and runs away. I am sure that no one will notice the theme that, at the end, is given to the timpani!'

"In the second movement, the young man roams about the world in a more robust, strong and confident way. The wonderful dance rhythms in the Trio are particularly noteworthy, 'because all music proceeds from the dance,' as Mahler once said. 'But everyone will condemn me as a thief because, in the first two bars, my memory failed me and they resemble a Bruckner symphony that is very well known in Vienna.'[59]

"Here a sentimental and rapturous piece was originally inserted, a love scene that Mahler jokingly called his hero's 'blunder of youth' and that he later eliminated. Of the third, *Bruder Martin*[60] movement, Mahler recently said: 'Now he (my hero) has found a hair in his soup and his entire meal is ruined.' . . . The situation can be imagined thus: A funeral procession passes by; all the misery and all the sorrow of the world strikes our hero with its biting contrasts and its dreadful irony. The *Bruder Martin* funeral march must be imagined played by a cheap band, such as one hears at country funerals; it draws near, takes shape and disappears, thus finally becoming what it is. In the midst of this, all the coarseness, the mirth and the banality of the world are heard in the sound of a Bohemian village band, together with the hero's terrible cries of pain. In its biting irony and contrasting polyphony, it is the most moving moment! Particularly when, after a wonderful interlude, the funeral procession returns and a soul-piercing 'gay tune' is heard.

"The last movement follows without pause, on a terrifying shriek. Our hero is now exposed to the most fearful combats and to all the sorrows of the world. He and his triumphant motifs are 'hit on the head again and again' by destiny. Once more he seems for a moment to get to his feet and become the master of his fate again. But only when he has triumphed over death, and when all the glorious memories of youth have returned with themes from the first movement, does he get the upper hand: and there is a great victorious chorale! . . ."

*JEAN PAUL:* Mahler's claim that the work's former title had nothing to do with Jean Paul is not entirely convincing, because he *must* have remembered the title of one of his favorite novels when applying it to a musical work. Nevertheless, there is little or no connection between Jean Paul's plot, the 1893 "program" and the symphony itself. In one movement only can one find something of Jean Paul's spirit: in the famous "Funeral March." As Bruno Walter pointed out, however, it is not the idealism of the novel's hero, Albano, but the negative and critical spirit of its "antihero," Roquairol, that is expressed.[61] Jean Paul's fascinating mind and tormented humor have left more obvious traces in the above "program": the subtitle to the first "part"—*i.e.*, the first three movements—(see above) and the title of the Andante (see below).

## VERSIONS AND PUBLICATION:

After the Weimar performance, Mahler eliminated the Andante, and the symphony was published in 1899 without it. Before the November 1906 Brno performance he made a few more alterations, prior to its republication by Universal Edition. Alma Mahler claims to have suggested one of them. According to her, Mahler took her advice and strengthened the orchestration of the first statement of the main theme, which was originally more brilliantly scored, when it later reappears, but this alteration cannot be traced in the various versions of the score.[62] Before the *Mahler Gesellschaft* edition appeared, it seems that some confusion arose from the fact that the 1943 Boosey & Hawkes score reproduced the 1899 Weinberger score rather than the definitive Universal Edition 1906 version.

## QUOTATIONS FROM LIEDER:

Mahler's *First* shares one important peculiarity with the two following symphonies: it is based in part on previously composed songs, in this case the 1884 *Lieder eines fahrenden Gesellen*. The simplest example of this borrowing is the quotation, in the second Trio of the "Funeral March," of the last section of the fourth *Gesellen Lied*. Aside from the Russian themes in Beethoven's *Rasumovsky Quartets,* there seem to be few previous examples of this procedure. As will be seen below, the transfer of material is less straightforward in the two first movements, and the Scherzo uses short motifs only from the earliest of Mahler's published songs, *"Hans und Grethe"* (or *"Maitanz"*). Both the idea of borrowing from a song and the method in which these *objets trouvés* ("borrowed objects")[63] are treated are original and significant. An examination of nineteenth-century symphonic literature reveals its main problem: how to combine two essentially different concepts of composition, the classical, dynamic development that is based on small melodic units, and romantic lyricism, using long melodies that are complete in themselves and are therefore easily spoiled by variation.

As early as 1822, Schubert was faced with this problem. Lyricism, which previously was to be found only in his slow movements, pervades the entire first Allegro of the *B Minor Symphony*. It has long been my conviction that his consciousness of having created something so revolutionary prevented him from searching for a suitable finale, because he did not at that time feel ready to compose it. Only in the last year of his life, in the great C *Major Symphony*, did he succeed triumphantly in unifying the two principles, by drawing the obvious conclusions from his earlier discovery. Yet Schubert was saved from failure thanks to that gift of the Gods, the unending flow of pure melodic invention which he possessed to a greater extent than any other composer.

The later history of the romantic symphony can be viewed as a series of semi-successes and half failures: Mendelssohn's neoclassical symphonies; Schumann's inspired but uneven works; Berlioz's orchestral productions in which his visionary genius imposes a kind of supralogical coherence; Dvořák's endless reiterations of simple folk tunes; and finally Bruckner's great processions of themes. By submitting his extensive melodic ideas to the strictest classical rules, Bruckner constructed great cathedrals of sound—but they are neoclassical monuments whose formalism and rigid symmetry do not always convince the modern mind, which often lacks his faith in the underlying order of the universe.

Consequently, Mahler's *First Symphony* is a keystone in the history of music, if only because it contains an entire movement based on a song theme, a long and characteristic melody in its original form, which is transformed into a continuous musical flow with practically no literal restatement. Not only is the outline of the melody varied, but its succession of motifs is combined, inverted, extended, and, to use Erwin Stein's brilliant image, shuffled like a pack of cards.[64] This technique was of course greatly improved and perfected in Mahler's later symphonies, but the very fact that he had already invented and used it in 1888 is highly significant.

a) *Langsam. Schleppend* (*"Wie ein Naturlaut"*); *Immer sehr gemächlich*
KEY: D minor, D major.
TIME SIGNATURE: 4/4 and Alla breve.
ORCHESTRATION: Mahler later admitted that he made one major change in orchestration at the time of the Budapest premiere: during the first rehearsals, the sound of the long pedal on A, covering all the registers in the strings, was too "material" and he decided that, except for a few double basses, they should use harmonics. Contrary to this statement reported by Natalie, the harmonics are not to be found at the beginning in the 1893 Hamburg score, and it must therefore have been made during the rehearsals preceding the second performance, in October of that year. They do appear, however, in the middle of the first movement, when the introduction is restated.
INTRODUCTION: A few obvious "models" must have been in Mahler's mind when he wrote the Introduction: the main theme of the first movement of Beethoven's *Ninth,* and that of Haydn's *Quartet* Op. 76, No. 2 ("Fifths"), and the long pedal points at the beginning of Bruckner's symphonies. Nonetheless, the "open air" atmosphere, the distant fanfares (played by offstage trumpets), the bird calls, the cuckoo singing in fourths, are all original, although inspired by a "theme" familiar to German romanticism, nature and the forest, with its polyphony of accompanying sounds. It is the same world as that of *Waldmärchen,* yet one cannot escape a feeling that Mahler has only now succeeded what he earlier attempted. The use of clarinets suggesting distant trumpets[65] is in itself a great innovation. Mahler the architect is already present in the stylized transposition of the cuckoo call into the main theme of the first movement.

FIRST MOVEMENT:

FORM: Mahler's transition theme to the Allegro proper is used again in the first movement of the following symphony. A thorough and detailed study of the development procedures would doubtless be extremely rewarding. The following example summarizes a few of the transformations undergone by the figures borrowed from *Ging' heut morgens über Feld.*

Various figures of Theme A and their transformations

There are three literal "quotations" from the song: eight bars in the beginning and, four bars later, thirty bars (transposed into A major) of the lied's B major passage (Figure 14 in the song), which is followed by an earlier passage from the song (at No. 11) and a brisk "new" coda.

A shortened restatement of the slow introduction presents a partly new secondary theme on the cellos but provides no real contrast, as it is closely connected to the main theme. As in the 1876 *Piano Quartet,* the development starts in the key of the exposition. Toward the middle (Figure 18), Mahler again borrows twenty-seven modulating bars from the song and introduces a new version of the transition motif (anticipating the main theme of the Finale). Restated fortissimo by all the brass, the distant fanfares of the introduction serve as climax for the development section. The recapitulation is equally unorthodox: after the first theme, Mahler restates the new secondary theme and ends with a short coda.

To summarize so briefly a highly complex symphonic movement is of course absurd; my intention is merely to show how freely Mahler handled the traditional symphonic form. This movement is more noteworthy for its liveliness and charm than for its organization. It has flaws (for instance the development section remains too long in the main key and quotes too extensively from the exposition), and it is probably more original than successful. Dika Newlin is justified in calling it a "Symphonic Fantasy on a theme from the *Gesellen Lieder.*" Yet Mahler's discovery of all the major elements of his new technique at so young an age is remarkable in itself. Only twelve years later, in the first Allegro of the *Fourth,* was he able to carry these new principles to their logical conclusion and write a wholly successful movement in the same style; he could never have done so without laying the essential groundwork in the *First Symphony.*

[b] *Andante Alegretto* (*sic*) (later suppressed and recently rediscovered)

At its first performances (1889, 1893, and 1894), the *First Symphony* (although not yet so called) included an Andante that Mahler in his "program" subtitled *"Blumine"* (the title given by Jean Paul to a collection of magazine articles, the first volume of which was published in 1810 in Tübingen, *"Herbst-Blumine oder gesammelte Werkchen"*). *"Herbst-Blumine"* can be approximately translated a "Collection of Autumn flowers." Mahler suppressed "autumn" but obviously meant to emphasize with this title the light and decorative character of the piece.

The dates on the 1893 manuscript in the Osborn Collection at Yale prove that Mahler recopied the Andante during the summer of that year, after having decided to leave it out of the symphony six months earlier. Mr. Perrin, the former owner of the autograph, has made two important statements about *"Blumine":* 1) That it expressed Mahler's tender feelings for Johanna Richter and 2) that Weinberger, Mahler's 1897 publisher, considered the symphony too long, and that Mahler "gave in very reluctantly . . . and, full of anger, suppressed the Andante." Neither of these statements can be taken any more seriously than Mr. Perrin's claim that the 1893 manuscript was given to his mother in 1891.[66]

The recent rediscovery of *"Blumine"* has revealed the identity of its theme, that of Werner's serenade in the 1884 stage music for *Der Trompeter von Säkkingen*. It seems possible that the whole eight-minute Andante is identical with the former Serenade, although Mahler undoubtedly improved and polished some of its details. He was probably already in love with Johanna in June 1884, but it is extremely unlikely that he should have composed as a "declaration of love" the mere accompaniment to a *tableau vivant,* which furthermore was based on a poem he despised. Even if his romantic attachment is reflected to a certain extent in the piece, Mahler's "innermost feelings" and his real confession of love to Johanna are to be found in the later *Gesellen Lieder*. It is a well-known fact that the whole *First Symphony* is, so to speak, a "declaration of love," but to Maria von Weber rather than to Johanna, the Kassel soprano whom Mahler had probably all but forgotten by 1888.

As to Weinberger's alleged influence on the suppression of *"Blumine,"* this is in my view even more improbable. In 1897, Mahler was already famous. He was then publishing the much longer *Third Symphony,* he was known for his uncompromising attitude toward his art, and he had resisted the suggestions of many friends and artists whom he admired (such as Strauss's advice to cut the Finale of the same symphony: see below). If Weinberger had recommended any deletion at all, it would probably have been that of the "shocking" and "scandalous" "Funeral March" rather than the innocuous eight-minute Andante.

Mahler himself later mentioned his suppressed Andante on two occasions, once in the text quoted above and sent to Karpath, in which he called it his hero's "Blunder of youth" (it is here mentioned as coming *after* the Scherzo), and again in 1900, when he spoke of the contrasts required within a work to avoid monotony and regretted not having planned such contrasts between the first movements of the *Second Symphony*. "It was mainly because of an excessive similarity in key that I eliminated the *'Blumine'* Andante from my *First.*"[67]

Was Mahler telling Natalie the whole truth? The entire movement could of course have been easily transposed, and there were obviously other reasons. Mahler could also have reinstated the movement later, particularly in 1906, but he never did, and he never revived *"Blumine"* after 1894.[68]

KEY: C major (with middle section in A minor).

TIME SIGNATURE: 6/8.

SCORING: Two flutes, two oboes, two C clarinets, two bassoons, four horns, one trumpet, one harp, timpani, and strings; consequently a much smaller group than for the rest of the symphony.

FORM: ABA. Section A is entirely dominated by the nine-bar melody stated by the solo trumpet, after a poetic pianissimo four-bar string prelude. The second phrase of the theme (before Figure 2) is taken up by the strings and quickly reveals its main weakness: an excessive symmetry in the heavily accented lower semitone appoggiaturas that precede every important note in the melody and become an exasperating mannerism. The contrasting episode (B) starts in A minor, with imitations on the first bar of theme A on two oboes. In the same middle section a second episode starts with a new version of A and returns to the main theme through a modulating passage combining yet another version of A with a counter melody on the violins. In only four bars Mahler returns from G flat, in which key high cellos and flutes have just restated A, to the first theme's concluding string phrase, opening the shortened reprise. This is followed by a simple coda, which is again based on A.

Another of the movement's obvious weaknesses is its abuse of A (the trumpet theme). There is no doubt as to the authorship of *"Blumine,"* and yet few other arguments can be stated in its favor. It is the music of a late-nineteenth-century Mendelssohn, pretty, charming, lightweight, urbane, and repetitious, just what Mahler's music never is. There are some lovely details, particularly in the transitions, for instance that between sections A and B, in which a long held note, E, the mediant of C major, becomes the dominant of the subsequent key, A minor, thanks to a glissando octave leap. The passage in which the first motif is used in imitations between the various instruments and later, when the harp plays delicious thirty-second-note tremolos (the harp is used extensively and very poetically throughout the movement), can be counted among its best moments. Yet these happy touches fail to give distinction to the whole. How strong any other music from Mahler's pen appears by comparison, particularly the nostalgic and stylized post-horn solo in the *Third Symphony!* In view of this, it is not surprising that Mahler suppressed *"Blumine."* It is harder to understand why he changed his mind and reinstated it after having recognized its weakness and sentimentality.]

c) *Kräftig bewegt, doch nicht zu schnell* (With energy and animation, but not too slowly); *Recht gemächlich* (Really moderate) in the Trio (1893 OR: id. and *Langsames Walzertempo* (In slow waltz tempo); in Trio: id. and *Etwas lansamer als zuvor* (Somewhat slower as before)

KEY: A major (modulating to E and C sharp minor and major)

Trio: F major (modulating to G, F sharp, and C).

TIME SIGNATURE: 3/4.

Mahler's first Scherzo (although not so named) is a ländler, the most straightforward and rustic of any that he wrote. Schubert's distant shadow and Bruckner's closer one are of course clearly discernible throughout, but the music is nevertheless thoroughly Mahlerian. The main theme is new, but Mahler has subtly used several different short motifs from *Hans und Grethe:*

The third and fourth motifs are closely related; after the first double bar and later in the Trio, they are used in a Bruckner type ostinato. The principal theme of the Scherzo starts, like most of the themes in the symphony, with a rising fourth. There is a striking similarity between the two bars before Figure 9 (repeated later) and the *Freischütz* waltz. The Trio has a more gracious, hesitant flavor. Its theme is divided between violins, violas, and oboes, with the same typical fourth and fifth intervals heard earlier, now in the bass. In the transition passage from Trio to Scherzo, Mahler shows his usual mastery and inexhaustible poetic imagination.

d) *Feierlich und gemessen, ohne zu schleppen* (Moderate and solemn, not too slow)

Trio 1: *id.*

Trio 2: *Sehr einfach und schlicht, wie eine Volksweise* (Very simple and modest like a folk song).

KEY: D minor (with many modulations: G minor in the first Trio, and major in the second; E flat minor in the reprise of the march).

TIME SIGNATURE: 4/4.

This is the most famous and the most extraordinary movement in the symphony, a piece of music so strange and so unique that it could not fail to amaze and horrify contemporary listeners. Why did Mahler decide to illustrate the "Huntsman's Funeral" with a minor version of the "Frère Jacques" melody? He himself has answered this question, stating that "even as a child, 'Bruder Martin' struck him not as being gay, as it was always sung, but rather deeply tragic, and that he already heard in it what it was later to become for him. While he was composing the latter part of the movement, he kept hearing the canon in his head, above the pedal point he needed, until he bravely reached out for it.[69]

Ernst Schulz, the son of Mahler's Prague landlord, remembered that the children of his house often sang "Bruder Martin" as a round while Mahler was there,[70] and Theodor Fischer, Mahler's childhood playmate, found a striking similarity between the first Trio and a typical dance of the Jihlava neighborhood, the *"Hatscho."*[71] So much for the "folklore" origins of this enigmatic movement. The famous "Huntsman's Funeral" engraving by Moritz von Schwind was indeed very popular throughout Germany and Austria.[72]

SCORING: The orchestral sound of this movement is as new as its general conception. Mahler devised it consciously for the following reasons: ". . . [The effect] results from the way in which I use the instruments. Whereas in the first piece, they disappear in a radiant sea of sounds, as a luminous source vanishes behind its own rays, in the third, the instruments are masked and hooded, and they appear in strange guises. Everything must sound dull and muffled, as if shadows were passing by. To make every entry in the canon clear and startling, its tone color, to draw attention to it, caused me many a headache, until I succeeded in creating this strange and uncanny effect. I don't think anyone has yet realized how I obtained this result. When I want a tortured and suppressed sound,[73] I produce it not with an instrument that plays it easily, but with one that can produce it only with considerable strain, by transgressing its natural limits. Thus double basses and bassoons must squeak in their highest register whereas flutes must blow in the lower registers and so on." (In the original 1893 score, the canon starts on a cello playing in unison with the double bass solo, which has remained alone in the final version.)

What is amazing is not that Mahler's music should have incensed listeners and critics for so many years, but that, at such an early date, he should have consciously pursued such a revolutionary goal. Only long afterward, in the music of such later masters of the orchestra as Ravel, Bartók, and Stravinsky, were effects of this kind to be achieved again.

FORM: The structure of the march is simple. It can be summed up as follows: ABACABA. "A" is the "Bruder Martin" canon (initiated by a solo muted double bass!), "B" a succession of two "vulgar" tunes played *"mit parodie"* (with a typical "beer parlor" glissando in the violins at the end) by a "village band" (flutes, oboes, clarinets in C and E flat, bassoons, horns, trumpets, Turkish cymbals, and big drum accompanied by strings pizzicato con legno); and "C" the last section of the fourth *Gesellen Lied "Die zwei blauen Augen,"* quoted complete even to the last recall of the song's main theme at the end, a theme unheard anywhere else in the symphony). Returning in the wholly unexpected tonality of E flat minor,[74] the march modulates back to the main key with the greatest of ease after the second "street tune" has been restated in the new key. Once again the coda, which recalls the theme of the second Trio and relates it to the second "village tune," is a masterpiece of poetic imagination.

e) *Stürmisch bewegt* (With stormy animation). *Energisch. Mit grosser Wildheit* (With violent fury). *Sehr gesangvoll* [In a very singing manner] for the second theme

The Finale of the *First Symphony* is the only big dramatic movement of the four. It lasts twenty minutes, as opposed to thirty minutes for the other three combined. Mahler took more trouble drawing up its over-all plan than he did later, when his structural devices became more instinctive than deliberate. A brief summary of its architecture follows:

INTRODUCTION:

| | |
|---|---|
| 1 to 54 | stating a group of important figures, two of which belong to the main theme: F minor |

EXPOSITION:

| | |
|---|---|
| 55 to 174 | A (First theme and various motifs from Introduction): F minor/D flat |
| 175 to 237 | B (Second theme): D flat |
| 238 to 253 | Quotation from first movement Introduction (called from here on "Introduction 1"); transition theme, with motif from Introduction to Finale (called from here on "Introduction F"): D flat/G minor |

DEVELOPMENT:

| | |
|---|---|
| 254 to 289 | 1. Initial tempo (motifs from Introduction F and theme A): G minor, A minor, D flat major and minor. |
| 290 to 316 | 2. (Theme A and its inversion): C major |
| 317 to 374 | 3. (Theme A and motifs from Introduction F): Fanfares from Introduction 1: C major and minor |
| 375 to 427 | 4. Sudden transition from C to D major (Pesante) Inverted Theme A and theme Introduction 1 |
| 428 to 457 | 5. *Sehr langsam* (Introduction 1 with its various motifs, its transition theme, Theme B and beginning of A from the first movement): D minor |

RECAPITULATION:

| 458 to 532 | B: *Sehr langsam.* F major on long dominant pedal |
| 533 to 622 | A: Tempo primo. Motifs from Introduction F, fanfares and quotation from first movement development: F minor/B flat |

CODA:

| 623 to 741 | Sudden transition to D major. Fanfares from Introduction A inverted, etc. General review of all former motifs. |

In the 1893 score, the beginning of Introduction F is repeated in Bar 509, with its startling cymbal clash, heard at the beginning of the Finale. In order no doubt to avoid a repetition of the surprise effect then achieved, Mahler crossed out about four pages and inserted six and a half new ones, the remarkable transition passage leading to the coda (Bars 509 to 587). Theme A's return is prepared by its first three notes, quickly reiterated by the violas in the lower register. Mahler selected them rather than the cellos because they produce a "strained, assertive" tone (*gepresst, gewaltsam*). This new transition is one of the best passages in the whole work. It was Mahler's only important afterthought, and posterity owes its knowledge of it to a mere chance: the presence in the 1893 manuscript of the crossed-out pages, which he did not take the trouble to remove. It illustrates his difficulty in achieving the movement's "final victory," a problem that he discussed in the following conversation reported by Natalie: ". . . One transition in my *First Symphony* gave me a lot of trouble. How was I to obtain the final, lasting victory after the music had fallen back again and again into the depths of despair, despite short intervals of light? After fumbling around in vain for a long time, I finally realized that I must modulate from one key to the key just above it (from C to D major, the main key of the piece). That could have been done very easily by using the intervening semitone, by modulating from C to C sharp and then to D. But everyone would then have known what my next step was going to be. I wanted my D chord to sound as if it came from heaven or from another world. At first. I could not understand this freest and boldest of modulations, and I resisted it, until I decided to use it. If there is now one truly great thing in the symphony, I know it is this passage."[75]

This conversation took place in the summer of 1893, shortly after Mahler had recopied the whole symphony. The passage discussed must be the one just before the coda, but, strangely enough, here Mahler jumps without transition not from C, but from B flat to D major, whereas earlier, between Sections 3 and 4 of the development, he does actually move from C to D major. The effect of these sudden modulations is tremendous in both cases.

At a first hearing this finale makes a very dense and somewhat confused impression, with its massive length and towering climaxes. Obviously, Mahler worked very hard on its structure, and no less obviously he did not entirely succeed in creating a unified whole out of such individual and sharply contrasted sections. The lyrical "Tchaikovskian" second theme, lovely as it is—and far less sentimental than the trumpet melody in *"Blumine"*—nonetheless has no part to play in the great conflict that is depicted in the movement. It provides only an extraneous moment of repose and quiet musing. Another and probably even graver weakness is the recurrence of the sudden modulation mentioned above and of the climactic D major passage. Both achieve the effect of a "final victory" and, in the first instance, the listener already feels that he is headed toward the final coda. Strauss wrote Mahler to this effect after the Weimar concert, and Mahler replied: "In the passage you mention, the denouement is only an illusion (in the true sense of the word a "false conclusion"). I needed to turn back, for the whole being to touch rock bottom, before a real victory could be obtained. The battle I was concerned with is the one in which victory is always furthest away when the fighter thinks it is at hand. That is the essence of any spiritual combat. It is not easy to be or to become a hero!" In the same letter Mahler adds that, rather than trying to improve a work in which his intentions were not adequately expressed, he preferred to write another. Strangely enough, he had already done so, and as early as 1888. The half-successful experience of this finale bore fruit only a few months later, in the first movement of the *Second Symphony*, an accomplished masterpiece in the same heroic style.

Regardless of its evident flaws, unavoidable in a youthful work of such vast proportions and daring style, it is hard to resist the tempestuous power of the *First Symphony*. Beethoven's influence is of course discernible in the conception, as is that of Weber, Berlioz, and Liszt. There are practically no traces of Wagner's in this particular work. However, despite such inevitable influences, almost everything in the *First Symphony* is both powerful and new. Mahler had become fully aware of his strength, both as an architect capable of raising great cathedrals of sound and as an artist concerned with the basic problems of human life and destiny.

When he wrote the *First Symphony*, Mahler naïvely thought that "neither the musicians nor the listeners would have any difficulty with it, that it would please them immediately and that he would be able to live and work for many years on the money it would earn him." In fact, at the time of its composition, the emotions he needed to express were so overpowering that he was not much concerned with his future listeners' reactions. Looking back on this period of his creative life, Mahler once explained to Richard Specht that Beethoven had originally been a Mozartian composer and Wagner an offspring of the Meyerbeerian tradition, whereas a cruel fate had condemned him to being himself from the start.

Many years later, in 1909, Mahler wrote to Bruno Walter from New York: "I performed my *First* here the day before yesterday, without any particular success with the public, it seems. I, on the contrary, was really pleased with my youthful efforts. What happens to me when I conduct these works is strange. A painful, burning sensation is crystallized within me: what kind of a world is this which (in the mirror of art) reflects such sounds and such shapes! Both the *Funeral March* and the storm that breaks out immediately afterward strike me as burning accusations hurled at the creator."

## 6) *9 WUNDERHORN LIEDER* with piano (1888–91)

### THE WUNDERHORN ANTHOLOGY

Mahler's discovery, early in 1888, of the "folk lieder" anthology *Des Knaben Wunderhorn* is one of those events that later seem miraculous so exactly did it fit his requirements at that stage of his career. What is most surprising and yet undeniably true is that he should not have encountered these poems before, for the publication of *Des Knaben Wunderhorn* in the first years of the nineteenth century was no mere literary event, but an important occurrence for German culture as a whole, and the result of specific political and historical circumstances. The rediscovery of the "people" that the anthology reflected can be traced back to the late eighteenth century. Strongly influenced by Jean-Jacques Rousseau's idea of man's idyllic life in the midst of nature, society and an urban existence were considered the source of all ills. At that time none were rated higher than the great "bards" Homer, Ossian, and Shakespeare. "Folk" art was praised at the expense of "literary" poetry, and several anthologies[76] of folk texts were published, which strongly influenced the contemporary German poets, Goethe, Uhland, and Rückert. The aim of the "editors" of these anthologies was not to transpose or "translate" the folk texts into contemporary poetic idiom, but to "rediscover and assimilate the early treasures" of German tradition.

Interpreted as an insult to German pride, the Lunéville Treaty of 1802 did much to reawaken the German national conscience. By immersing themselves in their past, the Germans sought to forget the bitter present and turned their attention toward a nobler time. In 1803, Ludwig Tieck published an anthology of *Minnelieder*. By then Brentano had already started questioning old people of all classes, peasants, servants, nurses, artisans, and schoolmasters and was writing down the poems that still lived in their memory.

The *Wunderhorn*'s two editors came from very different backgrounds and, at first, they had little in common other than their romantic leanings, their interest in folklore, and their literary talent. Achim von Arnim (1781–1831) was born in Berlin of an aristocratic Prussian family; he lived in Heidelberg, where in 1811 he married Bettina Brentano, Clemens' famous younger sister. Brentano (1778–1842) was a Rhinelander, the son of a Frankfurt merchant of Italian origin. A specialist in medieval studies, he was a very talented writer, but a changeable, tormented dilettante, never satisfied with his work. Both Arnim and Brentano were "wanderers" in the romantic sense, traveling incessantly from one city to another, thus ideally suited to the scholarly task of assembling the sources for such an anthology. Both were active in politics, supporting German Unity in the face of the Napoleonic threat. Their meeting in Halle before the turn of the century is a major event in the history of German letters, for, together with friends, they initiated what is often called the "Second German Romantic movement."

Gathering material for the *Wunderhorn*, Brentano and Bettina traveled through Swabia, North Germany, and the Rhineland. Not only did they write down many versions of the orally transmitted poems, but they read old prayer books, chronicles, and calendars and assembled a huge library of source material. The first volume was published in the autumn of 1805. It was dedicated to Goethe, who highly approved of the two authors' efforts and published a long and detailed review a year later in the *Jenaer Literaturzeitung*. The publication was tremendously successful, again largely for historical reasons. 1806 was the year of another military catastrophe, the Battle of Jena, a defeat that seemed to set the seal of doom upon the German Empire.

More than ever before, the discouraged and frustrated Germans turned toward the people, who seemed to represent the only hope for reunification after the country had been betrayed by the lack of patriotism of its princes. As a result, in 1808, the publication of the second volume of the *Wunderhorn* was hailed, even more than the first, as a patriotic act, a manifesto of the new romantic movement, and its influence soon became evident in German poetry. This volume is not as organized as the first, and the transcriptions are often freer. Endless controversies raged throughout Germany regarding the extent of the editors' own contributions. Today they seem utterly vain, for many of these poems have since been traced to other sources and the editors' changes can thus be easily recognized. In any case, the extent of the editors' rewriting seems of little consequence, as compared with the great debt that German letters owes to them.

The title *Des Knaben Wunderhorn* ("The Boy's Magic Horn") was simply that of the first poem, a short ballad of French origin. It is also usually associated with the style and contents of this anthology in which children, magic, and music play an important role. The *Wunderhorn* was immediately described as a collection of "German lieder," although no music accompanied the poems. Brentano was both a composer and a singer, Arnim sometimes expressed his desire to achieve a new unity between singing, dancing, and poetry, and neither of the two co-editors intended the assembled texts to be considered merely as poems. Their form and content vary considerably. There are many simple children's lullabies, but also romances, ballads, love songs, murder stories, and miracle legends. The tone alternates constantly between two extremes, the humorous and the elegiac. The length of the poems, their rhythms, and their verse forms also differ considerably.

A striking parallel may be drawn between Mahler's deep longing for simplicity, the naïve faith of children and saints, and the lost paradise of medieval Germany at a time when art was becoming conscious of its style and questioning its role in modern society, on the one hand, and, on the other, the early nineteenth century attempted a return to nature and simplicity and its quest for the soul of the people, as expressed in their spontaneous poetic creations. From the very beginning of his creative life, Mahler's musical imagination had been fired by the main themes of the *Wunderhorn*, although he did not yet know the anthology itself. The beauty of nature, the innocence of childhood, soldiers, ghosts, heroes, and saints were already familiar to him, as were the emotions dealt with in these poems: death, revolt, homesickness, and farewell. This is hardly surprising, for the spirit of the *Wunderhorn* penetrated practically every realm of German nineteenth-century literature, and Mahler was indirectly influenced by it long before he was aware of the fact. Strange as it may seem, however, few composers had set these poems to music before him; only Schumann in one song and Brahms in two songs and two duets. Thus in 1888, Mahler felt that he was discovering a new, unexplored, and magic world, in which he recognized himself at every turn. "It is now the book I prefer above all those I know," Arnim wrote in his 1805 postscript to the first volume of the *Wunderhorn*. "Not because of what my friend Brentano and I have done for it, although we did it with pleasure, but because of what exists and breathes deep down inside it, the fresh morning air and the old German manner. If I were a beekeeper, I would say: this was the last swarm; it was going to fly away. It took a lot of trouble and hard work to keep it in its old hive; take care of it, don't disturb it and enjoy its honey!"

## MAHLER'S EARLY *WUNDERHORN LIEDER:*

Altogether Mahler wrote twenty-two *Wunderhorn Lieder* (including those inserted in the *Second, Third,* and *Fourth Symphonies*). They constitute his entire song output between 1888 and 1901, with the exception of the *Nietzsche Lied* from the *Third Symphony*. The first group of nine songs with piano accompaniment was partly composed for the children of Karl and Marion von Weber in Leipzig.[77] None of these are dated, but the order is the same in the manuscript as it is in the first edition, and is probably chronological, as is usual with Mahler's song collections. The last songs were probably those composed in Hinterbrühl during the summer of 1890, for Mahler had no time to compose the following summer due to his Scandinavian journey. These early *Wunderhorn Lieder* are shorter and simpler than the later orchestral ones. Mahler was still pursuing his earlier efforts in a style based on the *Volkslied,* while borrowing from the art song many subtle and complex devices. Rather than simply restating, he often composed, for each stanza, music of roughly similar character, but in fact completely different, and created in each lied a new solution to the basic unity-diversity problem of music.

MANUSCRIPT: Alfred Rosé owns a complete manuscript of these songs, entitled *"Aus des Knaben Wunderhorn—9 Lieder von Gustav Mahler."* They are in the same order as in the first edition, but generally in different keys. I have mentioned, for each song, the difference between manuscript and edition.

a) *"UM SCHLIMME KINDER ARTIG ZU MACHEN"* [To Make Bad Children Good]

KEY: E major (in Rosé manuscript called from here on OR) (as in high voice edition).

TIME SIGNATURE: 4/4.

RHYTHM: Binary dance ("bourrée").

TEMPO: *Lustig* ("gay").

TEXT: Vol. I (Hempel ed.), page 390, under the title *"Um die Kinder still und artig zu machen."* The poem, in Swiss dialect, had already been published in Nicolai's 1776 *Almanach.* Mahler made very few alterations, other than increasing the number of *"Kukuk"* calls, repeating some lines and changing the original stanza structure from 4/4/4/4 to 6/6/6. Two lines were modified for the sake of the rhyme:

OR: *Und niemand heim als Kinder*      M: *Und niemand heim als meine Kind'*
    *Und's Mädchen auf der Winden.*          *Und's Mädchen ist auf der Wäsche-*
                                                                    *wind!*

Here are Mahler's two new lines, bringing the total number from sixteen, in the original poem, to eighteen in his version:

*In meiner Tasch' für folgsam Kind',*
*Da hab' ich manche Angebind,*

FORM: Strophic. The first and third stanzas are closely related, as are the second and fourth, both of which are in the minor mode. The only difference between the two pairs of stanzas are to be found in the accompaniment: there are a few octave doublings and the occasionally inverted counterpoint. The first stanza ends in the dominant. The text of the second requires an expressive crescendo, and thus the music is placed higher in the voice. There is a three-bar prelude, but both the interlude and postlude are four bars long. The melody is related to that of the folk original.[78]

b) *"ICH GING MIT LUST DURCH EINEN GRUENEN WALD"* (I Went Gaily Through a Green Forest")

KEY: D major (OR) (middle section in G) (as in high voice edition).

TIME SIGNATURE: 2/4.

TEMPO: *Träumerisch, durchaus zart* (Dreamily and tenderly); *Etwas langsamer* (A little slower).

TEXT: Vol. II, page 379, under the title *Waldvöglein*. As usual, Mahler repeated a few words, one whole line, and he also changed two words. He added the following line: *"Dann komm' zu mir"* (repeated), suppressed the last two stanzas of the original, and replaced them with six lines of his own, which end the poem on a dubious rather than a cheerful note:

> *Es schaut der Mond durch's Fensterlein*
> *Zum holden, süssen Lieben,*
> *Die Nachtigall sang die ganze Nacht.*
> *Du schlafselig' Mägdelein,*
> *Nimm dich in Acht!* [repeated]
> *Wo ist dein Herzliebster geblieben?*

> The moon shines through the window
> On a fine, sweet love,
> The nightingale sings the whole night
> O thou sleepy maiden
> O take care, take care!
> Where does thy sweetheart dally?

FORM: Simple da capo: AABA. The second stanza repeats the first with few alterations, whereas the third, in a slower tempo, introduces a new key (the subdominant). The stylized bird calls are typically Mahlerian. Like many folk songs, its principal melody is based on an arpeggio and related to that in the Erk-Böhme collection based on the same text (II, 390: *"Der Leichtfertige Liebhaber"*).

DER LEICHTFERTIGE LIEBHABER

Ich ging durch ei - nen gras - grü - nen — Wald, da
hört ich die Vö - ge-lein sin - gen; sie san-gen so jung, sie
san-gen so alt, die klei - nen Vö-ge-lein in dem Wald, die
hör ich so ger - ne wohl sin - gen.

c) *"AUS! AUS!"* (Over! Over!)

KEY: D flat major (OR) (E flat, in high; C major in low voice edition).
TIME SIGNATURE: 2/4.
RHYTHM: Quick march.
TEMPO: *Keckes Marschtempo* [In lively march tempo].
TEXT: Vol. I, page 474, under the title *"Abschied für immer"*, but so considerably altered that few lines have remained intact. By transforming the first line *"Heute marschieren wir,"* into a refrain and adding *"Juch-he, juch-he, im grünen Mai!"*, Mahler gave the whole song a rondo structure. The original poem has four short stanzas and a longer fifth one which Mahler suppressed, probably because it was known to have been written by the editors of the anthology. In the remaining stanzas, he added and cut several words, altered the position of two lines and deleted five. ("Ei, Du wacker schwarzbraun Mägdlein, Unsre Lieb ist noch nicht aus" originally concluded the first stanza.) Consequently, Mahler's poem has 5 stanzas of unequal length. The new last stanza and a half added by Mahler is as follows:

| | |
|---|---|
| "Gehst du fort, heut' schon fort? | "Are you leaving, leaving today? |
| Und kommst nimmer wieder? | And never coming back? |
| Ach! Wie wird's traurig sein | Oh! How sad it will be |
| Hier in dem Städtchen! | Here in the little town! |
| Wie bald vergisst du mein! | How quickly you will forget |
| Ich! armes Mädchen!" | Me, your poor sweetheart!" |
| | |
| "Morgen marschieren wir, | "Tomorrow we shall march, |
| Juch-he, juch-he, im grünen Mai! | High ho, high ho, in the green May! |
| Tröst dich, mein lieber Schatz, | Console yourself, my sweetheart, |
| Im Mai blüh'n gar viel Blümelein! | In May, may flowers bloom! |
| Die Lieb' ist noch nicht aus! | Love is not yet over! |
| Aus! Aus! Aus! Aus!" | Over! Over! Over! Over!" |

The repetition of *"Aus"* in the last line adds an ironic touch.
FORM: Rondo, on the following pattern: ABACADBA, modeled on Mahler's version of the text. The ritornello always returns in the same key and with the same words. This is Mahler's first song in quick march rhythm with military effects, horn fifths, and drumbeats. It can be viewed as a kind of sketch for the later *"Trost im Unglück."* Despite the simple folk style and elementary march rhythm, there are many subtleties, such as sudden modulations. The third stanza, in the contrasting submediant key, introduces a definite trio feeling. Further on, the girl's whining tone is humorously suggested by a chromatic descent over which Mahler has written "Plaintive, with Parody."

d) *"STARKE EINBILDUNGSKRAFT"* (Strong Imagination)
KEY: B flat major (OR) (C major in high, A in low voice ed.).
TIME SIGNATURE: 4/4.
RHYTHM: Binary dance (rustic "bourrée").
TEMPO: *Sehr gemächlich, mit humoristichem Ausdruck* (Very moderate, with humorous expression).
TEXT: Vol. I, page 402. Mahler made practically no alterations, except for re-

peating a few words and whole lines to enhance the "naïve" effect. The last line
is lengthened and transformed into a double line:

OR: *Ich mein', ich wär bei Dir.*                          M: *So mein' ich alle weile:*
                                                              *Ich wär schon bei dir!*

thus providing the song with a more effective ending. The poem is very close
in content to *Verlor'ne Müh'*, which immediately precedes it in the anthology
and which Mahler later set to an orchestral accompaniment.

FORM: Strophic, following the two-stanza structure of the poem. The first ends
in the dominant and the second in the tonic. This is one of the shortest and
simplest of all Mahler's lieder, yet its style is highly characteristic. There are
several delicate and subtle touches, such as the little pauses suggesting the boy's
hesitations (at *"so mein ich"*), the elision of two bars at the end of the second
stanza, and the voice ascending to a higher register in the last line to create the
crescendo effect required by the text. This poem, which is found only in the
*Wunderhorn,* has no known folk origin and no traditional musical setting.

e) *"ZU STRASSBURG AUF DER SCHANZ'"* (In Strasbourg on the Battle-
ment)

MANUSCRIPT: A two-page orchestration of the first quarter of this song exists,
but it breaks off abruptly at the end of the first page (of the piano edition)
(HLG Collection).

KEY: F sharp minor (G minor in high and F minor in low voice ed. and in the
orchestral version) ending in B minor.

TIME SIGNATURE: 4/4.

RHYTHM: Slow march.

TEMPO: *Im Volkston* (As a folk tune).

TEXT: Vol. I, page 180, under the title *"Der Schweizer"* (The Swiss). Mahler
has kept only four of the six stanzas and has changed their meter by repeating
all the last four-foot lines, while adding one foot to the first two. He has thus
increased the dramatic tension of the whole. The subject of the poem closely
resembles that of *Der Tamboursg'sell,* which Mahler later set to an orchestral
accompaniment. This is the earliest of Mahler's great military songs, in slow march
rhythm throughout. It it so expressive and powerful, so full of orchestral
effects in the accompaniment, that one can easily understand why he started
to orchestrate it. Like *"Revelge,"* the whole song is full of drumbeats and
military band effects.

FORM: There are four stanzas, although the song is not strictly strophic. The
second is practically a restatement of the first, but the third starts higher and
then moves to a lower register (*Schaudern* [Shuddering]) for expressive effect.
Wholly different in character, the last stanza starts in march rhythm, a new key
(subdominant) with a new, serene version of the original melody. Both accompaniment and melody are closely related to the final section of the last
*Gesellen Lied.* The original nostalgic "shawm solo" recurs twice, and the postlude
in the subdominant major key is again in march rhythm. The principal melody
borrows its typically Mahlerian portamento fourth upbeat from this solo. A folk
song set to nearly identical words and called "The Deserter" in Erk-Böhme's
collection (III, 261) is very similar, and Mahler must have been acquainted with it:

DER DESERTEUR

Zu Strass-burg auf der Schanz, da fing mein Un-glück
an; da __ wollt ich den Fran-zö-sen de-ser-
tieren, und __ wollt es bei den Preus-sen pro-
bieren, ei das ging nicht zu, _____ ei das ging nicht zu.

f) *"ABLÖESUNG IM SOMMER"* (Relief in Summer)

KEY: D flat minor (OR), as in high voice edition (A minor in low voice ed.) with major middle section.

TIME SIGNATURE: 2/4.

RHYTHM: Binary dance ("bourrée").

TEMPO: *Mit Humor* (With humor).

TEXT: Vol. II, page 406, under the title *"Ablöesung."* Mahler extended to twenty lines the original eight and altered three words. Six new lines are merely repetitions. Mahler wrote Lines 13 and 14: *"Die kleine, feine Nachtigall, Die liebe, süsse Nachtigall!"* but his only important contribution is in the last four lines:

*Wir warten auf Frau Nachtigall,*   We wait for the Lady Nightingale;
*Die wohnt im grünen Hage,*   She lives in the green grove,
*Und wenn der Kukuk zu Ende ist,*   And when the cuckoo is through,
*Dan fängt sie an zu schlagen!*   Then she starts her song!

Mahler's addition clarifies the poem's meaning and the "relief" of the cuckoo by the nightingale.

FORM: Like Mahler's version of the poem, the music is divided into four short stanzas, but despite the deliberately simple, almost crude folk style, the song is a free art lied rather than a strophic one. Small phrases and motifs are of course repeated (as in the later *Rheinlegendchen*), and the short postlude restates the initial motif, yet the symmetry is more apparent than real. The third stanza, in major, starts like a trio or contrasting middle section, but the earlier section is never literally restated. There are several delightful stylized birdcalls, beautifully integrated as usual in the thematic structure, and a startling sequence of descending perfect chords (on the words *"soll uns denn den Sommerlang"*), an archaic effect duplicated (but with sixth chords) in the choral movement of the *Third Symphony,* and the Finale of the *Fourth.* Rich in musical substance, this song has provided the great Scherzo of the *Third Symphony,* which also depicts animal life, with most of its thematic material. There is a 3/4 setting of the same text (1544) by Johann Ott, called "Kuckuck's Fall," but it need not be quoted, as it does not resemble Mahler's setting.[79]

g) *"SCHEIDEN UND MEIDEN"* (Parting and Fleeing) (Mahler's title in OR: *"Scheiden thut Weh!"*)

KEY: F major (OR, as in low voice ed.), alternating with minor.

TIME SIGNATURE: 6/8 (ending in 2/4 in the second section of both stanzas).

TEMPO: *Lustig* (Gay) (OR: *Frisch bewegt* [Lively and alert]).

TEXT: Vol. I, page 279, under the title *"Drei Ritter am Thor."* As usual, Mahler made many small changes, cutting, adding, and repeating occasional words. The "refrain" word *"Ade"* is repeated several times, and the entire last line once. Of the three original stanzas, Mahler has left out the second and has changed the words in the last line of the first stanza, which forms his title. In the original *"Scheiden und lassen"* (Parting and Leaving), he replaced *"lassen"* with *"meiden"* (to flee from) a more literary word that gives the poem a less naïve flavor than the original.

FORM: The song is made up of two pairs of stanzas that, although not identical musically, share the same accompaniment. To avoid monotony and uniformity, Mahler changed the order of the elements and subtly varied the two first stanzas. Thus once again he combined the strophic folk form with the *"durch-komponiert,"* art song. The last stanza (*"Ja, Scheiden"*) is simply an amplified version of the second part of the second stanza. The prevailing rhythm is that often used to imitate a horse's gallop, no doubt because of the poem's original title. The first bars of the accompaniment are marked *"wie Trompetenmusik,"* an effect further enhanced by the "horn" sixths, fifths, and thirds. The following quotation of the well-known German song, with much the same words, shows that Mahler knew it well. This song was based on an earlier melody published in Germany in 1774 and "sung four years ago in the streets of Rome by a German beggar.[80]

DREI RITTER AM TORE

TEDESCA

h) *"NICHT WIEDERSEHEN!"* (Never to Meet Again!)
KEY: C minor (OR), same as high voice ed. (B minor in low voice ed.).
TIME SIGNATURE: 4/4.
RHYTHM: Slow march.
TEMPO: *Schwermütig* [Sadly] (OR: id. with *"Ohne Sentimentalität"* added).
TEXT: Vol. I, page 317. For once, Mahler has scarcely altered the original text,
simply changing and repeating a few words and adding at the end of the first,
third, and fifth stanzas a refrain from the poem's last stanza: *"Ade, ade, mein
herzallerliebster Schatz."* A major difference between the poetic and musical
stanzas is that the song comprises three sections, each made up of two poetic
stanzas. Musically speaking, the two first sections are nearly identical, except
for some occasional octave doublings and a repeated bar creating an echo effect.
The alternation of major and minor gives the song a strong Mahlerian flavor. The
major mode conveys a more lyrical mood to the last stanza, but the coda, which
is again in minor, ends in the depths of despair. The final chord, prepared as it
is by a long tonic pedal, is inconclusive: it sounds like a dominant minor (in the
subdominant key).

This is another of Mahler's greatest songs, powerful and grief-laden, in which
his favorite slow march rhythm symbolizes man's tragic destiny. It is unfortunate
that he did not write an orchestral version, which would have greatly increased
the song's expressive power. There is a close connection between Mahler's melody
and the Kassel folk song *"Herzlieb im Grabe,"* set to the same words.[81]

HERZLIEB IM GRABE

i) *"SELBSTGEFÜHL"* (Odd Feeling)

KEY: F major (same as low voice ed.).

TIME SIGNATURE: 3/4.

RHYTHM: Ternary dance (ländler).

TEMPO: *In verdriesslichem Ton* [In a vexed tone] (OR: *In verdriesslich humoristichen Ton* [In a humorously vexed tone]).

TEXT: Vol. II, page 503. This is one of the very few poems in which Mahler has made no changes, aside from repeating a few lines and words and altering the original six three-line stanzas into four longer ones.

FORM: The last of the piano *Wunderhorn Lieder* is pure humor and charm. Without being a real ländler, it has a strong ländler flavor, and a nearly continuous eighth-note movement, which is used as a unifying principle in an otherwise very free composition. While the second and the fourth stanzas are nearly identical, the third, primarily in D minor, has little to do with the first. This song resembles *Hans und Grethe* more than any other Mahler composition, but shows what a long way he has traveled since 1880. The heavy octave basses are an obvious "folk" effect. There is no known traditional musical setting of this poem.

## 7) *10 WUNDERHORN LIEDER* with orchestra (1892–96)

COMPOSITION

The first four lieder of this group were composed and orchestrated in a very short time (January–February 1892), together with the future Finale of the *Fourth Symphony* (then called *"Das himmlische Leben"*). At that time Mahler searched for an original title for these unusual compositions and settled for a short time on *Humoresken*. The following year the songs were rechristened *Balladen und Humoresken aus "Des Knaben Wunderhorn."* In the concert program, only *"Das himmlische Leben," "Verlor'ne Müh'," and "Wer hat dies Liedlein erdacht?"* are entitled *Humoresken* (thus *"Der Schildwache Nachtlied," "Trost im Unglück,"* and *"Rheinlegendchen"* were presumably *Balladen*). One month later, in Wiesbaden, these three songs were entitled *Drei Gesänge aus den Knaben Wunderhorn.* The piano score, which is now in the Marburg Westdeutsche Staatsbibliothek, includes six songs (the five 1892 *Humoresken* and the 1893 *"Rheinlegendchen"*). The title reads *Des Knaben Wunderhorn.* Thus, Mahler had already done away with *Humoresken,* which he never used after 1893. As a matter of fact, these songs were not performed again until Selma Kurz sang three of them with the Vienna Philharmonic in 1900, when they were called *Gesänge.*

The orchestral *Wunderhorn Lieder* are "big" symphonic songs, in the same vein as the contemporary *Second* and *Third Symphonies,* and are so thoroughly orchestral in conception that they lose a great deal when accompanied on the piano. They do not, properly speaking, make up a cycle—*i.e.,* a logical integrated whole—and their sequence corresponds to the order of their composition. Yet they have so much in common—poems, themes, atmosphere, style—that, although the order can be changed at will, they are generally, and should be, performed together. Their style and dimensions place them in the tradition of the great ballads of Schubert and Löwe. Even more clearly than in the earlier, simpler songs, Mahler proves in this great and unique collection how much at home he felt in this world of naïveté and innocence. In it he found a complete image of man and his earthly destiny, both humorous and tragic, as well as a philosophical and mystical message more profound than that conveyed by most art poetry.

It has recently become the custom, both in concerts and on records, to divide the "duet" lieder between a male and a female voice. The performance obviously gains in liveliness and diversity, yet the songs were never meant to be performed in this way. The *répliques* are so short that the change of voice is not always convincing and is sometimes even detrimental to the music. Mahler himself wrote to the conductor Nicodé after 1903: "My songs are all conceived for male voices." This is true of most of the *Wunderhorn Lieder,* although, at the 1893 Hamburg performance, *"Wer hat dies Liedlein erdacht?"* and *"Verlor'ne Müh'"* were sung by Clementine Prosska, and in 1900 Selma Kurz sang the former song; as well as *"Das irdische Leben"* and *"Wo die schönen Trompeten blasen."* At the Vienna and Graz concerts in 1905 all the songs were sung by men. Why Mahler left out *"Lob des hohen Verstandes"* on this occasion is a mystery. Was he perhaps afraid of angering the critics once more?

In a letter of March 2, 1905, to Karpath, Mahler describes the *Wunderhorn* poems as "fundamentally different from any 'literary' poetry . . . They should be called nature and life (the source of all poetry) rather than art." Obviously the old anthology appeared to him more and more as a kind of lost paradise, inspiring a musical style that, although unique and supremely refined, is ideally suited to these simple folk texts.

MANUSCRIPTS: The piano score, most likely dating from 1893 and at present in the Marburg Westdeutsche Staatsbibliothek, includes a), b), c), d), and g), as well as *"Das himmlische Leben"* (see below No. 10, d). It was probably used for the rehearsals of the 1893 Hamburg concert, which included precisely these songs. There were sketches of a) and e) in Natalie Bauer-Lechner's collection (the first is now in the Library of Congress, Washington, D.C.); a piano sketch of f) in the Rosé Collection; and a short sketch of c) was formerly in Alma Mahler's collection. Orchestral scores of a), b), c), d), and *"Das himmlische Leben"* are in the Gesellschaft der Musikfreunde library in Vienna; orchestral scores of e) and g) formerly belonged to Alma Mahler; her orchestral score of f) was bought in 1948 by Rudolf Floersheim of Lugano.

No manuscripts of the last three songs are accessible at present, although Robin Lehmann possesses at least two of them.

a) *"DER SCHILDWACHE NACHTLIED"* (The Sentinel's Night Song)

The only song that Mahler sketched long before it was finished, this is, at least in part, his earliest known setting of a *Wunderhorn* text. Begun in 1888 for the opera that Mahler was then planning with Karl von Weber, it is the first consequence of the great revelation of the *Wunderhorn* anthology. It would be interesting to compare the two-page Leipzig sketch from Natalie's collection with the finished version, dated January 28, 1892.

MANUSCRIPTS: Sketch (Library of Congress) (It is composed of two separate sheets, the first one named as the song, and a further one bearing the title *"Verlorene Feldwacht"* and containing the last episode); piano (Berlin Staatsbibliothek); orchestra (Gesellschaft der Musikfreunde, Vienna).

KEY: B flat (ending on the dominant) (as in low voice ed.). 1st perf.: Paul Bulss, baritone (1893).

TIME SIGNATURE: 4/4, changing to 6/4 (mixed with 3/4 and 4/4).

RHYTHM: Quick march.

TEMPO: *Marschartig* (Like a march); *Etwas gemessener* (Somewhat slower); *Langsamer* (Slower).

TEXT: Vol. I, page 235. Mahler's alterations are very slight (*musst* instead of *sollst* in second stanza, first line; *geh'* instead of *komm* in third stanza, first line). Two groups of words are repeated. As Fritz Egon Pamer has pointed out, one of Mahler's alterations is more important than it looks: between Stanzas 4 and 5 the *Wunderhorn* reads:

| | |
|---|---|
| *An Gottes Segen* | On God's blessing |
| *Ist Alles gelegen,* | All is depending! |
| *Wer's glauben thut.* | [For] who may believe it. |

By changing the comma after *"gelegen"* into an exclamation mark, Mahler gave the last line an ironic rather than a direct meaning, and the whole following stanza about the condition of the powerful becomes bitter and sarcastic.

The last stanza's alteration undoubtedly makes it more "musical":

| OR: | MAHLER: |
|---|---|
| *Halt! Wer da?—Rund! Wer sang zur Stund?-* | *Halt! Wer da! Rund'!* |
| | *Bleib' mir vom Leib!* |
| | *Wer sang es hier! Wer sang zur Stund?* |
| *Verlor'ne Feldwacht* | *Verlor'ne Feldwacht* |
| *Sang es um Mitternacht.-* | *Sang es um Mitternacht.* |
| *Bleib mir vom Liebl* | *Mitternacht! Mitternacht!* |
| | *Feldwacht!* |

FORM: Like all those in dialogue form, this song is a rondo: the structure can be summed up as ABABAB, yet this simple pattern cannot suggest any of the subtle and delicate touches that Mahler has introduced, such as apparent restatements of the same passage retaining only characteristic rhythms, accompaniment figures or dynamics, but nothing more. Small orchestral intermezzos connect the various sections, and the last, very symphonic episode heightens the effect of *"Wer da! Rund! Bleib' mir vom Leib."* This is Mahler's first great orchestral "military" lied, bristling with drum rolls, trumpet calls, buoyant march rhythms, and rising fourths intervals. Even the sentinel's challenge is in the form of a trumpet call and plays an important part in the structure of the song as a whole. The voice's succeeding melody, in the relative minor key, is later restated in major. The girl's intervention is preceded by a caressing, lilting ostinato figure, which turns out to be the diminution of her melody and persists throughout her part. The melodic and harmonic sixths add to the feminine charm of these three episodes. As Fritz Egon Pamer has pointed out, the frequent rhythmic changes suggest a folk singer gasping for breath between the phrases of his song. The last lyrical section is extended into a short, serene coda based on earlier material. The girl takes over from her partner the trumpet call motif, which she sings pianissimo. Everything fades away into silence and midnight darkness with an inconclusive dominant chord.

Mahler violently disliked commentary or analysis of his music. When, in 1906, Paul Decsey pointed out this ending to him and emphasized the tension generated by the dominant pedal and the changing harmonies, he merely answered, "Oh! Dominant! Consider these things simply, as they were conceived!"[82]

There are several known folk songs based on this poem. One of them, of Westphalian origin, bears a certain likeness to Mahler's[83]:

WESTPHALIAN SONG

Ich kann und mag nicht trau-rig— sein,       wenn An - dre—

schla - fen so muss ich wa - chen, muss den - ken— dein.

b) *"VERLOR'NE MUEH' "* (Labor Lost) (Wasted Effort)

MANUSCRIPTS: Piano (Berlin Staatsbibliothek) dated February 1, 1892; orchestra (Gesellschaft, Vienna).

KEY: A major (and minor), as in high voice ed. (1st perf.: Amalie Joachim, alto [1892]; 2nd: Clementine Prosska, coloratura soprano [1893]).

TIME SIGNATURE: 3/8.

RHYTHM: Slow ländler.

TEMPO: *Gemächlich, heiter* (Moderate, gay) (on piano ms.: ♪=132).

TEXT: Vol. I, page 400, under the title: *"Verlor'ne Müh'."* This had already been published in Arnim's 1790 collection: *Fünf weltliche schöne neue Lieder.* Mahler kept only the first and last stanzas of the poem, in which he made few changes, aside from repeating lines and groups of words, adding question marks and exclamation points.

FORM: Strophic *Tanzlied.* Like all Mahler's other dialogue songs, this one has two separate musical sections for the boy's and girl's *répliques* and a short sixteenth note ritornello separating the first stanzas. Fritz Pamer has analyzed the means used by Mahler near the end to achieve a crescendo effect with un-expected modulations and a rising vocal line. In Bar 17 (*Unsere Lämmer*), Guido Adler noted the presence of Mahler's private "signal," which he borrowed from Beethoven's *Eighth Symphony* and often used in daily life. This is probably a deliberate quotation, connected in some way with the humor of the poem. There is no known original folk melody for this text.

c) *"TROST IM UNGLUECK"* (Comfort in Misfortune)

One of the five original *Humoresken.* Mahler's original title was *"Wir wissen uns zu trösten."*

MANUSCRIPTS: Sketch: Alma Mahler (one page); piano (Berlin Staatsbibliothek) dated February 22, 1892; orchestra (Gesellschaft, Vienna).

KEY: A major (as in high voice ed.: the girl's stanza is mostly in G major). (1st and 2nd perfs.: Paul Bulss, baritone [1893]; 3rd: Anton Moser, baritone [1905]).

TIME SIGNATURE: 6/8, 2/4. The most salient feature in this song is the constant alternation of binary and ternary rhythms, which are often used simultaneously, one in the voice and the other in the accompaniment, sometimes even in the two hands of the piano score.

TEMPO: *Verwegen. Durchaus mit prägnantestem Rhythmus* (Bold. Throughout with the most precise rhythm). (On piano ms.: ♩=100)

TEXT: Vol. I, page 399, under the title *"Geh Du nur hin, ich hab mein Theil."* The poem is another dialogue between a hussar and his girl, the last stanza being sung by both. The subject is very similar to that of the preceding song, and the two poems follow each other in the anthology. The *Wunderhorn* text is practically unchanged in the song. One word is suppressed and two are repeated. The four-line refrain *"Geh' Du nur hin,"* etc., returns five times in the poem but only three times in the song, and to different music.

FORM: There is a rondo feeling due to the recurrences of the original ritornello, but the form can be summarized as roughly AABA. B is the girl's stanza, which, although in 2/4 and in another key, is rhythmically connected to the first. The last stanza combines A with elements of B. Although this amusing dispute between a hussar and his fiancée has little to do with army life, it is full of quick triplet upbeats, horn and trumpet calls (even in the vocal line), military drums and triangle. In this song Mahler definitely quotes from the well-known Silesian folk setting of the same text: *Husarenliebe*[84]:

HUSARENLIEBE

Wohl - an die Zeit ist kom - men, mein Pferd das muss ge -
sat - telt sein; ich hab mir's vor - ge - nom - men, ge -
rit - ten muss es sein. Geh du nur hin, ich
hab' mein Theil, ich führ dich nur am Nar - ren seil; oh - ne
dich kann ich schon le - ben, oh - ne dich kann ich schon sein.

d) *"WER HAT DIES LIEDLEIN ERDACHT?"* (Who Made Up This Little Song?) (Third of the 1892 *Humoresken*)

MANUSCRIPTS: Piano (Berlin Staatsbibliothek) dated February 6, 1892; orchestra (Gesellschaft, Vienna).

KEY: F major (as in high voice ed.: 1st perf.: Clementine Prosska, coloratura soprano [1893]; 2nd: Selma Kurz, coloratura soprano [1900]).

TIME SIGNATURE: 3/8 (on piano ms.: ♪=160).

RHYTHM: Ländler.

TEMPO: *Mit heiterem Behagen* (With easy gaiety); *Gemächlich* (Moderate) for the middle stanza.

TEXT: Vol. I, page 243. Both the piano manuscript and the piano edition carry the above title, while for some unknown reason the miniature score has *"Liedel"* instead of *"Liedlein."* Mahler used the first and last stanzas verbatim, but replaced the middle one with a stanza that he no doubt took from another, unidentified poem (from *"Geh' nur hin"* to *"kann ich wohl sein"*). In addition to this major alteration, there are two smaller ones: *"wacker Mädel raus"* is changed into *"fein's lieb's Mädel heraus,"* and *"am Berg"* is added in the first line.

FORM: Strophic *Tanzlied*. The construction is far more subtle than at first appears, as is generally the case with Mahler's simplest and shortest lieder. The many different thematic fragments are unified by a nearly continuous sixteenth-note motion and by the first motif's return as a kind of refrain. Starting in D minor and modulating from there, the second stanza forms a contrasting element, and the last one restates only the conclusion of the first with many variants. Such techniques anticipate those Mahler used so brilliantly in the *Fourth Symphony*. The first and last stanzas end with a long sixteenth-note vocalise in which the influence of the Tyrolian yodel has been detected. It is often quoted as an example of Mahler's "instrumental" use of the voice.

### e) *"DAS IRDISCHE LEBEN"* (Earthly Life)

From Natalie's reference to this song in her Mahler diary in the summer of 1893, one can deduce that it was composed either before or, even more probably, at the same time as the *"Fischpredigt"* and *"Rheinlegendchen."*[85] Mahler himself explained why he changed the original title (see below): "The text only suggests the deeper meaning, the treasure that must be searched for. Thus, I picture as a symbol of human life the child's cry for bread and the mother's attempt to console him with promises. I named the song *'Das irdische Leben'* for precisely that reason. What I wished to express is that the necessities for one's physical and spiritual growth are long delayed, and finally come too late, as they do for the dead child. I believe I have expressed this in a characteristic and frightening way, thanks to the strange sounds of the accompaniment, which roars and whistles like a storm, to the tortured and anguished cries of the child, and to the slow, monotonous reply of the mother, Destiny, who does not always fulfill at the right time our anguished request for bread . . ." On another, symbolic level Mahler certainly considered this song an image of his own tragedy as a composer, who would be recognized only after his death.

MANUSCRIPTS: Sketch (Stanford University); orchestra (Alma Mahler, probably identical with ms. now in the Pierpont Morgan Library).

KEY: B flat minor, Lydian mode (with flattened surpratonic) (as in high voice ed.: 1st perf.: Selma Kurz, coloratura soprano [1900]; 2nd and 3rd: Fritz Weidemann, baritone [1905]).

TIME SIGNATURE: 2/4.

TEMPO: *Unheimlich bewegt* (With sinister animation).

TEXT: Vol. I, page 452, under the title *"Verspätung"* (Lateness). Mahler has made no alterations except to suppress two stanzas: the first in which the mother affirms that the wheat will be sown, and the next to last, in which she promises to grind the grains. His aim was to shorten this song and make it more dramatic. In the last line Mahler has replaced *"schon auf der Bahr"* with *"auf der Totenbahr."*

FORM: Strophic song. The intensity increases constantly until the tragic end. The child's cry, *"Gib' mir Brot,"* continually changes key (E flat minor, A flat minor, E flat minor, C flat minor, and F flat minor) until the final climactic high G flat, while the mother's *"warte nur"* symbolically remains the same. The child's anguish is suggested by a melodic minor ninth. With its archaic figures, the continuous sixteenth-note ostinato of the accompaniment evokes both feverish haste and the monotony of life proceeding mechanically, unconcerned by man's suffering, until the last muffled cymbal clash. Despite the simplicity of means employed, this is one of the most intensely gripping of all Mahler's songs. There are at least two folk songs based on this text,[86] but neither bears any resemblance to Mahler's setting.

f) *"DES ANTONIUS VON PADUA FISCHPREDIGT"* (St. Anthony of Padua's Sermon to the Fishes) (July–August 1893)

It is one of the most interesting facts in Mahler's creative life that here, rather than borrowing the substance of a symphonic movement from an earlier song, as he often did, he composed lied and symphonic scherzo practically at the same time (see Chapter XVIII). As to the song's symbolic meaning, Mahler explained his intentions to Natalie: "A somewhat sweet-sour humor reigns in the *'Fischpredigt.'* The blessed Anthony preaches to the fishes, but his speech sounds completely drunken, slurred (in the clarinet) and confused. And what a glittering multitude! The eels and carps and the sharp-nosed pikes, whose stupid expression as they look at Antonius, stretching their stiff, unbending necks out of the water, I can practically see in my music, and I nearly burst out laughing. Then, the sermon over, the assembly swims away in all directions

> The Sermon has pleased
> They remain as ever!

not an atom the wiser, although the saint has performed for them! Only very few people will understand the satire on humanity in this story!"

MANUSCRIPTS: Piano (Alfred Rosé, London, Ontario); orchestra (Gesellschaft, Vienna).

KEY: C minor (as in low voice ed., with one F major section) (1st and 2nd perfs.: Anton Moser, baritone [1905]; 3rd: Fritz Weidemann, baritone [1905]).

TIME SIGNATURE: 3/8.

RHYTHM: Slow ländler.

TEMPO: *Behäbig. Mit Humor* (Comfortable. With humor).

TEXT: Vol. I, page 375, reproduced by the *Wunderhorn* from Abraham a Sancta Clara's *Judas, der Erzschelm.* Mahler has made no changes except for omitting the second and fourth refrain *"Kein Predigt niemalen,"* changing three insignificant words and repeating the penultimate line at the end.

FORM: Strophic, rondo form, but, as usual, with considerable freedom of treatment. In the over-all AABA structure, each section is made up of two poetic stanzas. The B episode, in contrast, suggests a trio. As in *"Rheinlegendchen"* and *"Wer hat dies Liedlein erdacht?"*, there is a continuous sixteenth-note motion, sometimes in thirds. In this song Mahler's contrapuntal spirit is more than ever at work, and the design in thirds often runs on with complete disregard of the harmonies thus engendered. The many parallel fifths in the bass produce an archaic effect. The initial eighth-note motif (G-C-E flat-D-C), with its typical Mahlerian fourth on the upbeat, returns at the beginning of each poetic stanza like a refrain. The composition is full of subtle and interesting details, such as the anticipation of the vocal motif of B in the second A stanza, and the statement, in the middle of B, of a new short melody ("cantabile"), which plays an important part in the Scherzo. Mahler himself recognized in the *"Fischpredigt"* the "Bohemian music of his birthplace . . . The national feeling shows up in its crudest basic features, borrowed from the piping [*Gedudel*] of the itinerant Bohemian musicians."

### g) "RHEINLEGENDCHEN" (Little Rhine Legend)

Mahler told Natalie that the main theme for this lied sprang into his mind first and that he had searched the anthology for words to suit it; consequently the result differs greatly from the *Wunderhorn Lieder* composed earlier in Leipzig: "It is much more direct, that is, both childish, mischievous and heartfelt; you have never heard anything like it! And the instrumentation is both gentle and sunny, like the pure colors of a butterfly. But, despite its folklike simplicity, it is also highly unusual, especially as regards the harmony, so that people will not understand it and will call it farfetched. Nevertheless, the harmonies are the most natural imaginable, simply those which the melody required."[87]

MANUSCRIPTS: Piano (Marburg Staatsbibliothek), dated August 10, 1893; orchestra (Robin Lehman), dated August 9.

KEY: A major (high voice) (1st and 2nd perfs.: Paul Bulss, baritone [1893]; 3rd: Anton Moser [1905]).

TIME SIGNATURE: 3/8.

TEMPO: *Gemächlich* (At ease).

TEXT: Vol. I, page 458, under the title *"Rheinischer Bundesring."* Mahler's original title was *"Tanzreime,"* and later *"Tanzlegendchen."* He made practically no changes in the text, two stanzas of which are of Bavarian or Tyrolian folk origin, and the rest art poetry.

FORM: *Tanzlied* in Mahler's typically Austrian vein. The first notes of the vocal theme recur at the beginning of each of the three musical stanzas, together with several other melodic figures, but what follows is always different. There are a number of different motifs, but only one single continuous rhythmic flow and no real contrasts. Not only is the atmosphere similar to that of the *Fourth Symphony*, but so is the technique. Even the ritenuto upbeat (in the second bar), a typical dance music effect found in many Strauss waltzes, is present in the symphony in the main theme of the first movement.

Fritz Egon Pamer's detailed enumeration[88] of the purely "folk music" features in the song's principal melody is extremely interesting: they include the structure of the first phrase, its eight bar periods, the dance rhythms, the sequential appoggiaturas, and, in the accompaniment, the succession of simple chords, the *"Nachsatz"* (second part of the first phrase), modulating to the dominant. In addition, Pamer points out many other features that are quite foreign to the folk song, such as the highest note in the first vocal phrase appearing on an unaccented beat, the end of the first phrase, *"Was hilft mir,"* and its sudden return from the key of F sharp to E major. Most of the harmonies chosen too, as Mahler himself noted, are far from the obvious.

The well-known folk melody quoted by Pamer[89] has much in common with Mahler's:

DAS MÄRCHEN VOM RINGLEIN

Pamer has also quoted the *Trio* in ländler rhythm from Schubert's 1826 *G Major Sonata,* Op. 78, which is closely related to one of Mahler's melodic fragments:

RHEINLEGENDCHEN

SCHUBERT: Sonata in G, D. 894 (Trio)

h) *"LIED DES VERFOLGTEN IM TURM"* (Song of the Prisoner in the Tower)

For this lied and the following one, the manuscripts have not been found, and their dating must remain conjectural. They were probably composed during the summer of 1895, for the preceding summer Mahler was absorbed in the completion of the *Second Symphony,* and the following summer he seems to have composed only the last song in this collection, *"Lob des hohen Verstandes."*

MANUSCRIPTS: In the Robin Lehman Collection, London?

KEY: D minor (as in high voice ed.: 1st perf.: Anton Moser, baritone [1905]).

TIME SIGNATURE: 12/8 (changing to 6/8 for the girl's stanza).

TEMPO: *Leidenschaftlich, Eigenwillig* (Passionate, willfully obstinate), alternating with *Verzagt, Schmeichlerisch* (Despondent, flattering).

TEXT: Vol. II, page 338. In the original poem, of Swiss-German origin, quoted by Fritz Egon Pamer, there is no dialogue, and the exchange of questions between the prisoner and his girl was added by the editors. Mahler has made no changes other than to repeat two lines and cut out another.

FORM: ABABABA, rondo form, like all the dialogue songs, with two strongly contrasting episodes. The stanzas proceed from one key to another: D minor, G major, G minor, A flat major, C major, F major, D minor. Although the short, minor, A sections remain nearly identical despite their change of key, there are considerable differences between the girl's major and lyrical stanzas. The second, which is the longest, displays Mahler's most ingenious development and counterpoint techniques. The portamento upbeats are again inspired by the yodel singing style. The second A stanza in major is brilliantly accompanied by trumpets and horn. Another striking and archaic succession of "crude" fifths in the bass is found here, followed by a motif borrowed from the accompaniment of B. Given the subject, it is not surprising to find in this song a host of military such as march rhythm, fast triplet upbeats, and trumpet calls in arpeggio form (even in the vocal part). The music expresses the same bitterness and despair as the text, a feeling rarely found with such intensity in Mahler's lieder. The contrast to the "feminine" stanzas in the major mode is so sudden and so startling that it becomes an effect in itself. All of Mahler's skill was needed to unify such totally dissimilar elements.

i) *"WO DIE SCHOENEN TROMPETEN BLASEN"* (Where the Proud Trumpets Blow)

Like the preceding song, this one was in all likelihood composed in 1895. Mahler himself mentioned it only once, according to Natalie's unpublished Mahler diary of January 1900, just before the song's first performance. Lipiner and Spiegler both believed the poem's hero to be dead, appearing before his sweetheart as a ghost, while Mahler believed him alive and imagining his death on the battlefield.

MANUSCRIPT: In the Robin Lehman Collection, London?

KEY: D minor (as in high voice ed.) (1st perf.: Selma Kurz, soprano [1900]; 2nd: Anton Moser, baritone [1905]).

TIME SIGNATURE: 2/4 alternating with 3/4 in secondary sections.

TEMPO: *Verträumt. Leise* (Dreamy. Softly), *Sehr gehalten* (Much slower).

TEXT: Passages chosen from two poems from Vol. II (*Unbeschreibliche Freude*, page 406, and *Bildchen*, page 378), which have only a few lines in common. In fact Mahler practically invented a new poem. Stanzas 1, 2, and 3 of the first poem are quoted literally, while Nos. 5, 6, and 8 of the second are altered, particularly by the addition of the girl's lines (*"Willkommen lieber Knabe mein!"*). According to Pamer, the last stanzas of *Bildchen* are not true folk poetry, and Mahler replaced them with verses from another poem because of their somewhat artificial character. The words and lines added by him are even more naïve than the originals and therefore closer to the folk style. Pamer calls his work a "philological restoration."

FORM: Although not a true dialogue, the song is in rondo form with two alternating and sharply contrasted episodes, that of the soldier (2/4, minor) with wind accompaniment, and the girl (3/4, major) with a string background. The pattern is roughly the following: ABA(C)ABA, but the various episodes do not retain their original key; they change from D minor to D major, D major-minor, G flat, B minor, D major, and D minor. The whole song, a genuine tone poem in Mahler's most evocative and expressive vein, is based on the sound of the trumpet and the horn and their "signals." Nothing in the text suggests that the soldier is a ghost, yet the very character of the nocturnal and distant music implies it: the feelings expressed seem to be those of someone who has lost all contact with life's vanities.

The most amazing mastery of form and composition is evident throughout this song, in which the stylized military "signals" are endlessly transformed. Distant, ghostly drum rolls echo this time from the low strings. Mahler's use of rhythm is also highly refined. After the end of the instrumental prelude, the three bars in 3/4 are both a written out allargando and a suggestion of the later B section. The arpeggio intervals of the brass signals, on which the beginning of the vocal A section is based, contrast with the conjoint degrees of the B melody, accompanied by caressing strings playing in sixths. The expressive climax of the song, one of the finest passages in all of Mahler's music, is the melting G flat lullaby episode (C) with its muted string accompaniment. An extension of part of the A section, it is a musical episode of supreme simplicity and irresistible effect. Pamer finds a resemblance between both the oboe theme in the prelude and the Italian song by Denza *"Funiculì, funiculà,"* which Mahler loved, and, more striking still, Mahler's song and a *Mitteldeutsch* folk song, *"Die Freundenlose"*[90]:

DIE FREUDENLOSE

j) *"LOB DES HOHEN VERSTANDES"* (Praise of the Lofty Intellect)

This song, the last of the orchestral *Wunderhorn* collection, was composed in the middle of June 1896, while Mahler was waiting for the first movement sketches of the *Third Symphony,* which had been mailed to him from Hamburg. Like the other songs, it was certainly orchestrated immediately. Mahler's original title was *"Lob der Kritik."* He called it "a humorous mockery of the critics" and was delighted by the poem: "In this case, my problem was not to spoil anything, and to reproduce faithfully all that it contained, whereas elsewhere one can often add a great deal, deepen and enrich the poetic substance with music."

MANUSCRIPT: Unfinished sketch in E for voice and piano entitled *"Lob der Kritik,"* in Moldenhauer Archive, Spokane, Washington.

KEY: D major (same as high voice).

TIME SIGNATURE: 2/4.

RHYTHM: Binary dance ("bourrée").

TEMPO: *Keck* ("Audaciously").

TEXT: Vol. I, page 476, under the title *"Wettstreit des Kuckuks mit der Nachtigall"* (The Contest Between the Cuckoo and the Nightingale). The sixteenth-century five-voice setting of the poem by a Nuremberg Mastersinger was published as No. 14 in Jacob Regnart's anthology, *Neue kurtzweilige Teutsche Lieder* includes one stanza more than the *Wunderhorn* version. Mahler made many small alterations, cutting some words, adding or altering others, deleting two whole lines from the fourth stanza. At the end of the third stanza the *"Ija"* is his, as is the *"Kuckuk, Kuckuk, Ija!"* at the end, a combination of the two "languages," that of the victor and that of the judge.

FORM: Simple strophic structure: AAABA. The third A section starts in minor, to a grotesque accompaniment of horns, bassoons, and trombones. It is abruptly cut off at the end of the first phrase. The orchestra takes up and pursues the main line and the voice merely enters a few bars later for a single bar, in unison with the strings. The dimensions of the interludes somewhat upset the natural balance of the stanzas: they are real solos, which give to the simple and humorous lied a strong "art" flavor. The last stanza is a restatement of the first, but the short instrumental prelude is appended as a coda, this time accompanying the voice. Rather than singing in fourths, as in the Introduction to the *First Symphony,* the cuckoo now sings in thirds, as he does in nature. The dotted rhythms give the whole song an archaic flavor.

Pamer notes two interesting similarities, the first between the main theme of this lied and a fragment from a Tübingen folk song, itself similar to the *"Quodlibet"* from Bach's *Goldberg Variations:*

LOB DES HOHEN VERSTANDES

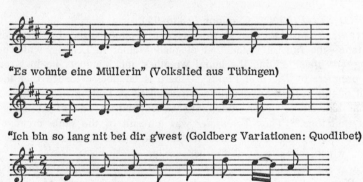

"Es wohnte eine Müllerin" (Volkslied aus Tübingen)

"Ich bin so lang nit bei dir g'west (Goldberg Variationen: Quodlibet)

The second is between a fragment from the last movement of the Schubert *D Major Sonata,* D. 850 (Bars 21 and 22), and one from the orchestral interludes in *Lob des hohen Verstandes* (Bars 70 and 71):

LOB DES HOHEN VERSTANDES

SCHUBERT: Sonata in G major, D. 894

Two further lieder are included in the voice and piano edition of the orchestral *Wunderhorn Lieder:*

k) *"ES SUNGEN DREI ENGEL EINEN SUESSEN GESANG"* [Three Angels Sang a Sweet Song] (See below the *Third Symphony,* 9e)

The song version is called "Transcription for one voice." The three first bars, *i.e.,* the children's chorus, *"Bim, Bam,"* are of course eliminated, as are the last ten decrescendo bars. The transcription is in E flat (low voice); or F (high voice, as in the symphony).

1) *"URLICHT"* [Primeval Light] (See below, the *Second Symphony,* 8d)

This is the piano original of the orchestral song that Mahler inserted in the *Second Symphony* as a slow introduction to the Finale (see below). The key is the same (D flat).

8) *SECOND SYMPHONY,* C minor (1888–94)

COMPOSITION: Thanks to one single anecdote, immortalized by the indispensable Natalie—the funeral vision that plagued Mahler in Leipzig, while he was composing *Totenfeier* among the laurel wreathes and bouquets he had received after the premiere of *Die drei Pintos*[91]—there is tangible evidence that the first movement of this *Second Symphony* was composed in Leipzig in February 1888, a fact that had already been stated by Max Steinitzer, one of Mahler's close friends at that time.[92] Thus *Totenfeier* was a result of the same creative urge (Mahler in one of his letters calls it "an impetuous torrent") as the *First Symphony,* which, however, was finished earlier.

Mahler was still working on his great "Funeral March" during the rehearsals of *Die drei Pintos* in Prague. The twenty-page autograph score of the original version of the movement, which used to belong to Natalie, is dated August 8, 1888.[93] Concerning the former title of this symphonic Allegro, an important fact seems to have escaped notice up to now. Siegfried Lipiner, Mahler's close friend from the Vegetarian Society days, published in Leipzig, where Mahler was then living, a complete translation, named *Totenfeier,* of Adam Mickiewicz's great poem *Dziady.*[94] It was the first appearance in print of any work by Lipiner, and it cannot have escaped Mahler's notice. Consequently, there must have been some connection in his mind between the Mickiewicz poem and the composition to which he gave the same title.

In the preface he wrote for the translation, Lipiner defines *Totenfeier* [Funeral Feast] as "a feast that is still held by people in many provinces of Lithuania, East Prussia and Kurlandia. Its origin can be traced back to the heroic age. It was then called *'Bockfest'* . . . These rites are still performed in chapels and deserted houses, not far from the cemetery." This funeral feast was, therefore, a very pagan ceremony, springing from man's ancient belief that banquets offered in honor of the dead can soothe them and better their condition. Although this feast plays an essential part in the poem, the exact translation of the Polish word *Dziady* is not "Funeral Feast," but "The Elders" or "The Forefathers."

Mickiewicz's poem is curiously divided into four different parts, the first of which is fragmentary and remained unpublished until after his death. Part 3, the longest, was written in France and published in 1830. Its main character is a patriotic hero called Conrad, while the earlier Parts 2 and 4 are about an ultra-romantic Werther figure, curiously named Gustav. Both heroes are known to be literary transpositions of the poet himself. In the Gustav poem, he tells the story of his own hopeless passion for Maria Wereszcak, a young girl who, although she was in love with him, married someone else. The shock was so great that it drove the poet to the brink of madness. Like his hero Gustav, he became obsessed with the idea of suicide, a recurrent theme in the poem. Knowing that literature (and particularly the works of his friend Siegfried Lipiner) was dear to Mahler's heart, one can be certain that Mickiewicz's poem was in his mind when he composed the great march or at least when he chose the title. It is also impossible not to draw a parallel between the poet's love for Maria Wereszcak (mentioned by Lipiner in his preface) and the composer's for Marion Mathilde von Weber, who was likewise married to another man. When Mahler had morbid visions of death in Leipzig while composing, it was Marion herself who dispelled them by visiting him and removing the flowers strewn around his room. Although there is no connection between Mickiewicz's poem and the program that Mahler later devised for the first movement of his symphony, Mahler probably secretly dedicated *Totenfeier*, like the *First Symphony*, to Marion, as a kind of requiem for their thwarted love affair.

*Totenfeier* was to remain an isolated work for five years. Mahler must have thought highly of it, as this is the piece he chose to play for Bülow when he arrived in Hamburg in 1891. Mahler had considered performing it on its own, for the *Prager Abendblatt* announced Dresden performances of both symphonic works when he left Prague at the end of August 1888. Only in 1893 did Mahler's symphonic conceptions mature: a symphony must be a world in sound, it must deliver some great message. And obviously in 1888 *Totenfeier*, grandiose as it was, could no longer remain on its own. It must be integrated into a larger composition. By that time he had already suppressed *Titan*, the original title of the *First Symphony*, and the very idea of "suggesting the contents of the work, or at least paraphrasing my intentions with words," no longer seemed feasible to him. "Let's call them both 'symphony' and nothing else! For the name 'symphonic poem' is old-fashioned, without any very precise meaning. One always thinks of Liszt's compositions, which rather attempt the description of detailed events. Whereas in my two symphonies, there is nothing except the complete substance of my whole life."[95]

When Mahler left for Steinbach in the middle of June 1893, he took with him not only the complete *Totenfeier* manuscript, but also two separate sheets of music paper; on one hand he had noted in Leipzig the complete A flat theme of the Andante (with, as a counter melody, the later cello song), practically complete until the double bar (Figure 3), and on the other the complete G sharp minor episode (with its own counter melody at Figure 4). The Andante was composed shortly after Mahler's arrival in Steinbach that summer, sometime around June 21[96] and the sketch took no more than a week to compose. According to

Natalie, by then Mahler had already completed the sketch of the Scherzo, and the first orchestral score likewise bears an earlier date (July 16) than that of the Andante (July 30). Strangely enough, the orchestration of the lied *"Fischpredigt"* was finished the next day (see Chapter XVIII). During the month of August that same summer (probably the most productive in Mahler's life), he also composed both *"Rheinlegendchen"* (see above, 7g) and *"Das irdische Leben"* (see 7e); copied the slow movement of the *First Symphony*, later suppressed, and searched in vain for suitable material for his finale.

During the early spring of 1894, Mahler revised *Totenfeier*, now the first movement of the symphony, and dated his revision April 29.[97] By that time the famous incident at Bülow's funeral had already provided inspiration for the *"Aufersteh'n"* Finale, and Mahler had noted down some of the material for this movement. It was sketched, again in Steinbach, between June 8 and June 29, 1894, and the orchestral score was finished on July 25, just before Mahler left for Bayreuth. It was later recopied by him during the autumn, and he wrote on the finished score, "December 18, 1894."

That *"Urlicht"* was composed before the second and third movements of the symphony is now an established fact. Josef Förster had already hinted as much,[98] and Mahler states, in a hitherto unknown letter to Hermann Behn, that he composed it with piano "before he even considered inserting it in the symphony."[99] It even seems probable that it preceded the 1892 *Wunderhorn Lieder*, for Mahler is hardly likely to have written such an important song with piano accompaniment after the orchestral *Wunderhorn* songs for that year. No clue exists as to the date of the orchestration of *"Urlicht,"* but it probably took place in Steinbach in the summer of 1893, unless of course Mahler decided to include it in the symphony only in 1894, when he composed his Finale and devised the final plan of the whole work.

ORDER OF THE MOVEMENTS: One of Mahler's problems when he completed the symphony was to decide the order of the various movements. He had originally placed the Scherzo second and the Andante third, but he found the lack of key contrast between the opening Allegro and the Scherzo unfortunate. Between the Andante and *"Urlicht"* the transition would have been equally unsatisfactory, no longer because of the keys, but because of the atmosphere and general character of the two movements.[100] Mahler often regretted the "overemphasized, sharp and inartistic contrast" between the "gay dance rhythms" of the Andante and the grandiose style of the preceding Allegro maestoso. Among other solutions he even considered revising the order of the various sections in the slow movement, to start with the cello melody that serves as countertheme (seven bars after Figure 5) in the restatement of A. But he finally gave up the idea of revising the composition of a work that was now "too far away from him." The trouble, he later remembered, came from the fact that he had sketched the first movements separately, without thinking of their respective positions. In the later symphonies this could not happen, the movements having been sketched in the right key and in their final order. All he could do to attenuate the contrast between the two first movements of the *Second Symphony* was to prescribe a five-minute pause, which he still insisted upon as late as 1903, claiming that otherwise the Andante appeared as a "mere discrepancy" after the first movement.

That Mahler was still concerned with this problem as late as 1903 is clear from the following extract from a letter to the Düsseldorf conductor Julius Buths: "Thus the main break in the concert will be between the fourth and fifth movement. I am amazed by the sensitivity of feeling that enabled you to find the natural division of the work, and this, contrary to my own indications. I have long been of the same opinion, and all the performances I have conducted have only strengthened it. Nevertheless, a pause must also be made after the first movement, because otherwise the second will seem like a mere discrepancy. It is I who am responsible for this, not any lack of comprehension on the part of the listener. Perhaps you felt it when you rehearsed the two pieces in succession. The Andante is a kind of intermezzo (like a last echo of bygone days in the life of the man who was carried to his grave in the first movement—'for the sun still smiles upon him').

"Whereas the first, third, fourth and fifth movements are connected as to theme and atmosphere, the second stands alone and somewhat interrupts the austere progression of events. Perhaps this is a weakness in the plan, but my intention is certainly clear to you by now, thanks to the explanation suggested above . . ."[101]

PUBLICATION: During her visit to Hamburg in 1896, Natalie claims that she enlisted the help of the rich industrialist Berkan for the publication of the score of the *Second Symphony*. Behn's two-piano transcription had already been published by Hofmeister in December 1895, together with the *"Urlicht,"* the fourth movement with piano accompaniment. The orchestral score was published in February 1897 by the same publisher (Hofmeister) in Leipzig.

MANUSCRIPTS: The complete score of the first version of the first movement called *Totenfeier* used to belong to Natalie Bauer-Lechner (now in the Rudolf Mengelberg collection). According to the catalogue of a 1930 Liepmannssohn autograph, it is an extensive orchestra sketch containing all the principal voices and some of the secondary ones, but there are substantial differences between it and the published version, especially in the first half of the piece. The latter part is practically identical to pages 43 to 56 of the published score, except for the end, where the last five bars are marked "Allegro" instead of "Tempo primo" in the printed score. Two pages (17 and 18) of this manuscript are crossed out in pencil, yet some of the material included in them has survived in the symphony. In all likelihood the score used by Mahler when he played the March for Bülow in 1891 was another one, which has vanished, at least for the moment. Twenty-eight pages of sketches, also from Natalie's collection, are now in the Vienna Stadtbibliothek. Most of them are from the first movement and date probably from 1893–94, when Mahler revised the movement. Two sheets dating from the Leipzig period and including the exposition of the Andante are to be found in the same library. In the sketches for the first movement one detail is of interest: the minor English horn "pastoral" melody that plays such an important part in the development (at Figure 8 in the score) is several times called by Mahler *"Meerestille"* (calm sea). The first orchestral scores of the second and third movements belong to an (at present) unidentified owner.

The first complete orchestral manuscript with *"1. Satz gezeichnet Sonntag, 29. April 94 renovatum"* inscribed at the end of the revised Allegro maestoso and *"18. Dezember 1894"* at the end of the Finale belonged to the late Rudolf Mengelberg. Lastly, there exists in the Osborn Collection at the Yale Library, a complete orchestral score in the hand of the Hamburg copyist (undoubtedly Weidich), with numerous additions and corrections in Mahler's handwriting. This was undoubtedly the copy used by him to conduct the 1895 premiere. It does not include *"Urlicht."* The first brass signal episode, with the backstage horn (at Figure 3) is called *"Der Rufer in der Wüste,"* while the parallel one, just before the entrance of the chorus, is named *"Der grosser Appell"* (Figure 29 in the score). Finally, Universal Edition owns a printed score with numerous other inscriptions in Mahler's hand.

PROGRAMS: To explain the meaning and structure of the *Second Symphony*, Mahler devised an elaborate "program," of which different versions exist. The first is included in a letter written to Max Marschalk[102] in December 1895 after the premiere of the work: "The original aim of this work was never to describe an event in detail; rather it concerns a feeling. Its spiritual message is clearly expressed in the words of the final chorus. The unexpected appearance of the alto solo casts a sudden illumination on the first movement. It is easy to understand that, because of the nature of music, I have imagined in certain passages something like the dramatic performance of a real event. The parallel between life and music is perhaps deeper and more extensive than can be drawn at present. Yet I ask no one to follow me along this track, and I leave the interpretation of details to the imagination of each individual listener . . ."

A few months later Mahler was already much more precise: "I have called the first movement *Totenfeier* [Funeral Feast] and, if you are interested, it is the hero of my *First D Major Symphony* who is being carried to his grave and whose life I imagine I can see reflected in a mirror from a high watchtower. At the same time the big question is being asked: Wherefore hast thou lived? Wherefore hast thou suffered? Is it all some great, fearful joke? We must answer these questions in some way if we are to continue living—yes, even if we must only continue dying. The man in whose life this call resounds must give an answer, and I give it in the last movement. The second and third movements are conceived as an interlude: the second, a memory! A ray of sun, clear and untroubled, from the hero's life. I am sure you have experienced this while you were carrying to his grave someone who was near to your heart; perhaps on the way back there suddenly appeared the image of an hour of happiness long passed, which lit up your soul and which no shadow can spoil. One practically forgets what has happened! That is the second movement!

"When you awaken from this melancholy dream and must return to life's confusion, it can easily happen that the ceaseless agitation, the meaningless bustle of life, seems to you unreal, like dancing forms in a brightly lit ballroom: you watch them from the darkness and from a distance, so that you cannot hear the accompanying music! And so life seems without meaning, a fearful nightmare from which you awaken with a cry of horror. This is the third movement! What follows afterwards is clear to you . . ."

In January 1896, after a two-piano performance of the symphony, Mahler gave Natalie and Bruno Walter another, slightly different program. "The first movement depicts the titanic struggle against life and destiny fought by a superman who is still a prisoner of the world; his endless, constant defeats and finally his death. The second and third movements are episodes from the life of the fallen hero. The Andante tells of his love. What I have expressed in the Scherzo can only be described visually. When one watches a dance from a distance, without hearing the music, the revolving motions of the partners seem absurd and pointless. Likewise, to someone who has lost himself and his happiness, the world seems crazy and confused, as if deformed by a concave mirror. The Scherzo ends with the fearful scream of a soul that has experienced this torture.

"In *'Urlicht'* the questions and struggle of the human soul for God, as well as its own divine nature and existence, come to the forefront. Whereas the first three movements are narrative, the last is altogether dramatic. Here, all is motion and occurrence. The movement starts with the same dreadful death cry which ended the Scherzo. And now, after these frightening questions, comes the answer, redemption. To begin with, as faith and the church picture it: the day of judgment, a huge tremor shakes the earth. The climax of this terrifying event is accompanied by drum rolls. Then the last trump sounds. The graves burst open, all the creatures struggle out of the ground, moaning and trembling. Now they march in mighty processions: rich and poor, peasants and kings, the whole church with bishops and popes. All have the same fear, all cry and tremble alike because, in the eyes of God, there are no just men. As though from another world, the last trump sounds again. Finally, after they have left their empty graves and the earth lies silent and deserted, there comes only the long-drawn note of the bird of death. Even he finally dies.

"What happens now is far from expected: no divine judgment, no blessed and no damned, no Good and no Evil, and no judge. Everything has ceased to exist. Soft and simple, the words gently swell up: 'Rise again, yes rise again, wilt thou, my dust, when rest is o'er.' Here the words suffice as commentary and I will not add one syllable. The big crescendo which starts at this point is so tremendous and unimaginable that I do not myself know how I achieved it."[103]

For the 1900 Munich performance and the 1901 Dresden concert, Mahler devised yet another program, which he suppressed at the last moment in Munich but was prevailed upon to publish in Dresden:

First Movement: Allegro maestoso. We are standing near the grave of a well-loved man. His whole life, his struggles, his sufferings and his accomplishments on earth pass before us. And now, in this solemn and deeply stirring moment, when the confusion and distractions of everyday life are lifted like a hood from our eyes, a voice of awe-inspiring solemnity chills our heart, a voice that, blinded by the mirage of everyday life, we usually ignore: "What next?" it says. "What is life and what is death? Will we live on eternally? Is it all an empty dream or do our life and death have a meaning?" And we must answer this question, if we are to go on living. The next three movements are conceived as intermezzi.

Second Movement: Andante. A blissful moment in the dear departed's life and a sad recollection of his youth and lost innocence.

Third Movement: Scherzo. A spirit of disbelief and negation has seized him. He is bewildered by the bustle of appearances and he loses his perception of childhood and the profound strength that love alone can give. He despairs both of himself and of God. The world and life begin to seem unreal. Utter disgust for every form of existence and evolution seizes him in an iron grasp, torments him until he utters a cry of despair.

Fourth Movement: Alto solo. *"Urlicht"* (Primeval Light) from the *Knaben Wunderhorn*. The stirring words of simple faith sound in his ears: "I come from God and I will return to God!"

Fifth Movement: Once more we must confront terrifying questions, and the atmosphere is the same as at the end of the third movement. The voice of the Caller is heard. The end of every living thing has come, the last judgment is at hand and the horror of the day of days has come upon us. The earth trembles, the graves burst open, the dead arise and march forth in endless procession. The great and the small of this earth, the kings and the beggars, the just and the godless, all press forward. The cry for mercy and forgiveness sounds fearful in our ears. The wailing becomes gradually more terrible. Our senses desert us, all consciousness dies as the Eternal Judge approaches. The last trump sounds; the trumpets of the Apocalypse ring out. In the eerie silence that follows, we can just barely make out a distant nightingale, a last tremulous echo of earthly life. The gentle sound of a chorus of saints and heavenly hosts is then heard: "Rise again, yes, rise again thou wilt!" Then God in all His glory comes into sight. A wondrous light strikes us to the heart. All is quiet and blissful. Lo and behold: there is no judgment, no sinners, no just men, no great and no small; there is no punishment and no reward. A feeling of overwhelming love fills us with blissful knowledge and illuminates our existence.

These various programs were surely devised after, rather than before, the symphony was completed: Mahler undoubtedly did not think of a "happy recollection" on the part of his symphonic hero when he took up the Leipzig sketches and composed the Andante in 1893. As in the *First Symphony,* certain images and ideas do remain attached to certain musical episodes. In a symphonic work starting with death and ending in resurrection, the middle movements could only be "memories of the past," as they were in the corresponding program for the *First Symphony.*

It has been pointed out that the very concept of resurrection is essentially foreign to the Jewish faith, but the idea of a last judgment with no judge and no recognition of Good and Evil is just as unorthodox for a Christian. If pantheistic leanings are definitely expressed in the *Third Symphony,* a very individual form of the Christian faith, to say the least, is expressed in the *Second.* One important difference between the first two versions of the program has been pointed out by Theodor Reik: in Janurary 1896, Mahler describes the first movement as "the titanic struggle of a superman," whereas later the hero is already dead and his life is relived and considered as a whole by some friend or relation. In the Finale all are merged, the narrator and the hero, the present and the past. Reik also underlines Mahler's obsession with death and with the senselessness of earthly life, as well as his feeling that he will be discovered and recognized as a composer posthumously. According to Reik, each one of Mahler's symphonies is a new attempt to answer the same burning question about life and death, about the meaning of life and the destiny of man. In Reik's view the very fact of asking these questions that reason cannot solve is a typical symptom of certain obsessive neuroses. None of the conquests or "victories" gained by Mahler in the Finales are ever final, and the next symphony once more asks the same fundamental questions and provides new answers. Again according to Reik, all of Mahler's works anticipate his own death in one way or another, as well as his posthumous recognition as a great symphonist.

a) *Allegro maestoso.* (OR: *Maestoso*). *Mit durchaus ernstem und feierlichem Ausdruck* (With a serious and solemn expression throughout) TEMPO: OR: $\text{♩} = 144$ for the sixteenth-note motifs in the first bars; yet Mahler requires the duration of the pauses between these motifs to be based on the main tempo of the movement, *i.e.,* $\text{♩} = 84$–$92$. He demands the fermata in the fourth bar to be interpreted as very brief, a mere breathing pause. There are several further metronomic tempo indications: 92 at Figure 2 (Bar 39); $\text{♩} =$

104 at Figure 18 (Bar 296); ♩=72 and *Im Tempo eines Trauermarsches* instead of *Tempo sostenuto* at Figure 24 (Bar 397). At Figure 13 (Bar 213): *Nicht zurückhaltend* instead of *Etwas drängend* (an interesting change of mind). And finally two bars before Figure 27 (Bar 444) *Zeit lassen zum crescendo und zum diminuendo* (*Oboen und 2 Trompeten*) (Leave time for crescendo and diminuendo [in oboe and 2 trumpets]).

KEY: C minor.

TIME SIGNATURE: 4/4.

RHYTHM: Slow funeral march.

FORM: Mahler's first great symphonic and dramatic opening movement retains most of the formal characteristics of sonata form, the only important innovations being the first appearance of the subsidiary theme in E major and the second development section in E flat minor. It can be summarized as follows:

EXPOSITION

Bars

| | | |
|---|---|---|
| 1 to 37 | Theme A (restated with countertheme A') : C minor |
| 38 to 42 | Transition Theme A2 : C minor |
| 43 to 58 | *Im Tempo nachgeben* (In slower tempo) : Theme B (with ostinato triplet fragment of A in the bass) : E major |
| 59 to 68 | *Wie zum Anfang* (In the initial tempo) shortened restatement of A and A' : C minor |
| 69 to 74 | Chorale theme C (*"Dies Irae"*) (to be restated in Finale) : A flat |
| 75 to 111 | Coda theme in the bass combined with A' (later alone) : C minor, ending in G |

DEVELOPMENT

| | |
|---|---|
| 112 to 142 | *Sehr mässig und zurückhaltend* (Very moderate and gradually slower) Theme B in C major alternating with new pastoral motif, *Meerestille*, combined with A2 (see above) : E minor |
| 143 to 174 | A (used as an ostinato bass) combined with A' : E minor and A minor |
| 175 to 212 | A' on Coda theme in bass and A : A and D major |
| 213 to 248 | *Etwas drängend* (Somewhat slower) B modulating from F to E flat and B major |

SECOND DEVELOPMENT

| | |
|---|---|
| 249 to 258 | *Schnell* (Fast). First bars of A : E flat minor |
| 259 to 333 | *Sehr langsam beginnend* (Very slow at the beginning) : A (as a bass ostinato), A' and C : E flat minor modulating to C minor |

RECAPITULATION

| | |
|---|---|
| 334 to 361 | Tempo primo : A and A' : C minor |
| 362 to 366 | A2 : C minor |
| 367 to 396 | *Zurückhaltend* (Slower) |

CODA

| | |
|---|---|
| 397 to 450 | *Tempo sostenuto* (gradually accelerated) : Coda theme, A' and A : C minor |

Undoubtedly inspired by Bruckner's great initial gestures, theme A, with its huge proposition, its dotted rhythm, broad declamation, and stirring tremolo background, is nevertheless wholly original.[104] To my knowledge, no one has as yet noticed the complete similarity of its measures 12 and 13 with Hunding's entrance in the first act of Wagner's *Die Walküre* (page 45 in the Schott miniature orchestral score): an unmistakable if probably unconscious reminiscence from one of the scores Mahler knew best and loved most. The most astonishing fact about this movement is Mahler's assumption, at such an early date, of such a self-assured, heroic, commanding tone and his ability to sustain it throughout the movement. Granting that it was only completed in 1894, the huge structure, with its alternating moments of light and shade, possesses a power, a unity of style, a richness of musical imagination that make it a worthy counterpart of other great funeral marches, such as the second movement of Beethoven's *"Eroica"* or Siegfried's Funeral March in *Die Götterdämmerung*.

b) *Andante moderato. Sehr gemächlich. Nicht eilen* (Very moderate. Without haste)
KEY: A flat (alternating with G sharp minor for B section).
TIME SIGNATURE: 3/8.
RHYTHM: Slow ländler.
TEMPO: There are far fewer metronomic tempo indications in OR for this movement than for the preceding one. Only ♪=84 at Figure 4; ♪=80 four bars later; ♪=83 four bars after 6; at Figure 12 Mahler recommends a very special type of pizzicato playing that gives the impression of a guitar.
FORM: ABABA. The last B section is a kind of development. The influence of the rustic and leisurely Austrian ländler is clearly discernible in this lovely movement, which Mahler found too graceful to follow the grim Allegro maestoso. At the end of the first theme he emphasizes its folk and dancelike character with "beerhouse" glissandos. The form is as simple as the style is idyllic. The G sharp minor B triplet episode is not unlike the corresponding theme in the slow movement of Brahms's *Fourth Symphony*. The principal melody A is restated, with a delightful cello counter melody. The second B section is much longer than the first: the melody is considerably extended and adorned with new counterpoints. When Theme A returns in string pizzicatos, it is also amplified into a lovely coda, ending pianissimo, again with plucked strings.

Mahler himself was never wholly satisfied with this movement. Shortly after completing it he exclaimed in Natalie's presence, "What I intended, what loomed before my eyes, I did not attain. Something has been lost, regardless of how successful I find the whole." Although this movement is far superior in quality to the suppressed Andante of the *First*—and no one in his right mind would like to dispense with it—there is a definite break in style after the first movement, which is why Mahler attempted to change the order of the movements, and finally prescribed a long pause after the Andante.[105]

c) *In ruhig fliessender Bewegung* [In calmly flowing movement]
KEY: C minor (with many modulations and a C major trio).
TIME SIGNATURE: 3/8.
RHYTHM: Slow ländler (nearly continuous sixteenth-note ostinato).
TEMPO: There are no metronomic tempo indications in OR.
FORM: A detailed comparison of this Scherzo with its companion piece, the lied *"Des Antonius von Padua Fischpredigt,"* reveals much concerning Mahler's composition procedures. The lied is long and substantial, and Mahler has quoted it practically in its entirety at two different moments.

After the two initial timpani dominant-tonic motifs (only the second appears in the song, but in the double basses) Mahler quotes 110 bars from the lied's 180.

(Here in OR four extra timpani bars were crossed out by Mahler. One of them is the extra dominant-tonic ostinato bar found in the song.)

Bars

| | | |
|---|---|---|
| 1 to 32 | Section A of the song *without* the vocal part : C minor | |
| 33 to 67 | A without the vocal part : C minor | |
| 68 to 102 | A with vocal part in the winds : C minor | |
| 103 to 148 | Section B : F major, modulating to E flat. There are considerable differences between this section and the song's contrasting major passage, particularly a new oboe theme at the end of the ninth bar | |
| 149 to 189 | Coda : A in *saltato* (as in the coda of the lied, but otherwise not identical) | |

TRIO

| | |
|---|---|
| 190 to 211 | Fugato effect starting in the basses with the same sixteenth-note ostinato as in Scherzo : C major |
| 212 to 256 | Trio theme with new counter melody : D major |
| 257 to 328 | Trio theme fortissimo, interrupted by nostalgic trumpet solo on sixteenth-note ostinato in the strings : E major |
| 329 to 347 | Trio theme divided between the strings : C major modulating to E flat |

SCHERZO

| | |
|---|---|
| 348 to 371 | A (staccato) : C minor |
| 372 to 406 | A restated in its entirety : C minor |
| 407 to 440 | B section shortened : F major |
| 441 to 464 | Second section of Trio, fortissimo, C major (stretto climax) |
| 465 to 480 | "Cry of despair" : B flat minor on a C pedal in the bass, ending with a long note scale motif in the treble |
| 481 to 544 | Trio theme : C major |
| 545 to 581 | Coda : Last statement of A ending with quotations of last twenty-nine bars of lied : C minor |

There are also many small differences between the scoring of the song and that of the Scherzo: the timpani in the beginning, the switch of birch twigs on the big drum (*"Ruthe"*), which is used more extensively in the symphonic movement, the lied's clarinet in B flat (at bar 48) which is replaced by the caricatural E flat instrument in the symphony (this alteration was made in OR, where the B flat clarinet part is erased and the new one added at the bottom of the page, etc.). The bassoon accompaniment at the beginning of the B section is not found in the *"Fischpredigt,"* either.

Rather than as a naïve and humorous picture of a holy man's wasted eloquence, Mahler interprets the Scherzo as an image of man's senseless restlessness. The "programs" of the two works are thus very different for the same music, but this is not as surprising as it appears, for tragedy and humor are never far apart in Mahler's romantic world. The sinister, rather than humorous, program does account for some of the changes in the scoring. The thematic material of the Scherzo proper is practically identical to that of the song, except for some counterthemes added by Mahler. He himself explained to Natalie how he had "been driven further and further from my original form" (see Chapter 18). A month later, after going through the movement again, Mahler was "amazed by it." "It is a big and remarkable piece," he added. "I had not realized this while I was composing it."[106]

While rehearsing the *Second Symphony* in 1899, Mahler was struck by the fact that "the loveliest passage, the calm theme of the middle section,[107] appears only once in the seething waves of the whole movement . . . This seems inexplicable at first sight, and it was not easy in fact to avoid elaborating the lovely motif and bringing it back in another key or in another version. But it would have been contrary to the essence of this passage, which, like the aloe, can bear only one single flower." The same day, Mahler compared this passage to a marriage (*"Hoch Zeit"* [Time of exaltation]), a celebration that a man can hold only once in a lifetime.

d) *"URLICHT"* (Primeval Light). *Sehr feierlich aber schlicht (Choralmässig)* (Very solemn but modestly simple [Like a chorale]) for alto solo, poem from *Des Knaben Wunderhorn*

KEY: D flat. The modulating middle section starts in B flat minor.

TIME SIGNATURE: 4/4 (changing to 2/4, 3/4, 5/4).

TEXT: *Knaben Wunderhorn*, I, 454, under the same title. The original folk poem from the Herzgebirge and Niederrochlitz is known: it is called *Der Todtensegen* and has two extra stanzas not reproduced by Arnim and Brentano. Mahler used the *Wunderhorn* text without making any alterations.

FORM: Free, *"durchkomponiert,"* *i.e.,* determined by the text. There are three well-defined parts. The voice, accompanied by the strings, starts with a motif of three ascending notes, while the brass solemnly pursues the choral theme. A second episode, starting in minor, belongs wholly to the voice. It ends in the major mode on a note of faith and hope, on the dominant of the main key of D flat.

The middle section (*Etwas bewegter* [Somewhat faster]) begins with an ostinato triplet figure in the clarinet, on which the solo violin states a new motif, which is later taken up by the flute and piccolo. There are several modulations that give to this episode the character of a miniature development: B flat minor, A major, A minor, F sharp minor, E flat minor, E minor (Pamer quotes this passage as one of the very few examples of chromatic modulations in Mahler's work), A flat, D flat. The first section returns, though much altered: *"Ich bin von Gott"* is based on the thematic material of the earlier *"Der Mensch liegt,"* while the last vocal phrase (*"Wird mir ein Lichtchen"*) is a shortened and altered recurrence of *"Je lieber möcht' ich."*

Mahler insisted on the singer using, for this song, "the tone and vocal expression of a child who thinks he is in heaven." Again Pamer considers the many changes in the time signature as a typical example of folk style and lists the archaic features in the harmony: the thirdless cadence in Bars 10 to 12, the drone bass effect in Bars 4 and 5, etc. Mahler undoubtedly composed this song before the last movements of the symphony, perhaps even before the 1892 *Wunderhorn Lieder*. Why he decided to use it as an introduction to the Finale is easy to understand: the naïve faith expressed in the poem was a first ray of hope, just what he needed as a contrast after the Scherzo. Musically, the chorale-like music and the ascending themes could also be adapted and transformed in the last movement. It also had the advantage of introducing the human voice before the choral climax of the Finale. "When I conceived a great musical fresco," he wrote, "a moment always comes when I must use words to support

my musical ideas. The same thing must have happened to Beethoven in his
*Ninth*."

e) *Im Tempo des Scherzos; Wild herausfahrend; Sehr zurückhaltend; Langsam*,
etc. (In the same tempo as the Scherzo; In a wild outburst; Much slower; slow,
etc.)
KEY: C minor/major at the beginning, with many modulations (see below).
Ending in E flat major.
TIME SIGNATURE: 3/8, 4/4, Alla breve, etc.
TEXT: The first two stanzas are borrowed from Klopstock's ode *Die Aufer-
stehung*, one of his *Geistliche Lieder* which is generally sung to the chorale
melody "*Jesus Christus, unser Heiland*." Mahler suppressed the three last stanzas
and, at the end of the first two, the refrain "*Halleluja*." The following stanzas
were added by him:

### Alto Solo

| | |
|---|---|
| *O glaube, mein Herz, o glaube:* | Believe, my heart, believe |
| *Es geht dir nichts verloren!* | Nothing is lost for thee! |
| *Dein ist, was du gesehnt!* | Thou hast what thou has longed for! |
| *Dein, was du geliebt, was du gestrit-*<br>*ten!* | What thou hast loved and fought for! |

### Soprano Solo

| | |
|---|---|
| *O glaube: du wardst nicht umsonst*<br>*geboren!* | Believe: thou wast not born in vain! |
| *Hast nicht umsonst gelebt, gelitten.* | Didst not live or suffer in vain. |

### Alto Solo and Chorus

| | |
|---|---|
| *Was enstanden ist, das musst ver-*<br>*gehen!* | What has been, must perish! |
| *Was vergangen, auferstehen!* | What has perished must rise again! |
| *Hör' auf zu beben!* | Cease to tremble! |
| *Bereite dich zu leben!* | Prepare to live! |

### Alto Solo and Soprano Solo

| | |
|---|---|
| *O Schmerz! Du Alldurchdringer!* | O pain, which penetrates all! |
| *Dir bin ich entrungen!* | I am free from thee! |
| *O Tod! Du Allbezwinger!* | O Death, who conquers all! |
| *Nun bist du bezwungen!* | Now thou art conquered! |

### Chorus

| | |
|---|---|
| *Mit Flügeln, die ich mir errungen,* | With wings I have won for myself |
| *In heissem Liebesstreben* | In fervent love |
| *Werd' ich entschweben* | I shall soar |
| *Zum Licht, zu dem kein Aug' ge-*<br>*drungen.* | To the light no eye has seen. |
| *Sterben werd' ich, um zu leben,* | To live anew, I shall die! |
| *Aufersteh'n, ja aufersteh'n* | Rise again, yes, rise again |
| *Wirst du, mein Herz, in einem Nu!* | Wilt thou, my heart, in an instant! |
| *Was du geschlagen* | Thy struggles and thy combats |
| *Zu Gott wird es dich tragen!* | Will bring thee to God! |

Mahler's new verses make the "message" much clearer. Their tone is more intense and personal than that of Klopstock's rather conventional ode.

FORM: Mahler himself admitted that his Finale was more "dramatic" than "narrative." The structure is in fact far removed from classical models, obviously influenced by the text and based on theatrical forms. The first orchestral section (Bars 1 to 192) can be considered a symphonic exposition (in the manner of an opera prelude) and the middle section (Bars 193 to 482), until the entrance of the chorus, has much in common with a development. Yet, while using only material that has already been stated earlier, the last (vocal) section is far from being a literal restatement. The movement was first sketched after Bülow's funeral, in March 1894, composed the following summer, and copied that winter.

Here is the over-all plan of the huge movement:

EXPOSITION
    or
PRELUDE
Bars

  1 to  25    Quotation of the Scherzo's "cry of despair" preceded by a scale (like the beginning of the 1st mvt. theme) (the trumpet and trombone motif at Bars 5 and 6 has been called by some authors "terror motif." It will recur later) : B flat minor chord on a sixty-one-bar C pedal and 3/8 (as in Scherzo).

26 to  42    *Sehr zurückhaltend* (Much slower) 4/4. First glimpse, in the winds, then in the horns, of Redemption Theme : C major.

43 to  96    *Langsam* (Slow) (OR : *"Der Rufer in der Wüste"* [The Call in the Desert]) : Brass signals and wind triplets (related to main theme of 1st mvt.); *"Dies Irae"* chorale from same mvt. on pizzicato string bass : F minor and major.

  97 to 141    *Im Anfang sehr zurückhaltend* (Very slow at the beginning) : Grief Motif recalling Amfortas' theme in *Parsifal :* B flat minor.

142 to 161    *Wieder sehr breit* (Very broad again): *"Dies Irae"* (and *Aufersteh'n* chorale) in the brass : D flat modulating to C.

162 to 192    Signals and *Aufersteh'n* Chorale Theme (This passage, suggesting the "end of the world," ends with the famous percussion crescendo anticipating that in *Wozzeck*) : C major/C Minor.

2ND SECTION or DEVELOPMENT

193 to 194    *Maestoso :* Terror Motif : F minor.

195 to 229    *Allegro energico :* March of the Resurrected : Chorale Theme and Redemption (related to B of 1st mvt.) : F minor and major.

230 to 298    *Kräftig* (Energetic) : Main section of March based on quick version of *"Dies Irae"* theme (*Kräftig :* F major modulating to E flat, D minor, F minor, etc.).

299 to 319    *Mit einem Mal etwas wuchtiger* (Suddenly more vigorous) : Climax of March in dotted rhythms ostinato; Chorale Theme (as in 1st mvt.). There is another literal quotation of a subsidiary motif from the same movement in the trumpets at Bars 311 to 314 (See 1st mvt. : Bars 287 to 290).

  , to 334    *Più Mosso :* Disintegration : Terror Motif and fragment of March Theme : F minor.

335 to 427  *Wieder zurückhaltend* (Slower again) : Grief passage extended into cello recitative, later taken up by violins with distant brass signals; Terror Theme and scale motif from "despair" passage of Scherzo. This episode gathers speed and modulates constantly : E flat minor, F minor, B minor, F sharp, etc.

428 to 482  *Sehr langsam und gedehnt* (Very slow and long drawn) (OR : *Der grosse Appell* [The Last Trump]) : Total destruction : Horn signals and trumpets answering from all directions with triplets motifs; "Bird of Death" (flutes) : F sharp (a semitone higher than *"Der Rufer in der Wüste"*).

FINAL SECTION (CHORALE)

483 to 546  *Langsam* (Slow) *Misterioso : Aufersteh'n* for *a cappella* chorus and soprano solo (based on 1st mvt. Chorale Theme). 1st and 2nd parts of the first stanza separated by return of brass signals and full statement of Redemption Theme combined with Chorale : G flat.

547 to 570  Redemption Theme in imitations between various orchestral groups : G flat.

571 to 628  *Etwas bewegter* (Somewhat more animated) Grief Theme : *"O glaube!"* (alto, then soprano solo), becoming increasingly confident (In OR, Mahler decided, but still as an alternative solution, to use the soprano for the second *"O glaube"* solo) : B flat minor/D flat.

629 to 650  *Langsamer* (Slower) *Misterioso : Aufersteh'n* (chorus, alto solo, and brass) : D flat/A flat.

651 to 682  *Mit Aufschwung, doch nicht eilen* (With impetus, but not too fast). Soprano and alto duet on new version of Grief soon combined with Redemption Theme, becoming more and more ecstatic (at Bar 671 there is a literal quotation of *"Ich bin von Gott"* from *"Urlicht"*) : B flat minor modulating to E flat.

683 to 723  *Langsam : "Auf Flügeln" :* Redemption Theme in imitations between the various choral groups, modulating to G minor and back to E flat.

CODA

724 to 775  *Pesante :* Climax (brass, chorus, organ) : *Aufersteh'n* chorale followed by orchestral conclusion on Redemption Theme : E flat.

There is no searching in this Finale for the unity of style, the classical grandeur, the concentration of thought, and the powerful architecture of the initial Allegro maestoso. Rather than seeing it as a large three-part symphonic structure, it should be viewed as a long sequence of metaphysical questions and answers. It is one of the rare instances in which Mahler's principal aim was to illustrate an idea, or rather to paint a huge apocalyptic fresco of doomsday, rather than to create a self-sufficient musical entity. Undeniably the succession of episodes is rather loose-jointed and sometimes even arbitrary: Mahler has rarely restated whole sections, as he did here, without attempting to vary or even to develop them. The whole movement is aimed at creating an overwhelming effect on the listener, an effect that is neither superficial nor theatrical: Mahler's true aim is to deliver as forcefully as possible a message of hope and faith to the universe. In this he has not only succeeded but even reaches heights seldom attained by a musician: the Finale contains many unforgettable moments, such as the "Last

Trump" episode, with the "Bird of Death" and the breath-taking choral entrance. To heighten this last effect, Mahler requires the chorus to remain seated, rising only for the *Auf Flügeln* fugato at Figure 46. Mahler has often been accused of an obsession with Beethoven's *Ninth Symphony*. He himself admitted as much in one of his letters to Seidl.[108] Yet his cyclic procedures are far more subtle and intricate than the flashbacks inserted by Beethoven at the beginning of his Finale to prepare the listener for the adoption of a new "style" and for the introduction of the human voice. Themes and motifs from the first, third, and fourth movements are used more or less extensively in the Finale, and the incorporation, as one of its two main themes, of the *"Dies Irae"* chorale from *Totenfeier* shows the importance that Mahler accorded to such architectural and structural details.

Considering the tremendous effect created by the Finale and the magnitude of its subject, the vast orchestral and choral forces used no longer call for any comment. They correspond to a certain historical evolution; in this respect, the *Second* is a milestone between Wagner's huge *Ring* orchestra, the 1906 *Eighth Symphony*, and the 1903–13 *Gurrelieder*. Such gigantism was once considered absurd and was long thought to have led to an impasse, Webern's extreme economy of means being considered as a kind of inevitable "return to reason." Yet Mahlerian length and vast forces have recently reappeared in music, and they can no longer be considered a momentary aberration. However, they should be used by great men to express great thoughts. The number of horns (ten) and trumpets (eight) is of course exceptional, and Mahler never repeated it, even in the *Eighth Symphony*. The two percussionists also have at their disposal a vast number of instruments, and the score demands that five musicians perform the percussion part, besides the timpanists.

Whether or not the *Second* is an accomplished masterpiece in the Beethovian manner and tradition will probably always be debated, although it has gained more whole-hearted admirers and more new listeners in the last ten years than ever before. Theodor Adorno's comment about Mahler having created a great symphonic art at an epoch that forbade the successful creation of such great symphonic art is brilliantly perceptive. Nor can the same author be accused of a paradox when he claims that Mahler's very "incapacity to begin" (to create) itself becomes a power, as if it had really achieved its aim.

In the *Second Symphony*, both Mahler's vision and the way in which he materialized it in sound are deeply stirring. It seems petty and even ridiculous, at this point in musical history, to wrangle about whether or not the form of its Finale is successful. It never fails to be effective and provides a stupendous conclusion to one of the most ambitious works ever conceived and composed. "Never again," Mahler said to Natalie in 1900, "will I attain such depths and heights, as Ulysses only once in his life returned from Tartarus. One can create only once or twice in a lifetime works on such a great subject. Beethoven with his *C minor* and his *Ninth*, Goethe with *Faust*, Dante with the *Divine Comedy*, etc. Without putting myself on their level, or comparing myself to them, I am amazed that I was able to write this that summer in Steinbach! It was only thanks to the long interruption that had been forced upon me, after which the waters gushed forth, as they do from any obstructed pipe . . ."[109]

## 9) *THIRD SYMPHONY,* D minor (1895–96)

COMPOSITION: After having "created with all the means at my disposal" his first "symphonic universe," Mahler undoubtedly found the conception and working out of another a much less problematic and arduous task. Thus, the actual composition of the *Third Symphony* absorbed him for only two successive summers, although he may have noted down a few themes beforehand (see below, Manuscripts). This was one of the happiest periods that Mahler spent composing. The work had no doubt been in his mind for quite some time, and nothing could stop or delay the creative flow, although it had not been forcibly interrupted for years, as had formerly been the case. During these two summers Mahler lived happily in the magic world of his creation: the *Third* is a great Hymn to Nature; in it he expressed a feeling that had stirred in him since childhood and that was echoed in the poems of Hölderlin and the novels of Jean Paul. That nature was not only the idyllic world as it is usually represented, not only "forest air, little birds and flowers," was not a recent discovery for him: "One always forgets that nature includes All, all that is great and terrifying as well as lovely (this is what I particularly wanted to express in the whole work, using a kind of evolutionary development) . . . No one knows the God Dionysus, the great Pan . . ."

Later in the same letter to Batka[110] Mahler claims that his music is "nothing but the sound of nature" (*"nur Naturlaut"*). Its aim is to express the very soul of nature, not, like Beethoven's *"Pastoral"* Symphony, the "emotions aroused in us by the pleasures of the country." When Bruno Walter arrived in Steinbach, Mahler told him not even to bother looking at the Attersee landscape and the rocky cliffs across the water, for "it is all in my music" (*"Das habe ich schon alles wegkomponiert"*). It is absolutely essential to bear this in mind while studying the *Third Symphony* and experiencing the raging hurricanes, the dionysiac marches, and the icy gales of the first movement, otherwise its tragedy, its wild exuberance, its reckless mixture of styles would remain absolutely enigmatic and unintelligible. The romantic artist invariably places himself in the center of the universe, or indeed of any subject he chooses to illustrate. Whether he evokes rocks, nature lying motionless in the icy grip of winter, the brightly colored spring flowers in a field, or the innocence of animals threatened by man, it is of course Mahler's own voice that speaks in his highly subjective and visionary musical style. Here, as in *Das Lied von der Erde,* Mahler's much later "Farewell to Nature," his philosophy has a definite pantheistic flavor. This form of mystical feeling was perhaps even more essential to his nature than either the Christian or the Jewish faith.

The last five movements of the *Third Symphony* were composed in the summer of 1895. The only manuscript that bears a precise date is that of the fifth, the *Wunderhorn* movement, which was completed on June 24. Mahler probably completed the sketches of the other movements during July and August. The first orchestral score of the fifth movement was finished just before he left Steinbach in early August. In the complete orchestral manuscript, which is Mahler's own fair copy, made during the winter, the movements are dated April 11, 1896 (second), April 25 (third), May 8 (fifth), June 21 (first) and November 22 (sixth).

MANUSCRIPTS: There are many pages of preliminary sketches for the first movement in the Stanford (California) Library, and in the Oesterreichische National Bibliothek. All came from Natalie's collection, while five further pages used to belong to Alma Mahler. One of these includes the theme of "Nature's Awakening" and is dated (but not in Mahler's hand) 1893. If this date is accurate, it would mean that some of the march themes were noted down while Mahler was starting work on the *Second Symphony*. Most of the other thematic material for the same opening movement is included in other sketches, which are dated 1895. The various manuscripts for the individual movements will be dealt with under each separate heading. The complete autograph orchestral score from Professor Rosé's collection now belongs to Mr. Robin Lehman. The Stanford Library also owns a copy of the first printed orchestral score, (Weinberger) with 185 pages corrected in Mahler's hand, while the Universal Edition in Vienna has a later copy of their first printed score, also corrected by Mahler.

PROGRAM: The programs for the *First* and *Second Symphonies* were devised after the music was composed; Mahler admitted this himself, but, even when he decided to suppress all "programs" or analyses of his work, he could not deny having written the titles of the various movements of the *Third* before the music. But this preconceived plan never took precedence in his mind over the music itself. It even had to be altered several times, because the musical reality did not always conform to the intended outline. In this respect Mahler was truly not a "program" musician. Nevertheless, the titles of the *Third* were undeniably of great importance to him while he was composing the work, otherwise he would not have altered them so often and sent the list to so many of his friends. They obviously expressed something very dear to his heart, and as late as 1907 he still thought enough of them to reproduce them in the program of the Berlin concert that he conducted at that time.

The evolution of the program of the *Third Symphony* is hard to summarize, because of the number of different versions, yet most of the changes are most interesting. The first two undated programs[111] were certainly devised in the early summer of 1895, *i.e.*, at a time when practically no music had been composed. They are the first "visions" of the great work and were doubtless drawn up together with the first musical sketches. The first movement was then entitled "What the Forest Tells Me" (it is the Scherzo that will later inherit this title, or rather a similar one: "What the Animals in the Forest Tell Me"). Mahler was soon dissatisfied with it, however, and substituted another, *Der Sommer marschiert ein* (Summer Marches In): *Fanfare und lustiger Marsch* (Fanfare and Joyous March). This was the origin of the present first movement, conceived originally for "winds and solo double basses" and still entitled "Introduction"; it was to become "The Entrance of Summer" in the final version. In September 1895, Mahler still called it "Procession of Dionysus" but finally preferred *Bacchuszug* (March of Bacchus). Upon his arrival in Steinbach in 1896, he composed the minor Introduction, which he first called "What the Rocks Tell Me" (*Was mir das Felsgebirge erzählt*). On June 21 he still thought of it as an introduction ("Pan Awakens") leading into the first movement.

The second movement bore its present title from the beginning, though it was originally conceived to be placed fourth.[112] At first Mahler had considered another second movement, "What the Twilight Tells Me," a "scherzo for strings," which became the *"Tierstück"* and took third place, with its final title, in the summer of 1895. The present fourth movement, "What the Night Tells Me,"

"Man," was immediately inserted in its present position. Early in the summer of 1896, the subtitle, "Man," permanently replaced the "Night."

The fifth movement, for contralto solo and chorus, is probably the "Scherzo" (No. 5: "What the Cuckoo Tells Me") of the preliminary program. It was named "What the Morning Bells Tell Me" in the third program. In the final version its subtitle, "The Bells," was replaced by "The Angels." As for the Finale, it bore its present title, "What Love Tells Me," from the start but was originally intended to be the third movement. The motto "My Father, see my wounds" did not make its appearance till late in the summer of 1895 and soon disappeared again.[113] On September 11 of that same year Mahler added "The Angels" as a subtitle, but this was later transferred to the preceding movement. "Das himmlische Leben," first intended as the Finale and entitled "What the Child Tells Me,"[114] disappeared from the symphony sometime between September 11, 1895, and June 21, 1896, to reappear later in the Fourth Symphony. Even the over-all title was altered several times.

Das glückliche Leben
Ein Sommernachtstraum
(Nicht nach Shakespeare, Anmerkungen eines Kritikers)[115]

This was changed at the end of the summer and replaced by the Nietzsche title: Meine fröhliche Wissenschaft, which later became Die fröliche Wissenschaft and finally Ein Sommermorgentraum. In 1896, Mahler finally considered "Pan, A Symphonic Poem,"[116] and suppressed the Nietzsche title. The finished work was thus an imposing fresco dedicated to the glory of creation, starting with inanimate nature and progressing step by step to its highest form, that is to say, to God. The following is the final program, sent to Marschalk on August 6, 1896, after Mahler had completed the symphony[117]:

A Midsummer Morning Dream

1st part:  Introduction: Pan's Awakening
           No. 1: Summer Marches In (Procession of Bacchus)
2nd part:  No. 2: What the Flowers of the Field Tell Me
           No. 3: What the Animals of the Forest Tell Me
           No. 4: What Man Tells Me
           No. 5: What the Angels Tell Me
           No. 6: What Love Tells Me

The following page is a further attempt to clarify the complex matter of the "programs" of the Third Symphony. It should be read chronologically from left to right. The figures in the first left-hand column are those at present attached to each movement in the symphony. The Introduction is now part of the first movement. Among Natalie's sketches are two sheets containing material for the "Blumenstück," one bearing the title "Was mir das Kind erzählt," and the other "Was mir der Abenderzählt." Mahler may have originally planned another "Blumenstück." More likely still, the above-mentioned sketch preceded the first program, and "Was mir das Kind erzählt" was intended for Das Himmlische Leben, which Mahler was later to place in the Fourth Symphony.

| TITLES MOVEMENTS OF FINAL VERSION | 1 DAS GLÜCKLICHE LEBEN EIN SOMMERNACHTS-TRAUM (early summer 1895) | 2 EIN SOMMERNACHTS-TRAUM | 3 MEINE FRÖHLICHE WISSENSCHAFT (summer 1895) | 4 DIE FRÖHLICHE WISSENSCHAFT EIN SOMMERNACHTS-TRAUM (Aug. 17, 1895) |
|---|---|---|---|---|
| (INTRODUCTION) | | Fanfare und lustiger Marsch DER SOMMER MARSCHIERT EIN | | |
| 1 *(Kräftig)* | WAS MIR DER WALD ERZÄHLT | WAS MIR DER WALD ERZÄHLT (2) | DER SOMMER MARSCHIERT EIN | DER SOMMER MARSCHIERT EIN |
| 2 *(Menuetto)* | WAS MIR DIE BAÜMEN ERZÄHLEN (4) | WAS MIR DIE BLUMEN ERZÄHLEN (Menuetto) (5) | WAS MIR DIE BLUMEN AUF DER WIESE ERZÄHLEN | WAS MIR DIE BLUMEN AUF DER WIESE ERZÄHLEN |
| 3 *(Scherzando)* | WAS MIR DIE DÄMMERUNG ERZÄHLT (nur Streicher) 2 oder 4 | WAS MIR DIE DÄMMERUNG ERZÄHLT (SCHERZO, nur Streicher) 4 | WAS MIR DIE TIERE IM WALDE ERZÄHLEN | WAS MIR DIE TIERE IM WALDE ERZÄHLEN |
| 4 *(Sehr Langsam)* | | | WAS MIR DIE NACHT ERZÄHLT (DER MENSCH) | WAS MIR DIE NACHT ERZÄHLT |
| 5 *(Lustig)* | WAS MIR DER KUCKUCK ERZÄHLT (SCHERZO) | WAS MIR DER KUCKUCK ERZÄHLT (SCHERZO) | WAS MIR DIE MORGEN-GLOCKEN ERZÄHLEN (DIE ENGEL) | WAS MIR DIE MORGEN-GLOCKEN ERZÄHLEN |
| 6 *(Langsam)* | | WAS MIR DIE LIEBE ERZÄHLT (3) (ADAGIO) | WAS MIR DIE LIEBE ERZÄHLT | WAS MIR DIE LIEBE ERZÄHLT |
| 7 *(Sehr behaglich)* | WAS MIR DAS KIND ERZÄHLT | WAS MIR DAS KIND ERZÄHLT | WAS MIR DAS KIND ERZÄHLT | DAS HIMMLISCHE LEBEN |

| 5 DIE FRÖHLICHE WISSENSCHAFT EIN SOMMERNACHTSTRAUM (Aug. 29, 1895) | 6 (Sept. 11, 1895) | 7 DIE FRÖHLICHE- WISSENSCHAFT EIN SOMMERMIT- TAGSTRAUM (June 21 to 28, 1896) | 8 EIN SOMMERMIT- TAGSTRAUM (Aug. 6, 1896) | |
|---|---|---|---|---|
| | | WAS MIR DAS FELDSGEBIRGE ERZÄHLT. | PAN ERWACHT | ERSTE ABTEILUNG |
| DER SOMMER MARSCHIERT EIN | ZUG DES DIONYSOS oder DER SOMMER MARSCHIERT EIN | DER SOMMER MARSCHIERT EIN | DER SOMMER MARSCHIERT EIN (BACCHUS ZUG) | |
| WAS MIR DIE BLUMEN AUF DER WIESE ERZÄHLEN | WAS MIR DIE BLUMEN AUF DER WIESE ERZÄHLEN | WAS MIR DIE BLUMEN AUF DER WIESE ERZÄHLEN | WAS MIR DIE BLUMEN AUF DER WIESE ERZÄHLEN | |
| WAS MIR DIE TIERE IM WALDE ERZÄHLEN | WAS MIR DIE TIERE IM WALDE ERZÄHLEN | WAS MIR DIE TIERE IM WALDE ERZÄHLEN | WAS MIR DIE TIERE IM WALDE ERZÄHLEN | |
| WAS MIR DIE NACHT ERZÄHLT (Alto solo) | WAS MIR DIE NACHT ERZÄHLT (DER MENSCH) | WAS MIR DER MENSCH ERZÄHLT | WAS MIR DER MENSCH ERZÄHLT | ZWEITE ABTEILUNG |
| WAS MIR DIE MORGEN- GLOCKEN ERZÄHLEN (Frauenchor mit Alto solo) | WAS MIR DIE MORGEN- GLOCKEN ERZÄHLEN | WAS MIR DIE ENGEL ERZÄHLEN | WAS MIR DIE ENGEL ERZÄHLEN | |
| WAS MIR DIE LIEBE ERZÄHLT MOTTO: Vater sieh'an die Wunden mein (Aus dem K.W.) | WAS MIR DIE LIEBE ERZÄHLT MOTTO: Vater sieh' an die Wunden mein (DIE ENGEL) | WAS MIR DIE LIEBE ERZÄHLT | WAS MIR DIE LIEBE ERZÄHLT | |
| DAS HIMMLISCHE LEBEN (Soprano solo, humoristich) | WAS MIR DAS KIND ERZÄHLT | (Deleted) | | |

Although the cuckoo's call is actually part of the thematic material of the *"Tierstück"* (borrowed from the song *"Ablösung im Sommer"* or "The Relief of the Nightingale by the Cuckoo"), *"Was mir der Kuckuck erzählt"* is probably the future fifth movement (*Wunderhorn*), and *"Was mir die Dämmerung erzählt"* the earlier title of the *"Tierstück."* This seems to be proved by the first complete sketch, which in Alma Mahler's former collection was entitled *"Was mir die Dämmerung. . . ."* This had been crossed out by Mahler and replaced by *"Was mir die Tiere im Walde . . .";* also the original Figure 2 (that of the first preliminary program) had been changed to 4 and then to 5!

The last versions of the program are undoubtedly more successful than the earlier ones. Even if one eventually chooses to let the music stand on its own, all listeners should at least be acquainted with them, for they throw a fascinating and essential light on Mahler's inner world. It is a well-known fact that Nietzsche strongly influenced Mahler's original conception of the symphony, even if this influence was short-lived. It is revealed by two details, the choice of the text for the fourth movement and the title *"Meine fröhliche Wissenschaft"* (changed to *"Die fröhliche Wissenschaft"*), later suppressed entirely, probably because of its very Nietzschean connotations.

At the end of 1901, Mahler urged his fiancée, Alma Schneider, to burn the complete works of Nietzsche, which lay on the floor of her bedroom, at least according to her sometimes highly unreliable memoirs. Thanks to this often-quoted passage, it is known that he was by then deeply opposed to Nietzsche's philosophy. This is not surprising, for Christianity and Judaism had so conditioned him that he could not endorse Nietzsche's total denial of the traditional concept of God. This denial is in fact one of the basic elements in all of Nietzsche's work: he refuted the dual God-man relationship present in most religions. Denying all idea of transcendency, he gradually evolved his own essential dogma of the "Eternal Recurrence."

Even admitting that he violently disapproved of Nietzsche in 1901, Mahler could not deny having read him, no doubt influenced by his friends in the Vegetarian Society, particularly Siegfried Lipiner, who was a disciple and lifelong admirer of Nietzsche. Already a fervent Wagnerian in those days, Mahler had undoubtedly been shocked when the poet-philosopher broke with Wagner in 1878 and attacked him in several books and pamphlets. He never mentioned Nietzsche in any of his letters or reported conversations, yet this very silence is puzzling, for he had undoubtedly read his books with much enthusiasm.

*Die fröhliche Wissenschaft,* the book whose title Mahler borrowed for his last programs of the *Third Symphony,* was written by Nietzsche in 1880–81, while he was recovering from a period of moral and physical stress, one of the darkest moments in his life. It bears witness to a great transformation within him: now he assumed a wholly positive, affirmative attitude, taking the responsibility and accepting the consequences of all his former breaks, whether with Wagner, with the romantic movement, with German philosophy or with society, which continued to ignore him. The poet's "Gay Science" reaches beyond Good and Evil, beyond questions and answers. It condemns man's eternal quest for God and the absolute, his traditional concept of "Truth" and his propensity to romantic unhappiness. To his mind, religious, philosophic, and scientific thought all reveal an attitude conditioned by suffering and disgust. By trying always to penetrate the essential truth and the mysteries of the world, they are the very negation of life. Instead, Nietzsche's "Gay Science" is nothing but happy questioning. It accepts its ignorance of essential truths. Its aim is to seize upon one thought, then leap to the next; to sing and dance, like Zarathustra, and to be joyous without seeking comfort or protection from any outside source.

The aphorisms in *Die fröhliche Wissenschaft* are as Nietzschean as anything in his work. Mahler cannot at that time have been shocked and repulsed by them, otherwise he would have selected a different title. Furthermore, the symphony itself contains other Nietzschean traits besides the 1896 title and the text for the fourth movement. The tragic undertones of the "nature" episodes in the first movement are thoroughly in keeping with Nietzsche's conception of a tragedy that is inherent to the cosmic principle and that surrounds man but is not created by him, a tragedy that is neither unhappy nor hopeless but cannot be "redeemed." In Nietzsche's work, as in Mahler's, humor is a consequence, an offspring of this tragic feeling; it is born of a deep affection for the things it mocks. Nietzsche reproached Wagner for his inevitably noble and serious approach to everything, for he believed that a light and humorous tone could equally well do justice to great subjects. The ruptures, the abrupt changes of tone in Mahler's music, are thus quite in keeping with Nietzsche's thought, as are the various glaring excesses in his music, its length, the dimension of the orchestral forces, and such insults to tradition as composing an adagio finale or a four-minute choral movement.[118]

Mahler's imagination continually produced new images, particularly while he was composing or revising his scores. It was never limited, even by the most carefully devised program. In the summer of 1896 he described the first movement to Natalie as "the whole defiant and blossoming life force fighting the 'immobility' [*Starrheit*] of the beginning of the world." Later that same summer he no longer saw in the introduction the winter sleep of nature, soon to be defeated by the full forces of summer, but rather the "burning furnace of midday, when no breath stirs . . ." while "the chained youth, life, grieves and moans and strives for salvation, lost as he is in the bottomless pit of still silent and disorganized nature, as in Hölderlin's 'Rhein.' "

*ERSTE ABTEILUNG* (FIRST PART)
  a) *Kräftig. Entschieden* (With force and decision)
KEY: D minor, ending in F major, with many modulations.
TIME SIGNATURE: 4/4, changing to 3/2, 2/2, etc.
RHYTHM: Slow and fast march.
FORM: The structure of the longest orchestral movement ever composed by Mahler is fairly simple. Without a text to work with, a fact that led him to adopt a dramatic, rather than symphonic, form in the Finale of the *Second*, Mahler here returns to the sonata form or something closely resembling it. Here is the plan of the huge movement:

INTRODUCTION
Bars
  1 to  26   Theme I (Nature's Inertia) : Its major-minor cadence is very characteristic and will be used again in the fourth movement : D minor/major.

EXPOSITION

27 to 131   Theme (or group) A : *Schwer und dumpf* (Heavy and muffled), including several short motifs separately used later on in this and in other movements, and a long cello recitative, later taken up by the trombones and later still by the trumpet : D minor.

132 to 163   *Immer das gleiche Tempo* (Always the same tempo). First transition passage introducing theme B′ (Pan or Nature's Awakening) as well as another important motif (at Bar 148) : D minor/major, D flat.

164 to 224   *Langsam, Schwer* (Slow, heavy). Varied restatements of A (trombone recitative) : D minor.

225 to 253   Tempo primo. 2nd transition passage (same motifs as in first) : D, D flat, C major.

254 to 368   Second group (B) : Triumphant March in dotted rhythm (Summer); B, B′, Theme I (Inertia) in a victorious major version, and later changed into a concluding theme (Figure 28) : F major, D major, D minor, C minor, E flat minor, E minor, etc.

2ND EXPOSITION

369 to 454   Group A introduced by the last motif of I (the recitative is taken up by the horns, trumpets, trombones, and finally by the English horn) : D minor/major, B major, F major, E flat minor.

455 to 491   Transition (same motifs as before) : D major, B major, F major, G minor, D flat.

492 to 529   Group B shortened and altered : G flat.

DEVELOPMENT
    or
2ND SECTION

530 to 641   *Immer dasselbe Tempo* (*Marsch*) (In the same march tempo) : Various themes and motifs from B group : B flat minor, E flat minor, C, D flat.[119]

RECAPITULATION

642 to 669   *Wie zum Anfang* (As in the beginning) : Introduction with cadence : D minor.

670 to 735   *Schwer* (Heavy) : Group A and trombone recitative : D minor

736 to 861   Tempo primo : Restatement of B : march episode ending with a twenty-three-bar stretto coda : F major.

Despite its unique style and proportions, the structure of this movement can be viewed as a large sonata form, with double exposition (as in the *Second Symphony,* 8a), and with a development exploiting only Group B (as in the *Second Symphony,* 8e, where the central or development section in quick march rhythm exploits only part of the earlier material). As in the Finale of the *Second Symphony,* and as in practically all Mahler's dramatic movements, two opposing forces are in conflict, nature's inertia and the tremendous strength of summer. Both participate in the final triumph, and the "inertia" themes themselves are transformed into victorious battle marches. As in the *First Symphony*'s Finale the finale victory is gained only at the very end, and there are several regressions. Just before the final stretto, the music shivers and trembles once more, as it did at the end of the exposition, but this makes the definitive victory all the more complete.

Several authors have traced the origin of the initial opening march theme to other well-known melodies; Křenek to an Austrian school children's march, others to the students' song *"Wir hatten gebaut ein stattliches Haus,"* used by Brahms in his Academic *Overture,* while its resemblances to the twin melodies of the finales of Beethoven's *Ninth Symphony* and Brahms's *First* are more obvious still.

The number of themes and motifs in Mahler's first movement is not particularly large, and its over-all length comes only from their massive size. In fact, the general construction is so clear and logical that the movement no longer seems long once one has learned to take in its whole breadth at one glance. Yet, although more than seventy years have elapsed since it was composed, this huge Allegro probably still has more admirers and more detractors than most of Mahler's other works. There is no text, no chorus, no offstage trumpets, as in the Finale of the *Second Symphony,* to conceal the highly "scandalous" changes of style. Instead of piously avoiding the subject, Theodor Adorno has stressed the "scandal" of Mahler's music and the fact that it never conforms, even super-ficially, to the concept of originality, as it was defined and demonstrated by the romantics. He has analyzed it as a rebellion against "culture" and "taste." Yet he was also the first to find in Mahler's greater movements a new unity, comparable to that of a novel, resulting from the individual character of the episodes, rather than from an abstract, preconceived plan.

In this movement the composer's vision is the essential driving force, and the doors of music are thrown wide open to all. Seen in this perspective, the "ruptures" in style cease to appear as such. Karlheinz Stockhausen, who has sought to introduce into his work the same universal approach, has pointed out, as perhaps the most striking moments in Mahler's works, those when "the gates fly open and a dancing mob bursts in." This happens in no other work of Mahler so often as in the opening movement of the *Third.* The contrasts in style are nowhere so glaring, or to my mind so convincing, as a revolutionary and sacrilegious effort to admit all styles and, perhaps for the first time in history, to allow the "banal," the "ugly," and the "vulgar" into the sacred precincts of symphonic form. Křenek defines the result as "surrealistic," for Mahler truly defies all rules, all criteria, all conventions. This is one of the principal reasons why he is classed today among the boldest explorers and pioneers and hailed as a precursor by so many of today's musicians.

The first movement of the *Third* is, according to Adorno, "the essential Mahlerian phenomenon [*Urphänomen*] . . . with its sequence of marches that seem to come from many different directions, that seize the ear and thus set it in motion, forcing it to listen simultaneously from several different locations. By the end of the development, the sounds have become just as wild as they were in the orchestra during the heroic phase of new music. Mahler renounces the inherited idea of the symphonic goal. He waits, without acting as stage director, until the uproar subsides. The fear that must have seized him at his own temerity has become productive: later, in the *Fourth Symphony,* and in the epilogue of the *Third,* all the different realms have been mastered . . ."

*ZWEITE ABTEILUNG* (SECOND PART)

   b) *Tempo di Menuetto. Sehr Mässig* (Very moderate)
KEY: A major (with contrasting section in F sharp minor).
TIME SIGNATURE: 3/4 (3/8, 2/4 and 9/8 in the contrasting section).

RHYTHM: Minuet (exceptional in Mahler's work).

MANUSCRIPTS: Complete sketch at Stanford University entitled *"Was der Abend mir erzählt"*; also seven-page sketch in same library entitled *"Was das Kind mir erzählt."*

COMPOSITION: Summer 1895.

FORM: ABABA. This symmetrical structure is identical with that of the corresponding Andante of the *Second Symphony*. Each section is made up of several episodes. The initial oboe theme is taken up by the violins and later returns to the woodwinds, but there is another episode (A') in C sharp minor and a concluding one (A") in the opening key. The B section is also composed of three episodes, each with its own rhythm. The last one modulates from E minor to D major, subdominant of the main key. There are many variations when A is restated in the original tonality, while the second B section is extended as a development, modulating from F sharp minor to G sharp minor and then back to D major, etc. At the beginning of the final A section, the main theme is played by the violas and the flutes in unison. The closing episode A" is extended into a coda of great lyrical beauty. In all Mahler's output there are few such idyllic pieces. It is hard to discern which episodes are intended as depicting "the icy autumn wind" breaking and withering the remaining flowers (cf. Chapter XXI).

c) *Comodo. Scherzando. Ohne Hast* (Without haste)

KEY: C minor (Trio in F major).

TIME SIGNATURE: 2/4 alternating with 6/8 in main section. 6/8 in Trio.

RHYTHM: Binary dance (bourrée) as in *"Ablösung."*

MANUSCRIPTS: 1-page sketch certified by Alma Mahler *"Einlage"* (C major); 2-page sketch in Stiftung Preussischer Kulturbesitz, Berlin; complete sketch: *"Was mir die Dämmerung erzählt"* crossed out and replaced by: *"Was mir die Tiere im Walde erzählen."* Original numbering "No. 2" crossed out and replaced by "No. 4."

COMPOSITION: June–July 1895.

FORM: The over-all structure is complex for a scherzo. It can be summarized as ABACABCA, in which C is the F major Trio. As in the *First Symphony*, 5a, and the *Fourth Symphony,* 10a, the little sixteenth-note melismas (here borrowed from the song *"Ablösung"*) are endlessly transformed. Here are a few of these transformations, taken only from the first two pages:

Except for the 6/8 contrasting section (B) and for the Trio (C) all the material for this movement is borrowed from *"Ablösung im Sommer"* (see above 6f), which is quoted verbatim at the beginning (with two extra bars of introduction and a new postlude). As in the Scherzo of the *Second Symphony*, Mahler inserted the humorous scene of St. Anthony preaching to the fishes, but placed a dissonant "cry of despair" at the end, he admitted in some of the texts written for the *Third Symphony* (see above Chapter 26) that he had meant to suggest the idyllic life of the animals of the forest and the panic that seizes them at man's approach. The long post-horn solo in the Trio is hard to fit into this program, for this essentially human sound seems to create no panic whatsoever among the animals, but rather a mood of happy nostalgia. The anguished outburst of the forest creatures mentioned by Mahler is undoubtedly the E flat minor triple fortissimo climax preceding the coda.

The first A section reproduces the entire song, with its contrasting major middle episode, but Mahler never quotes the vocal part literally: he simplifies it, either dividing it among various instruments or sometimes cutting it out entirely. In the new eight-bar transition passage between sections A and B of the Scherzo, Mahler borrows, from the last orchestral *Wunderhorn* song *"Lob des hohen Verstandes,"* a humorous musical imitation of the donkey's bray (in the violins). The contrasting 6/8 major episode has a solid rustic charm and a remarkable sequence of parallel fifths in the violins, just before the end. The first return of the A section, which is amplified and varied, modulates to E minor and E flat before returning to C minor, the original key. The violins embroider the main theme with a plaintive counter melody (this might have symbolized for Mahler the naïveté and helplessness of the animals). The following episode in major modulates (to A) and returns to the main key with the braying motif, while the 6/8 section also modulates and later returns to C. A last F minor pianissimo return of the A section serves as coda to the Scherzo proper, while a quick solo trumpet flourish announces the Trio.

The famous post-horn solo seems to have been suggested to Mahler by memories of Vlassim Park (see Chapter 32). In *Style and Idea,* Arnold Schönberg sings its praises, as it appears "at first with the divided high violins and then, even more beautiful, if possible, with the horns . . . This is a mood of nature," he adds, "of 'Greek serenity'—if one must express it in this way— or more simply, of the most wonderful beauty."[120] Once considered the very essence of Mahlerian banality, this Trio now appears utterly bewitching in its nostalgic simplicity and tender, innocent beauty. After the first solo, there is a dreamy interlude in the flutes, later taken up by the horns (its falling melody poetically recalls the trumpet melody from the first page of the Scherzo).

Another F minor recalls of theme A (2/4) leads to a shortened return of the post-horn solo and its horn interlude. A quick trumpet call then brings back the Scherzo, in F minor, with a new motif, none other than a faster version of the interlude: *"Mit geheimnisvoller Hast."* Mahler modulates to D minor and F minor before returning to the main key and the whole passage is completely "recomposed." The B section returns in a considerably varied form, although in its original key. Things seem to be moving toward a C minor climax when a high birdcall and the trumpet call announce a return of the post-horn solo (shortened) and of the interlude, this time in the divided first violins.

An accelerando version of A seems to be heading for an F minor climax, when a great E flat minor wave submerges the orchestra; it is the animals' "cry of terror," heard simultaneously with a horn and trombone fanfare, recalling those in the first and last movements of the *Second Symphony:* "A recurrence of the deep shadows of the Introduction," Mahler said in 1896. "Nature without life or light—the still uncrystallized, unorganized matter. But here it is more of a relapse into the deeply animal form of the All (PAN), before the huge leap into the 'spirit,' to that higher earthly creature, Man." Thereafter the end comes quickly, after a short stretto on the main motifs of A.

If anything, this short synopsis proves the complexity and asymmetry of the Scherzo, in which the character and alternation of the sections recur, more than the music itself. Mahler's growing skill led him to vary his motifs and episodes more and more, and literal recapitulation becomes the exception. The very briefness of *"Ablösung"* precluded long quotations from the song, such as those found in the Scherzo of the *Second Symphony*, and the labor of composition proper was therefore much greater. While revising this movement in 1899, Mahler was struck by its "mystical leaps" from "farcical to tragic" (see Chapter 30).

d) *Sehr langsam. Misterioso*, alto solo *"O Mensch!"* poem by Nietzsche
COMPOSITION: The original sketch of this movement, which was in Alma Mahler's collection, dates from the summer of 1895. It is called *"Was mir die Nacht erzählt,"* and the movement received its definitive title only after Mahler's arrival in Steinbach in June 1896. Whereas Mahler then prescribed eight minutes for the total duration of the piece, he extended it from ten and a half to eleven and a half in the copy made the following summer. He later remembered that the first bars were based on one of his earlier compositions (see Chapter 22).
KEY: D major/minor.
TIME SIGNATURE: 2/2, changing several times to 3/3 and once to 3/4.
MANUSCRIPT: *"Was mir die Nacht erzählt"* formerly in Alma Mahler's collection. Piano accompaniment. Fair copy (summer 1896) from NBL collection: Library of Congress.
TEXT: This song is the only one not composed on a *Wunderhorn* text by Mahler between 1884 and 1901. It is approximately contemporary with Strauss's tone poem *Also Sprach Zarathustra* and comes from the third part of the book, a chapter named *"Das andere Tanzlied."* Life is reproaching Zarathustra for his faithlessness and orders him to think between the twelve strokes of midnight. Life tells him his innermost thoughts, which he dares not express, and blames him for having contemplated suicide. The conclusion of the poem is optimistic, singing of the "Joys of Eternity" (which of course have nothing to do with the eternal bliss of Christian thought).

In the midnight poem, Nietzsche questions Light, Clarity, the Sun, all of which hold a privileged position in traditional art. He denounces the Search for Truth as something essentially nihilistic: instead of trying to see, Man, to his mind, should listen and discover a new sense with which to perceive the world. Midnight is the deepest, the darkest, the most opaque hour, an hour of doubt, that in which man comes closest to disowning life, and therefore closest to gaining access to a higher form of existence, Eternity, not in the Christian sense, but in that of the Nietzschean eternal recurrence. The poem consists of eleven lines, each sung between two strokes of the midnight bell. It appears again, just before the sun rises in the last chapter of the book. Having chosen a poem of such high literary worth, Mahler naturally did not alter a word of it. Its very brevity forced him to repeat a few lines and to entrust to the orchestra a bigger part than is usual in his songs.
FORM: In such a typically *"durchkomponiert"* song, it is difficult to find a definite plan or structure. There are no well-defined sections or literal restatements. In

the slow seventeen-bar introduction, the basses state the essential dominant-submediant motif and cadence, both borrowed from the Introduction to the first movement. The entrance of voice *"O Mensch,"* strongly recalls *"Röslein Roth"* from the beginning of *"Urlicht."* The first section proper remains essentially static but quotes the main ascending motif: *"Was spricht die tiefe Mitternacht"* (borrowed from the first movement recitative). Nature is not absent in this "human" piece, for immediately afterward the oboe three times sings *"Wie ein Naturlaut,"* an ascending minor third, which is later taken up by the English horn, before returning to the oboe in the next section and ending in a descending arpeggio, also borrowed from the first movement's recitative.

In the orchestral interlude (*Sehr breit und zurückhaltend*), the expression becomes more intense, and the continuous septuplet tonic-dominant bass motion is replaced by a viola tremolo. The ascending theme is then entrusted to the violins, to whom the horns reply. The *"Naturlaut"* in the oboe brings back the Introduction of the lied, followed by a shortened restatement of the opening. On the words *"Tief ist ihr Weh"* the voice quotes another motif from the first movement, the end of the introductory march theme, which already played a leading role in that movement (ABC here, instead of GAB flat originally). The following vocal passage (*"Lust, Lust!"*) anticipates the *Kindertotenlieder* and the later *Liebst du um Schönheit*. The voice quotes again from the first movement recitative (at *"will tiefe"*), and the introductory bass motif closes the song on a questioning dominant. As in Nietzsche's poem, the answer will be provided in the next episode by the morning bells. The intense atmosphere and deep emotion engendered by this Nietzsche lied is all the more amazing because it remains throughout in the piano and pianissimo dynamic range and comes as close as any piece by Mahler to being athematic.

e) *Lustig im Tempo und keck im Ausdruck,* alto solo, women's and children's choruses. *"Es sungen drei Engel"* from *Des Knaben Wunderhorn*

KEY: F major (modulating briefly to D minor).
TIME SIGNATURE: 4/4.
RHYTHM: Lively march.
TEXT: *Des Knaben Wunderhorn,* II, 375, under the title *"Armer Kinder Bettlerlied."* This very ancient, probably thirteenth-century *Judaslied* is already to be found in the 1605 *Mainzer Cantual* as *"Ein ander alt Gesang."* There is a musical setting of it, unrelated to Mahler's version, in Böhme's *Altdeutsches Liederbuch* (page 647). Mahler changed only a few words, omitted three repeated verses and the first line of the last stanza.
MANUSCRIPT: There is a first orchestral sketch in the Rosé Collection dated June 24, 1895. The first complete orchestral score used to be in Alma Mahler's collection. The following inscription is found at the end: *"Ferien Arbeit beschlossen. Sonntag August 1895."* Mahler having left Steinbach on the following Sunday (August 18), this must have been August 11. According to Mahler's own timing, the piece lasts four minutes. Its numbering was changed: No. 4 is crossed out and replaced by "6" in pencil.
ORCHESTRATION: The most striking feature is the very limited role of the strings and the complete absence of the violins. The texture always remains exquisitely transparent, although five clarinets and six horns sometimes perform together. The women's chorus nearly always sings in unison, while the children perform only one melodic phrase, besides imitating the bells (Bim-Bam).

COMPOSITION: According to Fritz Egon Pamer, who no doubt received this information from Guido Adler, the song was written before the rest of the symphony and transcribed without any alterations, except for the addition of the chorus part, two bars of "Bim-Bam" at the beginning, and ten others in the postlude. There is only one additional short phrase in the symphonic version, the women's chorus *"Du sollst ja nicht weinen."* Like *"Urlicht,"* whose position it shares as an introduction to the Finale, this was probably the earliest movement of the symphony.

FORM: Strophic *"durchkomponiert":* the third stanza restates the first with considerable variations. The middle stanza contains new elements, as well as some borrowed from the first. Since it is a celebration of the joys of heaven, it is not surprising that this lied should have several motifs in common with the *Fourth Symphony*'s *"Das Himmlische Leben"* (Heavenly Life), which was originally destined for the *Third*. Here are the three motifs used in both songs:

No. 1

No. 2

No. 3

The archaic character of the parallel sixths and octaves in the last quoted theme is of course intentional and suits the naïveté of the poem perfectly. What is surprising is that Mahler should have considered inserting in the same symphony two songs so much alike.

f) *Langsam, ruhevoll, empfunden.* (Slow, calm, deeply felt)

COMPOSITION: The final Adagio was most likely sketched in the early summer, as it is found in one of the preliminary programs, in third place, under its definitive title *"Was mir die Liebe erzählt. Adagio."* It was probably composed by the end of July 1895, for Mahler sketched *all* the movements except the first that summer and spent his last days in Steinbach in early August orchestrating the *Wunderhorn* movement.

After completing the initial movement the following summer, he simplified the conclusion of the Adagio: "It now ends the whole work with broad chords and in the one tonality of D major," he said to Natalie on July 31 of that year. Until the end of the summer of 1895, the Adagio was meant to be succeeded by the 1892 song *"Das Himmlische Leben,"* which was suppressed the following winter. In fact Mahler appears to be one of the first composers to end a symphony with an instrumental adagio. Liszt's two symphonies do close with slow movements, but in both cases a chorus joins in, providing the work with an oratorio-like conclusion. "In an adagio," Mahler said to Natalie, "all is resolved in peace and existence. The Ixion wheel of appearances is at last brought to a standstill" (see above Chapter XXIII).

KEY: D major (modulating to F sharp minor, C sharp minor, etc.).

TIME SIGNATURE: 4/4 (Mahler specifies that in the faster episodes the half-notes should be the time unit).

MANUSCRIPT: There seems to have been a ms. orchestral score in Alma Mahler's collection, but it had already disappeared by the time I inventoried it.

FORM: Certain authors have analyzed this movement as a kind of rondo, others as a sequence of variations on two themes (something like the parallel Adagio of the *Fourth Symphony*), and a case can be made for both. At this stage in his creative evolution Mahler's inexhaustible imagination never stopped transforming melodies and the task of the analyst thus becomes increasingly complex. The whole movement pours out in one great flow, and it is hard to determine sections. Here is an approximate synopsis of the Adagio:

EXPOSITION

Bars

1 to 40    Theme A (in three different phrases starting with same ascending fourth) : D major

41 to 50    *Nicht mehr so breit* (No longer so slow) : Theme B : F sharp minor (divided strings)

51 to 91    *Noch etwas bewegter* (A little faster still) : Theme B′ in the basses (always in gradually accelerating tempo, with B and a fragment of A, as well as a quotation from the first movement trombone recitative already quoted in fourth movement : C sharp minor modulating to F major, G minor and D minor

92 to 107    *Ruhevoll* (Peaceful) : Theme A varied : D major modulating to F sharp minor and back

108 to 123    *Sehr gesangvoll* (Very singing) : Theme A (with new counter melody in the treble) : D major

124 to 131    *Nicht mehr so breit* (No longer so broad) : B to D minor

132 to 148    *A tempo :* Theme B′ (with fragments from A) : C sharp minor modulating to F major/minor

149 to 167    Theme B (with new counter melody) : A flat minor, E flat minor, D flat major

168 to 197    *Etwas breiter wie vorher* (A little broader than before) : New variation of A (with G A B flat motif from the end of initial theme of first movement, also quoted in movement d) : E major, E flat, D major

198 to 251    *Tempo primo :* Theme A, varied and leading to a "mournful" climax in the minor mode on a fragment suggesting the first movement recitative : D major

RECAPITULATION

252 to 295   *Sehr langsam* (Very slow) : Theme A literally restated in the trum-
                   pet (with the original bass counter melody in the trombone) grad-
                   ually working up to a climax : D major

296 to 328   Coda. Theme A, gradually reduced to its main motifs. (The last
                   thirteen bars, as altered by Mahler, are nothing but a long tonic
                   chord held by the whole orchestra, while the string basses and
                   timpani relentlessly hammer out a succession of dominant-tonic
                   motifs.)

Hard as it is to discover any trace of symmetrical construction in this Finale, it
is nevertheless one of Mahler's most inspired and most successful movements. The
style is as grand and the tone as exalted as, in the first movement, it was full of
abrupt changes and unexpected contrasts. Even Bruckner never sustained such a
long and consistently sublime movement. The influence of Wagner's *Parsifal* is
undeniably present in the themes and the divided string writing. This movement
would obviously not have been written without *Parsifal,* and yet this fact detracts
nothing from its greatness. It is a fit counterpart and reply to the first movement,
and Mahler would have weakened the whole structure by attempting to duplicate
the marvelous choral ending of the preceding symphony. After Nature, Summer,
Flowers, Animals, Man, and Angelic Voices, he successfully climbed the last
step to Eternal Light in this great hymn to God, conceived as the supreme force
of Love.

## CYCLIC PROCEDURE

Although Mahler complained to Natalie in 1896 that "nothing has come of
the great cohesion I at first imagined between the various movements" and that
"each one stands on its own feet as a separate entity, without recapitulations or
reminiscences," several recurring motifs from the first movement have been
pointed out: G A B flat (from Bars 6, 7, and 8 of the first movement) in "d"; a
fragment of the trumpet recitative (Bars 84 to 86) in "d"; the third bar of the
same motif in "f" (after Figure 23). The trumpet and trombone fanfare theme
heard during the E flat minor climax at the end of the Scherzo can also be
traced to the first movement recitatives, and the main theme of the Finale may
be viewed as a major counterpart to the initial "Inertia" march, starting as it does
with the same ascending fourth.

It is no mere chance that all these thematic relationships exist only between
the first, fourth, and last movements. This proves that the others, the second,
third, and fifth, were less essential to Mahler's basic conception of the work and,
like the middle movements of the two preceding symphonies, could be considered as intermezzi. Even though the tone of the whole work is less passionate
and subjective than that of the *Second,* all the aspects of creation are viewed by
a man whose deeper feelings and emotions are stirred in these essential pieces,
whereas he remains a mere spectator in the Flower, Animal, and Angel movements. Yet the work's power does not lie in the affirmation of faith or in a victory
of the ego over destiny, as it did in the *First* and *Second Symphonies*. The first
movement, which Mahler himself considered the "maddest" he had composed
until then, has a certain impersonal granitic force that is Nietzschean, in that it

reaches beyond passion, whereas the *Totenfeier* movement, with all its grandeur, is still full of it.

On purely musical grounds—and Mahler himself wanted his listeners to forget about the program—the structure of the *Third Symphony* is very surprising indeed, but only if viewed in the light of the past. The succession of Minuet and Scherzo duplicates that of the corresponding movements in the *Second* and anticipates the same sequences in his three last symphonies (*Das Lied,* the *Ninth,* and the *Tenth*). The very brief and light choral movement, which comes between the two great meditations of the fourth movement and final Adagio, anticipates the *Tenth*'s *Purgatorio* or the small intermezzi in *Das Lied.* Although this is far less evident than in the *Second Symphony,* the whole can also be viewed as a sequence, not only of fast and slow movements, but also of questions and answers. The Finale is a reply to the terrifying restlessness and the titanic conflicts of the opening Allegro, while the daylight of the angel movement dispels the midnight darkness of the Nietzschean lied, and the deep faith and overpowering feeling of love that pervades the Finale answers all questions. It could even be claimed that none of Mahler's optimistic and victorious conclusions are as convincing as this one: the short moments of anxiety and grief only strengthen the complete serenity of the whole.

The *Third Symphony* brought Mahler his first, genuine success, and one of his very few, with the public. There can be little doubt that this was largely thanks to the final Adagio, for it is hard not be be moved by its tranquil power and sustained lyric profundity.

## 10) *FOURTH SYMPHONY,* G major (1899–1900)
### COMPOSITION

After having devoted four whole summers to the titanic task of building two great symphonic monuments, and after having accomplished his dearest wish, that of becoming director of the Vienna Opera, Mahler was forced to interrupt his composition for two successive summers because of poor health. When the creative urge seized him again, in Aussee, at the end of June 1899, it is understandable that he should have planned a shorter and lighter work. *Revelge* served as a rough tryout; the real work on the symphony started in mid-July and lasted until the end of the month, when Mahler was forced to return to Vienna and the opera. His depression and anxiety increased daily as the fatal date of his departure approached. He was forced to interrupt his work long before it was completed and at a time when new ideas were springing continuously to mind.

Remembering the title he had originally given to his first orchestral *Wunderhorn Lieder,* he decided that it suited the light character of the new work, and thus named it "Symphony No. 4 (*Humoreske*)." The original plan included three songs instead of one:

No. 1: *"Die Welt als ewige Jetztzeit"* (The World as Eternal Present), G major
No. 2: *"Das Irdische Leben"* (Earthly Life), E flat minor
No. 3: *"Caritas"* (Adagio), B major
No. 4: *"Morgenglocken"* (Morning Bells), F major
No. 5: *"Die Welt ohne Schwere"* (The World Without Gravity), D major (Scherzo)
No. 6: *"Das Himmlische Leben"*[121] (Heavenly Life)

This plan was obviously drawn up at the same time as those of the *Third*

*Symphony,* for Mahler still considered using in the *Fourth* the *Third*'s fifth movement (*"Morgenglocken"*), as well as *"Das Irdische Leben,"* which today belongs to the collection of orchestral songs. The *Fourth*'s minor Scherzo is absent from this original plan, and the D major one mentioned in it is undoubtedly the scherzo that was eventually placed in the *Fifth Symphony.*

The other movements are those of the present symphony, but was the great Adagio really the realization of the planned B major *"Caritas"* movement? It is of course as close in spirit to the Finale of the *Third,* as "Charity" is to "Love," but it is rare indeed to see Mahler change the key of a projected movement! In any case, the title *"Caritas"* reappears in 1906 in the original plan for the *Eighth Symphony.*

Upon arriving in Maiernigg the following summer, Mahler quickly adapted himself to life in his *Häuschen,* but he took quite some time to settle down to work again. When he finally succeeded (at the time of his birthday, *i.e.,* around July 7), he realized that the symphony had progressed in his mind, although he had not consciously been concentrating on it, thanks to the activity of his "second Me" (see Chapter 22). He later stated that all three movements had been left uncompleted in Aussee, but his main task during the second summer was probably the composition of the Adagio. It was interrupted by a four-day trip to the Dolomites, and, upon his return, he proceeded to complete the slow movement, which is dated "Sunday August 6, 1900."

Contrary to his earlier Steinbach custom, Mahler only spoke of the work in detail on August 1, when he was about to complete it. He knew by then that its performance would take about forty-five minutes. During the following winter he managed to spend some time each day working on the new symphony. In the Scherzo Natalie states that he "restored the first version of the music as he had originally sketched it" (although its first ending had been a tarentella that is not to be found in the final version). In January, while in bed with the flu, he worked on the first theme of the first movement and, immediately after recovering from a hemorrhage, received the score fresh from the copyist's hand. He was amazed to discover then that the Scherzo had been placed third instead of second and that two versions of one passage in the Adagio had been copied in succession rather than as alternative versions. What would have happened if he had died during the night?

It was in Abbazzia, where he went to rest and recover in April 1901, that he enlarged the orchestration of the Finale. Back in Vienna, he continued correcting the copied score, claiming that he was only really able to see it when it was no longer in his own handwriting, and that he would only be able to straighten out the last details on the printer's proofs. These he actually corrected at the end of October, after the first reading of the work by the Philharmonic orchestra.[122]

## MANUSCRIPTS AND DIFFERENT VERSIONS

These are fairly well covered in the introduction to the 1963 *Mahler Gesellschaft* edition of the work. To Professor Ratz's list should be added a four-page sketch of the Scherzo with seventeen bars of the solo violin on a separate sheet dated December 29, 1900, and dedicated by Mahler to his brother-in-law Arnold Rosé on January 11, 1902, the day before the Vienna premiere of the work.[123] It is clear that Mahler had worked with Rosé on the tuned-up violin solo.

A complete first orchestral score of the work was formerly in Alma Mahler's possession.[124] It did not include the Finale, which Mahler probably copied later, and ended with the sheet mentioned above: (*"Dritte Satz und somit die ganz Symphonie"* [The third movement and therewith the whole symphony], dated August 6, 1900). The first manuscript orchestral score copied by Mahler during the 1901–02 winter bears only one date, at the end of the Scherzo: January 5, 1901. There are also two pages of a short sketch, which came from Alma Mahler's collection, in the Stanford Library. This symphony seems to have been revised and retouched oftener than any other. The first printer's proofs have interesting metronomic markings. Mahler made many further alterations when Universal Edition republished the work in 1906, and still others during the summer of 1910 which were incorporated in the printed score. The final version, containing changes he made in New York after conducting the work there in January 1911, was discovered by Erwin Stein in 1929 in the cellars of Universal Edition and discussed by him in the magazine *Pult und Tacktstock* that year. The changes are both numerous and important, as Stein pointed out. They have been incorporated into the 1963 *Gesellschaft* edition.

Mahler's happiest and most carefree composition, the *Fourth Symphony*, not only was written during a period of ill-health and psychological strain, but it soon became Mahler's most misunderstood and decried work, at least during his lifetime. Only after his death did it achieve some success. Between the two World Wars, and again after the last one, it was, together with *Das Lied*, Mahler's most frequently performed and recorded work. The reason for the work's eclipse is easy to discern: both public and critics expected from Mahler other "titanic" symphonies like the *Second* and *Third*, and no one could make head or tail of the "humorous" style of the *Fourth*, which seemed just as artificial and lacking in authenticity as the earlier *Humoresken* or *Wunderhorn Lieder*.

PROGRAM: Although by 1899 Mahler had completely given up the idea of devising an explanatory program for his works, some of the remarks he made to Natalie come very close to resembling one (see Chapter 32). In the whole work he admitted attempting to render the "uniform blue of the sky in all its different hues," "an unheard-of gaiety, a supraterrestrial joy, which attracts and repels at the same time; an incredible light, an incredible air, in which very touching human sounds are also present," and also "the panic terror that sometimes seizes man on the most beautiful day." (As in the flower movement in the *Third Symphony*, it is hard to identify the passages that Mahler intended to illustrate this "panic terror.") Later in 1901, he described its gaiety "as coming from another sphere, so that it is terrifying for humans: only a child can understand and explain it, and a child does explain it in the end." He also compared the whole symphony to a primitive picture, painted on a gold background, and added that every small element and detail within it was varied, as happens with the human body and mind, "which from birth to the grave remains always identical and yet is always different" (October 1901).

In August 1900, Mahler admitted that he had thought up the most beautiful titles for each movement, in the manner of those of the *Third*, but that he had decided not to disclose them. He never ceased to emphasize the polyphonic complexity of the work, which he envisaged (in August 1900) as the close of a great Tetralogy of Symphonies. (It is still generally considered nowadays as the last of the *"Wunderhorn* Symphonies.") Mahler was right in believing that the symphony reflected all his present technical ability. He told Natalie (in January 1901) of the trouble he had had with the extremely simple opening theme, whose complete beauty is only later revealed ("like a dewdrop that, suddenly illuminated by the sun, bursts into a thousand lights and colors . . .") (see Chapter 34). According to the Dutch composer Alphonse Diepenbrock, who wrote an analysis of the *Fourth* after having discussed it often with Mahler,[125] Mahler sometimes described the first movement as representing the "supreme bliss" (*Ueberirdische Fröhlichkeit*) that has been conquered in the *Third Symphony*. The second movement (Scherzo) originally bore the subtitle *"Freund Hein spielt zum Tanz auf; der Tod streicht recht absonderlich die Fiedel und geigt uns in den Himmel hinauf"* [Death strikes up the dance for us; she scrapes her fiddle bizarrely and leads us up to heaven].[126]

The music is "mystic, confused [*verworren*], uncanny," Mahler said while composing this movement in 1900. "It will make your hair stand on the end, but its denouement [*Auflösung*] in the Adagio proves that its intentions were not so bad." In October 1901, Mahler speaks of its "terrifying humor" again, relating it to the Scherzo of the *Second Symphony* or the opening Allegro of the *First*. He was particularly proud of having created, with the Adagio, his first real variations (although they are of a very unconventional type: see below). Discussing the contrast between the two main sections, he adds that a melody both "divinely gay and deeply sad" pervades the whole. To this melody he often lent the features of one of the saints in the last movement: "St. Ursula herself, the most serious of all the saints, presides with a smile, so gay in this higher sphere. Her smile resembles that on the prone statues of old knights or prelates one sees lying in churches, their hands joined on their bosoms and with the peaceful gentle expressions of men who have gained access to a higher bliss; solemn, blessed peace; serious, gentle gaiety, such is the character of this movement, which also has deeply sad moments, comparable, if you wish, to reminiscences of earthly life, and other moments when gaiety becomes vivacity [*Steigerung der Heiterkeit ins Lebhafte*]."[127]

To Natalie, Mahler also privately admitted that, while composing the Adagio, he could sometimes see his mother's face, as she smiled through her tears, for she was able to "solve all suffering by love." In the big climax, the opening of the gates of heaven, just before the end of the Adagio, the atmosphere became "Catholic, almost churchlike." For the Finale, Mahler never gave any program other than the text itself: "When man, now full of wonder, asks what all this means, the child answers him with the fourth movement: 'This is Heavenly Life' . . ."

Using Mahler's unpublished early "titles" for the movement, Paul Bekker has suggested the following program as being that originally conceived by Mahler: "A dream excursion into the heavenly fields of Paradise, starting in the first movement with gay sleigh bells and leading through alternately smiling and melancholy landscapes to *Freund Hein* (Death), who is to be taken in a friendly, legendary sense, as gathering his flock and leading it with his fiddle from this world to the next. In the Adagio variations, which start peacefully and gain speed in a gradual crescendo, the new world becomes increasingly clear, spreading before the traveler's eyes, and progressing through a series of metamorphoses, until the last abode is reached, where all wishes are fulfilled, and where spirits dance and play and sing in everlasting bliss."[128]

The programs prove that Mahler believed, as we do today, that the transparent style of the *Fourth Symphony* was probably a higher achievement than anything in the earlier, grandiose symphonies. It was, in any case, anything but a regression to a sterile form of neoclassicism. Thanks to the battles of the preceding symphonies, Mahler felt that he had gained access to a higher sphere, to the simple faith and crystal-clear mirth of children.

a) *Bedächtig, nicht eilen* (Deliberate, without haste)
KEY: G major.
TIME SIGNATURE: 4/4 with a few 3/4 and 2/4 bars.
TEMPO: As usual in Mahler's later works there are countless tempo changes.
FORM: One of the shortest of Mahler's first or last movements, this is also one of the most complex. Mahler carried much further the effort initiated in the opening Allegro of the *First*. None of the published analyses cover the whole subject of the form of this movement, which would provide excellent material for a complete thesis. Having opted for the most concentrated style possible, and reached a point when his mature mind and polished technique constantly produced new variations, Mahler never ceased to invert, augment, and combine the original motifs and even to transfer them from one theme or group of themes to another. Erwin Stein describes this procedure in the following way: "Sometimes, he [Mahler] shuffles the motifs like a pack of cards, as it were, and makes them yield new melodies. The motifs of the theme reappear, but in a different arrangement."[129]

In the first movement of this "Classical Symphony," Mahler has of course retained all the main characteristics of sonata form:

EXPOSITION
Bars
  1 to   3  Introduction (I) : composed of three motifs (flutes and clarinet) : E minor (?)
  4 to  31  *Recht Gemächlich* (Very easygoing). Theme A in 3 parts (A : 1 to 7; A′ : 8 to 17; A in imitations with leading motif in future coda and development theme : 18 to 21; A″ : 22 to 31) : G major
 32 to  37  Bridge modulating from G to D major
 38 to  57  *Breit gesungen* (Broadly sung). Theme B in 3 parts : D major
 58 to  71  *Etwas fliessender* (Somewhat faster). Theme C (conclusive) : D major
 72 to  76  Theme I : E minor(?)
 77 to  90  *Tempo primo :* Theme A much varied (false recapitulation) : G major
 91 to 101  Coda : *Wieder sehr ruhig* (Very calm again)
DEVELOPMENT
102 to 108  *Tempo primo :* Theme I : E minor
109 to 116  Theme A′ : E minor
117 to 124  Theme A : A minor

125 to 154   *Fliessend aber ohne Hast* (Flowing, without haste) : New develop-
             ment theme (using a motif already introduced in the middle of A
             [Bar 20] and anticipating main theme of Finale)
155 to 166   Introduction and new motif derived from Bar 22 of A″, etc. : A flat
             minor
167 to 208   Theme I, Motif from A″, C, A, etc. : F minor, C minor, D minor
209 to 220   Fortissimo climax : Motif from A″ and bridge : C major
221 to 238   Motif from A″, I, trumpet call (which Mahler himself entitled
             *"Der kleiner Appell"*), return of beginning of A : F sharp major, C
             major

RECAPITULATION

239 to 253   *Wieder wie zum Anfang* (As in the beginning again) : restatement
             of A (with augmented motif from A″) starting one bar before A″ :
             G major
254 to 262   Bridge : G major
263 to 282   *Schwungvoll* (Energetic). Theme B in strings alone : G major
283 to 297   *Wieder plötzlich langsam* (Suddenly slow again) : Theme C
298 to 322   I, motif from A″, A, A′

CODA

323 to 340   *Ruhig und immer ruhiger werden* (Very calm, and always calmer) :
             A and development motif
341 to 349   *Sehr langsam* (Very slow), *poco a poco stringendo :* A and bridge

Even though the techniques used are very original, the structure and proportions of this movement remain close to traditional models, as the above plan
clearly shows. One of the most striking features is the evolutive character of the
developments, the various new versions of the themes being, so to speak, the
result of earlier ones. It is interesting, for instance, to note that the augmented
version of the motif from Bar 22 of A″, which has assumed an essential role in
the development (starting in the basses at Bar 148), appears as a counterpoint in
the trumpet over the original form of Theme A″ in the third bar of the recapitulation (Bar 241). The transformations of the themes and motifs are thus shown to
be irreversible. Among a vast number of other observations that could be made
about this movement is the fact that neither nature nor military music is absent
from it, as they practically never are from Mahler's music; there are birdcalls
(in Bars 186 and 187 of the development) derived from the flute motifs in the
second and third bars of the introduction, as well as trumpet calls before the
recapitulation. Mahler called this last passage *"Der kleiner Appell,"* as opposed
to the *"Grosser Appell"* of the *Second Symphony* (see Chapter 32). "It is," he
added, "as if the captain were calling his troops to order after the confusion of
the development."

From the point of view of classical sonata form, the only unusual features in
this movement are the recurrence of the main theme in its original key just before
the end of the exposition—a kind of "false recapitulation"—the uncertain tonality of the introduction (it is later revealed to be in E minor) and its rondo-like
recurrence several times in the same opening key (except for the A flat minor
episode, where it is combined with A′).

Mahler himself was conscious of the richness of his first theme, which, despite
its air of "old-fashioned simplicity," later "created six or even seven further

themes," all of which he played for Natalie on the piano.[180] An interesting and striking resemblance has been noted between the first bars of Mahler's main theme and a few bars in the exposition of the first movement of Schubert's *E Flat Sonata*, D. 568 (Bars 53 to 56).

SCHUBERT

MAHLER

b) *In gemächlicher Bewegung, ohne Hast* (In measured tempo, without haste)
KEY: C minor (with F major Trio).
TIME SIGNATURE: 3/8.
RHYTHM: slow ländler.
TEMPO: *Etwas gemächlicher* (A little slower) in the Trio.
INSTRUMENTATION: To suggest the crude sound of the fiddle, Mahler requires the concertmaster to play certain passages on a violin that is tuned a whole tone higher than usual. During the preliminary rehearsal, which he organized with the Vienna Philharmonic on October 12, 1901, he decided that the sound was not caricatured enough and planned to entrust the "fiddle passages" to a solo viola played by the same concertmaster, thinking that it would sound even shriller. He later reversed this decision and the score now calls for a violin.
FORM: The movement is composed in a sequence of short alternating sections, as befits a scherzo:

SCHERZO
Bars
1 to 33   Introduction (in horn : four bars) and A : C minor
34 to 45   B : C major
46 to 63   A : C minor
TRIO
64 to 109   Five-bar horn passage (as postlude to Scherzo or introduction to Trio and C : F major
SCHERZO
110 to 144   Introduction (horn : six bars) and A : C minor
145 to 156   B : C major
157 to 184   A : C minor (with one-bar introduction)
185 to 200   B : C major

TRIO

201 to 253   Two-bar introduction and C (varied) : F major
254 to 275   Development of C : D major

SCHERZO

276 to 313   Five-bar introduction and A : C minor
314 to 329   B : C major
330 to 364   Six-bar introduction and Coda derived from A (chromatically modu-
             lating) and introductory motif

Although much more sophisticated in every respect, this is Mahler's only real
dance movement since the Scherzo of the *First Symphony,* and it anticipates
future ländlers in the *Fifth* and *Ninth Symphonies:* several authors have found
a similarity between one of the Trio themes and *"Das Himmlische Leben"* (see
below, CYCLIC PROCEDURES), yet it is definitely an intermezzo. The contrast
in style is not so pronounced as it is in the *Second* and *Third Symphonies,*
because the outer movements are not so grandiose and heaven storming.

c) *Ruhevoll* (Calm) (*Poco Adagio*)
KEY: G major (Second theme in E minor).
TEMPO: Changing to *Viel langsamer* for the second theme and speeding up to
*Allegro molto* in variations.
TIME SIGNATURE: 4/4 changing to *alla breve,* 3/4, 3/8, 2/4 in the variations.
FORM: The variation form is one of the simplest and strictest inherited from
classical times, and Mahler proudly called this movement "my first real varia-
tions." The truth is that, even if he had been once, he was no longer capable of
blindly adhering to a traditional form, and this movement, which seems so
deceptively simple at first glance, is actually one of the hardest to analyze in
Mahler's whole production. Many authors have attempted to synthesize its structure; it is so complex that no one has, to my mind, wholly succeeded.
The essential facts are the following:

1) This Adagio is a variation movement, but on two contrasting themes, in the
manner of the slow movement of Beethoven's *Ninth Symphony.* The two themes
have motifs in common, both in the melody and the accompaniment. The first
creates a mood of serene meditation, while the second, in the relative minor key,
introduces a note of unrest and yearning. The definition "variation on two
themes" already proves inaccurate, for the second theme is not genuinely "varied,"
but only amplified when it is restated.

2) There is a strong passacaglia feeling throughout the major section of the
Adagio, because of the ostinato bass motif, which is always present in some form
or other. Matters are further complicated by the fact that the theme and its
bass seem to be constructed in sixteen-bar periods, while other features occasionally seem to point to an eight-bar construction. (There is a definite resemblance,
for instance, between the bass design of Bars 1 to 4 and 9 to 12, and Mahler uses
the same counter melody in Bars 25 to 28 as in 17 to 20.) Thus there are three
themes, A, B, and the bass motif, which are sometimes simultaneously varied;
for instance, Bars 151 to 156 are a variation in the treble of Bars 45 to 50,
while a variation of the bass theme starts two bars *before* the end of the same
period (at Bar 155) and continues after it has reached its conclusion.

3) The bass theme itself is melodically varied.

4) Bars 107 to 178 are a fairly strict variation of Bars 1 to 61.

5) The variations follow an evolutive process recognizable in all Mahler's music from now on (except perhaps in the scherzos). They are often variations of a previous variation, rather than of the theme.

To my mind, no one up to now has successfully analyzed the periodic structure of the theme, which is in three parts:

| | FIRST PERIOD | | | SECOND PERIOD | | | CLOSING PERIOD |
|---|---|---|---|---|---|---|---|
| original form Bars 1 to 8 | 1 to 8 | 9 to 16 | 17 to 24 | 25 to 36 | 37 to 44 | 45 to 51 | 52 to 61 |
| faster variations starting after B section | 107 to 114 | 115 to 122 | 123 to 130 | 131 to 142 | 143 to 150 | | |

The symmetry between theme and variations ends a few bars after 144, when the bass theme is introduced as a new subject for variation and is treated in imitations by the various orchestral groups. It is interesting to note that the first part of the second period (Bars 25 to 36) is ten bars rather than seven bars long, and that the same extension is found in the varied restatement (Bars 25 to 36). It can be attributed to the horn interlude (Bars 31 to 36), which is reproduced after Bar 137 (in clarinets and bassoons). One last detail should be noted: at Bar 123, while the cellos elaborate their long original melody (from Bar 25ff.), the oboe starts to elaborate on the original bass motif in the treble, although the same motif is already present in the pizzicato basses. A situation so complex that it makes one's mind whirl!

The bass theme has been called "bell motif" by Paul Bekker because of its intervals and because it is played on pizzicato strings. In the first sixty-one-bar statement of the theme, many elements are already elaborated in variation form. Here is a complete synopsis of the movement:

Bars

A    1 to   24  A (First period in three parts : see above) : G major
     25 to  50  A (Second period) (with horn and bassoon interlude)
     51 to  61  A (Closing period)

---

B   62 to   75  B : *Viel langsamer* (Much slower) (with fragments of initial bass motifs, diminished) : E minor
    76 to   91  B varied (on same bass) (Bar 80 anticipates a motif : *"Warum so dunkle Flammen"* from the second *Kindertotenlied*)
    92 to  106  B : Third section based on bass of theme (coda) : D minor

---

A  107 to  130  *Anmuthig bewegt* (Gracefully animated) : variation of first period of A (with bass motif appearing in the treble)
   131 to  150  Variation of beginning of second period, with horn and bassoon interlude in clarinet and bassoon : G major

151 to 178   *Sehr fliessend* (Very increasingly animated) free variation of the end of A

---

B   179 to 191   *Wieder wir vorher* (Again as before) : B (without ostinato bass) : G minor

192 to 204   *Fliessend* (Flowing : B : second period (fortissimo climax) : C sharp minor

205 to 221   *Leidenschaftlich und etwas drängend* (Passionate and somewhat slower) : B : last period (coda) : F sharp minor/major

---

A   222 to 237   *Andante* 3/4 : first variation proper of A : G major

238 to 262   *Allegretto subito* 3/8 : Second variation : G major

263 to 277   *Allegro subito* 2/4 : Third variation : E major

278 to 286   *Allegro molto* 2/4 : Fourth variation cut short (*Andante subito*) by horn interlude from first section : G major

287 to 314   *Poco Adagio :* Variation of the end of A (Bars 37 to 61) : G major

---

315 to 325   *Poco più mosso :* Triple fortissimo : anticipation in the brass of main theme of Finale (*Pesante*) (part of which was heard in development theme of first movement) : E major

---

326 to 353   Coda : ascending theme (based on motifs from both A and B) : E major, C major, G major (ending on the dominant).

Although very different in structure, this movement is closely related, not only in feeling but also in its variation techniques, to the Finale of the *Third Symphony*. It is also based on the contrast of a long and serene melody with another, more nostalgic one. In a work that he dedicated to the classical spirit, it is understandable that Mahler should have used the most classical of all forms, the variation. Nevertheless his use of it is as far removed from the model as Beethoven's fugal movements in sonata form are from the traditional fugue. Although possessing a complete poetic unity, these variations keep moving further and further away from the theme, each one being a logical result of the preceding one. In the third A section, the "senseless agitation" of everyday life gradually annihilates the serene mood of the opening, and the tempo becomes faster, like a spinning wheel gaining speed. The opening theme is gradually destroyed and distorted, but the nightmarish vision is brutally interrupted before the end of the last variation.

d) *Sehr behaglich* (At ease), soprano solo, *"Wir geniessen die Himmlischen Freuden"* from *Des Knaben Wunderhorn.*

It was a very original idea indeed in Mahler's time to close a symphony with a simple lied, yet it was the seed from which the whole work grew. As Mahler later remarked, *Das Himmlische Leben,* composed in Hamburg in 1892, had long been one of his favorite works, and it was one of the richest in substance, "having given birth to no less than five symphonic movements" (Mahler probably means the whole *Fourth Symphony* as well as the choral movement of the *Third*). In August 1900 he called his Finale the "pinnacle" of the symphony. That the song was the very source, the germ from which the whole work sprang, is proved by the fact that Mahler borrowed from its initial refrain to start the first movement and thus the whole symphony.

KEY: G major, ending in E major.

TIME SIGNATURE: 4/4 changing here and there to 2/4.

TEMPO: ♪=96 on 1892 ms.

TEXT: *Des Knaben Wunderhorn*, I, 335, under the title *"Der Himmel hängt voll Geigen."* Its origin is a folk song, well known throughout Bavaria and Bohemia, which can be traced to a late-eighteenth-century lied by Peter Marcellin Sturm, *"Nach Kreuz und ausgestandenen Leiden."* Mahler's only alteration was to suppress four lines from the fourth stanza. Thus the original poem has five ten-line stanzas, while Mahler's version has three ten-line stanzas and two of eight lines. There is a melody by Sturm himself set to this poem, but is has nothing in common with Mahler's setting. While working on this lied in Abbazia in April 1901 he expressed his delight at the "roguishness and deep mysticism" of the poem.

FORM: Strophic *"durchkomponiert."* There are three main sections, with a contrasting, self-sufficient middle episode (in minor) and a long coda that varies and prolongs the initial motifs. There are also two different "refrains": the fast ritornello used by Mahler in the first movement and the slow chorale common to this song and to the fifth movement of the *Third Symphony*.

Bars

| | | |
|---|---|---|
| 1 to | 11 | Orchestral introduction presenting first theme |
| 12 to | 35 | Main section A in two parts (A and A') |
| 36 to | 39 | *Plötzlich zurückhaltend* (Suddenly slower) : Chorale : E minor |
| 40 to | 56 | *Plötzlich frisch bewegt* (Suddenly sprightly and animated). Refrain developed : E minor |
| 57 to | 71 | *Etwas zurückhaltend* (A little slower) : Contrasting section : B : E minor |
| 72 to | 75 | *Wieder zurückhaltend* (Slower again) : Chorale : E minor |
| 76 to | 79 | *Wieder lebhaft* (Lively again) : Refrain : E minor |
| 80 to | 105 | *Tempo primo :* Section A (abridged) and A' (developed) : G major |
| 106 to | 114 | *Wieder plötzlich zurückhaltend* (Once again suddenly slower) : Chorale : D minor |
| 115 to | 121 | *Wieder lebhaft* (Lively once again) : Refrain : B minor |
| CODA | | |
| 122 to | 141 | *Tempo primo: Sehr zart und geheimnisvoll bis zum Schluss* (Very tender and mysterious until the end) : Orchestral introduction stating new theme based on A |
| 142 to | 168 | Theme A in E major (varied) |
| 169 to | 174 | Chorale (simplified) : E major |
| 175 to | 184 | Pianissimo orchestral conclusion |

No one, to my knowledge, has pointed out the striking similarity between Bars 32 and 33 of the Finale of Schubert's *D Major Sonata*, D. 850, and Bar 128 of the E major theme from the coda of *"Das Himmlische Leben"*—undoubtedly Mahler's subconscious memory at work—which proves once again how well Mahler knew

Schubert's sonatas, which he played in his childhood at the Vienna Conservatory, while studying under Epstein.

SCHUBERT

MAHLER

## CYCLIC PROCEDURES

In the *Fourth,* as in the earlier symphonies, Mahler deliberately attempted to unify the whole by establishing relationships between the first and last movements. The Leipzig conductor Georg Göhler did not mention them in the notes he drew up for the first performance in that city, and Mahler wrote to him a few days before he fell fatally ill: ". . . Did you overlook the thematic relationships that are of such importance even for the conception of the work? Or did you only feel that you must spare the public any technical explanations? In any case, I beg you to discover them in my work. Each of the three first movements is thematically related to the last, in the deepest and most significant way."[131]

Some of these thematic recurrences are obvious, like that of the opening wind ritornello in the Finale, and the anticipation of the main theme of *Das Himmlische Leben* in the first movement development and at the end of the Adagio. Others are more subtle, for instance, within the first movement, the small wind fragments in Bar 20, which later appear in the coda and become part of the new development theme, or the fragment of Bar 22 (A″), which, augmented, becomes one of the main features of the development section.

Between the other movements, the connections are more hidden. Some authors (Bekker, Diepenbrock, and Fritz Stiedry) have noticed a striking family air between the trios of the Scherzo and the main theme of the Finale (particularly the G sharp minor middle section of its E major version: Bar 159ff.).[132]

In Mahler's production as a whole, the *Fourth Symphony* appears as a diversion, a happy intermezzo, nonessential to the whole, yet there are many reasons for not maintaining this point of view. To begin with, Mahler expended more work, more time, and at least as much love on its forty-five minutes than on the ninety minutes of the two preceding works. As a result, the technical feat is even greater. Mahler's obvious intention was to return to more reasonable, more human proportions. Despite the fact that he had explicitly requested the soprano in the Finale to "assume joyous and childish tones, completely devoid of parody," contemporary listeners considered it a sacrilegious imitation and perversion of the folk style and the classical spirit. The "neoclassicism" of the *Fourth* is not a regression or an escape into the past, as is some of the music by the early-twentieth-century neoclassic composers. It is a new discovery by Mahler of himself, the revelation of a new, stricter, more concentrated style. In his "return to Haydn," Mahler borrows from inherited and traditional forms without ever adopting them completely. Today his "unreasoned and unreasonable gaiety" no longer appears as a grimace or a caricature, less so than Strauss, in his neoclassical scores such as *Le Bourgeois gentilhomme.*

One of the main problems with the *Fourth* is that it demands nothing less than a truly virtuoso orchestra, because of the extreme refinement of the chamber-music-like instrumental writing. In his remarkable article about the "contemporary" aspects of Mahler's music, Dieter Schnebel successfully demonstrates Mahler's early use of a kind of *"Klangfarbenmelodie"* and shows that timbre in his work is no mere decoration, but a basic part of the whole, of its thought, and of its conception. Any of his scores will reveal this on close examination, but nothing confirms it better than the extreme care that he lavished on the smallest instrumental detail of the score of the *Fourth,* and its two last revisions, made during the final ten months of his life.

# APPENDIX 4

## *Mahler's Poems*

I. Poems written for Josephine Poisl (1880)
    No. 1: *Vergessene Liebe* (March 3, 1880)
    No. 2: *Kam ein Sonnenstrahl* (undated)

The manuscript of *Vergessene Liebe* was sent to Anton Krisper, together with the text of the unpublished first part of *Das klagende Lied* in a letter dated March 3, 1880 (see Chapter V). It must have been written at the same time as the poems of the unpublished *Poisl Lieder* (see Appendix 3) and was first published by Hans Holländer in *Die Musik* (XX, 11, August 1928).

The manuscript of the second poem (*Kam ein Sonnenstrahl*) used to be in Alma Mahler's collection, which has now been dispersed. The poem is not dated, but its naïve style recalls that of the *Rübezahl* libretto. The small elves knocking on the beloved's door are found in many of Mahler's poems. They also appear in one of the letters he wrote to Josephine in March 1880. Thus, one may safely assume that the poem was written at about the same time.

No. 1                   *VERGESSENE LIEBE*

> *Wie öd' mein Herz! Wie leer das All'!*
>     *Wie gross mein Sehnen!*
> *O, wie die Fernen Tal zu Tal*
>     *sich endlos dehnen!*
> *Mein süsses Lieb! Zum letzten Mal!?*
> *Ach, muss ja ewig diese Qual*
>     *in meinem Herzen brennen!*
>
> *Wie strahlt' es einst so treu und klar*
>     *in ihren Blicken!*
> *Das Wandern liess ich ganz und gar*
>     *trotz Winters Tücken!*
> *Und als der Lenz vergangen war,*
> *Da tat mein Lieb ihr blondes Haar*
>     *wohl mit der Myrthe schmücken!*

*Mein Wanderstab! Noch einmal heut*
*komm aus der Ecken!*
*Schliefst du auch lang! Nun sei bereit!*
*Ich will dich wecken!*
*Ich trug es lang, mein Liebesleid,*
*Und ist die Erde doch so weit—*
*So komm, mein treuer Stecken!*

*Wie lieblich lächelt Berg und Tal*
*in Blütenwogen!*
*Kam ja mit seinem süssen Schall*
*der Lenz gezogen!*
*Und Blumen blühn ja überall*
*Und Kreuzlein steh'n ja überall—*
*die haben nicht gelogen!*

No. 1                                    FORGOTTEN LOVE

How desolate my heart! How empty the universe!
How great my longing!
O how endlessly the horizon stretches out
from vale to vale!
My sweetest! Is it farewell forever!?
Alas, this torment will enflame
my heart eternally!

How faithful and limpid was once
the look in her eyes!
For her I ceased my endless roaming
despite grim winter's malice!
And when Spring said farewell
My sweetest decked her golden hair
with white orange blossom!

My pilgrim's staff! Come forth, O come
once more today!
How long hast thou rested! Now be prepared!
for I shall rouse thee!
I have long born the pains of love
And be the world ne'er so wide—
Come forth, my trusty rod!

How sweetly hill and dale smile
amid billowing blossoms!
Spring has come at long last
with her silver laugh!
And flowers are blooming everywhere
And there are crosses everywhere—
they have not deceived me!

*No. 2*        *Kam ein Sonnenstrahl*
              *uns einzuladen*
              *zum Tannensaal.*
              *Lasst Euch rathen,*
              *einmal ist Keinmal.*

              *An einem golden Faden*
              *hat er uns hergezogen.*
              *Hei—wie sind wir geflogen*
              *Ueber die Matten—*
              *durch duftende Blumenwogen.*

              *Heiaha, heiaha,*
              *wir sind da—und*
              *an die grüne Thür wir pochen.*
              *Du lieber goldner Sonnenschein*
              *Lass uns ein—lass uns ein.*

No. 2         A ray of sunshine's
              come to invite us
              to the fir tree hall.
              Come along, do,
              Only for this once.

              It's pulled us hither
              on a golden thread.
              Hey—how we flew
              Over the meadows—
              through a sea of fragrant flowers.

              Heyaha, heyaha
              here we are
              a knocking on the green door.
              Dear golden sunshine
              Let us in—let us in!

II. Poems written for Johanna Richter (1884)

|        |                                        |                    |
|--------|----------------------------------------|--------------------|
| No. 3: | *Wir sind des Waldes . . .*            | (August 18, 1884)  |
| No. 4: | *Noch sitz' ich hier . . .*            | (September 1884)   |
| No. 5: | *Nach Tages Wechsel . . .*             | (October 1884)     |
| No. 6: | *Die Sonne spinnt ihr farbig Netz . . .* | (December 1884)  |
| No. 7: | *Die Nacht blickt mild . . .*          | (December 1884)    |
| No. 8: | *Es ist ein' holde Königin . . .*      | (undated)          |
| No. 8A:| *Du zürnest mir . . .*                 | (undated)          |
| No. 8B:| *Ja, ja! Und ja! Trotz Acht und Bann*  | (undated)          |

These poems may be considered as sketches for the *Lieder eines fahrenden Gesellen*. Mahler's self-criticism proves equally lucid in literature as in music, for the four poems he set to music are not only the best of the group, but also those best suited to a lieder cycle. Mahler wrote to Fritz Löhr stating that there would be *six* lieder. The two additional poems are probably No. 6 ("*Die Sonne spinnt . . .*") and No. 7 ("*Die Nacht blickt mild . . .*"), which are also dated

December 1884. This is all the more likely since each contains a reference to the cycle's title, while there is none in the four poems that Mahler set to music (*"Fahr' weiter . . . Gefährte"* in the first and *"den stummen fahrenden Gesellen"* in the second) (see Appendix 3 and Chapter IX).

The manuscript of Poems Nos. 3 and 4 used to be in Alma Mahler's collection together with two poems dated December 15 and 19, 1884: the texts for No. 3 and No. 4 of the *Lieder eines fahrenden Gesellen*, here marked as I and II. The manuscript of No. 5 was in the briefcase discovered by her in her library after Mahler's death. Here the style and "themes" bring to mind the famous letter to Josef Steiner of 1879 (see Chapter V). The manuscripts have disappeared, but a typewritten copy of all the documents were found among Alma Mahler's papers after her death. This poem is probably unfinished, and the last part was written on the same envelope as the first draft of a letter to Ernst von Schuch dated October 18, 1884 (see Chapter IX).

Poems Nos. 6 and 7, dated Kassel, December 1884, were copied by Natalie Bauer-Lechner in Hamburg (NBLS, February 1896). Both were written on the same manuscript page, which was given by Alma Mahler to Hermann Behn in later years. No. 7 contains the famous lines that Mahler later used in *Das Lied von der Erde*:

> *und müde Menschen schliessen ihre Lieder,*
> *Im Schlaf auf's Neu, vergess'nes Glück zu lernen!*

which become in the 1908 symphony:

> *die müden Menschen geh'n heimwärts,*
> *um im Schlaf vergess'nes Glück und Jugend neu zu lernen!*

No. 8 (8A & 8B) consists of fragments of an unfinished poem and written on the same sheet of paper. The undated autograph used to be in Alma Mahler's collection. The style of No. 8 strongly resembles that of the *Klagende Lied* text. No. 8A was crossed out in the manuscript. It was obviously intended for Mahler's beloved (Johanna?), who had apparently resented one of his letters. Both of these poems are preceded by the word *Ebenso* ("likewise"). No. 8B also recalls *Das klagende Lied* (particularly *"Sie spielen ein seltsam Spiel"*). Nevertheless, if only because of the feelings expressed, and the mild humor of 8A and 8B, which is entirely lacking in the 1880 poems, their most likely place is among the Kassel poems.

*No. 3*                        *Für den 18. August 84*

> *Wir sind des Waldes duftende Kinder*
> *und pochen an die Thür gar leise—*
> *wir hängen die Köpfchen wie arme Sünder,*
> *sind müd' und matt von der langen Reise.*
>
> *Wir mussten so lange suchen und fragen*
> *bei den Sternen und Wolken und bei den 4 Winden*
> *—wenn wir zur rechten Zeit Dich finden,*
> *sind uns viel Grüsse aufgetragen,*

*Wir können auch feine Mären erzählen*
*—lässt Du uns ein zu Deiner Pforte*
*von einem fernen stillen Orte*
*—von einsamen "fahrenden Gesellen"*

No. 4                         *IN DER NACHT!*                    September 1884

*Noch sitz' ich hier—kein Laut in weiter Runde!*
*Die Nacht ist lang und noch will es nicht tagen.*
*Ich bin so trunken—darf ich es Dir sagen?—*
*noch von der letzten süsserlebten Stunde!*

*Du bist so hold—es sagen's Dir ja Alle!*
*und ich bin ja so ganz in Dir verloren—*
*Mir stirbt das Wort in jener Worte Schwalle*
*noch eh's des Herzens heiss' Gefühl geboren!*

*Es ist so hart, im Dunkel zu verschwinden,*
*als Tropfen in dem Weltmeer zu verfliessen,*
*sich in die Kränze, die zu Deinen Füssen*
*verwelken, als ein stummes Blatt zu winden!*

*Und sieh'! Wie seltsam ist es doch hin nieden!*
*So viele Sterne blinken in der Nacht.*
*Und jedem Menschen ist ein Stern beschieden*
*Ach!—welcher ist doch wohl für mich entfacht!*

No. 3                         For August 18, 1884

We are the fragrant children of the forest
knocking oh so softly on the door—
We hang our little heads like poor devils,
weary and worn from our long journey.

We had to search and ask our way so long
among the stars, the clouds, and all four winds
—if we find these in good time,
we shall bring thee many greetings,

We also have rare tales to tell
—if thou wilst open thy door to us
of a far-off, peaceful land
—and of sad and lonely "wayfarers."

No. 4                         AT NIGHT                    (September 1884)

Still I sit here—not a sound for miles around!
The night is long and still the sun will not rise.
I'm still so drunk—may I say this to thee?—
from the last blissfully spent hour!

Thou art so fair—one and all they tell thee so!
and I'm so wholly wrapped up in thee—
Thy words are drowned, even before they're born,
In the great torrent of words of my heart's burning desire!

It's so hard to vanish into darkness,
To melt like drops of water into the ocean,
to twine myself like a silent leaf
into the garlands that lie fading at thy feet!

And lo! How strange this world is!
So many stars twinkle in the night.
And each human being is assigned a star
O—how I wonder which was lit for me!

*No. 5*                                                    *Kassel, October 1884*

1) *Nach Tages Wechsel sass ich stumm verloren*
   *Und dacht'an meines Lebens holde Sonne,*
   *In süssen Schauens ungestörte Wonne*
   *Ach—kühnster Wüsche, nicht zum Tag geboren.*

2) *Da leise, durch die unermessenen Räume*
   *Kam sacht der Freund der Sehnenden und Wunden*
   *Und löst' mir lind das Zauberband der Stunden,*
   *Und willig folgt ich ihm ins Land der Träume.*

3) *Die Welt sah ich entkleidet allen Scheins*
   *—Ein ungeheures Feuer war entzündet*
   *Am düstern Abgrund, den kein Mensch ergründet*
   *—Geöffnet weit das Thor des ew'gen Seins.*

4) *Und aus dem ungeheuern Meer der Flammen*
   *In dem mein Blick erblindet war versunken,*
   *Entrangen rastlos sich unzäh'ge Funken,*
   *Und schwebten auf, bis sie im Nichts verschwammen.*

5) *—Und ohne End'. Entschtehen und Verschwinden*
   *—Da klang plötzlich fern ein Ton der tiefsten Trauer*
   *So schmerzend wund—, des Seins geheimste Schauer.*
   *Als wollt' der Dinge Urgrund es verkünden.*

6) *Da fasste Angst mich, unaussprechlich Beben*
   *Im unermessen Leid—wollt ich vergehen.*
   *—Ach nein!—"Nicht sterben!—Nicht vergehn!"*
   *Nicht sein? Ja! Gott im Himmel!—Leben—Leben!! . . .*

   *Ich sah es wol—Du warst es—"Gnadenreiche"!*
   *Und beugtest mitleidsvoll Dich zu mir nieder!*
   *Und sprachst zu mir, noch klingts mir nach—*

*Da rauschte über mir schneeweiss Gefieder*
*Und einen Engel sah ich zu mir huldreich schweben.*
*Ich kannt' ihn wol—Ahnst Du mein süsses Leben!*
*Er beugte mitleidsvoll sich zu mir nieder.*

*Hier sitz ich wieder, (—quäl mich ab)*
*Für Dich was Schönes zu erfinden.*
*Sieh hin! Du Thor! Ernst ist das Menschenleben.*
*Ich sah im Traum mein armes stummes Leben*
*—Ein Funke, der der Esse keck entsprungen,*
*Muss er (sah ich) versprühend im All' verschweben.*

*(Da wacht' ich auf, mit Lachen und mit Weinen,*
*Da fasste mich ein ungeheures Sehnen.)*

No. 5                                                    Kassel, October 1884

1) I sat silent and forlorn after the close of day
   And thought of the sweet sun of my life,
   In the undisturbed rapture of blissful contemplation
   Oh!—of the wildest desires that do not see the light of day.

2) When softly, through immeasurable space,
   Came the friend of those who yearn and grieve
   And he gently freed me from the spell of time,
   And willingly I followed him into the land of dreams.

3) I saw the world stripped of all pretense
   —A tremendous fire was lit
   By the dark abyss that no man hath fathomed
   —The door of eternal life was opened wide.

4) And out of the gigantic sea of flames
   In which my blinded eyes were plunged,
   Countless sparks endlessly broke loose
   And soared upward, until they dissolved into nothingness.

5) —A soaring and a disintegration without end
   —Suddenly from far off came a sound of deepest sorrow
   So distressingly painful—the hiddenmost horror of existence.
   As though wishing to proclaim the source of all things.

6) I was seized with fear, and indefinable tremor,
   In boundless grief, I wanted to expire!
   Oh no!—"Not die!—Not perish!"
   Cease to be? Dear Lord in Heaven! To live—to live! . . .

   I could well see—it was thou—"rich in grace"!
   Thou bent down to me so compassionately!
   And spoke to me, thy voice still echoes in my ear—

Then snow-white plumage soared above me
And I saw an angel floating gracefully toward me.
I knew him well—can thou imagine, my sweet life!
He bent down to me, full of compassion.

Here I sit again and rack my brains
Trying to think up something nice for thee.
Take heed! You fool! Man's life is a serious thing.
I saw my poor dumb life in a dream
—A spark that has brazenly escaped from the forge
—Hardly has it come to burning being
Before it floats dying away into the universe.

(Then I awoke, laughing and crying,
And was seized with a tremendous longing.)

*No. 6*                                   *Kassel, December 1884*

*Die Sonne spinnt ihr farbig Netz,*
*Allmächtig über Wald und Flur.*
*Und goldene Fäden spinnen jetzt*
*Geheim um jede Creatur!*

*O lachende Thäler allerwärts,*
*O Blüten, die in den Lüften schweben,*
*Warum legt ihr euch an mein krankes Herz?*
*Ach! An dem süssen Kelch des lebens*

*Wie meine durstigen Lippen saugen!*
*Weh! Balsam wird zu Gift und Pein*
*Dem, der mit trocknen Schmerzensaugen*
*Muss blicken in den Lenz hinein!*

*Was ruhest Du mein müder Fuss?*
*Fahr' weiter stillen Leids Gefährte!*
*Über alle Schönheit ich wandern muss,*
*Ach, über die grüne, grüne Erde.*

*No. 7*                                   *Kassel, December 1884*

*Die Nacht blickt mild aus stummen, ew'gen Fernen*
*Mit ihren tausend goldnen Augen nieder—*
*Und müde Menschen schliessen ihre Lider,*
*Im Schlaf auf's Neu, vergess'nes Glück zu lernen!*

*Siehst Du den stummen fahrenden Gesellen?*
*Gar einsam und verloren ist sein Pfad,*
*Wohl Weg und Weiser er verloren hat,*
*Und ach! kein Stern will seinen Pfad erhellen.*

*Der Weg ist lang und Gottes Engel weit,*
*Und falsche Stimmen tönen lockend, leise—*

*"Ach wann,—ach wann soll enden meine Reise?"*
*Wann ruht der Wanderer von des Weges Leid?*

*Es starrt die Sphinx und droht mit Rätselqualen,*
*Und ihre grauen Augen schweigen, schweigen.*
*Kein rettend Wort, kein Lichtstrahl will sich zeigen,*
*Und lös' ichs nicht—muss es mein Leben zahlen*

No. 6                                              Kassel, December 1884

The sun weaves her colorful net,
Omnipotently over wood and field.
And golden threads now twirl
Invisibly around every creature!

O laughing valleys everywhere,
O blossoms floating in the air,
Why do you lie so heavy on my heart?
O how my thirsting lips suck

At the sweet cup of life!
Alas! Balsam turns to pain and poison
For him who looks at Spring
With eyes dried up and sorrowful!

Why dost thou rest, my weary foot?
Travel on, companion of my silent grief!
I must journey over all beauty
Oh, over the green, green earth.

No. 7                                              Kassel, December 1884

The night with her thousand golden eyes
Looks mildly down out of silent and eternal space—
And weary men close their heavy lids
To learn lost happiness anew in sleep!

Do you see the silent wayfarer?
All lonely and forsaken in his path,
His way and signpost he has doubtless lost
And alas! no star will light his path.

The way is long and God's angel far away
And deceitful voices call enticingly, softly—
"When, oh when, alas, will my journey end?"
When will the traveler rest from the pain of the way?

The sphinx stares and threatens with torments and enigmas
And her gray eyes remain silent, silent
Not a saving word I heard, not a ray of light I saw,
Yet should I not solve them—my life will be forfeit.

No. 8

### EBENSO

1) Es ist ein' holde Königin
   gerühmet weit und breit.
   Ihr hab' ich mich mit treuem Sinn
   zu stummen Dienst geweiht.

2) Ich dien' ihr nicht um Gut und Geld
   der Treue stolz und hehr,
   ich dien' ihr nicht um Minnesold,
   such' nicht um Ruhm und Ehr.

3) Ich möchte nur so unbewusst
   sie sehen in der Ferne,
   so wie man in der dunklen Nacht
   blickt auf zu einem Sterne.

4) Wie eine Schildwach will ich stehn
   ganz still auf ferner Stell',
   und seh ich sie vorüber gehn,
   so praesentir ich schnell.

No. 8A

### EBENSO

[Du zürnest mir, ich weiss es nun—
Ich fuehl's an Blick und Miene,
O hilf mir doch, was soll ich thun,
Dich wieder zu gewinnen.

War es so schlimm denn, was ich schrieb?
Was hab ich denn verbrochen,
Ich sprach ja nur: Ich hab Dich lieb!
Wie immer ich gesprochen!]

No. 8B

Ja, ja! Und ja! Trotz Acht und Bann!
und werd's Dir immer sagen!
Hab' ich Dich lieb—was geht's Dich an?
Muss ich's allein doch tragen!

Der Herrgott hat der Kinder viel
auf seiner Blumenweiden,
Sie spielen gar ein seltsam Spiel,
S'ist Leben oft auch Leiden.

Ich bin's einmal und bin grad' so,
Soll's recht Dir oder schlecht sein,
und sagt der Herrgott nichts ins Ohr!
muss's auch dem Engel recht sein!

No. 8                               LIKEWISE

1) There is a gracious queen
   Lauded far and wide.
   To serve her in silence
   I have loyally pledged myself.

2) I serve her not for money or possessions,
   I am not proud of my own loyalty,
   I serve her not for the reward of love,
   Neither for fame nor for honor.

3) I want only, as it were, unconsciously,
   To see her from afar
   just as on a dark night
   One looks up toward a star.

4) A sentinel, I want to stand
   Quite still on some distant spot,
   And if I see her passing by,
   I will quickly present arms.

No. 8A                              LIKEWISE

[Thou art angry with me, I know it now—
I feel it in thy look and attitude,
O help me please, what shall I do
To win thee back again.

Was it really so bad, what I wrote?
What have I done so wrong?
I only said: I love thee!
As I have always said!]

No. 8B  Yes, yes! And yes again! Despite outlawry and excommunication!
        And I shall continue to repeat it to thee!
        Why shouldst thou care if I love thee?
        I alone must bear it after all!

        The Lord God has many children
        in his flowering pastures,
        They play a strange game indeed,
        It's life and often also sorrow.

        It is true, I am this way
        Whether it pleases thee or not,
        And if the Lord God does not complain!
        Then his angel must be contented too!

III. Poem written in Prague for the anniversary of Wagner's death (1886)
     No. 9: *Im Park von Wahnfried* . . . (February 13, 1886)
   The manuscript of this poem formerly belonged to Ernst Schulz, the bookshop
owner in whose house Mahler lived in Prague. At the time of Mahler's death,

it was published by Ernst Rychnowsky, who claimed that it had been written
for a memorial performance in the Prague Landestheater planned by Angelo
Neumann to mark the third anniversary of Wagner's death. Whether Mahler
intended to set it to music or to have it read aloud during this performance is
not known. All that may seem surprising in this poem, its pompous and conventional style, its ecstatic praise of *"deutscher Kunst"* and *"deutscher Bühne"*
as opposed to *"fremde Melodie,"* is easily explained in view of the "circumstance" for which it was conceived and written.

*No. 9*                                    *Zum 13. Februar.*

> *Im Park von Wahnfried ruht ein stilles Grab*
> *Umgrünt von Trauerweiden und Zypressen,*
> *Dort senke Dich Dein Vaterland hinab,*
> *Im übergrossen Schmerze selbstvergessen.*
> *Bald zieht der Frühling über Berg und Tal,*
> *Und aus den Tränen, die voreinst geflossen,*
> *Da werden, aufgeweckt vom Sonnenstrahl,*
> *Vergissmeinnicht auf seinem Hügel sprossen.*
>
> *So ruh' denn sanft, du grosser Meister, du.*
> *Der deutschem Volk die deutsche Kunst gerettet,*
> *Dein Geist lebt fort, du hast zur kurzen Ruh'*
> *Die müden Glieder nur ins Grab gebettet.*
> *Ein Dornenröschen war die deutsche Kunst—*
> *Da nahtest du, der Kühne, Auserkor'ne,*
> *Und freie Bahn schlugst in die Dornen du,*
> *Und küsstest wach die schöne, traumverlor'ne.*
>
> *Was wir ersehnt in unbestimmtem Drange,*
> *Hast du zu festen Formen uns gestaltet.*
> *Der deutschen Bühne gabst du ihre Macht*
> *Zurück, wo fremde Melodie gewaltet.*
> *Du zeigst uns, was wir immer noch gesehen,*
> *Was wir geahnt, gefühlt im mächt'gen Glühen,*
> *Du liessest eine morsche Welt vergehen,*
> *Schufst eine junge Welt voll Melodien.*
>
> *Da zuckt die Parze—und der Faden reisst,*
> *Und deine mächt'ge Leier liegt zersprungen—*
> *Auf nach Walhalla flieht dein freier Geist,*
> *Von der so oft du deinem Volk gesungen!*
> *Doch wirkt er fort! Deutschland vergisst dich nicht*
> *Und wird sich ewig stolz an dir erheben,*
> *Solang als deutsch die Sprache deines Volk's,*
> *Wirst grosser Meister du im Volke leben.*

No. 9                              For February 13.

> In Wahnfried Park there lies a peaceful grave
> Surrounded by weeping willows and cypress trees,
> Thy Fatherland lowered thee into it,
> Forgetful of itself in its overwhelming grief.
> Soon Spring will advance o'er hill and dale,
> And from the tears that once did flow,
> Awakened by a ray of sunshine,
> Forget-me-nots will sprout upon thy knoll.
>
> So rest in peace, thou great master, thou
> Who hast redeemed German art for the German people,
> Thy spirit lives on, but for a brief rest
> Hast thou laid thy weary limbs down in the grave.
> Sleeping beauty was the art of Germany—
> Then thou, the brave, the chosen one, didst come,
> And hack a passageway among the thorns
> And kiss the Beauty lost in dreams awake.
>
> That for which we yearned with an undefined craving
> Thou didst mold into concrete forms for us.
> Thou didst give the German theater its former power
> Where foreign melody had reigned supreme.
> Thou hast shown us that which we had always sensed
> And foreseen with glowing ardor.
> Thou didst leave a decaying world to die out
> And didst create a young world full of melodies.
>
> Suddenly Fate quivers—and the thread is snapped,
> And thy mighty lyre lies broken in pieces—
> Thy free spirit flies up to Valhalla
> From whence thou hast so often to thy people sung!
> Yet it prevails! Germany will not forget thee
> And will forever be uplifted by thy memory,
> As long as German remains the language of thy people,
> Thou, great master, wilt live on in thy people's hearts.

IV. Poem written in Vienna to an unknown lady (1898)

No. 10: *Meiner lieben Unbekannten . . .* (July 11, 1898)

Mahler's last known poem (until 1910, when he wrote many to his wife) was probably composed in Vienna in answer to a woman admirer's gift or letter. The manuscript used to be in Alma Mahler's collection.

No. 10
> *Meiner lieben Unbekannten,*
> *Wenn auch nicht mehr Ungenannten,*
> *die so hold zu bitten weiss,*
> *Mag ein Gruss nun herzlich danken*
> *für die Treue sonder Wanken*
> *Und die Liebe, die so heiss!*

*Weiss ich mir auch nicht zu deuten*
*Ihres Herzens Heimlichkeiten*
*Und den Sinn der Schreiberin,*
*—Gilt's dem Künstler, gilt's dem Werke*
*—meiner Schwäche, seiner Stärke—*
*Scheinen Bied' nach ihrem Sinn!*

*11. Juli 1898*

No. 10                   My dear stranger,
                         Even though no longer nameless,
                         You who know how to beg most charmingly,
                         May a greeting now thank you warmly
                         For your unwavering loyalty
                         And for your love so fervent!

                         Although I am unable to penetrate
                         The secrets of her heart
                         And the mind of the writer,
                         —Whether she means the artist or the work
                         —My meanness or its strength—
                         Both seem to meet with her approval!

                         July 11, 1898

# NOTES

## CHAPTER 1

1. The *Kaiserliche Judensystemalpatent* promulgated by Joseph II on August 3, 1797, regulated the number of Jewish families in the empire, their marriages, etc.

2. In Mahler's lifetime the members of his family seem to have been uncertain whether July 1 or July 7 was the date of his birth. The later date has now been established definitely by his birth certificate, which survives in the Prague Archives (*Israelitische Kultusgemeinde Bezirk Unterkralowitz. Geburtsmatrikel. Register Nr. 120 a G. page 42 Nr. 16*).

3. On December 18, 1744, Maria Theresa had expelled all Jews from the Empire. Their individual residence permits, however, were extended upon payment of heavy fees.

4. *Musical Chronicle*, Harcourt, Brace and Company, 1923, pages 244–45.

5. Nothing is more unjust than to condemn Mahler the creator on the pretext that he was "an introvert" and "liked no one." For one thing, Mahler loved deeply and passionately at least once, and had many firm friendships; for another, all the great creators have been, like him, "introverts."

6. Stefan Zweig, *The World of Yesterday, An Autobiography*, Viking Press, New York, 1943, page 6. This quotation is from the original English version.

7. This is unfortunately no longer true because of the Nazis. There is now only one Mahler family in Svetla and another in Deutsch-Brod (Havlickuv Brod).

8. These hypotheses appear in a Nazi-inspired work, painstakingly documented since it was part of an effort to discover such Jewish families as had managed to remain in Germany (Konrad Krause *Die Jüdische Namenwelt*, Essen, 1943, page 65).

9. In 1782, Josef II authorized the Jews to take German names. He was the first European ruler to demand (1787) that the Jews should be registered. These registers were very negligently kept until about 1870.

10. If we are to believe the information that his family gave about his age. See *Staatsarchiv Telč. Bezirksgericht Deutsch-Brod. Verlassenschaft Simon Mahler*, IV, 282/1868.

11. *Repertorium Dolni Kralovice* (Unterkralowitz) *Protokolle Politicis* 1822–33. *Im Staatsarchiv Benešov*.

12. The Jewish registers were not kept properly, so the Catholic priests were also responsible for the Jewish community.

13. *Bauparzellen-Protokoll der Gemeinde Kalischt*. 1838. Staatsarchiv Prag.

14. *Staatsarchiv Prag. Pfarramt Kalischt bei Gumpolds. Judengeburtsbuch von Jahre 1810. Signatur:* HBM, 272.

15. The house (No. 41), situated in the Obervorstadt of Deutsch-Brod, cost 990 florins (*Staatsarchiv Telč. Bezirksgericht Deutsch-Brod*, VI, 290/1860).

16. Her daughter-in-law, Bernhard's wife and the composer's mother, was also called Maria. This anecdote may even have referred to Bernhard's grandmother, of whom nothing is known at present.

17. Or perhaps in Lipnitz. In a document in Iglau (*Anzeigezettel zur Zählung der Bevölkerung . . . nach dem Stande vom 31 Dez. 1869. Haus Nr. 265. I. Stock.*), Bernhard wrote down Lipnitz (Lipnice) as his birthplace. Later in 1848 he wrote to the Lipnitz authorities for some papers.

18. In an article written in Czech (*Jihlavské Listy*—Iglau, 1931, No. 12) Wladimir Urbanek, father of a friend of Mahler, affirms that Bernhard Mahler played the violin and never failed to take his violin with him on his business trips. He is the only one to mention this, but there seems no reason to doubt his testimony.

19. *Fremdenprotokoll*, 1858 (Stadtarchiv Iglau).

20. Cf. *Grundbuch zu Unterkralowitz* (*II, lit. H., folio 43v*) *Aussug aus dem Grundbuch* . . . Staatsarchiv Telč.) A *Wirtshaus* differed from a *Schank* (tavern) in that it served light refreshments—cold meals, for example—in addition to drinks.

21. The maiden name of Gustav Mahler's mother is given erroneously as Frank by AMM (page 13) and HFR. It was one of her sisters, Anna, who married a Frank.

22. See illustrations. Two photographs, one taken before the fire and one taken recently.

23. NBL, page 52.

24. J. G. Sommer: Böhmen (Saslauer Kreis.) Topography, page 97 (Prague, 1843).

25. The dates given up to now for this move have been largely fictitious. Happily, a police report still exists which establishes the exact date of Bernhard's arrival in Iglau. Cf. *Stadtarchiv Iglau: Vormerk über die Hierorts domicilirenden und Händel treibenden Judenfamilien, angefangen vom 14 Dez. 1859.*

26. The double number is explained as follows: in Iglau, as in Kalischt, and doubtless throughout the region, each building bore a number indicating the order of its construction. Only later did street numbers begin to be assigned. The Pirnitzergasse became the Wienergasse in 1878; after 1918, it was renamed Znaimergasse; and, after World War II, Malinowskigasse.

27. Johann Wenzel Anton Stamitz (or Steinmetz), violinist and conductor, founder of a renowned musical dynasty, and originator of the modern school of instrumentation, was born in 1717 in Deutsch-Brod. Son of a cantor there, he studied at the Iglau school in 1728–29 and in 1733–34. He later founded the famous "Mannheim School" and died in Mannheim in 1757. Johann Ladislaus Dussek (or Dušek), composer and virtuoso pianist, was born in Csaslau in 1760 and died in Paris in 1812. Friedrich Smetana, (1824–84), founder of the Czech nationalist school, became one of Mahler's favorite composers.

28. Cf. Theodor Fischer: *Das Musikleben Iglaus im 19. Jahrhundert: Zeitschrift dem deutschen Vereins f. d. Gesch. Mährens u. Schlesiens* (J. 36, Brünn, 1934, pages 105ff.).

29. *Stadtarchiv Iglau. Einreichsprotokolle in Politicis 1860ff.*

30. Successively those of Katharina Brabenz (née Rott), of Mathias Wilhelm, of Johann Friedl, and of Jakob Löwitt (Melion).

31. David Mahler ran successively a haberdashery (1863), a tavern (1864), a food store, and a perfumery.

32. *Gewerbsregister der k. Stadtgemeinde Iglau.*

33. An advertisement in the *Iglauer Sonntagsblatt* for January 7, 1866, announces to future clients that Bernhard Mahler's distillery can supply the best brands of French wines and liquors.

34. Biographers of Mahler up to now have written of only eleven or twelve children, but the list given here is taken from the Iglau archives. The total of fourteen is confirmed by NBLS and by a note in Justine Mahler's handwriting found by her son, Alfred Rosé, in Rudolf Mengelberg's notebook.

35. The exact date of Ernst's birth is not known. There is no trace of it either in the newspapers or in the Iglau official documents. According to one of the censuses made by the head of the family every ten years under the Habsburg monarchy (*Conscriptionsbogen*) he was born in 1861.

## CHAPTER 2

1. *Bezirksgericht Iglau. Grundbuch 256–92.* fol. 10a Haus No. 264 Stadtarchiv Iglau. *Verlassenschaft Familie Heinrich Fischer, Musikdirektor.* Heinrich Fischer, born June 28, 1828, in Iglau, studied at the Prague Conservatory, Master of the Städtische Musikkapelle in Iglau in 1870, head of the Männergesangverein (men's chorus) and the choirs of the two principal parishes of Iglau. He was one of Mahler's professors; he occupied the post of *Musikdirektor* at the theater for the season 1868/69, 1873/74, and 1875/76. Much of the information in this chapter comes from an article by Theodor Fischer, Heinrich's son, entitled *Aus Gustav Mahlers Jugendzeit* (Deutsche Heimat, VII, 1931).

2. The house still exists, the business premises being today occupied by a leather merchant. A detailed description of it exists, made at the time of Bernhard's death. *Staatsarchiv Telč Bezirksgericht Iglau IV 1889/17 Todfalls-Aufnahme Bernhard Mahler.*

3. Mahler's first biographers claimed that at the age of four he knew "more than two hundred" songs, but, according to Theodor Fischer, this estimate is a gross exaggeration.

4. Theodor Fischer finds a striking similarity between the third movement of the *First Symphony* and one of the most characteristic of the popular dances from the Iglau region, the Hatschô.

5. See Max Graf. *Legende einer Musikstadt* (page 71). Graf affirms that the traditional bugle calls of the Austrian army were the work of Michael Haydn, whose "Retreat" rings through Mahler's *Third Symphony* and is also in Berg's *Wozzeck*. It is tempting to believe that the brother of the great Haydn had an indirect influence on Mahler. Unfortunately it has now been proved that the Austrian army calls were composed by an unknown musician. (Cf. MGG, V, 1942.)

6. NBLS.

7. Ibid.

8. Cf. Theodor Fischer art. cit. Born November 1, 1859, Theodor Fischer was to become *Landesgerichts Direktor* and then *Kreisgerichtspräsident*. He died October 15, 1934.

9. GAM, page 8. Adler states that the parish priest of Sankt Jacob and the Rabbi Unger both considered tolerance a cardinal virtue.

10. Cf. Theodor Fischer: *Das Musikleben Iglaus in 19 Jahrhundert* ibid. These performances are mentioned in the Iglau paper (*Der Vermittler,* which became in 1872 *Mährische Grenzbote*); they took place in 1870 (*Christus am Ölberg*), 1872 and 1873 (*Stabat Mater*), and 1874 (*Die Sieben Worte*).

11. NBLS, MBR, page viii.

12. Mahler gave a public concert at the age of six, and it is probable that he had already been studying for at least one or two years.

13. ZNM adds to this list a professor called J. Ziska, a violinist and *Musikdirektor,* probably a friend of Fischer. Viktorin was first Kapellmeister at the Iglau Theater in 1864 and 1865, then again in 1868. In the article on the concert given by Mahler in 1870 we learn that he left the town, and in fact after 1868 he conducted in Budweis, Cracow, Bielitz and Budapest. It is thus possible that Pressburg replaced him as Mahler's teacher. In the *Iglauer Sonntagsblatt,* both Johannes Brosch and Viktorin announced the opening of a *Musik Institut* where piano and violin were taught.

14. Wenzel Pressburg (1842–1906), was born and died in Vienna. Contrary to the statement in the short biography published in the *Musikerziehung,* he never studied

under Bruckner, at any rate at the conservatory. On August 10, 1883, when Mahler was conductor at the Kassel Theater, Pressburg asked for and received a document certifying that he had been Pressburg's pupil for several years, and testifying to Pressburg's abilities as conductor, pianist, and teacher. A facsimile of this document was printed in Vienna in the *Musikerziehung* journal (1949). Pressburg seems to have been publicity-minded at the expense of truth, for unfortunately all the other information published about Pressburg, together with this testimonial, turned out to be untrue. On October 20, 1870, Bernhard Mahler inserted in the Iglau newspaper, *Der Vermittler*, a "public vote of thanks" to Pressburg, recommending him to "all parents who wish to have their children taught music." Later Pressburg settled in Vienna, continued teaching, and composed many waltzes (cf. *Illustriertes Wiener Extrablatt*, March 1, 1899).

15. NBLS.

16. Wurzinger: Geschichte des Iglauer Stadttheater.

17. NBLS.

18. NBLS quotes this poem almost word for word as it appears in Lessing's works: *Lessings Werke. Neu hrsg.v. Franz Muncker mit Einleitungen von Karl Goethe. 12*, Bände, Stuttgart, Göschen, 1890. Bd.I. S.56.

19. This affirmation, made by several biographers, has given rise to controversy (see Chapter 4). In NBLS, Mahler categorically states that he "jumped" these two classes, "to his great detriment."

20. NBLS.

21. NBLS.

22. RBM.

23. NBLS.

24. NBL, page 69.

25. For example, on December 12, 1878, he was elected by a large majority to the "Committee of the Iglau Jewish Community" and the School Committee. (Cf. *Mährischer Grenzbote*). Justine Mahler's godfather (she was born in 1868) was the cantor of the Iglau Jewish community, which was founded in 1861. The synagogue was built in 1862–63 and the cemetery site chosen in 1869. In 1880 Iglau had 1500 Jewish inhabitants.

26. This document used to be in the possession of Alma Mahler. Half a dozen other report cards still exist in the Iglau town archives.

27. NBLS.

28. Alfred Grünfeld (1852–1924) studied the piano under Kullak and was later a protégé of Liszt in Weimar: he taught the piano in Berlin and Vienna and made international tours both as a soloist and partnered by his brother Heinrich. Later he gave many concerts with the Rosé Quartet.

Heinrich Grünfeld (1855–1931), the cellist, taught in Berlin and together with Scharwenka founded a series of subscription concerts in the Prussian capital.

Ernestine Grünfeldova, daughter of Ernst Grünfeld, the youngest of the Grünfeld brothers, now teaches piano at the Prague Conservatory. Some of the information contained in these pages came from her.

The Grünfelds lived at 38, Zeltnergasse, Prague.

29. *Stadtarchiv Prag.*

30. Heinrich Grünfeld. *In Dur und Moll.* Page 19 (Leipzig, 1923).

31. NBLS.

32. Cf. Article in the *Mährische Grenzbote*.

33. Freud uses the term *Mutterbindung* in this respect (Oedipus complex).

34. See NBLS. Theodor Reik has an ingenious theory regarding the origin of the *Kindertotenlieder*. According to him, Mahler must have known that one of the dead children who inspired these odes to the poet Rückert was named Ernst. Thus Mahler, when setting them to music, was identifying himself with his father, who had lost a son called Ernst.

## CHAPTER 3

1. *Neues Wiener Journal*, August 6, 1905. The two letters from Mahler were re-published in the *Neue Freie Presse* of August 3, 1924, by Schwarz's granddaughter, an opera singer named Hanna Schwarz.

2. We know that for two years Mahler spent his vacations on the Morawan and Ronow estates, near Caslau (MBR, note, page 8).

3. Mahler later had a friend in Iglau named Josef Steiner, whose father, a merchant named Ignaz Steiner, was probably the one who introduced him to Schwarz.

4. Schwarz's testimony allows us to date the fragments of this opera, written in a notebook belonging to Josef Steiner but later destroyed, as were all Mahler's early works. Nonetheless, it is very improbable that the opera really was "completed" in 1875, as Schwarz asserted, since Mahler himself later declared that he had not completed a single one of his early works.

5. A celebrated ballad of the romantic period.

6. And it is you, O Werner, who must help me toward that.

7. *The World of Yesterday, op. cit.*, page 11.

8. Undoubtedly Epstein, who kept a friendly eye on Mahler during all his years at the conservatory.

9. *Illustriertes Wiener Extrablatt*, May 19, 1911.

10. *Handelsakademie*, a *Gymnasium* in which subjects on trade and commerce were emphasized. The sons of many well-to-do families who expected to join their fathers' businesses attended.

11. One son, a ballet orchestra conductor, was to succeed Mahler as conductor of the Vienna Philharmonic in 1901.

12. See the memoirs of the violinist Karl Flesch (New York, Macmillan Company, 1958, page 22), and those of the critic Ernst Decsey (EDM, page 44). Arnold Rosé, Mahler's future brother-in-law, was concertmaster of the Vienna Philharmonic Orchestra for fifty years.

13. It is thus not surprising that Mahler spoke of Hellmesberger so harshly. He incarnated those Viennese tendencies that most shocked Mahler. In NBLS, he is always referred to as *diese Schaf*—this silly ass.

14. Later, telling Natalie Bauer-Lechner of his conservatory memories, Mahler regretted not having followed Fuchs's classes in theory, and particularly in counterpoint, more assiduously. "It was a great loss to me," he said (NBLS).

15. Not Theodor Krenn as stated by PSM, GAM, and AMM.

16. Rudolf Krzyzanowski (1859–1911), born in Eger, Bohemia, the son of a china shop owner of Polish origin. (Krzyzanowski was the name of Chopin's mother.) He entered the Vienna Conservatory in 1872, studying violin, organ, composition, harmony, and piano. Kappelmeister in Halle (1887–89), Elberfeld, and Munich, successor to Muck in Prague (1892–95), and assistant to Mahler in Hamburg, he held the post of first conductor at the Weimar Theater from 1898 to 1907. He married a Wagnerian singer named Ida Doaxat and died shortly after Mahler, on June 20, 1911.

17. Heinrich Krzyzanowski, born in 1855, was for a while professor of German, then lived for many years in Starnberg and Vienna, making his living with difficulty by writing. He was the author of a novel entitled *Im Bruch* and translated several books from the Russian.

18. Karl Huby, a disciple of Bruckner and a friend of Rott, states that he looked like King Louis II of Bavaria (GAB, IV, 1, 446).

19. Mottl competed with Mahler for the post of director of the Vienna Opera in 1897 and almost succeeded him when he left in 1907.

20. This letter, dating from 1876 or 1877, is in the Rosé Collection. Born in

Wlaschim, Bohemia, on September 14, 1859, Gustav Frank was soon to study painting at the Vienna Royal Academy. He later became quite well known, especially for his engravings. In particular he was responsible for some of the illustrations in the official publication: *Oesterreichisch-ungarische Monarchie in Wort und Bild.* (Cf. L Eisenberg & R. Groner: *Das geistige Wien.* Künstler-und Schriftsteller-Lexikon, 1890, page 67.)

21. In the *Protokole* of the Gesellschaft der Musikfreunde for 1876, this document bears the number 518 and is marked as having been received on October 10. Two other letters, sent by Mahler for the same purpose on September 5, 1876, and September 10, 1877, have not survived.

22. Almost certainly, according to Wolf's letters, at Opernring 23. Later, according to Theodor Fischer, Mahler lived in the same Vienna district, at No 7 Margaretenstrasse (fourth floor, flat 40).

23. According to Frau Lorenz, Krzyzanowski's sister-in-law, quoted by Auer: *Bruckner*, IV, 1, 450.

24. See Alma Mahler, page 82. This anecdote proves that Mahler then composed at the piano, as he himself told Natalie Bauer-Lechner later. Was this a string quartet or one of the piano quartets? See Appendix 3.

25. NBL, page 65.

26. Perhaps this was the husband of Aunt Freischberger, mentioned by Stransky (see below). This letter is in the Rosé Collection. It is dated September 17, and may have been written in either 1876 or 1877. Perhaps it refers to the Symphony played by Hellmesberger—regarding which there is a well-known anecdote (see Appendix 3).

27. The extent of this triumph is indicated by the fact that no normal first prize was awarded that year, but only a second prize, which was divided between two students.

28. Formerly in Alma Mahler's collection.

29. NBLS.

30. NBLS. August 4, 1901.

31. NBL, page 1.

32. *Die Musik*, VII, May 15, 1908.

33. GAB, IV, page 450.

34. This is in a postscript, dated September 17 (1876 or 1877), that Mahler added to the letter, already mentioned, written by Gustav Frank, with whom he was then sharing lodgings.

35. Contrary to Donald Mitchell's deductions, the 1876 quintet, which won the first prize at the conservatory in July and was played in Iglau in September of that year, was certainly a quintet, and not the Quartet in A minor, of which the first movement has survived. Mahler said that a later piano quartet, sent to Moscow for a competition, was lost. The scherzo that won the composition prize in 1878 may have belonged to a second quintet, but was more probably another isolated movement (see below and Appendix 3).

36. Max Steinitzer, in his memories of Mahler in Leipzig (BSP, page 13), states that Mahler astonished one of the conservatory judges by his playing of a Sonata in D by Schubert. But the official documents clearly state that it was a Sonata in A minor.

37. NBLS, August 4, 1901.

38. Or quartet. See Appendix 3.

39. It will be recalled that Gustav Schwarz was the manager of a Morawan estate. The episode may have occurred during Mahler's first visit to Schwarz.

40. MBR, No. 1.

41. Josef Stransky later succeeded Mahler as the conductor of the New York Philharmonic Orchestra.

42. New York *Herald Tribune,* March 22, 1931. Josef Stransky: "Meeting with Gustav Mahler."

43. Siebert was a pupil of Hellmesberger and later, for two years, played second violin in the Rosé Quartet.

44. This is confirmed, word for word, by Mahler in NBLS. Alfred Cortot, who did me the honor of reading most of my manuscript and to whom I am endebted for much helpful advice, considered that this exploit was impossible and is the product of pure imagination.

45. BMG, page 99.

46. It is interesting to note that Brahms, in a letter of April 29, 1879, to Elisabeth von Herzogenberg, expressed an unfavorable opinion of the instruction at the conservatory during this period.

## CHAPTER 4

1. This is one of the three letters from Mahler to the conservatory authorities, still at the Gesellschaft der Musikfreunde. In the *Protokol* for 1876, it is indicated that Mahler re-entered the conservatory on March 15.

2. She was consulted on this subject by Göllerich, Bruckner's biographer (cf. Auer, *Bruckner,* IV, page 450).

3. The phrase "if the question of playing a work" proves this. Mahler did not conduct works by Bruckner until much later. Frau Lorenz was judging Mahler as an adult instead of judging him as he had been at the conservatory.

4. Schnürmann had turned the pages during the Iglau concert of September 1876. (Cf. article by Hans Holländer in *De Musiek,* 1928–29, page 216.) He was born in Iglau and seems to have been an amateur musician who later became a businessman.

5. GAM, page 7.

6. Later, in Hamburg, he compared them in Natalie's presence (see Chapter XVIII). Rubinstein gave two more Beethoven recitals in Vienna on February 25 and on March 3, 1878.

7. The Wagner Verein was founded in 1872 by Felix Mottl, then sixteen, and a young writer named Karl Wolf (cf. Guido Adler, *Wollen und Wirken,* Universal Edition, Vienna, 1935, pages 10–11).

8. An orphan, Guido Adler (1855–1941) was brought up by his uncle, a pharmacist on the Iglau market place. Like Mahler, he studied first with Johannes Brosch, then left for Vienna in 1854 to attend the conservatory and Bruckner's university courses. He left the conservatory in 1874.

9. Published for the first time in 1947 by Frank Walker in the review *"Music and Letters"* (XXVIII, I, 12).

10. December 12, 1875 (cf. Frank Walker, *Hugo Wolf*).

11. AML, page 35. This may have been after the Philharmonic concert of December 12, 1875, when Wolf finally managed to speak to Wagner. The dates of the first Wagnerian performances in Vienna were: *Das Rheingold* and *Siegfried* (1878), *Walküre* (1877), *Die Götterdämmerung* (1879), and *Tristan* (1883).

12. For reasons that seem to me insufficient DMM places this scene in 1879, after the Vienna premiere of *Die Götterdämmerung.* The three friends certainly read the score at the piano before that performance (cf. AMM, page 83, and DMM, page 33).

13. In fact, they were finally bought by the editor of the *Neue Freie Presse,* Michael Etienne, who later gave them to Spitzer. See the complete account of this curious episode in ENW, III, page 567.

14. This admiration was reciprocated, it seems, by Wagner, who in 1873 accepted the dedication of Bruckner's *Third Symphony.*

15. See Chapter VI regarding the two men's opinions of each other and Brahms's attitude toward Bruckner's pupils.

16. Cf. Auer, *Bruckner*, IV, I, pages 475–76.

17. It was published on January 1, 1880. Only Mahler's name is printed on the cover.

18. This manuscript, which belonged to Alma Mahler, was purchased by the Austrian Government at an auction in 1948. According to Alma Mahler (AML, page 334), Mahler did not transcribe the Finale, which was the work of Ferdinand Löwe. In fact, Schalk's and Löwe's transcription was later published anonymously by the same firm. Mahler later gave Bruckner's manuscript to his brother Otto, and Alma found it among the latter's possessions after her husband's death.

19. Hermann Behn (1859–1927). After completing his law studies he went to Vienna to work with Bruckner. He was a close friend of Mahler in Hamburg. In 1885 he transcribed Bruckner's *Seventh Symphony* for two pianos and later Mahler's *Second Symphony* (GAB, IV, 2, 380).

20. NBLS. Mahler told Natalie this on May 4, 1899.

21. GAB, IV, I, 448–49.

22. Mahler's Vienna address is written in Bruckner's diary for January 1880, and it was undoubtedly Bruckner who sent the young conductor the puzzle card now in the Rosé Collection. Ten years later, Mahler was to send his brother Otto to study harmony and counterpoint under Bruckner at the conservatory.

23. MAB, page 272. It must be remembered that Auer's book was published in 1941 under the Nazi regime.

24. MAB, page 323. See below.

25. On the title page of his score of the *Te Deum*, Mahler wrote (instead of "For soloists, chorus," etc.), "For the tongues of angels, the pure in heart, and souls cleansed by fire."

26. MBB, page 329.

27. This was the Piaristen Monastery (NBL and Maja Löhr, in an article on Rott: *Lebendige Stadt, Almanach der Stadt Wien*, 1958). Bruckner recommended Rott for a post as organist to Ignaz Traumihler, choirmaster at the Abbey of St. Florian, where he himself spent his youth. He also recommended him, unsuccessfully, to the Abbey of Klosterneuburg and to two churches in Vienna (GAB, IV, I, 445).

28. NBL, page 137.

29. When Rott died, his two closest friends, Fritz Löhr and Joseph Seemüller, inherited his manuscripts and papers. Those still in existence—a symphony, three movements of another, a string quintet, and some choral works—are now in the Viennese National Library.

30. Four prizes for excellence, a regular first prize (Mahler), and nine second prizes were awarded that year.

31. MBR, No. 2. The fact that Mahler almost never dated his letters raises numerous chronological problems for a biographer.

32. The letter of September 6, 1877, tells Schwarz that Mahler was about to present himself for the examination, which was to take place on September 12.

33. Reprinted in the *Neue Freie Presse* of June 26 and signed by Dr. Altrichter. The documents consulted by him seem to have disappeared, because only one document, dated July 14 and concerning Mahler's exemption from the mathematics oral examination is now to be found in the Iglau college archives (now kept in the town library).

34. Adolf Prosnitz (1829–1917), a native of Prague, was the author of a *Kompendium der Musikgeschichte*. Mahler's work in this history class must have been mediocre, as his name is not mentioned in the end-of-the-year lists either for this subject or for counterpoint.

35. According to Theodor Fischer, he was at that time an engraver. Mahler met him again many years later in Russia, where he and his family had emigrated.

36. A Fräulein von Kralik won the first prize for excellence in composition in July 1878 in the same contest in which Mahler obtained his conservatory diploma. Richard Kralik von Meyrswalden, a young man from an aristocratic Bohemian family, wrote poems in which he tried to combine the heroic German epic and the Christian mystery play. He soon left the socialist vegetarian society to which Lipiner and Mahler also belonged, and settled down into staid conservatism. His son Heinrich Kralik (1887–1965), a critic who studied under Robert Hirschfeld, wrote a monograph on Mahler, a biography of Richard Strauss, *Das Grosse Orchester* (Vienna 1952), *Das Opernhaus am Ring* (1955) and *Das Buch der Musikfreunde* (1951). The name Kralik is scribbled several times along with that of Steiner, in the margin of the sketch of the first part (*"Der Spielmann"*) of *Das klagende Lied* of March 1880.

37. NBLS. Summer 1898.

38. Out of interest, here is the program of the concert: 1. Hummel—Septet; 2. Harp pieces; 3. Mozart—aria from *Le Nozze di Figaro;* 4. Chopin—two Nocturnes; 5. Verdi—aria from *Un Ballo in maschera;* 6. Scharwenka—Concerto No. 1 in B flat minor, Opus 3 (*sic*), first movement (pianist, G. Mahler); 7. Mendelssohn—two romances; 8. Chopin—Concerto in E minor, first movement; 9. Brahms and Kirschner—lieder; 10. Bach-Gounod—Meditation for piano, cello, and organ. Xaver Scharwenka (1850–1924), well-known composer, virtuoso, and teacher, founded and directed several music schools. He composed a symphony and four concertos that have fallen into oblivion.

39. This assertion, made by most Mahler biographers, is confirmed by a phrase spoken by Mahler to Ernst Decsey (*Die Musik:* X, 18, 355). However, the final version bears few traces of this original conception.

40. Doubtless Mahler was referring to this quintet movement when he told Natalie, in 1900 "that he was short of time to finish the score and had written the four parts together, by placing them one on top of the other." He recalled this in order to make fun of his friend, the musicologist Guido Adler, who maintained that Mozart had composed the entire overture to *Don Giovanni* in a single night, writing each part separately.

41. Having abandoned the piano class at the beginning of this school year, Mahler made composition his "major class."

42. See BMG, page 62. Ludwig, after some time as a bank accountant, had become a professor of piano at the Vienna Conservatory and was one of Otto Mahler's many teachers.

## CHAPTER 5

1. Emil Freund relates this story (MBR, page 492).

2. NBL, page 147.

3. Josef Steiner, born August 31, 1857, in Habern, Bohemia, the son of a shop-keeper (no doubt the one who introduced Mahler to Gustav Schwarz). He also wrote the libretto of the opera sketched out by Mahler, *Ernst von Schwaben.*

4. The farm of Puszta Batta, near Teteny, was not far from Budapest. The Baumgartens, who had three sons, lived most of the time in Vienna. One of them, Ferdinand, wrote a mildly successful operetta entitled *Gräfin Kuni,* which was put on at the Theater an der Wien in 1899 (*Neue Freie Presse,* March 12, 1899).

5. This refers to the opera that Mahler had intended to compose to a liberetto by Steiner.

6. Ernst Mahler, who died in 1874.

7. MBR, No. 1.

8. Letter to Anna von Mildenburg (December 8, 1895).

9. The letter is in the possession of Alfred Rosé.

10. In a letter to Anton Krisper written the following year, there is an even more striking resemblance to a passage in *Das Lied von der Erde:* in this letter "Spring came during the night, and with it the *Sehnsucht* and ancient sorrow"; in *Das Lied "Der Lenz ist da, sei kommen über Nacht!"*

11. These bells held a particular significance for Mahler, who introduced them into the orchestra of his *Sixth* and *Seventh Symphonies.*

12. In his mazurkas, for instance, Chopin is much more "artistic," more refined, and thus further from the soul of the people.

13. Published by Hans Holländer (*Die Musik,* XX, 807, August 13, 1928). One of the typescripts of Frau Mahler's book also contained the copy of a seventh incomplete letter, which no doubt dated from 1879 and accompanied the *Ballade vom Blonden und Braunen Reitersmann.*

14. Anton Krisper, born December 28, 1858, son of Josef Krisper, a Laibach merchant, was a fellow-pupil of Mahler at the Vienna Conservatory for two years. Gifted in composition, he had an opera staged at the Prague Theater. Its failure made him abandon music and take up the study of philosophy in Leipzig in 1880. He wrote a thesis on "Musical Doctrines. Their Beginnings, Development, and Consequences" (1882). Later he entered the School of Mines in Laibach. He died in Graz in 1914 after a long mental illness.

15. This letter was no doubt written at the end of the fall or during the winter, since in it Mahler suggests meeting Anton again "at Easter." It cannot have been written in 1880, since four letters written by him to Krisper at this time exist and in the present letter Mahler apologizes for his "long silence." In 1881, once he had finished *Das klagende Lied,* Mahler would not have sent the "ballade" to Krisper, whose mind was already confused at that time. Thus this letter was no doubt written in 1879.

16. It seems that Mahler kept in touch with one of these two young girls for a considerable time. John Perrin, the former owner of one of the earliest (five movement) manuscripts of the *First Symphony,* received it from his mother, née Jenny Feld, who was given it by Mahler himself in 1894 or 1895.

17. In the *Neues Wiener Journal* of December 21, 1921, Rudolf Stefan Hoffmann published for the first time the lyrics of songs that had belonged to Mahler's sister Justine Rosé, thus revealing the identity of the dedicatee. Josefa Poisl was one of the six children of the Iglau postmaster Josef Poisl, born in Rohle, Moravia, in 1831. She was the same age as Mahler, having been born in Neusatz, Hungary, July 14, 1860. She married a professor from the Iglau College twenty years her senior, Julius Wallner, later director of the college. The Poisls were not Jews, which probably put an additional obstacle between the two young people.

18. Letter of December 14, 1879. In the lyric of the song *"Im Lenz"* (February 19, 1880) the same alternative occurs: *"Ich bin nicht blind und sehe doch nicht/ Mir ist nicht dunkel und ist nicht licht."*

19. From a typed note that preceded the copy of these letters in one of Frau Mahler's two original manuscripts (AMS). Only the originals of Mahler's letters to Josephine and Fanni (Josephine's mother) have survived in manuscript, and the card from Franz Melion, an assistant master at the Iglau College, who seems to have played the role of confidant and go-between in this affair.

20. This undated letter was clearly written at the start of March.

21. See the complete text in Appendix 4. Mahler also sent to Krisper, in a letter written about the same time, the poem entitled *"Ballade vom Blonden und Braunen Reitersmann,"* which, apart from some tiny variations, is the text of the first part of his first manuscript score of 1878.

22. See Appendix 3 for the texts of these songs.

23. See the above letter to Steiner. Franz Melion was an assistant tutor for young children at the Iglau College from 1877 to 1880.

24. The name Poisl is not mentioned on this card, but the initials "J." and "A." and the date leave no doubt as to the nature of the message.

25. See Chapter 4. The unpublished manuscript of these songs belongs to Alfred Rosé.

26. The sketch for the first part, "Der Spielmann," dated March 21, 1880, is in the Vienna National Library. In the original three-part version "Der Spielmann" was the second part.

27. See letter quoted above. Perhaps this was one of the symphonic scores that Mahler gave to Frau Weber when he left Leipzig (see Chapter 12).

28. His name heads the program as pianist only, for he played no work of his own. He also accompanied some songs (Cf. Mährischer Grenzbote).

29. Unfortunately this concert hall has kept no records, so it is impossible to find out the exact dates of the concerts and recitals that Mahler accompanied.

30. Rennweg No. 3, parterre, Tür 10b (see Mahler's letter to Krisper of September 22, 1879).

31. Fifteen florins per month. The villa is 24, Karl Ludwigstrasse.

32. It was in a letter of November 1, 1880, that Mahler told Freund he had become a vegetarian. The Ramharter was located at the corner of the Wallnerstrasse and the narrow Fahnengasse.

33. He later married the well-known singer Anna von Mildenburg, after she had had a liaison with Mahler in Hamburg.

34. Bayreuther Blätter, October 1880: "Religion und Kunst." In it Wagner, who was at work on Parsifal, condemned the eating of meat as being the essential cause of the decline of Christian civilization, and spoke of "the assassination of domestic animals."

35. Siegfried Lipiner (1856–1912). Prolific author of volumes of verse and of interminable obscure dramas: Prometheus Unbound, which some of his contemporaries compared to Faust; Der neue Don Juan; Adam (first part of the trilogy Christus); Renatus; Echo; Hippolytos; translator of the ballads of the Polish poet Adam Mickiewicz. Lipiner carried on a correspondence with such celebrated people as Nietzsche and Malwida von Meysenburg, and had numerous admirers. See the amusing story of his meeting with Wagner in R. von Kralik's Tage und Werke (Vienna, 1922, page 60). Little by little, Lipiner fell into obscurity. He finally accepted a position as librarian to the Vienna Parliament, which he occupied until his death in 1912.

36. See letters of Nietzsche to Rohde (II, 196, 1877).

37. Mahler, Krisper, and Krzyzanowski left the Wagner Verein in 1879 for reasons unknown.

38. See Max Ermers: Victor Adler, pages 94–101, and Richard Kralik: Tage und Werke, pages 62–63.

39. MBR, No. 27.

40. AMM, page 107. On that day Mahler accompanied the workers in a Labor Day rally.

41. NBLS.

42. Alte unnennbare Tage, page 112.

43. Mahler's close friends spoke of his "Böhmakeln" accent, the light singing Bohemian inflection common to all members of his family.

44. HFRM, page 112, note 2.

45. Die Bildnisse von Gustav Mahler, page 13. This small album of photographs is prefaced by Roller's introduction, which contains the most intelligent and complete physical and psychological description of Mahler in existence.

46. This refers to hemorrhoids, from which he suffered all his life. In 1901

they caused a hemorrhage from which he almost died. After this he had to undergo an operation.

47. The pericardium is the membrane that encloses the heart as the pleura envelops the lungs; it becomes inflamed and fills with liquid. It must be remembered that, according to contemporary newspaper reports, Ernst Mahler died of pericarditis.

48. This in fact attacks the valves on the left-hand side of the heart. They no longer close completely and the leakage of blood through the openings can be heard in the form of a whisper during auscultation. The blood from the aorta flows back into the left ventricle when it is dilated. This type of aortic valvular inadequacy is often "compensated," as was the case with Mahler, who was able to lead an extremely active life.

49. Friedrich Eckstein: *Alte unnennbare Tage,* page 113.

50. NBLS.

51. Once more Mahler had been inspired by E. T. A. Hoffmann, for the humor and the atmosphere of *Rübezahl* resembles one of that author's most lyrical stories, *Königsbraut.* This libretto, sent to Alfred Roller by Justi in 1908, gave rise to a great deal of confusion. Alma affirms in AMM that her husband threw the manuscript into the sea from the deck of the ship taking him to the United States. This has been proved to be inexact.

52. Robin Lehman Collection.

53. NBLS.

54. Hugo Wolf was tempted by the stage several times. He made two attempts in this realm: *Der Corregidor* (1895)—the initial cause of the final scene with Mahler in 1897—and an unfinished opera called *Manuel Venegas* (1897).

## CHAPTER 6

1. This plan is mentioned in a letter of March 3, 1880, to Krisper.

2. In Hamburg in 1896, at the time of the premiere of the *Lieder eines fahrenden Gesellen,* while describing how he had composed them (NBLS).

3. Among Guido Adler's papers was a short letter from an impresario named Schaumann, dated February 2, 1880. Adler must have suggested Mahler for a post as chorus master (*Chormeister*), for Schaumann had replied: "The post has not yet been officially filled, but we do have someone in mind. I already know of Mahler's accomplishments, and feel that here, except for conducting the concert, his talents would be wasted. On the whole, this is the kind of post for which practical craftsmanship rather than artistic knowledge is required. Since I like Mahler and admire his talent, I can only advise him not to apply for this post, solely because of his capabilities; from the very first he would be disappointed."

4. The manuscript of the first movement of a piano quartet belonging to Alma Mahler has Rättig's stamp on its first page, which seems to indicate that at one time Mahler had wanted Rättig to publish it.

5. The son of Richard Löwy, horn player at the Hofoper and professor at the conservatory, Gustav Löwy started his career as a singer and flutist. He was a pupil at the Commercial and Technical School at the same time as Johann Strauss and worked for four years for the Viennese music seller Müller, then at the "Musical Museum" of Petersburg. He returned to Vienna in 1852 and founded his own music shop. He followed in Otto Nicolaï's footsteps by organizing philharmonic concerts, brought Anton Rubinstein to Western Europe, arranged a concert tour in France for Johann Strauss in 1876, and finally founded the Vienna Singakademie, and also a concert agency—"the oldest in Austria"—in 1869. He died in 1901 "at an advanced age."

6. These details were published in an article on the Hall Theater (*Das Hei-*

*matland,* illustrated supplement to the *Linzer Volkblatt* No. 24, June 14, 1925, pages 196–97).

7. According to an "Inventory" preserved and quoted by Rudolf Baldrian (*Die Osterreichische Furche,* X, 42, October 16, 1954), in an article on "Mahler's First Engagement," which includes most of the information given here on the Hall Theater.

8. Perhaps this explains Mahler's predilection for Offenbach's operettas. Although they were diametrically opposed to his usual interests, he later added them to the Budapest Opera repertoire.

9. In the collection of Alfred Rosé.

10. This very famous tune was sung throughout the Germanic countries to invented words: *"Du bist verrückt mein Kind. Du musst nach Berlin."* The name of the city changed according to the locale, each region inserting the name of a rival city. Thus in Berlin it was *"Du musst nach Wien."*

11. See AMM, page 138. Mizzi (Marie) Zwerenz, born in 1880, was to become a celebrated operetta singer. She was a pupil of Rosa Papier, whom we shall meet several times in Mahler's later career.

12. Letter of June 21, 1880, to Albert Spiegler (Robin Lehman collection). Mahler also asks Spiegler to send him a book by Jean Paul, but unfortunately has not the five florins necessary to pay for it!

13. Heinrich von Angeli (1840–1925), son of an innkeeper; from 1876 professor at the Vienna Academy, painter of the crowned heads of Austria, England, and Russia. The conductor Felix Weingartner states in his memoirs that in 1907, when he had an audience with the Emperor Franz Josef, Professor Angeli preceded him into the imperial presence (WLE, II, page 166).

14. This anecdote is confirmed by a letter sent to Mahler by Fritz Löhr in June 1886: Löhr's sister Bertha and Nina Hoffmann had gone to take the waters in Bad Hall, and Fritz asks Mahler if it was in fact there that he had "lived such an aristocratic episode." (From a letter found by Frau Alma among Mahler's books in 1930.)

15. HLG Collection.

16. Mahler was no doubt alluding to the misfortunes of Rott in the monastery.

17. This episode would fit perfectly into one of Hoffmann's tales. The important role played by doubles in romantic literature must not be forgotten; for example Heine's famous *Doppelgänger,* immortalized by Schubert.

18. NBL, page 34.

19. NBLS, August 24, 1893. Mahler added that nevertheless he found this early work "a little too expansive and overloaded" and had revised it (this was before the definitive revision of 1898) in order to try and eliminate the "excessive decoration." This task turned out to be almost impossible, for "the main outlines were already too blurred."

20. He was also to submit *Das klagende Lied* later to the jury of the Allgemeiner Deutscher Musikverein. The Rosé Collection includes a letter of September 13, 1883, from Franz Liszt; a rather dryly expressed refusal to consider the work. Liszt was then president of the Musikverein.

21. See NBL, page 34.

22. See DMM, page 148.

23. We will meet Viktor von Herzfeld (1850–1920) again as a music critic in Budapest. Despite his friendly relations with Mahler, he published an entirely unfavorable review of Mahler's *First Symphony* after its premiere.

24. See Auer: *Bruckner,* IV, I, page 447.

25. Brahms's contempt for Bruckner's music was reciprocated. Bruckner used to say, "Brahms is an extraordinary musician, a great contrapuntist . . . One day I am going to say to him, 'Sir, you are not a composer, you are a manufacturer

of music.'" (GAB, IV, 2, 131.) However, Brahms, though dying himself, did attend the funeral of his illustrious colleague in the autumn of 1896.

26. GAB, IV, 1, page 447. According to Frau Löhr, this visit took place September 17, 1880, and Brahms added that Rott "could not have done all that alone."

27. Cf. Maja Löhr: Hans Rott (Lebendige Stadt, Almanach der Stadt Wien 1958).

28. For the whole story of Wolf's visit to Brahms, see Frank Walker, Hugo Wolf, page 84, and Max Kalbeck: Johannes Brahms, III, 2).

29. Mahler later discussed the jury's decision in the following terms (see Ernst Decsey, Die Musik, X, 18, page 355). "I don't hold it against those gentlemen (of the Deutscher Musikverein) at all. Imagine if today someone outdid me [in the matter of modernism], God knows what my attitude would be!"

30. See article by Hans Holländer in Muziek, 1928–29, page 212.

31. Alte unnennbare Tage, page 113.

32. This letter (MBR, No. 7) is wrongly dated 1882 in the collection. In it Mahler tells Freund that he is about to leave for Laibach to take up his post as conductor, but by September 1882, Mahler had left Laibach five months before.

33. These details, with many others concerning Mahler's stay in Laibach, were furnished by Janko Traven, director of the Slovenian Theatrical Museum. The theater building in which Mahler conducted was destroyed by fire on February 17, 1887.

34. It is impossible to determine the exact number of performances he conducted, since all the theater archives vanished in the 1887 fire, and the contemporary newspapers rarely mention the conductor's name. Some works were certainly conducted by Mahler's assistants—a second Kapellmeister named Steiner and an "orchestral conductor" named Georg Mayer, who was responsible for concerts given by the theater orchestra in the restaurant of the public library, before and after the opera season, as well as most of the incidental music in plays (except for that to A Midsummer Night's Dream) and some light operettas.

35. October 4, 1881.

36. AMM, page 139.

37. The Laibacher Zeitung mentions Mahler by name only in connection with the first three operettas, but he probably also conducted Boccaccio, since he put it on later in Iglau in September 1882.

38. Some remarkable recordings exist of Mahler playing on the piano the Finale of his Fourth Symphony, the Funeral March from the Fifth, and two songs. These are the only indications we have of Mahler's interpretation. Recorded by the German Welte-Mignon company, some of them can be found in the catalogues of two record firms in Germany and the United States (Telefunken and American Columbia).

39. This fact was discovered by Hans Holländer (The Musical Quarterly), XVII, 4, page 455.

40. AMM, page 139.

41. This postcard is in the British Museum. It is dated April 4, 1882. Catalogue number: 49597 B.

## CHAPTER 7

1. "Frühlingsmorgen" and "Erinnerung," set to poems by Leander, and "Serenade" and "Phantaisie" to texts from the Don Juan of Tirso de Molina. These are the first four songs in the collection published by Schott in 1892.

2. This card and letter from Marie Mahler were in the leather brief case that Alma Mahler found in 1930 among Mahler's books. Marie also suggests that Gustav visit his uncle Herrmann.

3. In January 1883, and very probably up to the time of his departure for Olmütz, he lived at No. 12 Wipplingerstrasse, second staircase, fourth floor, to

the right. This address is given in his last letter to Krisper (*Die Musik*, August 1928), which mentions the Iglau performance of *Boccaccio* and includes good wishes for the new year, thus making it possible to date it accurately.

4. This letter was among those discovered by Frau Mahler in her husband's library.

5. *Mährisches Tagblatt*, January 12, 1883.

6. AMM, page 139.

7. This correspondence survives in the Kassel Theater archives.

8. These facts, as well as many others that are given elsewhere in these chapters, come from the excellent article by Dagmar Kučerova published by the Czech review *Hudební Věda* (No. 4, 1968, page 627).

9. The newspaper *Die Neue Zeit* spoke of Kaiser's "hot-blooded temperament."

10. Mahler told this anecdote in Vienna in May 1899 when *Le Prophète* was being revived. It is almost certainly the source of the *Martha* anecdote told by Alma Mahler (AMM, page 139).

11. Cast: Fräulein Tanner (Alice), Milles (Isabelle), Fuchs (Bertram), Krüger (Robert).

12. Renamed Mahler street in 1962. A commemorative plaque was placed on the house in 1934 but disappeared during the German occupation.

13. This letter is in the Vienna Stadtbibliothek.

14. On February 13, the day of Wagner's death, Mahler conducted Méhul's *Joseph* in Olmütz.

15. The concert was given at the German Casino, and the singers were Fräulein Milles and Mayer and Herr Fuchs.

16. Cast: Fräulein Hild (Carmen), Milles (Micaëla), Herr Krüger (Don José), Herr Mannheit (Escamillo).

17. On this occasion the critic of the *Neue Zeit* wrote that "Mahler must have good reason to take the movement so slowly."

18. NBLS, May 8, 1899.

19. The three Olmütz performances of *Carmen* were on March 10, 11, and 17.

20. Ueberhorst's letter is in the Kassel Theater archives.

21. MBR, No. 31.

22. *Illustriertes Wiener Extrablatt*, March 3, 1883.

23. At the end of May, Mahler spent a week in Kassel to undergo the trials that led to his engagement.

24. On the second floor of the Eder House (MBR, note 13, page 473).

25. The Alfred Rosé Collection contains more than four hundred of them.

26. Years afterward in Hamburg, he would proudly show visitors the armchair that had belonged to his father.

27. In a letter to Löhr (MBR, No. 21, page 30) and in two letters to Justi dated May 8, 1885, and September 6, 1885. In the Rosé Collection.

28. Rosé Collection.

29. Rosé Collection.

30. The police reports speak of "meningitis." Poldi was then living at No. 7 Wallensteinstrasse, Vienna.

31. Letter of October 14, 1890, sold by a Vienna autograph dealer in 1929.

32. See in particular the vision he had in Leipzig while composing the *Totenfeier* (see Chapter 12).

33. In AMM, Otto is wrongly stated to be the elder of the brothers, but in reality he was born in 1873, and was thus six years younger than Alois.

34. This anecdote is told by Alma Mahler (AMM, page 18). The pension was almost certainly the Warnegg, to which some of Mahler's early 1893 letters to Justi are addressed.

35. See AMM, page 18. The affair of the check was probably not the cause of Alois's

move to New York. In fact, the Viennese confectionery of Gustav and Wilhelm Heller, which employed him until his departure from Vienna, later appointed Maldurmin (Mahler, Durson, and Minich), the business that he founded in New York, as its United States representative. They would scarcely have given such responsibility to their former bookkeeper if he had not given them satisfaction or if they knew he had a police record.

36. Information furnished by Anna Mahler.

37. Information furnished by Alfred Rosé.

38. Anna Hoffmann (known as Nina) née Matscheko) (1844–1914). A writer and philanthropist, who specialized in foreign languages and literature. She published translations from Polish, French, and Russian. In 1897 and 1898 she lived in Moscow. After 1900 she devoted her time to charities and theological study.

39. RHM, page 356.

40. MBR, No. 89.

41. See Chapter 3.

42. See MBR, page 126. Mahler thought that Schopenhauer's book contained the most profound analysis of music that had ever been made, comparable to Wagner's article on Beethoven.

43. Gustav Theodor Fechner (1801–1887), the son of a clergyman, studied medicine, physics, and natural science in Leipzig. Anthropologist and aesthetician, he expressed his idealistic and romantic philosophy of nature in a series of works that could not fail to gain the attention and enthusiasm of someone like Mahler, for the two men's conception of the universe was very similar. Fechner's work had a deep and lasting influence upon Mahler.

44. See BWM, pages 135ff. This is the source of most of the information about Mahler's reading mentioned here.

45. See MBR, No. 138.

46. Cf. MBR, No. 20.

47. MBR, Nos. 120 and 215.

48. MBR, No. 20.

49. MBR, No. 282.

50. Until 1893 Mahler's *First Symphony* bore the title *"Titan, Symphonic Poem."*

51. NBL, page 16.

52. See Mahler's letter to Steiner, Chapter 5.

53. Hoffmann: *Der Kater Murr.*

54. Ibid.

55. See Chapter 2.

56. Ibid.

57. AMM, page 257.

58. Frau Alma's library contained a copy of *Tristram Shandy* in English. In it many words and phrases have been translated, doubtless by Mahler, who used it to learn English before leaving for London in 1892.

59. One of his letters, MBR, No. 14, quotes Ibsen's *Peer Gynt.*

## CHAPTER 8

1. According to Wilhelm Kienzl, Mahler received this post only because he himself had refused to sign a three-year contract. Kienzl also states that there were, in all, forty-two candidates (WKL, page 150).

2. Karl Ueberhorst (1823–99), a Westphalian actor and singer, who was the head producer at the Dresden Theater from 1881 until his death.

3. See Auer: *Bruckner,* IV, 2, page 123.

4. See the letter that Mahler sent on June 21 to Zulauf, scenic designer of the Kassel Theater, who was temporarily deputizing for the intendant.

5. Eleven performances of *Parsifal* were given in Bayreuth between July 8 and July 30, 1883. The celebrated Amalie Materna sang Kundry, and the cast also included two singers whom Mahler encountered later at the Vienna Opera: the tenor Hermann Winkelmann (Parsifal) and the baritone Theodor Reichmann (Amfortas). As in the preceding year, the performances were under the direction of the Munich conductor Hermann Levi.

6. MBR, No. 13.

7. Hans Bruckmüller published this account in December 1932 in *Igel-Land*, a supplementary publication to the Iglau newspaper, *Mährischer Grenzbote*. The author tells us that he had known Mahler for many years and had played Beethoven symphonies with him as duets.

8. The violinist Mila von Ottenfeld was one of the six women in question, according to the newspapers.

9. At least this is the title given by Liszt in his reply. It is probable that Mahler sent him the whole score of *Das klagende Lied*. The letter is in the Rosé Collection.

10. For the period August 21 to October 1, which preceded his official nomination, Mahler received a salary of 235 marks.

11. Wilhelm Treiber, born in Graz in 1838, studied music with his father. After giving several concert tours in Austria and Germany as a pianist, he began a career as conductor. From 1876 he conducted the Euterpekonzerte of Leipzig and was made *Hofkapellmeister* in Kassel in 1881. He remained there till his death in 1889.

12. We possess only a very few criticisms of performances that Mahler conducted in Kassel: the newspapers of the period have almost all disappeared due to bombing. Criticism, furthermore, was in a rudimentary state there. Mahler told Justi in a letter dated May 9, 1885: "Pay no attention to the critics. It is exactly as if one had asked Emma [then ten years old] to judge a performance."

13. The allusion is to Ibsen's *Peer Gynt*, Act II, Scene 7.

14. It may seem astonishing that the conductor was supposed to be backstage also, but, as Mahler was the regular choirmaster, the fact that he conducted the performance did not free him from his usual duty, which was to beat time while the chorus sang in the wings.

15. Letter to Löwy (HLG Collection). The letter contained good wishes for the new year.

16. From a paragraph published on September 12 in the *Kasseler Journal*.

17. Called, as always in Germany, *Margarethe*. Cast on September 16: Fräulein Sieber (Marguerite), Hesse (Siebel), Zottmayer (Faust), Greef (Mephistopheles).

18. Cast: Johanna Richter (Leonore), Heuckeshoven (Stradella), Zottmayer and Schulze (bandits).

19. *Kasseler Journal*, December 28, 1883. Cast: Johanna Richter (Isabelle), Naumann-Gungl (Alice), Zottmayer (Robert), Greef (Bertram).

20. December 5, 1883. Cast: Naumann-Gungl (Queen of the Spirits), Sieber (Anna), Heuckeshoven (Konrad), Rathjens (Hans).

21. AMM, page 140.

22. He soon moved to new lodgings, in the apartment of Frau Frank, Mittlere Carlstrasse No. 17, second floor (MBR, No. 14).

23. Letter to Löwy (HLG Collection).

24. Mahler was to meet Rubinstein later. At both Hamburg and Vienna, he conducted Rubinstein's opera *The Demon*, which was always one of his favorite works.

25. See Krebs: *Meister des Taktstocks*, page 143.

26. A "fresh and lively performance," according to the *Kasseler Zeitung*, which added that on that occasion Mahler had conformed "to the tradition in effect in Kassel for the last three years." Cast of January 10, 1884: Sieber (Agathe), König (Ännchen), Zottmayer (Max), Greef (Kaspar).

27. Regarding the March 29 performance of this opera, the critic asserted that the

rehearsals had been insufficient for the interpreters to familiarize themselves with Mahler's intentions. Cast: Richter (Frau Fluth), Van Zanten (Frau Reich), Sieber (Anna), Hübbenett (Fenton), Schulze (Falstaff).

28. Viktor E. Nessler (1841–90), an Alsatian, who was studying theology in Leipzig when the success of his operetta *Fleurette* led him, at twenty-three, to leave the university and devote himself to music. An able composer, lacking originality and stylistic elegance, Nessler became *Musikdirektor* at the Leipzig Theater and won great popularity in Germany with *Der Rattenfänger von Hameln* (1879) and, above all, *Der Trompeter von Säkkingen* (1884). Against his wishes, Mahler was often obliged to conduct the latter opera in Prague and Leipzig.

29. Mittlere Carlstrasse 17.

30. This may have been an allusion to Klothilde Krzyzanowski, to whom Fritz Löhr paid "pompous" and "pedantic" court until he himself became engaged in 1886. This somewhat literary love affair seems to have exasperated Heinrich, Klothilde's husband.

31. The *tableaux vivants* had been staged by the director Ernold. Mahler used a single theme, written as a serenade, a march, an adagio, and battle music (see Appendix 3). This theme was quoted by Max Steinitzer (*Anbruch*, II, 718, 296). It has survived in the newly published slow movement (*Blumine*) of the *First Symphony*.

32. Cast for the act from *Les Huguenots*: Brandt-Goertz (Valentine), Zottmayer (Raoul), Ewald (Tavannes), Thümmel (Nevers), Schulze (St. Bris). Cast for the last act of *Il Trovatore*: Brandt-Goertz (Leonore), Koenig (Azucena), Heuckeshoven (Manrico), Thümmel (Luna), Pache (Ruiz). There were also recitations and lieder by Küken and Abt. For *Der Trompeter* the cast was: Pauli (Margaretha), Rinald (Werner), Müller (Mainau), Häser (Anton).

33. The Wiesbaden Theater still possesses archives from this period, but there is no reference to any performance of *Der Trompeter*. The Mannheim town and theater archives were entirely destroyed by bombing. Only at Karlsruhe is there any trace of a performance of this music—on June 6, 1885 (see below).

34. Appendix 3 contains all the available information about this lost score.

35. The story of this projected revision is to be found in a document written by Rättig and discovered by Auer in 1936. Schalk, Schönaich, Eckstein, and Baumgartner had helped the editor to persuade Bruckner.

36. MAB, page 323. In his work, Auer does not give the exact date of this incident, but places it between two other stories dated April 5 and May 28, 1884. It does not seem likely that Mahler was able to visit Vienna in the spring, and it is surprising that Bruckner considered an inexperienced young conductor of twenty-three a "professional" orchestral technician. But perhaps he formed this opinion after reading *Das klagende Lied*. Auer mentions that Bruckner had to pay four hundred gulden to his editor for the work not used.

37. Ernst von Schuch (1846–1914) was a well-known conductor. Born in Graz, he had studied law before devoting himself to music. He began conducting in Breslau and afterward went to Würzburg, Graz, and Basel. In 1873 he was conductor at the Dresden Theater and became director there from 1883 until his death.

38. Therese Malten (1855–1930), whose real name was Müller, was a famous dramatic soprano. Born in East Prussia, she made her debut in Dresden in 1873, remaining with the opera there until 1903. With Materna and Brandt, she created in Bayreuth in 1882 the role of Kundry in *Parsifal*.

39. MBR, No. 22.

## CHAPTER 9

1. This clearly refers to the Anna-Fenton duet (No. 7c in the score).

2. A draft of this letter, dated October 18, 1884, was in Alma Mahler's collection. No

addressee's name is mentioned, but the letter is addressed to "Herr Hofrath" (Schuch's title), and invites him to the first performance of *Un Ballo in maschera*. We know that Schuch had promised Mahler on August 24 that he would visit Kassel to hear him conduct.

3. A pun on his name. Faulpeltz means "lazybones."

4. A comic opera, probably in one act, by a now completely forgotten composer, given for the first time in 1831.

5. AMM, page 140.

6. This note reads: "Mahler's love for two actresses, Naumann and Johanna Elmblatt." The latter name is that of the Scandinavian baritone Mahler met in Prague, and for "Elmblatt" one should read "Richter." The signature has been mistakenly read by the copyist as Anna instead of "Johanna." But the latter is certainly the author of the letter, which alludes to her forthcoming engagement in Rotterdam.

7. This letter was found, with others, by Alma Mahler in 1930 in her library.

8. This expression is difficult to translate. In old German, *Gefährte* meant "traveling companion" (*Fahrt* meaning "trip"), and *Gesell* "table companion" (from *Saal*, "room"). Later, *Gesell* denoted a worker, an apprentice or agricultural worker who wandered about the country seeking employment. The word, then, can be translated as "companion," "comrade," or simply "boy." The best English rendering of *Lieder eines fahrenden Gesellen* is doubtless *Songs of a Wayfarer*.

9. See Appendix 4.

10. This poem was with the letters mentioned above in Alma Mahler's library (see Appendix 4).

11. This was the draft of a letter dated October 18 and no doubt intended for Schuch; in it Mahler invites him to the first performance of the *Masked Ball*.

12. The fourth and last poem seems to have been written first, since it is preceded by the numeral I and dated December 15, 1884. On the same handwritten page is the third, "*Ich hab' ein glühend Messer*," preceded by the numeral II and dated December 19. These manuscript pages were in the Alma Mahler collection.

13. Mahler used the word *Wegtafeln*, which can be translated more prosaically as "signpost."

14. It has been generally supposed that the *Lieder eines fahrenden Gesellen* were begun the preceding year. The dated manuscript of the poems in Alma Mahler's collection and the letter quoted above (MBR, No. 23) appear to prove that the lyrics and the music were composed almost simultaneously during the last two weeks of 1884.

15. Published in *Der Merker*, March 1912, page 183. See Appendix 4. The autograph copy of this poem was in the possession of Alma Mahler. Yet another precedes it in NBLS: Mahler showed both of them to Natalie on February 17, 1896, and she made copies of them. It is also dated December 1884 and once more describes the fatigue of the eternal traveler. These two poems are no doubt the two supplementary texts to which Mahler refers when he speaks of "six" lieder, but doubtless they were never set to music. (See Appendix 4: "*Die Sonne spinnt.*")

16. Letter of December 3, published with Neumann's reply in an article in the Prague paper *Bohemia* on March 5, 1898. Another article, published by Julius Steinberg in the *Prager Abendblatt*, the day before Mahler's death, suggested that he wrote to Neumann "at the instigation of someone in Prague," but no name is mentioned.

17. Neumann relates this episode in his article "*Mahler in Prag*," BSP, page 7.

18. Letter to Spiegler written on January 23.

19. NBL, page 14.

20. Also known as *Die Verschworenen*. Based on Aristophanes' *Lysistrata*.

21. See the article in the *Hessicher Blätter*, XVII, 1197, July 8, 1885.

22. MBR, No. 3, March 26, 1885.

23. MBR, No. 26.

24. It seems strange that he waited almost two months to do this, since he had already announced the news to his friend Albert Spiegler in January.

25. MBR, No. 24.

26. MBR, No. 25.

27. MBR, No. 26, May 1885.

28. MBR, No. 28, June 1885.

29. Cast: Naumann-Gungl (Rebekka), Zottmayer (Ivanhoe), Schaffganz (Guilbert), Heuckeshoven (Narr).

30. See Appendix 3 and the article by Fritz Egon Pamer.

31. WLE I, page 218.

32. Letter of April 10 in the archives of the Kassel Theater.

33. MBR, No. 26.

34. MBR, No. 27.

35. This letter is dated April 2, 1886, and no doubt refers to the conflict with Neumann that had taken place shortly before.

36. This letter was certainly among the documents that related to Mahler's youth and that Alma Mahler found in 1930.

37. Letter to Löwy, dated May 12, in the Vienna Stadtbibliothek.

38. *Karlsruher Zeitung,* July 7, 1885.

39. See NBL, page 113.

40. Exactly 450, according to the *Kasseler Zeitung,* although Mahler himself mentioned later 480.

41. Rosa Papier (1858–1932), mezzo-soprano at the Vienna Opera, was to become a well-known teacher of singing at the Vienna Conservatory.

42. In Hamburg on October 27, 1893, Paul Bulss later took part in the first performance of the lieder from *Des Knaben Wunderhorn,* then known as *Humoresken.*

43. Heinrich Gudehus (1845–1909), well-known Wagnerian tenor who alternated the role of Parsifal with Hermann Winkelmann in Bayreuth in July 1883, during Mahler's first visit there.

44. NBL, page 112. Carl Krebs (*Meister des Taktstocks*) states that Spontini also used a long ebony stick with an ivory tip when he conducted choruses and processional marches at the opera; for the arias he was content to use a baton (which, incidentally he held in the middle instead of at one end).

45. The *Kasseler Tageblatt* was a paper that was considered in Kassel to be pro-Jewish.

46. WLE, *ibid.*

47. Strauss was finally selected. See Maria von Bülow, *Hans von Bülow,* page 176.

48. All earlier biographers have asserted the contrary. Nevertheless, there was no place in Mahler's schedule that summer for a stay in Leipzig.

## CHAPTER 10

1. "The theater was known by a series of names: Gräflich-Nostitzsches National Theater auf dem Altmarkt (1783); Ständisches Theater (1799); Königliches Bömisches Landestheater (1861); Deutsches Landestheater (1864) and, finally, in 1918, Tschechisches Ständetheater. It is now called Tyl-Theater. See Richard Rosenheim: *Geschichte der Deutschen Bühnen in Prag, 1883–1918* (Prague, H. Mercy, 1938). The Neues Deutsches Theater, seating 2200, was not inaugurated by Angelo Neumann until January 1888, after which he directed the two German theaters until his death.

2. Angelo Neumann, born in Vienna on August 18, 1838, studied medicine and began a business career before he became an operatic lyric baritone. The first steps in this singing career were taken in Cologne, Krakov, Oldenburg, Pressburg, and Danzig. Before abandoning singing because of an inflammation of the vocal chords, Neumann was with the Vienna Hofoper for fourteen years, and sang there in *Lohengrin* under

Wagner's direction. In 1876 he became producer and co-director of the Leipzig Opera, and from there went to Bremen and then to Prague. From 1876 on, he organized a series of performances of *Der Ring des Nibelungen* in Berlin and London. In 1882, he organized another Wagnerian company for European tours. He welcomed Mahler to Prague again in 1898, and died there on December 20, 1910.

3. Many characteristic stories about Neumann are told, in particular an anecdote concerning an unfortunate soprano whom he once hung by one leg out a window in order to make her come around to his point of view.

4. Anton Seidl (1850–98), born in Budapest, studied at the Leipzig Conservatory, and then became a disciple of Wagner in Bayreuth, where he and other young musicians helped Wagner to copy and correct the parts of the *Ring*. In 1875, he was engaged by Neumann, at Wagner's suggestion, as chief conductor in Leipzig. He then conducted Neumann's Wagnerian tours, visited Bremen and Prague with him, and went to New York to take the place of Leopold Damrosch, who had just died, as director of German opera at the Metropolitan Opera House. He also later conducted the New York Philharmonic Orchestra. He died of food poisoning in 1898.

5. The cast of the *Lohengrin* conducted by Seidl was: Auguste Seidl-Kraus, his wife (Elsa), Marie Rochelle (Ortrud), Adolf Wallnöfer (Lohengrin), Josef Beck (Telramund), Hans Tomaschek (King), Felix Ehrl (Herald).

6. Ludwig Slansky, born in Haida in 1833, studied at the Prague Conservatory from 1852 to 1858 and was made director of the Prague Theater Orchestra in 1863. He retired in 1889 and died in 1905.

7. Mentioned in one of his letters to Mathilde Wesendonck.

8. For less important works an "assistant" named Stolz and a choirmaster named Rehbock were there to aid the *Kapellmeister*.

9. The list of conductors discovered by Neumann is impressive: Nikisch, Seidl, Mahler, and, much later, Otto Klemperer, not to mention Franz Schalk, Leo Blech, and Krzyzanowski.

10. See Angelo Neumann: *Mahler in Prag* (BSP, No. 7).

11. See BSP, page 8.

12. Letter to his parents dated September 6 (A. Rosé Collection).

13. Viktor Nessler's musical style was eclectic and strongly influenced by folklore.

14. During his first months in Prague, Mahler conducted these operas: August—*Der Wasserträger* (1); September—*Der Wasserträger* (1), *Don Giovanni* (1) *Der Trompeter von Säkkingen* (5), *Tannhäuser* (1); October—*Der Trompeter von Säkkingen* (4), *Die Meistersinger von Nürnberg* (2), *Don Giovanni* (1), *Norma* (1); December—*Der Trompeter von Säkkingen* (1), *Die Meistersinger von Nürnberg* (1), *Das Rheingold* (2), *Die Walküre* (2); January—*Der Trompeter von Säkkingen* (1), *Tannhäuser* (1), *Das Rheingold* (2), *Die Walküre* (2); February—*Der Trompeter von Säkkingen* (3), *Die Entführung aus dem Serail* (1), *Die Meistersinger von Nürnberg* (1), *Tannhäuser* (1), *Das Rheingold* (1), *Die Walküre* (1).

15. Tobisch attacked Mahler twice—on November 8, 1885, and May 9, 1886—for having, unlike Slansky, had the recitative accompanied by a string quartet. The critic of the *Abendblatt*, who praised the performance of the *recitativo secco*, does not seem to have realized that in this particular matter Mahler was further from Mozart than Slansky.

16. The Dresden critic Ludwig Hartmann (see BSP, page 9) said later that he never forgot these first performances of *Don Giovanni* conducted by Mahler.

17. Letter to his parents, September 5, 1885. In the Rosé Collection.

18. *Ibid.*

19. See Paul Nettl's article *"Gustav Mahler in Prag"* (*Sudetendeutsche Jahrbücher,* 1926). Some of the information contained in the present chapter is borrowed from this article.

20. Jahn attended the performance of October 19. *Der Trompeter* was given for the

first time in Vienna on January 30, 1886. No doubt the February 10 cast was the same as that for the premiere on September 12: Katharina Rosen (Maria); Hilgermann (Countess); Gustav Löwe (Damian); Joseph Beck (Kirchhofer); Felix Ehrl (Conradin); Hans Tomaschek (Wildenstein); Wenzel Dobsch (Schönau). According to the Prague newspaper, Maria, sister of the famous singer Lilli Lehmann, was present for the February 10 performance.

21. NBL, page 173. The Prague papers indicated that the great Viennese critic Eduard Hanslick attended the performance of *Der Trompeter von Säkkingen* conducted by Mahler on September 20.

22. Beim Goldenen Rad, Rittergasse 24.

23. See Paul Nettl, *ibid.*

24. Betty Frank, coloratura soprano, born in 1864 in Breslau, studied under the well-known Blanche Marchesi in Paris. She sang in Breslau from 1891 to 1893, then in Zurich in 1893 and Berlin in 1894. After this we lose track of her. Certain enigmatic phrases in Mahler's letters to Löhr probably refer to her (MBR, No. 35, 36, and 39).

25. Mahler's letter to his parents of November 1885, in the Rosé Collection.

26. See MBR, No. 31, of November 28, 1885.

27. Three letters that Mahler wrote in Leipzig (BR, 35, 36, and 39) suggest that Betty Frank had been very close to him.

28. This undated letter from Emil Freund was sent to Mahler in Prague probably at the start of 1886. It was among the papers discovered by Alma Mahler in her husband's library in 1930.

29. Letter written from Karlsbad to Gustav on May 6, 1886.

30. Letter from Marie Mahler dated May 31.

31. Letter from Justi (June 4, 1886). In the end Bernhard went back to Vienna on July 4 with the local Iglau doctor, Dr. Schwartz, in order to consult a specialist, Professor Bamberg.

32. Le Pirk (Eva), Hilgermann (Magdalena), Wallnöfer (Walther), Beck (Sachs), Tomaschek (Beckmesser), Elmblad (Pogner), Pirk (David).

33. *Neues Wiener Journal* (June 19 and 26, 1921).

34. Cast for the performances of February 15 and 17, 1886, attended by Fritz Löhr, and which were no doubt the same as the premiere (taken from the program in Löhr's collection). *Rheingold:* Frank (Woglinde), Sarolla Le Pirk (Wellgunde), Tomaschek (Freia), Rochelle (Fricka), Hilgermann (Flosshilde), Hoffmann (Erda), Wallnöfer (Loge), Engelbert Pirk (Mime), Warmuth (Froh), Beck (Alberich), Ehrl (Donner), Tomaschek (Wotan), Dobsch (Fasolt), Elmblad (Fafner). *Valkyries:* Frank (Gerhilde), Sarolla Le Pirk (Ortlinde), Tomaschek (Helmwige), Rosen (Sieglinde), Moser (Brünnhilde), Rochelle (Fricka), Hoffmann (Waltraute), Münk (Schwertleite), Heim (Siegrune), Plodek (Grimgerde), Hilgermann (Rossweise), Wallnöfer (Siegmund), Tomaschek (Wotan), Elmblad (Hunding).

35. See his letter to Baron von Gilsa, December 29, 1885, in the archives of the Kassel Theater.

36. These two extracts had the attraction of novelty, as *Parsifal* still could not be performed outside Bayreuth. Neumann had been the first to get permission from Wagner to present extracts from it in concerts.

37. The papers had announced that Saint-Saëns would conduct part of this concert. The singers in the *Götterdämmerung* excerpts were Adolf Wallnöfer and Marie Rochelle; those in the *Ninth Symphony* were Betty Frank, Laura Hilgermann, Adolf Wallnöfer and Johannes Elmblad. The theater orchestra had been augmented with well-known artists, amateurs, and conservatory students. The choirs were those of the Deutscher Männergesangsverein and the Gesangsverein Sankt Veit, plus the singers from the opera, in all, two hundred singers. According to the *Zwischenacts-Zeitung* (probably distributed to the audience instead of a program), the bells of the *Parsifal Verwand-*

*lungsmusik* were replaced by tuned kettledrums. The same paper speaks of Muck as being "one of the greatest Wagnerian conductors of his day" in its February 10 issue.

38. PSM, page 38.

39. See *Der Anbruch*, II, April 1920, page 303. According to Löhr, a discussion had broken out between Mahler and Neumann right after the concert of February 13 and seems to have caused a complete break between them. For this reason, Mahler did not learn until two days before the second concert that he would have to conduct it, and he had only one rehearsal with some of the strings for the Finale recitative. Despite this, Löhr asserts, Mahler got from the orchestra an interpretation wholly different from Muck's.

40. *Zum Fasching*. See Paul Nettl, *ibid.*, page 59.

41. GAM, page 13.

42. Langegasse 18. Cf. MBR, No. 32.

43. Johannes Elmblad (1853–1910) married twice, Maggie Menzies (who died in 1887) and Siegrid Petterson (who died in 1926). The first was probably not in Prague with her husband, since Schulz, the son of the Langegasse landlord, does not mention her (see below).

44. The "musician" was certainly the son of the printer Schulz, owner of the Langegasse house. The little book has no date, but only the name of the printer (Selbstverlag H. Schulz A.G. Prag VII).

45. Act I, Scene III (page 60 of the Peters piano score).

46. The melody in F sung by Sulamith to the words *"O, lass ihn durch dein Machtgebot die Freiheit, Herr!"*

47. Marie Renard had "come expressly from Berlin," where she was then singing at the opera. When Mahler took over the direction of the Vienna Hofoper, she was its reigning queen.

48. Most of the critics attended a performance of Haydn's *Die Jahreszeiten*, which took place the same evening, with Slansky conducting, and do not mention the benefit concert.

49. Löhr's assertion that this conflict broke out during his visit, before the second Wagner concert, fits in with the date of the first performance of the new production of *Faust*, which took place on February 22.

50. Julius Steinberg (1841–1916), orphaned at an early age, first played with a string orchestra, then in the orchestra of the German Opera in Prague under the direction of Wilhelm Jahn. This enabled him to continue studying music. He also contributed long articles to newspapers and covered the law courts as a reporter. He made the acquaintance of the lawyer-historian of music Wilhelm Ambros, whom he replaced in 1865 on the *Prager Zeitung*. His articles helped to launch a great many artists, among them Lilli and Marie Lehmann and Alfred Grünfeld (cf. Rudolf Freiherr Procházka: *Das romantische Musik-Prag. Charakterbilder*. Verlag Erben, Saaz in Böhmen, 1914).

51. Steinberg's daughter, Gisela Wien-Steinberg, who took over his position as musical critic in Prague, relates this scene in the *Neues Wiener Journal* of June 29, 1921. No doubt ignoring the fact that Mahler had had a second row with the director of the Prague Opera in August 1888, she confuses the two incidents and asserts that David Popper, the famous cellist, met Mahler the day of the *Faust* rehearsal, whereas this meeting actually took place in 1888.

52. See the article by Julius Steinberg, *Fremdenblatt*, Vienna, May 25, 1911.

53. In a letter written on March 3 and found by Alma Mahler among her husband's papers, Marie Mahler tells her son that she has read the text published by Neumann in *Bohemia*. Marie also asks him to pay a visit of condolence to his "Uncle Werner," whose wife had just died suddenly (AMS).

54. PSM, page 38.

55. Article in *Zum Fasching*, which also discusses the concert at which Mahler conducted Beethoven's *Ninth Symphony*. See Paul Nettl, *ibid.*, page 59.

56. *Taktfrage,* possibly a pun, as it means also "a matter of tact."

57. Letter to Baron von Gilsa, April 10, 1886, in the archives of the Kassel Theater. Like the Kassel and Hanover theaters, that in Wiesbaden was run by the Berlin General administration. Karl Reiss (1829–1908) was Kapellmeister in Kassel from 1856 to 1881, and then in Wiesbaden until 1886.

58. This letter from Von Gilsa, dated May 13, was with various other letters from Mahler's parents and his sister Justi in the brief case found in her library by Alma Mahler in 1930.

59. Letter to Baron von Gilsa, May 15, 1886, in the archives of the Kassel Theater.

60. March—*Der Trompeter von Säkkingen* (2), *Hans Heiling* (1), *Das Rheingold* and *Die Walküre* (1), April—*Der Trompeter von Säkkingen* (1), *Così fan tutte* (2), *Undine* (2), May—*Der Trompeter von Säkkingen* (1), *Don Giovanni* (1), *Undine* (2), June—*Der Trompeter von Säkkingen* (4), *Le Prophète* (1), *Tannhäuser* (1), July— *Iphigénie en Aulide* (2), *Fidelio* (1), *Le Prophète* (1), *Der Trompeter von Säkkingen* (1).

61. References exist from as early as 1850 to the playing of the overture before Act II. In about 1895, Anton Seidl remarked that the custom of playing it in the middle of Act II had arisen as a parallel with Siegfried's Funeral Music in *Die Götterdämmerung.*

62. MBR, No. 50.

63. In 1888 for *Die drei Pintos,* in 1898 for a concert, and in 1905 for the first performance of his own *Seventh Symphony.* In August 1886 he expressed nostalgia for Prague in a letter to his parents (in the Rosé Collection) written from Leipzig.

## CHAPTER 11

1. Max Staegemann (1843–1905), born in Freienwalde, studied in Dresden, and began his career as an operatic baritone in Hanover in 1863. He became director of the Königsberg Opera in 1876, leaving it three years later to live in Berlin, where he worked as a lieder singer and singing teacher. From 1882 until his death, he was director of the Leipzig Opera. He married a violinist named Hildegard Kirchner, and two of their children—Waldemar and Helene—became opera and lieder singers.

2. Letter to Justi, August 1886, in the Rosé Collection.

3. Henri Petri (1856–1914). Born in Utrecht, the son of an orchestral musician, he was a pupil of Joachim, among other teachers, and was leader of several orchestras, composer, professor, and founder of a famous quartet. Petri was also the father of a famous pianist and pupil of Busoni, Egon Petri.

4. See Max Steinitzer: *Der Anbruch.* II, 7/8, page 296.

5. MBR, No. 35, August 18.

6. Martin Krause (1853–1918) studied at the Leipzig Conservatory. He founded the Lisztverein, whose concerts were conducted by Nikisch, and later became a professor of piano and critic of the *Leipziger Neueste Nachrichten.*

7. Cast: Scherenberg (Elsa), Orlanda Riegler (Ortrud), Anton Schott (Lohengrin), Goldberg (Telramund).

8. This article was among those which Mahler sent to Löhr with MBR, No. 35. Vogel criticized Mahler for the rather too slow tempo of the prayer theme, but considered it nonetheless preferable to erring in the opposite direction.

9. Cast: (on August 2) Sthamer-Andriessen (Irene), Moran-Olden (Adriano), Schott (Rienzi), Artner (Messenger of Peace).

10. Cast: Wülsinghoff (Berthe), Moran-Olden (Fidès), Schott (Prophète), Goldberg (Oberthal).

11. Cast: Moran-Olden (Elisabeth), Baumann (Venus), Schott (Tannhäuser), Perron (Wolfram).

12. MBR, No. 35.

13. Anton Schott (1846–1913), a lyric tenor who became a dramatic tenor, was

famous for his Wagnerian interpretations and his participation in Angelo Neumann's tours. Krause reproached Staegemann for the presence, in nearly all of the same week's casts, of the baritone-stage manager Goldberg, "whose voice belongs to the past" (*Musikalisches Wochenblatt*, article of October 6 on *Tristan und Isolde*).

14. MBR, No. 35. In *La Juive* the Hungarian bass David Ney, a guest singer, sang the role of the Cardinal. Later he was a member of the Budapest Opera under Mahler's direction.

15. Cast: Baumann (Agathe), Artner (Annchen), Hübner (Max), Proft (Kuno), Ney (Caspar), Perron (Ottokar), Marian (Kilian), Köhler (Ermite).

16. Adolf Bernhard Vogel (1847–98) was, with Krause, the most important of the Leipzig critics. A composer, he also wrote some short biographies, notably on Robert Volkmann, Liszt, Wagner, Bülow, and Brahms.

17. Casts: *Der fliegende Holländer*—Sthamer-Andriessen (Senta), Hedmondt (Erik), Schelper (Holländer), Köhler (Daland); *Robert le Diable*—Sthamer-Andriessen (Alice), Baumann (Isabelle), Lederer (Robert), Ney (Bertram).

18. From *blamieren*, "to ridicule." See the article in the *Musikalisches Wochenblatt* on the September 10 premiere.

19. MBR, No. 36.

Max Steinitzer (1864–1937), critic and musicologist, was born in Innsbruck. He became an operatic conductor and a professor at the University of Freiburg. The future author of numerous musical books (notably on Beethoven, Tchaikovsky, and Richard Strauss) became a close friend of Mahler in Leipzig. He committed suicide in 1937 when the racial laws became operative in Germany. The information quoted above is taken from the monthly *Leipzig* (*hrsg.v. Rate der Stadt Leipzig, Jahr I, Heft 5*, October 1924, pages 97–98).

20. This statement is more than doubtful. It was obtained in Leipzig by my assistant Peter Riethus from a onetime oboist in the Gewandhaus Orchestra who was ninety-six years old in 1960.

21. Letter written early in October 1886 to Justi, in the Rosé Collection.

22. MBR, No. 39.

23. *Ibid.*

24. Karl Reinecke (1824–1910), famous conductor, composer, pedagogue, and pianist, was known particularly for his performances of Mozart.

25. MBR, No. 39.

26. In October, Mahler conducted *Tannhäuser, Der Trompeter von Säkkingen, Ramiro, Le Maçon* (2), *Der Templer und die Jüdin* (2), and the *Nachtlager*, not to mention a double performance of the two parts of Goethe's *Faust*, with incidental music by Eduard Lassen. In November, his repertoire included *Der Freischütz, Der fliegende Holländer* (2), *Tannhäuser, Robert le Diable, Das Nachtlager von Granada*, and *A Midsummer Night's Dream* (2) with Mendelssohn's incidental music.

27. MBR, No. 53.

28. Letter of November 25, 1889 to Baron von Gilsa, archives of the Kassel Theater.

29. The *Leipziger Tageblatt* of November 23 announced that Nikisch would leave for Budapest in January.

30. In a letter of December 26, Gilsa advised Mahler to write directly to the intendant. He himself would write to the intendant only when "asked for."

31. *Tannhäuser, Der fliegende Holländer, Templer, Der Trompeter von Säkkingen*, and Weber's *Preciosa* and *Abu Hassan* (a double bill), *Der Freischütz*, and *Oberon*.

32. *Neue Zeitschrift für Musik* (1886, S. 549) on the December 6 performance. The cast: Sthamer-Andriessen (Armide), Metzler-Loewy and Artner (Her Companions), Moran-Olden (Fury of Hate), Baumann (Lucinde), Lederer (Rinaldo), Köhler (Arant), Hedmondt (Artemidoro), Perron (Ubald), and Schelper (King of Damascus).

33. MBR, No. 40.

34. The *Leipziger Tageblatt* of January 9 announced that Nikisch would remain in Leipzig, but its January 11 issue contradicted this news.

35. In January, Mahler conducted *Tannhäuser, Rienzi, Les Huguenots, Le Prophète, Hans Heiling,* and *Faust* I and II.

36. MBR, No. 41.

37. See AMM, page 140.

38. See *Neue Zeitschrift für Musik.* Cast: Sthamer-Andriessen (Sieglinde), Moran-Olden (Brünnhilde), Scherenberg (Fricka), Lederer (Siegmund), Schelper (Wotan), Grengg (Hunding). During February, Mahler conducted ten performances: *Il Barbiere di Siviglia, Così fan tutte, Das Nachtlager von Granada,* Hermann Goetz's *Der Widerspenstigen Zähmung, Carmen, Der fliegende Holländer, Das Rheingold, Die Walküre* (3).

39. It has even been said (see RHM, page 347) that the various illnesses that had happy consequences for Mahler's career (that of Nikisch in Leipzig, of Bülow in Hamburg, and of Jahn in Vienna) finally gave Mahler a guilt complex.

40. In his book *Moderne Dirigenten,* published in Munich in 1900, the Munich critic Arthur Seidl recalls the performances of the *Ring* conducted by Mahler in Leipzig. According to him, at that time Mahler employed "a quite insupportably slow tempo in all the adagio passages, a real riot of slowness, to the extent that the wind instruments were left completely breathless."

41. Pauline Lucca (1841–1908), a Viennese soprano, specialized in the roles of Carmen, Zerlina, Selika in *L'Africaine.* She began her career in Olmütz and later sang in Prague, Berlin, and Vienna, where she was an honorary member of the opera. She toured all over the world giving concerts.

42. Casts: *Carmen*—Lucca (Carmen), Baumann (Micaëla), Metzler-Loewy (Mercedes), Artner (Frasquita), Hedmondt (Don José), Perron (Escamillo), Grengg (Zuniga); *Der Widerspenstigen Zähmung*—Lucca (Kätchen), Scherenberg (Bianca), Hedmondt (Lucentio), Schelper (Petrucchio).

43. *Musikalisches Wochenblatt,* 1887, pages 160–161. Cast of *Jean de Paris:* Baumann (Princesse de Navarre), Metzler-Loewy (Lorezza), Artner (Olivier), Hedmondt (Jean de Paris), Schelper (Senechal), Proft (Rodrigo).

44. *Les Contes d'Hoffmann* (4), *Der Templer und die Jüdin, Rienzi* (2), *Lohengrin* (2), *Das Rheingold* (2), *Die Walküre* (2), *Don Giovanni, Zar und Zimmermann, Fidelio.*

45. Letter to his parents of April 15. In the Rosé Collection.

46. MBR, No. 44.

47. Particularly the first finale, *"Leb'wohl du warmes Sonnenlicht."* The March 26 cast —Moran-Olden (Leonore), Artner (Marzelline), Lederer (Florestan), Schelper (Pizarro), Köhler (Rocco).

48. According to him, Bülow had first used this effect in the Finale to Beethoven's *Fifth Symphony.*

49. In 1892 in London Mahler incensed the critics by adopting a far slower tempo for the first bars than for the rest of the Allegro.

50. MBR, No. 44.

51. Letter of April 30 to his parents (Rosé Collection). The *Fidelio* cast as for March 26 except for: Sthamer-Andriessen (Leonore) and Grengg (Pizarro). The *Musikalisches Wochenblatt* declared that Mahler had conducted "with élan and fire." Three days after this performance of *Fidelio,* Mahler and Busoni took part in an evening's entertainment dedicated to the memory of the poet Uhland. Busoni was then living in Leipzig, but this is the only meeting of the two musicians about which we have any precise information.

52. Letter of April 15 to his parents. In the Rosé Collection.

53. Letter of May 13 to his parents. Rosé Collection.

54. Letter of May 13 to his parents. In the Rosé Collection.

55. *Neue Zeitschrift für Musik* (1887, page 213), *Leipziger Nachrichten* (May 15), and *Leipziger Tageblatt* (June 3). Cast: Moran-Olden (Brünnhilde) Metzler-Loewy

(Erda), Baumann (Waldvogel), Lederer (Siegfried), Perron (Wotan), Köhler (Albericht), Grengg (Fafner).

56. Mahler, in a letter to his parents, May 23. Rosé Collection.

57. It is curious to notice that from the time of Nikisch's return to Leipzig, the conductor's name was not indicated on the theater's announcements, so that it became impossible to know with certainty which of the two it was.

In May, Mahler conducted, besides *Siegfried, Jean de Paris* (2), *Don Giovanni, Der Templer und die Jüdin, Der Widerspenstigen Zähmung, Carmen, Les Contes d'Hoffmann, Der fliegende Holländer, Tannhäuser,* and *Die Walküre.*

58. Letter of early June to his parents. Rosé Collection.

59. The cast of *Siegfried* was that of the premiere with these exceptions: Sthamer-Andriessen (Brünnhilde) and a guest, Jaeger (Siegfried).

60. *Leipziger Abendzeitung,* May 20, 1911.

61. See Steinitzer, *Mahler in Leipzig* (*Anbruch: Mahler Heft,* 1920, page 296; BSP, page 10).

62. According to Steinitzer, Mahler thus designated the demoniac inspiration of certain music he composed in Leipzig—the principal theme of the *Totenfeier,* for example, and that of the finale of the *Titan.*

63. Busoni lived in Leipzig from December 1, 1886, and returned there after each of his concert tours. Grieg and Delius also lived in Leipzig at this period, but Mahler seems not to have been in touch with them.

64. See the *Leipziger Nachrichten* of May 2. At this concert, dedicated to the memory of the poet Uhland, Busoni played the Bach D Minor Toccata, transcribed by Tausig, and Liszt's Fantasia on *Lucrezia Borgia,* while Mahler accompanied the singers. Steinitzer did not recall seeing the two musicians talking together but noted that they belonged to the same circle. They met again in Hamburg and Vienna, where Busoni played several times when Mahler conducted, but they only became close friends in New York during the last two years of Mahler's life.

65. A striking similarity has never, to my knowledge, been noticed, between bars 32 and 33 of the final Rondo of the sonata and bar 7 of the Coda to the Finale of Mahler's *Fourth Symphony* (Mahler Gesellschaft ed., seventh bar after figure 12).

## CHAPTER 12

1. The history of *Die drei Pintos* was related in detail by Weber's grandson in an article published in the *Neue Zeitschrift für Musik* in 1888.

2. This became, in Mahler's version, the first number of Act II.

3. See NBL, pages 169–70. Mahler stated that he had made a certain number of changes in the libretto unknown to Karl von Weber.

4. See his letter to his parents from Reichenhall on July 28. In the Arnold Rosé Collection.

5. He was again assigned *Rienzi, Der fliegende Holländer, Tannhäuser, Lohengrin, Carmen,* and *Les Contes d'Hoffmann*—or at least these were the works in his repertoire which were given in August. As we have seen, the conductor's name was not mentioned on the programs except for premieres and a few other exceptional performances.

6. See Mahler's letters and postcards to his parents dated September 7, the end of September, the beginning of October, and October 8, 1887, in the Rosé Collection.

7. With Marcella Sembrich as guest artist.

8. This lied was probably composed about 1883 but contains a wind instrument accompaniment which implies that Mahler had the theater in mind when he composed it. This performance marked the occasion of the centenary of the first performance of *Don Giovanni.* The translation was by Ludwig Braunfels and the scenic adaptation by the Leipzig stage director Ernst Gettke.

9. Mahler and Strauss had been in contact, at least by letter, before this date, for a

card survives that Mahler wrote in Munich on January 2, 1886, to thank Strauss and send him New Year wishes. Nevertheless, the first important meeting of the two young masters can be considered that of October 1887, for the Strauss letter quoted here clearly says: "I have made the acquaintance . . ."

10. See Max Steinitzer: *Richard Strauss,* page 68, and the correspondence of Strauss and Bülow (*Strauss Jahrbuch,* 1954, Boosey and Hawkes, page 53).

11. Letter from Bülow to Strauss, March 27, 1888 (*ibid.,* page 59).

12. Strauss's letter to Bülow of April 7, 1888 (*ibid.,* page 60).

13. Letter to his parents, early November, in the Rosé Collection.

14. Mahler's letter to his parents, early November, in the Rosé Collection.

15. Mahler's letter to his parents at the end of November, in the Rosé Collection.

16. The first lieder from *Des Knaben Wunderhorn* are generally dated 1888, but Max Steinitzer (*Der Anbruch, Mahler Heft,* page 297) says that he saw together at Mahler's both the sketches of the *Titan* and the completed lieder from the *Wunderhorn,* notably *"Das Himmlische Leben"* (the future finale of the *Fourth Symphony,* completed in Hamburg in 1892).

17. The working titles of the *First Symphony* and the first movement of the *Second.*

18. AMM, page 140.

19. Alexander Eduard Carl Maria von Weber, born November 19, 1849, was the son of Max Maria Christian Philipp von Weber, a railway engineer and the biographer of his famous father, and of Catharina Huberta Cramer. Captain in the Saxon army, he married Marion Mathilde Schwalbe, who was of Jewish extraction (March 25, 1856–April 10, 1931). They had three children. One, Katharina Maria Maximiliane (1878–1946). Another, Adolf Eduard Carl Maria Herbert (1879–1914), who became an officer like his father and was killed at the start of the First World War. Karl von Weber died as the result of a riding accident in 1897. His sister Maria married Ernst von Wildenbuch and lived in Vienna.

20. Ethel Smyth considered Mahler "far and away the finest conductor I ever knew," a performer with "the most all-embracing musical instinct." However, she admits that she did not get on with him in Leipzig, being "too young and raw then to appreciate this good personality." All contact with him then seemed like "handling a bomb cased in razor-edges." (Ethel Smyth: *Impressions That Remained* (II page 165–166).

21. NBL, page 150.

22. December—*Jessonda* (2), *Der Freischütz, Il Trovatore, Lohengrin, Die Loreley,* and *Oberon;* January—*Rienzi, Aïda, Robert le Diable, Tannhäuser, Don Giovanni,* and *Die drei Pintos* (2).

23. At the twelfth Gewandhaus concert, on January 5, Tchaikovsky conducted his *First Suite* for orchestra. On the sixth, the Lisztverein organized an evening of his chamber music at the Gewandhaus with the violinist Carl Halir, the pianist Siloti and the Petri Quartet. The program included the *Trio Opus 50,* the *Quartet Opus 11* and a piano *Fantasy on Themes from Onegin.* The above information comes from the Russian composer's private diary, his letters to his brother Modeste, and a chronology of his life and works (Moscow 1940).

24. NBL, page 34.

25. In the magazine *Musical America* dated April 10, 1938, Paul Stefan published an article in which he mentions Mahler's "four youthful symphonies," which, according to him, still existed in Frau von Weber's library in Dresden. It seems that Joseph Willem Mengelberg and Max von Schillings spent the whole of one night sight reading them, and were "deeply moved." This is an astonishing statement, especially as far as Schillings was concerned, since he was notoriously anti-Semitic and was extremely scornful about both Mahler's music and personality. Mahler, upon giving the manuscripts to Marion von Weber, is supposed to have made her promise to oppose in every possible way any public performance of these works. Unfortunately the villa and the library were destroyed by Allied bombs on the night of February 13, 1945. It must be

noted that Alfredo Casella, the composer, in an article written no doubt after Mahler himself had given him the information, mentions "four youthful symphonies," the scores of which he had destroyed (SIM, 1910, VI, 4, 239).

26. MBR, No. 56.

27. Mahler, in a letter to his parents of January 21, in the Rosé Collection.

28. This assertion is not completely correct: in the students' chorus, only the melody sung by the tenor (Gaston) and, in the *"Kater Mansor,"* only the idea of the text were Mahler's (L. Hartmann, *Die Musik,* V, 17, page 303). At the time, Mahler appears to have been unaware that a detailed description of Weber's manuscript had appeared in Jahn's Weber catalogue in 1871.

29. Letter of January 23, 1888, to Heinrich Fischer (*Stadtarchiv Iglau, Schriftliche Verlassenschaften. Einzelpersonen*).

30. Letter to his parents of January 29, 1888, in the Rosé Collection.

31. Letter to his parents of February 1888, in the Rosé Collection.

32. *Ibid.*

33. Cast: Artner (Eva), Neuhaus (Magdalena), Hübner (Walther), Schelper (Sachs), Goldberg (Beckmesser).

34. Letter to his parents of February 14 or 21, in the Rosé Collection.

35. This untranslatable pun on the names of Mahler and Weber made the rounds of Germany. It is not likely, however, that the king really was the first to say it. (See the letter sent to Strauss by Bülow, mentioning *Die drei Pintos,* quoted above.)

36. In a letter to his parents of February 1888. All the letters that Mahler sent his parents in February and March 1888 seem to have survived, doubtless because all of them allude to *Die drei Pintos,* the biggest event in his life up to then.

37. The dates of the various *Drei Pintos* openings in 1888 are as follows: Hamburg (April 5), Munich (in two acts, April 10), Dresden (May 2), Kassel (October 2); in 1891: Berlin (July 4 in the Lessing Theater under Angelo Neumann's management). Mahler himself conducted the first Prague performance on September 18. In Hamburg the best-known critic, Josef Sittard, praised Mahler's skill and mastery but had several reservations, particularly regarding the orchestration, which he sometimes considered too heavy. Nevertheless he thought it impossible to distinguish between Weber's style and Mahler's and in his opinion the work was a happy addition to the repertoire. In Berlin almost all Neumann's singers were from the Prague Theater; the work was conducted by Muck and staged by Elmblad. The well-known musicologist Heinrich Reimann published a very unfavorable report in the *Musikalisches Wochenblatt.* He considered Mahler's effort a total failure, his work was "neither discrete nor skillful enough," the instrumentation was "often harsh and unlike Weber." He thought it "criminal" to have added an accompaniment to the well-known canon in Act III.

38. See NBL, page 150.

39. I have dated this important letter in the Rosé Collection as follows: Mahler announced for "Friday" the premiere of *Die drei Pintos* in Hamburg, and for the next Wednesday that in Munich. These performances took place on Saturday, April 5, and Wednesday, April 9. The letter, then, was written between Saturday, March 29, and Wednesday, April 1. On Friday, March 28, however, Mahler wrote to Bülow that he was about to complete the symphony and wanted to play it to him. This letter appears in one of the catalogues of the autograph dealer Liepmannsohn.

40. MBR, No. 47.

41. NBL, page 162.

42. This information, given to Natalie Bauer-Lechner by Mahler, is confirmed by the manuscript of the lied, which, coming from her collection, is now in the Stanford University Library in California. The paper is the same as that which Mahler used for other 1888 sketches, notably those of the *Totenfeier.*

43. An anonymous pamphlet published in Leipzig in 1889 (*Unser Stadttheater durch*

*ungefärbte Gläser besehen*) refers to the "scandals" of the previous years and criticizes the "cynicism" of Goldberg, Staegemann's principal adviser.

44. The bracketed phrase is not in the text.

45. MBR, No. 57.

46. *Leipziger Musik und Kunstzeitung* (V, 1888).

47. See *Neue Zeitschrift für Musik*, May 11, 1888. Cast of *Fernand Cortez:* Sthamer-Andriessen (Amazily), Lederer (Cortez).

48. Letter of May 12 to his parents, in the Rosé Collection. The projected performance never occurred, for on August 1, Mahler wrote his parents that he was to return to Dresden to play through his symphony for Schuch again.

49. Letter of May 12 to his parents, in the Rosé Collection.

50. He would have replaced the first *Kapellmeister*, Felix Otto Dessoff, who was retiring. This would have meant two months' vacation and a yearly salary of ten thousand marks.

51. Two letters to Staegemann (MBR, No. 59, and the HLG Collection) testify to the excellent relations that existed between Mahler and Staegemann after the former's departure from Leipzig.

52. Card of May 23 from Munich to his parents.

53. AMM, page 416.

54. Letter written to a Dresden friend, very probably Ludwig Hartmann, in the HLG Collection.

55. Mahler himself said that this finale expresses "the despair of a profoundly wounded heart."

56. Letter published in *Der Anbruch, Mahler Heft,* page 297.

57. The confirmation of this news was given on July 15 in the Prague paper *Bohemia,* which stated that Mahler had already arrived for the first rehearsals.

58. See Chapter 10.

59. Was it because of the new conflict (see below) between Mahler and Neumann that the Berlin performances were canceled and the *Pintos* only given there by the famous impresario three years later, with the Prague opera company?

60. Cast: Betty Frank (Clarissa), Le Pirk (Laura), Hilgermann (Inez), Wallnöfer (Gaston), Perluss (Gomez), Sieglitz (Ambrosio), Ehrl (Pinto), Dobsch (Pantaleone).

61. It is easy to calculate this date to within a few days, from a few short notices in the Prague papers, which on the second and the sixth announced that Mahler had started rehearsals and on the twelfth announced that his work in Prague was over.

62. Karl Muck finally conducted the *Barbier* instead of Mahler. It is surprising that, after once more leaving Neumann under such circumstances, ten years later Mahler conducted twice running at his invitation.

63. Paraphrase of a line by the poet August Platen.

64. David Popper (1843–1913) had been a professor at the Budapest Conservatory since 1886 and played an important part in the musical life of the city. He and the violinist Hubay founded the Hubay-Popper quartet. Popper was Hungarian by adoption but was spending a few days in Prague, his birthplace, on the way back from a concert tour in England. He had no doubt also heard about Mahler from their mutual friend, the musicologist Guido Adler. Popper was well known for his generosity in helping young musicians. In particular he arranged to teach at the Vienna Conservatory and sit on the board of directors of the Philharmonic Orchestra. It was also thanks to Popper that Arnold Rosé became the Philharmonic's *Konzertmeister* (Kretschmann: *Tempi passati*, II, page 190).

65. According to Steinberg's daughter, Gisela Steinberg-Wien, they waited from one to three o'clock. Mahler was finishing the *Totenfeier* at that time (*Neues Wiener Journal*—June 29, 1921).

66. Most of these facts come from an article published by Steinberg on May 17 and June 3, 1911, in the *Prager Abendblatt* at the time of Mahler's death.

67. According to the *Fremdenliste* (list of visitors) in the newspaper *Pester Lloyd,* Mahler arrived in Budapest on September 26 and stayed at the Jägerhorn Hotel; the period of uncertainty had lasted four whole months.

68. Letter to a friend in Dresden (HLG Collection). Mahler was not wrong in this conjecture, for during the two and a half years he spent in Budapest, he managed to compose only a few *Wunderhorn Lieder,* and these during his vacation.

69. It did not yet have the title *Titan.* Sometimes Mahler spoke of his "symphony" and sometimes of his "symphonic poem."

70. Catalogue of the autograph dealer Liepmannssohn.

71. Fritz Löhr has mistakenly dated letter No. 48 as 1888. Its contents clearly show that it was written later, no doubt in 1889.

72. *Bohemia* states clearly that the news was published in the Dresden newspapers.

73. *Prager Tagblatt* (August 23); *Bohemia* (July 20 and 22); *Prager Abendblatt* (August 2).

74. "Help me a little if you can," Mahler wrote in this letter of July or August 1888 (Dr. F. Strauss Collection).

75. He asks him to reply before the end of August, because he wishes to copy the score and the orchestra material for the Dresden, Viennese, Munich, and Prague orchestras before the start of the season (*Stadtarchiv,* Leipzig). Paul Bernhard Limburger, a businessman who was in turn consul in Frankfurt, Italy, Baden, and Leipzig, had been president of the Gewandhaus concerts since 1881.

## CHAPTER 13

1. Much of the information in this chapter comes from an important article by Alexander Jemnitz: *"Gustav Mahler als königlicher ungarischer Hofoperndirektor"* (*Der Auftakt, Musikblätter,* Prague, Jahr XVI, 1936, S. 7ff).

2. Beniczky was secretary of state to the minister of the interior until July 1889, when he was made intendant and *Geheimrat* (privy councilor).

3. Mahler and Mottl never knew each other well and probably had little mutual respect. Nevertheless it is interesting to note that three times Mottl almost got Mahler's jobs: in 1888 in Budapest and in 1897 and 1907 in Vienna. An article in the musical journal *Zenelap* published on September 30 states that Mottl had been approached, but refused the offer, knowing that "he could not succeed where Erkel had failed," that "the best conductors in Europe would be unable to surpass him," and that "a foreigner could not take his place successfully."

4. Probably Staegemann also recommended Mahler to Beniczky, doubtless preferring to see him work anywhere but Prague.

5. See BMG, page 13. At the time Karpath was considering a career as an operatic bass, but also acting as a critic. Mahler engaged him at the end of November, but Karpath left the opera after a few months.

6. Cf. F. Bonis: *Gustav Mahler and Ferenc Erkel* (*Studia musicologica* I, 3–4, 1961, page 478).

7. The music critics of these papers were Stefan Kereszty and Desider Ambrozovitz (*see* Jemnitz, *op. cit.*).

8. Kornél Ábrányi, Sr. (1822–1903), a mediocre composer, founded the Hungarian Conservatory, directed by Liszt, and also the first Hungarian musical review, *Zenészeti Lapok.* He also founded a choir. He was a fervent admirer of the great foreign musicians, Wagner, Berlioz, Bülow. With the help of the composer Erkel he arranged for the Hungarian Opera to invite Wagner to conduct one of his operas. He was the son of a Hungarian aristocrat and had incurred his father's wrath by studying music, first in Munich, where he met Liszt, then in Paris. Critic of the *Pesti Napló,* he was to write a long work on *Hungarian Music in the XIXth Century,* in which Mahler is unjustly treated.

9. The article in the *Zenelap* of September 29 deplored that "most of the orchestra" spoke German and talked that language more willingly than Hungarian, which should have made Mahler's task easier.

10. This is rather surprising, since Mahler wrote to a friend in Dresden, before leaving Vienna, in order to ask him what were "the intentions" of the Munich Opera intendant. Perhaps he had received an offer from him in the course of the preceding week. The *Neues Pester Journal* published the same information on October 2 but spoke of an engagement in Dresden rather than Munich.

11. Viktor von Herzfeld, the Budapest critic and fellow student of Mahler at the conservatory, in his October 11 account of this ceremony, noted the absence of Sándor Erkel and that of "many of the orchestral musicians." Could they have already heard of Mahler's difficult and demanding nature?

12. *Neues Pester Journal,* October 3. On October 22, Mahler was to be presented to Orczy, the minister of the interior.

13. She had created the role of Inez in *Die drei Pintos.* Mahler tried to engage her for Budapest, but, according to the anonymous pamphlet already mentioned (*Unser Stadttheater durch ungefärbte Gläser besehen,* see Chapter 12), Staegemann refused to release her before making sure it was too late for her to accept the offer.

14. From Dr. Anton Radó.

15. Bianca Bianchi (her real name was Bertha Schwartz) (1858–1947), a famous light soprano born in Heidelberg, was a pupil of Pauline Viardot-Garcia. She made her debut in 1873 in Karlsruhe. Later she married Bernhard Pollini, director of the Hamburg Opera. After his death, she taught singing in Munich and Strasbourg.

16. Alszeghy was introduced officially on November 15 (*Neues Pester Journal*). Another engagement that seems to have been considered was that of August Stoll, Mahler's future collaborator and stage director in Vienna (see *Zenelap,* September 29.)

17. Cf. F. Bonis (quoted earlier). Bonis proves, with the help of four letters from Mahler to Erkel and one statistic, that relations between the two musicians were much better than Ábrányi suggests in *Hungarian Music in the XIXth Century.* Of twenty-eight new works and revivals, eight of the works given at the Budapest Opera under Mahler's direction were Hungarian. This is all the more remarkable since, apart from Erkel, at that time Hungary had no important dramatic composer.

18. The search for new singers was particularly difficult in Hungary, which had only the Budapest Opera; thus no talent could be discovered easily from provincial scources.

19. Cf. Gisela Steinberg-Wien (see Chapter 12). After the first full rehearsal, during which the singer made several mistakes, forgetting pauses and fermatas, Mahler said to her, "You have a good voice, you're hired, but from a musical point of view you're only a baby."

20. Two letters were written to Alfred Fischhof, who was the brother of Robert, Mahler's fellow student and the husband of the well-known coloratura Sigrid Arnoldson, whom Mahler was to engage in 1889.

21. Two letters to the Vienna agent Wild, the first dated January 16, 1889. They were sold by auction by the Marburg firm of Stargardt in November 1965. They speak of the hiring of the soprano Ludmilla Kupfer-Berger. The new singers needed an extensive repertoire of at least twenty-five or thirty roles, for in Budapest "the public is so small that we can only give the works once a month!" They also had to accept short-term contracts and modest salaries, for economy was the order of the day.

22. The *Neues Pester Journal* of October 20 announced her engagement for the role of Brünnhilde.

23. After the first *Walküre* performance the critic Beer judged that this lowering was better for the spectator than for the listener.

24. Cf. "Mahler in Budapest," by Jenő Mohácsi (*Moderne Welt, Mahler Heft*, III, 7, 27).

25. BMG, page 22.

26. Cast on January 18: Beeth (Clarissa), Forster (Inez), Marie Renard (Laura), Schrödter (Gaston), Mayerhofer (Pantaleone), Müller (Gomez), Felix (Ambrosio), Reichenberg (Pinto), Hablawetz (Wirth).

27. Viktor von Herzfeld said that the cause of this fire, which almost started again the following day, was a badly insulated electric wire leading to the footlights.

28. Cast: *Das Rheingold:* Rotter (Freia), Heussler (Fricka), Broulik (Loge), Dalnoky (Mime), Ney (Wotan), Takáts (Alberich), Odry and Tallián (Giants); *Die Walküre:* Maleczky (Sieglinde), Szilágyi (Brünnhilde), Fleissig (Fricka), Broulik (Siegmund), Ney (Wotan), Szendrői (Hunding).

29. Edmund von Mihalovics (1842–1929), a Hungarian aristocrat and composer, a pupil of Liszt and Bülow, composer of four operas, including a *Wieland der Schmied,* (after Wagner's unfinished libretto). He succeeded Liszt as president-director of the Musical Academy of Budapest. Hans Kössler (1853–1926), German composer and organist, professor at the Budapest Conservatory, friend of Brahms. It was he who took Brahms to hear Mahler conduct *Don Giovanni.* Viktor von Herzfeld (1856–1920), Hungarian composer and music critic, second violin of the Hubay-Popper Quartet. He had been awarded the Beethoven Prize in 1881, one of the prizes that Mahler vainly had tried to win with *Das klagende Lied* (see Chapter VI). Jenő Hubay (1858–1937), celebrated Hungarian violin virtuoso, prolific composer, and founder with David Popper of the Hubay-Popper Quartet.

30. Dr. Max Falk, politician and editor in chief of the *Pester Lloyd.* Siegmund Singer, Budapest correspondent of the *Neue Freie Presse,* then Falk's successor as editor in chief of the *Pester Lloyd.*

31. The Iglau police records show that Mahler remained until at least February 22.

32. *György Brankovics* had not been performed for some fifteen years. Ferenc Erkel (1810–93), conductor, composer of nine Hungarian operas and his country's national anthem, was president of the Musical Academy before Mihalovics. His sons Sándor and Gyula were both conductors at the Budapest Opera after him. The second left the Budapest Opera in 1888. In a letter dated November 29, 1888, Mahler asks Erkel to let him know as soon as possible how he intends to cast *György Brankovics.*

33. On March 30, Mahler had written to his mother that he feared he would not get to Iglau to see Dr. Spitz, who was taking care of her. But we know from the *Pester Lloyd* that he was away from Budapest at the beginning of April.

34. Article in the *Pester Lloyd* of April 27. Cast: Bianchi (Susanna), Maleczky (Countess), Gabos (Cherubino), Ney (Figaro), Mannheit (Count).

35. MBR, page 479, note 47.

36. See MBR, No. 60.

37. The conflict must have been settled later, as Prevost was still at the Budapest Opera in 1890.

38. See articles of May 11 and 12 by Viktor von Herzfeld in the *Neues Pester Journal.*

## CHAPTER 14

1. MBR, page 480.

2. The light soprano Sigrid Arnoldson (1861–1943), a pupil of Désirée Artot,

quickly became successful in coloratura roles. She married the impresario Alfred Fischhof and at the end of her career taught singing in Vienna.

3. MBR, No. 48. This note was written on July 18 or 19, 1889, and not in 1888.

4. Pierson and Erkel corresponded that summer regarding the possibility of engaging the Hungarian conductor for the Berlin Opera (Hungarian National Library).

5. According to Fritz Löhr (MBR, page 480).

6. According to MBR, No. 48, and the note Mihalovics wrote to Erkel from Budapest on July 22, 1889 (Hungarian National Library).

7. Undated letter in the Hungarian National Library.

8. Letter from Mahler to Erkel in the Hungarian National Library.

9. See MBR, No. 48, probably written at the end of July 1889, and footnote 48.

10. Mahler's last letter to his mother, written after his return to Budapest late in August 1889, in the Rosé Collection.

11. See the *Pester Lloyd* of September 14. Mahler almost certainly learned this speech phonetically, as he does not ever seem to have spoken or understood Hungarian.

12. Cast: Bianchi (Elsa), Szilágyi (Ortrud), Broulik (Lohengrin), Takáts (Telramund), Mannheit (Herald), Ney (King).

13. At least according to an item published in the *Pester Lloyd*.

14. See MBR, footnote No. 50, page 480.

15. The police reports indicate that Poldi died at her home, Wallensteinstrasse 7, of "meningitis." Other sources indicate a cerebral tumor, and this hypothesis seems more likely.

16. At least the text of MBR, No. 64, gives this impression. Also it was Justi and not Mahler who signed the official documents when Marie died.

17. See MBR, No. 52, page 481.

18. Cast: Bianchi (Frau Fluth), Ábrányi, and Fleissig; Ney (Falstaff), Broulik, Takáts, Szendrői, Hegedűs, and Dalnoky.

19. On October 1 an article in the *Pester Lloyd* mentions that a *"Second Symphony"* by Mahler—*Totenfeier*—is to be given during the winter by the Munich Philharmonic, under the direction of General-Musikdirektor Levi. So at this time Mahler was thinking of having the *Totenfeier* performed as well.

20. This conclusion is nonetheless entirely faithful to the general style. Clearly, what worried Beer, though he did not wish to admit it, was the over-all conception and style of these lieder.

21. This letter was reproduced in facsimile in Béla Csuka's book *Kilenc évtizes a magyar zene*, pages 30 to 33.

22. This refers to the andante that Mahler later cut.

23. It was made up of Cherubini's overture to *Les Abencerages*, Mahler's "Symphonic Poem," two arias of Cherubino from *Le Nozze di Figaro* sung by Hermine Braga, and a *Prelude, Chorale, and Fugue* of Bach transcribed by d'Albert.

24. In a letter dated March 26, 1891, Justine Mahler asks the impresario Rosenberg, on her brother's behalf, to send him some caricatures that appeared in the newspaper *Bolond Istók*, and in particular the one that referred to the first performance of the "Symphonic Poem."

25. The italics are mine.

26. This critic maintained that in the Introduction Mahler had wished to describe stags and boars fleeing terrified before the huntsmen.

27. *Op. cit.*

28. NBL, page 152.

29. Cast on November 19 (according to the poster that Löhr took from Budapest,

HLG Collection): Radics (Rachel), Ábrányi (Eudoxie), Broulik (Eleazar), Szegedi (Major-domo), Ney (Brogni), Hegedűs (Albert).

30. Laura Hilgermann and her husband Rosenberg were shortly to settle in Budapest. Mahler remained on friendly terms with them and wrote them a certain number of letters. In 1899 he engaged Hilgermann for Vienna.

31. The doubling of the wind instruments, and in particular of the oboe solo, the introduction of the E flat clarinet, and the slow tempo of the Scherzo were always to be the most striking factors of Mahler's "version" of Beethoven's *Fifth*. Most of the critics greeted them with indignation.

32. This trip seems to have been prolonged from March 20 to the beginning of April. At Iglau, Mahler signed some documents concerned with his parents' wills.

33. Cast: Szilágyi (Die Jüdin), Rotter (Rowena), Broulik (Ivanhoë), Takáts (Der Templer), Ney (Bruder Tuck).

34. Letter to Staegemann written toward the close of 1889, in the HLG Collection.

35. MBR, No. 71.

36. See NBL, page 5.

37. In an article in the *Neues Pester Journal* of December 1, 1889, Herzfeld mentioned the rumors circulating in Budapest about the persistent refusal of the minister of the interior to "ratify" Mahler's contract. The contract had been drawn and signed by Orczky, the former minister: it was valid up to December 31, 1899, and needed no "ratification."

38. In the Hungarian National Library there is a letter from Mahler to Erkel dated March 10, 1890, concerning the performance of his operas *Bánk-bán* and *Hunyadi László,* only the first of which was performed during Mahler's directorship.

39. Early in the 1889–90 season, and again during the next season, Herzfeld had listed among the new productions Mihalovics' *Toldi Szerelme,* but Mahler never, in the end, could bring himself to give it its first performance.

40. Articles in the *Zenelap* of January 30 and March 1, 1890.

41. When Hilgermann left Prague, Neumann brought a suit against her for breach of contract.

42. It is impossible to determine exactly which performances in 1888–89 were conducted by Sándor Erkel and which by his brother Ladislaus: the only available sources mention only the family name.

43. See MBR, No. 74, and NBLS.

44. See MBR, page 482, note 59. This was the villa of a Frau Lehnart, located at No. 12 Weissenbachstrasse.

45. Mahler described his Budapest trip to Justi in a letter written shortly after his return to Hinterbrühl. In the Rosé Collection.

## CHAPTER 15

1. In the nineteenth century, cold-water cures had a reputation disproportionate to their therapeutic values. Fifty years earlier, Wagner almost killed himself with stubbornly inflicted orgies of cold water.

2. It would be interesting to know which lied this was, but Mahler does not mention the title to Justi, stating only that it is "quite pretty" [*ganz hübsch*].

3. Letter to Justi of June 1890 in the Rosé Collection.

4. These were the two last volumes published by Schott in 1892; nine lieder, of which the first were no doubt composed in 1887–88 (see Appendix 3).

5. Letter from Mahler to the Vienna agent Bernhard Wild (Stargardt Auction, November 1965).

6. NBLS.

7. Herzfeld's article (September 26, 1890) states that the Countess Vasquez, "finally reconciled to destiny and her velvet domino," this time sang the role of

Elvira. The singer, although one of Mahler's discoveries, seems to have incurred his wrath several times.

8. Before this they were replaced by spoken dialogue.

9. Wishing to speed up the action, Mahler cut two arias, Don Ottavio's "Il mio tesoro" and Donna Anna's "Non mi dir."

10. Cast: Szilágyi (Donna Anna), Maleczky (Donna Elivira), Bárdosy (Zerlina), Takáts (Don Giovanni), Broulik (Don Ottavio), Szendrői (Masetto), Odry (Commendatore).

11. See Alexander Jemnitz, op. cit.

12. See the article written by Beer two months before Mahler's departure (Pester Lloyd, January 30, 1891).

13. "The real reason for Újházy's departure must be entirely different from that given out by the intendant," Herzfeld wrote. He had read in the Pesti Napló that "experience showed this position to be unnecessary."

14. Count Zichy (1849–1924), son of a rich Hungarian magnate, lost an arm in a hunting accident when he was fourteen. This misfortune did not prevent him from continuing his musical education, and he acquired, under the direction of Mayrberger, Volkmann, and Liszt, a prodigious virtuosity with his left hand. At first an official at the National Hungarian Ministry of Education, Zichy wrote a comic play, a novel, and poems, and composed choral works and many virtuosic piano pieces. President of the Landes-Musikakademie, he made long tours each year giving charity recitals.

15. The rough draft of this letter is in the Rosé Collection. Two weeks later, "at a risk of breaking off the negotiations," Mahler repeated his demand in another letter, adding that the salary should be net and free from all deductions. By November 7 he had already received a draft contract, but before signing it he insisted that Pollini insert this clause. He also demanded that the salary be paid in nine monthly installments (MBR, No. 104 [dated October 14], 105, 106).

16. Lilli Lehmann (1848–1933) born in Würzburg, was able to continue singing a wide range of parts until quite late in life, thanks to her superb technical skill and her quite exceptional vocal gifts. She sang everything from Traviata, Norma, Philine (from Mignon), and even Konstanze (from Entführung), to Fidelio, Isolde, and Brünnhilde. She started her career as a coloratura singer in Berlin and before her Budapest appearance had just spent two years in the United States, where she married the tenor Kalisch. From then on she undertook long "guest star" tours each year and was universally acclaimed and admired.

Antonie Schläger (1860–1910) was an Austrian who sang in operetta before becoming leading dramatic soprano of the Vienna Opera, where she remained until 1896.

Luise von Ehrenstein (1867–1944) was a well-known Austrian singer who appeared at the Vienna Opera during Mahler's first years as director there. She left as the result of an unhappy incident (see Chapter 26) but ended her days as a teacher of singing in her home town.

Marie Schröder-Hanfstängel (1848–1917) was born in Breslau. After studying with Pauline Viardot-García, she sang in Paris, Stuttgart, New York, and Frankfurt, where she taught singing until her retirement in 1897.

17. The Szechenyi National Library archives still possess three letters from Mahler to Erkel. In the first, dated March 10, 1890, he asks the old composer to send him the piano scores of Bánk-bán and Hunyadi László, so that the singers need not work from orchestra scores (Archives No. 1253/90). The next letter concerns a gala performance given on the four hundredth anniversary of King Mathias (April 8, 1890, No. 1723/90), and the last mentions the first performance of a work of Erkel given at a concert at the opera.

18. Cast: Szilágyi (Amelia), Hilgermann (Ulrica), Bárdosy (Oscar), Prevost (Gustavo III), Mannheim (Renato), Veress (Silvano), Takáts (Samuele).

19. The *Neues Pester Journal,* quoting the *Pesti Napló,* printed a slightly different version of this incident. A dispute had broken out the preceding day between Mahler and the tenor Prevost, who had complained of the "too personal" way in which Mahler conducted, saying that "it could easily mislead the singers." As to the remark made next day by Szendrői to the stage director, it had been occasioned by a misunderstanding on Mahler's part. The stage director had stood in such a way as to hide Mahler's baton for a moment. Already displeased with the two singers because of their questionable jokes, Mahler may have thought that, like the day before, they were criticizing his conducting.

20. NBL, page 6.

21. Mahler's three letters to Natalie were sold in Vienna in 1929. Copies have survived in her unpublished manuscript.

22. Baron Alberto Franchetti (1860–1942), born in Turin, studied in Munich and Dresden. A rather mediocre composer of symphonic music and a dozen operas, he had a certain vogue in Germany and Italy at the turn of the century.

23. See the *Pester Lloyd* of November 20, 1890.

24. The correspondence that led up to this series of performances in Budapest survives in the Berlin Stadtbibliothek. We learn from it that Lehmann sang in *Lohengrin, Les Huguenots, Fidelio, Lucrezia Borgia, Mignon,* and *Don Giovanni.*

25. Clearly the trio following the duel at the start of Act I.

26. Lilli Lehmann, *Mein Weg,* page 366ff.

27. This version of the incident comes from an unsigned article in the *Neues Wiener Journal* of May 16, 1911, page 4.

28. Letter to Justi in the Rosé Collection.

29. MBR, No. 80.

30. Cast for the premiere on December 26, 1890. Szilágyi (Santuzza), Ábrányi (Lola), Heussler (Lucia), Szirovatka (Turiddu), Veres (Alfio). The performance was followed by the ballet *Csárdás.*

31. Mahler later told Natalie Bauer-Lechner that in his opinion the most important dramatic German composer after the three "greats" (Beethoven, Mozart, Wagner) was not Weber but Lortzing.

32. Cast: Ráday (Marie), Heussler (Governess), Takáts (Apprentice and Count), Ney (Armorer), Kiss (Georg), Hegedűs (Adelhof), Dalnoky (Innkeeper).

33. The rough draft of this letter was in Alma Mahler's collection. It was published in MBR as No. 108.

34. (WKL, page 135). Wilhelm Kienzl, who directed the Musikverein in Graz and had composed the then famous opera *Der Evangelimann,* had made Mahler's acquaintance in Hamburg and met him again in Budapest after rehearsal of *Le Nozze di Figaro.* On the latter occasion Mahler had talked to him about his nostalgia for Germany and "German singing."

35. See the article by Alexander Jemnitz, already mentioned.

36. The original text was by Emmanuel Geibel, with some modifications by a man named Gellart. The two leading female roles were sung by Arabella Szilágyi (Leonore) and Laura Hilgermann. The evening also included *Cavalleria rusticana* and the ballet *Sonne und Erde.*

37. See the article in the *Hamburger Signale,* March 20, 1891.

38. Ministry of the Interior, document No. 489/1891. Furthermore, Zichy's request was respected by the ministry (see article from the *Fővárosi Lapok* quoted below).

39. Herzfeld noted in an article on March 16 that Mahler and Beniczky had saved the opera a great deal more than this.

40. BMG, page 17. Mahler later learned that the arbitrary breaking of his contract

entitled him to a much larger sum in compensation. But this had not occurred to him, since no one had pointed out the legal strength of his position.

41. See "Gustav Mahler in Budapest," by Jenő Mohácsi (*Moderne Welt,* 1922, III, 7, 29).

42. See article by Jenő Mohácsi, *op. cit.*

43. Herzfeld claimed that Mahler had received, among other offers, one from the opera in New York.

44. Many of Mahler's Hungarian friends intervened on his behalf when he was being considered for the position of director of the Vienna Opera, in particular Beniczky, Max Falk, Singer, Mihalovics, and Apponyi.

45. See the article by Jenő Mohácsi, already mentioned.

46. A letter from Justi to Rosenberg, husband of the singer Laura Hilgermann, written from Vienna on March 26, gives this information.

47. Article in the *Pester Lloyd,* January 30, 1891.

48. "To interpret" in German is *nachschaffen*—"to create after" or "re-create"— and this is exactly how Mahler conceived his role as an interpreter.

## CHAPTER 16

1. Mahler's letters to Justi leave no possible doubt about this.

2. Heinrich Chevalley (in *Hundert Jahre Hamburger Stadt Theater,* page 32) states that this modernization cost 570,000 marks. Despite this, the auditorium had serious defects: it lacked access corridors, the acoustics were mediocre, and the décor was often shabby. Pollini's efforts were directed entirely toward vocal performance. Electric light was installed in the opera during the summer of 1891.

3. Up to 1892 the gulden equaled two marks. Mahler's salary was therefore equivalent to six thousand gulden, whereas at Budapest he had received ten thousand. In 1892 the rate of exchange was altered. Austria's official currency then became the crown (one gulden equaled two crowns) which was worth 0.85 mark. This new rate was unfavorable to Mahler.

4. Katharina Klafsky (1855–1896), daughter of a shoemaker from St. Johann, Hungary, made her debut as a mezzo-soprano. She had been a beggar and then a housemaid in Vienna before her employers sent her to the celebrated coach Mathilde Marchesi. She was finally discovered by Angelo Neumann, who instantly engaged her for the Leipzig Opera, and later for his traveling Wagnerian company.

5. Ernestine Schumann-Heink (1861–1936), daughter of an Austrian officer, was born near Prague. She made her debut in Dresden in 1878. Engaged for Hamburg in 1883, she went on many tours and sang each year in Bayreuth. She went to America in 1898, in Strauss's *Elektra.* Born Rössler, she used the names of her second and first husbands—the second was the actor Paul Schumann, whom she married in 1893.

6. Anna von Mildenburg mentions this constant hostility in her memoirs (*Erin-nerungen,* page 111), and relates a particularly violent quarrel between Mahler and Schumann-Heink that took place the day of the unveiling of Bülow's bust in the lobby of the Hamburg Opera. On this occasion, after Mahler had directed Sieg-fried's Funeral March, he started rehearsing the Waltraute scene from *Die Göt-terdämmerung.* During this rehearsal they exchanged bitter words, each claiming to be the one who had most respected, admired, and understood Bülow.

7. Max Alvary (1856–98) was the son of a well-known Düsseldorf painter, Andreas Achenbach. He became a singer only after completing his architectural studies—and then against his father's wishes; indeed his father demanded that Alvary change his name. After vocal studies in Italy, he fulfilled engagements in Weimar and

Munich before going to Hamburg. Chosen by Seidl, he had just sung his main Wagnerian roles at the New York Metropolitan Opera.

8. Letters of March and April 1891 to Justi, in the Rosé Collection.

9. Pollini then lived in the Rothenbaum district, at Heimhuderstrasse 54.

10. Mahler made two allusions to this in letters he wrote to Justi in April 1891 and to Laura Hilgermann early in 1892: "Don't address me as Director; it seems to irritate Pollini, who feels driven to the wall by it."

11. *Hamburgisches Fremdenblatt,* March 31, 1891. On March 29, Max Alvary was the Tannhäuser.

12. Carl F. Armbrust (1849–96), organist and son of a Hamburg organist, was at the same time director of the Bachverein and professor of piano and organ at the Hamburg Conservatory. His articles in the *Fremdenblatt,* devoted to operatic performances, were constantly favorable to Mahler, unlike those of Emil Krause, who covered concerts for the same newspaper.

13. Josef Sittard (1846–1903), born at Aix-la-Chapelle, was first a pupil, and then a professor, at the Stuttgart Conservatory. Critic of the Hamburg *Correspondent* from 1885 on, he wrote biographies, analyses, and many short books. He also composed. As soon as the subscription concerts began, he was to become Mahler's fiercest adversary.

14. Cast for the premiere: Klafsky (Brünnhilde), Max Alvary (Siegfried), Landau (Mime), Ritter (Alberich), Greve (Wanderer), Schumann-Heink (Erda), Gelber (Waldvogel), Wiegand (Fafner).

15. *Hamburgischer Correspondent,* April 1, 1891.

16. In English in the original.

17. Letter sold before World War II by the autograph dealer Liepmannssohn.

18. Hermann Wolff (1845–1902), born in Cologne, had been trained both as a businessman and a composer. After studying under Franz Kroll in Berlin, he became a composer, the music critic of the *Neue Berliner Musikzeitung* (1878–79), the co-editor of the review *Musikwelt,* and in 1881 founded his renowned concert agency. He made several concert tours with the celebrated pianist Anton Rubinstein and the no less celebrated Hans von Bülow. Having became a close friend of the latter, he organized his concert tours with the Meininger Hofkapelle as well as later those of the Berlin Philharmonic and Hamburg's New Subscription Concerts. His wife, Louise Wolff, took over the management of his agency after his death.

19. In the overture he noted the slow, measured tempo of the four measures preceding the entry of Agathe's theme; the rugged, marked accentuation of the quarter notes in the sixteenth measure of the same passage, before the fortissimo, as well as some other tempos that were taken faster than usual—for example, the introduction to the third act, Max's air and the terzetto *"O diese Sonne."*

20. Cast of the April 2 performance: Polna (Agathe), Lissmann (Aennchen), Cronberger (Max), Ritter (Ottokar), Wiegand (Caspar).

21. No other theatrical conductor seems to have had so large a salary at that time. Out of the ten thousand florins that he had received annually in Budapest, Mahler doubtless payed substantial deductions. His augmented Hamburg salary of fourteen thousand marks (seven thousand florins) was, then, only slightly smaller. According to Otto Klemperer (OKM, page 17), the increase in salary took place on the evening of his debut with *Tannhäuser:* Pollini was ill and had been obliged to remain at home. A telephone call from the opera had informed him, at the end of the second act, that the public's interest was wholly concentrated on the conductor, and it was then that he gave orders to grant this raise immediately.

22. He agreed with the tempo of the overture, a tempo that Mahler was to justify fully later in Vienna (see Chapter 26), as well as that of the Adagio of the Armed Man and the duet *"Könnte jeder brave Mann"* (at the end of the first act). Among other striking moments in this interpretation, Armbrust mentions the slowness

and mysterious pianissimo of *"Nur stille, stille"* (last scene), after which an immense forte produced a splendid effect; the slow tempo of the accompaniment of *"Die Stunde schlägt"* (Act II, terzetto, No. 19), and finally the very measured tempo of the Papageno-Papagena duet.

Cast of April 10, 1891: Polna (Pamina), Marie Katzmayr, of Rotterdam (Queen of the Night), Klafsky, Brandt, and Wiener (Three Ladies), Lissmann, Wolff, and Schumann-Heink (Three Spirits), Cronberger (Tamino), Ritter (Sarastro).

23. The Jaquino-Marcellina and Leonore-Rocco duets and the chorus *"Leb' wohl, du warmes Sonnenlicht."* Armbrust nonetheless conceded that Beethoven had marked these passages "Vivace . . . Allegro molto . . ."

24. Armbrust approved the moderate tempo of the *Fidelio* overture.

25. It is interesting to note that Mahler adopted from then on this habit, to which he remained faithful for the rest of his life. As for Armbrust, he preferred the more traditional insertion, between the two acts. Under Mahler's baton, the initial Adagio appeared as "calming oil" poured over the "furious waves" of the preceding scene. Some of Mahler's most daring innovations aroused his admiration, particularly the moderate tempo at the beginning of the Allegro and the thrice-repeated free and eloquent D G F motive, six measures before the Presto.

Cast for April 22: Klafsky (Leonore), Gritizinger (Florestan), Greve (Pizarro), Wiegand (Rocco).

26. The information given here comes from a text written by Adele Marcus's niece, Angele Mommsen.

27. Five short letters written by Mahler to Zinne can be seen at the Hamburg Library, but no reference whatsoever to any particular event allows us to establish their exact dates. It is possible that they were written during Mahler's short stay at the villa near Pollini's, for they bear an address found nowhere else in his correspondence: Oberstrasse 87.

28. The apartment they occupied that summer was at Hochstrasse 25.

29. In a letter written during the following autumn or winter to Laura Hilgermann, Mahler said that he had just composed six lieder. This letter can be dated because Mahler mentions the offer he had just received from Covent Garden.

30. Franz Jauner (1823–1900) was director of the Vienna Opera from 1877 to 1881. Ernst von Schuch was conductor and director of the Dresden Opera (see Chapter 12).

31. NBLS.

32. His 1890 trip to Italy had been undertaken mainly for business connected with the Budapest Opera.

33. On this subject, see MBR, No. 138, wrongly dated by Freund; it was written in November 1891.

34. *Ibid.*

35. MBR, No. 138.

## CHAPTER 17

1. Letter to Justine, November 22, 1891.

2. Letter to Natalie, autumn 1891.

3. Letter to Justine, September 1891.

4. The Hotel Royal, belonging to one A. Koch, was at Hohe Bleichen 12, in the center of Neustadt, a few steps from the opera (see also MBR, note page 129).

5. Letter to Justine of October 14, 1891.

6. *The Demon* had been sung in Hamburg eleven years earlier. Cast: Claus (Tamara), Lissmann (Demon).

7. This letter, dated September 13, 1891, belongs to a Hamburg lawyer named Hertz, the nephew of Hermann Behn, who was one of Mahler's closest friends in Hamburg. A letter from Löhr dated November 28 (MBR, No. 82) and a letter to Strauss refer to the visit to Bülow.

8. JFP, pages 356–57.

9. MBR, No. 82.

10. Letter of October 1891 to Richard Strauss.

11. See Chapter 8.

12. Doubtless the twelve variations for piano in A major on a *Russian Dance* by Wranitsky, composed in 1796–97.

13. JFP, page 364.

14. MBR, No. 82.

15. BWT, page 85.

16. This stormy concert was to close Bülow's activity as a conductor in Berlin, except for one last concert, in April 1893.

17. Anna Bernhardt's memories (*Neue Freie Presse,* May 8, 1927).

18. The program consisted of Berlioz's Overture to *King Lear,* Op. 4. Saint-Saëns' *Piano Concerto No. 4,* Op. 44 (soloist Teresa Carreño), Goldmark's Overture to *Sakuntala,* Op. 13, Liszt's *Hungarian Fantasy* for piano and orchestra (also with Teresa Carreño), and Beethoven's *Symphony No. 2.*

19. Letter of December 3, 1891, to Justi, in the Rosé Collection.

20. MBR, Nos. 81 and 138.

21. Letter to Justi at the end of October 1891.

22. JFP, pages 353–54.

23. The world premiere of *Eugene Onegin* had taken place in Moscow in 1879. That of Hamburg was postponed from December to January 19. The first cast of the Hamburg performance: Bettaque (Tatiana), Polna (Olga), Thomas (Larina), Cronberger (Lenski), Eichhorn (Onegin), Wiegand (Gremin).

24. Tchaikovsky came from Warsaw, where he had conducted a concert, and left for Paris on February 20.

25. Tchaikovsky, who spoke German badly, also feared that the translated libretto, which had surprised him during rehearsals, would handicap and mislead him. According to J. B. Förster, he "had already discovered Mahler's genius in Leipzig," (see Chapter 12), but this statement is in no way confirmed in the Russian master's correspondence.

26. Letter to N. G. Conradi dated January 20, 1892.

27. MBR, No. 82.

28. Letter of January 1892 to Justi.

29. Cf. Chapter 12 and Appendix 3. This was the opera for which Captain von Weber was to write the libretto, using a subject suggested by Mahler (NBL, page 162).

30. This was the future Finale of the *Fourth Symphony.*

31. NBLS, October 1900.

32. Cf. MBR, No. 47.

33. Letter of January 1892 to Justi.

34. A copy autographed in verse by Mahler ("old acquaintances newly dispatched") and dated February 1892 was sold in 1930 by the autograph dealer Liepmannssohn.

35. Letter of February 1892 to Justi.

36. Bundesstrasse 10, third floor. The building still stands. Mahler occupied two well-heated rooms in the apartment of a Widow Buchholz.

37. Karl Petersen (1809–92) was then eighty-three years old. Having studied law at Göttingen, Heidelberg, and Paris, he had begun his career as a lawyer in his native city, where he was later named senator (1855), chief of police (1860), and finally burgomaster of Hamburg (1876).

38. In a letter to Justi he mentions boxes of cigars, books, a piano lamp, and portraits of Beethoven and Wagner.

39. Mahler was particularly afraid that Muck's engagement for the following year would complicate the situation and force him to leave Hamburg. (Letter to Justi in April 1892.) But in fact this project was never carried through.

40. He was then composing a new opera, *L'Attaque du Moulin,* which Mahler conducted in Hamburg three years later. Bruneau was shown around Hamburg and introduced to Hamburg society by a Frenchman named Sylvain who lived in the city. He took him to the home of a millionaire patron of the theater who had reconstructed the entire battle of Sedan with toy soldiers; a remarkable lack of tact, since the visitor was a Frenchman!

41. A surprising detail, for Mahler was not tall and his mountain climber's legs certainly were not shaky.

42. According to Armbrust, shocked especially by some sequences of fifths. Cast: Bettaque (Angélique), Schumann-Heink (Hubertine), Cronberger (Felix), Greve (Hubert), Wiegand (Bishop).

43. He would consider himself satisfied "if the season's takings covered his expenses." This passage is taken from a letter sent by Mahler to the singer Laura Hilgermann, who remained in Budapest after his departure. It was written early in the year, and the financial conditions of this engagement may have improved later on, when Harris decided to increase the number of performances.

44. MBR, note page 129. Berliner was two years younger than Mahler. He was a member of the Allgemeine Elektrizitäts Gesellschaft and became a close friend of Albert Einstein. He committed suicide at the age of eighty, in 1942, during the Nazi regime.

45. In the *Kyrie* double fugue, it was Sittard's opinion that the chorus was incapable of singing the sixteenth notes clearly at the speed, and he had the same reproach to make regarding the *Requiem* and the *Domine Jesu,* especially during the passage *Quam olim Abrahae.* In the *Fremdenblatt,* Emil Krause was of the same opinion, particularly as far as the *Kyrie* fugue was concerned. The *Requiem* soloists were: M. Lissmann, Schumann-Heink, Cronberger, F. Lissmann. According to Zinne, the *Requiem,* conducted "with a nervous haste," was not very effective.

46. GAB (IV, 3, 222) and also MAB, page 387. According to Sittard, an original seating plan had been invented for the *Te Deum:* the chorus and soloists were placed on the stage, the members of the orchestra in the pit. Soloists: Bettaque, Schumann-Heink, Landau, Wiegand.

47. That winter Bruckner often spoke of his "dear Mahler" (*ibid.,* IV, 3, 247).

48. ABB, *ibid.* The Hamburg Theater's choirmaster was an old pupil of Bruckner named William Sichal. Zinne's letter is dated April 18.

49. AMM, page 138.

50. He referred to two passages in *"Nicht wiedersehen": "Dann komm ich wieder"* and *"Ade!"* Sittard also criticized Mahler for what he considered an undue resemblance between the theme in *"Aus! Aus!"* and the march from Suppé's *Boccaccio.*

51. This anonymous article was very probably by Armbrust, who might not have wanted to sign it because he had taken part in the concert as accompanist.

52. Keyser's Royal Hotel, then 69 Torrington Square, W.C., and finally 22 Alfred Place.

53. See Harold Rosenthal: *Two Centuries of Opera at Covent Garden,* from which much of the data given here on Mahler's London stay has been taken.

54. Hermann Klein: *Thirty Years of Musical Life in London (1870–1900),* page 365.

55. Hermann Klein: *The Golden Age of Opera,* pages 164–65.

56. *Ibid.*
There exists, in the Finlay Collection in London, a short note from Mahler to Hermann Klein written from St. Petersburg in 1907. He looks forward to seeing him again in New York after so many years.

57. Shaw noted that the public applauded enthusiastically after each act. He deplored the fact that Grengg sang Wotan with only one nuance, a "perpetual *fortissimo.*" He

considered Rosa Sucher a Brünnhilde "military rather than feminine," but she had a "solid, brilliant voice."

58. Bernard Shaw: *Music in London*, II, pages 111–45. Cast of the June 8 (Covent Garden) and June 13 (Drury Lane) *Siegfried:* Traubmann (Waldvogel), Sucher (Brünnhilde), Schumann-Heink (Erda), Alvary (Siegfried), Lieban (Mime), Lorent (Alberich), Grengg (Wotan), Wiegand (Fafner).

59. See *The Times* (June 9, 1892), the *Musical Times* (July 1, 1892), and the *Musical Standard* (June 18, 1892).

60. Casts: Covent Garden, June 15: Sucher (Isolde), Schumann-Heink (Brangäne), Alvary (Tristan), Landau (Shepherd), Knapp (Kurwenal), Simon (Melot), Lorent (Steuersman), Wiegand (Marke); June 25, Drury Lane: Ende-Andriessen (Isolde), Ralph (Brangäne), Bispham (Kurwenal); July 9, Drury Lane: Klafsky (Isolde), Ralph (Brangäne).

61. Casts: Covent Garden, June 22, and Drury Lane, June 27: Bettaque (Freia), Ende-Andriessen (Fricka), Schumann-Heink (Erda and Third Rhine Maiden), Alvary (Loge), Lieban (Mime), Lissmann (Alberich), Grengg (Wotan), Wiegand and Litter (Giants).

62. Casts: Covent Garden, June 29: Bettaque (Sieglinde), Ende-Andriessen (Brünnhilde), Schumann-Heink (Fricka), Alvary (Siegmund), Reichmann (Wotan); Drury Lane, July 4: Klafsky (Brünnhilde).

63. In *Siegfried*, Klafsky replaced Sucher on July 6 (Covent Garden) and Bettaque on July 11 (Drury Lane). Reichmann sang Wotan twice, in *Die Götterdämmerung* on July 13 (Covent Garden) and July 18 (Drury Lane). Cast: Klafsky (Brünnhilde), Bettaque (Gutrune), Schumann-Heink (Waltraute), Alvary (Siegfried), Reichmann (Wotan), Wiegand (Hagen).

64. The same critic also objected to the slow pace of the first act Quartet (in Hamburg, on the contrary, Armbrust found the tempo of this section too lively), and to the overloud kettledrums in the Finale. These detailed comments, contrasting with the vague praise in the other articles, proves that *Fidelio* was the only work this critic really knew well.

Casts: July 2, Drury Lane, and July 18, Covent Garden: Klafsky (Leonore), Traubmann (Marcellina), Seidel (Florestan), Landau (Jaquino), Lissmann (Pizarro), Wiegand (Rocco).

65. MBR, No. 112. This letter is incorrectly dated in the collection: it was written on July 4, not on June 15.

66. BSP, page 81.

67. Casts of July 16 and 22, Covent Garden: Klafsky (Elisabeth), Bettaque (Venus), Alvary (Tannhäuser), Reichmann (Wolfram), Wiegand (Landgraf).

68. This was the Villa Hechler am Salzberg.

## CHAPTER 18

1. NBLS.

2. Amalie Weiss-Joachim, a famous contralto, was born in Marburg, Styria, in 1839. Engaged by the Vienna Opera, she was also for a long time a member of the opera company in Hanover, where, in 1863, she married the great violinist Joseph Joachim. Thereafter, she had a brilliant career as recitalist and pedagogue. Her divorce from Joachim in 1884 occasioned the violinist's quarrel with Brahms, who took her part. Amalie Joachim spent the summer near Salzburg, where many of her students, and in particular her daughter Marie, gave a concert on September 1, 1892.

3. Mahler had spent two lonely days in Berlin, so he was particularly happy to run into three of Berliner's friends on the evening of Sunday the twenty-eighth. They were Löwenfeld, future founder of the Berlin Schillertheater, Lilienfeld, and Rosenfeld; the last two he had seen often at the café of the Royal Hotel in Hamburg the preceding

year. Before catching his train for Munich, Mahler spent a few hours with them, and together they wrote to Berliner to congratulate him on his courage during the epidemic. Only the part of this letter written by Mahler can be found in MBR, No. 115. The original was given to me, together with the other letters he wrote to Berliner, by Mrs. Anna Mahler.

4. AMM, page 416. In this letter Mahler talks of his various trips to Munich.

5. In the summer, Mahler almost always chose rooms that appealed to his taste for isolation and his desire to remain aloof from family activities.

6. Contemporary newspapers reveal that the epidemic, brought from Russia, was severe too at Le Havre, Paris, and Antwerp. Between August 16 and October 15, 17,000 persons suffered from cholera in Hamburg; 8600 died.

7. See Ferdinand Pfohl: *"Mahler und Nikisch"* (*Hundertjahrfeier des Hamburger Stadttheaters 1827–1927,* Hamburg, 1927, pages 72–79, Max Beck Verlag).

8. This short letter, which was formerly in the collection of Alma Mahler, must have been written at the beginning of November 1892, for it also mentions Bülow's recent refusal to conduct Mahler's lieder.

9. Eleven performances, sharing double bills with *Cavalleria rusticana, La Dame blanche,* Méhul's *Joseph,* and Auber's *Le Maçon.* Cast of the premiere (October 21): Traubmann (Djamileh), Landau (Splendiano), Seidel (Harun).

10. The letter in which Bülow asked Wolff to engage Mahler to conduct his own work does in fact state his regret at not being able to accompany the singer at the piano "because my hands tremble too much." See Marie von Bülow, *Hans von Bülow,* page 554, as well as the letter addressed to Mahler by Bülow on October 25, 1892 (in the Rosé Collection).

11. The two lieder were doubtless put in the Berlin Philharmonic program thanks to Bülow, who that year conducted both the Philharmonic concerts in Berlin and the subscription series in Hamburg. This was probably Bülow's way of carrying out the promise to Mahler that he had not kept in Hamburg in November.

12. In particular "an opera unknown" to Mahler, almost certainly Puccini's *Le Villi* (letter of December 8 or 9 to Justi), given in Hamburg for the first time on December 2.

13. The violinist Karl Halir took part in this concert as soloist in Lalo's *Symphonie espagnole* and the first movement of a Paganini concerto. He had long been second violinist in the Joachim Quartet, and was now *Kapellmeister* of the Berlin Opera (BWT, page 128).

14. See Carl Krebs: *Meister des Taktstocks,* page 150.

15. Emil Krause (1840–1916), who had studied at the Leipzig Conservatory, was a professor and composer. He was well known for his pedantry; Bülow often gave as an example Krause's habit, in all his articles, of giving the dates of composition of the works he discussed.

16. Bödecker's indignation was particularly aroused by the slow first bars and Mahler's huge crescendo on the E flat; Mahler never quite made up his mind as to the interpretation of these initial measures and the true value of the organ points (see Chapter 31).

17. The program of this concert consisted of Anton Rubinstein's *Ocean Symphony,* Tchaikovsky's *Violin Concerto* (with Joseph Sliwinski as soloist), the Brahms *Alto Rhapsody,* pieces by Paderewski and Liszt (Sliwinski), the Mahler lieder, Beethoven's *"Leonore" Overture No. 3.* The *Vossische Zeitung* did not even mention Mahler's name.

18. Letter to Mihalovics dated January 17, 1893 (Budapest National Library).

19. The latter died on December 19, and Pollini, upon Mahler's advice, engaged a young Austrian, Franz Erben, a former pupil of Epstein.

20. Cast of the January 3 premiere: Bettaque (Iolanta), Seidel (Vaudemont), Eichhorn (Robert), Wiegand (King). Tchaikovsky, who was then conducting in Paris, did not attend the premiere. He was informed of its success by telegram.

21. Nevertheless, the critics praised the high qualities of the music. The opera was again performed at the beginning of the 1893–1894 season, when Tchaikovsky visited Hamburg.

22. Letter of January 27, 1893, to Justi.

23. Article by Carl Armbrust in the *Fremdenblatt*. Cast of the January 16 premiere: Bettaque (Suzel), Schumann-Heink (Beppe), Bötel (Fritz), and Lissmann (David).

24. MBR, No. 36 (October 28, 1892).

25. Mahler advised them to travel first class, since the compartments were better heated, and begged them to make the most of their stay.

26. This no doubt refers to Löhr's three unmarried sisters.

27. Letter to Justi (October 1892), in the Rosé Collection.

28. Letter in spring 1893 to Justi.

29. This letter is listed in the catalogue of the autograph dealer Henrici (auction 39/1917). A letter to Justi in May also mentioned the *Lieder*, the manuscript of which Mahler had just presented to Amalie Joachim. These songs had been composed nine years earlier, probably with piano accompaniment. Either Mahler orchestrated them in the spring of 1893, or he revised the previous orchestration.

30. According to John Perrin, the son of the former owner of the original score (see Appendix 3 on the *First Symphony*).

31. Rubinstein's interpretation of the Finale of the *Concerto in E Flat*, he told Natalie in 1901, had seemed to Mahler more "light and gracious than stormy and powerful as it should be." He nevertheless recognized the man's "powerful, primitive force of nature ["*Steppennatur*"], a personality lacking all restraint of culture, in the sense that nature has no need of culture." Comparing Bülow, who weighed every detail with analytic and scientific precision, to Rubinstein, who never played the same sonata in the same way twice, Mahler preferred the latter, though he had not often heard either perform. In his opinion, the piano sonatas of the master should be played "with great liberty and an appearance of improvisation," which is impossible with an orchestra. Rubinstein always made an unforgettable impression on the audience, far greater than any left by Bülow. "In fact, an artistic experience deserving its name should never be repeated twice. It should always be new and always different, because, like life itself, it cannot start anew." NBL, page 167, August 20, 1901; NBLS, January 1901. During this last talk with Guido Adler, Mahler probably overemphasized his point of view, for he was frequently annoyed by the conventional and traditional ideas of the musicologist.

32. Besides this Mass, Bruckner had sent Mahler, through Zinne, the *Eighth Symphony* (GAB, IV, 3, 323). Zinne wrote to the old composer that Mahler had read Hanslick's review of this work and thought that a composition so "torn to pieces" could not be bad.

33. Soloists on March 31: in the *Mass*—Lissmann, Schumann-Heink, Seidel, Lissmann; in the *Te Deum*—Bettaque, Schumann-Heink, Landau, Wiegand.

34. Gemma Bellincioni (1864–1950), the Italian dramatic soprano, was born in Monza. She created roles in many "veristic" operas, notably with Stagno, *Cavalleria rusticana* and *Fedora*. She toured extensively, and later ran a singing school in Berlin. Roberto Stagno (1836–1897) was born in Palermo. He sang at the Metropolitan Opera, New York, during its opening season (1883–84).

35. MBR, No. 85.

36. In a letter to Mildenburg (July 25, 1896), Mahler mentions the salary offered to him by the American orchestra: forty thousand marks per year.

37. The *Fremdenblatt* announcement was dated June 17. It states that "according to the Berlin newspapers, Mahler was to be replaced by Kapellmeister Lohse." Mahler's denial was published by the same paper on the nineteenth.

38. See Alfred Rosé: "*Aus Gustav Mahlers Sturm und Drang Periode*," Hamburger

*Fremdenblatt,* October 5, 1928. Rosé received this information from his mother, Justine Mahler.

39. This letter, written on February 4, 1893, belongs to a New York collector, Walter Hinrichsen. It was published on May 10, 1958, by Paul Nettl in the *Neue Zürcher Zeitung.*

40. He was conducting *Die drei Pintos* there (NBLS).

41. NBLS, April 1899. Mahler later regretted the overly strong contrast between the two movements. It seems that the two main themes of this particular Andante had been noted on two different sheets of paper (NBLS, July 1893).

42. NBLS and NBL, page 7.

43. Judging from the first manuscript of the *Second Symphony,* it would seem that Mahler had initially intended to make the Scherzo the second movement and the Andante the fourth (see Appendix 3).

44. See below in this chapter.

45. "Parergon" is the precise, practical term used by Richard Strauss to designate a piece for piano and orchestra composed in 1925 on themes from the *Symphonia domestica.*

46. NBL, page 10. This is also why Mahler practically never used a poetic text for a musical score without making important changes.

47. NBL, page 17, and NBLS.

48. NBL, page 9.

49. NBL, pages 9 and 18.

50. NBL, page 15, and NBLS.

51. NBLS.

52. NBL, page 10, and NBLS.

53. Mahler had on the wall of his studio in Hamburg an engraving representing this scene (*Des Knaben Wunderhorn,* Ed. Killinger, 1876, with illustrations by H. Merté [Vol. I, page 376]).

54. The harmonies of the accompaniment, which were going to seem "strange", had flowed naturally from his pen, Mahler said, "as though the melody demanded them."

55. This explains Mahler's strong dislike for the songs of Hugo Wolf.

56. This letter of October–November 1895 belongs to James Osborn of New Haven, Connecticut (see Chapter 21). J. B. Förster had already implied that *"Urlicht"* was composed before 1892 and added to the *Second Symphony* after the composition of the Finale (JFP, page 406).

57. NBLS.

58. NBL, page 8.

59. NBLS.

60. NBL, page 16. This was Mahler the contrapuntalist and symphonic architect speaking. Mahler the artist and conductor was to show himself more accessible later on to Liszt's imagination and "modern" spirit. Several of Liszt's compositions figured in Mahler's programs, particularly *Les Préludes* and *Festklänge.*

61. Hölderlin: Hymn *Der Rhein* (line 50 *et seq.*).

62. NBL, page 17, and NBLS. On that same day, Mahler told Natalie about many very significant events from his childhood. These anecdotes, excised for unknown reasons from the published edition of Natalie's memoirs, luckily exist in her unpublished manuscript. They have been included above, in Chapters 1 to 4.

63. NBLS.

64. According to John Perrin, who inherited the original manuscript of the *First Symphony* from his mother, Mahler worked on it again during August, reinserting the Andante, which he had cut out a few months earlier and was definitively to eliminate later on (see Appendix 3).

## CHAPTER 19

1. 150 marks a month. Bülow lived in the center of town, at No. 10 Alsterglacis.

2. Cast: Artner (Ännchen), Klafsky (Agathe), Birrenkoven (Max), Wiegand (Caspar).

3. Josef Förster and his wife were also present that evening. Förster mistakenly dates this meeting after the first performance of *Iolanta*, which took place six months before.

4. This performance marked the first appearance of Birrenkoven, a new dramatic tenor whom Pollini had just engaged, and who is still remembered as a great Wagnerian singer.

5. NBLS states that Mahler fell ill "a year after the cholera epidemic in Hamburg" and "some days after his return from Steinbach."

6. According to Natalie, the prescription was for opiate sedatives rather than the traditional purge.

7. *Asrael* was one of the two new works that Mahler had "brought back from Italy" in 1890 and conducted in Budapest that winter; the other was *Cavalleria rusticana*.

8. Cast of the October 5 premiere: Bettaque (Queen), Vilman (Columbus), Seidel (Guevara).

9. During the same concert Lohse conducted excerpts from Mendelssohn's *Elijah*.

10. This orchestra was founded in 1877 by Julius Laube (born 1842), a Thuringian violinist who studied under Vieuxtemps and Wieniawski and later became a conductor. Each year, he gave a series of six "popular" concerts in the Ludwig Konzerthaus, near Altona. The programs, designed to appeal to a large public, were at first made up of selections from operettas, organ pieces, marches, and waltzes. Then Laube, having slowly won over the public, began to give symphonies and Wagnerian extracts as well. His name is among the first on the list of subscribers for Bayreuth, and he, more than anyone else, was responsible for making Wagner's music known in Hamburg. It is to his credit that he frequently entrusted his orchestra to young composers who wanted a hearing for their works. During the same season another concert of the same kind was conducted by the Danish organist Emil Hartmann.

11. Born in Vienna on February 12, 1853, a student at the conservatory, Clementine Prosska or Prochazka, when only twenty, had been engaged as a coloratura at the Dresden Theater. She later married its director and *Kapellmeister,* Ernst von Schuch.

12. Born in Priegnitz in 1847, Bulss had sung Mendelssohn's oratorio *Paulus* under Mahler's direction in the Kassel-Münden festival in 1885. In 1893 he was a member of the Berlin Opera.

13. Hermann Behn (1859–1927) read law before studying music with Bruckner in Vienna, Rheinberger in Munich, and Zumpe in Hamburg, where he settled in 1887. He composed several lieder, transcribed a number of orchestral works for two pianos, and taught the history of music from 1897 on.

14. Sittard lists the "picturesque" effects invented by Mahler to portray sheep, cattle, and even fish (sic) in *"Das himmlische Leben."*

15. That Sittard could detect a resemblance between the melody of this trio and that of the song *"Du, du liegst mir am Herzen"* is astonishing (see A. Härtel, *Deutsches Liederlexikon,* Leipzig, 1865).

16. Among the *Lieder,* Pfohl considered *"Das himmlische Leben"* a "real stroke of genius," which proves that he was a remarkably perceptive critic for his time.

17. *"Der Schildwache Nachtlied," "Trost im Unglück,"* and *Rheinlegendchen."*

18. The third subscription concert of the Kurhaus in Wiesbaden took place on November 13 with the following program: Beethoven: *Coriolan Overture;* Lachner: Gavotte from *Suite No. 6;* Reinecke: Prelude to Act V from *König Manfred;* Mahler: *Drei Humoresken;* Leoncavallo: Prologue to *Pagliacci;* Schubert: *Frühlingsgrüss;* Reinhold Becker: *Ganz leise* and *Erwartung;* Heinrich Hutter: *Bergfahrt;* Goldmark:

Symphony *"Ländliche Hochzeit."* The orchestral pieces as well as the accompaniments were conducted by Franz Nowak, and the lieder by Schubert, Becker, and Hutter were accompanied by Benno Voigt at the piano. Mahler himself conducted his *Humoresken*.

19. Letters from Natalie to Justi dated November 13 and 15 (Rosé Collection).

20. The *Nassauische Landesbibliotek* in Wiesbaden was unable to identify the origin of this article. It names Mahler as the conductor of his own *Humoresken*.

21. Mahler had offered Justi this vacation of rest and relaxation. After a short stay in Merano she went on to Rome.

22. NBLS, August 24, 1893.

23. Letter of December 9, 1893, to Natalie Bauer-Lechner.

24. In an article in the Vienna *Neue Freie Presse* of 1899 devoted to a Philharmonic concert conducted by Mahler, Eduard Hanslick stressed the fact that "for ten years Brahms constantly recommended that Mahler be engaged for the Vienna Opera."

25. See the article by Ferdinand Pfohl already quoted.

26. JFP, page 373.

27. Medical knowledge at that time was somewhat sketchy, and the disease from which Bülow suffered so terribly for years was identified only as "exhaustion and excessive irritation of the nervous system." In 1893 he underwent treatment at a hospital for nervous diseases in Pankow, near Berlin, and died of a brain tumor in 1894.

28. Bülow's letter of September 15, 1893, and Mahler's letter to Justi, are in the Rosé Collection.

29. Letter of August 28, 1893, to Justi.

30. Cast of the January 2 premiere: Förster-Lauterer (Mistress Ford), Artner (Anne), Felden (Mistress Page), Schumann-Heink (Dame Quickly), Vilmar (Falstaff), Birrenkoven (Fenton).

31. In March 1893 this young woman made a brilliant Hamburg debut as guest singer in the role of *Mignon;* Pollini immediately put her under contract.

32. Josef Bohuslav Förster (1859–1951), son of a Czech organist, was born in Prague, where he studied at the conservatory. After reviewing concerts for a Prague newspaper, he followed his wife to Hamburg in 1893 and became critic of the *Nachrichten*. From 1901 to 1918 he taught in Vienna, then returned to Prague, where he became director of the conservatory in 1920. His many compositions include music of all genres, and in particular several operas.

33. Cast of the January 17 premiere: Förster-Lauterer (Marie), Artner (Esmeralda), Bötel (Hans), Arden (Kezal), Weidmann (Wenzel).

34. JFP, page 351.

35. JFP, page 354ff.

36. The former director of the Vienna Opera had come to Hamburg to stage *The Bartered Bride*.

37. Förster's statement cannot be contested, but Mahler certainly did not speak Czech fluently. He made use of it, however, during his first trip to Russia, where few people he met could speak German.

38. Cast for the premiere of January 17: Förster-Lauterer (Marenka), Artner (Esmeralda), Bötel (Jenik), Arden (Kezal), who was later replaced by Hesch.

39. Karl Wagner (1865–1928), son of a well-known actor at the Vienna Burgtheater, made his debut in Kassel on June 5, 1884, in *Egmont*. Mahler had probably met him in Kassel, or earlier still in Vienna; they met again later in Leipzig. In Hamburg in 1892, Wagner was to become one of the public's favorite actors, the "Hamburg Kainz."

40. *Guntram* had been written by the young composer while convalescing in Sicily and Egypt. The first performance was originally planned for Munich and then Karlsruhe, but Mahler, foreseeing the difficulties that Strauss was to encounter, offered, as early as December 24, to induce Pollini to present the opera in his theater.

41. Strauss, *Briefe an die Eltern,* page 193. The concert of January 22 also included Liszt's *Mazeppa* and Beethoven's *Coriolan* Overture. In this letter Strauss added that

Mahler had promised to conduct *Guntram* at the beginning of the next season, with Birrenkoven, the Hamburg Opera's new Wagnerian tenor.

42. In a letter written the next day Mahler expressed his regret to Strauss at not being able to attend his Berlin concert on January 29, since he himself had to conduct *The Bartered Bride* that evening. Strauss did indeed replace Schuch at this seventh Philharmonic concert, conducting his own symphonic poem *Don Juan,* Liszt's *Piano Concerto in E Flat* (Moriz Rosenthal, soloist), an orchestral fantasy by Wilhelm Berger, and Beethoven's *"Pastoral" Symphony.*

43. Strauss had probably made the first move by approaching Pollini after he decided to leave Weimar. In a letter written as early as January 8 to his parents, he spoke of the possibility of a Hamburg contract (SBE, No. 191).

44. In the same letter of February 6, Mahler asked Strauss to send him as soon as possible his latest scores—*Don Juan, Macbeth,* and *Tod und Verklärung*—which he hoped to conduct in a concert soon.

45. In a letter to Behn dated June 12, 1895, Mahler's estimation of Strauss's conduct the year before appears clearly. It seems that this time Strauss had tried to replace Weingartner at the Königliche Kappelle in Berlin: "[Hermann] Wolff told me he has definitely turned down Strauss. When I think back on his behavior in Hamburg, it seems possible that he is now trying to increase his market value again. Weingartner will certainly remain."

46. Letter of late January to Justi. In a letter of February 1894, addressed to the composer Eugen Lindner, Mahler mentions some "slight tension" in his relationship with Strauss, the cause of which Lindner can easily guess (Stargardt sale, 1960).

47. The Gesellschafts Konzerte (not to be confused with the Orchesterverein der Gesellschaft der Musikfreunde, which was made up of amateurs) was an autonomous creation of the Gesellschaft der Musikfreunde. A few orchestral players from the Philharmonic Orchestra sometimes took part when additional musicians were needed. Four concerts were given every year, plus one special concert. Each included a choral work interpreted by the Singverein. The conductors of the Gesellschafts Konzerte were, from 1884 to 1890, Richter, from 1890 to 1895, Gericke, from 1895 to 1900, Perger, from 1900 to 1904, Löwe, and finally, until 1912, Frank Schalk. When Mahler was head of the Vienna Opera, the Gesellschaft asked him several times to conduct their concerts, but he always refused, no doubt because he had painful memories of being turned down in 1895 (cf. BMG, pages 139–41, and *Fremdenblatt,* November 8, 1906).

48. MBR, No. 89. This letter, wrongly dated, was written early in 1894, before Mahler signed the new contract with Pollini. The later date is confirmed by an allusion to the recent appointment of Otto Brahm (1856–1912) to the Lessing Theater in Berlin.

49. MBR, No. 118.

50. It was only during the autopsy that the doctors discovered the tumor of the brain that had caused his death.

51. Disgusted with Strauss's attitude, Fräulein Petersen remarked to Frau Wolff: "His latest telegrams are so childish that one would think he was 9 rather than 29 years old." (See Edith Stargardt-Wolff: *Wegbereiter grosser Musiker,* page 85.)

52. Theodor Reik, one of Freud's disciples, stresses Mahler's obsessional reaction to his colleagues' illnesses, which several times enabled him to advance his career: that of Nikisch in 1887, that of Erkel in Budapest, that of Bülow in 1892, that of Strauss in 1894. "Someone always has to fall ill before I can conduct a symphony," he wrote to Justi (Arnold Rosé, *"Mahler und Bülow," Leipziger neueste Nachrichten,* September 17, 1929, and Theodor Reik, *The Haunting Melody,* page 226ff.; see also Theodor Spiering, *Drei Jahre mit G. Mahler*).

53. This praise takes on very special value since it comes from an implacable enemy of Mahler's Beethovian interpretations.

54. There are three musical versions of this poem; by Karl Heinrich Graun (1704–

59), Johann Christian Kittel (1732–1809), and Johann Christoph Heinrich Rinck (1770–1846). The first is the best-known.

55. MBR, No. 209, February 17, 1897. In the German text we find that Mahler used, not the word *leben*, but *erleben*, roughly equivalent to "experience."

56. Letters of February 27, March 28 and 29, 1894, to Justi.

57. Marie von Bülow, *Hans von Bülow*, page 177.

58. Theodor Reik, born in Vienna in 1888, was a disciple and friend of Freud there. Not being a physician, he was prosecuted for practicing as a psychoanalyst; it was on his behalf that Freud wrote *The Question of Lay Analysis*. Reik wrote several books published in New York, where he settled in 1939 at the outbreak of the Second World War. The inferences drawn here are condensed from RHM, pages 259–70.

59. A French psychologist, to whom I showed the texts of both Reik and Ernest Jones (Freud's biographer), points to the striking coexistence of Mahler's conformism, that is total submission to the master, and his feeling of rebellion that is sometimes latent and sometimes expressed.

60. Letter of February 1894 to Justi.

61. In the introduction Sittard was shocked by the roughness of the great tutti chords, which, however, "more or less conformed to the indicated tempo"; he took even greater exception to the "unmotivated hesitations in the first movement, which started with the third and fourth bars of the *Vivace*, just before the beginning of the main theme on the flute." Later he objected to the passage in the development "where the woodwinds exchange a variation of the first theme, carried by an accompaniment of sostenuto chords from the strings." Sittard was also infuriated by the "Bayreuth" tempo of the Trio in the Scherzo, which he had never heard played so slowly; Mahler had slowed down even more in the transition that introduces the recapitulation of the Scherzo.

62. Otto Lohse, Mahler's chief assistant, finally conducted this London season.

63. Hearing that Bronsart, the intendant of the Weimar Opera, intended to use only ten first and eight second violins, Mahler insisted that the strings be reinforced, he himself bearing the added cost.

64. The Allgemeiner Deutscher Musikverein had been founded in 1859 by Franz Brendel and Ludwig Köhler on the occasion of the twenty-fifth jubilee of the *Neue Zeitschrift für Musik*, the organ of the Verein. This annual festival, presented each year in a different town, gave performances of important new compositions and little-known older works.

65. MBR, No. 134.

66. Ernst Otto Nodnagel: *Jenseits von Wagner und Liszt*, page 7.

67. Humperdinck's famous fairy-tale opera had had its premiere in Weimar on December 23, 1893. Richard Strauss's wife, Pauline de Ahna, sang Hänsel, as well as Freihild in her husband's *Guntram*. The festival also included a performance of *Christus*, by Liszt, the Verein's founder, and two chamber-music concerts made up of quartets by Brahms, Puchat and Sgambati; a *Piano Quartet* by Sinding: a Brahms *Trio;* a *String Quintet* by August Klughardt; some lieder by Liszt, Brahms, Cornelius Volkmann, and Margarethe Petersen.

68. According to Ernst Otto Nodnagel.

69. JFP, page 409.

70. Bernhard Stavenhagen (1862–1914) was at that time the court pianist of the Grand Duke of Weimar. He was named *Hofkapellmeister* there in 1895 and later held the same post in Munich, where Mahler came into contact with him on several occasions.

71. Carl Krebs: *Meister des Taktstocks*, page 186.

72. MBR, No. 119.

73. E. O. Nodnagel: *Jenseits von Wagner und Liszt*, page 7.

74. This last article is not signed, but the two texts are too similar not to have been written by the same man.

75. The future editor of the New York magazine *Musical Courier*, who published these memoirs in 1911, at the time of Mahler's death.

76. This letter is preserved in the Bayrische Staatsbibliothek.

77. Clearly Strauss thought that the Finale should end after its first major climax, which precedes the development and the recapitulation. But, if Strauss considered the passage in question to be the conclusion and the résumé of the movement, Mahler could only feel that he had expressed himself badly. This passage showed "the complete destruction of the soul," which one must experience in order to achieve real "victory." In fact he had wished to create in this Finale a combat in which victory is furthest away at the moment when one believes it closest, as happens always with inner struggles: "without this there is no hero." He had explained the general outline of this Finale to Natalie the summer before. After having repeatedly fallen back into "the depths of despair," he had wanted to *celebrate* the "triumphant and definitive" victory of the symphonic hero, and had then realized that, in order to do so, he would have to modulate from C to D "in a very free and bold way," so that the chord of D would appear to "fall out of the blue." All things considered, he found this the best and most "genuinely imposing" passage of the entire work.

78. Letter to Strauss dated July 19 (Collection of Dr. F. Strauss). In a letter addressed to the composer Eugen Lindner, a Verein committee member, Mahler announced his coming visit to Weimar and asked if Lindner had received his *First Symphony* score safely; this was because he was unable to get in touch with Strauss at that time: the latter had "withdrawn from the world." (Stargardt sale, 1960.)

CHAPTER 20

1. The building of this cabin cost Mahler three hundred gulden. It survived until the Second World War but had been transformed into a washhouse by the owners of the inn.

2. "In the past," he later told Natalie, "the piano encouraged me and allowed me to check my work. It was useful for nothing else, for composing on a piano had always seemed childish to me." It was difficult for him to understand how other composers, for instance Wagner, could compose on the piano, "which destroys all illusions" when employed for that purpose. Mahler used it even less in 1896, when composing the first movement of the *Third Symphony;* "It was impossible to get anything out of it for this music," so he preferred to dispense with it altogether (*Fremdenblatt:* February 18, 1912 and NBLS: July 25, 1896).

3. *Knaben Wunderhorn* (Ed. Hempel, Vol. II, page 264):
       *So geht es im Schnützelputz-Häusel*
       *Da singen und tanzen die Mäusel . . .*

4. This letter is in the Bayrische Staatsbibliothek.

5. Letter of May 6, 1894, to Justi in the Rosé Collection.

6. MBR, No. 87.

7. MBR, No. 120. Mahler wrote about half the texts, having in part used those of Klopstock.

8. NBLS, spring 1896.

9. NBLS.

10. In July 1894 he promised Berliner an account of one of his recent visits and probably gave it, verbally, upon his return from Hamburg (MBR, No. 120).

11. Ernst Decsey, *"Stunden mit Mahler"* (*Die Musik*, X, 21, 146).

12. In March she had written to ask him to coach Birrenkoven for the part of Parsifal. As soon as the tenor reached Bayreuth, she had written to thank and congratulate Mahler, saying that "no singer has ever arrived so perfectly prepared." No

corrections, no alterations, had been needed, and she had decided to assign to Birrenkoven the role of Parsifal for the opening of the festival, instead of giving it to the
famous Belgian tenor Ernest Van Dyck.

13. See Dietrich Mach: *Von der Christianisierung des Parsifal in Bayreuth* (*Neue
Zeitschrift für Musik,* October 1969, page 467).

14. These were the performances of July 29 and 30 and August 3. Casts: *Parsifal*
(conducted by Hermann Levi)—Sucher (Kundry), Birrenkoven (Parsifal), Plank
(Klingsor), Reichmann (Amfortas), Grengg (Gurnemanz); *Tannhäuser* (conducted by
Strauss)—Wiborg (Elisabeth), Mailhac (Venus), Grüning (Tannhäuser), Reichmann
(Wolfram); *Lohengrin* (conducted by Felix Mottl—its first appearance during a Bayreuth festival)—Nordica (Elsa), Brema (Ortrud), Gerhäuser or Van Dyck (Lohengrin), Popovici (Telramund), Grengg (König Heinrich).

15. Letter of May 6, 1894, to Justi.

16. This postcard was in the Löhr collection (HLG Collection).

17. See MBR, No. 121.

18. The house at 12 Parkallee has been destroyed. Its third floor was divided
between two owners, E. M. Chaplin and A. von Heyden.

19. See letter of September 1, 1894, to Justi.

20. BWT, page 77.

21. According to Alma Mahler, he disguised himself one day as a monk in order to
attend a masked ball, and looked so genuine that nobody dared to approach him (AMM,
page 126).

22. The famous tenor Hermann Winkelmann, one of the glories of the Vienna
Opera and the Bayreuth Festival, came to Hamburg to sing Lohengrin as guest star at the
beginning of Mahler's stay there. The latter tried to impose a new tempo for the theme
representing the hero in the passage of the last act of *"Nie sollst Du mich befragen."*
Mahler was forced to give in on this occasion because of the celebrity of the singer, but
he was to get even with him later on in Vienna, where Winkelmann no longer dared
say, "I sing this passage my way."

23. BWT, page 78, and BWM, pages 3–5.

24. Franz Bittong (1842–1904), born in Mainz, author of several plays, stage director
in Mainz, Stettin, Bremen, chief stage director of the Hamburg Opera after 1885. After Pollini's death in 1898, Bittong shared the direction of the opera with Max Bachur.

25. BWT, page 79.

26. NBLS, September 1901.

27. NBL, page 13.

28. See Ferdinand Pfohl's article already cited, *"Mahler und Nikisch."*

29. NBLS, page 13.

30. Petersen.

31. Pollini was the *Pächter*—the lessee-manager—of the Hamburg Opera (see H.
Pohle, *B. Pollini, Eine Beleuchtungsprobe,* Hamburg, 1896). Hugo Pohle, who seems to
have been related to Behn, was a bankrupt merchant; in this article he offended not
only Pollini, but also Burgomaster Petersen. As a result, he had to leave Hamburg.

32. The article *"Mahler und Nikisch,"* already cited.

33. Pfohl's testimony on these points somewhat contradicts that of others. What is
certain is that Mahler's conducting varied considerably according to the circumstances.
Later, in Vienna, he himself explained that he used smaller gestures for the Philharmonic concerts than for the operas, in which he often had to impose his personal conception of a work without having had rehearsals.

34. This is an untranslatable pun: *Zäsurenwahn-Caesarenwahn,* the latter word meaning Caesarean madness or megalomania.

35. Richard Specht, *"Mahler als Dirigent,"* Der Kunstwart, II, *Juliheft,* 1910, page
948.

36. Justi's move to Hamburg was to have an unfortunate consequence for posterity:

the interruption of the correspondence that gave us details of Mahler's life in Budapest and Hamburg.

37. BWM, page 18.

38. BWT, page 86.

39. *Ibid.,* page 85.

40. Cast for the premiere of September 25, 1894: Artner (Hänsel), Förster-Lauterer (Gretel), Schumann-Heink (Witch), Felden (Gertrud), Dörwald (Peter). Humperdinck's opera shared a double bill with a now forgotten opera, Vilém Blodek's *V Studni,* given in German as *Im Brunnen,* and at later performances with Ferdinand Hummel's *Mara, Cavalleria rusticana,* and *Pagliacci.* On November 24, Mahler conducted, after *Hänsel und Gretel,* a "Hymn to Apollo of the Third Century Before Christ, discovered at Delphi," which was sung by a male chorus on the stage and accompanied by harps and cellos. The hymn was followed by Mozart's *Bastien und Bastienne,* conducted by Bruno Walter.

41. JFP, page 444ff.

42. JFP, page 385.

43. It should be recalled that Steinitzer spoke in equally striking terms of the same interpretation that Mahler had already given in Leipzig.

44. JFP, page 499.

45. MBR, No. 122.

46. He especially praised, in the *Seventh Symphony,* the transition from the introduction and the Vivace (which had irritated Sittard six months earlier), as well as the great crescendo at the end of this movement (with double bass ostinato), and the Finale. Some of the tempos, however, aroused his "astonishment," among others those of the Allegretto and the trio of the Scherzo; he also disliked the excessive accentuation of the fortes.

47. Mahler only observed those repeats in the minuet, thus already anticipating today's practice.

48. Krause, on the other hand, said that Busoni's technique "had not attained its customary level," and held that he gave too many concerts and worked too little between them.

49. Mahler, he said, slowed down the quiet passages and picked up speed with every crescendo: the second theme of the first movement, for instance, had been taken more slowly than the first, in particular the triplets ending the themes. In the Andante, Mahler had, in his opinion, "destroyed the atmosphere and the poetry" by "detailing each episode" so that the movement seemed fragmented, as in the "mannered" ritardandos in the trio. However, Sittard found the rhythmic and dynamic vivacity of the Finale, like that of the Beethoven *Seventh,* altogether admirable.

50. At this concert Pablo de Sarasate played the solos in Lalo's *Symphonie espagnole,* and his own *Variations for Violin and Orchestra.* Although described by Krause as "a virtuoso in the most superficial sense of the word," Sarasate was praised warmly by Sittard.

51. Bloomfield Zeisler played Anton Rubinstein's *Concerto in D Minor;* Palloni sang old French airs and melodies.

52. Too slow in the third movement, too fast in the Finale. This was Mahler's first public performance of a Brahms symphony. The concert started with Beethoven's *Coriolan* Overture, and Mahler, before the symphony, conducted the minuet from Bizet's *Arlésienne.*

53. A poem in memory of Rubinstein was read before the concert by an actor from the theater. The lieder were sung by Raimund von Zur Mühlen.

54. The peasant dance had, according to Sittard, a slowness "worthy of grandmother and grandfather" and only the final Presto reached a tempo suitable for the initial allegro.

55. JFP, page 385.

56. The first Hamburg performance of this opera, the first of any Smetana opera in Germany, had taken place on December 28, 1881. Cast of the November 15, 1894, performance: Artner (Countess), Förster-Lauterer (Vilma), Bötel (Heinrich), Hesch (Peter), Traubmann (Minka), Weidmann (Hans). It shared a double bill with *Pagliacci*.

57. Cast of the February 20, 1895, premiere: Förster-Lauterer (Marinka), Artner (Clara), Schumann-Heink (Brigitte), Grüning (Hanno), Hesch (Zarkow), Dörwald (Janusch). It shared a double bill with Gluck's *Orfeo ed Euridice*.

58. Cast of *Fidelio*: Artner (Marzelline), Klafsky (Leonore), Weidmann (Jaquino), Grüning (Florestan), Dörwald (Pizarro), Vilmar (Minister), Lorent (Rocco).

59. Soloists: in *Die Schöpfung*—Saak (Eve), Artner (Gabriel), Grüning (Uriel), Vilmar (Adam); in the *Requiem*—Traubmann, Schumann-Heink, Weidmann, Hoffmann.

60. Hochberg had attended the Leipzig premiere of *Die drei Pintos* and had had some trouble with Mahler when he had tried to lure to Berlin Mahler's principal assistant in Budapest, Sándor Erkel.

61. These anecdotes were told by Mahler to Natalie Bauer-Lechner on July 30, 1899 (NBLS). Bruno Walter's anecdote about Bittong snapping his fingers during a scene with angels also refers to this opera. Cast: Artner (Elsbeth), Förster-Lauterer (Oda), Spielmann (Walther), Grüning (Eginhard).

62. *Tannhäuser* (11), *Tristan und Isolde* (5), *Die Meistersinger* (6), *Das Rheingold* (1), *Die Walküre* (4), *Siegfried* (5), *Götterdämmerung* (3).

63. JFP, page 406. Förster erred in saying that Anna von Mildenburg was also present: she reached Hamburg only the following autumn. Thanks to a letter of January 4, 1895, from Mahler to Strauss and to MBR, No. 124, the rehearsal can be dated with certainty.

64. NBL, page 53.

65. It has been often and wrongly stated that the performance had been conducted by Strauss. The rest of this ninth Philharmonic concert, which was actually conducted by Strauss, consisted of Mendelssohn's *Fingal's Cave* overture, the *Fourth Piano Concerto* of Saint-Saëns, and two solos by Chopin and Liszt played by the young pianist Josef Hofmann (replacing the ailing Moriz Rosenthal) before and after the Mahler movements. The concert ended with Weber's *Oberon* overture.

66. E. O. Nodnagel: *Jenseits von Wagner und Liszt*.

67. Justi cabled immediately afterward to Nina Hoffmann: "Great success, tell the others" (HLG Collection). According to Oskar Eichberg, the audience had warmly applauded, and the booing was only intended to calm the clapping and the bravos.

68. This anonymous critic found the Trio reminiscent of the episode of the two armed men in the *Zauberflöte*.

69. The first theme of the Allegro, in fact, is one of the longest in all symphonic literature.

70. WKL, page 143.

71. Postcard sent by Strauss to Mahler on February 22, 1897, which the latter gave to his friend Fritz Löhr (collection of Dr. Clemens Löhr).

72. MBR, No. 140.

73. MBR, No. 164.

74. In particular in the Beethoven overture the rallentando marking the entrance of the second theme and the general pause after the fanfare. In the Schumann symphony, he criticized both the rapidity of the Larghetto and the slowness of the Vivace at the end of the Scherzo. The holding of the first two notes of the theme of the Finale, finally, had seemed to him "most painful" and without any "musical basis."

75. The violinist Emile Sauret, soloist at this concert, played Moritz Moszkowski's *Concerto in C major*, op. 30, and his own *Elegy and Rondo for Violin and Orchestra*, op. 48. The 1956 catalogue of Willy Russ, a Neuchâtel autograph dealer,

contains an autograph by Mahler dedicated to Frau Sauret and dated January 22, 1895. It is the famous initial melodic descent from the introduction of *"Leonore" Overture No. 3,* with the following text: "To Frau Sauret, on the first day I have had the pleasure of making music with her husband." The nuance Mahler had jotted down over the last f sharp is characteristic: pppp.

76. Teresa Carreño (1853–1917), the celebrated Venezuelan pianist, was also a composer, conductor, and singer. She married in turn the violinist Emile Sauret, the Italian baritone Giovanni Tagliapietra, the composer-pianist Eugen d'Albert, who influenced her deeply, and finally Arturo Tagliapietra, a younger brother of her second husband.

77. Mahler sent the news of this performance to the old master, but the latter, feeling death close at hand, was no longer "interested in this world," where he had known so little joy. His only reaction was a "humble and fleeting smile." GAB, IV, 3, 303.

78. The idea of this documenting the interpretation of music seemed very original at the time, musicology being in its infancy. Such a study had also been the reason for his choice of a moderate tempo for the Finale of the *Fifth Symphony* and instrumental alterations in the same work.

79. JFP, page 386.

80. NBL, page 53.

81. Krause especially mentioned the "splitting up" of the theme of the Adagio, the "much too slow" tempo of the E minor passage in the Scherzo, and the "tasteless" interpretation of the recitatives in the Finale. The concert began with Beethoven's overture *Zur Namensfeier,* op. 115. Soloists in the *Ninth Symphony* were Josephine von Artner, Anna Bunz, Nicolo Boerter, and Hermann Gausche. The chorus was that of the Bach-Gesellschaft.

82. See Anna Bernhardt, article mentioned in Chapter XVII (*Neue Freie Presse,* 1927).

83. JFP, page 386.

84. *Wiener Tagblatt* (February 7, 1895), page 7. *Illustriertes Wiener Extrablatt* (same date). *Neues Wiener Tagblatt* (same date), page 5.

85. BWM, page 18, is our only source of information on this subject.

86. Otto's musical manuscripts disappeared in the bombing that damaged Alma Mahler's house during the First World War, but she claims that, before this happened, she had examined them and found them "mediocre." AML, page 204.

## CHAPTER 21

1. See letter of June 8 to Strauss (collection of Dr. Franz Strauss).

2. *Hamburger-Nachrichten,* May 19, 1911.

3. MBR, No. 93.

4. According to a letter written to Ernestine Löhr from Hamburg on May 31 (HLG Collection).

5. Mahler also considered calling the movement *"Was das Kind . . ."* or even *"Was der Abend erzählt"* (What the child or what the evening tells), but the "flowers" were more suited both to the character and the general plan of the symphony. The seventh movement, *"Das himmlische Leben,"* finally cut out, was also called *"Was das Kind erzählt"* at one time.

6. NBL, page 34.

7. These two programs might have been sketched before Mahler's arrival in Steinbach (collection of Alma Mahler; AMM, page 53).

8. Second program: 1. The entrance of summer (fanfare and gay march) (introduction) (for wind instruments with solo double basses). 2. What the forest tells me (first movement). 3. What love tells me (Adagio). 4. What twilight tells me

(Scherzo for strings). 5. What the flowers tell me (Minuet). 6. What the cuckoo tells me (Scherzo). 7. What the child tells me.

9. NBL, page 34.

10. NBL, page 118, summer 1899.

11. This movement also too closely resembled the preceding one both in spirit and thematic material.

12. See Appendix 3 for a complete picture of the changes in the *Third Symphony,* and its program as Mahler saw it.

13. NBL, page 19.

14. This epithet, which Mahler here applies to one of his greatest symphonic movements, might also be applied to a large portion of his work.

15. MBR, Nos. 93 and 127, letters to Natalie and Behn.

16. The letter, like most of the others to Behn, is with the Hamburg lawyer Hertz.

17. JFP, page 456.

18. This was doubtless Karl Wagner, who was more than the "actor-comedian" that Natalie describes here.

19. Alfred Rosé, *"Gustav Mahlers Sturm und Drang Periode";* article already mentioned in Chapter 18.

20. Max Kalbeck, *Brahms* (IV, 2, 454). From the evidence available it seems almost certain that Brahms received the first movements of the *Second Symphony* during the summer of 1895, and the Finale the following year. NBLS specifies that the first three movements were sent at this time.

21. The house and garden at Bismarckstrasse 86 no longer exist. The owner was a widow named Münch.

22. Pollini was to accompany the Hamburg Opera to St. Petersburg in March, and Mahler hoped to persuade Behn to go too (letter No. 14, collection of lawyer Hertz). In his next letter (collection of James M. Osborn) he asked Behn to return the manuscript of *Urlicht,* for it was not a "piano version," but "the original version of the composition, even before I decided to orchestrate it and insert it in the *Second Symphony."*

23. Rosa Papier had sung under Mahler's direction at the Kassel-Münden festival in 1885. She had abandoned her stage career in 1891 because illness attacked her vocal chords.

24. A surprising description, since all Mahler's other contemporaries speak of his eyes as dark.

25. Armbrust added that, as always, Mahler's tempos in this opera seemed too slow. Cast of the September 12 performance: Förster-Lauterer (Sieglinde), Mildenburg (Brünnhilde), Schumann-Heink (Fricka), Hoffmann (Wotan).

26. BMM, page 43.

27. MBR, No. 142, November 1895.

28. MBR, No. 141, January 1, 1896.

29. NBL, page 156, and NBLS.

30. Another of Mahler's letters written at this time suggests that one cause of this crisis was five hundred marks that he had lent Mildenburg and that she feared Justine might hear about.

31. NBLS. Cast of the October 10 premiere: Artner (Sophie), Förster-Lauterer (Charlotte), Birrenkoven (Werther), Vilmar (Albert).

32. The "version" given was that of the Vienna critic Robert Hirschfeld. Cast of the November 5 premiere: Artner (Grillette), Schumann-Heink (Volpino), Bötel (Mengone), Hesch (Sempronio).

33. Cast of the November 30 premiere: Förster-Lauterer (Françoise), Schumann-Heink (Marcelline), Giesswein (Dominique), Hoffmann (Merlier).

34. Edith Stargardt-Wolff: *Wegbereiter grosser Musiker,* p. 172.

35. Letter to Hermann Behn.

36. At the same time, he felt obliged to study all four of Gernsheim's own symphonies, which the composer had sent him in the hope that Mahler would conduct them in Hamburg. MBR, Nos. 165–71.

37. See MBR, No. 143, the final paragraph of which was deleted in the published version.

38. NBLS, April 1899.

39. MBR, No. 145.

40. This letter is in the Stadtbibliothek in Frankfurt.

41. Humperdinck's reply is in the Rosé Collection.

42. One hundred twenty instrumentalists took part in this performance—that is almost twice the normal complement of the Philharmonic—among them six percussionists (*National Zeitung*, December 15, 1895).

43. According to a letter Mahler wrote Behn a few weeks before the concert, he had first engaged the mezzo-soprano Marie Götze.

44. In a letter to Mildenburg he ascribed this headache to a deviation from his diet, all fatty food being forbidden to him.

45. BWM, page 20.

46. Cited by NBL, page 22.

47. NBL, *ibid.*

48. E. O. Nodnagel, *Jenseits von Wagner und Liszt*, page 5.

49. This critic admired only a few isolated passages, the Andante, and the entrance of the chorus in the Finale.

50. E. O. Nodnagel (*Biography of Mahler: Musikalisches Wochenblatt*), spring 1897, page 527.

51. He states, as he did in March, that the work had only just been finished.

52. This critic, like most of his colleagues, found the *Urlicht* superior to the rest of the work, but he blamed Mahler severely for the "improvements" he had brought to Klopstock's poem.

53. Max Marschalk (1863–1940) was born in Berlin. He composed a dozen operas and incidental music. Joining the *Vossische Zeitung* in 1895, he was to continue working for it most of his life. The article quoted above was doubtless written by his superior. Marschalk probably also wrote for other periodicals.

54. MBR, No. 172.

55. Letter to Frau Sommerfeld of March 2, 1896 (Private Collection, Bern).

56. NBL, page 21. Mahler had just given the manuscript orchestral score to Hermann Behn (orchestral score of twenty-nine pages—end of 1895). It had been heavily corrected.

57. The score of the second movement is dated April 11, that of the third the twenty-fifth, and the fifth the eighth of May.

58. Kienzl had attended the premiere of the *Second Symphony* in December. Austrian by birth, Wilhelm Kienzl (1857–1941) conducted at the Hamburg Opera from 1889 to 1891. *Der Evangelimann* was given its world premiere in Berlin on May 4, 1895. Cast of the Hamburg January 6 premiere: Förster-Lauterer (Martha), Birrenkoven (Evangelimann), Hoffmann (Johannes), Weidmann (Zitterbart).

59. Cast: Mildenburg (Norma), Wolff-Kauer (Adalgisa), Giesswein (Pollione).

60. See Ferdinand Pfohl, "*Mahler und Nikisch*" (article quoted) and Heinrich Chevalley.

61. NBLS.

62. Cast of the February 11 premiere: Artner (Jutta), Mildenburg (Mlada), Birrenkoven (Dalibor), Ungar (Veit), Dörwald (King).

63. A pupil of Reinecke in Leipzig, Kaskel was born in Dresden in 1866. His first opera, *Hochzeitsmorgen*, had been staged by Pollini in 1893. *Sjula* was given its

first two performances in Hamburg on a double bill with Offenbach's *Das Mädchen von Elizondo,* conducted by Bruno Walter. Cast of the February 27 premiere: Förster-Lauterer (Sjula), Schumann-Heink (Germa), Bötel (Merjid), Vilmar (Suleiman).

64. This was no doubt the glorious A flat *Variations,* or perhaps the *Andantino Varié* in B minor.

65. JFP, page 486.

66. Mahler was hard on Joachim because of his unjust attitude toward Wagner, but he was to see him again later in Vienna and show his respect in a particularly flattering way (see Chapter 35).

67. Natalie's first stay in Hamburg lasted from January 11 to 25, her second from February 16 to about February 20. She also met Mahler in Berlin in March, in order to attend the concert of his work, and returned to Hamburg again in April.

68. Behn, determined to reproduce everything in the orchestral score, had, in Mahler's opinion, often smothered the essential melodic lines. On November 19, 1896, Mahler borrowed three hundred marks from him (Stargardt, 1958).

## CHAPTER 22

1. In German this sentence reads: *"Weisst Du nicht, dass sich diese Worte wie glühende Messer in mein Herz bohren?"* It is interesting to note that this phrase is almost exactly the same as the first line of the third song in the *Lieder eines fahrenden Gesellen: "Ich hab ein glühend Messer, ein Messer in meiner Brust."*

2. When they separated, it was in fact Mahler who took the initiative.

3. The title is followed on the concert program by "First movement of the Symphony in C minor for full orchestra" (Löhr Collection, then HLG Collection). The "program" for the *First Symphony* was also omitted.

4. The concert took place on March 16 at 7:30 P.M. in the Philharmonic concert hall.

5. Anton Sistermanns (1865–1926), famous Dutch bass-baritone, was a pupil of Stockhausen in Frankfurt. He had a brilliant career as a singer in oratorio and recital, and also taught in Wiesbaden, Berlin, and finally in Holland.

6. The name is almost illegible in the original. The correspondence suggests that at some point in 1896 or 1897 Mildenburg became aware that Behn's admiration for her was passionate as well as artistic.

7. NBL, page 32.

8. *Berliner Neueste Nachrichten,* March 18, 1896. Paul Moos (1863–1952), a Swabian critic and musicologist, pursued his career in Berlin for many years before returning to his homeland in 1899. A pupil of Hartmann, he wrote a *"Philosophy of Music from Kant to Eduard von Hartmann"* and many other aesthetic works.

9. The *Tageblatt* critic Ernst Otto Nodnagel was on his "road to Damascus" from the first rehearsal onwards. In his opinion Mahler had been ill-advised to add a program after the work was finished, since it was "transparently clear" without one (*Jenseits von Wagner und Liszt,* page 9). Nodnagel discovered a striking resemblance between one of the themes of the symphony and Mendelssohn's *Hirtenlied,* which, he believed, was unknown to Mahler.

10. MBR, No. 177.

11. MBR, No. 209, to Seidl.

12. In particular an opera called *Lobetanz.* Mahler considered sending him his early libretto for *Rübezahl* but finally decided not to, having judged that it "belonged to the past."

13. MBR, No. 179.

14. NBL, page 35.

15. MBR, No. 95, spring or autumn 1896.

16. NBL, page 33. See above, Chapter 21.

17. NBLS.

18. Bruno Walter conducted in Breslau (1896–97), in Pressburg, in Riga (1898–1910), and finally in Berlin (1900–01) before rejoining Mahler in Vienna.

19. Cast for the opening on March 24: Förster-Lauterer (Laura), Artner (Bronislava), Schumann-Heink (Palmatica), Birrenkoven (Bettelstudent), Weidmann (Jan). Mahler conducted this work eight times during the season.

20. Cast for the March 21 performance: Förster-Lauterer (Sieglinde), Mildenburg (Brünnhilde), Schumann-Heink (Fricka), Birrenkoven (Siegmund), Hoffmann (Wotan), Lorent (Hunding).

21. On April 3 she wrote to Albert Spiegler, Mahler's childhood friend, from Hamburg to wish him a happy birthday, told him what concerts and operas she would attend (in particular *Fidelio*), and spoke of the "many walks" she took with Mahler (collection of R. Lehmann).

22. However, he praised his achievements with orchestra and singers. Soloists in the Mozart *Requiem,* April 3, 1896: Artner, Schumann-Heink, Giesswein, Hoffmann. According to Krause, Mahler had used a version "adapted" by Brahms in 1877 for the complete edition of Mozart's works.

23. Förster speaks of "two performances" of this symphony under Mahler, but the dates given in *Der Pilger* are incorrect.

24. Rosa Papier-Paumgartner, who had sung Mendelssohn's *Paulus* under Mahler's direction at the Kassel-Münden festival, had to leave the Vienna Opera and abandon her career due to a disease of the vocal cords. A friend of Brahms (who particularly admired her interpretation of the *Saphische Ode*), and of Wolf, she married one of Vienna's best accompanists, Hans Paumgartner. Their son is the well-known conductor and musicologist Bernhard Paumgartner. Rosa Papier taught many singers and knew how to give them stage sense as well as a thorough technical and musical training.

25. Intendant of the Vienna Opera.

26. BMG, page 35.

27. Letter of May 10 to Edmund von Mihalovics, the composer and director of the Budapest conservatory.

28. Steinberg had acted as mediator between Mahler and Neumann in Prague and had later introduced him to David Popper (cf. Chapter 12).

29. MBR, No. 184, to Max Marschalk.

30. BWM, page 12. Walter had often discussed this essential problem with Mahler, and they agreed that Italian operas were more suited to such liberties than German ones.

31. Cast of May 2: Prevosti (Violetta), Ungar (Alfredo), Hoffmann (Germont).

32. This letter was sent together with a photograph, which Mahler dedicated to his "Evangelist" with a few verses he had written himself.

33. *Tannhäuser* (4), *Tristan* (2), *Die Meistersinger* (4), *Die Walküre* (8), *Das Rheingold* (1), *Siegfried* (6), *Die Götterdämmerung* (3), *Fidelio* (6), *Der Freischütz* (7), *Oberon* (2), *Le Nozze di Figaro* (6), *Don Giovanni* (3), and *Die Zauberflöte* (2). *Tannhäuser* was probably conducted by Pohlig, but just possibly by Mahler.

34. Letters to Justi (June 1, Rosé Collection) and to Mildenburg (June 1 and 3).

35. In a conversation with Natalie Bauer-Lechner, Mahler said that it was impossible for him to approximate the sound of the first movement of the *Third* on the piano (NBLS, see Chapter 20). As soon as he heard the piano's short, tinny sounds, so puny compared to the storms he had imagined, his inspiration fled.

36. Letter of June 12.

37. Letter of June 13.

38. Letter of June 19.

39. Letter of June 20.

40. NBL, page 40.

41. Letter of June 23. In this description of his state of mind while working, Mahler, who was at that time upset by the forced interruption of his creative work, forgot how nervous and irritable he often became when composing.

42. MBR, No. 197.

43. NBL, page 40.

44. NBL, page 140.

45. *Ibid.*, pages 46–47.

46. NBLS.

47. The symphony now had only six movements, the original Finale—*"Das himmlische Leben"*—having already been cut.

48. The fourth and sixth movements of the symphony as we know it.

49. NBL, page 44ff.

50. NBLS.

51. NBL, pages 44–45.

52. NBL, page 44.

53. *Ibid.*, pages 45–46.

54. *Ibid.*, page 47.

55. *Ibid.*, page 42.

56. The letter published as MBR, No. 153, omits many sentences from the original.

57. MBR, No. 153, which is made up of passages from various letters of June 21, 28, and 29.

58. MBR, No. 149.

59. Among other things he had two servants in Steinbach.

60. Hermine Schwartz, in the book that she later wrote about her brother— *Ignaz Brüll und sein Freundekreis*, Rikola-Verlag, Vienna, 1922—confirms that during that summer Mahler paid several visits to Berghof, once with Bruno Walter, and that one day her brother and Mahler played the *Second Symphony,* she herself singing the *Urlicht.* On his next visit, Mahler brought her three albums of his *Lieder* with a "charming dedication."

61. The last part of this letter appears in MBR, No. 150.

62. NBL, page 51. The italics are the author's.

63. NBL, page 53.

64. Ernst Schulz, the author of the anonymous *"Memoirs of a Prague Musician"* (see Chapter 10), claims that this movement is an evocation of Vlassim Park, which lay between Schienenstrang and Benesov. According to him, Mahler often went there with Gustav Frank to visit the latter's parents. In the park were animals and birds of every kind that composed between them a "natural symphony." As in olden times, one could also hear the post horn of a coach on the nearby road, as in the Scherzo of the *Third Symphony.*

65. MBR, No. 151.

66. NBL, page 48.

## CHAPTER 23

1. MBR, No. 148.

2. BWT, page 90.

3. Karpath, Specht, NBL, and Max Kalbeck in his biography of Brahms all confirm that Mahler sent Brahms the complete score of the *Second Symphony.*

4. NBLS, February 1896. See Chapter 21.

5. *Neue Freie Presse,* January 8, 1907.

6. Ludwig Karpath confirms this equivocal judgment and states that Koessler went

expressly to Steinbach to fetch the score and take it to Brahms. Both these witnesses are reliable, for Specht and Karpath visited Ignaz Brüll in Unterach that summer (Richard Specht: *Johannes Brahms,* pages 352–53, and BMG, page 90).

7. He particularly admired the *Variations on a Theme by Haydn* (BMW, page 103), such chamber works as the sonatas for piano and clarinet (which he played with his brother-in-law Rosé in the summer of 1899, and the symphonies, which he conducted in Vienna and New York. In letters to his wife, Mahler twice expresses an unfavorable opinion of Brahms. Yet, even while recognizing Brahms's limitations, he never ceased performing his works. The only composers toward whom his attitude never changed were Mozart, Beethoven, and Wagner.

8. Mahler was later to compose a large part of the *Fourth Symphony* there during the summer of 1899.

9. MBR, No. 200.

10. On June 27, Mahler came out of the Häuschen and said to Natalie, "Who would have thought that I could put the Höllengebirge, with all its flowers, its forests, its animals, in my pocket . . . Now I have made all of Steinbach my own" (*zueigen*).

11. Walter states that he was already considered a "new Goethe."

12. The journalist Ludwig Karpath was present at this performance (BMG, pages 25–26).

13. NBLS, July 25.

14. NBL, page 49.

15. A surprisingly quick cure if it was a genuine sprain, but all those who knew Mahler well commented on the rapidity of his recoveries.

16. NBL, page 50.

17. It is interesting that Mahler should have already expressed this viewpoint: the *Sixth, Eighth,* and *Ninth Symphonies,* as well as *Das Lied von der Erde,* were to end in adagio tempo.

18. The sources for the programs are: AMM, page 53 (preliminary programs); BMS, page 106 (another version of the first preliminary program); NBL, page 20 (first program of the summer of 1895); MBR, No. 127, to Berliner (August 17, 1895); letter to Natalie of September 11, 1895; letter to Mildenburg of June 21 or 28, 1896; MBR, No. 184, to Marschalk, August 6, 1896; MBR, No. 93, to Fritz Löhr, August 29, 1895. See Appendix 3.

19. MBR, No. 184.

20. NBL, page 55.

21. In a letter to Mildenburg, Mahler commented on the various singers in the *Ring:* "Heink surpassed herself," Artner was "ordinary, as usual," and the tenor Burgstaller possessed the physical presence and the personality rather than the voice for Siegfried. Mildenburg, who was scheduled to sing at the next festival, had nothing to worry about: none of the singers had equaled her performances in any of her roles. Surprising as it may seem at first sight, Mahler does not mention the prima donna of the cycle, Lilli Lehmann, one of the singers he admired and respected most. No doubt he wished to avoid arousing Mildenburg's jealousy.

22. AMM, page 129.

23. MBR, No. 154. This phrase throws an interesting light upon Mildenburg's character.

24. According to the article in the *Neues Wiener Journal* of October 19, 1900, which mentions this incident, Mahler applied again at a later date, but when Levi left the Munich Opera, Strauss was engaged in his place.

Finally Possart and Perfall offered Mahler a job in April 1897, but he had by then been engaged by Vienna and cabled his reply: "Have agreed to another offer from those who think less of my nose than of my talent." Though it is difficult to date these events accurately, they are certainly true, for they were published in Vienna when Mahler was already well known there. Strauss stayed only a short time in Munich. He left at the end of 1896, to take Mottl's place in Berlin.

25. These offers had not been so numerous as Mahler suggested at this time.

26. Letter of August 16 to Mildenburg.

27. Klafsky (Elisabeth), Mildenburg (Venus), Schumann-Heink (Young Shepherd), Birrenkoven (Tannhäuser), Demuth (Wolfram), Endorf (Walther von der Vogelweide), Wittekopf (Landgraf).

28. Krzyzanowski had married her in Halle. Born in Senazac, she had studied under Luise Dustmann, then started her stage career in Halle, Elberfeld, and Leipzig. She seems to have been a mediocre singer who gravely imperiled her husband's career.

29. Armbrust, who had been this paper's opera critic, had died suddenly in Hanover that summer.

30. Cast of the September 9 performance: Wenz (Susanna), Klafsky (Countess), Förster-Lauterer (Cherubino), Schumann-Heink (Marcellina), Wittekopf (Figaro), Demuth (Count).

31. Three days after her forty-first birthday.

32. As it is generally the *"Leonore" No. 3* that is inserted at this point, Natalie is probably mistaken in this respect.

33. By virtue of these same principles, Mahler, in his last works, reached toward "total thematism" and tried to give the same interest to secondary parts as to principal ones.

34. NBL, page 59; JFP, page 489.

35. What was true of the Hamburg period doubtless was also true earlier when Mahler had no one to keep an eye on his clothes.

36. This is Natalie speaking. A great change was to occur in this respect in Mahler's life after his marriage.

37. NBL, page 121.

38. Natalie compared his profile to the heavy silhouette of an otter.

39. NBL, page 60.

40. Scrupulously truthful as she usually is, Natalie nonetheless here exaggerates her own part in the publication of the *Second Symphony* or is wrong about the date of her intervention. In a letter to Mildenburg the preceding summer, Mahler alludes to his "symphony," which is about to be published. The dinner at Berkan's could have occurred during Natalie's earlier visit, in February. On October 31, Mahler wrote Behn, telling him that the score and orchestral parts of the *Third* were with Nikisch. This letter proves that a publication was already being discussed.

41. Cast of the October 15 premiere: *Gloria:* Förster-Lauterer (Olympia), Moll (Silvia), Grüning (Marcel). *Runenzauber:* Wenz (Regisse), Horsten (Nanhild), Giesswein (Knight).

42. Cast of the December 4 premiere: Förster-Lauterer (Dot), Wenz (Cricket), Moll (May), Birrenkoven (Edward), Demuth (Postilion).

43. The complete program of this November 9 concert, in which the celebrated soprano Marcella Sembrich took part, was: Cherubini—Overture to *Anacreon;* Schumann—*Fourth Symphony in D minor;* from Mozart's *Don Giovanni*—"*Non mi dir*"; from Bellini's *Norma*—"*Casta diva*"; from Mozart's *Le Nozze di Figaro*—"*Deh vieni, non tardar*"; Mahler—*Blumenstück;* Dvořák—*Scherzo capriccioso.*

44. According to the letter he wrote to Frau Sommerfeld after the concert, her "exquisite" (*reizende*) article was poetry (*Nachdichtung*) rather than criticism.

45. Paul Bekker in *Allgemeine Musikzeitung* (June 9, 1905).

46. The program of the December 7 concert included two overtures—those to Wagner's *Rienzi* and Berlioz's *Benvenuto Cellini*—as well at Beethoven's *"Pastoral" Symphony.*

47. Letter of December 2, 1896, from Nikisch to Mahler.

48. Letter to Justi, in the Rosé Collection.

49. The Lisztverein was founded in 1885 by Nikisch and Martin Krause, Mahler's sworn enemy among the Leipzig journalists, in opposition to the staunchly conservative and traditional Gewandhaus concerts. Nikisch in fact became conductor of the Gewandhaus in October 1895; he also replaced Bülow with the Berlin Philharmonic in 1894. The Lisztverein orchestra was made up of the "Kapellen of Kappelmeister Winderstein and of the 134th Regiment."

50. A *Hofopersänger* in Schwerin. The Wolf songs were *"Verborgenheit," "Tambour," "Der Freund," "Das Ständchen," "Heimweh," "Der Genesene an die Hoffnung."* Emil Wagner accompanied at the piano.

51. This article was in Fritz Löhr's collection. Mahler must have sent it to him.

52. Gustav Schlemüller (1841–1900), born in Königsberg, was a pedagogue and a composer as well as a music critic.

53. Yet he asserted that he had tried to understand the work with the help of the piano transcription by Behn, published by Hofmeister.

54. Among the "borrowed" sources, Vogel mentions Beethoven's *Ninth Symphony* and *Die Walküre.* To my knowledge, no reference has ever been made to an unconscious resemblance of the first (Schott score, page 45) theme of the *Second Symphony,* to Hunding's entrance in Act I of *Die Walküre.* In an article published a month later, on the *Blumenstück,* Vogel called the first movement "an uneven, nervous pastiche," the second a collection of "eclectic winks, a witty French *Pikanterie!"* Wolf is no better treated in the same article.

55. MBR, No. 189.

56. Letter to Goldmark, BMG, page 45.

57. In fact, Mahler had only just decided to become a convert. He did not actually take this step until February 1897 (see Chapter 24). On January 13, 1897, the *Hamburger Nachrichten* stated that Jahn had resigned and that Mottl and Schuch were the leading candidates. Even though Mahler had been converted, "it was impossible to call upon him in the present circumstances."

58. Letter of December 22, 1896, to Mihalovics, who replied from Abbazia, regretting that he was unable to approach Prince Liechtenstein personally, since he did not know him. However, he asked his friend Count Julius Szechenyi, who was a close friend of the prince's sister, Countess Trautmansdorf, to act in his place. He advised Mahler to write to their mutual friends, the journalists Singer and Max Falk, who personally knew Liechtenstein. Max Falk wrote to Prince Liechtenstein to recommend Mahler. On January 3 the latter approached Mihalovics for the third time, once more asking him to contact Bezecny and Wlassack on his behalf, since the decision lay in their hands. Mihalovics proved his friendship by writing yet another letter to the intendant.

59. Letters of January 4 and 12 to Goldmark (BMG, pages 43 and 46). On Christmas night, Natalie had called on Goldmark to ask for advice as to what steps should be taken. Goldmark, who lacked both energy and courage, gave only halfhearted help, for which Mahler never forgave him.

60. *Haus- Hof- und Staatsarchiv Wien.* Nr. 1610, ex. 1896.

61. MBR, No. 190, January 14.

62. His contract did in fact make this possible after the second year (letter to Rosa Papier dated February 5, 1897. BMG, page 41).

63. MBR, No. 132.

64. Letter from Schuch, January 10, 1897 (Rosé Collection).

65. The program also included Beethoven's *Fourth Piano Concerto,* Liszt's *Totentanz* (soloist Otto Neitzel) and Richard Heuberger's *Nachtmusik.* The *Urlicht* was sung by Frau Chavanne.

66. Neitzel was anticipating somewhat, for the comparison with Meyerbeer was only made later, when Mahler began to be successful as a composer (*Der Anbruch* II 7/8, 257). Otto Neitzel (1852–1920) was the son of a Pomeranian professor.

He studied at the Joachim School in Berlin, became a doctor of philosophy at the university there, and accompanied Pauline Lucca and Sarasate on their concert tours. Director of the Strasbourg Musikverein in 1878, then conductor and professor in the city, he later taught at the Moscow Conservatory before settling in Cologne, where he was music critic on the *Kölnische Zeitung* and professor at the conservatory. He wrote a few operas and several works on musicology.

67. This unusually penetrating critic was Friedrich Brandes. Born in Aschersleben, he studied literature, philosophy, and music in Halle, Berlin, and Leipzig. Critic on the *Anzeiger* from 1895, he conducted from 1898 the Dresdner Lehrergesangverein, and in 1908 succeeded Max Reger as director of the music department at the University of Leipzig. He later became editor of the *Neue Zeitschrift für Musik* and died in Dresden in 1940.

68. Arthur Seidl (1863–1928), born in Munich, studied music and philosophy there and in Leipzig, where he obtained a doctorate in philosophy with a thesis on musical aesthetics. Critic in Dresden and Hamburg from 1893 to 1899, he later settled in Weimar, where he collaborated with Peter Gast, editing Nietzsche's complete works. Professor of musical history and aesthetics at the Leipzig Conservatory from 1904 on, he was the author of many books on Wagner, Strauss, Pfitzner, Jaques-Dalcroze, etc. There are chapters on Mahler in *Moderne Dirigenten* (1902) and *Moderner Geist in der deutschen Tonkunst* (1900–13).

69. *Der Merker, Mahler Heft*, page 192.

70. MBR, No. 208.

71. In the same letter Mahler announces to Frau Sommerfeld the date of the Berlin premiere of three movements from the *Third Symphony* and quotes the titles of the various movements.

72. Letter of February 5, 1897, to Rosa Papier (BMG, page 41).

73. Letter of January 25 to Mihalovics (Hungarian National Library). Jahn had handed in his resignation unwillingly, just before leaving for Dresden, and Bezecny had aroused the wrath of his superior, the First Lord Chamberlain, by refusing to accept it.

74. BMG, page 79. See also Chapter 3.

75. Once more Karpath seems well informed as to what was going on behind the scenes in the opera, as Hanslick's letter quoted below shows.

76. *Staatsarchiv/Oper*, No. 491/1897.


# CHAPTER 24

1. Cast: Doxat (Constance), Giesswein (Armand).

2. See Chapter 10.

3. Cast of the February 5 premiere: Mildenburg (Madeleine), Birrenkoven (Andrea), Demuth (Gérard).

4. Sittard found the first movement "too agitated" but admitted that the performance was perfectly "in place."

5. Next Krzyzanowski conducted an unfinished *Spingspiel* called *Der Vierjährige Posten*, in an arrangement by Robert Hirschfeld. *Am Meer* and *Du bist die Ruhi* were sung by Demuth, *Suleikas Gesang* by Mildenburg, and *Trock'ne Blumen, Wanderers Nachtlied,* and *Horch! Horch!* by Birrenkoven, the piano accompanist for all three being Mahler. The performance ended with a *Festspiel* by Gustav Burchard, "Franz Schubert."

6. It seems that Nikisch considered conducting the Scherzo, the final Adagio, or possibly even the whole symphony, at the Berlin Philharmonic. In a letter to Weingartner in December, Mahler requested him to announce his projected performance of part of the *Third Symphony* at the Königliche Kapelle, so that Nikisch could not reproach him for refusing him the first performance. According to another

letter to Weingartner (January 27, HLG Collection), Nikisch did indeed hold a grudge against Mahler for this reason. Several others letters to Weingartner accompanied some lists of minor alterations in orchestration, particularly following the first sight-reading of the score by Mahler's Hamburg orchestra, which took place on February 5 or 6, after which Mahler declared himself "quite satisfied" with his work.

7. Letter in the Rosé Collection.

8. The program also included Brahms's *Akademische Festouvertüre* and Tchaikovsky's *Fifth Symphony*. The Parisian violinist Sophie Jaffé also played Vieuxtemps's *Fifth Violin Concerto,* an Anton Rubinstein *Romance,* and Wieniawski's *Souvenir de Moscou.*

9. Letter from Mahler to Kaim of February 15, 1897, in the Stadtbibliothek, Munich.

10. Weingartner was conductor of the Berlin Opera Orchestra and of the Königliche Kapelle from 1891 on. He conducted four subscription concerts in Hamburg during the 1895–96 season and eight during the following one.

11. In the letter he wrote to Weingartner on November 14, Mahler informed him that Wolff had nonetheless expressed his intention of giving the *Blumenstück* again, perhaps together with another movement from the *Third.* The last two movements were in the hands of a copyist and should be ready by January (HLG Collection).

12. With this in mind, Mahler invited the critic Josef Sittard to dinner with Weingartner, and also gave the score to Mildenburg and Birrenkoven, whom he considered suitable for the two main roles.

13. Many of Mahler's contemporaries did likewise in their memoirs, and for this reason Natalie Bauer-Lechner deserves all our gratitude for having adopted so modest and scrupulous an attitude.

14. Cf. Nodnagel's article in the *Musikalisches Wochenblatt* of April 1897, page 299.

15. Weingartner gave this lecture in Berlin on February 11, 1897, in Bremen on March 15, in Munich on March 26, and in Hamburg on April 11. It was published the next year in a slightly enlarged version as *Die Symphonie nach Beethoven* by S. Fischer Verlag, Berlin (1898).

16. According to Weingartner, those who condemned the first theme of the *Second Symphony* in Berlin had, because of its mighty proportions, failed to "consider it as a whole" and to "follow its developments."

17. A letter from Mahler to Weingartner dated March 6 announces his arrival in Berlin for the following day and his intention of attending a performance of Gerhard Hauptmann's play *Die Versunkene Glocke* (HLG Collection).

18. On April 25, 1897, Weingartner wrote Mahler a letter in which he wished him good luck for Vienna and spoke of his opera *Genesius,* the score of which Mahler had given to Mildenburg, for Pollini was supposed to perform it with Birrenkoven (Rosé Collection). By then the failure of the first movements of the *Third Symphony* had made Weingartner drop the complete performance he had planned.

19. Ludwig Bussler states in his *National Zeitung* article that the two factions continued to clash long after the departure of most of the audience, but that Mahler's opponents finally withdrew, leaving the field to his supporters.

20. Letters to Mildenburg dated March 7, 8, and 9. In his biography of Mahler published sometime later in the *Musikalisches Wochenblatt* (1897, pages 526–27, 544–45, 562–63), E. O. Nodnagel, then one of Mahler's most fervent disciples, claims that most of the public present that night showed such enthusiasm that Mahler took five curtain calls. Nodnagel is equally unrealistic when he states that Richard Strauss later said he "admired Berliners" that evening. His testimony carries little weight when set against Mahler's.

21. MBR, No. 194.

22. This "program" was undoubtedly written by Mahler for the occasion, to help the listeners through the difficulties of the Scherzo. It was often reprinted later.

23. The post horn's sentimental solo reminded this anonymous critic of the *Trompeter* by Nessler, a comparison that must have cut Mahler to the quick, considering his scorn for that composer.

24. Because of the fragmentary performances certain critics maintained that Mahler did not finish his compositions. In the Philharmonic Program, Heinrich Reimann, the famous musicologist, had in fact reprinted, in March 1895 (when the first part of the *Second Symphony* was originally performed), the date that appeared on the score— February 8, 1895—actually the date on which the manuscript copy had been completed. Some critics, including Ludwig Bussler in the *National Zeitung,* had taken advantage of this to state that the *Second Symphony* was still incomplete.

25. Nodnagel thought the complete performance of the symphony, planned for the following year, would doubtless prove impossible because of this Finale; this was all the more regrettable, since the work could only be understood after several hearings.

26. Letters to Mildenburg and to Justi.

27. The society had been founded in 1859 by Nikolai Rubinstein. Its concerts took place at 9 P.M.

28. This information was supplied by the Soviet musicologist D. E. Rabinovich.

29. Letters to Mildenburg and Justi dated March 22.

30. Letter of March 18 to Justi, in the Rosé Collection.

31. Is Mahler alluding to Richard Strauss? Letter to Weingartner, March 31 (HLG Collection).

32. NBL, page 118, and NBLS, July 1899.

33. Son of a piano manufacturer, Franz Kaim (1856–1935), a philologist and literary historian, founded in 1893 the "Kaim-Konzerte," which were held in the large Kaimsaal (later called the Tonhalle), built expressly for these concerts. The orchestra, composed of seventy-five musicians, played in Munich during the winter and in Kissingen during the summer. The twelve annual "Kaim-Konzerte" took place on Monday evenings from November to March. Twenty "popular" symphonic concerts on Wednesday evenings, conducted by Bernhard Stavenhagen, and fifty popular concerts made up the orchestra's schedule. The programs of the Kaim Orchestra were usually more modern than those of the other Munich symphonic orchestras, especially the 'Hofopernkonzerte," conducted by Mottl.

34. *Neues Wiener Journal,* October 19, 1900.

35. NBL, page 62.

36. Hermann Zumpe (1850–1903), born in Taubenheim (Saxony), studied music in Leipzig before going to Bayreuth, where, like many other young musicians, he collaborated on copying and checking the orchestral parts of Wagner's *Ring.* After being *Kapellmeister* in Salzburg, Würzburg, Magdeburg, Frankfurt, and Hamburg, he was made *Hofkapellmeister* in Stuttgart in 1891. He became conductor of the Kaim Concerts in 1895, but soon left them for the Schwerin Opera. In 1900 he returned to Munich as general music director and conducted the inaugural performance of the *Prinzregenten Theater.* He composed several operas. If he really was the excellent all-around conductor the *Allgemeine Zeitung* thought him to be, posterity had done him a cruel injustice by forgetting him almost entirely.

37. NBL, page 63.

38. An article published in *Das Kleine Journal* of Berlin, on May 7, 1897, accused Wetschel of having "reformed to death" many things at the Opera and of having provoked the departure of the Intendant so as to reinforce his own authority in the management of the two theaters.

39. Burckhard did everything he could to keep his post, even asking his mistress, Frau Schratt of the Burgtheater, to intervene, because she knew the Emperor, but the latter said any such request would be useless, for on no account would he try to influence his subordinates, more competent than himself in theatrical matters. So

Burckhard, like Bezecny, was forced to give in. Bezecny later pretended to forget his promise to resign, but he was forcefully reminded of it.

40. This news, published in the *Hamburger Nachrichten* on January 13, had been picked up from the Vienna press.

41. BMG, pages 47 and 48. The article in *Das Kleine Journal* of Berlin, dated May 7, 1897, confirms all Ludwig Karpath's statements in every detail.

42. Bezecny was in fact governor of the bank of the Bodenkreditanstalt, and it was supposed that the deficit (fifty thousand florins) had humiliated him, though it was smaller than that of preceding years. The *Deutsche Zeitung* also mentioned as a reason for his departure his opposition to the reconstruction of the Burgtheater and the difference of opinion between Prince Liechtenstein and himself over a vaudeville that had been performed at Schönbrunn—*Madame et Monsieur Denis*—and that was "anti-French" in tone.

43. Mahler conducted this *Invitation to the Dance* out of gratitude to Weingartner, although the critics Beer and Herzfeld found the orchestration much inferior to Berlioz's. Weingartner himself had called Mahler's attention to his version of Weber's piano piece (letter from Mahler to Weingartner of March 15. HLG Collection).

44. According to Hanslick, Jahn's scouting trips had been fruitless, for since the beginning of the year no new work had been heard except for Smetana's *Bartered Bride*, which was not really new, and André Messager's *Le Chevalier d'Harmental*, which had been a failure. Jahn immediately wrote to the intendant to defend himself and to complain of the "intentionally misleading" facts in Hanslick's article: other new premieres had in fact been planned but had had to be postponed for various reasons; as for singers, there were none to be found. This defense was as weak as it was unconvincing: it was clear that Jahn was exhausted and nearing the end of the road.

45. The account in BMG is exact down to the smallest detail.

46. Karpath wrongly gives April 6, the day of Brahm's funeral, as the date of this communiqué.

47. BMG, page 42, and MBR, No. 218.

48. MBR, Nos. 99 and 220.

49. In a letter to Jahn, who was then in Karlsbad, Mahler expressed the hope that these attacks in the anti-Semitic press would not "spoil his vacation."

50. MBR, Nos. 99 and 220. On the same day he sent a telegram to Wlassack and Bezecny saying that he would reach Vienna on the twenty-seventh. Karpath was requested to announce the news and did so immediately.

51. Letter to Weingartner, April 15 (HLG Collection).

52. Soloists in the *Requiem:* Artner, Schumann-Heink, Giesswein, Demuth; in the *Te Deum:* Mildenburg, Birrenkoven, Wittekopf.

53. In order to draw the attention of the Viennese toward their new conductor, Karpath had ordered the Hamburg correspondent of his paper (the *Neues Wiener Tagblatt*) to telegraph him an account of this farewell performance.

54. When Ferdinand Pfohl wrote to Mahler in 1901 to recommend a singer, he ended his letter by mentioning the decline of the Hamburg Opera. "You would not even recognize the orchestra any more."

55. Letter from Mahler to Cosima dated December 9 (*ibid.*). In it Mahler apologizes for not having coached Mildenburg in this role, but Pollini had just made her learn another in only a few days, and all to no purpose. Mahler also sets down his conception of the essential dramatic progression in the role of Kundry. Act I: struggle for redemption. Act II: Kundry unwillingly succumbs to Klingsor's enchantment and then becomes the demoniac temptress of Parsifal. Act III: after the destruction of her will power, redemption through grace. The three stages can be reduced to two, thus expressing the dualism of the human soul: the opposition between the first and third acts and between the two scenes of the second act. In an undated letter Mahler advises Frau Wagner not to give Mildenburg any roles other than Kundry and Brünnhilde—the only

ones that suit her temperament. For Sieglinde she has not enough "femininity (in the passive sense)." He also mentions the conducting debut of Cosima's son Siegfried (Wahnfried Archives).

56. This letter (No. 155) was not written in December 1896, as stated in MBR. The other letters to Mildenburg show that her first stay in Bayreuth took place at the end of February.

57. The composer Förster, in answer to questions put to him by the musicologist Alfred Mathis, asserted that Alma Mahler had been the first physically consummated love of Mahler's life. But it seems that all of Mahler's contemporaries underestimated the importance of his affair with Mildenburg. The letters he wrote her leave no doubt as to the character of their relationship.

58. Letter of December 1896 to Mihalovics and BMG, page 102.

59. Mahler's baptismal notice is No. 29 in the register of that parish. The vicar who baptized him was named Swider and his godfather Theodor Meynberg. All we know of the latter is that he was first the "confidential agent" of a committee for the Protection of German Emigrants in Offenbach-am-Main, and then, in 1896, of the "St. Raphael-Vereins," and that he lived at No. 52 Kleine Reichenstrasse. Mahler gave, as the birthplace of his father, Deutsch Brod. On the day of his marriage at the Church of St. Carlo Borromeo in Vienna he had to give the exact date of his conversion, which appears in the register of that church.

60. The word "Christian" is underlined in the documents mentioned, a proof of the importance the Austrian officials attached to this matter.

61. BMG, page 102.

62. See in AM, page 289, his remarks after watching the Jews in the Lemberg ghetto.

63. See BMG, *ibid.*

64. See *Les Voies d'Israël* by André Siegfried (Hachette, Paris, 1958), *Jésus et Israël*, by Jules Isaac, and *The Last of the Just*, André Schwarz-Bart's novel (New York, English translation, 1961).

65. In his famous biography Ernest Newman shows clearly that Wagner was incapable of understanding any point of view other than his own.

66. Cf. André Siegfried, *op. cit.*, page 166.

67. Psalms, CIII, 15, 16, quoted by Siegfried, page 167. The similarity of expression between these verses and the Chinese poems of *Das Lied von der Erde* is striking, though the biblical accent is more metaphysical.

68. *Ibid.*, page 79.

69. *Ibid.*, page 99. I am indebted to Mr. Manès-Sperber for some valuable suggestions on this point.

70. AMM, page 60.

71. See the program written for the first performance of the *Second Symphony* in Munich, October 1900 (WRM, page 22).

72. Specht had several discussions with Mahler in Hamburg in the spring of 1895.

73. RSM, page 50.

74. MBR, No. 73, of June 22, 1901.

75. Mahler expressed himself almost identically in 1901 in a letter to his fiancée Alma, who had been brought up an atheist.

## CHAPTER 25

1. Johann Schrammel (1850–93) made his debut in 1878, founding the Schrammel Quartet with his brother (a violinist like himself), a guitar player, and a clarinet player. In 1891 the clarinet was replaced by an accordion. The voluptuous, sensual strings of the Schrammel Quartet made it famous. They played in a Viennese restaurant, much frequented by the royal family and the aristocracy, and toured the world with a repertoire of marches, waltzes, and popular Viennese songs, some of which Schrammel

composed himself. Professional whistlers and yodelers were often soloists with the Schrammel Quartet.

2. The Austrian aristocracy had, in the eighteenth century, played an essential role in this respect, right up to the time of Beethoven. Maria Theresa had patronized Gluck; Josef II, Mozart; and Leopold III was himself a composer. Beethoven had several generous artistic patrons, but the taste for culture was gradually lost in that stratum of society.

3. As early as April 10, 1897, two days after the announcement of Mahler's appointment, the anti-Semitic papers attacked the choice of a Jew for *Kappellmeister* at the opera, when so many "young men of talent" were vainly awaiting a post and Viennese art was already so completely "Jewified."

4. See Chapter 1.

5. After the Italian defeats and during the ill-fated war against Prussia.

6. Exactly 6,116,747 gulden according to Franz Farga (*Die Wiener Oper*).

7. Thanks to an unusual subscription plan, one could make a down payment in advance and thus have a seat reserved for all performances, subject to confirmation the evening before.

8. The concerts took place at 12:30 P.M. When Mahler arrived, their conductor for over twenty years had been Hans Richter.

9. The Philharmonic supplementary concert, called the Nicolaï Concert, generally took place at the end of the season and presented a large choral work.

10. This three-hundred-member group of amateurs rehearsed on Monday evenings and regularly presented masses, passions, and oratorios by Bach, Handel, Haydn, and Mozart.

11. Montenuovo is the Italian translation of Neipperg (Neuberg—that is, "new mountain").

12. Hans Richter, born on April 4, 1843, in Györ, Hungary, was the son of a *Kappellmeister* at the cathedral there and of the singer who created the role of Venus in *Tannhäuser* in Vienna. Having completed his studies at the Vienna Conservatory, he was recommended to Wagner, who summoned him to Lucerne in 1866–67 to copy the score of *Die Meistersinger*. A conductor at the Munich Opera, he also conducted in Paris and Brussels before returning to Lucerne, where he took part in the first performance of the *Siegfried Idyll* and copied the *Ring* scores. First conductor of the Budapest Opera from 1871 to 1875, he was then engaged as a conductor in Vienna and was later elected head of the Philharmonic Concerts. The only conductor in Bayreuth in 1876, he presented in turn the Viennese premieres of the big Wagner dramas. He was also head of the Richter Concerts in London.

13. BMG, page 66. This letter and Richter's reply were published for the first time in MKW (*Wagners Kampf und Sieg*) in 1930.

14. MBR, No. 100.

15. MBR, No. 133.

16. MBR, No. 210.

17. Letter to Justi of April 28. Mahler traveled with a "childhood friend from Iglau" named Grünfeld. Was this one of the Grünfeld brothers from Prague?

18. BMG, page 55. Once he became director, apart from a few exceptions, he had no further contact with journalists.

19. Bahr, who was to read Romain Rolland's novel *Jean Christophe* a few years later, considered its hero both the physical and moral incarnation of Mahler. He also compared him to a Neapolitan musican called Pisani, described by the novelist Bulwer-Lytton in *Zanoni* (Hermann Bahr, "Mahler" in *Neue Freie Presse,* March 22, 1914).

20. In a note dated April 29, Mahler announced his arrival in Vienna to the prince and asks him to set a time for their meeting. (Robert Lehmann collection).

21. Letter from Mahler to Jahn (*Staatsarchiv,* Wien, Z 256–1897).

22. Puccini's *La Bohème* was staged at the Hofoper by Mahler five years later.

23. BMG, page 377.

24. NBL, page 77. The passage indicates that this performance of *Die Meistersinger* occurred during rehearsals for *Der fliegende Holländer* and *Die Zauberflöte*. The performance on May 8 was the only one given that spring.

25. BMG, pages 54–55, and NBL, page 73.

26. Mahler was certainly alluding to the very mediocre acoustics of the Hamburg Opera.

27. Richard Heuberger (1850–1914), born in Graz, studied as an engineer before devoting himself to music at the age of twenty-six. *Chordirektor* of the Akademischer Gesangverein in Vienna, then leader of the *Singakademie* in 1878, he first became music critic for the *Wiener Tagblatt*, then for the *Münchner Allgemeine Zeitung* and finally for the *Neue Freie Presse*, where he remained from 1896 to 1901. A professor at the conservatory and leader of the Männergesangverein, he became editor of the *Neue Musikalische Presse* in 1904. He also published some critical and biographical works as well as operas, operettas, and choral works.

28. Max Kalbeck (1850–1921) born in Breslau, studied law and philosophy and published several books of verse before studying music at the Munich Musikschule. Music critic in Breslau from 1875 to 1880, he then became, on Hanslick's recommendation, critic on the *Wiener Allgemeine Zeitung*, then on the *Presse* in 1883, and on the *Montags Revue* in 1890. He joined the *Neues Wiener Tagblatt* in 1886. He and Hanslick were the principal adversaries of the new school of music, that is, of Wagner and Bruckner. The author of several biographies and other works, and translator of many operatic librettos presented in Vienna, Kalbeck published between 1904 and 1914 a huge four-volume biography of Brahms. Mahler himself commissioned several opera translations from him.

29. Robert Hirschfeld (1858–1914) came from a Moravian Jewish family and studied music at the conservatories of Breslau and Vienna. In the latter he also taught musical aesthetics from 1884. In 1885 he published a polemic work criticizing Hanslick. He arranged for the stage Haydn's *Der Apotheker* (*Lo Speziale*) and Schubert's *Der Vierjahrige Posten*, which Mahler conducted in Hamburg. Two years before his death he took over the direction of the Mozarteum in Salzburg.

30. Hirschfeld ends by complaining of the behavior of Winkelmann's admirers, who "shout their heads off, even when the curtain has risen."

31. Cast: Ehrenstein (Elsa), Kaulich (Ortrud), Winkelmann (Lohengrin), Reichmann (Telramund), Grengg (King), Felix (Herald). Heuberger also regretted the disgraceful behavior of the paid applauders, whom Mahler was shortly to attack.

32. In the middle of the Act I "prayer" Helm noted that Mahler had cut the accompaniment added by Richter in order to help the soprano.

33. The slowness of the Prelude, the amazing pianissimo of the chorus after the hero's farewell to the swan and in the passage *"Seht, seht, welch seltsam Wunder,"* the superb crescendo of the Prayer, and many other moments—all earned the anonymous writer's enthusiastic admiration, as did the rallentando discreetly employed by Mahler in the passage *"Rauschen des Festes, seid nun entronnen,"* in the wedding chorus of Act III.

34. NBL, page 75.

35. Universitätstrasse No. 6, second floor, Door No. 5.

36. MBR, No. 161.

37. In addition, Pollini would demand damages for the breaking of her contract, for he had told Mahler that he did not intend to let her go for at least a year.

38. Anton Rückauf (1855–1903), a Czech composer who lived in Vienna, where he had been given much advice by Brahms. His only opera, *Die Rosenthalerin,* had some success in Dresden but was never staged in Vienna.

39. NBL, page 77. Mahler also once said that the "delicate pollen of a Mozart flower does not survive too large an orchestra."

40. Mahler added that he wanted to follow the lead already given by the Munich Shakespeare Theater.

41. According to a letter to Justi that is easy to date, since in it Mahler mentions that the performance of *Die Walküre,* scheduled for the following day, has been canceled due to the illness of Luise von Ehrenstein.

42. In a letter to Justi, Mahler complained that Natalie "watches over me like a hawk; if it were up to her, she'd keep me from seeing any woman under fifty."

43. NBL, page 80.

44. Here we encounter one of the least convincing reproaches that Helm addressed to Mahler, solely to comply with the anti-Semitic views of his paper. He specifies that the Moor (Monostatos) expressed his delight with Papageno's bells by means of murmurs that "deprived the scene of part of its humor," adding that "as in *Lohengrin,* the chorus could have sung more forcefully." Nevertheless, he congratulates Mahler for having re-established the Mozartean truth throughout, and particularly for having suppressed the traditional cadence at the end of Pamina's aria. Cast of the May 29 performance: Teleky (Queen of the Night), Förster (Pamina), Mora, Ehrenstein, Kaulich (Three Ladies), Elizza (Papagena), Dippel (Tamino), Felix (Papageno), Reichenberg (Sarastro).

45. NBL, No. 163.

46. NBL, page 74. Mahler confused artistic qualities and personality to such an extent that he fell in love in turn with Johanna Richter, Betti Frank, Mildenburg, and later in Vienna with Gutheil-Schoder and Selma Kurz.

47. Cast of the June 5 performance: Mora (Senta), Schrödter (Erik), Neidel (Holländer), Reichenberg (Daland).

48. Had Mahler followed this excellent advice, he might have lived longer, for his final illness originated as a tonsil infection.

49. At the Reformhotel (Habsburgerhof).

50. The Villa Zirnheim. On June 19, Mahler wrote a letter of sympathy from there to his onetime teacher Heinrich Fischer, whose wife had just died (*Stadtarchiv* Iglau).

51. Letter of June 1897 to Rosa Papier (BMG, page 72).

52. Sterzing is now known in Italy as Vipiteno.

53. On July 8, Mahler climbed the nine-thousand-foot Amthorspitze.

## CHAPTER 26

1. Rosa Papier had no illusions about her former pupil's character, as is shown by her letter quoted below.

2. MBR, No. 212, and letter to Mildenburg.

3. Her first performance as Kundry in *Parsifal.*

4. Letter to Rosa Papier, dated June 19 (Z 983/1897).

5. BMG, page 75.

6. Letter of September 24, 1897, from Rosa Papier to Mildenburg (Nationalbibliothek, Vienna).

7. One of Mildenburg's "admirers" was Mahler's friend, Hermann Behn, and another the critic Ludwig Karpath, who wrote her on October 3, 1900, reproaching her for being nothing but "a vain prima donna," only interested in herself and her own comfort. He added that Mahler had been right to say that "one would need the soul of a *valet de chambre* in order to live with her . . . And now you complain of your loneliness!" he concluded. (Letters to Anna Bahr-Mildenburg, *ibid.*)

8. The official archives contain a letter Mahler wrote to Hofrath Doczi, Johann Strauss's librettist, concerning a revival of *Ritter Pázmán,* the Waltz King's only serious opera.

9. Letter of June 19 (Z 983/1897).

10. BMG, page 75.

11. The circular was sent from Nauheim, where Bezecny was spending the summer. The same day the intendant wrote to Jahn to congratulate him on the success of his operation and to give him the news: "It is essential that in your absence, the directorship be entrusted to a firm hand."

12. BMG, page 77.

13. BMG, page 77.

14. BMG, page 79 (letter of July 30 to Rosa Papier).

15. *Ibid*.

16. *Ibid*, page 57.

17. Letter of July 30 to Justi.

18. Cast of the August 1 *Lohengrin:* Ehrenstein (Elsa), Winkelmann (Lohengrin), Kaulich (Ortrud), Hesch (King).

19. BMG, page 63. Cast of the August 14 *Le Nozze di Figaro:* Förstel (Susanna), Sedlmair (Countess), Pohlner (Cherubino), Thann (Marcellina), Neidel (Figaro), Ritter (Count).

20. The *Neue Freie Presse* article is unsigned, but its style and content clearly indicate that Hanslick was the author. Probably that same year, Mahler wrote to the famous critic, thanking him for having "dealt so often and so seriously with his work" (in a letter sold some years ago by the Viennese autograph dealer Heck).

21. Hanslick also congratulated Mahler for having restored to Act II the short Susanna-Cherubino duet, and for adding drama to the latter's second aria by making the singer strike a "stiff, yet pleasing" attitude. The whole performance, "delightfully accompanied by a small orchestra," was the "most exciting" he had ever heard.

22. "Unholy halls," a reference to Sarastro's *"In diesen heilg'n Hallen"* ("Within these sacred halls") in *Die Zauberflöte*.

23. Wolf's opera based on Alarcón's *El Sombrero de tres picos*.

24. On August 12, Mahler wrote to Richard Strauss to ask for information about the tenor who was to sing Loge in *Das Rheingold,* and about the "wooden trumpet" that the Munich Opera used for the *"Lustige Weise"* in the final act of *Tristan und Isolde.* That same day he sent the administration a detailed outline of the season's programs. At the end of the month he wrote a series of letters to the Munich Opera and to the elderly conductor Hermann Levi, concerning Levi's new version of Mozart's *Così fan tutte.*

25. NBL, page 83.

26. After *Die Walküre,* the Brünnhilde, Sophie Sedlmair, thanked him for having mouthed every syllable of her role to her throughout the performance.

27. According to Ernst Decsey, the musician left at a quarter to ten.

28. In relating this incident, Mahler complained that in order to show his anger he had had to rise at six in the morning so as to reach the opera ahead of the culprit (NBL, page 85). Paul Decsey, in his article *"Stunden mit Mahler"* (*Die Musik*, X, 21, 144), speaks of a "trumpeter" when telling this story, but Natalie's account is more precise and detailed.

29. The musicians' salaries varied between 660 and 900 gulden per year, but in addition they received "activity pay" of between 120 and 200 gulden a year, which was reduced when they did not play.

30. Wolf expressed the same admiration in a letter written on September 1, 1897, to Oskar Grohe: "We have recently had magnificent performances of the *Ring* under the direction of Mahler, who is creating a sensation here."

31. Most of the opera's best singers were in fact absent in August, either on holiday or appearing as guest singers abroad.

32. In *Das Rheingold,* Leitich approved the suppression of the intermission but deplored the fact that the staging and mechanical effects—such as the Rhine in the first scene—were not more "modern." Also according to him, the Valkyries, for the first

time, "sang and acted well together in their final scene." Cast of *Das Rheingold* on August 25: Ehrenstein (Freia), Walker (Fricka), Van Dyck (Loge), Ritter (Alberich), Reichmann (Wotan). *Die Walküre,* on August 26: Ehrenstein (Sieglinde), Sedlmair (Brünnhilde), Walker (Fricka), Winkelmann (Siegmund), Reichmann (Wotan), Hesch (Hunding). *Siegfried,* on August 28: Sedlmair (Brünnhilde), Winkelmann (Siegfried), Schmitt (Mime), Ritter (Alberich), Grengg (Wotan). *Die Götterdämmerung* on August 29: Sedlmair (Brünnhilde), Abendroth, Pohlner, Kaulich (Rhine maidens), Winkelmann (Siegfried), Horwitz (Alberich), Reichenberg (Hagen).

33. Almost blind for months, Jahn could no longer read new scores. Instead he learned them by heart by having them played on the piano by the *Korrepetitor* Raoul Mader, composer of the ballet *Rothe Schuhe* and future director of the Budapest Opera.

34. Letter to Justi of August 11.

35. BMG, page 58.

36. A few additional clauses specified the travel expenses to which Mahler would be entitled, as well as the pension increases he would receive periodically: three thousand florins immediately; four thousand after ten years of service, five thousand after fifteen years, and six thousand after twenty.

37. Although he had conferred it upon Dr. Schlenther a few years before, when the latter resigned the directorship of the Burgtheater.

38. It is interesting to note that Vienna was one of the last German-speaking cities to stage the great Wagnerian dramas.

39. MBR, No. 196.

40. Born in Hof, Moravia, in 1835, Jahn first became a chorister, then a conductor in Budapest from 1854 on. He pursued his conducting career in Amsterdam, Prague, and Wiesbaden and was named director of the Vienna Opera in 1881.

41. It was rumored in Vienna that Jahn once, in order to finish a game of cards he was playing with the Austrian war minister and two singers from the opera (the baritone Reichmann and the tenor Schrödter), changed the opera scheduled to be performed that evening at the very last moment. Cf. Leo Slezak: *Mein Lebensmärchen* (page 122).

42. Both the *Neues Wiener Tagblatt* of June 14, 1907, and the *Fremdenblatt* of July 4 declared that Richter had been offered Jahn's post but had refused to accept it because of his experiences in Budapest. Apart from the fact that he had already been retired by the Vienna Opera, which would have raised untold administrative problems, he also felt he was hardly qualified to head an opera.

43. Son of a piano manufacturer, Hermann Winkelmann (1849–1912) studied singing in Paris and Hanover, after which he was engaged successively in Altenburg, Darmstadt, and Hamburg. First dramatic tenor at the Vienna Opera from 1883 to 1906, he created the role of Parsifal in Bayreuth in 1882; in 1883 he became the first Vienna Tristan. By the time Mahler arrived, his voice had become undependable, his breath short, and his diction often distorted the vowels. He was famous, like many other aging tenors, for his interpretation of the last-act Tristan. He was an intelligent and cultured man and a gifted actor who could take a wide variety of roles.

44. Theodor Reichmann (1849–1903) studied music and singing in Berlin, Prague, and Milan, then set out upon a brilliant career as a baritone in Magdeburg, Berlin, Rotterdam, Strasbourg, Hamburg, and Munich. His two engagements at the Vienna Opera (1882–89 and 1893–1903) were separated by long tours. In Bayreuth in 1882 he created the role of Amfortas in *Parsifal*. He sang at the Metropolitan Opera in New York 1889–91.

45. Mahler was to meet Dippel (1866–1932) again at the Metropolitan Opera in New York, where for a short time he held an important administrative post.

46. Marie Renard (1863–1939), whose real name was Marie Pölz, was born into a peasant family in Graz. She made her debut there in 1882 as a mezzo-soprano in the role of Azucena in *Il Trovatore*. Engaged in Prague and then Berlin, she joined the

Vienna Opera in 1888, and left it as a *Kammersängerin* in 1900 to marry Count Rudolf Kinsky.

47. Ernest Van Dyck (1861–1923), born in Antwerp, took vocal lessons in Brussels and Paris, where he became famous after a debut with the Lamoureux Orchestra. For many years he sang the role of Parsifal in Bayreuth. He joined the Vienna Opera in 1888 and left in 1899 to sing many Wagnerian performances in Paris. After four years (1898–1902) at the Metropolitan Opera, New York, Van Dyck became director of the Théâtre des Champs-Elysées, Paris. In 1914 he gave up singing to become a teacher. His farewell performance was *Parsifal* in Paris.

48. When Mahler heard Van Dyck's interpretation of *Tristan und Isolde* in Paris in 1909, he flew into such a rage that he left the commissioner of police's box without a word.

49. *Montags Revue*, May 4, 1897. This article, numbered 2991/97, is in the opera archives, which proves that the authorities had taken notice of it. It states that "on paper, the chorus is larger than ever, but in fact, it has never been so mediocre. Also, since many of the choristers' voices are too weak, the opera is frequently obliged to call in supplementary singers at the last moment, a costly procedure." Wondra is accused of favoring certain of the singers by granting them long sick leaves; this had caused deep resentment among the less favored. Wondra remained at the opera throughout Mahler's tenure and was secretly one of his most dangerous enemies.

50. In particular three sopranos: Mora, Teleky, and Abendroth. Ehrenstein and Elizza were also attacked violently by the anti-Semitic papers.

51. In particular André Messager's *Le Chevalier d'Harmenthal* and Albert Kauders' *Walther von der Vogelweide*.

52. See Chapter 28 for the visit paid by the leader of the claque to Emil von Reznicek, the composer of *Donna Diana*.

53. BMG, pages 60–61.

54. BMG, pages 60–61.

55. See BMG, page 92, and LEM, page 142. Karpath was mistaken in saying that this had to do with "the engagement" of Karin, since she was a member of the Vienna Opera from October 1, 1900, to September 30, 1901. Graf was therefore correct in speaking of her "re-engagement" but wrong in affirming that Mahler went from Steinbach to Ischl to see the Emperor, for he had left Steinbach long before.

56. Man's memory can be short when his own interests are at stake!

57. The lady-in-waiting returned to the charge, but the Emperor let the matter drop. NBL, page 103; BMG, page 63, and an article by Edgar Istel, *Münchner Neueste Nachrichten*, March 23, 1911: *Wie Gustav Mahler eine Protectionsoper ablehnte*. Max Graf quotes a similar incident that arose over an opera composed by the young Archduke Peter Ferdinand, which Mahler refused to perform unless expressly ordered to do so by the Emperor (LEM, page 143).

58. Both Luise and her sister, the pianist Gisela von Ehrenstein, had long frequented her salon.

59. See BMG, pages 113–14. Ehrenstein resigned in 1899. The reasons for Mahler's lack of consideration toward her were doubtless more artistic than personal. Judging from articles by Leitich and Hirschfeld, Ehrenstein was no great singer.

60. BMG, page 88.

61. Letters to Leopold Demuth, on December 17, 1897, and to Fräulein Mackrott, on November 14 (Archives of the Vienna Opera).

## CHAPTER 27

1. Mahler, it seems, grouped the violins around him to improve the orchestral sound.

2. Cast of the September 11 performance: Forster (Marie), Schrödter (Ivanov), Dippel (Chateauneuf), Reichmann (Zaar), Hesch (Bürgermeister).

3. This correspondence is in the National Museum in Prague. Since he was unable to attend a Prague performance on August 24, Mahler sent the stage director Stoll and the painter Brioschi. He also got from Prague models of the sets and sketches of the costumes.

4. NBL, page 88.

5. Natalie notes that Mahler succeeded in producing this performance most economically: the staging and scenery cost three thousand gulden, the costumes three hundred. At the first performance, Kalbeck states, the ovations resembled a Czech nationalist manifestation, for the audience included all the Viennese Czechs (as well as Giacomo Puccini, in Vienna to attend performances of his *La Bohème* at the Theater an der Wien).

6. This libretto, written originally in German by Joseph Wenzig, has been translated into Czech for the composer by Erwin Spindler and translated back into German by Kalbeck.

7. Cast of the first (October 4) performance: Sedlmair (Milada), Michalek (Jutta), Winkelmann (Dalibor), Dippel (Vitek), Felix (Budivoj), Hesch (Benĕs).

8. NBL, page 173.

9. He continued to do this throughout his whole career in Vienna, even after the important premieres.

10. NBL, page 89.

11. Letter from Mahler to Weingartner (September–October 1897) (HLG Collection).

12. Wolf's letter quoted above (cf. Chapter XXVI) confirms that Mahler probably did make such a promise.

13. The first Vienna performance of this work took place on October 23, 1899, with Mahler conducting.

14. Alma Mahler's version of this incident differs from that given by Frank Walker: she claims that Wolf "believed himself to be Mahler" and wanted "to enter his own house."

15. See Frank Walker: *Hugo Wolf,* page 420; AMM, page 84; and Ernst Decsey (*Die Musik* I, page 139).

16. NBL, page 91.

17. In the *Deutsche Zeitung,* Helm compared the staging of this procession to the Bayreuth staging of the entrance of the knights in *Parsifal.*

18. In particular the passage *"Kommet, lasst uns auf die Seite geh'n, damit wir, was sie machen sehn?"* caused such uproarious laughter at the first performance that Wlassack advised Mahler to suppress it, fearing that it would be judged "too risqué." The phrase *"auf die Seite geh'n"* is a German euphemism meaning to go to the bathroom.

19. NBL, page 92. Despite Mildenburg's vocal agility, it is certain that she could never have sung the acrobatic role of the Queen of the Night. Mahler was thinking only of her physical appearance.

20. Kalbeck noted that even the smaller roles had been assigned to first-class singers. Cast of the October 16 performance: Abendroth (Queen of the Night), Forster (Pamina), Michalek (Papagena), Sedlmair, Pohlner, Kaulich (Three Ladies), Dippel (Tamino), Schrödter (Monostatos), Ritter (Papageno), Neidel (Speaker), Grengg (Sarastro). Marie Renard sang Papagena in the November 10 performance.

21. Above all in the ballroom scene at Larina's and in the final duet.

22. Like Hanslick, Helm discussed at length the weaknesses of the libretto, especially in the last scene; the "old-fashioned" construction of the work reminded him of the "early operas, divided into numbers." Cast of the first performance (November 19): Michalek (Olga), Renard (Tatiana), Schrödter (Lenski), Schittenhelm (Triquet), Ritter (Onegin), Hesch (Gremin).

23. Mahler put back one of the traditional cuts, the passage in the love duet where

Wagner comments on the meaning of the word *und* (and) (pages 147–50 in the Breitkopf piano score), but he made the usual cut eighteen pages earlier in the same duet.

24. Hirschfeld is more to be trusted here than Kalbeck, whose love for Brahms blinded him when judging Wagner.

25. He notes that certain of Mahler's tempos were slower than Richter's; for example, in the Prelude; while others, like Isolde's curse, were faster.

26. Cast of the October 24 performance: Sedlmair (Isolde), Kaulich (Brangäne), Winkelmann (Tristan), Neidel (Kurwenal), Grengg (King Mark).

27. The previous cast had been partly altered by Mahler as follows: Ehrenstein (Elisabeth), Sedlmair (Venus), Michalek (Shepherd), Winkelmann (Tannhäuser), Schrödter (Walter), Reichmann (Wolfram), Grengg (Heinrich), Marion (Bitterolf). Helm on this occasion was astonished by the fact that the passage *"Zum Heil den Sündigen"* in the second finale had previously been cut: it now seemed to be the high spot of Tannhäuser's role.

28. In particular the slowness of the Hymn to Venus and the speed of the Act II March, which he felt exceeded Wagner's intention. (Helm recalled that Wagner, in his short book on orchestral conducting, had complained that this heroic march was too often conducted "in a clerical tempo.")

29. NBL, page 95.

30. BMG, page 275. Richter was to express his point of view to Karpath in an interview published in the *Neues Wiener Tagblatt* on September 28, 1902. In it he also restated his admiration for Mahler. Cast of the first night of *Der fliegende Holländer:* Sedlmair (Senta), Winkelmann (Erik), Dippel (Steersman), Reichmann (Dutchman).

31. This letter was written between the first *Dalibor* (October 4) and the first *Eugene Onegin* (November 19) and was probably addressed to the German composer Karl von Kaskel (whose *Sjula* and *Hochzeitsmorgen* Mahler had conducted in Hamburg), for it alludes to an opera called *Die Bettlerin,* and Kaskel had composed an opera of this name (HLG Collection).

32. Letter to Behn dated November 26, 1897 (Notar Hertz Collection). In the same letter Mahler assured Behn that "nothing has changed between us" and invited him to Vienna.

33. Mahler wrote this to an unknown correspondent (Nicolas Rauch sale, Geneva, 1957), upon whom he feared his works had made a bad impression, which might prejudice their friendship.

34. At the Philipphof on Lobkowitzplatz (see BMG, page 176).

35. BMG, page 177.

36. See in Chapter 26 the letter of September 24. Mahler must have revealed to Papier some of the facts about the liaison to which the letter referred.

37. Mahler wrote again to Mildenburg a few days later, discussing the dates of her various performances. He was prepared to delay her guest appearance, if she were not in good health, until early December. In a final, affectionate note he promised to meet her at the station or, if held up at the last moment, to visit her immediately after her arrival.

38. It is possible that this prolongation was obtained for medical reasons, for one of Mahler's notes to Mildenburg, apparently dating from this period, mentions a friend of his, Dr. Boer, the Vienna Opera doctor. (If Mildenburg had not just arrived, she would already have met Dr. Boer.) Mahler advises her to let him examine her and to sing if he pronounces her fit, so as not to disappoint the public with a last-minute cancellation.

39. Schönaich noted that her "joyful" interpretation of Brünnhilde's cry was new and untraditional.

40. For this performance Mahler changed the staging of the church scene so that the chorus participated in the action; Hirschfeld thought this a considerable improvement.

Cast of the December 14 *Lohengrin:* Ehrenstein (Elsa), Mildenburg (Ortrud), Winkelmann (Lohengrin), Popovici (Telramund), Grengg (King).

41. The singer's final five-year contract, dated December 20, was to take effect from June 1, 1898. Mahler had passed on to the administration Mildenburg's letter of November 5 in which she asked for a higher salary than that proposed, "having received brilliant offers from various theaters, certain of which are offering over 50,000 marks per year." Her salary in Vienna was finally set at 14,000 florins for the first two years, 15,000 for the third year, 16,000 for the last two years.

42. Cast of the October 31 performance: Renard (Rosalinda), Forster (Adele), Abendroth (Orlofsky), Schrödter (Eisenstein), Dippel (Alfred), Felix (Falk), Ritter (Frank), Hesch (Frosch).

43. NBL, page 117.

44. See Chapter 31.

45. Letter to Behn of January 22, 1898 (HLG Collection). According to Hofmeister's *Musikalisch-literarischer Monatsbericht,* it was Weinberger who published the *Lieder eines fahrenden Gesellen* in December 1897, the *First Symphony* in February 1899, and the *Knaben Wunderhorn* in March 1900. The score of the *Third Symphony* was not published until July 1902. In a letter written at the end of the year to Weingartner, Mahler informed his colleague that the printed scores of both symphonies were now at his disposal (HLG Collection).

46. NBL, page 97.

47. Born in Liège in 1856, Sylvain Dupuis founded La Légia, a choral society, as well as the Nouveaux Concerts. Conductor at the Théâtre de la Monnaie in Brussels from 1900 to 1911, then director of the conservatory in Liège, Dupuis composed several operas. He died in 1931.

48. Brahms, Smetana, Franck, and Chausson were all performed at these concerts, as well as Duparc, Chabrier, and Debussy.

49. The soloists were Marthe Lignière (soprano) and Frieda Lautmann (contralto). The chorus consisted of *"Dames amateurs et de la Société Royale La Légia."* The concert ended with an aria from Max Bruch's oratorio *Odysseus* (with Lautmann as soloist), followed by Beethoven's *Egmont* Overture.

50. Mahler concluded by expressing to Dupuis his wish to attend the second performance should it take place at a time when he could get away. In fact, Dupuis later asked Mahler to conduct the performance himself in January 1899 (see Chapter 30). (Collection of Mme. Roskam Dupuis, Liège.)

51. Postcard sent to Justi from Semmering on December 22, 1897.

52. The dance was usually entrusted to a ballerina rather than to the singer.

53. Bruno Walter was chief conductor at the Pressburg Theater during this 1897–98 season. He was in Vienna to show Mahler the piano four-hand transcription of the *Second Symphony* which Mahler had asked him to make.

54. See NBLS.

55. Cast of the first performance (January 22, 1898): Renard (Djamileh), Schrödter (Haroun), Schittenhelm (Splendiano). This last role was transposed; in the original score it was for a baritone. Heuberger in the *Wiener Tagblatt* said that Renard and Schrödter had been surpassed only by Mahler on the podium. The evening also included the performance of a ballet by Josef Bayer, *Rund um Wien.*

56. In those days the final sextet was cut, as it had been by Mozart for the Vienna performance.

57. NBL, page 97.

58. As early as April 12, 1897, the *Neue Freie Presse* had announced Bezecny's resignation and the appointment of Plappart, adding that the new intendant would work much more closely with the lord chamberlain.

59. BMG, page 101. Karpath was given the original of Mahler's letter by Rolleder, who, being a rabid anti-Semite, did not wish to keep it.

60. The *Dienst-Instruktion*, or Service Instructions, of November 1885 received two official modifications dated February and May 1898 (Opera Archives, No. 308).

61. NBL, page 102.

62. The letter Mahler sent to Jahn when he returned from Venice on May 8, 1897, clearly states his preference for Puccini's opera.

63. This refers to Leoncavallo's opera *I Medici*.

64. Leoncavallo had few scruples when his interests were at stake. Some years earlier, during another trip to Vienna, he had not hesitated to pretend that he was a Jew in order to win the support of the Viennese press, mainly in Jewish hands (see BMG, page 369).

65. Van Dyck himself was in part responsible for Leoncavallo's intervention.

66. The rough draft of this letter is in the opera archives. At the bottom of the page appears the phrase "If the premiere is deferred, Mahler will entrust the baton to one of his colleagues." Leoncavallo's reply indicates that this phrase was also in the letter he received.

67. The *Neue Freie Presse* stated that the lawyer was Oskar Eirich, representing the Parisian Society of Authors, Composers, and Editors.

68. This of course refers to *Pagliacci*.

69. Van Dyck's contract was to terminate in March and had not yet been renewed. As it turned out, he stayed on at the opera for another year.

70. Helm reported that the auditorium emptied noticeably during the fourth act.

71. Cast of the February 23 premiere: Forster (Mimi), Renard (Musetta), Dippel (Marcello), Neidel (Rodolfo), Hesch (Schaunard).

72. See BMG, page 379, and the *Neue Freie Presse* of October 19, 1898. Leoncavallo's letters are in the Opera Archives.

## CHAPTER 28

1. In an undated letter, undoubtedly written in 1897, Mahler urgently requested his friend and lawyer Emil Freund to send his curriculum vitae to Adler, who was then acting on his behalf in Prague. MBR, No. 233.

2. This report is to be found among Adler's papers, now at the University of Georgia. I am greatly indebted to Professor Edward R. Reilly for sending me a copy of Adler's letter to Mahler and a copy of his unpublished article on "Mahler and Guido Adler." Among Mahler's early works Adler lists: chamber music and lieder, the opera *Die Argonauten* (prior to 1880); *Rübezahl*, a *Märschenspiel* with text by the composer (1880–90); the *Lieder eines fahrenden Gesellen*, the *Humoresken;* and of course the three symphonies, following "early symphonic essays."

3. A single page of notes on this symphony written on the official notepaper of the Vienna Opera suggests that Adler discussed the work with Mahler himself before writing the report. Adler's papers also contain a draft of a brief review, probably intended for one of the Prague newspapers.

4. The second half of this fourth and last subscription concert, which began at 7:30 P.M., was directed by Franz Schalk, a friend of Mahler who studied under Bruckner at the conservatory. The program was as follows: 1. Beethoven: *An die Hoffnung.* 2. Berlioz: Minuet and Danse of the Sylphs from the *Damnation of Faust.* 3. Heinrich Hermann, Schumann, and Schubert: Three lieder. 4. Beethoven: *"Leonore" Ouverture No. 3.* The vocal pieces were sung by Karl Scheidemantel. The fifty-seven-man orchestra of the German Opera House was augmented for the occasion by twenty-five musicians from the Czech Theater. Mahler's *First Symphony* comprised the four movements we know today, as the Andante had been suppressed in a previous revision.

5. On this occasion Mahler met Josef Stransky, who later succeeded him at the head of the New York Philharmonic Orchestra. Stransky wrote a long and highly enthusiastic letter to Mahler on the day after the concert, for which Mahler thanked him warmly, as

"he had for a long time doubted that he would live to see the day when his music would find an echo in a few men's hearts." As Mozart had been called the "singer of love" he hoped that he might claim to be the "singer of nature." (New York *Herald-Tribune*, March 22, 1931.)

6. Born in Vienna in 1861, he was doubtless the father of the well-known tenor of the same name. Formerly an actor in Graz and later in Berlin, he became superintendant of the Chernowitz theater in 1912. Later that evening, the tenor Gustav Löwe reminded Mahler that he had sung in *Trompeter von Säkkingen* under his direction. Arias from operas and lieder were also performed and some society ladies sang Tyrolean duets.

7. The concert program also included the overture to Cornelius' *Der Barbier von Bagdad;* Beethoven's *Violin Concerto* (soloist Rettig, concertmaster of the orchestra); Brahms's *Variations on a Theme by Haydn;* and Beethoven's *Fifth Symphony.*

Ferdinand Löwe (1865–1925) was born in Vienna, studied at the conservatory there, and later became professor of choral singing. He was appointed conductor of the Kaim Orchestra in 1897 (Mahler was also considered for this post) and at the same time director of the Wiener Singakademie; he conducted the Konzertverein from 1900 to 1904; from 1908 until 1914 he was the director of the Munich Konzertverein, then of the Vienna Musikakademie. He published a large number of Bruckner's works. After the concert with the Kaim Orchestra he was engaged for a year by the Vienna Opera.

8. Mahler gave his consent. The first performance took place on April 14 in Budapest.

9. Bruno Walter had been extremely unhappy conducting the Breslau Theater Orchestra, owing to the "authoritarian and paradoxical" character of the director, Theodor Löwe, to whom Mahler had recommended him. When Walter resigned, Mahler sent him a letter full of advice and the sum of twelve thousand marks—almost a year's salary. But Walter probably returned this generous gift, because he had accepted a temporary appointment in Pressburg while waiting to take up his new engagement with the Riga Opera.

10. It was then that Mahler told the story of *Das klagende Lied* and the Beethoven Prize which Natalie later noted down and which contains so many inaccuracies (see Chapter 5).

11. As compared with Verdi's interpretation when he conducted the opera in Vienna in June 1875. According to Helm, it should never be forgotten that *Aïda* is the work of a "warm-blooded Mediterranean."

12. Cast for the performance on April 20: Sedlmair (Aïda), Edyth Walker (Amneris), Winkelmann (Radames), Reichmann (Amonasro).

13. The two main stars, Marie Renard and Ernest Van Dyck, both resigned in 1900, but Van Dyck returned frequently to sing as a guest artist, particularly in Massenet's operas.

14. These incidents occurred during a Christmas Eve performance in 1898 (*Deutsche Zeitung,* December 28).

15. Cf. Erwin Stein (*Opera* magazine).

16. This diary later came into the hands of the Viennese critic Felix Salten: (*Gestalten und Erscheinungen.* S. Fischer, Berlin, 1913, page 133). See also L. Karpath: *Lachende Musiker,* page 95.

17. RSM, page 76 (first edition), and Felix Salten (*op. cit.*).

18. NBLS.

19. He gave the part of Kaspar in *Der Freischütz* (see below) to Josef Ritter, the baritone, and was condemned by all the critics except Kalbeck.

20. *Neue Musikalische Presse* (June 19, 1898).

21. Mahler conducted 111 performances, Richter 39, and Fuchs 57 during the 1898–99 season.

22. The most frequently performed works during this season were: *Lohengrin, Dalibor, Pagliacci,* and *Onegin* (12); *Hänsel* and *Cavalleria* (10); *Faust* and *Zar und Zimmermann* (10); *Meistersinger, Tannhäuser, Walkyrie, Djamileh, Le Grillon au*

*foyer,* and *Magic Flute* (7). Below is Specht's table comparing the length of the Wagnerian performances under Mahler and Jahn.

|                    | JAHN          | MAHLER   |
| ------------------ | ------------- | -------- |
| *Lohengrin*        | 7–10:26 P.M.  | 7–11     |
| *Tannhäuser*       | *Idem.*       |          |
| *Götterdämmerung*  | 7–10:30       | 7–11:50  |
| *Meistersinger*    | 7–10:52       | 7–11:50  |
| *Tristan*          |               | 7–11:50  |

(Richard Specht: *Das Wiener Operntheater, Erinnerungen aus 50 Jahren.* Paul Knepler, Wien 1919, page 36.)

23. NBLS, 1899 (see below).

24. NBLS, summer of 1899 (see Chapter 30).

25. Natalie continued vacationing there after Mahler's return to Vienna and wrote him long letters full of every kind of suggestion; to bathe, to go cycling, and to breathe country air.

26. In a letter to Nina Spiegler written from Vahrn on August 1, Mahler states that he was in pain every morning from nine-thirty to about two o'clock and then from three to four in the afternoon.

27. Unfortunately Natalie does not name them, but there seems little doubt that they were the *Lied des Verfolgten im Turm, Wo die schönen Trompeten blasen,* and possibly the sketch of *Revelge,* which was not finished until the following year. In fact all the other pieces in the collection are dated earlier. The "furious" song might well be the *Lied des Verfolgten im Turm,* which well fits the description of Mahler's mood. He gave the manuscript of these lieder to Nina Spiegler the following year and wrote on the first page in dedication: "Conceived in pain, I hope my children do not bear its traces." It seems he was annoyed with his friend Natalie for thinking that he was referring to mental anguish when he had only meant physical suffering (NBLS). On July 30 he wrote to Behn that his pain "had not yet ceased," so that he had not "been able to work much."

28. Letter to Nina Spiegler (see above).

29. A letter from Richter dated August 27 thanks Mahler for having granted him leave of absence because of pain in his arms; this had been his only reason for giving up *Die Meistersinger.* Cast for the performance on the twenty-sixth: Forster (Eva), Spielmann (David), Winkelmann (Walther), Reichmann (Sachs), Reichenberg (Pogner), Horwith (Kothner).

30. Erik Schmedes (1868–1931) was born near Copenhagen. He studied in Berlin and Vienna as a baritone and sang in Wiesbaden, Nuremberg, and Hanover. On Pollini's advice he became a tenor, at first singing lyric parts. Mahler engaged him as a *Heldentenor,* and his first appearance on the Viennese stage was as a guest artist in *Siegfried* on February 11. His contract came into force on June 1.

31. In a letter to Albert Spiegler dated August 27, Mahler informed him that his pains were "getting no better" and that they were accompanied by "a rage against powers of the subterranean world."

32. NBLS.

33. Cast in the September 20 performance: Sedlmair (Fricka), Michalek, Kusmitsch and Kaulich (Rhine maidens), Schmedes (Froh), Van Dyck (Loge), Ritter (Alberich), Reichmann (Wotan), Demuth (Donner), Grengg and Reichenberg (Giants).

34. Cast of *Die Walküre* on September 22: Sedlmair (Sieglinde), Mildenburg (Brünnhilde), Reichmann (Wotan). After an earlier performance on May 7, Helm wrote in the *Deutsche Zeitung* that Mahler's *Walküre* had "less style" than Richter's because his "nervous haste" destroyed "the highly poetic atmosphere." Although some passages were "nobly and expressively interpreted," Helm felt it would have been better

to "follow Richter's example," in particular "his admirable broadening of the tempo in the closing phases."

35. Alfred Kauders, writing in the *Neues Wiener Tagblatt*, considered that Spielmann's Mime was "the caricature of a caricature." He also criticized the slowness of some of Mahler's tempos.

36. Cast of the performance on September 23: Mildenburg (Brünnhilde), Schmedes (Siegfried), Spielmann (Mime), Demuth (Wanderer).

37. Cast of the performance on September 25, 1898: Mildenburg (Brünnhilde), Walker (Waltraute), Schmedes (Siegfried), Demuth (Gunther), Reichenberg (Hagen). Mahler invited Guido Adler to the performance on September 4, emphasizing "the new (and excellent) cast."

38. NBL, page 108. This incident did not affect Mahler's relations with the Wagner family. Cosima Wagner wrote to him in early summer to say she would be delighted to attend the performance of *Rienzi* that he was planning for the following winter. In any case she was far too diplomatic to quarrel with the director of the Vienna Opera at a time when she was trying to impose on Germany the mediocre dramatic efforts of her son Siegfried.

39. Letter from Mahler to the intendant (September 22) (Document No. 547).

40. NBLS. That same day, Mahler told Natalie that he often "readily paid out small sums" and that after each rehearsal he bought sausages and beer for the children playing the dwarfs of Nibelheim, which cost him about nine gulden each time.

41. In an article on the first Philharmonic concert in November, Hanslick suggests that Richter's ills were not perhaps as serious as he claimed, since they did not prevent him from conducting a considerable number of operas and concerts, particularly in England.

42. Mahler was certainly not unaware of Richter's intentions, and he must have guessed that he would be chosen to succeed him. On November 12 he had written to Guido Adler asking to borrow a score of Berlioz's *Symphonie fantastique*, which shows that he intended to conduct it. But most of the papers regarded Richter's decision as temporary and recalled that he had already resigned from the Philharmonic during the 1881–82 season.

43. The *Deutsche Zeitung*, as usual, regretted the Philharmonic's choice and Richter's departure, which it hoped would not be permanent. Mahler was the first "non-German" conductor of the orchestra and could not be expected to defend German music properly. The "Jewish press" was accused of speaking of Richter as though he were "dead or finished."

44. In a farewell article, written on the occasion of Mahler's first concert, Kalbeck stated: "He didn't always want to do what he could, but he could always do what he wanted." (*Neues Wiener Tagblatt*).

45. NBLS, May 29, 1899.

46. NBL, page 99. Mahler also thought that the sense of tempo and phrasing had been lost and that conducting had been reduced to beating time. Only dramatic music had been spared to some extent, because the words and actions facilitated its comprehension. "Orchestral music, on the contrary, gives full rein to stupidity and ignorance, or, at best, subjectivity."

47. According to NBL (page 110), it was "a desperate attempt by a few of the singers and musicians at the opera to get rid of Mahler."

48. The author acknowledges "Mahler's great success as director of the opera" and approves the uncut productions of Wagner.

49. Most conductors today attach great importance on the independence of their hands, regarding this as an essential feature of their art.

50. This malicious description does not have the effect the author intended, for it gives a striking and by no means unfavorable impression of Mahler conducting.

51. The author of this article considered that the recent *Der Freischütz* revealed

"an absolutely new and unusual conception for musicians impregnated with the spirit of Weber, and this at a time when a certain stability had just been reached in the interpretation of his work." Mahler had "turned it into a caricature, changing, for example, the last Allegro into an Allegretto! Atrocious!" This same tempo aroused Kalbeck's admiration (see below).

52. One of Mahler's most "scandalous innovations" had in fact been to introduce an E flat clarinet into Beethoven's *"Eroica" Symphony.* Unitl then this instrument had been confined to military music and Berlioz's *Symphonie fantastique.* According to Helm, Mahler suppressed the famous clarinet before the concert. Among other things, he had attempted an orchestral performance of the slow movement of Beethoven's *Quartet in A minor,* op. 132.

53. Steinfeld: a military training area.

54. Mahler got the opera to pay one graphologist, Professor Skallipitzky, but he had to pay a second expert out of his own pocket (see Chapter 29).

55. Letter to the intendant dated December 9.

56. The correspondent of the *Neue Zeitschrift für Musik* described Mahler's reception as one of "glacial silence."

57. According to Mahler, they should not be played (though they always are) as five equal beats, but should be interpreted expressively, as an ascension to a climax that then ebbs away to the two final chords. He also criticized those who interpreted the passage that follows as a "gracious acquiescence": The sixteenth notes in the violins, he claimed, should not be played with bravura but with "thunderous power." (NBL, page 109.)

58. NBL, page 99, February 1898. On the same day, Mahler spoke feelingly of the symphony's second movement, which evoked "the hero's funeral procession in all its power and tragedy."

59. In Kalbeck's view Mahler had apparently "decided to concentrate all the feeling into the secondary movements, keeping the main ones as short, taut and severe as possible."

60. The nuances and phrasing of the Andante greatly pleased him, as did the flow of the melodies, "personal, songlike, set free from the beat" and "without the hysteria of the new German school!"

61. As in Hamburg, this "concentration on detail" found many detractors among the critics; the *Neue Zeitschrift* correspondent, for instance, felt that general effect had been compromised.

62. NBL and NBLS.

63. Despite this the *Deutsche Zeitung* criticized the slowness of the overture's initial Adagio and the frequent changes of tempo on the subsequent Allegro and the *Unfinished,* whose "unity and charm were destroyed in a plethora of nuances."

64. Anti-Czech as well as anti-Semitic, the *Deutsche Zeitung* remarked that, in spite of tepid applause, Dvořák appeared immediately to thank the orchestra and the audience. He later reappeared twice more, thus giving the Vienna correspondent of the Czech newspaper *Narodni Listy* occasion to "cable the news of the national hero's great triumph to his paper." Three letters from Mahler to Dvořák, dated October 3 and 5 and November 17 (Prague, Anton Dvořák, Bequest), originated this performance of *Heldenlied.* In them Mahler asked for a recent, unperformed orchestral work, and Dvořák sent *Die Waldtaube* and *Heldenlied* (letter from Dvořák to Mahler: Rosé Collection).

65. Cast of the first performance on October 4: Michalek (Margarete), Sedlmair (Anna), Naval (Georges Brown), Spielmann (Dickson), Grengg (Gaveston). Kalbeck wrote that Naval and Sedlmair were "ideal heroes" for the work and that Mahler had been right to restore the period balance of the orchestra by reducing the string section.

66. Born in 1859 in Salzburg, Ritter started his theatrical career in Munich.

There followed an engagement by Pollini in Hamburg. He joined the Vienna Opera in 1889, where he was highly successful in most of the big baritone roles: Don Giovanni, Pizarro, Rigoletto, Alberich, etc. Unfortunately his voice tired early and from 1901 he could no longer manage the leading roles. Nevertheless Mahler kept him on at the opera until 1905, considering him still indispensable for certain parts. In 1907 Ritter became afflicted with religious mania, and ended his days in an asylum.

67. According to Helm (*Musikalisches Wochenblatt,* 1899, page 101), Mahler was later forced to replace some of the "apparitions" he had cut. Cast of the first performance on October 22: Michalek (Aennchen), Forster (Agathe), Schrödter (Max), Spielmann (Kilian), Ritter (Kaspar), Neidel (Fürst), Hesch (Eremit).

68. According to Helm, Mahler conducted the overture "in the manner of Wagner or Bülow." Great slowness and gentleness in the Introduction led to many pathetic changes of tempo in the *Allegro.*

69. The performance lasted from 7 to 11:30 P.M. Cast: Sedlmair (Isolde), Winkelmann (Tristan).

70. Four complete cycles in the 1898–99 season. Mahler had ordered a new red velvet curtain, which opened in the center, as in Bayreuth, to enable the singers to take their bows. Helm mentioned in the *Wochenblatt* that the intendant had refused to agree to an earlier start, but that, though *Die Götterdämmerung* lasted from 7 till 11:45 P.M., no one left their seats before the final chord.

71. Cast for the performance of November 4: Mildenburg (Donna Anna), Demuth (Don Giovanni).

72. Emil Nikolaus von Reznicek was born in Vienna on May 4, 1860. He studied law before taking up music on the advice of Busoni and Weingartner. After studying under Reinecke at the Leipzig Conservatory, he embarked on a career as an opera conductor. He took the libretto of *Donna Diana,* his fourth opera, from a Spanish play by Agustín Moreto called *"El desdén con el desdén,"* which had been successfully produced at the Vienna Burgtheater. His opera was first performed in Prague on December 16, 1894, and had considerable success in Germany.

73. Mahler wrote to Bruno Walter in August: "You'll be interested to learn that I am putting on Reznicek's *Donna Diana.* Its freshness attracts me to the work as a whole, and I think it will be a big success."

74. The lines in question are: *"So lass mich denn . . ."* The letter is in the manuscript collection of Louis Koch, in Stuttgart.

75. *Der Anbruch,* Mahler Heft (1920), page 298.

76. Cast of the premiere on December 9: Renard (Diana), Michalek (Floretta), Naval (Cesar), Demuth (Perin). Renard and Naval were later replaced by Mildenburg and Schmedes; Helm considered them both too "heroic" for their parts and thought that Schrödter would have been better than Van Dyck. This, he complained, was a typical example of Mahler's "arbitrary casting."

77. MBR, No. 244.

78. MBR, No. 245.

## CHAPTER 29

1. Karpath asserts that Theodor Helm had been "obliged" to attack Mahler despite the respect he felt for him, and that sometime later he sent Mahler one of his works with this inscription: "To the faithful upholder of the Wagner and Mozart traditions, to the unsurpassed interpreter of *Tristan"* (BMG, pages 172–73).

2. The *Deutsche Zeitung* devoted no less than five articles to this "scandal." That of January 11 announced that the mayor had canceled the concert; that of

January 17 stigmatized "Jewish tyranny" and the "lies of the Jewish press." It also underlined the fact that, properly speaking, Mahler was not the head of the orchestra, but only of the Philharmonic Concerts.

3. Quoted by Hanslick in the *Neue Freie Presse*, January 17, 1899.

4. NBL, pages 107–8. Hanslick's article gives the impression that Mahler "did occasionally strengthen the cellos with double basses."

5. NBL, page 111.

6. NBLS.

7. NBLS, February 1898. Mahler also mentioned at this time how important it was for the string instruments to be perfectly tuned.

8. According to Helm, it was Arnold Rosé who influenced Mahler in his choice of the *Quartet in F Minor* rather than any other.

9. *Neue Freie Presse*, January 17, 1899.

10. The same thing had been tried before, Helm stated, by Habeneck, with the Orchestra of the Paris Conservatory, and by Liszt, who had orchestrated Beethoven's *"Archduke" Trio.*

11. The original title of the work was the same as that of Chabrier's opera, but Goldmark later changed it when he heard of the French composer's *Briséis.*

12. Cast of the January 17 premiere: Renard (Briseis), Walker (Thetis), Pacal (Antomedon), Reichmann (Achilles), Neidel (Agamemnon), Hesch (Priam).

13. January 27, 1899, page 68.

14. NBLS, February 1898.

15. The *Neue Musikalische Presse* of January 1, 1899, printed a quite favorable article on the new edition signed by Hans Geissler.

16. The program of this concert, which took place in the Königliche Kapelle on December 16, 1898, consisted of the Mahler *First Symphony;* an aria from Paisiello's *Proserpina* (soloist Nina Faliero); the *Suite miniature* by César Cui; the *Chanson sarrasine* by Victorin de Joncières; Saint-Saëns's *Chanson florentine* (both sung by Nina Faliero); and Beethoven's *"Leonore" Overture No. 3.*

17. According to Mahler, the *Dresdner Zeitung* tried to define the atmosphere of this Funeral March, not by quoting the text of the last of the *Lieder eines fahrenden Gesellen,* the theme of which is used for the trio, but by quoting the third, *"Ich hab' ein glühend Messer."*

18. Sylvain Dupuis asked Mahler to conduct his own work in a letter dated October 27. Mme. Roskam Dupuis, the musician's daughter, has in her possession a rough copy of this letter, as well as that of another, dated January 9, 1899, in which Dupuis promises Mahler a rehearsal at one o'clock on January 20 and invites him to stay at his home in Liège. She also has four Mahler letters, one dated October 29, in which he asks Dupuis to place his symphony at the start of the concert because it needed an audience with "freshness of spirit." He agreed to come without remuneration and to pay his own traveling expenses.

19. See NBLS, April 1899. Mahler added that he also lacked a harp.

20. Letter of January 21 to Justi.

21. The second part of the program, conducted by Sylvain Dupuis, included the Weber *Konzerstück* (soloist, Ferruccio Busoni), the Saint-Saëns *Danse macabre,* and Liszt's *Second Piano Concerto* (Busoni). The Mahler soloists were Marthe Lignière (soprano), who had sung the preceding year, and Mme. Caro-Lucas (contralto).

22. Here the Liège critic seems to have lacked insight, for the Scherzo is grimacing rather than good-humored, and the Andante more dancing than moving.

23. Mahler had to take the train the evening of the Liège concert. In the same letter he enthusiastically approved Frau Sommerfeld's idea of having one of his works performed in Paris by the Lamoureux Orchestra. He even proposed conducting it himself.

24. Hermann Götz (1840–76), organist and composer, born in Königsberg, studied in Berlin under Hans von Bülow. A rather prolix composer of instrumental and orchestral music, he taught in Switzerland for a long time, dying at thirty-six after having added to the modern German repertoire one of its best-known operas.

25. This *Novitäten Konzert* took place at twelve-thirty on Sunday, February 19, 1899, in the Grosse Musikvereins Saal, in aid of the Vienna Society of Authors-Composers. Siegfried Wagner first conducted the overture to *Bärenhäuter;* after this Humperdinck performed his own *Maurische Rhapsodie,* and Wilhelm Kienzl the interludes from the first and third acts of his opera *Don Quixote,* followed by the extracts from *Guntram.*

26. According to Wilhelm Kienzl, the well-known caricatures and silhouettes of Otto Böhler and Oscar Garvens were sketched during this concert.

27. Sixteen years earlier Jahn had given the first, incomplete performance, consisting of the two middle movements—all that the composer heard before his death. The work was still in manuscript form.

28. GAB: IV, 1, page 660.

29. The *First Symphony* formed the first part of the concert. It was followed by an aria from Haydn's *Die Schöpfung* (soloist Fräulein Schacko) and Beethoven's *Eighth Symphony* under the baton of the local conductor, Ludwig Rottenberg.

30. NBLS.

31. NBLS.

32. Perosi, at twenty-six, had already composed three oratorios to Latin texts: *La Trasfigurazione del Nostro Signore Gesù Cristo, La Risurrezione di Lazzaro,* and *La Risurrezione di Cristo.* His main skill lay in "bringing back to life the austere melodic formulas of Palestrina and Bach by investing them with all the attractive assets of the modern orchestra."

33. Soloists at the performances of March 13 and 14: Amelia Fusco (Martha), Lotte von Bärensfeld (Mary), Guido Vaccari (Evangelist), Silla Carobbi (Christ), Emil Vaupel (Servant). The *Neue Freie Presse* critic thought them all, the baritone excepted, mediocre. The three-hundred-voice choir was drawn from various choral societies.

34. NBL, pages 113–14.

35. *Busoni: Briefe an seine Frau* (page 25, June 22, 1899).

36. The article in the *Deutsche Zeitung* (April 8, 1899) adds that Mahler "seemed to want to throw at his head the music stand that he had just had built at the orchestra's expense during his trip to Frankfurt."

37. This claim by Mahler is confirmed by a document in the opera archives (General Intendanz 544; 1898, March–May 1898). Accepted on May 24, a 20-per-cent increase in the salary of the singers and orchestral musicians was accompanied by an equivalent increase in their pensions.

38. BMG, page 174. At first Mahler had thought of paying out of his own pocket for the additional musicians needed for the *Second Symphony,* particularly the four double-bass players who had to be added to the ten Philharmonic musicians. Karpath and other friends had dissuaded him, telling him that the anti-Semitic press would take advantage of such an action to assert that he had paid the orchestra to perform his symphony, whereas in reality the orchestral committee had asked him for this first performance.

39. This episode, related by Natalie, was also reported—in almost identical terms in the article (quoted above) that the *Deutsche Zeitung* published during the rehearsals.

40. This was the long cello melody beginning on the seventh bar after the No. 5 in the score. The long-drawn-out sentimentality displayed by certain orchestral conductors in this movement is thus condemned by Mahler himself.

41. Five months later, after hearing an eight-hand piano performance of the *Second,*

Mahler remarked that "the most beautiful passage" in the Scherzo, the peaceful central theme, which is the only contrast to the "restless brazier" of the movement, disappears completely: he had not been able to bring himself to reintroduce the theme in another key. That would have been contrary to its nature, for, like the aloe, it flowers only once.

42. The solo soprano engaged for this concert was Lotte von Bärensfeld.

43. Helm was in Italy at the time of the concert, and his article in the *Musikalisches Wochenblatt* reflects only what he was told upon his return. The success had been "enormous" but the various critical opinions had been "totally divergent."

44. No doubt Bruno Walter.

45. NBL, page 132.

46. NBLS.

47. It had already been performed once in the Vienna Karltheater in 1895 for a benefit performance.

48. Cast of the February 10 first performance: *Der Apotheker* (sung five times): Michalek (Griletta), Pohlner (Volpino), Schrödter (Mengone), Hesch (Sempronio); *Die Opernprobe* (sung ten times): Michalek (Louise), Baier (Countess), Forster (Hannchen), Naval (Adolf), Demuth (Johann), Felix (Christopher), Hesch (Count).

49. This was a time in which a composer's rights were so badly protected that the most famous and honored musicians could not manage to live on them. See Wagner's terribly difficult early life and Weber's whole lifetime.

50. After the eleventh performance (May 12), given to a full house Mahler listed its faults to Natalie. In one of the two surviving copies of her manuscript this passage has been scratched through to make it illegible. One of the censors who "edited" Natalie's work after her death wanted to hide this "severe" judgment from posterity.

51. No doubt on December 11, 1899, the day Siegfried was due to conduct his own opera. In the letter Mahler assures him that he is "as angry as you are" and that this "fine flower of bureaucracy" will show him "what I, the director, have to suffer here. . . . Don't let it, I beg of you, spoil this splendid evening" he concludes. "Remember, my dear friend, that all Vienna, and especially all of us here at the opera, are thinking of you today with affection and gratitude . . ." No doubt the opera administration had decided to cancel the opera, or perhaps to lower the conductor-composer's fee.

52. Frau Wagner's correspondence with Prince Ernst zu Hohenhofe—Langenburg (Stuttgart, Cotta, 1937, page 183).

53. Cast of the March 27 premiere: Michalek (Luise), Schmedes (Hans Kraft), Hesch (Devil).

54. NBL, page 106. Mahler complained that day of having "lost the original version." Perhaps this referred to the first score, now in the Rosé Collection, which had already been put aside by Justi, or perhaps he found it later and presented it to her.

55. NBLS: see Chapter 4.

56. The hostility of the Philharmonic musicians continued to grow. More than one fourth of them voted against Mahler at the time of his re-election in August. A new anti-Semitic campaign was to be unleashed later in the year by the *Deutsche Zeitung*, and there was then much talk of his "tyranny" and his "brutality."

57. The first is called the "artist's line" and the second the "police limit." One step further and Neidel would have found himself in front of the curtain, facing the laughter of the audience.

58. *Neue Freie Presse* and *Neues Wiener Journal,* January 29, 1905.

59. NBLS.

60. May 25, performance of Pedro Calderón's *El Alcalde de Zalamea.*

## CHAPTER 30

1. Wlassack made most of the important decisions for his superior Plappart, as did Prince Montenuovo for Prince Liechtenstein. Rosa Papier seems to have shared Wlassack's feelings about Mahler, to judge from the following paragraph in a letter to Mildenburg written on January 4, 1903: "It would be small-minded to insist that Mahler show some gratitude for my having so enthusiastically helped him to become Opera Director. But it is really very rude of him to dare to treat me as if I didn't exist, just because he no longer needs me; he does not even show me the common politeness due to any woman. At one time he spent hours in my waiting room, but now that he is married, he never comes to see me; he hasn't even introduced his wife to me, etc. You yourself wrote to me from Hamburg: 'He would walk over dead bodies,' and you were right."

2. Twenty-four thousand florins (see opera documents Nos. 308/X/1898 and 33.363/484).

3. In particular he has distributed, under the heading "daily expenses," small remunerations to the salaried employees. That he was not officially entitled to use opera funds in this way is proved by his long letter to the lord chamberlain quoted earlier.

4. Opera Archives: No. 1560/1898 (October 12, 15, 25) and Nos. 1873, 2241, and 381 of 1899.

5. Opera Archives (No. 156/1899 and No. 311 of February 14 and 24, 1899).

6. Opera documents (No. 156/1899).

7. *Schleunigst:* This is the exact word used by the intendant in his note, quoted here from the letter sent to Mahler by the administration.

8. King Edward VII of England was said to have personally recommended this young singer (BMG, pages 379–80). She made her Vienna debut at the Theater an der Wien in September 1897 in Puccini's *La Bohème.*

9. She was to receive her full salary of nine hundred gulden during this time.

10. Mahler: letter of March 27 (Opera Archives No. 233/1899).

11. As Stritt had found a post in Strasbourg, Mahler felt that it should have been possible to cancel his contract by mutual agreement and without indemnity. It is essential in this case to make a distinction between the terms *Übersiedlungsbeitrag* (contribution to moving expenses), which Mahler should have proposed, and *Abfertigung* (an indemnity), which the intendant was free to grant without consultation.

12. This was a veiled but justified criticism of the intendant. All the newspaper articles of the time state that Plappart "had no theatrical experience."

13. *Rienzi* was finally restaged in January 1902.

14. Mahler is careful to note in this respect that, "resolutely opposed as always to needless expenditure," he had reduced to forty-five gulden the costumer's original estimate of 140.

15. See Chapter 28 and Mahler's letter to the intendant of November 23, 1898.

16. Mahler then detailed the net cost of each of the year's new productions: 736 gulden (*Die Kriegsgefangene*). 58 gulden (*Der Apotheker* and *Die Opernprobe*), and 3727 gulden (*Der Bärenhäuter*), a total of 4521 gulden.

17. The administration also considered as too high the sum of 700 gulden claimed by the publisher Sanzogno for renting orchestral parts for this production. This surprised Mahler, because most of the other recent productions had cost more. Three figures he furnished in this regard are: 1800 gulden (Smetana's *Tajemství*), 1800 gulden (*Hubička,* by the same composer), 2000 gulden (Leoncavallo's *I Medici*).

18. When Weingartner was appointed to replace Mahler in 1907, he found the 1889

*Dienst-Instruktion* "an old and outdated" document. Wetschel advised him "to let it subsist" because it had never been applied.

19. New York *Herald Tribune,* March 22, 1931. Seated in Neumann's box, Mahler heard Stransky conduct the overture to *Parsifal,* and, to mark the occasion, presented him with the dedicated score of his *First Symphony.*

20. The *Second Symphony* was not performed in Prague until long after the *Third,* which Mahler conducted there in 1904.

21. Laussa is situated near Losenstein and Steyr.

22. NBLS.

23. Writing to Selma Kurz on July 5, Mahler was so cold he could barely hold his pen.

24. Mahler may have used this outline for the lied written in 1901, unless he had destroyed it in the meantime.

25. NBL, page 119.

26. NBLS.

27. "One volume of the *Kunst,*" Natalie specified, but there is no work of this title in Goethe's writings.

28. He had "discovered" and played them with Arnold Rosé during the summer of 1898.

29. Emma had just married Eduard Rosé and the former "disturbance" may either have come from her infatuation for him or from her difficulties in adapting to family life.

30. NBL, page 119.

31. Josef Venantius von Wöss (1863–1943), son of an army officer, studied music at the Vienna Conservatory. Piano teacher in Moravia, then professor of harmony in Vienna, and a fairly prolific composer, he made the piano transcription of Mahler's *Third, Fourth, Eighth,* and *Ninth Symphonies.* The Mahler Gesellschaft in Vienna has a copy of the letter of thanks sent to Wöss that summer.

32. Besides being disturbed by the local band, Mahler was often bothered by the yodeling of the happy mountaineers, who were encouraged and wildly applauded by the tourists; he was certain that "these people would surely not otherwise, without reason, dream of screaming like this after a hard working day."

33. *Kuhgäste,* a pun on *Kurgäste* (cure guests) and *Kuh* (cow).

34. On May 5, 1899, Mahler, who was reading Ludwig Nohl's great biography of Beethoven, spoke of this solitude, which had been the source of some of the most beautiful musical movements in the world, comparing it to Christ's stations of the cross, with the difference that Beethoven's suffering lasted for years (NBLS).

35. NBL, page 120.

36. NBL, page 125.

37. Among others, the incident at the Stadtwäldchen Café (see Chapter 15).

38. Opera documents No. 413/1899 (July 13).

39. This was a quotation from his long letter to Prince Liechtenstein.

40. This occurred during a performance conducted by Mahler himself on September 20 (see the Opera Archives, No. 1521 ex 1899).

41. Letter to Justi, August 1899.

42. This large Carinthian lake, with its particularly mild climate, is in a sense the Austrian Mediterranean.

43. Daughter of a Viennese schoolteacher, Laura Hilgermann (1869–1937) had studied music in Vienna. She made her stage debut in Prague in 1885 while Mahler was there, and was engaged for Budapest by him in 1890. Later she toured with Grieg, singing his lieder, and taught singing at the Budapest Conservatory.

44. Born in Galicia, a pupil of Johannes Reiss in Vienna and Mathilde Marchesi in Paris, Selma Kurz (1877–1933) made her debut at the Frankfurt Opera. Under

Mahler's direction she became one of the most famous virtuoso singers of her time, and later married a Viennese gynecologist, Professor Halban. Selma Kurz's letters to Mahler were kindly lent to the author by her daughter, Frau Desi Halban Saher. The early ones concern her studies with Frau Hanfstängl and her Vienna appointment. Mahler asked her to arrive by the middle of August, so that he could judge whether she was capable of singing the principal role in Rubinstein's *The Demon* (which was ultimately sung by Mildenburg).

45. Another of Mahler's reforms had less success that year: he tried to get the members of the orchestra to wear evening clothes during the performances and thus give the auditorium a gala appearance. But he had to abandon this project after meeting insurmountable resistance.

46. Cast of the performance of September 6: Michalek (Marie), Baier (Marchesa), Schrödter (Tonio), Frauscher (Sulpice), Schmitt (Hortensio).

47. Cast of the first performance, September 29: Michalek (Zerline), Walker (Pamela), Schrödter (Fra Diavolo), Pacal (Lorenzo), Neidel (Lord Koolbaum), Stoll and Hesch (Bandits).

48. The affair was reported in the *Musikalisches Wochenblatt* by Helm, who accused Mahler of another momentary infatuation.

49. NBL, pages 129–30.

50. Born on May 27, 1863, Franz Schalk had been a fellow student of Mahler at the conservatory. Bruckner called him "Franzisce" and nicknamed the two brothers "Cylinder Bruarn" (colloquial German) because of their collapsible hats. Schalk had conducted in Graz and Prague before joining the Berlin Opera in 1898. Conductor of a Wagnerian season at Covent Garden, London, he then succeeded Anton Seidl as conductor at the Metropolitan Opera, New York. Later he became director of the Vienna Opera (1918–29). His letters to Mahler, dated November 4 and 8, 1899, and December 13, 1899, as well as a reply from Mahler dated November 6, are listed as No. 2640 in the Opera Archives. Schalk died in Edlach, near Vienna, in 1931.

51. This anonymous critic found the range of the role of Edgar too high for Schrödter and judged the bass Preuss, recently engaged by Mahler, scarcely worthy of a provincial theater. Cast of the October 9 performance: Saville (Lucia), Schrödter (Edgar), Demuth (Ashton), Frauscher (Raymond), Preuss (Arturo).

52. Luise von Ehrenstein's last performance on the Viennese stage in 1899 was in one of her best parts, the title role in Liszt's *Die Legende von der heiligen Elisabeth,* which was given each year on November 19, anniversary of the death of the Empress Elisabeth.

53. Although Rubinstein himself had visited Vienna to conduct the first performances of some of his operas, according to Hanslick he was never successful there as a dramatic composer.

54. Hans Geissler wrote in the *Neue Musikalische Presse* that Richter had already replaced some of the cuts. The following episodes were reinstated by Mahler: in the second act, the second stanza of Sachs's lied and that of Beckmesser's serenade; in the last act the second stanza of the lieder sung by Beckmesser and Walter, as well as Sachs's monologue, *"Hat man mit dem Schuhwerk nicht seine Not"*; the comic intermezzo accompanying Beckmesser's appearance, and part of the scene with Sachs and the chorus at the end of the last act. The total cuts, about one hundred pages in the score, only added twenty minutes to the performance.

Cast of the first performance on October 23: Mildenburg (Tamara), Kaulich (Nurse), Walker (Angel), Naval (Sinodal), Pacal (Messenger), Reichmann (Demon), Grengg (Gudal), Hesch (Servant).

55. Cast of the performance of November 26, 1899: Kurz (Eva), Schrödter (David), Winkelmann (Walther), Demuth (Sachs), Felix (Beckmesser), Rellé (Magdalene), Frauscher (Pogner), Stehmann (Kothner).

56. Miniature score, Schott ed., page 322.

57. This in any case was Mahler's opinion, colored perhaps by his personal feelings, because most critics did not share his admiration for the new Eva.

58. Felix Salten: *Gestalten und Erscheinungen,* page 127.

59. The first act chorale had been too perfectly performed, since it is supposedly sung by a church congregation.

60. Although the Prelude had been played too rapidly, many passages had been deprived of their gaiety by a slow tempo, including the chorus of apprentices, the chorus at the beginning of the second act (*Johannistag*), and Sachs's two monologues.

61. Judging from his letter to Justi at the end of August, Mahler had seriously considered not continuing as Philharmonic conductor.

62. Mahler presented this work in 1904, and its reception was lukewarm.

63. Mahler did not have much esteem for these three works.

64. Hellmesberger was without a doubt one of the worst conductors in German-speaking Europe.

## CHAPTER 31

1. The orchestra consisted of 110 members. Of the other votes cast nineteen were for Hellmesberger, one was for Mottl, and three were invalidated.

2. *Neue Freie Presse,* September 10, 1899.

3. Taken from an article in the *Neue Freie Presse* at the time of the first seasonal concert. Its prediction came true two years later, when Hellmesberger took over the Philharmonic. Mahler wrote to Justi at the end of August, saying that he would probably not accept the post.

4. The first held note followed by a fermata is one bar long, the second, two.

5. NBL, page 130.

6. NBLS.

7. A typical pun: *heruntergespült* means "flushed down the drain" and *heruntergespielt* "massacred."

8. NBL, page 130.

9. AMM, page 126.

10. In particular, he asked the violas to drag their bows during the bar's opening eighth-note instead of accentuating it heavily, and to observe the duration of the dotted notes very carefully.

11. NBL, page 130, and NBLS. This passage from Natalie's manuscript shows that the accusations brought against Mahler were to some extent justified.

12. In the Finale, particularly just before the coda presto, Beethoven assigns the theme (G, C, G, E, D, C, G) first to bassoons, then to horns. Mahler had the horns enter with the bassoons and entrusted the famous solos of the first movement to two oboes. Karpath tells us that the orchestra had pointed out the changes to the critics before the concert via the editors of the important newspapers (BMG, page 131).

13. Particularly the doubling of the piccolo in the Finale. However, he objected to the muting of the horns at the beginning of the Scherzo and the doubling of the bassoons by the horns in the Finale, for although he had merely tried to soften their tone, Mahler had in fact altered their actual sound (see above). Schönaich claimed that such doubling was "accepted by all the famous conductors in Germany."

14. He singled out the rapid tempo of the first movement of the *Fifth Symphony,* the "celestial passage" of the Andante, to which Mahler, taking it with excessive slowness, gave "a sentimental and Mendelssohnian flavor," and the instrumental modifications in the Finale.

15. Clearly, Mahler did not know that the composer of *"Funiculì, funiculà"* was Luigi Denza (1846–1922).

16. NBL, page 126.

17. *Ibid.*, page 121. Mahler's striving for contrasts of atmosphere within a work, charm versus emotion or gentleness versus violence, differed radically from Richter's more "architectural" performances and was one of the essential characteristics of his conducting, a characteristic stressed by many of his contemporaries.

18. NBL, page 133.

19. NBLS, November 14, 1900. The manuscript mentions the *"Symphony in B flat."* Does this mean the second in D or the third in F?

20. Dvořák had sent this score to Mahler the preceding year together with that of his *Heldenlied.* On September 23, 1899, Mahler had written to announce that, if Dvořák had no newer work to give him, he would conduct *Die Waldtaube* (Prague, Anton Dvořák Bequest).

21. NBL, page 100. January 1898.

22. In Munich in 1910, when the *Eighth Symphony* was given its first performance (OKE, page 13).

23. In fact Mahler had never signed a contract, since he had been appointed by the Emperor.

24. A veiled allusion to Mahler's morals, albeit there is no proof that they were ever loose.

25. Undoubtedly Count Apponyi.

26. Both the *Deutsche Zeitung* and the *Deutsches Volksblatt* were organs of the anti-Semitic Christian Democratic Party, of which Mayor Lueger was the leader.

27. Learning that Count Apponyi was in Vienna, Karpath went to catch him at the end of a session held by the Magyar delegation at the Hungarian Palace in the Bankgasse. But when Karpath finally encountered him on the staircase, the count brushed him off with "I haven't a moment to spare and won't raise a finger for Mahler." Later on, however, he included a eulogy of Mahler's activities in Budapest in his memoirs. Moreover, in 1930, in the hope of clearing up the whole affair, Karpath himself wrote to the director of the Budapest Opera, Desider Vidor, who was composing a history of the establishment. Vidor affirmed that he had never come across anything in the course of his labors to justify the *Volksblatt*'s accusations: "There is absolutely no question of Mahler's ever having profited financially from directorship of the Budapest Opera, especially as he never had anything to do with its finances." Since all the records of the Budapest Opera were destroyed during the Hungarian rebellion of 1956, it is no longer possible to check the research carried out by Vidor in 1930.

28. Marie Renard was only thirty-seven and still at the height of her powers. She was leaving to marry Count Kinsky and had chosen as her farewell role that of *Carmen,* in which she had made her debut in Vienna on August 18, 1887. She took over fifteen curtain calls at the end of Act I and nearly forty at the end of the opera. Thereafter, she took leave of the public with a short speech improvised amid a sea of flowers and wreaths. The final ovation lasted almost forty-five minutes. Helm swore, in the *Musikalisches Wochenblatt,* that she took 130 curtain calls.

29. Richter in fact had only twenty-eight years to his credit, since he had been away from Vienna during several seasons.

30. In Manchester, Birmingham and London, Richter continued to conduct for another eleven years.

31. Since Richter was Siegfried Wagner's godfather, Mahler had tried in vain to get him to conduct the first performance of *Der Bärenhäuter.* He was nevertheless accused of robbing his illustrious senior of "the joy of guiding Richard Wagner's son's first steps in the theater."

32. Vienna Opera Archives (Praes, March 19, 1900).

33. A few years ago the English autograph dealer Otto Haas sold a letter

written by Mahler to Richter, doubtless before the latter left Vienna. In cordial, even friendly terms, Mahler asks the well-known conductor for his advice on two Wagnerian singers and pleads in favor of certain of the opera musicians: "It would be exceedingly unkind of me not to take into account the justified claims of these men, who have carried out their tasks enthusiastically and spent the best years of their lives in our institution. I feel sure you will agree with me."

34. Some of Mahler's innovations, notably his instrumental alterations to *Tannhäuser*, had angered Richter, who found them "contrary to the spirit of the work" (MKW, page 251). In a letter to Karpath written on February 24, 1902 (and which the latter published in the *Neues Wiener Tagblatt* on September 28 of the same year), he praised Mahler's "phenomenal talent" and prodigious activity and said that, apart from Mottl, nobody was worthier of conducting the Vienna Opera than he. He added that his relations with Mahler were always extremely cordial and condemned those who denigrated him. His (Richter's) only objections were to Mahler's introduction of "improvements" into such masterpieces as *Tannhäuser* and *Der fliegende Holländer*. "He is brilliant enough not to have to stoop to such methods in order to draw attention to himself."

35. This statement is not true. Schalk does not figure in any of the lists of "non-Aryans" published by the Nazi authorities.

36. See below.

37. Born in Vienna on October 4, 1872, and, like Mahler, a pupil of Fuchs and Krenn at the conservatory, Zemlinsky, in 1897, had won Munich's Leopold Prize for his first opera, *Sarema*, with a libretto by Arnold Schönberg, which was forthwith performed in Munich. As a conductor of operettas, he attracted the attention of Brahms. He was engaged by the Volksoper in 1906 and by Mahler at the Hofoper in 1907. Together with Schönberg, he later became one of Mahler's closest friends. In 1927 he was appointed conductor of the opera and professor at the conservatory in Prague. He subsequently conducted the Kroll Opera in Berlin and then immigrated to America, where he died on March 16, 1942. His compositions include chamber music, symphonic music, and six operas.

38. The Danish poet Holger Drachmann had already turned Andersen's tale into a play, for which a Danish composer had provided incidental music.

39. See *Neue Freie Presse*, April 29, 1917. *Aus der Mahler Zeit Zemlinskys.*

40. NBLS. This remark proves that, despite the accusations so frequently leveled against him, Mahler had never knowingly been guilty of plagiarism and believed every composer should avoid the obvious "reminiscences" that he himself was so often accused of.

41. According to his paper, the first act of *Es war einmal* was nothing but an "elaboration of the flower girls' theme from *Parsifal*" and was only applauded by the composer's friends. The cast of the first performance, on January 22, was as follows: Kurz (Princess), Pohlner, Schmedes (Prince), Hesch (Emperor).

42. According to the *Fremdenblatt*, Mildenburg had also been studying the part with Cosima Wagner. At the opening performance, Mahler had been greeted with a barrage of both applause and catcalls, the latter doubtless due to Richter's departure. Cast of the performance of February 13, 1900, the seventeenth anniversary of Wagner's death: Mildenburg (Isolde), Edyth Walker (Brangäne), Winkelmann (Tristan), Grengg (Marke), Demuth (Kurwenal).

43. According to Helm, Franz Pacal sang most of the part standing behind Naval, who merely struck the attitudes and went through the motions. The *Fremdenblatt* disagreed entirely and claimed that the audience had laughed and that Pacal had later been reprimanded.

44. Cast of the performance of March 22, 1900: Kurz (Iolanta), Rellé (Martha), Pohlner (Brigitta), Kusmitsch (Laura), Naval (Vaudemont), Pacal (Almerich), Demuth (Robert), Neidel (Ebn Jahia), Hesch (King). The evening had been completed with Delibes' ballet *Sylvia*.

45. On March 22, Mahler wrote to the intendant asking that Schalk's salary be paid from March 20, since he had made himself available to the opera, where he urgently needed an assistant conductor. He added that Schalk's contract would only become effective on September 1 and that he would have to be granted a few days' leave to go to Berlin.

46. NBLS.

47. The text of these notes was imparted to me by Selma Kurz's daughter, Frau Desi Halban Saher. According to her, Mahler wanted to marry the singer, but at that time the director of the Vienna Opera could not be married to a member of the company; besides which, Selma herself would never have given up the career she had just begun.

48. The bass singer Gerhard Stehmann had been permitted to hear the concert from the stage, where Mahler had placed a chair for him. Stehmann's opinion of the lieder was reserved but favorable, and after the concert Mahler invited him to the Bristol Café to discuss musical life in the United States (*Blätter des Operntheaters*, I, 3).

49. Kalbeck particularly emphasized the beauty of the Funeral March in the last song of the cycle and, in *Das irdische Leben,* "the monotonous throbbing of the accompaniment" to illustrate hunger. Only one aspect of the cycle bothered him: its conclusion in a key other than that in which it began.

50. The paper found that the passage *"nimmer, nimmer mehr"* in the second song of the cycle expressed no sorrow whatsoever, whereas the music accompanying the words *"alles wieder gut"* in the last song was "almost a groan." Moreover, this song and *Wo die schönen Trompeten blasen* were "mannered and affected."

51. According to Helm, Mahler's success was far greater than that of other "daring secessionists" such as Strauss. The opinions expressed in the articles of the *Volksblatt* and the *Deutsche Zeitung* are very similar, and Helm was doubtless the anonymous author (H.) of the first.

52. This irate critic wrote that Michalek had sung the songs, but since she was ill, he had obviously not even bothered to attend the concert.

53. For Selma Kurz, Hanslick had nothing but praise: her voice was pleasant, she showed complete mastery of the words and sounds and sang with warmth and constantly spontaneous feeling. Hirschfeld, on the other hand, felt she had sung "disjointedly, with no sense of continuity, and her diction was careless, passive and dull." Helm also raised certain objections to her diction.

54. Hirschfeld was nonetheless perceptive enough to point out the relationship between Mahler's music and that of Berlioz, with whose *Carnaval romain* the concert ended.

55. They also congratulated Mahler on having respected Schumann's intentions by conducting the symphony without pauses between the movements. The *Deutsche Zeitung* disapproved of several features in Mahler's interpretation of this work, particularly the slow tempo of the first allegro and its acceleration at the beginning of the development.

56. The unusual order of Mahler's programs proceeded as before from his desire to play the longest and most difficult work while the audience was still fresh enough to listen to it. In this way, he hoped to stop the Viennese public from leaving en masse before the finales of the symphonies, which it was rather apt to do, even with Brahms. The correspondent of the *Neue Zeitschrift* reproached Mahler for having conducted the *Kaisermarsch* in honor of Kaiser Wilhelm II's birthday, whereas he had discontinued the custom of giving a new opera each year on Franz Joseph's birthday. The initial adagio of the Mendelssohn overture, was condemned by some critics as too slow. Mahler had a deep fondness for this work, and stated during the rehearsals that Mendelssohn would still be a great composer even if

he had composed only three works, this one, the *Hebrides Overture* and the *Fourth Symphony*.

57. LEM, page 144.

58. According to Kalbeck, Mahler's markedly slow tempo in the Scherzo restored the importance and balance of the woodwinds. It also destroyed the comic effect of their duets (bassoon-clarinet and oboe-flute) and rendered the kettledrums more thunderous. Wagner had already introduced some necessary modifications, such as the addition of the horns in the D major return of the second theme of the Scherzo. Only one feature bothered Kalbeck in Mahler's version: the roll of the kettledrums in the last fortissimo of the main theme and the omission of the eight opening bars in the return of the Scherzo.

59. Hirschfeld complains of Mahler's tendency to neglect certain lesser passages and overemphasize others (a principle of interpretation that Mahler had deliberately evolved). He said that too many cataclysms (*Überströmungen*) had impeded the flow of the first movement, that the Scherzo lacked vigor (*Wucht*), which even a Beethoven pianissimo should have, and that, because of the cuts in the latter, the Trio had assumed too much importance. The soloists at the concerts of February 18 and 20 were: Marie Katzmayr (soprano), Franz Pacal (tenor), Rellé (mezzo-soprano), and Hesch (bass). On the evening of February 22, the *Ninth Symphony* was preceded by the *Weihe des Hauses* overture and the chorus was made up of members of the Singakademie and Schubertbund.

60. BMG, page 136. I have been unable to trace the source of this article quoted by Karpath. In the *Wiener Abendpost* of February 23, Hirschfeld methodically refuted Mahler's declarations of principles, accusing him of "making music perversely" and of wanting to "defy the critics."

61. BMG, page 138.

62. Stauber's pamphlet is far from being consistently convincing, but it nevertheless proves Stefan wrong on this particular point (SWE).

## CHAPTER 32

1. Three months later, in his *Fourth Symphony*, Mahler completed the only genuine variations he ever composed. He may even have made a rough draft of this movement at Aussee.

2. Mahler also drew Natalie's attention to the fact that, since the score of the C major symphony, unlike the *Unfinished Symphony*, contained no indications of expression, these had to be added to make its performance possible.

3. Emilie Herzog (1859–1923), who was of Russian origin, had sung at the Munich Opera and had made a name for herself as a Mozart singer in Berlin.

4. Rosé Collection. Strauss was shortly to devote himself to the theater, and this important period in his development abounds in half-finished works, including, it seems, a ballet mentioned in this letter.

5. *Manus manum lavat*, meaning "one hand washes the other," i.e., one good turn deserves another.

6. A reference to the articles in the Berlin press.

7. NBLS. This assertion is particularly noteworthy in view of the fact that Mahler was so frequently accused of being an "analytic" conductor and of overemphasizing details.

8. NBLS.

9. When Mahler first met Henriette Mankiewicz, Natalie Bauer-Lechner was touring France with her quartet. Upon her return, she soon made a friend of Henriette and copied out the first notebooks of the *Mahleriana* for her, in order that she should understand Mahler better. According to the *Neues Wiener Tagblatt* of June 24, 1900, Henriette Mankiewicz, "painter in embroidery," achieved exceptionally felici-

tous results in this unusual art, her sense of nature and of color making her a "creator" rather than a decorator. In 1900 she won a gold medal at the Paris Exposition.

10. Since the first of these cycles was given during the final rehearsals of Tchaikovsky's *Iolanta*, Mahler must indeed have been up to his ears during that week. He conducted the complete and unabridged *Ring* cycle five times during the season, to a full house each time. In all, the season included fifty-eight performances of Wagner, of which ten were of *Lohengrin*.

11. According to the *Musikalische Presse*, Mildenburg had been an ideal Brünnhilde and Schmedes a superb Loge; Wotan had been sung by three different people, Demuth having fallen ill after *Das Rheingold* and only recovered in time for *Siegfried*. Cast of *Das Rheingold* (March 20): Ritter (Alberich), Stehmann (Donner), Demuth (Wotan), Grengg (Fasolt), Reichenberg (Fafner), Korb, Kusmitch, Rellé (Rhine maidens), Forster (Freia), Sedlmair (Fricka), Walker (Erda), Schmedes (Loge), Schittenhelm (Mime). *Die Walküre* (March 21): Hilgermann (Sieglinde), Mildenburg (Brünnhilde), Walker (Fricka and Rossweise), Winkelmann (Siegmund), Reichmann (Wotan), Reichenberg (Hunding). *Siegfried* (March 23): Korb (Forest Bird), Mildenburg (Brünnhilde), Walker (Erda), Schmedes (Siegfried), Liebau (Mime), Ritter (Alberich), Stehmann (Wotan), Reichenberg (Fafner). *Die Götter-dämmerung* (March 26): Kusmitch (Gutrune), Mildenburg (Brünnhilde), Walker (Waltraute), Schmedes (Siegfried), Reichenberg (Hagen).

12. Letters to Lilli Lehmann: *Staatsarchiv*, Vienna, and *Staatsarchiv*, Berlin.

13. Lilli Lehmann's "invitation" was for six different performances: *Le Nozze di Figaro* (April 23), *Aïda* (April 26), *Fidelio* (April 28), *Don Giovanni* (May 1), and *Norma* (April 24 and May 3). One of Lehmann's letters, dated November 16, 1899, is in the Rosé Collection, and the others are in the Vienna Opera Archives. She warmly recommended both Charpentier's *Louise* and Erlanger's *Le Juif polonais* to Mahler, who gave the latter in Vienna six years later. The letter he wrote to Lehmann in February is in the Berlin Library.

14. NBL, page 128. The following year Natalie also heard him express his admiration for Verdi as an orchestrator (see Chapter 35).

15. NBLS.

16. *Ibid.*

17. Marie Gutheil-Schoder was born in Weimar on February 17, 1874, and studied at the Weimar Conservatory. From 1891 to 1900 she sang at the Weimar Opera under the baton of Richard Strauss, and from 1900 until 1926 was one of the most popular members of the Vienna Opera, where she was later active as a stage director. Her first husband, the violinist Gustav Gutheil, conducted in Strasbourg and Weimar and later went to Vienna, where he conducted the popular concerts of the Konzertverein. Marie Gutheil-Schoder subsequently married a Viennese photographer, Franz Setzer, and died on October 19, 1935.

18. Gemma Bellincioni, who had sung in *Cavalleria rusticana* with her in Weimar, had also drawn Mahler's attention to Gutheil-Schoder.

19. We have already noted that this supposition was entirely gratuitous as far as Schalk was concerned.

20. Cast of the performance of February 19: Gutheil-Schoder (Nedda), Schrödter (Canio), Demuth (Tonio).

21. It is obvious that Helm greatly admired Gutheil-Schoder from the start and had made these reservations solely in order to conform to the anti-Semitic line of his paper.

22. NBL, page 135.

23. NBLS.

24. Cast of the performance of May 26, 1900: Michalek (Micaela), Gutheil-Schoder (Carmen), Pohlner (Mercédès), Kusmitch (Frasquita), Naval (José), Neidel (Escamillo), Frauscher (Zuniga).

25. GWO, page 80.

26. The article published on April 5, 1900, in the *Illustriertes Wiener Extrablatt* mentioned both Leffler and Kolo Moser as possible successors to Gaul, but it was still too early for the Vienna Opera to engage a member of the scandalous "Secession" to which Moser belonged, together with Alfred Roller, who succeeded Leffler in 1903. Gaul died in July 1906.

27. Only the correspondent of the *Neue Zeitschrift* asserted that Mahler had "prompted" his musicians to undertake this tour, but the systematically hostile attitude of this magazine renders the statement totally unreliable.

28. In an interview published on June 7 in the *Neues Wiener Tagblatt,* Princess Metternich complained that she had had to pay innumerable visits to all the important members of Parisian society for the sake of ensuring the success of the concerts, not a single impresario having been entrusted with their publicity. She had contacted the Société de Charité Maternelle, for whose benefit the concert of the Männergesangverein was to be given, in order that its patronesses would at least attend that concert. Justifiably concerned about the competition of the legion other events at the exposition, she had also been to several newspaper directors to persuade them to publish advance notices.

29. Letters to Justi in the Rosé Collection.

30. Maurel had created the title role in Erlanger's *Le Juif polonais,* which Mahler heard at the Opéra Comique during his stay in Paris.

31. In an interview published on June 19 in the *Gaulois*, he enumerated the French composers most frequently played in Vienna. The same paper described the stream of admirers who went to congratulate Malher (*sic*) backstage after the first concert, among whom was the "talented pianist" Madame Roger-Miolos, who said she had been "moved to tears."

32. The concert drew 2800 people and brought in 20,000 francs, which, according to Karpath, was remitted to the Société Maternelle.

33. According to Karpath, who sent a daily report to the *Neues Wiener Tagblatt,* Mahler had been suffering from a violent migraine for two days and had already arrived backstage when he almost fainted and fell into the arms of Rosé.

34. L'Ouvreuse (Willy), *La Ronde des blanches,* page 104.

35. Karpath supplies this detail, thereby proving that a score could indeed remain a "dead letter," even for someone like Mahler, who was to produce *Louise* in Vienna in 1903.

36. BMG, page 153, and AMM, page 132. The bells in question are the Jew's sleigh bells.

37. Before leaving the podium Mahler made a short speech of thanks to Princess Metternich.

38. This letter was originally written in French and obviously neither very accurately nor very elegantly translated into German. The present approximate translation from the German therefore leaves much to be desired.

39. NBLS.

40. Mahler added that the Viennese papers certainly ought to have made a greater effort to bring such an important event to the public's notice, but that the Paris critics had nonetheless saved what could be saved of the unfortunate tour.

41. See below the psychological conclusions that Theodor Reik drew from this period of sterility and from the terms in which Mahler confided his anguish to Natalie.

42. NBLS.

43. Twenty years after the letter to Steiner and eight years before *Das Lied von der Erde,* it is interesting to see Mahler refer to earth as a pagan divinity.

44. NBL, page 138. Mahler thus implicitly confirms that his teachers at the Vienna Conservatory always considered his contrapuntal gifts good enough to allow a less

thorough study of this discipline. It is somewhat surprising, however, that he should have been granted the conservatory diploma despite this lack.

45. MBR, Nos. 262, 263, 264.

46. NBLS.

47. He discovered only the following year that some of the birds had made their nests in the roof of the Häuschen.

48. NBL, page 146.

49. *Verjüngende Spitze*—the image is that of a church spire that forms the light and airy summit of the edifice.

50. NBL, page 120. That same day Mahler also mentioned how difficult it had been to end his *First Symphony* in D, while his first theme had really been in A. "It would have been quite different," he added, "if I had guided the conclusion toward this key."

51. This passage and another concerning Zemlinsky and his *Es war einmal* (see Chapter 31) prove that Mahler sometimes plagiarized deliberately, but more often had to be on his guard against doing so unconsciously.

52. NBL, pages 143–46.

53. NBLS.

54. RHM, page 320. Theodor Reik compares this "obsession" to one Mahler had expressed the year before: "The day my house is ready, inspiration will fail me and I won't be able to work any more." According to Reik, such obsessions have hidden meaning: the building of the house and its completion represented a reward for the completion of the symphony, and Mahler perhaps felt guilty for having ordered the house before he had finished his work. In other respects, the house symbolized woman, and the obsession about a completed house in which it would be impossible to work reveals, Reik says, an impotence complex that he juxtaposes to Mahler's latent desire to marry. Mahler frequently relates creative fecundity to physical fecundity.

55. NBLS.

56. NBL, page 141. The sentence means literally, "one is composed."

57. See Chapter 2.

## CHAPTER 33

1. This last sheet of the manuscript of the Adagio is presently in my possession.

2. Levi had suggested this to him in 1897, not knowing that he had already done it in Prague, Budapest, and Hamburg.

3. According to Karl Maria Kolb, however, this revolving stage had a serious drawback: when the singers went upstage, one could no longer see them from the fourth balcony. Moreover, he said, the acoustics were not as good because the curtain hung down lower than usual over the proscenium (KMO, page 81).

4. Cast of the performance of October 4, 1900: Gutheil-Schoder (Despina), Saville (Fiordiligi), Hilgermann (Dorabella), Naval (Ferrando), Demuth (Guglielmo), Hesch (Alfonso).

5. Joseph Reiter (1862–June 2, 1939), born in Braunau am Inn, the son of an organist, studied at Linz. Teacher and choirmaster in Vienna from 1886 to 1907, later director of the Mozarteum in Salzburg and still later conductor at the Hofburgtheater. Reiter composed four operas, of which *Der Bundschuh* was the first, as well as chamber music and numerous choral works.

6. Mahler wrote to Mildenburg in 1900: "I hope you're relieved to see what a bootee this 'sandal' is!"

7. Opera documents, (No. 951).

8. Cast of the premiere on November 13: Mildenburg (Ehrengard), Sedlmair (Ulrike), Walker and Schmedes (Hans), Breuer (Schneider), Grengg (Weber), Stehmann (Hartmann).

9. Born in Vienna on May 27, 1863, the son of a Viennese merchant, Franz Schalk,

together with his brother Josef, had been a pupil of Bruckner, who, despite their youth, had entrusted them with the correction and copying out of his manuscripts. He had been a fellow student of Mahler at the conservatory and, like the latter, had studied piano with Epstein and violin with Hellmesberger. He began his conducting career at Czernowitz and Reichenberg and then spent five years (1890–95) in Graz. He had already managed to perform both Wagner and Bruckner uncut. He conducted the symphonic concerts and the opera in Prague from 1895 to 1898 and replaced Weingartner in Berlin before conducting in London and then New York, where he replaced Anton Seidl for one season. Owing to his brother's illness, he subsequently returned to Europe and was again conducting in Berlin when Mahler engaged him for the Vienna Opera, where he made his debut on February 8, 1900, with a performance of *Lohengrin* and was to remain for twenty-nine years. In 1904 he succeeded Löwe as conductor of the concerts of the Gesellschaft der Musikfreunde, a post that he held until 1921. He became professor of conducting at the Vienna Conservatory in 1909 and shared the directorship of the Vienna Opera with Richard Strauss after the First World War. He died on September 3, 1931.

10. MBR, No. 248. Mahler offered him an opening salary of five thousand florins a year, a sum which he increased some weeks later to six thousand.

11. The article was reprinted in the *Neue Freie Presse* of November 7, 1900. Among the singers Mahler had thus "enticed" the paper named two who were relatively unknown, Elise Feinhals and Klopfer, and the celebrated Olive Fremstad, Mahler's future Isolde at the Metropolitan Opera in New York. Mahler conducted his *Second Symphony* in Munich on October 20.

12. NBL, page 154.

13. See *Opera* magazine (Vol. 4, No. 1, January 1953, page 10).

14. Reichmann was singing the role of Telramund. The anecdote was told by the tenor Schmedes.

15. Mahler had engaged both Naval and Saville after the first Theater an der Wien performance of Puccini's *La Bohème* in 1897 (BMG, page 380).

16. Erik Schmedes (1868–1931) born in Gjentofte, Denmark, studied singing in Berlin and Vienna and first appeared in lyric tenor parts in Wiesbaden in 1891. After singing at the Nuremburg and Hamburg opera houses, he was engaged by Mahler for the Vienna Opera in 1898. He remained there till 1924.

17. GWO, page 80, and LEM, page 313.

18. GWO, page 80, and LEM, page 313.

19. Cast of *Il Trovatore:* Kurz (Leonora), Walker (Azucena), Schrödter (Manrico), Demuth (Conte di Luna).

20. According to the *Allgemeine Musik Zeitung* of November 2, 1900, during a general assembly on October 23, the Verein had decided to change its name to Münchner Gesellschaft für moderne Tonkunst (Munich Society for Modern Music), any "exclusive propaganda" for Wolf's music having become unnecessary.

21. It seems that he also resented Mahler's having "borrowed" the idea of the revolving stage from the Munich Opera. That the misunderstanding between Mahler and Possart was short-lived is proved by a series of letters of 1903, preserved in the Opera Archives, about the engagement of the latter's daughter at the Vienna Opera. Possart begged Mahler to give Poppi (von Possart) a one-year contract and have her make her debut under his direction. Mahler was obliged to refuse the request, because "I would never obtain the consent of my superiors" to an engagement without a "preliminary invitation." (Opera documents, June–July 1903, No. 2635.)

22. See the article by Paula Reber, Munich correspondent of the *Zeitschrift für Musik.*

23. MBR, No. 209, of February 17, 1897. Seidl had published the letter in the *Allgemeine Zeitung.* In it Mahler had expatiated on his *Second Symphony,* its program,

and the inspiration of its finale, as well as on that which he owed to Strauss's success (see above, Chapter 23).

24. NBLS does not indicate which performance, but it could only have been that of 1895 in Berlin or that of 1899 in Vienna.

25. Adler's testimony is unreliable here, at least as far as the exact words are concerned, for it is unlikely that Strauss would have accused himself if gratuitous cacophony except as a joke. Natalie may well have twisted Adler's words slightly.

26. Various versions of this plan have been preserved (see Chapter 26). Mahler said that he had removed the Andante from his *First Symphony* for the same reasons, but he had in fact had far more important reasons for doing so.

27. Louis obviously subscribed to the fable, all too prevalent in the nineteenth and twentieth centuries, of Jewish "materialism." In a book published in 1909 (*Die Deutsche Musik der Gegenwart*) he again succumbed to the temptation of treating Mahler's "case" from the point of view of his Jewishness, claiming that he "speaks musical German with the accent, the cadence and above all the gestures of the too oriental Jew."

28. Arthur Seidl: *Moderner Geist in Deutscher Tonkunst*, page 62.

29. Program of the concert of October 20: Berlioz's *Rob Roy Overture;* Richard Strauss's *Hymnus*, Op. 33, No. 3, for voice and orchestra (soloist Elise Feinhals). This first half of the concert was conducted by Siegmund von Hausegger; the second half consisted entirely of Mahler's *Second Symphony*. The chorus was made up of members of the Porges'schen Chorverein and the Lehrergesangverein.

30. Letter to Justi of October 24, 1900 (Rosé Collection).

31. Letter of October 25 (*ibid.*). The symphony was played again on November 8 at the Allerheiligen Konzert of the Münchner Musikalische Akademie and conducted by Stavenhagen, to whom Mahler afterward sent a telegram of thanks and congratulations.

32. According to an article published in the *Wiener Allgemeine Zeitung* on November 20, the commotion had begun even before the concert, because the police had refused to allow some of the young people who had been queuing for standing room to install themselves, as they usually did, on the stage behind the orchestra, so that many of them had had to remain outside.

33. NBLS.

34. According to Helm, however, one could easily find them in the score, since it had already been published.

35. It was performed each year at the Hofoper on the anniversary of Empress Elisabeth's assassination. The title role had been sung in 1900 by the Munich soprano Agnes Stavenhagen, who had just participated in the Munich performance of Mahler's *Second Symphony* (NBLS).

36. NBL, page 175, November 19, 1901.

37. As usual, Helm fulminated against certain of Mahler's tempos after this concert, and particularly the slowness of the Scherzo and the Trio, as well as denouncing the "overloading of the instruments and the exaggerated explosion of the brasses in the Finale." Hans Geissler, in the *Neue musikalische Presse*, reported that Mahler repeatedly had them played with their bells up during this concert.

38. In a letter of September 13, 1899, to František Adolf Šubert, the director of the Czech Theater in Prague, Mahler wrote that he intended to put on three Russian operas at the Hofoper: Dargomizhsky's *Russalka*, Glinka's *Ruslan and Ludmilla* and Rimsky-Korsakov's *May Night*. On May 7 of that year he had already sent Šubert a telegram concerning *Libuše*, since he had hoped to be able to attend a performance of it at the Prague Opera.

39. The second item on the program, between Bach's *Concerto in D Minor* and Franck's *Variations symphoniques*. The concert ended with Smetana's two works.

40. The quotation from Hanslick figures in NBLS, and its accuracy shows that Mahler read criticisms far more attentively than he would usually admit.

41. Carl Friedberg (1872–1955), born in Bingen am Rhein, studied at the Frankfurt Conservatory and Heidelberg University and began his career as a piano virtuoso in 1901. He was a professor at the Cologne Conservatory from 1904–14 and spent the years 1916–18 in the United States. Thereafter, he became assistant conductor to Eugène Ysaÿe in Brussels, returning to America in 1923 to the New York Institute of Musical Art and to teach at the Juilliard School. He later formed a trio with Karl Flesch and Hugo Becker.

42. Kalbeck questioned the "staccato" style of the introduction to the Finale of the *First Symphony*, resulting from Mahler's "insertion of short breathings between the different fragments of the theme." He also objected to the rapid tempo in the Finale of the *Fourth*, which had made it impossible for the bassoons to play the principal theme at the restatement, and wondered whether Mahler had sought to create a comic effect in the belief that that was what Beethoven had intended. The *Neue Zeitschrift* opposed the slowness of the Andante and the speed of the Finale in the *First Symphony*.

## CHAPTER 34

1. See Ernst Decsey, *Stunden mit Mahler* (*Die Musik:* X, 21, 147) and GWO, page 79. Max Graf asserts in the latter that it was he who was asked this extraordinary question.

2. Max Graf in the *Neues Wiener Journal* (June 26, 1921). Mahler often referred to the critics as *die Herren Vorgesetzten* (the superiors).

3. The first performance of *Rienzi* (on January 21) was given for the benefit of the Opera Retirement Fund. Cast: Pohlner (Messenger), Mildenburg (Irene), Walker (Adriano), Schmedes (Rienzi), Neidel (Orsini), Breuer (Baroncelli), Felix (Cecco), Hesch (Cardinal), Reichenberg (Colonna).

4. Hanslick pronounced Mahler's performance "exquisite" but found the tempo of the Introduction "a little too slow," while Helm reproached Mahler with having disregarded Mendelssohn's indications by pausing between the movements.

5. Max Graf saw the score thus marked in blue pencil in Mahler's office before the concert (GWO, page 84).

6. The Nicolai Concert of January 27 was given with the following singers: Elizza (soprano), Kusmitsch (mezzo-soprano), Naval (tenor) and Frauscher (bass).

7. The Koncertverein, founded in 1900, to which Mahler entrusted the Vienna premiere of his *Fifth* and *Sixth Symphonies*.

8. Son of a well-known Viennese piano manufacturer, Friedrich Ehrbar had just taken over the directorship of the Singakademic, which, founded in 1888 to perform the *a cappella* works of the old Italian composers, had since run into difficulties. In order to restore it to its former glory, Ehrbar himself had invested large sums of money in the enterprise. The concert of February 17 brought in a considerable sum, despite the fact that it had meant enlisting and paying five hundred performers, including not only the extra musicians but also the Schubertbund, to reinforce the rather weak male contingent of the Singverein. The repeat performance planned for March was postponed until the following year, Mahler having fallen ill shortly before it.

9. According to Helm, the typically Mahlerian theme of *Der Spielmann*, was merely an old-fashioned gavotte, and the piece as a whole "constantly changed style" and "showed just how thoroughly young Mahler had studied Wagner's scores."

10. Soloists for the first performance on February 17, 1901: Elizza and Mildenburg (sopranos), Walker (contralto), Schrödter (tenor). The orchestra was that of the opera.

11. The complete list of the crimes of which Helm accused him reads as follows: cutting about two hundred bars in the first two movements, inverting certain elements in the first, cutting the third theme and the characteristic unison passage that follows it, inserting transitions of his own invention; cutting the restatement of the great 4/4

melody, the most beautiful passage in the Adagio according to Helm, so that the final crescendo of the principal theme had come far too early, and, finally, of accelerating several tempos and particularly that of the Scherzo, in which, disregarding the indications in the score, Mahler had slowed down the tempo for the second theme. The critic also recalled the unabridged performance Löwe had conducted in Vienna, on March, 1898, and April 15, 1899.

12. NBLS, February 1901.

13. *Der Mann is z'klan für die G'schicht"* (NBLS, January 1900). The words are Natalie's, but it is clear from the context that Mahler shared her opinion.

14. NBLS, September 29, 1901.

15. AMM, page 23. Deceived by her memory, Alma Mahler says that it was a performance of *Die Meistersinger.*

16. Justine wrote to Berliner on March 2 to give him news of her brother and said that Mahler would have to be re-examined and possibly operated on the following Monday (HLG Collection).

17. The eleven thousand florins comprised an additional emolument (*Functionszulage*) of five thousand florins (including an allowance for his rent), a "fixed allowance" payable, like the rest of his income, in monthly installments, of three thousand florins, and an annual "carriage allowance" of three thousand florins (see opera documents, letter of March 2, 1901, signed by Plappart). The Emperor's decree is dated February 22 and was therefore promulgated before Mahler's illness.

18. Mahler was still to be entitled to a pension of three thousand florins a year after ten years of service, but the amount of the pension was thereafter to increase by one thousand florins every year instead of every five years (see Chapter 26). The decree also stipulated that he would be retired only if he were incapable of continuing his activities or dismissed by the lord chamberlain.

19. See Chapter 33.

20. Made up of movements taken from two orchestral suites, the Bach suite that Mahler was to conduct and publish in New York includes a carefully noted realization of the figured bass "for organ and clavicembalo." In it he specified that it was "to be regarded as a rough draft, with the richest possible harmonies in the tuttis and delicate nuances in the *piano* passages." The organ plays only in the overture.

21. Throughout his life Mahler had a pronounced aversion to the violin, which he expressed at Aussee in 1899: "As a solo instrument, the violin stands out above all for the insignificance of its literature, which, with a few exceptions, consists of nothing but 'dances on a tightrope' and is devoid of art." (NBLS.)

22. The cantata to which Mahler was referring was either *Ich elender Mensch* (No. 48) or *Ich armer Mensch, ich Sünderknecht* (No. 55).

23. NBL, page 112. In this, as in many other instances, Mahler proved a forerunner, since this preoccupation with "stereophony," this contrasting of different orchestral and choral groups which prevailed during the Renaissance, baroque, and classical eras, was rediscovered long after his death.

24. Cast of the first performance (March 18): Gutheil-Schoder (Princess), Pohlner (First Young Girl), Thann (spoken part), Naval (Lobetanz), Preuss (Student), Frauscher (King), Stehmann, Ritter, and Grengg (spoken parts).

25. NBLS and NBL, page 158. This last undated passage is missing in NBLS and comes immediately after the account of a discussion with Guido Adler (on Tchaikovsky's *Pathétique*) which took place in Vienna on April 18.

26. The dream concerned his mother and his brother Ernst and ended with an apparition of the Wandering Jew (see Chapter 3).

27. See Chapter 16.

28. In the unpublished portion of her manuscript, needless to say, for the published portion was carefully "purged" of all "personal" notes.

29. Letter of late March to Guido Adler and card of April 3 to Nanna, the wife of Albert Spiegler.

30. BMG, pages 168–69, and Perger: *Fünfzig Jahre Wiener Philharmoniker,* page 42.

31. Mahler's decision was evidently not made public immediately, for the *Neue Freie Presse* of May 14, 1901, announced that the Philharmonic committee had just approached him again and that he had replied that "his doctor had categorically forbidden him to resume the direction of the concerts."

32. Born on April 9, 1855, Josef, Jr., was an infant prodigy and a son and namesake of the director of the conservatory and founder of the renowned quartet, and a ballet conductor at the opera. Hellmesberger succeeded his father as first violinist of the Hellmesberger Quartet. He conducted the Hofkapelle, taught at the conservatory, composed some pleasant but lightweight ballet music, became a *Konzertmeister* in 1866 and a *Kapellmeister* in 1900. He conducted the Philharmonic concerts for only two years and was then obliged to leave Vienna because of a violent quarrel with the mother of a young ballerina he had seduced. He subsequently conducted at the Stuttgart Opera and died in Vienna on April 26, 1907.

33. These figures are taken from an article published in the *Neue Freie Presse* on October 10, 1903.

34. Mahler was to conduct the Philharmonic on three more occasions, namely the Vienna premiere of his *Fourth Symphony,* on January 12, 1902, that of his *Third Symphony,* given at a "special concert" on December 14, 1904, and his farewell concert to Vienna, the Gesellschafts Konzert of November 26, 1907, at which he conducted his *Second Symphony.* Between 1904 and 1907 he preferred to entrust the first performances of his symphonies to the Konzertverein orchestra.

35. Theobald Kretschmann: *Tempi passati,* Vol. II, page 157ff. Kretschmann then recalled the "scandal" of the sixty-string performance of Beethoven's *Quartet in F Minor* and reproached Mahler for his "sacrilegious attitude" toward composers like Beethoven and Schumann, his preference for the "extreme registers" of the bass tuba and the E flat clarinet, and finally and most vehemently for his tempos in *Die Walküre.* When he conducted it, everything was "dragging and disjointed" (*verschleppt und zerrissen*), while the Magic Fire of the third act completely lacked grandeur and blessed inspiration (*Weihe*). Its performance even became technically impossible.

36. Cf. Karl Blessinger: *Judentum in der Musik.*

37. He was referring, of course, to Demuth.

38. Ludwig Karpath: *Lachende Musiker,* page 95.

39. Born in Schönberg, Moravia, Leo Slezak (1873–1946) studied to be an engineer before taking up singing as a career. His first appearance was in *Lohengrin,* at Brno in 1896, after which he was engaged by the Berlin Opera. Despite his great success as guest singer in Vienna, Slezak's firm engagement there was delayed owing to an indiscretion on the part of the critic Karpath. The Berlin opera director, Löwe, was later decorated by the Austrian Emperor for consenting to free him some months before the end of his contract. The famous tenor remained with the Vienna Opera until 1911. In 1907 he improved his technique by studying in Paris with the well-known Jean de Reszke. After Mahler's death he pursued his triumphant career by appearing in most of the great opera houses of the world, particularly in the United States.

40. That evening Slezak and the soprano had a difference of opinion. The latter wished to incorporate a cadenza into their duet, a kind of "exotic Kakezerei" that she would perform while he just crossed his arms and "served only to supply a musical background." But Slezak refused, declaring that he was incapable of learning anything new only two days before his "guest" performance.

41. According to Schönaich, Mahler's negotiations with the publisher of the Paris version had come to nothing because the latter had demanded payment of an extra

copyright fee, whereas Helm attributed his decision not to give the Paris version to his dislike of ballet. Certain of Mahler's "improvements" were far from appreciated by the Viennese Wagnerians, and particularly Richter, who, in a letter to Karpath of February 20, 1902, which the latter published in the *Neues Wiener Tagblatt* of September 28, summed up the "crimes" he had committed in *Der fliegende Holländer* (see Chapter 27) and *Tannhäuser.* In the latter opera, he said, the wind instruments symbolized the serious, virtuous, and religious elements, and the violins personified sensuality. Thus, in the prelude to the second act, the pure joy of Elisabeth (oboes) contrasted with the ironic laughter of Venus (violins). Yet, at the end of the final act, Mahler had omitted the woodwinds in the Pilgrims' Chorus when the flowering staff is brought in! He was far too talented, Richter said, to perpetrate such atrocities and should know better than to give the impression that he was "trying to push himself forward at all costs."

42. Schönaich admitted that Wagner had declared he would "definitely give up this type of indications," for every time he heard a tempo that was inexact or contrary to his intentions in either *Der fliegende Holländer* or *Tannhäuser,* it almost always turned out to be "that of the metronome," but maintained that, transformed into an adagio, the Landgraf's monologue (*"Noch bleibe denn . . ."*) had lost all its effect, the singer having been, as it were, imprisoned in brass walls; that, in the official address that followed, the contrasts between "fury" and "excessive gentleness" had been "exaggerated and contrary to reason" and that the "rigid precision of the rendition was unsuited to the lyric and poetic passages," for it had made them sound "more like expressions of anger." As far as the abolishment of the former cuts was concerned, Schönaich was happy to hear the Finale of the second act and Elisabeth's prayer in their entirety, but not the duet of the two heroes, which he considered one of the weakest and most outmoded passages of Wagner's music. (Mahler had also restored the middle verse of Tannhäuser's hymn to Venus.) In Kalbeck's view none of the passages thus salvaged were worth the honor.

43. Cast of the performance of May 12, 1901: Kurz (Elisabeth), Mildenburg (Venus), Kusmitsch (Shepherd), Winkelmann (Tannhäuser), Preuss (Vogelweide), Demuth (Wolfram), Frauscher (Landgrave). In this performance, Helm objected to the "intolerable slowness" of the hymn to Venus as well as that of a few other passages, such as *"Gegrüsst sei uns"* in the first act.

44. Mahler, however, had no personal feeling for Goldmark, who had refused to intervene on his behalf when he was hoping to be appointed to the Vienna Opera. A letter Goldmark wrote him in May 1900, in reply to a telegram of good wishes on his seventieth birthday, shows that their relations were far from cordial: "Notwithstanding I am frequently too loquacious in my operas, forgive me for being brief today," he began, doubtless alluding to Mahler's criticisms of his works, and ended up in the deliberately ambiguous tone that characterizes the whole letter: "You are well acquainted with my opinion of the genius of Gustav Mahler." (Rosé Collection.) Mahler subsequently refused to give his latest opera, *Götz von Berlichingen,* which was not performed in Vienna until 1910, and then only in a "new version."

45. Cast of the first performance (April 20, 1901): Mildenburg (Queen of Sheba), Schrödter (Assad), Demuth (Solomon), Hesch (High Priest).

46. Cast of the performance of May 4, 1901: Saville (Martha), Hilgermann (Nancy), Naval (Lionel), Felix (Lord Tristan), Hesch (Plunkett).

47. Gustav Brecher (1878–1940) was born in Teplitz and studied in Leipzig. While still a schoolboy, he composed a symphonic poem, *Rosmersholm,* which led to his being discovered by Richard Strauss. Later on, he made his theatrical debut as a volunteer in Leipzig. Mahler got him a job at the Olmütz Theater, where he himself had conducted. Brecher subsequently pursued his career in Hamburg, Cologne, Frankfurt-am-Main, Leipzig, and Berlin and became one of the most celebrated conductors in Germany.

48. The 1900–01 season topped all its predecessors in the number of performances of

Wagner: seventy as compared to the previous record of fifty-eight, including six complete *Ring* cycles and a series of chronological performances of all his works from *Rienzi* to *Die Götterdämmerung*.

49. Hermann Kretzschmar (1848–1924) was a celebrated Berlin musicologist. He studied at the conservatories of Leipzig and Dresden, had a brief career as a conductor, and then taught history of music at the University of Leipzig, where he directed both the Bachgesellschaft and the chorus of the Riedelverein. He wrote many books and articles and, together with Hugo Riemann, was regarded as one of the most eminent musicologists of his time.

50. NBL, page 163.

51. Rudolf Braun (1869–1925), who had quite a reputation at that time. Mahler had given three of his pantomimes at the Vienna Opera.

52. Mahler may indeed have used the possessive adjective "ours," which figures in Natalie's text. However, it should be noted that at that moment his faithful friend still thought she would succeed in becoming his wife.

53. Letter of September 20 to Nanna Spiegler (R. Lehmann Collection). On June 26 he had sent her a postcard of Pörtschach am Wörthersee via Natalie.

54. NBLS, July 12, 1897.

55. NBL, page 121, July 30, 1899.

56. NBL, page 82, and NBLS. In this statement Mahler delivers up the key to the notorious mixture of style with which the critics so untiringly reproached him. The statement is therefore of cardinal importance to the understanding of his musical style.

57. The importance of this passage needs hardly be stressed considering the subsequent evolution of music. It is amazing to see Mahler so confidently drawing conclusions of paramount significance to the future of his art. From the point of view of sound, the *Fifth Symphony* long continued to present problems, and he was obliged to alter its orchestration several times.

58. Mahler calls it the "second movement," but the preceding passage clearly refers to the "third movement" of the symphony. Doubtless he had not yet split the first movement in two.

59. Thomas Koschat (1845–1914), a Carinthian composer, was the author of numerous folkloric waltzes for male chorus and of their text in Carinthian dialect. His *"Liederspiel" Am Wörthersee* had just been given at the Vienna Opera.

60. Mahler had therefore not yet decided to divide the first movement into Funeral March and Allegro.

61. This incident is almost identical to one that occurred while he was composing his *Eighth Symphony* (see Volume II).

62. Natalie does not indicate how many of the *Kindertotenlieder* were composed during this summer. However, before he returned to Vienna, he gave her, in token of friendship, a manuscript of seven lieder which included three *Kindertotenlieder*. Alma Mahler incorrectly asserts that three others were composed in 1904, for only the last two date from that year. Theodor Reik thinks that Mahler had been toying with the idea of getting married for over a year and that this had revived the memory of certain of his parents' anxieties. Moreover, the psychologist says, he must have known that one of Rückert's children was called Ernst and thus, while composing the *Kindertotenlieder*, "identified himself with his father by putting himself into the frame of mind of a man who had lost a son named Ernst." This, according to Reik, would explain his intense emotion. A number of people have pointed out the striking thematic similarity between one of the *Kindertotenlieder* and the Funeral March of the *Fifth Symphony*.

63. In the manuscript of *"Um Mitternacht"* with piano accompaniment, from the collection of William Ritter, Mahler wrote "composed in 1899 or 1900" (HLG Collection). However, Natalie was always so scrupulous and precise that we can be sure it was Mahler who was mistaken.

64. Letter to Henriette Mankiewicz written the day Mahler left Maiernigg around August 21 (see Chapter 35).

65. Letter of August 20, 1901, to Nanna Spiegler (R. Lehmann Collection).

66. Letter to Henriette Mankiewicz.

## CHAPTER 35

1. This letter, which belongs to the Amsterdam collector Marius Slothuis, must have been written in March 1901, because Mahler mentions his hemorrhage in February. *Feuersnot* had its world premiere in Dresden on November 2, 1901.

2. Since the fourth and last Philharmonic concert had otherwise consisted exclusively of his own works, Strauss had done Mahler a great honor by including his lieder cycle in the program, which had comprised the prelude to the second act of *Guntram*, three lieder with orchestral accompaniment (*"Meinem Kinde," "Muttertändelei," and "Wiegenlied"*), sung by Pauline de Ahna Strauss, and, as the highlight of the concert, the symphonic poem *Also sprach Zarathustra*. Mahler's second lied had been encored. The newspaper *Bohemia* had said that, because of their labored naïveté, the poems were less interesting than "the musical construction and spicy orchestration" of the lieder.

3. NBLS stresses the fact that this inscription had "several meanings," doubtless including both "What do you make of this?" and "How much of this will you swallow?" Mahler was not wrong in thinking that the symphony would not really appeal to Strauss, who nevertheless persuaded the committee of the Allgemeiner Deutscher Musikverein to give it its first performance.

4. These and the following letters from Mahler to Strauss are owned by Dr. Franz Strauss.

5. Letter of July 11, 1901 (Rosé Collection).

6. Postcard of August 17, 1901 (Rosé Collection). The performance was eventually postponed to December 16, probably because the Munich premiere had been postponed to November 25.

7. Richard Sternfeld (1858–1926) professor of musical history at the University of Berlin, composer, critic, and author of many books.

8. Letter to Weingartner, written in August or September 1901 (HLG Collection). In it Mahler states that the score will be published in October.

9. Letter to Weingartner (*ibid.*).

10. He must have left Maiernigg between August 20 and 25, since Natalie's memoirs contain an account of a walk and a discussion on Beethoven on the twentieth, and the Rosé Collection a letter he wrote Justi on August 27, from which it appears that he had been back in Vienna at least two days.

11. Theodor Bertram had already sung under Mahler's baton in Hamburg. During the summer of 1901, he had made a tremendous hit as Wotan at Bayreuth. He had made his first appearance in Vienna as a guest artist the preceding spring, singing the Count in *Le Nozze di Figaro* and Mephistopheles in *Faust*, and he had immediately been engaged. He apparently had "a voice like a trumpet" but too frequently forced it and, according to Graf, was "too realistic" as the Dutchman (*Die Musik*, I, 3, 260).

12. NBLS.

13. See *Die Musik*, I, 3, page 261. Cast of the first performance conducted by Bruno Walter in Vienna on September 27, 1901: Mildenburg (Aïda), Walker (Amneris), Slezak (Radames), Reichmann (Amonasro), Grengg (Ramfis).

14. BWT, pages 161–64.

15. The following passage from a letter Mahler wrote to Weingartner proves that Bruno Walter seriously considered leaving Vienna; "Schlesinger is still talking of leaving! It's not impossible that he may go when his temporary contract ends. But nothing can be settled before the summer." (Letter of January or February 1902. HLG Collection.)

16. Between September 1901 and December 1907, when Mahler left Vienna, Walter conducted almost five hundred performances.

17. In a letter to Justi (Rosé Collection), Mahler himself described her interpretation as *grossartig* (superb).

18. See Chapter 34.

19. Letter to the intendant of November 25, 1900 (Opera documents, Z. 1862).

20. Cast of the performance of October 4, 1901: Michalek (Anna), Gutheil-Schoder (Frau Fluth), Hilgermann (Frau Reich), Naval (Fenton), Breuer (Spärlich), Demuth (Fluth), Ritter (Cajus), Frauscher (Reich), Grengg (Falstaff).

21. Located on the Schottenring, the Ringtheater, which had opened its doors on January 17, 1874, burned down at around seven-thirty in the evening on December 8, 1881, just before the performance of *Les Contes d'Hoffmann*. About three hundred people died, and Bruckner was terrified because the window of the room where he kept all the manuscripts of his unpublished symphonies gave onto the theater.

22. Cast of the first performance on November 11, 1901: Gutheil-Schoder (Olympia, Giulietta, Antonia), Kusmitsch (Niklaus), Schrödter (Hoffmann), Schittenhelm (Spalanzani), Breuer (Andreas, Cochenille, Pitinacchio), Neidel (Schlemihl), Ritter (Lindorf, Coppelius, Dapertutto, Dr. Miracle), Frauscher (Krespel). In the second cast the minor roles were sung by the same people, but Saville and Kurz alternated with Gutheil-Schoder, Naval with Schrödter, and Ritter with Hesch.

23. Letter of October 9, 1901 (Opera documents).

24. Although virtually unknown outside Germany, Lortzing is in fact a dramatic composer of outstanding merit, and there is therefore nothing surprising about Mahler's judgment.

25. NBL, page 168, and NBLS.

26. This passage might lead one to believe that Mahler had conducted the *Missa Solemnis*. However, this is not so and he undoubtedly made the "mistakes" he mentions while reading it at the piano.

27. NBLS.

28. This structural complexity has not escaped any attentive musician. Once again, Mahler proved more lucid than most other composers are about their own work.

29. It was precisely these patchings and mendings that Mahler censured in Bruckner's symphonies. This "organic unity," even in the most complex developments, constituted one of the main virtues of his own mature works.

30. Natalie says that "he decided" (*beschloss*), but the score itself proves that he later gave up this idea (NBL, page 171).

31. This statement will not surprise those who have studied the at once original and phenomenally effective orchestrations of *Otello, Falstaff,* and the *Requiem*.

32. Hence the unusual indications in Mahler's scores. He had already complained to Natalie in late 1900 about the way in which his indications were misconstrued. For instance, the Scherzo of his *Second Symphony* was played slowly, like an étude, because he had noted *mit ruhiger, fliessender Bewegung* (with calm, flowing motion). It was for the same reason that he had done away with such indications as *mit innigster Empfindung* (with intense feeling) at the beginning of the Adagio of his *Third Symphony*. He used laughingly to recall the indication *mit teuflischer Wildheit* (with demoniac savagery) he had noted above the second movement of *Das klagende Lied* when he was twenty.

33. The Kaim Orchestra was co-directed by Felix Weingartner, then one of the "moderns," and Siegmund von Hausegger.

34. Letter to Weingartner written in September or October 1901 (HLG Collection). Mahler added that Margarete Michalek would accept any "reasonable" fee offered by Kaim. She would attend "out of enthusiasm" and had even agreed not to sing a solo. In the end the young soprano received only "traveling expenses" of two hundred florins.

All Mahler's requests were not granted, for Weingartner placed his *Wallfahrt nach Kevlaar* for orchestra and alto voice in the program before the *Fourth*.

35. This reminded Mahler of the evening when he himself had had to conduct a performance in Budapest immediately after being informed of his mother's death.

36. In a letter written in October, Mahler asked Weingartner for at least fourteen first violins, twelve second violins, eight second violins, as many cellos, and at least six double basses for the first performance, begging him to "understand the anxiety of a creator who, for the first time, launches his work into the world." (HLG Collection).

37. William Ritter (May 31, 1867–March 19, 1955), Swiss writer, painter, and art critic. After completing his studies, first in his home town of Neuchâtel, then in Dôle, and finally at the University of Vienna, Ritter traveled widely, dividing his interests between music and the fine arts. He crossed Europe several times, as far as Rumania, in search of new methods of expression and national traditions. He became a specialist on Czech art thanks to the influence of his collaborator and friend Janko Cadra, and he settled in Munich from 1900 to 1914, where he was reader in French to Prince Ruprecht of Bavaria. He wrote articles for many music and art reviews, counted many famous painters and composers among his friends, and in 1906 the *Mercure de France* published his collection of articles entitled *Études d'art étranger.*" He also wrote an important biography of Smetana (Alcan, 1907). After 1914 he settled in Switzerland, where he continued to paint and write articles until his death in Melide (Tessino) in 1955.

38. *"Souvenirs sur Gustav Mahler," Schweizerische Musikzeitung*, 101, 1, 30/31.

39. The concert consisted of a little Mozart *Symphony in G Major*, "composed when he was thirteen years old" (doubtless K. 74 or K. 129), a work for contralto and orchestra by Weingartner, *Wallfahrt nach Kevlaar*, Mahler's symphony, a group of lieder (Brahms's *"Immer leise,"* Schumann's *"Waldesgespräch,"* Reisenauer's *"Der Ritter,"* and Cornelius' *"Wiegenlied"*), sung, like the *Wallfahrt*, by Therese Behr and accompanied at the piano by Weingartner, and Beethoven's *Egmont Overture*.

40. WRE, page 271.

41. *Die Musik*, I, 6, 549.

42. *Aufsätze und Skizzen*, page 287.

43. *Le Courrier Musical:* July 1, 1904.

44. This same critic maintained that Weingartner's reputation had been badly damaged by this enterprise and that he had only given the work "out of friendship for a highly placed musician," while the Nuremberg correspondent of *Die Musik* stated that Mahler had promised to reward Weingartner by giving the latter's *Oreste* in Vienna.

45. The programs of the four concerts were as follows: Nuremberg (November 27), Berlioz: *Roi Lear Overture*, Mahler: *Fourth Symphony*, Brahms: *Fourth Symphony*, Beethoven: *Egmont Overture;* Frankfurt (November 28), Mahler: *Fourth Symphony*, Brahms: *Fourth Symphony*, Berlioz: *Roi Lear Overture;* Karlsruhe (November 29), Berlioz: *Roi Lear Overture*, Mahler: Finale of the *Fourth Symphony*, Beethoven: *First Symphony* and *"Leonore" Overture No. 3;* Stuttgart (November 30), Mahler: *Fourth Symphony*, Brahms: *Fourth Symphony*, Beethoven: *"Leonore" Overture No. 3*.

46. "If I remember rightly, do I really owe you a letter?" wrote Mahler. "You promised me a report on your activities, but alas, I never received it . . . You cannot imagine how nervous and tense I am! I don't even have the time to think of myself, let alone my friends . . . !" (Letter of March or April 1902. HLG Collection. Weingartner's letters to Mahler have unfortunately disappeared, as have most of the other letters he received.)

47. In this letter, which is now in the Gemeente Museum in The Hague, Mahler also informed Strauss that *Feuersnot* had finally been passed by the Viennese censorship.

48. This letter belongs to Dr. Franz Strauss. In it Mahler tells Strauss that the bells required for the performance will be sent directly to Berlin by Weingartner. Mahler also wrote to Destinn to admonish her not to assume the "parodic tone" that the text, at

first glance, appeared to call for but "the most naïve and modest tone possible." This last letter forms part of the Emmy Destinn bequest, which is preserved in the Prague Museum (Theatrical Section, 1884/26).

49. This letter was given to me by Professor Alfred Rosé.

50. MBR, No. 279 (August 29, 1901).

51. *"Bekenntnis," "Wie wundersam,"* and *"Lied vom Winde."* Born in Memmingen in 1862, Rösch conducted the Berlin Akademischer Gesangverein, for which he composed several choral works. Together with Strauss and Hans Sommer, he had founded the Genossenschaft Deutscher Tonsetzer, which made it its business to look after the interests of German composers. He died in 1925.

52. See Arthur Seidl: *Aufsätze, Studien und Skizzen,* I, 296.

53. *Allgemeine Musikzeitung.*

54. *Musikalischers Wochenblatt.*

55. NBL, page 178. Strauss subsequently sent Mahler signed copies of all his scores in token of his admiration.

56. AMM, page 275.

57. Mahler was obliged to agree to let the program be published in the *Dresdner Nachrichten,* where it appeared on December 20 with the following preamble: "At the very special request of the direction, Gustav Mahler, who is averse to all explanations and all programs of any kind or description, has written the following general comments in order to make the world of emotions expressed in his work more understandable to the audience of the premiere." The program is reproduced in Alma Mahler's book (AMM, page 267) (see Appendix 3).

58. The Dresden concert of December 20 consisted of Mahler's *Second Symphony,* the overture to Cherubini's *Anacréon,* two of Sarastro's arias from *Die Zauberflöte,* an aria from Verdi's *Simone Boccanegra* and a song by Rotole, *"La mia bandiera,"* all of which were sung by the Italian bass Vittorio Arimondi. The soloists in Mahler's symphony were Frau Wedekind and Fräulein von Chavanne.

59. Wilhelm Kienzl: *Im Konzert,* page 49.

## CHAPTER 36

1. AMM, page 272.

2. He doubtless wrote letters of an intimate nature to Selma Kurz, Rita Michalek and Gutheil-Schoder, but these, if they still exist, have never been published.

3. It is easy to ascertain the date of this first meeting, for Alma Mahler tells of the late arrival of a guest who had just come from "a Jan Kubelik concert," and it was on the evening of November 7 that the great violinist was the soloist in a concert of the Konzertverein conducted by Alexander von Zemlinsky.

4. Max Burckhard (1854–1912), author and drama critic, was director of the Burgtheater from 1890 to 1897, after which he held an important office in the magistracy.

5. This part of the conversation is related in Frau Zuckerkandl's manuscript.

6. The Hohe Warte is a hill on the outskirts of Vienna, near Grinzing, where modern villas were being built.

7. Born in Vienna in 1842, Jakob Emil Schindler studied at the Akademie under the aegis of Albert Zimmermann. He devoted himself from his earliest youth to landscape painting, and five of his larger canvases now adorn Vienna's Museum of Natural History. He won several prizes, was made an honorary member of the Vienna Akademie in 1888 and later of the Munich Akademie, and is still considered one of the few Austrian painters of international stature. He died of appendicitis in 1892.

8. These details of Alma's childhood are all taken from her autobiography (AML).

9. In one respect her dreams were curiously prophetic, for not only did a large number of famous men become her intimate friends, but she also divided her life among four of

them: Mahler, the architect Walter Gropius, the painter Oskar Kokoschka, and the writer Franz Werfel.

10. Alma Mahler had good reason to be angry with her stepfather when she wrote her book on Mahler, for he apparently adopted the Nazi ideology after the Anschluss. However, it is unlikely that in her youth she hated him quite as much as she maintained.

11. Zemlinsky was to influence a whole generation of musicians, headed by Arnold Schoenberg, his future brother-in-law.

12. It is not easy to ascertain the precise meaning of the word *"Unacht."* Alma may have meant *"Unachtsamkeit,"* negligence.

13. Frau Mahler's books betray her irritation at this mutual liking, an irritation that undoubtedly sprang from her deep-seated aversion to her mother.

14. Frau Mahler toned down Burckhard's anti-Semitic remarks in AMM. In the two original manuscripts, she wrote *"verderben"* or *"verschweindeln"* instead of *"verdunkeln"* and *"degenerierten rachitischen Juden"* instead of *"degenerierten älteren Mann."*

15. Alma copied out this letter in her diary. After Mahler's death, she destroyed all her letters to him.

16. L was probably the young architect who had also been at dinner.

17. Probably of one of Zemlinsky's operas.

18. Mahler was doubtless referring to the clay and terra-cotta figures that abounded in Viennese drawing rooms at that time.

19. Letter of December 5 (see Chapters 7 and 35).

20. AMM, page 258.

21. This sentence, and in fact all Mahler's later allusions to her singularly illegible writing, has been cut out of the printed text (AMM, page 259).

22. According to Alma, Justi did not know the truth when she joined her brother in Dresden and could not understand why Mahler asked her things like: "Can an elderly man marry a young girl?" In point of fact, Justi had already met Alma before she went to Dresden. As for the questions, which Mahler was asking himself as much as his sister, they appear in the letter (quoted below) he wrote to Justi from Berlin.

23. This letter from Berlin, dated "Thursday, December 14," was doubtless written on the twelfth. In her book, Frau Mahler omitted the whole of the first part of it, quoted above, as well as most of the references to her private life and her handwriting.

24. AMM, page 266.

25. In her anxiey to hide her uneasiness, Alma had undoubtedly misunderstood what Mahler had written, for, in the passage quoted at the beginning of this chapter, he advises her not to underestimate success. Two pages of this same letter, written on the morning of December 16, have been inverted. The unpublished first part of it directly precedes the passage beginning *"Schütte das Kind"* (AMM, page 272) and ending *"der wir geizen."* The passage *"Eigentlich kommt es mir"* (AMM, page 271) is both preceded and followed by a few more unpublished lines, then comes the passage *"Ich bitte dich auch,"* which is in turn followed by the last paragraph of AMM, page 271, which ends on page 272.

26. See the preceding chapter.

27. "Must I give way?" she had written in her diary that day. "I can't and won't. And yet I feel I'm on a lower level and it wouldn't hurt me to be pulled up a bit."

28. In the absence of Alma's letter, this sentence is completely obscure. "Third party" is therefore merely a guess on the part of the translator, for *"4. Fall"* means accusative case.

29. Frau Mahler destroyed the original of this letter but fortunately left a copy of it in one of the typed manuscripts of *Ein Leben mit Gustav Mahler.*

30. Freud remarked that Mahler's habit of calling his wife by his mother's Christian name was a symptom of the Oedipus complex.

31. There is a slight discrepancy here between Karpath's account and Alma's, for she claims that the composer Goldschmidt took part in the discussion.

32. BMG, pages 104–9. If one reads *Begegnung mit dem Genius* and compares Karpath's writings with those of other contemporary witnesses, one is indeed impressed with the strict accuracy of the facts he reports.

33. In the same letter, Behn went on to complain that Mahler had completely dropped him, since they had last seen one another at Lipiner's house in November 1899, and said he had even heard that Mahler had complained of his transcription of the *Second Symphony,* although, at the time, he had told Behn that it was "a model for all piano transcriptions." In fact, we know from Natalie that Mahler had never liked this transcription and was often irritated by Behn's vanity.

34. Another letter, which Behn wrote to Mildenburg two years later, shows that her relations with Mahler had become more "harmonious" but were now artistic rather than social. The same letter also indicates Behn's anger at the fact that Mahler had turned his back on Lipiner.

35. Just before the end, there is an entry, dated November 15, describing a long walk along the Danube with Mahler and Lipiner, during which the two men discussed Plato.

36. Indeed, in a letter Natalie wrote to Mildenburg on November 4, 1909, she even asked the latter to save her old clothes for her.

# APPENDIX I

1. No. 51 in the *Grundbuch Humpolec* 112, fol. 35 (*Staatsarchiv Prag*).

2. This son, like Markus, Barbara, and Sophie, was not mentioned in Simon's "act of succession" prepared in 1868.

3. The register contains only the date on which the declaration of his birth was made, not that of his birth, which certainly was earlier.

4. The register contains only the date on which the declaration of her birth was made, not that of her birth, which certainly was earlier.

# THEATRICAL WORKS

1. June 1880. Robin Lehman collection.
2. NBLS, VII, 93.
3. MBR, No. 183.
4. Rosé Collection.
5. NBL, 104.
6. MBR, No. 15.
7. RSM 1, 17.
8. NBL, 162.
9. Mahler gave Natalie a sketch of this song (now in the Library of Congress, Washington, D.C.). It dates from the Leipzig period.
10. Jan Löwenbach, the wife of a well-known Czech lawyer. Frau Löwenbach's family were close friends of Emil Freund, from whom she received this information.
11. MBR, No. 23. There is no trace of a performance of the *tableaux* either in the Wiesbaden Theater archives or in the contemporary newspapers.
12. *Der Anbruch,* II, 7/8, 296.
13. *Die Musik,* VII, May 15, 1908.
14. GAB, IV, 450.
15. The letter is dated July 27 and was sent from Cortina. Natalie was then touring the south Tyrol with Lipiner. Copies of all her letters to Mahler had been placed in an envelope that I found in one of the original volumes of the "Mahleriana."
16. The concert was announced by the *Mährischer Grenzbote,* but no criticism appeared afterward. The Städtische Musikkapelle participated in the concert, during which Mahler also performed the Schubert *C Major Fantasy.*
17. NBLS, July 1893.
18. Hermann Graedener (1844–1929), organist, violinist, conductor, and composer, taught harmony and counterpoint at the conservatory and succeeded Bruckner as lecturer on music at the University of Vienna.
19. Theodor Billroth. A well-known physician and amateur musician who was an intimate friend of Brahms.
20. Vol. III, 46/7. See "Chord and Discord," 1969, "Notes on some Mahler Juvenilia."
21. NBL, page 118.
22. NBL, page 142.
23. Now in the Osborn Collection at Yale University Library.
24. As Mahler himself stated to Paul Decsey (*Die Musik,* X, 18, 355).
25. See MBR, No. 5, and the original sketch of *Hochzeitstück,* formerly in Alma Mahler's collection.
26. At the Vienna Stadtbibliothek.

27. GAM, page 97. The same author (page 75) suggests that the first revision dates from 1888.

28. NBL, pages 106–7.

29. *Die Musik*, X, 18, 355.

30. *Die Musik*, XX, 11, 807.

31. *The Musical Quarterly*, XVII, 4, 453.

32. DMM wrongly spells his name "Graf."

33. *Gedichte von Martin Greif* (Amelangs Verlag, Leipzig, 1895, page 256).

34. Wilhelm Kosch: *Martin Greif und seinen Werken* (Leipzig, 1907).

35. Letter to Mahler dated September 13, 1883, in the Rosé Collection. In it Liszt calls the work *"Waldmärchen,"* but Mahler had certainly sent the complete score.

36. HFR, PSM, and GAM.

37. *Die Musik*, X, 18, 355.

38. The second stanza in the third section of Greif's poems starts:

*O Hirte mein, O Hirte mein,*
*Du flötest auf meinem Totenbein!*

and Mahler has in the first flute song:

*O Spielmann, lieber Spielmann mein . . .*

and in the third:

*Nun bläst du auf meinem Totenbein . . .*

39. "Chord and Discord," 1969, page 13ff.

40. Could these hidden motivations account for the uncanny experiences that plagued Mahler while he was working on the score? NBL, 34. See Chapter V.

41. In my opinion, Diether is also mistaken in believing that the *Tenth Symphony's* unfinished state can be explained by Mahler's superstitious fears regarding his wife. In fact, the compulsion must have been very strong and the inspiration very abundant to allow him to compose so much of it during a summer occupied by the Gropius crisis, the preliminary rehearsals of the *Eighth Symphony* and also his trip to Leyden. There is every reason to believe that he worked on the *Tenth* until just before his death.

42. HLG Collection. Two different sopranos and two altos took part in the 1902 performance.

43. NBL, page 106.

44. In his commentary, written for the Columbia recording of *Das klagende Lied*.

45. Leipzig, Year 64, May 5, 1892.

46. Breitkopf und Härtel.

47. The keys given for all the early songs are those in Alfred Rosé's manuscript version.

48. *Spanische Dramen*, Berlin, 1841, Vol. I.

49. Bibliotek Ausländer Klassiker Spanisches Theater (ed. Moritz Rapp). Vol. V (Hildburghausen, Verlag des bibliographischen Instituts, 1870). By comparing Mahler's text with a much later translation of the play, Fritz Egon Pamer wrongly deduced that Mahler had altered it himself.

50. In the catalogue of the autograph dealer Henrici (No. 39. 1917).

51. For the meaning of the words *"fahrenden Gesellen"* ("wayfarer" or "traveling *Gesell"*) see Chapter 9.

52. According to Professor Rosé, it was given to the contralto Amalie Joachim, to whom Mahler played his cycle in Salzburg in 1892.

53. *Knaben Wunderhorn*, Ed. Zeitschrift für Wissen, XXX, I, 93; Ed. Hempel, II, 417.

54. Dr. Ernst was related through his mother, née Singer, to the family of Siegmund Singer, a Hungarian journalist who was a close friend of Mahler.

55. I am extremely grateful to Mr. Osborn for having allowed the complete manuscript to be photostated for me.

56. *"Blumen-, Frucht- und Dornenstücke oder Ehestand, Tod und Hochzeit des Armenadvokaten F. St. Siebenkäs"* is the complete original title of Jean Paul's famous novel *Siebenkäs*.

57. *"Blumine"* was also borrowed by Mahler from Jean Paul (see below).

58. MBR, 177.

59. Natalie claims that for this reason Mahler made slight alterations in the beginning of the Scherzo for the Vienna performance.

60. The entire piece is based on this well-known student canon, which is the same as *"Frère Jacques."*

61. BWM, page 137.

62. AMM, page 95.

63. This term is used by avant-garde composers who make such borrowing their occasional practice.

64. *Orpheus in New Guises,* page 7.

65. In the first 1893 score the muted horns play the first fanfares and the clarinets were substituted in a later version.

66. There is of course no doubt about Mr. Perrin's story of the manuscript's origin. Mahler did see Jenny Feld in Belgium in 1899, not, as Mr. Perrin suggests, in Brussels, but in Liège, where she attended the last rehearsals and the performance of the *Second Symphony* (see letter to Justi).

67. NBLS, October 1900.

68. The first performance of *"Blumine"* since the Weimar Festival was conducted by Benjamin Britten at the Aldeburgh Festival on June 18, 1967, and that of the whole symphony with the hitherto unknown Andante in New Haven, Connecticut, by Frank Brief on April 9, 1968.

69. NBL, page 149.

70. See Chapter 10.

71. *Deutsche Heimat,* VII, 1931.

72. *Der Jägers Leichenbegräbnis* (Münchner Bilderbogen, 1848–54, No. 44), later reproduced in the Schwind album (Braun & Schneider, Munich, 1880).

73. The original version of Natalie's manuscript has, instead of *leisen, gequälten,* which undoubtedly is much closer to Mahler's meaning.

74. In the 1893 OR, the staccato woodwind notes in the two bars before Figure 16 (return to the main key) are marked *"Wie Unkenrufe"* (Imitating the toad calls).

75. NBL, page 9.

76. Herder's anthology *Volkslieder* or *Stimmen der Völker in Liedern* (Voices of the People in Lieder) was published in 1778–79, Fritz Nicolai's *Ein feiner kleiner Almanach voll schöner echter lieblichen Volkslieder* in 1777–78. Friedrich D. Gräter (whom Arnim visited in 1805) also assembled and published folk poems in the magazine *Bragur* in 1791.

77. NBL, page 12.

78. Erk-Böhme: DLH (*Deutsche Liederhort*), II, 390.

79. Böhme: *Altdeutsches Liederbuch,* page 261.

80. Erk-Böhme, DLH, II, 561.

81. DLH, I, 606.

82. *Die Musik,* X, 21, 144.

83. DLH, II, 568.

84. DLH, III, 281.

85. NBL, page 10.

86. DLH, I, 580.

87. NBL, page 12.

88. Pamer thesis, page 221.

89. Serig's anthology (Leipzig, 1830, page 193).

90. DLH, II, page 396.

91. NBL, page 34.

92. *Der Anbruch:* II, Nos. 7/8, page 296.

93. It is now in the Rudolf Mengelberg Collection in Amsterdam.

94. *Poetische Werke von Adam Mickiewicz, übersetzt von Siegfried Lipiner, Band 2* (Breitkopf und Härtel, Leipzig, 1887).

95. NBL, July 1893.

96. MBR, page 117.

97. In the complete manuscript score, which used to belong to Rudolf Mengelberg.

98. JFP, page 406. Förster claims that it was composed in 1892.

99. This letter, from the Osborn Collection at Yale University, is numbered like the other letters to Hermann Behn.

100. NBL, page 116, and NBLS, October 1900.

101. MBR, No. 293.

102. MBR, No. 172.

103. NBL, page 22, and NBLS, April 1899.

104. While preparing the October 1900 Munich performance, Mahler had to rehearse the cellos and basses very carefully, for, from the fifth bar on, their rhythm became imprecise: he insisted on their emphasizing the difference between the eighth and sixteenth note value (NBLS).

105. While rehearsing this movement in Munich in August 1900, Mahler explained that he wanted it to sound both "old-fashioned, comfortable and measured." He took the cellos to task for their interpretation of the countertheme in the second B section: "You play expressivo throughout," he said, "whereas I have clearly prescribed two bars with expression, after which you must return immediately to private life and leave the melody to the violas."

106. NBLS, August 1893.

107. Obviously the trumpet theme at the end of the Trio (Bar 272), which is only once restated in the winds.

108. MBR, No. 209.

109. NBLS, July 1900.

110. MBR, 197.

111. AMM, page 53. I shall henceforth call them "preliminary."

112. After "The Forest" (1), "The Twilight" (2), and "Love" (3).

113. This motto, taken from the *Wunderhorn,* was nevertheless quoted in the program of the first performance of this work (Berlin, February 9, 1897):

*Vater, sieh' an die Wunden mein,*     Father, see my wounds,
*Kein Wesen lass' verloren sein.*      Let no being be lost.

114. Except in the programs for August 17 and August 29, 1895, when Mahler preferred the original title, *"Das himmlische Leben."*

115. *"The Happy Life, A Midsummer Night's Dream* (Not after Shakespeare, as one critic remarked)."

116. See Chapter XXII: the idea of Pan was suggested to Mahler by the envelope of a letter from Mildenburg.

117. MBR, No. 184.

118. For most of the ideas concerning Nietzsche and his work I am indebted to a young writer, Jean-Louis Lenfant, who has made a long and thorough study of the great German poet-philosopher.

119. According to Bruno Walter, Mahler used to call the beginning of this episode *"Das Gesindel"* (The Rabble, or The Mob), and the fortissimo scale motifs in the strings starting two bars before Figure 51 *"Südsturm"* (Southern Storm).

120. Arnold Schönberg: *Style and Idea,* page 18.

121. The sheet on which this plan is outlined once belonged to Paul Bekker, the author of the most important book written to date on Mahler's symphonies (Schuster & Loeffler, Berlin 1920).

122. NBL and NBLS.

123. Now in the Rosé Collection: *"Eurrinere dich bei diesem Blatte an unsere gemeinschaftliche Appretur dieses solos! Zur Zeit meiner Reconvalescenz,"* the dedication reads. ("This sheet will remind you of our common work on this solo at the time of my convalescence.")

124. Only the last three pages are in my collection. The rest of the manuscript has probably been dispersed.

125. It was published for the first time in the program of the Amsterdam Concertgebouw Orchestra for the April 14, 1910, concert, and later included in the complete writings of Diepenbrock (E. Reeser, Utrecht-Brussels, 1950).

126. From Bruno Walter's December 1901 letter to Ludwig Schiedelmair, in which he discusses programs at length and suggests one for the *Fourth,* obviously dictated by Mahler himself.

127. Letter from Bruno Walter to Ludwig Schiedelmair, December 5, 1901.

128. Paul Bekker, *op. cit.,* page 146.

129. *Orpheus in New Guises,* page 7.

130. NBL, page 171. See above, Chapter 35.

131. MBR, No. 420.

132. This is particularly noticeable in Bars 78 and 79 and Bars 212ff. of the Scherzo.

# BIBLIOGRAPHY

## I. ALPHABETICAL LIST OF KEYS

ABB BRUCKNER ANTON: *Gesammelte Briefe*

AML MAHLER ALMA: *Mein Leben*

AMM MAHLER ALMA: *Gustav Mahler. Erinnerungen und Briefe*

BME BAHR-MILDENBURG ANNA: *Erinnerungen*

BMG KARPATH LUDWIG: *Begegnung mit dem Genius*

BSP STEFAN PAUL (ED.): *Gustav Mahler. Ein Bild seiner Persönlichkeit in Widmungen*

DMM MITCHELL DONALD: *Gustav Mahler. The Early Years*

DNM NEWLIN DIKA: *Bruckner, Mahler and Schönberg*

ENW NEWMAN ERNEST: *The Life of Richard Wagner*

EON NODNAGEL ERNST OTTO: *Jenseits von Wagner und Liszt*

GAB GOELLERICH AUGUST: *Anton Bruckner. Ein Lebens und Schaffensbild*

GAM ADLER GUIDO: *Gustav Mahler*

GEM ENGEL GABRIEL: *Gustav Mahler, Song Symphonist*

GWO GRAF MAX: *Die Wiener Oper*

HFR REDLICH HANS FERDINAND: *Bruckner and Mahler*

JFP FOERSTER JOSEF BOHUSLAV: *Der Pilger*

KMO KOLB KARL MARIA: *Musik und Oper. Kritische Gänge*

MAB AUER MAX: *Anton Bruckner*

MBR MAHLER GUSTAV: *Briefe. 1879–1911*

MKB KALBECK MAX: *Johannes Brahms*

MKW MOROLD MAX: *Wagners Kampf und Sieg*

MMR MELL MAX: *Alfred Roller*

NBL BAUER-LECHNER NATALIE: *Erinnerungen an Gustav Mahler*

OKM KLEMPERER OTTO: *Erinnerungen an Gustav Mahler*

PSM STEFAN PAUL: *Gustav Mahler*

RBM ROLLER ALFRED: *Die Bildnisse von Gustav Mahler*

RHM REIK THEODOR: *The Haunting Melody*

RSM SPECHT RICHARD: *Gustav Mahler* (1913–18)

RSM 1 SPECHT RICHARD: *Gustav Mahler* (1905)

RWM Collection of articles on Mahler by Schoenberg, Bloch, Klemperer, Ratz, Mayer, Schnebel, Adorno (Rainer Wunderlich Verlag)

SBE STRAUSS RICHARD: *Briefe an die Eltern*

SWE STAUBER PAUL: *Das wahre Erbe Mahlers*

SWO    SPECHT RICHARD: *Das Wiener Operntheater*
TAM    ADORNO THEODOR WIESENGRUND: *Gustav Mahler. Eine musikalische Physiognomik*
WKL    KIENZL WILHELM: *Meine Lebenswanderung. Erlebtes und Erlauschtes*


## II. KEYS TO UNPUBLISHED SOURCES
(See also "Sources" in Introduction)


AMS    MAHLER ALMA: *Ein Leben mit Gustav Mahler* (Unpublished ms. belonging to Frau Anna Mahler and containing many unpublished passages and letters)
AMT    MAHLER ALMA: *Tagebuch* (Excerpts from Alma's diary that have survived in her daughter's collection)
NBLS   BAUER-LECHNER NATALIE: *Mahleriana* (surviving ms. of which selections were published by Tal in 1923) (HLG Collection)


## III. GENERAL BIBLIOGRAPHY
of all books and leading magazine articles


ABENDROTH WALTER: *Vier Meister der Musik* (*Bruckner, Mahler, Reger, Pfitzner*). (Prestel, Munich, 1952)
GAM    ADLER GUIDO: *Gustav Mahler* (Universal Edition, Vienna, 1911–16)
———: *Wollen und Wirken. Aus dem Leben eines Musikhistorikers* (Universal Edition, Vienna, 1935)
TAM    ADORNO THEODOR WIESENGRUND: *Mahler, eine musikalische Physiognomik* (Suhrkamp, Frankfurt, 1960)
RWM    ———: in *Gustav Mahler,* by Schoenberg, Bloch, Klemperer, Ratz, Mayer, Schnebel, Adorno (Rainer Wunderlich, Hermann Leins, Tübingen, 1966)
ANBRUCH MUSIKBLÄTTER DES: Mahler issue: II, 7 and 8 (Universal Edition, Vienna, April 1920)
———: Mahler issue: XII, 3 (Universal Edition, Vienna, March 1930)
APPIA ADOLPHE: *Die Musik und die Inscenierung* (Bruckmann, Munich, 1899)
———: *L'Oeuvre d'art vivant* (Atar, Geneva-Paris, 1921)
MAB    AUER MAX: *Anton Bruckner* (Musikwissenschaftlicher Verlag, Leipzig, 1941)
BAHR HERMANN: *Meister und Meisterbriefe* (ed. Joseph Gregor) (Bauer, Vienna, 1947)
BME    BAHR-MILDENBURG ANNA: *Erinnerungen* (Wiener Literarische Anstalt, Vienna-Berlin, 1921)
BALAN GEORGE: *Gustav Mahler sau cum exprima muzica idei* (Editura Musicala, Bucharest, 1964)
BARSOVA L. (ED.): *Gustav Mahler, Letters and Memories* (Musica, Moscow, 1964)
BARTOŠ FRANTIŠEK (ED.): *Mahler. Correspondence, Documents* (Statni Hudebni Vydavatelstvi, Prague, 1962)

NBL    BAUER-LECHNER NATALIE: *Erinnerungen an Gustav Mahler* (Tal, Vienna-Zurich, 1923)

BEETZ WILHELM: *Das Wiener Opernhaus 1869–1945* (Panorama, Zurich, 1949)

BEKKER PAUL: *Gustav Mahler's Sinfonien* (Schuster, Berlin, 1921)

————: *Die Sinfonie von Beethoven bis Mahler* (Schuster, Berlin, 1922)

BERG ALBAN: *Briefe an seine Frau* (Langen-Müller, Vienna, 1965)

BERL HEINRICH: *Das Judentum in der Musik* (Deutsche Verlaganstalt, Stuttgart, 1926)

BETHGE HANS: *Die Chinesische Flöte* (Inselverlag, Leipzig, 1907)

BIE OSKAR: *Die Moderne Musik und Richard Strauss* (Giegels, Leipzig, 1907)

BLAUKOPF KURT: *Gustav Mahler oder der Zeitgenosse der Zukunft* (Molden, Vienna, 1969)

BLESSINGER KARL: *Mendelssohn, Meyerbeer, Mahler. Drei Kapitel Judentum in der Musik als Schlüssel zur Musikgeschichte des 19. Jahrhunderts* (Hahnefeld, Berlin, 1939)

RWM    BLOCH ERNEST: in *Gustav Mahler,* by Schoenberg, Bloch, Klemperer, Ratz, Mayer, Schnebel, Adorno (Rainer Wunderlich, Hermann Leins, Tübingen, 1966)

ABB    BRUCKNER ANTON: *Gesammelte Briefe* (Ed. Max Auer) (Bosse, Regensburg, 1924)

BRUNEAU ALFRED: *A l'Ombre d'un Grand Coeur* (Fasquelle, Paris, 1932)

BÜLOW HANS VON: *Ausgewählte Briefe* (Ed. Marie von Bülow) (Breitkopf, Leipzig, 1919)

BÜLOW MARIE VON: *Hans von Bülow* (Engelhorn, Stuttgart, 1925)

BUSONI FERRUCIO: *Briefe an seine Frau* (Rotapfel, Erlenbach, Zurich, 1935)

CARDUS NEVILLE: *Gustav Mahler. The Man and His Music* (Vol. I, Gollancz, London, 1965)

CARNER MOSCO: *Of Men and Music* (Joseph Williams, London, 1944)

CHEVALLEY HEINRICH: *Hundert Jahre Hamburger Stadt Theater* (Broschek, Hamburg, 1927)

CHORD AND DISCORD: Vol. I (10 issues) (Bruckner Society of America, New York, 1932–39)

————: Vol. II (10 issues) (Bruckner Society of America, New York, 1940–63)

————: Vol. III: No. 1 (Bruckner Society of America, New York, 1969)

COOKE DERYCK: *Gustav Mahler (1860–1911)* (BBC, London, 1960)

DAMROSCH WALTER: *My Musical Life* (Scribner, New York, 1926)

DAVENPORT MARCIA: *Too Strong for Fantasy* (Collins, London, 1968)

————: *Of Lena Geyer* (Grosset & Dunlap, New York, 1936)

DECSEY ERNST: *Musik war sein Leben. Lebenserinnerungen* (Hans Deutsch, Vienna, 1962)

————: *Die Spieldose* (Tal, Leipzig, 1922)

————: *"Stunden mit Mahler"* in *Die Musik,* X, 18 and 21 (June–August 1911)

DIEPENBROCK ALPHONS: *Verzamelde Geschriften* (Het Spectrum, Utrecht, 1950)

DUSE UGO: *Studio sulla poetica liederistica di Gustav Mahler* (Istituto Veneto di Scienze, Lettere ed Arti, 1960–61, Vol. CXIX)

————: *Gustav Mahler. Introduzione allo studio della vita e delle opere* (Marsilio, Padua, 1962)

ECKSTEIN FRIEDRICH: *Alte Unnennbare Tage* (Herbert Reichner, Vienna, 1936)

EFFENBERGER RUDOLF: *Fünfundzwanzig Jahre Dienstbarer Geist im Reiche der Frau Musika* (Vienna, n.d.)

ELSON LOUIS C.: *The History of American Music* (Macmillan, New York, 1925)

GEM    ENGEL GABRIEL: *Gustav Mahler, Song Symphonist* (Bruckner Society of America, New York, 1932)

ERMERS MAX: *Victor Adler* (Epstein, Vienna, 1932)

ERSKINE JOHN: *The Philharmonic Society of New York. Its First Hundred Years* (Macmillan, New York, 1943)

EWEN DAVID: *Music Comes to America* (Allen, Towne & Heath, New York, 1947)

FARGA FRANZ: *Die Wiener Oper* (Franz Göth, Vienna, 1947)

FERGUSON DONALD N.: *Masterworks of the Orchestral Repertoire* (University of Minnesota, Minneapolis, 1954)

FISCHHOF ROBERT: *Begegnungen auf meinem Lebensweg* (Hugo Heller, Vienna, 1916)

FLESCH KARL: *The Memoirs of Karl Flesch* (Macmillan, New York, 1958)

JFP    FOERSTER JOSEF BOHUSLAV: *Der Pilger* (Artia, Prague, 1955)

FOURNIER AUGUST: *Erinerrungen* (Drei Masken, Munich, 1923)

GAB    GOELLERICH AUGUST: *Anton Bruckner, ein Lebens- und Schaffensbild* (ergänzt und herausgegeben von Max Auer) (Bosse, Regensburg, 1936)

GRADENWITZ PETER: *The Music of Israel* (Norton, New York, 1949)

GRAF MAX: *Legende einer Musikstadt* (Oesterreichische Buchgemeinschaft, Vienna, 1949)

————: *Wagner Probleme und andere Studien* (Wiener Verlag, Vienna, 1900)

————: *Geschichte und Geist der Modernen Musik* (Humboldt, Stuttgart, 1953)

GWO    ————: *Die Wiener Oper* (Humboldt, Vienna, 1955)

GRASBERGER FRANZ: *Richard Strauss und die Wiener Oper* (Hans Schneider, Tutzing, 1969)

————: (ED.) *Die Welt um Richard Strauss in Briefen* (id.)

GRUENFELD HEINRICH: *In Dur und Moll* (Grethlein, Leipzig, 1923)

GUTHEIL-SCHODER MARIE: *Erlebtes und Erstebtes, Rolle und Gestaltung* (Rudolf Krey, Vienna, 1937)

HADAMOVSKY FRANZ: *Gustav Mahler und seine Zeit*. Katalog der Austellung (Wiener Festwochen, Vienna, 1960)

HAHN REYNALDO: *Thèmes Variés* (Janin, Paris, 1946)

HANSLIK EDUARD: *Am Ende des Jahrhunderts 1895–1899* (Allgemeiner Verein für Deutsche Litteratur, Berlin, 1899)

———: *Concerte, Componisten und Virtuosen der letzten fünfzehn Jahren 1870–1885* (id., 1896)

———: *Musikalisches und Literarisches* (id., 1890)

———: *Aus Neuer und Neuester Zeit* (id., 1900)

HARCOURT EUGÈNE D': *La Musique en Allemagne et en Autriche-Hongrie* (F. Durdilly, Paris, 1908)

HEUBERGER RICHARD: *Im Foyer* (Hermann Seemann, Leipzig, 1901)

HOLDE ARTUR: *Jews in Music* (Peter Owen, London, 1959)

HUNEKER JAMES GIBBONS: *The Philharmonic Society of New York and Its 75th Anniversary. A Retrospect* (New York, 1917)

———: *Letters* (Ed. Josephine Huneker) (Scribner, New York, 1922)

HUTSCHENRUYTER WOUTER: *Mahler* (Kruseman, The Hague, n.d.)

ISTEL EDGAR (ED.): *Mahlers Symphonien* (Meisterführer No. 10, Schlesingersche Buch- und Musikhandlung, Berlin, n.d.)

JOLIZZA W. K. VON: *Das Lied und seine Geschichte* (Hartleben, Vienna, 1910)

JONES ERNEST: *The Life and Work of Siegmund Freud* (2 vols., Basic Books, New York, 1953)

MKB   KALBECK MAX: *Johannes Brahms* (8 vols., Deutsche Brahms-gesellschaft, Berlin, 1921)

———: (ED.) *Johannes Brahms im Briefwechsel mit Heinrich und Elisabeth von Herzogenberg* (2 vols., Deutsche Brahms-gesellschaft, Berlin, 1907)

BMG   KARPATH LUDWIG: *Begegnung mit dem Genius* (Fiba, Vienna, 1934)

———: *Lachende Musiker* (Knorr & Hirth GMBH, Munich, 1929)

KERNER DIETER: *Krankheiten Grosser Musiker* (Karl Schattauer, Stuttgart, 1963)

WKL   KIENZL WILHELM: *Meine Lebenswanderung. Erlebtes und Erlauschtes* (Engelhorn, Stuttgart, 1926)

OKM   KLEMPERER OTTO: *Erinnerungen an Gustav Mahler* (Atlantis, Zurich, 1960)

———: in *Gustav Mahler* by Schoenberg, Bloch, Klemperer, Ratz, Mayer, Schnebel, Adorno (Rainer Wunderlich, Hermann Leins, Tübingen, 1966)

KMO   KOLB KARL MARIA: *Musik und Oper. Kritische Gänge* (Heinrich Kerler, Ulm, 1953)

KOLODIN IRVING: *The Story of the Metropolitan Opera* (Knopf, New York, 1966)

KRALIK HEINRICH: *Gustav Mahler* (Ed. Friedrich Keller) (Elisabeth Lafite, Vienna, 1968)

———: *Das Buch der Musikfreunde* (Amalthea, Zurich, 1951)

———: *Die Wiener Philharmoniker* (Wilhelm Frick, Vienna, 1938)

———: Translation of same: *The Great Orchestra* (Wilhelm Frick, Vienna, 1955)

———: *Mahler: Das Lied von der Erde.* Thematic Analysis (Steyermühl, Vienna, n.d.)

KRALIK RICHARD: *Tage und Werke, Lebenserinnerungen* (Vogelsangverlag, Vienna, 1922)

KRAUS HEDWIG AND SCHREINZER KARL: *Statistik der Wiener Philharmoniker 1842–1942* (Universal Edition, Vienna, 1942)

KREBS CARL: *Meister des Taktstocks* (Schuster & Loeffler, Berlin, 1919)

KREHBIEL HENRY EDWARD: *More Chapters of Opera* (Henry Holt, New York, 1919)

KRETSCHMANN THEOBALD: *Tempi Passati. Aus den Erinnerungen eines Musikanten* (Karl Prohaska, Vienna, 1910)

————: *ETC* (2nd vol. of same) (id., 1913)

KRUG WALTHER: *Die Neue Musik* (Eugen Rentsch, Erlenbach bei Zürich, 1920)

KUČEROVA DAGMAR: *Gustav Mahler a Olomouc in Hudebni Veda* (Academia, Prague, 1968)

KUFFERATH MAURICE: *L'Art de diriger* (Fischbacher, Paris, 1909)

KUNZ OTTO: *Richard Mayr* (Bergland, Vienna, 1933)

LA GRANGE HENRY-LOUIS DE: "Mahler. A New Image," in *Saturday Review* (New York, March 29, 1969)

————: *Mahler prigionero della leggenda,* in *Nuova Rivista Musicale Italiana,* III, 2 (Turin, March–April 1969)

————: *Mahler Today,* in *The World of Music,* XI, 2 (Bärenreiter, Kassel, March 1969)

————: *Redécouverte de Mahler* (Gustav Mahler Gesellschaft, Berlin, 1967)

————: "Mistakes about Mahler," in *Music and Musicians,* XXI, 2 (London, October 1972)

LEA HENRY A.: *Gustav Mahler und der Expressionismus* (in *Aspekte des Expressionismus:* Lothar Stiehm, Heidelberg, 1969)

LOCHNER LOUIS P.: *Fritz Kreisler* (Macmillan, New York, 1950)

LOESER NORBERT: *Gustav Mahler* (Gottner, Haarlem, 1968)

LOUIS RUDOLF: *Die Deutsche Musik der Gegenwart* (Georg Müller, Munich, 1909)

AML  MAHLER ALMA: *Mein Leben* (Fischer, Frankfurt am Main, 1960)

————: Abridged version translated into English in collaboration with E. B. Ashton: *And the Bridge Is Love* (Harcourt Brace, New York, 1958)

AMM  ————: *Gustav Mahler. Erinnerungen und Briefe* (Bermann Fischer, Vienna, 1949)

————: (same book translated and abridged) *Gustav Mahler. Memories and Letters.* Tr. Basil Creighton (Viking Press, New York, 1946)

————: (id.) Tr. Basil Creighton (John Murray, London, 1946)

————: (id.) Same, translation introduction, and footnotes by Donald Mitchell (John Murray, London, 1968)

MBR  MAHLER GUSTAV: *Briefe. 1879–1911* (Ed. Alma Mahler) (Zsolnay, Vienna, 1924)

————: *Gustav Mahler und seine Zeit.* Katalog der Austellung (Wiener Festwochen, Vienna, 1960)

————: *Mahler Feestboek* (May 6 to 21, 1920) (Concertgebouw, Amsterdam, 1920)

MANN THOMAS: *Briefe 1889–1936* (Aufbau, Berlin, 1965)

MARLIAVE JOSEPH DE: *Études musicales* (Alcan, Paris, 1917)

MARX JOSEPH: *Betrachtungen eines Romantischen Realisten* (Gerlach & Wiedling, Vienna, 1947)

MATTER JEAN: *Mahler le démoniaque* (Foma, Lausanne, 1959)

RWM   MAYER HANS: in *Mahler* by Schoenberg, Bloch, Klemperer, Ratz, Mayer, Schnebel, Adorno (Rainer Wunderlich, Hermann Leins, Tübingen, 1966)

MMR   MELL MAX: *Alfred Roller* (Wiener Literarische Anstalt, Vienna, 1922)

MELLERS WILFRID: *Studies in Contemporary Music* (Dobson, London, 1947)

MENGELBERG C. RUDOLF: *Gustav Mahler* (Breitkopf, Leipzig, 1923)

————: *Das Mahler-Fest. Amsterdam Mai 1920* (Universal Edition, Vienna, 1920)

MERKER DER: Mahler issue: III, 5 (Vienna, March 1912)

DMM   MITCHELL DONALD: *Mahler. The Early Years* (Rockliffe, London, 1958)

MITTAG ERWIN: *Aus der Geschichte der Wiener Philharmoniker* (Gerlach & Wiedling, Vienna, 1950)

MODERNE WELT: Mahler issue: III, 7 (Vienna, 1921–22)

MKW   MOROLD MAX: *Wagners Kampf und Sieg* (2 vols., Amalthea, Zurich, 1930)

MOSES MONTROSE J.: *Heinrich Conried* (Thomas Crowell, New York, 1916)

MOULIN ECKART GRAF RICHARD DU: *Hans von Bülow* (Rösl, Munich, 1921)

MUSIK DIE: Mahler issue: X, 18 (Schuster & Loeffler, Berlin, June 1911)

————: *Gustav Mahler Literatur:* X, 18, 21 (Schuster & Loeffler, Berlin, June–August 1911)

NEISSER ARTHUR: *Gustav Mahler* (Philipp Reclam, Leipzig, 1918)

NEJEDLY ZDENEK: *Gustav Mahler* (Statni Nakladatelstvi Krasne Literatury, Hudby a Umeni, Prague, 1958)

DNM   NEWLIN DIKA: *Bruckner, Mahler and Schönberg* (King's Crown Press, Morningside Heights, New York, 1947)

ENW   NEWMAN ERNEST: *The Life of Richard Wagner* (4 vols., Knopf, New York, 1933–47)

NIEMANN WALTER: *Die Musik der Gegenwart* (Schuster & Loeffler, Berlin, 1913)

NIKISCH ARTUR: *Leben und Wirken* (Ed. Heinrich Chevalley) (Bote, Berlin, 1922)

EON   NODNAGEL ERNST OTTO: *Jenseits von Wagner und Liszt* (Ostpreussichen Druckerei, Königsberg, 1902)

————: *Mahler: Symphonie No V:* Thematische Analyse (Peters, Leipzig, 1905)

OESTERREICHISCHE MUSIKZEITSCHRIFT: Mahler issue: XV, 6 (Vienna, June 1960)

OREL ALFRED: *Ein Harmonielehrekolleg bei Anton Bruckner* (Payer, Berlin, 1940)

PAMER FRITZ EGON: *Gustav Mahlers Lieder. Eine Stilkritische Studie* (Dissertation, Vienna, 1922)

PAUMGARTNER BERNHARD: *Erinnerungen* (Residenz, Salzburg, 1969)

PERGER RICHARD VON: *Fünfzig Jahre Wiener Philharmoniker. 1860–1910* (Fromme, Vienna, 1910)

PFITZNER HANS: *Reden, Schriften, Briefe* (Hermann Luchterhand, Berlin, 1955)

PONNELLE LAZARE: *A Munich. Gustav Mahler, Richard Strauss, Ferruccio Busoni* (Fischbacher, Paris, 1913)

RACHMANINOFF SERGEI: *Rachmaninoff's Recollections told to Oskar von Riesemann* (Allen & Unwin, London, 1934)

RATZ ERWIN: in *Gustav Mahler* by Schoenberg, Bloch, Klemperer, Ratz, Mayer, Schnebel, Adorno (Rainer Wunderlich, Hermann Leins, Tübingen, 1966)

RAUPP WILHELM: *Max von Schillings* (Hanseatischer Verlag, Hamburg, 1935)

REDLICH HANS FERDINAND: *Gustav Mahler. Eine Erkenntnis* (Hans Carl, Nürenberg, 1919)

HFR ———: *Bruckner and Mahler* (Dent, London, 1955)

———: *Alban Berg* (Universal Edition, Vienna, 1957)

REICH WILLI (ED.): *Gustav Mahler. Im eigenen Wort. Im Worte der Freunde* (Die Arche, Zurich, 1958)

RHM REIK THEODOR: *The Haunting Melody* (Farrar, Strauss & Young, New York, 1953)

REZNICEK FELICITAS VON: *Gegen den Strom* (Amalthea, Zurich, 1960)

RICHOLSON-SOLLITT EDNA: *Mengelberg spreekt* (J. Philip Kruseman, The Hague, n.d.)

RITTER WILLIAM: *Études d'Art Étranger* (Mercure de France, Paris, 1911)

———: *Souvenirs sur Gustav Mahler* in *Revue Musicale Suisse*, 101, 1, 29 (Hug, Zurich, January–February 1961)

———: *Pélerinage à la Neuvième Symphonie et à la tombe de Gustav Mahler* in *Revue Française de Musique*, X, 7 and 8 (Paris, July–August 1912)

ROBERT GUSTAVE: *La Musique à Paris 1898–1900* (Vols. V and VI) (Delagrave, Paris, 1901)

ROLLAND ROMAIN: *Musiciens d'aujourd'hui* (Hachette, Paris, 1922)

———: *Fräulein Elsa. Lettres à Elsa Wolff* (Albin Michel, Paris, 1964)

———: (et Richard Strauss): *Correspondance. Fragments de journal* (Albin Michel, Paris, 1951)

RBM ROLLER ALFRED: *Die Bildnisse von Gustav Mahler* (Tal, Leipzig, 1922)

ROSENFELD PAUL: *Musical Chronicle* (Harcourt Brace, New York, 1923)

ROTHMULLER ARON MARKO: *The Music of the Jews* (Beechhurst, New York, 1954)

RUTTERS HERMAN: *Gustav Mahler* (Hollandia, 1919)

SACHAR ABRAM LEON: *A History of the Jews* (Knopf, New York, 1955)

SALTEN FELIX: *Gestalten und Erscheinungen* (Fischer, Berlin, 1913)

SCHAEFER HANS JOACHIM: "Gustav Mahlers Wirken in Kassel" in *Musica*, XIV, 6 (Bärenreiter, Kassel, June 1960)

SCHAEFERS ANTON: *Gustav Mahlers Instrumentation* (Dissertation, Nolte, Düsseldorf, 1935)

SCHALK FRANZ: *Briefe und Betrachtungen* (Musikwissenschaftlicher Verlag, Vienna, 1935)

SCHARWENKA XAVIER: *Klänge aus meinem Leben. Erinnerungen eines Musikers* (Koehler, Leipzig, 1922)

SCHIBLER ARMIN: *Zum Werk Gustav Mahlers* (Kahnt, Lindau, 1955)

SCHIEDERMAIR LUDWIG: *Gustav Mahler* (Hermann Seemann, Leipzig, 1900)

———: *Musikalische Begegnungen* (Staufen, Cologne, 1948)

SCHMIDT HEINRICH: *Formprobleme und Entwicklungslinien in Gustav Mahlers Symphonien. Ein Beitrag zur Formenlehre der musikalischen Romantik* (Dissertation, Vienna, 1929)

SCHMIDT LEOPOLD: *Erlebnisse und Betrachtungen* (Hofmann, Berlin, 1913)

———: *Aus dem Musikleben der Gegenwart* (Hofmann, Berlin, 1909)

RWM　SCHNEBEL DIETER: in *Gustav Mahler* by Schoenberg, Bloch, Klemperer, Ratz, Mayer, Schnebel, Adorno (Rainer Wunderlich, Hermann Leins, Tübingen, 1966)

SCHOENBERG ARNOLD: *Briefe* (Ed. Erwin Stein) (Schott, Mainz, 1958)

———: *Style and Idea* (Philosophical Library, New York, 1950)

RWM　———: Original version of same article in *Gustav Mahler* by Schoenberg, Bloch, Klemperer, Ratz, Mayer, Schnebel, Adorno (Rainer Wunderlich, Hermann Leins, Tübingen, 1966)

———: *Harmonielehre* (Universal Edition, Vienna, 1922)

SCHROTT LUDWIG: *Hans Pfitzner* (Atlantis Verlag, Zurich, 1959)

SCHÜNEMANN GEORG: *Geschichte des Dirigierens* (Breitkopf, Leipzig, 1913)

SCHUH WILLI (ED.): *Richard Strauss, Jahrbuch 1954* (Boosey & Hawkes, Bonn, 1953)

SCHUMANN KARL: *Das Kleine Gustav Mahler Buch* (Residenz, Salzburg, 1972)

SEIDL ARTHUR: *Moderne Dirigenten* (Schuster & Loeffler, Berlin, 1902)

———: *Moderner Geist in der deutschen Tonkunst* (Gustav Bosse, Regensburg, 1912)

———: *Aufsätze, Studien und Skizzen* (2 vols., Gustav Bosse, Regensburg, 1926)

SELTSAM WILLIAM H. (ED.): *Metropolitan Opera Annals* (H. W. Wilson, New York, 1947)

SIEGFRIED ANDRÉ: *Les Voies d'Israël* (Hachette, Paris, 1958)

SITTARD JOSEPH: *Alte und Neue Opern*, etc. (Dotz, Hamburg, 1889)

SLEZAK LEO: *Mein Lebensmärchen* (Piper, Munich, 1948)

RSM I　SPECHT RICHARD: *Gustav Mahler* (Gose und Tetzlaff, Berlin, 1905)

———: *Gustav Mahler:* 1st Ed. Illustr. (Schuster & Loeffler, Berlin, 1913)

———: *Gustav Mahler:* 2nd Ed. (Schuster & Loeffler, Berlin, 1918)

———: *Johannes Brahms* (Avalun, Hellerau, 1928)

SWO ————: *Das Wiener Operntheater. Erinnerung aus 50 Jahren* (Paul Knepler, Vienna, 1919)

————: *Mahler: Symphonies I, II, III, IV, VII:* Thematische Analyse (Universal Edition, Vienna, n.d.)

————: *Mahler: Symphony VI:* Thematic analysis (Kahnt, Leipzig, 1906)

————: *Gustav Mahler. Nachgelassene Zehnte Symphonie. Einführende Bemerkungen* (Zsolnay, Vienna, 1925)

STARGARDT-WOLFF EDITH: *Wegbereiter grosser Musiker (unter Verwendung von Tagebuchblättern, Briefen und vielen persönlichen Erinnerungen von Hermann und Louise Wolff, den Gründern der ersten Konzertdirektion 1880–1935)* (Bote & Bock, Wiesbaden, 1954)

SWE STAUBER PAUL: *Das wahre Erbe Mahlers* (Hubert & Lahme, Vienna, 1909)

PSE STEFAN PAUL: *Gustav Mahlers Erbe* (H. von Weber, Munich, 1908)

————: *Gustav Mahler* (1st Ed., Piper & Co., Munich, 1910)

————: *Gustav Mahler* (2nd Ed., Piper & Co., Munich, 1913)

————: *Gustav Mahler:* Tr. T. E. Clark (Schirmer, New York, 1913)

BSP ————: (ED.) *Gustav Mahler. Ein Bild seiner Persönlichkeit in Widmungen* (Piper, Munich, 1910)

————: *Bruno Walter* (Herbert Reichner, Vienna, 1936)

————: *Das Neue Haus* (Ed. Strache, Vienna, 1919)

STEIN ERWIN: *Orpheus in New Guises* (Rockliffe, London, 1953)

————: *Mahler and the Vienna Opera* in *Opera* magazine, IV, 1, 3, 4, 5 (London, January, March, April, May, 1953)

STEIN LEON: *The Racial Thinking of Richard Wagner* (Philosophical Library, New York, 1950)

STEINITZER MAX: *Richard Strauss* (Schuster & Loeffler, Berlin, 1914)

STEPHAN RUDOLPH: *Mahler: Symphonie IV, G Dur* (Wilhelm Fink, Munich, 1966)

STEPHENSON KURT: *Hundert Jahre Philharmonische Gesellschaft in Hamburg* (Broschek, Hamburg, 1928)

STORCK KARL: *Die Musik der Gegenwart* (J. B. Metzlersche, Stuttgart, 1922)

SBE STRAUSS RICHARD: *Briefe an die Eltern* (Atlantis, Zurich, 1954)

————: und Hugo von Hofmannsthal: *Briefwechsel* (Atlantis, Zurich, 1952)

————: Same: Eng. Tr. by Hans Hammelmann & Ewald Osers (Random House, New York, 1961)

————: et Romain Rolland: *Correspondance. Fragments de journal* (Albin Michel, Paris, 1951)

TANZBERGER ERNST: *Jan Sibelius* (Breitkopf & Härtel, Wiesbaden, 1962)

TENNER FRANZ (ED.): *Richard Strauss. Dokumente seines Lebens und Schaffens* (C. H. Beck, Munich, 1954)

TIBBE MONIKA: *Über die Verwendung von Liedern und Liedelementen in instrumentalen Symphoniesätzen Gustav Mahlers* (Katzbichler, Munich, 1971)

TISCHLER HANS: *Die Harmonik in den Werken Gustav Mahlers* (Dissertation, Vienna, 1937)

VESTDIJK S.: *Gustav Mahler. Over de Structuur van zijn symfonisch Oeuvre* (Bert Bakker, The Hague, 1960)

VIGNAL MARC: *Mahler* (Seuil, Paris, 1966)

VOGEL JAROSLAV: *Leos Janacek. Leben und Werk* (Artia, Prague, 1958)

VOLBACH WALTHER R.: *Adolphe Appia. Prophet of the Modern Theater. A Profile.* (Wesleyan University Press, Middletown, Conn., 1968)

WAGNER COSIMA: *Briefwechsel mit Prinz Ernst zu Hohenlohe Langenburg* (Cotta, Stuttgart, 1937)

WALKER FRANK: *Hugo Wolf* (Knopf, New York, 1952)

WALTER BRUNO: *Gustav Mahler* (Orig. German: Fischer, Berlin, 1957)

————: *Gustav Mahler* (Tr. Lotte Walter Lindt: 1st Ed., Greystone, New York, 1947)

————: *Gustav Mahler* (Revised, Ed. & Tr. Lotte Walter Lindt: Knopf, New York, 1958)

————: *Thema und Variationen* (Orig. German: Fischer, Berlin, 1950)

————: *Theme and Variations* (Tr. James A. Galston: Knopf, New York, 1946)

————: *Briefe 1894–1962* (Fischer, Frankfurt am Main, 1969)

WEBERN ANTON VON: *Briefe an Hildegard Jone und Josef Humplik* (Ed. Josef Polnauer) (Universal Edition, Vienna, 1959)

————: *Der Weg zu Neuen Musik* (Ed. Willi Reich) (Universal Edition, Vienna, 1960)

————: (Ed. Herbert Eimert & K. H. Stockhausen) *Die Reihe*, No. 2 (Universal Edition, Vienna, 1955)

WEINGARTNER FELIX: *Die Symphonie nach Beethoven* (Fischer, Berlin, 1898)

————: *Lebens erinnerungen* (2 vols., Orell Füssli, Zurich, 1928–29)

WELLESZ EGON: *Die neue Instrumentation* (2 vols., Max Hesse, Berlin, 1928)

WESSEM CONSTANT VON: *Gustav Mahler* (Van Loghum Slaterus, Arnhem, 1920)

WOESS JOSEPH VENANTIUS VON: *Mahler: Das Lied von der Erde.* Thematic analysis (Universal Edition, Vienna, 1912)

WORBS HANS CHRISTIAN: *Gustav Mahler* (Max Hesse, Berlin Halensee, 1960)

ZWEIG STEFAN: *The World of Yesterday* (Viking Press, New York, 1943)

# INDEX